GLEIM®

20TH EDITION

FINANCIAL ACCOUNTING

EXAM QUESTIONS & EXPLANATIONS

by

Irvin N. Gleim, Ph.D., CPA, CIA, CMA, CFM

with the assistance of
Grady M. Irwin, J.D.

Gleim Publications, Inc.
PO Box 12848
University Station
Gainesville, Florida 32604
(800) 87-GLEIM or (800) 874-5346
(352) 375-0772
Website: www.gleim.com
Email: admin@gleim.com

For updates to the first printing of the twentieth edition of *Financial Accounting Exam Questions and Explanations*

Go To: www.gleim.com/updates

Or: Email update@gleim.com with **FIN EQE 20-1** in the subject line. You will receive our current update as a reply.

Updates are available until the next edition is published.

ISSN: 1091-451X
ISBN: 978-1-61854-179-6

First Printing: July 2018

ACKNOWLEDGMENTS

Material from Uniform Certified Public Accountant Examination questions and unofficial answers, Copyright © 1972-2018 by the American Institute of Certified Public Accountants, Inc., is reprinted and/or adapted with permission.

The authors also appreciate and thank The Institute of Internal Auditors, Inc., for permission to use The Institute's Certified Internal Auditor Examination questions, Copyright © 1978-2018 by The Institute of Internal Auditors, Inc.

The authors also appreciate and thank the Institute of Certified Management Accountants for permission to use questions from past CMA examinations, Copyright © 1979-2018 by the Institute of Management Accountants.

The authors also acknowledge the Florida State Board of Accountancy and its written professional examination as a source of questions.

The authors appreciate questions contributed by the following individuals: Ken M. Boze, O. Whitfield Broome, Jr., H. Francis Bush, John Cerepak, Robert P. Derstine, James M. Emig, D.L. Flesher, J.O. Hall, Alene G. Helling, Wayne M. Higley, Judith A. Hora, Donald G. Kame, LaVern E. Krueger, Pete Lockett, J.W. Mantooth, Phil McBrayer, E. Milacek, Tim Miller, Alfonso R. Oddo, Ruth R. O'Keefe, T.J. Phillips, Jr., Roderick B. Posey, Karl Putnam, Sally Schultz, C.J. Skender, Edward C. Spede, John B. Sperry, James P. Trebby, and Sankaran Venkateswar.

Environmental Statement -- This book is printed on recyclable, environmentally friendly groundwood paper, sourced from certified sustainable forests and produced either TCF (totally chlorine-free) or ECF (elementally chlorine-free).

ABOUT THE AUTHOR

Irvin N. Gleim is Professor Emeritus in the Fisher School of Accounting at the University of Florida and is a member of the American Accounting Association, Academy of Legal Studies in Business, American Institute of Certified Public Accountants, Association of Government Accountants, Florida Institute of Certified Public Accountants, The Institute of Internal Auditors, and the Institute of Management Accountants. He has had articles published in the *Journal of Accountancy*, *The Accounting Review*, and *The American Business Law Journal* and is author/coauthor of numerous accounting books, aviation books, and CPE courses.

REVIEWERS AND CONTRIBUTORS

Garrett W. Gleim, B.S., CGMA, received a Bachelor of Science degree from the University of Pennsylvania, The Wharton School. He also holds a CPA certificate issued by the State of Delaware. Mr. Gleim coordinated the production staff, reviewed the manuscript, and provided production assistance throughout the project.

Grady M. Irwin, J.D., is a graduate of the University of Florida College of Law, and he has taught in the University of Florida College of Business. Mr. Irwin provided substantial editorial assistance throughout the project.

Michael Kustanovich, M.A., CPA, is a Senior Lecturer of Accountancy in the Department of Accountancy at the University of Illinois at Urbana-Champaign. He teaches advanced financial accounting courses at both undergraduate and graduate levels, and he is the instructor of the CPA Exam Review Course. Previously, Mr. Kustanovich worked in the assurance departments of KPMG and PWC. He provided substantial editorial assistance throughout the project.

Mark S. Modas, M.S.T., CPA, received a Bachelor of Arts in Accounting from Florida Atlantic University and a Master of Science in Taxation from Nova Southeastern University. He was the Sarbanes-Oxley project manager and internal audit department manager at Perry Ellis International, and the former Acting Director of Accounting and Financial Reporting for the School Board of Broward County, Florida. Mr. Modas provided substantial editorial assistance throughout the project.

iv

A PERSONAL THANKS

This manual would not have been possible without the extraordinary effort and dedication of Jacob Bennett, Julie Cutlip, Ethan Good, Blaine Hatton, Kelsey Hughes, Fernanda Martinez, Bree Rodriguez, Teresa Soard, Justin Stephenson, Joanne Strong, Elmer Tucker, and Candace Van Doren, who typed the entire manuscript and all revisions and drafted and laid out the diagrams, illustrations, and cover for this book.

The authors also appreciate the production and editorial assistance of Sirene Dagher, Jessica Hatker, Kristen Hennen, Belea Keeney, Katie Larson, Diana León, Bryce Owen, Jake Pettifor, Shane Rapp, Drew Sheppard, and Alyssa Thomas.

The authors also appreciate the critical reading assistance of Matthew Blockus, Felix Chen, Corey Connell, Cole Gabriel, Dean Kingston, Melissa Leonard, Monica Metz, Kelly Meyer, Timothy Murphy, Cristian Prieto, Crystal Quach, Martin Salazar, and Diana Weng.

Finally, we appreciate the encouragement, support, and tolerance of our families throughout this project.

IF YOU HAVE QUESTIONS

Gleim has an efficient and effective way for users to submit an inquiry and receive a response regarding Gleim materials directly through their Test Prep. This system also allows you to view your Q&A session in your Gleim Personal Classroom.

Questions regarding the information in the Introduction (study suggestions, studying plans, exam specifics) should be emailed to personalcounselor@gleim.com.

Questions concerning orders, prices, shipments, or payments should be sent via email to customerservice@gleim.com and will be promptly handled by our competent and courteous customer service staff.

For technical support, you may use our automated technical support service at www.gleim.com/support, email us at support@gleim.com, or call us at (800) 874-5346.

Returns of books purchased from bookstores and other resellers should be made to the respective bookstore or reseller. For more information regarding the Gleim Return Policy, please contact our offices at (800) 874-5346 or visit www.gleim.com/returnpolicy.

TABLE OF CONTENTS

DETAILED TABLE OF CONTENTS

PREFACE FOR ACCOUNTING STUDENTS

The purpose of this book is to help you understand financial accounting principles and procedures and their applications. In turn, these skills will enable you to perform better on your undergraduate exams, as well as look ahead to (and prepare for) professional exams.

One of the major benefits of this study manual is comprehensive coverage of financial accounting topics. Accordingly, when you use this study manual to help prepare for financial accounting courses and exams, you are assured of covering virtually all topics that could reasonably be expected to be studied in typical college or university intermediate and advanced financial accounting courses. See Appendix A for a comprehensive list of cross-references.

The signature Gleim answer and explanation format is designed to facilitate effective study and learning. The Gleim EQE Test Prep is packed with features that allow you to customize quizzes to focus on the areas with the biggest opportunity for improvement and review detailed answer explanations for questions you missed.

The majority of the questions are from past CIA, CMA, and CPA exams. Although a citation for the source of each question is provided, a substantial number have been modified to accommodate changes in professional pronouncements, to clarify questions, and/or to emphasize a financial accounting concept or its application. In addition, hundreds of publisher-written questions test areas covered in current textbooks but not directly tested on accounting certification exams. Finally, we are pleased to use questions submitted by accounting professors.

Note that this study manual should not be relied upon exclusively to prepare for the professional exams. You should primarily use review systems specifically developed for each exam. The Gleim CIA, CMA, CPA, and EA Review Systems are up-to-date and comprehensively cover all material necessary for successful completion of these exams. Further descriptions of these exams and our review materials are provided in the Introduction. To obtain any of these materials, order online at www.gleim.com or call us at (800) 874-5346.

Thank you for your interest in this book. We deeply appreciate the many letters and suggestions received from accounting students and educators during the past years, as well as from CIA, CMA, and CPA candidates. Please go to www.gleim.com/feedbackFIN to share your suggestions on how we can improve this edition.

Please read the Introduction carefully. It is very short but very important.

Good Luck on Your Exams,

Irvin N. Gleim

July 2018

INTRODUCTION

This innovative accounting text provides students with a well-organized, extensive collection of multiple-choice questions covering the topics taught in typical financial accounting courses.

The Gleim *Exam Questions and Explanations* (EQE) series will help you to pretest yourself before class to determine whether you are strong or weak in the assigned area. Then test yourself after class to reinforce the concepts. The questions in these books cover **all** topics in your related courses, so you will encounter few questions on your exams for which you will not be well prepared.

The titles and organization of Study Units 1 through 28 are based on the current financial accounting textbooks listed in Appendix A, which contains a comprehensive cross-reference of your textbook to Gleim study units and subunits. If you are using a textbook that is not included in our list or if you have any suggestions on how we can improve these cross-references to make them more useful, please submit your request/feedback at www.gleim.com/crossreferences/FIN or email them to FINcrossreferences@gleim.com.

FEATURES

The Gleim EQE series will ensure your understanding of each topic you study in your courses with access to the largest bank of exam questions (including thousands from past certification exams) that is widely used by professors. This series provides immediate feedback on your study effort while you take your practice tests.

- Each book or EQE Test Prep question bank contains over 1,000 multiple-choice questions with correct and incorrect answer explanations and can be used in two or more classes.
- Exhaustive cross-references are presented for all related textbooks so that you can easily determine which group of questions pertains to a given chapter in your textbook.
- Questions taken directly from professional certification exams demonstrate the standards to which you will be held as a professional accountant and help prepare you for certification exams later.
- Titles include Auditing & Systems, Cost/Managerial Accounting, Financial Accounting, Federal Tax, and Business Law & Legal Studies. They thoroughly cover the topics you are presented with while pursuing your accounting degree. Go to www.gleim.com/eqe for more details.

After graduation, you will compete with graduates from schools across the country in the accounting job market. Make sure you measure up to standards that are as demanding as the standards of your counterparts at other schools. These standards will be tested on professional certification exams.

USE OF SUBUNITS

Each study unit of this book is divided into subunits to portion overwhelming topics into more manageable, bite-size learning components.

Topics and questions may overlap among subunits. The number of questions offers comprehensive coverage but does not present an insurmountable task. We define each subunit narrowly enough to cover a single topic but broadly enough to prevent questions from being repetitive.

QUESTION SOURCES

Past CIA, CMA, and CPA exams and sample questions are the primary sources of questions included in this study guide.

In addition, Gleim Exam Prep prepares questions (coded in this text as *Publisher, adapted*) based on the content of financial accounting textbooks, pronouncements, etc. Professionals and professors from schools around the country also have contributed to provide a more thorough and the largest bank of questions. See page ii for a list of their names.

The source of each question appears in the first line of its answer explanation in the column to the right of the question. Summary of source codes:

CIA	Certified Internal Auditor Examination
CMA	Certified Management Accountant Examination
CPA	Uniform Certified Public Accountant Examination
Publisher	EQE FIN author
Individual's name	Name of professional or professor who contributed the question

If you, your professor, or your classmates wish to submit questions, we will consider using them in future editions. Please email questions you develop, complete with answers and explanations, to professor.relations@gleim.com.

Writing and analyzing multiple-choice questions is an excellent way to prepare yourself for your exams. We will make every effort to consider, edit, and use questions you submit. However, we ask that you send us only serious, complete, carefully considered efforts.

MULTIPLE-CHOICE QUESTIONS

The major advantage of multiple-choice questions is their ability to cover a large number of topics with little time and effort in comparison to essay questions and/or computational problems.

The advantage of multiple-choice questions over true/false questions is that they require more analysis and result in a lower score for those with little or no knowledge.

Students and professors both like multiple-choice questions. Students find them relatively easy to answer because only one of the answer choices needs to be selected. Professors like them because they are easy to grade and much more material can be tested in the same period of time. Most professors also will ask students to complete essays or computational questions.

Note that the detailed Gleim answer explanations also can help students prepare for the inevitable essay questions.

ANSWER EXPLANATIONS ALONGSIDE THE QUESTIONS

The format of our book presents multiple-choice questions side by side with their answer explanations. The example below is from the CPA exam.

According to the FASB's conceptual framework, the objective of general-purpose financial reporting is most likely based on

A. Generally accepted accounting principles.

B. Reporting on how well management has discharged its responsibilities.

C. The need for conservatism.

D. The needs of the users of the information.

Answer (D) is correct. *(CPA, adapted)*

REQUIRED: The objectives of financial reporting for business enterprises.

DISCUSSION: The objective of general-purpose financial reporting is to provide information that is useful to existing and potential investors, lenders, and other creditors in making decisions about providing resources to the entity.

Answer (A) is incorrect. GAAP govern how to account for items in the financial statements. Answer (B) is incorrect. Financial reporting provides information that is helpful, among other things, in evaluating how well management has discharged its responsibilities to make effective and efficient use of entity resources. Answer (C) is incorrect. Conservatism is a constraint on recognition in the statements.

This format is designed to make studying more efficient by eliminating the need to turn pages back and forth from questions to answers.

Be careful, however. Do not misuse this format by consulting the answers before you have answered the questions. Misuse of the readily available answers will give you a false sense of security and will result in poor performance on your actual exams.

STUDY SUGGESTIONS

The emphasis in the next few pages is on developing strategies, approaches, and procedures to learn and retain the material in less time.

Using Tests to Study

Tests, especially quizzes and midterms, provide feedback on your study and test-taking procedures. It is extremely important to identify your opportunities for improvement on quizzes and tests at the beginning of the term so you can take corrective action on subsequent tests, including your final exam.

When your test is returned, determine how you did relative to the rest of your class and your professor's grading standards. Next, analyze your relative performance between types of questions (essay vs. multiple-choice) and types of subject matter (topics or study units). The objective is to identify the areas where you can improve.

Using Multiple-Choice Questions to Study

Experts on testing continue to favor multiple-choice questions as a valid means of evaluating various levels of knowledge. Using these questions to study for academic exams is an important tool not only for obtaining good grades, but also for long-range preparation for certification and professional exams. The following suggestions will help you study in conjunction with each Gleim *Exam Questions and Explanations* book and EQE Test Prep (visit www.gleim.com/students):

1. Locate the study unit that contains questions on the topic you are currently studying. Each *Exam Questions and Explanations* book and EQE Test Prep contains cross-references to the tables of contents of the most commonly used textbooks.

2. Work through a series of questions, selecting the answers you think are correct. Follow the Gleim multiple-choice question-answering technique outlined in the next section of this introduction.

3. **If you are using the Gleim book, do not consult the answer or answer explanations on the right side of the page until after you have chosen and written down an answer.**

    a.   It is crucial that you cover the answer explanations and intellectually commit yourself to an answer. This method will help you understand the concept much better, even if you answered the question incorrectly. Our EQE Test Prep prevents you from consulting the answer, which allows you to study in an exam-like environment.

4. Study the explanations to the correct and incorrect answer choices for each question you answered incorrectly. In addition to learning and understanding the concept tested, analyze **why** you missed the question. Reasons for missing questions include

    - Misreading the requirement (stem)
    - Not understanding what is required
    - Making a math error
    - Applying the wrong rule or concept
    - Being distracted by one or more of the answers
    - Incorrectly eliminating answers from consideration
    - Not having any knowledge of the topic tested
    - Employing bad intuition when guessing

    Studying the important concepts that we provide in our answer explanations will help you understand the principles to the point that you can answer that question (or any other like it) successfully.

5. Identify your weaknesses in answering multiple-choice questions and take corrective action (before you take a test). The EQE Test Prep provides a detailed performance analysis.

    The analysis will show your weaknesses (areas needing more study) and also your strengths (areas of confidence). You can improve your performance on multiple-choice questions both by increasing your percentage of correct answers and by decreasing the time spent per question.

Multiple-Choice Question-Answering Technique

The following series of steps is suggested for answering multiple-choice questions. The important point is that you need to devote attention to and develop **the technique that works for you**. Personalize and practice your answering technique on questions in this study guide. Begin now to develop **your** control system.

1. **Budget your time.**

    a.   We make this point with emphasis – **finish your exam before time expires**.
    b.   Calculate the time allowed for each multiple-choice question after you have allocated time to the other questions (e.g., essays) on the exam. If 20 multiple-choice questions are allocated 40 minutes on your exam, you should spend a little under 2 minutes per question (always budget extra time for transferring answers to answer sheets, interruptions, etc.).
    c.   Before beginning a series of multiple-choice questions, write the starting time on the exam near the first question.
    d.   As you work through the questions, check your time. Assuming a time allocation of 120 minutes for 60 questions, you are fine if you worked 5 questions in 9 minutes. If you spent 11 minutes on 5 questions, you need to speed up. Remember that your goal is to answer all questions and achieve the maximum score possible.

2. **Answer the items in consecutive order.**

    a.   Do **not** agonize over any one item. Stay within your time budget.
    b.   Mark any questions you are unsure of and return to them later as time allows.
    c.   Never leave a question unanswered **if** you will not be penalized for incorrect answers. Make your best guess in the time allowed.

3. **For each multiple-choice question,**

   a. **Ignore the answer choices.** Do not allow the answer choices to affect your reading of the question.

      1) If four answer choices are presented, three of them are incorrect. These incorrect choices are called **distractors** for good reason. Often, distractors are written to appear correct at first glance.

      2) In computational items, distractors are carefully calculated so they are the result of common mistakes. Be careful and double-check your computations if time permits.

   b. **Read the question carefully** to determine the precise requirement.

      1) Focusing on what is required enables you to ignore extraneous information and to proceed directly to determining the correct answer.

         a) Be especially careful to note when the requirement is an **exception**; e.g., "Which of the following payments is **not** an investing cash flow?"

   c. **Determine the correct answer** before looking at the answer choices.

   d. **Read the answer choices carefully.**

      1) Even if the first answer appears to be the correct choice, do **not** skip the remaining answer choices. Questions often ask for the "best" choice provided. Thus, each choice requires your consideration.

      2) Treat each answer choice as a true/false question as you analyze it.

   e. **Select the best answer.**

      1) If you are uncertain, guess intelligently (see "If You Don't Know the Answer" below). Improve on your 25% chance of getting the correct answer with blind guessing.

      2) For many multiple-choice questions, two answer choices can be eliminated with minimal effort, thereby increasing your educated guess to a 50-50 proposition.

4. **Transfer your answers to the answer sheet**, if one is provided.

   a. Make sure you are within your time budget so you will be able to perform this vital step in an unhurried manner.

   b. Do not wait to transfer answers until the very end of the exam session because you may run out of time.

   c. Double-check that you have transferred the answers correctly; e.g., recheck every 5th or 10th answer from your test paper to your answer sheet to ensure that you have not fallen out of sequence.

If You Don't Know the Answer

If the exam you are taking does not penalize incorrect answers, you should make an educated guess. First, rule out answers that you think are incorrect. Second, speculate on what the examiner is looking for and/or the rationale behind the question. Third, select the best answer or guess between equally appealing answers. Mark the question with a "?" in case you have time to return to it for further analysis.

If you cannot make an educated guess, read the stem and each answer, and pick the best or most intuitive answer. It's just a guess! Do **not** look at the previous answer to try to detect an answer. Answers are usually random, and it is possible to have four or more consecutive questions with the same answer letter, e.g., answer (B).

NOTE: Do not waste time beyond the amount you budgeted for each question. Move forward and stay on or ahead of schedule.

Examination Summary

	CPA (Certified Public Accountant)	CIA (Certified Internal Auditor)*	CMA (Certified Management Accountant)	EA (IRS Enrolled Agent)
Sponsoring Organization	American Institute of Certified Public Accountants	Institute of Internal Auditors	Institute of Certified Management Accountants	Internal Revenue Service
Contact Information	www.aicpa.org (888) 777-7077	www.theiia.org (407) 937-1111	www.imanet.org (800) 638-4427	www.irs.gov (313) 234-1280
Exam Parts	Auditing and Attestation (4 hrs.) / Business Environment and Concepts (4 hrs.) / Financial Accounting and Reporting (4 hrs.) / Regulation (4 hrs.)	1 – Essentials of Internal Auditing (2.5 hrs.) / 2 – Practice of Internal Auditing (2 hrs.) / 3 – Business Knowledge for Internal Auditing (2 hrs.)	1 – Financial Reporting, Planning, Performance, and Control (4 hrs.) / 2 – Financial Decision Making (4 hrs.)	1 – Individuals (3.5 hrs.) / 2 – Businesses (3.5 hrs.) / 3 – Representation, Practices, and Procedures (3.5 hrs.)
Exam Format	AUD: 72 multiple-choice questions 8 TBS / BEC: 62 multiple-choice questions 4 TBS 3 written communications / FAR: 66 multiple-choice questions 8 TBS / REG: 76 multiple-choice questions 8 TBS	Part 1: 125 multiple-choice questions / Parts 2 and 3: 100 multiple-choice questions	Parts 1 and 2: 100 multiple-choice questions 2 essays	Parts 1, 2, and 3: 100 multiple-choice questions
Avg. Pass Rate	AUD – 49% / BEC – 53% / FAR – 44% / REG – 47%	Pass rates are not yet available for the reorganized exam.	1 – 40% / 2 – 50%	1 – 61% / 2 – 64% / 3 – 86%
Testing Windows	January-March 10 / April-June 10 / July-September 10 / October-December 10	On demand throughout the year	January-February / May-June / September-October	May-February (e.g., 5/01/2018-2/28/2019)
Resources	gleimcpa.com	gleimcia.com	gleimcma.com	gleimea.com
Available Prep Course Student Discounts	Up to 20%	Up to 20%	Up to 20%	Up to 10%

*Reflects the information for the reorganized 2019 exam.

ACCOUNTING CERTIFICATION PROGRAMS--OVERVIEW

The CPA (Certified Public Accountant) exam is the grandparent of all professional accounting exams. Its origin was in the 1896 public accounting legislation of New York. In 1917, the American Institute of CPAs (AICPA) began to prepare and grade a uniform CPA exam. It is currently used to measure the technical competence of those applying to be licensed as CPAs in all 50 states, Guam, Puerto Rico, the Virgin Islands, the District of Columbia, the Commonwealth of the Northern Mariana Islands, and an ever-expanding list of international locations.

The CIA (Certified Internal Auditor), CMA (Certified Management Accountant), and EA (IRS Enrolled Agent) exams are relatively new certification programs compared to the CPA. The CMA exam was first administered in 1972 and the first CIA exam in 1974. The EA exam dates back to 1959. Why were these other exams initially created? Generally, the requirements of the CPA designation instituted by the boards of accountancy (especially the necessity for public accounting experience) led to the development of the CIA and CMA programs, which allow for professionals to show proficiency in specific job functions. The EA designation is available for persons specializing in tax.

The table of selected CPA, CIA, CMA, and EA exam data on the preceding page provides an overview of these accounting exams.

ACCOUNTING CERTIFICATION PROGRAMS--PURPOSE

The primary purpose of professional exams is to measure the technical competence of candidates. Competence includes technical knowledge, the ability to apply such knowledge with good judgment, comprehension of professional responsibility, and ethical considerations. Additionally, the nature of these exams (low pass rate, broad and rigorous coverage, etc.) has several very important effects:

1. Candidates are forced to learn all of the material that should have been presented and learned in a good accounting education program.

2. Relatedly, candidates must integrate the topics and concepts that are presented in individual courses in accounting education programs.

3. The content of each exam provides direction to accounting education programs; i.e., what is tested on the exams will be taught to accounting students.

Certification is important to professional accountants because it provides

1. Participation in a recognized professional group
2. An improved professional training program arising out of the certification program
3. Recognition among peers for attaining the professional designation
4. An extra credential to enhance career opportunities
5. The personal satisfaction of attaining a recognized degree of competency

These reasons hold true in the accounting field due to wide recognition of the CPA designation. Accountants and accounting students are often asked whether they are CPAs when people learn they are accountants. Thus, there is considerable pressure for accountants to become **certified.**

A newer development is multiple certifications, which are important for the same reasons as initial certification. Accounting students and recent graduates should look ahead and obtain multiple certifications to broaden their career opportunities.

The CIA and CMA are now globally recognized certifications, making them appealing designations for multi-national companies.

When to Sit for the Certification Exams

Sit for all exams as soon as you can. Candidates are allowed to sit for the exam and then complete the requirements within a certain time period. The CIA program allows full-time students in their senior year to sit for the exam, and the CMA program offers a 7-year window for submission of educational credentials. The CIA and CMA exams are offered at a reduced fee for students. The requirements for the CPA vary by jurisdiction, but many state boards allow candidates to sit for the exam before they have completed the required hours. However, you will not be certified until you have met all requirements.

Register to take the parts of each exam that best match up to the courses you are currently taking. For example, if you are taking a Business Law course and a Federal Tax course this semester, schedule your CPA Regulation date for the week after classes end.

Dual certification can greatly enhance your career. Visit www.gleim.com/cmablog to find out why the CPA and CMA is an especially beneficial combination and to learn the steps on how to achieve dual certification.

Steps to Passing Certification Exams

1   Become knowledgeable about the exam you will be taking, and determine which part you will take first.

2   Purchase the complete Gleim Review System to thoroughly prepare yourself. Commit to systematic preparation for the exam as described in our review materials.

3   Communicate with your Personal Counselor to design a study plan that meets your needs. Call (800) 874-5346 or email personalcounselor@gleim.com.

4   Apply for membership in the exam's governing body and/or in the certification program as required.

5   Register online to take the desired part of the exam.

6   Schedule your test with the testing center in the location of your choice.

7   Work systematically through each study unit in the Gleim Review System.

8   Sit for and PASS the exam. Gleim guarantees success!

9   Email or call Gleim with your comments on our study materials and how well they prepared you for the exam.

10 Enjoy your career, pursue multiple certifications (CPA, CIA, CMA, EA, etc.), and recommend Gleim to others who are also taking these exams. Stay up-to-date on your Continuing Professional Education requirements with Gleim CPE.

CITATIONS TO AUTHORITATIVE PRONOUNCEMENTS

Throughout the book and software, we refer to certain authoritative accounting pronouncements by the following abbreviations:

ASC – The FASB's Accounting Standards Codification is "the single source of authoritative nongovernmental U.S. generally accepted accounting principles." The Codification organizes the many pronouncements that constitute U.S. GAAP into a consistent, searchable format accessible through the Internet.

GAAP – The sources of authoritative U.S. generally accepted accounting principles (GAAP) recognized by the FASB as applicable by nongovernmental entities are (1) the FASB's Accounting Standards Codification™ and (2) (for SEC registrants only) pronouncements of the SEC. All guidance in the codification is equally authoritative. SEC pronouncements must be followed by registrants regardless of whether they are reflected in the codification.

GASBS – The Governmental Accounting Standards Board issues Statements of Governmental Accounting Standards and other pronouncements. They apply to state and local governments.

IFRS and IASs – International Financial Reporting Standards (IFRS) are issued by the current standard-setter, the International Accounting Standards Board (IASB). International Accounting Standards (IASs), related Interpretations, and the framework for the preparation and presentation of financial statements were issued by the predecessor entity. IFRS also is the collective term for IFRS and IASs.

SEC – The Securities and Exchange Commission (SEC) was created by the Securities Exchange Act of 1934 to regulate the trading of securities and otherwise to enforce securities legislation. The basic purposes of the securities laws are to prevent fraud and misrepresentation and to require full and fair disclosure so investors can evaluate investments.

SFAC – FASB Statements of Financial Accounting Concepts establish financial accounting and reporting objectives and concepts. SFACs are other accounting literature. They are considered only in the absence of applicable authoritative guidance (the FASB Accounting Standards Codification™ or SEC pronouncements). They are used by the FASB to develop its authoritative pronouncements.

STUDY UNIT ONE
THE FINANCIAL REPORTING ENVIRONMENT

The first major subject area in this study unit is the **conceptual framework** that underlies financial accounting and reporting in accordance with U.S. generally accepted accounting principles **(GAAP)** issued by the Financial Accounting Standards Board **(FASB)**. The components of the FASB's conceptual framework are summarized in the following table:

Objective of Financial Reporting
Provide information • Useful in investment and credit decisions • Useful in assessing cash-flow prospects • About entity resources, claims to those resources, and changes in them

Qualitative Characteristics	**Elements of Financial Statements**

Fundamental
 Relevance
  Materiality (entity specific)
  Predictive or confirmatory value
 Faithful representation
  Completeness
  Freedom from error
  Neutrality
Enhancing
 Comparability
 Verifiability
 Timeliness
 Understandability
Cost constraint
	Assets
	Liabilities
	Equity or net assets
	Investments by owners
	Distributions to owners
	Comprehensive income
	Revenues
	Expenses
	Gains
	Losses

Recognition and Measurement Concepts	
Financial statements	Expense recognition
Revenue recognition	Measurement attributes
Cash flows and present value (SU 4)	

Assumptions	**Principles**	**Constraints**
Economic entity	Historical cost	Industry practice
Going concern	Revenue recognition	Conservatism
Monetary unit	Expense recognition	
Periodicity	Full disclosure	

The second major subject area addresses standard setting by the FASB (U.S. GAAP) and the International Accounting Standards Board (IASB). The IASB issues International Financial Reporting Standards **(IFRS)**. Other important topics included in this study unit are SEC reporting, the framework for measurement of fair value, and first time adoption of IFRS.

QUESTIONS

1.1 Introduction to the Conceptual Framework

1.1.1. What are the *Statements of Financial Accounting Concepts* intended to establish?

A. Generally accepted accounting principles in financial reporting by business enterprises.

B. The meaning of "present fairly in accordance with generally accepted accounting principles."

C. The objectives and concepts for use in developing standards of financial accounting and reporting.

D. The hierarchy of sources of generally accepted accounting principles.

Answer (C) is correct. *(CPA, adapted)*

DISCUSSION: SFACs do not establish accounting and reporting requirements. They are nonauthoritative guidance for nongovernmental entities. SFACs describe the objectives, qualitative characteristics, elements, and other fundamental concepts that guide the FASB in developing sound accounting principles.

Answer (A) is incorrect. SFACs are intended to guide the development of accounting standards by the FASB. Answer (B) is incorrect. This language is from a Statement on Auditing Standards. Answer (D) is incorrect. The ASC contains the only authoritative guidance issued by the FASB.

1.1.2. During the lifetime of an entity, accountants produce financial statements at arbitrary moments in time in accordance with which basic accounting concept?

A. Verifiability.

B. Periodicity.

C. Conservatism.

D. Matching.

Answer (B) is correct. *(CPA, adapted)*

REQUIRED: The basic accounting concept requiring financial statements to be issued at arbitrary moments in time.

DISCUSSION: A basic feature of the financial accounting process is that information about the economic activities of the business should be issued at regular intervals. These time periods should be of equal length to facilitate comparability. They also should be of relatively short duration, e.g., 1 year, to provide business information useful for decision making.

Answer (A) is incorrect. Information is verifiable if knowledgeable and independent observers can reach a consensus that it is faithfully represented. Answer (C) is incorrect. Under the conservatism constraint, when alternative accounting methods are appropriate, the one having the less favorable effect on net income and total assets is preferable. However, conservatism does not permit a deliberate understatement of total assets and net income. Furthermore, SFAC 5 describes "a general tendency to emphasize purchase and sale transactions and to apply conservative procedures in accounting recognition." This tendency is a response to uncertainty. Answer (D) is incorrect. Matching (another term for associating cause and effect) requires costs to be recognized as expenses on the basis of their direct association with specific revenues to the extent possible.

1.1.3. Continuation of an accounting entity in the absence of evidence to the contrary is an example of the basic concept of

A. Accounting entity.

B. Consistency.

C. Going concern.

D. Substance over form.

Answer (C) is correct. *(CPA, adapted)*

REQUIRED: The concept related to continuation of a business entity.

DISCUSSION: A basic feature of financial accounting is that a business is assumed to be a going concern in the absence of evidence to the contrary. The going-concern concept is based on the empirical observation that many entities have an indefinite life.

Answer (A) is incorrect. The accounting entity (economic or reporting) is the business entity, which may or may not be synonymous with the legal entity. The emphasis is on the separation of the entity from its ownership. Answer (B) is incorrect. Consistency is a means of achieving the enhancing qualitative characteristic of comparability. Answer (D) is incorrect. Substance over form was specifically excluded from the conceptual framework as a vague and redundant idea. The fundamental qualitative characteristic of faithful representation does not permit subordinating substance to form.

1.1.4. Reporting LIFO inventory at the lower of cost or market (LCM) is a departure from the accounting principle of

A. Historical cost.

B. Consistency.

C. Conservatism.

D. Full disclosure.

Answer (A) is correct. *(CPA, adapted)*
    REQUIRED: The principle not followed when reporting LIFO inventory at the lower of cost or market.
    DISCUSSION: Historical cost is the amount of cash, or its equivalent, paid to acquire an asset. Thus, the LCM rule departs from the historical cost principle when the utility of the inventory is judged no longer to be as great as its cost.
    Answer (B) is incorrect. Consistency is a means of achieving the enhancing qualitative characteristic of comparability. Consistent application of LCM to appropriate items is not a departure from an accounting principle. Answer (C) is incorrect. LCM yields a conservative inventory measurement. Answer (D) is incorrect. If the basis of stating inventories is disclosed, LCM does not violate the full disclosure principle.

1.2 Objective of Financial Reporting (SFAC 8)

1.2.1. According to the FASB's conceptual framework, the objective of general-purpose financial reporting is most likely based on

A. Generally accepted accounting principles.

B. Reporting on how well management has discharged its responsibilities.

C. The need for conservatism.

D. The needs of the users of the information.

Answer (D) is correct. *(CPA, adapted)*
    REQUIRED: The objectives of financial reporting for business enterprises.
    DISCUSSION: The objective of general-purpose financial reporting is to provide information that is useful to existing and potential investors, lenders, and other creditors in making decisions about providing resources to the entity.
    Answer (A) is incorrect. GAAP govern how to account for items in the financial statements. Answer (B) is incorrect. Financial reporting provides information that is helpful in evaluating management's performance. But entity performance is affected by many factors other than management. Answer (C) is incorrect. Conservatism is a constraint on recognition in the statements.

1.2.2. Which of the following best reflects the objective of general-purpose financial reporting?

A. The primary focus of financial reporting is information about an entity's resources.

B. The best indication of an entity's ability to generate favorable cash flows is information based on previous cash flows.

C. Financial accounting is expressly designed to accurately measure the value of a business.

D. Investment and credit decisions often are based, at least in part, on evaluations of the past performance of an entity.

Answer (D) is correct. *(Publisher, adapted)*
    REQUIRED: The true statement about the objective of general-purpose financial reporting.
    DISCUSSION: Although investment and credit decisions reflect investors' and creditors' expectations about future performance, those expectations are commonly based, at least in part, on evaluations of past performance. Information about financial performance helps users to understand the return on the entity's economic resources and how well management has discharged its responsibilities.
    Answer (A) is incorrect. General-purpose financial reporting provides information about (1) the entity's economic resources and claims to them (financial position) and (2) changes in those resources and claims. Answer (B) is incorrect. Accrual accounting is preferable to cash basis accounting for predicting future performance. Answer (C) is incorrect. General-purpose financial reports do not suffice to measure the value of the entity. But the information provided may be helpful to those who wish to estimate its value.

1.2.3. Which of the following is a true statement about the objective of general-purpose financial reporting?

A. Financial reporting is ordinarily focused on industries rather than individual entities.

B. The objective applies only to information that is useful for investment professionals.

C. Financial reporting directly measures management performance.

D. The information provided relates to the entity's economic resources and claims.

Answer (D) is correct. *(Publisher, adapted)*
    REQUIRED: The true statement about the objective of general-purpose financial reporting.
    DISCUSSION: The information reported relates to the entity's economic resources and claims to them (financial position) and to changes in those resources and claims.
    Answer (A) is incorrect. Financial reporting is focused on individual entities. Answer (B) is incorrect. The objectives apply to information that is useful for current and potential investors, creditors, and other users in making rational investment, credit, and other decisions. Answer (C) is incorrect. Entity performance is affected by many factors other than management.

1.2.4. Which of the following is least likely to be accomplished by providing general-purpose financial information useful for making decisions about providing resources to an entity?

    A. To provide information about changes in an entity's economic resources and claims to them.

    B. To provide information to help investors and creditors assess the amount, timing, and uncertainty of prospective net cash inflows to the entity.

    C. To provide sufficient information to determine the value of the entity.

    D. To provide information about management's performance.

Answer (C) is correct. *(Publisher, adapted)*
    REQUIRED: The least likely benefit of general-purpose financial information.
    DISCUSSION: General-purpose financial reports are significantly based on estimates and do not suffice to determine the value of the entity.
    Answer (A) is incorrect. General-purpose financial reports include information useful for differentiating between changes in economic resources and claims to them resulting from (1) the entity's performance and (2) other events and transactions. Answer (B) is incorrect. General-purpose financial reports include information to help investors and creditors assess cash flows. Answer (D) is incorrect. General-purpose financial reports include information useful for evaluating management's performance.

1.2.5. Determining periodic earnings and financial position depends on measuring economic resources and obligations and changes in them as these changes occur. This explanation pertains to

    A. Disclosure.

    B. Accrual accounting.

    C. Materiality.

    D. The matching concept.

Answer (B) is correct. *(CPA, adapted)*
    REQUIRED: The accounting concept described.
    DISCUSSION: A basic feature of financial accounting is that it is an accrual system. The determination of periodic earnings and financial position depends on measuring all economic resources and obligations (e.g., receivables and payables) and changes in them as the changes occur.
    Answer (A) is incorrect. Disclosure pertains to the requirement that the user of financial statements be provided with sufficient information to avoid being misled. Answer (C) is incorrect. Accounting data are material if their omission or misstatement can influence user decisions. Answer (D) is incorrect. The matching concept associates cause and effect, that is, costs with revenues.

1.3 Qualitative Characteristics (SFAC 8)

1.3.1. According to the FASB's conceptual framework, the two fundamental qualitative characteristics that make accounting information useful for decision making are

    A. Neutrality and completeness.

    B. Fairness and precision.

    C. Relevance and faithful representation.

    D. Consistency and comparability.

Answer (C) is correct. *(Publisher, adapted)*
    REQUIRED: The two fundamental qualitative characteristics of accounting information.
    DISCUSSION: Relevance and faithful representation are the fundamental qualities that make accounting information useful for decision making. Relevance is the capacity of information to make a difference in the user's decision. A representation is perfectly faithful if it is complete, neutral, and free from error.
    Answer (A) is incorrect. Neutrality and completeness are aspects of faithful representation. Answer (B) is incorrect. Accounting information should be fairly presented, but precision (perfect accuracy) is not always possible when estimates are necessary. Answer (D) is incorrect. Comparability is a qualitative characteristic that enhances the usefulness of relevant and faithfully represented information. Consistency helps achieve comparability.

1.3.2. According to the FASB's conceptual framework, neutrality relates to

	Faithful Representation	Relevance
A.	Yes	Yes
B.	Yes	No
C.	No	Yes
D.	No	No

Answer (B) is correct. *(CPA, adapted)*
    REQUIRED: The quality to which neutrality relates.
    DISCUSSION: A representation is perfectly faithful if it is (1) complete (containing what is needed for user understanding), (2) neutral (unbiased in its selection or presentation), and (3) free from error (but not necessarily perfectly accurate). Relevant information is able to make a difference in user decisions. To do so, it must have predictive value, confirmatory value, or both.

1.3.3. According to the FASB conceptual framework, which of the following correctly pairs a fundamental qualitative characteristic of useful financial information with one of its aspects?

A. Relevance and materiality.

B. Relevance and neutrality.

C. Faithful representation and predictive value.

D. Faithful representation and confirmatory value.

Answer (A) is correct. *(CPA, adapted)*
REQUIRED: The pairing of a fundamental qualitative characteristic and one of its aspects.
DISCUSSION: Relevance is a fundamental qualitative characteristic, and materiality is an entity-specific aspect of relevance. Relevant information is able to make a difference in user decisions. To do so, it must have predictive value, confirmatory value, or both. Information is material if its omission or misstatement can influence user decisions based on a specific entity's financial information.
Answer (B) is incorrect. Relevance and faithful representation are the fundamental qualitative characteristics. A representation is perfectly faithful if it is complete, neutral, and free from error. Answer (C) is incorrect. Relevant information has predictive value, confirmatory value, or both. Answer (D) is incorrect. Relevant information has predictive value, confirmatory value, or both.

1.3.4. Which of the following is considered a pervasive constraint by the FASB's conceptual framework?

A. Cost.

B. Conservatism.

C. Timeliness.

D. Verifiability.

Answer (A) is correct. *(CPA, adapted)*
REQUIRED: The accounting quality that is a pervasive constraint.
DISCUSSION: Cost is a pervasive constraint on the information provided by financial reporting. The benefits of financial information should exceed the costs of reporting.
Answer (B) is incorrect. Under the conservatism constraint, when alternative accounting methods are appropriate, the one having the less favorable effect on net income and total assets is preferable. However, conservatism does not permit a deliberate understatement of total assets and net income. Furthermore, SFAC 5 describes "a general tendency to emphasize purchase and sale transactions and to apply conservative procedures in accounting recognition." This tendency is a response to uncertainty. Answer (C) is incorrect. Timeliness is an enhancing qualitative characteristic. Answer (D) is incorrect. Verifiability is an enhancing qualitative characteristic.

1.3.5. According to *Statements of Financial Accounting Concepts*, predictive value relates to

	Relevance	Faithful Representation
A.	No	No
B.	Yes	Yes
C.	No	Yes
D.	Yes	No

Answer (D) is correct. *(CPA, adapted)*
REQUIRED: The qualitative characteristic to which predictive value relates.
DISCUSSION: Relevance is a fundamental qualitative characteristic of useful financial information. It is the capacity of information to make a difference in a decision. It must have (1) predictive value, (2) confirmatory value, or both. Moreover, materiality is an entity-specific aspect of relevance. Something has predictive value if it can be used in a predictive process. Something has confirmatory value with respect to prior evaluations if it provides feedback that confirms or changes (corrects) them.

1.3.6. According to the FASB's conceptual framework, what does the concept of faithful representation in financial reporting include?

A. Predictive value.

B. Certainty.

C. Perfect accuracy.

D. Neutrality.

Answer (D) is correct. *(CPA, adapted)*
REQUIRED: The item included in the concept of faithful representation.
DISCUSSION: Faithful representation and relevance are the fundamental qualitative characteristics of accounting information. A perfectly faithful representation is complete, neutral, and free from error. Faithfully represented information is neutral if it is unbiased in its selection or presentation of information.
Answer (A) is incorrect. Relevant information has predictive value, confirmatory value, or both. Faithfully represented information is not necessarily relevant. Answer (B) is incorrect. Certainty and perfect accuracy are not implied by faithful representation. The financial statements are a model of the reporting entity. This model may be representationally faithful for its intended purposes without corresponding precisely to the real-world original. Thus, immaterial uncertainty does not impair faithful representation. Answer (C) is incorrect. Faithful representation includes the concept of perfect faithfulness, not perfect accuracy.

1.3.7. According to the FASB's conceptual framework, the usefulness of providing information in financial statements is subject to the constraint of

A. Consistency.

B. Cost.

C. Relevance.

D. Representational faithfulness.

Answer (B) is correct. *(CPA, adapted)*
REQUIRED: The constraint on financial reporting.
DISCUSSION: Cost is a pervasive constraint on the information provided by financial reporting. The benefits of financial information should exceed the costs of reporting.
    Answer (A) is incorrect. Consistency is a means of achieving comparability, an enhancing qualitative characteristic. It is the use of the same methods, for example, accounting principles, for the same items. Answer (C) is incorrect. Relevance is a fundamental qualitative characteristic of useful information, not a constraint. Answer (D) is incorrect. Faithful representation is a fundamental qualitative characteristic of useful information, not a constraint.

1.3.8. According to the FASB's conceptual framework, which of the following most likely does not violate the concept of faithful representation?

A. Financial statements were issued 9 months late.

B. Report data on segments having the same expected risks and growth rates to analysts estimating future profits.

C. Financial statements included property with a carrying amount increased to management's estimate of market value.

D. Management reports to shareholders regularly refer to new projects undertaken, but the financial statements never report project results.

Answer (B) is correct. *(CPA, adapted)*
REQUIRED: The item that does not violate the concept of faithful representation.
DISCUSSION: A representation is perfectly faithful if it is (1) complete (containing what is needed for user understanding), (2) neutral (unbiased in its selection or presentation), and (3) free from error. The faithful representation of any given information is logically unrelated to whether the segments have the same expected risks and growth rates (assuming freedom from error) or the identity of the users.
    Answer (A) is incorrect. Late issuance is a matter of timeliness. Timeliness is a qualitative characteristic that enhances relevance and faithful representation. Information is timely when it is available in time to influence decisions. Answer (C) is incorrect. Management's estimate of market value may not be verifiable. Verifiability is a qualitative characteristic that enhances relevance and faithful representation. Information is verifiable (directly or indirectly) if knowledgeable and independent observers can reach a consensus (not necessarily unanimity) that it is faithfully represented. Answer (D) is incorrect. Failure to report results is a matter of timeliness. Timeliness is a qualitative characteristic that enhances relevance and faithful representation. Information is timely when it is available in time to influence decisions.

1.3.9. Under SFAC 8, the ability, through consensus among measurers, to ensure that information represents what it purports to represent is an example of the concept of

A. Relevance.

B. Verifiability.

C. Comparability.

D. Predictive value.

Answer (B) is correct. *(CPA, adapted)*
REQUIRED: The ability to ensure that information represents what it purports to represent.
DISCUSSION: Verifiability is a qualitative characteristic that enhances relevance and faithful representation. Information is verifiable (directly or indirectly) if knowledgeable and independent observers can reach a consensus (not necessarily unanimity) that it is faithfully represented.
    Answer (A) is incorrect. Relevance (a fundamental qualitative characteristic) is the capacity of information to make a difference in a decision. Answer (C) is incorrect. Comparability (an enhancing qualitative characteristic) is the quality of information that enables users to identify similarities and differences among items. Answer (D) is incorrect. Relevant information is able to make a difference in user decisions. To do so, it must have predictive value, confirmatory value, or both. Something has predictive value if it can be used as an input in a predictive process.

1.3.10. According to the FASB's conceptual framework, which of the following enhances information that is relevant and faithfully represented?

A. Comparability.

B. Confirmatory value.

C. Neutrality.

D. Materiality.

Answer (A) is correct. *(CPA, adapted)*
REQUIRED: The item that enhances information that is relevant and faithfully represented.
DISCUSSION: Comparability is a qualitative characteristic that enhances the usefulness of relevant and faithfully represented information. It enables users to identify similarities in and differences among items.
Answer (B) is incorrect. Relevance is a fundamental qualitative characteristic. Relevant information is able to make a difference in user decisions. To do so, it must have predictive value, confirmatory value, or both. Something has confirmatory value with respect to prior evaluations if it provides feedback that confirms or changes (corrects) them. Answer (C) is incorrect. Faithful representation is a fundamental qualitative characteristic. A perfectly faithful representation is complete, neutral, and free from error. Faithfully represented information is neutral if it is unbiased in its selection or presentation of information. Answer (D) is incorrect. Information is material if its omission or misstatement can influence user decisions based on a specific entity's financial information. Thus, it is an entity-specific aspect of relevance.

1.3.11. Which of the following accounting concepts states that an accounting transaction should be supported by sufficient evidence to allow two or more qualified individuals to arrive at essentially similar measures and conclusions?

A. Matching.

B. Verifiability.

C. Periodicity.

D. Stable monetary unit.

Answer (B) is correct. *(CPA, adapted)*
REQUIRED: The accounting concept described.
DISCUSSION: Verifiability is a qualitative characteristic that enhances relevance and faithful representation. Information is verifiable (directly or indirectly) if knowledgeable and independent observers can reach a consensus (but not necessarily unanimity) that it is faithfully represented.
Answer (A) is incorrect. Matching associates cause and effect, for example, recognition in the same period of revenues and the expenses incurred to produce them. Answer (C) is incorrect. Periodicity is the assumption that accounting information is reported at regular intervals to provide comparability and at relatively short intervals to provide useful information. Answer (D) is incorrect. The stable monetary unit assumption is that the purchasing power of the unit of measure (e.g., the U.S. dollar) does not fluctuate.

1.3.12. Financial information is most likely to be verifiable when an accounting transaction occurs that

A. Involves an arm's-length transaction between two independent parties.

B. Furthers the objectives of the entity.

C. Is promptly recorded in a fixed amount of monetary units.

D. Allocates revenues or expense items in a rational and systematic manner.

Answer (A) is correct. *(CPA, adapted)*
REQUIRED: The accounting transaction that most likely is verifiable.
DISCUSSION: Verifiability is an enhancing qualitative characteristic of relevant and faithfully represented financial information. Information is verifiable (directly or indirectly) if knowledgeable and independent observers can reach a consensus (but not necessarily unanimity) that it is faithfully represented. The existence of an arm's-length transaction between independent interests suggests that the transaction is verifiable.
Answer (B) is incorrect. Verifiability enhances relevant and faithfully represented accounting measures, not the objectives of any entity. Answer (C) is incorrect. Recording at a fixed amount of monetary units does not ensure that the measurement is faithfully represented. Answer (D) is incorrect. Rational and systematic allocation is a specific means of expense recognition. Systematic and rational allocation of expenses is undertaken when a direct means of associating cause and effect (expense and revenue) is lacking.

1.3.13. The concept of consistency is sacrificed in the accounting for which of the following income statement items?

A. Discontinued operations.

B. Loss on disposal of a component of an entity.

C. Gain from bargain purchase.

D. Change in accounting principle when the cumulative effect on any prior period is not known.

Answer (D) is correct. *(CPA, adapted)*
REQUIRED: The income statement item that sacrifices consistency.
DISCUSSION: Changes in accounting principles ordinarily are accounted for by retrospective application. However, if it is impracticable to determine the cumulative effect of applying the change to any prior period, the change is applied prospectively. Thus, similar events are not accounted for in the same way in succeeding accounting periods.
Answer (A) is incorrect. Principles may be consistently observed in the current period in relation to the preceding period even though operations have been discontinued. Substantially different transactions or events do not result in lack of consistency. Answer (B) is incorrect. Principles may be consistently observed in the current period in relation to the preceding period even though a component of an entity has been disposed of. Substantially different transactions or events do not result in lack of consistency. Answer (C) is incorrect. Principles may be consistently observed in the current period in relation to the preceding period even though a gain on a bargain purchase has been recognized on the business combination date. Substantially different transactions or events do not result in lack of consistency.

1.3.14. According to the FASB's conceptual framework, the quality of information that enables users to identify similarities in and differences between two sets of economic phenomena is

A. Conservatism.

B. Neutrality.

C. Matching.

D. Comparability.

Answer (D) is correct. *(Publisher, adapted)*
REQUIRED: The quality of information that enables users to identify similarities in, and differences between, two sets of economic phenomena.
DISCUSSION: Comparability is an enhancing qualitative characteristic. Information should be comparable with similar information for (1) other entities and (2) the same entity for another period or date. Thus, comparability allows users to understand similarities and differences.
Answer (A) is incorrect. Under the conservatism constraint, when alternative accounting methods are appropriate, the one having the less favorable effect on net income and total assets is preferable. However, conservatism does not permit a deliberate understatement of total assets and net income. Furthermore, SFAC 5 describes "a general tendency to emphasize purchase and sale transactions and to apply conservative procedures in accounting recognition." Answer (B) is incorrect. Useful information faithfully represents economic events. A representation is perfectly faithful if it is (1) complete (containing what is needed for user understanding), (2) neutral (unbiased in its selection or presentation), and (3) free from error (but not necessarily perfectly accurate). Answer (C) is incorrect. Matching associates cause and effect, for example, recognition in the same period of revenues and the expenses incurred to produce them.

1.3.15. According to the FASB's conceptual framework, the quality of information that helps users increase the likelihood of correctly forecasting the outcome of past or present events is called

A. Confirmatory value.

B. Predictive value.

C. Representational faithfulness.

D. Comparability.

Answer (B) is correct. *(CPA, adapted)*
REQUIRED: The quality of information that helps increase the likelihood of correct forecasts.
DISCUSSION: Relevant information is able to make a difference in user decisions. To do so, it must have predictive value, confirmatory value, or both. Financial information has predictive value if it can be used as an input in a predictive process.
Answer (A) is incorrect. Relevant information must have predictive value, confirmatory value, or both. Something has confirmatory value with respect to prior evaluations if it provides feedback that confirms or changes (corrects) them. Answer (C) is incorrect. Faithful representation is a fundamental qualitative characteristic. A perfectly faithful representation is complete, neutral, and free from error. Answer (D) is incorrect. Comparability is an enhancing qualitative characteristic. Information should be comparable with similar information for (1) other entities and (2) the same entity for another period or date. Thus, comparability allows users to understand similarities and differences.

1.3.16. To be relevant, financial information should have which of the following?

  A. Neutrality.

  B. Confirmatory value.

  C. Understandability.

  D. Costs and benefits.

Answer (B) is correct. *(CPA, adapted)*
  REQUIRED: The characteristic of relevance.
  DISCUSSION: Relevance is a fundamental qualitative characteristic. Relevant information is able to make a difference in user decisions. To do so, it must have predictive value, confirmatory value, or both. Something has confirmatory value with respect to prior evaluations if it provides feedback that confirms or changes (corrects) them.
  Answer (A) is incorrect. Neutrality is an aspect of faithful representation. Answer (C) is incorrect. Understandability is an enhancing qualitative characteristic. Understandable information is clearly and concisely classified, characterized, and presented. Information should be readily understandable by reasonably knowledgeable and diligent users, but information should not be excluded because of its complexity. Answer (D) is incorrect. Cost is the pervasive constraint in the hierarchy of accounting qualities.

1.3.17. Which of the following characteristics relates to both accounting relevance and faithful representation?

  A. Verifiability.

  B. Timeliness.

  C. Comparability.

  D. All of the answers are correct.

Answer (D) is correct. *(CPA, adapted)*
  REQUIRED: The characteristic(s) relating to relevance and faithful representation.
  DISCUSSION: Verifiability, timeliness, comparability, and understandability are qualitative characteristics that enhance the relevance and faithful representation of accounting information.
  Answer (A) is incorrect. Verifiability is an enhancing qualitative characteristic. Information is verifiable (directly or indirectly) if knowledgeable and independent observers can reach a consensus (but not necessarily unanimity) that it is faithfully represented. Answer (B) is incorrect. Timeliness is an enhancing qualitative characteristic. Information is timely when it is available in time to influence decisions. Answer (C) is incorrect. Comparability is an an enhancing qualitative characteristic. It is the quality of information that enables users to identify similarities in and differences among items.

1.4 Elements (SFAC 6)

1.4.1. According to the FASB's conceptual framework, which of the following is an essential characteristic of an asset?

  A. The claims to an asset's benefits are legally enforceable.

  B. An asset is tangible.

  C. An asset is obtained at a cost.

  D. An asset provides future benefits.

Answer (D) is correct. *(CPA, adapted)*
  REQUIRED: The essential characteristic of an asset.
  DISCUSSION: One of the three essential characteristics of an asset is that the transaction or event giving rise to the entity's right to or control of its assets has already occurred. It is not expected to occur in the future. A second essential characteristic of an asset is that an entity can obtain the benefits of and control others' access to the asset. The third essential characteristic is that an asset must embody a probable future benefit that involves a capacity to contribute to future net cash inflows.
  Answer (A) is incorrect. Claims to an asset's benefits may not be legally enforceable. Goodwill is an example. Answer (B) is incorrect. Some assets are intangible. Answer (C) is incorrect. Assets may be obtained through donations or investments by owners.

1.4.2. Under SFAC No. 6, *Elements of Financial Statements*, interrelated elements of financial statements include

	Distribution to Owners	Notes to Financial Statements
A.	Yes	Yes
B.	Yes	No
C.	No	Yes
D.	No	No

Answer (B) is correct. *(CPA, adapted)*
   REQUIRED: The interrelated element(s), if any, directly related to measuring performance and status.
   DISCUSSION: The elements of financial statements directly related to measuring the performance and status of business enterprises and nonbusiness organizations are (1) assets, (2) liabilities, (3) equity of a business or net assets of a nonbusiness organization, (4) revenues, (5) expenses, (6) gains, and (7) losses. The elements of (1) investments by owners, (2) distributions to owners, and (3) comprehensive income relate only to business enterprises. Information disclosed in notes or parenthetically on the face of financial statements amplifies or explains information recognized in the financial statements.
   Answer (A) is incorrect. The notes to financial statements supplement and amplify the information contained in the statements. They are not directly related to measuring the performance and status of an enterprise. Answer (C) is incorrect. Distributions to owners are directly related to measuring the performance and status of a business enterprise. The notes to financial statements supplement and amplify the information contained in the statements. Answer (D) is incorrect. Distributions to owners are directly related to measuring the performance and status of a business enterprise.

1.4.3. According to the FASB's conceptual framework, which of the following is an essential characteristic of a liability?

A. Liabilities must require the obligated entity to pay cash to a recipient entity.

B. Liabilities must be legally enforceable.

C. The identity of the recipient entity must be known to the obligated entity before the time of settlement.

D. Liabilities are obligations resulting from previous transactions or events.

Answer (D) is correct. *(Publisher, adapted)*
   REQUIRED: The characteristic that is essential to the existence of a liability.
   DISCUSSION: A liability has three essential characteristics: (1) It represents an obligation that requires settlement by a probable future transfer or use of assets, (2) the entity has little or no discretion to avoid the obligation, and (3) the transaction or other event resulting in the obligation has already occurred.
   Answer (A) is incorrect. Liabilities often require the payment of cash, but they also may be settled through the use of other assets or the provision of services. Answer (B) is incorrect. Although liabilities are usually legally enforceable, that is not an essential characteristic. Answer (C) is incorrect. The identity of the recipient must be known only by the time of settlement, not before.

1.4.4. According to the FASB's conceptual framework, asset valuation accounts are

A. Assets.

B. Neither assets nor liabilities.

C. Part of equity.

D. Liabilities.

Answer (B) is correct. *(CPA, adapted)*
   REQUIRED: The conceptual framework's definition of asset valuation accounts.
   DISCUSSION: Asset valuation accounts are separate items sometimes found in financial statements that reduce or increase the carrying amount of an asset. The conceptual framework considers asset valuation accounts to be part of the related asset account. They are not considered to be assets or liabilities in their own right.
   Answer (A) is incorrect. Asset valuation accounts are not assets. Answer (C) is incorrect. An asset valuation account is part of the related asset account. Answer (D) is incorrect. Asset valuation accounts are not liabilities.

1.4.5. A stated purpose of SFAC 6, *Elements of Financial Statements*, is to

A. Define three classes of net assets for businesses.

B. Define the elements necessary for presentation of financial statements of both business and not-for-profit entities.

C. Apply the comprehensive income concept to not-for-profit entities.

D. Apply its principles to reporting by state and local governmental units.

Answer (B) is correct. *(Publisher, adapted)*
REQUIRED: The stated purpose of SFAC 6.
DISCUSSION: SFAC 6 defines 10 interrelated elements of financial statements that are directly related to measuring the performance and status of an entity. Of these, seven are found in statements of both business and not-for-profit entities: (1) assets, (2) liabilities, (3) equity or net assets, (4) revenues, (5) expenses, (6) gains, and (7) losses. Investments by owners, distributions to owners, and comprehensive income are elements of financial statements of businesses only.
Answer (A) is incorrect. SFAC 6 defines three classes of net assets of not-for-profit entities and the changes therein during the period. Answer (C) is incorrect. The comprehensive income concept is not applicable to not-for-profit entities. Answer (D) is incorrect. SFAC 6 does not apply its principles to reporting by state and local governmental units. GASB Concepts Statements apply to such entities.

1.4.6. Which of the following statements about accrual accounting is false?

A. Accrual accounting is concerned with the process by which cash expended on resources and activities is returned as more (or perhaps less) cash to the entity, not just with the beginning and end of that process.

B. Accrual accounting recognizes that buying, producing, selling, and other operations of an entity during a period often do not coincide with the cash receipts and payments of the period.

C. Accrual accounting attempts to record the financial effects on an entity of transactions and other events and circumstances that have cash consequences for an entity.

D. Accrual accounting primarily addresses the cash receipts and cash payments of an entity.

Answer (D) is correct. *(Publisher, adapted)*
REQUIRED: The false statement about accrual accounting.
DISCUSSION: Accrual accounting attempts to record the financial effects on an entity of transactions and other events and circumstances that have cash consequences in the periods in which those transactions, events, and circumstances occur, rather than only in the periods in which cash is received or paid by the entity. Thus, the focus of accrual accounting is not primarily on the actual cash receipts and cash payments. It addresses the process by which cash expended on resources is returned as more (or perhaps less) cash to the entity, not just with the beginning and end of the process.
Answer (A) is incorrect. Accrual accounting is concerned with the process by which cash expended on resources and activities is returned as more (or perhaps less) cash to the entity, not just with the beginning and end of that process. Answer (B) is incorrect. Accrual accounting recognizes that buying, producing, selling, and other operations of an entity during a period often do not coincide with the cash receipts and payments of the period. Answer (C) is incorrect. Accrual accounting attempts to record the financial effects on an entity of transactions and other events and circumstances that have cash consequences for an entity.

1.4.7. According to the FASB's conceptual framework, an entity's revenue may result from a(n)

A. Decrease in an asset from primary operations.

B. Increase in an asset from incidental transactions.

C. Increase in a liability from incidental transactions.

D. Decrease in a liability from primary operations.

Answer (D) is correct. *(CPA, adapted)*
REQUIRED: The possible source of revenue.
DISCUSSION: Revenues are inflows or other enhancements of assets or settlements of liabilities from activities that constitute the entity's ongoing major or central operations. Thus, a revenue may result from a decrease in a liability from primary operations, for example, by delivering goods that were paid for in advance.
Answer (A) is incorrect. A decrease in an asset from primary operations results in an expense. Answer (B) is incorrect. An increase in an asset from incidental transactions results in a gain. Answer (C) is incorrect. An increase in a liability from incidental transactions results in a loss.

1.4.8. According to the FASB's conceptual framework, which of the following best describes the distinction between expenses and losses?

A. Losses are reported net of related tax effect, and expenses are not.

B. Losses are decreases in net assets, and expenses are not.

C. Losses are material, and expenses are immaterial.

D. Losses result from peripheral or incidental transactions, and expenses result from ongoing major or central operations of the entity.

Answer (D) is correct. *(CIA, adapted)*
REQUIRED: The distinction between expenses and losses.
DISCUSSION: According to the FASB's conceptual framework, expenses are outflows or other uses of assets or incurrences of liabilities (or both) from (1) delivering or producing goods, (2) providing services, or (3) other activities that qualify as ongoing major or central operations. Losses are decreases in equity (net assets) from peripheral or incidental transactions or other events and circumstances except expenses or distributions to owners.

1.4.9. The FASB's conceptual framework explains both financial and physical capital maintenance concepts. Which capital maintenance concept is applied to currently reported net income, and which is applied to comprehensive income?

	Currently Reported Net Income	Comprehensive Income
A.	Financial capital	Physical capital
B.	Physical capital	Physical capital
C.	Financial capital	Financial capital
D.	Physical capital	Financial capital

Answer (C) is correct. *(CPA, adapted)*
　　REQUIRED: The capital maintenance concept(s) applicable to currently reported net income and comprehensive income.
　　DISCUSSION: The financial capital maintenance concept is the basis of (1) traditional financial statements (including net income) and (2) the full set of financial statements (including comprehensive income), discussed in the conceptual framework. Under this concept, a return on investment (defined in terms of financial capital) results only if the financial amount of net assets at the end of the period exceeds the amount at the beginning after excluding the effects of transactions with owners. Under a physical capital concept, a return on investment (in terms of physical capital) results only if the physical productive capacity (or the resources needed to achieve that capacity) at the end of the period exceeds the capacity at the beginning after excluding the effects of transactions with owners. The physical capital concept requires many assets to be measured at current (replacement) cost.

1.4.10. The primary purpose of the statement of financial position of a business is to reflect

A. The fair value of the entity's assets at some moment in time.

B. The status of the entity's assets in case of forced liquidation.

C. The entity's potential for growth in stock values in the stock market.

D. Items of value, debts, and net worth.

Answer (D) is correct. *(CMA, adapted)*
　　REQUIRED: The primary purpose of the statement of financial position (balance sheet).
　　DISCUSSION: In conformity with GAAP, the statement of financial position or balance sheet of a business presents three major financial accounting elements: assets (items of value), liabilities (debts), and equity (net worth). According to SFAC 6, *Elements of Financial Statements*, "Assets are probable future economic benefits obtained or controlled by a particular entity as a result of past transactions or events." SFAC 6 defines liabilities as "probable future sacrifices of economic benefits arising from present obligations of a particular entity to transfer assets or provide services to other entities in the future as a result of past transactions or events." SFAC 6 defines the equity of a business as "the residual interest in the assets of an entity that remains after deducting its liabilities."
　　Answer (A) is incorrect. Assets are reported in the balance sheet using various measurement attributes, including but not limited to fair values. Answer (B) is incorrect. The balance sheet usually does not report forced liquidation values. Answer (C) is incorrect. The future value of an entity's stock is more dependent upon future operations and investors' expectations than on the data found in the balance sheet.

1.4.11. Consolidated financial statements are prepared when a parent-subsidiary relationship exists in recognition of the accounting concept of

A. Materiality.

B. Entity.

C. Verifiability.

D. Going concern.

Answer (B) is correct. *(CPA, adapted)*
　　REQUIRED: The accounting concept recognized in consolidated financial statements.
　　DISCUSSION: Accounting information pertains to a business entity, the boundaries of which are not necessarily those of the legal entity. For example, a parent and subsidiary are legally separate but are treated as a single business entity in consolidated statements.
　　Answer (A) is incorrect. Information is material if its omission or misstatement can influence user decisions based on a specific entity's financial information. Answer (C) is incorrect. Information is verifiable if knowledgeable and independent observers can reach a consensus that it is faithfully represented. Answer (D) is incorrect. The going-concern concept assumes that the business entity will continue to operate in the absence of evidence to the contrary, but it is not a reason for preparing consolidated statements.

1.5 Recognition and Measurement (SFAC 5)

1.5.1. According to the FASB's conceptual framework, recognition is the process of formally incorporating an element into the financial statements of an entity. Recognition criteria include all of the following except

    A. Measurability with sufficient reliability.

    B. Definitions of elements of financial statements.

    C. Decision usefulness.

    D. Relevance.

Answer (C) is correct. *(CMA, adapted)*
    REQUIRED: The item not included in recognition criteria.
    DISCUSSION: An item and information about the item should be recognized when the following four fundamental recognition criteria are met: (1) The item meets the definition of an element of financial statements; (2) it has a relevant attribute measurable with sufficient reliability; (3) the information about the item is capable of making a difference in user decisions; and (4) the information is representationally faithful, verifiable, and neutral. Decision usefulness is the objective of general-purpose financial reporting.
    Answer (A) is incorrect. Measurability with sufficient reliability is included in the recognition criteria. Answer (B) is incorrect. Definitions of elements of financial statements are included in the recognition criteria. Answer (D) is incorrect. Relevance is included in the recognition criteria.

1.5.2. According to the FASB's conceptual framework, which of the following statements conforms to the realization concept?

    A. Equipment depreciation was assigned to a production department and then to product unit costs.

    B. Depreciated equipment was sold in exchange for a note receivable.

    C. Cash was collected on accounts receivable.

    D. Product unit costs were assigned to cost of goods sold when the units were sold.

Answer (B) is correct. *(CPA, adapted)*
    REQUIRED: The statement that conforms to the realization concept.
    DISCUSSION: The term "realization" is used most precisely in accounting and financial reporting with regard to sales of assets for cash or claims to cash. The terms "realized" and "unrealized" identify revenues or gains and losses on assets sold and unsold, respectively. Thus, the sale of depreciated equipment results in realization.
    Answer (A) is incorrect. Assigning costs based on depreciation is allocation, not realization. Answer (C) is incorrect. Realization occurred when the accounts receivable (claims to cash) were recognized. Answer (D) is incorrect. Assigning costs to products is allocation, not realization.

1.5.3. Revenues of an entity are usually measured by the exchange values of the assets or liabilities involved. According to the FASB's conceptual framework, recognition of revenue does not occur until

    A. The revenue is realizable.

    B. The revenue is realized and earned.

    C. Products or services are exchanged for cash or claims to cash.

    D. The entity has substantially accomplished what it agreed to do.

Answer (B) is correct. *(CMA, adapted)*
    REQUIRED: The appropriate timing of the recognition of revenue.
    DISCUSSION: According to the FASB's conceptual framework, revenues should be recognized when they are realized or realizable and earned. Revenues are realized when products, merchandise, or other assets are exchanged for cash or claims to cash. Revenues are realizable when related assets received or held are readily convertible to known amounts of cash or claims to cash. Revenues are earned when the entity has substantially accomplished what it must do to be entitled to the benefits represented by the revenues.
    Answer (A) is incorrect. Revenue also must be earned. Answer (C) is incorrect. Exchange for cash or claims to cash does not suffice for revenue recognition. Answer (D) is incorrect. Revenue must be realized or realizable as well as earned.

1.5.4. The Star Company is a service entity that requires customers to place their orders 2 weeks in advance. Star bills its customers on the 15th day of the month following the date of service and requires that payment be made within 30 days of the billing date. Conceptually, Star should recognize revenue from its services at the date when

    A. A customer places an order.

    B. The service is provided.

    C. A billing is mailed.

    D. A customer's payment is received.

Answer (B) is correct. *(CIA, adapted)*
    REQUIRED: The date at which a catering service should recognize revenue.
    DISCUSSION: Revenue is recognized when (or as) the performance obligation is satisfied by transferring a promised good or service to a customer.
    Answer (A) is incorrect. When a customer places an order, the services have not yet been provided. Answer (C) is incorrect. Mailing a bill is not necessary for the recognition of revenue. Star should recognize revenue from performing services when the performance obligation is satisfied, that is, as soon as the service has been performed. Answer (D) is incorrect. Star need not wait for payment to be received from the customer. Revenue is recognized once Star has substantially completed the earning process, i.e., performed its service for the customer, and exchanged its service for a claim to cash (e.g., a receivable).

1.5.5. For $50 a month, Rawl Co. visits its customers' premises and performs insect control services. If customers experience problems between regularly scheduled visits, Rawl makes service calls at no additional charge. Instead of paying monthly, customers may pay an annual fee of $540 in advance. For a customer who pays the annual fee in advance, Rawl should recognize the related revenue

    A. When the cash is collected.

    B. At the end of the fiscal year.

    C. At the end of the contract year after all of the services have been performed.

    D. Evenly over the contract year as the services are performed.

Answer (D) is correct. *(CPA, adapted)*
    REQUIRED: The timing of recognition of revenue.
    DISCUSSION: The performance obligation is satisfied over time because the customer simultaneously receives and consumes the benefits as the entity performs. The entity recognizes revenue based on a transaction price in the form of an annual fee as it satisfies the performance obligation to deliver insect control services for 1 year. Accordingly, the entity must recognize revenue over time by measuring the progress toward satisfaction of the 1-year performance obligation. That progress is measured by time elapsed (an example of an input method). Because inputs are incurred evenly over time (one scheduled visit every month), recognition of revenue on a straight-line basis is appropriate in this case.

1.5.6. Under a contract with another entity, a company will receive sales-based royalties from the assignment of a patent for 3 years. The royalties received should be reported as revenue

    A. At the date of the royalty agreement.

    B. In the period earned as sales occur.

    C. In the period received.

    D. Evenly over the life of the royalty agreement.

Answer (B) is correct. *(CPA, adapted)*
    REQUIRED: The timing of recognition of sales-based royalty revenue.
    DISCUSSION: Assuming the entity satisfied the performance obligation to which the sales-based royalties relate, revenue for sales-based royalties from licensed intellectual property, such as a patent, is recognized as the subsequent sales occur.
    Answer (A) is incorrect. At the date of the royalty agreement, the contract is wholly executory. The recognition criteria have not been met, and no asset, revenue, or liability is recognized. Answer (C) is incorrect. Royalties received before they are earned are credited to a liability. Answer (D) is incorrect. Revenue is recognized evenly over the life of the royalty agreement only if earned evenly over that period.

1.5.7. Which of the following is not a theoretical basis for the allocation of expenses?

    A. Systematic allocation.

    B. Cause and effect.

    C. Profit maximization.

    D. Immediate recognition.

Answer (C) is correct. *(CPA, adapted)*
    REQUIRED: The accounting concept not a theoretical basis for allocation of expenses.
    DISCUSSION: Profit maximization is not a theoretical basis for the allocation of expense. The allocation of expenses on such a basis would subvert the purpose of GAAP to present fairly the results of operations and financial position because expenses would not be reported.
    Answer (A) is incorrect. Expenses are to be recognized by a systematic and rational allocation if causal relations are generally identifiable but particular amounts cannot be related directly to specific revenues or periods. Answer (B) is incorrect. Expenses should be recognized in a particular period if they have a direct association with that period or with specific revenues recognized in that period. Answer (D) is incorrect. Immediate recognition is appropriate when costs have no discernible future benefits, or no other theoretically sound basis exists for allocation of the expenses.

1.5.8. Some costs cannot be directly related to particular revenues but are incurred to obtain benefits that are exhausted in the period in which the costs are incurred. An example of such a cost is

    A. Salespersons' monthly salaries.

    B. Salespersons' commissions.

    C. Transportation to customers' places of business.

    D. Prepaid insurance.

Answer (A) is correct. *(CPA, adapted)*
    REQUIRED: The costs not directly related to particular revenues but incurred to obtain benefits exhausted in the same period in which they are incurred.
    DISCUSSION: Expenses should be recognized when a benefit has been consumed. The consumption of benefit may occur when (1) the expenses are matched with the revenues, (2) they are allocated on a systematic and rational basis to the periods in which the related assets are expected to provide benefits, or (3) the cash is spent or liabilities are incurred for goods and services that are used up either simultaneously with the acquisition or soon after. An example of a cost that (1) cannot be directly related to particular revenues but (2) is incurred to obtain benefits that are exhausted in the same period in which the cost is incurred is salespersons' monthly salaries.
    Answer (B) is incorrect. Salespersons' commissions (not salaries) are recognized upon recognition of revenues that result directly and jointly from the same transactions or other events as the cost. Answer (C) is incorrect. Transportation to customers' places of business is recognized upon recognition of revenues that result directly and jointly from the same transactions or other events as the cost. Answer (D) is incorrect. Prepaid insurance benefits more than one accounting period. Its cost should be allocated on a systematic and rational basis to the accounting periods benefited.

1.5.9. Ande Co. estimates uncollectible accounts expense using the ratio of past actual losses from uncollectible accounts to past net credit sales, adjusted for anticipated conditions. The practice follows the accounting concept of

    A. Consistency.

    B. Going-concern.

    C. Matching.

    D. Substance over form.

Answer (C) is correct. *(CPA, adapted)*
    REQUIRED: The accounting concept that is the basis for estimating an expense using the ratio of losses to credit sales.
    DISCUSSION: Matching bad debt expense with related revenues is an application of the matching principle. Matching is synonymous with associating cause and effect. It is based on a direct relationship between the expense and the revenue.
    Answer (A) is incorrect. Consistency is a means of achieving comparability, an enhancing qualitative characteristic of useful financial information. Consistency is the use of the same methods, e.g., accounting principles, for the same items. Answer (B) is incorrect. Going-concern is an assumption underlying the environment in which the reporting entity operates. It is the assumption that the entity will continue operating indefinitely. Answer (D) is incorrect. The concept of substance over form guides accountants to present the financial reality of a transaction over its legal form. An example is the consolidation of a legally separate subsidiary by a parent. Presenting a parent and a separate entity that it controls as one reporting entity is faithfully representational. Thus, substance over form is more closely related to a fundamental qualitative characteristic than to an expense recognition principle.

1.5.10. Why are certain costs of doing business capitalized when incurred and then depreciated or amortized over subsequent accounting cycles?

    A. To reduce the federal income tax liability.

    B. To aid management in the decision-making process.

    C. To match the costs of production with revenues as earned.

    D. To adhere to the accounting concept of conservatism.

Answer (C) is correct. *(CPA, adapted)*
    REQUIRED: The reason certain costs are capitalized and then depreciated or amortized.
    DISCUSSION: If costs benefit more than one accounting period, they should be systematically and rationally allocated to all periods benefited. This is done by capitalizing the costs and depreciating or amortizing them over the periods in which the asset helps generate revenue. The term "matching" is most narrowly defined as the expense recognition principle of associating cause and effect, but it is sometimes used more broadly (as here) to apply to the entire process of expense recognition or even of income determination.
    Answer (A) is incorrect. Capitalization and depreciation of costs on the financial statements have no effect on federal income tax liability. Answer (B) is incorrect. Expense recognition principles are applied to benefit all users of financial statements, not merely management. Answer (D) is incorrect. The accounting concept of conservatism requires a prudent approach to uncertainty but without the introduction of bias into financial reporting. Thus, the more conservative approach might be to recognize all costs immediately.

1.5.11. Which of the following is an example of the expense recognition principle of associating cause and effect?

    A. Allocation of insurance cost.

    B. Sales commissions.

    C. Depreciation of fixed assets.

    D. Officers' salaries.

Answer (B) is correct. *(CPA, adapted)*
    REQUIRED: The example of associating cause and effect for expense recognition.
    DISCUSSION: If a direct cause-and-effect relationship can be established between costs and revenues, the costs should be recognized as expenses when the related revenue is recognized. Costs of products sold or services provided and sales commissions are examples of costs that can be associated with specific revenues.
    Answer (A) is incorrect. Allocation of insurance cost is an example of allocating costs among several periods on a systematic and rational basis. Answer (C) is incorrect. Depreciation is an example of allocating costs among several periods on a systematic and rational basis. Answer (D) is incorrect. Officers' salaries are expenses that are recognized immediately. They provide no discernible future benefits.

1.5.12. Which of the following is an application of the principle of systematic and rational allocation?

    A. Amortization of intangible assets.

    B. Sales commissions.

    C. Research and development costs.

    D. Officers' salaries.

Answer (A) is correct. *(CPA, adapted)*
    REQUIRED: The application of systematic and rational allocation.
    DISCUSSION: The expense recognition principle of systematic and rational allocation is applied to the amortization of intangible assets because of the absence of a direct means of associating cause and effect. The costs benefit two or more periods (they generate revenue in those periods) and should be systematically and rationally allocated.
    Answer (B) is incorrect. Sales commissions directly relate to particular revenues and should be recognized as an expense when the related revenues are recognized. Answer (C) is incorrect. R&D costs are expensed in the period incurred. Answer (D) is incorrect. Officers' salaries are expensed in the period incurred.

1.5.13. A patent, purchased in Year 1 and amortized over a 15-year life, was determined to be worthless in Year 6. The write-off of the asset in Year 6 is an application of which of the following principles?

    A. Associating cause and effect.

    B. Immediate recognition.

    C. Systematic and rational allocation.

    D. Objectivity.

Answer (B) is correct. *(CPA, adapted)*
    REQUIRED: The accounting principle of which the write-off of a patent is an example.
    DISCUSSION: The patent was being amortized in a systematic and rational manner. When it was determined that the costs associated with the patent (recorded as an asset) no longer provided discernible benefits, the remaining unamortized costs were written off; that is, the loss was recognized immediately.
    Answer (A) is incorrect. Associating cause and effect is a method of deferring costs to future periods that is not appropriate when a cost has no discernible future benefit. Answer (C) is incorrect. Systematic and rational allocation is a method of amortizing the patent. Answer (D) is incorrect. Objectivity is neither a quality of accounting information nor an accounting principle.

1.5.14. Items reported in financial statements must have a relevant attribute that can be measured in monetary units. According to the conceptual framework,

    A. The unit of measure should have constant general purchasing power.

    B. One attribute should be used for measuring all assets and one for all liabilities.

    C. Different measurement attributes are used for different items depending on the nature of the item.

    D. The unit of measure should be current cost.

Answer (C) is correct. *(Publisher, adapted)*
    REQUIRED: The approach to measurement.
    DISCUSSION: Current accounting practice is based on (1) nominal units of money (unadjusted for changes in purchasing power) and (2) quantifiable attributes. Attributes used in practice include (1) historical cost (historical proceeds), (2) current cost, (3) current market value, (4) net realizable (settlement) value, and (5) present (or discounted) value of future cash flows. The use of different attributes will continue.
    Answer (A) is incorrect. Unless inflation increases to an intolerable level, measurement will continue to be in nominal units of money. Answer (B) is incorrect. Use of different attributes will continue. Answer (D) is incorrect. Current cost is an attribute, not a unit of measure.

1.5.15. Which of the following is not a basis for the immediate recognition of a cost during a period?

A. The cost provides no discernible future benefit.

B. The cost recorded in a prior period no longer produces discernible benefits.

C. The federal income tax savings using the immediate write-off method exceed the savings obtained by allocating the cost to several periods.

D. Allocation of the cost on the basis of association with revenue or among several accounting periods is considered to serve no useful purpose.

Answer (C) is correct. *(CPA, adapted)*
REQUIRED: The item that should not be immediately recognized as an expense.
DISCUSSION: In applying the principles of expense recognition, costs are analyzed to determine whether they can be associated with revenue on a cause-and-effect basis, e.g., cost of goods sold. If not, a systematic and rational allocation should be attempted, e.g., depreciation. If neither principle applies, costs are recognized immediately. Accordingly, even though federal income tax savings could be obtained by the immediate write-off method, GAAP might require another treatment of the expense.
Answer (A) is incorrect. A cost with no discernible future benefit is not capitalized. It does not meet the definition of an asset. Answer (B) is incorrect. The matching principle requires costs to be matched with their associated revenues. If a particular cost will no longer produce benefits, it does not meet the definition of an asset and must be expensed. Answer (D) is incorrect. Allocation of a cost for the sake of allocation does not provide the user of financial statements with useful information. In this case, the cost should be expensed immediately.

1.5.16. Items currently reported in financial statements are measured by different attributes. The amount of cash or its equivalent that would have to be paid if the same or an equivalent asset were acquired currently defines the attribute of

A. Historical cost.

B. Current cost.

C. Current market value.

D. Net realizable value.

Answer (B) is correct. *(Publisher, adapted)*
REQUIRED: The measurement attribute defined as the cash or equivalent to be paid if the same or an equivalent asset were acquired currently.
DISCUSSION: The amount of cash or its equivalent that would have to be paid if the same or an equivalent asset were acquired currently is the measurement attribute of current (replacement) cost. Some inventories are reported in accordance with this attribute (SFAC 5).
Answer (A) is incorrect. Historical cost is the amount of cash or its equivalent paid to acquire an asset. Answer (C) is incorrect. Current market value is the amount of cash or its equivalent that could be obtained by selling an asset in orderly liquidation. Answer (D) is incorrect. Net realizable value is the nondiscounted amount of cash or its equivalent into which an asset is expected to be converted in due course of business minus any direct cost necessary to make that conversion.

1.5.17. The appropriate attribute for measuring noncurrent payables is

A. Historical cost.

B. Current cost.

C. Net realizable value.

D. Present value of future cash flows.

Answer (D) is correct. *(CMA, adapted)*
REQUIRED: The appropriate attribute to use when measuring noncurrent payables.
DISCUSSION: According to SFAC 5, the appropriate measurement attribute for noncurrent liabilities is "the present or discounted value of future cash outflows expected to be required to satisfy the liability in due course of business."
Answer (A) is incorrect. Historical cost is an attribute of assets, not liabilities. Assets are generally purchased in a marketplace or in a transaction in which "cost" is quantifiable. Liabilities are not "purchased" in the same way assets are. The attribute of a liability to provide goods or services is historical proceeds. Answer (B) is incorrect. Current cost is a concept used in assessing the outlays that would be required to replace assets. It is not a concept related to liabilities, such as noncurrent payables. Answer (C) is incorrect. Net realizable value is a valuation concept applied to current receivables and some inventories, not payables.

1.5.18. What is the purpose of information presented in notes to the financial statements?

A. To provide disclosures required by generally accepted accounting principles.

B. To correct improper presentation in the financial statements.

C. To provide recognition of amounts not included in the totals of the financial statements.

D. To present management's responses to auditor comments.

Answer (A) is correct. *(CPA, adapted)*
   REQUIRED: The purpose of information presented in notes to the financial statements.
   DISCUSSION: Notes are an integral part of the basic financial statements. Notes provide information essential to understanding the financial statements, including disclosures required by GAAP.
   Answer (B) is incorrect. Notes may not be used to correct an improper presentation. Answer (C) is incorrect. Disclosure in notes is not a substitute for recognition in financial statements for items that meet recognition criteria. Answer (D) is incorrect. Management's responses to auditor comments are not an appropriate subject of financial reporting.

1.5.19. According to the FASB's conceptual framework, certain assets are reported in financial statements at the amount of cash or its equivalent that would have to be paid if the same or equivalent assets were acquired currently. What is the name of the reporting concept?

A. Replacement cost.

B. Current market value.

C. Historical cost.

D. Net realizable value.

Answer (A) is correct. *(CPA, adapted)*
   REQUIRED: The measurement attribute that results in reporting assets at the cash amount (or equivalent) that would have to be paid currently for them.
   DISCUSSION: Replacement (current) cost is the amount of cash that would have to be paid for a current acquisition of the same or an equivalent asset.
   Answer (B) is incorrect. Current market value is the cash or equivalent realizable in an ordinary liquidation (not a forced sale). Answer (C) is incorrect. Historical cost is the price paid for an asset adjusted for amortization and other allocations. Answer (D) is incorrect. Net realizable value is the cash or cash equivalent expected to be received for the asset in the due course of business, minus costs of completion and sale.

1.6 Fair Value

1.6.1. According to the FASB, fair value is

A. An entry price.

B. An exit price.

C. Based on an actual transaction.

D. An entity-specific measurement.

Answer (B) is correct. *(Publisher, adapted)*
   REQUIRED: The nature of fair value.
   DISCUSSION: "Fair value is the price that would be received to sell an asset or paid to transfer a liability in an orderly transaction between market participants at the measurement date." Thus, fair value is an exit price.
   Answer (A) is incorrect. An entry price is what is paid or received in an orderly exchange to acquire an asset or assume a liability, respectively. Answer (C) is incorrect. Fair value is an exit price paid or received in a hypothetical transaction considered from the perspective of a market participant. Answer (D) is incorrect. Fair value is market-based. It is based on pricing assumptions of market participants.

1.6.2. For the purpose of a fair value measurement (FVM) of an asset or liability, a transaction is assumed to occur in the

A. Principal market if one exists.

B. Most advantageous market.

C. Market in which the result is optimized.

D. Principal market or most advantageous market at the election of the reporting entity.

Answer (A) is correct. *(Publisher, adapted)*
   REQUIRED: The market in which a transaction is assumed to occur.
   DISCUSSION: For FVM purposes, a transaction is assumed to occur in the principal market for an asset or liability if one exists. The principal market has the greatest volume or level of activity. If no such market exists, the transaction is assumed to occur in the most advantageous market.

1.6.3. The fair value measurement (FVM) of an asset

A. Assumes transfer, not a settlement.

B. Is based on the expected use by the reporting entity.

C. Reflects the highest and best use by market participants.

D. Includes the entity's own credit risk.

Answer (C) is correct. *(Publisher, adapted)*
　　REQUIRED: The true statement about the FVM of an asset.
　　DISCUSSION: The FVM is based on the highest and best use (HBU) by market participants. This use maximizes the value of the asset. The HBU is in-use if the value-maximizing use is in combination with other assets in a group. An example is machinery. The HBU is in-exchange if the value-maximizing use is as a standalone asset. An example is a financial asset.
　　Answer (A) is incorrect. The FVM of a liability, not an asset, assumes transfer without settlement. Answer (B) is incorrect. The FVM assumes use by market participants. Answer (D) is incorrect. The FVM of a liability includes nonperformance risk. An element of nonperformance risk is the entity's own credit risk.

1.6.4. Which of the following items would best enable Driver Co. to determine whether the fair value of its investment in Favre Corp. is properly stated in the balance sheet?

A. Discounted cash flow of Favre's operations.

B. Quoted market prices available from a business broker for a similar asset.

C. Quoted market prices on a stock exchange for an identical asset.

D. Historical performance and return on Driver's investment in Favre.

Answer (C) is correct. *(CPA, adapted)*
　　REQUIRED: The item best enabling an investor to measure the fair value of an investment.
　　DISCUSSION: In the fair value hierarchy, Level 1 inputs are the most reliable. They are unadjusted quoted prices in active markets for identical assets or liabilities that the entity can access at the measurement date.
　　Answer (A) is incorrect. Discounted cash flow is consistent with the income approach to valuation. It is based on current market expectations, e.g., about earnings or cash flows. Discounted cash flow is a Level 2 input, so it is observable, that is, based on market data from independent sources. But it is less reliable than a Level 1 input. Answer (B) is incorrect. Quoted market prices available from a business broker for a similar asset are Level 2 inputs, that is, observable but less reliable than Level 1 inputs. Answer (D) is incorrect. Historical performance and return on Driver's investment in Favre are Level 3 inputs (unobservable). They are based on the entity's own assumptions about the assumptions of market participants that reflect the best available information. The use of Level 3 inputs should be minimized.

1.6.5. Each of the following would be considered a Level 2 observable input that could be used to determine an asset or liability's fair value except

A. Quoted prices for identical assets and liabilities in markets that are not active.

B. Quoted prices for similar assets and liabilities in markets that are active.

C. Internally generated cash flow projections for a related asset or liability.

D. Interest rates that are observable at commonly quoted intervals.

Answer (C) is correct. *(CPA, adapted)*
　　REQUIRED: The Level 2 observable inputs.
　　DISCUSSION: Internally generated cash flow projections are not observable and would be considered a Level 3 input. Level 3 inputs are unobservable inputs that are used in the absence of observable inputs. They should be based on the best available information in the circumstances.
　　Answer (A) is incorrect. Quoted prices for identical assets and liabilities in markets that are not active is an example of a Level 2 input. Level 2 inputs are observable. Answer (B) is incorrect. Quoted prices for similar assets and liabilities in markets that are active is an example of a Level 2 input. Level 2 inputs are observable. Answer (D) is incorrect. Interest rates that are observable at commonly quoted intervals are an example of a Level 2 input. Level 2 inputs are observable.

1.7 Standards

1.7.1. Arpco, Inc., a for-profit provider of healthcare services, recently purchased two smaller companies and is researching accounting issues arising from the two business combinations. Which of the following accounting pronouncements are the most authoritative?

A. FASB Accounting Standards Updates.

B. FASB Statements of Financial Accounting Concepts.

C. FASB Statements of Financial Accounting Standards.

D. The Accounting Standards Codification.

Answer (D) is correct. *(CPA, adapted)*
　　REQUIRED: The most authoritative pronouncements.
　　DISCUSSION: The FASB's Accounting Standards Codification and SEC pronouncements are the only sources of authoritative financial accounting guidance for nongovernmental entities in the U.S. All other sources of guidance are nonauthoritative.
　　Answer (A) is incorrect. Accounting Standards Updates are authoritative only to the extent they have been incorporated in the Accounting Standards Codification. Answer (B) is incorrect. Statements of Financial Accounting Concepts are nonauthoritative. Answer (C) is incorrect. Statements of Financial Accounting Standards are no longer issued. Their guidance is authoritative only to the extent it has been incorporated in the Accounting Standards Codification.

1.7.2. Which of the following documents is typically issued as part of the due-process activities of the Financial Accounting Standards Board (FASB) for amending the FASB Accounting Standards Codification?

    A.   A proposed statement of position.

    B.   A proposed accounting standards update.

    C.   A proposed accounting research bulletin.

    D.   A proposed staff accounting bulletin.

Answer (B) is correct. *(CPA, adapted)*
    REQUIRED: The document issued as part of the FASB's due-process activities.
    DISCUSSION: The FASB follows a due-process procedure before issuing final pronouncements: After discussing the issues and considering input from interested parties (e.g., business, academia, and the accounting profession), the FASB votes on a final draft proposal. If a majority of the board members approves, an Accounting Standard Update (ASU) is issued. Once an ASU has been incorporated into the FASB's Accounting Standards Codification, it has the status of U.S. GAAP.
    Answer (A) is incorrect. A proposed statement of position is not a part of the due-process activities of the FASB for amending the Codification. Answer (C) is incorrect. A proposed accounting research bulletin is not a part of the due-process activities of the FASB for amending the Codification. Answer (D) is incorrect. Staff accounting bulletins are issued as interpretations to be followed by the SEC staff in administering disclosure requirements.

1.8 SEC Reporting

1.8.1. Which of the following statements is correct concerning corporations subject to the reporting requirements of the Securities Exchange Act of 1934?

    A.   The annual report (Form 10-K) need not include audited financial statements.

    B.   The annual report (Form 10-K) must be filed with the SEC within 20 days of the end of the corporation's fiscal year.

    C.   A quarterly report (Form 10-Q) need only be filed with the SEC by those corporations that are also subject to the registration requirements of the Securities Act of 1933.

    D.   A report (Form 8-K) must be filed with the SEC after a materially important event occurs.

Answer (D) is correct. *(CPA, adapted)*
    REQUIRED: The reporting required under the Securities Exchange Act of 1934.
    DISCUSSION: Current reports must be filed on Form 8-K describing specified material events. Examples are (1) changes in control of the registrant, (2) the acquisition or disposition of a significant amount of assets not in the ordinary course of business, (3) bankruptcy or receivership, (4) resignation of a director, and (5) a change in the registrant's certifying accountant.
    Answer (A) is incorrect. Form 10-K must include audited comparative balance sheets and statements of income, cash flows, and changes in equity. Answer (B) is incorrect. Form 10-K is due within 60, 75, or 90 days (depending on the filer) after the entity's fiscal year end. Answer (C) is incorrect. An entity required to file Form 10-K also must file Form 10-Q for each of the first three quarters.

1.8.2. Integral Corp. is subject to the reporting provisions of the Securities Exchange Act of 1934. For its current fiscal year, Integral filed the following with the SEC: quarterly reports, an annual report, and a periodic report listing newly appointed officers of the corporation. Integral did not notify the SEC of shareholder "short-swing" profits, did not report that a competitor made a tender offer to Integral's shareholders, and did not report changes in the price of its stock as sold on the New York Stock Exchange. Under the SEC reporting requirements, which of the following was Integral required to do?

    A.   Report the tender offer to the SEC.

    B.   Notify the SEC of shareholder "short-swing" profits.

    C.   File the periodic report listing newly appointed officers.

    D.   Report the changes in the market price of its stock.

Answer (C) is correct. *(CPA, adapted)*
    REQUIRED: The reporting required of a covered corporation under the 1934 act.
    DISCUSSION: A covered corporation is required to file annual (10-K), quarterly (10-Q), and current events (8-K) reports with the SEC. Similar reports are sent to shareholders. The 10-K report contains information about the entity's business activities, securities, management, related parties, disagreements about accounting principles and disclosure, audited financial statements, etc. It is intended to bring the information in the registration statement up to date. Thus, newly appointed officers will be listed.
    Answer (A) is incorrect. The target must file a statement with the SEC only if the tender offer is hostile (unsolicited). Answer (B) is incorrect. Insiders are liable to the corporation for short-swing profits. These are from sale and purchase (or purchase and sale) of the issuer's stock within a 6-month period. Insiders include directors, officers, and persons owning more than 10% of the corporation's stock. They must report transactions in their holdings within 2 business days. Answer (D) is incorrect. Although the annual report (Form 10-K) requires disclosure of the market price of the common stock of the registrant (including the high and low sales prices) for each quarter of the last 2 fiscal years and any subsequent interim periods, not every change in the market price of its stock need be reported.

1.9 IFRS

1.9.1. On July 1, Year 2, a company decided to adopt IFRS. The company's first IFRS reporting period is as of and for the year ended December 31, Year 2. The company will present 1 year of comparative information. What is the company's date of transition to IFRS?

A. January 1, Year 1.

B. January 1, Year 2.

C. July 1, Year 2.

D. December 31, Year 2.

Answer (A) is correct. *(CPA, adapted)*
REQUIRED: The date of transition to IFRS.
DISCUSSION: The date of transition is "the beginning of the earliest period for which an entity presents full comparative information under IFRS in its first IFRS financial statements" (IFRS 1). Thus, the date of transition is January 1, Year 1. In the entity's first IFRS financial statements, it must present at least (1) three statements of financial position, (2) two statements of comprehensive income, (3) two separate income statements (if presented), (4) two statements of cash flows, and (5) two statements of changes in equity and related notes.
Answer (B) is incorrect. January 1, Year 2, is the beginning of the entity's first IFRS reporting period. Answer (C) is incorrect. July 1, Year 2, is the date the entity decided to adopt IFRS. The transition date is the beginning of the earliest period presented. Answer (D) is incorrect. December 31, Year 2, is the end of the entity's first IFRS reporting period.

1.9.2. Under IFRS, which of the following is the first step within the hierarchy of guidance to which management refers, and whose applicability it considers, when selecting accounting policies?

A. Consider the most recent pronouncements of other standard-setting bodies to the extent that do not conflict with the IFRS or the IASB Framework.

B. Apply a standard from IFRS if it specifically relates to the transaction, other event, or condition.

C. Consider the applicability of the definitions, recognition criteria, and measurement concepts in the IASB Framework.

D. Apply the requirements in IFRS dealing with similar and related issues.

Answer (B) is correct. *(CPA, adapted)*
REQUIRED: The first step in the IFRS hierarchy.
DISCUSSION: When an IASB Standard or Interpretation specifically applies to a transaction, other event, or condition, it must be selected if the effect is material. Any Implementation Guidance also must be considered. Absent such a standard or Interpretation, management considers (1) guidance for similar and related issues in other IASB Standards and Interpretations and (2) the content of the Framework for the Preparation and Presentation of Financial Statements.
Answer (A) is incorrect. The IFRS hierarchy does not refer to pronouncements of other standard setters. Answer (C) is incorrect. The content of the Framework is considered only when a specific IASB Standard or Interpretation does not apply. Answer (D) is incorrect. An entity may apply the requirements in IFRS dealing with similar and related issues only when a specific IASB Standard or Interpretation does not apply.

1.9.3. A company's first IFRS reporting period is for the year ended December 31, Year 2. While preparing the Year 2 statement of financial position, management identified an error in which a $90,000 loss accrual was not recorded: $40,000 of the loss accrual related to a Year 1 event, and $50,000 related to a Year 2 event. What amount of loss accrual should the company report in its December 31, Year 1, IFRS statement of financial position?

A. $0

B. $40,000

C. $50,000

D. $90,000

Answer (B) is correct. *(CPA, adapted)*
REQUIRED: The adjustment required for the correction of an error in a company's first IFRS reporting period.
DISCUSSION: In a company's first IFRS reporting period, it must present full comparative information under IFRS. This company would include full comparative information for Year 1. Thus, the company would merely correct the error in the Year 1 financial statements and record the amount of the loss accrual related to a Year 1 event of $40,000.
Answer (A) is incorrect. The Year 1 financial statements will be presented and should be adjusted for the error. Answer (C) is incorrect. The Year 1 financial statements should report a loss accrual related to an event in Year 1, not Year 2. The Year 2 event will be accounted for in the Year 2 financial statements. Answer (D) is incorrect. The Year 1 financial statements should not include a loss accrual related to a Year 2 event.

STUDY UNIT TWO
THE ACCOUNTING PROCESS

This study unit covers the accounting cycle. It consists of procedures for recording, classifying, summarizing, and reporting financial information in accordance with the accrual basis of accounting. Special attention is given to recording journal entries to adjust accrued and deferred accounts. This chapter also includes questions on personal financial statements and other bases of accounting. **Special purpose frameworks** for financial reporting include (1) income tax basis, (2) a cash basis, (3) a basis required by a regulator, (4) a basis required by a contract, and (5) a definite set of logical and reasonable criteria applied to all material items.

QUESTIONS
2.1 The Accounting System

2.1.1. A chart of accounts is

A. A flowchart of all transactions.

B. An accounting procedures manual.

C. A journal.

D. A list of names of all account titles.

Answer (D) is correct. *(Publisher, adapted)*
REQUIRED: The definition of a chart of accounts.
DISCUSSION: A chart of accounts is a listing of all account titles used within an accounting system. Business transactions affecting these accounts are initially recorded by journal entries and then posted to the individual accounts maintained in the ledger.
Answer (A) is incorrect. Actual transactions are not flowcharted. Flowcharts of accounting procedures are developed by auditors and systems analysts (but are not called charts of accounts). Answer (B) is incorrect. An accounting procedures manual explains how to use the chart of accounts, e.g., whether to make adjusting entries, reversing entries, etc. Answer (C) is incorrect. A journal contains the initial recording of the transactions that affect the accounts contained in the chart of accounts.

2.1.2. As commonly used, the term "net assets" of a business enterprise represents

A. Retained earnings of a corporation.

B. Current assets minus current liabilities.

C. Total paid-in (contributed) capital of a corporation.

D. Total assets minus total liabilities.

Answer (D) is correct. *(CPA, adapted)*
REQUIRED: The definition of net assets.
DISCUSSION: Net assets of a business enterprise is equal to total assets minus total liabilities. It is synonymous with the net worth of an entity as expressed in the balance sheet equation: assets – liabilities = equity.
Answer (A) is incorrect. Retained earnings is the cumulative income earned by a corporation minus amounts declared as dividends. Answer (B) is incorrect. Current assets minus current liabilities is working capital. Answer (C) is incorrect. Total paid-in (contributed) capital of a corporation is the sum of all money and property received from investors. In addition to total paid-in (contributed) capital, net assets includes retained earnings and accumulated other comprehensive income.

2.1.3. What are real accounts?

A. Nonfictitious accounts.

B. Accounts in existence.

C. Balance sheet accounts.

D. Income statement accounts.

Answer (C) is correct. *(Publisher, adapted)*
REQUIRED: The definition of real accounts.
DISCUSSION: Real accounts are not closed at the end of the year and can carry forward nonzero balances from one accounting period to the next. Real accounts are typically balance sheet accounts and are also called permanent accounts.
Answer (A) is incorrect. The term "nonfictitious accounts" has no accounting meaning. Answer (B) is incorrect. Nominal accounts can also exist. Answer (D) is incorrect. Income statement accounts are nominal accounts.

2.1.4. What is the purpose of nominal accounts?

A. To provide temporary accumulations of certain account balances for a meaningful period of time.

B. To facilitate accounting for small amounts.

C. To correct errors as they are detected.

D. To record all transactions initially.

Answer (A) is correct. *(Publisher, adapted)*
REQUIRED: The purpose of nominal accounts.
DISCUSSION: The primary focus of financial reporting is to account for earnings. To facilitate the calculation of earnings, nominal revenue and expense accounts are created to accumulate temporarily the components of earnings during an accounting period. At the end of the period, they are usually aggregated to determine net income. Each nominal account is reduced to a zero balance by closing it to retained earnings, a balance sheet account.
Answer (B) is incorrect. Small amounts are recorded in real as well as nominal accounts. Answer (C) is incorrect. Errors are corrected wherever they are found, e.g., in real accounts, nominal accounts, ledgers, or journals. Answer (D) is incorrect. All transactions are initially recorded in the books of original entry called journals.

2.1.5. In the equation, assets + expenses + losses = liabilities + revenues + gains + equity, the expenses and revenues are

A. Contra asset and contra liability accounts, respectively, that assist analysis of the financial progress of the firm.

B. Incorrectly stated because their signs are reversed. Both are contra items that should have negative signs in the formula.

C. Adjustments to equity that are postponed until the end of a specific accounting period to determine their net effect on equity for that period.

D. Incorrectly included in the formula because assets = liabilities + equity.

Answer (C) is correct. *(Publisher, adapted)*
REQUIRED: The status of expenses and revenues in the basic accounting equation.
DISCUSSION: Expenses and revenues are adjustments to retained earnings (an equity account of a business) that are not made immediately upon their occurrence. Instead, they are postponed until the end of a specific accounting period to determine their net effect on equity for that period, i.e., at the time of computation of net income (revenues + gains – expenses – losses). They are initially recorded in nominal accounts.
Answer (A) is incorrect. Contra asset and contra liability accounts reduce the related accounts. For example, accumulated depreciation offsets the related asset. Answer (B) is incorrect. Expenses are debits (positive) on the left-hand side of the equation. Revenues are credits (positive) on the right-hand side of the equation. Answer (D) is incorrect. The debits to assets equal the sum of the credits to liabilities and equity accounts, but the given equation is also correct.

2.1.6. The basic accounting equation (assets – liabilities = equity) for a business reflects the

A. Entity point of view.

B. Fund theory.

C. Proprietary point of view.

D. Enterprise theory.

Answer (C) is correct. *(Publisher, adapted)*
REQUIRED: The concept reflected by the basic accounting equation.
DISCUSSION: The equation is based on the proprietary theory: The owners' interest (residual equity) is what remains after the economic obligations of the entity are subtracted from its economic resources.
Answer (A) is incorrect. The entity concept limits accounting information to that related to a specific entity (possibly not the same as the legal entity). Answer (B) is incorrect. Fund theory stresses that assets equal obligations (equity and liabilities are sources of assets). Answer (D) is incorrect. The enterprise concept stresses ownership of the assets. The emphasis is on the credit side of the balance sheet.

2.1.7. A subsidiary ledger is

A. A listing of the components of account balances.

B. A backup system to protect against record destruction.

C. A listing of account balances just before closing entries are prepared.

D. All accounts of a subsidiary.

Answer (A) is correct. *(Publisher, adapted)*
REQUIRED: The definition of a subsidiary ledger.
DISCUSSION: A general or controlling ledger contains the balance for each asset, liability, and equity account. A subsidiary ledger consists of the detail of a general ledger account, e.g., the individual receivables making up accounts receivable in the aggregate.
Answer (B) is incorrect. A subsidiary ledger is not a supplementary accounting system. Answer (C) is incorrect. A listing of account balances just before closing entries are prepared is a trial balance. Answer (D) is incorrect. The term "subsidiary ledger" relates to a specific general ledger account, not the accounting systems of a subsidiary company.

2.1.8. Which of the following statements is a true description of reversing entries?

A. The recording of reversing entries is a mandatory step in the accounting cycle.

B. Reversing entries are made at the end of the next accounting period, after recording regular transactions of the period.

C. Reversing entries are identical to the adjusting entries made in the previous period.

D. Reversing entries are the exact opposite of the adjustments made in the previous period.

Answer (D) is correct. *(CIA, adapted)*
   REQUIRED: The true description of reversing entries.
   DISCUSSION: Reversing entries are made at the beginning of a period to reverse the effects of adjusting entries made at the end of the preceding period. They are optional entries made for the sake of convenience in recording the transactions of the period. In order for reversing entries to reverse the prior adjustments, they must be the exact opposite of the adjustments made in the previous period.
   Answer (A) is incorrect. Reversing entries are optional. Answer (B) is incorrect. Reversing entries are made at the beginning of the next accounting period. Answer (C) is incorrect. Reversing entries are the exact opposite of the adjustments made in the previous period.

2.1.9. The business reason usually given for a business to select a fiscal year different from the calendar year is that

A. The firm's owners may have a personal preference.

B. Tax laws favor firms that employ a fiscal year other than the calendar year.

C. The fiscal year end is selected to coincide with the low points in sales, production, and inventories, which may occur at some period other than the calendar year end.

D. Public accounting firms might not be able to handle the workload if all their clients were to report on a calendar-year basis.

Answer (C) is correct. *(CMA, adapted)*
   REQUIRED: The most common reason for selecting a fiscal year different from the calendar year.
   DISCUSSION: A fiscal year is a 12-month period that ends at a date other than December 31. The business's natural business year is normally chosen. A natural year runs from one low point in a firm's business activity to the same low point 12 months later.
   Answer (A) is incorrect. Personal preference is a less compelling reason than matching the period chosen with the entity's normal business cycle. Answer (B) is incorrect. In the long term, choice of a fiscal year provides no tax advantage. Answer (D) is incorrect. An entity should choose a reporting period based on its normal business cycle, not the convenience of accounting firms.

2.2 Accruals and Deferrals

2.2.1. How would the proceeds received from the advance sale of nonrefundable tickets for a theatrical performance be reported in the seller's financial statements before the performance?

A. Revenue for the entire proceeds.

B. Revenue to the extent of related costs expended.

C. Unearned revenue to the extent of related costs expended.

D. Unearned revenue for the entire proceeds.

Answer (D) is correct. *(CPA, adapted)*
   REQUIRED: The reporting of the proceeds received from the advance sale of nonrefundable tickets.
   DISCUSSION: Revenue is recognized when (or as) the entity satisfies a performance obligation by transferring a promised good or service to a customer. The good or service is transferred when the customer obtains control of that good or service. The entire proceeds therefore should be credited to a contract liability (deferred or unearned revenue) because the performance obligation will not be satisfied until the performance has been given even though the tickets are not refundable.
   Answer (A) is incorrect. Revenue is recognized when (or as) the entity satisfies a performance obligation by transferring a promised good or service to a customer. The good or service is transferred when the customer obtains control of that good or service. Answer (B) is incorrect. Revenue is recognized when (or as) the entity satisfies a performance obligation by transferring a promised good or service to a customer. The good or service is transferred when the customer obtains control of that good or service. Answer (C) is incorrect. The entire proceeds should be credited to unearned revenue.

2.2.2. An adjusting entry that records the earned portion of unearned revenue previously recorded always includes a

A. Debit to an account in the asset category.

B. Credit to an account in the asset category.

C. Credit to an account in the equity category.

D. Credit to an account in the liability category.

Answer (C) is correct. *(CMA, adapted)*
REQUIRED: The effect of an adjusting entry that records the earned portion of unearned revenue previously recorded.
DISCUSSION: When cash from customers is collected in advance, a credit is made to the unearned revenue account. When the revenue is earned, usually on the basis of production and delivery, the unearned revenue account must then be debited, with a corresponding credit to a revenue account (an equity account).
Answer (A) is incorrect. The debit in any entry to reclassify unearned revenue to earned revenue is to unearned revenue. Answer (B) is incorrect. When unearned revenue is reclassified to earned revenue, the credit must be to earned revenue. Answer (D) is incorrect. The liability is unearned revenue, and it must be decreased (debited) when a portion of it is reclassified to earned revenue.

2.2.3. On February 12, Goal Publishing, Inc., purchased the copyright to a book for $15,000 and agreed to pay royalties equal to 10% of book sales, with a guaranteed minimum royalty of $60,000. Goal had book sales of $750,000 during the year. In its income statement, what amount should Goal report as royalty expense for the year?

A. $60,000

B. $75,000

C. $76,500

D. $90,000

Answer (B) is correct. *(CPA, adapted)*
REQUIRED: The royalty expense for the year.
DISCUSSION: The royalty expense is equal to 10% of book sales, with a guaranteed minimum royalty of $60,000. Thus, royalty expense is $75,000 ($750,000 book sales × 10%).
Answer (A) is incorrect. The guaranteed minimum royalty is $60,000, which is less than 10% of book sales. Answer (C) is incorrect. The amount of $76,500 includes 10% of the purchase price of the copyright. Answer (D) is incorrect. The copyright purchase price is not included in royalty expense.

2.2.4. A company that sprays chemicals in residences to eliminate or prevent infestation of insects requires that customers prepay for 3 months' service at the beginning of each new quarter. Which term appropriately describes the prepayment from the perspective of the service provider?

A. Unearned revenue.

B. Earned revenue.

C. Accrued revenue.

D. Prepaid expense.

Answer (A) is correct. *(CIA, adapted)*
REQUIRED: The classification of collected fees that pertain to a future period.
DISCUSSION: Under the revenue recognition principle, revenue is recognized (reported as revenue) in the period in which it is earned. Thus, when it is received in advance of its being earned, the amount applicable to future periods is deferred. The amount unearned (received in advance) is considered a liability because it represents an obligation to perform a service in the future arising from a past transaction. Unearned revenue is revenue that has been received but not earned.
Answer (B) is incorrect. The revenue is not earned. The company has not performed the related services for the customer. Answer (C) is incorrect. Accrued revenue is revenue that has been earned but not received. The company reports revenue that has been received but not earned. Answer (D) is incorrect. The customer reports a prepaid expense (expense paid but not incurred). The company reports unearned revenue (revenue received but not earned).

2.2.5. On November 1, Year 1, Key Co. paid $3,600 to renew its now-expired insurance policy for 3 years. It recorded this payment as an expense. At December 31, Year 1, Key's unadjusted trial balance showed a balance of $90 for prepaid insurance and $4,410 for insurance expense. What amounts should be reported for prepaid insurance and insurance expense in Key's December 31, Year 1, financial statements?

	Prepaid Expense	Insurance Expense
A.	$3,400	$1,100
B.	$3,490	$1,010
C.	$3,300	$1,200
D.	$3,400	$1,200

Answer (A) is correct. *(CPA, adapted)*
REQUIRED: The amounts reported for prepaid insurance and insurance expense.
DISCUSSION: Key Co. renewed its policy on November 1. Thus, (1) the prior policy had expired and (2) the only insurance expense properly recognized for the last 2 months of Year 1 for accrual accounting purposes was $200 [($3,600 cost of the new 3-year policy ÷ 36 months) × 2 months]. Accordingly, the asset prepaid insurance should be adjusted at year-end to $3,400 ($3,600 – $200). Moreover, annual insurance expense should equal $1,100 [$90 of pre-November 1 prepaid insurance not previously expensed + $200 expired amount of the November 1 payment + ($4,410 – $3,600 amount expensed on November 1)].
Answer (B) is incorrect. The unadjusted prepaid insurance balance ($90) is an expired amount. Answer (C) is incorrect. An asset balance of $3,300 and an expense of $1,200 assume the renewed policy has been in effect for 3 months. Answer (D) is incorrect. An expense of $1,200 assumes the renewed policy has been in effect for 3 months.

2.2.6. An analysis of Thrift Corp.'s unadjusted prepaid expense account at December 31, Year 4, revealed the following:

- An opening balance at $1,500 for Thrift's comprehensive insurance policy. Thrift had paid an annual premium of $3,000 on July 1, Year 3.
- A $3,200 annual insurance premium payment made July 1, Year 4.
- A $2,000 advance rental payment for a warehouse Thrift leased for 1 year beginning January 1, Year 5.

In its December 31, Year 4, balance sheet, what amount should Thrift report as prepaid expenses?

- A. $5,200
- B. $3,600
- C. $2,000
- D. $1,600

Answer (B) is correct. *(CPA, adapted)*
REQUIRED: The amount reported for prepaid expenses.
DISCUSSION: The $1,500 beginning balance of prepaid insurance expired on 6/30/Yr 4, leaving a $0 balance. The $3,200 annual insurance premium paid on 7/1/Yr 4 should be allocated equally to Year 4 and Year 5, leaving a $1,600 prepaid insurance balance. The $2,000 advance rental payment is an expense that is wholly deferred until Year 5. Consequently, the total of prepaid expenses at year end is $3,600 ($1,600 + $2,000).
Answer (A) is incorrect. Half of the $3,200 of prepaid insurance should be expensed in Year 4. Answer (C) is incorrect. Only half of the $3,200 of prepaid insurance should be expensed in Year 4. Answer (D) is incorrect. The prepaid rent is deferred until Year 5.

2.2.7. Cathay Co. owns a royalty interest in an oil well. The contract stipulates that Cathay will receive royalty payments semiannually on January 31 and July 31. The January 31 payment will be for 20% of the oil sold to jobbers between the previous June 1 and November 30, and the July 31 payment will be for oil sold between the previous December 1 and May 31. Royalty receipts for Year 2 amounted to $80,000 and $100,000 on January 31 and July 31, respectively. On December 31, Year 1, accrued royalty revenue receivable amounted to $15,000. Production reports show the following oil sales:

June 1, Year 1-November 30, Year 1	$400,000
December 1, Year 1-May 31, Year 2	500,000
June 1, Year 2-November 30, Year 2	425,000
December 1, Year 2-December 31, Year 2	70,000

What amount should Cathay report as royalty revenue for Year 2?

- A. $179,000
- B. $180,000
- C. $184,000
- D. $194,000

Answer (C) is correct. *(CPA, adapted)*
REQUIRED: The royalty revenue for Year 2.
DISCUSSION: The royalty revenue for Year 2 is 20% of Year 2 oil sales. Given that 12/1/Year 1-5/31/Year 2 oil sales equaled $500,000 and that the accrued royalty for December Year 1 was $15,000, oil sales for that month must have been $75,000 ($15,000 accrued ÷ 20%). Hence, oil sales for Year 2 are $920,000 [($500,000 – $75,000) + $425,000 + $70,000]. Thus, royalty revenue for Year 2 is $184,000 ($920,000 × 20%).
Answer (A) is incorrect. The amount of $179,000 incorrectly computes part of the revenue with the sales from 6/1/Year 1-11/30/Year 1 instead of 1/1/Year 1-5/31/Year 2. Answer (B) is incorrect. The royalty payments received in Year 2 are $180,000. Answer (D) is incorrect. The amount of $194,000 is the royalty payments received in Year 2, plus 20% of December Year 2's sales.

2.2.8. Windy Co. must determine the December 31, Year 2, year-end accruals for advertising and rent expenses. A $500 advertising bill was received January 7, Year 3. It related to costs of $375 for advertisements in December Year 2 issues and $125 for advertisements in January Year 3 issues of the newspaper. A store lease, effective December 16, Year 1, calls for fixed rent of $1,200 per month, payable 1 month from the effective date and monthly thereafter. In addition, rent equal to 5% of net sales over $300,000 per calendar year is payable on January 31 of the following year. Net sales for Year 2 were $550,000. In its December 31, Year 2, balance sheet, Windy should report accrued liabilities of

A. $12,500

B. $12,875

C. $13,100

D. $13,475

Answer (D) is correct. *(CPA, adapted)*
REQUIRED: The accrued liabilities reported at year-end.
DISCUSSION: The $375 of advertising expense should be accrued in Year 2 because this amount can be directly related to events in that period. The $125 amount is related to events in Year 3 and should not be accrued in Year 2. The fixed rental is due at mid-month. Thus, the fixed rental for the last half month of Year 2 ($1,200 ÷ 2 = $600) and the rental based on annual sales [($550,000 – $300,000) × 5% = $12,500] should also be accrued, for a total of $13,475 ($375 + $600 + $12,500).
Answer (A) is incorrect. The amount of $12,500 omits the half-month of the fixed rental and the advertising bill for December. Answer (B) is incorrect. The amount of $12,875 omits the half-month of the fixed rental. Answer (C) is incorrect. The amount of $13,100 excludes the advertising bill for December.

2.2.9. Zach Corp. pays commissions to its sales staff at the rate of 3% of net sales. Sales staff are not paid salaries but are given monthly advances of $15,000. Advances are charged to commission expense, and reconciliations against commissions are prepared quarterly. Net sales for the year ended March 31, Year 1, were $15 million. The unadjusted balance in the commissions expense account on March 31, Year 1, was $400,000. March advances were paid on April 3, Year 1. In its income statement for the year ended March 31, Year 1, what amount should Zach report as commission expense?

A. $465,000

B. $450,000

C. $415,000

D. $400,000

Answer (B) is correct. *(CPA, adapted)*
REQUIRED: The commission expense for the year.
DISCUSSION: Sales commissions should be recognized as an expense when the related revenues are earned. Commission expense is thus $450,000 ($15,000,000 net sales × 3%).
Answer (A) is incorrect. The amount of $465,000 is the sum of commission expense and one monthly advance. Answer (C) is incorrect. The amount of $415,000 equals the unadjusted balance in the commissions expense account plus one monthly advance. Answer (D) is incorrect. The amount of $400,000 is the unadjusted balance in the commissions expense account.

2.2.10. Jay Corp.'s trademark was licensed to John Co. for royalties of 15% of sales of the trademarked items. Royalties are payable semiannually on March 15 for sales in July through December of the prior year, and on September 15 for sales in January through June of the same year. Jay received the following royalties from John:

	March 15	September 15
Year 1	$10,000	$15,000
Year 2	12,000	18,000

John estimated that sales of the trademarked items would total $90,000 for July through December Year 2. In Jay's Year 2 income statement, the royalty revenue should be

A. $31,500

B. $30,000

C. $43,500

D. $46,500

Answer (A) is correct. *(CPA, adapted)*
REQUIRED: The amount of royalty revenue to be reported.
DISCUSSION: The royalty revenue for Year 2 is $31,500 [$18,000 received in September Year 2 + ($90,000 × 15%) to be received in March Year 3 for sales in Year 2].
Answer (B) is incorrect. The amount of $30,000 includes $12,000 that was received in March Year 2 but was applicable to Year 1 sales and omits the $13,500 ($90,000 × 15%) attributable to sales for July through December Year 2. Answer (C) is incorrect. The amount of $43,500 includes $12,000 that was received in March Year 2 but was applicable to Year 1 sales. Answer (D) is incorrect. The amount of $46,500 includes $15,000 that was received in September Year 1 and was applicable to Year 1 sales.

2.2.11. Seri Co.'s professional fees expense account had a balance of $92,000 at December 31, Year 1, before considering year-end adjustments relating to the following:

- Consultants were hired for a special project at a total fee not to exceed $65,000. Seri has recorded $55,000 of this fee based on billings for work performed in Year 1.
- The attorney's letter requested by the auditors, dated January 28, Year 2, indicated that legal fees of $6,000 were billed on January 15, Year 2, for work performed in November Year 1 and that unbilled fees for December Year 1 were $9,000.

What amount should Seri report for professional fees expense for the year ended December 31, Year 1?

   A. $117,000

   B. $107,000

   C. $98,000

   D. $92,000

Answer (B) is correct. *(CPA, adapted)*
   REQUIRED: The professional fees expense for the year.
   DISCUSSION: The entity should recognize an expense only for the work done by the consultants and attorneys in Year 1. Thus, no adjustment is necessary for the consulting fees, but the legal fees, billed and unbilled, for November and December Year 1 should be debited to the account. The professional fees expense for the year is therefore $107,000 ($92,000 + $6,000 + $9,000).
   Answer (A) is incorrect. The amount of $117,000 includes the maximum fee that may be payable to the consultants. Answer (C) is incorrect. The amount of $98,000 excludes the attorneys' fees for December. Answer (D) is incorrect. The amount of $92,000 excludes the attorney's fees for November and December.

2.2.12. Dix Company sells subscriptions to a specialized directory that is published semiannually and shipped to subscribers on April 15 and October 15. Subscriptions received after the March 31 and September 30 cutoff dates are held for the next publication. Cash from subscribers is received evenly during the year and is credited to deferred revenues from subscriptions. Data relating to Year 2 are as follows:

Deferred revenues from subscriptions, balance 12/31/Year 1	$1,500,000
Cash receipts from subscribers	7,200,000

In its December 31, Year 2, balance sheet, Dix should report deferred revenues from subscriptions of

   A. $1,800,000

   B. $3,300,000

   C. $3,600,000

   D. $5,400,000

Answer (A) is correct. *(CPA, adapted)*
   REQUIRED: The balance to be reported as deferred revenues from subscriptions at year end.
   DISCUSSION: The deferred revenues from subscriptions account records subscription fees received that have not been earned. The balance in this account in the December 31, Year 2, balance sheet should reflect the subscription fees received after the September 30 cutoff date. Because cash from subscribers is received evenly during the year, $1,800,000 [$7,200,000 × (3 months ÷ 12 months)] should be reported as deferred revenues from subscriptions.
   Answer (B) is incorrect. The amount of $3,300,000 is the sum of the existing deferred revenues balance and the fees received after the September 30 cutoff. Answer (C) is incorrect. Six months of fees equals $3,600,000. Answer (D) is incorrect. Nine months of fees equals $5,400,000.

2.2.13. Based on current year sales of music recorded by an artist under a contract with Cyber Music, the artist earned $200,000 after an adjustment of $16,000 for anticipated returns. In addition, Cyber paid the artist $150,000 in the current year as a reasonable estimate of the amount recoverable from future royalties to be earned by the artist. What amount should Cyber report in its current year income statement for royalty expense?

   A. $200,000

   B. $216,000

   C. $350,000

   D. $366,000

Answer (A) is correct. *(CPA, adapted)*
   REQUIRED: The royalty expense.
   DISCUSSION: Income is earned by the artist and an expense is incurred by Cyber based on net sales (sales – returns). Amounts paid in advance and recoverable from future royalties are classified as prepaid expenses. Thus, Cyber should report royalty expense of $200,000.
   Answer (B) is incorrect. The amount of $216,000 includes the adjustment of $16,000 for anticipated returns. Answer (C) is incorrect. The amount of $350,000 includes the prepayment. Answer (D) is incorrect. The amount of $366,000 includes the prepayment and the adjustment of $16,000 for anticipated returns.

2.2.14. Aneen's Video Mart sells 1- and 2-year mail order subscriptions for its video-of-the-month business. Subscriptions are collected in advance and credited to sales. An analysis of the recorded sales activity revealed the following:

	Year 1	Year 2
Sales	$420,000	$500,000
Cancelations	(20,000)	(30,000)
Net sales	$400,000	$470,000
Subscriptions expirations:		
Year 1	$120,000	
Year 2	155,000	$130,000
Year 3	125,000	200,000
Year 4		140,000
	$400,000	$470,000

In Aneen's December 31, Year 2, balance sheet, the balance for unearned subscription revenue should be

A. $495,000

B. $470,000

C. $465,000

D. $340,000

Answer (C) is correct. *(CPA, adapted)*
   REQUIRED: The balance for unearned subscription revenue.
   DISCUSSION: An entity recognizes revenue when (or as) it satisfies a performance obligation by transferring a promised good or service to a customer. The balance for unearned subscription revenue (a contract liability) should reflect the advance collections for which the performance obligation is not satisfied. Thus, the unexpired subscriptions as of 12/31/Yr 2 total $465,000 ($125,000 + $200,000 + $140,000), which is the balance for unearned subscription revenue.
   Answer (A) is incorrect. The amount of $495,000 results from adding Year 1 sales of subscriptions that expired in Year 2 to the unexpired subscriptions. Also, the amount omits the Year 1 sales of subscriptions that will expire in Year 3. Answer (B) is incorrect. The amount of $470,000 equals net sales for Year 2. Answer (D) is incorrect. The amount of $340,000 omits the Year 1 sales of subscriptions that will expire in Year 3.

2.2.15. In its Year 4 financial statements, Cris Co. reported interest expense of $85,000 in its income statement and cash paid for interest of $68,000 in its cash flow statement. There was no prepaid interest or interest capitalization at either the beginning or the end of Year 4. Accrued interest at December 31, Year 3, was $15,000. What amount should Cris report as accrued interest payable in its December 31, Year 4, balance sheet?

A. $2,000

B. $15,000

C. $17,000

D. $32,000

Answer (D) is correct. *(CPA, adapted)*
   REQUIRED: The accrued interest payable at year end.
   DISCUSSION: The cash paid for interest was $68,000, including $15,000 of interest paid for Year 3. Consequently, $53,000 ($68,000 – $15,000) of the cash paid for interest related to Year 4. Interest payable is therefore $32,000 ($85,000 – $53,000).
   Answer (A) is incorrect. The amount of $2,000 results from adding the $15,000 to $68,000 and subtracting that sum from the $85,000 interest expense. Answer (B) is incorrect. The interest paid for Year 3 is $15,000. Answer (C) is incorrect. The difference between the interest expense and cash paid out is $17,000.

2.2.16. Dana Co.'s officers' compensation expense account had a balance of $490,000 at December 31, Year 1, before any appropriate year-end adjustment relating to the following:

- No salary accrual was made for the week of December 25-31, Year 1. Officers' salaries for this period totaled $18,000 and were paid on January 5, Year 2.

- Bonuses to officers for Year 1 were paid on January 31, Year 2, in the total amount of $175,000.

The adjusted balance for officers' compensation expense for the year ended December 31, Year 1, should be

A. $683,000

B. $665,000

C. $508,000

D. $490,000

Answer (A) is correct. *(CPA, adapted)*
   REQUIRED: The adjusted balance in the officers' compensation expense account.
   DISCUSSION: The officers' compensation expense account should include the entire compensation expense incurred in Year 1. Accordingly, it should include the $490,000 previously recorded in the account, the $18,000 of accrued salaries, and the $175,000 of accrued bonuses. The adjusted balance should therefore be $683,000 ($490,000 + $18,000 + $175,000).
   Answer (B) is incorrect. The amount of $665,000 does not include salaries accrued at year end. Answer (C) is incorrect. The amount of $508,000 does not include the bonuses. Answer (D) is incorrect. The amount of $490,000 does not include the bonuses and the accrued salaries.

2.2.17. Kiddie Kare Co. offers three payment plans on its 12-month contracts. Information on the three plans and the number of children enrolled in each plan for the June 1, Year 1, through May 31, Year 2, contract year follows:

Plan	Initial Payment per Child	Monthly Fees per Child	Number of Children
#1	$500	$ --	15
#2	200	30	12
#3	--	50	9
			36

Kiddie received $9,900 of initial payments on June 1, Year 1, and $5,670 of monthly fees during the period June 1 through December 31, Year 1. In its December 31, Year 1, balance sheet, what amount should Kiddie report as deferred revenues?

A. $5,670

B. $5,775

C. $4,125

D. $9,900

Answer (C) is correct. *(CPA, adapted)*
REQUIRED: The amount reported as deferred revenues.
DISCUSSION: Unearned (deferred) revenues relate to the portion of the contracts for which services have not been performed (the earning process has not been completed). At December 31, Year 1, deferred revenues should equal $4,125 [9,900 prepayments received × (5 months ÷ 12 months)].
Answer (A) is incorrect. The total of monthly fees collected in Year 1 is $5,670. Answer (B) is incorrect. The portion of prepayments earned in Year 1 is $5,775. Answer (D) is incorrect. The total prepayments equal $9,900.

2.2.18. O'Hara Co. owns an office building and leases the offices under a variety of rental agreements involving rent paid in advance monthly or annually. Not all tenants make timely payments of their rent. O'Hara's balance sheets contained the following data:

	Year 1	Year 2
Rentals receivable	$19,200	$24,800
Unearned rentals	64,000	48,000

During Year 2, O'Hara received $160,000 cash from tenants. What amount of rental revenue should O'Hara record for Year 2?

A. $181,600

B. $170,800

C. $144,000

D. $133,200

Answer (A) is correct. *(CPA, adapted)*
REQUIRED: The rental revenue for the current year.
DISCUSSION: The ending balance in the rental receivable was $5,600 higher than the beginning balance ($24,800 – $19,200). Thus, revenues exceeded cash receipts. The ending balance in unearned rent was $16,000 less than the beginning balance ($64,000 – $48,000), again indicating that revenues exceeded cash receipts. Rental revenue is $181,600 ($160,000 + $5,600 + $16,000).
Answer (B) is incorrect. The amount of $170,800 equals the cash received plus 50% of the sum of the increase in rentals receivable and the decrease in unearned rentals. Answer (C) is incorrect. The amount of $144,000 equals the cash received minus the decrease in unearned rentals. Answer (D) is incorrect. The amount of $133,200 equals the cash received, minus the decrease in unearned rentals, minus 50% of the sum of the increase in rentals receivable and the decrease in unearned rentals.

2.2.19. Under Best Co.'s accounting system, all insurance premiums paid are debited to prepaid insurance. For interim financial reports, Best makes monthly estimated charges to insurance expense with credits to prepaid insurance. Additional information for the year ended December 31, Year 2, is as follows:

Prepaid insurance at December 31, Year 1	$110,000
Charges to insurance expense during Year 2 (including a year-end adjustment of $10,500)	437,500
Prepaid insurance at December 31, Year 2	120,500

What was the total amount of insurance premiums paid by Best during Year 2?

A. $327,500

B. $427,000

C. $437,500

D. $448,000

Answer (D) is correct. *(CPA, adapted)*
REQUIRED: The total amount of insurance premiums paid.
DISCUSSION: The company debits prepaid insurance for all insurance premiums paid and credits the account when it charges insurance expense. Thus, total debits equal insurance premiums paid. The asset account had total credits (charges to expense) of $437,500 and increased by $10,500 ($120,500 ending balance – $110,000 beginning balance). Consequently, total debits (premiums paid) must have been $448,000 ($437,500 total charges to insurance expense + $10,500 increase in the asset account).
Answer (A) is incorrect. Total credits minus the beginning balance is $327,500. Answer (B) is incorrect. The amount of $427,000 results from subtracting, not adding, the difference between the beginning and ending balances. Answer (C) is incorrect. Total credits to the account equal $437,500.

2.2.20. A company provides the following information:

Cash receipts from customers:	Year 1	Year 2	Year 3
From Year 1 sales	$95,000	$120,000	
From Year 2 sales		200,000	$ 75,000
From Year 3 sales		50,000	225,000

What is the accrual-based revenue for Year 2?

A. $200,000

B. $275,000

C. $320,000

D. $370,000

Answer (B) is correct. *(CPA, adapted)*
REQUIRED: The accrual-based revenue for Year 2.
DISCUSSION: Under the accrual method, revenues and gains are realized when goods or services have been exchanged for cash or claims to cash, not when that cash is collected. Consequently, given that total cash collected for Year 2 sales is $275,000 ($200,000 Year 2 + $75,000 Year 3), revenue for Year 2 is $275,000.
Answer (A) is incorrect. The amount of $200,000 equals cash collected in Year 2 for sales from Year 2. Answer (C) is incorrect. The amount of $320,000 equals cash collected in Year 2 for sales from Year 1 and Year 2. Answer (D) is incorrect. The amount of $370,000 equals cash collected in Year 2.

2.2.21. Dunne Co. sells equipment service contracts that cover a 2-year period. The sales price of each contract is $600. Dunne's past experience is that, of the total dollars spent for repairs on service contracts, 40% is incurred evenly during the first contract year and 60% evenly during the second contract year. Dunne sold 1,000 contracts evenly throughout the year. In its December 31 balance sheet, what amount should Dunne report as deferred service contract revenue?

A. $540,000

B. $480,000

C. $360,000

D. $300,000

Answer (B) is correct. *(CPA, adapted)*
REQUIRED: The amount of deferred service contract revenue reported on the balance sheet.
DISCUSSION: Revenue should be recognized when (or as) the entity satisfies a performance obligation by transferring a promised good or service to a customer. The good or service is transferred when the customer obtains control of that good or service. Service contract revenue should be recognized over time as the services are provided. An appropriate measure of the entity's progress to complete satisfaction of the performance obligation also must be selected. Assuming that services are provided in proportion to the incurrence of expenses, 40% of revenue should be recognized in the first year of a service contract. Given that expenses are incurred evenly throughout the year, revenue also will be recognized evenly. Moreover, given that Dunne sold 1,000 contracts evenly throughout the year, total revenue will be $600,000 (1,000 contracts × $600), and the average contract must have been sold at mid-year. Thus, the elapsed time of the average contract must be half a year, and revenue recognized for the year must equal $120,000 ($600,000 total revenue × 40% × .5 year). Deferred revenue (a contract liability) at year end will equal $480,000 ($600,000 – $120,000).
Answer (A) is incorrect. The amount of $540,000 assumes the average contract has been outstanding for 3 months. Answer (C) is incorrect. The second year's revenue for all contracts is $360,000. Answer (D) is incorrect. This is the amount deferred if 50% of expenses are expected to be incurred each year and the average contract has been outstanding for 1 year.

2.2.22. Delect Co. provides repair services for the AZ195 TV set. Customers prepay the fee on the standard 1-year service contract. The Year 1 and Year 2 contracts were identical, and the number of contracts outstanding was substantially the same at the end of each year. However, Delect's December 31, Year 2, deferred revenue balance on unperformed service contracts was significantly less than the balance at December 31, Year 1. Which of the following situations might account for this reduction in the deferred revenue balance?

A. Most Year 2 contracts were signed later in the calendar year than were the Year 1 contracts.

B. Most Year 2 contracts were signed earlier in the calendar year than were the Year 1 contracts.

C. The Year 2 contract contribution margin was greater than the Year 1 contract contribution margin.

D. The Year 2 contribution margin was less than the Year 1 contract contribution margin.

Answer (B) is correct. *(CPA, adapted)*
REQUIRED: The situation that might explain the reduction in the deferred revenue balance.
DISCUSSION: Revenue should be recognized when (or as) the entity satisfies a performance obligation by transferring a promised good or service to a customer. The good or service is transferred when the customer obtains control of that good or service. Service contract revenue should be recognized over time as the services are provided. An appropriate measure of the entity's progress to complete satisfaction of the performance obligation also must be selected. Service contract fees are not recognized until the services are provided and the performance obligation is satisfied. Thus, the fees collected in advance should be reported as unearned (deferred) revenue (a contract liability) in the liability section of the balance sheet until the services are provided. The earlier a service contract is signed, the longer the time to provide the service and satisfy the performance obligation. Thus, if most contracts outstanding on December 31, Year 2, were signed earlier in the period than those outstanding a year earlier, the deferred revenue balance should have decreased.
Answer (A) is incorrect. If most Year 2 contracts were signed later in the calendar year than were the Year 1 contracts, the deferred revenue balance would have increased. Answer (C) is incorrect. The contribution margin relates to profit, not revenue. Answer (D) is incorrect. The contribution margin relates to profit, not revenue.

2.2.23. Ina Co. had the following beginning and ending balances in its prepaid expenses and accrued liabilities accounts for the current year:

	Prepaid Expenses	Accrued Liabilities
Beginning balance	$ 5,000	$ 8,000
Ending balance	10,000	20,000

Debits to operating expenses totaled $100,000. What amount did Ina pay for operating expenses during the current year?

A. $83,000

B. $93,000

C. $107,000

D. $117,000

Answer (B) is correct. *(CPA, adapted)*
REQUIRED: The amount of operating expenses paid.
DISCUSSION: Debits to operating expenses totaled $100,000 for the year. The accrued liabilities account increased by $12,000 ($20,000 ending – $8,000 beginning). This means that $12,000 of the debited operating expenses were not paid in the current year and must be subtracted from the $100,000. The prepaid expenses account increased by $5,000 ($10,000 ending – $5,000 beginning). This means $5,000 of operating expenses were prepaid in the current year but not included in debited operating expenses because the prepaid expense account was debited instead; these must be added to the $100,000. Thus, Ina paid $93,000 total in operating expenses during the current year ($100,000 – $12,000 + $5,000).
Answer (A) is incorrect. An amount of $83,000 results from subtracting, rather than adding, the increase in prepaid expenses. This expense represents $5,000 of operating expenses that were paid in the current year but not included in debited operating expenses because the prepaid expense account was debited instead. Answer (C) is incorrect. The increase in the accrued liabilities account should be subtracted from the debited operating expenses as it represents $12,000 of the debited operating expenses that were not paid in the current year. The increase in the prepaid expenses account should be added as it represents $5,000 of operating expenses that were paid in the current year and not included in debited operating expenses. Answer (D) is incorrect. The increase in the accrued liabilities account should be subtracted from, not added to, the amount of operating expenses recognized because it represents $12,000 of debited operating expenses that were not paid in the current year.

2.3 Journal Entries

2.3.1. In reviewing a set of journal entries, an auditor encounters an entry composed of a debit to interest expense and a credit to interest payable. The purpose of this journal entry is to record

    A. An accrued expense.

    B. A deferred expense.

    C. A contingent liability.

    D. An unexpired cost.

Answer (A) is correct. *(CIA, adapted)*
    REQUIRED: The purpose of a journal entry that debits an expense and credits a payable.
    DISCUSSION: An accrued expense is one that has been incurred in the current period but has not yet been paid. The journal entry to record an accrued expense requires a debit to an expense account and a credit to a payable account.
    Answer (B) is incorrect. A deferred expense is a prepayment and is recorded as an asset. Answer (C) is incorrect. Interest expense is not a contingent liability. Answer (D) is incorrect. An unexpired cost is an asset.

2.3.2. In performing an audit, an auditor encounters an adjusting journal entry recorded at year end that contains a debit to rental revenue and a credit to unearned rental revenue. The purpose of this journal entry is to record

    A. An accrued revenue.

    B. An unexpired cost.

    C. An expired cost.

    D. A deferred revenue.

Answer (D) is correct. *(CIA, adapted)*
    REQUIRED: The purpose of a journal entry that debits rental revenue and credits unearned rental revenue.
    DISCUSSION: Revenues should be recognized when realized or realizable and earned. If rental fees are collected before the revenue is earned and a credit is made to rental revenue, an adjusting entry may be necessary at year end. The purpose of the journal entry is to adjust both rental revenue and unearned rental revenue to reflect the rental fees collected that had not been earned during this accounting period.
    Answer (A) is incorrect. An accrued revenue is reflected as a receivable. Answer (B) is incorrect. An unexpired cost is recorded as an asset. Answer (C) is incorrect. An expired cost is charged to expense.

2.3.3. The correct order of the following steps of the accounting cycle is

    A. Posting, closing, adjusting, reversing.

    B. Posting, adjusting, closing, reversing.

    C. Posting, reversing, adjusting, closing.

    D. Adjusting, posting, closing, reversing.

Answer (B) is correct. *(CIA, adapted)*
    REQUIRED: The proper sequence of steps in the accounting cycle.
    DISCUSSION: The order of the steps in the accounting cycle is (1) journalization of transactions, events, and other circumstances required to be recognized; (2) posting from the journals to the ledgers; (3) the development of an unadjusted trial balance; (4) adjustments to produce an adjusted trial balance; (5) statement preparation; (6) closing; (7) taking a postclosing trial balance (optional); and (8) making reversing entries (optional).
    Answer (A) is incorrect. Adjusting entries are made prior to closing. Answer (C) is incorrect. Reversing entries are made after adjustments and closing entries. Answer (D) is incorrect. Posting is done prior to adjusting.

2.3.4. Why are adjusting entries necessary?

    A. To record revenues and expenses.

    B. To make debits equal credits.

    C. To close nominal accounts at year end.

    D. To correct erroneous balances in accounts.

Answer (A) is correct. *(Publisher, adapted)*
    REQUIRED: The reason for adjusting entries.
    DISCUSSION: Adjusting entries are used to adjust expenses (and the related asset or liability accounts) or revenues (and the related asset or liability accounts) to year-end amounts. Adjusting entries are needed to properly reflect revenues recognized when they are realized or realizable and earned and expenses recognized in accordance with the expense recognition principles. Accrual adjusting entries are made when the expense or revenue is recognized prior to the payment or receipt of cash. Deferral adjusting entries are necessary when the expense or revenue is recognized after the payment or receipt of cash.
    Answer (B) is incorrect. All transactions result in equal debits and credits, and the cumulative balances of debits and credits are always equal. Answer (C) is incorrect. Closing nominal accounts at year end is the function of closing entries, not adjusting entries. Answer (D) is incorrect. Correcting erroneous account balances is the function of correcting entries, not adjusting entries.

2.3.5. On October 1, Year 1, a company sold services to a customer and accepted a note in exchange with a $120,000 face amount and an interest rate of 10%. The note requires that both the principal and interest be paid at the maturity date, December 1, Year 2. The company's accounting period is the calendar year. What adjusting entry (related to this note) will be required at December 31, Year 1, on the company's books?

A. Deferred interest income $3,000
     Interest receivable $3,000

B. Interest income $3,000
     Interest receivable $3,000

C. Interest receivable $3,000
     Deferred interest income $3,000

D. Interest receivable $3,000
     Interest income $3,000

Answer (D) is correct. *(CIA, adapted)*
     REQUIRED: The adjusting entry related to a note receivable.
     DISCUSSION: Interest receivable should be debited and interest income credited for the interest on the note accrued (earned but not paid) at year end [$120,000 × 10% × (3 months ÷ 12 months) = $3,000].
     Answer (A) is incorrect. The entry on December 31, Year 1, should reflect the interest earned by the passage of 3 months since the issuance of the note. The entry is to debit interest receivable (an asset) and credit interest income (a revenue). Answer (B) is incorrect. A debit to interest income and a credit to interest receivable is a reversing entry. Answer (C) is incorrect. Interest of $3,000 is not deferred. It has been earned by the passage of 3 months since the issuance of the note.

2.3.6. What is the purpose of the following entry?

Supplies $XXX
     Supplies expense $XXX

A. To recognize supplies used, if purchases of supplies are recorded in supplies.

B. To recognize supplies on hand, if purchases of supplies are recorded in supplies expense.

C. To record the purchase of supplies during or at the end of the period.

D. To close the expense account for supplies at the end of the period.

Answer (B) is correct. *(CIA, adapted)*
     REQUIRED: The purpose of the given entry.
     DISCUSSION: The debit to supplies and credit to supplies expense is an end-of-period adjusting entry. Assuming the acquisition of supplies was debited to expense, an adjusting entry is needed to record the supplies on hand and to recognize the correct amount of expense.
     Answer (A) is incorrect. If purchases are initially recorded in a real account, the entry to record use of supplies is

Supplies expense $XXX
     Supplies $XXX

Answer (C) is incorrect. The correct entry to record the purchase of supplies is

Supplies or Supplies expense $XXX
     Cash or Accounts payable $XXX

Answer (D) is incorrect. The entry to close supplies expense is

Income summary $XXX
     Supplies expense $XXX

2.3.7. On December 31, earned but unpaid wages amounted to $15,000. What reversing entry could be made on January 1?

A. Wages expense $15,000
     Wages payable $15,000

B. Prepaid wages $15,000
     Wages expense $15,000

C. Wages expense $15,000
     Prepaid wages $15,000

D. Wages payable $15,000
     Wages expense $15,000

Answer (D) is correct. *(Publisher, adapted)*
     REQUIRED: The reversing entry for an accrual of wages expense.
     DISCUSSION: The accrual of an expense requires a debit to expense and a credit to a liability. Accordingly, the reversing entry is to debit the liability and credit expense. The purpose of reversing this accrual of expense is to avoid having to apportion the first cash disbursement in the next period between the liability and expense accounts.
     Answer (A) is incorrect. A debit to wages expense and a credit to wages payable is the adjusting entry. Answer (B) is incorrect. A debit to prepaid wages and a credit to wages expense is an adjusting entry when wages have been prepaid and the original debit was to an expense (a method not frequently found in practice). Answer (C) is incorrect. A debit to wages expense and a credit to prepaid wages is the reversing entry for an adjusting entry made when wages have been prepaid and the original debit was to an expense account.

2.3.8. A consulting firm started and completed a project for a client in December of Year 1. The project has not been recorded on the consulting firm's books, and the firm will not receive payment from the client until February Year 2. The adjusting entry that should be made on the books of the consulting firm on December 31, Year 1, the last day of the firm's fiscal year, is

A. Cash in transit $XXX
　　　Consulting revenue　　　　　　　　$XXX

B. Consulting revenue receivable　$XXX
　　　Consulting revenue　　　　　　　　$XXX

C. Unearned consulting revenue　$XXX
　　　Consulting revenue　　　　　　　　$XXX

D. Consulting revenue receivable　$XXX
　　　Unearned consulting revenue　　$XXX

Answer (B) is correct. *(CMA, adapted)*
　　REQUIRED: The adjusting entry necessary to record consulting revenue.
　　DISCUSSION: Revenues should be recognized when they are realized or realizable and earned. Consulting revenue is realized and earned when the consulting service has been performed. Thus, for a consulting project that was started and completed during Year 1, an adjusting entry should be made at year end to record both a receivable and the revenue. The journal entry is a debit to consulting revenue receivable and a credit to consulting revenue.
　　Answer (A) is incorrect. Cash in transit is not an account. Answer (C) is incorrect. The unearned revenue account is used only if the client prepays. Answer (D) is incorrect. The revenue was earned during the period.

2.3.9. A 3-year insurance policy was purchased on October 1 for $6,000, and prepaid insurance was debited. Assuming a December 31 year end, what is the reversing entry at the beginning of the next period?

A. None is required.

B. Cash　　　　　　　$6,000
　　　Prepaid insurance　　　　　$6,000

C. Prepaid insurance　$5,500
　　　Insurance expense　　　　　$5,500

D. Insurance expense　$500
　　　Prepaid insurance　　　　　　$500

Answer (A) is correct. *(Publisher, adapted)*
　　REQUIRED: The reversing entry when a prepaid expense was debited to an asset account.
　　DISCUSSION: Given that the original entry recorded the prepaid insurance as an asset, the adjusting entry will debit expense and credit the asset for the amount of insurance that has expired. Accordingly, at the beginning of the year, the unexpired insurance will be in an asset account. Thus, no reversing entry is required.
　　Answer (B) is incorrect. Debit cash and credit prepaid insurance is the opposite (not a reversing entry) of the entry made to record the purchase of the 3-year insurance policy. Answer (C) is incorrect. Debit prepaid insurance and credit expense is the correct adjusting entry if the original entry had debited insurance expense rather than prepaid insurance. Answer (D) is incorrect. Debit expense and credit prepaid insurance is the correct adjusting entry (which requires no reversing entry).

2.3.10. Hurlburt Corporation renewed an insurance policy for 3 years beginning July 1 and recorded the $81,000 premium in the prepaid insurance account. The $81,000 premium represents an increase of $23,400 from the $57,600 premium charged 3 years ago. Assuming Hurlburt's records its insurance adjustments only at the end of the calendar year, the adjusting entry required to reflect the proper balances in the insurance accounts at December 31 Hurlburt's year end is to

A. Debit insurance expense for $13,500 and credit prepaid insurance for $13,500.

B. Debit prepaid insurance for $13,500 and credit insurance expense for $13,500.

C. Debit insurance expense for $67,500 and credit prepaid insurance for $67,500.

D. Debit insurance expense for $23,100 and credit prepaid insurance for $23,100.

Answer (D) is correct. *(CMA, adapted)*
　　REQUIRED: The entry to adjust the prepaid insurance account assuming annual adjustments.
　　DISCUSSION: The $57,600 premium paid 3 years ago was equivalent to a rate of $1,600 per month ($57,600 ÷ 36 months). On January 1, the prepaid insurance account would have had a balance of $9,600 ($1,600 × 6 months). On July 1, the prepaid insurance account would have been debited for an additional $81,000 covering the next 36 months at a monthly rate of $2,250 ($81,000 ÷ 36 months). The expense is therefore $23,100 [$9,600 + ($2,250 × 6 months)]. The adjusting entry is to debit insurance expense and credit prepaid insurance for $23,100.
　　Answer (A) is incorrect. The expense for the last 6 months of the year is $13,500. Answer (B) is incorrect. If the initial payment is debited to a real account, the adjustment requires a debit to a nominal account and a credit to the real account. Answer (C) is incorrect. The ending balance in prepaid insurance is $67,500.

Questions 2.3.11 and 2.3.12 are based on the following information. Louviere Co. prepares monthly financial statements. The clerical staff is paid every 2 weeks on the Monday following the end of the 2-week (10 working days) pay period ending on the prior Friday. The last pay period ended on Friday, November 19. The next payday is Monday, December 6, for the pay period ending December 3. The total clerical payroll for a 2-week period is $30,000, income tax withholding averages 15%, and Social Security taxes amount to 7.65%. None of the clerical staff's earnings will exceed the maximum limit for Social Security taxes.

2.3.11. The adjusting entry required to accrue Louviere's payroll as of November 30 is to

A. Debit wage expense for $21,000 and credit wages payable for $21,000.

B. Debit wage expense for $30,000, credit payroll tax expense for $1,950, and credit wages payable for $28,050.

C. Debit wage expense for $21,000, credit income tax withholding payable for $3,150, credit payroll taxes payable for $1,606.50, and credit wages payable for $16,243.50.

D. Debit wage expense for $30,000, credit income tax withholding payable for $4,500, credit payroll taxes payable for $1,950, and credit wages payable for $23,550.

Answer (C) is correct. *(CMA, adapted)*
REQUIRED: The adjusting entry necessary to accrue the payroll.
DISCUSSION: The 7 days included in the period from November 20 through November 30 represents 70% of the 10 working days in a 2-week pay period. Thus, $21,000 in wages expense should be accrued ($30,000 × 70%). Of this amount, $3,150 ($21,000 × 15%) must be credited to income tax withholding payable, $1,606.50 ($21,000 × 7.65%) to payroll tax payable, and the remainder, $16,243.50, to wages payable.
Answer (A) is incorrect. Wages payable must be reduced by income tax withholding and Social Security. Answer (B) is incorrect. The period from November 20 through November 30 includes only 7 working days, not the full 2-week period. Answer (D) is incorrect. The period from November 20 through November 30 includes only 7 working days, not the full 2-week period.

2.3.12. Louviere also is required to record an accrual for its obligation for payroll tax expenses. This adjusting entry should be to

A. Debit payroll tax expense for $4,756.50 and credit payroll taxes payable for $4,756.50.

B. Debit payroll tax expense for $1,606.50 and credit payroll taxes payable for $1,606.50.

C. Debit payroll tax expense for $2,295 and credit payroll taxes payable for $2,295.

D. Debit payroll tax expense for $4,515 and credit payroll taxes payable for $4,515.

Answer (B) is correct. *(CMA, adapted)*
REQUIRED: The adjusting entry necessary to accrue the company's obligation for Social Security taxes.
DISCUSSION: In addition to the Social Security taxes that must be withheld from employees' wages and remitted to the tax collection agency, the employer also must accrue and remit an equivalent amount as the employer's share. Thus, an additional expense of $1,606.50 ($21,000 × 7.65%) must be accrued.
Answer (A) is incorrect. The amount of $4,756.50 includes the employee withholding tax. Answer (C) is incorrect. The amount of $2,295 ($30,000 × 7.65%) mistakenly accrues payroll taxes for the entire 2-week (10-day) period instead of just the 7 working days from November 20 to November 30. Answer (D) is incorrect. Only the employer's share of Social Security ($21,000 × 7.65% = $1,606.50) is an expense of the employer.

2.3.13. Dunlap Company sublet a portion of its warehouse for 5 years at an annual rental of $15,000, beginning on March 1. The tenant paid 1 year's rent in advance, which Dunlap recorded as a credit to unearned rental income. Dunlap reports on a calendar-year basis. The adjustment on December 31 of the first year should be

A. No entry.

B. Unearned rental income $2,500
    Rental income $2,500

C. Rental income $2,500
    Unearned rental income $2,500

D. Unearned rental income $12,500
    Rental income $12,500

Answer (D) is correct. *(CPA, adapted)*
REQUIRED: The adjusting entry at year end for unearned rental income.
DISCUSSION: Given that the sublessor originally recorded the $15,000 received as a credit to a liability account, the adjusting entry is to debit the liability account and credit revenue for the revenue earned, which equals $1,250 a month ($12,500) for 10 months.
Answer (A) is incorrect. An adjusting entry is needed for all deferrals and accruals. Answer (B) is incorrect. The rental income to be recognized is for 10 months at $1,250 a month, not for 2 months. Answer (C) is incorrect. The debit and credit entries are switched, and the rental income to be recognized should be for 10 months, not 2 months.

2.3.14. After a successful drive aimed at members of a specific national association, Online Publishing Company received a total of $180,000 for 3-year subscriptions beginning April 1 and recorded this amount in the unearned revenue account. Assuming Online records adjustments only at the end of the calendar year, the adjusting entry required to reflect the proper balances in the accounts at December 31 is to

A. Debit subscription revenue for $135,000 and credit unearned revenue for $135,000.

B. Debit unearned revenue for $135,000 and credit subscription revenue for $135,000.

C. Debit subscription revenue for $45,000 and credit unearned revenue for $45,000.

D. Debit unearned revenue for $45,000 and credit subscription revenue for $45,000.

Answer (D) is correct. *(CMA, adapted)*
REQUIRED: The year-end adjusting entry.
DISCUSSION: The company initially debited cash and credited unearned revenue, a liability account, for $180,000. Subscriptions revenue should be recognized when it is realized or realizable and the earning process is substantially complete. Because 25% (9 months ÷ 36 months) of the subscription period has expired, 25% of the realized but unearned revenue should be recognized. Thus, the adjusting entry is to debit unearned revenue and credit subscription revenue for $45,000.
Answer (A) is incorrect. The amount of $135,000 would be the debit to the revenue account if it had been credited initially. Answer (B) is incorrect. A $135,000 debit to the unearned revenue account would be appropriate if 75% of the subscription period had elapsed. Answer (C) is incorrect. The amount of $45,000 would be the debit to the revenue account if it had been credited initially and if 75% of the subscription period had elapsed.

2.3.15. A machine costing $27,000 with a residual value of $2,000 is to be depreciated on a straight-line basis over 5 years. What is the adjusting entry for a full year of depreciation?

A. Depreciation expense　　$5,000
　　Machine　　　　　　　　　　　　$5,000

B. Depreciation expense　　$5,000
　　Cash　　　　　　　　　　　　　　$5,000

C. Machine　　　　　　　　　$27,000
　　Cash　　　　　　　　　　　　　$20,000
　　Depreciation expense　　　　　5,000
　　Residual value　　　　　　　　　2,000

D. Depreciation expense　　$5,000
　　Accumulated depreciation　　　$5,000

Answer (D) is correct. *(Publisher, adapted)*
REQUIRED: The year-end adjusting entry to depreciate a machine.
DISCUSSION: At year end, depreciation expense is debited, and accumulated depreciation (a contra asset) is credited. The amount of depreciation is 20% (1 year ÷ 5 years) of the depreciation base of $25,000 ($27,000 machine cost – $2,000 residual value).
Answer (A) is incorrect. The credit is not made directly to the asset but to the contra account, accumulated depreciation. Answer (B) is incorrect. Cash is paid when the machine is purchased, not each year when depreciation is recorded. Answer (C) is incorrect. The machine's cost was $27,000, depreciation expense is a debit rather than a credit, and residual value is not separately recorded.

2.3.16. On October 31, Year 1, a company with a calendar year end paid $90,000 for services that will be performed evenly over a 6-month period from November 1, Year 1, through April 30, Year 2. The company expensed the $90,000 cash payment in October Year 1 to its services expense general ledger account. The company did not record any additional journal entries in Year 1 related to the payment. What is the adjusting journal entry that the company should record to properly report the prepayment in its Year 1 financial statements?

A. Debit prepaid services and credit services expense for $30,000.

B. Debit prepaid services and credit services expense for $60,000.

C. Debit services expense and credit prepaid services for $30,000.

D. Debit services expense and credit prepaid services for $60,000.

Answer (B) is correct. *(CPA, adapted)*
REQUIRED: The adjusting entry needed to properly report a prepayment.
DISCUSSION: The full payment of $90,000 for services was initially recorded as an expense. Thus, the year-end adjusting entry is to debit an asset (prepaid service) and credit (decrease) services expense for the unexpired portion. At year end, $30,000 of the prepaid expense had expired [$90,000 × (2 months ÷ 6 months)]. The unexpired portion is equal to $60,000 ($90,000 – $30,000 expired). The appropriate adjusting entry is to debit prepaid services (to recognize the asset) and credit services expense (to lower the expense recognized) for $60,000, or the unexpired portion.
Answer (A) is incorrect. Only 2 months of services were performed in the current year (Nov.-Dec.), and 4 months were prepaid. Thus, at year-end, the company should recognize $60,000 as prepaid services [$90,000 × (4 months ÷ 6 months)]. Answer (C) is incorrect. This adjusting journal entry would be recorded if the company had initially recognized the entire payment of $90,000 as an asset (prepaid services). Answer (D) is incorrect. The company recorded the entire $90,000 as a services expense. However, only 2 months of services were performed in the current year (Nov.-Dec.), and 4 months were prepaid. Thus, services expenses are overstated (and prepaid services are understated) by year-end. Debiting service expenses by $60,000 would further overstate the expense account.

2.4 Other Comprehensive Basis of Accounting (OCBOA)

2.4.1. Which of the following is not a comprehensive basis of accounting other than generally accepted accounting principles?

A. Cash receipts and disbursements basis of accounting.

B. Basis of accounting used by an entity to file its income tax returns.

C. Basis of accounting used by an entity to comply with the financial reporting requirements of a government regulatory agency.

D. Basis of accounting used by an entity to comply with the financial reporting requirements of a lending institution.

Answer (D) is correct. *(CPA, adapted)*
REQUIRED: The item not a comprehensive basis of accounting other than GAAP.
DISCUSSION: A comprehensive basis of accounting other than GAAP may be (1) a basis that the reporting entity uses to comply with the requirements or financial reporting provisions of a regulatory agency; (2) a basis used for tax purposes; (3) the cash basis, and modifications of the cash basis having substantial support, such as recording depreciation on fixed assets or accruing income taxes; or (4) a definite set of criteria having substantial support that is applied to all material items, for example, the price-level basis. However, a basis of accounting used by an entity to comply with the financial reporting requirements of a lending institution does not qualify as governmentally mandated or as having substantial support.
Answer (A) is incorrect. The cash basis is a comprehensive basis of accounting other than GAAP. Answer (B) is incorrect. The tax basis is a comprehensive basis of accounting other than GAAP. Answer (C) is incorrect. A basis required by a regulator is a comprehensive basis of accounting other than GAAP.

2.4.2. Compared with the accrual basis of accounting, the cash basis of accounting understates income by the net decrease during the accounting period of

	Accounts Receivable	Accrued Expenses
A.	Yes	Yes
B.	Yes	No
C.	No	No
D.	No	Yes

Answer (D) is correct. *(CPA, adapted)*
REQUIRED: The cash-basis item(s), if any, the net decrease of which understates income compared with accrual-basis accounting.
DISCUSSION: A net decrease in accounts receivable indicates that cash collected exceeded accrual-basis revenue from receivables in the current period. A net decrease in accrued expenses indicates that cash paid for expenses exceeded the current period's accrual-basis expenses. Thus, a net decrease in receivables results in an overstatement of cash-basis income compared with accrual-basis income, and a net decrease in accrued expenses results in an understatement.
Answer (A) is incorrect. A net decrease in receivables results in an overstatement of cash-basis income compared with accrual-basis income. Answer (B) is incorrect. The net decrease in accrued expenses understates cash-basis compared with accrual-basis income, but accounts receivable does not. Answer (C) is incorrect. A net decrease in accrued expenses results in an understatement.

2.4.3. On April 1, Julie began operating a service proprietorship with an initial cash investment of $1,000. The proprietorship provided $3,200 of services in April and received a payment of $2,500 in May. The proprietorship incurred expenses of $1,500 in April that were paid in June. During May, Julie drew $500 from her capital account. What was the proprietorship's income for the 2 months ended May 31 under the following methods of accounting?

	Cash-Basis	Accrual-Basis
A.	$500	$1,200
B.	$1,000	$1,700
C.	$2,000	$1,200
D.	$2,500	$1,700

Answer (D) is correct. *(CPA, adapted)*
REQUIRED: The income for a proprietorship under the cash basis and accrual basis.
DISCUSSION: Under the cash basis, $2,500 of income is recognized for the payments received in May for the services rendered in April. The $1,500 of expenses is not recognized until June. Under the accrual basis, the $3,200 of income and the $1,500 of expenses incurred in April but not paid until June are recognized. The net income is $1,700 under the accrual basis. The cash investment and capital withdrawal are ignored because they do not affect net income.
Answer (A) is incorrect. The $500 withdrawal should not be recognized in the computation of net income under either method, and the $1,500 of expenses should not be recognized under the cash basis. Answer (B) is incorrect. The cash basis does not recognize the $1,500 in expenses until June. Answer (C) is incorrect. The $500 withdrawal should not be recognized in the computation of net income under either method.

2.4.4. Hahn Co. prepared financial statements on the cash basis of accounting. The cash basis was modified so that an accrual of income taxes was reported. Are these financial statements in accordance with the modified cash basis of accounting?

A. Yes.

B. No, because the modifications are illogical.

C. No, because there is no substantial support for recording income taxes.

D. No, because the modifications result in financial statements equivalent to those prepared under the accrual basis of accounting.

Answer (A) is correct. *(CPA, adapted)*
REQUIRED: The true statement about whether cash-basis statements may be modified for accrual of income taxes.
DISCUSSION: A comprehensive basis of accounting other than GAAP includes the cash basis. Modifications of the cash basis having substantial support, such as accruing income taxes or recording depreciation on fixed assets, may be made when preparing financial statements on the cash basis (AU-C 800).
Answer (B) is incorrect. Accrual of quarterly income taxes is a logical modification of the cash basis of accounting. Answer (C) is incorrect. Substantial support exists for accrual of a reasonably estimable expense such as income taxes. Answer (D) is incorrect. A modification of the cash basis that accrues income taxes but incorporates no other accruals or deferrals will not result in financial statements equivalent to those prepared under the accrual basis.

2.4.5. Income-tax-basis financial statements differ from those prepared under GAAP because they

A. Do not include nontaxable revenues and nondeductible expenses in determining income.

B. Include detailed information about current and deferred income tax expense.

C. Contain no disclosures about finance and operating lease transactions.

D. Recognize certain revenues and expenses in different reporting periods.

Answer (D) is correct. *(CPA, adapted)*
REQUIRED: The difference between income tax-basis and GAAP financial statements.
DISCUSSION: Financial statements prepared under the income tax basis of accounting and financial statements prepared under GAAP differ when the tax basis of an asset or a liability and its reported amount in the GAAP-based financial statements are not the same. The result will be taxable or deductible amounts in future years when the reported amount of the asset is recovered or the liability is settled. Thus, certain revenues and expenses are recognized in different periods. An example is subscriptions revenue received in advance, which is recognized in taxable income when received and recognized in financial income when earned in a later period. Another example is an assurance-type warranty liability, which is recognized as an expense in financial income when a product is sold and recognized in taxable income when the expenditures are made in a later period.
Answer (A) is incorrect. Even when financial statements are prepared on the income tax basis, permanent difference items, e.g., nondeductible expenses, are included as revenues or expenses in the income statement. They do not have to be presented in a special category of the income statement. Answer (B) is incorrect. Detailed information about current and deferred income tax expense is necessary in financial statements prepared on the income-tax basis and in conformity with GAAP. Temporary differences, which result in deferred tax amounts, arise under either basis of accounting. Answer (C) is incorrect. Lease disclosures would be the same under either basis of accounting.

2.4.6. To calculate net sales, <List A> must be <List B> cash receipts from customers.

	List A	List B
A.	An increase in net accounts receivable	Added to
B.	An increase in net accounts receivable	Subtracted from
C.	An increase in net accounts payable	Added to
D.	A decrease in net accounts receivable	Neither added to nor subtracted from

Answer (A) is correct. *(CIA, adapted)*
REQUIRED: The calculation of net sales.
DISCUSSION: To convert from the cash basis (cash receipts) to the accrual basis (net sales), the increase in net accounts receivable must be added to cash receipts from customers.
Answer (B) is incorrect. An increase in net accounts receivable is added to cash receipts. Answer (C) is incorrect. Changes in accounts payable are not included in the conversion of cash receipts to net sales. Answer (D) is incorrect. A decrease in net accounts receivable is subtracted from cash receipts.

2.4.7. Young & Jamison's modified cash-basis financial statements indicate cash paid for operating expenses of $150,000, end-of-year prepaid expenses of $15,000, and accrued liabilities of $25,000. At the beginning of the year, Young & Jamison had prepaid expenses of $10,000, while accrued liabilities were $5,000. If cash paid for operating expenses is converted to accrual-basis operating expenses, what would be the amount of operating expenses?

A. $125,000

B. $135,000

C. $165,000

D. $175,000

Answer (C) is correct. *(CPA, adapted)*
REQUIRED: The amount of operating expenses reported under the accrual basis.
DISCUSSION: During the year, prepaid expenses increased by $5,000 ($15,000 – $10,000), and accrued liabilities increased by $20,000 ($25,000 – $5,000). The increase in prepaid expenses is a cash outflow without accrual of an expense. It indicates that accrual-basis expenses were $5,000 lower than cash-basis expenses. The increase in accrued liabilities results in accrual of an expense without a cash outflow. It indicates that accrual-basis expenses were $20,000 higher than cash-basis expenses. Thus, the adjustments of cash-basis operating expenses are a $5,000 decrease and a $20,000 increase, respectively.

Cash-basis operating expenses	$150,000
Increase in prepaid expenses	(5,000)
Increase in accrued liabilities	20,000
Accrual-basis operating expenses	$165,000

Answer (A) is incorrect. The amount of $125,000 results from subtracting the $20,000 increase in accrued liabilities. Answer (B) is incorrect. The amount of $135,000 results from adding the $5,000 increase in prepaid expenses and subtracting the $20,000 increase in accrued liabilities. Answer (D) is incorrect. The amount of $175,000 results from adding the $5,000 in prepaid expenses.

2.4.8. The following information pertains to Falcon Co.'s current year sales:

Cash sales

Gross	$160,000
Returns and allowances	7,000

Credit sales

Gross	$240,000
Discounts	11,000

On January 1, customers owed Falcon $70,000. On December 31, customers owed Falcon $60,000. Falcon uses the direct write-off method for bad debts. No bad debts were recorded in the current year. Under the cash basis of accounting, what amount of net revenue should Falcon report for the current year?

A. $153,000

B. $340,000

C. $382,000

D. $392,000

Answer (D) is correct. *(CPA, adapted)*
REQUIRED: The revenue under the cash basis of accounting.
DISCUSSION: Under the cash basis of accounting, revenue is recognized when cash is received. Falcon had $153,000 ($160,000 – $7,000) in net cash sales and $229,000 ($240,000 – $11,000) in net credit sales. Given that accounts receivable decreased, cash collections thereon must have exceeded net credit sales by $10,000 ($70,000 – $60,000). No adjustment for bad debts is needed because no bad debts were recorded. Accordingly, net revenue is $392,000 ($153,000 + $229,000 + $10,000).
Answer (A) is incorrect. Net cash sales equals $153,000. Answer (B) is incorrect. Total gross sales minus ending accounts receivable is $340,000. Answer (C) is incorrect. The amount of $382,000 does not reflect an adjustment for the change in receivables.

2.4.9. A company records items on the cash basis throughout the year and converts to an accrual basis for year-end reporting. Its cash-basis net income for the year is $70,000. The company has gathered the following comparative balance sheet information:

	Beginning of Year	End of Year
Accounts payable	$3,000	$1,000
Unearned revenue	300	500
Wages payable	300	400
Prepaid rent	1,200	1,500
Accounts receivable	1,400	600

What amount should the company report as its accrual-based net income for the current year?

A. $68,800

B. $70,200

C. $71,200

D. $73,200

Answer (C) is correct. *(CPA, adapted)*
REQUIRED: The accrual-based net income given cash-basis net income.
DISCUSSION: The decrease in accounts payable implies that cash paid to suppliers exceeded purchases. The decrease ($3,000 – $1,000 = $2,000) is included in the calculation of cash-basis net income but not accrual-basis net income. The increase in the liability for unearned revenue ($500 – $300 = $200) implies a cash inflow that increased cash-basis net income but not accrual-basis net income. The increase in wages payable ($400 – $300 = $100) implies an accrual-basis expense not recognized in cash-basis net income. The increase in prepaid rent ($1,500 – $1,200 = $300) implies reduced cash-basis net income with no effect on accrual-basis net income. The decrease in accounts receivable ($1,400 – $600 = $800) implies that cash collections exceeded accrual-basis revenue. Accrual-basis net income based on these adjustments is therefore $71,200.

Cash-basis net income	$70,000
A/P decrease	2,000
Unearned revenue increase	(200)
Wages payable increase	(100)
Prepaid rent increase	300
A/R decrease	(800)
	$71,200

Answer (A) is incorrect. The amount of $68,800 equals cash-basis net income, minus the decrease in accounts payable, plus the decrease in accounts receivable. Answer (B) is incorrect. The amount of $70,200 equals cash-basis net income, plus the increase in unearned revenue. Answer (D) is incorrect. The amount of $73,200 equals cash-basis net income, plus the decrease in accounts payable, plus the decrease in accounts receivable, plus the increase in wages payable, plus the increase in prepaid rent.

2.5 Personal Financial Statements

2.5.1. Personal financial statements usually consist of

A. A statement of net worth and a statement of changes in net worth.

B. A statement of net worth, an income statement, and a statement of changes in net worth.

C. A statement of financial condition and a statement of changes in net worth.

D. A statement of financial condition, a statement of changes in net worth, and a statement of cash flows.

Answer (C) is correct. *(CPA, adapted)*
REQUIRED: The basic financial statements that should be included in personal financial statements.
DISCUSSION: According to GAAP, personal financial statements include at least a statement of financial condition. A statement of changes in net worth and comparative financial statements are recommended but not required. A personal statement of cash flows is neither required nor recommended.

2.5.2. Mrs. Taft owns a $150,000 insurance policy on her husband's life. The cash value of the policy is $125,000, and a $50,000 loan is secured by the policy. In the Tafts' personal statement of financial condition at December 31, what amount should be shown as an investment in life insurance?

A. $150,000

B. $125,000

C. $100,000

D. $75,000

Answer (D) is correct. *(CPA, adapted)*
REQUIRED: The amount at which an investment in life insurance should be presented in a personal statement of financial condition.
DISCUSSION: Assets are presented at their estimated current values in a personal statement of financial condition. Furthermore, investments in life insurance must be reported at their cash values minus the amount of any outstanding loans. Thus, the amount that should be reported in Mrs. Taft's personal financial statement is $75,000 ($125,000 cash value – $50,000 loan).
Answer (A) is incorrect. The amount of the policy is $150,000. Answer (B) is incorrect. The cash value is $125,000. Answer (C) is incorrect. The amount of the policy minus the loan is $100,000.

2.5.3. Green, a calendar-year taxpayer, is preparing a personal statement of financial condition as of April 30, Year 4. Green's Year 3 income tax liability was paid in full on April 15, Year 4. Green's tax on income earned between January and April Year 4 is estimated at $20,000. In addition, $40,000 is estimated for income tax on the differences between the estimated current values and current amounts of Green's assets and liabilities and their tax bases at April 30, Year 4. No withholdings or payments have been made towards the Year 4 income tax liability. In Green's April 30, Year 4, statement of financial condition, what amount should be reported for income taxes?

A. $0

B. $20,000

C. $40,000

D. $60,000

Answer (D) is correct. *(CPA, adapted)*
REQUIRED: The reported amount of estimated income taxes.
DISCUSSION: No amount should be reported for Year 3 taxes because the Year 3 liability was paid in full. Thus, Green will report estimated income taxes for amounts earned through April Year 4 and for the differences between the estimated current values of assets and the estimated current amounts of liabilities and their tax bases, a sum of $60,000 ($20,000 + $40,000).
Answer (A) is incorrect. Green must report estimated income taxes. Answer (B) is incorrect. This amount excludes estimated income taxes for the differences between the estimated current values of assets and the estimated current amounts of liabilities and their tax bases. Answer (C) is incorrect. This amount excludes the estimated income taxes on Year 4 income earned to date.

2.5.4. On December 31, Year 4, Shane is a fully vested participant in a company-sponsored pension plan. According to the plan's administrator, Shane has at that date the nonforfeitable right to receive a lump sum of $100,000 on December 28, Year 5. The discounted amount of $100,000 is $90,000 at December 31, Year 4. The right is not contingent on Shane's life expectancy and requires no future performance on Shane's part. In Shane's December 31, Year 4, personal statement of financial condition, the vested interest in the pension plan should be reported at

A. $0

B. $90,000

C. $95,000

D. $100,000

Answer (B) is correct. *(CPA, adapted)*
REQUIRED: The amount at which the vested interest in a pension plan should be reported in a personal statement of financial condition.
DISCUSSION: Noncancelable rights to receive future sums be presented at their estimated current value as assets in personal financial statements if they (1) are for fixed or determinable amounts; (2) are not contingent on the holder's life expectancy or the occurrence of a particular event, such as disability or death; and (3) do not require the future performance of service by the holder. The fully vested rights in the company-sponsored pension plan therefore should be reported at their current value, which is equal to the $90,000 discounted amount.
Answer (A) is incorrect. The current value of the right should be reported. Answer (C) is incorrect. It is a nonsense amount. Answer (D) is incorrect. The undiscounted amount is $100,000.

2.5.5. Quinn is preparing a personal statement of financial condition as of April 30. Included in Quinn's assets are the following:

- 50% of the voting stock of Ink Corp. A shareholders' agreement restricts the sale of the stock and, under certain circumstances, requires Ink to repurchase the stock. Quinn's tax basis for the stock is $430,000, and at April 30, the buyout value is $675,000.

- Jewelry with a fair value aggregating $70,000 based on an independent appraisal on April 30 for insurance purposes. This jewelry was acquired by purchase and gift over a 10-year period and has a total tax basis of $40,000.

What is the total amount at which the Ink stock and jewelry should be reported in Quinn's April 30 personal statement of financial condition?

A. $470,000

B. $500,000

C. $715,000

D. $745,000

Answer (D) is correct. *(CPA, adapted)*
REQUIRED: The amount at which stock and jewelry should be reported in a personal statement of financial condition.
DISCUSSION: All assets must be reported at estimated current value. An interest in a closely held business is an asset and should be shown at its estimated current value. The buyout value is a better representation of the current value of the Ink stock than the tax basis. The appraisal value is the appropriate basis for reporting the jewelry. Thus, the stock and jewelry should be reported at $745,000 ($675,000 + $70,000).
Answer (A) is incorrect. The amount of $470,000 reports both assets at their tax basis. Answer (B) is incorrect. The amount of $500,000 includes the stock at its tax basis. Answer (C) is incorrect. The amount of $715,000 includes the jewelry's tax basis rather than its fair value.

2.5.6. On December 31, Year 5, Mr. and Mrs. Blake owned a parcel of land held as an investment. The land was purchased for $95,000 in Year 1, and was encumbered by a mortgage with a principal balance of $60,000 at December 31, Year 5. On this date, the fair value of the land was $150,000. In the Blakes' December 31, Year 5, personal statement of financial condition, at what amount should the land investment and mortgage payable be reported?

	Land Investment	Mortgage Payable
A.	$150,000	$60,000
B.	$95,000	$60,000
C.	$90,000	$0
D.	$35,000	$0

Answer (A) is correct. *(CPA, adapted)*
REQUIRED: The amounts at which the land investment and mortgage payable should be reported.
DISCUSSION: For an investment in a limited business activity not conducted in a separate business entity (such as an investment in real estate and a related mortgage), the assets and liabilities must not be presented as a net amount. Instead, they should be presented as separate assets at their estimated current values and separate liabilities at their estimated current amounts. This presentation is particularly important if a large portion of the liabilities may be satisfied with funds from sources unrelated to the investments. Thus, the land should be reported at its $150,000 fair value and the mortgage principal at $60,000 (the amount at which the debt could currently be discharged).
Answer (B) is incorrect. The cost of the land was $95,000. Answer (C) is incorrect. The asset and liability should be presented separately and not as a net amount. Answer (D) is incorrect. The cost minus the mortgage balance equals $35,000.

2.5.7. A business interest that constitutes a large part of an individual's total assets should be presented in a personal statement of financial condition as

A. A separate listing of the individual assets and liabilities at cost.

B. Separate line items of both total assets and total liabilities at cost.

C. A single amount equal to the proprietorship equity.

D. A single amount equal to the estimated current value of the business interest.

Answer (D) is correct. *(CPA, adapted)*
REQUIRED: The amount at which a business interest constituting a large part of an individual's total assets should be presented in a personal financial statement.
DISCUSSION: A business interest constituting a large part of an individual's total assets be presented in a personal statement of financial condition as a single amount equal to the estimated current value of the business interest. This investment should be disclosed separately from other investments if the entity is marketable as a going concern.
Answer (A) is incorrect. The business interest should be reported as a net amount. Answer (B) is incorrect. The business interest should be reported as a net amount. Answer (C) is incorrect. The business interest should be reported at its estimated current value.

☑ ≡
☐ ≡   Use **Gleim Test Prep** for interactive study and easy-to-use detailed analytics!
☐ ≡

STUDY UNIT THREE
REPORTING INCOME

To increase the usefulness of the **statement of income**, different classifications of income are used. The major classifications are (1) income from continuing operations (or other proper title) and (2) discontinued operations. The components of **net income** may be presented as follows in an income statement using the multiple-step format:

Net sales revenue		$ XXX,XXX
Cost of goods sold		(XXX,XXX)
Gross profit		$ XX,XXX
Operating expenses		(X,XXX)
Operating income		$ XX,XXX
Other revenues and gains		X,XXX
Other expenses and losses		(X,XXX)
Income from continuing operations before income taxes		$ XX,XXX
Income taxes		(X,XXX)
Income from continuing operations*		$ XX,XXX
Discontinued operations:		
Income from operations of discontinued component unit (net of loss on disposal of $XXX)	$X,XXX	
Income tax expense	(XXX)	X,XXX
Net income		$ XX,XXX

*NOTE: This title is used when the entity reports a discontinued operation. If it does not report a discontinued operation, the title is modified.

An entity that presents a full set of financial statements also must report comprehensive income if it has items of other comprehensive income (OCI). This presentation may be in (1) one continuous statement with two sections (net income and OCI) or (2) two separate but consecutive statements (income statement and statement of OCI).

The following is an example of the **single-statement** presentation for reporting comprehensive income of an entity with no noncontrolling interest:

CI Company
Statement of
Comprehensive Income (in millions)
Year Ended December 31, Year 1

Statement of Income	Revenues and gains:		
	Net revenues	$250	
	Gain on sale of available-for-sale securities	10	
	Gains reclassified from OCI	14	$274
	Expenses and losses:		
	Expenses	$122	
	Amortized prior service cost reclassified from OCI	12	(134)
	Income from continuing operations		$140
	Income tax expense		(30)
	Net income		**$110**
Statement of OCI	OCI, net of tax:		
	Foreign currency translation adjustments		20
	Unrealized holding gains	40	
	Minus: Reclassification of gains included in net income	(14)	26
	Defined benefit pension plan:		
	Prior service cost	(33)	
	Minus: Amortization of prior service cost	12	(21)
	OCI		$ 25
	Comprehensive income		**$135**

A **two-statement** presentation is easily derived from the example above. The final component of the **statement of net income** is net income. The first component of the **statement of OCI** is net income, and the final component is comprehensive income. If a **noncontrolling interest** exists, amounts for net income and comprehensive income attributable to the parent and to the subsidiary must be reported in the appropriate statements.

QUESTIONS

3.1 Income from Continuing Operations

3.1.1. On January 1, Year 1, Brecon Co. installed cabinets to display its merchandise in customers' stores. Brecon expects to use these cabinets for 5 years. Brecon's Year 1 multi-step income statement should include

A. One-fifth of the cabinet costs in cost of goods sold.

B. One-fifth of the cabinet costs in selling expenses.

C. All of the cabinet costs in cost of goods sold.

D. All of the cabinet costs in selling expenses.

Answer (B) is correct. *(CPA, adapted)*
REQUIRED: The cabinet costs included in the determination of current net income.
DISCUSSION: The cost of the cabinets is a selling expense. However, because the cabinets will provide benefits over a 5-year period, their cost should be allocated systematically and rationally over that period, for example, by the straight-line method. In effect, periodic depreciation of the cabinets should be recognized as a selling expense.
Answer (A) is incorrect. Selling costs are not inventoried.
Answer (C) is incorrect. Selling costs are not inventoried.
Answer (D) is incorrect. The costs should be allocated to the periods benefited.

3.1.2. Under GAAP, comparative financial statements are

A. Required for at least the current and the prior year.

B. Required for at least the current and the prior 2 years.

C. Recommended for at least the current and the prior year.

D. Neither required nor recommended.

Answer (C) is correct. *(S. Rubin)*
REQUIRED: The position of GAAP regarding comparative financial statements.
DISCUSSION: Presenting financial statements of two or more periods is ordinarily desirable. This position is commonly understood to be a recommendation rather than a requirement. However, public companies must file comparative statements with the SEC.
Answer (A) is incorrect. Although not required, comparative financial statements ordinarily should be presented. Answer (B) is incorrect. Comparative financial statements are not required. Answer (D) is incorrect. Comparative financial statements are recommended.

3.1.3. The all-inclusive income statement concept

A. Is synonymous with the current operating concept, and both are acceptable under GAAP.

B. Is generally more appropriate than the current operating concept.

C. Is not appropriate. The current operating concept is a generally accepted accounting principle.

D. Produces an interactive income statement that avoids the problems associated with the changing value of currencies.

Answer (B) is correct. *(Publisher, adapted)*
REQUIRED: The true statement about the all-inclusive income statement concept.
DISCUSSION: In the calculation of net income, the all-inclusive approach includes all transactions that affect equity during the current period except (1) transactions with owners, (2) prior-period adjustments, and (3) certain items that are reported initially in other comprehensive income. The current operating concept includes only the ordinary, normal, recurring operations in the net income of the current period. Other items are direct adjustments to retained earnings. GAAP adopt the all-inclusive approach. The all-inclusive concept was strengthened by the limitation of prior-period adjustments to corrections of errors. As a result, most revenue, expense, gain, and loss items are included in continuing operations in the income statement.
Answer (A) is incorrect. GAAP reject the current operating concept. Answer (C) is incorrect. GAAP reject the current operating concept. Answer (D) is incorrect. An "interactive income statement" does not exist in financial accounting.

3.1.4. Select the best order for the following items in income statements:

1. Income from continuing operations
2. Discontinued operations
3. Prior-period adjustments
4. Taxes on income from continuing operations
5. Dividends
6. Net income
7. Revenues
8. Expenses
9. Income from continuing operations before income tax

A. 8 - 9 - 7 - 6 - 5 - 1 - 3

B. 7 - 5 - 6 - 1 - 4

C. 8 - 9 - 7 - 5 - 2 - 1 - 3

D. 7 - 8 - 9 - 4 - 1 - 2 - 6

Answer (D) is correct. *(Publisher, adapted)*
REQUIRED: The order of items in income statements.
DISCUSSION: The order of appearance in income statements of the items is

7. Revenues
8. Expenses
9. Income from continuing operations before income tax
4. Taxes on income from continuing operations
1. Income from continuing operations
2. Discontinued operations
6. Net income

Prior-period adjustments (4) and dividends (6) appear only in retained earnings statements.
Answer (A) is incorrect. The list begins with expenses, which cannot be the first item on a GAAP-based income statement. Answer (B) is incorrect. Although the first item (revenues) is correct, the other items are not in the right order. Answer (C) is incorrect. Among other things, prior-period adjustments and dividends affect retained earnings directly. They are not components of net income.

3.1.5. Brock Corp. reports operating expenses in two categories: (1) selling and (2) general and administrative. The adjusted trial balance at December 31 included the following expenses and losses:

Accounting and legal fees	$120,000
Advertising	150,000
Freight-out	80,000
Interest	70,000
Loss on sale of long-term investment	30,000
Officers' salaries	225,000
Rent for office space	220,000
Sales salaries and commissions	140,000

One-half of the rented premises is occupied by the sales department. Brock's total selling expenses are

A. $480,000

B. $400,000

C. $370,000

D. $340,000

Answer (A) is correct. *(Publisher, adapted)*
REQUIRED: The total selling expenses.
DISCUSSION: Within the categories of expenses presented, the $150,000 of advertising, the $80,000 of freight-out, 50% of the $220,000 rent for office space, and the $140,000 of sales salaries and commissions should be classified as selling expenses. Total selling expenses are therefore $480,000.
Answer (B) is incorrect. The amount of $400,000 omits freight-out. Answer (C) is incorrect. The amount of $370,000 omits rent. Answer (D) is incorrect. The amount of $340,000 omits sales salaries and commissions.

150 000
80,000
110,000
140,000
$ 480,000

3.1.6. On December 31, Salo Corp.'s balance sheet accounts increased by the following amounts compared with those at the end of the prior year:

Assets	$178,000
Liabilities	62,000
Capital stock	125,000
Additional paid-in capital	17,000

Salo had no accumulated other comprehensive income (OCI), and the only charge to retained earnings during the year was for a dividend payment of $34,000. Net income for the year was

A. $60,000

B. $34,000

C. $8,000

D. $26,000

Answer (C) is correct. *(CPA, adapted)*
    REQUIRED: The net income for the year given the increases in assets, liabilities, and paid-in capital.
    DISCUSSION: Assets equal the sum of liabilities and equity (contributed capital, retained earnings, and accumulated other comprehensive income). To calculate net income, the first step is to add the dividend payment ($34,000) to the increase in assets ($178,000). The excess of this sum ($212,000) over the increase in liabilities ($62,000) gives the total increase in equity ($150,000). Given no accumulated OCI, the excess of this amount over the combined increases in the capital accounts ($142,000) equals the increase in retained earnings ($8,000) arising from net income.
    Answer (A) is incorrect. The amount of $60,000 equals the dividend payment plus the excess of the sum of the increases in liabilities, capital stock, and additional paid-in capital over the increase in assets. Answer (B) is incorrect. The dividend payment is $34,000. Answer (D) is incorrect. The amount of $26,000 is the excess of the sum of the increases in liabilities, capital stock, and additional paid-in capital over the increase in assets.

3.1.7. In Baer Food Co.'s Year 3 single-step income statement, the section titled *Revenues* consisted of the following:

Net sales revenue	$187,000
Discontinued operations:	
Income from operations of component unit (including gain on disposal of $21,600)	18,000
Income tax	(6,000)
Interest revenue	10,200
Gain on sale of equipment	4,700
Total revenues	$213,900

In the revenues section of the Year 3 income statement, Baer Food should have reported total revenues of

A. $213,900

B. $209,200

C. $203,700

D. $201,900

Answer (D) is correct. *(CPA, adapted)*
    REQUIRED: The total revenues.
    DISCUSSION: This single-step income statement classifies the items included in income from continuing operations as either revenues or expenses. Discontinued operations is a classification in the income statement separate from continuing operations. Thus, total revenues (including interest and the gain) were $201,900 ($213,900 – $12,000 after-tax results from discontinued operations).
    Answer (A) is incorrect. The amount of $213,900 equals reported total revenues. Answer (B) is incorrect. The amount of $209,200 excludes the gain. Answer (C) is incorrect. The amount of $203,700 excludes the interest.

3.1.8. The effect of a material transaction that is infrequent in occurrence and unusual in nature should be presented separately as a component of income from continuing operations when the transaction results in a

	Gain	Loss
A.	Yes	Yes
B.	Yes	No
C.	No	No
D.	No	Yes

Answer (A) is correct. *(CPA, adapted)*
    REQUIRED: The circumstances in which an infrequent and unusual transaction is presented in a separate component of income from continuing operations.
    DISCUSSION: A material event or transaction that is unusual in nature, infrequent in occurrence, or both must be reported as a separate component of income from continuing operations. Whether the item is a gain or loss is irrelevant to the presentation.
    Answer (B) is incorrect. A loss from an infrequent and unusual transaction should be presented as a component of income from continuing operations. Answer (C) is incorrect. A gain from an infrequent and unusual transaction should be presented as a component of income from continuing operations. Answer (D) is incorrect. A gain or loss from an infrequent and unusual transaction should be presented as a component of income from continuing operations.

3.1.9. The major distinction made between the multiple-step and single-step income statement formats is the separation of

A. Operating and nonoperating data.

B. Income tax expense and administrative expenses.

C. Cost of goods sold expense and administrative expenses.

D. The effect on income taxes due to extraordinary items and the effect on income taxes due to income before extraordinary items.

Answer (A) is correct. *(CIA, adapted)*
REQUIRED: The major distinction between the multiple-step and single-step income statement formats.
DISCUSSION: Within the income from continuing operations classification, the single-step income statement provides one grouping for revenue items and one for expense items. The single-step is the one subtraction necessary to arrive at income from continuing operations prior to the effect of income taxes. In contrast, the multiple-step income statement matches operating revenues and expenses separately from nonoperating items. This format emphasizes subtotals, such as gross profit or loss and operating income or loss, within the presentation of income from continuing operations.
Answer (B) is incorrect. Either format separates income tax expense and administrative expenses. Answer (C) is incorrect. Cost of goods sold and administrative expenses cannot be combined under GAAP reporting. Answer (D) is incorrect. Extraordinary items are not reported under U.S. GAAP or IFRS. Items that are unusual in nature or infrequent in occurrence or both are presented separately as a component of income from continuing operations. However, such items must not be reported on the face of the income statement net of income taxes. Moreover, their EPS effects are not presented on the face of the income statement.

3.1.10. A company's activities for Year 2 included the following:

Gross sales	$3,600,000
Cost of goods sold	1,200,000
Selling and administrative expense	500,000
Adjustment for a prior-year understatement of amortization expense	59,000
Sales returns	34,000
Gain on sale of available-for-sale securities	8,000
Gain on disposal of a discontinued business segment	4,000
Unrealized gain on available-for-sale securities	2,000

The company has a 30% effective income tax rate. What is the company's net income for Year 2?

A. $1,267,700

B. $1,273,300

C. $1,314,600

D. $1,316,000

Answer (C) is correct. *(CPA, adapted)*
REQUIRED: The net income.
DISCUSSION: Net sales equal $3,566,000 ($3,600,000 gross sales – $34,000 sales returns). The adjustment for a prior-year understatement of amortization expense is the basis for restatement of a prior-year income statement (if comparative statements are presented) or is made to beginning retained earnings (if single-year statements are presented). It has no effect on the current income statement. The unrealized gain on available-for-sale securities is recognized in other comprehensive income (OCI). Net income for Year 2 is calculated as follows:

Net sales		$3,566,000
Cost of goods sold		(1,200,000)
Gross profit		$2,366,000
Selling and administrative		(500,000)
Income from operations		$1,866,000
Gain on sale of available-for-sale securities		8,000
Income from continuing operations before taxes		$1,874,000
Income taxes ($1,874,000 × 30%)		(562,200)
Income from continuing operations		$1,311,800
Discontinued operations:		
Gain on disposal	$4,000	
Income taxes ($4,000 × 30%)	(1,200)	2,800
Net income		$1,314,600

Answer (A) is incorrect. The amount of $1,267,700 results from recognizing the adjustment for a prior-year understatement of amortization expense as an expense in the calculation of current-year net income and omitting the gain on sale of available-for-sale securities. Answer (B) is incorrect. The amount of $1,273,300 results from recognizing the adjustment for a prior-year understatement of amortization expense as an expense in the calculation of current-year net income. Answer (D) is incorrect. The amount of $1,316,000 results from including the unrealized gain on available-for-sale securities in the calculation of net income.

3.1.11. A company has a 40% gross margin, general and administrative expenses of $50, interest expense of $20, and net income of $70 for the year just ended. If the corporate tax rate is 30%, the level of sales revenue for the year just ended was

A. $170

B. $255

C. $350

D. $425

Answer (D) is correct. *(CIA, adapted)*
REQUIRED: The sales revenue for the year.
DISCUSSION: Net income before taxes is $100 [$70 NI ÷ (1.0 − .3 tax rate)]. Thus, the gross margin (sales − cost of sales) is $170 ($100 NI before taxes + $20 interest + $50 G&A expenses). Sales must then be $425 ($170 gross margin ÷ 40% gross margin ratio).
Answer (A) is incorrect. The gross margin is $170.
Answer (B) is incorrect. The cost of goods sold is $255.
Answer (C) is incorrect. The amount of $350 assumes pre-tax net income was $70.

3.1.12. A transaction that is unusual in nature and infrequent in occurrence is presented

A. After income from continuing operations and before discontinued operations.

B. As a separate component of income from continuing operations.

C. In the notes but not in the income statement.

D. After discontinued operations and before net income.

Answer (B) is correct. *(CPA, adapted)*
REQUIRED: The reporting of a transaction that is unusual in nature and infrequent in occurrence.
DISCUSSION: A material event or transaction that is unusual in nature and infrequent in occurrence in the environment in which the reporting entity operates is presented as a separate component of income from continuing operations.
Answer (A) is incorrect. No items may be reported between income from continuing operations and discontinued operations. Answer (C) is incorrect. The transaction is reported in the income statement. Its nature and financial effects may be disclosed in the notes. Answer (D) is incorrect. A material transaction that is unusual in nature and infrequent in occurrence in the environment in which the entity operates is presented as a separate component of income from continuing operations.

3.1.13. A material event that is unusual in nature or infrequent in occurrence should be reported separately on the income statement as a component of income

	Net of Income Taxes	Before Results of Discontinued Operations
A.	Yes	Yes
B.	Yes	No
C.	No	No
D.	No	Yes

Answer (D) is correct. *(CPA, adapted)*
REQUIRED: The presentation of a material event that is unusual in nature or infrequent in occurrence.
DISCUSSION: A material event or transaction that is unusual in nature or infrequent in occurrence must be reported as a separate component of income from continuing operations. Such items must not be reported on the face of the income statement net of income taxes.
Answer (A) is incorrect. Separate components of income from continuing operations must not be reported on the face of the income statement net of income taxes. Answer (B) is incorrect. A material event or transaction that is unusual in nature or infrequent in occurrence is reported in continuing operations but not net of tax. Answer (C) is incorrect. A material event or transaction that is unusual in nature or infrequent in occurrence must be reported as a separate component of income from continuing operations.

3.1.14. In Year 4, hail damaged several of Toncan Co.'s vans. Hailstorms had frequently inflicted similar damage to Toncan's vans. Over the years, Toncan had saved money by not buying hail insurance and either paying for repairs or selling damaged vans and then replacing them. In Year 4, the damaged vans were sold for less than their carrying amount. How should the hail damage cost be reported in Toncan's Year 4 financial statements?

A. The actual Year 4 hail damage loss as a discontinued operation, net of income taxes.

B. The actual Year 4 hail damage loss in continuing operations, with no separate disclosure.

C. The expected average hail damage loss in continuing operations, with no separate disclosure.

D. The expected average hail damage loss in continuing operations, with separate disclosure.

Answer (B) is correct. *(CPA, adapted)*
REQUIRED: The reporting of hail damage costs when a company is uninsured and sells the damaged item for a loss.
DISCUSSION: Because Toncan sold its damaged vans for less than their carrying amount, the company suffered a loss. The actual loss should be reported even though the company is uninsured against future hail damage and a contingency exists. With respect to future hailstorms, no asset has been impaired and no contingent loss should be recorded. Furthermore, this occurrence is not unusual or infrequent, and a separate disclosure is not needed.
Answer (A) is incorrect. Hail damage does not meet the definition of a discontinued operation. Answer (C) is incorrect. Toncan should report the actual loss incurred in Year 4. Answer (D) is incorrect. Toncan should report the actual loss, and a separate disclosure is not needed because this occurrence is not unusual or infrequent.

3.1.15. During the current year, both Raim Co. and Cane Co. suffered material losses due to the flooding of the Mississippi River. Raim is located 2 miles from the river and sustains flood losses every 2 to 3 years. Cane, which has been located 50 miles from the river for the past 20 years, has never before had flood losses. How should the flood losses be reported in each company's current-year income statement?

	Raim	Cane
A.	As ordinary losses	As a separate component of income from continuing operations
B.	As ordinary losses	As ordinary losses
C.	As an unusual and infrequent item	As a separate component of income from continuing operations
D.	As an extraordinary item	As ordinary losses

Answer (A) is correct. *(CPA, adapted)*
    REQUIRED: The reporting of flood losses in the income statement.
    DISCUSSION: For Raim, flood losses are neither unusual nor infrequent in the environment in which it operates. Thus, these material losses should be classified as ordinary losses. Ordinary income or loss is income or loss from continuing operations excluding (1) significant unusual or infrequent items, (2) discontinued operations, and (3) cumulative effects of changes in accounting principles. For Cane, the flood losses are unusual and infrequent. Cane had never before suffered flood losses. Thus, they should be reported as a separate component of income from continuing operations.
    Answer (B) is incorrect. For Cane, located 50 miles from the river, a flood is unusual in nature and infrequent in occurrence. This requires treatment as a separate component of income from continuing operations. Furthermore, given that Cane's losses are unusual and infrequent, they cannot be ordinary. Answer (C) is incorrect. Raim, which has floods every 2 to 3 years, cannot reasonably consider this event to be unusual or infrequent. But a flood is unusual and infrequent to Cane, making reporting as a separate component of income from continuing operations appropriate. Answer (D) is incorrect. Ordinary income or loss is income or loss from continuing operations excluding (1) significant unusual or infrequent items, (2) discontinued operations, and (3) cumulative effects of changes in accounting principles. Accordingly, Cane reports the losses as a separate component of income from continuing operations. Also, extraordinary items are never reported.

3.1.16. Kent is a technology company that does business worldwide. It incurred the following losses during the current year:

- A $300,000 loss was incurred on disposal of a component of the entity in a strategic shift.
- A major currency devaluation caused a $120,000 foreign currency transaction loss on an amount remitted by one of Kent's international customers.
- High-tech FIFO inventory with a cost of $190,000 had a net realizable value of $0 because of a competitor's unexpected product innovation.

In its current-year income statement, what amount should Kent report as losses that are not considered infrequent or unusual or both?

A. $610,000

B. $490,000

C. $420,000

D. $310,000

Answer (A) is correct. *(CPA, adapted)*
    REQUIRED: The amount of losses not considered unusual or infrequent.
    DISCUSSION: An event or transaction that is infrequent of occurrence should be a type that is not reasonably expected to recur in the foreseeable future, considering the environment in which the entity operates. An event or transaction that is unusual in nature should have a high degree of abnormality and be of a type clearly unrelated to, or only incidentally related to, the ordinary and typical activities of the entity, considering the environment in which the entity operates. If an event or transaction is unusual or infrequent or both, it is reported as a separate component of income from continuing operations. However, the disposal of a component of the entity that is a strategic shift is reported as a discontinued operation. Furthermore, a foreign currency transaction loss incurred by an entity that does business with customers in other countries is neither unusual nor infrequent. It does not have a high degree of abnormality and is reasonably expected to recur. Obsolescence resulting in a writedown of FIFO inventory to NRV also does not meet the criteria for treatment as unusual or infrequent. Thus, the amount of losses that is not infrequent or unusual or both is $610,000 ($300,000 + $120,000 + $190,000).
    Answer (B) is incorrect. The amount of $490,000 omits the foreign currency transaction loss. Answer (C) is incorrect. The amount of $420,000 omits the inventory write-off. Answer (D) is incorrect. The amount of $310,000 omits the loss on disposal of the factory.

3.1.17. In the current year, Teller Co. incurred material losses from its guilty plea in its first antitrust action and from a substantial increase in production costs caused when a major supplier's unionized workers went on strike after their current contracts expired. Which of these losses most likely should be reported as an unusual or infrequent item?

	Antitrust Action	Production Costs
A.	No	No
B.	No	Yes
C.	Yes	No
D.	Yes	Yes

Answer (C) is correct. *(CPA, adapted)*
REQUIRED: The loss(es), if any, reported as an unusual or infrequent item.
DISCUSSION: The effects of a strike most likely are not unusual in nature or infrequent in occurrence. They are not unusual because they (1) do not have a high degree of abnormality and (2) are not (a) unrelated or (b) incidentally related to the entity's typical activities. Also, the effects of the strike are not infrequent because they may be reasonably expected to recur in the foreseeable future. However, a material loss from the entity's first antitrust action is clearly infrequent and most likely unusual. It is unusual because it is abnormal and of a type unrelated to the typical activities of the entity in the environment in which it operates. Thus, the loss from the antitrust action should be reported separately as a component of income from continuing operations.
Answer (A) is incorrect. The litigation loss most likely is unusual and infrequent. Answer (B) is incorrect. The litigation loss most likely is unusual and infrequent, but the effects of the strike are not. Answer (D) is incorrect. The effects of a strike most likely are not unusual or infrequent.

3.1.18. A transaction that is unusual in nature or infrequent in occurrence should be reported as a(n)

A. Component of income from continuing operations, net of applicable income taxes.

B. Item of other comprehensive income.

C. Component of income from continuing operations, but not net of applicable income taxes.

D. Discontinued operations, net of applicable income tax.

Answer (C) is correct. *(CPA, adapted)*
REQUIRED: The reporting of a transaction that is unusual in nature or infrequent in occurrence.
DISCUSSION: A material event or transaction that is unusual in nature or infrequent in occurrence must be reported as a separate component of income from continuing operations. Such items must not be reported on the face of the income statement net of income taxes.
Answer (A) is incorrect. Separate components of income from continuing operations should not be reported net of applicable income taxes. Answer (B) is incorrect. A material event or transaction that is unusual in nature or infrequent in occurrence must be reported as a separate component of income from continuing operations. Such items must not be reported on the face of the income statement net of income taxes. Answer (D) is incorrect. A material event or transaction that is unusual in nature or infrequent in occurrence must be reported as a separate component of income from continuing operations. Such items must not be reported on the face of the income statement net of income taxes.

3.1.19. Which of the following items is not subject to the application of intraperiod income tax allocation?

A. Discontinued operations.

B. Income from continuing operations.

C. Other comprehensive income.

D. Operating Income.

Answer (D) is correct. *(CPA, adapted)*
REQUIRED: The item not subject to intraperiod income tax allocation.
DISCUSSION: Items included in the determination of taxable income may be presented in different sections of the financial statements. Accordingly, intraperiod tax allocation is required. Income tax expense or benefit is allocated to (1) continuing operations, (2) discontinued operations, (3) other comprehensive income, and (4) items debited or credited directly to shareholders' equity. Operating income is not one of the categories of income subject to intra-period income tax allocation.
Answer (A) is incorrect. Income tax expense or benefit is allocated to several categories of income, including discontinued operations. Answer (B) is incorrect. Items included in the determination of taxable income may be presented in different sections of the financial statements. Accordingly, intraperiod tax allocation is required. Income tax expense or benefit is allocated to several categories of income, including income from continuing operations. Answer (C) is incorrect. Income tax expense or benefit is allocated to several categories of income, including other comprehensive income.

3.2 Discontinued Operations

3.2.1. Which of the following transactions most likely qualifies as a discontinued operation?

- A. Disposal of part of a line of business.
- B. Planned and approved sale of a reporting segment.
- C. Phasing out of a production line.
- D. Changes related to technological improvements.

Answer (B) is correct. *(CPA, adapted)*
REQUIRED: The most likely discontinued operation.
DISCUSSION: The operating results of a discontinued operation are reported separately if (1) a component of the entity has been disposed of or is classified as held for sale and (2) disposal is a strategic shift. A strategic shift has (or will have) a major effect on operations and financial results. A component of an entity has operations and cash flows that are clearly distinguishable for operating and financial reporting purposes. A component may be a(n) (1) reporting segment, (2) operating segment, (3) reporting unit, (4) subsidiary, or (5) asset group (a disposal group if it is to be disposed of). Accordingly, a reporting segment approved for sale is most likely to meet the criteria for a component of an entity classified as held for sale in a disposal that is a strategic shift.

Answer (A) is incorrect. Part of a line of business is most likely below the lowest level at which a strategic shift occurs involving disposal of a component of the entity. Answer (C) is incorrect. Phasing out of a production line is not a disposal or a classification of a component of an entity as held for sale. A gradual reduction in use is not a discontinuance of an operation. Answer (D) is incorrect. Changes related to technological improvements do not meet any of the criteria for reporting a discontinued operation.

3.2.2. Newt Co. sold a warehouse and used the proceeds to acquire a new warehouse. The excess of the proceeds over the carrying amount of the warehouse sold should be reported as a(n):

- A. Reduction of the cost of the new warehouse.
- B. Gain from discontinued operations, net of income taxes.
- C. Part of continuing operations.
- D. Item of other comprehensive income net of taxes.

Answer (C) is correct. *(CPA, adapted)*
REQUIRED: The reporting of the excess of the proceeds from the sale of real property over its carrying amount.
DISCUSSION: When property, plant, or equipment is disposed of other than by an exchange, the gain or loss is included in the results of continuing operations unless the disposal is reported in discontinued operations. The operating results of discontinued operations are presented in a separate component of the income statement following continuing operations. However, the facts do not indicate that the warehouse sold is (1) a component of the entity or (2) a business or nonprofit activity. For example, a component of an entity must have operations and cash flows clearly distinguishable for operating and financial reporting purposes. Moreover, disposal of a component of an entity must be a strategic shift (e.g., a major part of the entity). Thus, the gain on the sale is not from a discontinued operation.

Answer (A) is incorrect. The excess proceeds do not reduce the cost of the new warehouse. This transaction was not a nonmonetary exchange accounted for based on the carrying amount of the assets given up. The new warehouse is recorded at its initial cost. Answer (B) is incorrect. The criteria for reporting a discontinued operation, e.g., disposal of a component of the entity, have not been met. Answer (D) is incorrect. Gain on disposal of an item of property, plant, and equipment is not reported in OCI.

3.2.3. On April 30, Deer Corp. committed to a plan to sell a component of the entity. This sale represents a strategic shift that has a major effect on Deer's operations and financial results. For the period January 1 through April 30, the component had revenues of $500,000 and expenses of $800,000. The assets of the component were sold on October 15 at a loss for which no tax benefit is available. In its income statement for the year ended December 31, how should Deer report the component's operations from January 1 to April 30?

A. $500,000 and $800,000 should be included with revenues and expenses, respectively, as part of continuing operations.

B. $300,000 should be reported as part of the loss on disposal of a component.

C. $300,000 should be reported as an item of other comprehensive income.

D. $300,000 should be included in the determination of income or loss from operations of a discontinued component.

Answer (D) is correct. *(CPA, adapted)*
REQUIRED: The reporting of a loss related to operations of a discontinued component.
DISCUSSION: The results of operations of a component that meets the definition of a discontinued operation and any loss on a writedown to fair value minus cost to sell, net of applicable income taxes (benefit), should be reported separately as a component of income (discontinued operations) after the results of continuing operations. These results should be reported in the period(s) when they occur. Thus, the operating results of the component from January 1 through October 15 and the loss on disposal are included in the determination of income or loss from operations of the discontinued component.
Answer (A) is incorrect. Discontinued operations should not be reported as part of continuing operations. Answer (B) is incorrect. Discontinued operations should be presented in two categories: income or loss from operations of the discontinued component and the applicable income taxes (benefit). The loss on disposal is included in the determination of income or loss from the discontinued component. Answer (C) is incorrect. Income or loss from discontinued operations should be reported separately as a component of income after the results of continuing operations. Discontinued operations are not an item of other comprehensive income.

3.2.4. A company decided to sell an unprofitable major line of its business. The company can sell the entire operation for $800,000, and the buyer will assume all assets and liabilities of the operations. The tax rate is 30%. The assets and liabilities of the discontinued operation are as follows:

Buildings	$5,000,000
Accumulated depreciation	3,000,000
Mortgage on buildings	1,100,000
Inventory	500,000
Accounts payable	600,000
Accounts receivable	200,000

What is the after-tax net loss on the disposal of the division?

A. $140,000

B. $200,000

C. $1,540,000

D. $2,200,000

Answer (A) is correct. *(CPA, adapted)*
REQUIRED: The after-tax net loss on the disposal of an operation.
DISCUSSION: None of the items is measured at fair value under U.S. GAAP, assuming that the fair value option was not elected for the mortgage. Thus, the after-tax loss is calculated as follows based on the carrying amounts given:

Sale price		$ 800,000
Buildings, net ($5,000,000 –		
$3,000,000 acc. dep.)	$2,000,000	
Inventory	500,000	
Accounts receivable	200,000	
Mortgage	(1,100,000)	
Accounts payable	(600,000)	
Net carrying amount		1,000,000
Pre-tax loss		$ (200,000)
Tax benefit ($200,000 × 30%)		60,000
After-tax loss		$ (140,000)

Answer (B) is incorrect. The amount of $200,000 is the pre-tax loss. Answer (C) is incorrect. The amount of $1,540,000 equals the sum of the net carrying amount of the building, minus accounts payable, plus the after-tax loss. Answer (D) is incorrect. The amount of $2,200,000 equals the sum of the net carrying amount of the building and accounts receivable.

3.2.5. During January of Year 6, Doe Corp. agreed to sell the assets and product line of its Hart division. The sale was completed on January 15, Year 7, and resulted in a gain on disposal of $900,000. Hart's operating losses were $600,000 for Year 6 and $50,000 for the period January 1 through January 15, Year 7. Disregarding income taxes and assuming that the criteria for reporting a discontinued operation are met, what amount of net gain (loss) should be reported in Doe's comparative Year 7 and Year 6 income statements?

	Year 7	Year 6
A.	$0	$250,000
B.	$250,000	$0
C.	$850,000	$(600,000)
D.	$900,000	$(650,000)

Answer (C) is correct. *(CPA, adapted)*
REQUIRED: The amounts reported in comparative statements for discontinued operations.
DISCUSSION: The results of operations of a component that meets the definition of a discontinued operation are reported separately in the income statement under discontinued operations in the periods when they occur. Thus, in its Year 6 income statement, Doe should recognize a $600,000 loss. For Year 7, a gain of $850,000 should be recognized ($900,000 – $50,000).
Answer (A) is incorrect. The amount of $250,000 is the net gain for Year 6 and Year 7. However, the results for Year 7 may not be anticipated. Answer (B) is incorrect. The results for Year 6 should not be deferred. Answer (D) is incorrect. The operating loss for January Year 7 should be recognized in Year 7.

3.2.6. A company recently moved to a new building. The old building is being actively marketed for sale, and the company expects to complete the sale in 4 months. Each of the following statements is correct regarding the old building, except:

A. It will be reclassified as an asset held for sale.

B. It will be classified as a current asset.

C. It will no longer be depreciated.

D. It will be valued at historical cost.

Answer (D) is correct. *(CPA, adapted)*
REQUIRED: The false statement about an asset that is being sold.
DISCUSSION: The building will be reclassified as an asset held for sale. Under GAAP, an asset classified as held for sale is measured at the lower of carrying amount or fair value minus cost to sell.
Answer (A) is incorrect. This is a true statement. The old building will be reclassified as an asset held for sale because the company has moved to a new building (an action to complete the plan to sell), the old building is being actively marketed for sale, and it is expected to be sold in 4 months (within 1 year). Based on this information (and the absence of any contradictory information), we can assume that the other requirements have been met (management has committed to a plan to sell, it is available for sale in the present condition, and the likelihood is low of a significant change in, or withdrawal of, the plan). Answer (B) is incorrect. This is a true statement. The building will be reclassified as an asset held for sale. Assets held for sale are presented separately on the balance sheet as current assets. Answer (C) is incorrect. This is a true statement. The building will be reclassified as an asset held for sale. An asset classified as held for sale is not depreciated or amortized.

3.3 Comprehensive Income

3.3.1. When a full set of general-purpose financial statements is presented, comprehensive income and its components

    A. Appear as a part of discontinued operations.

    B. Must be reported net of related income tax effects in total and individually.

    C. Appear only in a supplemental schedule in the notes to the financial statements.

    D. Must be reported in a presentation that includes the components of other comprehensive income and their total.

Answer (D) is correct. *(CPA, adapted)*
    REQUIRED: The presentation of comprehensive income and its components.
    DISCUSSION: If an entity that reports a full set of financial statements has items of other comprehensive income (OCI), it must report comprehensive income in one continuous statement or in two separate but consecutive statements. One continuous statement has two sections: net income and OCI. It must include (1) a total of net income with its components, (2) a total of OCI with its components, and (3) a total of comprehensive income. In separate but consecutive statements, the first statement (the income statement) must present the components of net income and total net income. The second statement (the statement of OCI) must be presented immediately after the first. It presents (1) the components of OCI, (2) the total of OCI, and (3) a total for comprehensive income. The entity may begin the second statement with net income.
    Answer (A) is incorrect. Discontinued operations is a component of net income, a component of comprehensive income. Answer (B) is incorrect. The components of OCI must be presented either (1) net of related tax effects or (2) pretax, with one amount shown for the aggregate tax effect related to the total of OCI. No amount is displayed for the tax effect related to total comprehensive income. Answer (C) is incorrect. Comprehensive income must be reported in one continuous statement or in two separate but consecutive statements.

3.3.2. What is the purpose of reporting comprehensive income?

    A. To summarize all changes in equity from nonowner sources.

    B. To reconcile the difference between net income and cash flows provided from operating activities.

    C. To provide a consolidation of the income of the firm's segments.

    D. To provide information for each segment of the business.

Answer (A) is correct. *(CPA, adapted)*
    REQUIRED: The purpose of reporting comprehensive income.
    DISCUSSION: Comprehensive income includes all changes in equity of a business during a period except those from investments by and distributions to owners. It includes all components of (1) net income and (2) other comprehensive income (OCI).
    Answer (B) is incorrect. A statement of cash flows (direct or indirect method) includes a reconciliation of net income to net operating cash flow. Answer (C) is incorrect. The income statement presents aggregated information about revenues, gains, expenses, and losses. Answer (D) is incorrect. Information about specific segments is presented in the notes.

3.3.3. On December 31, Year 4, the last day of its fiscal year, OCI Company purchased 2,000 available-for-sale debt securities at a price of $10 per security. These securities had a fair value of $24,000 and $30,000 on December 31, Year 5, and December 31, Year 6, respectively. All of the securities were sold on December 31, Year 6. OCI recognizes all holding gains and losses on available-for-sale securities before recognizing realized gain. If OCI's tax rate is 25%, the total after-tax effect on comprehensive income in Year 6 of the foregoing transactions was

    A. $10,000

    B. $7,500

    C. $4,500

    D. $3,000

Answer (C) is correct. *(Publisher, adapted)*
    REQUIRED: The total after-tax effect on comprehensive income of a sale of available-for-sale securities in Year 3.
    DISCUSSION: OCI paid $20,000 for the debt securities. Thus, its after-tax holding gain in Year 5 was $3,000 [($24,000 fair value – $20,000) × (1.0 – .25 tax rate)]. Because the securities were classified as available-for-sale, the $3,000 holding gain was credited to other comprehensive income, not net income. OCI's after-tax holding gain in Year 6 was $4,500 [($30,000 – $24,000) × (1.0 – .25)]. Moreover, its realized after-tax gain in Year 6 included in net income was $7,500 [($30,000 – $20,000) × (1.0 – .25)]. The recognition of these amounts in Year 5 and Year 6 necessitates a reclassification adjustment to prevent double counting. This adjustment to other comprehensive income (a debit) is equal to the realized gain recognized in net income. Accordingly, the after-tax effect on comprehensive income in Year 6 of the sale of the available-for-sale securities is $4,500 ($7,500 realized gain + $4,500 holding gain – $7,500 reclassification adjustment).
    Answer (A) is incorrect. The amount of $10,000 is the pretax realized gain recognized in net income in Year 6. Answer (B) is incorrect. The amount of $7,500 is the reclassification adjustment and the realized after-tax gain. Answer (D) is incorrect. The amount of $3,000 is the after-tax holding gain in Year 5.

3.3.4. Which of the following is a component of other comprehensive income?

A. Minimum accrual of vacation pay.

B. Cumulative currency-translation adjustments.

C. Changes in market value of inventory.

D. Unrealized gain or loss on trading debt securities.

Answer (B) is correct. *(CPA, adapted)*
REQUIRED: The component of OCI.
DISCUSSION: Foreign currency translation adjustments for a foreign operation that is relatively self-contained and integrated within its environment do not affect cash flows of the reporting entity. They should be excluded from earnings. Accordingly, translation adjustments are reported in other comprehensive income (OCI).
Answer (A) is incorrect. Accrual of vacation pay affects earnings directly. Answer (C) is incorrect. A write-down to lower of cost or market affects earnings directly. Answer (D) is incorrect. Unrealized gain or loss on trading debt securities affects earnings directly.

3.3.5. Rock Co.'s financial statements had the following balances at December 31:

Infrequently occurring gain	$ 50,000
Foreign currency translation gain	100,000
Net income	400,000
Unrealized gain on available-for-sale debt securities	20,000

What amount should Rock report as comprehensive income for the year ended December 31?

A. $400,000

B. $420,000

C. $520,000

D. $570,000

Answer (C) is correct. *(Publisher, adapted)*
REQUIRED: The amount to report as comprehensive income.
DISCUSSION: Comprehensive income includes all changes in equity of a business entity except those changes resulting from investments by owners and distributions to owners. Comprehensive income includes two major categories: net income and other comprehensive income (OCI). Net income includes the results of continuing and discontinued operations. Components of comprehensive income not included in the determination of net income are included in OCI, for example, unrealized gains and losses on available-for-sale debt securities and certain foreign currency items, such as a translation adjustment. The infrequently occurring gain of $50,000 has already been included in the determination of net income. Thus, comprehensive income equals $520,000 ($400,000 net income + $100,000 translation gain + $20,000 unrealized gain on available-for-sale securities).
Answer (A) is incorrect. Certain foreign currency items and unrealized gains on available-for-sale debt securities are components of OCI. Answer (B) is incorrect. A foreign currency translation gain is a component of OCI. Answer (D) is incorrect. The infrequently occurring gain already is included in the net income amount of $400,000.

3.3.6. Palmyra Co. has net income of $11,000, a positive $1,000 net cumulative effect of a change in accounting principle, a $3,000 unrealized loss on available-for-sale debt securities, a positive $2,000 foreign currency translation adjustment, and a $6,000 increase in its common stock. What amount is Palmyra's comprehensive income?

A. $4,000

B. $10,000

C. $11,000

D. $17,000

Answer (B) is correct. *(CPA, adapted)*
REQUIRED: The total comprehensive income.
DISCUSSION: Comprehensive income includes all changes in equity of a business during a period except those from investments by and distributions to owners. It includes all elements of (1) net income and (2) other comprehensive income (OCI). Comprehensive income thus includes net income of $11,000, the unrealized loss on available-for-sale debt securities of $3,000 (component of OCI), and the $2,000 foreign currency translation adjustment (component of OCI). Thus, total comprehensive income is $10,000 ($11,000 − $3,000 + $2,000).
Answer (A) is incorrect. Comprehensive income includes all components of net income and other comprehensive income. It does not include an increase in the company's common stock. Answer (C) is incorrect. Comprehensive income includes all components of net income and other comprehensive income. A change in accounting principle is accounted for retrospectively, and the cumulative effect of the change is not included in comprehensive income. The carrying amount of assets, liabilities, and retained earnings at the beginning of the first period reported are adjusted for the cumulative effect of the new principle. Answer (D) is incorrect. Comprehensive income does not include changes in entity's common stock. Furthermore, a change in accounting principle is generally accounted for retrospectively, and the cumulative effect of the change is not included in comprehensive income.

3.4 IFRS

3.4.1. During the current year, both Raim Co. and Cane Co. suffered material losses due to the flooding of the Mississippi River. Raim is located 2 miles from the river and sustains flood losses every 2 to 3 years. Cane, which has been located 50 miles from the river for the past 20 years, has never before had flood losses. In accordance with IFRS, how should the flood losses be reported in each company's current-year income statement?

	Raim	Cane
A.	As a separate component of income from continuing operations	As an extraordinary item net of tax after results of discontinued operations
B.	As a separate component of income from continuing operations	As another expense in continuing operations
C.	As an extraordinary item	As another expense in continuing operations
D.	As an extraordinary item	As an extraordinary item

Answer (B) is correct. *(Publisher, adapted)*
REQUIRED: The reporting of flood losses in the income statement under IFRS.
DISCUSSION: Neither IFRS nor U.S. GAAP classify events or transactions as extraordinary. Thus, the flood losses should be classified as a separate component of income from continuing operations by Raim and Cane.
Answer (A) is incorrect. Neither IFRS nor U.S. GAAP classify events or transactions as extraordinary. Thus, Cane should recognize the flood loss in continuing operations. Answer (C) is incorrect. Neither IFRS nor U.S. GAAP classify events or transactions as extraordinary. Thus, Raim should recognize flood loss in continuing operations. Answer (D) is incorrect. Neither IFRS nor U.S. GAAP classify events or transactions as extraordinary.

3.4.2. A company that operates in Vermont incurred hurricane damage of $10 million. How is this loss reported in the financial statements prepared under IFRS and U.S. GAAP?

A. Under IFRS and U.S. GAAP as an extraordinary item.

B. Under IFRS and U.S. GAAP as a loss from continuing operations.

C. Under IFRS and U.S. GAAP as an item of other comprehensive income (OCI).

D. Under U.S. GAAP as an infrequent and unusual item and under IFRS as an other expense in the continuing operations section.

Answer (D) is correct. *(Publisher, adapted)*
REQUIRED: The reporting of a natural disaster loss under IFRS and U.S. GAAP.
DISCUSSION: The loss as a result of a hurricane is a material transaction that is (1) unusual in nature and (2) infrequent in occurrence in the environment in which the entity operates. Thus, under U.S. GAAP, this loss is reported as a separate component of income from continuing operations in the income statement. Under IFRS, this loss is reported as an other expense in the continuing operations section of the income statement.
Answer (A) is incorrect. Under IFRS and U.S. GAAP, no items are classified as extraordinary. Answer (B) is incorrect. Under U.S. GAAP, this loss is reported as an infrequent and unusual item. It is unusual in nature and infrequent in occurrence in the environment in which the company operates. Answer (C) is incorrect. A loss as a result of a hurricane must not be classified as an item of OCI. Instead, it must be recognized in the income statement as an infrequent and unusual item under U.S. GAAP or as a loss from continuing operations under IFRS.

Use **Gleim Test Prep** for interactive study and easy-to-use detailed analytics!

STUDY UNIT FOUR
THE TIME VALUE OF MONEY

The time value of money is essential to many accounting measurements. A quantity of money to be received or paid in the future is worth less than the same amount now. The difference is measured in terms of interest calculated using the appropriate discount rate. **Interest** is the payment received by an owner of money from the borrower as a fee for its use. It is stated as a percentage of the amount borrowed or invested.

The majority of the questions in this study unit require the calculation of the following: (1) the present value of a single amount (the value today of some future single payment), (2) the future value of a single amount (the amount available at a specified time in the future based on a single investment today), (3) the present value of an annuity (the value today of a series of future equal payments at equal intervals discounted at a given rate), and (4) the future value of an annuity (the amount available at a specified time in the future based on an annuity of payments). Standard tables have been developed to facilitate the calculation of present and future values of both single amounts and annuities.

QUESTIONS

4.1 Present Value

4.1.1. On July 1, Dichter Company obtained a $2,000,000, 180-day bank loan at an annual rate of 12%. The loan agreement requires Dichter to maintain a $400,000 compensating balance in its checking account at the lending bank. Dichter would otherwise maintain a balance of only $200,000 in this account. The checking account earns interest at an annual rate of 6%. Based on a 360-day year, the effective interest rate on the borrowing is

A. 6%

B. 12%

C. 12.67%

D. 13.33%

Answer (C) is correct. *(CPA, adapted)*
REQUIRED: The annual effective interest rate on a loan requiring a compensating balance.
DISCUSSION: The effective interest rate on the 180-day borrowing is equal to the net interest cost divided by the net available proceeds of $1,800,000 ($2,000,000 loan – $200,000 increase in the compensating balance). The net interest cost is equal to the gross interest cost minus the incremental interest revenue. The gross interest cost is $120,000 [$2,000,000 × 12% × (6 months ÷ 12 months)]. Because the incremental interest revenue is $6,000 [$200,000 × 6% × (6 months ÷ 12 months)], the net interest cost is $114,000 ($120,000 – $6,000). The 6-month effective interest rate is therefore 6.33% ($114,000 ÷ $1,800,000). The annual effective interest rate is 12.67% (6.33% × 2).
Answer (A) is incorrect. The checking account earns interest at an annual rate of 6%. Answer (B) is incorrect. Twelve percent is the annual rate. Answer (D) is incorrect. The interest revenue from the checking account must be included in the calculations.

4.1.2. The relationship between the present value of a future sum and the future value of a present sum can be expressed in terms of their respective interest factors. If the present value of $200,000 due at the end of 8 years, at 10%, is $93,300, what is the approximate future value of $200,000 invested for the same length of time and at the same rate?

A. $93,300

B. $200,000

C. $293,300

D. $428,724

Answer (D) is correct. *(CIA, adapted)*
REQUIRED: The approximate future value of an amount.
DISCUSSION: The interest factor for the future value of a present sum is equal to the reciprocal of the interest factor for the present value of a future sum. Thus, the future value is $428,724 [($200,000 ÷ $93,300) × $200,000].
Answer (A) is incorrect. The amount of $93,300 is the present value of $200,000 to be received in 8 years. Answer (B) is incorrect. The amount of $200,000 is the present value, not the future value, of $200,000 invested today. Answer (C) is incorrect. The addition of the present and future values has no accounting meaning.

4.1.3. A company purchased some large machinery on a deferred payment plan. The contract calls for $40,000 down on January 1 and $40,000 at the beginning of each of the next 4 years. There is no stated interest rate in the contract, and there is no established exchange price for the machinery. What should be recorded as the cost of the machinery?

A. $200,000.

B. $200,000 plus the added implicit interest.

C. Future value of an annuity due for 5 years at an imputed interest rate.

D. Present value of an annuity due for 5 years at an imputed interest rate.

Answer (D) is correct. *(CIA, adapted)*
REQUIRED: The cost of machinery acquired under a deferred payment plan.
DISCUSSION: The contract calls for an annuity due because the first annuity payment is due immediately. In an ordinary annuity (annuity in arrears), each payment is due at the end of the period. According to GAAP, an interest rate must be imputed in the given circumstances to arrive at the present value of the machinery.
Answer (A) is incorrect. The undiscounted sum of the payments is $200,000. Answer (B) is incorrect. The implicit interest should be subtracted from the $200,000 in total payments. Answer (C) is incorrect. The present value, not the future value, is the appropriate concept.

4.1.4. On September 1, Year 1, an entity purchased a new machine that it does not have to pay for until September 1, Year 3. The total payment on September 1, Year 3, will include both principal and interest. Assuming interest at a 10% rate, the cost of the machine will be the total payment multiplied by what time value of money factor?

A. Present value of annuity of $1.

B. Present value of $1.

C. Future amount of annuity of $1.

D. Future amount of $1.

Answer (B) is correct. *(CPA, adapted)*
REQUIRED: The time value of money factor to compute current cost when payment is to be made in a lump sum at a future date.
DISCUSSION: The cost of the machine on 9/1/Year 1 is the present value of the payment to be made on 9/1/Year 3. To obtain the present value, i.e., today's price, the future payment is multiplied by the present value of $1 for two periods at 10%.
Answer (A) is incorrect. The present value of an annuity is the value today of a series of future payments, not merely one payment. Answer (C) is incorrect. The future value of an annuity is the amount available at a specified time in the future after a series of deposits (investments). Answer (D) is incorrect. The future value of a dollar is the amount that will be available at a specified time in the future based on a single investment (deposit) today.

4.1.5. The computation of the current value of an asset using the present value of future cash flows method does not include the

A. Cost of alternate uses of funds given up.

B. Productive life of the asset.

C. Applicable interest rate.

D. Future amounts of cash receipts or cash savings.

Answer (A) is correct. *(CPA, adapted)*
REQUIRED: The information not used in computing current value using the present value of future cash flows method.
DISCUSSION: The calculation of the current value of an asset using the present value method requires (1) the discount period (the productive life of the asset), (2) the discount rate (the applicable interest rate), and (3) the future values (the future amounts of cash receipts or cash savings). This method does not consider opportunity costs (benefits of the best alternative use of funds).
Answer (B) is incorrect. The productive life of the asset is the number of periods used in calculating the asset's present value. Answer (C) is incorrect. The applicable interest rate is the discount rate in the present value computation. Answer (D) is incorrect. The future amounts of cash receipts or cash savings are the cash flows to be discounted.

4.1.6. In the determination of a present value, which of the following relationships is true?

A. The lower the discount rate and the shorter the discount period, the lower the present value.

B. The lower the future cash flow and the shorter the discount period, the lower the present value.

C. The higher the discount rate and the longer the discount period, the lower the present value.

D. The higher the future cash flow and the longer the discount period, the lower the present value.

Answer (C) is correct. *(Publisher, adapted)*
REQUIRED: The true relationship between the discount period, discount rate, and present value.
DISCUSSION: As the discount rate increases, the present value decreases. Also, as the discount period increases, the present value decreases.
Answer (A) is incorrect. Both conditions are untrue. As the discount rate decreases, present value increases. Also, as the discount period gets shorter, the present value increases. Answer (B) is incorrect. As the discount period gets shorter, the present value increases. Answer (D) is incorrect. Increased future cash flows increase the present value.

4.1.7. On July 1, Goblette Company sold some machinery to another company. The two companies entered into an installment sales contract at a predetermined interest rate. The contract required 5 equal annual payments with the first payment due on July 1, the date of sale. What present value concept is appropriate for this situation?

A. Present value of an annuity due of $1 for 5 periods.

B. Present value of an ordinary annuity of $1 for 5 periods.

C. Future amount of an annuity due of $1 for 5 periods.

D. Future amount of $1 for 5 periods.

Answer (A) is correct. *(CPA, adapted)*
REQUIRED: The present value concept appropriate for an installment sale with the first payment due immediately.
DISCUSSION: The contract calls for 5 equal annual payments with the first due immediately. Ordinary annuity tables assume the first payment occurs at the end of the first time period. An annuity in which the first payment occurs at the beginning of the first period is called an "annuity due" or an "annuity in advance." The number of payments earning interest in an annuity due is one less than the number earning interest in an ordinary annuity because there is no interest on the first payment. Accordingly, the present value of an annuity due of $1 for 5 periods can be calculated by taking the present value of an ordinary annuity of $1 for 4 periods and adding $1. Hence, either a special table for an annuity due or the method described above can be used in this situation.
Answer (B) is incorrect. The question describes an annuity due (not an ordinary annuity) for 5 periods. Answer (C) is incorrect. Although the question involves an annuity due, the present value, not the future amount, is required. Answer (D) is incorrect. The present value of an annuity due, not the future amount of a single sum, will provide the correct answer.

4.1.8. For which of the following transactions would the use of the present value of an annuity due concept be appropriate in calculating the present value of the asset obtained or liability owed at the date of incurrence?

A. A finance lease is entered into with the initial lease payment due 1 month subsequent to the signing of the lease agreement.

B. A finance lease is entered into with the initial lease payment due upon the signing of the lease agreement.

C. A 10-year, 8% bond is issued on January 2 with interest payable semiannually on July 1 and January 1, yielding 7%.

D. A 10-year, 8% bond is issued on January 2 with interest payable semiannually on July 1 and January 1, yielding 9%.

Answer (B) is correct. *(CPA, adapted)*
REQUIRED: The transaction for which the present value of an annuity due concept would be appropriate.
DISCUSSION: In an annuity due, the first payment is made at the beginning of the first period and is therefore not discounted. In an ordinary annuity, the first payment is made at the end of the first period and therefore is discounted. For annuities due, the first payment is included in the computation at its face value.
Answer (A) is incorrect. Given that the first payment is due 1 month from signing and not on the day of signing, an ordinary annuity, not an annuity due, is the relevant model. Answer (C) is incorrect. The bonds have just passed an interest payment (coupon) date. The next one is not for another 6 months. Given no immediate payment, the annuity is ordinary. Furthermore, the yield percentage is irrelevant to annuity. Answer (D) is incorrect. The initial payment is not due immediately.

4.1.9. Chambers Company bought Machine 1 on March 5, Year 1, for $5,000 cash. The estimated salvage was $200 and the estimated life was 11 years. On March 5, Year 2, the company learned that it could purchase a different machine for $8,000 cash. It would save the company an estimated $250 per year. The new machine would have no estimated salvage and an estimated life of 10 years. The company could sell Machine 1 for $3,000 on March 5, Year 2. Ignoring income taxes, which of the following calculations would best assist the company in deciding whether to purchase the new machine?

A. (Present value of an annuity of $250) + $3,000 − $8,000.

B. (Present value of an annuity of $250) − $8,000.

C. (Present value of an annuity of $250) + $3,000 − $8,000 − $5,000.

D. (Present value of an annuity of $250) + $3,000 − $8,000 − $4,800.

Answer (A) is correct. *(CPA, adapted)*
REQUIRED: The calculation that would best assist the company in deciding whether to purchase the new machine.
DISCUSSION: The sale of the first machine for $3,000 and the purchase of the new machine for $8,000 on 3/5/Year 2 results in an incremental cost to the company of $5,000. If the present value of the future savings from the second machine (present value of an annuity of $250) exceeds $5,000, the company should purchase the new machine. Note that the remaining estimated useful life of the first machine is the same as that of the second. Note also that the cost of Machine 1 should be ignored because it is a sunk cost.
Answer (B) is incorrect. (Present value of an annuity of $250) − $8,000 fails to consider the resale value of Machine 1 on 3/5/Year 2. Answer (C) is incorrect. (Present value of an annuity of $250) + $3,000 − $8,000 − $5,000 improperly considers the sunk cost of Machine 1 ($5,000). Answer (D) is incorrect. (Present value of an annuity of $250) + $3,000 − $8,000 − $4,800 improperly considers the sunk cost of Machine 1 and its salvage value [$4,800 ($5,000 − $200)].

4.1.10. Stone Co. is considering the acquisition of equipment. To buy the equipment, the cost is $15,192. To lease the equipment, Stone must sign a noncancelable lease and make five payments of $4,000 each. The first payment will be paid on the first day of the lease. At the time of the last payment, Stone will receive title to the equipment. The present value of an ordinary annuity of $1 is as follows:

No. of Periods	Present Value		
	10%	12%	16%
1	0.909	0.893	0.862
2	1.736	1.690	1.605
3	2.487	2.402	2.246
4	3.170	3.037	2.798
5	3.791	3.605	3.274

The interest rate implicit in this lease is approximately

A. 10%.

B. 12%.

C. Between 10% and 12%.

D. 16%.

Answer (D) is correct. *(CPA, adapted)*
    REQUIRED: The interest rate implicit in a lease.
    DISCUSSION: To perform this computation, a present value factor must be derived and compared with those in the table. The factor can be calculated by dividing the relevant present value by the periodic payment.

Full cost of equipment (present value)	$15,192
Minus: First payment, due immediately	(4,000)
Amount financed (present value of an ordinary annuity of 4 $4,000 payments)	$11,192
Divided by: Periodic payment	÷ 4,000
Present value factor	2.798

Consulting the table reveals that the factor inherent in this calculation for a 4-period annuity is 16%.
    Answer (A) is incorrect. A 10% discount rate does not yield the appropriate cash flows. The amount financed is $11,192 ($15,192 – $4,000). The table reveals that the 10% factor for four periods is 3.17. The result of multiplying $4,000 by 3.170 is $12,680, not $11,192. Answer (B) is incorrect. A 12% discount rate does not yield the appropriate cash flows. The amount financed is $11,192 ($15,192 – $4,000). The table reveals that the 12% factor for four periods is 3.037. The result of multiplying $4,000 by 3.037 is $12,148, not $11,192. Answer (C) is incorrect. A discount rate between 10% and 12% does not yield the appropriate cash flows. The table reveals that the 12% factor for four periods is 3.037. The result of multiplying $4,000 by 3.037 is $12,148, not $11,192. Accordingly, a discount rate higher than 12% must be used because 12% gives an amount greater than $11,192.

4.1.11. On July 1, Year 4, Ahmed signed an agreement to operate as a franchisee of Teacake Pastries, Inc., for an initial franchise fee of $240,000. On the same date, Ahmed paid $80,000 and agreed to pay the balance in four equal annual payments of $40,000 beginning July 1, Year 5. The down payment is not refundable, and no future services are required of the franchisor. Ahmed can borrow at 14% for a loan of this type.

Present value of $1 at 14% for 4 periods	0.59
Future amount of $1 at 14% for 4 periods	1.69
Present value of an ordinary annuity of $1 at 14% for 4 periods	2.91

Ahmed should record the acquisition cost of the franchise on July 1, Year 4, at

A. $270,400

B. $240,000

C. $196,400

D. $174,400

Answer (C) is correct. *(CPA, adapted)*
    REQUIRED: The acquisition cost of a franchise to be paid for in installments.
    DISCUSSION: The acquisition cost would have been recorded at $240,000 if this amount of cash had been paid immediately. Given that the $240,000 is to be paid in installments, the acquisition cost is equal to the down payment of $80,000 plus the present value of the series of 4 annuity payments beginning 1 year after the date of purchase. The proper interest factor to be employed is the present value of an ordinary annuity of $1 at 14% for 4 periods, or 2.91.

Periodic payment	$ 40,000
Times: PV factor	× 2.91
PV of periodic payments	$116,400
Plus: Down payment	+ 80,000
PV of franchise fee	$196,400

Answer (A) is incorrect. The amount of $270,400 results from using the factor for the future amount, rather than an ordinary annuity, of $1 at 14% for 4 periods. Answer (B) is incorrect. The amount of $240,000 results from failing to account for the time value of money. Answer (D) is incorrect. The amount of $174,000 results from using the factor for a single amount, rather than an ordinary annuity, of $1 at 14% for 4 periods.

4.1.12. Harry Rawlings wants to withdraw $10,000 (including principal) from an investment fund at the end of each year for 5 years. How should he compute his required initial investment at the beginning of the first year if the fund earns 6% compounded annually?

A. $10,000 times the amount of an annuity of $1 at 6% at the end of each year for 5 years.

B. $10,000 divided by the amount of an annuity of $1 at 6% at the end of each year for 5 years.

C. $10,000 times the present value of an annuity of $1 at 6% at the end of each year for 5 years.

D. $10,000 divided by the present value of an annuity of $1 at 6% at the end of each year for 5 years.

Answer (C) is correct. *(CPA, adapted)*
REQUIRED: The computation for the initial investment required at a given rate to permit withdrawal of a fixed amount at the end of each of a series of years.
DISCUSSION: The question requires a present value rather than a future value, i.e., today's equivalent of $10,000 at the end of each of the next 5 years. The table used is for the present value of an ordinary annuity. The interest factor corresponding to 6% for 5 periods is multiplied by $10,000 to provide the answer.
Answer (A) is incorrect. The question requires a present value rather than a future value calculation. "Amount of an annuity" is synonymous with future value of an annuity. Answer (B) is incorrect. A present value computation is required. Moreover, the payment should be multiplied by the relevant interest factor. Answer (D) is incorrect. The amount of $10,000 must be multiplied (rather than divided) by the present value of an ordinary annuity of $1 for 6% and 5 periods.

4.1.13. On January 1, Year 3, Orr Company bought a building with an assessed value of $220,000 on the date of purchase. Orr gave as consideration a $400,000 noninterest-bearing note due on January 1, Year 6. There was no established exchange price for the building, and the note had no ready market. The prevailing rate of interest for a note of this type at January 1, Year 3, was 10%. The present value of $1 at 10% for three periods is 0.75. What amount of interest expense should be included in Orr's Year 3 income statement?

A. $22,000

B. $30,000

C. $33,333

D. $40,000

Answer (B) is correct. *(CPA, adapted)*
REQUIRED: The interest expense on a noninterest-bearing note.
DISCUSSION: The purchase of a building without an established exchange price should be recorded at the fair value of the consideration given. A noninterest-bearing note receivable or payable should be recorded at the present value of the future cash flows discounted at the prevailing rate of interest. This note payable and building should therefore be recorded at $300,000 ($400,000 × 0.75). The difference between the face amount (a liability) and the present value is recorded as a discount and amortized to interest expense over the life of the note payable using the effective interest method. The amount of interest expense for the first year is $30,000 ($300,000 discounted note × 10% effective rate).
Answer (A) is incorrect. The amount of $22,000 results from applying the interest rate to the assessment value of the building. Answer (C) is incorrect. The amount of $33,333 results from applying the straight-line method of amortizing the discount. Answer (D) is incorrect. The amount of $40,000 fails to consider the present value of the note.

4.1.14. Risoner Company plans to purchase a machine with the following conditions:

● Purchase price = $300,000.
● The down payment = 10% of purchase price with remainder financed at an annual interest rate of 16%.
● The financing period is 8 years with equal annual payments made every year.
● The present value of an annuity of $1 per year for 8 years at 16% is 4.3436.
● The present value of $1 due at the end of 8 years at 16% is .3050.

The annual payment (rounded to the nearest dollar) is

A. $39,150

B. $43,200

C. $62,160

D. $82,350

Answer (C) is correct. *(CIA, adapted)*
REQUIRED: The annual payment (rounded to the nearest dollar).
DISCUSSION: The periodic payment is found by dividing the amount to be accumulated ($300,000 price – $30,000 down payment = $270,000) by the interest factor for the present value of an ordinary annuity for 8 years at 16%. Consequently, the payment is $62,160 ($270,000 ÷ 4.3436).
Answer (A) is incorrect. The amount of $39,150 is based on dividing ($270,000 × 1.16) by 8 (years). Answer (B) is incorrect. The amount of $43,200 is 16% of $270,000. Answer (D) is incorrect. The amount of $82,350 reflects multiplication by the present value of a sum due (.305) instead of dividing by the present value of an annuity (4.3436).

4.1.15. On December 30 of the current year, Azrael, Inc., purchased a machine from Abiss Corp. in exchange for a noninterest-bearing note requiring 8 payments of $20,000. The first payment was made on December 30, and the others are due annually on December 30. At date of issuance, the prevailing rate of interest for this type of note was 11%. Present value factors are as follows:

Period	Present Value of Ordinary Annuity of $1 at 11%	Present Value of Annuity in Advance of $1 at 11%
7	4.712	5.231
8	5.146	5.712

On Azrael's current year December 31 balance sheet, the note payable to Abiss was

A. $94,240

B. $102,920

C. $104,620

D. $114,240

Answer (A) is correct. *(CPA, adapted)*
REQUIRED: The carrying amount of a noninterest-bearing note payable at the date of issuance.
DISCUSSION: The payment terms of this purchase agreement provide for a $20,000 initial payment and seven equal payments of $20,000 to be received at the end of each of the next 7 years. The note payable, however, should reflect only the present value of the 7 future payments. The present value factor to be used is the present value of an ordinary annuity for 7 periods at 11%, or 4.712. The note payable should be recorded at $94,240 ($20,000 × 4.712).
Answer (B) is incorrect. The amount of $102,920 uses the factor for 8 periods rather than 7. Answer (C) is incorrect. The factor for an ordinary annuity should be used. Answer (D) is incorrect. The factor used should be for an ordinary annuity of 7 periods, not an annuity in advance for 8 periods.

4.1.16. Based on 8% interest compounded annually from day of deposit to day of withdrawal, what is the present value today of $4,000 to be received 6 years from today?

Periods	Present Value of $1 Discounted at 8% per Period
1	.926
2	.857
3	.794
4	.735
5	.681

A. $4,000 × 0.926 × 6.

B. $4,000 × 0.794 × 2.

C. $4,000 × 0.681 × 0.926.

D. Cannot be determined from the information given.

Answer (C) is correct. *(CPA, adapted)*
REQUIRED: The present value today of an amount to be received at a given future date.
DISCUSSION: To calculate the present value of an amount to be received 6 years from today when present value factors for only 5 periods are available, multiply $4,000 by the present value of $1 factor for 5 periods. This discounts the $4,000 back 5 years. This result should then be discounted back 1 additional year, i.e., multiplied by the present value factor for one period.
Answer (A) is incorrect. The $4,000 should first be discounted for 5 years; then that amount should be discounted for 1 additional year. Answer (B) is incorrect. The $4,000 should first be discounted for 5 years; then that amount should be discounted for 1 additional year. Answer (D) is incorrect. The present value can be determined from the information given.

4.1.17. Potter Corporation is contemplating the purchase of a new piece of equipment with a purchase price of $500,000. It plans to make a 10% down payment and will receive a loan for 25 years at 10% interest. The present value interest factor for an annuity of $1 per year for 25 years at 10% is 9.0770. The annual payment required on the loan will be

A. $18,000

B. $49,576

C. $45,000

D. $55,084

Answer (B) is correct. *(CIA, adapted)*
REQUIRED: The annual payment required on the loan.
DISCUSSION: The corporation plans a 10% down payment on equipment with a purchase price of $500,000. The amount of the loan will therefore equal $450,000. Because the loan will be financed at 10% for 25 years, the annual payments can be calculated by dividing the amount of the initial loan by the present value interest factor for an annuity of $1 per year for 25 years at 10%. The annual payment required is equal to $49,576 ($450,000 ÷ 9.0770).
Answer (A) is incorrect. This amount results from allocating the $450,000 equally over 25 years. Answer (C) is incorrect. This amount results from multiplying $450,000 by the 10% interest. Answer (D) is incorrect. This amount results if the $50,000 down payment is not removed before the annual payment is calculated.

4.1.18. Murray is planning a project that will cost $22,000. The annual cash inflow, net of income taxes, will be $5,000 a year for 7 years. The present value of $1 at 12% is as follows:

Period	Present Value of $1 at 12%
1	.893
2	.797
3	.712
4	.636
5	.567
6	.507
7	.452

Using a rate of return of 12%, what is the present value of the cash flow generated by this project?

A. $22,600

B. $22,820

C. $34,180

D. $35,000

Answer (B) is correct. *(CPA, adapted)*
REQUIRED: The present value of the cash flow generated by the project.
DISCUSSION: If the cash inflow, net of taxes, at the end of each of 7 years is $5,000, and if the discount rate is 12%, the present value of this series of cash flows will be equal to the present value of an ordinary annuity of $5,000 for 7 years at 12%. The interest factor for the present value of an ordinary annuity is equal to the sum of the interest factors for the present value of $1 for the same period. The interest factor for an ordinary annuity of $5,000 for 7 periods is 4.564. The present value is $22,820 ($5,000 × 4.564).
The alternative is to calculate the present value of each $5,000 cash flow using the interest factor for the present value of $1 at 12% for each of the periods 1 through 7. The sum of these products is equal to the present value of an ordinary annuity of $5,000 for 7 periods at 12%.

$5,000	×	.893	=	$ 4,465
5,000	×	.797	=	3,985
5,000	×	.712	=	3,560
5,000	×	.636	=	3,180
5,000	×	.567	=	2,835
5,000	×	.507	=	2,535
5,000	×	.452	=	2,260
5,000	×	4.564	=	$22,820

Answer (A) is incorrect. The amount of $22,600 results from adding 12% of $5,000 to the project cost of $22,000. Answer (C) is incorrect. The amount of $34,180 results from subtracting the difference between the present value of the cash flows and the project cost ($22,820 – $22,000 = $820) from the $35,000 ($5,000 × 7 years) undiscounted total cash flows ($35,000 – $820 = $34,180). Answer (D) is incorrect. The amount of $35,000 fails to consider the time value of money.

4.1.19. A loan is to be repaid in eight annual installments of $1,875. The interest rate is 10%. The present value of an ordinary annuity for eight periods at 10% is 5.33. Identify the computation that approximates the outstanding loan balance at the end of the first year.

A. $1,875 × 5.33 = $9,994.

B. $1,875 × 5.33 = $9,994;
$9,994 – $1,875 = $8,119.

C. $1,875 × 5.33 = $9,994;
$1,875 – $999 = $876;
$9,994 – $876 = $9,118.

D. $1,875 × 8 = $15,000;
$15,000 – ($1,875 – $1,500) = $14,625.

Answer (C) is correct. *(CIA, adapted)*
REQUIRED: The computation approximating the outstanding loan balance at the end of Year 1.
DISCUSSION: The present value of an ordinary annuity of $1 for 8 periods at 10% is 5.33. Thus, the present value of an ordinary annuity of $1,875 is $9,994 (5.33 × $1,875), the original balance of the loan. If the interest rate is 10%, the interest on the principal for Year 1 will be approximately $999. Accordingly, the first installment has an interest component of $999 and a principal component of $876 ($1,875 – $999 interest). The first payment therefore reduces the principal balance of $9,994 by $876 to $9,118.
Answer (A) is incorrect. This computation ($1,875 × 5.33 = $9,994) determines the present value of the annuity at the beginning of Year 1, not the loan balance at the end of Year 1. Answer (B) is incorrect. These computations ($1,875 × 5.33 = $9,994; $9,994 – $1,875 = $8,119) improperly subtract both principal and interest for Year 1 in arriving at the principal balance. Answer (D) is incorrect. These computations [$1,875 × 8 = $15,000; $15,000 – ($1,875 – $1,500) = $14,625] do not consider the time value of money.

4.2 Future Value

Questions 4.2.1 and 4.2.2 are based on the following information. Present value, amount of $1, and ordinary annuity information are presented below. All values are for four periods with an interest rate of 8%.

Amount of $1	1.36
Present value of $1	0.74
Amount of an ordinary annuity of $1	4.51
Present value of an ordinary annuity of $1	3.31

4.2.1. Cara Galadon decides to create a fund to earn 8% compounded annually that will enable her to withdraw $5,000 per year each June 30, beginning in Year 4 and continuing through Year 7. Cara wishes to make equal contributions on June 30 of each year from Year 0 through Year 3. Which equation would be used to compute the balance that must be in the fund on June 30, Year 3, for Cara to meet her objective?

- A. $X = $5,000 × 3.31.
- B. $X = $5,000 × (3.31 + 1.00).
- C. $X = $5,000 × 1.36.
- D. $X = $5,000 × 4.51.

Answer (A) is correct. *(CIA, adapted)*
REQUIRED: The equation to compute the balance in the fund on a given date to permit withdrawals at equal intervals over a stated period.
DISCUSSION: The fund balance on 6/30/Year 3 should be equal to the present value of four equal annual payments of $5,000 each discounted at a rate of 8%. If the factor for the present value of an ordinary annuity of $1 for 4 periods at 8% is 3.31, the present value of an ordinary annuity of $5,000 for four periods discounted at 8% is $5,000 × 3.31.
Answer (B) is incorrect. The equation $X = $5,000 × (3.31 + 1.00) gives the present value of an annuity due for 5 periods. Answer (C) is incorrect. The equation $X = $5,000 × 1.36 gives the future value in 4 periods of $5,000 invested today. Answer (D) is incorrect. The equation $X = $5,000 × 4.51 is the future value of an annuity of four annual deposits of $5,000.

4.2.2. Pippen wants to accumulate $50,000 by making equal contributions at the end of each of 4 succeeding years. Which equation would be used to compute Pippen's annual contribution to achieve the $50,000 goal at the end of the fourth year?

- A. $X = $50,000 ÷ 4.51.
- B. $X = $50,000 ÷ 4.00.
- C. $X = $12,500 ÷ 1.36.
- D. $X = $50,000 ÷ 3.31.

Answer (A) is correct. *(CIA, adapted)*
REQUIRED: The equation to compute the annual year-end payment necessary to accumulate a stated amount at the end of a stated period.
DISCUSSION: The factor for the amount of an ordinary annuity of $1 for four periods at 8% (4.51) is used. If an investment of $1 at 8% at the end of each of 4 periods would generate a future amount of 4.51, an investment of $X per period for 4 periods at 8% would generate the necessary $50,000. The required annual payment is equal to $50,000 ÷ 4.51.
Answer (B) is incorrect. The equation $X = $50,000 ÷ 4.00 does not take into account interest to be earned. Answer (C) is incorrect. The equation $X = $12,500 ÷ 1.36 gives the present value of $12,500 to be received four periods hence. Answer (D) is incorrect. The equation $X = $50,000 ÷ 3.31 gives the amount of the periodic payment needed to produce an ordinary annuity with a present value of $50,000.

4.2.3. Jarvis wants to invest equal semiannual payments in order to have $10,000 at the end of 20 years. Assuming that Jarvis will earn interest at an annual rate of 6% compounded semi-annually, how would the periodic payment be calculated?

- A. $10,000 divided by the future amount of an ordinary annuity of 40 payments of $1 each at an interest rate of 3% per period.
- B. $10,000 divided by the present value of an ordinary annuity of 40 payments of $1 each at an interest rate of 3% per period.
- C.   The future amount of an ordinary annuity of 20 payments of $1 each at an interest rate of 6% per period divided into $10,000.
- D.   The present value of an ordinary annuity of 40 payments of $1 each at an interest rate of 3% per period divided by $10,000.

Answer (A) is correct. *(CPA, adapted)*
REQUIRED: The method of calculating the periodic payment to accumulate a known future amount.
DISCUSSION: The question involves future value because it requires computation of the periodic amount of an annuity that must be invested to produce a given future amount. Accordingly, the appropriate factor reflecting the compound interest effect will be derived from the formula for the future value of an ordinary annuity of $1. This factor multiplied by the periodic payment is equal to the desired future amount. If the payment is unknown, it may be calculated by dividing the known future amount ($10,000) by the appropriate factor derived from the future value of an ordinary annuity formula. If the payments are to be made semiannually for 20 years, 40 compounding periods are involved. If the interest rate is 6% per annum, the semiannual interest rate is 3%.
Answer (B) is incorrect. The question calls for a future value computation. Answer (C) is incorrect. The number of semiannual payments to be made at an interest rate of 3% per period is 40 (not 20 payments at 6%). Answer (D) is incorrect. The future amount should be divided by the relevant interest factor for the future amount of an ordinary annuity.

4.2.4. On March 15, Year 1, Kathleen Corp. adopted a plan to accumulate $1,000,000 by September 1, Year 5. Kathleen plans to make 4 equal annual deposits to a fund that will earn interest at 10% compounded annually. Kathleen made the first deposit on September 1, Year 1. Future value and future amount factors are as follows:

Future value of $1 at 10% for 4 periods	1.46
Future amount of ordinary annuity of $1 at 10% for 4 periods	4.64
Future amount of annuity in advance of $1 at 10% for 4 periods	5.11

Kathleen should make 4 annual deposits (rounded) of

A. $250,000

B. $215,500

C. $195,700

D. $684,930

Answer (C) is correct. *(CPA, adapted)*
REQUIRED: The amount of an annuity in advance that would generate a future sum.
DISCUSSION: The depositor wishes to have $1,000,000 at the end of a 4-year period (from 9/1/Year 1 to 9/1/Year 5). The amount will be generated from 4 equal annual payments (an annuity) to be made starting at the beginning of the 4-year period. The annual payment needed to reach this goal can be calculated by dividing the desired future amount of $1,000,000 by the factor for the future amount of an annuity in advance of $1 at 10% for 4 periods. Each annual deposit should therefore equal $195,700 ($1,000,000 ÷ 5.11).
Answer (A) is incorrect. The amount of $250,000 does not take into account the interest. Answer (B) is incorrect. The amount of $215,500 is computed using the future value factor of an ordinary annuity instead of an annuity in advance (annuity due). Answer (D) is incorrect. The amount of $684,930 is computed using the future value factor of $1 instead of the future value factor of an annuity in advance.

4.2.5. If the amount to be received in 4 years is $137,350, and given the correct factor from the 10% time-value-of-money table below, what is the current investment?

Interest Factors for 10%

Periods	FV	PV	FV of Ordinary Annuity	PV of Ordinary Annuity
1	1.1000	.9091	1.0000	.9091
2	1.2100	.8264	2.1000	1.7355
3	1.3310	.7513	3.3100	2.4869
4	1.4641	.6830	4.6410	3.1699
5	1.6105	.6029	6.1051	3.7908

A. $30,034.33

B. $43,329.44

C. $93,810.05

D. $201,094.14

Answer (C) is correct. *(CIA, adapted)*
REQUIRED: The current investment required to receive a future amount of money at a given interest rate.
DISCUSSION: The current investment is the present value of the given future amount. It equals the future amount multiplied by the factor for the present value of $1 for 4 periods at 10%. Accordingly, the current investment is $93,810.05 ($137,350 × .6830).
Answer (A) is incorrect. This amount cannot be derived from any of the time value factors given. Answer (B) is incorrect. The amount of $43,329.44 results from incorrectly dividing by the factor for the present value of an ordinary annuity for 4 periods. Answer (D) is incorrect. The amount of $201,094.14 results from incorrectly using the factor for the future value of $1 for 4 periods.

4.2.6. A pension fund is projecting the amount necessary today to fund a retiree's pension benefits. The retiree's first annual pension check will be in 10 years. Payments are expected to last for a total of 20 annual payments. Which of the following best describes the computation of the amount needed today to fund the retiree's annuity?

A. Present value of $1 for 10 periods, times the present value of an ordinary annuity of 20 payments, times the annual annuity payment.

B. Present value of $1 for nine periods, times the present value of an ordinary annuity of 20 payments, times the annual annuity payment.

C. Future value of $1 for 10 periods, times the present value of an ordinary annuity of 20 payments, times the annual annuity payment.

D. Future value of $1 for nine periods, times the present value of an ordinary annuity of 20 payments, times the annual annuity payment.

Answer (B) is correct. *(CIA, adapted)*
REQUIRED: The formula to compute the amount needed today to fund a pension that will begin in the future.
DISCUSSION: Multiplying the annual annuity pension payment times the present value of an ordinary annuity of 20 payments factor results in a present value determination 1 year prior to the start of the payments, or 9 years hence. Multiplying the present value of ordinary annuity pension payments by a present value of $1 factor for 9 years results in the amount needed today to fund the retiree's annuity.
Answer (A) is incorrect. The present value factor for nine periods should be used to determine the amount needed to fund the pension plan. Answer (C) is incorrect. A future value fact is not used to determine the amount needed to fund the pension plan. Answer (D) is incorrect. A present value factor should be used.

4.2.7. An actuary has determined that Jaykay Company should have $90,000,000 accumulated in a fund 20 years from now to be able to meet its pension obligations. An interest rate of 8% is considered appropriate for all pension fund calculations involving an interest component. Jaykay wishes to calculate how much it should contribute at the end of each of the next 20 years for the pension fund to have its required balance in 20 years. Which set of instructions correctly describes the procedures necessary to compute the annual amount the company should contribute to the fund?

A. Divide $90,000,000 by the interest factor for the present value of an ordinary annuity for n=20, i=8%.

B. Multiply $90,000,000 by the interest factor for the present value of an ordinary annuity for n=20, i=8%.

C. Divide $90,000,000 by the interest factor for the future value of an ordinary annuity for n=20, i=8%.

D. Multiply $90,000,000 by the interest factor for the future value of an ordinary annuity for n=20, i=8%.

Answer (C) is correct. *(CIA, adapted)*
REQUIRED: The set of instructions that correctly describes the procedures necessary to compute the annual amount the company should contribute to the fund.
DISCUSSION: The future value of an annuity equals the appropriate interest factor (for n periods at an interest rate of i), which is derived from standard tables, times the periodic payment. The $90,000,000 amount is the future value of the funding payments. The amount of each funding payment can be calculated by dividing the future value of the funding payments by the interest factor for future value of an ordinary annuity for n equals 20 and i equals 8%.
Answer (A) is incorrect. The $90,000,000 is a future value figure. The interest factor to be used for the division process should be a future value factor, not a present value factor. Answer (B) is incorrect. The $90,000,000 is a future value figure. The factor to be used should be a future value factor. That factor should be used in a division, rather than a multiplication, process. Answer (D) is incorrect. The $90,000,000 should be divided by the appropriate interest factor.

☑ ≡
☐ ≡   Use **Gleim Test Prep** for interactive study and easy-to-use detailed analytics!
☐ ≡

STUDY UNIT FIVE
CURRENT ASSETS, CASH,
ACCOUNTS RECEIVABLE, AND NOTES RECEIVABLE

This study unit contains questions on certain specific assets included in working capital (cash and current receivables). **Working capital** equals current assets minus current liabilities. **Current assets** are expected to be realized in cash, sold, or consumed within 1 year from the balance sheet date or the operating cycle, whichever is longer.

Cash is the most liquid of assets. It includes **cash equivalents**, a special category of assets so close to conversion to cash that they are classified with cash on the balance sheet. **Accounts receivable** ordinarily consist of unwritten promises by credit customers and do not include an interest component unless overdue. **Notes receivable** customarily are formal written agreements that may include an interest component. The majority of the receivables questions are about their measurement and presentation in the financial statements. Current receivables are measured at net realizable value (net of allowance for uncollectible accounts, allowance for sales returns, and billing adjustments). Noncurrent receivables are measured at the net present value of the future cash flows. Some questions relate to the accounting for **transfers of financial assets**. These transfers may be in the form of secured borrowings or sales.

QUESTIONS
5.1 Current Assets and Working Capital

5.1.1. At October 31, Dingo, Inc., had cash accounts at three different banks. One account balance is segregated solely for a November 15 payment into a bond sinking fund. A second account, used for branch operations, is overdrawn. The third account, used for regular corporate operations, has a positive balance. How should these accounts be reported in Dingo's October 31 classified balance sheet?

A. The segregated account should be reported as a noncurrent asset, the regular account should be reported as a current asset, and the overdraft should be reported as a current liability.

B. The segregated and regular accounts should be reported as current assets, and the overdraft should be reported as a current liability.

C. The segregated account should be reported as a noncurrent asset, and the regular account should be reported as a current asset net of the overdraft.

D. The segregated and regular accounts should be reported as current assets net of the overdraft.

Answer (A) is correct. *(CPA, adapted)*
REQUIRED: The proper reporting of three cash accounts.
DISCUSSION: Current assets include cash available for current operations and items that are the equivalent of cash. Hence, the account used for regular operations is current. Cash that is restricted to use for other than current operations is designated for the acquisition or construction of noncurrent assets or segregated for the liquidation of noncurrent debt. Amounts that are clearly to be used in the near term (1) to liquidate noncurrent debt, (2) to make payments to a sinking fund, or (3) for similar purposes also should be classified as noncurrent. Moreover, they need not be recorded in a special account. The overdraft should be treated as a current liability and not netted against the other cash balances. If the company had another account in the same bank with a positive balance, netting would be appropriate because the bank would have a right of offset.
Answer (B) is incorrect. The segregated account is noncurrent. Answer (C) is incorrect. The overdraft should not be netted. Answer (D) is incorrect. The overdraft should not be netted and the segregated account is noncurrent.

5.1.2. On Geo's April 30, Year 3, balance sheet, a note receivable was reported as a noncurrent asset, and its accrued interest for 10 months was reported as a current asset. Which of the following terms would fit Geo's note receivable?

A. Both principal and interest amounts are payable on June 30, Year 3 and Year 4.

B. Principal and interest are due December 31, Year 3.

C. Both principal and interest amounts are payable on December 31, Year 3 and Year 4.

D. Principal is due June 30, Year 4, and interest is due June 30, Year 3 and Year 4.

Answer (D) is correct. *(CPA, adapted)*
REQUIRED: The terms explaining classification of a note receivable as a noncurrent asset and its accrued interest as a current asset.
DISCUSSION: A noncurrent note receivable is not expected to be converted into cash within 1 year or one operating cycle, whichever is longer. Because the principal is due more than 1 year from the balance sheet date, it must be regarded as noncurrent. However, the accrued interest is a current asset because it is due in 2 months.
Answer (A) is incorrect. The portion of principal due in 2 months would be considered current. Answer (B) is incorrect. Principal amounts due in less than 1 year are current assets. Answer (C) is incorrect. Only the principal due at the end of Year 4 is noncurrent.

5.1.3. The following is Gold Corp.'s June 30, Year 6, trial balance:

	Dr.	Cr.
Cash overdraft		$ 10,000
Accounts receivable, net	$ 35,000	
Inventory	58,000	
Prepaid expenses	12,000	
Land held for resale	100,000	
Property, plant, and equipment, net	95,000	
Accounts payable and accrued expenses		32,000
Common stock		25,000
Additional paid-in capital		150,000
Retained earnings		83,000
	$300,000	$300,000

Additional information:

- Checks amounting to $30,000 were written to vendors and recorded on June 29, Year 6, resulting in a cash overdraft of $10,000. The checks were mailed on July 9, Year 6.

- Land held for resale was sold for cash on July 15, Year 6.

- Gold issued its financial statements on July 31, Year 6.

In its June 30, Year 6 balance sheet, what amount should Gold report as current assets?

A. $225,000

B. $205,000

C. $195,000

D. $125,000

Answer (A) is correct. *(CPA, adapted)*
REQUIRED: The amount reported for current assets on the balance sheet.
DISCUSSION: Current assets include, in descending order of liquidity, (1) cash and cash equivalents; (2) certain individual trading, available-for-sale, and held-to-maturity debt securities; (3) receivables; (4) inventories; (5) prepaid expenses; and (6) certain individual investments in equity securities. Current assets are reasonably expected to be realized in cash, sold, or consumed within 1 year or the normal operating cycle of the business, whichever is longer. Thus, Gold's current assets include $20,000 of cash ($30,000 of checks mailed in the next period but prematurely recorded – $10,000 overdraft), net accounts receivable ($35,000), inventory ($58,000), prepaid expenses ($12,000), and the land held for resale (treated as a $100,000 inventory item unless held for use in the business or as a long-term investment). The total is $225,000.
Answer (B) is incorrect. The amount of $205,000 does not include the $20,000 in cash. Answer (C) is incorrect. The amount of $195,000 reflects the $30,000 of checks not mailed at June 30, Year 6. Answer (D) is incorrect. The amount of $125,000 does not include the land held for resale, which was realized in cash after the balance sheet date.

5.1.4. A characteristic of all assets and liabilities included in working capital is that they are

A. Cash equivalents.

B. Current.

C. Monetary.

D. Marketable.

Answer (B) is correct. *(CPA, adapted)*
REQUIRED: The characteristic of all assets and liabilities included in working capital.
DISCUSSION: Working capital is the excess of current assets over current liabilities. Working capital identifies the relatively liquid portion of the capital of the entity available for meeting obligations within the operating cycle of the firm.
Answer (A) is incorrect. The assets and liabilities included in working capital are not limited to cash equivalents. Answer (C) is incorrect. Although assets and liabilities may be any combination of monetary, marketable, or cash equivalents in addition to cash, they must be current to be part of working capital. Answer (D) is incorrect. Assets need not be marketable to be current.

5.1.5. The operating cycle of a business is the span of time that

A. Coincides with the economy's business cycle, which runs from one trough of the economy's business activity to the next.

B. Corresponds with its natural business year, which runs from one trough of the particular entity's business activity to the next.

C. Is set by the industry's trade association, usually on an average length of time for all entities that are members of the association.

D. Runs from cash disbursement for items of inventory through their sale to the realization of cash from sale.

Answer (D) is correct. *(CPA, adapted)*
REQUIRED: The operating cycle of a business.
DISCUSSION: Operations usually follow a cycle that begins with cash payments and ends with cash receipts. The average amount of time from cash payment to the realization of cash from the sale is the operating cycle of the entity.
Answer (A) is incorrect. Financial reporting is based on an entity's business cycle, not the economy's. Answer (B) is incorrect. An entity's fiscal year is not normally its operating cycle. One operating cycle may last 12 months or more, although usually the fiscal year of the entity includes a number of operating cycles. Answer (C) is incorrect. The operating cycle is determined by an entity's transactions, not by an industry trade association estimate.

5.1.6. Griffin Corp. declared a $50,000 cash dividend on May 19, Year 1, to shareholders of record on May 30, Year 1, payable on June 9, Year 1. As a result of this cash dividend, working capital

A. Was not affected.

B. Decreased on June 9.

C. Decreased on May 30.

D. Decreased on May 19.

Answer (D) is correct. *(CPA, adapted)*
REQUIRED: The effect of a cash dividend on working capital.
DISCUSSION: On May 19, the date of declaration, retained earnings is debited and dividends payable credited. The declaration decreases working capital because a current liability is increased.
Answer (A) is incorrect. Working capital was decreased on May 19. Answer (B) is incorrect. When payment is made, both a current liability (dividends payable) and a current asset (cash) are decreased, which has no net effect on working capital. Answer (C) is incorrect. No entry is made on the record date.

5.1.7. The following transactions occurred during a company's first year of operations:

I. Purchased a delivery van for cash
II. Borrowed money by issuance of short-term debt
III. Purchased treasury stock

Which of the items above caused a change in the amount of working capital?

A. I only.

B. II and III only.

C. I and III only.

D. I, II, and III.

Answer (C) is correct. *(CIA, adapted)*
REQUIRED: The items that caused a change in the amount of working capital.
DISCUSSION: Working capital is computed by deducting total current liabilities from total current assets. The purchase of a delivery van for cash reduces current assets and has no effect on current liabilities. The borrowing of cash by incurring short-term debt increases current assets by the same amount as it increases current liabilities; hence, it will have no effect on working capital. The purchase of treasury stock decreases current assets but has no effect on current liabilities. Thus, the purchases of the van and treasury stock affect working capital.
Answer (A) is incorrect. The purchase of the treasury stock also affects working capital. Answer (B) is incorrect. The purchase of the van affects working capital, but not the issuance of short-term debt. Answer (D) is incorrect. The issuance of short-term debt does not affect working capital.

5.1.8. Current liabilities are best defined as those obligations

A. The liquidation of which will require the use of resources properly classifiable as current assets within the next operating cycle or 1 year, whichever is longer.

B. The liquidation of which will require the use of cash or increase current liabilities within the next operating cycle or 1 year, whichever is longer.

C. The liquidation of which is reasonably expected to require the use of current assets or the creation of other current liabilities within the next operating cycle or 1 year, whichever is longer.

D. Involving commitments made within the next operating cycle or 1 year, whichever is longer.

Answer (C) is correct. *(Publisher, adapted)*
REQUIRED: The correct description of current liabilities.
DISCUSSION: Current liabilities are obligations the liquidation of which is reasonably expected to require the use of existing resources properly classifiable as current assets or the creation of other current liabilities during the next operating cycle or year, whichever is longer. Current liabilities also include (1) obligations that by their terms are or will be due on demand within 1 year (or the operating cycle, if longer) and (2) obligations that are or will be callable by the creditor because of a violation of a debt covenant at the balance sheet date.
Answer (A) is incorrect. Liabilities also are current if their liquidation requires creation of other current liabilities. Answer (B) is incorrect. Liabilities are current if they are settled with any current assets, not just cash. Answer (D) is incorrect. Commitments made during the longer of the next year or the operating cycle may not even be liabilities at the balance sheet date.

5.1.9. Which of the following items enter into the determination of working capital?

A. Inventory of finished products that as of the balance sheet date has been held by a manufacturer for 1 year of a 3-year aging cycle.

B. Cash value of life insurance policies pledged as collateral against 90-day bank notes.

C. Cash held by an investment banker to be used to acquire in the open market an additional 25% of a 55%-owned subsidiary.

D. U.S. Treasury bills maturing 60 days after the balance sheet date, the proceeds of which, by direction of the board of directors, will be used to retire long-term debts.

Answer (A) is correct. *(Publisher, adapted)*
REQUIRED: The item that is considered part of working capital.
DISCUSSION: Working capital is the excess of current assets over current liabilities. An asset is current if it is reasonably expected to be realized in cash, sold, or consumed during the longer of 1 year or the normal operating cycle of the business. The operating cycle is the average time elapsing between the acquisition of materials or services entering into the earning process and the final cash realization. If a manufacturer's inventory must undergo a 3-year aging process before it can be sold, the inventory should be classified as a current asset because it will be sold during the current operating cycle.
Answer (B) is incorrect. The cash surrender value of life insurance policies is a long-term investment. Answer (C) is incorrect. Cash is not a current asset if it is restricted to purchase noncurrent assets. Answer (D) is incorrect. Treasury bills are not current assets if they are restricted to pay long-term debts.

5.1.10. Comparative balance sheets for a company are presented below:

Assets	12/31/Yr 2	12/31/Yr 1
Cash	$ 35,000	$ 30,000
Accounts receivable	80,000	75,000
Inventory	230,000	240,000
Equipment	620,000	600,000
Accumulated depreciation	(220,000)	(200,000)
Intangibles	150,000	140,000
Total assets	$895,000	$885,000

Liabilities and equity		
Accounts payable	$ 50,000	$ 60,000
Taxes payable	30,000	25,000
Salaries payable	55,000	70,000
Bonds payable (due Year 5)	400,000	400,000
Discount on bonds payable	(4,000)	(5,000)
Common stock	270,000	250,000
Retained earnings	94,000	85,000
Total liabilities and equity	$895,000	$885,000

What is the increase in working capital for the year ended December 31, Year 2?

A. $5,000

B. $10,000

C. $20,000

D. $29,000

Answer (C) is correct. *(CIA, adapted)*
REQUIRED: The increase in working capital for the current year.
DISCUSSION: Working capital is the excess of current assets over current liabilities. The change in working capital is equal to the aggregate change in those accounts classified as current assets and current liabilities. Increases in current assets and decreases in current liabilities increase (are sources of) working capital. Decreases in current assets and increases in current liabilities decrease (are uses of) working capital. The change in working capital for the year is presented below:

Working Capital Accounts	Increase (Decrease)
Cash	$ 5,000
Accounts receivable	5,000
Inventory	(10,000)
Accounts payable	10,000
Taxes payable	(5,000)
Salaries payable	15,000
Increase in working capital	$20,000

Answer (A) is incorrect. The amount of $5,000 does not include the change in salaries payable. Answer (B) is incorrect. The amount of $10,000 is the increase in total assets. Answer (D) is incorrect. The amount of $29,000 is the increase in working capital plus the increase in retained earnings.

5.1.11. A service company's working capital at the beginning of May of the current year was $70,000. The following transactions occurred during May:

Performed services on account	$30,000
Purchased supplies on account	5,000
Consumed supplies	4,000
Purchased office equipment for cash	2,000
Paid short-term bank loan	6,500
Paid salaries	10,000
Accrued salaries	3,500

What is the amount of working capital at the end of May?

A. $80,500

B. $78,500

C. $50,500

D. $47,500

Answer (A) is correct. *(CIA, adapted)*
REQUIRED: The amount of working capital.
DISCUSSION: Working capital is the excess of total current assets (CA) over total current liabilities (CL). Thus, working capital at the end of May equals $80,500 computed as follows:

		CA*	CL*
Beginning working capital	$70,000		
Performed services on account	30,000	I	N
Purchased supplies on account	--	I	I
Consumed supplies	(4,000)	D	N
Purchased office equipment	(2,000)	D	N
Paid short-term bank loan	--	D	D
Paid salaries	(10,000)	D	N
Accrued salaries	(3,500)	N	I
Working capital, end of January	$80,500		

* N = no effect; I = increase; D = decrease

Answer (B) is incorrect. The amount of $78,500 does not include the consumed supplies, the cash purchase of office equipment, and the accrued salaries, and it includes the supplies purchased on account and the repayment of the short-term bank loan. Answer (C) is incorrect. The amount of $50,500 does not include the services performed on account. Answer (D) is incorrect. The amount of $47,500 does not include the services performed on account and accrued salaries and includes the repayment of short-term loan.

5.2 Cash

5.2.1. The objective of a petty cash system is to

A. Facilitate office payment of small, miscellaneous items.

B. Cash checks for employees.

C. Account for cash sales.

D. Account for all cash receipts and disbursements.

Answer (A) is correct. *(Publisher, adapted)*
REQUIRED: The objective of a petty cash system.
DISCUSSION: In a petty cash system, a specific amount of money, e.g., $1,000, is set aside in the care of a petty cash custodian to pay office expenses that are too small to pay by check or to record in the accounting system as they occur. The entry is to debit petty cash and to credit cash. Periodically, the fund is reimbursed for all expenditures based on expense receipts, and journal entries are made to reflect the transactions. However, entries are made to the petty cash account only to establish the fund, to change its amount, or to adjust the balance if it has not been reimbursed at year end.

Answer (B) is incorrect. If necessary, a separate check-cashing fund should be established with daily bank deposits of checks cashed. Answer (C) is incorrect. Petty cash systems are for cash disbursements, not cash sales. Answer (D) is incorrect. Petty cash systems are for cash disbursements, not cash receipts.

5.2.2. Usually, if the petty cash fund is not reimbursed just prior to year end and an appropriate adjusting entry is not made,

A. A complete audit is necessary.

B. The petty cash account should be returned to the company cashier.

C. Expenses will be overstated and cash will be understated.

D. Cash will be overstated and expenses understated.

Answer (D) is correct. *(Publisher, adapted)*
REQUIRED: The effect of not reimbursing the petty cash fund prior to year end and not making the appropriate adjusting entry.
DISCUSSION: When the petty cash fund is established, petty cash is debited and cash credited. As monies are expended, expense receipts are obtained. The petty cash fund consists of the cash and expense receipts. Upon reimbursement of the petty cash fund, the various expenses are debited, and cash is credited. If the petty cash fund is not reimbursed at year end and an adjusting entry debiting expenses and crediting cash is not made, the cash account will be overstated and expenses understated because petty cash is a component of the cash account.

Answer (A) is incorrect. Complete audits are usually undertaken only if fraud is suspected. Petty cash is ordinarily not material. Answer (B) is incorrect. The petty cash cannot be returned to the cashier. At least some of the cash will usually have been expended. Answer (C) is incorrect. Expenses will be understated and cash overstated.

5.2.3. On January 1, a company establishes a petty cash account and designates one employee as petty cash custodian. The original amount included in the petty cash fund is $500, and it will be used to make small cash disbursements. The fund will be replenished on the first of each month, after the petty cash custodian presents receipts for disbursements to the general cashier. The following disbursements are made in January:

Office supplies	$127
Postage	83
Entertainment	84

The balance in the petty cash box at the end of January is $196.

The entry required at the end of January is

A. Office supplies expense $127
   Postage expense   83
   Entertainment expense   84
       Cash $294

B. Office supplies expense $127
   Postage expense   83
   Entertainment expense   84
       Petty cash $294

C. Office supplies expense $127
   Postage expense   83
   Entertainment expense   84
   Cash over and short   10
       Cash $304

D. Office supplies expense $127
   Postage expense   83
   Entertainment expense   84
       Cash $284
       Cash over and short   10

Answer (C) is correct. *(CIA, adapted)*
REQUIRED: The entry for petty cash fund disbursements.
DISCUSSION: Each expense item is recognized, cash is credited for the total expenditures plus the cash shortage ($127 + $83 + $84 + $10 = $304), and the discrepancy is debited to the cash over and short account. The discrepancy is the original balance of the fund, minus total documented expenditures, minus the ending balance of the fund ($500 – $294 – $196 = $10).
   Answer (A) is incorrect. This entry does not recognize that $10 is missing from the petty cash fund. Answer (B) is incorrect. This entry credits petty cash rather than cash and does not recognize that $10 is missing from the petty cash fund. Answer (D) is incorrect. This entry credits the cash account for the wrong amount ($284 rather than $304) and credits the cash over and short account rather than debiting it.

5.2.4. Nefertiti Corporation had the following transactions in its first year of operations:

Sales (90% collected in first year)	$1,500,000
Bad debt write-offs	60,000
Disbursements for costs and expenses	1,200,000
Disbursements for income taxes	90,000
Purchases of fixed assets	400,000
Depreciation on fixed assets	80,000
Proceeds from issuance of common stock	500,000
Proceeds from short-term borrowings	100,000
Payments on short-term borrowings	50,000

What is the cash balance at the end of the first year?

A. $150,000

B. $170,000

C. $210,000

D. $280,000

Answer (C) is correct. *(CPA, adapted)*
REQUIRED: The cash balance at year end.
DISCUSSION: The cash balance may be determined by setting up a T account and appropriately debiting or crediting the account for each of the transactions listed. The beginning balance is $0 for the first year of operations. The sales collections result in a debit of $1,350,000 ($1,500,000 × 90%). The bad debt write-offs and depreciation on fixed assets are not cash transactions. The disbursements for costs and expenses, taxes, fixed assets, and debt service are credits. The proceeds from stock and short-term borrowings are debits. Thus, the account has a year-end debit balance of $210,000.

Cash (in 000s)			
Sales	$1,350	$1,200	Disbursements
Stock	500	90	Taxes
Loan	100	400	FA
		50	Loan
	$ 210		

   Answer (A) is incorrect. The amount of $150,000 results from a credit to the cash account for the bad debt write-offs. Answer (B) is incorrect. The amount of $170,000 results from debiting bad debt write-offs and not debiting proceeds from short-term borrowings to cash. Answer (D) is incorrect. The amount of $280,000 incorrectly debits cash for 100% of sales for the year and credits cash for depreciation on fixed assets.

5.2.5. Bank reconciliations are usually prepared on a monthly basis upon receipt of the bank statement to identify either bank errors or items that need to be adjusted on the depositor's books. The adjustments should be made for

A. Deposits in transit and outstanding checks.

B. All items except deposits in transit, outstanding checks, and bank errors.

C. Deposits in transit, outstanding checks, and bank errors.

D. All items except bank errors, NSF checks, outstanding checks, and deposits in transit.

Answer (B) is correct. *(Publisher, adapted)*
   REQUIRED: The adjustments made as a result of a bank reconciliation.
   DISCUSSION: Deposits in transit and outstanding checks are reconciling items that have no effect on the correctness of either the depositor's or the bank's accounting records. They reflect a timing difference between the two sets of books as to when cash receipts and disbursements are recognized. Thus, they require no adjustment by the bank or the depositor. Bank errors must be corrected by the bank, not the depositor. All other items must be adjusted on the depositor's books.
   Answer (A) is incorrect. Deposits in transit and outstanding checks do not require adjustment on either the bank's or depositor's books. Answer (C) is incorrect. Deposits in transit and outstanding checks do not require adjustment on either the bank's or depositor's books. Answer (D) is incorrect. NSF checks require a debit to a receivable and a credit to cash on the depositor's books.

5.2.6. Hilltop Co.'s monthly bank statement shows a balance of $54,200. Reconciliation of the statement with company books reveals the following information:

Bank service charge	$ 10
Insufficient funds check	650
Checks outstanding	1,500
Deposits in transit	350
Check deposited by Hilltop and cleared by the bank for $125, but improperly recorded by Hilltop as $152	

What is the net cash balance after the reconciliation?

A. $52,363

B. $53,023

C. $53,050

D. $53,077

Answer (C) is correct. *(CPA, adapted)*
   REQUIRED: The net cash balance after reconciling the bank statement with the books.
   DISCUSSION: The bank balance is given ($54,200). The procedure is to adjust this amount for reconciling items. The bank balance includes the effects of the NSF check and the service charge. Thus, the reconciling adjustments are for the checks that have not yet cleared the bank and deposits in transit.

Bank balance	$54,200
Checks outstanding	(1,500)
Deposits in transit	350
True balance	$53,050

The error by Hilltop affects only the reconciliation from its book balance to the true balance.
   Answer (A) is incorrect. The amount of $52,363 results from subtracting the service charge, NSF check, and recording error. Answer (B) is incorrect. The amount of $53,023 results from subtracting the recording error. Answer (D) is incorrect. The amount of $53,077 results from adding the recording error.

5.2.7. Piquet Corp.'s checkbook balance on December 31, Year 1, was $5,000. In addition, Piquet held the following items in its safe on that date:

Check payable to Piquet Corp., dated January 2, Year 2, in payment of a sale made in December Year 1, not included in December 31 checkbook balance.	$1,000
Check payable to Piquet Corp., deposited December 15 and included in December 31 checkbook balance, but returned by Bank on December 30 stamped "NSF." The check was redeposited on January 2, Year 2, and cleared on January 9.	600
Check drawn on Piquet Corp.'s account, payable to a vendor, dated and recorded in Piquet's books on December 31 but not mailed until January 10, Year 2.	700

The proper amount to be shown as cash on Piquet's balance sheet at December 31, Year 1, is

A. $5,100

B. $5,700

C. $5,400

D. $6,100

Answer (A) is correct. *(CPA, adapted)*
   REQUIRED: The amount to be recorded as cash on the year-end balance sheet.
   DISCUSSION: The December 31 checkbook balance is $5,000. The $1,000 check dated 1/2/Year 2 is properly not included in this balance because it is not negotiable at year end. The $600 NSF check should not be included in cash because it is a receivable. The $700 check that was not mailed until January 10 should be added to the balance. This predated check is still within the control of the company and should not decrease the cash account. Consequently, the cash balance to be reported on the 12/31/Year 1 balance sheet is $5,100.

Balance per checkbook	$5,000
Add: Predated check	700
Deduct: NSF check	(600)
Cash balance 12/31/Year 1	$5,100

   Answer (B) is incorrect. The amount of $5,700 does not include the deduction for the NSF check. Answer (C) is incorrect. The amount of $5,400 includes the postdated check but not the predated check. Answer (D) is incorrect. The amount of $6,100 includes the postdated check.

5.2.8. Puddie Company maintains two checking accounts. A special account is used for the weekly payroll only, and the general account is used for all other disbursements. Every week, a check in the amount of the net payroll is drawn on the general account and deposited in the payroll account. The company maintains a $10,000 minimum balance in the payroll account. On a monthly bank reconciliation, the payroll account should

A. Show a zero balance per the bank statement.

B. Show a $10,000 balance per the bank statement.

C. Reconcile to $10,000.

D. Be reconciled jointly with the general account in a single reconciliation.

Answer (C) is correct. *(CPA, adapted)*
REQUIRED: The true statement concerning the monthly bank reconciliation of the payroll account.
DISCUSSION: Because a minimum balance of $10,000 is maintained, the check drawn on the general account is deposited to the special account before any payroll checks are written. The balance in the special account recorded by the bank, minus any outstanding checks, plus any bank charges not yet recorded on the company's books should equal $10,000.
Answer (A) is incorrect. The balance per bank statement should be equal to at least $10,000, less any bank charges. Answer (B) is incorrect. The balance per bank statement should be equal to $10,000, plus the amount of any outstanding checks, minus any bank charges not recorded in the company's books. Answer (D) is incorrect. Each checking account reflected in the formal accounting system should be separately reconciled with the related bank statement.

5.2.9. The following information is shown in the accounting records of a company:

Balances as of January 1, Year 1

Cash	$62,000
Merchandise inventory	86,000
Accounts receivable	67,000
Accounts payable	53,000

Balances as of December 31, Year 1

Merchandise inventory	$78,000
Accounts receivable	91,000
Accounts payable	48,000

Total sales and cost of goods sold for Year 1 were $798,000 and $583,000, respectively. All sales and all merchandise purchases were made on credit. Various operating expenses of $107,000 were paid in cash. Assume that there were no other pertinent transactions. The cash balance on December 31, Year 1, is

A. $108,000

B. $149,000

C. $256,000

D. $305,000

Answer (B) is correct. *(CIA, adapted)*
REQUIRED: The cash balance at year end.
DISCUSSION: Cash collected from customers equals $774,000 ($798,000 credit sales – $24,000 increase in A/R). The amount of credit purchases is $575,000 ($583,000 COGS – $8,000 decrease in inventory). Disbursements to suppliers totaled $580,000 ($575,000 Pur. + $5,000 decrease in A/P). The cash collected is added to the beginning balance in the cash account. The disbursements to suppliers and for operating expenses are subtracted to arrive at an ending cash balance of $149,000.

Accounts Receivable

Beg. Bal.	$ 67,000		
Sales	798,000	$774,000	Collections
End. Bal.	$ 91,000		

Merchandise Inventory

Beg. Bal.	$ 86,000		
Purchases	575,000	$583,000	COGS
End. Bal.	$ 78,000		

Accounts Payable

		$ 53,000	Beg. Bal.
Disburse.	$580,000	575,000	Purchases
		$ 48,000	End. Bal.

Cash

Beg. Bal.	$ 62,000		
Collections	774,000	$580,000	Disb.–Merchandise
		107,000	Disb.–Operating Exps.
End. Bal.	$149,000		

Answer (A) is incorrect. The amount of $108,000 is the excess of total sales over cost of goods sold and operating expenses. Answer (C) is incorrect. The amount of $256,000 does not include a credit to cash for the operating expenses. Answer (D) is incorrect. The amount of $305,000 appears to be a random number.

5.2.10. An entity is reconciling its bank statement with internal records. The cash balance per the bank statement is $20,000, while the cash balance per the entity's books is $18,000. There are $2,000 of bank charges not yet recorded, $3,000 of outstanding checks, $5,000 of deposits in transit, and $6,000 of bank credits and collections not yet recorded in the entity's books. If there are no bank or book errors, what is the entity's actual cash balance?

A. $20,000

B. $22,000

C. $24,000

D. $29,000

Answer (B) is correct. *(CIA, adapted)*
REQUIRED: The cash balance given no bank or book errors.
DISCUSSION: The balance per bank is $20,000, which includes the bank charges, credits, and collections not recorded on the books. Adding deposits in transit and subtracting outstanding checks results in an actual cash balance of $22,000 ($20,000 + $5,000 – $3,000). This amount equals the adjusted balance per the entity's books ($18,000 + $6,000 of bank credits and collections not recorded in the books – $2,000 of bank charges).
Answer (A) is incorrect. The amount of $20,000 is the balance per bank before the reconciliation. Answer (C) is incorrect. The amount of $24,000 equals the balance per the entity's books, plus bank credits and collections. Answer (D) is incorrect. The amount of $29,000 results from adding outstanding checks, outstanding bank credits, and collections to the balance per bank.

5.2.11. A company shows a cash balance of $35,000 on its bank statement dated November 1. As of November 1, there are $11,000 of outstanding checks and $7,500 of deposits in transit. The cash balance on the company books as of November 1 is

A. $24,000

B. $31,500

C. $42,500

D. $53,500

Answer (B) is correct. *(CIA, adapted)*
REQUIRED: The cash balance on the company books.
DISCUSSION: The $35,000 cash balance on the November 1 bank statement does not reflect either the $11,000 of outstanding checks or the $7,500 of deposits in transit. Adding the deposits in transit and subtracting the outstanding checks result in a cash balance per books of $31,500 ($35,000 + $7,500 – $11,000).
Answer (A) is incorrect. The amount of $24,000 does not include the $7,500 of deposits in transit. Answer (C) is incorrect. The amount of $42,500 does not include the $11,000 of outstanding checks. Answer (D) is incorrect. The amount of $53,500 results from adding the $11,000 of outstanding checks and the $7,500 of deposits in transit.

5.2.12. In preparing its bank reconciliation at December 31, Case Company has the following data available:

Balance per bank statement, 12/31	$38,075
Deposit in transit, 12/31	5,200
Outstanding checks, 12/31	6,750
Amount erroneously credited by bank to Case's account, 12/28	400
Bank service charges for December	75

Case's adjusted cash in bank balance at December 31 is

A. $36,525

B. $36,450

C. $36,125

D. $36,050

Answer (C) is correct. *(CPA, adapted)*
REQUIRED: The adjusted cash in bank balance at year-end.
DISCUSSION: The balance per bank statement at December 31 is $38,075. As indicated below, the $5,200 deposit in transit should be added to this amount. The $6,750 in outstanding checks and the $400 that was erroneously credited by the bank to Case's account should be deducted. The $75 bank service charges are already included in the December 31 bank statement balance. The adjusted cash in bank balance at December 31 is therefore $36,125.

Balance per statement	$38,075
Add: Deposit in transit	5,200
Deduct: Outstanding checks	(6,750)
Bank error	(400)
Adjusted cash in bank	$36,125

Answer (A) is incorrect. The amount of $36,525 omits the adjustment for the bank error. Answer (B) is incorrect. The amount of $36,450 omits the adjustment for the bank error and subtracts the service charges from the balance per book. Answer (D) is incorrect. The amount of $36,050 subtracts the service charges from the balance per book.

5.3 Accounts Receivable

5.3.1. Which of the following is a false statement about balance sheet disclosure of accounts receivable?

A. Accounts receivable should be identified on the balance sheet as pledged if they are used as security for a loan even though the loan is shown on the same balance sheet as a liability.

B. That portion of installment accounts receivable from customers which falls due more than 12 months from the balance sheet date usually would be excluded from current assets.

C. Allowances may be deducted from the gross amount of accounts receivable for uncollectible accounts and adjustments to be made in the future on accounts shown in the current balance sheet.

D. Trade receivables are best shown separately from nontrade receivables where amounts of each are material.

Answer (B) is correct. *(CPA, adapted)*
REQUIRED: The invalid statement concerning balance sheet disclosure of accounts receivable.
DISCUSSION: Current assets are reasonably expected to be realized in cash or to be sold or consumed within 12 months or the operating cycle of the business, whichever is longer. If the ordinary trade receivables of the business fall due more than 12 months from the balance sheet date, then the operating cycle is clearly longer than 12 months and the receivables should be included in current assets.
Answer (A) is incorrect. Accounts receivable pledged or used as security for a loan should be presented with relevant information disclosed in a note or in a parenthetical explanation. Answer (C) is incorrect. Various allowance or valuation accounts may be set up as contra accounts to receivables to arrive at the net realizable value of receivables in the balance sheet. Allowance may be made for uncollectible accounts. Answer (D) is incorrect. If the different categories of receivables are material in amount, they should be segregated in the balance sheet.

5.3.2. On a balance sheet, what is the preferable presentation of notes receivable or accounts receivable from officers, employees, or affiliated companies?

A. As trade notes and accounts receivable if they otherwise qualify as current assets.

B. As assets but separately from other receivables.

C. As offsets to capital.

D. By means of disclosure in the notes.

Answer (B) is correct. *(CPA, adapted)*
REQUIRED: The preferable balance sheet presentation of receivables from officers, employees, or affiliated companies.
DISCUSSION: The basic principle is that, if the different categories of receivables are material in amount, they should be presented separately in the balance sheet. Receivables from officers, employees, or affiliated companies are assets and should be presented in the balance sheet as such. If these receivables are material, they should be segregated from other classifications of receivables.
Answer (A) is incorrect. Such receivables, if material, should be separately classified even though they qualify as current assets. Answer (C) is incorrect. Such receivables are assets and should not be presented in the equity section. Answer (D) is incorrect. Such receivables are assets that should be included in the body of the balance sheet. Presentation by note disclosure would understate financial position.

5.3.3. Henry Stores, Inc., had sales of $2,000,000 during December. Experience has shown that merchandise equaling 7% of sales will be returned within 30 days and an additional 3% will be returned within 90 days. Returned merchandise is readily resalable. The cost of sales was $1,500,000. What amount should Henry report for sales revenue in its income statement for the month of December?

A. $1,800,000

B. $500,000

C. $2,000,000

D. $450,000

Answer (A) is correct. *(CPA, adapted)*
REQUIRED: The amount of sales revenue.
DISCUSSION: Sales revenue is recognized only for the amount of consideration to which an entity is expected to be entitled. Thus, no sales are recognized for the 10% of merchandise expected to be returned. Accordingly, sales revenue equals $1,800,000 [$2,000,000 – ($2,000,000 × 10%)].
Answer (B) is incorrect. The amount of $500,000 is the gross profit assuming no right of return. Answer (C) is incorrect. The amount of $2,000,000 assumes no right of return. Answer (D) is incorrect. The amount of $450,000 is the gross profit recognized.

5.4 Accounts Receivable -- Measurement

5.4.1. When may an asset valuation allowance, such as the allowance for uncollectible accounts, be shown on the credit side of the balance sheet?

A. Never.

B. When they have to be repaid.

C. In the airline industry.

D. When it exceeds 10% of the accounts receivable balance.

Answer (A) is correct. *(Publisher, adapted)*
REQUIRED: The circumstances in which an asset valuation allowance may be shown on the credit side of the balance sheet.
DISCUSSION: All allowance accounts must be displayed contra to the related asset accounts. Thus, they are never reported as liabilities or elsewhere on the credit side of the balance sheet. They are subtracted from the related assets (or asset groups), with proper disclosure.
Answer (B) is incorrect. Valuation accounts are not repaid. Answer (C) is incorrect. There are no industry exceptions for presentation of asset valuation accounts. Answer (D) is incorrect. The materiality of the account does not affect its classification as a contra asset.

5.4.2. When the allowance method of recognizing uncollectible accounts is used, the entries at the time of collection of a small account previously written off

A. Increase the allowance for uncollectible accounts.

B. Increase net income.

C. Decrease the allowance for uncollectible accounts.

D. Have no effect on the allowance for uncollectible accounts.

Answer (A) is correct. *(CPA, adapted)*
REQUIRED: The effect of the collection of an account previously written off.
DISCUSSION: When an account receivable is written off, both accounts receivable and the allowance for uncollectible accounts are decreased. When an account previously written off is collected, the account must be reinstated by increasing both accounts receivable and the allowance. Accounts receivable is then decreased by the amount of cash collected.
Answer (B) is incorrect. Neither write-off nor reinstatement and collection affects bad debt expense or net income. Answer (C) is incorrect. The allowance is increased. Answer (D) is incorrect. The allowance is increased.

5.4.3. When the allowance method of recognizing uncollectible accounts is used, the entry to record the write-off of a specific account

A. Decreases both accounts receivable and the allowance for uncollectible accounts.

B. Decreases accounts receivable and increases the allowance for uncollectible accounts.

C. Increases the allowance for uncollectible accounts and decreases net income.

D. Decreases both accounts receivable and net income.

Answer (A) is correct. *(CPA, adapted)*
REQUIRED: The effect of the collection of an account previously written off.
DISCUSSION: When an account receivable is written off, both accounts receivable and the allowance for uncollectible accounts are decreased. If an account previously written off is collected, the account must be reinstated by increasing both accounts receivable and the allowance. The account receivable is then decreased by the amount of cash collected.
Answer (B) is incorrect. The write-off also decreases the allowance account. Answer (C) is incorrect. The write-off decreases the allowance, and does not affect net income. Answer (D) is incorrect. The write-off does not affect net income.

5.4.4. A method of estimating uncollectible accounts that emphasizes asset valuation rather than income measurement is the allowance method based on

A. Aging the receivables.

B. Direct write-off.

C. Gross sales.

D. Credit sales less returns and allowances.

Answer (A) is correct. *(CPA, adapted)*
REQUIRED: The method of estimating uncollectible accounts that emphasizes asset valuation.
DISCUSSION: Under the allowance method, uncollectible accounts are estimated in two ways. The method that emphasizes asset valuation is based on an aging of the receivables to determine the balance in the allowance for uncollectible accounts. Bad debt expense is the amount necessary to adjust the allowance account to this estimated balance. The method emphasizing the income statement calculates bad debt expense as a percentage of sales.
Answer (B) is incorrect. The direct write-off method is not a means of estimation. Answer (C) is incorrect. An estimate based on gross sales focuses on the income statement. Answer (D) is incorrect. An estimate based on credit sales less returns and allowances focuses on the income statement.

5.4.5. Which method of recording uncollectible accounts expense is consistent with accrual accounting?

	Allowance	Direct Write-Off
A.	Yes	Yes
B.	Yes	No
C.	No	Yes
D.	No	No

Answer (B) is correct. *(CPA, adapted)*
REQUIRED: The method(s) of recording uncollectible accounts expense consistent with accrual accounting.
DISCUSSION: The allowance method attempts both to match the expense with the related revenue and to determine the NRV of the accounts receivable. This method is acceptable under GAAP. The direct write-off method debits expense and credits accounts receivable at the time uncollectibility is established. This method does not match revenue and expense or state receivables at NRV. It is not acceptable under GAAP.
Answer (A) is incorrect. The direct write-off method is not consistent with accrual accounting. Answer (C) is incorrect. The direct write-off method is not consistent with accrual accounting. Answer (D) is incorrect. The allowance method is consistent with accrual accounting.

5.4.6. William Co. determined that the net realizable value (NRV) of its accounts receivable at December 31, based on an aging of the receivables, was $650,000. Additional information is as follows:

Allowance for uncollectible accounts -- 1/1	$ 60,000
Uncollectible accounts written off during the year	36,000
Uncollectible accounts recovered during the year	4,000
Accounts receivable at 12/31	700,000

What is William's bad debt expense for the year?

- A. $10,000
- B. $22,000
- C. $30,000
- D. $42,000

Answer (B) is correct. *(CPA, adapted)*
REQUIRED: The bad debt expense.
DISCUSSION: The allowance for uncollectible accounts before year-end adjustment is $28,000 ($60,000 beginning balance – $36,000 write-offs + $4,000 recovered). The balance should be $50,000 ($700,000 year-end A/R – $650,000 NRV based on aging). Thus, the allowance account should be credited and bad debt expense debited for $22,000 ($50,000 desired balance – $28,000).
Answer (A) is incorrect. The amount of $10,000 is the difference between gross and net accounts receivable ($50,000) and the balance in the allowance account at the beginning of the year ($60,000). Answer (C) is incorrect. The amount of $30,000 equals $50,000 minus the difference between the $60,000 allowance and the $36,000 written off, reduced by the $4,000 recovered. Answer (D) is incorrect. The amount of $42,000 equals the $60,000 allowance, plus $36,000 written off, reduced by $4,000 recovered, minus $50,000.

5.4.7. The following information relates to Soward Co.'s accounts receivable for the year just ended:

Accounts receivable, 1/1	$1,300,000
Credit sales for the year	2,700,000
Sales returns for the year	75,000
Accounts written off during the year	40,000
Collections from customers during the year	2,150,000
Estimated future sales returns at 12/31	50,000
Estimated uncollectible accounts at 12/31	220,000

What amount should Soward report for gross accounts receivable, before allowances for sales returns and uncollectible accounts, at December 31?

- A. $1,850,000
- B. $1,775,000
- C. $1,735,000
- D. $1,465,000

Answer (C) is correct. *(CPA, adapted)*
REQUIRED: The year-end balance in gross accounts receivable.
DISCUSSION: The $1,735,000 ending balance in accounts receivable is equal to the $1,300,000 beginning debit balance, plus debits for $2,700,000 of credit sales, minus credits for $2,150,000 of collections, $40,000 of accounts written off, and $75,000 of sales returns. The $220,000 of estimated uncollectible receivables and the $50,000 of estimated sales returns are not relevant because they affect the allowance accounts but not gross accounts receivable.

Gross Accounts Receivable (in 000s)

1/1	$1,300		$ 75	Sales returns
Credit sales	2,700		2,150	Collections
			40	Write-off
	$1,735			

Answer (A) is incorrect. The amount of $1,850,000 does not subtract write-offs and sales returns from accounts receivable. Answer (B) is incorrect. The amount of $1,775,000 does not subtract write-offs from accounts receivable. Answer (D) is incorrect. Estimated future sales returns and uncollectible accounts affect their respective allowance accounts, not gross accounts receivable.

5.4.8. Ward Co. estimates its uncollectible accounts expense to be 2% of credit sales. Ward's credit sales for the current year were $1 million. During the year, Ward wrote off $18,000 of uncollectible accounts. Ward's allowance for uncollectible accounts had a $15,000 balance on January 1. In its December 31 income statement, what amount should Ward report as uncollectible accounts expense?

A. $23,000

B. $20,000

C. $18,000

D. $17,000

Answer (B) is correct. *(CPA, adapted)*
REQUIRED: The uncollectible accounts expense as a percentage of sales.
DISCUSSION: When bad debt expense is estimated on the basis of net credit sales, a cost (bad debt expense) is being directly associated with a revenue of the period (net credit sales). Thus, uncollectible accounts expense is $20,000 ($1,000,000 credit sales × 2%).
Answer (A) is incorrect. The amount of $23,000 assumes that $20,000 is the required ending balance in the allowance account (expense = write-offs + the change in the allowance). Answer (C) is incorrect. The write-offs for this year equal $18,000. Answer (D) is incorrect. The ending balance in the allowance account is $17,000.

5.4.9. The following information pertains to Eire Co.'s accounts receivable at December 31, Year 2:

Days Outstanding	Amount	Estimated % Uncollectible
0 - 60	$240,000	1%
61 - 120	180,000	2%
Over 120	200,000	6%
	$620,000	

During Year 2, Eire wrote off $14,000 in receivables and recovered $8,000 that was written off in prior years. Its December 31, Year 1, allowance for uncollectible accounts was $44,000. Under the aging method, what amount of allowance for uncollectible accounts should Eire report at December 31, Year 2?

A. $18,000

B. $20,000

C. $26,000

D. $38,000

Answer (A) is correct. *(CPA, adapted)*
REQUIRED: The allowance for uncollectible accounts under the aging method.
DISCUSSION: The aging schedule determines the allowance for uncollectible accounts based on year-end accounts receivable, their age, and their estimated collectibility. This year-end amount is $18,000 [($240,000 × 1%) + ($180,000 × 2%) + ($200,000 × 6%)].
Answer (B) is incorrect. The amount of $20,000 equals the beginning balance, plus the recovery, minus write-offs, minus the amount determined by the aging schedule ($44,000 + $8,000 – $14,000 – $18,000). Answer (C) is incorrect. The amount of $26,000 equals the beginning balance minus the amount determined by the aging schedule ($44,000 – $18,000). Answer (D) is incorrect. The amount of $38,000 equals the beginning balance, plus the recovery, minus write-offs ($44,000 + $8,000 – $14,000).

5.4.10. The following accounts were abstracted from Pika Co.'s unadjusted trial balance at December 31:

	Debit	Credit
Accounts receivable	$2,000,000	
Allowance for uncollectible accounts	16,000	
Net credit sales		$6,000,000

Pika estimates that 3% of the gross accounts receivable will become uncollectible. After adjustment at December 31, the allowance for uncollectible accounts should have a credit balance of

A. $180,000

B. $164,000

C. $44,000

D. $60,000

Answer (D) is correct. *(CPA, adapted)*
REQUIRED: The ending balance in the allowance for uncollectible accounts.
DISCUSSION: The allowance for uncollectible accounts at year end should have a credit balance of $60,000. This amount is equal to the $2,000,000 of accounts receivable multiplied by the 3% that is estimated to become uncollectible.
Answer (A) is incorrect. The amount of $180,000 is equal to 3% of net credit sales. Answer (B) is incorrect. The amount of $164,000 equals 3% of net credit sales minus the unadjusted balance in the allowance account. Answer (C) is incorrect. The amount of $44,000 equals 3% of accounts receivable minus the unadjusted balance in the allowance account.

5.4.11. An analysis and aging of Hom Company's accounts receivable at December 31 disclosed the following:

Accounts receivable	$850,000
Allowance for uncollectible accounts	
per books	50,000
Amounts deemed uncollectible	64,000

The net realizable value (NRV) of the accounts receivable at December 31 should be

A. $836,000

B. $800,000

C. $786,000

D. $736,000

Answer (C) is correct. *(CPA, adapted)*
   REQUIRED: The NRV of accounts receivable.
   DISCUSSION: The NRV of accounts receivable is equal to the $850,000 gross accounts receivable minus the $64,000 estimate of the accounts estimated to be uncollectible. The $50,000 balance in the allowance account is not used because it is an unadjusted balance.
   Answer (A) is incorrect. The amount of $836,000 is the gross accounts receivable account, minus the amount deemed uncollectible, plus the allowance for uncollectible accounts. Answer (B) is incorrect. The amount of $800,000 is the gross accounts receivable account minus the allowance for uncollectible accounts. Answer (D) is incorrect. The amount of $736,000 is the gross accounts receivable account minus the allowance for uncollectible accounts and the amount deemed uncollectible.

5.5 Notes Receivable

5.5.1. How should unearned discounts, finance charges, and unearned interest included in the face amount of notes receivable be presented in the balance sheet?

A. As a deferred credit.

B. As deductions from the related receivables.

C. In the notes to the financial statements.

D. As a current liability.

Answer (B) is correct. *(Publisher, adapted)*
   REQUIRED: The proper presentation of unearned discounts, finance charges, and unearned interest.
   DISCUSSION: Unearned discounts (except for cash discounts, quantity discounts, etc.), finance charges, and unearned interest included in the face amount of notes receivable should be displayed contra to the face amounts of the related receivables in the balance sheet. Thus, a note receivable should be recorded at its net amount, that is, as a debit for the face amount and a credit for the unearned discount, finance charge, or unearned interest.
   Answer (A) is incorrect. Unearned discounts, finance charges, and unearned interest are displayed as deductions from the related receivables, not as a deferred credit. Answer (C) is incorrect. Unearned discounts, finance charges, and unearned interest are displayed as deductions from the related receivables, not in the notes. Answer (D) is incorrect. Unearned discounts, finance charges, and unearned interest are displayed as deductions from the related receivables, not as a current liability.

5.5.2. On August 15, Benet Co. sold goods for which it received a note bearing the market rate of interest on that date. The 4-month note was dated July 15. Note principal, together with all interest, is due November 15. When the note was recorded on August 15, which of the following accounts increased?

A. Unearned discount.

B. Interest receivable.

C. Prepaid interest.

D. Interest revenue.

Answer (B) is correct. *(CPA, adapted)*
   REQUIRED: The account that increased when the note was recorded.
   DISCUSSION: Because the note bears interest at a reasonable rate (in this case, the market rate), its present value at the date of issuance is the face amount. Accordingly, the note should be recorded at this amount. Interest receivable also may be debited, and unearned interest revenue may be credited. The simple alternative is to debit cash and credit interest revenue when payment is received. If the reporting period ends prior to November 15, the period-end entry is to debit interest receivable and credit accrued interest revenue.
   Answer (A) is incorrect. The note bears interest at the market rate. Thus, no discount from its face amount is recorded. Answer (C) is incorrect. No prepayment of interest has been made. Answer (D) is incorrect. Interest revenue has not yet been earned.

5.5.3. United Refinery Company, a refiner of peanut oil, lent $500,000 to James Barter, a peanut farmer, interest free for 5 years. The day after the loan agreement, Barter guaranteed that United Refinery could purchase up to 1 million pounds of shucked peanuts per year for the next 6 years at a price 5¢ less per pound than the prevailing market price. Barter asked for nothing in return for this price concession. United should record the loan at

A. Its face amount with no recognition of interest income over the 5-year period.

B. A discount using the average cost of capital as the rate for imputing interest.

C. Its face amount with interest income recognized each year in the amount of the price concession realized during that year.

D. A discount equal to the expected value of the price concession granted.

Answer (D) is correct. *(Publisher, adapted)*
REQUIRED: The accounting for an interest-free loan related to an unstated right or privilege.
DISCUSSION: Even though the price concession was not explicitly part of the loan agreement, the economic reality is that the noninterest-bearing loan is partial consideration for the purchase of products at less than the prevailing market price. The expected value of the price concession should be the measure of the loan discount. It is the difference between the amount of the loan and the present value of the note. The discount should be recorded as a debit to prepaid purchases and a credit to discount on notes receivable. The prepaid asset will be written off proportionally to the purchases made (debit purchases, credit prepaid purchases) during the contract term. The discount should be amortized using the interest method as interest income over the 5-year life of the loan.
Answer (A) is incorrect. The economic substance of the transaction must be explicitly recognized in the accounts by recognizing the unstated right as an asset and a discount to the note receivable. Answer (B) is incorrect. The present value of the price concession should be used to discount the note. Answer (C) is incorrect. The discount on the note should be recognized as a direct deduction from the note receivable.

5.5.4. The Brown Company received a 2-year, $190,000 note on January 1, Year 1, in exchange for property it sold to Gray Company. According to the terms of the note, interest of 5% is payable annually on January 1, Year 2, and January 1, Year 3, when the face amount is also due. There was no established exchange price for the property. The prevailing rate of interest for a note of this type was 12% at the beginning of Year 1 and 14% at the beginning of Year 2. What interest rates should be used to calculate the amount of interest revenue from this transaction for the years ended December 31, Year 1 and Year 2, respectively?

A. 0% and 5%.

B. 5% and 5%.

C. 12% and 12%.

D. 12% and 14%.

Answer (C) is correct. *(CIA, adapted)*
REQUIRED: The interest rates used to calculate interest revenue for successive years if the prevailing rate changes.
DISCUSSION: When the nominal interest rate on a note is not equal to the prevailing market rate for this type of note, the face amount of the note is not equal to its fair value or present value. In this case, the present value of the note should be determined by discounting the $190,000 maturity amount and the $9,500 annual interest payments using an appropriately imputed rate of interest. Given that 12% was the prevailing rate of interest for a note of that type at the issuance date, 12% should be used to determine both the fair market value and the interest revenue during the life of the note, regardless of fluctuations in prevailing interest rates.
Answer (A) is incorrect. Five percent is the nominal rate. Zero percent is not appropriate given that the note states a rate and that a rate may be imputed. Answer (B) is incorrect. The market rate of interest at the issuance date (12%) should be used to calculate the amount of interest revenue. Answer (D) is incorrect. Fourteen percent was not the prevailing rate at the issuance date.

5.5.5. Holder Co. has an 8% note receivable dated June 30, Year 1, in the original amount of $300,000. Payments of $100,000 in principal plus accrued interest are due annually on July 1, Year 2, Year 3, and Year 4. In its June 30, Year 3, balance sheet, what amount should Holder report as a current asset for interest on the note receivable?

A. $0

B. $8,000

C. $16,000

D. $24,000

Answer (C) is correct. *(CPA, adapted)*
REQUIRED: The amount reported as a current asset for interest on a note receivable.
DISCUSSION: Current assets are those reasonably expected to be realized in cash, sold, or consumed during the longer of the operating cycle of a business or 1 year. Given that the date of the balance sheet is 6/30/Year 3, the interest to be paid on the next day, 7/1/Year 3, of $16,000 ($200,000 principal × 8% stated interest rate) should be classified as a current asset.
Answer (A) is incorrect. An interest amount of $16,000 is reported as a current asset. Answer (B) is incorrect. The amount of $8,000 is the interest to be earned in Year 4. Answer (D) is incorrect. The amount of $24,000 is the interest earned in Year 2.

5.5.6. On January 1, the Fulmar Company sold personal property to the Austin Company. The personal property had cost Fulmar $40,000. Fulmar frequently sells similar items of property for $44,000. Austin gave Fulmar a noninterest-bearing note payable in six equal annual installments of $10,000 with the first payment due this December 31. Collection of the note is reasonably assured. A reasonable rate of interest for a note of this type is 10%. The present value of an annuity of $1 in arrears at 10% for six periods is 4.355. What amount of sales revenue from this transaction should be reported in Fulmar's income statement for the year ended December 31?

A. $10,000

B. $40,000

C. $43,550

D. $44,000

Answer (D) is correct. *(CPA, adapted)*
REQUIRED: The amount of sales revenue to be reported in the income statement of the recipient of a noninterest-bearing note.
DISCUSSION: When a noninterest-bearing note is exchanged for property, the note, the sales price, and the cost of the property exchanged for the note should be recorded at the fair value of the property or at the market value of the note, whichever is more clearly determinable. Here, the $44,000 fair value of the property is clearly determinable because Fulmar frequently sells similar items for that amount. Consequently, $44,000 is the proper amount to be recorded as sales revenue from this transaction.
Answer (A) is incorrect. The amount of $10,000 is the annual installment. Answer (B) is incorrect. The amount of $40,000 is the original cost of the property. Answer (C) is incorrect. The amount of $43,550 is the present value of the note, but the fair value of the property is more clearly determinable.

5.5.7. A 90-day, 15% interest-bearing note receivable is sold to a bank after being held for 30 days. The proceeds are calculated using an 18% interest rate. The note receivable has been

	Discounted	Pledged
A.	No	Yes
B.	No	No
C.	Yes	No
D.	Yes	Yes

Answer (C) is correct. *(CPA, adapted)*
REQUIRED: The proper description of the sale of a note receivable.
DISCUSSION: A note receivable sold before maturity has been discounted. A pledge is a security transaction in which the collateral to secure a debt is held by the secured party. No security has been given in this case.

5.5.8. On November 1, Year 4, Davis Co. discounted with recourse at 10% a 1-year, noninterest-bearing, $20,500 note receivable maturing on January 31, Year 5. What amount of contingent liability for this note must Davis disclose in its financial statements for the year ended December 31, Year 4?

A. $0

B. $20,000

C. $20,333

D. $20,500

Answer (D) is correct. *(CPA, adapted)*
REQUIRED: The amount to be disclosed in the financial statements for a contingent liability.
DISCUSSION: When a note receivable is discounted, the receivable is removed from the accounts, a gain or loss is recognized, and a contingent liability is disclosed in a note. If the receivables are not paid, Davis Co. may be responsible for the full amount of the note $(20,500). Consequently, this amount should be disclosed in the notes.
Answer (A) is incorrect. The notes to the financial statements should disclose the full potential liability. Answer (B) is incorrect. Davis may be responsible for the full amount of the note $(20,500). Answer (C) is incorrect. Davis may be responsible for the full amount of the note $(20,500).

5.5.9. Jayne Corp. discounted its own $50,000, 1-year note at a bank, at a discount rate of 12%, when the prime rate was 10%. In reporting the note on Jayne's balance sheet prior to the note's maturity, what rate should Jayne use for the accrual of interest?

A. 10.0%

B. 10.7%

C. 12.0%

D. 13.6%

Answer (D) is correct. *(CPA, adapted)*
REQUIRED: The effective rate of interest on a discounted note.
DISCUSSION: The note had a face amount of $50,000. The proceeds from discounting the note were $44,000 [$50,000 – ($50,000 × 12% × 1 year)]. Thus, Jayne paid $6,000 interest ($50,000 – $44,000) on $44,000 for 1 year. The effective interest rate was thus 13.6% ($6,000 ÷ $44,000).
Answer (A) is incorrect. The prime rate is not used for accruals. Answer (B) is incorrect. The rate used for the accrual of interest is the effective interest rate. Answer (C) is incorrect. The discount rate is not used for accruals.

5.5.10. Ayn, Inc., accepted from a customer an $80,000, 90-day, 12% interest-bearing note dated August 31. On September 30, Ayn discounted the note at the Nadir State Bank at 15%. However, the proceeds were not received until October 1. In Ayn's September 30 balance sheet, the amount receivable from the bank, based on a 360-day year, includes accrued interest revenue of

A. $340

B. $400

C. $600

D. $800

Answer (A) is correct. *(CPA, adapted)*
REQUIRED: The accrued interest revenue recognized when a note is discounted.
DISCUSSION: As determined below, the interest received by Ayn if it had held the 90-day note to maturity would have been $2,400. The discount fee charged on a note with a maturity amount of $82,400 ($80,000 face amount + $2,400 interest) discounted at 15% for 60 days is $2,060. The difference of $340 ($2,400 interest – $2,060 discount fee) should be reflected as accrued interest revenue at the balance sheet date because the cash proceeds were not received until the next period.

$80,000 × 12% × (90 days ÷ 360 days) = $2,400 interest
$82,400 × 15% × (60 days ÷ 360 days) = (2,060) discount fee
Accrued interest revenue $ 340

Answer (B) is incorrect. Incorrectly calculating the discount fee based on the $80,000 face amount rather than the $82,400 maturity amount results in $400. Answer (C) is incorrect. The accrued interest revenue is the difference between the interest on the note if held to maturity minus the discounted amount of the note. Answer (D) is incorrect. The amount of $800 incorrectly assumes no discount fee.

5.5.11. Halen, Inc., received from a customer a 1-year, $500,000 note bearing annual interest of 8%. After holding the note for 4 months, Halen discounted the note at Regional Bank at an effective interest rate of 10%. What amount of cash did Halen receive from the bank?

A. $540,000

B. $520,667

C. $504,000

D. $486,000

Answer (C) is correct. *(CPA, adapted)*
REQUIRED: The amount of cash received when a note is discounted.
DISCUSSION: The maturity amount of the note is $540,000 [$500,000 face amount + ($500,000 × 8%)]. The discount fee is $36,000 [$540,000 × 10% × (8 months ÷ 12 months)]. Consequently, the proceeds equal $504,000 ($540,000 – $36,000).
Answer (A) is incorrect. The amount of $540,000 is the maturity value. Answer (B) is incorrect. The amount of $520,667 assumes a nominal rate of 10% and a discount rate of 8%. Answer (D) is incorrect. The amount of $486,000 results from discounting the note for 1 year.

5.5.12. On August 1, Year 1, Vann Corp.'s $500,000 1-year, noninterest-bearing note due July 31, Year 2, was discounted at Homestead Bank at 10.8%. Vann uses the straight-line method of amortizing bond discount. What carrying amount should Vann report for notes payable in its December 31, Year 1, balance sheet?

A. $500,000

B. $477,500

C. $468,500

D. $446,000

Answer (C) is correct. *(CPA, adapted)*
REQUIRED: The carrying amount reported for notes payable.
DISCUSSION: The discount is $54,000 ($500,000 ×10.8%). Hence, the carrying amount on August 1 was $446,000. Given straight-line amortization of the discount, the carrying amount at year end is $468,500 [$500,000 – $54,000 + ($54,000 × 5 ÷ 12)].
Answer (A) is incorrect. This figure is the face amount of the note payable. Answer (B) is incorrect. This figure will be the carrying amount after 7 months. Answer (D) is incorrect. This figure was the carrying value on August 1.

5.5.13. Leaf Co. purchased from Oak Co. a $20,000, 8%, 5-year note that required five equal, annual year-end payments of $5,009. The note was discounted to yield a 9% rate to Leaf. At the date of purchase, Leaf recorded the note at its present value of $19,485. What should be the total interest revenue earned by Leaf over the life of this note?

A. $5,045

B. $5,560

C. $8,000

D. $9,000

Answer (B) is correct. *(CPA, adapted)*
REQUIRED: The total interest revenue earned on a discounted note receivable.
DISCUSSION: Leaf Co. will receive cash of $25,045 ($5,009 × 5). Hence, interest revenue is $5,560 ($25,045 – $19,485 present value).
Answer (A) is incorrect. The amount of $5,045 does not include the discount amortization. Answer (C) is incorrect. The amount of $8,000 equals $20,000 times 8% nominal interest for 5 years. Answer (D) is incorrect. The amount of $9,000 equals $20,000 times the 9% yield rate for 5 years.

5.5.14. Punn Co. has been forced into bankruptcy and liquidated. Unsecured claims will be paid at the rate of $.30 on the dollar. Mega Co. holds a noninterest-bearing note receivable from Punn in the amount of $50,000, collateralized by machinery with a liquidation value of $10,000. The total amount to be realized by Mega on this note receivable is

A. $25,000

B. $22,000

C. $15,000

D. $10,000

Answer (B) is correct. *(CPA, adapted)*
   REQUIRED: The amount to be realized from a liquidation claim.
   DISCUSSION: The $50,000 note receivable is secured to the extent of $10,000. The remaining $40,000 is unsecured, and Mega will be paid on this claim at the rate of $.30 on the dollar.

Secured claim	$10,000
Unsecured ($40,000 × .3)	12,000
	$22,000

   Answer (A) is incorrect. The amount of $25,000 equals 30% of the note receivable plus the liquidation value of the collateral [($50,000 × .3) + $10,000]. Answer (C) is incorrect. The amount of $15,000 is what would be realized if no collateral had been pledged ($50,000 × 3%). Answer (D) is incorrect. The amount of $10,000 is the liquidation value of the collateral.

5.6 Transfers of Financial Assets

5.6.1. Which of the following is a method to generate cash from accounts receivable?

	Assignment	Factoring
A.	Yes	No
B.	Yes	Yes
C.	No	Yes
D.	No	No

Answer (B) is correct. *(CPA, adapted)*
   REQUIRED: The method(s) of generating cash from accounts receivable.
   DISCUSSION: Methods of generating cash from accounts receivable include both assignment and factoring. Assignment occurs when specifically named accounts receivable are pledged as collateral for a loan. The accounts receivable remain those of the assignor. However, when cash is collected from these accounts receivable, the cash must be remitted to the assignee. Accounts receivable are factored when they are sold outright to a third party. This sale may be with or without recourse.
   Answer (A) is incorrect. Factoring is a way to generate cash from accounts receivable. Answer (C) is incorrect. Assignment is a way to generate cash from accounts receivable. Answer (D) is incorrect. Both assignment and factoring are ways to generate cash from accounts receivable.

5.6.2. On April 1, Aloe, Inc., factored $80,000 of its accounts receivable without recourse. The factor retained 10% of the accounts receivable as an allowance for sales returns and charged a 5% commission on the gross amount of the factored receivables. What amount of cash did Aloe receive from the factored receivables?

A. $68,000

B. $68,400

C. $72,000

D. $76,000

Answer (A) is correct. *(CPA, adapted)*
   REQUIRED: The cash received for accounts receivable factored without recourse if the factor retained a percentage as an allowance for sales returns and charges a commission.
   DISCUSSION: Factoring is a transfer of receivables to a third party (a factor) who assumes the responsibility of collection. Factoring discounts receivables on a nonrecourse, notification basis. If a sale is without recourse, the transferee (the factor) assumes the risks and rewards of collection. The factor retained 10% of the receivables ($80,000 × 10% = $8,000) as a reserve (an allowance for returns) and charged a 5% commission on the gross receivables ($80,000 × 5% = $4,000). Accordingly, the transferor received $68,000 ($80,000 – $8,000 – $4,000).
   Answer (B) is incorrect. The amount of $68,400 equals the commission rate times the excess of the receivables factored over the receivables retained. Answer (C) is incorrect. The amount of $72,000 does not include the 5% commission. Answer (D) is incorrect. The amount of $76,000 does not include the allowance for the 10% of accounts receivable retained as an allowance for sales returns.

5.6.3. Milton Co. pledged some of its accounts receivable to Good Neighbor Financing Corporation in return for a loan. Which of the following statements is correct?

A. Good Neighbor Financing cannot take title to the receivables if Milton does not repay the loan. Title can only be taken if the receivables are factored.

B. Good Neighbor Financing will assume the responsibility of collecting the receivables.

C. Milton will retain control of the receivables.

D. Good Neighbor Financing will take title to the receivables and will return title to Milton after the loan is paid.

Answer (C) is correct. *(CPA, adapted)*
REQUIRED: The true statement about a pledge of accounts receivable for a loan.
DISCUSSION: A pledge (a general assignment) is the use of receivables as collateral (security) for a loan. The borrower agrees to use collections of receivables to repay the loan. Upon default, the lender can sell the receivables to recover the loan proceeds. Because a pledge is a relatively informal arrangement, it is not reflected in the accounts. A transfer of financial assets is a sale only when the transferor relinquishes control. If the transfer (e.g., a pledge) of accounts receivable is not a sale, the transaction is a secured borrowing. The transferor becomes a debtor, and the transferee, a creditor in possession of collateral. However, absent default, the collateral remains an asset of the transferor.
Answer (A) is incorrect. If the transferor defaults, the transferor loses its right of redemption, and the title remains with the transferee. Title to receivables can therefore be taken by means other than factoring. Answer (B) is incorrect. The risks and rewards of collection are passed to the transferee when the sale of receivables is without recourse. In this case, because the pledge is not a sale, the debtor retains the responsibility of collecting the receivables. Answer (D) is incorrect. The transfer of receivables is not a sale. The debtor retains title unless it defaults.

5.6.4. On January 1, Davis College transferred $500,000 of accounts receivable to the Scholastic Finance Company. Davis gave a 14% note for $450,000 representing 90% of the transferred accounts and received proceeds of $432,000 after payment of a 4% fee. On February 1, Davis remitted $80,000 to Scholastic, including interest for 1 month on the unpaid balance. As a result of this $80,000 remittance, accounts receivable transferred and notes payable will be decreased by what amounts?

	A/R Transferred	Notes Payable
A.	$80,000	$74,750
B.	$80,000	$80,000
C.	$72,000	$74,750
D.	$74,750	$80,000

Answer (A) is correct. *(A.G. Helling)*
REQUIRED: The decrease in assigned accounts receivable and notes payable when cash is collected and remitted to the assignor.
DISCUSSION: When transferred accounts receivable are collected, the cash should be remitted to the transferee. The accounts receivable transferred account should be decreased for the amount collected ($80,000), and the note should be decreased by the amount remitted ($80,000) minus interest [$450,000 × 14% × (1 month ÷ 12 months) = $5,250].
Answer (B) is incorrect. Notes payable should be decreased by the amount remitted minus the interest payment. Answer (C) is incorrect. Accounts receivable should be decreased by the amount collected. Answer (D) is incorrect. Notes payable should be decreased by the amount remitted minus the interest payment, and accounts receivable should be decreased by the amount collected.

5.6.5. In accounting for the transfer of financial assets, which of the following is the approach underlying the accounting prescribed by GAAP?

A. Financial-components approach.

B. The risks-and-rewards approach.

C. Inseparable-unit approach.

D. Linked-presentation approach.

Answer (A) is correct. *(Publisher, adapted)*
REQUIRED: The approach underlying the accounting for transfers of financial assets.
DISCUSSION: The accounting for the transfer of financial assets follows a financial-components approach based on control. The objective is for each party to the transaction to (1) recognize the assets it controls and the liabilities it has incurred, (2) derecognize assets when control has been given up, and (3) derecognize liabilities when they have been extinguished. Thus, it must be determined whether the transferor has given up control of the transferred financial assets.
Answer (B) is incorrect. The risks-and-rewards approach was rejected by the FASB. It is consistent with viewing each financial asset as an indivisible unit. Answer (C) is incorrect. The inseparable-unit approach was rejected by the FASB. It is consistent with viewing each financial asset as an indivisible unit. Answer (D) is incorrect. The linked-presentation approach was rejected by the FASB. It is consistent with viewing each financial asset as an indivisible unit.

5.6.6. A transfer of financial assets may be treated as a sale if the transferor surrenders control of the assets. Which of the following is one of the criteria that must be met before control is deemed to be surrendered?

A. The transferred assets are isolated from the transferor and its creditors except in bankruptcy.

B. The transferee cannot pledge or exchange the transferred assets.

C. The transferor is not a party to an agreement that both entitles and obligates it to repurchase or redeem the securities prior to maturity.

D. An entire financial asset is transferred.

Answer (C) is correct. *(Publisher, adapted)*
REQUIRED: The criterion that must be met before control over transferred financial assets is deemed to be surrendered.
DISCUSSION: Three criteria must be met: (1) The transferred assets are beyond the reach of the transferor and its creditors; (2) transferees may pledge or exchange the assets or interests; and (3) the transferor does not maintain effective control through, for example, (a) an agreement to repurchase or redeem the assets prior to maturity, (b) an ability unilaterally to benefit from causing the holder to return specific assets, or (c) an agreement making it probable that the transferee will require repurchase.
Answer (A) is incorrect. Control is not surrendered if the transferor's creditors can reach the assets in bankruptcy. Answer (B) is incorrect. The transferee is able to pledge or exchange the assets if control is surrendered. Answer (D) is incorrect. A transfer may be accounted for as a sale if it involves a participating interest in an entire financial asset.

5.6.7. Seller Co. transferred entire loans to Buyer Co. in a sale transaction. It did not retain a servicing interest. The loans had a fair value of $1,650 and a carrying amount of $1,500. Seller also undertook to repurchase delinquent loans. Furthermore, the loans had a fixed rate, but Seller agreed to provide Buyer a return at a variable rate. Thus, the transaction effectively included an interest rate swap. The following are the relevant fair values:

Cash received $1,575
Interest rate swap asset   60
Recourse obligation   90

Seller should recognize a gain of

A. $45

B. $90

C. $150

D. $225

Answer (A) is correct. *(Publisher, adapted)*
REQUIRED: The gain on a sale of financial assets.
DISCUSSION: The gain equals the net proceeds (cash or other assets obtained in a transfer of financial assets, minus liabilities incurred) minus the carrying amount of the assets derecognized. Any asset obtained that is not an interest in the transferred assets is included in the proceeds. Thus, the cash received and the fair value of the interest rate swap asset are debited as part of the proceeds. Any liability incurred, even if related to the assets transferred, reduces the proceeds, so the recourse obligation should be credited. After crediting the carrying amount of the loans sold and measuring assets and liabilities at fair value, Seller should recognize a gain on sale (a credit) of $45 ($1,575 cash + $60 interest rate swap − $90 recourse obligation − $1,500 carrying amount).
Answer (B) is incorrect. The fair value of the recourse obligation is $90. Answer (C) is incorrect. The sum of the recourse obligation and the interest rate swap asset is $150. Answer (D) is incorrect. The recourse obligation is a liability.

5.6.8. Lender Bank made a large loan to a major borrower and then transferred a participating interest in this loan to Student Union Bank. The transfer was on a nonrecourse basis, and Lender continued to service the loan. Student Union is not a major competitor of Lender. Lender should account for this transfer as a secured borrowing if the agreement

A. Allows Student Union Bank to pledge its participating interest.

B. Does not grant Lender the right of first refusal on the sale of Student Union's participating interest.

C. Does not allow Student Union to sell its participating interest.

D. Prohibits Student Union from selling its participating interest to banks that are direct, major competitors of Lender.

Answer (C) is correct. *(Publisher, adapted)*
REQUIRED: The condition under which a participating interest in a loan should be accounted for as a secured borrowing.
DISCUSSION: A transfer of financial assets, such as a participating interest in a loan, should be accounted for as a sale if the transferor surrenders control over the participating interest transferred to the transferee. If control is not surrendered, the transfer should be accounted for as a secured borrowing. Control is not surrendered if the agreement prevents the transferee from pledging or exchanging its participating interest.
Answer (A) is incorrect. The right to exchange or pledge participating interests is consistent with the relinquishment of control. Answer (B) is incorrect. Failing to grant Lender the right of first refusal on the sale of Student Union's participating interest is not a constraint on the transferee that permits the transferor to retain control. Indeed, a right of first refusal is not such a constraint. Answer (D) is incorrect. A prohibition on sale to the transferor's competitors is not a constraint on the transferee if other willing buyers exist.

5.6.9. Athens Corporation sold an 80% pro rata interest in a $2,000,000 note receivable to Sparta Company for $1,920,000. The note was originally issued at its face amount. Future benefits and costs of servicing the note are immaterial. The amount of gain or loss Athens should recognize on this transfer of a partial interest is

A. $(80,000)

B. $0

C. $320,000

D. $400,000

Answer (C) is correct. *(Publisher, adapted)*
REQUIRED: The amount of gain or loss to be recognized on a transfer of a partial interest in a loan.
DISCUSSION: The fair value of the note is $2,400,000 ($1,920,000 ÷ 80%). The carrying amount is $2,000,000. Given no servicing asset or liability, Athens should debit cash for $1,920,000, reduce the carrying amount of the note receivable by $1,600,000 ($2,000,000 × 80%), and recognize a gain of $320,000 ($1,920,000 – $1,600,000).
Answer (A) is incorrect. A loss of $80,000 is equal to the $1,920,000 cash received minus the $2,000,000 carrying amount of the note. Answer (B) is incorrect. A gain should be recognized equal to the pro rata (80%) difference between the fair value and the carrying amount of the note. Answer (D) is incorrect. The amount of $400,000 is equal to 100% of the difference between the fair value and the carrying amount of the note.

5.6.10. On the last day of its fiscal year, Originator Co. transferred noncurrent loans to Transferee Co. in a transaction appropriately accounted for as a sale and retained a servicing asset. These loans have a 10% yield, a fair value of $220,000 (including servicing), and a carrying amount of $200,000. Originator sold the entire principal and the right to receive interest income at 8% for $198,000. The fee for continuing to service the loans is a portion of the interest income not transferred. This fee is not subordinate to any other interest and is equal to fair compensation for a substitute service provider. The remainder of the interest income not transferred is an interest-only strip receivable. The following are the relevant fair values:

Cash	$198,000
Interest-only strip receivable	13,200
Servicing asset	8,800
	$220,000

The gain on the sale is

A. $800

B. $1,200

C. $18,000

D. $20,000

Answer (D) is correct. *(Publisher, adapted)*
REQUIRED: The gain on the sale of noncurrent loans given retention of an interest-only strip receivable and a servicing asset.
DISCUSSION: The interests retained by the transferor do not qualify as participating interests. Thus, the interest-only strip receivable does not satisfy the requirement that all cash flows be divided in proportion to shares of ownership. The reason is that the transferor does not share in principal payments. Moreover, the servicing asset does not qualify because cash flows received as compensation for services ordinarily are excluded from proportionate cash flows. Accordingly, the carrying amount of the entire asset is not allocated among participating interests by the transferor. The entry based on fair values is

Cash	$198,000	
Interest-only strip receivable	13,200	
Servicing asset	8,800	
Loans		$200,000
Gain on sale		20,000

Answer (A) is incorrect. The amount of $800 equals the $8,800 fair value of the servicing asset minus an $8,000 allocation of the carrying amount. Answer (B) is incorrect. The amount of $1,200 equals the $13,200 fair value of the interest-only strip receivable minus a $12,000 allocation of the carrying amount. Answer (C) is incorrect. The amount of $18,000 equals the cash received ($198,000) minus a $180,000 allocation of the carrying amount to the loans.

5.6.11. If a transfer of an entire financial asset meets the criteria for recognition as a sale, the transferor should

A. Account for any gain or loss in other comprehensive income.

B. Initially measure at fair value any assets obtained and liabilities incurred.

C. Allocate the previous carrying amount to the assets obtained and liabilities incurred.

D. Recognize liabilities in accordance with the accounting for contingencies.

Answer (B) is correct. *(Publisher, adapted)*
REQUIRED: The accounting for a transfer of an entire financial asset that meets the criteria for recognition as a sale.
DISCUSSION: The transferor should (1) derecognize assets when control has been relinquished, (2) recognize assets controlled and liabilities incurred, (3) derecognize liabilities when they have been extinguished, and (4) recognize gain or loss in earnings.
Answer (A) is incorrect. The transferor should recognize any gain or loss in earnings. Answer (C) is incorrect. Fair value accounting should be used. Answer (D) is incorrect. Under prior guidance that has been superseded, if fair value measurement of liabilities is not practicable, no gain is recognized, and the liabilities are recorded at the greater of (1) the excess, if any, of (a) the fair value of assets obtained minus the fair value of other liabilities incurred over (b) the sum of the carrying amounts of the assets transferred or (2) the amount determined under GAAP for contingencies.

STUDY UNIT SIX
INVENTORIES

Inventory consists of the tangible goods intended to be sold to produce revenue. The **cost** of inventory is a deferral because it is not included in earnings until the reporting period in which the inventory is sold. Financial accounting for inventory includes (1) initial determination of the costs to be recognized as inventory and (2) measurement of inventory until the related revenues are recognized. Most questions are about these issues. Specific topics include (1) the perpetual and periodic inventory accounting systems, (2) calculation of inventory under different cost flow methods (FIFO, LIFO, average, and dollar-value LIFO), (3) measurement of losses when the utility of goods is impaired at either (a) the lower-of-cost-or-market (LCM) or (b) the lower-of-cost-or-net-realizable-value (depending on the cost flow method applied), and (4) use of the gross profit and retail inventory methods to estimate ending inventory. Moreover, financial accounting for inventory requires recognition of an expense (cost of goods sold) and revenue from its sale.

QUESTIONS

6.1 Inventory Fundamentals

6.1.1. The following information pertains to Hague Corp.'s Year 2 cost of goods sold:

Inventory, 12/31/Year 1	$180,000
Year 2 purchases	248,000
Year 2 write-off of obsolete inventory	68,000
Inventory, 12/31/Year 2	60,000

The inventory written off became obsolete because of an unexpected and unusual technological advance by a competitor. In its Year 2 income statement, what amount should Hague report as cost of goods sold?

A. $436,000

B. $368,000

C. $300,000

D. $248,000

Answer (C) is correct. *(CPA, adapted)*
  REQUIRED: The cost of goods sold for the year.
  DISCUSSION: As indicated in the T-account analysis below, cost of goods sold equals purchases plus any decrease in inventory or minus any increase in inventory (purchases minus the change in inventory). The write-off of obsolete inventory is a loss, not a component of COGS. Thus, cost of goods sold is $300,000.

Inventory			
12/31/Year 1	$180,000	$ 68,000	Obsolescence
Purchases	248,000	300,000	COGS
	$ 60,000		

Answer (A) is incorrect. The amount of $436,000 results from adding obsolete inventory to, not subtracting it from, beginning inventory. Answer (B) is incorrect. The amount of $368,000 includes the obsolete inventory in COGS. Answer (D) is incorrect. The amount of $248,000 equals purchases.

6.1.2. In a retailer's periodic inventory system that uses the weighted-average cost flow method, the beginning inventory is the

A. Net purchases minus the ending inventory.

B. Net purchases minus the cost of goods sold.

C. Total goods available for sale minus the net purchases.

D. Total goods available for sale minus the cost of goods sold.

Answer (C) is correct. *(CPA, adapted)*
  REQUIRED: The beginning inventory in a periodic system using weighted average cost.
  DISCUSSION: In a retailer's periodic inventory system, goods available for sale is the sum of beginning inventory and net purchases. Thus, the beginning inventory equals the total goods available for sale minus the net purchases, regardless of the cost flow method used.
  Answer (A) is incorrect. It states the difference between the beginning inventory and the cost of goods sold. Answer (B) is incorrect. This difference is the change in inventory valuation during the period. Answer (D) is incorrect. Goods available minus cost of sales equals ending inventory.

6.1.3. Application rates for fixed production overheads best reflect anticipated fluctuations in production over a cycle of years when they are computed under the concept of

    A. Maximum capacity.

    B. Normal capacity.

    C. Practical capacity.

    D. Expected actual capacity.

Answer (B) is correct. *(CPA, adapted)*
    REQUIRED: The concept of capacity for best applying overheads over a cycle of years.
    DISCUSSION: Normal capacity is the production level that will approximate demand over a period of years that includes seasonal, cyclical, and trend variations. Deviations in one year will be offset in other years. Moreover, normal capacity is expected to be achieved under normal circumstances, including loss of capacity because of planned maintenance. Consequently, GAAP require allocation of fixed production overheads to conversion cost based on normal capacity.
    Answer (A) is incorrect. Maximum (theoretical or ideal) capacity is the level at which output is maximized assuming perfectly efficient operations at all times. This level is impossible to maintain and results in underapplied overheads. Answer (C) is incorrect. Practical capacity is the maximum level at which output is produced efficiently. It usually also results in underapplied overheads. Answer (D) is incorrect. Expected actual capacity is a short-run output level. It minimizes under- or overapplied overheads but does not provide a consistent basis for assigning overhead cost. Per-unit overheads will fluctuate because of short-term changes in the expected production level.

6.1.4. During December of Year 1, Nile Co. incurred special insurance costs but did not record these costs until payment was made during the following year. These insurance costs related to inventory that had been sold by December 31, Year 1. What is the effect of the omission on Nile's accrued liabilities and retained earnings at December 31, Year 1?

	Accrued Liabilities	Retained Earnings
A.	No effect	No effect
B.	No effect	Overstated
C.	Understated	Overstated
D.	Understated	No effect

Answer (C) is correct. *(CPA, adapted)*
    REQUIRED: The effect on accrued liabilities and retained earnings of omitting insurance costs of inventory.
    DISCUSSION: A liability must be recognized when (1) an item meets the definition of a liability (probable future sacrifice of economic benefits arising from a current obligation of the entity as a result of a past event or transaction), (2) it is measurable, and (3) the information about it is relevant and reliable. These criteria were met in Year 1 with respect to the insurance obligation. The insurance is a cost of inventory and theoretically should be accounted for as a product cost. Thus, the entry in Year 1 should have been to debit inventory and credit a liability. The omission of this entry understated accrued liabilities. Given that the related inventory was sold in Year 1, it also overstated net income and retained earnings by understating cost of goods sold. Moreover, the same effects would occur if the insurance costs were chargeable to expense as a period cost.

6.1.5. If ending inventory is underestimated due to an error in the physical count of items on hand, cost of goods sold for the period will be <List A> and net earnings will be <List B>.

	List A	List B
A.	Underestimated	Underestimated
B.	Underestimated	Overestimated
C.	Overestimated	Underestimated
D.	Overestimated	Overestimated

Answer (C) is correct. *(CIA, adapted)*
    REQUIRED: The effect on cost of goods sold and net earnings of an error in counting inventory.
    DISCUSSION: Cost of goods sold equals beginning inventory, plus purchases, minus ending inventory. If the ending inventory is underestimated, the cost of goods sold will be overestimated. If cost of goods sold is overestimated, net earnings will be underestimated.
    Answer (A) is incorrect. The cost of goods sold will be overestimated. Answer (B) is incorrect. The cost of goods sold will be overestimated and net earnings will be underestimated. Answer (D) is incorrect. Net earnings will be underestimated.

6.1.6. Heidelberg Co.'s beginning inventory at January 1 was understated by $52,000, and its ending inventory was overstated by $104,000. As a result, Heidelberg's cost of goods sold for the year was

    A. Understated by $52,000.

    B. Overstated by $52,000.

    C. Understated by $156,000.

    D. Overstated by $156,000.

Answer (C) is correct. *(CPA, adapted)*
    REQUIRED: The misstatement of cost of goods sold.
    DISCUSSION: When beginning inventory is understated, cost of goods sold will be understated. When ending inventory is overstated, cost of goods sold will be understated. Thus, Heidelberg Co.'s inventory is understated by $156,000 ($52,000 + $104,000).
    Answer (A) is incorrect. The overstatement of ending inventory also understates cost of goods sold. Answer (B) is incorrect. The error understates cost of goods sold. Answer (D) is incorrect. The error understates cost of goods sold.

6.1.7. The following inventory errors have been discovered for Lithuania Corporation:

- The Year 1 year-end inventory was overstated by $23,000.
- The Year 2 year-end inventory was understated by $61,000.
- The Year 3 year-end inventory was understated by $17,000.

The reported income before taxes for Lithuania was

Year	Income before Taxes
Year 1	$138,000
Year 2	254,000
Year 3	168,000

Reported income before taxes for Year 1, Year 2, and Year 3, respectively, should have been

- A. $161,000, $170,000, and $212,000.
- B. $115,000, $338,000, and $124,000.
- C. $161,000, $338,000, and $90,000.
- D. $115,000, $338,000, and $212,000.

Answer (B) is correct. *(CMA, adapted)*
REQUIRED: The reported income after correction of inventory errors.
DISCUSSION: Cost of sales equals beginning inventory, plus purchases or cost of goods manufactured, minus ending inventory. Hence, over (under) statement of inventory affects cost of sales and income. The Year 1 pretax income was affected by the $23,000 Year 1 overstatement of year-end inventory. This error understated Year 1 cost of sales and overstated pretax income. The corrected income is $115,000 ($138,000 – $23,000). The same $23,000 error caused Year 2 income to be understated by overstating beginning inventory. In addition, the $61,000 understatement of Year 2 year-end inventory also caused Year 2 income to be understated. Thus, the corrected Year 2 pretax income is $338,000 ($254,000 + $23,000 + $61,000). The $61,000 understatement at the end of Year 2 caused Year 3 income to be overstated by understating beginning inventory. Income for Year 3 is understated by the $17,000 of year-end inventory understatement. Accordingly, the corrected income is $124,000 ($168,000 – $61,000 + $17,000).
Answer (A) is incorrect. Year 1 income of $161,000 results from adding, not subtracting, the $23,000 overstatement of ending inventory. Similarly, Year 2 income of $170,000 results from subtracting, not adding, the $23,000 overstatement of beginning inventory and the $61,000 understatement of ending inventory. Finally, Year 3 income of $212,000 results from adding, not subtracting, the $61,000 understatement of beginning inventory and subtracting, not adding, the understatement of ending inventory. Answer (C) is incorrect. Year 3 income of $90,000 results from subtracting, not adding, the $17,000 understatement of ending inventory. Answer (D) is incorrect. Year 3 pre-tax income should be $124,000.

6.1.8. According to the net method, which of the following items should be included in the cost of inventory?

	Freight Costs	Purchase Discounts Not Taken
A.	Yes	No
B.	Yes	Yes
C.	No	Yes
D.	No	No

Answer (A) is correct. *(CPA, adapted)*
REQUIRED: The items that should be included as inventoriable cost.
DISCUSSION: Cost is the total of the expenses directly or indirectly incurred in bringing an item to its existing condition and location. Freight costs are therefore an inventoriable cost to the extent they are not abnormal. Under the net method, purchase discounts are treated as reductions in the invoice prices of specific purchases. Accordingly, goods available for sale reflects the purchase price net of the discount, and a purchase discount not taken is recognized as an item of interest expense.
Answer (B) is incorrect. Purchase discounts not taken are not included in inventory under the net method. Answer (C) is incorrect. Freight costs, but not purchase discounts not taken, are included in inventory under the net method. Answer (D) is incorrect. Freight costs are included in inventory under the net method.

6.1.9. On July 1, Clio Company recorded purchases of inventory of $40,000 and $50,000 under credit terms of 2/15, net 30. The payment due on the $40,000 purchase was remitted on July 14. The payment due on the $50,000 purchase was remitted on July 25. Under the net method and the gross method, these purchases should be included at what respective net amounts in the determination of cost of goods available for sale?

	Net Method	Gross Method
A.	$90,000	$90,000
B.	$89,200	$88,200
C.	$88,200	$89,200
D.	$88,200	$88,200

Answer (C) is correct. *(Publisher, adapted)*
REQUIRED: The amounts at which net purchases should be measured under the net and gross methods.
DISCUSSION: The 2/15, net 30 credit term indicates that a 2% discount may be taken if payment is made within 15 days of the invoice date and that payment is overdue if not made within 30 days. The net method records purchases net of any discount. It is used when the purchaser expects to pay soon enough to take advantage of the discount provision. Accordingly, these two purchases should be recorded under the net method at $88,200 [($40,000 + $50,000) × 98%]. When the July 25 payment is made after the discount period, the purchases account is unaffected. The gross method records purchases at their gross amount. It is used when the purchaser does not expect to pay within the discount period. In this case, the July 14 payment was made within the discount period, but the July 25 payment was not. Accordingly, these two purchases should be recorded under the gross method at $89,200 [($40,000 × 98%) + $50,000]. This amount is net of the purchase discount taken, an item subtracted from purchases on the income statement.
Answer (A) is incorrect. The amount of $90,000 does not reflect the discount taken (gross method) or the discounts expected to be taken (net method). Answer (B) is incorrect. The net method and gross method amounts are $88,200 and $89,200, respectively. Answer (D) is incorrect. The two purchases should be recorded under the gross method at $89,200 [($40,000 × 98%) + $50,000].

6.1.10. The following costs were incurred by Parthos Co., a manufacturer, during the current year:

Accounting and legal fees	$ 50,000
Freight-in	350,000
Freight-out	320,000
Officers' salaries	300,000
Insurance	170,000
Sales representatives' salaries	430,000

What amount of these costs should be reported as general and administrative expenses for the current year?

A. $520,000

B. $1,100,000

C. $1,270,000

D. $1,620,000

Answer (A) is correct. *(CPA, adapted)*
REQUIRED: The amount to be reported as general and administrative expenses for the year.
DISCUSSION: General and administrative expenses are incurred for the direction of the entity as a whole and are not related wholly to a specific function, e.g., selling or manufacturing. They include (1) accounting, legal, and other fees for professional services; (2) officers' salaries; (3) insurance; (4) wages of office staff; (5) miscellaneous supplies; (6) utilities' costs; and (7) office occupancy costs. Thus, the general and administrative expenses for Parthos equaled $520,000 ($50,000 + $300,000 + $170,000).
Answer (B) is incorrect. The amount of $1,100,000 does not include insurance and incorrectly includes the sales representatives' salaries and freight-out (selling costs). Answer (C) is incorrect. Freight-out costs and sales representatives' salaries are included. Answer (D) is incorrect. Freight costs and sales representatives' salaries are not considered general and administrative costs.

6.1.11. In theory, the cash discounts allowed on purchased merchandise (purchase discounts) in a periodic inventory system should be

A. Deducted from purchases in determination of goods available for sale.

B. Deducted from cost of goods sold in the income statement.

C. Shown as other income in the income statement.

D. Deducted from inventory on the balance sheet at year end.

Answer (A) is correct. *(D.G. Kame)*
REQUIRED: The theoretically correct treatment of cash discounts earned on the purchase of merchandise.
DISCUSSION: In theory, cash discounts on purchases should be treated as reductions in the invoiced prices of specific purchases so that goods available for sale reflects the purchase price net of the discounts. It is consistent with this approach to record any purchase discounts not taken as a financial expense in the income statement.
Answer (B) is incorrect. Purchase discounts should be matched with the purchases with which they were associated, i.e., shown as a contra-account to purchases. Deducting them from cost of goods sold is therefore inappropriate. Answer (C) is incorrect. Under the net method, purchase discounts taken are not recognized. Under the gross method, they reduce purchases. Answer (D) is incorrect. Purchase discounts should be matched with the purchases with which they were associated, i.e., shown as a contra-account to purchases. They cannot be assigned in full to ending inventory.

6.1.12. West Retailers purchased merchandise with a list price of $20,000, subject to trade discounts of 20% and 10%, with no cash discounts allowable. West should record the cost of this merchandise as

A. $14,000

B. $14,400

C. $15,600

D. $20,000

Answer (B) is correct. *(CPA, adapted)*
REQUIRED: The amount to be recorded as cost of inventory subject to trade discounts.
DISCUSSION: When inventory is subject to cash discounts, the purchases may be reflected either net of these discounts or at the gross prices. However, purchases should always be recorded net of trade discounts. A chain discount is the application of more than one trade discount to a list price. Chain discounts should be applied in steps as indicated below.

List price	$20,000
20% discount	(4,000)
After 1st discount	$16,000
10% discount	(1,600)
Cost of merchandise	$14,400

Answer (A) is incorrect. The amount of $14,000 results from applying both discount percentages to the list price. Answer (C) is incorrect. The amount of $15,600 results from applying the second discount percentage to the first discount amount. Answer (D) is incorrect. Purchases should be recorded net of trade discounts.

6.1.13. On December 28, Kerr Manufacturing Co. purchased goods costing $50,000. The terms were FOB destination. Some of the costs incurred in connection with the sale and delivery of the goods were as follows:

Packaging for shipment	$1,000
Shipping	1,500
Special handling charges	2,000

These goods were received on December 31. In Kerr's December 31 balance sheet, what amount of cost for these goods should be included in inventory?

A. $54,500

B. $53,500

C. $52,000

D. $50,000

Answer (D) is correct. *(CPA, adapted)*
REQUIRED: The amount of cost for goods included in inventory.
DISCUSSION: FOB destination means that title passes upon delivery at the destination, the seller bears the risk of loss during transit, and the seller is responsible for the expense of delivering the goods to the designated point. Consequently, the packaging, shipping, and handling costs are not included in the buyer's inventory. The amount that Kerr should include is therefore the purchase price of $50,000.
Answer (A) is incorrect. The amount of $54,500 includes the packaging, shipping, and handling costs. Answer (B) is incorrect. The amount of $53,500 includes the shipping and handling costs. Answer (C) is incorrect. The amount of $52,000 includes the handling costs.

6.1.14. Madrid Corp.'s trial balance for the year ended December 31, Year 1, included the following:

	Debit	Credit
Sales		$600,000
Cost of sales	$240,000	
Administrative expenses	60,000	
Loss on sale of equipment	36,000	
Sales commissions	40,000	
Interest revenue		20,000
Freight-out	12,000	
Loss on early retirement of long-term debt	40,000	
Bad debt expense	12,000	
Totals	$440,000	$620,000

Other information:

Finished goods inventory:
January 1, Year 1	$400,000
December 31, Year 1	360,000

In Madrid's Year 1 multiple-step income statement, the cost of goods manufactured was

A. $200,000

B. $212,000

C. $280,000

D. $292,000

Answer (A) is correct. *(CPA, adapted)*
REQUIRED: The cost of goods manufactured.
DISCUSSION: Cost of goods sold equals beginning finished goods inventory, plus cost of goods manufactured, minus ending finished goods inventory. Hence, cost of goods manufactured equals cost of goods sold, plus ending finished goods inventory, minus beginning finished goods inventory, or $200,000 ($240,000 cost of goods sold + $360,000 ending finished goods inventory – $400,000 beginning finished goods inventory).
Answer (B) is incorrect. The amount of $212,000 includes the freight-out. Answer (C) is incorrect. The amount of $280,000 subtracts ending finished goods and adds beginning finished goods. Answer (D) is incorrect. The amount of $292,000 subtracts ending finished goods inventory and adds beginning finished goods. It also includes the freight-out.

6.2 Items Counted in Inventory

6.2.1. Naples Company bought a product on behalf of Rome Corporation. In a related transaction, Rome agreed to buy the product from Naples at a specified price at a specified date in the future. Rome should record an asset and a related obligation at the date that

A. The agreement is signed.

B. Naples acquires the product.

C. Naples ships the product to Rome.

D. Rome receives the product.

Answer (B) is correct. *(Publisher, adapted)*
REQUIRED: The date on which a product financing arrangement should be recorded.
DISCUSSION: The transaction is essentially a financing arrangement because Rome has acquired rights in the product without an immediate expenditure. Rome should record the asset and the related liability when Naples acquires the product. Naples is acting for Rome, and Rome should treat the goods received by Naples as if Rome itself had received them.
Answer (A) is incorrect. Purchases are not ordinarily recorded until title to the goods passes. Answer (C) is incorrect. Rome should record the inventory and liability when Naples acquires the product, not later. Answer (D) is incorrect. Recognition should not be deferred until Rome receives the product.

6.2.2. A sponsoring entity enters into an agreement by which it sells a product to another entity and agrees to repurchase that product at specified prices at later dates. If the specified prices fluctuate solely because of changes in purchasing, financing, and holding costs, the transaction should be treated as which of the following?

A. A borrowing.

B. A consignment.

C. A sale and repurchase.

D. Not recorded.

Answer (A) is correct. *(Publisher, adapted)*
REQUIRED: The correct accounting treatment of a product financing arrangement.
DISCUSSION: This arrangement is a transaction in which an entity sells and agrees to repurchase inventory, with the repurchase price equal to the original price plus carrying and financing costs. It should be treated as a borrowing if the specified prices do not fluctuate except to cover changes in purchasing, financing, and holding costs.
Answer (B) is incorrect. A consignment is the consignor's inventory physically located at the consignee's place of operations. Answer (C) is incorrect. A sale and repurchase describes the form of the transaction, not the substance. Answer (D) is incorrect. Liabilities must be recorded.

6.2.3. Herc Co.'s inventory at December 31, Year 1, was $1.5 million based on a physical count priced at cost, and before any necessary adjustment for the following:

● Merchandise costing $90,000 was shipped FOB shipping point from a vendor on December 30, Year 1, and was received and recorded on January 5, Year 2.

● Goods in the shipping area were excluded from inventory although shipment was not made until January 4, Year 2. The goods, billed to the customer FOB shipping point on December 30, Year 1, had a cost of $120,000.

What amount should Herc report as inventory in its December 31, Year 1, balance sheet?

A. $1,500,000

B. $1,590,000

C. $1,620,000

D. $1,710,000

Answer (D) is correct. *(CPA, adapted)*
REQUIRED: The year-end inventory.
DISCUSSION: The inventory balance prior to adjustments was $1.5 million. The merchandise shipped FOB shipping point to Herc should be included because title passed when the goods were shipped. The goods in the shipping area should be included because title did not pass until the goods were shipped in Year 2. Thus, inventory reported at December 31, Year 1, should be $1,710,000 ($1,500,000 + $90,000 + $120,000).
Answer (A) is incorrect. The amount of $1,500,000 excludes the $90,000 of goods shipped by a vendor and the $120,000 of goods not shipped until January 4. Answer (B) is incorrect. The amount of $1,590,000 results from failing to include the $120,000 of goods not shipped until January 4. Answer (C) is incorrect. The amount of $1,620,000 does not include the $90,000 of goods shipped by a vendor FOB shipping point.

6.2.4. On December 30, Year 1, Astor Corp. sold merchandise for $75,000 to Day Co. The terms of the sale were net 30, FOB shipping point. The merchandise was shipped on December 31, Year 1, and arrived at Day on January 5, Year 2. Due to a clerical error, the sale was not recorded until January Year 2, and the merchandise, sold at a 25% markup, was included in Astor's inventory at December 31, Year 1. As a result, Astor's cost of goods sold for the year ended December 31, Year 1, was

A. Understated by $75,000.

B. Understated by $60,000.

C. Understated by $15,000.

D. Correctly stated.

Answer (B) is correct. *(CPA, adapted)*
REQUIRED: The cost of goods sold given delayed recording of a sale.
DISCUSSION: Astor should have debited a receivable and credited sales for $75,000, the net amount, on the date of shipment. Astor also should have debited cost of sales and credited inventory at cost on the same date. Under the shipping terms, the sale should have been recognized on December 31, Year 1, because title and risk of loss passed to the buyer on that date; that is, an earning process was complete. The error therefore understated cost sales by $60,000 ($75,000 sales price ÷ 125% of cost).
Answer (A) is incorrect. The selling price is $75,000. Answer (C) is incorrect. The amount of the markup is $15,000. Answer (D) is incorrect. Cost of goods was understated by $60,000.

6.2.5. On June 1, Pitt Corp. sold merchandise with a list price of $5,000 to Burr on account. Pitt allowed trade discounts of 30% and 20%. Credit terms were 2/15, n/40, and the sale was made FOB shipping point. Pitt prepaid $200 of delivery costs for Burr as an accommodation. On June 12, Pitt received from Burr a remittance in full payment amounting to

A. $2,744

B. $2,912

C. $2,944

D. $3,112

Answer (C) is correct. *(CPA, adapted)*
REQUIRED: The amount of the full payment.
DISCUSSION: A trade discount is a means of establishing a price for a certain quantity or for a particular class of customers. Neither the buyer nor the seller reflects trade discounts in the accounts. Assuming that the 30% discount is applied first, the initial discount is $1,500 ($5,000 × 30%), and the second discount is $700 [($5,000 – $1,500) × 20%]. Thus, the base price is $2,800. (If both discounts apply, it makes no difference which is taken first.) Because the buyer paid within the discount period, the cash equivalent price is $2,744 ($2,800 × 98%). Given that the goods were shipped FOB shipping point, title passed when they were put in the possession of the carrier, and the buyer is responsible for payment of delivery costs. Accordingly, the full amount owed by the buyer was $2,944 ($2,744 + $200 delivery costs).
Answer (A) is incorrect. The amount of $2,744 does not include the delivery costs. Answer (B) is incorrect. The amount of $2,912 assumes that the delivery costs are part of the list price. It also ignores the cash discount. Answer (D) is incorrect. The amount of $3,112 assumes that the delivery costs are part of the list price. It also ignores the cash discount but adds back the delivery costs.

6.2.6. Seller Co. is a calendar-year retailer. Its year-end physical count of inventory on hand did not consider the effects of the following transactions:

- Goods with a cost of $50,000 were shipped by Seller FOB shipping point on December 30 and were accepted by the buyer on January 4.
- Goods with a cost of $40,000 were shipped FOB destination by a vendor on December 30 and were accepted by Seller on January 4.
- Goods were sold on the installment basis by Seller. Installment receivables representing sales of goods with a cost of $30,000 were reported at year end. Seller retains title to such goods until full payment is made.
- Goods with a cost of $20,000 were held on consignment for a vendor. These goods were not counted although they were sold in January.

If inventory based solely on the physical count of items on hand equaled $1 million, what amount of inventory should Seller report at year end?

- A. $1,000,000
- B. $1,090,000
- C. $1,120,000
- D. $1,140,000

Answer (A) is correct. *(Publisher, adapted)*
REQUIRED: The year-end inventory.
DISCUSSION: Goods shipped FOB shipping point become the property of the buyer when shipped. Thus, they were properly excluded from inventory. Goods shipped FOB destination become the property of the buyer (Seller Co.) when tender of delivery is made, so these goods were also properly excluded. Although title is retained to goods sold on the installment basis, the goods are excluded from inventory because dominion over the goods has passed to the buyer, assuming a reasonable expectation of payment in the ordinary course of business. Finally, in a consignment, the consignor ships merchandise to the consignee, who acts as an agent for the consignor in selling the goods. The goods are held by the consignee but remain the property of the consignor and are included in the consignor's inventory at cost. Accordingly, the physical count requires no adjustment for any of the listed transactions. Ending inventory is $1 million.
Answer (B) is incorrect. The amount of $1,090,000 reflects the goods Seller shipped FOB shipping point and the goods Seller received that were shipped FOB destination. Answer (C) is incorrect. The amount of $1,120,000 reflects all the listed transactions except the consignment. Answer (D) is incorrect. The amount of $1,140,000 reflects all the listed transactions.

6.2.7. Lew Co. sold 200,000 corrugated boxes for $2 each. Lew's cost was $1 per unit. The sales agreement gave the customer the right to return up to 60% of the boxes within the first 6 months, provided an appropriate reason was given. It was reasonably estimated that 5% of the boxes would be returned. Lew expects an additional $3,000 of costs to recover those boxes. What amount should Lew report as gross profit from this transaction?

- A. $380,000
- B. $190,000
- C. $187,000
- D. $200,000

Answer (C) is correct. *(CPA, adapted)*
REQUIRED: The amount reported as operating profit.
DISCUSSION: No sales are recorded for the products expected to be returned. Thus, sales of $380,000 (200,000 × $2 × 0.95) are recognized. A return asset also is recognized for the entity's right to recover products from customers. The return asset is measured initially at the former carrying amount of the products expected to be returned of $10,000 [(200,000 × 0.05) × $1] minus the $3,000 of expected recovery costs. A return asset is therefore recognized at $7,000 ($10,000 – $3,000). Cost of goods sold is measured at the carrying amount of the products sold of $200,000 (200,000 × $1) minus the return asset of $7,000. Accordingly, cost of goods sold is $193,000 ($200,000 – $7,000). The gross profit for this transaction is $187,000 ($380,000 – $193,000).
Answer (A) is incorrect. The amount of $380,000 is the amount of sales recognized. Answer (B) is incorrect. The amount of $190,000 ignores the expected recovery costs. Answer (D) is incorrect. The amount of $200,000 ignores the right of return.

6.2.8. Lin Co., a distributor of machinery, bought a machine from the manufacturer in November for $10,000. On December 30, Lin sold this machine to Zee Hardware for $15,000, under the following terms: 2% discount if paid within 30 days, 1% discount if paid after 30 days but within 60 days, or payable in full within 90 days if not paid within the discount periods. However, Zee had the right to return this machine to Lin if Zee was unable to resell the machine before expiration of the 90-day payment period, in which case Zee's obligation to Lin would be canceled. Based on its past experience, Lin concludes that it is probable that (1) Zee will not be able to sell the machine and (2) it will be returned. In Lin's net sales for the year ended December 31, how much should be included for the sale to Zee?

A. $0

B. $14,700

C. $14,850

D. $15,000

Answer (A) is correct. *(CPA, adapted)*
REQUIRED: The sales revenue to be recognized when a right of return exists.
DISCUSSION: Sales revenue is recognized only for the amount of consideration to which the company expects to be entitled. Accordingly, no sales are recognized for products expected to be returned. Because it is probable that Zee will return the machine, no sales revenue for the current year is recognized by Lin.

6.2.9. Net losses on firm purchase commitments to acquire goods for inventory result from a contract price that exceeds the current market price. If a firm expects that losses will occur when the purchase occurs, expected losses, if material,

A. Should be recognized in the accounts and separately disclosed as losses on the income statement of the period during which the decline in price takes place.

B. Should be recognized in the accounts and separately disclosed as net unrealized losses on the balance sheet at the end of the period during which the decline in price takes place.

C. Should be recognized in the accounts and separately disclosed as net unrealized losses on the balance sheet at the end of the period during which the contract is executed.

D. Should not be recognized in the accounts until the contract is executed and need not be separately disclosed in the financial statements.

Answer (A) is correct. *(CMA, adapted)*
REQUIRED: The accounting treatment of losses arising from a firm (noncancelable) purchase commitment not yet exercised.
DISCUSSION: A loss is accrued in the income statement on goods subject to a firm purchase commitment if the market price of these goods declines below the commitment price. This loss should be measured in the same manner as inventory losses. Disclosure of the loss is also required.
Answer (B) is incorrect. The losses should be recognized in the determination of net income. Answer (C) is incorrect. The losses should be recognized in the determination of net income during the period in which the decline in price occurs. Answer (D) is incorrect. If a loss arises out of a firm, noncancelable, and unhedged commitment, it should be recognized in the current year.

6.2.10. On January 1, Year 4, Card Corp. signed a 3-year, noncancelable purchase contract that allows Card to purchase up to 500,000 units of a computer part annually from Hart Supply Co. The price is $.10 per unit, and the contract guarantees a minimum annual purchase of 100,000 units. During Year 4, the part unexpectedly became obsolete. Card had 250,000 units of this inventory at December 31, Year 4, and believes these parts can be sold as scrap for $.02 per unit. What amount of probable loss from the purchase commitment should Card report in its Year 4 income statement?

A. $24,000

B. $20,000

C. $16,000

D. $8,000

Answer (C) is correct. *(CPA, adapted)*
REQUIRED: The amount of probable loss from the purchase commitment.
DISCUSSION: The entity must accrue a loss in the current year on goods subject to a firm purchase commitment if their market price declines below the commitment price. This loss should be measured in the same manner as inventory losses. Disclosure of the loss also is required. Consequently, given that 200,000 units must be purchased over the next 2 years for $20,000 (200,000 × $.10), and the parts can be sold as scrap for $4,000 (200,000 × $.02), the amount of probable loss for Year 4 is $16,000 ($20,000 – $4,000).
Answer (A) is incorrect. The amount of $24,000 includes the purchase commitment for the current year. Answer (B) is incorrect. The amount of $20,000 excludes the net realizable value of the parts from the calculation. Answer (D) is incorrect. The amount of $8,000 excludes the probable loss expected in the last year of the purchase commitment.

6.2.11. During Year 4, R Corp., a manufacturer of chocolate candies, contracted to purchase 100,000 pounds of cocoa beans at $1.00 per pound, with delivery to be made in the spring of Year 5. Because a record harvest is predicted for Year 5, the price per pound for cocoa beans had fallen to $.80 by December 31, Year 4. Of the following journal entries, the one that would properly reflect in Year 4 the effect of the commitment of R Corp. to purchase the 100,000 pounds of cocoa is

A. Cocoa inventory $100,000
      Accounts payable $100,000

B. Cocoa inventory $80,000
    Loss on purchase
      commitments   20,000
      Accounts payable $100,000

C. Loss on purchase
      commitments $20,000
      Accrued loss
        on purchase
        commitments $20,000

D. No entry is necessary in Year 4.

Answer (C) is correct. *(CPA, adapted)*
    REQUIRED: The journal entries to reflect the purchase commitment.
    DISCUSSION: Recognition of the loss in the income statement and accrual of a liability in Year 4 are required (assuming the purchase commitment is noncancelable). The loss on purchase commitments is an expense. Accrued loss on purchase commitments is a liability.
    Answer (A) is incorrect. The entry does not recognize a loss and improperly records an asset. Answer (B) is incorrect. The entry prematurely records the cocoa as an asset prior to acquisition. The loss on purchase commitments is an expense account. Answer (D) is incorrect. An entry is needed to recognize the loss.

6.2.12. What is the appropriate treatment for goods held on consignment?

A. The goods should be included in ending inventory of the consignor.

B. The goods should be included in ending inventory of the consignee.

C. The goods should be included in cost of goods sold of the consignee only when sold.

D. The goods should be included in cost of goods sold of the consignor when transferred to the consignee.

Answer (A) is correct. *(CPA, adapted)*
    REQUIRED: The accounting for goods held on consignment.
    DISCUSSION: A consignment sale is an arrangement between the owner of goods and a sales agent. Consigned goods are not sold but rather transferred to the agent (consignee) for possible sale. The consignor records sales only when the goods are sold to third parties by the consignee. Thus, unsold consigned goods are included in inventory at cost.
    Answer (B) is incorrect. The consignee never records the consigned goods as an asset, but it does record an asset for the amount receivable from the consignor. Answer (C) is incorrect. The goods are not an asset of the consignee, so it cannot recognize cost of goods sold. Answer (D) is incorrect. The transfer to the consignee is not a sale. Hence, the goods are included in the cost of goods sold of the consignor only when sold to a third party.

6.2.13. Southgate Co. paid the in-transit insurance premium for consignment goods shipped to Hendon Co., the consignee. In addition, Southgate advanced part of the commissions that will be due when Hendon sells the goods. Should Southgate include the in-transit insurance premium and the advanced commissions in inventory costs?

	Insurance Premiums	Advanced Commissions
A.	Yes	Yes
B.	No	No
C.	Yes	No
D.	No	Yes

Answer (C) is correct. *(CPA, adapted)*
    REQUIRED: The item(s) included in a consignor's inventory costs.
    DISCUSSION: Inventoriable costs include all costs of making the inventory ready for sale. Costs incurred by a consignor on the transfer of goods to a consignee are costs necessary to make the inventory ready for sale. Consequently, they are inventoriable. Thus, the in-transit insurance premium is inventoried. The advanced commissions constitute a receivable or prepaid expense, not an element of inventory cost.
    Answer (A) is incorrect. The advanced commissions constitute a receivable, not an element of inventory cost. Answer (B) is incorrect. The in-transit insurance premium is inventoried. Answer (D) is incorrect. The in-transit insurance premium is inventoried, but the advanced commissions constitute a receivable, not an element of inventory cost.

Questions 6.2.14 and 6.2.15 are based on the following information. Glazier Co. sells all of its glassware on a consignment basis. The consignees receive reimbursement of expenses plus a sales commission of 10% of retail value. During the current year, Glazier shipped 11,800 units with a cost of $24 per unit and a retail value of $44 per unit to the Glass Retailers. Freight paid by Glazier on these shipments totaled $26,600. Glass reported that it sold 9,500 units and incurred expenses relating to the sold units, exclusive of commissions, in the amount of $19,200. Glass remitted cash for the units sold minus commissions and expenses.

6.2.14. The cash collected during the year by Glazier from Glass is

A. $208,800

B. $357,000

C. $186,000

D. $398,800

Answer (B) is correct. *(CMA, adapted)*
REQUIRED: The cash collected by the consignor.
DISCUSSION: The consignor will receive cash equal to the sales price of the units sold, minus expenses of $19,200, minus a 10% sales commission. The units sold for $418,000 (9,500 units × $44). Cash collected equaled $357,000 [$418,000 − ($418,000 × 10%) − $19,200].
Answer (A) is incorrect. The amount of $208,800 is based on the cost of $24 per unit, not the retail selling price, and ignores the sales commissions. Answer (C) is incorrect. The amount of $186,000 is based on the cost of $24 per unit, not the retail selling price of $44. Answer (D) is incorrect. The amount of $398,800 omits the 10% sales commission.

6.2.15. Glazier's profit before taxes from consignment sales made by Glass for the current year is

A. $129,000

B. $138,280

C. $102,400

D. $107,585

Answer (D) is correct. *(CMA, adapted)*
REQUIRED: The consignor's profit before taxes.
DISCUSSION: The consignor will receive cash equal to the sales price of the units sold, minus expenses of $19,200, minus a 10% sales commission. The units sold for $418,000 (9,500 units × $44). Cash collected equaled $357,000 [$418,000 − ($418,000 × 10%) − $19,200]. Freight costs attributable to the units sold were $21,415 [(9,500 units sold ÷ 11,800 units consigned) × $26,600]. Thus, pretax profit is $107,585 [$357,000 − $21,415 freight costs − (9,500 units × $24 unit cost)].
Answer (A) is incorrect. The amount of $129,000 ignores the freight costs of $26,600. Answer (B) is incorrect. The amount of $138,280 assumes 11,800 units were sold. Answer (C) is incorrect. The amount of $102,400 expenses all of the freight costs (inventoriable costs).

6.2.16. In accounting for sales on consignment, sales revenue and the related cost of goods sold should be recognized by the

A. Consignor when the goods are shipped to the consignee.

B. Consignee when the goods are shipped to the third party.

C. Consignor when notification is received that the consignee has sold the goods.

D. Consignee when cash is received from the customer.

Answer (C) is correct. *(CIA, adapted)*
REQUIRED: The basis for recognition of sales revenue and related cost of goods sold for goods on consignment.
DISCUSSION: Under a consignment sales arrangement, the consignor ships merchandise to the consignee, who acts as agent for the consignor in selling the goods. The goods are in the physical possession of the consignee but remain the property of the consignor and are included in the consignor's inventory count. Sales revenue and the related cost of goods sold from these consigned goods should be recognized by the consignor only when the merchandise is sold and delivered to the ultimate customer. Accordingly, recognition occurs when notification is received that the consignee has sold the goods.
Answer (A) is incorrect. At the date of shipment to the consignee, the goods are still the property of the consignor. Answer (B) is incorrect. The consignee does not recognize sales revenue or cost of goods sold for these goods. The consignee recognizes commission revenue only. Answer (D) is incorrect. The consignee does not recognize sales revenue or cost of goods sold for these goods. The consignee recognizes commission revenue only when the goods are sold and delivered to the third party.

6.2.17. Jel Co., a consignee, paid the freight costs for goods shipped from Dale Co., a consignor. These freight costs are to be deducted from Jel's payment to Dale when the consignment goods are sold. Until Jel sells the goods, the freight costs should be included in Jel's

A. Cost of goods sold.

B. Freight-out costs.

C. Selling expenses.

D. Accounts receivable.

Answer (D) is correct. *(CPA, adapted)*
REQUIRED: The consignee's classification of freight costs paid by the consignee on behalf of the consignor.
DISCUSSION: The consignee should debit consignment-in for the freight costs. Consignment-in is a receivable/payable account used by consignees. It represents the amount payable to the consignor if it has a credit balance. If it has a debit balance, it reflects the amount receivable from the consignor. Before consigned goods are sold, expenditures chargeable to the consignor are recorded in the consignment-in account as a receivable. After the consigned goods are sold, the consignee's net liability to the consignor is reflected in the account.

6.2.18. Stone Co. had the following consignment transactions during December:

Inventory shipped on consignment to Beta Co.	$18,000
Freight paid by Stone	900
Inventory received on consignment from Alpha Co.	12,000
Freight paid by Alpha	500

No sales of consigned goods were made through December 31. Stone's December 31 balance sheet should include consigned inventory at

A. $12,000

B. $12,500

C. $18,000

D. $18,900

Answer (D) is correct. *(CPA, adapted)*
REQUIRED: The recognition of inventory for consignment sales.
DISCUSSION: In a consignment, the consignor ships merchandise to the consignee, who acts as agent for the consignor in selling the goods. The goods are in the physical possession of the consignee but remain the physical property of the consignor and are included in the consignor's inventory. Costs incurred by a consignor on the transfer of goods to a consignee are inventoriable. Thus, Stone's inventory account should include $18,900 equal to the $18,000 inventory shipped to Beta on consignment and the $900 associated freight charges.
Answer (A) is incorrect. The amount of $12,000 is the inventory received from Alpha, which is not the property of Stone. Answer (B) is incorrect. The amount of $12,500 is the inventory received from Alpha and the associated freight charges. Answer (C) is incorrect. The amount of $18,000 does not include the $900 freight cost.

6.2.19. On October 1, the Ajax Company consigned 100 television sets to M&R Retailers, Inc. Each television set had a cost of $150. Freight on the shipment was paid by Ajax in the amount of $200. On December 1, M&R submitted an "account sales" stating that it had sold 60 sets, and it remitted the $12,840 balance due. The remittance was net of the following deductions from the sales price of the televisions sold:

Commission	20% of sales price
Advertising	$500
Delivery and installation charges	$100

What was the total sales price of the television sets sold by M&R?

A. $13,440

B. $15,000

C. $16,800

D. $17,000

Answer (C) is correct. *(CPA, adapted)*
REQUIRED: The total sales price of the consigned goods sold during the period.
DISCUSSION: Because the television sets are on consignment from Ajax, M&R should make no accounting entry to record the receipt of the sets. The inventory should remain on the books of Ajax. A consignment-in account is used by M&R to record reimbursable expenses in connection with the consignment and sales of the consigned goods. Assuming the advertising and delivery and installation charges are expenses of Ajax, they are debits to consignment-in (reimbursable cash outlays). Moreover, the commission of 20% of the sales price due M&R should be debited to the account. The calculation of sales price is given below:

Consignment-In			
Adv.	$ 500	X	Sales
Del. & inst.	100		
Commission	.2X		
Remit to Ajax	$12,840		

$$\$500 + \$100 + .2X + \$12,840 = X$$
$$\$13,440 = X - .2X$$
$$\$13,440 = .8X$$
$$\$16,800 = X$$

Answer (A) is incorrect. The total sales price if the amount of commission is excluded is $13,440. Answer (B) is incorrect. The amount of consigned television sets multiplied by the cost per set (100 × $150) is $15,000. Answer (D) is incorrect. The total sales price plus the freight costs paid by Ajax ($16,800 + $200) is $17,000.

6.2.20. The following information was derived from the current year accounting records of Clem Co.:

	Clem's Central Warehouse	Clem's Goods Held By Consignees
Beginning inventory	$110,000	$12,000
Purchases	480,000	60,000
Freight-in	10,000	
Transportation to consignees		5,000
Freight-out	30,000	8,000
Ending inventory	145,000	20,000

Clem's cost of sales was

A. $455,000

B. $485,000

C. $507,000

D. $512,000

Answer (D) is correct. *(Publisher, adapted)*
    REQUIRED: The cost of sales.
    DISCUSSION: Cost of sales is equal to beginning inventory, plus purchases, plus additional costs (such as freight-in and transportation to consignees) necessary to prepare the inventory for sale, minus ending inventory. Cost of sales for inventory in the central warehouse and for inventory held by consignees are calculated below:

	Central Warehouse Inventory	Consigned Inventory
Beginning inventory	$110,000	$12,000
Purchases	480,000	60,000
Freight-in	10,000	
Transportation to consignees		5,000
Cost of sales	(455,000)	(57,000)
Ending inventory	$145,000	$20,000

Hence, total cost of sales equals $512,000 ($455,000 + $57,000). Freight-out is a selling cost. It is not included in the determination of cost of sales.
    Answer (A) is incorrect. The amount of $455,000 is the cost of sales for items held in the central warehouse. Answer (B) is incorrect. The amount of $485,000 omits transportation to consignees, the beginning consigned inventory, and freight-in. Answer (C) is incorrect. The amount of $507,000 omits transportation to consignees.

6.2.21. On December 1, Alt Department Store received 505 sweaters on consignment from Todd. Todd's cost for the sweaters was $80 each, and they were priced to sell at $100. Alt's commission on consigned goods is 10%. At December 31, 5 sweaters remained. In its December 31 balance sheet, what amount should Alt report as payable for consigned goods?

A. $49,000

B. $45,400

C. $45,000

D. $40,400

Answer (C) is correct. *(CPA, adapted)*
    REQUIRED: The payable reported by the consignee for consigned goods.
    DISCUSSION: Consignment-in is a receivable/payable account used by consignees. It is the amount payable to the consignor if it has a credit balance. The amount of the payable equals total sales minus 10% commission on the goods sold, or $45,000 [(500 × $100) sales – (500 × $100 × 10%)].
    Answer (A) is incorrect. The amount of $49,000 equals sales minus 10% of total gross margin [500 × ($100 – $80) = $10,000]. Answer (B) is incorrect. The amount of $45,400 equals the cost of the 505 sweaters, plus the markup on the sweaters sold, minus commissions. Answer (D) is incorrect. The amount of $40,400 is the cost of 505 sweaters.

6.2.22. Mare Co.'s December 31 balance sheet reported the following current assets:

Cash	$ 70,000
Accounts receivable	120,000
Inventories	60,000
Total	$250,000

An analysis of the accounts disclosed that accounts receivable consisted of the following:

Trade accounts	$ 96,000
Allowance for uncollectible accounts	(2,000)
Selling price of Mare's unsold goods out on consignment, at 130% of cost, not included in Mare's ending inventory	26,000
Total	$120,000

At December 31, the total of Mare's current assets is

A. $224,000

B. $230,000

C. $244,000

D. $270,000

Answer (C) is correct. *(CPA, adapted)*
    REQUIRED: The amount of total current assets to be reported at year-end.
    DISCUSSION: Under a consignment sales agreement, the goods are in the physical possession of the consignee but remain the property of the consignor and are included in the consignor's inventory. Thus, unsold consigned goods should be included in inventory at cost ($26,000 ÷ 130% = $20,000), not in receivables at their sale price. Current assets should therefore be $244,000 ($70,000 cash + $94,000 net receivables + $80,000 inventory).
    Answer (A) is incorrect. The amount of $224,000 does not include the cost of the consigned goods in inventory. Answer (B) is incorrect. The amount of $230,000 results from subtracting the cost of the consigned goods from the total reported current assets. Answer (D) is incorrect. The amount of $270,000 results from adding the cost of the consigned goods to the total reported current assets.

6.3 Cost Flow Methods -- FIFO, LIFO, Weighted Average

Questions 6.3.1 through 6.3.5 are based on the following information. Toulouse Co. began the month of November with 150 baubles on hand at a cost of $4.00 each. These baubles sell for $7.00 each. The following schedule presents the sales and purchases of this item during the month of November.

Date of Transaction	Purchases		Units Sold
	Quantity Received	Unit Cost	
November 5			100
November 7	200	$4.20	
November 9			150
November 11	200	4.40	
November 17			220
November 22	250	4.80	
November 29			100

6.3.1. If Toulouse uses FIFO inventory pricing, the inventory on November 30 will be

A. $936

B. $1,012

C. $1,046

D. $1,104

Answer (D) is correct. *(CMA, adapted)*
REQUIRED: The value of the ending inventory using the FIFO method of inventory costing.
DISCUSSION: Under FIFO, the ending inventory consists of the most recent inventory purchased. The beginning inventory included 150 units and purchases totaled 650 units, a total of 800 units. Sales equaled 570 units (100 + 150 + 220 + 100). Thus, ending inventory was 230 units (800 – 570). Under FIFO, these units are valued at the cost of the most recent 230 units purchased, or $4.80. Ending inventory is therefore $1,104 (230 × $4.80).
Answer (A) is incorrect. The amount of $936 is based on periodic LIFO. Answer (B) is incorrect. The amount of $1,012 is based on the weighted-average unit cost of $4.40, not $4.80. Answer (C) is incorrect. The amount of $1,046 is the ending inventory under perpetual LIFO.

6.3.2. If Toulouse uses perpetual moving-average inventory pricing, the sale of 220 items on November 17 will be recorded at a unit cost of

A. $4.00

B. $4.16

C. $4.20

D. $4.32

Answer (D) is correct. *(CMA, adapted)*
REQUIRED: The unit cost of the items sold on November 17 under the perpetual moving-average method.
DISCUSSION: The beginning inventory consisted of 150 units at $4.00 each. Following the November 5 sale, the inventory valuation was $200 (50 units × $4). The November 7 purchase added 200 units at $4.20, after which the moving average unit cost was $4.16 {[$200 + (200 units × $4.20)] ÷ (50 units + 200 units)}. The November 9 sale of 150 units left 100 units at $4.16. Adding $416 (100 units × $4.16) to the $880 purchase on November 11 brought the total inventory to 300 units with a total cost of $1,296, or $4.32 each. Thus, $4.32 was the unit cost of items sold on November 17.
Answer (A) is incorrect. The amount of $4.00 was the cost of the beginning inventory. Answer (B) is incorrect. The amount of $4.16 was the unit cost of the items sold on November 9. Answer (C) is incorrect. The amount of $4.20 would have been the cost if the perpetual LIFO method had been used for the November 9 sale.

6.3.3. If Toulouse uses weighted-average inventory pricing, the gross profit for November will be

A. $1,046

B. $1,482

C. $1,516

D. $1,528

Answer (B) is correct. *(CMA, adapted)*
REQUIRED: The gross profit if the weighted-average method is used.
DISCUSSION: The total goods available for sale is determined as follows:

Beginning inventory	150 × $4.00 =	$ 600.00
Nov. 7 purchase	200 × $4.20 =	840.00
Nov. 11 purchase	200 × $4.40 =	880.00
Nov. 22 purchase	250 × $4.80 =	1,200.00
Total available	800	$3,520.00

The weighted-average unit cost is $4.40 ($3,520 ÷ 800 units available). The cost of goods sold and total sales are therefore $2,508 (570 units sold × $4.40) and $3,990 (570 units × $7), respectively. Consequently, gross profit is $1,482 ($3,990 − $2,508).
    Answer (A) is incorrect. The amount of $1,046 is the ending inventory under perpetual LIFO. Answer (C) is incorrect. The amount of $1,516 is based on perpetual LIFO. Answer (D) is incorrect. The amount of $1,528 is based on the moving-average method.

6.3.4. If Toulouse uses periodic LIFO inventory pricing, the cost of goods sold for November will be

A. $2,416

B. $2,444

C. $2,474

D. $2,584

Answer (D) is correct. *(CMA, adapted)*
REQUIRED: The cost of goods sold using periodic LIFO.
DISCUSSION: The goods available for sale are as follows:

Beginning inventory	150 × $4.00 =	$ 600.00
Nov. 7 purchase	200 × $4.20 =	840.00
Nov. 11 purchase	200 × $4.40 =	880.00
Nov. 22 purchase	250 × $4.80 =	1,200.00
Total available	800	$3,520.00

The ending inventory consists of 230 units. Under periodic LIFO, these are costed at the prices paid for the earliest 230 units purchased, or 150 units at $4.00 and 80 units at $4.20, a total of $936. Hence, cost of goods sold is $2,584 ($3,520 goods available − $936 EI).
    Answer (A) is incorrect. The amount of $2,416 is based on the FIFO method. Answer (B) is incorrect. The amount of $2,444 is based on the moving-average method. Answer (C) is incorrect. The amount of $2,474 is based on perpetual LIFO.

6.3.5. If Toulouse uses perpetual LIFO inventory pricing, the inventory at November 30 will be

A. $936

B. $1,012

C. $1,046

D. $1,076

Answer (C) is correct. *(CMA, adapted)*
REQUIRED: The value of the inventory.
DISCUSSION: Under perpetual LIFO, the inventory valuation is recalculated as follows after every purchase and sale. The 230 units in ending inventory consist of 150 units at $4.80 each, 30 units at $4.20 each, and 50 units from the beginning inventory at $4.00 each.

Date	Receipts	Sales	Ending Inventory
11-1	150 × $4.00 = $600		$ 600.00
11-5		100 × $4.00 = $400	200.00
11-7	200 × $4.20 = $840		1,040.00
11-9		150 × $4.20 = $630	410.00
11-11	200 × $4.40 = $880		1,290.00
11-17		200 × $4.40 = $880	
		20 × $4.20 = $84	326.00
11-22	250 × $4.80 = $1,200		1,526.00
11-29		100 × $4.80 = $480	1,046.00

Answer (A) is incorrect. The amount of $936 is based on periodic LIFO. Answer (B) is incorrect. The amount of $1,012 is based on the weighted-average method. Answer (D) is incorrect. The amount of $1,076 is based on the moving-average method.

6.3.6. The weighted average for the year inventory cost flow method is applicable to which of the following inventory systems?

	Periodic	Perpetual
A.	Yes	Yes
B.	Yes	No
C.	No	Yes
D.	No	No

Answer (B) is correct. *(CPA, adapted)*
REQUIRED: The applicability of the weighted-average cost flow method to periodic and perpetual inventory systems.
DISCUSSION: The weighted-average method determines an average cost only once (at the end of the period) and is therefore applicable only to a periodic system. In contrast, the moving-average method requires determination of a new weighted-average cost after each purchase and thus applies only to a perpetual system.
    Answer (A) is incorrect. The weighted-average method does not apply to the perpetual inventory system. Answer (C) is incorrect. The weighted-average method applies to the periodic inventory system. The moving-average method applies to a perpetual system. Answer (D) is incorrect. The weighted average applies to the periodic inventory system.

6.3.7. Assuming constant inventory quantities, which of the following inventory-costing methods will produce a lower inventory turnover ratio in an inflationary economy?

A. FIFO (first-in, first-out).

B. LIFO (last-in, first-out).

C. Moving average.

D. Weighted average.

Answer (A) is correct. *(CPA, adapted)*
REQUIRED: The inventory costing method producing a lower inventory turnover ratio in an inflationary economy.
DISCUSSION: The inventory turnover ratio equals cost of goods sold divided by the average of beginning and ending inventory. Under FIFO, ending inventory is assumed to contain the most recently purchased items, and cost of goods sold is assumed to contain the costs of the earliest purchased items. Under LIFO, the opposite assumptions are made. In an inflationary economy, costs are increasing. Thus, FIFO cost of goods sold is lower, and FIFO ending or average inventory is higher than under LIFO. The inventory methods based on average costs produce results that lie between those of FIFO and LIFO. Accordingly, inventory turnover is lowest under FIFO because the numerator is lower and the denominator is higher than under other methods.
    Answer (B) is incorrect. Use of LIFO results in the highest inventory turnover (highest COGS, lowest inventory). Answer (C) is incorrect. The moving average inventory costing method results in an inventory turnover ratio between those calculated using FIFO and LIFO. Answer (D) is incorrect. The weighted average inventory costing method results in an inventory turnover ratio between those calculated using FIFO and LIFO.

6.3.8. Sackett Corporation had a beginning inventory of 10,000 units, which were purchased in the prior year as follows:

	Units	Unit Price
September	4,000	$2.00
October	4,000	$2.10
December	2,000	$2.30

In the current year, Sackett purchases an additional 12,000 units (7,000 in June at $2.50 and 5,000 in November at $2.70) and sells 16,000 units. Using the FIFO method, what is Sackett's ending inventory?

A. $12,200 (4,000 @ $2.00 and 2,000 @ $2.10)

B. $13,000 (4,000 @ $2.10 and 2,000 @ $2.30)

C. $15,600 (6,000 @ $2.60 – average of $2.50 and $2.70)

D. $16,000 (5,000 @ $2.70 and 1,000 @ $2.50)

Answer (D) is correct. *(CPA, adapted)*
REQUIRED: The ending inventory using the FIFO method.
DISCUSSION: Under FIFO, the first goods purchased are assumed to be the first sold. Using FIFO, all of the 10,000 units of inventory in beginning inventory were sold and 6,000 (16,000 sold – 10,000 beginning inventory) of the units purchased in June for $2.50 each were sold. This leaves in ending inventory 1,000 units purchased in June for $2.50 each and all 5,000 units purchased in November for $2.70 each.
    Answer (A) is incorrect. This is Sackett's ending inventory applying the LIFO method. Answer (B) is incorrect. This answer assumes all the inventory purchased in the current year is sold before beginning inventory and that FIFO is then applied to the units in beginning inventory. Answer (C) is incorrect. This answer assumes that the average price paid for the last two purchases is averaged and applied to the remaining units in inventory.

6.3.9. The LIFO inventory cost flow method may be applied to which of the following inventory systems?

	Periodic	Perpetual
A.	No	No
B.	No	Yes
C.	Yes	Yes
D.	Yes	No

Answer (C) is correct. *(CPA, adapted)*
REQUIRED: The applicability of LIFO to periodic and perpetual inventory systems.
DISCUSSION: In a periodic system, a purchases account is used, and the beginning inventory remains unchanged during the accounting period. Cost of goods sold is determined at year-end. It is the difference between the goods available for sale (beginning inventory + purchases) and ending inventory.
In a perpetual system, purchases are directly recorded in the inventory account. Cost of goods sold is determined as the goods are sold. LIFO may be applied to both a periodic and a perpetual system, but the amount of cost of goods sold may vary with the system chosen.
Answer (A) is incorrect. LIFO may be used under both a periodic and a perpetual inventory system. Answer (B) is incorrect. LIFO may be used under a periodic inventory system. Answer (D) is incorrect. LIFO may be used under a perpetual inventory system.

6.3.10. The operations of a firm may be viewed as a continual series of transactions or as a series of separate ventures. The inventory cost flow method that views a firm as a series of separate ventures is

A. First-in, first-out.

B. Last-in, first-out.

C. Weighted average.

D. Specific identification.

Answer (D) is correct. *(CMA, adapted)*
REQUIRED: The inventory cost flow assumption that views a firm as a series of separate ventures.
DISCUSSION: When specific inventory is clearly identified from the time of purchase through the time of sale and is costed on that basis, the firm's operations may be viewed as a series of separate ventures or transactions. Much business activity, however, involves goods whose identity is lost between the time of acquisition and the time of sale. Moreover, if items of inventory are interchangeable, the use of specific identification may not result in the most useful financial information. For these reasons, other inventory cost flow assumptions essentially view the firm as a continual series of transactions.
Answer (A) is incorrect. FIFO views the firm's activities as a continual series of transactions. Answer (B) is incorrect. LIFO views the firm's activities as a continual series of transactions. Answer (C) is incorrect. Weighted average views the firm's activities as a continual series of transactions.

6.3.11. During periods of rising prices, a perpetual inventory system would result in the same dollar amount of ending inventory as a periodic inventory system under which of the following inventory cost flow methods?

	FIFO	LIFO
A.	Yes	No
B.	Yes	Yes
C.	No	Yes
D.	No	No

Answer (A) is correct. *(CPA, adapted)*
REQUIRED: The effect of perpetual and periodic inventory systems on the dollar amount of ending inventory.
DISCUSSION: Under a FIFO cost flow, ending inventory and cost of goods sold are the same regardless of whether a perpetual or periodic system is used. Under a LIFO cost flow, on the other hand, a perpetual inventory system will generate dollar amounts different from those of a periodic inventory system. During a time of rising prices, goods sold and ending inventory will consist of units bearing different costs. The periodic system determines the cost of sales only at year end. The perpetual system determines cost of sales as the sale takes place. Thus, the perpetual system assumes that layers of inventory may be liquidated during a year even though inventory quantities are restored by later purchases. The periodic system does not make this assumption.
Answer (B) is incorrect. FIFO periodic and FIFO perpetual do not produce different ending inventory valuations. Answer (C) is incorrect. LIFO periodic and LIFO perpetual produce different ending inventory valuations. FIFO periodic and FIFO perpetual do not. Answer (D) is incorrect. LIFO periodic and LIFO perpetual produce different ending inventory valuations.

6.3.12. A company had 2,000 units of opening inventory that cost $20 per unit. On May 1, 2,000 units were purchased at a cost of $22 each, and on September 1, another 2,000 units were purchased at a cost of $24 each. If 4,000 units were sold during the year, the company will report cost of goods sold of <List A> if the <List B> method of inventory valuation is used.

	List A	List B
A.	$88,000	LIFO
B.	$92,000	Weighted-average
C.	$84,000	FIFO
D.	$88,000	FIFO

Answer (C) is correct. *(CIA, adapted)*
REQUIRED: The proper match of cost of goods sold and inventory cost flow assumption.
DISCUSSION: Under FIFO, the first items purchased are presumed to be the first sold. Furthermore, under FIFO, perpetual and periodic systems produce the same ending inventory and cost of goods sold. If 6,000 units were available and 4,000 units were sold, FIFO cost of goods sold equals $84,000 [(2,000 × $20) BI + (2,000 × $22) May 1 purchase].
Answer (A) is incorrect. Cost of goods sold is $88,000 under the weighted-average method. Under LIFO (assuming a periodic system), cost of goods sold is $92,000 ($48,000 + $44,000). The 2,000 most recently purchased units are presumed to have been sold. Answer (B) is incorrect. The weighted-average unit cost of all items available for sale is $22 [($40,000 + $44,000 + $48,000) ÷ 6,000]. Given that 4,000 units were sold, cost of goods sold is $88,000 (4,000 × $22) under this method. Answer (D) is incorrect. FIFO cost of goods sold is $84,000. Under the weighted-average method, cost of goods sold is $88,000.

6.3.13. Generally, which inventory costing method most closely approximates the current cost for each of the following?

	Cost of Goods Sold	Ending Inventory
A.	LIFO	FIFO
B.	LIFO	LIFO
C.	FIFO	FIFO
D.	FIFO	LIFO

Answer (A) is correct. *(CPA, adapted)*
REQUIRED: The appropriate inventory costing method.
DISCUSSION: The LIFO basis assumes that the most recently purchased items are the first to be sold. Thus, LIFO is a better approximation of current cost of goods sold than FIFO. Assuming that turnover is rapid and material amounts of depreciation are not allocated to inventory, LIFO cost of goods sold may be an acceptable alternative to cost of goods sold measured at current cost. However, the effect of any LIFO inventory liquidations (decreases in earlier years' LIFO layers) must be excluded. Nevertheless, the FIFO basis more closely approximates the current cost of ending inventory because it assumes the most recent purchases are the last to be sold.
Answer (B) is incorrect. Current cost of ending inventory is most closely approximated by FIFO. Answer (C) is incorrect. Current cost of goods sold is most closely approximated by LIFO. Answer (D) is incorrect. Current cost of goods sold and current cost of ending inventory are most closely approximated by LIFO and FIFO, respectively.

6.3.14. The acquisition cost of a heavily used raw material changes frequently. The carrying amount of the inventory of this material at year end will be the same if perpetual records are kept as it would be under a periodic inventory method only if the carrying amount is computed under the

A. Weighted-average method.

B. First-in, first-out method.

C. Last-in, first-out method.

D. Base-stock method.

Answer (B) is correct. *(CPA, adapted)*
REQUIRED: The cost flow assumption giving the same year-end carrying amount under both perpetual and periodic inventory systems.
DISCUSSION: Under FIFO, the oldest goods are assumed to have been sold first, and it would not matter whether the cost of goods sold was determined at the point of sale (perpetual) or at year end (periodic).
Answer (A) is incorrect. Under the weighted-average method, different goods are assumed to be sold if the determination is made at the time of sale (perpetual) rather than at year end (periodic). Answer (C) is incorrect. Under the last-in, first-out method, different goods are assumed to be sold if the determination is made at the time of sale (perpetual) rather than at year end (periodic). Answer (D) is incorrect. The base-stock method is not acceptable under GAAP or for tax purposes. The base-stock method assumes that a minimum amount of inventory is always required. Accordingly, the inventory base or minimum amount is considered a long-term investment to be recorded at its original cost. Last-in, first-out (LIFO) has the same effect if base levels of inventory are not sold.

6.3.15. Munich Co. uses the average-cost inventory method for internal reporting purposes and LIFO for financial statement and income tax reporting. At December 31, the inventory was $750,000 using average cost and $640,000 using LIFO. The unadjusted credit balance in the LIFO reserve account on the same date was $70,000. What adjusting entry should Munich record to adjust from average cost to LIFO at December 31?

Cost of Goods Sold	Debit	Credit
A. Cost of goods sold	$110,000	
Inventory		$110,000
B. Cost of goods sold	$110,000	
LIFO reserve		$110,000
C. Cost of goods sold	$40,000	
Inventory		$40,000
D. Cost of goods sold	$40,000	
LIFO reserve		$40,000

Answer (D) is correct. *(CPA, adapted)*
REQUIRED: The journal entry to adjust from average cost to LIFO.
DISCUSSION: The LIFO reserve account is an allowance that adjusts the inventory balance stated according to the method used for internal reporting purposes to the LIFO amount appropriate for external reporting. If the LIFO effect is $110,000 ($750,000 average cost – $640,000 LIFO cost) and the account has a $70,000 credit balance, it must be credited for $40,000, with a corresponding debit to cost of goods sold.
Answer (A) is incorrect. The balance in the reserve account should equal $110,000, and inventory should not be adjusted. Answer (B) is incorrect. The balance in the reserve account should be $110,000. Answer (C) is incorrect. Inventory should not be adjusted.

6.3.16. Which of the following is not valid as it applies to inventory costing methods?

A. If inventory quantities are to be maintained, part of the earnings must be invested (plowed back) in inventories when FIFO is used during a period of rising prices.

B. LIFO tends to smooth out the net income pattern since it matches current cost of goods sold with current revenue when inventories remain at constant quantities.

C. When a firm using the LIFO method fails to maintain its usual inventory position (reduces stock on hand below customary levels), there may be a matching of old costs with current revenue.

D. The use of FIFO permits some control by management over the amount of net income for a period through controlled purchases, which is not true with LIFO.

Answer (D) is correct. *(CPA, adapted)*
REQUIRED: The invalid statement concerning inventory valuation.
DISCUSSION: Under LIFO, the most recent purchases are included in cost of goods sold. Management could affect net income with an end-of-period purchase that would immediately alter cost of goods sold. A last-minute FIFO purchase included in the ending inventory would have no such effect.
Answer (A) is incorrect. Maintenance of inventory quantities results in an increased dollar investment in inventory when FIFO is used during inflationary times. Answer (B) is incorrect. LIFO smooths income in a period of rising prices. The inflated current costs are matched with current sales prices. Answer (C) is incorrect. LIFO results in matching old, lower costs with current revenues when inventory is liquidated. If sales exceed purchases, a firm liquidates earlier, lower-priced LIFO layers.

6.3.17. The Hastings Company began operations on January 1, Year 1, and uses the FIFO method in costing its raw material inventory. Management is contemplating a change to the LIFO method and is interested in determining what effect such a change will have on net income. Accordingly, the following information has been developed:

Final Inventory	Year 1	Year 2
FIFO	$240,000	$270,000
LIFO	200,000	210,000
Net Income per FIFO	$120,000	$170,000

Based upon the above information, a change to the LIFO method in Year 2 results in net income for Year 2 of

A. $110,000

B. $150,000

C. $170,000

D. $230,000

Answer (B) is correct. *(CPA, adapted)*
REQUIRED: The second-year net income after a change from FIFO to LIFO in the second year of operations.
DISCUSSION: A change in accounting principle requires retrospective application. All periods reported must be individually adjusted for the period specific effects of applying the new principle. The difference in income in the second year is equal to the $20,000 difference between the FIFO inventory change and the LIFO inventory change (FIFO: $270,000 – $240,000 = $30,000 change; LIFO: $210,000 – $200,000 = $10,000 change; $30,000 – $10,000 = $20,000 difference). The $170,000 FIFO net income will decrease by $20,000. Net LIFO income will therefore be $150,000 ($170,000 – $20,000).
Answer (A) is incorrect. The amount of $110,000 incorrectly subtracts the difference from Year 1 from the net income under LIFO for Year 2. Answer (C) is incorrect. The amount of $170,000 is the income for Year 2 under FIFO. Answer (D) is incorrect. The amount of $230,000 incorrectly adds the cumulative difference between LIFO and FIFO to FIFO net income instead of subtracting the difference from FIFO net income.

6.4 Cost Flow Methods -- Dollar-Value LIFO

6.4.1. The double-extension method and the link-chain method are two variations of which of the following inventory cost flow methods?

    A.   Moving average.

    B.   FIFO.

    C.   Dollar-value LIFO.

    D.   Conventional (lower-of-cost-or-market) retail.

Answer (C) is correct. *(CPA, adapted)*
    REQUIRED: The inventory cost flow method of which the double-extension method and the link-chain method are variations.
    DISCUSSION: The double-extension method and the link-chain method are variations of dollar-value LIFO. In dollar-value LIFO, similar (rather than identical) dollar-value pools of inventory are accumulated. Each layer of inventory is stated in dollar-value terms based on the price index for the relevant year. The link-chain version uses beginning-of-the-year costs as the denominator of the index for each year after the base year. Each successive year's index is multiplied by the cumulative index. The double-extension version uses the base-year prices in the annual index. The two methods are mutually exclusive.
    Answer (A) is incorrect. The moving-average method calculates a new weighted-average unit inventory cost after each purchase. Answer (B) is incorrect. First-in, first-out (FIFO) is a basic inventory flow assumption. Answer (D) is incorrect. The lower-of-average-cost-or-market retail method includes net markups but not net markdowns in the determination of goods available for sale. The approximate LACM (conventional) retail method is a weighted-average method.

6.4.2. Estimates of price-level changes for specific inventories are required for which of the following inventory methods?

    A.   Conventional retail.

    B.   Dollar-value LIFO.

    C.   Weighted-average cost.

    D.   Average cost retail.

Answer (B) is correct. *(CPA, adapted)*
    REQUIRED: The inventory method for which estimates of price-level changes for specific inventories are required.
    DISCUSSION: Dollar-value LIFO accumulates inventoriable costs of similar (not identical) items. These items should be similar in the sense of being interchangeable, having similar uses, belonging to the same product line, or constituting the raw materials for a given product. Dollar value LIFO determines changes in ending inventory in terms of dollars of constant purchasing power rather than units of physical inventory. This calculation uses a specific price index for each year.
    Answer (A) is incorrect. The conventional retail method calculates ending inventory at retail and then adjusts it to cost by applying a cost-retail ratio. Answer (C) is incorrect. The weighted-average method determines an average cost that is not adjusted for general price-level changes. Answer (D) is incorrect. The average cost retail method calculates ending inventory at retail and then adjusts it to cost by applying a cost-retail ratio.

6.4.3. Which of the following inventory cost flow methods could use dollar-value pools?

    A.   Conventional (lower-of-cost-or-market) retail.

    B.   Weighted average.

    C.   FIFO.

    D.   LIFO.

Answer (D) is correct. *(CPA, adapted)*
    REQUIRED: The cost flow assumption using dollar-value pools.
    DISCUSSION: A modification of LIFO may be employed to account for dollar-value pools of similar items rather than identical items. This method overcomes a difficulty with traditional LIFO: Some items may be liquidated below the LIFO base while the value of similar items may increase. Dollar-value LIFO prevents the loss of the advantages of LIFO when the mixture of similar items changes.
    Answer (A) is incorrect. The lower-of-average-cost-or-market retail method includes net markups but not net markdowns in the determination of goods available for sale. The approximate LACM (conventional) retail method is a weighted-average method. The dollar-value pool approach has been used only with LIFO. Answer (B) is incorrect. The weighted-average method determines an average unit inventory cost only at period-end. The dollar-value pool approach has been used only with LIFO. Answer (C) is incorrect. First-in, first-out (FIFO) is a basic inventory flow assumption. The dollar-value pool approach has been used only with LIFO.

6.4.4. When the double-extension approach to the dollar-value LIFO inventory method is used, the inventory layer added in the current year is multiplied by an index number. Which of the following correctly states how components are used in the calculation of this index number?

A. In the numerator, the average of the ending inventory at base-year cost and at current-year cost.

B. In the numerator, the ending inventory at current-year cost and in the denominator, the ending inventory at base-year cost.

C. In the numerator, the ending inventory at base-year cost and in the denominator, the ending inventory at current-year cost.

D. In the denominator, the average of the ending inventory at base-year cost and at current-year cost.

Answer (B) is correct. *(CPA, adapted)*
   REQUIRED: The true statement of how components are used in the calculation of an index number under the double-extension method.
   DISCUSSION: An entity applying dollar-value LIFO may choose to calculate price indexes rather than use externally determined numbers. The double-extension approach states ending inventory at current-year cost and then divides that amount by the base-year cost to determine the index for the current year. Hence, this method extends the quantity of the inventory at both current-year and base-year unit cost. The indexes determined in this way are then multiplied by the appropriate inventory layers stated at base-year cost.
   Answer (A) is incorrect. The numerator is the current-year cost. Answer (C) is incorrect. The numerator is the current-year cost and the denominator is the base-year cost. Answer (D) is incorrect. The denominator is the base-year cost.

6.4.5. The dollar-value LIFO inventory cost flow method involves computations based on

	Inventory Pools of Similar Items	A Specific Price Index for Each Year
A.	No	Yes
B.	No	No
C.	Yes	No
D.	Yes	Yes

Answer (D) is correct. *(CPA, adapted)*
   REQUIRED: The computations required for dollar-value LIFO inventory.
   DISCUSSION: Dollar-value LIFO accumulates inventoriable costs of similar (not identical) items. These items should be similar in the sense of being interchangeable, having similar uses, belonging to the same product line, or constituting the raw materials for a given product. Dollar-value LIFO determines changes in ending inventory in terms of dollars of constant purchasing power rather than units of physical inventory. This calculation uses a specific price index for each year. The ending inventory is deflated by the current-year index to arrive at base-year cost. This amount is then compared to the beginning inventory stated at base-year cost to determine what layers are to be in the ending inventory. Each layer is then inflated by the relevant price index for the year it was created to determine the aggregate ending inventory valuation.
   Answer (A) is incorrect. Dollar-value LIFO uses inventory pools of similar items. Answer (B) is incorrect. Dollar-value LIFO uses inventory pools and a price index. Answer (C) is incorrect. Dollar-value LIFO uses a price index for each year.

6.4.6. In January, Stitch, Inc., adopted the dollar-value LIFO method of inventory valuation. At adoption, inventory was valued at $50,000. During the year, inventory increased $30,000 using base-year prices, and prices increased 10%. The designated market value of Stitch's inventory exceeded its cost at year end. What amount of inventory should Stitch report in its year-end balance sheet?

A. $80,000

B. $83,000

C. $85,000

D. $88,000

Answer (B) is correct. *(CPA, adapted)*
   REQUIRED: The ending inventory measured at dollar-value LIFO.
   DISCUSSION: Dollar-value LIFO determines changes in inventory in terms of dollars of constant purchasing power, not units of physical inventory. The first step is to determine the inventory layers at base-year prices by dividing current-year (year-end) cost amounts by the relevant respective annual price indexes. These layers are calculated using a LIFO assumption. The second step is to restate the layers by multiplying by the relevant indexes. In this case, the layers stated at base-year prices ($50,000 and $30,000) are given, and the relevant indexes are 1.0 for the base year and 1.1 (1 + .10) for the second year. The dollar-value LIFO measurement is $83,000.

Base layer	$50,000 × 1.0 =	$50,000
Second layer	30,000 × 1.1 =	33,000
	$80,000	$83,000

   Answer (A) is incorrect. The amount of $80,000 does not include an adjustment for the price change. Answer (C) is incorrect. The amount of $85,000 results from multiplying the base layer but not the second layer by the current-year price index. Answer (D) is incorrect. The amount of $88,000 results from multiplying both layers by the current-year price index.

6.4.7. Which of the following is an advantage of the dollar-value LIFO method over the specific-goods LIFO method?

A. The dollar-value LIFO method may be used only for identical inventory items.

B. Under dollar-value LIFO, new inventory items are entered into the inventory pool at their entry year cost.

C. Under dollar-value LIFO, a given inventory item may experience a unit count decrease, but no liquidation need be recorded.

D. Under dollar-value LIFO, updating of the cost basis of old inventory items is facilitated.

Answer (C) is correct. *(D.L. Flesher)*
REQUIRED: The advantage of the dollar-value LIFO method.
DISCUSSION: The dollar-value LIFO method is applicable to pools of similar but not identical inventory items. The method deals with layers of inventory, not with individual inventory items. Thus, when a given inventory item experiences a unit count decrease, but the overall pool of inventory does not decrease, no liquidation is recorded.
Answer (A) is incorrect. Dollar-value LIFO is used for inventory pools composed of similar but not identical items. Answer (B) is incorrect. New inventory items are placed in the pool at the substituted item's base-year price. Answer (D) is incorrect. No LIFO method permits an updating of old inventory items.

Questions 6.4.8 and 6.4.9 are based on the following information. Minsk Company adopted the dollar-value last-in, first-out (LIFO) method of inventory valuation at December 31, Year 1. Inventory balances and price indices are shown below.

December 31	Ending Inventory at End-of-Year Prices	Price Index at December 31
Year 1	$240,000	100
Year 2	275,000	110
Year 3	300,000	120

6.4.8. Minsk Company's ending inventory as of December 31, Year 2, computed by the dollar-value LIFO method was

A. $240,000

B. $250,000

C. $251,000

D. $275,000

Answer (C) is correct. *(CMA, adapted)*
REQUIRED: The dollar-value LIFO inventory for Year 2.
DISCUSSION: The first step is to convert the Year 2 ending inventory into base-year prices. Dividing by the price index for Year 2 results in an inventory measure of $250,000 ($275,000 ÷ 1.1). This amount consists of two layers: $240,000 purchased during the base year (Year 1) and $10,000 acquired in the current year (Year 2). The second amount must be converted back into year-end prices because this merchandise was not purchased during the base year. The Year 2 increment therefore has a dollar-value LIFO measure of $11,000 (1.1 × $10,000). Total inventory is $251,000 ($240,000 + $11,000).
Answer (A) is incorrect. The amount of $240,000 does not include the Year 2 layer. Answer (B) is incorrect. The amount of $250,000 includes the Year 2 layer at base-year prices. Answer (D) is incorrect. The amount of $275,000 is the ending inventory at end-of-year prices.

6.4.9. Minsk Company ending inventory as of December 31, Year 3, computed by the dollar-value LIFO method would be

A. $240,000

B. $250,000

C. $251,000

D. $300,000

Answer (C) is correct. *(CMA, adapted)*
REQUIRED: The dollar-value LIFO inventory for Year 3.
DISCUSSION: The first step is to convert the Year 3 ending inventory at year end prices into base-year prices. Dividing by the price index for Year 3 results in an inventory measure at base-year prices of $250,000 ($300,000 ÷ 1.2). This amount is the same as that for Year 2. Thus, no increment was added during Year 3, and the dollar-value LIFO ending inventory for Year 3 is the same as at the end of Year 2 ($251,000). This amount consists of a $240,000 layer purchased in Year 1 and an $11,000 layer purchased in Year 2. Under LIFO, the assumption is that nothing is still on hand from Year 3 purchases because the inventory stated in base-year prices is the same as at the end of the preceding year.
Answer (A) is incorrect. The amount of $240,000 does not include the Year 2 layer. Answer (B) is incorrect. The amount of $250,000 includes the Year 2 layer at base-year prices. Answer (D) is incorrect. The amount of $300,000 is the ending inventory at end-of-year prices.

6.5 Measurement of Inventory Subsequent to Initial Recognition

6.5.1. The lower-of-cost-or-market rule for inventories may be applied to total inventory, to groups of similar items, or to each item. Which application generally results in the lowest inventory amount?

A. All applications result in the same amount.

B. Total inventory.

C. Groups of similar items.

D. Separately to each item.

Answer (D) is correct. *(CPA, adapted)*
REQUIRED: The application of the LCM rule that usually results in the lowest amount.
DISCUSSION: Applying the LCM rule to each item of inventory produces the lowest amount for each item and therefore the lowest and most conservative measurement for the total inventory. The reason is that aggregating items results in the inclusion of some items at amounts greater than LCM. For example, if item A (cost $2, market $1) and item B (cost $3, market $4) are aggregated for LCM purposes, the inventory measurement is $5. If the rule is applied separately to A and B, the LCM measurement is $4.
Answer (A) is incorrect. Each application results in a different amount. Answer (B) is incorrect. Grouping all items results in a higher measurement than applying the LCM rule to individual items. Answer (C) is incorrect. Grouping some items results in a higher measurement than applying the LCM rule to individual items.

6.5.2. The replacement cost of a LIFO basis inventory item is below the net realizable value and above the net realizable value minus the normal profit margin. The original cost of the inventory item is below the net realizable value minus the normal profit margin. Under the lower-of-cost-or-market (LCM) method, the inventory item should be measured at

A. Net realizable value.

B. Net realizable value minus the normal profit margin.

C. Original cost.

D. Replacement cost.

Answer (C) is correct. *(CPA, adapted)*
REQUIRED: The measurement of an inventory item under the lower-of-cost-or-market method.
DISCUSSION: Inventory accounted for using LIFO or the retail inventory method is measured at the lower of cost or market. When replacement cost is below the NRV and above the NRV minus the normal profit margin, market equals replacement cost. Given that the original cost of the inventory item is below market, the original cost should be used to measure the inventory item under the LCM method.
Answer (A) is incorrect. The replacement cost, given the circumstances, is designated as market. Answer (B) is incorrect. The replacement cost is above net realizable value minus the normal profit margin and cost but below net realizable value. Answer (D) is incorrect. Cost is below market.

6.5.3. The original cost of an inventory item is both below replacement cost and net realizable value. The net realizable value minus normal profit margin is below the original cost. Under the lower-of-cost-or-market (LCM) method, the inventory item that is accounted for using the LIFO method should be measured at

A. Replacement cost.

B. Net realizable value.

C. Net realizable value minus normal profit margin.

D. Original cost.

Answer (D) is correct. *(CPA, adapted)*
REQUIRED: The measurement of inventory under the LCM method.
DISCUSSION: Inventory accounted for using LIFO or the retail inventory method is measured at the lower of cost or market. Market is current replacement cost subject to a ceiling and a floor. The maximum is net realizable value, and the minimum is net realizable value minus normal profit. When replacement cost is within this range, it is used as market. The original cost is above the NRV minus normal profit margin but below the NRV and the replacement cost. Thus, market must be the NRV (if it is less than replacement cost) or the replacement cost (which is greater than NRV minus normal profit), and LCM is equal to original cost.
Answer (A) is incorrect. Replacement cost is greater than original cost. Answer (B) is incorrect. The NRV is greater than original cost. Answer (C) is incorrect. Net realizable value minus a normal profit margin is the LCM measure of inventory only if it is (1) below original cost and (2) equal to or greater than replacement cost.

6.5.4. Lorraine Co. has determined its fiscal year-end inventory on a LIFO basis to be $400,000. Information pertaining to that inventory follows:

Estimated selling price	$408,000
Estimated cost of disposal	20,000
Normal profit margin	60,000
Current replacement cost	360,000

Lorraine records losses that result from applying the lower-of-cost-or-market (LCM) rule. At its year end, what should be the net carrying value of Lorraine's inventory?

A. $400,000

B. $388,000

C. $360,000

D. $328,000

Answer (C) is correct. *(CPA, adapted)*
    REQUIRED: The net carrying amount of the ending inventory.
    DISCUSSION: Inventory accounted for using LIFO or the retail inventory method is measured at the lower of cost or market. Under the LCM method, market is current replacement cost subject to a maximum (ceiling) equal to net realizable value and a minimum (floor) equal to net realizable value minus a normal profit. NRV equals selling price minus costs of completion and disposal. Here, original cost is $400,000 and replacement cost is $360,000. The LCM method uses the lower of the two, $360,000, to measure inventory. However, the inventory measure cannot exceed the NRV of $388,000 ($408,000 selling price – $20,000 cost of disposal). Furthermore, the inventory carrying amount cannot be lower than NRV minus normal profit, or $328,000 ($388,000 NRV – $60,000 normal profit). Because the lower of cost or market ($360,000) is between $388,000 (ceiling) and $328,000 (floor), the net carrying amount is $360,000.
    Answer (A) is incorrect. The amount of $400,000 is the original cost. Answer (B) is incorrect. The amount of $388,000 is the NRV (ceiling). Answer (D) is incorrect. The amount of $328,000 is the NRV minus normal profit (floor).

Questions 6.5.5 through 6.5.7 are based on the following information. Stockholm Co. accounts for its inventory using the last-in, first-out (LIFO) method. The data below concern items in Stockholm Co.'s inventory.

Per Unit	Gear	Stuff	Wickets
Historical cost	$190.00	$106.00	$53.00
Selling price	217.00	145.00	73.75
Cost to complete and sell	19.00	8.00	2.50
Current replacement cost	203.00	105.00	51.00
Normal profit margin	32.00	29.00	21.25

6.5.5. The limits to the market measurement (i.e., the ceiling and the floor) that Stockholm Co. should use in the lower-of-cost-or-market (LCM) comparison of gear are

A. $217 and $198.

B. $217 and $185.

C. $198 and $166.

D. $185 and $166.

Answer (C) is correct. *(CMA, adapted)*
    REQUIRED: The limits of the market measurement for gear.
    DISCUSSION: Inventory accounted for using LIFO or retail inventory method is measured at the lower of cost or market (LCM). Market is current replacement cost subject to a ceiling equal to net realizable value and a floor equal to net realizable value minus a normal profit. Net realizable value is the estimated selling price minus costs of completion and disposal. For gear, the net realizable value is $198 ($217 selling price – $19 completion and disposal costs). Net realizable value minus normal profit is $166 ($198 net realizable value – $32 normal profit).
    Answer (A) is incorrect. The amount of $217 is the selling price, and $198 is the NRV. Answer (B) is incorrect. The amount of $217 is the selling price, and $185 is the selling price minus normal profit. Answer (D) is incorrect. The ceiling equals the net realizable value, not selling price minus normal profit.

6.5.6. The cost amount that Stockholm Co. should use in the lower-of-cost-or-market (LCM) comparison of stuff is

A. $105

B. $106

C. $108

D. $137

Answer (B) is correct. *(CMA, adapted)*
    REQUIRED: The cost amount for stuff.
    DISCUSSION: The cost amount used in the LCM comparison is the historical cost of an item. Thus, for stuff, the historical cost of $106 is compared with market.
    Answer (A) is incorrect. The amount of $105 is the current replacement cost, not the historical cost. Answer (C) is incorrect. The amount of $108 is the net realizable value minus the normal profit margin, not the historical cost. Answer (D) is incorrect. Net realizable value ($137) is not used in the calculation of historical cost.

6.5.7. The market amount that Stockholm Co. should use to measure the wickets on the basis of the lower-of-cost-or-market (LCM) rule is

A. $51.00

B. $53.00

C. $50.00

D. $71.25

Answer (A) is correct. *(CMA, adapted)*
REQUIRED: The market amount for wickets.
DISCUSSION: Inventory accounted for using LIFO or retail inventory method is measured at the lower of cost or market (LCM). Market is the current cost to replace the inventory, subject to certain limitations. Market should not exceed a ceiling equal to net realizable value (NRV) or be less than a floor equal to NRV minus normal profit margin. Net realizable value for wickets is $71.25 ($73.75 selling price – $2.50 completion and disposal costs). The net realizable value minus normal profit is $50 ($71.25 net realizable value – $21.25 normal profit margin). The $51 replacement cost falls between the $71.25 ceiling and the $50 floor and is the appropriate market value. Because the $51 market value is lower than the $53 historical cost, it should be the basis of valuation for the wickets.
Answer (B) is incorrect. The amount of $53 is the historical cost. Answer (C) is incorrect. The amount of $50 is the floor. It is used only if replacement cost is lower. Answer (D) is incorrect. The amount of $71.25 is the net realizable value. It is used as the market amount only if replacement cost is greater.

6.5.8. Based on a physical inventory taken on December 31, Chewy Co. determined its chocolate inventory on a LIFO basis at $26,000 with a replacement cost of $20,000. Chewy estimated that, after further processing costs of $12,000, the chocolate could be sold as finished candy bars for $40,000. Chewy's normal profit margin is 10% of sales. Under the lower-of-cost-or-market rule, what amount should Chewy report as chocolate inventory in its December 31 balance sheet?

A. $28,000

B. $26,000

C. $24,000

D. $20,000

Answer (C) is correct. *(CPA, adapted)*
REQUIRED: The LCM value of inventory.
DISCUSSION: Under LIFO, inventory is measured at the lower of cost or market (LCM). Market equals current replacement cost subject to maximum and minimum values. The maximum is NRV, and the minimum is NRV minus normal profit. When replacement cost is within this range, it is used as market. Cost is given as $26,000. NRV is $28,000 ($40,000 selling price – $12,000 additional processing costs), and NRV minus a normal profit equals $24,000 [$28,000 – ($40,000 × 10%)]. Because the lowest amount in the range ($24,000) exceeds replacement cost ($20,000), it is used as market. Because market value ($24,000) is less than cost ($26,000), it is also the inventory amount.
Answer (A) is incorrect. The NRV is $28,000. Answer (B) is incorrect. The cost is $26,000. Answer (D) is incorrect. The replacement cost is $20,000.

6.5.9. The original cost of an inventory item is above the replacement cost. The inventory item's replacement cost is above the net realizable value. Under the lower-of-cost-or-market method, the inventory item accounted for using the retail inventory method should be valued at

A. Original cost.

B. Replacement cost.

C. Net realizable value.

D. Net realizable value less normal profit margin.

Answer (C) is correct. *(CPA, adapted)*
REQUIRED: The measurement of an inventory item under the LCM method given that cost exceeds replacement cost and replacement cost exceeds NRV.
DISCUSSION: Inventory accounted for using LIFO or the retail inventory method is measured at the lower of cost or market. Market is the current cost to replace inventory, subject to certain limitations. Market should not exceed a ceiling equal to net realizable value (NRV) or be less than a floor equal to NRV minus a normal profit margin. Because replacement cost exceeds NRV, the ceiling is NRV.
Answer (A) is incorrect. The inventory item should be written down to market if its utility is no longer as great as its cost. Answer (B) is incorrect. Market should not exceed a ceiling equal to NRV. Answer (D) is incorrect. Net realizable value minus a normal profit margin is the minimum amount (the floor) for market.

6.5.10. Pine City owned a vacant plot of land zoned for industrial use. Pine gave this land to Medi Corp. solely as an incentive for Medi to build a factory on the site. The land had a fair value of $300,000 at the date of the gift. This nonmonetary transaction is most likely to be reported by Medi as

A. Other comprehensive income.

B. Contribution revenue.

C. A credit to retained earnings.

D. A memorandum entry.

Answer (B) is correct. *(CPA, adapted)*
REQUIRED: The accounting for a donated asset.
DISCUSSION: In general, contributions received ordinarily should be accounted for as revenues and gains at fair value.
Answer (A) is incorrect. A contribution received should be recognized as a revenue or gain in the period of receipt. It is not classified as an item of OCI. Answer (C) is incorrect. A contribution from a government is not recorded directly in retained earnings. It should be reported in the income statement or as contributed capital. Answer (D) is incorrect. A contribution should be recognized in the accounts.

6.5.11. Inventory accounted for under which of the following cost flow methods is not measured at the lower of cost or net realizable value?

A. First-in, first-out (FIFO).

B. Moving average.

C. Last-in, first-out (LIFO).

D. Specific identification.

Answer (C) is correct. *(Publisher, adapted)*
REQUIRED: The cost flow method that does not measure inventory at lower of cost or NRV.
DISCUSSION: Inventory accounted for using LIFO or the retail inventory method is measured at the lower of cost or market (LCM). Inventory accounted for using any other cost method (e.g., FIFO or average cost) is measured at the lower of cost or net realizable value (NRV).

6.5.12. A company accounts for its inventory using the first-in, first-out (FIFO) method. The following information pertains to the inventory at the end of the fiscal year:

Historical cost	$150,000
Current replacement cost	120,000
Net realizable value (NRV)	125,000
Normal profit margin	15,000
Fair value	140,000

What amount should the company report as inventory on its year-end balance sheet?

A. $150,000

B. $125,000

C. $120,000

D. $140,000

Answer (B) is correct. *(Publisher, adapted)*
REQUIRED: The ending balance of inventory measured using FIFO.
DISCUSSION: Inventory accounted for using the FIFO method (or any cost method other than LIFO or retail) is measured at the lower of cost or net realizable value (NRV). Because the NRV ($125,000) is lower than the historical cost ($150,000), the inventory is reported on the year-end balance sheet at its NRV of $125,000.
Answer (A) is incorrect. The inventory should be reported at its NRV because it is lower than the historical cost. Answer (C) is incorrect. If the inventory were accounted for under the LIFO or the retail inventory method, it would have been reported at its current replacement cost of $120,000. Answer (D) is incorrect. Certain investments in securities, such as trading or available-for-sale securities are measured at fair value. Inventory accounted for using the FIFO method (or any cost method other than LIFO or retail) is measured at the lower of cost or NRV.

6.5.13. Lialia Co. has determined the cost of its fiscal year-end unfinished FIFO inventory to be $300,000. Information pertaining to that inventory at year-end is as follows:

Estimated selling price	$330,000
Estimated cost of disposal	20,000
Normal profit margin	15%
Current replacement cost	280,000
Estimated completion costs	15,000

What amount should Lialia report as inventory on its year-end balance sheet?

A. $295,000

B. $280,000

C. $300,000

D. $330,000

Answer (A) is correct. *(Publisher, adapted)*
REQUIRED: The ending balance of inventory measured using FIFO.
DISCUSSION: Inventory accounted for using the FIFO method (or any cost method other than LIFO or retail) is measured at the lower of cost or net realizable value (NRV). NRV is the estimated selling price in the ordinary course of business, minus reasonably predictable costs of completion, disposal, and transportation. At year-end, the NRV of the inventory of $295,000 ($330,000 estimated selling price – $15,000 estimated completion costs – $20,000 estimated costs of disposal) is lower than its cost of $300,000. Thus, the inventory is reported at its NRV of $295,000.
Answer (B) is incorrect. If the inventory were accounted for under the LIFO or the retail inventory method, it would have been reported at its current replacement cost of $280,000. Answer (C) is incorrect. Inventory accounted for using the FIFO method is measured at the lower of cost or net realizable value (NRV). The NRV is lower than cost, so the inventory must be reported at its NRV. Answer (D) is incorrect. Inventory should not be reported at an amount greater than its historical cost.

6.5.14. Gail Co. has determined the cost of its 12/31/Year 1 inventory on a moving-average basis to be $200,000. Information pertaining to that inventory at year-end is as follows:

Estimated selling price	$215,000
Estimated cost of disposal	10,000
Normal profit margin	20,000
Current replacement cost	190,000

What loss on inventory write-down, if any, should be recognized in Gail's Year 1 income statement?

- A. $10,000
- B. $15,000
- C. $20,000
- D. $0

Answer (D) is correct. *(Publisher, adapted)*
REQUIRED: The loss, if any, on a write-down of inventory measured on a moving-average basis.
DISCUSSION: Inventory accounted for using the average method (or any cost method other than LIFO or retail) is measured at the lower of cost or net realizable value (NRV). NRV is the estimated selling price in the ordinary course of business, minus reasonably predictable costs of completion, disposal, and transportation. The cost of the inventory of $200,000 is lower than its NRV of $205,000 ($215,000 selling price – $10,000 estimated cost of disposal). Thus, the inventory is reported at its cost and no loss on write-down of inventory is recognized.
Answer (A) is incorrect. The amount of $10,000 is the loss under the LCM method. If the inventory were accounted for under the LIFO or the retail inventory method, it would be accounted for using the LCM method. Cost is $200,000. Market is replacement cost subject to a ceiling (NRV) and a floor (NRV – normal profit margin). Replacement cost ($190,000) is above the floor ($205,000 NRV – $20,000 normal profit = $185,000) and lower than NRV ($205,000). Market therefore is $190,000. Lower of cost ($200,000) or market ($190,000) is $190,000, and the loss under the LCM method is $10,000 ($200,000 cost – $190,000 market). Answer (B) is incorrect. The amount of $15,000 equals selling price ($215,000) minus cost ($200,000), not lower of cost or NRV. Answer (C) is incorrect. The amount of $20,000 is the normal profit margin.

6.5.15. How should inventory that is accounted for under the average-cost method be measured in the financial statements?

- A. Lower of cost or market (LCM).
- B. Lower of cost of fair value minus cost to sell.
- C. Lower of cost or net realizable value (NRV).
- D. Fair value.

Answer (C) is correct. *(Publisher, adapted)*
REQUIRED: The measurement of inventory under the average-cost method
DISCUSSION: Inventory accounted for using the average-cost method (or any cost method other than LIFO or retail) is measured at the lower of cost or NRV. NRV is the estimated selling price in the ordinary course of business, minus reasonably predictable costs of completion, disposal, and transportation.
Answer (A) is incorrect. Inventory accounted for using LIFO or the retail inventory method is measured at the LCM. Inventory accounted for using any other cost method (e.g., FIFO or average cost) is measured at the lower of cost or net realizable value (NRV). Answer (B) is incorrect. An asset that is classified as held for sale is measured at the lower of its carrying amount or fair value minus cost to sell. Inventory accounted for using the average-cost method is measured at the lower of cost or net realizable value (NRV). Answer (D) is incorrect. Certain investments in debt securities, such as those that are classified as trading or available-for-sale, are measured at fair value in the financial statements. Inventory accounted for using the average-cost method is measured at the lower of cost or net realizable value (NRV).

6.5.16. Which of the following statements regarding fiscal year-end accounting for inventory under IFRS and U.S. GAAP is true?

A. Under both IFRS and U.S. GAAP, losses on write-down of inventory that are accounted for using the average-cost method can be reversed in subsequent periods.

B. Under both IFRS and U.S. GAAP, inventory that is accounted for using the first-in, first-out (FIFO) cost method is measured at the lower of cost or net realizable value (NRV).

C. Under both IFRS and U.S. GAAP, inventory that is accounted for using the last-in, first-out (LIFO) cost method is measured at the lower of cost or market (LCM).

D. Under both IFRS and U.S. GAAP, inventory that is accounted for using the retail cost method is measured at the lower of cost or market (LCM).

Answer (B) is correct. *(Publisher, adapted)*
REQUIRED: The true statement about accounting for inventory under IFRS and U.S. GAAP.
DISCUSSION: Under U.S. GAAP, inventory accounted for using the FIFO method (or any cost method other than LIFO or retail) is measured at the lower of cost or NRV. Under IFRS, inventory is measured at the lower of cost or NRV, regardless of the cost method used.
Answer (A) is incorrect. Under U.S. GAAP, regardless of the cost method used to account for inventory, losses on inventory write-down must not be reversed in subsequent fiscal years. Under IFRS, a write-down may be reversed but not above original cost. Answer (C) is incorrect. Under U.S. GAAP, inventory accounted for using LIFO or the retail inventory method is measured at the lower of cost or market. Under IFRS, the LIFO method is not permitted. In addition, under IFRS, inventory is measured at the lower of cost or NRV. Answer (D) is incorrect. Under U.S. GAAP, inventory accounted for using LIFO or the retail inventory method is measured at the lower of cost or market. Under IFRS, inventory is measured at the lower of cost or NRV, regardless of the cost method used.

6.5.17. A company determined the following values for its inventory as of the end of the fiscal year:

Historical cost	$300,000
Current replacement cost	280,000
Selling price	308,000
Normal profit margin	13,000
Cost to sell	10,000

What amount should the company report as inventory on its year-end balance sheet under the following cost methods?

	Last-in, first-out (LIFO)	First-in, first-out (FIFO)
A.	$280,000	$298,000
B.	$285,000	$298,000
C.	$298,000	$300,000
D.	$285,000	$285,000

Answer (B) is correct. *(Publisher, adapted)*
REQUIRED: The ending inventory under LIFO and FIFO.
DISCUSSION: Inventory accounted for using LIFO or the retail inventory method is measured at the lower of cost or market (LCM). Market is the current cost to replace inventory, subject to certain limitations. Market cannot be greater than a ceiling equal to net realizable value (NRV) of $298,000 ($308,000 estimated selling price – $10,000 cost of disposal). It cannot be less than a floor equal to NRV reduced by a normal profit margin of $285,000 ($298,000 NRV – $13,000 normal profit margin). Because the current replacement cost ($280,000) is lower than the floor ($285,000), market is $285,000. Thus, under the LIFO method, the inventory is reported at $285,000, which is lower than the $300,000 cost. Inventory accounted for using the FIFO method (or any cost method other than LIFO or retail) is measured at the lower of cost or net realizable value (NRV). Thus, under FIFO method, the inventory is reported at its NRV of $298,000, which is lower than the $300,000 cost.
Answer (A) is incorrect. The current replacement cost of inventory is lower than NRV minus the normal profit margin (floor). Thus, under the LIFO method, the inventory must not be reported at its current replacement cost. Answer (C) is incorrect. The NRV of inventory is lower than its historical cost. Thus, under the FIFO method, the inventory must not be reported at its cost. Also, inventory accounted for using the LIFO method is measured at the lower of cost or market (LCM). Answer (D) is incorrect. Inventory accounted for using the FIFO method is measured at the lower of cost or net realizable value (NRV). Normal profit margin is not included in the estimation of NRV of inventory.

6.5.18. In accounting for inventories, GAAP require departure from the historical cost principle when the utility of inventory has fallen below cost. Inventory accounted for under certain cost flow methods can be measured at the lower of cost or net realizable value (NRV). The term "net realizable value (NRV)" as defined here means

A. Fair value minus cost to sell.

B. Original cost minus normal profit margin.

C. Estimated selling price minus estimated costs of completion and disposal.

D. Fair value minus normal profit margin.

Answer (C) is correct. *(Publisher, adapted)*
　　REQUIRED: The meaning of NRV.
　　DISCUSSION: Inventory measured using any cost method other than LIFO or retail (e.g., FIFO or average cost) must be measured at the lower of cost or NRV. NRV is the estimated selling price in the ordinary course of business, minus reasonably predictable costs of completion, disposal, and transportation.
　　Answer (A) is incorrect. An asset that is classified as held for sale is measured at the lower of its carrying amount or fair value minus cost to sell. The NRV of inventory is the estimated selling price in the ordinary course of business, minus reasonably predictable costs of completion, disposal, and transportation. Answer (B) is incorrect. NRV of inventory is the estimated selling price in the ordinary course of business, minus reasonably predictable costs of completion, disposal, and transportation. Answer (D) is incorrect. NRV of inventory is the estimated selling price in the ordinary course of business, minus reasonably predictable costs of completion, disposal, and transportation.

6.5.19. Inventory accounted for under which cost flow methods is measured subsequent to acquisition at lower of cost or market (LCM)?

	LIFO	FIFO	Retail	Weighted-Average
A.	Yes	No	Yes	No
B.	Yes	Yes	No	No
C.	No	Yes	No	Yes
D.	No	No	Yes	Yes

Answer (A) is correct. *(Publisher, adapted)*
　　REQUIRED: The cost flow methods under which inventory is measured at LCM.
　　DISCUSSION: Inventory accounted for using LIFO or the retail inventory method is measured at the lower of cost or market (LCM). Inventory accounted for using any other cost method (e.g., FIFO, average cost, or specific identification) is measured at the lower of cost or net realizable value (NRV).
　　Answer (B) is incorrect. FIFO inventory is measured at lower of cost or net realizable value. Retail inventory is measured at LCM. Answer (C) is incorrect. LIFO inventory is measured at LCM. FIFO and weighted-average inventory are measured at lower of cost or net realizable value. Answer (D) is incorrect. LIFO inventory is measured at LCM. Weighted-average inventory is measured at lower of cost or net realizable value.

6.5.20. Kusta Company measures its year-end inventory using the weighted-average method. The following is relevant information:

Costs of completion, disposal, and transportation	$ 25,000
Estimated selling price	450,000
Current replacement cost	420,000
Normal profit margin	40,000
Cost	400,000

The amount of ending inventory reported in the statement of financial position is

A. $400,000

B. $420,000

C. $425,000

D. $450,000

Answer (A) is correct. *(Publisher, adapted)*
　　REQUIRED: The year-end amount of weighted-average inventory.
　　DISCUSSION: Inventory accounted for using a method other than LIFO or retail (e.g., FIFO, average cost, or specific identification) is measured subsequent to acquisition at lower of cost or net realizable value (NRV). NRV equals (1) the estimated selling price in the ordinary course of business minus (2) reasonably predictable costs of completion, disposal, and transportation. Accordingly, the year-end weighted-average inventory is measured at the lower of cost ($400,000) or NRV [($450,000 sales price – $25,000 costs to complete, etc.) = $425,000], that is, the $400,000 historical cost.
　　Answer (B) is incorrect. The amount of $420,000 is the current replacement cost. Inventory accounted for using the weighted-average method is measured at the lower of cost or net realizable value. Answer (C) is incorrect. The amount of $425,000 is the NRV. Inventory accounted for using the weighted-average method is measured at the lower of cost or net realizable value. Answer (D) is incorrect. The amount of $450,000 is the estimated selling price. Inventory accounted for using the weighted-average method is measured at the lower of cost or net realizable value.

6.6 Inventory Estimation -- Gross Profit Method

6.6.1. Which of the following methods of inventory valuation is allowable at interim dates but not at year end?

A. Weighted average.

B. Estimated gross profit.

C. Retail method.

D. Specific identification.

Answer (B) is correct. *(CPA, adapted)*
REQUIRED: The inventory valuation method permitted at interim dates but not at year end.
DISCUSSION: The estimated gross profit method may be used to determine inventory for interim statements provided that adequate disclosure is made of reconciliations with the annual physical inventory at year end. Any other method allowable at year end is also allowable at an interim date.
Answer (A) is incorrect. Weighted average is allowable at year end. Answer (C) is incorrect. Retail method is allowable at year end. Answer (D) is incorrect. Specific identification is allowable at year end.

6.6.2. Zeno Menswear, Inc., maintains a markup of 60% based on cost. The company's selling and administrative expenses average 30% of sales. Annual sales amounted to $960,000. Zeno's cost of goods sold and operating profit for the year are

	Cost of Goods Sold	Operating Profit
A.	$576,000	$96,000
B.	$576,000	$288,000
C.	$600,000	$72,000
D.	$600,000	$288,000

Answer (C) is correct. *(CPA, adapted)*
REQUIRED: The estimated cost of goods sold and operating profit.
DISCUSSION: A markup of 60% based on cost is equal to the fraction 60% markup ÷ 100% cost. Because retail is equal to markup plus cost, a markup on retail is equal to the 60% markup divided by the total of the 100% cost plus the 60% markup. Zeno's markup on retail is therefore 37.5% [60% ÷ (100% + 60%)]. If the markup on retail is 37.5%, cost of goods sold must be 62.5% (1.0 – .375) of sales. Thus, cost of goods sold must be $600,000 ($960,000 sales × 62.5%). Selling and administrative expenses average 30% of sales and are estimated to be $288,000 ($960,000 sales × 30%). Accordingly, operating profit is $72,000 ($960,000 sales – $600,000 COGS – $288,000 S&A expenses).
Answer (A) is incorrect. Cost of goods sold is based on a 60% markup from cost, not sales, and the $96,000 operating profit is based on the incorrect cost of goods sold. Answer (B) is incorrect. Cost of goods sold is based on a 60% markup from cost, not sales, and the $288,000 is the selling and administrative expenses. Answer (D) is incorrect. The amount of $288,000 is the selling and administrative expenses.

6.6.3. The following information is available for Sweden Company for its most recent year:

Net sales	$3,600,000
Freight-in	90,000
Purchase discounts	50,000
Ending inventory	240,000

The gross margin is 40% of net sales. What is the cost of goods available for sale?

A. $1,680,000

B. $1,920,000

C. $2,400,000

D. $2,440,000

Answer (C) is correct. *(CPA, adapted)*
REQUIRED: The cost of goods available for sale.
DISCUSSION: Because the gross margin equals 40% of net sales, cost of goods sold equals 60% of net sales, or $2,160,000. Cost of goods available for sale equals the cost of goods sold plus the cost of the goods in ending inventory. Hence, cost of goods available for sale equals $2,160,000 plus $240,000, or $2,400,000 (BI + PUR = GAFS* = COGS + EI). Freight-in and purchase discounts are not used to estimate COGS or GAFS in the gross margin approach.

Ending inventory	$ 240,000
Cost of goods sold	2,160,000
Goods available for sale*	$2,400,000

Answer (A) is incorrect. The amount of $1,680,000 is gross margin plus ending inventory. Answer (B) is incorrect. The amount of $1,920,000 is cost of goods sold minus ending inventory. Answer (D) is incorrect. The amount of $2,440,000 is cost of goods available for sale plus freight-in and minus purchase discounts.

6.6.4. The following information is available for the Silver Company for the 3 months ended March 31 of this year:

Merchandise inventory,	
January 1 of this year	$ 900,000
Purchases	3,400,000
Freight-in	200,000
Sales	4,800,000

The gross margin recorded was 25% of sales. What should be the merchandise inventory at March 31?

A. $700,000

B. $900,000

C. $1,125,000

D. $1,200,000

Answer (B) is correct. *(CPA, adapted)*
REQUIRED: The estimated ending inventory using the gross profit method.
DISCUSSION: If the gross profit margin is 25% of sales, cost of goods sold equals 75% of sales. Ending inventory is equal to goods available for sale minus cost of goods sold.

Beginning inventory	$ 900,000
Purchases	3,400,000
Freight-in	200,000
Goods available for sale	$4,500,000
COGS [($4,800,000) × (1.0 − .25)]	(3,600,000)
Ending inventory	$ 900,000

Answer (A) is incorrect. The amount of $700,000 omits freight-in from the calculation. Answer (C) is incorrect. The amount of $1,125,000 is 25% of goods available for sale. Answer (D) is incorrect. The amount of $1,200,000 is the gross margin.

6.6.5. A store uses the gross profit method to estimate inventory and cost of goods sold for interim reporting purposes. Past experience indicates that the average gross profit rate is 25% of sales. The following data relate to the month of March:

Inventory cost, March 1	$25,000
Purchases during the month at cost	67,000
Sales	84,000
Sales returns	3,000

Using the data above, what is the estimated ending inventory at March 31?

A. $20,250

B. $21,000

C. $29,000

D. $31,250

Answer (D) is correct. *(CIA, adapted)*
REQUIRED: The estimated ending inventory value based on a 25% gross margin ratio.
DISCUSSION: The gross profit rate is 25% of sales. Thus, estimated cost of goods sold is 75% (1.0 − .25) of sales. Subtracting estimated cost of goods sold from total goods available for sale leaves an estimated ending inventory of $31,250.

Beginning inventory	$25,000
Purchases	67,000
Goods available for sale	$92,000
Estimated COGS [($84,000 − $3,000) × (1.0 − .25)]	(60,750)
Estimated ending inventory	$31,250

Answer (A) is incorrect. The amount of $20,250 is the gross margin. Answer (B) is incorrect. The amount of $21,000 is the gross margin without considering sales returns. Answer (C) is incorrect. The amount of $29,000 fails to consider sales returns.

6.6.6. Finland Co. prepares monthly income statements. A physical inventory is taken only at year end; hence, month-end inventories must be estimated. All sales are made on account. The rate of markup on cost is 50%. The following information relates to the month of June:

Accounts receivable, June 1	$20,000
Accounts receivable, June 30	30,000
Collection of accounts receivable during June	50,000
Inventory, June 1	36,000
Purchases of inventory during June	32,000

The estimated cost of the June 30 inventory is

A. $24,000

B. $28,000

C. $38,000

D. $44,000

Answer (B) is correct. *(CPA, adapted)*
REQUIRED: The estimated cost of ending inventory assuming a 50% markup on cost.
DISCUSSION: To determine inventory cost, cost of sales must be determined. Sales can be derived from a T-account analysis of accounts receivable; that is, the beginning balance ($20,000) plus credit sales equals the collections ($50,000) plus the ending balance ($30,000). Thus, sales equal $60,000 ($50,000 + $30,000 − $20,000). Because sales equal cost of sales plus the 50% markup on cost, sales equal 150% of cost. Cost of sales therefore equals $40,000 ($60,000 sales ÷ 1.5). Cost of sales deducted from the cost of goods available for sale equals the ending inventory.

Beginning inventory	$36,000
Purchases	32,000
Goods available for sale	$68,000
Cost of goods sold	(40,000)
Ending inventory	$28,000

Answer (A) is incorrect. Sales are incorrectly computed. Answer (C) is incorrect. The amount of $38,000 results from a markup based on sales instead of cost. Answer (D) is incorrect. Sales are incorrectly computed.

6.6.7. Dart Company's accounting records indicated the following information:

Beginning inventory	$ 500,000
Purchases during the year	2,500,000
Sales during the year	3,200,000

A physical inventory taken at year end resulted in an ending inventory of $575,000. Dart's gross profit on sales has remained constant at 25% in recent years. Dart suspects some inventory may have been taken by a new employee. At the balance sheet date, what is the estimated cost of missing inventory?

A. $25,000

B. $100,000

C. $175,000

D. $225,000

Answer (A) is correct. *(CPA, adapted)*
REQUIRED: The missing inventory estimated based on a gross margin ratio.
DISCUSSION: To estimate the missing inventory, the estimated cost of goods sold is subtracted from the cost of goods available for sale to estimate the amount of inventory that should be on hand. Given that the gross margin is 25% of sales, 75% of sales, or $2,400,000, is the estimated cost of goods sold.

Beginning balance	$ 500,000
Purchases	2,500,000
Cost of goods available	$3,000,000
Estimated cost of goods sold	
[$3,200,000 sales × (1.0 – .25)]	(2,400,000)
Estimated year-end balance	$ 600,000
Physical inventory year end	(575,000)
Estimated theft loss	$ 25,000

Answer (B) is incorrect. The amount of $100,000 is the difference between estimated ending inventory and actual beginning inventory. Answer (C) is incorrect. The amount of $175,000 is the ending physical inventory minus beginning inventory, plus purchases, minus cost of goods sold. Answer (D) is incorrect. The amount of $225,000 is the gross margin minus actual ending inventory.

6.6.8. A firm experienced a flood loss in the current year that destroyed all but $6,000 of inventory (at cost). Data available are below:

	Prior Year	Current (to Date of Flood)
Sales	$100,000	$40,000
Purchases	70,000	35,000
Cost of goods sold	60,000	
Ending inventory	10,000	

What is the approximate inventory lost?

A. $10,000

B. $15,000

C. $16,000

D. $21,000

Answer (B) is correct. *(CIA, adapted)*
REQUIRED: The approximate inventory lost to flood.
DISCUSSION: Based on the prior-year figures, the ratio of cost of goods sold to sales is 60% ($60,000 ÷ $100,000). This ratio can be used to approximate current-year cost of goods sold ($40,000 current-year sales × 60% = $24,000). As indicated below, this estimate is subtracted from goods available for sale to the date of the flood to determine estimated inventory at the time of the flood ($21,000). Given actual remaining inventory of $6,000, the inventory lost to flood is $15,000.

Beginning inventory	$10,000
Purchases	35,000
Cost of goods available	$45,000
Estimated cost of goods sold	(24,000)
Estimated inventory	$21,000
Actual inventory	(6,000)
Approximate inventory destroyed	$15,000

Answer (A) is incorrect. The amount of $10,000 is the ending inventory for the prior year and the beginning inventory in the current year. Answer (C) is incorrect. The amount of $16,000 is the current year beginning inventory plus the actual ending inventory of $6,000. Answer (D) is incorrect. The amount of $21,000 is the estimated ending inventory.

6.7 Inventory Estimation -- Retail Inventory Method

6.7.1. With regard to the retail inventory method, which of the following is the most accurate statement?

A. Generally, accountants ignore net markups and net markdowns in computing the cost-price percentage.

B. Generally, accountants include both net markups and net markdowns in computing the cost-price percentage.

C. This method results in a lower ending inventory cost if net markups are included but net markdowns are excluded in computing the cost-price percentage.

D. It is not adaptable to LIFO costing.

Answer (C) is correct. *(CPA, adapted)*
REQUIRED: The most accurate statement concerning the retail inventory method.
DISCUSSION: The cost-retail ratio is lower if retail (the denominator) is increased. Excluding markdowns increases the denominator, thus decreasing the ratio applied to ending inventory stated at retail and also decreasing ending inventory stated at cost. Excluding markdowns approximates lower of cost or market and is characteristic of the conventional retail method.
Answer (A) is incorrect. Accountants usually include net markups but not net markdowns in the denominator of the cost-retail ratio. Answer (B) is incorrect. The LIFO version includes net markups and markdowns in the denominator of the cost-retail ratio, but it is not the most widely used method. Answer (D) is incorrect. Among the variations of the retail method are (1) LIFO retail, (2) dollar-value LIFO retail, (3) lower-of-average-cost-or-market, (4) FIFO cost, (5) FIFO LCM, and (6) average cost.

6.7.2. Under the retail inventory method, freight-in would be included in the calculation of the goods available for sale for which of the following?

	Cost	Retail
A.	No	No
B.	No	Yes
C.	Yes	No
D.	Yes	Yes

Answer (C) is correct. *(CPA, adapted)*
REQUIRED: The calculation that includes freight-in when determining goods available for sale.
DISCUSSION: In the retail inventory method, records of the components of net purchases (purchases, freight-in, and purchase returns and allowances) are kept at cost and are included with beginning inventory in the calculation of the goods available for sale at cost. Records are kept at retail only for net purchases, not its components, because retail prices are usually set to cover a variety of costs, such as freight-in. Consequently, freight-in, a component of net purchases, is explicitly and directly included only in the calculation of goods available for sale at cost.
Answer (A) is incorrect. Freight-in is used in the calculation of cost. Answer (B) is incorrect. Freight-in is used in the calculation of cost, and it is not used in the calculation of retail. Answer (D) is incorrect. Freight-in is not used in the calculation of retail.

6.7.3. The retail inventory method includes which of the following in the calculation of both cost and retail amounts of goods available for sale?

A. Purchase returns.

B. Sales returns.

C. Net markups.

D. Freight-in.

Answer (A) is correct. *(CPA, adapted)*
REQUIRED: The element common to calculation of goods available for sale at cost and at retail.
DISCUSSION: In the retail inventory method, records are kept of beginning inventory and net purchases at both cost and retail. Purchase returns are deducted in the calculation of net purchases at both cost and retail because the return of goods reduces both total cost and the total sales price of the purchased goods.
Answer (B) is incorrect. Sales returns is an element of retail only. Answer (C) is incorrect. Markups and markdowns affect retail only. Answer (D) is incorrect. Freight-in is an element of cost.

6.7.4. If the retail method is used to approximate a lower-of-average-cost-or-market (LACM) measurement, which of the following describes the proper treatment of net additional markups and markdowns in the cost-retail ratio calculation?

A. Net markups should be included, and net markdowns should be excluded.

B. Net markups should be excluded, and net markdowns should be included.

C. Net markups and markdowns should be included.

D. Net markups and markdowns should be excluded.

Answer (A) is correct. *(S. Venkateswar)*
REQUIRED: The treatment of markups and markdowns in computing the cost-retail ratio under a lower-of-average-cost-or-market approach.
DISCUSSION: The cost-retail ratio based on a lower-of-average-cost-or-market measurement approach should include net markups but not net markdowns. Including net markups and excluding net markdowns approximates lower of cost or market. The reason is that increasing the denominator of the ratio (BI at retail + Pur at retail + Markups) while holding the numerator (BI at cost + Pur at cost) constant gives a more conservative (a lower) measurement.
Answer (B) is incorrect. Under the LACM retail method, net markups are included in the cost-retail ratio. Net markdowns are excluded. Answer (C) is incorrect. Net markdowns are excluded. Answer (D) is incorrect. Net markups are included.

6.7.5. In the retail inventory method, when computing the cost-retail ratio, under what flow assumption(s) is beginning inventory excluded from both cost and retail?

A. FIFO only.

B. LIFO only.

C. Weighted-average cost or weighted-average lower of cost or market.

D. Both FIFO and LIFO.

6.7.6. The accounting records of Seraphina Co. contain the following amounts on November 30, the end of its fiscal year:

	Cost	Retail
Beginning inventory	$ 68,000	$100,000
Purchases	262,000	400,000
Net markups		50,000
Net markdowns		110,000
Sales		360,000

Seraphina's ending inventory as of November 30, computed by the conventional retail method, is

A. $80,000

B. $60,000

C. $54,400

D. $48,000

6.7.7. Hutch, Inc., uses the conventional (lower of average cost or market) retail inventory method to account for inventory. The following information relates to current year operations:

	Average	
	Cost	Retail
Beginning inventory and purchases	$600,000	$920,000
Net markups		40,000
Net markdowns		60,000
Sales		780,000

What amount should be reported as cost of sales for the current year?

A. $480,000

B. $487,500

C. $520,000

D. $525,000

Answer (D) is correct. *(Publisher, adapted)*
REQUIRED: The flow assumption(s) requiring that beginning inventory be excluded in determining the cost-retail ratio.
DISCUSSION: Under both FIFO and LIFO, the cost-retail ratio must be computed for purchases, not goods available for sale. For FIFO, beginning inventory is excluded because ending inventory includes only goods from current purchases. For LIFO, the layers of goods from the purchases of separate accounting periods must be considered separately.
Answer (A) is incorrect. FIFO excludes beginning inventory in determining the cost-retail ratio. Answer (B) is incorrect. LIFO excludes beginning inventory in determining the cost-retail ratio. Answer (C) is incorrect. Weighted average includes beginning inventory as well as purchases.

Answer (D) is correct. *(CMA, adapted)*
REQUIRED: The ending inventory under the conventional retail method.
DISCUSSION: The lower-of-average-cost-or-market retail method includes net markups but not net markdowns in the determination of goods available for sale. The approximate LACM (conventional) retail method is a weighted-average method. Accordingly, the numerator of the cost-retail ratio is the sum of the beginning inventory at cost plus purchases at cost, and the denominator is the sum of beginning inventory at retail, purchases at retail, and net markups.

	Cost	Retail
Beginning inventory	$ 68,000	$100,000
Purchases	262,000	400,000
Markups, net		50,000
Goods available	$330,000	$550,000
Sales		(360,000)
Markdowns, net		(110,000)
Ending inventory -- retail		$ 80,000
Cost-retail ratio ($330 ÷ $550 = 60%)		× .6
Ending inventory at cost		$ 48,000

Answer (A) is incorrect. The amount of $80,000 is ending inventory at retail. Answer (B) is incorrect. The amount of $60,000 incorrectly uses a 75% cost-retail ratio. Answer (C) is incorrect. The amount of $54,400 incorrectly uses a 68% cost-retail ratio.

Answer (D) is correct. *(CPA, adapted)*
REQUIRED: The cost of sales based on the conventional retail inventory method.
DISCUSSION: The lower-of-cost-or-market retail method includes net markups but not net markdowns in the determination of goods available for sale. The approximate LACM (conventional) retail method is a weighted-average method. Accordingly, the numerator of the cost-retail ratio is the sum of the beginning inventory at cost plus purchases at cost, and the denominator is the sum of beginning inventory at retail, purchases at retail, and net markups. The numerator of the ratio (goods available at cost) is given as $600,000, and the denominator (goods available at retail) is $960,000 ($920,000 BI and purchases + $40,000 net markups). Ending inventory at retail is $120,000 ($960,000 goods available at retail – $60,000 net markdowns – $780,000 sales). Hence, ending inventory at cost is $75,000 [$120,000 EI at retail × ($600,000 ÷ $960,000) cost-retail ratio], and cost of sales must be $525,000 ($600,000 BI and purchases at cost – $75,000 EI at cost).
Answer (A) is incorrect. The amount of $480,000 results from subtracting ending inventory at retail from the sum of beginning inventory and purchases at cost. Answer (B) is incorrect. The amount of $487,500 omits net markdowns from the computation. Answer (C) is incorrect. The amount of $520,000 assumes net markdowns are deducted in determining the cost-retail ratio.

6.7.8. The Good Trader Company values its inventory by using the retail method (FIFO basis, lower of cost or market). The following information is available for the year just ended:

	Cost	Retail
Beginning inventory	$ 80,000	$140,000
Purchases	297,000	420,000
Freight-in	4,000	
Shortages		8,000
Markups (net)		10,000
Markdowns (net)		2,000
Sales		400,000

At what amount would The Good Trader Company report its ending inventory?

A. $112,000

B. $113,400

C. $117,600

D. $119,000

Answer (A) is correct. *(CPA, adapted)*
REQUIRED: The ending inventory at cost using the retail method (FIFO basis, LCM).
DISCUSSION: Under FIFO, ending inventory is composed of the latest purchases. Thus, in calculating the cost-retail ratio, only current purchases are included. To approximate the lower of cost or market, the denominator of the ratio includes net markups but not net markdowns.

	Cost	Retail
Purchases	$297,000	$420,000
Freight-in	4,000	
Markups, net		10,000
Adjusted purchases	$301,000	$430,000
Beginning inventory	80,000	140,000
Goods available	$381,000	$570,000
Net markdowns		(2,000)
Shortages		(8,000)
Sales		(400,000)
Ending inventory -- retail		$160,000
Cost-retail ratio ($301,000 ÷ $430,000 = 70%)		× .7
Ending inventory		$112,000

Answer (B) is incorrect. The amount of $113,400 fails to consider net markdowns in retail ending inventory. Answer (C) is incorrect. The amount of $117,600 ignores the effects of shortages in retail ending inventory. Answer (D) is incorrect. The amount of $119,000 incorrectly includes net markups in retail ending inventory.

6.7.9. Riga PLC uses a calendar year and the LIFO retail inventory method (assuming stable prices). Information relating to the computation of the inventory at December 31 is as follows:

	Cost	Retail
Beginning inventory	$ 150	$ 300
Purchases (net)	1,650	4,860
Net markups		830
Net markdowns		970
Sales		4,180

What should be the ending inventory at cost at December 31 using the LIFO retail inventory method?

A. $252

B. $333

C. $339

D. $840

Answer (C) is correct. *(K. Boze)*
REQUIRED: The ending inventory at cost using the LIFO retail inventory method.
DISCUSSION: Under the LIFO retail method (assuming stable prices), markups and markdowns are included in the calculation of the cost-retail ratio because the lower of cost or market is not being approximated. The markups and markdowns are usually assumed to apply only to purchases, and the ratio applies only to the LIFO layer added from the current purchases. Hence, the cost-retail ratio excludes beginning inventory and includes only purchases, markups, and markdowns. As indicated below, this ratio is 35%. The ending inventory will consist of a layer at 35% and a layer at the previous year's ratio.

	Cost	Retail
Purchases	$1,650	$4,860
Markups		830
Markdowns		(970)
Adjusted purchases	$1,650	$4,720
Beginning inventory	150	300
Goods available	$1,800	$5,020
Sales		(4,180)
Ending inventory -- retail		$ 840

Current cost-retail ratio ($1,650 ÷ $4,720 = 35%)

BI layer at cost	$ 150
Current layer at cost = ($840 – $300) × 35%	189
Ending inventory at cost	$ 339

Answer (A) is incorrect. The amount of $252 is the ending inventory based on the conventional retail method. Answer (B) is incorrect. The amount of $333 results from using a cost-retail ratio equal to purchases at cost divided by purchases at retail. Answer (D) is incorrect. The amount of $840 is the retail ending inventory.

6.7.10. Union Corp. uses the first-in, first-out retail method of inventory valuation. The following information is available:

	Cost	Retail
Beginning inventory	$12,000	$ 30,000
Purchases	60,000	110,000
Net additional markups		10,000
Net markdowns		20,000
Sales revenue		90,000

If the lower-of-cost-or-market rule is disregarded, what would be the estimated cost of the ending inventory?

A. $24,000

B. $20,000

C. $19,200

D. $18,000

Answer (A) is correct. *(CPA, adapted)*
REQUIRED: The ending inventory using the FIFO version of the retail inventory method.
DISCUSSION: Under FIFO, ending inventory consists of purchases because beginning inventory is assumed to be sold first. Both markdowns and markups are used to calculate the cost-retail ratio because LCM is not being approximated.

	Cost	Retail
Purchases	$60,000	$110,000
Markups		10,000
Markdowns		(20,000)
Adjusted purchases	$60,000	$100,000
Beg. inv. 1/1	12,000	30,000
Goods available	$72,000	$130,000
Sales		(90,000)
Ending inventory -- retail		$ 40,000
Cost-retail ratio ($60,000 ÷ $100,000)		× .6
Ending inventory -- FIFO		$ 24,000

Answer (B) is incorrect. The amount of $20,000 results from applying the LCM rule (not deducting markdowns in determining the cost-retail ratio) and using the FIFO version of the retail method. Answer (C) is incorrect. The amount of $19,200 results from applying the approximate LCM (conventional) retail method. Answer (D) is incorrect. The amount of $18,000 results from applying the LIFO retail method (assuming stable prices).

6.7.11. The following information is available for Sportworld, Inc., at year end:

	Cost	Retail
Inventory, January 1	$153,000	$221,000
Purchases, net	591,000	828,000
Markups, net		30,000
Markdowns, net		70,000
Sales, net		900,000

Assuming lower of cost or market is to be approximated, the estimated ending inventory under the FIFO version of the retail method is

A. $75,158

B. $75,080

C. $77,800

D. $109,000

Answer (B) is correct. *(Publisher, adapted)*
REQUIRED: The ending inventory at cost using the retail method (FIFO basis, LCM).
DISCUSSION: Under FIFO, ending inventory is composed of the latest purchases. Thus, in calculating the cost-retail ratio, only current purchases are included. To approximate the lower of cost or market, the denominator of the ratio includes net markups but not net markdowns.

	Cost	Retail
Purchases, net	$591,000	$ 828,000
Markups, net		30,000
Adjusted purchases, net	$591,000	$ 858,000
Beginning inventory	153,000	221,000
Goods available	$744,000	$1,079,000
Net markdowns		(70,000)
Sales		(900,000)
Ending inventory -- retail		$ 109,000
Cost-retail ratio ($591 ÷ $858)		× 68.88%
Ending inventory at cost		$ 75,080

Answer (A) is incorrect. The amount of $75,158 uses goods available for sale in the cost-retail ratio. Answer (C) is incorrect. The amount of $77,800 does not use net markups in the cost-retail ratio. Answer (D) is incorrect. The amount of $109,000 is ending inventory at retail.

6.8 IFRS

6.8.1. A company determined the following values for its inventory as of the end of the fiscal year:

Historical cost	$100,000
Current replacement cost	70,000
Net realizable value	90,000
Net realizable value minus a normal profit margin	85,000
Fair value	95,000

Under IFRS, what amount should the company report as inventory on its balance sheet?

   A. $70,000

   B. $85,000

   C. $90,000

   D. $95,000

Answer (C) is correct. *(CPA, adapted)*
   REQUIRED: The year-end inventory.
   DISCUSSION: Under IFRS, inventory is measured at the lower of cost or NRV (estimated selling price in the ordinary course of business – estimated costs of completion and sale). Given cost of $100,000 and NRV of $90,000, inventory should be reported at $90,000.
   Answer (A) is incorrect. Current replacement cost ($70,000) is neither cost nor NRV. Answer (B) is incorrect. The lower of cost or market ($85,000) is the appropriate measure under U.S. GAAP of inventory measured using LIFO or the retail method. Answer (D) is incorrect. Fair value is greater than NRV.

6.8.2. According to IFRS, a write-down of inventory is recognized in <List A>, and it <List B> reversed in subsequent periods.

	List A	List B
A.	Profit or loss	May be
B.	Other comprehensive income	Must not be
C.	Directly in equity	May be
D.	Profit or loss	Must not be

Answer (A) is correct. *(Publisher, adapted)*
   REQUIRED: The accounting for a write-down of inventory under IFRS.
   DISCUSSION: Under IFRS, a write-down of inventory may be reversed in subsequent periods but not above the original cost. The write-down and reversal of inventory are recognized in profit or loss.
   Answer (B) is incorrect. A write-down of inventory is recognized in profit or loss, not in OCI, and it may be reversed in subsequent periods. Answer (C) is incorrect. The write-down of inventory is recognized as a loss in profit or loss and therefore ultimately decreases retained earnings (an equity amount). Answer (D) is incorrect. Under IFRS, a write-down of inventory may be reversed in subsequent periods.

6.8.3. A company determined the following amounts for its inventory at the end of the fiscal year:

Historical cost	$100,000
Selling price	140,000
Cost of disposal	10,000
Cost of completion	5,000
Normal profit margin	17,000

What is the net realizable value (NRV) of the inventory at year end?

   A. $125,000

   B. $108,000

   C. $130,000

   D. $135,000

Answer (A) is correct. *(Publisher, adapted)*
   REQUIRED: The NRV of inventory.
   DISCUSSION: NRV is the estimated selling price in the ordinary course of business ($140,000), minus reasonably predictable costs of completion ($5,000) and disposal ($10,000). NRV is $125,000 ($140,000 – $10,000 – $5,000).
   Answer (B) is incorrect. The normal profit margin should not be considered in calculating NRV. Answer (C) is incorrect. The cost of disposal of inventory must be considered in calculating its NRV. Answer (D) is incorrect. The cost of completion of inventory must be considered in calculating its NRV.

6.8.4. Which inventory cost flow method is prohibited according to IFRS?

   A. First-in, first-out (FIFO) method.

   B. Specific identification method.

   C. Weighted-average cost method.

   D. Last-in, first-out (LIFO) method.

Answer (D) is correct. *(Publisher, adapted)*
   REQUIRED: The inventory method that is prohibited under IFRS.
   DISCUSSION: The last-in, first-out (LIFO) method is prohibited by IFRS. This method is based on the assumption that the newest items are sold first. Its effect is to include current prices in cost of goods sold. But the LIFO assumption ordinarily does not match actual inventory use.
   Answer (A) is incorrect. The first-in, first-out method is permitted by IFRS. Answer (B) is incorrect. The specific identification method is permitted by IFRS. Answer (C) is incorrect. The weighted-average cost method is permitted by IFRS.

6.8.5. A company manufactures and distributes replacement parts for various industries. As of December 31, Year 1, the following amounts pertain to the company's inventory:

Item	Cost	Net Replace-ment Cost	Sale Price	Cost to Sell or Dispose	Normal Profit Margin
Blades	$41,000	$ 38,000	$ 50,000	$ 2,000	$15,000
Towers	52,000	40,000	54,000	4,000	14,000
Generators	20,000	24,000	30,000	2,000	6,000
Gearboxes	80,000	105,000	120,000	12,000	8,000

What is the total carrying value of the company's inventory as of December 31, Year 1, under IFRS?

A. $178,000

B. $191,000

C. $193,000

D. $207,000

Answer (B) is correct. *(CPA, adapted)*
REQUIRED: The carrying value of inventory under IFRS.
DISCUSSION: Under IFRS, inventories are measured at the lower of cost or net realizable value (NRV). NRV is the estimated selling price minus reasonably predictable costs of completion and disposal. Blades, generators, and gearboxes are measured at their costs of $41,000, $20,000, and $80,000, respectively, because these amounts are lower than their NRVs of $48,000 ($50,000 – $2,000), $28,000 ($30,000 – $2,000), and $108,000 ($120,000 – $12,000). Towers are measured at their NRV of $50,000 ($54,000 – $4,000) because this amount is lower than cost ($52,000). Thus, the total carrying value of the company's inventory is equal to $191,000 ($41,000 + $20,000 + $80,000 + $50,000).

Answer (A) is incorrect. A carrying value of $178,000 results from improperly including net replacement cost among the possible values. Under IFRS, inventories are measured at the lower of cost or net realizable value; net replacement cost is generally not considered. Answer (C) is incorrect. A carrying value of $193,000 results from measuring inventory at cost. Under IFRS, inventories are measured at the lower of cost or net realizable value. Answer (D) is incorrect. A carrying value of $207,000 results from measuring inventory at net replacement cost. Under IFRS, inventories are measured at the lower of cost or net realizable value.

Use **Gleim Test Prep** for interactive study and easy-to-use detailed analytics!

STUDY UNIT SEVEN
PROPERTY, PLANT, AND EQUIPMENT

The accounting for items of property, plant, and equipment (PPE) has three phases:

Initial measurement. Purchased items of PPE are initially measured at historical cost, that is, all costs needed to bring the asset to the condition and location necessary for its intended use. The initial measurement of internally constructed items of PPE also might require capitalization of additional costs such as interest.

Measurement after initial recognition. Items of PPE are reported in the financial statements at their carrying amount.

Carrying amount = Historical cost − Accumulated depreciation − Impairment losses

This phase includes the two-step impairment test for items of PPE and how to distinguish between the subsequent costs that should be expensed and the costs that should be capitalized. Study Unit 8 addresses the related topics of depreciation and depletion.

Disposal or exchange. Most questions in this phase require computation of a gain or loss on disposal and understanding the accounting for monetary and nonmonetary exchanges of assets.

This study unit also covers the accounting models that are permitted under IFRS but not U.S. GAAP. These models include (1) the revaluation model and (2) the fair value model that can be applied only to investment property.

QUESTIONS

7.1 Definition and Initial Measurement

7.1.1. Property, plant, and equipment are conventionally presented in the balance sheet at

A. Replacement cost less accumulated depreciation.

B. Historical cost less salvage value.

C. Original cost adjusted for general price-level changes.

D. Historical cost less depreciated portion thereof.

Answer (D) is correct. *(CPA, adapted)*

REQUIRED: The conventional balance sheet presentation of property, plant, and equipment.

DISCUSSION: Property, plant, and equipment are recorded at their acquisition cost. They are then measured at their historical cost attribute. When property, plant, and equipment are used in normal operations, this historical cost must be allocated (depreciated) on a systematic and rational basis to the accounting periods in which they are used. Land is an exception because it is not depreciated.

Answer (A) is incorrect. Historical cost rather than replacement cost is the attribute at which property, plant, and equipment are measured. Answer (B) is incorrect. Assets appear in the balance sheet at historical cost with an offset for accumulated depreciation (not salvage value). Answer (C) is incorrect. The basic financial statements are not adjusted for price-level changes.

7.1.2. A contributed plant asset for which the fair value has been determined, and for which incidental costs were incurred in acceptance of the asset, should be recorded at an amount equal to its

A. Incidental costs incurred.

B. Fair value and incidental costs incurred.

C. Carrying amount on books of donor and incidental costs incurred.

D. Carrying amount on books of donor.

Answer (B) is correct. *(CPA, adapted)*
REQUIRED: The amount at which a contributed plant asset should be recorded.
DISCUSSION: A contributed plant asset should be debited at its fair value plus any incidental costs necessary to make the asset ready for its intended use. Contributions received ordinarily should be credited as revenues or gains in the periods they are received. However, a credit to a revenue or gain is not required for contributions by governments to business enterprises.
Answer (A) is incorrect. Any plant asset, including a contributed plant asset, should be recorded at fair value in addition to any incidental costs incurred. Answer (C) is incorrect. Any plant asset, including a contributed plant asset, should be debited at fair value plus costs necessary to render the asset operational. Answer (D) is incorrect. The carrying amount on the books of the donor has no impact on the recorded value of the asset.

7.1.3. When fixed assets are self-constructed, which costs should be expensed in the period of construction?

A. Excess of construction costs over third-party selling price.

B. Fixed and variable overhead costs.

C. Fees paid to outside consultants.

D. Cost of safety devices required by government agencies.

Answer (A) is correct. *(Publisher, adapted)*
REQUIRED: The costs of self-constructed fixed assets that should be expensed in the period of construction.
DISCUSSION: An asset should not be recorded in excess of its fair value. Thus, a self-constructed fixed asset should not be capitalized at an amount greater than that at which the asset could be purchased from a third party. Any excess cost is a loss that should not be deferred to future periods and should be expensed.
Answer (B) is incorrect. Some fixed costs may be expensed rather than capitalized when the construction reduces normal production. Answer (C) is incorrect. Fees paid to outside consultants are directly related to the construction of fixed assets and should be capitalized. Answer (D) is incorrect. The cost of safety devices required by government agencies are directly related to the construction of fixed assets and should be capitalized.

7.1.4. Merry Co. purchased a machine costing $125,000 for its manufacturing operations and paid shipping costs of $20,000. Merry spent an additional $10,000 testing and preparing the machine for use. What amount should Merry record as the cost of the machine?

A. $155,000

B. $145,000

C. $135,000

D. $125,000

Answer (A) is correct. *(CPA, adapted)*
REQUIRED: The amount to be recorded as the acquisition cost.
DISCUSSION: The amount to be recorded as the acquisition cost of a machine includes all costs necessary to prepare it for its intended use. Thus, the cost of a machine used in the manufacturing operations of a company includes the cost of testing and preparing the machine for use and the shipping costs. The acquisition cost is $155,000 ($125,000 + $20,000 + $10,000).
Answer (B) is incorrect. The amount of $145,000 does not include the $10,000 cost of testing and preparation. Answer (C) is incorrect. The amount of $135,000 does not include the shipping costs. Answer (D) is incorrect. The amount of $125,000 does not include the shipping, testing, and preparation costs.

7.1.5. Land was purchased to be used as the site for the construction of a plant. A building on the property was sold and removed by the buyer so that construction on the plant could begin. The proceeds from the sale of the building should be

A. Classified as other income.

B. Deducted from the cost of the land.

C. Netted against the costs to clear the land and expensed as incurred.

D. Netted against the costs to clear the land and amortized over the life of the plant.

Answer (B) is correct. *(CPA, adapted)*
REQUIRED: The treatment of proceeds from the sale of a building removed to prepare for construction.
DISCUSSION: Land obtained as a plant site should be recorded at its acquisition cost. This cost includes the purchase price of the land and any additional expenses such as legal fees, title insurance, recording fees, assumption of encumbrances on the property, and any other costs incurred in preparing the property for its intended use. Because the intended use of the land was as a site for the construction of a plant, the proceeds from the sale of the building removed to prepare the land for construction should be deducted from the cost of the land.
Answer (A) is incorrect. The proceeds affect the cost of the land, not income. Answer (C) is incorrect. The proceeds affect the cost of the land, not income. Answer (D) is incorrect. The proceeds affect the cost of the land, not income.

7.1.6. On December 1 of the current year, Horton Co. purchased a tract of land as a factory site for $300,000. The old building on the property was razed, and salvaged materials resulting from demolition were sold. Additional costs incurred and salvage proceeds realized during December were as follows:

Cost to raze old building	$25,000
Legal fees for purchase contract and to record ownership	5,000
Title guarantee insurance	6,000
Proceeds from sale of salvaged materials	4,000

In Horton's current-year balance sheet dated December 31, what amount should be reported as land?

A. $311,000

B. $321,000

C. $332,000

D. $336,000

Answer (C) is correct. *(CPA, adapted)*
REQUIRED: The amount to be reported as the cost of land.
DISCUSSION: When land is acquired as a factory site, the cost of the land should include the purchase price of the land and such additional expenses as legal fees, title insurance, recording fees, subsequent assumption of encumbrances on the property, and the costs incurred in preparing the property for its intended use. Because the land was purchased as a factory site, the cost of razing the old building minus any proceeds received from the sale of salvaged materials, should be capitalized as part of the land account. Thus, the amount to be reported as land is $332,000 ($300,000 + $5,000 + $6,000 + $25,000 – $4,000).
Answer (A) is incorrect. The amount of $311,000 excludes the net cost of razing the old building. Answer (B) is incorrect. The amount of $321,000 excludes the legal fees and title insurance. Answer (D) is incorrect. The amount of $336,000 excludes the proceeds of razing the old building.

7.1.7. During the current year, Hamilton Co. had the following transactions pertaining to its new office building:

Purchase price of land	$120,000
Legal fees for contracts to purchase land	4,000
Architects' fees	16,000
Demolition of the old building on site	10,000
Sale of scrap from old building	6,000
Construction cost of new building (fully completed)	700,000

In Hamilton's current year balance sheet dated December 31, what amounts should be reported as the cost of land and cost of building?

	Land	Building
A.	$120,000	$720,000
B.	$124,000	$720,000
C.	$128,000	$716,000
D.	$130,000	$724,000

Answer (C) is correct. *(CPA, adapted)*
REQUIRED: The amounts reported as the cost of land and cost of building.
DISCUSSION: The cost of the land should include the purchase price of the land and additional expenses such as legal fees, title insurance, recording fees, subsequent assumption of encumbrances on the property, and the costs incurred in preparing the property for its intended use. Because the land was purchased as the site of an office building, the cost of razing the old building, minus any proceeds received from the sale of salvaged materials, should be capitalized as part of the land account. Thus, land should be reported as $128,000 ($120,000 + $4,000 + $10,000 – $6,000). The architects' fees are included in the cost of the building, which should be reported as $716,000 ($700,000 + $16,000).
Answer (A) is incorrect. A $120,000 land cost omits the legal fees and the net demolition cost, and a $720,000 building cost improperly includes the legal fees. Answer (B) is incorrect. A $124,000 land cost omits the legal fees or the net demolition cost, and a $720,000 building cost improperly includes the legal fees. Answer (D) is incorrect. A $130,000 land cost includes the gross demolition cost but not the legal fees. A $724,000 building cost includes the legal fees and the net demolition cost.

7.1.8. On July 1, Casa Development Co. purchased a tract of land for $1.2 million. Casa incurred additional costs of $300,000 during the remainder of the year in preparing the land for sale. The tract was subdivided into residential lots as follows:

Lot Class	Number of Lots	Sales Price per Lot
A	100	$24,000
B	100	16,000
C	200	10,000

Using the relative sales value method, what amount of costs should be allocated to the Class A lots?

A. $300,000

B. $375,000

C. $600,000

D. $720,000

Answer (C) is correct. *(CPA, adapted)*
REQUIRED: The amount of costs allocated using the relative sales value method.
DISCUSSION: The relative sales value method allocates cost based on the relative value of assets in a group. The total sales value of the lots is $6,000,000 [(100 × $24,000) + (100 × $16,000) + (200 × $10,000)]. Class A represents 40% of the total value ($2,400,000 ÷ $6,000,000). Total costs equal $1,500,000 ($1,200,000 + $300,000). Thus, the amount of costs allocated to Class A is $600,000 ($1,500,000 × .40).
Answer (A) is incorrect. The amount of $300,000 equals the additional costs incurred. Answer (B) is incorrect. The amount of $375,000 equals 25% of the total cost. Class A represents 25% of the lots but 40% of the total value. Answer (D) is incorrect. The amount of $720,000 equals 48% of the total cost. Class A's sales price per lot is 48% of the sum of the unit sales prices of Classes A, B, and C.

7.1.9. A company purchased a building for $45,000 cash and recorded its cost on the books at that amount. However, the fair value of the building was $46,500 on the date of purchase. How should the company account for this $1,500 difference?

A. Amortize it over the useful life of the building.

B. Capitalize it as goodwill.

C. Debit it to the building account.

D. Do not record the amount.

Answer (D) is correct. *(CIA, adapted)*
REQUIRED: The accounting treatment for an unrealized gain on a building.
DISCUSSION: Property, plant, and equipment should not be written up by an entity to reflect the appraisal, market, or current values that are above cost to the entity. The company should not recognize the unrealized gain of $1,500.
Answer (A) is incorrect. The unrealized gain should not be amortized. Answer (B) is incorrect. The unrealized gain is not goodwill. Answer (C) is incorrect. The recorded amount of the building should not exceed its acquisition cost.

7.1.10. On July 1, Year 1, Colman Company sold land with a carrying amount of $75,000 to Monte Company in exchange for $50,000 in cash and a note calling for five annual $10,000 payments beginning on June 30, Year 2, and ending on June 30, Year 6. The fair value of the land is uncertain, and Monte can borrow long-term funds at 11%. What should be the amount capitalized as acquisition cost of the land by Monte Company? (The present value of $1 for five periods at 11% is 0.59345, and the present value of an ordinary annuity of $1 for five periods at 11% is 3.6959.)

A. $55,935

B. $75,000

C. $86,959

D. $100,000

Answer (C) is correct. *(S. Schultz)*
REQUIRED: The cost at which an asset should be capitalized when acquired under a financing agreement.
DISCUSSION: If an item of PPE is acquired in exchange for a noncurrent note, its cost is the present value of the consideration paid (the note). But the note's interest rate may be unstated or unreasonable, or the face amount may differ materially from the cash price of the PPE or the market value of the note. In these cases, the cost of the PPE should be the more clearly determinable of the cash price of the PPE or the market value of the note. The assets transferred included $50,000 in cash and a note with no stated interest rate. Given that Monte can borrow long-term funds at 11%, the market value of the note can be approximated by imputing an 11% rate and using it to calculate the present value of the five equal annual payments. The present value of this ordinary annuity is $36,959 ($10,000 payment × 3.6959), and the land should be recorded at $86,959 ($50,000 + $36,959).
Answer (A) is incorrect. The amount of $55,935 is the $50,000 in cash plus the present value of $10,000 to be received in 5 years. Answer (B) is incorrect. Colman Company's carrying amount of the land is $75,000. Answer (D) is incorrect. The amount of $100,000 is the $50,000 in cash plus $50,000 of payments that should have been calculated at present value.

7.1.11. Talton Co. installed new assembly line production equipment at a cost of $185,000. Talton had to rearrange the assembly line and remove a wall to install the equipment. The rearrangement cost $12,000, and the wall removal cost $3,000. The rearrangement did not increase the life of the assembly line, but it did make it more efficient. What amount of these costs should be capitalized by Talton?

A. $185,000

B. $188,000

C. $197,000

D. $200,000

Answer (D) is correct. *(CPA, adapted)*
REQUIRED: The costs capitalized for new equipment.
DISCUSSION: Property, plant, and equipment are measured initially at historical cost. This amount includes the price of the asset and the costs needed to bring it to the condition and location necessary for its intended use, e.g., shipping and installation costs. Furthermore, capital (asset) expenditures for acquisition or enhancement of service potential are included in the historical cost. However, revenue expenditures (expenses) maintain an asset's normal service capacity. Consequently, the amount capitalized is $200,000 ($185,000 installation costs + $12,000 rearrangement cost that increased efficiency + $3,000 wall removal cost necessary for the intended use of the asset).
Answer (A) is incorrect. The amount of $185,000 does not include the rearrangement cost and wall removal cost. Answer (B) is incorrect. The amount of $188,000 does not include the rearrangement cost. Answer (C) is incorrect. The amount of $197,000 does not include the wall removal cost.

7.2 Capitalization of Interest

7.2.1. Interest should be capitalized for assets that are

A. In use or ready for their intended use in the earning activities of the entity.

B. Being constructed or otherwise being produced as discrete projects for an entity's own use.

C. Not being used in the earning activities of the entity and not undergoing the activities necessary to get them ready for use.

D. Routinely produced.

Answer (B) is correct. *(CMA, adapted)*
REQUIRED: The types of assets for which interest should be capitalized.
DISCUSSION: GAAP require capitalization of material interest costs for assets constructed for internal use and those constructed for sale or lease as discrete projects. It does not apply to products routinely produced for inventory, assets in use or ready for use, assets not being used or being prepared for use, and idle land.
Answer (A) is incorrect. Interest is not capitalized for assets in use or ready for use. Answer (C) is incorrect. Assets not being used and being prepared for use are not subject to interest capitalization rules. Answer (D) is incorrect. Capitalized interest should not be added to routinely produced inventory.

7.2.2. Which one of the following ways of determining an interest rate should be used when the average accumulated expenditures for the constructed asset exceed the amounts of specific new borrowings associated with the asset?

A. Average rate of return on equity for the last 5 years.

B. Cost of capital rate for the entity.

C. Prime interest rate.

D. Weighted average of the interest rates applicable to the other borrowings of the entity.

Answer (D) is correct. *(CMA, adapted)*
REQUIRED: The method of determining the interest rate.
DISCUSSION: The actual interest rate on specific new borrowings is used to capitalize construction expenditures to the extent of the new borrowings. If average accumulated construction expenditures for the period exceed the specific new borrowings related to the construction, interest on other borrowings must be capitalized. A weighted-average interest rate must be used to capitalize interest costs on accumulated construction expenditures in excess of the specific new borrowings associated with the asset.

7.2.3. Which of the following is not an accurate statement of a criterion that must be met before interest is required to be capitalized?

A. Expenditures relative to a qualifying asset have been made.

B. Activities necessary to prepare the asset for its intended use are in progress.

C. Interest cost is incurred on borrowings.

D. Debt is incurred for the project.

Answer (D) is correct. *(Publisher, adapted)*
REQUIRED: The item not a criterion for capitalization of interest.
DISCUSSION: Capitalization of interest for a qualifying asset is required when expenditures have been made, activities are in progress to ready the asset for its intended use, and interest cost is being incurred. The mere incurrence of debt is not sufficient. Capitalized interest is limited to interest on borrowings. Accordingly, the incurrence of debt, such as trade payables, upon which no interest cost is being incurred, is not sufficient to meet the required criteria, even if qualifying expenditures have been made and the appropriate activities are in progress.
Answer (A) is incorrect. Having actually made expenditures is one of the qualifying criteria for capitalization of interest. Answer (B) is incorrect. Activities being underway to prepare the asset for its intended use is one of the qualifying criteria for interest capitalization. Answer (C) is incorrect. Incurring debt for the project is one of the qualifying criteria for interest capitalization.

7.2.4. Harbor Co. began constructing a building for its own use in January of the current year. During the current year, Harbor incurred interest of $100,000 on specific construction debt and $40,000 on other borrowings. Interest computed on the weighted-average amount of accumulated expenditures for the building during the current year was $80,000. What amount of interest cost should Harbor capitalize?

A. $40,000

B. $80,000

C. $100,000

D. $140,000

Answer (B) is correct. *(CPA, adapted)*
REQUIRED: The amount of interest capitalized.
DISCUSSION: Material interest costs incurred for the construction of certain assets for internal use are capitalized. The interest to be capitalized is determined by applying an interest rate (the capitalization rate) to the average qualifying expenditures accumulated during a given period. Thus, $80,000 of the interest incurred on the construction is capitalized.
Answer (A) is incorrect. Interest on other borrowings equals $40,000. Answer (C) is incorrect. The total interest on specific construction debt equals $100,000. Answer (D) is incorrect. The sum of interest on other borrowings and the total interest on specific construction debt equals $140,000.

7.2.5. During the year, Bay Co. constructed machinery for its own use and for sale to customers. Bank loans financed these assets both during construction and after construction was complete. How much of the interest incurred should be reported as interest expense in the income statement?

	Interest Incurred for Machinery for Own Use	Interest Incurred for Machinery Held for Sale
A.	All interest incurred	All interest incurred
B.	All interest incurred	Interest incurred after completion
C.	Interest incurred after completion	Interest incurred after completion
D.	Interest incurred after completion	All interest incurred

Answer (D) is correct. *(CPA, adapted)*
REQUIRED: The interest incurred reported as interest expense.
DISCUSSION: Interest should be capitalized for (1) assets constructed or otherwise produced for an entity's own use, including those constructed or produced by others; (2) assets intended for sale or lease that are constructed or produced as discrete projects (e.g., ships); and (3) certain equity-based investments. An asset constructed for an entity's own use qualifies for capitalization of interest if (1) relevant expenditures have been made, (2) activities necessary to prepare the asset for its intended use are in progress, and (3) interest is being incurred. Thus, all other interest incurred, e.g., interest incurred for machinery held for sale and interest incurred after an asset has been completed, should be expensed.
Answer (A) is incorrect. All interest incurred for machinery held for sale and interest incurred for machinery for Bay's own use after completion should be expensed. Answer (B) is incorrect. All interest incurred for machinery held for sale and interest incurred for machinery for Bay's own use after completion should be expensed. Answer (C) is incorrect. All interest incurred for machinery held for sale and interest incurred for machinery for Bay's own use after completion should be expensed.

7.2.6. Sun Co. was constructing fixed assets that qualified for interest capitalization. Sun had the following outstanding debt issuances during the entire year of construction:

- $6,000,000 face value, 8% interest
- $8,000,000 face value, 9% interest

None of the borrowings were specified for the construction of the qualified fixed asset. Average expenditures for the year were $1,000,000. What interest rate should Sun use to calculate capitalized interest on the construction?

A. 8.00%

B. 8.50%

C. 8.57%

D. 9.00%

Answer (C) is correct. *(CPA, adapted)*
REQUIRED: The interest rate used to calculate capitalized interest given average expenditures and outstanding debt issuances.
DISCUSSION: The costs necessary to bring an asset to the condition and location of its intended use are part of the historical cost. Interest incurred during construction is such a cost and must be debited to the internally constructed asset. No new borrowings were outstanding during the period that can be identified with the ICA. Thus, the interest rate used is the weighted-average rate on other borrowings outstanding during the period. It is calculated as follows:

$$[\$6,000,000 \div (\$6,000,000 + \$8,000,000)] \times 8\% = \quad 3.43\%$$
$$[\$8,000,000 \div (\$6,000,000 + \$8,000,000)] \times 9\% = \quad \underline{5.14\%}$$
$$\overline{8.57\%}$$

Answer (A) is incorrect. This interest rate (8.00%) is for the $6,000,000 face amount debt issuance. Answer (B) is incorrect. This interest rate (8.50%) is the average of the two rates. The weighted-average rate on other borrowings is used to calculate the amount of interest that must be capitalized when no specific borrowing can be identified with the asset. Answer (D) is incorrect. This interest rate (9.00%) is for the $8,000,000 face amount debt issuance.

7.2.7. Which of the following items should not have been capitalized?

A. The cost of reinstalling or rearranging equipment to facilitate more efficient future production.

B. The cost of removing an old building from land that was purchased with the intent of constructing a new office building on the site.

C. The estimated cost of equity capital during the construction period of a new office building.

D. The cost of a new hospital wing.

Answer (C) is correct. *(CIA, adapted)*
REQUIRED: The item that should not have been capitalized.
DISCUSSION: GAAP require the capitalization of interest on debt incurred as a cost of acquiring an asset during the period in which an asset is being constructed for the company's own use. Imputed interest on equity capital is not capitalized. The view of the FASB is that recognizing the cost of equity capital would not conform to the current accounting framework.
Answer (A) is incorrect. Such a cost will benefit future periods and thus should be capitalized. Answer (B) is incorrect. The removal cost is associated with preparing land for its intended use and therefore should be capitalized. Answer (D) is incorrect. A new hospital wing is an addition and should be capitalized.

7.2.8. A company obtained a $300,000 loan with a 10% interest rate on January 1, Year 1, to finance the construction of an office building for its own use. Building construction began on January 1, Year 1, and the project was not completed as of December 31, Year 1. The following payments were made in Year 1 related to the construction project:

January 1	Purchased land for $120,000
September 1	Progress payment to contractor for $150,000

What amount of interest should be capitalized for the year ended December 31, Year 1?

   A. $13,500

   B. $15,000

   C. $17,000

   D. $30,000

Answer (C) is correct. *(CPA, adapted)*
   REQUIRED: The amount of interest on debt used to finance construction that should be capitalized.
   DISCUSSION: The costs necessary to bring an asset to the condition and location of its intended use, such as interest incurred during construction, are capitalized as part of the historical cost of the asset. Capitalized interest equals the weighted-average accumulated expenditures for the qualifying asset during the capitalization period times the interest rate. For the year, the weighted-average accumulated expenditures includes the full $120,000 cost of land [$120,000 × (12 months ÷ 12 months)] and $50,000 of the progress payment [$150,000 × (4 months ÷ 12 months)]. Thus, total weighted-average accumulated expenditures is $170,000 ($120,000 + $50,000). Multiplying this amount by the interest rate of the loan (10%) results in the amount of interest that should be capitalized of $17,000 ($170,000 × 10%).
   Answer (A) is incorrect. Capitalized interest equals the weighted-average accumulated expenditures for the qualifying asset during the capitalization period times the interest rate. Accumulated expenditures must be weighted based on the time the expenditures incurred interest. The cost of land incurred interest for the full 12 months, while the progress payment only incurred interest for 4 out of 12 months in the period (September – December). Answer (B) is incorrect. Capitalized interest equals the weighted-average accumulated expenditures for the qualifying asset during the capitalization period times the interest rate. Accumulated expenditures for the asset include both the cost of land and the progress payment. However, these amounts must be weighted based on the time the expenditures incurred interest (which otherwise could have been avoided by repaying the debt). Answer (D) is incorrect. The amount of $30,000 incorrectly capitalizes the total interest expense for the loan. Capitalized interest should equal the weighted-average accumulated expenditures for the qualifying asset during the capitalization period times the interest rate.

7.3 Costs Subsequent to Acquisition

7.3.1. Charging the cost of ordinary repairs to the machinery and equipment asset account during the current year

   A. Understates net income for the current year.

   B. Understates equity at the end of the current year.

   C. Does not affect the total assets at the end of the current year.

   D. Does not affect the total liabilities at the end of the current year.

Answer (D) is correct. *(CMA, adapted)*
   REQUIRED: The effect of charging the cost of ordinary repairs to the machinery and equipment asset account.
   DISCUSSION: When an asset is acquired, the expenses of maintaining the asset are expenses of the period in which the ordinary repairs are rendered. Charging such ordinary repairs to the machinery and equipment asset account overstates total assets, the current year's net income, and equity. Liabilities are not affected.
   Answer (A) is incorrect. Net income is overstated (not understated). Answer (B) is incorrect. Equity is overstated (not understated). Answer (C) is incorrect. Assets are overstated.

7.3.2. A machine with an original estimated useful life of 10 years is moved to another location in the factory after it had been in service for 3 years. The efficiency of the machine is increased for its remaining useful life. The reinstallation costs should be capitalized if the remaining useful life of the machine is

	5 Years	10 Years
A.	No	No
B.	No	Yes
C.	Yes	No
D.	Yes	Yes

Answer (D) is correct. *(CPA, adapted)*
   REQUIRED: The proper treatment of reinstallation costs that increase a machine's efficiency.
   DISCUSSION: Costs that significantly improve the future service potential of an asset by increasing the quality or quantity of its output should be capitalized even though the machine's useful life is not extended. The reinstallation cost should be capitalized whether the remaining useful life is 5 or 10 years.
   Answer (A) is incorrect. The reinstallation costs also should be capitalized when the remaining useful life is 5 or 10 years. Answer (B) is incorrect. The reinstallation costs should also be capitalized when the remaining useful life is 5 years. Answer (C) is incorrect. The reinstallation costs should also be capitalized if the remaining useful life is 10 years.

7.3.3. On January 2, Novation Corp. replaced its boiler with a more efficient one. The following information was available on that date:

Purchase price of new boiler	$120,000
Carrying amount of old boiler	10,000
Fair value of old boiler	4,000
Installation cost of new boiler	16,000

The old boiler was sold for $4,000. What amount should Novation capitalize as the cost of the new boiler?

  A. $136,000

  B. $132,000

  C. $126,000

  D. $120,000

Answer (A) is correct. *(CPA, adapted)*
REQUIRED: The amount to be capitalized as the cost of the replacement asset.
DISCUSSION: When a fixed asset is replaced, the new asset should be recorded at its purchase price plus any incidental costs necessary to make the asset ready for its intended use. Consequently, the replacement boiler should be recorded at $136,000 ($120,000 purchase price + $16,000 installation cost). In addition, the $10,000 carrying amount of the old boiler should be removed from the accounts, and a loss of $6,000 ($4,000 proceeds – $10,000 carrying amount) should be recognized.
Answer (B) is incorrect. The amount of $132,000 improperly deducts the fair value of the old boiler. Answer (C) is incorrect. This figure results from deducting the carrying amount of the old boiler. Answer (D) is incorrect. The amount of $120,000 does not consider the installation costs.

7.3.4. Derby Co. incurred costs to modify its building and to rearrange its production line. As a result, an overall reduction in production costs is expected. However, the modifications did not increase the building's market value, and the rearrangement did not extend the production line's life. Should the building modification costs and the production line rearrangement costs be capitalized?

	Building Modification Costs	Production Line Rearrangement Costs
A.	Yes	No
B.	Yes	Yes
C.	No	No
D.	No	Yes

Answer (B) is correct. *(CPA, adapted)*
REQUIRED: The accounting for building modification costs and production line rearrangement costs.
DISCUSSION: A rearrangement is the movement of existing assets to provide greater efficiency or to reduce production costs. If the rearrangement expenditure benefits future periods, it should be capitalized. If the building modification costs likewise improve future service potential, they too should be capitalized.
Answer (A) is incorrect. The production line rearrangement costs should be capitalized. Answer (C) is incorrect. The building modification costs and production line rearrangement costs should be capitalized. Answer (D) is incorrect. The building modification costs should be capitalized.

7.3.5. A building suffered uninsured fire damage. The damaged portion of the building was refurbished with higher-quality materials. The cost and related accumulated depreciation of the damaged portion are identifiable. The owner should

  A. Reduce accumulated depreciation equal to the cost of refurbishing.

  B. Record a loss in the current period equal to the sum of the cost of refurbishing and the carrying amount of the damaged part of the building.

  C. Capitalize the cost of refurbishing and record a loss in the current period equal to the carrying amount of the damaged part of the building.

  D. Capitalize the cost of refurbishing by adding the cost to the carrying amount of the building.

Answer (C) is correct. *(CPA, adapted)*
REQUIRED: The proper accounting for a substitution.
DISCUSSION: When a substantial portion of a productive asset is replaced and the cost and related accumulated depreciation associated with the old component are identifiable, the substitution method of accounting is used. Under this approach, the asset account and accumulated depreciation should be reduced by the appropriate amounts, and a gain or loss should be recognized. In this instance, the damages were uninsured, and a loss equal to the carrying amount of the damaged portion of the building should be recognized. In addition, the cost of refurbishing should be capitalized in the asset account.
Answer (A) is incorrect. The cost of refurbishing should be capitalized, and a loss equal to the carrying amount of the damaged portion of the building should be recognized. Answer (B) is incorrect. The cost of refurbishing should be capitalized, and a loss equal to the carrying amount of the damaged portion of the building should be recognized. Answer (D) is incorrect. The cost of refurbishing should be capitalized, and a loss equal to the carrying amount of the damaged portion of the building should be recognized.

7.3.6. An expenditure subsequent to acquisition of assembly-line manufacturing equipment benefits future periods. The expenditure should be capitalized if it is a

	Betterment	Rearrangement
A.	No	No
B.	No	Yes
C.	Yes	No
D.	Yes	Yes

Answer (D) is correct. *(CPA, adapted)*
REQUIRED: The type(s) of expenditure that should be capitalized.
DISCUSSION: A betterment occurs when a replacement asset is substituted for an existing asset, and the result is increased productivity, capacity, or expected useful life. A rearrangement is the movement of existing assets to provide greater efficiency or to reduce production costs. If the betterment or rearrangement expenditure benefits future periods, it should be capitalized.

7.3.7. During the current year, Murdock Company made the following expenditures relating to plant machinery and equipment:

- Renovation of a group of machines at a cost of $100,000 to secure greater efficiency in production over their remaining 5-year useful lives. The project was completed on December 31.
- Continuing, frequent, and low-cost repairs at a cost of $70,000.
- Replacement of a broken gear on a machine at a cost of $10,000.

What total amount should be charged to repairs and maintenance for the current year?

- A. $70,000
- B. $80,000
- C. $170,000
- D. $180,000

Answer (B) is correct. *(CPA, adapted)*
REQUIRED: The amount to be charged to repair and maintenance expense.
DISCUSSION: Repair and maintenance costs are incurred to maintain plant assets in operating condition. The continuing, frequent, and low-cost repairs and the replacement of a broken gear meet the definition of repairs and maintenance expense. Accordingly, the amount that should be charged to repairs and maintenance is $80,000 ($70,000 + $10,000). The renovation cost increased the quality of production during the expected useful life of the group of machines. Hence, this $100,000 cost should be capitalized.
    Answer (A) is incorrect. The cost of a broken gear should also be charged to repairs and maintenance. Answer (C) is incorrect. The renovation of machines should not be charged to repairs and maintenance; it should be capitalized. The broken gear should be included in repairs and maintenance. Answer (D) is incorrect. The renovation of machines should be capitalized, not charged to repairs and maintenance.

7.3.8. On November 2, Corley Co. incurred the following costs for one of its printing presses:

Purchase of collating and stapling attachment	$168,000
Installation of attachment	72,000
Replacement parts for overhaul of press	52,000
Labor and overhead in connection with overhaul	28,000

The overhaul resulted in a significant increase in production. Neither the attachment nor the overhaul increased the estimated useful life of the press. What amount of the above costs should be capitalized?

- A. $0
- B. $168,000
- C. $240,000
- D. $320,000

Answer (D) is correct. *(CPA, adapted)*
REQUIRED: The amount of costs to be capitalized.
DISCUSSION: Expenditures that increase the quality or quantity of a machine's output should be capitalized whether or not its useful life is extended. Thus, the amount of the cost to be capitalized equals $320,000 ($168,000 + $72,000 + $52,000 + $28,000).
    Answer (A) is incorrect. Costs in the amount of $320,000 should be capitalized. Answer (B) is incorrect. All of the costs associated with the purchase of the parts and the overhaul should be capitalized. Answer (C) is incorrect. The cost of replacement parts and labor and overhead should also be capitalized.

7.3.9. During Year 1, Kapital Company spent $2,700,000 to rearrange and $1,200,000 to reinstall the assembly line at one of its plants in order to convert the plant over to the manufacture of a new company product beginning in Year 2. The $1,200,000 in reinstallation costs were charged to the related machinery and equipment, which has an average remaining useful life of 15 years. The new product has an expected life of 9 years. The $2,700,000 in rearrangement costs should be charged in Year 1 to

A. A deferred expense account and expensed at a rate of $300,000 per year beginning in Year 2.

B. A deferred expense account that is never amortized.

C. An expense account.

D. Factory machinery and equipment and depreciated over 15 years.

Answer (A) is correct. *(CIA, adapted)*
REQUIRED: The proper accounting for rearrangement costs.
DISCUSSION: Costs that significantly improve the future service potential of an asset by increasing the quality or quantity of its output should be capitalized. Because the rearrangement and reinstallation costs were incurred to increase the productivity of the assembly line, both costs should be capitalized as part of the related machinery and equipment. These capitalized costs should then be amortized over the expected 9-year life of the new product. Thus, the $2,700,000 in rearrangement costs should be debited to either the asset account or a deferred expense account and then expensed over the 9 years at a rate of $300,000 per year.
Answer (B) is incorrect. The rearrangement costs should be capitalized and amortized over 9 years. Answer (C) is incorrect. The rearrangement costs increase the quality or quantity of output so the costs should not be treated as an expense. Answer (D) is incorrect. The rearrangement costs benefit the new product, which has an expected life of 9 years; therefore, the cost should not be amortized over 15 years (the life of the old equipment).

7.4 Impairment and Disposal

7.4.1. When should a long-lived asset be tested for recoverability?

A. When external financial statements are being prepared.

B. When events or changes in circumstances indicate that its carrying amount may not be recoverable.

C. When the asset's carrying amount is less than its fair value.

D. When the asset's fair value has decreased, and the decrease is judged to be permanent.

Answer (B) is correct. *(CPA, adapted)*
REQUIRED: The time when a long-lived asset should be tested for recoverability.
DISCUSSION: A long-lived asset is impaired when its carrying amount is greater than its fair value. However, a loss equal to this excess is recognized for the impairment only when the carrying amount is not recoverable. The carrying amount is not recoverable when it exceeds the sum of the undiscounted cash flows expected from the use and disposition of the asset. Testing should occur when events or changes in circumstances indicate that the carrying amount may not be recoverable.
Answer (A) is incorrect. Under U.S. GAAP, preparation of the external financial statements is not a reason to test for recoverability. Examples of events or changes in circumstances indicating nonrecoverability are a significant decrease in market price or a significant adverse change in use or condition of the asset. Answer (C) is incorrect. When the asset's carrying amount is less than its fair value, the asset is not impaired. Thus, the excess of the fair value over the carrying amount cannot be an indicator of impairment. Answer (D) is incorrect. Even though the asset's fair value has decreased permanently, the fair value may still exceed the carrying amount.

7.4.2. On January 2, Year 5, Clarinette Co. purchased assets for $400,000 that were to be depreciated over 5 years using the straight-line method with no salvage value. Taken together, these assets have identifiable cash flows that are largely independent of the cash flows of other asset groups. At the end of Year 6, Clarinette, as the result of certain changes in circumstances indicating that the carrying amount of these assets may not be recoverable, tested them for impairment. It estimated that it will receive net future cash inflows (undiscounted) of $100,000 as a result of continuing to hold and use these assets, which had a fair value of $80,000 at the end of Year 6. Thus, the impairment loss to be reported at December 31, Year 6, is

A. $0

B. $140,000

C. $160,000

D. $400,000

Answer (C) is correct. *(Publisher, adapted)*
REQUIRED: The carrying amount given estimated future net cash inflows and the fair value.
DISCUSSION: The carrying amount at December 31, Year 6, is $240,000 {$400,000 cost − [2 years × ($400,000 ÷ 5 years)]}, but the recoverable amount is only $100,000. Hence, the test for recognition of an impairment loss has been met. This loss is measured by the excess of the carrying amount over the fair value. Clarinette should therefore recognize a loss of $160,000 ($240,000 − $80,000 fair value).
Answer (A) is incorrect. The test for recognition of impairment has been met. Answer (B) is incorrect. The amount of $140,000 is the excess of the carrying amount over the undiscounted future net cash inflows. Answer (D) is incorrect. The purchase price of the assets is $400,000.

7.4.3. Tera Corporation owns a plant that produces baubles for a specialized market niche. This plant is part of an asset group that is the lowest level at which identifiable cash flows are largely independent of those of Tera's other holdings. The asset group includes long-lived assets X, Y, and Z, which are to be held and used. It also includes current assets and liabilities that are not subject to the guidance on accounting for the impairment or disposal of long-lived assets. The sum of the undiscounted cash flows expected to result from the use and eventual disposition of the asset group is $3,200,000, and its fair value is $2,900,000. The following are the carrying amounts ($000 omitted) of the assets and liabilities included in the asset group:

Current assets	$ 600
Liabilities	(200)
Long-lived asset	
X	1,500
Y	900
Z	600

If the fair value of X is determinable as $1,400,000 without undue cost and effort, what should be the carrying amount of Z?

A. $440,000

B. $500,000

C. $600,000

D. $660,000

Answer (A) is correct. *(Publisher, adapted)*
REQUIRED: The carrying amount of Z.
DISCUSSION: An impairment loss decreases only the carrying amounts of the long-lived assets in the group on a pro rata basis according to their relative carrying amounts. However, the carrying amount of a given long-lived asset is not reduced below its fair value if that fair value is determinable without undue cost and effort. Because the total carrying amount of the asset group of $3.4 million ($600 − $200 + $1,500 + $900 + $600) exceeds the $3.2 million sum of the undiscounted cash flows expected to result from the use and eventual disposition of the asset group, the carrying amount is not recoverable. Hence, an impairment loss equal to the excess of the total carrying amount of the group over its fair value ($3.4 million − $2.9 million = $500,000) must be recognized and allocated pro rata to the long-lived assets. The amounts allocated to X, Y, and Z are $250,000 [($1,500 ÷ $3,000) × $500], $150,000 [($900 ÷ $3,000) × $500], and $100,000 [($600 ÷ $3,000) × $500], respectively. The preliminary adjusted carrying amounts of X, Y, and Z are therefore $1,250,000 ($1,500 − $250), $750,000 ($900 − $150), and $500,000 ($600 − $100), respectively. However, the fair value of X determined without undue cost and effort is $1,400,000. Accordingly, $150,000 ($1,400 fair value of X − $1,250 preliminary adjusted carrying amount of X) must be reallocated to Y and Z. The amounts reallocated to Y and Z are $90,000 [($750 ÷ $1,250) × $150] and $60,000 [($500 ÷ $1,250) × $150], respectively. Thus, the carrying amount of Z should be $440,000 ($600 − $100 − $60).
Answer (B) is incorrect. The preliminary adjusted carrying amount of Z is $500,000. Answer (C) is incorrect. The carrying amount of Z before reduction for a proportionate share of the impairment loss is $600,000. Answer (D) is incorrect. The carrying amount of Z before reduction for a proportionate share of the impairment loss plus (rather than minus) Z's share of the reallocated amount is $660,000.

7.4.4. An impairment loss on a long-lived asset (asset group) to be held and used is reported by a business enterprise in

A. Discontinued operations.

B. The equity section of the balance sheet as a direct reduction of retained earnings.

C. Other comprehensive income.

D. Income from continuing operations.

Answer (D) is correct. *(Publisher, adapted)*
REQUIRED: The reporting of an impairment loss on a long-lived asset (asset group) to be held and used.
DISCUSSION: An impairment loss is included in income from continuing operations before income taxes by a business enterprise (income from continuing operations in the statement of activities by a not-for-profit organization). When a subtotal for "income from operations" is reported, the impairment loss is included.
Answer (A) is incorrect. A long-lived asset (asset group) to be held and used is not a discontinued operation. Answer (B) is incorrect. An impairment loss decreases retained earnings only after it is recognized in income from continuing operations. It is not separately reported in the equity section. Answer (C) is incorrect. An impairment loss is reported in the income statement. Items reported in OCI have bypassed the income statement.

7.4.5. A long-lived asset (disposal group) classified as held for sale should be accounted for by

A. Subtracting expected future operating losses from its fair value.

B. Recognizing a write-down to fair value minus cost to sell as a credit to other comprehensive income.

C. Recognizing a gain for any increase in fair value minus cost to sale.

D. Adjusting only a long-lived asset for write-downs to fair value minus cost to sell or the reversal of such an adjustment.

Answer (D) is correct. *(Publisher, adapted)*
REQUIRED: The accounting for a long-lived asset classified as held for sale.
DISCUSSION: A loss is recognized for a write-down to fair value minus cost to sell. A gain is recognized for any subsequent increase but only to the extent of previously recognized losses for write-downs. The loss or gain adjusts only the carrying amount of a long-lived asset even if it is included in a disposal group.
Answer (A) is incorrect. A long-lived asset (disposal group) is measured at fair value minus cost to sell. Answer (B) is incorrect. A write-down to fair value minus cost to sell is recognized as a loss (a debit) in the income statement. Answer (C) is incorrect. The gain is limited to the cumulative loss previously recognized for write-downs.

7.4.6. According to U.S. GAAP, restorations of carrying value for long-lived assets are permitted if an asset's fair value increases subsequent to recording an impairment loss for which of the following?

	Held for use	Held for disposal
A.	Yes	Yes
B.	Yes	No
C.	No	Yes
D.	No	No

Answer (C) is correct. *(CPA, adapted)*
REQUIRED: The long-lived assets for which an increase in the carrying amount is permitted if their fair value increases subsequent to recognition of an impairment loss.
DISCUSSION: Under U.S. GAAP, a previously recognized impairment loss on a long-lived asset to be held and used must not be reversed. The carrying amount of the long-lived asset adjusted for an impairment loss is its new cost basis. However, if the long-lived asset is held for sale, a gain is recognized for a subsequent increase in fair value minus cost to sell. But the gain is limited to the extent of prior write-downs. Furthermore, if the long-lived asset is held to be disposed of other than by sale, it is classified as held and used until disposal.
Answer (A) is incorrect. Under U.S. GAAP, a previously recognized impairment loss on a long-lived asset to be held and used must not be reversed. Answer (B) is incorrect. Under U.S. GAAP, a previously recognized impairment loss on a long-lived asset to be held and used must not be reversed. However, if the long-lived asset is held for sale, a gain is recognized for a subsequent increase in fair value minus cost to sell. But the gain is limited to the extent of prior write-downs. Answer (D) is incorrect. Under U.S. GAAP, if the long-lived asset is held for sale, a gain is recognized for a subsequent increase in fair value minus cost to sell. But the gain is limited to the extent of prior write-downs.

7.4.7. Four years ago on January 2, Randall Co. purchased a long-lived asset. The purchase price of the asset was $250,000, with no salvage value. The estimated useful life of the asset was 10 years. Randall used the straight-line method to calculate depreciation expense. An impairment loss on the asset of $30,000 was recognized on December 31 of the current year. The estimated useful life of the asset at December 31 of the current year did not change. What amount should Randall report as depreciation expense in its income statement for the next year?

A. $20,000

B. $22,000

C. $25,000

D. $30,000

Answer (A) is correct. *(CPA, adapted)*
    REQUIRED: The depreciation expense reported in the year following recognition of an impairment loss.
    DISCUSSION: The asset's initial depreciable base was $250,000 ($250,000 purchase price – $0 salvage value), and accumulated depreciation after 4 years was $100,000 [($250,000 ÷ 10 years) × 4 years]. The asset's carrying amount on December 31 was therefore $120,000 ($250,000 depreciable base – $100,000 accumulated depreciation – $30,000 impairment loss). Allocating this amount over the remaining useful life results in a revised annual depreciation expense of $20,000 ($120,000 ÷ 6 years).
    Answer (B) is incorrect. The amount of $22,000 is based on the assumption that the impairment loss was $18,000. Answer (C) is incorrect. The amount of $25,000 is the annual depreciation expense reported prior to recognition of the impairment loss. Answer (D) is incorrect. The amount of $30,000 equals $180,000 recognized over a remaining useful life of 6 years. This calculation is based on the assumption that a $30,000 revaluation increase was recognized. A revaluation increase is permitted under IFRS, not U.S. GAAP.

7.4.8. If a long-lived asset satisfies the criteria for classification as held for sale,

A. Its carrying amount is the cost at the acquisition date if the asset is newly acquired.

B. It is not depreciated.

C. Interest attributable to liabilities of a disposal group to which the asset belongs is not accrued.

D. It is classified as held for sale even if the criteria are not met until after the balance sheet date but before issuance of the financial statements.

Answer (B) is correct. *(Publisher, adapted)*
    REQUIRED: The treatment of a long-lived asset that meets the criteria for classification as held for sale.
    DISCUSSION: A long-lived asset is not depreciated (amortized) while it is classified as held for sale and measured at the lower of carrying amount or fair value minus cost to sell. The reason is that depreciation (amortization) would reduce the carrying amount below fair value minus cost to sell. Furthermore, fair value minus cost to sell must be evaluated each period, so any future decline will be recognized in the period of decline.
    Answer (A) is incorrect. The carrying amount of a newly acquired long-lived asset classified as held for sale is its fair value minus cost to sell at the acquisition date. Answer (C) is incorrect. Interest and other expenses attributable to liabilities of a disposal group to which the asset belongs are accrued. Answer (D) is incorrect. If the criteria are not met until after the balance sheet date but before issuance of the financial statements, the long-lived asset continues to be classified as held and used in those statements.

7.4.9. The guidance for the recognition and measurement of impairment losses on long-lived assets to be held and used applies to

A. Goodwill.

B. An asset group.

C. A financial instrument.

D. Any intangible asset not being amortized.

Answer (B) is correct. *(Publisher, adapted)*
    REQUIRED: The item to which the guidance for the recognition and measurement of impairment losses on long-lived assets to be held and used applies.
    DISCUSSION: Such guidance applies to the long-lived assets of an entity that are to be held and used or disposed of, including those that are part of a group with other assets and liabilities not subject to such guidance. The unit of accounting for such a long-lived asset is the asset group. If a long-lived asset(s) is to be held and used, the asset group is the lowest level at which identifiable cash flows are largely independent of those of other groups. If the carrying amount of a long-lived asset (asset group) is not recoverable, a loss equal to the excess of that carrying amount over the fair value is recognized.
    Answer (A) is incorrect. The guidance does not apply to goodwill, which is tested for impairment at the reporting unit level. Answer (C) is incorrect. The guidance does not apply to financial instruments, servicing assets, deferred tax assets, and certain long-lived assets subject to Codification sections applicable to specialized industries (such as marketed software or oil and gas). Answer (D) is incorrect. The guidance does not apply to an intangible asset not being amortized that is to be held and used.

7.4.10. A long-lived asset is measured at the lower of carrying amount or fair value minus cost to sell if it is to be

I. Held for sale
II. Abandoned
III. Exchanged for a similar productive asset
IV. Distributed to owners in a spinoff

    A. I only.

    B. I and III only.

    C. II, III, and IV only.

    D. I, II, III, and IV.

Answer (A) is correct. *(Publisher, adapted)*
    REQUIRED: The circumstances in which a long-lived asset is measured at the lower of carrying amount or fair value minus cost to sell.
    DISCUSSION: Disposal of a long-lived asset may be other than by sale, e.g., by abandonment, exchange, or distribution to owners in a spinoff. When disposal is to be other than by sale, the asset continues to be classified as held and used until disposal. A long-lived asset to be held and used is measured at the lower of its carrying amount or fair value, but an impairment is recognized prior to disposal only if the carrying amount is not recoverable. An asset that meets the criteria for classification as held for sale is measured at the lower of its carrying amount or fair value minus cost to sell.
    Answer (B) is incorrect. A long-lived asset to be disposed of other than by sale is classified as held and used and is measured at the lower of carrying amount or fair value. Answer (C) is incorrect. A long-lived asset to be disposed of other than by sale is classified as held and used and is measured at the lower of carrying amount or fair value. Answer (D) is incorrect. A long-lived asset to be disposed of other than by sale is classified as held and used and is measured at the lower of carrying amount or fair value.

7.4.11. An entity may decide not to sell a long-lived asset (disposal group) classified as held for sale. It should therefore reclassify the long-lived asset (disposal group) as held and used. As a result of reclassification,

    A. The disposal group will be measured at the lower of carrying amount or fair value at the date of the decision not to sell.

    B. The results of operations of a reclassified component of an entity will be reported prospectively in continuing operations.

    C. Depreciation on individual reclassified long-lived assets is reflected in their measurement.

    D. Any assets removed from a disposal group that are to be sold must continue to be measured as a group.

Answer (C) is correct. *(Publisher, adapted)*
    REQUIRED: The result of reclassifying a long-lived asset (disposal group) after a decision not to sell.
    DISCUSSION: Changes to a plan of sale may occur because of circumstances previously regarded as unlikely that result in a decision not to sell. In these circumstances, the asset (disposal group) is reclassified as held and used. A reclassified long-lived asset is measured individually at the lower of (1) carrying amount before the asset (disposal group) was classified as held for sale, minus any depreciation (amortization) that would have been recognized if it had always been classified as held and used, or (2) fair value at the date of the decision not to sell.
    Answer (A) is incorrect. Individual long-lived assets are measured at the lower of (1) carrying amount before classification as held for sale, adjusted for depreciation (amortization) that would otherwise have been recognized, or (2) fair value at the date of the decision not to sell. Answer (B) is incorrect. When a component of an entity is reclassified as held and used, its results of operations previously reported in discontinued operations are reclassified and included in income from continuing operations for all periods presented. Answer (D) is incorrect. If the assets removed from a disposal group that are to be sold do not meet the criteria for classification as held for sale as a group, they are measured individually at the lower of their carrying amounts or fair values minus cost to sell at the date of removal.

7.4.12. How should a long-lived asset or disposal group classified as held for sale be reported?

    A. The major classes of assets and liabilities must be separately disclosed on the face of the balance sheet.

    B. Assets and liabilities of a disposal group may not be presented as one amount.

    C. A long-lived asset may be aggregated with similar items on the balance sheet if separate disclosure is made in the notes.

    D. The income statement must separately present a loss for a write-down to fair value minus cost to sell.

Answer (B) is correct. *(Publisher, adapted)*
    REQUIRED: The reporting of a long-lived asset or disposal group classified as held for sale.
    DISCUSSION: If a disposal group is held for sale, its assets and liabilities are reported separately in the balance sheet and are not offset and presented as a single amount.
    Answer (A) is incorrect. The major classes of assets and liabilities held for sale are separately disclosed on the face of the balance sheet or in the notes. Answer (C) is incorrect. If a long-lived asset is held for sale, it is reported separately in the balance sheet. Answer (D) is incorrect. The entity must disclose in the notes a loss recognized for a write-down to fair value minus cost to sell, and, if not separately presented on the income statement, the caption that includes the loss.

7.4.13. An entity disposes of a nonmonetary asset in a nonreciprocal transfer. A gain or loss should be recognized on the disposition of the asset when the fair value of the asset transferred is determinable and the nonreciprocal transfer is to

	Another Entity	A Shareholder of the Entity
A.	No	Yes
B.	No	No
C.	Yes	No
D.	Yes	Yes

Answer (D) is correct. *(CPA, adapted)*
REQUIRED: The circumstances under which gain or loss should be recorded in a nonreciprocal transfer.
DISCUSSION: A nonreciprocal transfer is a transfer of assets or services in one direction. A nonreciprocal transfer of a nonmonetary asset to a shareholder or to another entity should be recorded at the fair value of the asset transferred. A gain or loss should be recognized on the transfer. However, an exception to this general rule is provided for distributions of nonmonetary assets to owners in (1) a spin-off or other form of reorganization or liquidation or (2) a plan that is in substance the rescission of a prior business combination.

7.4.14. A state government condemned Epirus Co.'s parcel of real estate. Epirus will receive $1,500,000 for this property, which has a carrying amount of $1,150,000. Epirus incurred the following costs as a result of the condemnation:

Appraisal fees to support a $1,500,000 value	$5,000
Attorney fees for the closing with the state	7,000
Attorney fees to review contract to acquire replacement property	6,000
Title insurance on replacement property	8,000

What amount of cost should Epirus use to determine the gain on the condemnation?

- A. $1,162,000
- B. $1,164,000
- C. $1,168,000
- D. $1,176,000

Answer (A) is correct. *(CPA, adapted)*
REQUIRED: The amount of cost used to determine the gain on the condemnation.
DISCUSSION: Gain or loss must be recognized even though an enterprise reinvests or is obligated to reinvest the monetary assets in replacement nonmonetary assets. The determination of the gain is based on the carrying amount ($1,150,000) and the costs incurred as a direct result of the condemnation ($5,000 appraisal fees and $7,000 attorney fees), a total of $1,162,000. Because the recipient is not obligated to reinvest the condemnation proceeds in other nonmonetary assets, the costs associated with the acquisition of the replacement property (attorney fees and title insurance) should be treated as part of the consideration paid for that property.
Answer (B) is incorrect. The amount of $1,164,000 includes the costs associated with the replacement property but not the costs incurred as a direct result of the condemnation. Answer (C) is incorrect. The amount of $1,168,000 includes the attorney fees associated with the replacement property. Answer (D) is incorrect. The amount of $1,176,000 includes the costs associated with the replacement property.

7.4.15. On July 1, one of Rudd Co.'s delivery vans was destroyed in an accident. On that date, the van's carrying value was $2,500. On July 15, Rudd received and recorded a $700 invoice for a new engine installed in the van in May and another $500 invoice for various repairs. In August, Rudd received $3,500 under its insurance policy on the van, which it plans to use to replace the van. What amount should Rudd report as gain (loss) on disposal of the van in its income statement for the year?

- A. $1,000
- B. $300
- C. $0
- D. $(200)

Answer (B) is correct. *(CPA, adapted)*
REQUIRED: The gain (loss) on disposal of the van.
DISCUSSION: Gain (loss) is recognized on an involuntary conversion equal to the difference between the proceeds and the carrying amount. The carrying amount includes the carrying value at July 1 ($2,500) plus the capitalizable cost ($700) of the engine installed in May. This cost increased the carrying amount because it improved the future service potential of the asset. Ordinary repairs, however, are expensed. Consequently, the gain is $300 [$3,500 – ($2,500 + $700)].
Answer (A) is incorrect. The amount of $1,000 results from expensing the cost of the engine. Answer (C) is incorrect. Gain (loss) is recognized on an involuntary conversion. Answer (D) is incorrect. The amount of $(200) assumes the cost of repairs increased the carrying amount.

7.4.16. Ocean Corp.'s comprehensive insurance policy allows its assets to be replaced at current value. The policy has a $50,000 deductible clause. One of Ocean's waterfront warehouses was destroyed in a winter storm. Such storms occur approximately every 4 years. Ocean incurred $20,000 of costs in dismantling the warehouse and plans to replace it. The following data relate to the warehouse:

Current carrying amount $ 300,000
Replacement cost   1,100,000

The gain Ocean should report in its income statement is

A. $1,030,000

B. $780,000

C. $730,000

D. $0

Answer (C) is correct. *(CPA, adapted)*
REQUIRED: The gain reported in the income statement.
DISCUSSION: Ocean should separately recognize a gain from continuing operations equal to $730,000 ($1,100,000 current value – $50,000 deductible – $300,000 carrying amount – $20,000 costs of dismantling).
Answer (A) is incorrect. The amount of $1,030,000 disregards the $300,000 carrying amount. Answer (B) is incorrect. The amount of $780,000 omits the deductible. Answer (D) is incorrect. A gain (loss) should be recognized for an involuntary conversion.

7.5 Exchanges of Nonmonetary Assets

7.5.1. Which of the following statements correctly describes the proper accounting for nonmonetary exchanges that are deemed to have commercial substance?

A. It defers any gains and losses.

B. It defers losses to the extent of any gains.

C. It recognizes gains and losses immediately.

D. It defers gains and recognizes losses immediately.

Answer (C) is correct. *(CPA, adapted)*
REQUIRED: The accounting for nonmonetary exchanges that have commercial substance.
DISCUSSION: When the fair value of both assets in a nonmonetary exchange is determinable, the transaction is treated as a monetary exchange. Thus, it is measured at the fair value of the assets given up, and any gain or loss is recognized immediately. When certain exceptions apply, the accounting for a nonmonetary exchange is based on the carrying amount of the assets given up. Unless boot is received, no gain is recognized. The following are the exceptions: (1) neither the fair value of the assets given up nor the fair value of the assets received is reasonably determinable; (2) the exchange involves inventory sold in the same line of business that facilitates sales to customers, not parties to the exchange; or the exchange lacks commercial substance; that is, an entity's cash flows are not expected to change significantly.
Answer (A) is incorrect. Unless an exception applies, gains are recognized in full immediately. Losses always are recognized in full immediately. Answer (B) is incorrect. The full amount of a loss on a nonmonetary exchange always is recognized in full. Answer (D) is incorrect. All or part of a gain (but not a loss) is deferred if the transaction is measured at the carrying amount of the assets given up.

7.5.2. Campbell Corp. exchanged delivery trucks with Highway, Inc. Campbell's truck originally cost $23,000, its accumulated depreciation was $20,000, and its fair value was $5,000. Highway's truck originally cost $23,500, its accumulated depreciation was $19,900, and its fair value was $5,700. Campbell also paid Highway $700 in cash as part of the transaction. The transaction lacks commercial substance. What amount is the new book value for the truck Campbell received?

A. $5,700

B. $5,000

C. $3,700

D. $3,000

Answer (C) is correct. *(CPA, adapted)*
REQUIRED: The carrying amount of the asset received by the payor or boot in a nonmonetary exchange that lacks commercial substance.
DISCUSSION: If a nonmonetary exchange lacks commercial substance, it is measured at the carrying amount of the assets given up. Accordingly, unless boot is received, no gain is recognized. Campbell gave boot of $700 and a truck with a carrying amount of $3,000 ($23,000 cost – $20,000 accumulated depreciation). The carrying amount of the new truck is therefore $3,700.
Answer (A) is incorrect. The amount of $5,700 is the fair value of the truck received. Answer (B) is incorrect. The amount of $5,000 is the fair value of the truck given. Answer (D) is incorrect. The amount of $3,000 is the carrying amount of the truck given up.

7.5.3. Bensol Co. and Sable Co. exchanged similar trucks with fair values in excess of carrying amounts. In addition, Bensol paid Sable to compensate for the difference in fair values. The boot paid was less than 25% of the fair value of the exchange. If the exchange lacked commercial substance, Sable recognizes

A. A gain equal to the difference between the fair value and carrying amount of the truck given up.

B. A gain determined by the proportion of the cash received to the total consideration.

C. A loss determined by the proportion of the cash received to the total consideration.

D. Neither a gain nor a loss.

Answer (B) is correct. *(CPA, adapted)*
REQUIRED: The consequences of exchanging similar nonmonetary assets when boot is given.
DISCUSSION: The receipt of boot is considered a partial culmination of an earning process requiring recognition of a partial gain. A gain is realized because the carrying amount of Sable's truck was less than its fair value, and the total consideration received apparently equaled the fair value. The recognized gain equals the realized gain times the ratio of boot to total consideration received. However, if the boot is 25% or more of the fair value of the exchange, both parties record the transaction as a monetary exchange at fair value, with gains and losses recognized in full.
Answer (A) is incorrect. The amount of gain recognized is in proportion to the amount of boot (cash) received. Answer (C) is incorrect. A gain should be recognized. Answer (D) is incorrect. Sable recognizes a gain.

7.5.4. Amble, Inc., exchanged a truck with a carrying amount of $12,000 and a fair value of $20,000 for another truck and $5,000 cash. The fair value of the truck received was $15,000. The exchange was not considered to have commercial substance. At what amount should Amble record the truck received in the exchange?

A. $7,000

B. $9,000

C. $12,000

D. $15,000

Answer (D) is correct. *(CPA, adapted)*
REQUIRED: The amount at which a nonmonetary asset should be recorded in a transaction involving boot.
DISCUSSION: A transaction involving nonmonetary assets and boot is monetary if the boot equals or exceeds 25% of the fair value of the exchange. In this exchange, the $5,000 of boot equals 25% of the $20,000 ($5,000 + $15,000) fair value of the exchange. Thus, the exchange is monetary. Accounting for monetary transactions should be based on the fair value of the assets involved, with gain or loss recognized immediately. The party receiving boot measures the asset received at the fair value of the asset given up minus boot. Accordingly, Amble should record the truck received at $15,000 ($20,000 fair value of truck given up – $5,000 boot received).
Answer (A) is incorrect. The amount of $7,000 is the $12,000 carrying amount of the asset given up minus the $5,000 boot received. Answer (B) is incorrect. The amount of $9,000 is the $12,000 carrying amount of the truck given up, minus the $5,000 boot received, plus the $2,000 ($8,000 × 25%) proportionate gain that would have been recognized had the transaction been nonmonetary. Answer (C) is incorrect. The amount of $12,000 is the carrying amount of the truck given up.

7.5.5. Horn Co. and Book Co. exchanged nonmonetary assets in a transaction that did not have commercial substance for either party. Horn paid cash to Book that was equal to 15% of the fair value of the exchange. To the extent that the amount of cash exceeds a proportionate share of the carrying amount of the asset surrendered, a realized gain on the exchange should be recognized by

	Horn	Book
A.	Yes	Yes
B.	Yes	No
C.	No	Yes
D.	No	No

Answer (C) is correct. *(CPA, adapted)*
REQUIRED: The party(ies), if any, that should recognize a realized gain on a nonmonetary transaction involving boot that lacked commercial substance.
DISCUSSION: The accounting for a nonmonetary transaction should be based on the carrying amount of the asset(s) relinquished when the exchange lacks commercial substance. In addition, when the transaction includes a cash component (termed boot), if the boot is less than 25% of the fair value of the exchange, the recipient of the boot should adjust the carryover basis for the portion of the gain equal to the total gain times the ratio of the boot to the sum of the boot and the fair value of the asset received. However, the full amount of a loss is recognized as an adjustment of the carryover basis. In contrast, the payor of boot should measure the asset received at an amount equal to the carrying amount of the asset relinquished plus the amount of boot.
Answer (A) is incorrect. Horn does not recognize a proportionate gain. Answer (B) is incorrect. Book recognizes a proportionate gain, but Horn does not. Answer (D) is incorrect. The recipient of boot should recognize a gain.

7.5.6. In an exchange of assets, Junger Co. received equipment with a fair value equal to the carrying amount of the equipment given up. Junger also contributed cash equal to 10% of the fair value of the exchange. If the exchange is not considered to have commercial substance, Junger should recognize

A. A loss equal to the cash (boot) given up.

B. A loss determined by the proportion of cash paid to the total transaction value.

C. A gain determined by the proportion of cash paid to the total transaction value.

D. Neither gain nor loss.

Answer (A) is correct. *(CPA, adapted)*
REQUIRED: The gain or loss in a nonmonetary transaction involving boot that lacked commercial substance.
DISCUSSION: The accounting for a nonmonetary transaction should be based on the carrying amount of the asset(s) given up when the exchange lacks commercial substance. Because the boot in the transaction is less than 25% of the fair value of the exchange, the exchange is based on the carrying amount of assets given up.
Answer (B) is incorrect. When a loss is indicated, the entire loss should be recognized. Answer (C) is incorrect. A loss equal to the amount of cash given up should be recognized. Answer (D) is incorrect. A loss equal to the amount of cash given up should be recognized.

7.5.7. Minor Baseball Company had a player contract with Doe that was recorded in its accounting records at $145,000. Better Baseball Company had a player contract with Smith that was recorded in its accounting records at $140,000. Minor traded Doe to Better for Smith by exchanging player contracts. The fair value of each contract was $150,000. Evidence suggested that the contract exchange lacked commercial substance. At what amount should the contracts be valued in accordance with generally accepted accounting principles at the time of the exchange of the player contracts?

	Minor	Better
A.	$140,000	$140,000
B.	$140,000	$145,000
C.	$145,000	$140,000
D.	$150,000	$150,000

Answer (C) is correct. *(CPA, adapted)*
REQUIRED: The amount at which to record an asset received in a nonmonetary exchange transaction that lacked commercial substance.
DISCUSSION: The accounting for a nonmonetary transaction should be based on the carrying amount of the asset(s) given up when the exchange lacks commercial substance. An exchange lacks commercial substance when an entity's cash flows are not expected to change significantly. Thus, Minor should record its contract with Smith at $145,000, and Better should record its contract with Doe at $140,000.
Answer (A) is incorrect. Minor should record its contract with Smith at $145,000, its previously recorded (carryover) amount for its contract with Doe. Answer (B) is incorrect. Minor should record its contract with Smith at $145,000, and Better should record its contract with Doe at $140,000. Answer (D) is incorrect. The amount of $150,000, the fair value of each contract, should be recorded if the exchange has commercial substance.

7.5.8. Bell and Mayo are independent entities. Each owns a tract of land being held for development. However, each would prefer to build on the other's land. Accordingly, they agreed to exchange their land. From an independent appraisal report and the entities' records, the following information was obtained:

	Bell's Land	Mayo's Land
Cost and carrying amount	$ 80,000	$50,000
Fair value	100,000	85,000

Based on the difference in fair values, Mayo paid $15,000 to Bell. If Mayo did not consider the exchange to have commercial substance, at what amount should Mayo record the receipt of land?

A. $100,000

B. $85,000

C. $65,000

D. $50,000

Answer (C) is correct. *(Publisher, adapted)*
REQUIRED: The amount at which the asset received should be recorded by the payer of boot in a nonmonetary exchange lacking commercial substance.
DISCUSSION: Accounting for a nonmonetary transaction should be based on the carrying amount of the asset(s) given up when the exchange lacks commercial substance. In addition, when the transaction includes monetary consideration (boot), if the boot is less than 25% of the fair value of the exchange, the recipient (but not the payer) of the boot should adjust the carryover basis for a portion of the gain. The payer of boot should record the asset received at an amount equal to the carryover basis of the nonmonetary asset given up plus the boot paid. In this situation, because the boot equals 15% ($15,000 ÷ $100,000) of the fair value of the exchange, Mayo should record the land received from Bell at $65,000 ($50,000 carrying amount + $15,000 boot).
Answer (A) is incorrect. The amount of $100,000 is the fair value of the land received, the amount at which the land would be recorded if the exchange had commercial substance. Answer (B) is incorrect. The fair value of the land Mayo exchanged is $85,000. Answer (D) is incorrect. The carrying amount of the land Mayo exchanged is $50,000.

7.5.9. On July 1 of the current year, Trey Co. exchanged a truck for 25 shares of Deuce Corp.'s common stock. The fair value of this stock is not readily determinable. On that date, the truck's carrying amount was $2,500, and its fair value was $3,000. Also, the carrying amount of Deuce's stock was $50 per share. Trey cannot exercise significant influence over Deuce. What amount should Trey report in its December 31 current-year balance sheet as investment in Deuce?

A. $3,000

B. $2,500

C. $1,250

D. $1,750

Answer (A) is correct. *(CPA, adapted)*
REQUIRED: The amount reported for stock received in exchange for a nonmonetary asset.
DISCUSSION: Accounting for nonmonetary transactions usually should be based on the fair values of the assets or services involved. The exceptions arise when (1) the fair value of neither the asset(s) received nor the asset(s) relinquished is determinable within reasonable limits, (2) the exchange facilitates sales of inventory to customers, or (3) the exchange lacks commercial substance. No exception applies because the fair value of the asset relinquished is known, inventory is not involved, and no facts indicate that the exchange lacks commercial substance. Accordingly, the exchange is measured on July 1 at the $3,000 fair value of the asset relinquished. Moreover, this investment in equity securities is subsequently reported at cost (the fair value of the truck on July 1) because (1) their fair value is not readily determinable and (2) the equity method does not apply because Trey cannot exercise significant influence over Deuce.
Answer (B) is incorrect. The truck's carrying amount, not its fair value, is $2,500. Answer (C) is incorrect. The carrying amount of 25 shares of Deuce's stock on July 1 on Deuce's books was $1,250. Answer (D) is incorrect. The fair value of the truck minus the carrying amount of 25 shares of Deuce's stock on July 1 is $1,750.

7.5.10. Markson Co. traded a concrete-mixing truck with a book value of $10,000 to Pro Co. for a cement-mixing machine with a fair value of $11,000. Markson needs to know the answer to which of the following questions in order to determine whether the exchange has commercial substance?

A. Does the book value of the asset given up exceed the fair value of the asset received?

B. Is the gain on the exchange less than the increase in future cash flows?

C. Are the future cash flows expected to change significantly as a result of the exchange?

D. Is the exchange nontaxable?

Answer (C) is correct. *(CPA, adapted)*
REQUIRED: The requirement for determining whether an exchange has commercial substance.
DISCUSSION: An exchange has commercial substance if it is expected to change the entity's cash flows significantly.
Answer (A) is incorrect. Whether or not the book value of the asset given up exceeds the fair value of the asset received does not determine if the exchange has commercial substance. Answer (B) is incorrect. Whether or not the gain on the exchange is less than the increase in future cash flows does not determine if the exchange has commercial substance. Answer (D) is incorrect. Whether or not the exchange is taxable does not (in itself) determine if the exchange has commercial substance.

7.5.11. A company exchanged land with an appraised value of $50,000 and an original cost of $20,000 for machinery with a fair value of $55,000. Assuming that the transaction has commercial substance, what is the gain on the exchange?

A. $0

B. $5,000

C. $30,000

D. $35,000

Answer (C) is correct. *(CPA, adapted)*
REQUIRED: The gain on a nonmonetary exchange having commercial substance.
DISCUSSION: As the transaction has commercial substance and the fair value of both assets in a nonmonetary exchange is determinable, the transaction is measured at the fair value of the asset(s) given up, and any gain or loss is recognized immediately (accounted for as a monetary exchange). The gain on the exchange is $30,000, which is the difference between the fair value of the land given up and its carrying value ($50,000 – $20,000). The company will record the following journal entry:

Machinery	$50,000	
Land		$20,000
Gain on exchange		30,000

Answer (A) is incorrect. As no exceptions apply, this nonmonetary exchange is measured at the fair value of the asset(s) given up and any gain or loss is recognized immediately. Answer (B) is incorrect. As no exceptions apply, the amount realized on the nonmonetary exchange is considered the fair value of the asset(s) given up. The gain on the exchange is the difference between the fair value of the land given up and its carrying value. The fair value of the machinery is not included. Answer (D) is incorrect. The amount realized on the nonmonetary exchange is considered the fair value of the asset(s) given up, not the fair value of the asset(s) received.

7.6 IFRS

7.6.1. Under IFRS, when an entity chooses the revaluation model as its accounting policy for measuring property, plant, and equipment, which of the following statements is correct?

A. When an asset is revalued, the entire class of property, plant, and equipment to which that asset belongs must be revalued.

B. When an asset is revalued, individual assets within a class of property, plant, and equipment to which that asset belongs can be revalued.

C. Revaluations of property, plant, and equipment must be made at least every 3 years.

D. Increases in an asset's carrying amount as a result of the first revaluation must be recognized as a component of profit or loss.

Answer (A) is correct. *(CPA, adapted)*
REQUIRED: The true statement about revaluation of PPE.
DISCUSSION: Under IFRS, measurement of PPE subsequent to initial recognition may be at fair value at the revaluation date (minus subsequent depreciation and impairment losses). The assumption is that the PPE can be reliably measured. If an item of PPE is revalued, every item in its class also should be revalued.
Answer (B) is incorrect. If an item of PPE is revalued, every item in its class also should be revalued. Answer (C) is incorrect. Revaluation is needed whenever an asset's fair value and carrying amount differ materially. Answer (D) is incorrect. A revaluation increase (surplus) is credited directly to equity.

7.6.2. An entity bought a building for administrative purposes on January 1, Year 1, for $260,000. Its useful life is 20 years, with no residual value. The entity depreciates its items of PPE according to the straight-line (S-L) depreciation method, and its accounting policy for the building is the revaluation model with annual revaluations. The entity transfers the revaluation surplus directly to retained earnings as the asset is used by the entity. The fair values of the building on December 31, Year 1, and December 31, Year 2, are $285,000 and $261,000, respectively. On December 31, Year 1, the revaluation surplus is <List A> and the building's carrying amount is <List B>.

	List A	List B
A.	$13,000	$247,000
B.	$38,000	$285,000
C.	$25,000	$285,000
D.	$13,000	$261,000

Answer (B) is correct. *(Publisher, adapted)*
REQUIRED: The revaluation surplus and carrying amount at the end of the first year of the building's useful life.
DISCUSSION: The carrying amount of the building on December 31, Year 1, is $285,000 because it is the fair value on the revaluation date. The depreciation for Year 1 is $13,000 [($260,000 – $0 residual value) ÷ 20 years]. Thus, the carrying amount just prior to the revaluation is $247,000 ($260,000 – $13,000), and the revaluation surplus is $38,000 ($285,000 – $247,000).
Answer (A) is incorrect. The depreciation for Year 1 is $13,000. The carrying amount of the building is $247,000 ($260,000 – $13,000) on December 31, Year 1, before the revaluation. Answer (C) is incorrect. The difference between the fair value of the building on December 31, Year 1 ($285,000), and its cost ($260,000) is $25,000. Answer (D) is incorrect. The depreciation for Year 1 is $13,000, and the fair value at December 31, Year 2, is $261,000.

7.6.3. On December 31, Year 1, a company determined the following information for a long-lived asset:

Carrying amount	$80,000
Fair value	78,000
Costs to sell	3,000
Value in use	74,000
Undiscounted expected future cash flows	77,000

According to IFRS, what amount of impairment loss should the company recognize in the year-end financial statements?

A. $0

B. $6,000

C. $2,000

D. $5,000

Answer (D) is correct. *(Publisher, adapted)*
REQUIRED: The impairment loss.
DISCUSSION: Under IFRS, an impairment loss equals the excess of the carrying amount of the asset ($80,000) over its recoverable amount. The recoverable amount of the asset is the greater of its fair value minus costs to sell ($78,000 – $3,000 = $75,000) or its value in use ($74,000). Thus, the recoverable amount of the asset is $75,000, and the impairment loss is $5,000 ($80,000 – $75,000).
Answer (A) is incorrect. The carrying amount of the asset is higher than its recoverable amount. Thus, an impairment loss must be recognized. Answer (B) is incorrect. The recoverable amount of an asset is the greater, not the lower, of its fair value minus costs to sell or value in use. Answer (C) is incorrect. Under IFRS, an impairment loss of an asset is not the excess of the carrying amount and the fair value.

7.6.4. According to IFRS, which accounting policy may an entity apply to measure investment property in periods subsequent to initial recognition?

A. Cost model or revaluation model.

B. Cost model or fair value model.

C. Fair value model only.

D. Fair value model or revaluation model.

Answer (B) is correct. *(Publisher, adapted)*
REQUIRED: The accounting policy(ies) applicable to investment property.
DISCUSSION: An entity may choose either the cost model or the fair value model as its accounting policy. But it must apply that policy to all of its investment property. Under the cost model, investment property is carried at its cost minus any accumulated depreciation and impairment losses. Under the fair value model, investment property is measured at fair value, and gain or loss from a change in its fair value is recognized immediately in profit or loss.
Answer (A) is incorrect. Owner-occupied (not investment) property that is accounted for in accordance with IAS 16, *Property, Plant, and Equipment*, is measured in periods subsequent to initial recognition using the cost model or the revaluation model. Answer (C) is incorrect. An entity has a choice of models to use as its accounting policy for measuring investment property. Answer (D) is incorrect. The revaluation model may be applied to measure owner-occupied (not investment) property that is accounted for in accordance with IAS 16, *Property, Plant, and Equipment*.

7.6.5. Under IFRS, according to the revaluation model, an item of property, plant, and equipment must be carried at

A. Cost minus any accumulated depreciation.

B. Cost minus residual value.

C. Fair value minus any subsequent accumulated depreciation and impairment losses.

D. The lower of cost or net realizable value.

Answer (C) is correct. *(Publisher, adapted)*
REQUIRED: The measure of PPE according to the revaluation model.
DISCUSSION: Under the revaluation model, if the fair value of an item of property, plant, and equipment can be reliably measured, it must be carried subsequent to initial recognition at a revalued amount. This amount is fair value at the date of the revaluation minus any subsequent accumulated depreciation and impairment losses. The revaluation model is permitted by IFRS, not U.S. GAAP.
Answer (A) is incorrect. According to the cost model, an item of property, plant, and equipment must be carried at its cost minus any accumulated depreciation and impairment losses. Answer (B) is incorrect. Cost minus residual value is the depreciable amount of an item of property, plant, and equipment. Answer (D) is incorrect. Under IFRS, inventory must be measured at the lower of cost and net realizable value.

7.6.6. Under IFRS, an increase in the carrying amount of an item of property, plant, and equipment as a result of a first revaluation must be <List A> under the heading of <List B>.

	List A	List B
A.	Recognized in profit or loss	Gain on disposal
B.	Accumulated in equity	Revaluation surplus
C.	Accumulated in equity	Retained earnings
D.	Accumulated in current liabilities	Revaluation surplus

Answer (B) is correct. *(Publisher, adapted)*
REQUIRED: The accounting for an increase in the carrying amount after a first revaluation.
DISCUSSION: The net carrying amount of an item of property, plant, and equipment may increase as a result of a revaluation (fair value at the revaluation date – net carrying amount before revaluation). Given no prior revaluation, the increase must be credited directly to revaluation surplus in the equity section of the statement of financial position.
Answer (A) is incorrect. A revaluation decrease is recognized in profit or loss. A gain on disposal is recognized in profit or loss when the entity derecognizes the asset if the net proceeds are greater than the carrying amount of the asset. Answer (C) is incorrect. The increase in an asset's carrying amount as a result of revaluation may be transferred directly to retained earnings from revaluation surplus as the asset is used by the entity. But this transfer is not at the moment of the revaluation. Answer (D) is incorrect. Revaluation surplus is an equity item, not a current liability.

7.6.7. Which of the following statements is false about an item of property, plant, and equipment (PPE)?

A. Under U.S. GAAP, such an item may be carried at an amount above its historical cost.

B. Under IFRS, such an item may be carried at an amount above its historical cost.

C. Under IFRS, such an item may be carried at its fair value.

D. Under U.S. GAAP, such an item may be carried at its historical cost.

Answer (A) is correct. *(Publisher, adapted)*
REQUIRED: The false statement about PPE.
DISCUSSION: Under U.S. GAAP, items of PPE cannot be carried above their historical cost. They are carried at historical cost minus accumulated depreciation and impairment losses.
Answer (B) is incorrect. Under IFRS, according to the revaluation model, an item of PPE is carried at its revalued amount, which can be greater than the historical cost. Answer (C) is incorrect. Under IFRS, according to the revaluation model, an item of PPE is measured at fair value on the revaluation date. Answer (D) is incorrect. If an item of PPE is acquired on the financial reporting date, it is carried at its historical cost because depreciation of the item has not yet begun.

7.6.8. Under IFRS, the recoverable amount of an asset is

A. The higher of an asset's value in use or its fair value minus costs to sell.

B. The estimated selling price in the ordinary course of business minus the estimated costs of completion and the estimated costs necessary to make the sale.

C. The present value of the future cash flows expected to be derived from an asset.

D. The amount obtainable from the sale of an asset in an arm's length transaction between knowledgeable, willing parties, minus the costs of disposal.

Answer (A) is correct. *(Publisher, adapted)*
REQUIRED: The recoverable amount of an asset.
DISCUSSION: Any indication that an asset may be impaired requires the entity to estimate its recoverable amount. The recoverable amount is the higher of an asset's fair value minus costs to sell and its value in use. Value in use is the present value of estimated future cash flows expected from (1) continuing use of an asset and (2) its disposal at the end of its useful life. Fair value minus costs to sell is the amount obtainable from the sale of an asset in an arm's length transaction between knowledgeable, willing parties, minus costs of disposal.
Answer (B) is incorrect. The estimated selling price in the ordinary course of business minus the estimated costs of completion and the estimated costs necessary to make the sale is the net realizable value. Answer (C) is incorrect. The present value of the future cash flows expected to be derived from an asset is the value in use. Answer (D) is incorrect. Under IFRS, the amount obtainable from the sale of an asset in an arm's length transaction between knowledgeable, willing parties, minus the costs of disposal, is the fair value minus costs to sell, not the recoverable amount.

7.6.9. On January 1, Year 1, a company purchased a building for the purpose of earning rental income. The price paid was $100,000. The company classified the building as investment property and accounts for it using the fair value model. The fair values of the property on December 31, Year 1, and December 31, Year 2, are $80,000 and $110,000, respectively. Under IFRS, what effect does this property have on the company's Year 2 profit or loss?

A. No effect on profit or loss.

B. Appreciation gain of $10,000.

C. Appreciation gain of $20,000.

D. Appreciation gain of $30,000.

Answer (D) is correct. *(Publisher, adapted)*
REQUIRED: The effect on profit or loss of property purchased to earn rental income.
DISCUSSION: The changes in the fair value of investment property that is accounted for according to the fair value model are recognized as gain or loss in profit or loss for the period in which they occur. An appreciation gain of $30,000 ($110,000 – $80,000) is recognized for the Year 2 increase in the fair value of the investment property.
Answer (A) is incorrect. The fair value of the property on December 31, Year 2, differs from the fair value on December 31, Year 1. Thus, the property affects profit or loss. Answer (B) is incorrect. Over the 2-year period, the total effect on the company's profit or loss is an appreciation gain of $10,000 ($110,000 – $100,000). Answer (C) is incorrect. The impairment loss recognized in Year 1 is $20,000. Under the fair value model, changes in the fair value of investment property are recognized in profit or loss. The gain recognized is not limited to impairment loss previously recognized.

7.6.10. On December 31, Year 1, indications are that an entity's asset may be impaired. The recoverable amount of that asset is $50,000. The entity applies the revaluation model for its assets and depreciates them using the straight-line method. The carrying amount of the asset on December 31, Year 1, before the test for impairment is $80,000 ($100,000 cost – $20,000 accumulated depreciation). The entity also has recognized a revaluation surplus from previous revaluations of the asset equal to $25,000. What impairment loss, if any, must be recognized in the entity's profit or loss on December 31, Year 1?

A. No impairment loss.

B. Impairment loss of $30,000.

C. Impairment loss of $10,000.

D. Impairment loss of $5,000.

Answer (D) is correct. *(Publisher, adapted)*
REQUIRED: The impairment loss on a depreciable asset accounted for using the revaluation model.
DISCUSSION: The reduction of the carrying amount of the asset to its recoverable amount results in an impairment loss of $30,000 ($80,000 carrying amount before impairment – $50,000 recoverable amount). An impairment loss on a revalued asset is recognized as a decrease in the credit balance of the revaluation surplus related to that asset. Any remainder after elimination of the revaluation surplus is recognized as a loss in profit or loss of $5,000 ($30,000 impairment of the asset – $25,000 revaluation surplus).
Answer (A) is incorrect. The decrease in the carrying amount of the asset as a result of impairment is greater than the carrying amount of the revaluation surplus for the same asset. Thus, an impairment loss must be recognized in profit or loss. Answer (B) is incorrect. The difference between the recoverable amount and the carrying amount of the asset is $30,000. But an impairment loss on a revalued asset is first recognized as a decrease in the credit balance of any revaluation surplus related to the asset. Answer (C) is incorrect. The loss recognized in profit or loss for a revalued asset is the decrease in the carrying amount as a result of an impairment minus the credit balance of the revaluation surplus related to the asset. The amount of $10,000 is the difference between the $30,000 decrease in the carrying amount of the asset as a result of impairment and the $20,000 of accumulated depreciation.

7.6.11. A company has a parcel of land to be used for a future production facility. The company applies the revaluation model under IFRS to this class of assets. In Year 1, the company acquired the land for $100,000. At the end of Year 1, the carrying amount was reduced to $90,000, which represented the fair value at that date. At the end of Year 2, the land was revalued, and the fair value increased to $105,000. How should the company account for the Year 2 change in fair value?

A. By recognizing $10,000 in other comprehensive income.

B. By recognizing $15,000 in other comprehensive income.

C. By recognizing $15,000 in profit or loss.

D. By recognizing $10,000 in profit or loss and $5,000 in other comprehensive income.

Answer (D) is correct. *(CPA, adapted)*
REQUIRED: The treatment of a change in fair value under the IFRS revaluation model.
DISCUSSION: In Year 2, the revaluation increase for the land is $15,000 ($105,000 fair value – $90,000 carrying amount). A revaluation increase must be recognized in other comprehensive income and accumulated in equity as a revaluation surplus. However, the increase must be recognized in profit or loss to the extent it reverses a decrease of the same asset that was recognized in profit or loss. In Year 1, the carrying amount of the asset was reduced by $10,000 ($100,000 – $90,000). This reduction was recognized in profit or loss (as there was no credit in revaluation surplus for the asset at that time). Thus, $10,000 of the increase in Year 2 must be recognized in profit or loss. The remaining $5,000 ($15,000 – $10,000) of the increase is recognized in other comprehensive income as a revaluation surplus.
Answer (A) is incorrect. Under the revaluation model, an item of PPE may be carried at a revalued amount equal to fair value at the revaluation date. In Year 2, the revaluation increase is $15,000 ($105,000 fair value – $90,000 carrying amount). A revaluation increase must be recognized in other comprehensive income and accumulated in equity as a revaluation surplus. However, the increase must be recognized in profit or loss to the extent it reverses a decrease of the same asset that was recognized in profit or loss. Answer (B) is incorrect. The increase must be recognized in profit or loss to the extent it reverses a decrease of the same asset that was recognized in profit or loss. Answer (C) is incorrect. The revaluation increase is only recognized in profit or loss to the extent it reverses a decrease of the same asset that was recognized in profit or loss. The remainder is recognized in other comprehensive income.

STUDY UNIT EIGHT
DEPRECIATION AND DEPLETION

Depreciation is a noncash expense reflecting the consumption of the economic benefits represented by an asset's recorded amount. It results from the systematic and rational allocation of the **historical cost** of a long-lived, tangible, productive asset to the service (useful) life of the asset. Depreciation may be calculated using straight-line, usage-centered, and accelerated methods (e.g., sum-of-the-years'-digits and declining balance). The method chosen should reflect the pattern in which economic benefits (services) from the assets are expected to be received. **Depletion** of natural resources (wasted assets) ordinarily is determined by applying the units-of-output (production) method.

QUESTIONS

8.1 Depreciation Concepts

8.1.1. A depreciable asset has an estimated 15% salvage value. At the end of its estimated useful life, the accumulated depreciation would equal the original cost of the asset under which of the following depreciation methods?

	Straight-Line	Productive-Output
A.	Yes	No
B.	Yes	Yes
C.	No	Yes
D.	No	No

Answer (D) is correct. *(CPA, adapted)*
REQUIRED: The method(s) under which accumulated depreciation will equal cost at the end of a salvageable asset's useful life.
DISCUSSION: The straight-line and productive-output depreciation methods both deduct estimated salvage value from the original cost to determine the depreciable base. At the end of the asset's estimated useful life, the accumulated depreciation will therefore equal the depreciable base under both methods.
Answer (A) is incorrect. The productive-output method also deducts salvage value to determine the depreciable base. Answer (B) is incorrect. Both methods deduct salvage value to determine the depreciable base. Answer (C) is incorrect. The straight-line method also deducts salvage value to determine the depreciable base.

8.1.2. Net income is understated if, in the first year, estimated salvage value is excluded from the depreciation computation when using the

	Straight-Line Method	Activity (Production-or-Use) Method
A.	Yes	No
B.	Yes	Yes
C.	No	No
D.	No	Yes

Answer (B) is correct. *(CPA, adapted)*
REQUIRED: The depreciation method(s) that understate(s) net income if estimated salvage value is excluded from the computation.
DISCUSSION: Under the straight-line method, the depreciable base of an asset is allocated uniformly over the time periods of the estimated use of the asset. Under the activity (production-or-use) method, the depreciable base is allocated as a constant per-unit amount as goods are produced. For both methods, the depreciable base is equal to the original cost minus the salvage value. Thus, if the estimated salvage value is excluded from the depreciable base calculated using either method, the amount of depreciation will be overstated. The result will be an understatement of net income.
Answer (A) is incorrect. For both methods, the depreciable base is equal to the original cost minus the salvage value. Answer (C) is incorrect. For both methods, the depreciable base is equal to the original cost minus the salvage value. Answer (D) is incorrect. For both methods, the depreciable base is equal to the original cost minus the salvage value.

8.1.3. Depreciation of a plant asset is the process of

A. Asset valuation for statement of financial position purposes.

B. Allocation of the asset's cost to the periods of use.

C. Fund accumulation for the replacement of the asset.

D. Asset valuation based on current replacement cost data.

Answer (B) is correct. *(CMA, adapted)*
REQUIRED: The purpose of depreciation of fixed assets.
DISCUSSION: In accounting, depreciation is the systematic and rational allocation of the cost of the productive capacity of a fixed asset to the accounting periods the asset benefits. The asset's historical cost minus expected salvage value is the basis for the allocation.
Answer (A) is incorrect. Depreciation is the allocation of a cost, not a process of valuation. Answer (C) is incorrect. Depreciation allocates cost. It does not provide for replacement. Answer (D) is incorrect. Plant assets are reported at historical cost rather than current replacement costs.

8.1.4. Depreciation is computed on the original cost less estimated salvage value under which of the following depreciation methods?

	Double-Declining-Balance	Productive-Output
A.	No	No
B.	No	Yes
C.	Yes	Yes
D.	Yes	No

Answer (B) is correct. *(CPA, adapted)*
REQUIRED: The method(s) under which depreciation is computed on original cost minus estimated salvage value.
DISCUSSION: Under the productive-output method, depreciation is determined by allocating the original cost less the estimated salvage value to the projected units of output during the expected life of the asset. Under the double-declining-balance method, depreciation is determined by multiplying the carrying amount at the beginning of each period by a constant rate that is equal to twice the straight-line rate of depreciation. Each year the carrying amount of the asset decreases by the depreciation expense recognized. The double-declining-balance calculation does not include salvage value in calculating depreciation. However, the asset may not be depreciated below the amount of the estimated salvage value.
Answer (A) is incorrect. The productive-output method but not the DDB method includes salvage in the calculation. Answer (C) is incorrect. The productive-output method but not the DDB method includes salvage in the calculation. Answer (D) is incorrect. The productive-output method but not the DDB method includes salvage in the calculation.

8.1.5. In which of the following situations is the units-of-production method of depreciation most appropriate?

A. An asset's service potential declines with use.

B. An asset's service potential declines with the passage of time.

C. An asset is subject to rapid obsolescence.

D. An asset incurs increasing repairs and maintenance with use.

Answer (A) is correct. *(CPA, adapted)*
REQUIRED: The situation in which the units-of-production method of depreciation is most appropriate.
DISCUSSION: The units-of-production depreciation method allocates asset cost based on the level of production. As production varies, so will the credit to accumulated depreciation. Consequently, when an asset's service potential declines with use, the units-of-production method is the most appropriate method.
Answer (B) is incorrect. The straight-line method is appropriate when an asset's service potential declines with the passage of time. Answer (C) is incorrect. An accelerated method is best when an asset is subject to rapid obsolescence. Answer (D) is incorrect. The units-of-production method does not allow for increasing repairs and maintenance.

8.1.6. Which of the following reasons provides the best theoretical support for accelerated depreciation?

A. Assets are more efficient in early years and initially generate more revenue.

B. Expenses should be allocated in a manner that "smooths" earnings.

C. Repairs and maintenance costs will probably increase in later periods, so depreciation should decline.

D. Accelerated depreciation provides easier replacement because of the time value of money.

Answer (A) is correct. *(CPA, adapted)*
REQUIRED: The best theoretical basis for accelerated depreciation.
DISCUSSION: Accelerated depreciation methods result in decreasing depreciation charges over the life of the asset. Depreciation charges are greatest in the early years when the asset is presumably more efficient and generates more revenue. The effect of accelerated depreciation under this assumption is to match expenses and revenues more realistically.
Answer (B) is incorrect. The smoothing of earnings is not a proper justification for making a choice among generally accepted accounting principles. Accounting theory requires that the results of operations be presented fairly, even though such presentation might produce considerable fluctuations in earnings. Answer (C) is incorrect. Although an anticipated increase in maintenance costs is a practical justification for accelerated depreciation, it is not the best theoretical support. Answer (D) is incorrect. Depreciation for financial reporting purposes has no effect on cash flow.

8.1.7. Which of the following statements is the assumption on which straight-line depreciation is based?

- A. The operating efficiency of the asset decreases in later years.

- B. Service value declines as a function of time rather than use.

- C. Service value declines as a function of obsolescence rather than time.

- D. Physical wear and tear are more important than economic obsolescence.

Answer (B) is correct. *(CPA, adapted)*
    REQUIRED: The assumption on which straight-line depreciation is based.
    DISCUSSION: Under the straight-line method, depreciation expense is a constant amount for each period of the estimated useful life of the asset. The straight-line method ignores fluctuations in the use of an asset and in maintenance and service charges. The carrying amount is dependent upon the length of time the asset has been held rather than the amount of use.
    Answer (A) is incorrect. If operating efficiency declines over time, an accelerated depreciation method may be appropriate. Answer (C) is incorrect. If obsolescence determines service value, a write-down method based on market values may be appropriate. Answer (D) is incorrect. Physical wear and tear is a justification for an activity method of depreciation, e.g., depreciation based on hours of machine use.

8.1.8. Under which of the following depreciation methods is it possible for depreciation expense to be higher in the later years of an asset's useful life?

- A. Straight-line.

- B. Activity method based on units of production.

- C. Sum-of-the-years'-digits.

- D. Declining-balance.

Answer (B) is correct. *(CIA, adapted)*
    REQUIRED: The depreciation method under which higher depreciation is possible later in an asset's useful life.
    DISCUSSION: Under the activity method, depreciation is a function of use, not the passage of time. If the estimated activity level (stated, for example, in units of production) is higher in the later years of the asset's useful life, depreciation expense will be higher.
    Answer (A) is incorrect. The straight-line method results in a constant depreciation expense. Answer (C) is incorrect. Depreciation expense diminishes over time when an accelerated method, such as SYD, is used. Answer (D) is incorrect. Depreciation expense diminishes over time when an accelerated method, such as declining-balance method, is used.

8.1.9. Ottawa Corp. uses the sum-of-the-years'-digits method of depreciation. In the third year of use of an asset with a 4-year estimated useful life, the portion of the depreciation cost for the asset that the entity will expense is

- A. 10%

- B. 20%

- C. 30%

- D. 33.33%

Answer (B) is correct. *(CIA, adapted)*
    REQUIRED: The SYD depreciation in the third year.
    DISCUSSION: The SYD fraction (remaining years of the useful life at the beginning of the year ÷ the sum of the years of the useful life) is applied to the constant depreciable base (cost – salvage). For the third year of use of an asset with a 4-year life, the percentage of the depreciable base to be recognized is 20% [2 years ÷ (1 + 2 + 3 + 4)].
    Answer (A) is incorrect. This percentage results from calculating the portion of depreciable cost to expense in any given year using the end of the current year in the numerator. Answer (C) is incorrect. This percentage uses the digit of the current year in the numerator. Answer (D) is incorrect. This percentage calculates the denominator as the sum of the years up to the end of the current year and uses the digit of the current year in the numerator.

8.1.10. A machine with a 5-year estimated useful life and an estimated 10% salvage value was acquired on January 1, Year 1. On December 31, Year 4, accumulated depreciation using the sum-of-the-years'-digits method would be

- A. (Original cost less salvage value) multiplied by 1/15.

- B. (Original cost less salvage value) multiplied by 14/15.

- C. Original cost multiplied by 14/15.

- D. Original cost multiplied by 1/15.

Answer (B) is correct. *(CPA, adapted)*
    REQUIRED: The accumulated depreciation at the end of 4 years under the SYD method.
    DISCUSSION: SYD depreciation is calculated on a constant depreciable base equal to the original cost minus the salvage value, multiplied by the SYD fraction. The SYD fraction's numerator is the number of years of remaining useful life of the asset. The denominator is the sum of the digits of the total years of the expected useful life. In this case, the denominator is 15 (1 + 2 + 3 + 4 + 5). Thus, the accumulated depreciation at the end of Year 4 is the sum of the depreciation calculated in each of the 4 years, or 14/15 [(5 ÷ 15) + (4 ÷ 15) + (3 ÷ 15) + (2 ÷ 15)] times the depreciable base, which is the original cost minus the salvage value.
    Answer (A) is incorrect. The depreciation for Year 5 is (original cost minus salvage value) multiplied by 1/15. Answer (C) is incorrect. Original cost multiplied by 14/15 is the depreciation at December 31, Year 4, assuming no salvage value. Answer (D) is incorrect. Original cost multiplied by 1/15 is the depreciation for Year 5, assuming no salvage value.

8.1.11. Quito Co. acquired a fixed asset with an estimated useful life of 5 years and no salvage value for $15,000 at the beginning of Year 1. For financial statement purposes, how would the depreciation expense calculated using the double-declining-balance (DDB) method compare with that calculated using the sum-of-the-years'-digits (SYD) method in Year 1 and Year 2, respectively?

	Year 1	Year 2
A.	Lower	Lower
B.	Lower	Higher
C.	Higher	Lower
D.	Higher	Higher

Answer (C) is correct. *(CIA, adapted)*
REQUIRED: The comparison for 2 years of DDB and SYD depreciation expense.
DISCUSSION: DDB is an accelerated depreciation method that determines periodic depreciation expense by multiplying the carrying amount at the beginning of each period by a constant rate that is equal to twice the straight-line rate of depreciation. Each year the carrying amount of the asset decreases by the depreciation expense recognized. Salvage value is ignored in determining the carrying amount except as a floor beneath which the asset may not be depreciated. SYD depreciation multiplies a constant depreciable base (cost – salvage value) by the SYD fraction. The SYD fraction's numerator is the number of years of the useful life (n) minus the prior years elapsed. The formula to compute the denominator in the SYD method is

$$n\left[\frac{(n+1)}{2}\right]$$

For a 5-year estimated useful life, the denominator of the fraction is 15 {5 × [(5 + 1) ÷ 2]}.

DDB: Year 1 = $15,000(.4) = $6,000
      Year 2 = $9,000(.4) = $3,600

SYD: Year 1 = $15,000(5 ÷ 15) = $5,000
      Year 2 = $15,000(4 ÷ 15) = $4,000

Answer (A) is incorrect. DDB depreciation is higher in Year 1. Answer (B) is incorrect. DDB depreciation is higher in Year 1 and lower in Year 2. Answer (D) is incorrect. DDB depreciation is lower in Year 2.

8.1.12. Tunis Company purchased a van for $45,000. The estimated useful life of the van is 5 years or 80,000 miles, and the salvage value is $5,000. Actual mileage driven in the first year was 20,000 miles. Which of the following methods will result in the highest depreciation for the first year?

A. Straight-line.

B. Activity.

C. Sum-of-the-years'-digits.

D. Double-declining-balance.

Answer (D) is correct. *(J. Emig)*
REQUIRED: The method that will result in the highest depreciation for the first year.
DISCUSSION: Under the straight-line, activity, and SYD methods, the depreciable base is $40,000 ($45,000 original cost – $5,000 estimated salvage value). Under the straight-line method, this base is allocated equally to the 5 years, resulting in a depreciation expense of $8,000. Under the units-of-output method, the $40,000 is allocated evenly across the estimated mileage to produce a depreciation charge of $.50 per mile. Thus, first-year depreciation expense is $10,000 (20,000 miles × $.50). Under SYD, the depreciable base is multiplied by the SYD factor (years remaining at the beginning of the year ÷ the sum of the digits). SYD depreciation expense in the first year is therefore $13,333 [$40,000 × (5 ÷ 15)]. Under the DDB method, the $45,000 original cost is multiplied by a rate that is equal to twice the straight-line rate (2 × 20% = 40%). The result is a depreciation expense of $18,000 ($45,000 × 40%) in the first year.
Answer (A) is incorrect. Straight-line depreciation is $8,000. Answer (B) is incorrect. Activity method depreciation is $10,000. Answer (C) is incorrect. SYD depreciation is $13,333.

8.1.13. On January 1, Year 5, Crater, Inc., purchased equipment having an estimated salvage value equal to 20% of its original cost at the end of a 10-year life. The equipment was sold December 31, Year 9, for 50% of its original cost. If the equipment's disposition resulted in a reported loss, which of the following depreciation methods did Crater use?

A. Double-declining balance.

B. Sum-of-the-years'-digits.

C. Straight-line.

D. Composite.

Answer (C) is correct. *(CPA, adapted)*
REQUIRED: The method that results in a reported loss upon disposition.
DISCUSSION: The straight-line method of depreciation is the only one of the generally accepted methods that is not an accelerated method. It thus yields the lowest amount of depreciation for the early part of the depreciable life of the asset. Because only 50% of the original cost was received and straight-line accumulated depreciation equaled 40% of cost {[(100% − 20%) ÷ 10 years] × 5 years} at the time of sale, a 10% loss [50% − (100% − 40%)] results.
Answer (A) is incorrect. The DDB method results in 5-year accumulated depreciation that is greater than 50% of cost. Answer (B) is incorrect. The SYD method results in 5-year accumulated depreciation that is greater than 50% of cost. Answer (D) is incorrect. The composite method of depreciation applies to the weighted average of multiple useful lives of assets, whereas only one asset is mentioned in this question. Moreover, it recognizes no gain or loss on disposition.

8.2 Depreciation Calculations

8.2.1. Pretoria Company acquired a new machine at a cost of $400,000 and incurred costs of $4,000 to have the machine shipped to its factory. Pretoria also paid $9,000 to construct and prepare a site for the new machine and $7,000 to install the necessary electrical connections. Pretoria estimates that the useful life of this new machine will be 5 years and that it will have a salvage value of $30,000 at the end of that period. Assuming that Pretoria acquired the machine on January 1 and will take a full year's depreciation, the proper amount of depreciation expense to be recorded by Pretoria if it uses the double-declining-balance method is

A. $148,000

B. $168,000

C. $160,000

D. $161,600

Answer (B) is correct. *(CMA, adapted)*
REQUIRED: The proper amount of depreciation under the double-declining-balance (DDB) method.
DISCUSSION: The acquisition cost of the machine includes all costs necessary to prepare it for its intended use. Hence, the depreciable cost is $420,000 ($400,000 invoice price + $4,000 delivery expense + $9,000 site preparation + $7,000 electrical work). Under the DDB method, salvage value is ignored at the beginning. Thus, the full $420,000 is subject to depreciation. Given a 5-year life, the annual straight-line rate is 20%, and the DDB rate is 40%. Depreciation for the first year is therefore $168,000 ($420,000 × 40%).
Answer (A) is incorrect. The amount of $148,000 assumes that the depreciable cost is the invoice price minus salvage value. Answer (C) is incorrect. The depreciable cost of the machine was $420,000, not the $400,000 invoice price. Answer (D) is incorrect. The amount of $161,600 assumes a depreciable cost of $404,000, which does not include the site preparation and electrical costs.

8.2.2. Sydney Co. purchased a machine that was installed and placed in service on January 1, Year 1, at a cost of $480,000. Salvage value was estimated at $80,000. The machine is being depreciated over 10 years by the double-declining-balance method. For the year ended December 31, Year 2, what amount should Sydney report as depreciation expense?

A. $96,000

B. $76,800

C. $64,000

D. $61,440

Answer (B) is correct. *(CPA, adapted)*
REQUIRED: The DDB depreciation expense reported in the second year.
DISCUSSION: DDB is an accelerated depreciation method that determines periodic depreciation expense by multiplying the carrying amount at the beginning of each period by a constant rate that is equal to twice the straight-line rate of depreciation. Given that this machine has a 10-year useful life, the DDB rate is 20%. Each year the carrying amount of the asset decreases by the depreciation expense recognized. Salvage value is ignored in determining the carrying amount except as a minimum below which the asset may not be depreciated. The carrying amount at the end of the first year was $384,000 [$480,000 cost × (100% − 20%)]. Thus, second-year depreciation is $76,800 ($384,000 × 20%).
Answer (A) is incorrect. The first-year depreciation was $96,000. Answer (C) is incorrect. The amount of $64,000 assumes that salvage value is included in the calculation. Answer (D) is incorrect. The third-year depreciation will be $61,440.

Questions 8.2.3 and 8.2.4 are based on the following information.

Since Year 1, Canberra Company has replaced all of its major manufacturing equipment and now has the following equipment recorded in the appropriate accounts. Canberra uses a calendar year as its fiscal year.

- A forge purchased January 1, Year 1, for $100,000. Installation costs were $20,000, and the forge has an estimated 5-year life with a salvage value of $10,000.
- A grinding machine costing $45,000 purchased January 1, Year 2. The machine has an estimated 5-year life with a salvage value of $5,000.
- A lathe purchased January 1, Year 4, for $60,000. The lathe has an estimated 5-year life with a salvage value of $7,000.

8.2.3. Using the straight-line depreciation method, Canberra's Year 4 depreciation expense is

　A.　$45,000

　B.　$40,334

　C.　$40,600

　D.　$40,848

Answer (C) is correct. *(CMA, adapted)*
　REQUIRED: The Year 4 depreciation expense using the straight-line method.
　DISCUSSION: The straight-line method allocates the depreciation evenly over the estimated useful life of an asset. The depreciable cost equals cost minus salvage value for each asset, and dividing that amount by the life of the asset gives the periodic depreciation as follows:

Asset	Cost	Salvage	C – S	Life	Expense
Forge	$120,000	$10,000	$110,000	5	$22,000
Grind	45,000	5,000	40,000	5	8,000
Lathe	60,000	7,000	53,000	5	10,600
Total					$40,600

　Answer (A) is incorrect. The amount of $45,000 does not take into account the deduction for salvage value. Answer (B) is incorrect. The amount of $40,334 is based on the sum-of-the-years'-digits method. Answer (D) is incorrect. The amount of $40,848 is based on the double-declining-balance method.

8.2.4. Using the double-declining-balance method, Canberra's Year 4 depreciation expense is

　A.　$36,464

　B.　$40,334

　C.　$40,600

　D.　$40,848

Answer (D) is correct. *(CMA, adapted)*
　REQUIRED: The Year 4 depreciation expense using the double-declining-balance method.
　DISCUSSION: The DDB method allocates a series of decreasing depreciation charges over an asset's life. A percentage that is double the straight-line rate is multiplied each year by an asset's remaining carrying amount at the beginning of the year. Given that each asset has a 5-year life, the straight-line rate is 20%. The DDB rate is therefore 40%. The forge was purchased in Year 1 at a total cost of $120,000. The depreciation for each year is calculated as follows:

Year	Carrying Amount	%	Expense
Year 1	$120,000	40%	$48,000
Year 2	72,000	40%	28,800
Year 3	43,200	40%	17,280
Year 4	25,920	40%	10,368

For the grinding machine, the calculations are

Year	Carrying Amount	%	Expense
Year 2	$45,000	40%	$18,000
Year 3	27,000	40%	10,800
Year 4	16,200	40%	6,480

The Year 4 calculation for the new lathe requires multiplying the $60,000 cost by 40% to yield a $24,000 expense. Adding the Year 4 expense for each of the three machines ($10,368 + $6,480 + $24,000) produces total depreciation of $40,848.
　Answer (A) is incorrect. The amount of $36,464 is based on the double-declining-balance method, but with salvage value deducted from the initial depreciable base. Answer (B) is incorrect. The amount of $40,334 is based on the sum-of-the-years'-digits method. Answer (C) is incorrect. The amount of $40,600 is based on the straight-line method.

Questions 8.2.5 through 8.2.7 are based on the following information.

Samoa Corporation's schedule of depreciable assets at December 31, Year 3, is shown in the next column. Samoa takes a full year's depreciation expense in the year of an asset's acquisition and no depreciation expense in the year of an asset's disposition. The estimated useful life of each depreciable asset is 5 years.

Asset	Cost	Accumulated Depreciation	Acquisition Date	Salvage Value
A	$100,000	$ 64,000	Year 2	$20,000
B	55,000	36,000	Year 1	10,000
C	70,000	33,600	Year 1	14,000
	$225,000	$133,600		$44,000

8.2.5. Samoa depreciates asset A on the double-declining-balance method. How much depreciation expense should Samoa record in Year 4 for asset A?

A. $32,000

B. $24,000

C. $14,400

D. $1,600

Answer (C) is correct. *(CPA, adapted)*
REQUIRED: The current depreciation expense.
DISCUSSION: DDB depreciation equals carrying amount at the beginning of the year times twice the straight-line rate. Salvage value is considered only as a minimum below which the carrying amount may be reduced. Asset A has a useful life of 5 years, so the straight-line rate is 20%. The DDB rate is 40% (2 × 20%). The carrying amount is $36,000 ($100,000 cost – $64,000 accumulated depreciation). Annual depreciation expense for its third year is thus $14,400 ($36,000 × 40%).
Answer (A) is incorrect. First-year depreciation after subtracting salvage value from the depreciable base is $32,000. Answer (B) is incorrect. The Year 2 depreciation was $24,000. Answer (D) is incorrect. The difference between 12/31/Year 4 carrying amount and the salvage value that will be the Year 5 depreciation will be $1,600.

8.2.6. Using the same depreciation method as used in Year 1, Year 2, and Year 3, how much depreciation expense should Samoa record in Year 4 for asset B?

A. $6,000

B. $9,000

C. $12,000

D. $15,000

Answer (A) is correct. *(CPA, adapted)*
REQUIRED: The current depreciation expense.
DISCUSSION: The cost of asset B was $55,000, and the depreciation accumulated after 3 years of its 5-year life is $36,000. Under the straight-line method, depreciation would have totaled $27,000 [($55,000 – $10,000 salvage value) × 3 × 20%]. DDB depreciation would have been $43,120 (40% of a declining carrying amount each year). The SYD method multiplies a fraction (the years remaining ÷ the SYD) by a constant depreciable base (cost – salvage). The SYD is 15 [n(n + 1) ÷ 2 = 5(5 + 1) ÷ 2]. Total SYD depreciation after 3 years is $36,000. Thus, SYD should be used and Year 4 depreciation is $6,000 [$45,000 × (2 ÷ 15)].

Year 1:	[(5 ÷ 15) × ($55,000 – $10,000)]	=	$15,000
Year 2:	[(4 ÷ 15) × ($55,000 – $10,000)]	=	12,000
Year 3:	[(3 ÷ 15) × ($55,000 – $10,000)]	=	9,000
			$36,000

Answer (B) is incorrect. The third-year SYD depreciation was $9,000. Answer (C) is incorrect. The second-year depreciation was $12,000. Answer (D) is incorrect. The first-year depreciation was $15,000.

8.2.7. Samoa depreciates asset C by the straight-line method. On June 30, Year 4, Samoa sold asset C for $28,000 cash. How much gain or (loss) should Samoa record in Year 4 on the disposal of asset C?

A. $2,800

B. $(2,800)

C. $(5,600)

D. $(8,400)

Answer (D) is correct. *(CPA, adapted)*
REQUIRED: The gain (loss) on disposal of asset C.
DISCUSSION: Asset C had a carrying amount at the time of its disposition of $36,400 ($70,000 cost – $33,600 accumulated depreciation), given that no depreciation was recognized in the year of sale. The loss on the transaction was $8,400 ($36,400 carrying amount – $28,000 cash received).
Answer (A) is incorrect. The amount of $2,800 assumes that a year's depreciation was taken in Year 4. Answer (B) is incorrect. The amount of $(2,800) assumes depreciation was taken for the first half of the year. Answer (C) is incorrect. The amount of $(5,600) equals the accumulated depreciation balance minus the cash received.

Questions 8.2.8 and 8.2.9 are based on the following information. Roswell Company has the following information on one of its vehicles purchased on January 1, Year 1:

Vehicle cost	$50,000
Useful life, years, estimated	5
Useful life, miles, estimated	100,000
Salvage value, estimated	$10,000
Actual miles driven: Year 1	30,000
Year 2	20,000
Year 3	15,000
Year 4	25,000
Year 5	12,000

No estimates were changed during the life of the asset.

8.2.8. The Year 3 depreciation expense for Roswell's vehicle using the sum-of-the-years'-digits (SYD) method was

A. $6,000

B. $8,000

C. $10,000

D. $16,000

Answer (B) is correct. *(CMA, adapted)*
REQUIRED: The Year 3 depreciation expense under the SYD method.
DISCUSSION: Under the SYD method, the amount to be depreciated is $40,000 ($50,000 original cost – $10,000 salvage). The portion expensed each year is based on a fraction, the denominator of which is the summation of the years of life of the asset being depreciated. For an asset with a 5-year life, the denominator is 15 (5 + 4 + 3 + 2 + 1). The numerator equals the years remaining at the beginning of the year. For Year 3, the fraction is 3 ÷ 15, and depreciation expense is $8,000 [$40,000 × (3 ÷ 15)].
Answer (A) is incorrect. The amount of $6,000 is based on the units-of-production method. Answer (C) is incorrect. The amount of $10,000 omits the vehicle's salvage value from the calculation. Answer (D) is incorrect. The amount of $16,000 is the double-declining-balance method depreciation for Year 1 if the salvage value is subtracted from the cost.

8.2.9. Using the activity method, what was Roswell's Year 5 depreciation expense?

A. $4,000

B. $4,800

C. $5,000

D. $6,000

Answer (A) is correct. *(CMA, adapted)*
REQUIRED: The depreciation expense for Year 5 under the units-of-production method.
DISCUSSION: Under the activity method, periodic depreciation is based on the proportion of expected total production that occurred. For Years 1 through 4, the total depreciation was $36,000 {($50,000 – $10,000) × [(30,000 + 20,000 + 15,000 + 25,000) ÷ 100,000]}. Hence, the remaining depreciable base was $4,000 ($50,000 cost – $10,000 salvage – $36,000). Given that the 12,000 miles driven in Year 5 exceeded the remaining estimated production of 10,000 miles (100,000 – 30,000 – 20,000 – 15,000 – 25,000), only the $4,000 of the remaining depreciable base should be recognized in Year 5.
Answer (B) is incorrect. The amount of $4,800 is based on a Year 5 rate of 12% (12,000 miles ÷ 100,000 miles of estimated usage). It ignores the effects of depreciation expense deducted in prior years. Answer (C) is incorrect. The amount of $5,000 assumes that depreciation is based on original cost without regard to salvage value. Answer (D) is incorrect. The amount of $6,000 is based on a 12% rate and ignores salvage value.

8.2.10. Turtle Co. purchased equipment on January 2, Year 1, for $50,000. The equipment had an estimated 5-year service life. Turtle's policy for 5-year assets is to use the 200% double-declining-balance depreciation method for the first 2 years of the asset's life, and then switch to the straight-line depreciation method. In its December 31, Year 3, balance sheet, what amount should Turtle report as accumulated depreciation for equipment?

A. $30,000

B. $38,000

C. $39,200

D. $42,000

Answer (B) is correct. *(CPA, adapted)*
REQUIRED: The amount of accumulated depreciation to be reported in the balance sheet.
DISCUSSION: Under the DDB method, the assets are depreciated at a constant rate of 40% (200% × 20% straight-line rate). This rate is applied in both of the first 2 years. For Year 3, straight-line is used based on the remaining carrying amount. The calculation is as follows:

Year 1: $50,000 × 40%	$20,000
Year 2: ($50,000 − $20,000) × 40%	12,000
Year 3: ($50,000 − $20,000 − $12,000) ÷ 3	6,000
Accumulated depreciation, 12/31/Year 3	$38,000

Answer (A) is incorrect. The accumulated straight-line deprecation equals $30,000. Answer (C) is incorrect. DDB depreciation for 3 years equals $39,200. Answer (D) is incorrect. The amount of $42,000 includes third-year straight-line depreciation calculated without regard to DDB depreciation previously taken.

8.2.11. Weir Co. uses straight-line depreciation for its property, plant, and equipment, which, stated at cost, consisted of the following:

	12/31/Yr 2	12/31/Yr 1
Land	$ 25,000	$ 25,000
Buildings	195,000	195,000
Machinery and equipment	695,000	650,000
PPE -- gross	$915,000	$870,000
Less: Accumulated depreciation	400,000	370,000
PPE -- net	$515,000	$500,000

Weir's depreciation expense for Year 2 and Year 1 was $55,000 and $50,000, respectively. What amount was debited to accumulated depreciation during Year 2 because of property, plant, and equipment retirements?

A. $40,000

B. $25,000

C. $20,000

D. $10,000

Answer (B) is correct. *(CPA, adapted)*
REQUIRED: The amount that was debited to accumulated depreciation because of retirements.
DISCUSSION: When an asset is depreciated, a debit is made to depreciation expense and a credit to accumulated depreciation. An equipment retirement results in a debit to accumulated depreciation. During Year 2, accumulated depreciation increased by $30,000 despite recognition of a $55,000 expense (a credit). Consequently, a $25,000 ($55,000 − $30,000) debit must have been made to the accumulated depreciation account.
Answer (A) is incorrect. The amount of $40,000 subtracts the difference between depreciation expense for Year 1 and Year 2 from the increase in the machinery and equipment account. Answer (C) is incorrect. The amount of $20,000 is based on Year 1 depreciation ($50,000). Answer (D) is incorrect. The amount of $10,000 is based on the increase in the machinery and equipment account, not the accumulated depreciation.

8.2.12. Spiro Corp. uses the sum-of-the-years'-digits method to depreciate equipment purchased in January Year 2 for $20,000. The estimated salvage value of the equipment is $2,000, and the estimated useful life is 4 years. What should Spiro report as the asset's carrying amount as of December 31, Year 4?

A. $1,800

B. $2,000

C. $3,800

D. $4,500

Answer (C) is correct. *(CPA, adapted)*
REQUIRED: The asset's carrying amount as of December 31, Year 2.
DISCUSSION: The sum-of-the-years'-digits (SYD) method multiplies a constant depreciable base (cost minus salvage value) by a declining fraction. It is a declining-rate, declining-charge method. Consequently, the depreciable base is $18,000 ($20,000 − $2,000). The SYD fraction's numerator is the number of years of useful life minus the prior years elapsed. The denominator is the sum of the digits of all the years in the asset's life. The numerator is 1 year (4 − 3), and the denominator is 10 (1 + 2 + 3 + 4). The depreciation for the last year is $1,800 [$18,000 × (1 ÷ 10)], so the declining balance after 3 years of the 4-year period (Year 2-Year 4) is $3,800 ($1,800 remaining depreciable base + $2,000 salvage value).
Answer (A) is incorrect. The final-year SYD depreciation is $1,800. Answer (B) is incorrect. The salvage value is $2,000. Answer (D) is incorrect. The annual straight-line depreciation is $4,500.

8.2.13. On January 2, Year 1, Reed Co. purchased a machine for $800,000 and established an annual depreciation charge of $100,000 over an 8-year life. At the beginning of Year 4, after issuing its Year 3 financial statements, Reed concluded that $250,000 was a reasonable estimate of the sum of the undiscounted net cash inflows expected to be recovered through use of the machine for the period January 1, Year 4, through December 31, Year 8. The machine's fair value was $200,000 at the beginning of Year 4. In Reed's December 31, Year 4, balance sheet, the machine should be reported at a carrying amount of

A. $0

B. $100,000

C. $160,000

D. $400,000

Answer (C) is correct. *(CPA, adapted)*
REQUIRED: The carrying amount of an asset.
DISCUSSION: The asset should be written down to fair value if the carrying amount is not recoverable. Because the carrying amount ($800,000 cost – $300,000 accumulated depreciation = $500,000) exceeded the recoverable amount ($250,000) at the beginning of Year 4, Reed should have recognized an impairment loss of $300,000 ($500,000 carrying amount – $200,000 fair value at the beginning of Year 4). Accordingly, the new carrying amount was $200,000, and the new annual depreciation expense for the remaining 5-year useful life (Year 4 - Year 8) was $40,000 ($200,000 ÷ 5 years). The machine should be reported at a carrying amount of $160,000 ($200,000 – $40,000 depreciation) on December 31, Year 4.
Answer (A) is incorrect. The machine still has a carrying amount. Answer (B) is incorrect. The amount of $100,000 results from subtracting the originally computed annual depreciation from the new carrying amount. Answer (D) is incorrect. The amount of $400,000 assumes no impairment.

8.2.14. Auckland Co. determined that, because of obsolescence, equipment with an original cost of $1,800,000 and accumulated depreciation on the first day of the current fiscal year of $840,000 had suffered impairment and, as a result, should have a carrying amount of only $600,000 (the fair value) as of the beginning of the year. In addition, the remaining useful life of the equipment was reduced from 8 years to 3. In its year-end balance sheet, what amount should Auckland report as accumulated depreciation?

A. $200,000

B. $1,040,000

C. $1,200,000

D. $1,400,000

Answer (D) is correct. *(CPA, adapted)*
REQUIRED: The accumulated depreciation given on impairment loss and a change in estimate.
DISCUSSION: The carrying amount of the equipment before the impairment was $960,000 ($1,800,000 – $840,000). After the impairment, the carrying amount should be $600,000; therefore, $360,000 ($960,000 – $600,000) of additional accumulated depreciation should be recorded to reflect the impairment loss (assuming the entry is to debit the loss and credit accumulated depreciation). In addition, the depreciation for the year should be $200,000 ($600,000 ÷ 3). Hence, the accumulated depreciation in the year-end balance sheet is $1,400,000 ($840,000 + $360,000 impairment loss + $200,000 depreciation for the year).
Answer (A) is incorrect. The depreciation for the year is $200,000. Answer (B) is incorrect. The sum of the accumulated depreciation at the beginning of the year and the revised annual depreciation is $1,040,000. Answer (C) is incorrect. The accumulated depreciation before adjusting the useful life and claiming current-year depreciation is $1,200,000.

8.2.15. On January 2, Lem Corp. bought machinery under a contract that required a down payment of $10,000, plus 24 monthly payments of $5,000 each, for total cash payments of $130,000. The cash equivalent price of the machinery was $110,000. The machinery has an estimated useful life of 10 years and estimated salvage value of $5,000. Lem uses straight-line depreciation. In its income statement for the year, what amount should Lem report as depreciation for this machinery?

A. $10,500

B. $11,000

C. $12,500

D. $13,000

Answer (A) is correct. *(CPA, adapted)*
REQUIRED: The depreciation on the machinery.
DISCUSSION: The cash equivalent price of the machinery (present value), reduced by the salvage value, equals the depreciable base. The excess of the total cash to be paid over the cash equivalent price of the machinery will be recognized as interest expense, not depreciation. Accordingly, straight-line depreciation is $10,500 [($110,000 cash equivalent price – $5,000 salvage value) ÷ 10 years].
Answer (B) is incorrect. The amount of $11,000 does not allow for the salvage value. Answer (C) is incorrect. The amount of $12,500 is based on the total cash payments minus salvage value. Answer (D) is incorrect. The amount of $13,000 is based on the total cash payments with no allowance for salvage value.

8.2.16. Caracas Corp. purchased a computer on January 1 for $108,000. It was estimated to have a 4-year useful life and a salvage value of $18,000. The double-declining-balance (DDB) method is to be used. The amount of depreciation to be reported at the end of the first year is

A.   ($108,000 – $18,000) × (25% × 2)

B.   ($108,000 – $18,000) × (25% × 1/2)

C.   ($108,000) × (25% × 2)

D.   ($108,000) × (25% × 1/2)

Answer (C) is correct. *(CIA, adapted)*
   REQUIRED: The computation to calculate the amount of depreciation under the double-declining-balance method.
   DISCUSSION: When using a declining-balance method, a constant rate is applied to the changing carrying amount of the asset. The carrying amount for the first period's calculation is the acquisition cost ($108,000). The constant rate for the DDB method is twice the straight-line rate [(100% ÷ 4 years) × 2].
   Answer (A) is incorrect. The salvage value is ignored in computing depreciation by use of a declining-balance method until the later years of the life. The asset should not be depreciated below its salvage value. Answer (B) is incorrect. The salvage value is ignored. Furthermore, the rate used should be twice the straight-line rate. Answer (D) is incorrect. The rate used should be twice the straight-line rate.

8.2.17. On the first day of its current fiscal year, Santiago Corporation purchased equipment costing $400,000 with a salvage value of $80,000. Depreciation expense for the year was $160,000. If Santiago uses the double-declining-balance (DDB) method of depreciation, what is the estimated useful life of the asset?

A.   5

B.   4

C.   2.5

D.   2

Answer (A) is correct. *(J. Hora)*
   REQUIRED: The estimated useful life of an asset being depreciated using the DDB method.
   DISCUSSION: DDB uses a depreciation rate that is twice the straight-line rate. In the first year of this equipment's life, the DDB depreciation rate is 40% ($160,000 ÷ $400,000). The straight-line rate is therefore 20% (40% ÷ 2). Accordingly, the expected useful life of the asset is 5 years.
   Answer (B) is incorrect. Four years assumes salvage value is subtracted from the cost to determine the depreciable base used to calculate DDB depreciation. Answer (C) is incorrect. A straight-line rate of 40% and a DDB rate of 80% is equivalent to 2.5 years. Hence, DDB depreciation would be $320,000 ($400,000 × 80%). Answer (D) is incorrect. If the useful life were 2 years, the depreciation expense would be $320,000 [($400,000 cost × 100%) – $80,000 salvage].

8.2.18. Lima Company is depreciating an asset with a 5-year useful life. It cost $100,000 and has no salvage value. If the <List A> method is used, depreciation expense in the second year will be <List B>.

	List A	List B
A.	Sum-of-years'-digits	$20,000
B.	Sum-of-years'-digits	$40,000
C.	Double-declining-balance	$16,000
D.	Double-declining-balance	$24,000

Answer (D) is correct. *(CIA, adapted)*
   REQUIRED: The proper match of depreciation method and expense amount.
   DISCUSSION: The DDB method uses twice the straight-line rate. In the first year of the asset's life, depreciation expense was $40,000 ($100,000 × 20% × 2 years). In the second year, the depreciation base is reduced by the amount of depreciation expense already taken in the first year, so depreciation expense in the second year is $24,000 [($100,000 – $40,000) × 20% × 2 years].
   Answer (A) is incorrect. Depreciation in the second year will be $20,000 under the straight-line method of depreciation. Under the SYD method, it is $26,667 [$100,000 × (4 ÷ 15)]. Answer (B) is incorrect. SYD depreciation in the second year is $26,667. Answer (C) is incorrect. The amount of $16,000 assumes the declining-balance method is used with the straight-line rate.

8.2.19. A depreciable asset has an estimated 15% salvage value. Under which of the following methods, properly applied, would the accumulated depreciation equal the original cost at the end of the asset's estimated useful life?

	Straight-line	Double-declining-balance (DDB)
A.	Yes	Yes
B.	Yes	No
C.	No	Yes
D.	No	No

Answer (D) is correct. *(CPA, adapted)*
   REQUIRED: The method(s), if any, under which accumulated depreciation ultimately equals original cost.
   DISCUSSION: Neither method results in an accumulated depreciation balance equal to the original cost of the asset. The straight-line method allocates the depreciable base (historical cost – salvage value). DDB depreciates the full historical cost of the asset without regard to salvage value but not below the salvage value.
   Answer (A) is incorrect. Neither method depreciates the asset below its salvage value. Answer (B) is incorrect. The straight-line method does not depreciate the asset below its salvage value. Answer (C) is incorrect. DDB does not depreciate the asset below its salvage value.

8.3 Group and Composite Depreciation Methods

Questions 8.3.1 through 8.3.3 are based on the following information.

For its first year of operations, Falkland Co. decided to use the composite method of depreciation and prepared the schedule of machinery owned presented in the opposite column.

	Total Cost	Estimated Salvage Value	Estimated Life in Years
Machine X	$550,000	$50,000	20
Machine Y	200,000	20,000	15
Machine Z	40,000	--	5

8.3.1. Falkland computes depreciation on the straight-line method. Based upon the information presented, the composite life of these assets (in years) should be

A. 13.3

B. 16.0

C. 17.6

D. 20.0

Answer (B) is correct. *(CPA, adapted)*
REQUIRED: The composite life of the assets in years.
DISCUSSION: The composite or average useful life of the assets is essentially a weighted average. As illustrated below, the annual straight-line depreciation for each asset should be calculated. The total cost, estimated salvage value, and depreciable base of the assets should then be computed. Dividing the composite depreciable base ($720) by the total annual straight-line depreciation ($45) gives the composite life (16 years) of these assets.

	Total Cost	Salvage Value	Dep. Base	Est. Life	Annual S-L Dep.
X	$550	$50	$500	20	$25
Y	200	20	180	15	12
Z	40	0	40	5	8
	$790	$70	$720		$45

Answer (A) is incorrect. The average useful life of the three assets is 13.3. Answer (C) is incorrect. The amount of 17.6 ignores salvage value in the calculation of total depreciable cost. Answer (D) is incorrect. The estimated life of asset X is 20.

8.3.2. At the start of the fifth year of operations, Falkland sold machine Z for $10,000. Assume that this change is not material. What are the depreciation expense and the ending balance in the accumulated depreciation account recorded for Year 5?

A. $45,000 and $225,000.

B. $45,000 and $195,000.

C. $42,750 and $222,750.

D. $42,750 and $192,750.

Answer (D) is correct. *(Publisher, adapted)*
REQUIRED: The depreciation expense and accumulated depreciation under the composite method when an asset is sold.
DISCUSSION: The straight-line depreciation rate is 5.70% ($45,000 annual depreciation ÷ $790,000 total cost). When an asset included in a composite group is sold, the original cost of that asset minus the amount received for it is debited to the accumulated depreciation account. No gain or loss is recorded. The depreciation rate is multiplied by the total cost of the remaining assets to determine the depreciation expense. Given that the asset disposal was not material to the total depreciable cost and the useful life composition of the group, the original depreciation rate continues to be used.

Thus, the depreciation expense for the fifth year is equal to $42,750 [($790,000 – $40,000) × 5.70%]. The accumulated depreciation at the start of Year 5 ($180,000) is increased by a credit for $42,750 of depreciation expense and decreased by a debit of $30,000 ($40,000 original cost – $10,000 cash received), leaving a year-end balance of $192,750.

Answer (A) is incorrect. The annual depreciation before the disposal is $45,000, and $225,000 is the ending accumulated depreciation for Year 5, assuming no disposal. Answer (B) is incorrect. The original annual depreciation is $45,000, and $195,000 equals the accumulated depreciation after 4 years, plus the original annual depreciation, minus $30,000 ($40,000 cost of Z – $10,000 sale price). Answer (C) is incorrect. The amount of $222,750 results from not adjusting accumulated depreciation for the difference between the cost and selling price of machine Z.

8.3.3. Assume that, in addition to the sale of machine Z for $10,000 at the start of Year 5, Falkland purchased machine W for $60,000 to replace the machine that was sold. Machine W is expected to last 5 years with an expected salvage value of $10,000. If machine W is included in the composite asset group, the depreciation expense for the fifth year should be equal to which of the following amounts?

- A. $42,750
- B. $45,000
- C. $45,600
- D. $46,170

Answer (D) is correct. *(Publisher, adapted)*
REQUIRED: The depreciation expense under the composite method when a new asset is added.
DISCUSSION: When machine Z was sold, the total cost of the composite group was decreased from $790,000 to $750,000. The purchase of machine W adds $60,000 to the total cost. The new total cost ($810,000) is multiplied by the straight-line depreciation rate (5.70%), resulting in Year 5 depreciation of $46,170. Once a composite rate has been set, it continues to be used unless significant changes occur in the estimated lives or the composition of the assets through additions and retirements.
Answer (A) is incorrect. The depreciation expense excluding the new asset is $42,750. Answer (B) is incorrect. The amount of $45,000 fails to consider the effects of both the sale of Z and the purchase of W. Answer (C) is incorrect. The amount of $45,600 results from subtracting the salvage value of the new asset from the new total cost.

8.3.4. A company using the composite depreciation method for its fleet of trucks, cars, and campers retired one of its trucks and received cash from a salvage company. The net carrying amount of these composite asset accounts was decreased by the

- A. Cash proceeds received and original cost of the truck.
- B. Cash proceeds received.
- C. Original cost of the truck minus the cash proceeds.
- D. Original cost of the truck.

Answer (B) is correct. *(CPA, adapted)*
REQUIRED: The effect of a retirement on the net carrying amount of a composite asset account.
DISCUSSION: Because both composite and group methods use weighted averages of useful lives and depreciation rates, early and late retirements are expected to offset each other. Consequently, gains and losses on retirements of single assets are treated as adjustments of accumulated depreciation. The entry is to credit the asset at cost, debit cash for any proceeds received, and debit accumulated depreciation for the difference. Thus, the net carrying amount of the composite asset accounts is decreased by the amount of cash received. The net carrying amount of total assets is unchanged.
Answer (A) is incorrect. The net carrying amount of the composite asset accounts is decreased only by the cash proceeds received. Answer (C) is incorrect. The net carrying amount of the composite asset accounts is decreased only by the cash proceeds received. Answer (D) is incorrect. The net carrying amount of the composite asset accounts is decreased only by the cash proceeds received.

8.3.5. Which of the following uses the straight-line depreciation method?

	Group Depreciation	Composite Depreciation
A.	No	No
B.	Yes	No
C.	Yes	Yes
D.	No	Yes

Answer (C) is correct. *(CPA, adapted)*
REQUIRED: The method(s) using straight-line depreciation.
DISCUSSION: Both composite and group depreciation use the straight-line method. Both methods aggregate groups of assets. The composite method is used for a collection of dissimilar assets with varying useful lives, whereas the group method deals with similar assets. Each method involves the calculation of a total depreciable cost for all the assets included in one account and of a weighted-average estimated useful life.
Answer (A) is incorrect. Both methods use the straight-line method of depreciation. Answer (B) is incorrect. Both methods use the straight-line method of depreciation. Answer (D) is incorrect. Both methods use the straight-line method of depreciation.

8.4 Depletion

8.4.1. Miller Mining, a calendar-year corporation, purchased the rights to a copper mine on July 1, Year 1. Of the total purchase price, $2.8 million was appropriately allocable to the copper. Estimated reserves were 800,000 tons of copper. Miller expects to extract and sell 10,000 tons of copper per month. Production began immediately. The selling price is $25 per ton. Miller uses percentage depletion (15%) for tax purposes. To aid production, Miller also purchased some new equipment on July 1, Year 1. The equipment cost $76,000 and had an estimated useful life of 8 years. After all the copper is removed from this mine, however, the equipment will be of no use to Miller and will be sold for an estimated $4,000. If sales and production conform to expectations, what is Miller's depletion expense on this mine for financial accounting purposes for the Year 1 calendar year?

A. $105,000

B. $210,000

C. $215,400

D. $420,000

Answer (B) is correct. *(CPA, adapted)*
REQUIRED: The depletion expense for financial accounting purposes assuming accurate estimates of sales and production.
DISCUSSION: Miller's depletion base is $2.8 million (the equipment cost is not included in the depletion base and is depreciated separately), resulting in a depletion charge per ton of $3.50 ($2,800,000 ÷ 800,000 estimated recoverable tons). If 10,000 tons is extracted in each of the last 6 months of Year 1, the depletion charge should be $210,000 [(10,000 tons × 6 months) × $3.50 per ton].
Answer (A) is incorrect. Depletion for 3 months equals $105,000. Answer (C) is incorrect. The amount of $215,400 includes depreciation of the new equipment. Answer (D) is incorrect. The amount of $420,000 is 15% of the purchase price.

8.4.2. In January, Vorst Co. purchased a mineral mine with removable ore estimated at 1.2 million tons for $2,640,000. After it has extracted all the ore, Vorst will be required by law to restore the land to its original condition at an estimated cost of $180,000. Vorst believes it will be able to sell the property afterwards for $300,000. During the year, Vorst incurred $360,000 of development costs preparing the mine for production and removed and sold 60,000 tons of ore. In its income statement for the year, what amount should Vorst report as depletion?

A. $135,000

B. $144,000

C. $150,000

D. $159,000

Answer (B) is correct. *(CPA, adapted)*
REQUIRED: The amount of depletion to be reported.
DISCUSSION: Vorst's per-ton depletion charge is calculated as follows:

Purchase price	$2,640,000
Add: Restoration costs	180,000
Minus: Residual value	(300,000)
Add: Preparation costs	360,000
Depletion base	$2,880,000
Divided by: Estimated removable tons	÷1,200,000
Depletion charge per ton	$ 2.40

Accordingly, Vorst should report $144,000 (60,000 tons sold × $2.40 per ton) as depletion in its income statement for the year.
Answer (A) is incorrect. The amount of $135,000 does not include the $180,000 restoration costs. Answer (C) is incorrect. The amount of $150,000 does not consider the restoration costs and the residual value of the land. Answer (D) is incorrect. The amount of $159,000 adds the $180,000 restoration cost instead of deducting the $120,000 net residual value of the land.

8.5 IFRS

8.5.1. On January 1, Year 1, an entity acquires for $100,000 a new piece of machinery with an estimated useful life of 10 years. The machine has a drum that must be replaced every 5 years and costs $20,000 to replace. Continued operations of the machine requires an inspection every 4 years after purchase; the inspection cost is $8,000. The company uses the straight-line method of depreciation. Under IFRS, what is the depreciation expense for Year 1?

A. $10,000

B. $10,800

C. $12,000

D. $13,200

Answer (D) is correct. *(CPA, adapted)*
REQUIRED: The depreciation expense.
DISCUSSION: Under IFRS, each significant part of the item must be depreciated. For the machinery, the significant parts are (1) the inspection cost presumed to be included in the initial cost ($8,000 with a 4-year life), (2) the drum ($20,000 with a 5-year life), and (3) the machine parts excluding the drum ($100,000 – $8,000 – $20,000 = $72,000 with a 10-year life). Thus, first-year straight-line depreciation expense is $13,200 [($72,000 ÷ 10 years) + ($20,000 ÷ 5 years) + ($8,000 ÷ 4 years)].
Answer (A) is incorrect. The amount of $10,000 results from not separately depreciating the costs of the drum and the inspection. Answer (B) is incorrect. The amount of $10,800 equals $108,000 divided by 10 years. Answer (C) is incorrect. The amount of $12,000 equals $120,000 divided by 10 years.

STUDY UNIT NINE
INTANGIBLE ASSETS AND
RESEARCH AND DEVELOPMENT COSTS

Intangible assets are nonfinancial assets that lack physical substance. The major categories of intangible assets are (1) marketing-related (e.g., trademarks), (2) customer-related (e.g., customer lists), (3) artistic-related (e.g., copyrights), (4) contract-related (e.g., franchise rights), (5) technology-related (e.g., computer software), and (6) goodwill (only in business combinations). Some intangible assets (such as goodwill or computer software) may require special accounting treatment.

Intangible assets with a **finite useful life** are amortized over that life, and a two-step impairment test is used.

Determination of an Impairment Loss
1. Events or changes in circumstances indicate a possible loss
2. Carrying amount > Sum of undiscounted cash flows
3. Loss = Carrying amount – Fair value

Intangible assets with an **indefinite useful life** are not amortized. Testing for impairment is not needed if an optional qualitative assessment indicates that it is **not** more likely than not to be impaired. Otherwise, a one-step impairment test is used.

Determination of an Impairment Loss
1. Review for impairment (at least annually)
2. Loss = Carrying amount – Fair value

Also, some questions in this study unit relate to issues unique to specific types of intangible assets, for example, revenue recognition under franchise accounting or capitalization of costs related to legal defense of a patent.

QUESTIONS

9.1 Accounting for Intangible Assets

9.1.1. Amortization of intangible assets, such as copyrights or patents, is the accounting process of

A. Determining the cash flow from operations for the current period.

B. Systematically allocating the cost of the intangible asset to the periods of use.

C. Accumulating a fund for the replacement of the asset at the end of its useful life.

D. Systematically reflecting the change in general price levels over the current period.

Answer (B) is correct. *(CMA, adapted)*
REQUIRED: The meaning of amortization.
DISCUSSION: Amortization is a means of allocating an initial cost to the periods that benefit from that cost. It is similar to depreciation, a term associated with long-lived tangible assets, and depletion, which is associated with natural resources.
Answer (A) is incorrect. Amortization is an allocation process that is not cash-based. Answer (C) is incorrect. No funding is associated with amortization. Answer (D) is incorrect. Amortization has nothing to do with changes in price levels.

9.1.2. A company recognized an intangible asset. The intangible asset is amortized over its useful life

A. Unless the pattern of consumption of the economic benefits of the asset is not reliably determinable.

B. If that life is determined to be finite.

C. Unless the precise length of that life is not known.

D. If that life is indefinite but not infinite.

Answer (B) is correct. *(Publisher, adapted)*
REQUIRED: The circumstances in which a recognized intangible asset is amortized.
DISCUSSION: A recognized intangible asset is amortized over its useful life if that useful life is finite, that is, unless the useful life is determined to be indefinite. The useful life of an intangible asset is indefinite if no foreseeable limit exists on the period over which it will contribute, directly or indirectly, to the reporting entity's cash flows.
Answer (A) is incorrect. An intangible asset is amortizable if its useful life is finite. If the pattern of consumption of the economic benefits of such an intangible asset is not reliably determinable, the straight-line amortization method is applied. Answer (C) is incorrect. If the precise length of the useful life is not known, an intangible asset with a finite useful life is amortized over the best estimate of its useful life. Answer (D) is incorrect. A recognized intangible asset is not amortized if its useful life is indefinite.

9.1.3. Which of the following assets, if any, acquired this year in an exchange transaction is(are) potentially amortizable?

	Goodwill	Trademarks
A.	No	No
B.	No	Yes
C.	Yes	Yes
D.	Yes	No

Answer (B) is correct. *(CPA, adapted)*
REQUIRED: The currently acquired assets that are potentially amortizable.
DISCUSSION: Goodwill is tested for impairment at least annually but is never amortized. Trademarks, however, may be amortized but only if they have finite useful lives.
Answer (A) is incorrect. Only trademarks are amortizable. Answer (C) is incorrect. Only trademarks are amortizable. Answer (D) is incorrect. Only trademarks are amortizable.

9.1.4. In accordance with generally accepted accounting principles, which of the following methods of amortization is required for amortizable intangible assets if the pattern of consumption of economic benefits is not reliably determinable?

A. Sum-of-the-years'-digits.

B. Straight-line.

C. Units-of-production.

D. Double-declining-balance.

Answer (B) is correct. *(CPA, adapted)*
REQUIRED: The method of amortization of intangible assets if the pattern of consumption of economic benefits is not reliably determinable.
DISCUSSION: The default method of amortization of intangible assets is the straight-line method.
Answer (A) is incorrect. Sum-of-the-years'-digits may be used only if it is reliably determined to reflect the pattern of consumption of the economic benefits of the intangible asset. Answer (C) is incorrect. Units-of-production may be used only if it is reliably determined to reflect the pattern of consumption of the economic benefits of the intangible asset. Answer (D) is incorrect. Double-declining-balance may be used only if it is reliably determined to reflect the pattern of consumption of the economic benefits of the intangible asset.

9.1.5. Intangible assets acquired solely from other entities or individuals should be recorded at cost at date of acquisition. Cost may not be measured by which of the following?

    A. Net carrying amount of the previous owner.

    B. Amount of cash disbursed.

    C. Present value of amounts to be paid for liabilities incurred.

    D. Fair value of other assets distributed.

Answer (A) is correct. *(Publisher, adapted)*
    REQUIRED: The method not allowed to measure cost of intangible assets.
    DISCUSSION: If cash is the consideration given in an exchange transaction, the cash paid is the measure of the transaction. If noncash consideration (noncash assets, liabilities incurred, or equity interests issued) is given, the measure is based on the more reliably determinable of the fair value of the consideration given or the fair value of the asset or net assets acquired. Furthermore, the only objective of present value used in initial recognition and fresh-start measurements is to estimate fair value in the absence of a market price. Consequently, only the carrying amount of the previous owner is not a proper measure of cost.
    Answer (B) is incorrect. The amount of cash disbursed is an allowable measure of fair value depending on the consideration given. Answer (C) is incorrect. The present value of amounts to be paid for liabilities incurred is an allowable measure of fair value depending on the consideration given. Answer (D) is incorrect. The fair value of other assets distributed is an allowable measure of fair value depending on the consideration given.

9.1.6. Which of the following is not a consideration in determining the useful life of an intangible asset?

    A. Legal, regulatory, or contractual provisions.

    B. Provisions for renewal or extension.

    C. Expected actions of competitors.

    D. Initial cost.

Answer (D) is correct. *(CPA, adapted)*
    REQUIRED: The item not a consideration in determining the useful life of an intangible asset.
    DISCUSSION: Initial cost is not a factor relevant to estimating the useful life of an intangible asset because it has no causal connection with the asset's contribution to the future cash flows of the reporting entity. The relevant factors for determining the useful life of an intangible asset include the expected use of the asset; the useful life of a related asset or assets; legal, regulatory, or contractual provisions that may limit the useful life or that may permit renewal or extension without substantial cost; economic factors (e.g., obsolescence, competition, or demand); and expenditures for maintenance.
    Answer (A) is incorrect. The relevant factors for determining the useful life of an intangible asset include legal, regulatory, or contractual provisions that may limit the useful life or that may permit renewal or extension without substantial cost. Answer (B) is incorrect. The relevant factors for determining the useful life of an intangible asset include provisions that may limit the useful life or that may permit renewal or extension without substantial cost. Answer (C) is incorrect. The relevant factors for determining the useful life of an intangible asset include economic factors (e.g., obsolescence, competition, or demand).

9.1.7. When should leaseholds and leasehold improvements be amortized over different periods?

    A. When the useful life of the leasehold improvement is less than the term of the leasehold.

    B. When the term of the leasehold exceeds 40 years.

    C. When the term of the leasehold is less than the useful life of the leasehold improvement.

    D. If the company is in the development stage.

Answer (A) is correct. *(Publisher, adapted)*
    REQUIRED: The reason the amortization periods of leaseholds and leasehold improvements may differ.
    DISCUSSION: A leasehold is the property under lease. Leasehold improvements should be amortized over their useful life if it is less than the term of the lease. But if the useful life is greater than the term of the lease, the improvement should be amortized over the life of the lease because the property will revert to the lessor at the end of the lease. If an option exists for renewal of the lease and the lessee intends to renew, the leasehold improvements should be amortized over the option period as well, but not to exceed their useful life.
    Answer (B) is incorrect. A leasehold should be amortized in the same way as other similar property. There is no minimum or maximum period. Answer (C) is incorrect. When the term of the lease is less than the improvement's useful life, amortization should occur over the shorter period. Answer (D) is incorrect. Development stage companies and established operating companies apply the same GAAP.

9.2 Subsequent Accounting for Goodwill

9.2.1. Which of the following costs of goodwill should be capitalized and amortized?

	Maintaining Goodwill	Developing Goodwill
A.	Yes	No
B.	No	No
C.	Yes	Yes
D.	No	Yes

Answer (B) is correct. *(CPA, adapted)*
REQUIRED: The cost(s) of goodwill, if any, that should be capitalized and amortized.
DISCUSSION: Goodwill arising from a business combination must be capitalized. However, amortization of goodwill is prohibited. Moreover, the cost of developing, maintaining, or restoring intangible assets (including goodwill) that (1) are not specifically identifiable, (2) have indeterminate useful lives, or (3) are inherent in a continuing business and related to an entity as a whole are expensed as incurred.
Answer (A) is incorrect. Costs of maintaining and developing goodwill should not be capitalized. Answer (C) is incorrect. Costs of maintaining and developing goodwill should not be capitalized. Answer (D) is incorrect. Costs of maintaining and developing goodwill should not be capitalized.

9.2.2. Say Co. purchased Ivy Co. at a cost that resulted in recognition of goodwill having an expected 10-year benefit period. However, Say plans to make additional expenditures to maintain goodwill for a total of 40 years. What costs should be capitalized and over how many years should they be amortized?

	Costs Capitalized	Amortization Period
A.	Acquisition costs only	0 years
B.	Acquisition costs only	40 years
C.	Acquisition and maintenance costs	10 years
D.	Acquisition and maintenance costs	40 years

Answer (A) is correct. *(CPA, adapted)*
REQUIRED: The costs to be capitalized and the amortization period.
DISCUSSION: Goodwill is capitalized and tested for impairment, but not amortized. In contrast, the cost of developing, maintaining, or restoring intangible assets (including goodwill) that are not specifically identifiable, have indeterminate lives, or are inherent in a continuing business and related to an entity as a whole are expensed as incurred.
Answer (B) is incorrect. Goodwill is not amortized. Answer (C) is incorrect. The costs of maintaining goodwill should be expensed as incurred, and goodwill is not amortized. Answer (D) is incorrect. Goodwill is not amortized. The costs of maintaining goodwill are expensed as incurred.

9.2.3. A company reported $6 million of goodwill in last year's statement of financial position. How should the company account for the reported goodwill in the current year?

A. Determine the current year's amortizable amount and report the current year's amortization expense.

B. Determine whether the fair value of the reporting unit is greater than the carrying amount and report a gain on goodwill in the income statement.

C. Determine whether the fair value of the reporting unit is less than the carrying amount and report an impairment loss on goodwill in the income statement.

D. Determine whether the fair value of the reporting unit is greater than the carrying amount and report the recovery of any previous impairment in the income statement.

Answer (C) is correct. *(CPA, adapted)*
REQUIRED: The current accounting for goodwill reported in the prior year's statements.
DISCUSSION: Potential impairment of goodwill is deemed to exist only if the carrying amount of a reporting unit is greater than its fair value. The accounting for goodwill is based on the units of the combined entity into which the acquiree was absorbed. The goodwill impairment test includes an optional qualitative test and a two-step quantitative test.
Answer (A) is incorrect. Goodwill is not amortized. Answer (B) is incorrect. Goodwill is recognized only after applying the acquisition method to account for a business combination. Thus, recognition of impairment but not appreciation is allowed. Answer (D) is incorrect. An impairment of goodwill is not reversible.

9.2.4. On January 2, Paye Co. acquired Shef Co. in a business combination that resulted in recognition of goodwill of $200,000 having an expected benefit period of 10 years. Shef is treated as a reporting unit, and the entire amount of the recognized goodwill is assigned to it. During the first quarter of the year, Shef spent an additional $80,000 on expenditures designed to maintain goodwill. Due to these expenditures, at December 31, Shef estimated that the benefit period of goodwill was 40 years. In its consolidated December 31 balance sheet, what amount should Paye report as goodwill?

A. $180,000

B. $200,000

C. $252,000

D. $280,000

Answer (B) is correct. *(CPA, adapted)*
REQUIRED: The amount of goodwill in the balance sheet.
DISCUSSION: Goodwill is not recorded except in a business combination. Thus, only the $200,000 recognized at the acquisition date should be recorded as goodwill. It should not be amortized but should be tested for impairment at the reporting-unit level. The facts given suggest that the fair value of the reporting unit (Shef) is not less than its carrying amount. Hence, no impairment of goodwill has occurred, and goodwill is unchanged at $200,000. Moreover, the cost of internally developing, maintaining, or restoring intangible assets (including goodwill) that are not specifically identifiable, have indeterminate useful lives, or are inherent in a continuing business and related to an entity as a whole should be expensed as incurred.
Answer (A) is incorrect. The amount of $180,000 results when goodwill is amortized on the straight-line basis over 10 years. Answer (C) is incorrect. The amount of $252,000 results from amortizing an additional $80,000 of expenditures to maintain goodwill over 10 years. Answer (D) is incorrect. The amount of $280,000 results from adding $80,000 of expenditures for the maintenance of goodwill.

9.2.5. What is the proper treatment of the recorded goodwill when an entity disposes of a portion of a reporting unit that constitutes a stand-alone acquired business?

A. All of the carrying amount of the goodwill of the reporting unit should be considered part of the cost of the assets sold.

B. The total carrying amount of the goodwill acquired with the business should be considered part of the cost of the assets sold.

C. Goodwill cannot be considered sold; it should be written off as a loss.

D. Goodwill cannot be sold; it should be amortized over its original useful life.

Answer (B) is correct. *(Publisher, adapted)*
REQUIRED: The true statement about goodwill when a portion of a reporting unit is sold.
DISCUSSION: If part of a reporting unit is to be disposed of and that part constitutes a business, goodwill related to the business is included in the carrying amount to be disposed of. The goodwill of the business and the goodwill retained by the reporting unit are determined based on relative fair values. However, when the business was not integrated with the other activities of the reporting unit, for example, because it is operated as a stand-alone entity, no allocation of the goodwill acquired with the business is made, and its carrying amount should be included in the carrying amount of the business to be disposed of.
Answer (A) is incorrect. The carrying amount of the goodwill acquired with the business should be considered sold. Answer (C) is incorrect. Goodwill can be considered sold as part of the business. Answer (D) is incorrect. Goodwill can be sold and cannot ever be amortized.

9.2.6. An entire acquired entity is sold. The goodwill remaining from the acquisition should be

A. Included in the carrying amount of the net assets sold.

B. Charged to retained earnings of the current period.

C. Expensed in the period sold.

D. Charged to retained earnings of prior periods.

Answer (A) is correct. *(Publisher, adapted)*
REQUIRED: The accounting for goodwill when an acquired entity is sold.
DISCUSSION: When a reporting unit is disposed of in its entirety, goodwill of that reporting unit (to the extent an impairment loss has not been recognized) is included in the carrying amount of the reporting unit to determine the gain or loss on disposal. Consequently, the unimpaired goodwill of each reporting unit of the acquired entity is included in the total carrying amount of that entity.
Answer (B) is incorrect. Unimpaired goodwill of a reporting unit disposed of in its entirety is included in its carrying amount. Answer (C) is incorrect. Unimpaired goodwill of a reporting unit disposed of in its entirety is included in its carrying amount. Answer (D) is incorrect. Unimpaired goodwill of a reporting unit disposed of in its entirety is included in its carrying amount.

9.3 Patents and Other Intangible Assets

9.3.1. A purchased patent has a remaining legal life of 15 years. It should be

   A. Expensed in the year of acquisition.

   B. Amortized over 15 years regardless of its useful life.

   C. Amortized over its useful life if less than 15 years.

   D. Amortized over 40 years.

Answer (C) is correct. *(CPA, adapted)*
   REQUIRED: The period over which a patent should be amortized.
   DISCUSSION: The amortization period for an intangible asset distinct from goodwill is the shorter of its useful life or the legal life remaining after acquisition.
   Answer (A) is incorrect. An intangible asset acquired from another entity should be recorded as an asset. Answer (B) is incorrect. The amortization period is not to exceed the useful life. Answer (D) is incorrect. The remaining legal life of the patent is only 15 years.

9.3.2. Grayson Co. incurred significant costs in defending its patent rights. Which of the following is the appropriate treatment of the related litigation costs?

   A. Litigation costs would be capitalized regardless of the outcome of the litigation.

   B. Litigation costs would be expensed regardless of the outcome of the litigation.

   C. Litigation costs would be capitalized if the patent right is successfully defended.

   D. Litigation costs would be capitalized only if the patent was purchased rather than internally developed.

Answer (C) is correct. *(CPA, adapted)*
   REQUIRED: The accounting for litigation costs related to defending patent rights.
   DISCUSSION: Subsequent to the grant of a patent, its owner may need to bring or defend a suit for patent infringement. The unrecovered costs of successful litigation are capitalized because they will benefit future periods. They are amortized over the shorter of the remaining legal life or the estimated useful life of the patent. The costs of unsuccessful litigation (damages, attorneys' fees) are expensed. An unsuccessful suit also indicates that the unamortized cost of the patent has no value and should be recognized as a loss.
   Answer (A) is incorrect. The costs of unsuccessful litigation are expensed. Answer (B) is incorrect. The costs of successful litigation are capitalized. Answer (D) is incorrect. Whether the costs of litigation are capitalized does not depend on whether the patent was purchased or developed internally. This distinction is significant only for measurement at initial recognition. The costs of purchase but not internal development are capitalized under U.S. GAAP.

9.3.3. Espion Corp. bought Patent X for $80,000 and Patent Z for $120,000. Espion also paid acquisition costs of $10,000 for Patent X and $14,000 for Patent Z. Both patents were challenged in legal actions. Espion paid $40,000 in legal fees for a successful defense of Patent X and $60,000 in legal fees for an unsuccessful defense of Patent Z. What amounts should Espion capitalize for patents?

   A. $324,000

   B. $224,000

   C. $130,000

   D. $90,000

Answer (C) is correct. *(CPA, adapted)*
   REQUIRED: The amount capitalized for patents.
   DISCUSSION: When an intangible asset is acquired externally, it should be recorded at its cost at the date of acquisition. Cost is measured by the more reliably determinable of the fair value of the consideration given or the fair value of the net assets acquired. Moreover, an exchange transaction for which the consideration is cash is measured by the amount paid. Legal fees incurred in the successful defense of a patent should be capitalized as part of the cost of the patent and then amortized over its remaining useful life. Amortization is appropriate for a patent because its useful life is finite. Legal fees incurred in an unsuccessful defense should be expensed as the costs are incurred. Hence, the cost of Patent X ($80,000 + $10,000) and the legal fees for its successful defense ($40,000) should be capitalized in the amount of $130,000. The costs associated with Patent Z should be written off immediately. The unsuccessful defense suggests that no asset exists.
   Answer (A) is incorrect. The amount of $324,000 includes all costs associated with Patent Z. Answer (B) is incorrect. The amount of $224,000 equals the total acquisition costs for Patents X and Z but excludes legal fees. Answer (D) is incorrect. The amount of $90,000 excludes the legal fees for a successful defense of Patent X.

9.3.4. On January 2, Year 1, Valhalla Corp. purchased a utility patent for a new consumer product for $180,000. At the time of purchase, the patent was valid for 15 years. However, the patent's useful life was estimated to be only 10 years due to the competitive nature of the product, with no residual value. On December 31, Year 4, the product was permanently withdrawn from sale under governmental order because of a potential health hazard in the product. Thus, no future positive cash flows will result from use of the patent, and its fair value is zero. What amount should Valhalla charge against income during Year 4, assuming straight-line amortization is appropriately recorded at the end of each year?

A. $18,000

B. $108,000

C. $126,000

D. $144,000

Answer (C) is correct. *(CPA, adapted)*
   REQUIRED: The amount charged against income when a product is permanently withdrawn from sale.
   DISCUSSION: A patent is an amortizable intangible asset because its useful life is finite. The straight-line method of amortization is used if the pattern of consumption of the economic benefits cannot be reliably determined. Because the patent was written off at the end of Year 4, the amount charged against income is equal to amortization expense plus the carrying amount of the asset at the time of the write-off. Amortization expense is $18,000 ($180,000 cost ÷ 10 years useful life). The remaining carrying amount of the asset is $108,000 ($180,000 cost – 4 years of amortization expense). This amount reflects an impairment loss ($108,000 carrying amount – $0 fair value). It is calculated in accordance with the principles of accounting for the impairment of long-lived assets when (1) the carrying amount is not recoverable and (2) the fair value of the asset is zero. Thus, the amount charged against income is $126,000 ($18,000 + $108,000).
   Answer (A) is incorrect. The amount of $18,000 includes only amortization expense. Answer (B) is incorrect. The amount of $108,000 includes only the carrying amount of the asset before recognition of the impairment loss. Answer (D) is incorrect. The amount of $144,000 is based on a 15-year useful life.

9.3.5. Freya Co. has two patents that have allegedly been infringed by competitors. After investigation, legal counsel informed Freya that it had a weak case for Patent A34 and a strong case in regard to Patent B19. Freya incurred additional legal fees to stop infringement on Patent B19. Both patents have a remaining legal life of 8 years. How should Freya account for these legal costs incurred relating to the two patents?

A. Expense costs for Patent A34 and capitalize costs for Patent B19.

B. Expense costs for both Patent A34 and Patent B19.

C. Capitalize costs for both Patent A34 and Patent B19.

D. Capitalize costs for Patent A34 and expense costs for Patent B19.

Answer (A) is correct. *(CPA, adapted)*
   REQUIRED: The accounting for legal costs incurred.
   DISCUSSION: Legal fees incurred in a successful defense of a patent should be capitalized and amortized. Legal fees incurred in an unsuccessful defense should be expensed as incurred. Hence, Freya should expense costs for Patent A34 and capitalize costs for Patent B19.
   Answer (B) is incorrect. Freya should capitalize costs for Patent B19. Answer (C) is incorrect. Freya should expense costs for Patent A34. Answer (D) is incorrect. Freya should expense costs for Patent A34 and capitalize costs for Patent B19.

9.3.6. A company recently acquired a copyright that now has a remaining legal life of 30 years. The copyright initially had a 38-year useful life assigned to it. An analysis of market trends and consumer habits indicated that the copyrighted material will generate positive cash flows for approximately 25 years. What is the remaining useful life, if any, over which the company can amortize the copyright for accounting purposes?

A. 0 years.

B. 25 years.

C. 30 years.

D. 38 years.

Answer (B) is correct. *(CPA, adapted)*
   REQUIRED: The remaining useful life, if any, over which an entity amortizes a copyright.
   DISCUSSION: An intangible asset distinct from goodwill with a finite useful life to the reporting entity is amortized over that useful life. Because the entity expects the copyrighted material to generate positive cash flows for approximately 25 years, the copyright is amortized over 25 years.
   Answer (A) is incorrect. An intangible asset is not amortized if it has an indefinite useful life. The copyright does not have an indefinite useful life. Answer (C) is incorrect. The remaining legal life is not the useful life of the copyright. Answer (D) is incorrect. The useful life should be reevaluated each reporting period. Thus, the initial useful life is subject to revision.

9.3.7. Northstar Co. acquired a registered trademark for $600,000. The trademark has a remaining legal life of 5 years but can be renewed every 10 years for a nominal fee. Northstar expects to renew the trademark indefinitely. What amount of amortization expense should Northstar record for the trademark in the current year?

A. $0

B. $15,000

C. $40,000

D. $120,000

Answer (A) is correct. *(CPA, adapted)*
REQUIRED: The amortization expense for a trademark expected to be renewed indefinitely.
DISCUSSION: The trademark is expected to be renewed indefinitely. Thus, it has an indefinite useful life and is not amortized. Amortization is recorded only for an intangible asset with a finite useful life.
Answer (B) is incorrect. The amount of $15,000 equals annual amortization over 40 years. Answer (C) is incorrect. The amount of $40,000 is the annual amortization over a 15-year useful life (5-year remaining legal life + the first 10-year renewal). Answer (D) is incorrect. The amount of $120,000 equals annual amortization over the 5-year remaining legal life.

9.4 Franchises

9.4.1. On January 2, Fafnir Co. purchased a franchise with a finite useful life of 10 years for $50,000. An additional franchise fee of 3% of franchise operation revenues must be paid each year to the franchisor. Revenues from franchise operations amounted to $400,000 during the year, and the pattern of consumption of benefits of the franchise is not reliably determinable. In its December 31 balance sheet, what amount should Fafnir report as an intangible asset-franchise?

A. $33,000

B. $43,800

C. $45,000

D. $50,000

Answer (C) is correct. *(CPA, adapted)*
REQUIRED: The amount of the intangible asset that is recorded for a franchise.
DISCUSSION: Intangible assets acquired other than in a business combination are initially recognized and measured based on their fair value. This "cost" should be based on the more reliably measurable of the fair value of the consideration given or the fair value of the assets acquired. Franchise fees are capitalized and amortized over the finite useful life. Absent information about the fair value of the assets acquired, the capitalizable amount equals the consideration given, that is, the initial fee and other expenditures necessary to acquire the franchise. Future franchise fees are expensed as incurred. Given that the pattern of consumption of benefits of the franchise is not reliably determinable, the straight-line method of amortization is used. Thus, given no residual value, the amount that should be reported as an intangible asset is $45,000 [$50,000 − ($50,000 ÷ 10)].
Answer (A) is incorrect. The amount of $33,000 results from subtracting the additional franchise fee. Answer (B) is incorrect. The amount of $43,800 includes amortization of the additional franchise fee. Answer (D) is incorrect. The unamortized initial fee is $50,000.

9.4.2. Helsing Co. bought a franchise from Anya Co. on January 1 for $204,000. An independent consultant retained by Helsing estimated that the remaining useful life of the franchise was a finite period of 50 years and that the pattern of consumption of benefits of the franchise is not reliably determinable. Its unamortized cost on Anya's books on January 1 was $68,000. What amount should be amortized for the year ended December 31, assuming no residual value?

A. $5,100

B. $4,080

C. $3,400

D. $1,700

Answer (B) is correct. *(CPA, adapted)*
REQUIRED: The first-year amortization expense of the cost of a franchise.
DISCUSSION: A franchise is an intangible asset. The initial measurement of an intangible asset acquired other than in a business combination is at fair value. Thus, the "cost" to be amortized should be based on the more reliably measurable of the fair value of the consideration given or the fair value of the assets acquired. If the useful life is finite, the intangible asset is amortized over that period. Moreover, if the consumption pattern of benefits of the intangible asset is not reliably determinable, the straight-line method of amortization is used. Accordingly, given no residual value, the amortization expense is $4,080 ($204,000 consideration given ÷ 50-year finite useful life).
Answer (A) is incorrect. The amount of $5,100 is based on a 40-year period. Answer (C) is incorrect. The amount of $3,400 is the difference between the $204,000 franchise price and Anya's $68,000 unamortized cost, divided by 40 years. Answer (D) is incorrect. The amount of $1,700 equals the unamortized cost on Anya's books amortized over 40 years.

9.4.3. Which of the following should be expensed as incurred by the franchisee for a franchise with an estimated useful life of 10 years?

A. Amount paid to the franchisor for the franchise.

B. Periodic payments to a company, other than the franchisor, for that company's franchise.

C. Legal fees paid to the franchisee's lawyers to obtain the franchise.

D. Periodic payments to the franchisor based on the franchisee's revenues.

Answer (D) is correct. *(CPA, adapted)*
REQUIRED: The payment that should be expensed as incurred by the franchisee.
DISCUSSION: Payments under a franchise agreement made to a franchisor based on the franchisee's revenues do not create benefits in future periods and should not be treated as an asset. These payments should be treated as operating expenses in the period in which they are incurred.
Answer (A) is incorrect. Amount paid to the franchisor for the franchise is a cost of acquiring the franchise. Answer (B) is incorrect. Periodic payments to a company, other than the franchisor, for that company's franchise is a cost of acquiring the franchise. Answer (C) is incorrect. Legal fees paid to the franchisee's lawyers to obtain the franchise is a cost of acquiring the franchise.

9.5 R&D

9.5.1. Which one of the following is not considered a research and development activity?

A. Laboratory research intended for the discovery of a new product.

B. Testing in search of product processing alternatives.

C. Modification of the design of a process.

D. Periodic design changes to existing products.

Answer (D) is correct. *(CMA, adapted)*
REQUIRED: The item not considered an R&D activity.
DISCUSSION: R&D costs must be expensed as incurred. Research is planned search or critical investigation aimed at discovery of new knowledge with the hope that such knowledge will be useful in developing a new product or service or a new process or technique or in bringing about a significant improvement in an existing product or process. Development is the translation of research findings or other knowledge into a plan or design for a new product or process or for a significant improvement in an existing product or process whether intended for use. Seasonal or other periodic design changes in existing products do not meet either of these definitions.
Answer (A) is incorrect. Laboratory research aimed at discovery of a new product is an R&D activity. Answer (B) is incorrect. Testing in search of product or process alternatives is an R&D activity. Answer (C) is incorrect. Modification of the formulation or design of a product or process is an R&D activity.

9.5.2. West, Inc., made the following expenditures relating to Product Y:

- Legal costs to file a patent on Product Y -- $10,000. Production of the finished product would not have been undertaken without the patent.
- Special equipment to be used solely for development of Product Y -- $60,000. The equipment has no other use and has an estimated useful life of 4 years.
- Labor and material costs incurred in producing a prototype model -- $200,000.
- Cost of testing the prototype -- $80,000.

What is the total amount of costs that will be expensed when incurred?

A. $280,000

B. $295,000

C. $340,000

D. $350,000

Answer (C) is correct. *(CPA, adapted)*
REQUIRED: The total amount of costs that will be expensed when incurred.
DISCUSSION: R&D costs are expensed as incurred. However, legal work in connection with patent applications or litigation and the sale or licensing of patents are specifically excluded from the definition of R&D. The legal costs of filing a patent should be capitalized. West's R&D costs include those incurred for the design, construction, and testing of preproduction prototypes. Moreover, the cost of equipment used solely for a specific project is also expensed immediately. Thus, the total amount of costs that will be expensed when incurred is $340,000.
Answer (A) is incorrect. The amount of $280,000 omits the cost of the special equipment. Answer (B) is incorrect. The amount of $295,000 includes 1 year's straight-line depreciation on the special equipment instead of the full cost. Answer (D) is incorrect. The amount of $350,000 includes the legal costs of filing a patent.

9.5.3. During the current year, Beta Motor Co. incurred the following costs related to a new solar-powered car:

Salaries of laboratory employees researching how to build the new car	$250,000
Legal fees for the patent application for the new car	20,000
Engineering follow-up during the early stages of commercial production (the follow-up occurred during the current year)	50,000
Marketing research to promote the new car	30,000
Design, testing, and construction of a prototype	400,000

What amount should Beta Motor report as research and development expense in its income statement for the current year?

A. $250,000

B. $650,000

C. $720,000

D. $750,000

Answer (B) is correct. *(CPA, adapted)*
REQUIRED: The research and development (R&D) expense.
DISCUSSION: Salaries, wages, and other related costs of personnel engaged in R&D and the design, construction, and testing of preproduction prototypes and models are activities typically included in R&D. These costs are expensed when incurred. Thus, R&D expense for the current year is $650,000 ($250,000 + $400,000).
Answer (A) is incorrect. Costs for design, testing, and construction of a prototype are included in R&D costs and expensed when incurred. Answer (C) is incorrect. Legal work in connection with patent applications and engineering follow-through in an early phase of commercial production are not R&D activities. Answer (D) is incorrect. Legal work in connection with patent applications, engineering follow-through in an early phase of commercial production, and marketing research are not R&D activities.

9.5.4. During the year just ended, Orr Co. incurred the following costs:

Research and development services performed by Key Corp. for Orr	$150,000
Design, construction, and testing of preproduction prototypes and models	200,000
Testing in search for new products or process alternatives	175,000

In its income statement for the year, what should Orr report as research and development expense?

A. $150,000

B. $200,000

C. $350,000

D. $525,000

Answer (D) is correct. *(CPA, adapted)*
REQUIRED: The R&D expense.
DISCUSSION: Research is planned search or critical investigation aimed at discovery of new knowledge useful in developing a new product, service, process, or technique or in bringing about a significant improvement to an existing product, etc. Development is translation of research findings or other knowledge into a plan or design for a new or improved product or process. R&D expenses include R&D performed under contract by others; design, construction, and testing of prototypes; and testing in search for new products.
Answer (A) is incorrect. The amount of $150,000 does not include design, construction, and testing of preproduction prototypes or testing in search of new products. Answer (B) is incorrect. The amount of $200,000 does not include R&D performed under contract by others or testing in search for new products. Answer (C) is incorrect. The amount of $350,000 does not include testing in search for new products.

9.5.5. Brill Co. made the following expenditures during Year 1:

Costs to develop computer software for internal use in Brill's general management information system	$100,000
Costs of market research activities	75,000

What amount of these expenditures should Brill report in its Year 1 income statement as research and development expenses?

A. $175,000

B. $100,000

C. $75,000

D. $0

Answer (D) is correct. *(CPA, adapted)*
REQUIRED: The amount of research and development expenses.
DISCUSSION: Costs of market research are not R&D costs. Furthermore, general and administrative costs not clearly related to R&D activities are not included as R&D costs. Thus, costs to develop software for the company's own general management information system are also not R&D costs.
Answer (A) is incorrect. R&D expenses do not include costs to develop software for internal use in a general management information system or the costs of market research. Answer (B) is incorrect. R&D costs do not include costs to develop software for internal use in a general management information system. Answer (C) is incorrect. R&D costs do not include market research costs.

9.5.6. Corporation B accounts for the $1 million as

A. A liability.

B. Income from operations.

C. Deferred contract revenue.

D. Shareholders' equity.

Answer (C) is correct. *(E. Spede/J. Sperry)*
    REQUIRED: The classification of an R&D advance in the accounts of the recipient.
    DISCUSSION: If the entity is obligated to repay any of the funds provided by the other party, regardless of the outcome of the project, it recognizes a liability. If repayment depends solely on the results of the R&D having future economic benefit, the entity accounts for its obligation as a contract to perform R&D for others. Given that B must repay only on successful completion of the project, the advance should be recorded as deferred contract revenue.
    Answer (A) is incorrect. The entity is not obligated to repay if the R&D has no future economic benefit. Answer (B) is incorrect. No services have yet been performed. Answer (D) is incorrect. The transaction is a contract to perform services, not an investment by Partnership A.

9.5.7. Partnership A accounts for the $1 million as

A. Accounts receivable.

B. Research and development expense.

C. Deferred research and development costs.

D. Advances on contract.

Answer (B) is correct. *(E. Spede/J. Sperry)*
    REQUIRED: The classification of the advance in the accounts of the lender.
    DISCUSSION: If repayment to the entity of any advance to other parties depends solely on the results of the R&D having future economic benefits, the advance is accounted for as a cost incurred. Furthermore, the costs are charged to R&D expense. B's repayment depends solely on the successful completion of the R&D, and Partnership A should treat the advance as R&D expense.
    Answer (A) is incorrect. Corporation B does not have an unconditional obligation to repay the advance. Answer (C) is incorrect. The $1 million must be expensed. Answer (D) is incorrect. When repayment depends solely on the results of the R&D having future economic benefits, the advance must be expensed.

9.5.8. Which of the following is the proper treatment of the cost of equipment used in research and development activities that will have alternative future uses?

A. Expensed in the year in which the research and development project started.

B. Capitalized and depreciated over the term of the research and development project.

C. Capitalized and depreciated over its estimated useful life.

D. Either capitalized or expensed, but not both, depending on the term of the research and development project.

Answer (C) is correct. *(CPA, adapted)*
    REQUIRED: The proper treatment of the cost of equipment used in R&D activities.
    DISCUSSION: The costs of equipment acquired or constructed for R&D and having alternative future uses are capitalized as tangible assets and depreciated over its estimated useful life.
    Answer (A) is incorrect. The cost of equipment for a particular project that has no alternative future uses is classified as an R&D cost and expensed when incurred. However, the question states that the equipment has alternative future uses. Therefore, it is capitalized and depreciated over its estimated useful life. Answer (B) is incorrect. The life and use of the equipment extends beyond the term of the research and development project. The equipment should be depreciated over its estimated useful life since it will be used beyond the term of the project. Answer (D) is incorrect. The term of the project does not determine whether the cost of the equipment is capitalized or expensed. This is determined by the fact that the equipment will have alternative future uses.

9.5.9. During the current year ended December 31, Metal, Inc., incurred the following costs:

Laboratory research aimed at discovery of new knowledge	$ 75,000
Design of tools, jigs, molds, and dies involving new technology	22,000
Quality control during commercial production, including routine testing	35,000
Equipment acquired 2 years ago, having an estimated useful life of 5 years with no salvage value, used in various R&D projects	150,000
Research and development services performed by Stone Co. for Metal, Inc.	23,000
Research and development services performed by Metal, Inc., for Clay Co.	32,000

What amount of research and development expenses should Metal report in its current-year income statement?

A. $120,000

B. $150,000

C. $187,000

D. $217,000

Answer (B) is correct. *(CPA, adapted)*
REQUIRED: The amount of R&D costs that should be reported in the current period.
DISCUSSION: Research and development (R&D) costs must be expensed as incurred. The following items are considered R&D costs of Metal:

1. Laboratory research aimed at discovery of new knowledge.
2. Design of tools, jigs, molds, and dies involving new technology.
3. Research and development services performed by Stone for Metal. The costs of services performed by others in connection with the R&D activities of an entity, including R&D conducted by others on behalf of the entity, are R&D costs and are expensed as incurred.
4. The depreciation on the equipment with alternative uses used in R&D projects. The costs of materials, equipment, and facilities acquired or constructed for R&D and having alternative uses (in R&D projects or otherwise) are capitalized as tangible assets and depreciated over their estimated useful lives. The depreciation on the equipment is $30,000 ($150,000 ÷ 5-year useful life). Thus, the R&D expenses total $150,000 ($75,000 + $22,000 + $23,000 + $30,000). Quality control during commercial production, including routine testing, is not considered an R&D cost.

Answer (A) is incorrect. The depreciation on the equipment used in R&D projects is considered an R&D expense in the current period. Answer (C) is incorrect. The depreciation on the equipment used in R&D projects is considered an R&D cost in the current period. Furthermore, the research and development services performed by Metal, for Clay are not considered R&D costs of Metal. Quality control during commercial production, including routine testing, is not considered an R&D cost. Answer (D) is incorrect. The research and development services performed by Metal for Clay are not considered R&D costs of Metal. Quality control during commercial production, including routine testing, is not considered an R&D cost.

9.5.10. During the current year, Lyle Co. incurred $204,000 of research and development costs in its laboratory to develop a patent that was granted on July 1. Legal fees and other costs associated with registration of the patent totaled $41,000. The estimated useful life of the patent is 10 years. What amount should Lyle capitalize for the patent on July 1?

A. $0

B. $41,000

C. $204,000

D. $245,000

Answer (B) is correct. *(CPA, adapted)*
REQUIRED: The amount to be capitalized for an internally developed patent.
DISCUSSION: R&D costs are required to be expensed as they are incurred. Legal fees and registration fees are excluded from the definition of R&D. Thus, the $41,000 in legal fees and other costs associated with the registration of the patent should be capitalized. The $204,000 in R&D costs should be expensed.

Answer (A) is incorrect. Legal fees and other costs associated with the registration of the patent should be capitalized. Answer (C) is incorrect. Legal fees and other costs associated with the registration of the patent should be capitalized, whereas R&D costs must be expensed as incurred. Answer (D) is incorrect. R&D costs must be expensed as incurred.

9.5.11. On January 1, Year 1, Jambon purchased equipment for use in developing a new product. Jambon uses the straight-line depreciation method. The equipment could provide benefits over a 10-year period. However, the new product development is expected to take 5 years, and the equipment can be used only for this project. Jambon's Year 1 expense equals

A. The total cost of the equipment.

B. One-fifth of the cost of the equipment.

C. One-tenth of the cost of the equipment.

D. Zero.

Answer (A) is correct. *(CPA, adapted)*
REQUIRED: The expense for equipment usable only for developing a new product.
DISCUSSION: The costs of materials, equipment, or facilities that are acquired or constructed for a particular R&D project and that have no alternative future uses and therefore no separate economic values are R&D costs when incurred. R&D costs are expensed in full when incurred.

Answer (B) is incorrect. The total cost of the equipment should be expensed in Year 1. Answer (C) is incorrect. The total cost of the equipment should be expensed in Year 1. Answer (D) is incorrect. The total cost of the equipment should be expensed in Year 1.

9.6 Computer Software and Other Costs

9.6.1. On December 31, Year 7, Byte Co. had capitalized software costs of $600,000 with an economic life of 4 years. Sales for Year 8 were 10% of expected total sales of the software. At December 31, Year 8, the software had a net realizable value of $480,000. In its December 31, Year 8, balance sheet, what amount should Byte report as net capitalized cost of computer software?

A. $432,000

B. $450,000

C. $480,000

D. $540,000

Answer (B) is correct. *(CPA, adapted)*
REQUIRED: The net capitalized cost of computer software at year end.
DISCUSSION: The annual amortization is the greater of the amount determined using (1) the ratio of current gross revenues to the sum of current gross revenues and anticipated future gross revenues, or (2) the straight-line method over the remaining estimated economic life, including the current reporting period. At year end, the unamortized cost of each software product must be compared with the net realizable value (NRV) of that software product. Any excess of unamortized cost over NRV must be written off. The amount of amortization under the straight-line method is used because it is greater than the amount determined using the 10% ratio of current sales to expected total sales. Thus, Byte Co. had an unamortized cost of software of $450,000 [$600,000 capitalized cost – ($600,000 ÷ 4)] at December 31, Year 8. The $450,000 unamortized cost is lower than the $480,000 NRV, so $450,000 is the amount reported in the year-end balance sheet.
Answer (A) is incorrect. The amount of $432,000 equals the NRV at December 31, Year 8, minus amortization calculated as 10% of NRV. Answer (C) is incorrect. The NRV at December 31, Year 8, is $480,000. Answer (D) is incorrect. The amount of $540,000 assumes amortization at 10% with no adjustment for NRV.

9.6.2. Miller Co. incurred the following computer software costs for the development and sale of software programs during the current year:

Planning costs	$ 50,000
Design of the software	150,000
Substantial testing of the project's initial stages	75,000
Production and packaging costs for the first month's sales	500,000
Costs of producing product masters after technological feasibility was established	200,000

The project was not under any contractual arrangement when these expenditures were incurred. What amount should Miller report as research and development expense for the current year?

A. $200,000

B. $275,000

C. $500,000

D. $975,000

Answer (B) is correct. *(CPA, adapted)*
REQUIRED: The R&D expense.
DISCUSSION: R&D costs of software are all costs incurred to establish technological feasibility. Technological feasibility is established when the enterprise has completed all planning, designing, coding, and testing necessary to establish that the product can be produced to meet its design specifications, including functions, features, and technical performance requirements. Consequently, Miller's R&D cost is $275,000 ($50,000 planning + $150,000 design + $75,000 initial testing).
Answer (A) is incorrect. The amount of $200,000 does not include the cost for substantial testing of the project's initial stages. Answer (C) is incorrect. Production and packaging costs for the first month's sales are capitalized as inventory. Answer (D) is incorrect. The amount of $975,000 includes production and packaging costs for the first month's sales that should be inventoried. Costs of producing product masters after technological feasibility was established should be capitalized as software costs.

9.6.3. Neue Co. incurred the following costs during its first year of operations:

Legal fees for incorporation and other related matters	$55,000
Underwriters' fees for initial stock offering	40,000
Exploration costs and purchases of mineral rights	60,000

Neue had no revenue during its first year of operation. What amount must Neue expense as organizational costs?

A. $155,000

B. $100,000

C. $95,000

D. $55,000

Answer (D) is correct. *(CPA, adapted)*
REQUIRED: The organizational costs to be expensed.
DISCUSSION: Organization costs are those incurred in the formation of a business entity. For financial accounting purposes, nongovernmental entities must expense all start-up and organization costs as incurred. Thus, the legal fees should be expensed because they are organization costs. Fees for an initial stock offering are customarily treated as a reduction in the proceeds rather than as organization costs, and exploration costs and purchases of mineral rights are capitalizable items that are not organization costs.
Answer (A) is incorrect. Fees for an initial stock offering are customarily treated as a reduction in the proceeds rather than as organization costs. Answer (B) is incorrect. Fees for an initial stock offering are customarily treated as a reduction in the proceeds rather than as organization costs, and exploration costs and purchases of mineral rights are capitalizable items that are not organization costs. The legal fees should be expensed because they are organization costs. Answer (C) is incorrect. Fees for an initial stock offering are customarily treated as a reduction in the proceeds rather than as organization costs.

9.6.4. Wind Co. incurred organization costs of $6,000 at the beginning of its first year of operations. How should Wind treat the organization costs in its financial statements in accordance with GAAP?

A. Never amortized.

B. Amortized over 180 months.

C. Amortized over 40 years.

D. Expensed immediately.

Answer (D) is correct. *(CPA, adapted)*
REQUIRED: The accounting for organization costs.
DISCUSSION: Organization costs are those incurred in the formation of a business entity. Under the federal tax code, organization and start-up costs must be capitalized and amortized over a period of not less than 15 years. However, for financial accounting purposes, nongovernmental entities must expense all start-up and organization costs as incurred.
Answer (A) is incorrect. Organization costs are never capitalized. Answer (B) is incorrect. Organization costs are amortized over a minimum of 15 years (180 months) for federal income tax purposes. Answer (C) is incorrect. Organization costs are expensed as incurred.

9.6.5. On January 1, Year 1, Alpha Co. signed an annual maintenance agreement with a software provider for $15,000, and the maintenance period begins on March 1, Year 1. Alpha also incurred $5,000 of costs on January 1, Year 1, related to software modification requests that will increase the functionality of the software. Alpha depreciates and amortizes its computer and software assets over 5 years using the straight-line method. What amount is the total expense that Alpha should recognize related to the maintenance agreement and the software modifications for the year ended December 31, Year 1?

A. $5,000

B. $13,500

C. $16,000

D. $20,000

Answer (B) is correct. *(CPA, adapted)*
REQUIRED: The amounts that should be expensed instead of capitalized.
DISCUSSION: Maintenance should be expensed in the period it is used. The maintenance period began on March 1, which means 10 months of maintenance were used in the current year. Thus, Alpha Co. recognizes $12,500 in maintenance expense for the current period [$15,000 × (10 months ÷ 12 months)] due to the maintenance agreement. The $5,000 in software modifications should be capitalized because it will benefit more than one period. This amount will be amortized over 5 years using the straight-line method. Amortization expense relating to the software modifications for the current period is $1,000 ($5,000 ÷ 5 years). Thus, total expense that Alpha should recognize related to the maintenance agreement and the software modifications for the year totals $13,500 ($12,500 + $1,000), expense that was incurred from March to December of the current year.
Answer (A) is incorrect. The $5,000 in software modifications should be capitalized and amortized, not expensed. Furthermore, Alpha Co. must also recognize the maintenance expense. Answer (C) is incorrect. Alpha Co. will only recognize maintenance expense for the 10-month period of the agreement that occurred during the current year (March-December). Answer (D) is incorrect. The $5,000 in software modifications should be capitalized and amortized, not expensed. Furthermore, Alpha Co. will only recognize maintenance expense for the 10-month period of the agreement that occurred during the current year (March-December).

Questions 9.6.6 and 9.6.7 are based on the following information. During Year 1, Microcomp Corp. incurred costs to develop and produce a routine, low-risk computer software product, as described below.

Completion of detail program design	$13,000
Costs incurred for coding and testing to establish technological feasibility	10,000
Other coding costs after establishment of technological feasibility	24,000
Other testing costs after establishment of technological feasibility	20,000
Costs of producing product masters for training materials	15,000
Duplication of computer software and training materials from product masters (1,000 units)	25,000
Packaging product (500 units)	9,000

9.6.6. In Microcomp's December 31, Year 1, balance sheet, what amount should be reported in inventory?

A. $25,000

B. $34,000

C. $40,000

D. $49,000

Answer (B) is correct. *(CPA, adapted)*
REQUIRED: The amount reported in inventory.
DISCUSSION: Costs incurred internally in creating a computer software product must be charged to expense when incurred as R&D until technological feasibility has been established. Thereafter, all software production costs incurred until the product is available for general release to customers must be capitalized and amortized. The costs of duplicating the software, documentation, and training materials from the product masters and of physically packaging the product for distribution are capitalized as inventory. Hence, inventory should be reported at $34,000 ($25,000 duplication costs + $9,000 packaging costs).
Answer (A) is incorrect. The amount of $25,000 excludes packaging costs. Answer (C) is incorrect. The amount of $40,000 excludes packaging costs but includes costs of producing product masters. Answer (D) is incorrect. The amount of $49,000 includes costs of producing product masters.

9.6.7. In Microcomp's December 31, Year 1, balance sheet, what amount should be capitalized as software cost subject to amortization?

A. $54,000

B. $57,000

C. $59,000

D. $69,000

Answer (C) is correct. *(CPA, adapted)*
REQUIRED: The amount capitalized as software cost subject to amortization.
DISCUSSION: Costs incurred internally in creating a computer software product shall be charged to expense when incurred as research and development until technological feasibility has been established for the product. Thereafter, all software production costs incurred until the product is available for general release to customers shall be capitalized and subsequently reported at the lower of unamortized cost or net realizable value. Hence, the costs of completing the detail program design and establishing technological feasibility are expensed, the costs of duplicating software and training materials and packaging the product are inventoried, and the costs of coding and other testing after establishing technological feasibility and the costs of producing product masters are capitalized and amortized. The amount capitalized as software cost subject to amortization is therefore $59,000 ($24,000 + $20,000 + $15,000).
Answer (A) is incorrect. The amount of $54,000 equals inventoriable costs plus the other testing costs. Answer (B) is incorrect. The amount of $57,000 is the sum of the costs expensed and the costs inventoried. Answer (D) is incorrect. The amount of $69,000 assumes the costs of coding and testing to establish feasibility are capitalized and amortized.

9.7 IFRS

9.7.1. Under IFRS, an entity that acquires an intangible asset may use the revaluation model for subsequent measurement only if

- A. The useful life of the intangible asset can be reliably determined.
- B. An active market exists for the intangible asset.
- C. The cost of the intangible asset can be measured reliably.
- D. The intangible asset is a monetary asset.

Answer (B) is correct. *(CPA, adapted)*
REQUIRED: The condition for use of the revaluation model for subsequent measurement of an intangible asset.
DISCUSSION: An intangible asset is carried at cost minus any accumulated amortization and impairment losses, or at a revalued amount. The revaluation model is similar to that for items of PPE (initial recognition of an asset at cost). However, fair value must be determined based on an active market.
Answer (A) is incorrect. An intangible asset may have an indefinite life. Answer (C) is incorrect. Initial recognition of an intangible asset is at cost. Recognition is permitted only when it is probable that the entity will receive the expected economic benefits, and the cost is reliably measurable. Answer (D) is incorrect. An intangible asset is nonmonetary.

9.7.2. Under IFRS, which of the following is a criterion that must be met in order for an item to be recognized as an intangible asset other than goodwill?

- A. The item's fair value can be measured reliably.
- B. The item is part of the entity's activities aimed at gaining new scientific or technical knowledge.
- C. The item is expected to be used in the production or supply of goods or services.
- D. The item is identifiable and lacks physical substance.

Answer (D) is correct. *(CPA, adapted)*
REQUIRED: The criterion for recognizing an intangible asset other than goodwill.
DISCUSSION: IAS 38, *Intangible Assets*, defines an intangible asset as an identifiable nonmonetary asset without physical substance.
Answer (A) is incorrect. Initial recognition of an intangible asset is at cost. Recognition is permitted only when it is probable that the entity will receive the expected economic benefits, and the cost is reliably measurable. Answer (B) is incorrect. Research is undertaken to gain new scientific or technical knowledge and understanding. Expenditures for research are expensed as incurred. Answer (C) is incorrect. Property, plant, and equipment are expected to be used in the production or supply of goods or services.

9.7.3. An entity purchases a trademark and incurs the following costs in connection with the trademark:

One-time trademark purchase price	$100,000
Nonrefundable VAT taxes	5,000
Training sales personnel on the use of the new trademark	7,000
Research expenditures associated with the purchase of the new trademark	24,000
Legal costs incurred to register the trademark	10,500
Salaries of the administrative personnel	12,000

Assuming that the trademark meets all of the applicable initial asset recognition criteria, the entity should recognize an asset in the amount of

- A. $100,000
- B. $115,500
- C. $146,500
- D. $158,500

Answer (B) is correct. *(CPA, adapted)*
REQUIRED: The initial amount recognized for an intangible asset.
DISCUSSION: Cost includes the purchase price (including purchase taxes and import duties) and any directly attributable costs to prepare the asset for its intended use, such as legal fees. Thus, the intangible asset is initially recognized at $115,500 ($100,000 price + $5,000 value-added taxes + $10,500 of legal costs).
Answer (A) is incorrect. Purchase taxes and legal fees for registration also are capitalized. Answer (C) is incorrect. Training and research costs are expensed as incurred. Answer (D) is incorrect. Training and research costs and administrative salaries and other overhead costs are not directly attributable costs.

STUDY UNIT TEN
INVESTMENTS

Investments in debt securities are classified as held-to-maturity, available-for-sale, or trading. Many questions about debt securities relate to bonds classified as **held-to-maturity**. The accounting for investments in equity securities (e.g., common stock) depends on the investor's presumed influence based on the ownership interest held.

Election of the **fair value option** allows entities to (1) measure most financial assets and liabilities at fair value and (2) report unrealized gains and losses in earnings. This method of accounting also is applied to debt securities classified as **trading**. Debt securities classified as **available-for-sale** are measured at fair value, but unrealized gains and losses are reported in other comprehensive income (OCI).

An investment in equity securities that does not result in control or significant influence over the investee is measured at fair value through the income statement. An entity may elect the measurement alternative for an investment in equity securities without a readily determinable fair value. This alternative is cost minus impairment (if any), plus or minus changes resulting from observable price changes for an identical or a similar security of the same issuer.

When the investor controls the investee, consolidation is required. Business combinations and consolidated reporting are covered in Study Unit 24.

Other topics in this study unit are (1) derivatives and hedges, (2) cash surrender value, and (3) disclosures about financial instruments.

QUESTIONS

10.1 Held-to-Maturity, Trading, and Available-for-Sale Debt Securities

10.1.1. Investments in debt securities may be classified as

I.   Available-for-sale securities
II. Held-to-maturity securities
III. Trading securities

A. I only.

B. I and II only.

C. I and III only.

D. I, II, and III.

Answer (D) is correct. *(Publisher, adapted)*
REQUIRED: The possible classification(s) of debt securities.
DISCUSSION: An investment in debt securities may be classified as (1) trading (if held for sale in the near term), (2) held-to-maturity (if the holder has the positive intent and ability to hold until the maturity date), or (3) available-for-sale (if not classified as trading or held-to-maturity).
Answer (A) is incorrect. Debt securities also may be classified as trading or as held-to-maturity. Answer (B) is incorrect. Debt securities also may be classified as trading. Answer (C) is incorrect. Debt securities also may be classified as held-to-maturity.

10.1.2. At year end, Rim Co. held several investments with the intent of selling them in the near term. The investments consisted of $100,000, 8%, 5-year bonds, purchased for $92,000, and short-term notes purchased for $35,000. At year end, the bonds were selling on the open market for $105,000, and the short-term notes had a market value of $50,000. What amount should Rim report as trading securities in its year-end balance sheet?

A. $50,000

B. $127,000

C. $142,000

D. $155,000

Answer (D) is correct. *(CPA, adapted)*
REQUIRED: The amount of trading securities at year end.
DISCUSSION: Debt securities that are bought and held primarily for sale in the near term are classified as trading securities. Consequently, the bonds and the short-term notes are trading securities. They are initially recorded at cost but are subsequently measured at fair value at each balance sheet date. Quoted market prices in active markets are the best evidence of fair value. Based on market quotes at year end, the bonds had a fair value of $105,000, and the short-term notes had a fair value of $50,000. The total is $155,000.
Answer (A) is incorrect. The fair value of the bonds is also included. Answer (B) is incorrect. Trading securities are reported at their fair value, not historical cost. Answer (C) is incorrect. The bonds should be measured at fair value, not historical cost.

10.1.3. Investments classified as held-to-maturity securities should be measured at

A. Acquisition cost.

B. Amortized cost.

C. Lower of cost or market.

D. Fair value.

Answer (B) is correct. *(Publisher, adapted)*
REQUIRED: The attribute for measuring held-to-maturity securities.
DISCUSSION: Debt securities classified as held-to-maturity are measured at amortized cost if the reporting entity has the positive intent and ability to hold them to maturity.
Answer (A) is incorrect. The acquisition cost of held-to-maturity securities is adjusted for amortization. Answer (C) is incorrect. Inventory accounted for using the LIFO or retail inventory method is measured at the lower of cost or market. Held-to-maturity securities are written down below amortized cost only when a decline in fair value below amortized cost is other than temporary. Answer (D) is incorrect. Debt securities classified as held-to-maturity are reported at amortized cost.

10.1.4. On July 2, Year 4, Wynn, Inc., purchased as a short-term investment a $1 million face-value Kean Co. 8% bond for $910,000 plus accrued interest to yield 10%. The bonds mature on January 1, Year 11, and pay interest annually on January 1. On December 31, Year 4, the bonds had a fair value of $945,000. On February 13, Year 5, Wynn sold the bonds for $920,000. In its December 31, Year 4, balance sheet, what amount should Wynn report for the bond if it is classified as an available-for-sale security?

A. $910,000

B. $920,000

C. $945,000

D. $950,000

Answer (C) is correct. *(CPA, adapted)*
REQUIRED: The amount to be reported for a bond classified as an available-for-sale security.
DISCUSSION: Available-for-sale debt securities should be measured at fair value in the balance sheet. Thus, the bond should be reported at its fair value of $945,000 to reflect the unrealized holding gain (change in fair value).
Answer (A) is incorrect. The amount of $910,000 is the cost (accrued interest is not recorded as part of the cost but as an adjustment of interest income). Answer (B) is incorrect. The sale price is $920,000. Answer (D) is incorrect. The amount of $950,000 equals the cost plus accrued interest (the total price paid) on July 2, Year 4.

10.1.5. When the fair value of an investment in debt securities exceeds its amortized cost, how should each of the following debt securities be reported at the end of the year, given no election of the fair value option?

	Debt Securities Classified As	
	Held-to-Maturity	Available-for-Sale
A.	Amortized cost	Amortized cost
B.	Amortized cost	Fair value
C.	Fair value	Fair value
D.	Fair value	Amortized cost

Answer (B) is correct. *(CPA, adapted)*
REQUIRED: The reporting of debt securities classified as held-to-maturity and available-for-sale.
DISCUSSION: Investments in debt securities must be classified as held-to-maturity and measured at amortized cost in the balance sheet if the reporting entity has the positive intent and ability to hold them to maturity. Debt securities that are not expected to be sold in the near term and that are not held-to-maturity should be classified as available-for-sale. Available-for-sale debt securities should be reported at fair value, with unrealized holding gains and losses (except those on securities designated as being hedged in a fair value hedge) excluded from net income and reported in OCI.
Answer (A) is incorrect. Debt securities classified as held-to-maturity and available-for-sale are reported at amortized cost and fair value, respectively. Answer (C) is incorrect. Debt securities classified as held-to-maturity and available-for-sale are reported at amortized cost and fair value, respectively. Answer (D) is incorrect. Debt securities classified as held-to-maturity and available-for-sale are reported at amortized cost and fair value, respectively.

10.1.6. A decline in the fair value of an available-for-sale security below its amortized cost basis that is deemed to be other than temporary should

A. Be accumulated in a valuation allowance.

B. Be treated as a realized loss and included in the determination of net income for the period.

C. Not be realized until the security is sold.

D. Be treated as an unrealized loss and included in the equity section of the balance sheet as a separate item.

Answer (B) is correct. *(CMA, adapted)*
REQUIRED: The accounting for a nontemporary impairment of an available-for-sale security.
DISCUSSION: Any other-than-temporary decline in the fair value of an available-for-sale security below its amortized cost basis should be considered a realized loss. The amortized cost basis should be written down to fair value and is not adjusted for subsequent recoveries in fair value. Realized gains and losses should be included in income in the period in which they occur. However, if a security has been the hedged item in a fair value hedge, its amortized cost basis will reflect adjustments in its carrying amount for changes in fair value attributable to the hedged risk. The amortized cost basis should be distinguished from the fair value, which equals the cost basis plus or minus the net unrealized holding gain or loss. The cost basis, not the fair value, is used to determine the amount of any other-than-temporary decline in fair value that will be treated as a realized loss.
Answer (A) is incorrect. A valuation allowance is used to record changes in fair value regarded as temporary. Answer (C) is incorrect. A permanent decline in fair value is treated as a realized loss. Answer (D) is incorrect. A temporary decline in fair value is debited to other comprehensive income (OCI). Accumulated OCI is a component of equity on the balance sheet.

10.1.7. The following information pertains to Lark Corp.'s available-for-sale debt securities:

	December 31	
	Year 2	Year 3
Cost	$100,000	$100,000
Fair value	90,000	120,000

Differences between cost and fair values are considered to be temporary. The decline in fair value was properly accounted for at December 31, Year 2. Ignoring tax effects, by what amount should other comprehensive income (OCI) be credited at December 31, Year 3?

A. $0

B. $10,000

C. $20,000

D. $30,000

Answer (D) is correct. *(CPA, adapted)*
REQUIRED: The credit to OCI if fair value exceeds cost.
DISCUSSION: Unrealized holding gains and losses on available-for-sale debt securities, including those classified as current assets, are not included in earnings but ordinarily are reported in OCI, net of tax effects (ignored in this question). At December 31, Year 2, OCI should have been debited for $10,000 for the excess of cost over fair value to reflect an unrealized holding loss. At December 31, Year 3, OCI should be credited to reflect a $30,000 unrealized holding gain ($120,000 fair value at 12/31/Year 3 – $90,000 fair value at 12/31/Year 2).
Answer (A) is incorrect. Unrealized holding gains on available-for-sale securities are recognized. Answer (B) is incorrect. The amount of $10,000 is the recovery of the previously recognized unrealized holding loss. The recognition of gain is not limited to that amount. Answer (C) is incorrect. The excess of fair value over cost is $20,000.

10.1.8. For available-for-sale debt securities included in noncurrent assets, which of the following amounts should be included in the period's net income?

I.   Unrealized holding losses during the period
II. Realized gains during the period
III. Changes in fair value during the period

    A.   III only.

    B.   II only.

    C.   I and II.

    D.   I, II, and III.

Answer (B) is correct. *(CPA, adapted)*
    REQUIRED: The amounts included in the period's net income for available-for-sale debt securities included in noncurrent assets.
    DISCUSSION: The temporary decline below cost of the fair value of available-for-sale debt securities is recorded in OCI, assuming they are not designated as being hedged in a fair value hedge. Thus, temporary changes in the valuation of these securities do not flow through net income. A realized gain occurs when securities are sold at an amount greater than their cost basis. Realized gains are included in net income regardless of the classification of the securities.
    Answer (A) is incorrect. Changes in the fair value of available-for-sale debt securities (unrealized holding gains and losses) are excluded from the determination of net income. Answer (C) is incorrect. Changes in the fair value of available-for-sale debt securities (unrealized holding gains and losses) are excluded from the determination of net income. Answer (D) is incorrect. Changes in the fair value of available-for-sale debt securities (unrealized holding gains and losses) are excluded from the determination of net income.

10.1.9. On January 2, Year 1, Adam Co. purchased as a long-term investment 10,000 Mill Corp. bonds for $40 per bond. These securities were properly classified as available for sale. On December 31, Year 1, the market price of the bonds was $35 per bond, reflecting a temporary decline in market price. On January 28, Year 2, Adam sold 8,000 of the bonds for $30 per bond. For the year ended December 31, Year 2, Adam should report a realized loss on disposal of a long-term investment of

    A. $100,000

    B. $80,000

    C. $60,000

    D. $40,000

Answer (B) is correct. *(CPA, adapted)*
    REQUIRED: The loss on disposal of a noncurrent investment.
    DISCUSSION: A realized loss or gain is recognized when an individual security is sold or otherwise disposed of. The investment was acquired for $40 per bond. The temporary decline in fair value at 12/31/Year 1 was debited to other comprehensive income and was not included in earnings. Accordingly, the realized loss included in earnings at 12/31/Year 2 was $80,000 [8,000 shares × ($40 – $30)].
    Answer (A) is incorrect. The amount of $100,000 assumes disposal of 10,000 bonds. Answer (C) is incorrect. The amount of $60,000 is the fair value of the remaining bonds. Answer (D) is incorrect. The amount of $40,000 was the temporary decline in value of 8,000 bonds at 12/31/Year 1.

10.1.10. In Year 1, a company reported in other comprehensive income an unrealized holding loss on an investment in available-for-sale debt securities. During Year 2, these securities were sold at a loss equal to the unrealized loss previously recognized. The reclassification adjustment should include which of the following?

    A.   The unrealized loss should be credited to the investment account.

    B.   The unrealized loss should be credited to the other comprehensive income account.

    C.   The unrealized loss should be debited to the other comprehensive income account.

    D.   The unrealized loss should be credited to beginning retained earnings.

Answer (B) is correct. *(CPA, adapted)*
    REQUIRED: The reclassification adjustment after sale of available-for-sale debt securities on which an unrealized holding loss was reported in OCI.
    DISCUSSION: Available-for-sale debt securities are measured at fair value, with unrealized holding gains and losses recognized in OCI. The Year 1 entry to recognize the loss was a debit to OCI for a loss and a credit to the allowance for securities fair value adjustments (or directly to available-for-sale securities). The Year 2 sale of the securities was at a loss equal to the recognized unrealized loss. Accordingly, the sale was at their carrying amount. Assuming the securities had a cost of $100 and the unrealized loss was $10, the Year 2 entry was

Cash	$90	
Allowance	10	
Loss	10	
Securities		$100
OCI		10

This entry reclassifies the loss from OCI to earnings.
    Answer (A) is incorrect. The investment is credited for the initial cost, assuming an allowance account is used. Answer (C) is incorrect. The now-realized loss must be reclassified by crediting OCI to remove the effect of the previously recognized unrealized loss. Answer (D) is incorrect. Retained earnings is not directly affected by the loss.

10.1.11. The following information was extracted from Gil Co.'s December 31 balance sheet:

Noncurrent assets:
Available-for-sale debt securities
(carried at fair value) $96,450
Equity:
Accumulated other comprehensive
income (OCI)
Unrealized gains and losses on
available-for-sale debt securities   (19,800)

Historical cost of the available-for-sale debt securities was

A. $63,595

B. $76,650

C. $96,450

D. $116,250

Answer (D) is correct. *(CPA, adapted)*
REQUIRED: The historical cost of the available-for-sale debt securities.
DISCUSSION: The existence of an equity account with a debit balance signifies that the available-for-sale debt securities are reported at fair value that is less than historical cost. The difference is the net unrealized loss balance. Thus, historical cost must have been $116,250 ($96,450 available-for-sale securities at fair value + $19,800 net unrealized loss).
Answer (A) is incorrect. The amount of $63,595 is a nonsense figure. Answer (B) is incorrect. The amount of $76,650 results from subtracting the unrealized loss instead of adding. Answer (C) is incorrect. The amount of $96,450 ignores the unrealized loss balance.

10.1.12. Jay Company acquired a wholly owned foreign subsidiary on January 1. The equity section of the December 31 consolidated balance sheet follows:

Common stock	$ 500,000
Additional paid-in capital	200,000
Retained earnings	900,000
Accumulated other comprehensive income	(600,000)
Total equity	$1,000,000

The balance in accumulated OCI appropriately represents adjustments in translating the foreign subsidiary's financial statements into U.S. dollars.

The consolidated income statement included the excess of cost of investments in certain debt and equity securities over their fair values, which is considered temporary, as follows:

Available-for-sale debt securities	$200,000
Trading securities	100,000

Ignoring tax effects, the amounts for retained earnings and accumulated OCI in the consolidated statement of financial position for the year ended December 31 are

	Retained Earnings	Accumulated OCI
A.	$900,000	$(600,000)
B.	$1,000,000	$(700,000)
C.	$1,100,000	$(800,000)
D.	$1,200,000	$(900,000)

Answer (C) is correct. *(CPA, adapted)*
REQUIRED: The amounts of retained earnings and accumulated OCI in the consolidated statement of equity.
DISCUSSION: An investment in equity securities that does not result in significant influence or control over the investee is measured at fair value through net income. The unrealized holding loss on available-for-sale debt securities does not affect earnings (unless the securities are designated as being hedged in a fair value hedge). Instead, it is debited to OCI. This amount is closed to accumulated OCI, a permanent account reported in the equity section. Accordingly, retained earnings was understated by $200,000, and accumulated OCI was overstated by $200,000. Their amounts should be $1,100,000 and $800,000, respectively.
Answer (A) is incorrect. The amounts of $900,000 and $600,000 are the unadjusted amounts of retained earnings and accumulated OCI, respectively. Answer (B) is incorrect. The amount of $1,000,000 equals total equity. Moreover, $700,000 assumes that the unrealized holding loss on the equity securities, not the available-for-sale debt securities, is debited to an equity account. Answer (D) is incorrect. The amount of $1,200,000 assumes that the unrealized holding losses on both classes of securities are charged to equity. An accumulated OCI balance of $900,000 reflects the same assumption.

10.1.13. Data regarding Ball Corp.'s available-for-sale debt securities follow:

	Cost	Fair Value
December 31, Year 3	$150,000	$130,000
December 31, Year 4	150,000	160,000

Differences between cost and fair values are considered temporary. The decline in fair value was considered temporary and was properly accounted for at December 31, Year 3. Ball's Year 4 statement of changes in equity should report an increase of

A. $30,000

B. $20,000

C. $10,000

D. $0

Answer (A) is correct. *(CPA, adapted)*
REQUIRED: The increase reported in the statement of changes in equity because of a change in the fair value of available-for-sale securities.
DISCUSSION: Unrealized holding losses on available-for-sale debt securities that are deemed to be temporary are ordinarily excluded from earnings and reported in other comprehensive income (OCI). Nontemporary losses are treated as realized and included in earnings, and the fair value is the new cost basis. At 12/31/Year 3, the net amount reported (an unrealized holding loss) was a debit to OCI of $20,000 ($150,000 cost – $130,000 fair value). The $20,000 credit was to the fair value adjustment account for available-for-sale securities. The carrying amount at 12/31/Year 3 was therefore $130,000 ($150,000 – $20,000). At 12/31/Year 4, the $30,000 unrealized gain ($160,000 fair value – $130,000 carrying amount) is credited to OCI and debited to the fair value adjustment account. The statement of comprehensive income reports OCI, and the statement of changes in equity reports changes in accumulated OCI.
Answer (B) is incorrect. The amount of $20,000 is the excess of cost over fair value on 12/31/Year 3. Answer (C) is incorrect. The amount of $10,000 is the excess of fair value over cost on 12/31/Year 4. Answer (D) is incorrect. Equity increases when the unrealized holding gain is reported in other comprehensive income.

10.1.14. On December 1, Wall Company purchased trading debt securities. Pertinent data are as follows:

Debt Security	Cost	Fair Value at 12/31
A	$39,000	$36,000
B	50,000	55,000
C	96,000	85,000

On December 31, Wall reclassified its investment in security C from trading to available-for-sale because Wall intends to retain security C. What net loss on its securities should be included in Wall's income statement for the year ended December 31?

A. $0

B. $9,000

C. $11,000

D. $14,000

Answer (B) is correct. *(CPA, adapted)*
REQUIRED: The net loss to be included in net income when a trading debt security is reclassified.
DISCUSSION: Unrealized holding gains and losses on trading debt securities are included in earnings, and reclassification is at fair value. Furthermore, if a security is transferred from the trading category, the unrealized holding gain or loss at the date of transfer has already been recognized in earnings and is not reversed. Thus, the net unrealized holding loss at 12/31 is $9,000 ($3,000 loss on A – $5,000 gain on B + $11,000 loss on C).
Answer (A) is incorrect. The amount of $0 results from the assumption that A, B, and C are not trading securities. Answer (C) is incorrect. The amount of $11,000 ignores the loss on A and the gain on B. Answer (D) is incorrect. The amount of $14,000 ignores the gain on B.

10.1.15. A reclassification of available-for-sale debt securities to the held-to-maturity category results in

A. The amortization of an unrealized gain or loss existing at the transfer date.

B. The recognition in earnings on the transfer date of an unrealized gain or loss.

C. The reversal of any unrealized gain or loss previously recognized in earnings.

D. The reversal of any unrealized gain or loss previously recognized in other comprehensive income.

Answer (A) is correct. *(Publisher, adapted)*
REQUIRED: The true statement about a reclassification of available-for-sale debt securities to the held-to-maturity category.
DISCUSSION: The unrealized holding gain or loss on the date of transfer for available-for-sale debt securities transferred to the held-to-maturity category continues to be reported in OCI. However, it is amortized as an adjustment of yield in the same manner as the amortization of any discount or premium. This amortization offsets or mitigates the effect on interest income of the amortization of the premium or discount. Fair value accounting may result in a premium or discount when a debt security is transferred to the held-to-maturity category.
Answer (B) is incorrect. Only transfers to the trading debt securities category result in immediate recognition in earnings of an unrealized gain or loss. Answer (C) is incorrect. No reversals are required by reclassification. Answer (D) is incorrect. The reclassification does not require reversal of any previously recognized amounts.

10.2 The Fair Value Option

10.2.1. Election of the fair value option (FVO) for financial assets

A. Permits only for-profit entities to measure eligible items at fair value.

B. Results in recognition of unrealized gains and losses in earnings of a business entity.

C. Requires deferral of related upfront costs.

D. Results in recognition of unrealized gains and losses in other comprehensive income of a business entity.

Answer (B) is correct. *(Publisher, adapted)*
REQUIRED: The accounting for the FVO.
DISCUSSION: A business measures at fair value the eligible items for which the FVO election was made at a specified election date. The unrealized gains and losses on financial assets are reported in earnings at each subsequent reporting date.
Answer (A) is incorrect. The FVO may be elected by all entities. Answer (C) is incorrect. Upfront costs and fees are recognized in earnings of a business as they are incurred if they relate to eligible items for which the FVO election was made. Answer (D) is incorrect. The unrealized gains and losses on financial assets are recognized in earnings, not OCI. A portion of the total change in fair value of financial liabilities accounted for under the FVO may be attributable to the change in instrument-specific credit risk. This portion is recognized in OCI.

10.2.2. The decision to elect the fair value option (FVO)

A. Is irrevocable until the next election date, if any.

B. May be applied to a portion of a financial instrument.

C. Must be applied only to classes of financial instruments.

D. Must be applied to all instruments issued in a single transaction.

Answer (A) is correct. *(Publisher, adapted)*
REQUIRED: The scope of the decision to elect the FVO.
DISCUSSION: The decision to elect the FVO is final and cannot be revoked unless a new election date occurs. For example, an election date occurs when an entity recognizes an investment in equity securities with readily determinable fair values issued by another entity. A second election date occurs if the accounting changes because the investment later becomes subject to equity-method accounting.
Answer (B) is incorrect. The decision to elect the FVO applies "only to an entire instrument and not to only specified risks, specific cash flows, or portions of that instrument." Answer (C) is incorrect. The decision to elect the FVO ordinarily may be applied to individual eligible items. Answer (D) is incorrect. With certain exceptions, the FVO need not be applied to all eligible items acquired or issued in the same transaction. For example, an acquirer of registered bonds may apply the FVO to only some of the bonds.

10.2.3. Which of the following is an election date for the purpose of determining whether to elect the fair value option (FVO)?

A. The accounting treatment of an equity investment changes because the entity no longer has significant influence.

B. The entity enters into a firm commitment to purchase soybeans in 3 months.

C. The accounting for an equity investment changes because the entity no longer consolidates a subsidiary.

D. The accounting treatment of an equity investment changes because the entity must consolidate the investee.

Answer (C) is correct. *(Publisher, adapted)*
REQUIRED: The election date.
DISCUSSION: An entity may choose the FVO only on an election date. For example, an election date occurs when the accounting for an equity investment in another entity changes because the investor retains an interest but no longer consolidates a subsidiary or a variable interest entity.
Answer (A) is incorrect. An election date occurs when the accounting changes because the investment becomes subject to equity-method accounting. Loss of significant influence does not result in an election date. Answer (B) is incorrect. A firm commitment is not an eligible item unless it involves financial instruments only. Answer (D) is incorrect. The FVO is not an alternative to consolidation.

10.3 Fair Value Method for Investments in Equity Securities

10.3.1. On December 31, Ott Co. had investments in equity securities as follows:

	Cost	Fair Value
Man Co.	$10,000	$ 8,000
Kemo, Inc.	9,000	11,000
Fenn Corp.	11,000	9,000
	$30,000	$28,000

Ott's December 31 balance sheet should report the equity securities as

- A. $26,000
- B. $28,000
- C. $29,000
- D. $30,000

Answer (B) is correct. *(CPA, adapted)*
REQUIRED: The amount at which the trading securities should be reported.
DISCUSSION: An investment in equity securities that does not result in significant influence or control over the investee is reported at fair value, and unrealized holding gains and losses are included in earnings. Consequently, the securities should be reported as $28,000.
Answer (A) is incorrect. The amount of $26,000 is the lower of cost or fair value determined on an individual security basis. Answer (C) is incorrect. The amount of $29,000 is the average of the aggregate cost and aggregate fair value. Answer (D) is incorrect. The aggregate cost is $30,000.

10.3.2. An entity should report an investment in marketable equity securities that does not result in significant influence or control over the investee at

- A. Lower of cost or market, with holding gains and losses included in earnings.
- B. Lower of cost or market, with holding gains included in earnings only to the extent of previously recognized holding losses.
- C. Fair value, with holding gains included in earnings only to the extent of previously recognized holding losses.
- D. Fair value, with holding gains and losses included in earnings.

Answer (D) is correct. *(CPA, adapted)*
REQUIRED: The reporting method for marketable equity securities not giving significant influence or control over the investee.
DISCUSSION: Unrealized holding gains and losses on an investment in equity securities that do not result in significant influence or control over the investee are reported in earnings. On a statement of financial position, these securities are reported at fair value.

10.3.3. During Year 6, Wall Co. purchased 2,000 shares of Hemp Corp. common stock for $31,500. They represent 2% of ownership in Hemp Corp. The fair value of this investment was $29,500 at December 31, Year 6. Wall sold all of the Hemp common stock for $14 per share on December 15, Year 7, incurring $1,400 in brokerage commissions and taxes. In its income statement for the year ended December 31, Year 7, Wall should report a recognized loss of

- A. $4,900
- B. $3,500
- C. $2,900
- D. $1,500

Answer (C) is correct. *(CPA, adapted)*
REQUIRED: The realized loss on the sale of equity securities.
DISCUSSION: A realized loss or gain is recognized when an individual equity security is sold or otherwise disposed of. Wall would have included the $2,000 ($31,500 – $29,500) decline in the fair value of the equity securities (an unrealized holding loss) in earnings at 12/31/Yr 6. Consequently, the realized loss on disposal at 12/15/Yr 7 is $2,900 {$29,500 carrying amount – [(2,000 shares × $14) – $1,400]}.
Answer (A) is incorrect. The sum of the recognized losses for Year 6 and Year 7 is $4,900. Answer (B) is incorrect. The sum of the recognized losses for Year 6 and Year 7 without regard to the commissions and taxes is $3,500. Answer (D) is incorrect. Ignoring the commissions and taxes results in $1,500.

10.3.4. Janson traded stock in Flax Co. marketable equity securities during Year 1 as follows:

	Number of shares purchased (sold)	Price per share
February 3, Year 1	1,100	$11
April 15, Year 1	2,500	9
May 28, Year 1	(750)	13
July 5, Year 1	1,400	12
September 30, Year 1	(4,000)	15

No other transactions took place for Flax during the remainder of the year. At December 31, Year 1, Flax is trading at $10 per share. Janson trades securities on a last in, first out basis. What amount is the net value of the investment in Flax at year end?

   A. $(250)

   B. $2,500

   C. $2,750

   D. $3,750

Answer (B) is correct. *(CPA, adapted)*
   REQUIRED: The net value of the investment.
   DISCUSSION: At each balance sheet date, an investment in equity securities that does not result in significant influence or control over the investee is measured at fair value. During the year, Janson purchased 5,000 shares and sold 4,750 shares for an ending balance of 250 shares. At year end, the fair value of each share is $10, so the year-end balance is $2,500 (250 shares × $10 per share).
   Answer (A) is incorrect. Janson purchased 5,000 shares and sold 4,750 shares for an ending balance of 250 shares. Answer (C) is incorrect. An investment in equity securities is measured at fair value each balance sheet date. The amount of $2,750 incorrectly uses the February 3, Year 1, price per share instead of the December 31, Year 1, price per share. Answer (D) is incorrect. The amount of $3,750 incorrectly uses the September 30, Year 1, price per share instead of the December 31, Year 1, price per share.

10.3.5. The measurement alternative may be elected for an investment in equity securities if the

   A. Fair value of the investment is not readily determinable and the investment does not result in control or significant influence over the investee.

   B. Investment allows significant influence over the investee.

   C. Listed prices of the investment are not available and the investment allows control over the investee.

   D. Listed prices of the investment are available and the investment does not result in control or significant influence over the investee.

Answer (A) is correct. *(Publisher, adapted)*
   REQUIRED: The basis for election of the measurement alternative.
   DISCUSSION: An investment in equity securities that does not result in control or significant influence over the investee is measured at fair value through net income. However, an entity may elect the measurement alternative for an investment in equity securities without a readily determinable fair value. This alternative is cost minus impairment (if any), plus or minus changes resulting from observable price changes for the identical or a similar investment of the same issuer.
   Answer (B) is incorrect. An investment in equity securities that allows significant influence over the investee is accounted for using either the fair value option or equity method. The measurement alternative is not used. Answer (C) is incorrect. An investment in equity securities that allows control over the investee requires presentation of consolidated financial statements subsequent to the business combination date. The measurement alternative is not used. Answer (D) is incorrect. An investment in equity securities that does not result in control or significant influence over the investee is measured at fair value through net income. Because the listed prices of the investment are available, the measurement alternative cannot be used.

10.3.6. Under the measurement alternative for an investment in equity securities, the investment is measured at

   A. Cost minus subsequent impairment, plus or minus changes resulting from observable price changes for the identical or a similar investment of the same issuer.

   B. Fair value minus subsequent impairment.

   C. Lower of cost or net realizable value.

   D. Amortized cost.

Answer (A) is correct. *(Publisher, adapted)*
   REQUIRED: The measure of an investment under the measurement alternative.
   DISCUSSION: An investment in equity securities that does not result in control or significant influence over the investee is measured at fair value through net income. However, an entity may elect the measurement alternative for an investment in equity securities without a readily determinable fair value. This alternative is cost minus impairment (if any), plus or minus changes resulting from observable price changes for the identical or a similar investment of the same issuer.
   Answer (B) is incorrect. The measurement alternative may be elected for an investment in equity securities for which the fair value is not readily determinable. Thus, under the measurement alternative, the investment is not measured at fair value. Answer (C) is incorrect. Inventory not measured using the LIFO or retail method, not an investment in equity securities, can be measured at the lower of cost or net realizable value. Answer (D) is incorrect. An investment in debt securities classified as held-to-maturity is measured at amortized cost.

10.4 Equity Method

10.4.1. If the reporting entity has not elected the fair value option, the equity method of accounting for investments in common stock

   A. Should be used in accounting for investments in common stock of corporate joint ventures.

   B. Should be used only for investments in common stock of unconsolidated domestic subsidiaries reported in consolidated financial statements.

   C. Is a valid substitute for consolidation.

   D. May not be used when accounting for an investment of less than 25% of the voting stock of an investee.

Answer (A) is correct. *(Publisher, adapted)*
   REQUIRED: The true statement about the equity method.
   DISCUSSION: Investors should account for investments in common stock of corporate joint ventures by the equity method because it best enables them to reflect the underlying nature of their investments. Usually, the investors have the ability to exert significant influence on the operation of the joint venture.
   Answer (B) is incorrect. Investments in which the investor has significant influence must be accounted for by the equity method whether the unconsolidated subsidiaries are domestic or foreign. Answer (C) is incorrect. Application of the equity method is not a valid substitute for consolidation. Answer (D) is incorrect. The equity method would most likely be used if ownership were 20% or greater.

10.4.2. X Company owns 15% of the voting stock of Y Co. and 25% of the voting stock of Z Co. X has not elected the fair value option. Under what circumstances should X account for each investment using the equity method?

	Investment in Y	Investment in Z
A.	In all cases	In all cases
B.	Never	In all cases
C.	Never	Only if X has the ability to exercise significant influence over Z
D.	Only if X has the ability to exercise significant influence over Y	Only if X has the ability to exercise significant influence over Z

Answer (D) is correct. *(S. Rubin)*
   REQUIRED: The circumstances in which the equity method of accounting for a stock investment should be used.
   DISCUSSION: The equity method is used when an investee has the ability to exercise significant influence. An investment of 20% or more of the voting stock of an investee leads to a presumption that an investor has the ability to exercise significant influence. An investment of less than 20% leads to a presumption that an investor does not have such ability. However, those presumptions can be overcome by predominant evidence to the contrary. See the guidance on the criteria for applying the equity method.
   Answer (A) is incorrect. The equity method should be used only if X has the ability to exercise significant influence over Y or Z. Answer (B) is incorrect. The equity method should be used if X has the ability to exercise significant influence over Y even though its holding is below the 20% threshold. The equity method should not be used if X cannot exercise significant influence over Y even though its holding exceeds the 20% threshold. Answer (C) is incorrect. The equity method should be used if X has the ability to exercise significant influence over Y even though its holding is below the 20% threshold.

10.4.3. When the equity method is used to account for investments in common stock, which of the following affects the investor's reported investment income?

	Goodwill Amortization Related to the Purchase	Cash Dividends from Investee
A.	Yes	Yes
B.	No	Yes
C.	No	No
D.	Yes	No

Answer (C) is correct. *(CPA, adapted)*
   REQUIRED: The transaction(s) affecting the investor's reported investment income when the equity method is used.
   DISCUSSION: Amortization of goodwill is prohibited and therefore does not reduce investment income. Moreover, equity method goodwill is not separately reviewed for impairment because it is not separate from the investment. The receipt of a cash dividend from the investee also does not affect equity-based earnings. The entry is to debit cash and credit the investment.
   Answer (A) is incorrect. Goodwill related to the purchase is not amortized, and cash dividends do not affect investment income. Answer (B) is incorrect. Cash dividends do not affect investment income. Answer (D) is incorrect. Goodwill is not amortized.

10.4.4. In its financial statements, Pulham Corp. uses the equity method of accounting for its 30% ownership of Angles Corp. At December 31, Year 4, Pulham has a receivable from Angles. How should the receivable be reported in Pulham's Year 4 financial statements?

A. None of the receivable should be reported, but the entire receivable should be offset against Angles's payment to Pulham.

B. 70% of the receivable should be separately reported, with the balance offset against 30% of Angles's payment to Pulham.

C. The total receivable should be disclosed separately.

D. The total receivable should be included as part of the investment in Angles, without separate disclosure.

Answer (C) is correct. *(CPA, adapted)*
REQUIRED: The method of reporting a receivable from a related party.
DISCUSSION: Related parties include an entity and its equity-based investees. A receivable from a related party should be separately and fully disclosed. Indeed, nontrade receivables generally are subject to separate treatment.
Answer (A) is incorrect. Elimination of interentity transactions is inappropriate except in the case of combined or consolidated statements. Answer (B) is incorrect. None of the receivable should be separately reported or offset. Answer (D) is incorrect. The investment balance equals cost plus the investor's share of earnings and losses, minus any return of the investment. Also, adjustments may be necessary for acquisition differentials. Furthermore, separate disclosure is required.

10.4.5. The criterion for determining whether an entity may apply the equity method is the ability to exercise significant influence over the investee. An investor who owns 30% of the voting common stock of the investee is most likely to exercise significant influence when

A. The investor and investee sign an agreement under which the investor surrenders significant rights.

B. The investor tries and fails to obtain representation on the investee's board of directors.

C. Opposition by the investee, such as litigation, challenges the investor's exercise of significant influence.

D. The majority ownership of the investee is spread among a large group of shareholders who have objectives with respect to the investee that differ from those of the investor.

Answer (D) is correct. *(Publisher, adapted)*
REQUIRED: The situation that indicates ability to exercise significant influence.
DISCUSSION: If the investor owns 20% to 50% of an investee and the remainder of the ownership is spread among a large group of shareholders, the investee will be able to exert significant influence even though most of the other owners have objectives contrary to those of the investor. The presumption of significant influence can be overcome by evidence that majority ownership is held by a small number of shareholders who operate the investee without regard to the investor's views.
Answer (A) is incorrect. When the investor and investee sign an agreement under which the investor surrenders significant rights, the investor cannot exercise significant influence. Answer (B) is incorrect. When the investor tries and fails to obtain representation on the investee's board of directors, the investor cannot exercise significant influence. Answer (C) is incorrect. When opposition by the investee, such as litigation or complaints to governmental regulatory authorities, challenges the investor's exercise of significant influence, the investor cannot exercise significant influence.

10.4.6. On January 2, Well Co. purchased 10% of Rea, Inc.'s outstanding common shares for $400,000, which equaled the carrying amount and the fair value of the interest purchased in Rea's net assets. Well did not elect the fair value option. Because Well is the largest single shareholder in Rea, and Well's officers are a majority on Rea's board of directors, Well exercises significant influence over Rea. Rea reported net income of $500,000 for the year and paid dividends of $150,000. In its December 31 balance sheet, what amount should Well report as investment in Rea?

A. $450,000

B. $435,000

C. $400,000

D. $385,000

Answer (B) is correct. *(CPA, adapted)*
REQUIRED: The amount reported in the investment account.
DISCUSSION: The equity method should be used because Well Co. exercises significant influence over Rea. The investment in Rea equals $435,000 [$400,000 investment + ($500,000 net income × 10%) – ($150,000 of dividends × 10%)].
Answer (A) is incorrect. The amount of $450,000 does not subtract Well's dividends. Answer (C) is incorrect. The amount of $400,000 does not include Well's share of net income or deduct Well's dividends. Answer (D) is incorrect. The amount of $385,000 does not include Well's share of net income.

10.4.7. An investor uses the equity method to account for an investment in common stock. After the date of acquisition, the investment account of the investor is

A. Not affected by its share of the earnings or losses of the investee.

B. Not affected by its share of the earnings of the investee, but is decreased by its share of the losses of the investee.

C. Increased by its share of the earnings of the investee, but is not affected by its share of the losses of the investee.

D. Increased by its share of the earnings of the investee, and is decreased by its share of the losses of the investee.

Answer (D) is correct. *(CPA, adapted)*
REQUIRED: The effect(s) on an equity-based investment in common stock of investee earnings and losses.
DISCUSSION: After the date of acquisition, an equity-based investment in common stock account of an investor is increased by its share of the earnings of the investee, decreased by its share of the losses of the investee, and decreased by its share of cash dividends received from the investee.
Answer (A) is incorrect. The investment account is affected by the investor's share of both earnings and losses of the investee. Answer (B) is incorrect. The investment account is affected by the investor's share of both earnings and losses of the investee. Answer (C) is incorrect. The investment account is affected by the investor's share of both earnings and losses of the investee.

10.4.8. Peel Co. received a cash dividend from a common stock investment. Should Peel report an increase in the investment balance if it uses the fair value method or the equity method of accounting?

	Fair Value	Equity
A.	No	No
B.	Yes	Yes
C.	Yes	No
D.	No	Yes

Answer (A) is correct. *(CPA, adapted)*
REQUIRED: The effect of a cash dividend on the investment balance under the fair value and equity methods.
DISCUSSION: Under the fair value method, dividends from an investment in equity securities should be accounted for by the investor as dividend income unless a liquidating dividend is received. Thus, assuming that the dividend is not liquidating, it has no effect on the investment balance under the fair value method. Under the equity method, the investor recognizes its equity in the undistributed earnings of the investee. Consequently, cash dividends decrease the investment balance because the dividend is considered to be a return of investment.

10.4.9. On January 1, Point, Inc., purchased 10% of Iona Co.'s common stock. Point purchased additional shares bringing its ownership up to 40% of Iona's common stock outstanding on August 1. During October, Iona declared and paid a cash dividend on all of its outstanding common stock. How much income from the Iona investment should Point's income statement report?

A. 10% of Iona's income for January 1 to July 31 plus 40% of Iona's income for August 1 to December 31.

B. 40% of Iona's income for August 1 to December 31.

C. 40% of Iona's full-year income.

D. Amount equal to dividends received from Iona.

Answer (B) is correct. *(CPA, adapted)*
REQUIRED: The income from an investment that has increased from less than 20% to more than 20% during the period.
DISCUSSION: Once the ownership percentage increased from 10% to 40%, Point was presumed to exercise significant influence over Iona. Thus, Point applies the equity method prospectively from the moment significant influence is achieved (August 1). Given that Point held 40% of Iona's common stock beginning August 1, it should recognize its share (40%) of Iona's income for the period August 1 to December 31.
Answer (A) is incorrect. The equity method should be applied prospectively beginning August 1, not retrospectively from January 1. Answer (C) is incorrect. Point held 40% of Iona's common stock only from August 1. Answer (D) is incorrect. Iona's dividends do not affect Point's net income.

10.4.10. A corporation that uses the equity method of accounting for its investment in a 40%-owned investee that earned $20,000 and paid $5,000 in dividends made the following entries:

Investment in subsidiary	$8,000	
Equity in earnings of subsidiary		$8,000
Cash	$2,000	
Dividend revenue		$2,000

What effect will these entries have on the parent's statement of financial position?

A. Investment understated, retained earnings understated.

B. Investment overstated, retained earnings overstated.

C. Investment overstated, retained earnings understated.

D. Financial position will be fairly stated.

Answer (B) is correct. *(CPA, adapted)*
REQUIRED: The effect of an error in recording investment income or dividends received.
DISCUSSION: In the case of 40% ownership, the equity method of accounting for the investment in the investor's books should be applied. The 40% share of the investee's $20,000 net income ($8,000) is correctly recorded.
Dividends received from an investee must be recorded in the books of the investor as a decrease in the carrying amount of the investment and an increase in assets (cash). Hence, dividend revenue was incorrectly credited with the $2,000 dividend resulting in an overstatement of retained earnings. The investment should have been credited for $2,000. Thus, the effect on the investment is also an overstatement.
Answer (A) is incorrect. The $2,000 of dividend revenue should have been credited to the investment in subsidiary. Thus, both the investment and retained earnings are overstated. Answer (C) is incorrect. The entries overstated retained earnings. Answer (D) is incorrect. Financial position is misstated. The investment (an asset) and retained earnings (an equity account) are overstated.

10.4.11. Park Co. uses the equity method to account for its January 1 purchase of Tun, Inc.'s common stock. On January 1, the fair values of Tun's FIFO inventory and land exceeded their carrying amounts. How do these excesses of fair values over carrying amounts affect Park's reported equity in Tun's earnings for the year?

	Inventory Excess	Land Excess
A.	Decrease	Decrease
B.	Decrease	No effect
C.	Increase	Increase
D.	Increase	No effect

Answer (B) is correct. *(CPA, adapted)*
REQUIRED: The effect on equity in investee earnings of the excess of the fair values of the investee's FIFO inventory and land over their carrying amounts.
DISCUSSION: The equity method of accounting requires the investor's proportionate share of the investee's reported net income to be adjusted for acquisition differentials. Thus, the difference at the date of acquisition of the investee's stock between the fair value and carrying amount of inventory is such an adjustment when the inventory is sold. A similar adjustment for items of property, plant, and equipment is required when the assets are depreciated or sold. Assuming that the FIFO inventory was sold during the year and the land was not, Park's proportionate share of Tun's reported net income is decreased by the inventory differential allocated at the date of acquisition.

10.4.12. On January 2, Year 1, Kean Co. purchased a 30% interest in Pod Co. for $250,000. On this date, Pod's equity was $500,000. The carrying amounts of Pod's identifiable net assets approximated their fair values, except for land whose fair value exceeded its carrying amount by $200,000. Pod reported net income of $100,000 for Year 1, and paid no dividends. Kean accounts for this investment using the equity method. In its December 31, Year 1, balance sheet, what amount should Kean report as investment in Pod Co.?

A. $210,000

B. $220,000

C. $276,000

D. $280,000

Answer (D) is correct. *(CPA, adapted)*
REQUIRED: The amount reported as investment in subsidiary under the equity method.
DISCUSSION: The purchase price is allocated to the fair value of the net assets acquired, with the remainder allocated to goodwill. The fair value of Kean's 30% interest in Pod's net assets is $210,000 [($500,000 + $200,000) × 30%]. Goodwill is $40,000 ($250,000 – $210,000). The equity method requires the investor's share of subsequent net income reported by the investee to be adjusted for the difference at acquisition between the fair value and the carrying amount of the investee's net assets when the net assets are sold or consumed in operations. The land is assumed not to be sold, and the equity method goodwill is not amortized or separately reviewed for impairment. Thus, Kean's share of Pod's net income is $30,000 ($100,000 declared income × 30%), and the investment account at year-end is $280,000 ($250,000 acquisition balance + $30,000 investment income).
Answer (A) is incorrect. The amount of $210,000 equals the fair value of the identifiable net assets acquired. Answer (B) is incorrect. The amount of $220,000 equals the price minus Kean's equity in Pod's net income. Answer (C) is incorrect. The amount of $276,000 assumes amortization of goodwill over 10 years.

10.4.13. Green Corp. owns 30% of the outstanding common stock and 100% of the outstanding noncumulative nonvoting preferred stock of Axel Corp. In Year 1, Axel declared dividends of $100,000 on its common stock and $60,000 on its preferred stock. Green exercises significant influence over Axel's operations and uses the equity method to account for the investment in the common stock. What amount of dividend revenue should Green report in its income statement for the year ended December 31, Year 1?

A. $0

B. $30,000

C. $60,000

D. $90,000

Answer (C) is correct. *(CPA, adapted)*
REQUIRED: The dividend revenue reported given declaration of common and preferred dividends by an investee.
DISCUSSION: Under the equity method, the receipt of a cash dividend from the investee should be credited to the investment account. It is a return of, not a return on, the investment. However, the equity method is not applicable to preferred stock. Thus, Green should report $60,000 of revenue when the preferred dividends are declared.
Answer (A) is incorrect. The preferred, not the common, dividends should be credited to revenue. Answer (B) is incorrect. The amount of $30,000 is Green's share of the common dividends. The cash dividends on common stock should be credited to the investment account. Answer (D) is incorrect. The amount of $90,000 is the sum of the preferred dividends ($60,000) and 30% of the common dividends ($100,000 × 30%).

10.4.14. Sage, Inc., bought 40% of Adams Corp.'s outstanding voting common stock on January 2 for $400,000, which equaled a proportionate share of the fair value of the net assets. The carrying amount of the net assets at the purchase date was $900,000. Fair values and carrying amounts were the same for all items except for plant and inventory, for which fair values exceeded their carrying amounts by $90,000 and $10,000, respectively. The plant has an 18-year life. All inventory was sold during the year. During the year, Adams reported net income of $120,000 and paid a $20,000 cash dividend. What amount should Sage report in its income statement from its investment in Adams for the year ended December 31?

A. $48,000

B. $42,000

C. $36,000

D. $34,000

Answer (B) is correct. *(CPA, adapted)*
REQUIRED: The investment income.
DISCUSSION: Sage holds 40% of the investee's voting common stock and is assumed to exercise significant influence. It should therefore account for the investment on the equity basis by recognizing its proportionate share of the investee's net income. For this purpose, the investee's net income of $120,000 should be adjusted for the $10,000 excess of fair value over the carrying amount of the inventory sold and for the portion of the difference between the fair value and carrying amount of the plant that has been consumed (depreciated). This adjustment equals $5,000 ($90,000 difference ÷ 18 years). Thus, Sage should report investment income of $42,000 [($120,000 – $10,000 – $5,000) × 40%].
Answer (A) is incorrect. The amount of $48,000 equals 40% of the investee's unadjusted reported net income. Answer (C) is incorrect. The amount of $36,000 results from adjusting the reported net income for the inventory differential and the dividend but not for the depreciation. Answer (D) is incorrect. The amount of $34,000 equals the increase in the investment balance.

10.4.15. Pare, Inc., purchased 10% of Tot Co.'s 100,000 outstanding shares of common stock on January 2 for $50,000. On December 31, Pare purchased an additional 20,000 shares of Tot for $150,000. There was no equity method goodwill or other acquisition differential as a result of either purchase, and Tot did not issue any additional stock during the year. Tot reported earnings of $300,000 for the year. What amount should Pare report in its December 31 balance sheet as investment in Tot?

A. $150,000

B. $200,000

C. $230,000

D. $290,000

Answer (B) is correct. *(CPA, adapted)*
REQUIRED: The amount reported in the investment account.
DISCUSSION: When significant influence is achieved in stages (step-by-step), the investor applies the equity method prospectively from the moment significant influence is achieved. On the date the investment becomes qualified for the equity method, the equity method investment equals (1) the cost of acquiring the additional equity interest in Tot of $150,000 plus (2) the current basis of the previously held equity interest in Tot of $50,000. Thus, investment in Tot equals $200,000.
Answer (A) is incorrect. On the date the investment becomes qualified for the equity method, the equity method investment equals (1) the cost of acquiring the additional equity interest in the investee plus (2) the current basis of the previously held equity interest in the investee. Answer (C) is incorrect. When significant influence is achieved in stages (step-by-step), the equity method is applied prospectively from the moment significant influence is achieved. Answer (D) is incorrect. The amount of $290,000 assumes Pare held a 30% interest throughout the year.

10.4.16. On July 1, Year 1, Denver Corp. purchased 3,000 shares of Eagle Co.'s 10,000 outstanding shares of common stock for $20 per share but did not elect the fair value option. On December 15, Year 1, Eagle paid $40,000 in dividends to its common shareholders. Eagle's net income for the year ended December 31, Year 1, was $120,000, earned evenly throughout the year. In its Year 1 income statement, what amount of income from this investment should Denver report?

    A. $36,000

    B. $18,000

    C. $12,000

    D. $6,000

Answer (B) is correct. *(CPA, adapted)*
    REQUIRED: The income reported from an investment in common stock.
    DISCUSSION: Denver Corp.'s purchase of 30% of Eagle presumably allows it to exercise significant influence. Thus, it should apply the equity method. The investor's share of the investee's income is a function of the percentage of ownership and the length of time the investment was held. The income from this investment was therefore $18,000 [$120,000 × 30% × (6 months ÷ 12 months)].
    Answer (A) is incorrect. The amount of $36,000 assumes Denver owned the stock for the full year. Answer (C) is incorrect. The amount of $12,000 equals 30% of the dividend. Dividends do not affect income under the equity method. Answer (D) is incorrect. The amount of $6,000 equals 50% of 30% of the dividends.

10.4.17. On January 1, Year 1, Mega Corp. acquired 10% of the outstanding voting stock of Penny, Inc. On January 2, Year 2, Mega gained the ability to exercise significant influence over financial and operating control of Penny by acquiring an additional 20% of Penny's outstanding stock. Mega did not elect the fair value option for its investment in Penny. The two purchases were made at prices proportionate to the value assigned to Penny's net assets, which equaled their carrying amounts. Hence, no adjustment to investment income for acquisition differentials is necessary. For the years ended December 31, Year 1 and Year 2, Penny reported the following:

	Year 1	Year 2
Dividends paid	$200,000	$300,000
Net income	600,000	650,000

In Year 2, what amounts should Mega report as current year investment income and as an adjustment, before income taxes, to Year 1 investment income?

	Year 2 Investment Income	Adjustment to Year 1 Investment Income
A.	$195,000	$40,000
B.	$195,000	$120,000
C.	$195,000	$0
D.	$105,000	$40,000

Answer (C) is correct. *(CPA, adapted)*
    REQUIRED: The amounts reported as current-year investment income and as an adjustment, before income taxes, to the previous year's investment income.
    DISCUSSION: When significant influence is achieved in stages, the investor applies the equity method prospectively from the moment significant influence is achieved. Under the equity method, the investor recognizes in income its share of the investee's earnings or losses for the period. Consequently, Mega should report Year 2 investment income before taxes equal to $195,000 ($650,000 net income reported by Penny for Year 2 × 30%). Because the equity income is applied prospectively, no adjustment to Year 1 investment income is needed.
    Answer (A) is incorrect. When significant influence is achieved in stages, the investor applies the equity method prospectively from the moment significant influence is achieved. Answer (B) is incorrect. When significant influence is achieved in stages, the investor applies the equity method prospectively from the moment significant influence is achieved. Answer (D) is incorrect. The amount of $105,000 equals Mega's share of Year 2 net income minus its share of dividends. Furthermore, the equity method must be applied prospectively from the moment the significant influence was achieved.

10.4.18. Pear Co.'s income statement for the year ended December 31, as prepared by Pear's controller, reported income before taxes of $125,000. The auditor questioned the following amounts that had been included in income before taxes:

Equity in earnings of Cinn Co.	$40,000
Dividends received from Cinn	8,000
Adjustments to profits of prior years for arithmetical errors in depreciation	(35,000)

Pear owns 40% of Cinn's common stock, and no acquisition differentials are relevant. Pear's December 31 income statement should report income before taxes of

   A. $85,000

   B. $117,000

   C. $120,000

   D. $152,000

Answer (D) is correct. *(CPA, adapted)*
   REQUIRED: The amount reported as income before taxes on the income statement.
   DISCUSSION: Under the equity method, the investor's share of the investee's net income (adjusted for any acquisition differentials, such as impairment of goodwill) is accounted for as an addition to, and losses and dividends are reflected as reductions of, the carrying amount of the investment. Consequently, the equity in earnings of Cinn Co. was correctly included in income, but the dividends received should have been excluded. In addition, error corrections related to earlier periods are treated as prior-period adjustments and are not included in net income. Thus, income before taxes should have been $152,000 ($125,000 – $8,000 dividends + $35,000 depreciation error).
   Answer (A) is incorrect. The amount of $85,000 subtracts the equity in earnings of Cinn Co. and includes the dividends and the effects of the prior-period adjustment. Answer (B) is incorrect. The amount of $117,000 includes the prior-period adjustment. Answer (C) is incorrect. The amount of $120,000 equals the computed income, minus the equity in the earnings of Cinn, plus the depreciation error.

10.4.19. Band Co. uses the equity method to account for its investment in Guard, Inc., common stock. How should Band record a 2% stock dividend received from Guard?

   A. As dividend revenue at Guard's carrying amount of the stock.

   B. As dividend revenue at the market value of the stock.

   C. As a reduction in the total cost of Guard stock owned.

   D. As a memorandum entry reducing the unit cost of all Guard stock owned.

Answer (D) is correct. *(CPA, adapted)*
   REQUIRED: The entry to record a stock dividend received from an equity investee.
   DISCUSSION: No entries are made to record the receipt of stock dividends. However, a memorandum entry should be made in the investment account to record additional shares owned. This treatment applies whether the investment is accounted for by the fair-value method or the equity method.
   Answer (A) is incorrect. The receipt of a stock dividend is not a revenue. The shareholder has the same proportionate interest in the investee. Answer (B) is incorrect. The stock dividend does not result in revenue. Answer (C) is incorrect. The cost per share, not the total cost, is reduced.

10.4.20. Larkin Co. has owned 25% of the common stock of Devon Co. for a number of years and has the ability to exercise significant influence over Devon. The following information relates to Larkin's investment in Devon during the most recent year:

Carrying amount of Larkin's investment in Devon at the beginning of the year	$200,000
Net income of Devon for the year	600,000
Total dividends paid to Devon's stockholders during the year	400,000

What is the carrying amount of Larkin's investment in Devon at year end?

   A. $100,000

   B. $200,000

   C. $250,000

   D. $350,000

Answer (C) is correct. *(CPA, adapted)*
   REQUIRED: The carrying amount of an investment if the investor has significant influence over the investee.
   DISCUSSION: If an investor with significant influence over an investee has not elected to account for the investment using the fair value option, it must apply the equity method. Thus, the carrying amount of the investment is increased (decreased) by the investor's share of the investee's net income (dividends paid). The year-end carrying amount is $250,000 [$200,000 + ($600,000 × 25%) – ($400,000 × 25%)].
   Answer (A) is incorrect. The amount of $100,000 is the investor's share of the investee's dividends paid. Answer (B) is incorrect. The amount of $200,000 is the beginning balance of the investment. Answer (D) is incorrect. The amount of $350,000 omits the investor's share of dividends paid.

10.4.21. A company has a 22% investment in another company that it accounts for using the equity method. Which of the following disclosures should be included in the company's annual financial statements?

A. The names and ownership percentages of the other stockholders in the investee company.

B. The reason for the company's decision to invest in the investee company.

C. The company's accounting policy for the investment.

D. Whether the investee company is involved in any litigation.

Answer (C) is correct. *(CPA, adapted)*
REQUIRED: The required disclosure under the equity method.
DISCUSSION: A company is required to disclose its accounting policies for equity method investees. Disclosures for an investment accounted for under the equity method should also include (1) the names and company's percentage of ownership in each investee; (2) the difference, if any, between the carrying amount of the investment and the underlying equity in the net assets of the investee; and (3) the accounting method applied to the difference.
Answer (A) is incorrect. A company is required to disclose the names and its (not other stockholders) percentage of ownership in each equity method investee. Answer (B) is incorrect. The company is not required to disclose the reason for the company's decision to invest in the investee company. Answer (D) is incorrect. A company is not required to disclose whether an investee company accounted for under the equity method is involved in any litigation.

10.5 Investments in Bonds

10.5.1. When bond interest payments are sent to the owner of the bonds by the debtor, the bonds are called

A. Participating bonds.

B. Coupon bonds.

C. Registered bonds.

D. Debenture bonds.

Answer (C) is correct. *(Publisher, adapted)*
REQUIRED: The bonds on which interest payments are sent to the owner by the debtor.
DISCUSSION: Registered bonds are issued in the name of the owner. Thus, interest payments are sent directly to the owner. When the owner sells registered bonds, the bond certificates must be surrendered and new certificates issued. They differ from coupon (bearer) bonds, which can be freely transferred and have a detachable coupon for each interest payment.
Answer (A) is incorrect. Participating bonds participate in excess earnings of the debtor as defined in the contractual agreement. Answer (B) is incorrect. The debtor does not keep records of the owners of coupon (bearer) bonds. Answer (D) is incorrect. Debenture bonds are unsecured bonds.

10.5.2. Bonds that investors may present for payment prior to maturity are

A. Callable bonds.

B. Redeemable bonds.

C. Convertible bonds.

D. Income bonds.

Answer (B) is correct. *(Publisher, adapted)*
REQUIRED: The type of bond that may be presented for payment prior to maturity.
DISCUSSION: Redeemable bonds may be presented for payment by the creditor prior to the maturity date. The bonds usually are redeemable only after a specified period of time.
Answer (A) is incorrect. Callable bonds may be redeemed by the debtor. Answer (C) is incorrect. Convertible bonds may be exchanged, usually at the option of the creditor, for common stock or other equity securities. Answer (D) is incorrect. The distinctive feature of income bonds is that interest is paid only if income is earned by the debtor.

10.5.3. On January 1, Welling Company purchased 100 of the $1,000 face value, 8%, 10-year bonds of Mann, Inc. The bonds mature on January 1 in 10 years, and pay interest annually on January 1. Welling purchased the bonds to yield 10% interest. Information on present value factors is as follows:

Present value of $1 at 8% for 10 periods	0.4632
Present value of $1 at 10% for 10 periods	0.3855
Present value of an annuity of $1 at 8% for 10 periods	6.7101
Present value of an annuity of $1 at 10% for 10 periods	6.1446

How much did Welling pay for the bonds?

A. $87,707

B. $92,230

C. $95,477

D. $100,000

Answer (A) is correct. *(CPA, adapted)*
REQUIRED: The present value to the investor (price paid) of an investment in long-term bonds.
DISCUSSION: An investment in a bond should be recorded at its fair value, i.e., the present value of its cash flows discounted at the market (yield) rate of interest. The present value of the investment has two components: the value of the periodic cash interest payments and the value of the bond proceeds at maturity. The interest payment at 8% on each bond will be $80 per year for 10 years. Applying a present value factor of 6.1446 (annuity, 10 periods, 10%) gives a present value of the periodic interest payments of $491.57. The proceeds of each bond at maturity of $1,000 are multiplied by a factor of .3855 (10%, 10 periods) for a present value of $385.50. The resulting total price per bond of $877.07 ($491.57 + $385.50) multiplied by 100 bonds gives a total payment of $87,707.
Answer (B) is incorrect. The amount of $92,230 is based on a present value of an annuity factor of 6.7101. Answer (C) is incorrect. The amount of $95,477 results from using a present value factor of .4632. Answer (D) is incorrect. The amount of $100,000 is the face amount of the bonds, which were purchased at a discount.

10.5.4. Loan origination fees are charged to the borrower in connection with originating, refinancing, or restructuring a loan (e.g., points, lending fees, etc.). Loan origination fees should be

A. Recognized in income when collected.

B. Recognized in income on a straight-line basis during the life of the loan but over no more than 5 years.

C. Deferred and recognized in income over the life of the loan using the straight-line method.

D. Deferred and recognized in income over the life of the loan by the interest method.

Answer (D) is correct. *(Publisher, adapted)*
REQUIRED: The lender accounting procedure for loan origination fees.
DISCUSSION: Loan origination fees must be recognized in income over the life of the loan using the interest method. The objective is to achieve a constant effective yield over the life of the loan.
Answer (A) is incorrect. The fees are deferred, not recognized immediately. Answer (B) is incorrect. The effective interest method is used and no 5-year maximum is prescribed. Answer (C) is incorrect. The effective interest method is used, not straight-line amortization.

10.5.5. An investor purchased a bond classified as a long-term investment between interest dates at a discount. At the purchase date, the carrying amount of the bond is more than the

	Cash Paid to Seller	Face Amount of Bond
A.	No	Yes
B.	No	No
C.	Yes	No
D.	Yes	Yes

Answer (B) is correct. *(CPA, adapted)*
REQUIRED: The carrying amount of a bond purchased at a discount between interest dates.
DISCUSSION: At the date of purchase, the carrying amount of the bond equals its face amount minus the discount. The cash paid equals the initial carrying amount plus accrued interest. Hence, the initial carrying amount is less than the cash paid by the amount of the accrued interest.

10.5.6. On September 1, the Consul Company acquired $10,000 face value, 8% bonds of Envoy Corporation at 104. The bonds were dated May 1 and mature in 5 years on April 30, with interest payable each October 31 and April 30. What entry should Consul make to record the purchase of the bonds?

A. Investment in bonds $10,400
    Interest receivable   266
      Cash $10,666

B. Investment in bonds $10,666
      Cash $10,666

C. Investment in bonds $10,666
      Accrued interest receivable $ 266
      Cash   10,400

D. Investment in bonds $10,000
    Premium on bonds   666
      Cash $10,666

Answer (A) is correct. *(CPA, adapted)*
REQUIRED: The entry to record a bond purchased at a premium with accrued interest.
DISCUSSION: At 104, the price paid for the bonds is $10,400 in the absence of any accrued interest. Because the bonds were purchased between interest dates, cash interest accrued for the 4 months from May 1 to September 1 (date of purchase) must be computed and included in the purchase price. The interest for 4 months at 8% is $266.67 [$10,000 × 8% × (4 months ÷ 12 months)], which is recorded as interest receivable and added to the $10,400 purchase price, for a total amount paid of $10,666. When interest is received on October 31, the $266 in interest receivable will be credited.
Answer (B) is incorrect. Interest receivable should be recognized in the amount of $266. The purchase was between interest dates. Answer (C) is incorrect. Interest receivable should be debited. Answer (D) is incorrect. The premium paid was $400. The interest receivable of $266 should be recorded separately from bond premium.

10.5.7. Cap Corp. reported accrued investment interest receivable of $38,000 and $46,500 at January 1 and December 31, Year 1, respectively. During Year 1, cash collections from the investments included the following:

Capital gains distributions $145,000
Interest   152,000

What amount should Cap report as interest revenue from investments for Year 1?

A. $160,500

B. $153,500

C. $152,000

D. $143,500

Answer (A) is correct. *(CPA, adapted)*
REQUIRED: The interest revenue from debt investments.
DISCUSSION: When a receivable increases, revenue exceeds collections. Given that the accrued interest receivable balance increased by $8,500 ($46,500 – $38,000), and interest collected equaled $152,000, interest revenue equals $160,500 ($152,000 + $8,500). Capital gains distributions do not affect interest.
Answer (B) is incorrect. The amount of $153,500 equals capital gains plus the increase in accrued interest receivable. Answer (C) is incorrect. The amount of $152,000 equals collections. Answer (D) is incorrect. The amount of $143,500 equals collections of interest minus the increase in accrued interest receivable.

10.5.8. On July 1, Year 2, York Co. purchased as a long-term investment $1 million of Park, Inc.'s 8% bonds for $946,000, including accrued interest of $40,000. The bonds were purchased to yield 10% interest. The bonds mature on January 1, Year 8, and pay interest annually on January 1. York uses the effective interest method of amortization. In its December 31, Year 2, balance sheet, what amount should York report as investment in bonds?

A. $911,300

B. $916,600

C. $953,300

D. $960,600

Answer (A) is correct. *(CPA, adapted)*
REQUIRED: The amount reported as bond investment at year-end.
DISCUSSION: The bond investment's original balance was $906,000 ($946,000 price – $40,000 accrued interest) because the carrying amount does not include accrued interest paid. Under the effective interest method, interest income equals the yield or effective interest rate times the carrying amount of the bonds at the beginning of the interest period. The amortization of premium or discount is the difference between this interest income and the periodic cash payments. For Year 2, interest income is $45,300 [$906,000 × 10% × (6 ÷ 12)], and the actual interest is $40,000 [$1,000,000 × 8% × (6 ÷ 12)]. Hence, the carrying amount at year-end is $911,300 [$906,000 + ($45,300 – $40,000)].
Answer (B) is incorrect. The amount of $916,600 amortizes the discount for 12 months. Answer (C) is incorrect. The amount of $953,300 includes the accrued interest paid. Answer (D) is incorrect. The amount of $960,600 includes the accrued interest paid and amortizes the discount for 12 months.

10.5.9. On July 1, Year 1, Cody Co. paid $1,198,000 for 10%, 20-year bonds with a face amount of $1 million. Interest is paid on December 31 and June 30. The bonds were purchased to yield 8%. Cody uses the effective interest rate method to recognize interest income from this investment. The bonds are properly classified as held-to-maturity. What should be reported as the carrying amount of the bonds in Cody's December 31, Year 1, balance sheet?

    A. $1,207,900

    B. $1,198,000

    C. $1,195,920

    D. $1,193,050

Answer (C) is correct. *(CPA, adapted)*
    REQUIRED: The amount reported as bond investment at year-end.
    DISCUSSION: Under the effective interest method, interest income equals the yield or effective interest rate times the carrying amount of the bonds at the beginning of the interest period. The amortization of premium or discount is the difference between this interest income and the periodic cash payments. For Year 1, interest income is $47,920 [$1,198,000 × 8% × (6 months ÷ 12 months)], and interest received is $50,000 [$1,000,000 × 10% × (6 months ÷ 12 months)]. Hence, the carrying amount at year end is $1,195,920 [$1,198,000 – ($50,000 – $47,920)].
    Answer (A) is incorrect. The amount of $1,207,900 equals the investment if interest income is determined using a 10% rate, and the difference between actual interest and interest income is added to the carrying amount. Answer (B) is incorrect. The amount of $1,198,000 is the carrying amount before adjustment for the premium amortization. Answer (D) is incorrect. The amount of $1,193,050 assumes that interest income is based on a 10% rate and that the bonds have been outstanding for 3 months.

10.5.10. On July 1, Year 4, Pell Co. purchased Green Corp. 10-year, 8% bonds with a face amount of $500,000 for $420,000. The bonds are classified as held-to-maturity, mature on June 30, Year 14, and pay interest semiannually on June 30 and December 31. Using the interest method, Pell recorded bond discount amortization of $1,800 for the 6 months ended December 31, Year 4. From this long-term investment, Pell should report Year 4 revenue of

    A. $16,800

    B. $18,200

    C. $20,000

    D. $21,800

Answer (D) is correct. *(CPA, adapted)*
    REQUIRED: The interest revenue when amortization of bond discount is known.
    DISCUSSION: Interest income for a bond issued at a discount is equal to the sum of the periodic cash flows and the amount of bond discount amortized during the interest period. The periodic cash flows are equal to $20,000 ($500,000 face amount × 8% coupon rate × 1/2 year). The discount amortization is given as $1,800. Thus, revenue for the 6-month period from July 1 to December 31, Year 4, is $21,800 ($20,000 + $1,800).
    Answer (A) is incorrect. The amount of $16,800 is 50% of 8% of $420,000. Answer (B) is incorrect. The amount of $18,200 equals the cash flow minus discount amortization. Answer (C) is incorrect. The amount of $20,000 equals the cash flow.

10.5.11. In Year 5, Lee Co. acquired, at a premium, Enfield, Inc., 10-year bonds as a long-term investment. At December 31, Year 6, Enfield's bonds were quoted at a small discount. Which of the following situations is the most likely cause of the decline in the bonds' fair value?

    A. Enfield issued a stock dividend.

    B. Enfield is expected to call the bonds at a premium, which is less than Lee's carrying amount.

    C. Interest rates have declined since Lee purchased the bonds.

    D. Interest rates have increased since Lee purchased the bonds.

Answer (D) is correct. *(CPA, adapted)*
    REQUIRED: The most likely cause of a decline in a bond's fair value.
    DISCUSSION: To adjust the yield on a bond investment to equal the market rate, the price of the bond must fluctuate inversely with the market rate because the nominal interest rate is fixed. Bonds selling at a premium have a nominal rate in excess of the market rate. If the market rate subsequently increases, the price of the bonds must decrease to provide a yield equal to the new market rate.
    Answer (A) is incorrect. A stock dividend has no effect on quoted fair values of bonds. Answer (B) is incorrect. Bonds expected to be called at a premium will not be quoted at a discount. Answer (C) is incorrect. If interest rates decline below the stated rate, the bonds will be quoted at an even higher premium.

10.5.12. When bonds with detachable stock warrants are purchased, the amount debited to investment in stock warrants relative to the total amount paid

A. Increases the premium on the investment in bonds.

B. Increases the discount on investment in bonds.

C. Increases any premium or decreases any discount on the bonds.

D. Has no effect on the investment of bond premium or discount because the warrants are purchased separately.

Answer (B) is correct. *(Publisher, adapted)*
REQUIRED: The effect on the carrying amount of bonds of debiting investment in stock warrants.
DISCUSSION: The portion of the price allocated to the detachable stock warrants decreases the allocation to investment in bonds. Thus, amounts debited to investment in stock warrants increase the discount or decrease the premium recorded for the investment in bonds.
Answer (A) is incorrect. The allocation to detachable stock warrants decreases the premium. Answer (C) is incorrect. The allocation to detachable stock warrants decreases the premium or increases any discount. Answer (D) is incorrect. The price should be allocated between the warrants and the bonds based upon their relative market values at issuance. The allocation to detachable stock warrants decreases the premium or increases any discount.

10.6 Cash Surrender Value

10.6.1. On January 2, Year 1, Beal, Inc., acquired a $70,000 whole-life insurance policy on its president. The annual premium is $2,000. The company is the owner and beneficiary. Beal charged officer's life insurance expense as follows:

Year	Life Insurance Expense
1	$2,000
2	1,800
3	1,500
4	1,100
Total	$6,400

In Beal's December 31, Year 4, balance sheet, the investment in cash surrender value should be

A. $0

B. $1,600

C. $6,400

D. $8,000

Answer (B) is correct. *(CPA, adapted)*
REQUIRED: The investment in cash surrender value.
DISCUSSION: Cash surrender value is the loan value or surrender value of a whole-life insurance policy. It is equal to the difference between the premiums paid and the life insurance expense recognized. Because the total of premiums paid is $8,000 ($2,000 × 4 years) and the total life insurance expense is $6,400, the investment in cash surrender value is $1,600. This amount is classified as a noncurrent asset on a classified balance sheet because management purchases life insurance policies for the life insurance aspect rather than as a short-term investment.
Answer (A) is incorrect. The excess of the premiums over the expenses is the cash surrender value. Answer (C) is incorrect. The amount of $6,400 is the total insurance expense for 4 years. Answer (D) is incorrect. The amount of $8,000 is the sum of the premiums for 4 years.

10.6.2. An increase in the cash surrender value of a life insurance policy owned by a company is recorded by

A. Decreasing annual insurance expense.

B. Increasing investment income.

C. Recording a memorandum entry only.

D. Decreasing a deferred charge.

Answer (A) is correct. *(CPA, adapted)*
REQUIRED: The proper recording of an increase.
DISCUSSION: The cash surrender value of the policy is an asset of the company. Thus, part of the premium paid is not expense. As the cash surrender value increases, the annual insurance expense decreases, assuming a constant premium.
Answer (B) is incorrect. Investment income is not affected by life insurance. Answer (C) is incorrect. As the cash surrender value increases, the annual insurance expense decreases. Answer (D) is incorrect. Cash surrender value should be classified as an asset, not a deferred charge. The deferred charge category should be avoided.

10.6.3. In Year 1, Chain, Inc., purchased a $1 million life insurance policy on its president, of which Chain is the beneficiary. Information regarding the policy for the year ended December 31, Year 6, follows:

Cash surrender value, 1/1/Year 6	$ 87,000
Cash surrender value, 12/31/Year 6	108,000
Annual advance premium paid 1/1/Year 6	40,000

During Year 6, dividends of $6,000 were applied to increase the cash surrender value of the policy. What amount should Chain report as life insurance expense for Year 6?

- A. $40,000
- B. $21,000
- C. $19,000
- D. $13,000

Answer (C) is correct. *(CPA, adapted)*
REQUIRED: The life insurance expense to be reported.
DISCUSSION: Life insurance expense is equal to the excess of the premiums paid over the increase in cash surrender value and dividends received. Because the dividends were applied to increase the cash surrender value, they were therefore not received. Hence, Chain's life insurance expense is $19,000.

Premium	$40,000
Less:	
Increase in cash surrender value ($108,000 – $87,000)	(21,000)
Life insurance expense	$19,000

Answer (A) is incorrect. The amount of $40,000 is the premium paid. Answer (B) is incorrect. The amount of $21,000 is the change in the cash surrender value. Answer (D) is incorrect. The amount of $13,000 results from subtracting the dividends applied.

10.6.4. In Year 1, Gar Corp. collected $300,000 as beneficiary of a key person life insurance policy carried on the life of Gar's controller, who had died in Year 1. The life insurance proceeds are not subject to income tax. At the date of the controller's death, the policy's cash surrender value was $90,000. What amount should Gar report as revenue in its Year 1 income statement?

- A. $0
- B. $90,000
- C. $210,000
- D. $300,000

Answer (C) is correct. *(CPA, adapted)*
REQUIRED: The revenue reported from collection of life insurance.
DISCUSSION: Upon receipt of life insurance proceeds, cash is debited for the amount received. Cash surrender value is credited for the amount of the asset on the books, and the balancing credit is to insurance income (a revenue account). Hence, revenue equals $210,000 ($300,000 cash – $90,000 cash surrender value).
Answer (A) is incorrect. Cash collected exceeded the asset. Answer (B) is incorrect. The amount of $90,000 is the cash surrender value. Answer (D) is incorrect. The amount of $300,000 equals the cash collected.

10.7 Derivatives and Hedges

10.7.1. A derivative financial instrument is best described as

- A. Evidence of an ownership interest in an entity such as shares of common stock.
- B. A contract that has its settlement value tied to an underlying notional amount.
- C. A contract that conveys to a second entity a right to receive cash from a first entity.
- D. A contract that conveys to a second entity a right to future collections on accounts receivable from a first entity.

Answer (B) is correct. *(CPA, adapted)*
REQUIRED: The best description of a derivative financial instrument.
DISCUSSION: A derivative is a bet on whether the value of something (underlying notional amount) will go up or down. A derivative has at least one underlying (interest rate, currency exchange rate, price of a specific financial instrument, etc.) and at least one notional amount (number of units specified in the contract) or payment provision, or both. No initial net investment, or one smaller than that necessary for contracts with similar responses to the market, is required. Furthermore, a derivative's terms require or permit net settlement or provide for the equivalent. Net settlement means that the derivative can be readily settled with only a net delivery of assets. Thus, neither party must deliver (1) an asset associated with its underlying or (2) an asset that has a principal, stated amount, etc., equal to the notional amount.
Answer (A) is incorrect. Financial instruments include cash, evidence of an ownership interest in an entity, and certain contracts. A derivative is a contract. Answer (C) is incorrect. Any financial instrument (not just a derivative) that is a contract conveys to a second entity a right to receive cash or another financial instrument from a first entity or to exchange other financial instruments on potentially favorable terms with the first entity. Answer (D) is incorrect. A contract that conveys to a second entity a right to future collections on accounts receivable from a first entity is not, by itself, a derivative. It is not a bet on whether the price of something will go up or down. Instead, it may be a factoring arrangement.

10.7.2. Garcia Corporation has entered into a binding agreement with Hernandez Company to purchase 400,000 pounds of Colombian coffee at $2.53 per pound for delivery in 90 days. This contract is accounted for as a

A. Financial instrument.

B. Firm commitment.

C. Forecasted transaction.

D. Fair value hedge.

Answer (B) is correct. *(Publisher, adapted)*
REQUIRED: The type of transaction defined.
DISCUSSION: A firm commitment is an agreement with an unrelated party, binding on both parties and usually legally enforceable, that specifies all significant terms and includes a disincentive for nonperformance.
Answer (A) is incorrect. A financial instrument does not involve the delivery of a product. Answer (C) is incorrect. A forecasted transaction is a transaction that is expected to occur for which no firm commitment exists. Answer (D) is incorrect. The purchase commitment is an exposure to risk, not a hedge of an exposure to risk.

10.7.3. Neron Co. has two derivatives related to two different financial instruments, instrument A and instrument B, both of which are debt instruments. The derivative related to instrument A is a fair value hedge, and the derivative related to instrument B is a cash flow hedge. Neron experienced gains in the value of instruments A and B due to a change in interest rates. Which of the gains should be reported by Neron in its income statement?

	Gain in Value of Debt Instrument A	Gain in Value of Debt Instrument B
A.	Yes	Yes
B.	Yes	No
C.	No	Yes
D.	No	No

Answer (B) is correct. *(CPA, adapted)*
REQUIRED: The gain(s), if any, on the hedged items reported in the income statement.
DISCUSSION: In a fair value hedge, the change in fair value of the hedged item (instrument A) is an adjustment to the carrying amount that is recognized currently in earnings. The same treatment applies to the change in fair value of the hedging instrument. The earnings effect of (gain on) the hedged item (instrument B) in this cash flow hedge occurs in a future reporting period.
Answer (A) is incorrect. The earnings effect of (gain on) the hedged item (instrument B) in this cash flow hedge occurs in a future reporting period. Answer (C) is incorrect. The gain in fair value of instrument B is recognized in a future period. The gain in fair value of instrument A is recognized currently in earnings. Answer (D) is incorrect. The gain in fair value of instrument A is recognized currently in earnings.

10.7.4. When the hedge is highly effective, a loss arising from the decrease in fair value of a derivative is included in current earnings if the derivative qualifies and is designated as a

	Fair-Value Hedge	Cash-Flow Hedge
A.	Yes	No
B.	No	Yes
C.	Yes	Yes
D.	No	No

Answer (A) is correct. *(Publisher, adapted)*
REQUIRED: The treatment of a loss from a decrease in fair value of a derivative qualified and designated as either a fair-value or a cash-flow hedge that is highly effective.
DISCUSSION: A fair-value hedge includes a hedge of an exposure to changes in the fair value of a recognized asset or liability or of an unrecognized firm commitment. Changes in both (1) the fair value of a derivative that qualifies and is designated as a fair-value hedge and (2) the fair value of the hedged item attributable to the hedged risk are included in earnings in the period of change. Thus, the net effect on earnings is limited to the difference between the changes in fair value. A cash-flow hedge includes a hedge of an exposure to variability in the cash flows of a recognized asset or liability or a forecasted transaction. When the hedge is determined to be highly effective, the entire change in the fair value of the hedging instrument (derivative) is reported in OCI. The amounts accumulated in OCI are reclassified to earnings in the period(s) the hedged transaction affects earnings. For example, accumulated amounts related to a forecasted purchase of equipment are reclassified as the equipment is depreciated.
Answer (B) is incorrect. When the hedge is highly effective, the changes in fair value of a hedge qualified and designated as a fair-value hedge are included in earnings in the periods the changes take place. The changes in the fair value of a derivative that qualifies and is designated as a cash-flow hedge are recognized as in OCI. Answer (C) is incorrect. When the hedge is highly effective, changes in the fair value of a derivative that qualifies and is designated as a cash-flow hedge are recognized in OCI. Answer (D) is incorrect. The changes in fair value of a hedge qualified, designated, and effective as a fair-value hedge are included in earnings in the periods when they occur.

10.7.5. On October 1, Bordeaux, Inc., a calendar year-end firm, invested in a derivative designed to hedge the risk of changes in fair value of certain assets, currently valued at $1.5 million. The derivative is structured to result in a highly effective hedge. On December 31, the fair value of the hedged assets decreased by $350,000, and the fair value of the derivative increased by $345,000. Bordeaux should recognize a net effect on earnings for the year of

A. $0

B. $5,000

C. $345,000

D. $350,000

Answer (B) is correct. *(Publisher, adapted)*
REQUIRED: The net effect on earnings of a highly effective hedge of changes in fair value of a recognized asset.
DISCUSSION: A hedge of an exposure to changes in the fair value of a recognized asset or liability is classified as a fair value hedge. Gains and losses from changes in fair value of a derivative classified as a fair value hedge are included in the determination of earnings in the period of change. They are offset by losses or gains on the hedged item attributable to the risk being hedged. Thus, earnings of the period of change are affected only by the net gain or loss attributable to the ineffective aspect of the hedge. The ineffective portion is equal to $5,000 ($350,000 – $345,000).
Answer (A) is incorrect. The effect on earnings is equal to the ineffective portion of the hedge. Answer (C) is incorrect. The increase in the fair value of the derivative is a gross effect. Answer (D) is incorrect. The decrease in the fair value of the hedged assets is a gross effect.

10.8 Financial Instrument Disclosures

10.8.1. Which of the following is a financial instrument?

A. Merchandise inventory.

B. Deferred subscription revenue.

C. A note payable in U.S. Treasury bonds.

D. A warranty payable.

Answer (C) is correct. *(Publisher, adapted)*
REQUIRED: The item meeting the definition of a financial instrument.
DISCUSSION: A financial instrument is cash, evidence of an ownership interest in an entity, or a contract that both (1) imposes on one entity a contractual obligation (a) to deliver cash or another financial instrument to a second entity or (b) to exchange financial instruments on potentially unfavorable terms with the second entity, and (2) conveys to that second entity a contractual right (a) to receive cash or another financial instrument from the first entity or (b) to exchange other financial instruments on potentially favorable terms with the first entity. A note payable in U.S. Treasury bonds gives the holder the contractual right to receive and imposes on the issuer the contractual obligation to deliver bonds that are themselves financial instruments. Thus, given that one entity has a contractual obligation to deliver another financial instrument and the second entity has a contractual right to receive another financial instrument, the note payable in U.S. Treasury bonds meets the definition of a financial instrument.
Answer (A) is incorrect. Although the sale of inventory could result in the receipt of cash, the holder of the inventory has no current contractual right to receive cash. Answer (B) is incorrect. Deferred subscription revenue will result in the delivery of goods or services. Answer (D) is incorrect. A warranty payable will result in the delivery of goods or services.

10.8.2. Whether recognized or unrecognized in an entity's financial statements, disclosure of the fair values of the entity's financial instruments is required when

A. It is feasible to estimate those values and aggregated fair values are material to the entity.

B. The entity maintains accurate cost records and aggregated fair values are material to the entity.

C. Aggregated fair values are material to the entity and credit risk has been appropriately hedged.

D. Individual fair values are material to the entity or any of the instruments are accounted for as derivatives.

Answer (A) is correct. *(CPA, adapted)*
REQUIRED: The circumstances in which disclosure of the fair values of the entity's financial instruments is required.
DISCUSSION: Certain entities must disclose the fair value of financial instruments, whether or not they are recognized in the balance sheet, if it is feasible to estimate such fair values and aggregated fair values are material to the entity. If estimating fair value is not feasible, disclosures include information pertinent to estimating the fair value of the financial instrument or class of financial instruments, such as the carrying amount, effective interest rate, and maturity. The reasons that estimating the fair value is not feasible also should be disclosed.
Answer (B) is incorrect. The disclosure requirement is based on practicability and aggregate materiality, not record keeping and aggregate materiality. Answer (C) is incorrect. The disclosure requirement is based on practicability and aggregate materiality, not aggregate materiality and credit risk hedging. Answer (D) is incorrect. The disclosure requirement is based on practicability and aggregate materiality, not individual materiality or derivative accounting.

10.8.3. Disclosure of information about significant concentrations of credit risk is required for

- A. Most financial instruments.
- B. Financial instruments with off-balance-sheet credit risk only.
- C. Financial instruments with off-balance-sheet market risk only.
- D. Financial instruments with off-balance-sheet risk of accounting loss only.

Answer (A) is correct. *(CPA, adapted)*

REQUIRED: The financial instruments for which disclosure of significant concentrations of credit risk is required.

DISCUSSION: GAAP require the disclosure of information about the fair value of financial instruments, whether recognized or not (certain nonpublic entities and certain instruments, such as leases and insurance contracts, are exempt from the disclosure requirements). GAAP also require disclosure of all significant concentrations of credit risk for most financial instruments (except for obligations for deferred compensation, certain instruments of a pension plan, insurance contracts, warranty obligations and rights, and unconditional purchase obligations).

Use **Gleim Test Prep** for interactive study and easy-to-use detailed analytics!

STUDY UNIT ELEVEN
CURRENT LIABILITIES, COMPENSATED ABSENCES, AND CONTINGENCIES

Current liabilities are expected to be (1) paid using current assets or (2) replaced with other current liabilities within 1 year from the balance sheet date (or operating cycle if longer). They include (1) accounts payable, (2) notes payable, (3) current maturities of long-term debt, (4) unearned revenues, (5) taxes payable, (6) wages payable, and (7) other accruals. Questions on current liabilities test basic accrual accounting procedures for recognition and reporting of liabilities in the balance sheet.

A contingency involves uncertainty about possible loss (loss contingency) or gain (gain contingency). Contingencies also are classified as (1) probable (likely to occur), (2) reasonably possible (more than remote but less probable), and (3) remote (slight chance of occurrence). Gain contingencies are disclosed but are recognized only when realized. Loss contingencies (other than guarantees) are recognized only when (1) it is probable that a liability has been incurred or an asset impaired and (2) the loss can be reasonably estimated.

Chance of Future Event(s)	Probable Liability or Impaired Asset	Reasonably Estimable	Accrual	Disclosure Required
Probable	Yes	Yes	Yes	Yes
Reasonably possible	Yes	No	No	Yes
Reasonably possible	No	Yes	No	Yes
Reasonably possible	No	No	No	Yes
Remote	--	--	No	No

Most questions on contingencies test the conditions that must be met to accrue a contingent liability.

QUESTIONS

11.1 Current Liabilities

11.1.1. Acme Co.'s accounts payable balance at December 31 was $850,000 before necessary year-end adjustments, if any, related to the following information:

- At December 31, Acme has a $50,000 debit balance in its accounts payable resulting from a payment to a supplier for goods to be manufactured to Acme's specifications.
- Goods shipped FOB destination on December 20 were received and recorded by Acme on January 2. The invoice cost was $45,000.

In its December 31 balance sheet, what amount should Acme report as accounts payable?

A. $850,000

B. $895,000

C. $900,000

D. $945,000

Answer (C) is correct. *(CPA, adapted)*
REQUIRED: The balance in accounts payable given a prepayment to a supplier and a shipment FOB destination.
DISCUSSION: The payment to a supplier for goods to be manufactured to specifications should have been recorded by a debit to a prepaid asset, not accounts payable. Accordingly, accounts payable should be $900,000 ($850,000 + $50,000 error correction). The goods shipped FOB destination were not received until January 2, so they were appropriately excluded from accounts payable at year end. When the shipping term is FOB destination, the buyer records inventory and a payable when the goods are tendered at the destination (when title and risk of loss pass).
Answer (A) is incorrect. The amount of $850,000 does not reflect the necessary year-end adjustment to remove the erroneous charge for the prepayment. Answer (B) is incorrect. The amount of $895,000 includes $45,000 for the goods shipped FOB destination and received after the cutoff date. It does not include the adjustment for the erroneous charge to accounts payable for the prepayment. Answer (D) is incorrect. The amount of $945,000 includes $45,000 for the goods shipped FOB destination and received after the cutoff date.

11.1.2. Seoul Corp. had the following liabilities at December 31, Year 1:

Accounts payable	$ 110,000
Unsecured notes, 8%, due 7/1/Year 2	800,000
Accrued expenses	70,000
Contingent liability	900,000
Deferred income tax liability	50,000
Senior bonds, 7%, due 3/31/Year 2	2,000,000

The contingent liability is an accrual for possible losses on a $2 million lawsuit filed against Seoul. Seoul's legal counsel expects the suit to be settled in Year 3 and has estimated that Seoul will be liable for damages in the range of $900,000 to $1,500,000. The deferred income tax liability is not related to an asset for financial reporting and is expected to reverse in Year 3. What amount should Seoul report in its December 31, Year 1, balance sheet for current liabilities?

A. $1,030,000

B. $1,880,000

C. $2,980,000

D. $3,030,000

Answer (C) is correct. *(CPA, adapted)*
REQUIRED: The amount reported for current liabilities.
DISCUSSION: A current liability is an obligation that will be either liquidated using a current asset or replaced by another current liability. The following are current liabilities: (1) obligations that, by their terms, are due on demand within 1 year (or the operating cycle if longer) and (2) obligations that are callable by the creditor within 1 year because of a violation of a debt covenant. Thus, the current liabilities are calculated as follows:

Accounts payable	$ 110,000
Unsecured notes, 8%, due 7/1/Year 2	800,000
Accrued expenses	70,000
Senior bonds, 7%, due 3/31/Year 2	2,000,000
	$2,980,000

Answer (A) is incorrect. The amount of $1,030,000 excludes the senior bonds due within 1 year and includes the deferred tax liability that will not reverse within 1 year. Whether a deferred tax asset or liability is current depends on the classification of the related asset or liability. If it is not related to an asset or liability, the expected reversal date of the temporary difference determines the classification. Answer (B) is incorrect. The amount of $1,880,000 includes the contingent liability not expected to be settled until Year 3 and excludes the senior bonds. Answer (D) is incorrect. The amount of $3,030,000 includes the deferred income tax liability not expected to reverse until Year 3.

11.1.3. On September 30, World Co. borrowed $1,000,000 on a 9% note payable. World paid the first of four quarterly payments of $264,200 when due on December 30. In its December 31 balance sheet, what amount should World report as note payable?

A. $735,800

B. $750,000

C. $758,300

D. $825,800

Answer (C) is correct. *(CPA, adapted)*
REQUIRED: The year-end note payable balance after the initial payment.
DISCUSSION: This interest-bearing 1-year note with four quarterly payments is a current liability because it is expected to be liquidated using current assets. Each payment of $264,200 consists of interest and principal. Only the principal component reduces the liability. The interest component equals $22,500 [$1,000,000 face amount × 9% × (1 ÷ 4 quarters)]. Thus, the principal is reduced by $241,700 ($264,200 payment – $22,500 interest). The note payable is reported as $758,300 ($1,000,000 carrying amount – $241,700 principal reduction) at year end.
Answer (A) is incorrect. The amount of $735,800 results from treating the entire payment as principal. Answer (B) is incorrect. The amount of $750,000 is simply 75% of the face amount of the note. Answer (D) is incorrect. The amount of $825,800 is based on the assumption that the annual interest of $90,000 is included in the first payment.

11.1.4. Wilk Co. reported the following liabilities at December 31, Year 1:

Accounts payable-trade	$ 750,000
Short-term borrowings	400,000
Bank loan, current portion $100,000	3,500,000
Other bank loan, matures June 30, Year 2	1,000,000

The bank loan of $3,500,000 was in violation of the loan agreement. The creditor had not waived the rights under the loan. What amount should Wilk report as current liabilities at December 31, Year 1?

A. $1,250,000

B. $2,150,000

C. $2,250,000

D. $5,650,000

Answer (D) is correct. *(CPA, adapted)*
REQUIRED: The current liabilities to be reported at year end.
DISCUSSION: Obligations are liabilities when they are callable by the creditor within 1 year because of a violation of a debt covenant. Noncurrent debt need not be classified as current if it is probable that a violation existing at the balance sheet date will be remedied within a specified period. With no probable remedy of Wilk's violation of the loan agreement, current liabilities to be reported at year end are $5,650,000 ($750,000 trade payables + $400,000 current borrowings + $3,500,000 bank loan + $1,000,000 other bank loan due within 1 year).
Answer (A) is incorrect. Both the entire $3,500,000 bank loan and the other bank loan must be included as current liabilities. Answer (B) is incorrect. The $3,500,000 bank loan must be included as a current liability. Answer (C) is incorrect. The entire $3,500,000 bank loan must be recorded as a current liability.

11.1.5. On March 31, Dallas Co. received an advance payment of 60% of the sales price for special order goods to be manufactured and delivered within 5 months. At the same time, Dallas subcontracted for production of the special order goods at a price equal to 40% of the main contract price. What liabilities should be reported in Dallas's March 31 balance sheet?

	Deferred Revenues	Payables to Subcontractor
A.	None	None
B.	60% of main contract price	40% of main contract price
C.	60% of main contract price	None
D.	None	40% of main contract price

Answer (C) is correct. *(CPA, adapted)*
REQUIRED: The liabilities to be reported in the balance sheet.
DISCUSSION: The 60% advance payment is a deferred revenue (a contract liability) because it is an obligation to transfer goods to a customer for which consideration already has been received from the customer. The agreement with the subcontractor does not create a liability because the entity has no performance obligation to transfer goods or provide services. That obligation will not arise until the subcontractor has performed.
Answer (A) is incorrect. The 60% prepayment should be credited to deferred revenue. Answer (B) is incorrect. Dallas has no liability to the subcontractor. Answer (D) is incorrect. The 60% prepayment should be credited to deferred revenue, and Dallas has no liability to the subcontractor.

11.1.6. Nepal Co. requires advance payments with special orders for machinery constructed to customer specifications. These advances are nonrefundable. Information for Year 2 is as follows:

Customer advances--balance 12/31/Year 1	$236,000
Advances received with orders in Year 2	368,000
Advances applied to orders shipped in Year 2	328,000
Advances applicable to orders canceled in Year 2	100,000

In Nepal's December 31, Year 2, balance sheet, what amount should be reported as a current liability for advances from customers?

- A. $0
- B. $176,000
- C. $276,000
- D. $296,000

Answer (B) is correct. *(CPA, adapted)*
REQUIRED: The current liability for advances.
DISCUSSION: The amount of $176,000 ($236,000 beginning balance + $368,000 advances received – $328,000 advances credited to revenue after shipment of orders – $100,000 for canceled orders) should be reported as a current liability for customer advances. Deposits or other advance payments are liabilities because they involve a probable future sacrifice of economic benefits arising from a current obligation. The advances applicable to canceled orders are not refundable. Thus, no future sacrifice of economic benefits is necessary.
Answer (A) is incorrect. Deposits or other advance payments should be recognized as liabilities. Answer (C) is incorrect. The amount of $276,000 includes $100,000 applicable to orders canceled. Answer (D) is incorrect. The amount of $296,000 results from subtracting advances received and adding advances applied to shipments and advances for canceled orders.

11.1.7. Kent Co., a division of National Realty, Inc., maintains escrow accounts and pays real estate taxes for National's mortgage customers. Escrow funds are kept in interest-bearing accounts. Interest, less a 10% service fee, is credited to the mortgagee's account and used to reduce future escrow payments. Additional information follows:

Escrow accounts liability, 1/1	$ 700,000
Escrow payments received during the year	1,580,000
Real estate taxes paid during the year	1,720,000
Interest on escrow funds during the year	50,000

What amount should Kent report as escrow accounts liability in its December 31 balance sheet?

- A. $510,000
- B. $515,000
- C. $605,000
- D. $610,000

Answer (C) is correct. *(CPA, adapted)*
REQUIRED: The amount of escrow accounts liability.
DISCUSSION: The liability at the beginning of the year was $700,000. Escrow payments of $1,580,000 were credited and taxes paid of $1,720,000 were debited to the account during the year. Furthermore, interest of $45,000 [$50,000 – ($50,000 × 10%) service fee] was credited. Thus, the year-end balance was $605,000 ($700,000 + $1,580,000 – $1,720,000 + $45,000).
Answer (A) is incorrect. The amount of $510,000 results from debiting $50,000 rather than crediting $45,000. Answer (B) is incorrect. The amount of $515,000 results from debiting $45,000 rather than crediting $45,000. Answer (D) is incorrect. The amount of $610,000 omits the adjustment for the service fee.

11.1.8. Sudan Co. sells major household appliance service contracts for cash. The service contracts are for a 1-year, 2-year, or 3-year period. Cash receipts from contracts are credited to unearned service contract revenues. This account had a balance of $1,440,000 at December 31, Year 1, before year-end adjustment. Service contract costs are charged as incurred to the service contract expense account, which had a balance of $360,000 at December 31, Year 1. Outstanding service contracts at December 31, Year 1, expire as follows:

During Year 2	$300,000
During Year 3	450,000
During Year 4	200,000

What amount should be reported as unearned service contract revenues in Sudan's December 31, Year 1, balance sheet?

- A. $1,080,000
- B. $950,000
- C. $590,000
- D. $490,000

Answer (B) is correct. *(CPA, adapted)*
REQUIRED: The amount to be reported as unearned service contract revenues at year end.
DISCUSSION: Unearned service contract revenues relate to outstanding contracts for which the agreed service has not yet been provided. Thus, the amount to be reported as unearned service contract revenues is the $950,000 ($300,000 + $450,000 + $200,000) of service contracts outstanding at 12/31/Year 1.
Answer (A) is incorrect. The amount of $1,080,000 is the difference between the unearned service contract revenue before adjustment and the balance in the service contract expense account. Answer (C) is incorrect. The amount of $590,000 is the difference between the $360,000 balance in service contract expense and the $950,000 of unearned service contract revenue reported in the 12/31/Year 1 balance sheet. Answer (D) is incorrect. The amount of $490,000 is the change in the unearned service contract revenue account ($1,440,000 – $950,000).

11.1.9. On January 3, Year 1, North Company issued noncurrent bonds due January 3, Year 6. The bond agreement includes a call provision that is effective if the firm's current ratio falls below 2:1. On June 30, Year 1, the fiscal year end for the company, its current ratio was 1.5:1. The bonds should be reported on the financial statements as a

A. Noncurrent liability because their maturity date is January 3, Year 6.

B. Noncurrent liability if it is reasonably possible that North can remedy the violation of the agreement before the end of any allowed grace period.

C. Current liability if the violation of the agreement is not remedied.

D. Current liability, regardless of any action by the bondholder, because the company was in violation of the agreement on the balance sheet date.

Answer (C) is correct. *(R.B. Posey)*
REQUIRED: The proper classification of callable obligations.
DISCUSSION: Noncurrent liabilities that are callable by the creditor because of the debtor's violation of the debt agreement at the balance sheet date must be classified as current.
Answer (A) is incorrect. The violation of the debt agreement allows the creditor to accelerate the maturity date. Answer (B) is incorrect. The debt should be classified as current unless it is probable that the violation will be remedied within any specified period. Answer (D) is incorrect. A creditor's waiver of the right to demand repayment of the debt allows North to classify the bonds as noncurrent.

11.1.10. As of December 15, Year 4, Aviator had dividends in arrears of $200,000 on its cumulative preferred stock. Dividends for Year 4 of $100,000 have not yet been declared. The board of directors plans to declare cash dividends on its preferred and common stock on January 16, Year 5. Aviator paid an annual bonus to its CEO based on the company's annual profits. The bonus for Year 4 was $50,000, and it will be paid on February 10, Year 5. What amount should Aviator report as current liabilities on its balance sheet at December 31, Year 4?

A. $50,000

B. $150,000

C. $200,000

D. $350,000

Answer (A) is correct. *(CPA, adapted)*
REQUIRED: The current liabilities for a bonus and dividends reported on the balance sheet for Year 4.
DISCUSSION: The $50,000 bonus payable to the CEO is an obligation incurred in Year 4 based on profits for that year. Moreover, it will be paid within 12 months, so it should be classified as a current liability. However, dividends do not become a legal obligation of the entity until declared. The entity incurs no liability in Year 4 because it has no obligation to declare dividends on common stock or preferred stock (whether or not cumulative).
Answer (B) is incorrect. Dividends have not been declared. Thus, the Year 4 dividend of $100,000 is not a current liability. Answer (C) is incorrect. Dividends in arrears are not a legal obligation until authorization from the board of directors to distribute earnings is established. Answer (D) is incorrect. Dividends in arrears and other undeclared dividends are not current liabilities.

11.2 Certain Taxes Payable

11.2.1. Lime Co.'s payroll for the month ended January 31, Year 4, is summarized as follows:

Total wages	$10,000
Federal income tax withheld	1,200

All wages paid were subject to FICA. FICA tax rates were 7% each for employee and employer. Lime remits payroll taxes on the 15th of the following month. In its financial statements for the month ended January 31, Year 4, what amounts should Lime report as total payroll tax liability and as payroll tax expense?

	Liability	Expense
A.	$1,200	$1,400
B.	$1,900	$1,400
C.	$1,900	$700
D.	$2,600	$700

Answer (D) is correct. *(CPA, adapted)*
REQUIRED: The amounts reported as total payroll tax liability and as payroll tax expense.
DISCUSSION: The payroll liability is $2,600 ($1,200 federal income tax withheld + $700 employer's FICA + $700 employees' FICA). The payroll tax expense consists of the employer's share of FICA. The employees' share is considered a withholding, not an expense.
Answer (A) is incorrect. The amount of $1,200 does not include employer and employee shares of current FICA taxes, and $1,400 includes the employees' share of FICA taxes. Answer (B) is incorrect. The amount of $1,900 does not include $700 of FICA taxes, and $1,400 includes the employees' share of FICA taxes. Answer (C) is incorrect. The amount of $1,900 does not include $700 of FICA taxes.

11.2.2. Hudson Hotel collects 15% in city sales taxes on room rentals, in addition to a $2 per room, per night, occupancy tax. Sales taxes for each month are due at the end of the following month, and occupancy taxes are due 15 days after the end of each calendar quarter. On January 3, Year 5, Hudson paid its November Year 4 sales taxes and its fourth quarter Year 4 occupancy taxes. Additional information pertaining to Hudson's operations is

Year 4	Room Rentals	Room Nights
October	$100,000	1,100
November	110,000	1,200
December	150,000	1,800

What amounts should Hudson report as sales taxes payable and occupancy taxes payable in its December 31, Year 4, balance sheet?

	Sales Taxes	Occupancy Taxes
A.	$39,000	$6,000
B.	$39,000	$8,200
C.	$54,000	$6,000
D.	$54,000	$8,200

Answer (B) is correct. *(CPA, adapted)*
REQUIRED: The sales taxes payable and occupancy taxes payable.
DISCUSSION: Hudson presumably paid its October sales taxes during Year 4, but it did not pay sales taxes for November and December and occupancy taxes for October, November, and December until Year 5. Consequently, it should accrue a liability for sales taxes in the amount of $39,000 [($110,000 November rentals + $150,000 December rentals) × 15%] and a liability for occupancy taxes in the amount of $8,200 [(1,100 + 1,200 + 1,800) room nights × $2].
Answer (A) is incorrect. The amount of $6,000 excludes October room nights. Answer (C) is incorrect. The amount of $54,000 includes October room rentals, and $6,000 excludes October room nights. Answer (D) is incorrect. The amount of $54,000 includes October room rentals.

11.2.3. On July 1, Year 1, Wessex County issued real estate tax assessments for its fiscal year ended June 30, Year 2. On September 1, Year 1, Milan Co. purchased a warehouse in Wessex County. The purchase price was reduced by a credit for accrued realty taxes. Milan did not record the entire year's real estate tax obligation but instead records tax expenses at the end of each month by adjusting prepaid real estate taxes or real estate taxes payable, as appropriate. On November 1, Year 1, Milan paid the first of two equal installments of $24,000 for real estate taxes. What amount of this payment should Milan record as a debit to real estate taxes payable?

A. $8,000

B. $16,000

C. $20,000

D. $24,000

Answer (B) is correct. *(CPA, adapted)*
REQUIRED: The amount to be debited to real estate taxes payable.
DISCUSSION: The credit balance in real estate taxes payable at 11/1/Year 1 is $16,000. This amount reflects accrued real estate taxes of $4,000 a month [(2 × $24,000) ÷ 12 months] for 4 months (July through October). This payable should be debited for $16,000 when the real estate taxes are paid.
Answer (A) is incorrect. The amount of $8,000 includes real estate taxes for September and October only. Answer (C) is incorrect. The amount of $20,000 includes real estate taxes for November. Answer (D) is incorrect. The amount of $24,000 equals 6 months of real estate taxes.

11.3 Refinancing of Current Debt

11.3.1. At December 31, Year 1, Telemark Co. owed notes payable of $1,750,000, due on May 15, Year 2. Telemark expects to retire this debt with proceeds from the sale of 100,000 shares of its common stock. The stock was sold for $15 per share on March 10, Year 2, prior to the issuance of the year-end financial statements. In Telemark's December 31, Year 1, balance sheet, what amount of the notes payable should be excluded from current liabilities?

A. $0

B. $250,000

C. $1,500,000

D. $1,750,000

Answer (C) is correct. *(CPA, adapted)*
REQUIRED: The amount of notes payable that should be excluded from current liabilities.
DISCUSSION: If an entity intends to refinance current obligations on a noncurrent basis and demonstrates an ability to do so, the obligation should be excluded from current liabilities and reclassified as noncurrent. The ability to refinance may be demonstrated by issuing noncurrent obligations or equity securities after the end of the reporting period but before issuance of the balance sheet. Thus, $1,500,000 (100,000 shares × $15) of the notes payable should be excluded from current liabilities and reclassified as noncurrent.
Answer (A) is incorrect. The amount of $1,500,000 should be excluded from current liabilities. Answer (B) is incorrect. The amount that should be classified as a current liability is $250,000. Answer (D) is incorrect. The full amount of notes payable, which should be allocated between current and noncurrent liabilities, is $1,750,000.

11.3.2. On December 31, Year 4, Largo, Inc., had a $750,000 note payable outstanding due July 31, Year 5. Largo borrowed the money to finance construction of a new plant. Largo planned to refinance the note by issuing noncurrent bonds. Because Largo temporarily had excess cash, it prepaid $250,000 of the note on January 12, Year 5. In February Year 5, Largo completed a $1.5 million bond offering. Largo will use the bond offering proceeds to repay the note payable at its maturity and to pay construction costs during Year 5. On March 3, Year 5, Largo issued its Year 4 financial statements. What amount of the note payable should Largo include in the current liabilities section of its December 31, Year 4, balance sheet?

A. $750,000

B. $500,000

C. $250,000

D. $0

Answer (C) is correct. *(CPA, adapted)*
REQUIRED: The amount that should be classified as current obligations.
DISCUSSION: The portion of debt scheduled to mature in the following fiscal year ordinarily should be classified as a current liability. However, if an entity intends to refinance current obligations on a noncurrent basis and demonstrates an ability to consummate the refinancing, the obligation should be excluded from current liabilities and classified as noncurrent. One method of demonstrating the ability to refinance is to issue noncurrent obligations or equity securities after the balance sheet date but before the financial statements are issued. Largo demonstrated an intention to refinance $500,000 of the note payable. Thus, the portion prepaid ($250,000) is a current liability, and the remaining $500,000 should be classified as noncurrent.
Answer (A) is incorrect. The amount of $750,000 includes the $500,000 that was refinanced. Answer (B) is incorrect. The amount of $500,000 is the amount that should be reclassified as noncurrent. Answer (D) is incorrect. A portion of the debt should be classified as a current liability.

11.3.3. Ames, Inc., has $1 million of notes payable due June 15, Year 2. At the financial statement date of December 31, Year 1, Ames signed an agreement to borrow up to $1 million to refinance the notes payable on a long-term basis. The financing agreement called for borrowings not to exceed 80% of the value of the collateral Ames was providing. At the date of issue of the December 31, Year 1, financial statements, the value of the collateral was $1.2 million and was not expected to fall below this amount during Year 2. In its December 31, Year 1, balance sheet, Ames should classify the notes payable as

	Short-Term Obligations	Long-Term Obligations
A.	$0	$1,000,000
B.	$40,000	$960,000
C.	$200,000	$800,000
D.	$1,000,000	$0

Answer (B) is correct. *(CPA, adapted)*
REQUIRED: The proper classification of notes payable subject to a refinancing agreement.
DISCUSSION: The portion of debt scheduled to mature in the following fiscal year ordinarily should be classified as a current liability. However, if an enterprise intends to refinance short-term obligations on a long-term basis and demonstrates an ability to consummate the refinancing, the obligation should be excluded from current liabilities and classified as noncurrent. Ames has signed an agreement to borrow up to $1 million to refinance the notes payable on a long-term basis, but the borrowings may not exceed 80% of the value of the collateral. Consequently, Ames has demonstrated an ability to refinance $960,000 ($1,200,000 collateral × 80% ceiling) of the notes payable. This amount should be classified as a long-term obligation. The remaining $40,000 ($1,000,000 – $960,000) should be reported as a short-term obligation.
Answer (A) is incorrect. Ames has not demonstrated an ability to refinance $40,000 of the notes payable. Answer (C) is incorrect. Ames has demonstrated an ability to refinance $960,000 of the notes payable. Answer (D) is incorrect. Ames has demonstrated an ability to refinance $960,000 of the notes payable.

11.3.4. Included in Lee Corp.'s liability account balances at December 31, Year 4, were the following:

14% note payable issued October 1, Year 4, maturing September 30, Year 5	$125,000
16% note payable issued April 1, Year 2, payable in six equal annual installments of $50,000 beginning April 1, Year 3	200,000

Lee's December 31, Year 4, financial statements were issued on March 31, Year 5. On January 15, Year 5, the entire $200,000 balance of the 16% note was refinanced by issuance of a long-term obligation payable in a lump sum. In addition, on March 10, Year 5, Lee consummated a noncancelable agreement with the lender to refinance the 14%, $125,000 note on a long-term basis, on readily determinable terms that have not yet been implemented. Both parties are financially capable of honoring the agreement, and there have been no violations of the agreement's provisions. On the December 31, Year 4, balance sheet, the amount of the notes payable that Lee should classify as short-term obligations is

A. $175,000

B. $125,000

C. $50,000

D. $0

Answer (D) is correct. *(CPA, adapted)*
REQUIRED: The amount that should be classified as short-term obligations.
DISCUSSION: If an entity intends to refinance short-term obligations on a long-term basis and demonstrates an ability to consummate the refinancing, the obligation should be excluded from current liabilities and reclassified as noncurrent. The ability to consummate the refinancing may be demonstrated by a post-balance-sheet-date issuance of long-term obligations or equity securities. Thus, the 16% note payable should be classified as noncurrent. The ability to refinance may also be shown by entering into a financing agreement that meets the following criteria: (1) the agreement does not expire within the longer of 1 year or the operating cycle, (2) it is noncancelable by the lender, (3) no violation of the agreement exists at the balance sheet date, and (4) the lender is financially capable of honoring the agreement. For this reason, the 14% note payable is also excluded from short-term obligations. The amount of the notes payable classified as short-term is therefore $0.
Answer (A) is incorrect. Neither of the notes payable should be classified as short-term. Answer (B) is incorrect. Neither of the notes payable should be classified as short-term. Answer (C) is incorrect. Neither of the notes payable should be classified as short-term.

11.4 Compensated Absences and Postemployment Benefits

11.4.1. If the payment of employees' compensation for future absences is probable, the amount can be reasonably estimated, and the obligation relates to rights that vest, the compensation should be

A. Recognized when paid.

B. Accrued if attributable to employees' services whether or not already rendered.

C. Accrued if attributable to employees' services already rendered.

D. Accrued if attributable to employees' services not already rendered.

Answer (C) is correct. *(CPA, adapted)*
REQUIRED: The additional criterion to be met to accrue an expense for compensated absences.
DISCUSSION: GAAP require an accrual when four criteria are met: (1) The payment of compensation is probable, (2) the amount can be reasonably estimated, (3) the benefits either vest or accumulate, and (4) the compensation relates to employees' services that have already been rendered.
Answer (A) is incorrect. The cash basis is not appropriate for recognizing expenses related to compensated absences. Answer (B) is incorrect. The services must have been previously rendered. Answer (D) is incorrect. The services must have been previously rendered.

11.4.2. At December 31, Year 2, Taos Co. estimates that its employees have earned vacation pay of $100,000. Employees will receive their vacation pay in Year 3. Should Taos accrue a liability at December 31, Year 2, if the rights to this compensation accumulated over time or if the rights are vested?

	Accumulated	Vested
A.	Yes	No
B.	No	No
C.	Yes	Yes
D.	No	Yes

Answer (C) is correct. *(CPA, adapted)*
REQUIRED: The effect of accumulation and vesting on accrual of a liability for vacation pay.
DISCUSSION: GAAP require an accrual for compensated services when the compensation relates to services previously provided, the benefits either vest or accumulate, and payment is both probable and reasonably estimable. The single exception is for sick pay benefits, which must be accrued only if the rights vest.
Answer (A) is incorrect. Vesting meets one of the criteria for accrual of a liability. Answer (B) is incorrect. Either vesting or accumulation meets one of the criteria for accrual of a liability. Answer (D) is incorrect. Accumulation meets one of the criteria for accrual of a liability.

11.4.3. Employers must accrue a liability for employees' compensation for future absences. The item that requires accrual is

A. Stock compensation.

B. Termination benefits.

C. Postretirement benefits.

D. Vacation pay based on past service.

Answer (D) is correct. *(CMA, adapted)*
REQUIRED: The item that requires accrual.
DISCUSSION: The accounting for compensated absences applies to such items as sick pay benefits, holidays, and vacations. The criteria for accrual are that the obligation arose from past services, the employees' rights vest or accumulate, payment is probable, and an amount can be reasonably estimated.
Answer (A) is incorrect. The GAAP for compensated absences does not apply to stock compensation plans, which are addressed by GAAP for share-based payment. Answer (B) is incorrect. The GAAP for compensated absences does not apply to special or contractual termination benefits. Answer (C) is incorrect. The GAAP for compensated absences does not apply to pension and other postretirement benefits.

11.4.4. On January 1, Year 1, Baker Co. decided to grant its employees 10 vacation days and 5 sick days each year. Vacation days, but not sick days, may be carried over to the next year. However, sick pay benefits are vested. Each employee received payment for an average of 3 sick days in Year 1. During Year 1, each of Baker's six employees earned $100 per day and earned 10 vacation days. These vacation days were taken during Year 2. What amount should Baker report for accrued compensated absence expense for the year ended December 31, Year 1?

A. $0

B. $6,000

C. $7,200

D. $9,000

Answer (C) is correct. *(CPA, adapted)*
REQUIRED: The accrued compensated absence expense.
DISCUSSION: An accrual is required for compensated services when the compensation relates to services previously provided, the benefits either vest or accumulate, and payment is both probable and reasonably estimable. The single exception is for sick pay benefits, which must be accrued only if the rights vest. Accordingly, Baker should report accrued compensated absence expense of $7,200 [(6 employees × $100 × 10 days) vacation pay + (6 employees × $100 × 2 days) sick pay].
Answer (A) is incorrect. Baker must accrue accumulated vacation pay and vested sick pay benefits. Answer (B) is incorrect. The amount of $6,000 omits sick pay. Answer (D) is incorrect. The amount of $9,000 includes 5 days of sick pay per employee.

11.4.5. Employers' accounting for postemployment benefits applies to

A. Pension benefits provided to spouses of retired employees.

B. Salary continuation benefits provided to employees on disability leave.

C. Counseling benefits provided to employees nearing retirement age.

D. Healthcare benefits provided to dependents of retired employees.

Answer (B) is correct. *(Publisher, adapted)*
REQUIRED: The type of benefits to which employers' accounting applies.
DISCUSSION: Benefits to former or inactive employees, their beneficiaries, and their covered dependents after employment but before retirement include, but are not limited to, (1) salary continuation, (2) supplemental unemployment benefits, (3) severance benefits, (4) disability-related benefits (including workers' compensation), (5) job training and counseling, and (6) continuation of benefits, such as healthcare and life insurance coverage.
Answer (A) is incorrect. The former employees have retired and thus are not covered. Answer (C) is incorrect. The employees are still employed. Answer (D) is incorrect. Healthcare benefits provided to dependents of retired employees are not covered.

11.4.6. Sanders Co. has determined that its payment of postemployment benefits is probable, the amount can be reasonably estimated, and the obligation relates to rights that vest or accumulate. The company's obligation for postemployment benefits should

A. Be recognized when the benefits are paid.

B. Be accrued at the date of the event giving rise to the payment of benefits.

C. Be accrued if attributable to employees' services already rendered.

D. Not be recognized.

Answer (C) is correct. *(Publisher, adapted)*
REQUIRED: The treatment of postemployment benefits by the employer.
DISCUSSION: Employers must recognize the obligation to provide postemployment benefits if (1) the obligation is attributable to employees' services already rendered, (2) employees' rights accumulate or vest, (3) payment is probable, and (4) the amount of the benefits can be reasonably estimated.
Answer (A) is incorrect. If the services have been performed, a liability must be recognized. Answer (B) is incorrect. If the definition of a liability is met, an obligation is accrued even if an event triggering payment (e.g., severance) has not occurred. Answer (D) is incorrect. The obligation should be accrued.

11.4.7. North Corp. has an employee benefit plan for compensated absences that gives employees 10 paid vacation days and 10 paid sick days. Both vacation and sick days can be carried over indefinitely. Employees can elect to receive payment in lieu of vacation days; however, no payment is given for sick days not taken. At December 31 of the current year, North's unadjusted balance of liability for compensated absences was $21,000. North estimated that there were 150 vacation days and 75 sick days available at December 31. North's employees earn an average of $100 per day. In its December 31 balance sheet, what amount of liability for compensated absences is North required to report?

    A. $36,000

    B. $22,500

    C. $21,000

    D. $15,000

Answer (D) is correct. *(CPA, adapted)*
    REQUIRED: The amount of liability for compensated absences.
    DISCUSSION: Vacation benefits earned but not yet taken must be accrued. However, a liability is not accrued for future sick pay unless the rights are vested. Thus, the estimated vacation days available at December 31 require a liability of $15,000 ($100 × 150 days).
    Answer (A) is incorrect. The amount of $36,000 is the sum of the $15,000 liability for compensated absences and the unadjusted balance of liability for compensated absences. Answer (B) is incorrect. The sick days are not required to be included in the liability for compensated absences. Answer (C) is incorrect. The amount of $21,000 is the unadjusted balance of liability for compensated absences.

11.4.8. At December 31 of this year, Medina Corporation reasonably estimates that its obligations for postemployment benefits include

Severance pay	$120,000
Job training benefits	90,000

These benefits relate to employees' services already rendered, and payment is probable. The severance pay benefits vest; the job training benefits accumulate. In its December 31 balance sheet, Medina should report a liability for postemployment benefits of

    A. $0

    B. $90,000

    C. $120,000

    D. $210,000

Answer (D) is correct. *(Publisher, adapted)*
    REQUIRED: The amount of liability that should be recorded for postemployment benefits.
    DISCUSSION: If postemployment benefits are attributable to employees' services already rendered, employees' rights accumulate or vest, payment is probable, and the amount of the benefits can be reasonably estimated, the employer should recognize a liability for the obligation. Thus, the full amount of the severance pay and job training benefits of $210,000 ($120,000 + $90,000) should be reported as a liability.
    Answer (A) is incorrect. The full amount of both benefits should be included in the liability. Answer (B) is incorrect. The amount of $90,000 excludes the severance pay. Answer (C) is incorrect. The amount of $120,000 excludes the training benefits.

11.5 Contingencies

11.5.1. A loss contingency should be accrued on an entity's records only if it is

    A. Reasonably possible that a liability has been incurred and the amount of the loss is known.

    B. Probable that a liability has been incurred and the amount of the loss is unknown.

    C. Probable that a liability has been incurred and the amount of the loss can be reasonably estimated.

    D. Remotely probable that a liability has been incurred but the amount of the loss can be reasonably estimated.

Answer (C) is correct. *(CMA, adapted)*
    REQUIRED: The circumstance under which a loss contingency should be accrued.
    DISCUSSION: Loss contingencies should be accrued when information available prior to issuance of financial statements indicates that it is probable that an asset has been impaired or a liability has been incurred, and the amount of loss can be reasonably estimated. Probable is defined as a condition in which future events are likely to occur.
    Answer (A) is incorrect. An event is reasonably possible if the chance of occurrence is more than remote but less than probable. Accrual requires that the event be probable. Answer (B) is incorrect. The amount of the loss must be capable of reasonable estimation. Answer (D) is incorrect. An event is remote if the chance of occurrence is slight.

11.5.2. Conlon Co. is the plaintiff in a patent-infringement case. Conlon has a high probability of a favorable outcome and can reasonably estimate the amount of the settlement. What is the proper accounting treatment of the patent infringement case?

A. A gain contingency for the minimum estimated amount of the settlement.

B. A gain contingency for the estimated probable settlement.

C. Disclosure in the notes only.

D. No reporting is required at this time.

Answer (C) is correct. *(CPA, adapted)*
REQUIRED: The accounting if a plaintiff has a high probability of winning and the settlement can be reasonably estimated.
DISCUSSION: Under the conservatism restraint, when alternative accounting methods are appropriate, the one having the less favorable effect on net income and total assets is preferable. Thus, a loss, not a gain, contingency may be recorded in the financial statements. If the probability of realization of a gain is high, the contingency is disclosed in the notes.
Answer (A) is incorrect. A gain contingency is never recognized. Answer (B) is incorrect. A gain contingency is never recognized. Answer (D) is incorrect. Although contingencies that might result in gains are not accrued, some minimum disclosure is required.

11.5.3. Management can estimate the amount of loss that will occur if a foreign government expropriates some company assets. If expropriation is reasonably possible, a loss contingency should be

A. Disclosed but not accrued as a liability.

B. Disclosed and accrued as a liability.

C. Accrued as a liability but not disclosed.

D. Neither accrued as a liability nor disclosed.

Answer (A) is correct. *(CPA, adapted)*
REQUIRED: The reporting of a loss contingency that is reasonably possible.
DISCUSSION: A contingent loss that is reasonably possible but not probable is disclosed but not accrued. The disclosure indicates the nature of the contingency and gives an estimate of the loss or range of loss or states that an estimate cannot be made.
Answer (B) is incorrect. A contingent loss is accrued only if it is probable and reasonably estimable. Answer (C) is incorrect. If a loss is reasonably possible, it is disclosed but not accrued. Answer (D) is incorrect. A loss that is reasonably possible should be disclosed.

11.5.4. A manufacturer of household appliances may incur a loss due to the discovery of a defect in one of its products. The occurrence of the loss is reasonably possible and the resulting costs can be reasonably estimated. This possible loss should be

	Accrued	Disclosed in Notes
A.	Yes	No
B.	Yes	Yes
C.	No	Yes
D.	No	No

Answer (C) is correct. *(CPA, adapted)*
REQUIRED: The proper accounting for a contingent loss that is reasonably possible and reasonably estimable.
DISCUSSION: A contingent loss is accrued when two conditions are met: It is probable that at a balance sheet date an asset is overstated or a liability has been incurred, and the amount of the loss can be reasonably estimated. If both conditions are not met, but the probability of the loss is at least reasonably possible, the amount of the loss must be disclosed. This loss is reasonably possible and reasonably estimable, and it therefore should be disclosed but not accrued as a liability. The financial statements should disclose the nature of the loss contingency and the amount or range of the possible loss. If an estimate cannot be made, the notes should state this.
Answer (A) is incorrect. The contingent loss should be disclosed but not accrued. Answer (B) is incorrect. The contingent loss should not be accrued. Answer (D) is incorrect. The contingent loss should be disclosed.

11.5.5. When reporting contingencies,

A. A guarantee of another's indebtedness is accrued as a loss contingency only if the loss is considered imminent.

B. Disclosure of a loss contingency is to be made if there is a remote possibility that the loss has been incurred.

C. Disclosure of a loss contingency must include a dollar estimate of the loss.

D. A loss that is probable but not estimable must be disclosed with a notation that the amount of the loss cannot be estimated.

Answer (D) is correct. *(CMA, adapted)*
REQUIRED: The true statement about reporting contingencies.
DISCUSSION: Contingencies are probable (likely to occur), reasonably possible, or remote. When contingent losses are probable and the amount can be reasonably estimated, the amount of the loss should be recognized. If the amount cannot be reasonably estimated but the loss is at least reasonably possible, full disclosure should be made, including a statement that an estimate cannot be made.
Answer (A) is incorrect. A loss contingency is accrued when (1) it is probable (not necessarily imminent) that an asset has been impaired or a liability incurred and (2) the loss is reasonably estimable. Moreover, a guarantee of another's indebtedness must be disclosed even if the possibility of loss is remote. Answer (B) is incorrect. Remote contingencies ordinarily need not be disclosed. Answer (C) is incorrect. Disclosure need not include an amount when that amount cannot be reasonably estimated.

11.5.6. On December 20, Year 6, an uninsured property damage loss was caused by a company car being driven on company business by a company sales agent. The company did not become aware of the loss until January 25, Year 7, but the amount of the loss was reasonably estimable before the financial statements were issued. The company's December 31, Year 6, financial statements should report an estimated loss as

   A. A disclosure but not an accrual.

   B. An accrual.

   C. Neither an accrual nor a disclosure.

   D. An appropriation of retained earnings.

Answer (B) is correct. *(CPA, adapted)*
   REQUIRED: The manner of disclosure of a loss contingency.
   DISCUSSION: A loss contingency is an existing condition, situation, or set of circumstances involving uncertainty as to the impairment of an asset's value or the incurrence of a liability as of the balance sheet date. Resolution of the uncertainty depends on the occurrence or nonoccurence of one or more future events. A loss should be debited and either an asset valuation allowance or a liability credited when the loss contingency is both probable and reasonably estimable. The loss should be accrued even though the company was not aware of the contingency at the balance sheet date.
   Answer (A) is incorrect. Disclosure alone would suffice only if the loss had occurred after December 31. Answer (C) is incorrect. A loss that is both probable and reasonably estimable must always be disclosed. Accrual depends on the timing of the loss. Answer (D) is incorrect. The loss must be charged to income.

11.5.7. Ace Co. settled litigation on February 1, Year 2, for an event that occurred during Year 1. An estimated liability was determined as of December 31, Year 1. This estimate was significantly less than the final settlement. The transaction is considered to be material. The year-end financial statements for Year 1 have not been issued. How should the settlement be reported in Ace's Year 1 financial statements?

   A. Disclosure only of the settlement.

   B. Only an accrual of the settlement.

   C. Neither a disclosure nor an accrual.

   D. Both a disclosure and an accrual.

Answer (D) is correct. *(CPA, adapted)*
   REQUIRED: The treatment of a loss contingency.
   DISCUSSION: A contingent loss must be accrued when, based on information available prior to the issuance of the financial statements, two conditions are met: (1) It is probable that an asset has been impaired or a liability has been incurred at a balance sheet date, and (2) the amount of the loss can be reasonably estimated. Because the liability was settled before the financial statements were issued, it was certain that a liability had been incurred, and the amount could be specifically determined. Thus, the contingent loss must be accrued. Disclosure of the amount of the accrual is necessary to keep the financial statements from being misleading, given that the settlement was significantly greater than expected.
   Answer (A) is incorrect. The settlement amount must also be accrued. Answer (B) is incorrect. The settlement must also be disclosed. Answer (C) is incorrect. The settlement must be disclosed and accrued.

11.5.8. During Year 3, Manfred Corp. guaranteed a supplier's $500,000 loan from a bank. On October 1, Year 4, Manfred was notified that the supplier had defaulted on the loan and filed for bankruptcy protection. Counsel believes Manfred will probably have to pay between $250,000 and $450,000 under its guarantee. As a result of the supplier's bankruptcy, Manfred entered into a contract in December Year 4 to retool its machines so that Manfred could accept parts from other suppliers. Retooling costs are estimated to be $300,000. What amount should Manfred report as a liability in its December 31, Year 4, balance sheet?

   A. $250,000

   B. $450,000

   C. $550,000

   D. $750,000

Answer (A) is correct. *(CPA, adapted)*
   REQUIRED: The amount reported as a liability.
   DISCUSSION: A contingent loss is accrued when two conditions are met: It is probable that, at a balance sheet date, an asset is overstated or a liability has been incurred, and the amount of the loss can be reasonably estimated. If the estimate is stated within a given range and no amount within that range appears to be a better estimate than any other, the minimum of the range should be accrued. Hence, the minimum amount ($250,000) of the probable payment under the guarantee should be accrued as a liability. The retooling costs will be charged to the equipment account when incurred because they significantly improve the future service of the machines.
   Answer (B) is incorrect. This figure is the maximum amount of the estimated range of loss. Answer (C) is incorrect. The amount of $550,000 includes the retooling costs. Answer (D) is incorrect. The amount of $750,000 equals the retooling costs plus the maximum amount of the estimated range of loss.

11.5.9. In January Year 2, an explosion occurred at Slim Co.'s plant, causing damage to area properties. By March 10, Year 2, no claims had yet been asserted against Slim. However, Slim's management and legal counsel concluded that it was reasonably possible that Slim would be held responsible for negligence, and that $3 million would be a reasonable estimate of the damages. Slim's $5 million comprehensive public liability policy contains a $300,000 deductible clause. In Slim's December 31, Year 1, financial statements, for which the auditor's field work was completed in April Year 2, how should this casualty be reported?

A. As a note to the financial statements disclosing a possible liability of $3 million.

B. As an accrued liability of $300,000.

C. As a note to the financial statements disclosing a possible liability of $300,000.

D. No disclosure in the notes or accrual is required for Year 1 because the event occurred in Year 2.

Answer (C) is correct. *(CPA, adapted)*
REQUIRED: The accounting for a reasonably possible contingent loss covered by a liability policy.
DISCUSSION: If a loss contingency is not both probable and reasonably estimable but is at least reasonably possible, it should be disclosed but not accrued. This requirement applies when no claims have been asserted if management believes that the loss may occur. Moreover, the condition for accrual that an asset be impaired or a liability be incurred at the date of the financial statements has not been met. The amount of the loss to be disclosed by Slim Co. equals the amount of the company's potential liability. The comprehensive public liability policy has a $300,000 deductible clause, and the policy is sufficient to cover the reasonable estimate of the liability. The company should therefore disclose in a note the possible loss of $300,000.
Answer (A) is incorrect. The possible loss to the company is limited to the $300,000 deductible. Answer (B) is incorrect. A reasonably possible loss should not be accrued. Answer (D) is incorrect. Disclosure in the notes is required to prevent the financial statements from being misleading even though no asset was impaired and no liability was incurred at the balance sheet date.

11.5.10. On February 5, Year 2, an employee filed a $2 million lawsuit against Steel Co. for damages suffered when one of Steel's plants exploded on December 29, Year 1. Steel's legal counsel expects the company will lose the lawsuit and estimates the loss to be between $500,000 and $1 million. The employee has offered to settle the lawsuit out of court for $900,000, but Steel will not agree to the settlement. In its December 31, Year 1, balance sheet, what amount should Steel report as liability from lawsuit?

A. $2,000,000

B. $1,000,000

C. $900,000

D. $500,000

Answer (D) is correct. *(CPA, adapted)*
REQUIRED: The contingent loss that should be accrued when a range of estimates is provided.
DISCUSSION: Because the loss is probable and can be reasonably estimated, it should be accrued if the amount is material. If the estimate is stated within a given range, and no amount within that range appears to be a better estimate than any other, the minimum of the range should be accrued. Thus, Steel should report a $500,000 contingent liability.
Answer (A) is incorrect. The minimum of the range should be accrued. Answer (B) is incorrect. The minimum of the range should be accrued. Answer (C) is incorrect. The amount of $900,000 is the proposed settlement amount.

11.5.11. On November 10, Year 4, a Garry Corp. truck was in an accident with an auto driven by Dacey. On January 10, Year 5, Garry received notice of a lawsuit seeking $800,000 in damages for personal injuries suffered by Dacey. Garry Corp.'s counsel believes it is reasonably possible that Dacey will be awarded an estimated amount in the range between $250,000 and $500,000, and that $400,000 is a better estimate of potential liability than any other amount. Garry's accounting year ends on December 31, and the Year 4 financial statements were issued on March 6, Year 5. What amount of loss should Garry accrue at December 31, Year 4?

A. $0

B. $250,000

C. $400,000

D. $500,000

Answer (A) is correct. *(CPA, adapted)*
REQUIRED: The proper accounting for a contingent loss that is reasonably possible and can be estimated within a range.
DISCUSSION: A contingent loss is accrued when it is probable that, at a balance sheet date, an asset is overstated or a liability has been incurred and the amount of the loss can be reasonably estimated. If both conditions are not met but the probability of the loss is at least reasonably possible, the amount of the loss must be disclosed. This loss is reasonably possible and reasonably estimable. Hence, it should be disclosed but not accrued.
Answer (B) is incorrect. No loss should be accrued. Answer (C) is incorrect. No loss should be accrued. Answer (D) is incorrect. No loss should be accrued.

11.5.12. Invern, Inc., has a self-insurance plan. Each year, retained earnings is appropriated for contingencies in an amount equal to insurance premiums saved less recognized losses from lawsuits and other claims. As a result of a Year 4 accident, Invern is a defendant in a lawsuit in which it will probably have to pay damages of $190,000. What are the effects of this lawsuit's probable outcome on Invern's Year 4 financial statements?

A. An increase in expenses and no effect on liabilities.

B. An increase in both expenses and liabilities.

C. No effect on expenses and an increase in liabilities.

D. No effect on either expenses or liabilities.

Answer (B) is correct. *(CPA, adapted)*
REQUIRED: The effect on the financial statements of litigation with a probable unfavorable outcome.
DISCUSSION: A loss contingency is an existing condition, situation, or set of circumstances involving uncertainty as to the impairment of an asset's value or the incurrence of a liability as of the balance sheet date. Resolution of the uncertainty depends on the occurrence or nonoccurence of one or more future events. A loss should be debited and either an asset valuation allowance or a liability credited when the loss contingency is both probable and reasonably estimable. Thus, the company should accrue a loss and a liability.
Answer (A) is incorrect. The company should also accrue a liability. Answer (C) is incorrect. The company should accrue a loss and a liability. Answer (D) is incorrect. The company should also accrue a loss.

11.5.13. Seller-Guarantor sold an asset with a carrying amount at the time of sale of $500,000 to Buyer for $650,000 in cash. Seller also provided a guarantee to Guarantee Bank of the $600,000 loan that Guarantee made to Buyer to finance the sale. The probability that Seller will become liable under the guarantee is remote. In a stand-alone arm's-length transaction with an unrelated party, the premium required by Seller to provide the same guarantee would have been $40,000. The entry made by Seller at the time of the sale should include a

A. Gain of $150,000.

B. Noncontingent liability of $40,000.

C. Contingent liability of $600,000.

D. Loss of $450,000.

Answer (B) is correct. *(Publisher, adapted)*
REQUIRED: The entry made to reflect sale of an asset and the seller's guarantee of the buyer's debt.
DISCUSSION: No contingent liability results because the likelihood of payment by the guarantor is remote. However, a noncontingent liability is recognized at the inception of the seller's obligation to stand ready to perform during the term of the guarantee. This liability is initially measured at fair value. In a multiple-element transaction with an unrelated party, the fair value is estimated, for example, as the premium required by the guarantor to provide the same guarantee in a stand-alone arm's-length transaction with an unrelated party. The amount of that premium is given as $40,000. Hence, Seller debits cash for the total received ($650,000), credits the asset sold for its carrying amount ($500,000), credits the noncontingent liability for its estimated fair value ($40,000), and credits a gain for $110,000 ($650,000 – $500,000 – $40,000).
Answer (A) is incorrect. A gain of $150,000 assumes neither a noncontingent nor a contingent liability is recognized. Answer (C) is incorrect. No contingent liability is recognized. The likelihood of payment is remote, not probable. Answer (D) is incorrect. A loss of $450,000 assumes recognition of a contingent liability of $600,000.

11.5.14. In Year 4, a contract dispute between Doll Co. and Brooker Co. was submitted to binding arbitration. In Year 4, each party's attorney indicated privately that the probable award in Doll's favor could be reasonably estimated. In Year 5, the arbitrator decided in favor of Doll. When should Doll and Brooker recognize their respective gain and loss?

	Doll's Gain	Brooker's Loss
A.	Year 4	Year 4
B.	Year 4	Year 5
C.	Year 5	Year 4
D.	Year 5	Year 5

Answer (C) is correct. *(CPA, adapted)*
REQUIRED: The proper accounting for a contingent gain or loss that is probable and capable of reasonable estimation.
DISCUSSION: A contingent loss is accrued when two conditions are met: (1) It is probable that at a balance sheet date an asset is overstated or a liability has been incurred, and (2) the amount of the loss can be reasonably estimated. Gain contingencies should not be recognized until they are realized. A gain contingency should be disclosed, but care should be taken to avoid misleading implications as to the likelihood of realization. Because the award in favor of Doll is probable and can be reasonably estimated, a loss should be recognized in Year 4 by Brooker. However, Doll should not recognize the gain until Year 5.

11.5.15. During January, Haze Corp. won a litigation award for $15,000 that was tripled to $45,000 to include punitive damages. The defendant, who is financially stable, has appealed only the $30,000 punitive damages. Haze was awarded $50,000 in an unrelated suit it filed, which is being appealed by the defendant. Counsel is unable to estimate the outcome of these appeals. In its current year financial statements, Haze should report what amount of pretax gain?

A. $15,000

B. $45,000

C. $50,000

D. $95,000

Answer (A) is correct. *(CPA, adapted)*
REQUIRED: The amount of pretax gain from litigation.
DISCUSSION: Gain contingencies should not be recognized until they are realized. A gain contingency should be disclosed, but care should be taken to avoid misleading implications as to the likelihood of realization. Consequently, the only litigation award to be recognized in income in the current year is the $15,000 amount that has not been appealed. The other awards have not been realized because they have been appealed.
Answer (B) is incorrect. The amount of $45,000 includes the punitive damages that have been appealed. Answer (C) is incorrect. This figure is the amount of the award in the unrelated suit that has been appealed. Answer (D) is incorrect. The amount of $95,000 includes the punitive damages and the amount of the award in the unrelated suit. Both have been appealed.

11.5.16. In May Year 1, Caso Co. filed suit against Wayne, Inc., seeking $1.9 million damages for patent infringement. A court verdict in November Year 4 awarded Caso $1.5 million in damages, but Wayne's appeal is not expected to be decided before Year 6. Caso's counsel believes it is probable that Caso will be successful against Wayne for an estimated amount in the range between $800,000 and $1.1 million, with $1 million considered the most likely amount. What amount should Caso record as income from the lawsuit in the year ended December 31, Year 4?

A. $0

B. $800,000

C. $1,000,000

D. $1,500,000

Answer (A) is correct. *(CPA, adapted)*
REQUIRED: The amount of income recorded from the lawsuit.
DISCUSSION: Gain contingencies are not recognized until they are realized. Because the appeal is not expected to be decided before Year 6, Caso should not record any revenue from the lawsuit in the Year 4 income statement. This gain contingency should be disclosed; however, care should be taken to avoid misleading implications as to the likelihood of realization.
Answer (B) is incorrect. Gains should not be recognized until they are realized. Answer (C) is incorrect. Gains should not be recognized until they are realized. Answer (D) is incorrect. Gains should not be recognized until they are realized.

11.5.17. Green Co. was preparing its year-end financial statements. Green had a pending lawsuit against a competitor for $5,000,000 in damages. Green's attorneys indicate that obtaining a favorable judgment was probable and the amount of damages is reasonably estimated. Green incurred $100,000 in legal fees. The income tax rate was 30%. What amount, if any, should Green recognize as a contingency gain in its financial statements?

A. $0

B. $3,430,000

C. $3,500,000

D. $4,900,000

Answer (A) is correct. *(CPA, adapted)*
REQUIRED: The contingency gain recognized.
DISCUSSION: Gain contingencies are recognized only when realized. A probable favorable judgment and reasonably estimated amount of damages may be disclosed in the notes to the financial statements, but no amount should be recognized as a contingency gain until realized.
Answer (B) is incorrect. The amount of $3,430,000 includes the full $5,000,000 of damages expected from the lawsuit, less the $100,000 in legal fess, less the 30% income tax expense. However, gain contingencies are recognized only when realized. Answer (C) is incorrect. The amount of $3,500,000 includes the full $5,000,000 of damages expected from the lawsuit, net of tax. However, gain contingencies are recognized only when realized. Answer (D) is incorrect. The amount of $4,900,000 includes the full $5,000,000 of damages expected from the lawsuit, less the $100,000 in legal fees. However, gain contingencies are recognized only when realized.

11.6 Warranties

11.6.1. Kamchatka sells a durable good on January 1, Year 1, and the customer is automatically given a 1-year standard warranty against manufacturing defects. The customer also buys an extended warranty package, extending the coverage for an additional 2 years to the end of Year 3. At the time of the original sale, the company expects warranty costs to be incurred evenly over the life of the warranty contracts. The customer has only one warranty claim during the 3-year period, and the claim occurs during Year 2. The company will recognize revenue from the sale of the extended warranty

A. On January 1, Year 1.

B. In Years 2 and 3.

C. At the time of the claim in Year 2.

D. December 31, Year 3, when the warranty expires.

Answer (B) is correct. *(CIA, adapted)*
REQUIRED: The recognition of revenue from the sale of an extended warranty.
DISCUSSION: Because the extended warranty was purchased separately, it is classified as a service-type warranty. Revenue from a service-type warranty is recognized over the coverage period. Because warranty costs are expected to be incurred evenly over the life of the warranty contracts, the revenue should be recognized on the straight-line basis over the life of the extended warranty contract.
Answer (A) is incorrect. The recognition of revenue from the sale of the extended warranty is deferred until the extended warranty period begins. Answer (C) is incorrect. The revenue should be recognized evenly over the life of the contract. It is not related to the timing of the claims. Answer (D) is incorrect. Revenue is recognized over the life of the warranty, not at expiration.

11.6.2. Vadis Co. sells appliances that include a standard 3-year assurance-type warranty. Service calls under the warranty are performed by an independent mechanic under a contract with Vadis. Based on experience, warranty costs are estimated at $30 for each machine sold. When should Vadis recognize these warranty costs?

A. Evenly over the life of the warranty.

B. When the service calls are performed.

C. When payments are made to the mechanic.

D. When the machines are sold.

Answer (D) is correct. *(CPA, adapted)*
REQUIRED: The recording of warranty costs.
DISCUSSION: An assurance-type warranty creates a loss contingency. Under the accrual method, a provision for warranty costs is made when the related revenue is recognized.
Answer (A) is incorrect. The accrual method matches the costs and the related revenues. Answer (B) is incorrect. When the warranty costs can be reasonably estimated, the accrual method should be used. Recognizing the costs when the service calls are performed is the cash basis. Answer (C) is incorrect. Recognizing costs when paid is the cash basis.

11.6.3. Salvador Co. sold 800,000 electronic can openers in Year 1. Based on past experience, the company estimated that 10,000 of the 800,000 would prove to be defective and that 60% of these would be returned for replacement under the company's standard warranty against manufacturing defects. The cost to replace an electronic can opener is $6.00.

On January 1, Year 1, the balance in the company's estimated liability for warranties account was $3,000. During Year 1, 5,000 electronic can openers were replaced under the warranty. The estimated liability for warranties reported on December 31, Year 1, should be

A. $6,000

B. $9,000

C. $36,000

D. $39,000

Answer (B) is correct. *(O. Broome, Jr.)*
REQUIRED: The year-end estimated liability for warranties.
DISCUSSION: A standard warranty against manufacturing defects is an assurance-type warranty. This warranty creates a loss contingency. A liability for warranty costs is recognized on the date the product is sold. At the time of the sale of each electronic can opener, it is probable that a warranty liability has been incurred and its amount can be reasonably estimated. Consequently, a warranty expense should be recognized with a corresponding credit to an estimated liability for warranties account. As indicated below, the 1/1/Year 1 balance in this account is $3,000. It was increased during Year 1 by $36,000 (10,000 estimated defective can openers × $6 replacement fee × 60% estimated replacement rate). The account should be decreased by $30,000 (5,000 openers replaced × $6). Thus, the ending balance is $9,000.

Estimated Liability for Warranties		
	$ 3,000	1/1/Year 1
Replacements $30,000	36,000	Warranty expense
	$ 9,000	12/31/Year 1

Answer (A) is incorrect. The amount of $6,000 is the balance if you ignore the $3,000 balance already in the account. Answer (C) is incorrect. The amount of $36,000 is the estimated liability recorded when the can openers are sold. Answer (D) is incorrect. The amount of $39,000 is the balance in the estimated liability for warranties account before it is adjusted for the actual replacement costs incurred.

11.6.4. During Year 1, Gum Co. introduced a new product carrying a standard 2-year warranty against defects. The estimated warranty costs related to dollar sales are 2% within 12 months following the sale and 4% in the second 12 months following the sale. Sales and actual warranty expenditures for the years ended December 31, Year 1 and Year 2, are as follows:

	Sales	Actual Warranty Expenditures
Year 1	$150,000	$2,250
Year 2	250,000	7,500
	$400,000	$9,750

What amount should Gum report as estimated warranty liability in its December 31, Year 2, balance sheet?

A. $2,500

B. $3,250

C. $11,250

D. $14,250

Answer (D) is correct. *(CPA, adapted)*
REQUIRED: The estimated warranty liability at the end of the second year.
DISCUSSION: A standard warranty against manufacturing defects is an assurance-type warranty. This warranty creates a loss contingency. A liability for warranty costs is recognized on the date the product is sold. Because this product is new, the beginning balance in the estimated warranty liability account at the beginning of Year 1 is $0. For Year 1, the estimated warranty costs related to dollar sales are 6% (2% + 4%) of sales, or $9,000 ($150,000 × 6%). For Year 2, the estimated warranty costs are $15,000 ($250,000 × 6%). These amounts are charged to warranty expense and credited to the estimated warranty liability account. This liability account is debited for expenditures of $2,250 and $7,500 in Year 1 and Year 2, respectively. Hence, the estimated warranty liability at 12/31/Year 2 is $14,250.

Estimated Liability for Warranties			
		$ 0	1/1/Year 2
Year 1 expenditures	$2,250	9,000	Year 1 expense
Year 2 expenditures	$7,500	15,000	Year 2 expense
		$14,250	12/31/Year 2

Answer (A) is incorrect. The amount of $2,500 is equal to 10% of Year 2 sales. Answer (B) is incorrect. The amount of $3,250 is equal to 2% of Year 1 sales, plus 4% of Year 2 sales, minus the $9,750 in actual expenses incurred. Answer (C) is incorrect. The amount of $11,250 is the sum of Year 1's actual expenditures of $2,250 and the Year 1 warranty expense of $9,000.

11.6.5. The selling price of a new company's units is $20,000 each. The buyers are provided with a 2-year assurance-type warranty that is expected to cost the company $500 per unit in the year of the sale and $1,500 per unit in the year following the sale. The company sold 160 units in the first year of operation and 200 units in the second year. Actual payments for warranty claims were $40,000 and $260,000 in Years 1 and 2, respectively. The amount charged to warranty expense during the second year of operation is

A. $100,000

B. $260,000

C. $340,000

D. $400,000

Answer (D) is correct. *(CIA, adapted)*
REQUIRED: The amount charged to warranty expense during the second year of operation.
DISCUSSION: Under the accrual method, the total estimated warranty costs are charged to operating expense in the year of sale. The total estimated warranty cost per unit is $2,000 ($500 + $1,500). In Year 2, 200 units were sold, so the warranty expense recognized is $400,000.
Answer (A) is incorrect. The expected amount of warranty claims for the first year of the warranty from second-year sales is $100,000. Answer (B) is incorrect. The actual amount of claims in the second year is $260,000. Answer (C) is incorrect. The expected amount of warranty claims in the second year is $340,000.

11.7 Coupons and Premiums

11.7.1. A department store sells gift cards that may be redeemed for merchandise. Each card expires 3 years after issuance. The revenue from the gift cards should be recognized

A. Evenly over 3 years from the date of issuance.

B. In the period the cards are sold.

C. In the period the cards expire.

D. In the period the cards are redeemed or in the period they expire if they are allowed to lapse.

Answer (D) is correct. *(CIA, adapted)*
REQUIRED: The timing of revenue recognition for gift cards.
DISCUSSION: A deposit or other advance is initially recognized as a contract liability. Revenue from gift cards is realized when the cash is received. It is earned (the performance obligation is satisfied) when the cards are redeemed or allowed to lapse. Thus, the criteria of being both realized and earned are satisfied when the cards are redeemed or allowed to lapse.
Answer (A) is incorrect. The revenue from the cards is not earned evenly over 3 years. Answer (B) is incorrect. The revenue from the cards is not earned when the cards are sold. Answer (C) is incorrect. The revenue is also recognized in the period the cards are redeemed.

11.7.2. Conch Shell Company sells gift cards, redeemable for merchandise, that expire 1 year after their issuance. Conch Shell has the following information pertaining to its gift cards sales and redemptions:

Unredeemed at 12/31/Year 1	$150,000
Year 2 sales	500,000
Year 2 redemptions of prior-year sales	50,000
Year 2 redemptions of current-year sales	350,000

Conch Shell's experience indicates that 10% of gift certificates sold will not be redeemed. In its December 31, Year 2, balance sheet, what amount should Conch Shell report as deferred revenue?

- A. $250,000
- B. $200,000
- C. $150,000
- D. $100,000

Answer (D) is correct. *(CPA, adapted)*
REQUIRED: The amount reported as deferred revenue at year end.
DISCUSSION: Because the cards expire after 1 year, all revenue from sales prior to Year 2 has been earned. Thus, the unearned revenue balance for gift card sales at the end of Year 2 relates solely to Year 2 sales. Given Year 2 sales of $500,000 and redemptions of $350,000, $150,000 of cards are unredeemed at year end. However, 10% of total cards sold in Year 2 ($500,000 × 10% = $50,000) are not expected to be redeemed. Accordingly, deferred revenue is $100,000 ($150,000 – $50,000).
Answer (A) is incorrect. The amount of $250,000 is the sum of the beginning and ending balances. Answer (B) is incorrect. The amount of $200,000 assumes that none of the cards reflected in the beginning balance have lapsed but that 10% of the cards sold in Year 2 are expected to lapse. Answer (C) is incorrect. The amount of $150,000 does not consider the 10% of cards sold in Year 2 that are estimated not to be redeemed.

11.7.3. Dunn Trading Stamp Company records stamp service revenue and provides for the cost of redemptions in the year stamps are sold to licensees. Dunn's past experience indicates that only 80% of the stamps sold to licensees will be redeemed. Dunn's liability for stamp redemptions was $6 million at December 31, Year 3. Additional information for Year 4 is as follows:

Stamp service revenue from stamps sold to licensees	$4,000,000
Cost of redemptions (stamps sold prior to 1/1/Yr 4)	2,750,000

If all the stamps sold in Year 4 were presented for redemption in Year 5, the redemption cost would be $2,250,000. What amount should Dunn report as a liability for stamp redemptions at December 31, Year 4?

- A. $7,250,000
- B. $5,500,000
- C. $5,050,000
- D. $3,250,000

Answer (C) is correct. *(CPA, adapted)*
REQUIRED: The reported liability for stamp redemptions at year end.
DISCUSSION: The liability for stamp redemptions at the beginning of Year 4 is given as $6 million. This liability would be increased in Year 4 by $2,250,000 if all stamps sold in Year 4 were presented for redemption. However, because only 80% are expected to be redeemed, the liability should be increased by $1,800,000 ($2,250,000 × 80%). The liability was decreased by the $2,750,000 attributable to the costs of redemptions. Thus, the liability for stamp redemptions at December 31, Year 4, is $5,050,000 ($6,000,000 + $1,800,000 – $2,750,000).
Answer (A) is incorrect. The amount of $7,250,000 equals the beginning balance, plus stamp service revenue, minus redemptions of stamps sold before Year 4. Answer (B) is incorrect. The amount of $5,500,000 is based on an expected 100% redemption rate. Answer (D) is incorrect. The amount of $3,250,000 assumes that no stamps were sold in Year 4.

11.7.4. In June Year 1, Northan Retailers sold refundable merchandise coupons. Northan received $10 for each coupon redeemable from July 1 to December 31, Year 1, for merchandise with a retail price of $11. At June 30, Year 1, how should Northan report these coupon transactions?

- A. Unearned revenues at the merchandise's retail price.
- B. Unearned revenues at the cash received amount.
- C. Revenues at the merchandise's retail price.
- D. Revenues at the cash received amount.

Answer (B) is correct. *(CPA, adapted)*
REQUIRED: The reporting of refundable merchandise coupons.
DISCUSSION: Revenue should be recognized when (or as) the related performance obligation is satisfied (e.g., when the coupons lapse or are redeemed). An unearned revenue (a contract liability) should be credited at the time of sale for the amount received.
Answer (A) is incorrect. The transaction is measured at the amount received, not the nominal retail price. Answer (C) is incorrect. Revenue is not realized or realizable and earned at June 30, Year 1, so it cannot be recognized. Answer (D) is incorrect. Revenue should not be recognized until it is realized or realizable and earned.

11.8 IFRS

11.8.1. Because of a defect discovered in its seat belts in December Year 1, an automobile manufacturer believes it is probable that it will be required to recall its products. The final decision on the recall is expected to be made in March Year 2. The cost of the recall is reliably estimated to be $2.5 million. How should this information be reported in the December 31, Year 1, financial statements?

A. As a loss of $2.5 million and a provision of $2.5 million.

B. As an adjustment of the opening balance of retained earnings equal to $2.5 million.

C. As an appropriation of retained earnings of $2.5 million.

D. It should not be disclosed because it has not yet happened.

Answer (A) is correct. *(CIA, adapted)*
REQUIRED: The reporting of a probable loss from a product recall.
DISCUSSION: A provision is a liability of uncertain timing or amount. Recognition of provisions is appropriate when (1) the entity has a legal or constructive present obligation resulting from a past event (called an obligating event), (2) it is probable that an outflow of economic benefits will be necessary to settle the obligation, and (3) its amount can be reliably estimated. Consequently, the entity must recognize a loss and a liability for $2.5 million.
Answer (B) is incorrect. An adjustment of beginning retained earnings is not appropriate. A loss should be recognized because it is probable and can be reliably estimated. Answer (C) is incorrect. An appropriation of retained earnings is permissible although not required, but the entity must still recognize a loss and a provision. Moreover, no part of the appropriation may be transferred to income, and no loss may be charged to an appropriation of retained earnings. Answer (D) is incorrect. If the loss is probable and can be reliably estimated, it should be recognized by a charge to income.

11.8.2. An entity is currently being sued by a customer. A reliable estimate can be made of the costs that would result from a ruling unfavorable to the entity, and the amount involved is material. The entity's managers, lawyers, and auditors agree that the likelihood of an unfavorable ruling is remote. This contingent liability

A. Should be disclosed in a note.

B. Should be disclosed as a parenthetical comment in the balance sheet.

C. Need not be disclosed.

D. Should be disclosed by an appropriation of retained earnings.

Answer (C) is correct. *(Publisher, adapted)*
REQUIRED: The treatment of a contingent liability that is reliably estimable but remote in probability.
DISCUSSION: A contingent liability includes a present obligation for which an outflow of resources embodying economic benefits is not probable. A contingent liability is not recognized but is disclosed unless the possibility of the outflow is remote.

11.8.3. A company had $100,000 in current liabilities at the end of the current year. The company refinanced this liability on a noncurrent basis subsequent to the end of the year but before the financial statements were issued. How should this liability be presented, according to IFRS and U.S. GAAP, in the company's year-end financial statements?

A. In current liabilities under IFRS and in noncurrent liabilities under U.S. GAAP.

B. In current liabilities under IFRS and U.S. GAAP.

C. In noncurrent liabilities under IFRS and U.S. GAAP.

D. In noncurrent liabilities under IFRS and in current liabilities under U.S. GAAP.

Answer (A) is correct. *(Publisher, adapted)*
REQUIRED: The presentation of current and noncurrent liabilities.
DISCUSSION: Under U.S. GAAP, a current liability is classified as noncurrent if the entity (1) intends to refinance on a noncurrent basis and (2) demonstrates an ability to complete such refinancing. The ability to refinance may be demonstrated by entering into an agreement to refinance or to reschedule payments on a long-term basis. Such an agreement may be completed after the reporting date but before the financial statements are issued. Under IFRS, a current liability may be classified as noncurrent only if the agreement to refinance or reschedule payments on a noncurrent basis is completed before the reporting date.
Answer (B) is incorrect. Under U.S. GAAP, the liability should be reported as noncurrent. The refinancing agreement was completed before the financial statements were issued. Answer (C) is incorrect. Under IFRS, the liability must continue to be presented in current liabilities. The refinancing agreement was completed after the reporting date. Answer (D) is incorrect. The refinancing agreement was completed after the reporting date. Thus, the liability must continue to be reported in current liabilities under IFRS. The liability is reported in noncurrent liabilities under U.S. GAAP. It was refinanced before the financial statements were issued.

STUDY UNIT TWELVE
NONCURRENT LIABILITIES

This study unit covers traditional noncurrent liabilities (bonds and notes), including some securities that have characteristics of debt and equity. A **bond** is a formal contract to pay an amount of money (called the par value, maturity amount, or face amount) to the holder of the bond at a certain date. Also, a bond ordinarily pays cash interest at specified intervals based on a percentage (the stated rate or coupon rate) of the face amount. The following topics related to bonds are commonly tested: (1) calculation of the proceeds from issuing the bonds, (2) presentation of bonds in the financial statements, (3) calculation of interest costs on bonds using the effective interest method, and (4) conversion of debt to equity.

Other topics related to noncurrent liabilities are (1) extinguishment of debt, (2) noncurrent notes payable with different patterns of repayment, (3) troubled debt restructuring, and (4) asset retirement obligations.

QUESTIONS
12.1 Bonds

12.1.1. When purchasing a bond, the present value of the bond's expected net future cash inflows discounted at the market rate of interest provides what information about the bond?

A. Price.

B. Par.

C. Yield.

D. Interest.

Answer (A) is correct. *(CPA, adapted)*
REQUIRED: The present value of a bond's expected net future cash inflows discounted at the market rate.
DISCUSSION: The issue price of a bond is based on the market interest rate and reflects its fair value. The proceeds received from the sale of a bond equal the sum of the present values of the face amount and the interest payment (if the bond is interest-bearing). When bonds are issued between interest payment dates, the buyer includes accrued interest in the purchase price.
Answer (B) is incorrect. Par is the maturity amount. Answer (C) is incorrect. Yield is the effective interest rate. Answer (D) is incorrect. Interest is the amount of cash paid as interest.

12.1.2. When the effective interest method of amortization is used for bonds issued at a premium, the amount of interest payable for an interest period is calculated by multiplying the

A. Face value of the bonds at the beginning of the period by the contractual interest rate.

B. Face value of the bonds at the beginning of the period by the effective interest rates.

C. Carrying value of the bonds at the beginning of the period by the contractual interest rate.

D. Carrying value of the bonds at the beginning of the period by the effective interest rates.

Answer (A) is correct. *(CPA, adapted)*
REQUIRED: The calculation of interest payable for bonds issued at a premium using the effective interest method.
DISCUSSION: Interest payable does not vary with the issue price of bonds. It equals their face amount times the stated (contractual) rate at the beginning of the period.
Answer (B) is incorrect. The contractual rate and the face amount determine the amount payable. The effective rate and the carrying amount determine the amount of interest expense. Answer (C) is incorrect. The contractual rate and nominal (face) amount determine the amount of bonds payable. The carrying amount and the effective rate determine the amount of interest expense. Answer (D) is incorrect. The carrying amount and the effective rate determine the amount of interest expense.

12.1.3. Perk, Inc., issued $500,000, 10% bonds to yield 8%. Bond issuance costs were $10,000. How should Perk calculate the net proceeds to be received from the issuance?

A. Discount the bonds at the stated rate of interest.

B. Discount the bonds at the market rate of interest.

C. Discount the bonds at the stated rate of interest and deduct bond issuance costs.

D. Discount the bonds at the market rate of interest and deduct bond issuance costs.

Answer (D) is correct. *(CPA, adapted)*
REQUIRED: The net proceeds to be received from the issuance.
DISCUSSION: The gross proceeds from the sale of bonds consist of the sum of the present values of the maturity amount and the interest payments discounted using the market rate of interest. The net proceeds equal the price of the bonds minus the issue costs. Issue costs are incurred to bring a bond to market and include printing and engraving costs, legal fees, accountants' fees, underwriters' commissions, registration fees, and promotion costs.
Answer (A) is incorrect. The bonds should be discounted at the market rate, and the net proceeds equal the price (cash flows discounted at the market rate) minus the issue costs. Answer (B) is incorrect. The net proceeds equal the price (cash flows discounted at the market rate) minus the issue costs. Answer (C) is incorrect. The bonds should be discounted at the market rate.

12.1.4. York Corp.'s December 31, Year 3, balance sheet contained the following items in the noncurrent liabilities section:

9 3/4% registered debentures, callable in Year 14, due in Year 19	$1,400,000
9 1/2% collateral trust bonds, convertible into common stock beginning in Year 12, due in Year 22	1,200,000
10% subordinated debentures ($60,000 maturing annually beginning in Year 9)	600,000

What is the total amount of York's term bonds?

A. $1,200,000

B. $1,400,000

C. $2,000,000

D. $2,600,000

Answer (D) is correct. *(CPA, adapted)*
REQUIRED: The total amount of term bonds.
DISCUSSION: Term bonds mature on a single date. Hence, the registered bonds and the collateral trust bonds are term bonds, a total of $2,600,000 ($1,400,000 + $1,200,000).
Answer (A) is incorrect. The registered bonds are also term bonds. Answer (B) is incorrect. The collateral trust bonds are also term bonds. Answer (C) is incorrect. The collateral trust bonds, not the subordinated debentures, are term bonds.

12.1.5. A bond issued on June 1, Year 1, has interest payment dates of April 1 and October 1. Bond interest expense for the year ended December 31, Year 1, is for a period of

A. Three months.

B. Four months.

C. Six months.

D. Seven months.

Answer (D) is correct. *(CPA, adapted)*
REQUIRED: The period for which interest expense is recognized when a bond is issued between interest payment dates.
DISCUSSION: Bond interest expense is for the 7 months from June 1, Year 1, through December 31, Year 1, that the bond was outstanding. When bonds are sold between interest payment dates, the buyer pays the issuer the interest accrued since the last payment date. The bond was issued on June 1, Year 1, with interest payment dates of April 1 and October 1. Because the issuer will pay 6 months of interest on October 1, the buyer pays the 2 months of interest (April and May of Year 1) since the last payment date (April 1).
Answer (A) is incorrect. Bond interest is not paid for the 3 months prior to the first interest payment date (April 1). Answer (B) is incorrect. The bond was outstanding for 4 months between April 1, Year 1, and October 1, Year 1. Answer (C) is incorrect. Bond interest is paid every 6 months for the term of the bond.

12.1.6. Cornwall Co.'s December 31, Year 3, balance sheet contained the following items in the noncurrent liabilities section:

Unsecured

9.375% registered bonds ($50,000 maturing annually beginning in Year 7)	$550,000
11.5% convertible bonds, callable beginning in Year 12, due Year 23	250,000

Secured

9.875% guaranty security bonds, due Year 23	$500,000
10.0% commodity-backed bonds ($100,000 maturing annually beginning in Year 8)	400,000

What are the total amounts of serial bonds and debenture bonds?

	Serial Bonds	Debenture Bonds
A.	$950,000	$800,000
B.	$950,000	$250,000
C.	$900,000	$800,000
D.	$400,000	$1,300,000

Answer (A) is correct. *(CPA, adapted)*
REQUIRED: The total amounts of serial bonds and debenture bonds.
DISCUSSION: Serial bonds mature in installments at various dates. Debentures are unsecured bonds. The commodity-backed bonds and the registered bonds are serial bonds. They total $950,000 ($550,000 + $400,000). The registered bonds and the convertible bonds are debentures. They total $800,000 ($550,000 + $250,000).
Answer (B) is incorrect. The registered bonds also are debentures. Answer (C) is incorrect. The registered bonds, not the guaranty security bonds, are serial bonds. Answer (D) is incorrect. The registered bonds are serial bonds, and the guaranty security bonds are not debentures.

12.1.7. Unamortized bond discount should be reported on the balance sheet of the issuer as a

A. Direct deduction from the face amount of the debt.

B. Direct deduction from the present value of the debt.

C. Deferred charge.

D. Part of the issue costs.

Answer (A) is correct. *(CPA, adapted)*
REQUIRED: The issuer's balance sheet presentation of unamortized discount.
DISCUSSION: Bond discount must appear as a direct deduction from the face amount of the bond payable to report the effective liability for the bonds. Thus, the bond liability is shown net of unamortized discount.
Answer (B) is incorrect. The face amount minus the unamortized discount is equal to the present value (carrying amount) of the bond. Answer (C) is incorrect. Deferred charges are not recognized for debt discounts or issue costs in the balance sheet. Answer (D) is incorrect. Unamortized discount and unamortized debt issue costs are reported as a direct deduction from the face amount of the debt. However, unamortized discount is segregated from debt issue costs.

12.1.8. The following information pertains to Camp Corp.'s issuance of bonds on July 1, Year 4:

Face amount	$800,000
Term	10 years
Stated interest rate	6%
Interest payment dates	Annually on July 1
Yield	9%

	At 6%	At 9%
Present value of 1 for 10 periods	0.558	0.422
Future value of 1 for 10 periods	1.791	2.367
Present value of ordinary annuity of 1 for 10 periods	7.360	6.418

What should the issue price be for each $1,000 bond?

A. $1,000

B. $943

C. $864

D. $807

Answer (D) is correct. *(CPA, adapted)*
REQUIRED: The issue price for each bond.
DISCUSSION: The issue price of a bond equals the sum of the present values of the future cash flows (principal + interest). This amount is $807 [($1,000 face amount × .422 PV of 1 for 10 periods at 9%) principal + ($1,000 face amount × 6% stated rate × 6.418 PV of an ordinary annuity for 10 periods at 9%) interest].
Answer (A) is incorrect. The face amount is $1,000. Answer (B) is incorrect. The amount of $943 is the result of discounting the interest payments at 9% and the face amount at 6%. Answer (C) is incorrect. The amount of $864 is the result of discounting the interest payments at 6% and the face amount at 9%.

12.1.9. On January 2, Year 4, Nast Co. issued 8% bonds with a face amount of $1 million that mature on January 2, Year 10. The bonds were issued to yield 12%, resulting in a discount of $150,000. Nast incorrectly used the straight-line method instead of the effective-interest method to amortize the discount. How is the carrying amount of the bonds affected by the error?

	At December 31, Year 4	At January 2, Year 10
A.	Overstated	Understated
B.	Overstated	No effect
C.	Understated	Overstated
D.	Understated	No effect

Answer (B) is correct. *(CPA, adapted)*
REQUIRED: The effect of amortizing bond discount using the straight-line method.
DISCUSSION: When bond discount is amortized using the effective-interest method, the carrying amount of the bonds increases by a greater amount every period. Under the straight-line method, however, discount amortized is a constant periodic amount. Thus, in the first year, straight-line amortization of the discount exceeds the amount determined under the interest method. The effect of the error is to overstate the carrying amount by this excess. At the due date of the bonds, the discount is fully amortized, and the carrying amount is the same under both methods.
Answer (A) is incorrect. This error has no effect at January 2, Year 10. Answer (C) is incorrect. This error overstates the carrying amount at December 31, Year 4, but it has no effect at January 2, Year 10. Answer (D) is incorrect. This error overstates the carrying amount at December 31, Year 4.

12.1.10. Kent Co. issued 6,000 of its 9%, $1,000 face amount bonds at 101 1/2. In connection with the sale of these bonds, Kent paid the following expenses:

Promotion costs	$ 40,000
Engraving and printing	50,000
Underwriters' commissions	400,000

What amount should Kent recognize as bond issue costs to be amortized over the term of the bonds?

A. $0

B. $440,000

C. $450,000

D. $490,000

Answer (D) is correct. *(CPA, adapted)*
REQUIRED: The amount to be recognized as bond issue costs.
DISCUSSION: Costs to issue debt securities are reported as direct deductions from the face amount of the debt. Debt issue costs should be amortized over the term of the debt. These costs include printing costs, underwriters' commissions, attorney's fees, and promotion costs (including preparation of a prospectus). The issue costs to be amortized equal $490,000 ($40,000 promotion costs + $50,000 printing costs + $400,000 underwriters' commissions).
Answer (A) is incorrect. The amount of $490,000 of bond issue costs should be amortized. Answer (B) is incorrect. The $50,000 printing cost should be amortized. Answer (C) is incorrect. The $40,000 promotion costs should be amortized.

12.1.11. On May 1, Year 1, a company issued, at 103 plus accrued interest, 500 of its 12%, $1,000 bonds. The bonds are dated January 1, Year 1, and mature on January 1, Year 5. Interest is payable semiannually on January 1 and July 1. The journal entry to record the issuance of the bonds and the receipt of the cash proceeds is

A.
Cash	$515,000	
Interest payable	20,000	
Bonds payable		$500,000
Premium on bonds payable		35,000

B.
Cash	$525,000	
Bonds payable		$500,000
Premium on bonds payable		15,000
Interest payable		10,000

C.
Cash	$535,000	
Bonds payable		$500,000
Premium on bonds payable		15,000
Interest payable		20,000

D.
Cash	$535,000	
Bonds payable		$500,000
Premium on bonds payable		35,000

Answer (C) is correct. *(CIA, adapted)*
REQUIRED: The journal entry to record the issuance of a bond at a premium plus accrued interest.
DISCUSSION: The face amount of the 500 bonds is equal to $500,000 (500 × $1,000). The cash proceeds excluding interest from the issuance of the bonds are $515,000 ($500,000 × 103%). The $15,000 premium is the difference between the cash issuance proceeds and the face amount of the bonds. Because the bonds were issued between interest payment dates, the issuer is also entitled to receive cash for the accrued interest for the 4 months between the prior interest date and the issuance date. The accrued interest is $20,000 [500 bonds × $1,000 face amount × 12% stated rate × (4 months ÷ 12 months)]. The issuing company will therefore receive $535,000 in cash ($515,000 + $20,000). The resulting journal entry includes a $535,000 debit to cash, a $500,000 credit to bonds payable, a $15,000 credit to premium, and a $20,000 credit to either interest payable or interest expense.
Answer (A) is incorrect. The bond premium is $15,000 ($500,000 × 3%), and interest payable should be credited. Answer (B) is incorrect. Interest payable should be $20,000 [$500,000 × 12% × (4 months ÷ 12 months)]. Answer (D) is incorrect. The premium on bonds payable should not include interest payable.

12.1.12. If the market rate of interest is <List A> the coupon rate when bonds are issued, then the bonds will sell in the market at a price <List B> the face amount, and the issuing firm will record a <List C> on bonds payable.

	List A	List B	List C
A.	Equal to	Equal to	Premium
B.	Greater than	Greater than	Premium
C.	Greater than	Less than	Discount
D.	Less than	Greater than	Discount

Answer (C) is correct. *(CIA, adapted)*
    REQUIRED: The relationship of the market rate, the coupon rate, and the recording of a discount or premium.
    DISCUSSION: If the market rate exceeds the coupon rate, the price of the bonds must decline to a level that equates the yield on the bonds with the market rate of interest. Accordingly, the bonds will be recorded by a debit to cash for the proceeds, a debit to discount on bonds payable, and a credit to bonds payable at face amount.
    Answer (A) is incorrect. If the market rate equals the coupon rate, the bonds will not sell at a premium or discount. Answer (B) is incorrect. If the market rate exceeds the coupon rate, the bond issue will sell at a discount. Answer (D) is incorrect. If the market rate is less than the coupon rate, the bonds will sell at a premium.

12.1.13. How is the carrying amount of a bond payable affected by amortization of the following?

	Discount	Premium
A.	Increase	Increase
B.	Decrease	Decrease
C.	Increase	Decrease
D.	Decrease	Increase

Answer (C) is correct. *(CPA, adapted)*
    REQUIRED: The effect of discount and premium amortization on the carrying value of a bond payable.
    DISCUSSION: The carrying amount of a bond payable is equal to its maturity (face) amount plus any unamortized premium or minus any unamortized discount. Amortization results in a reduction of the discount or premium. Consequently, the carrying amount of a bond is increased when discount is amortized and decreased when premium is amortized.
    Answer (A) is incorrect. Amortization of discount increases and amortization of premium decreases the carrying amount of a bond payable. Answer (B) is incorrect. Amortization of discount increases and amortization of premium decreases the carrying amount of a bond payable. Answer (D) is incorrect. Amortization of discount increases and amortization of premium decreases the carrying amount of a bond payable.

12.1.14. Midland, Inc., had the following amounts of noncurrent debt outstanding at December 31, Year 1:

14 1/2% term note, due Year 2	$ 6,000
11 1/8% term note, due Year 4	214,000
8% note, due in 11 equal annual principal payments, plus interest beginning December 31, Year 2	220,000
7% guaranteed debentures, due Year 5	200,000
Total	$640,000

Midland's annual sinking-fund requirement on the guaranteed debentures is $8,000 per year. What amount should Midland report as current maturities of noncurrent debt in its December 31, Year 1, balance sheet?

    A. $8,000

    B. $14,000

    C. $20,000

    D. $26,000

Answer (D) is correct. *(CPA, adapted)*
    REQUIRED: The amount to be reported as current maturities of noncurrent debt in the balance sheet.
    DISCUSSION: A noncurrent liability that will become due within 1 year or the firm's operating cycle, whichever is longer, should be reclassified as a current liability, except when (1) the portion currently due will be refinanced on a noncurrent basis, (2) the assets that will be used to retire the currently due portion are classified as noncurrent assets, or (3) capital stock will be issued to retire the portion currently due. In this case, the obligations that should be reclassified as current are the $6,000 balance of the 14 1/2% term note due in Year 2 and $20,000 of the 8% note (the payment is made to reduce principal in 11 equal payments), a total of $26,000. No exception applies.
    Answer (A) is incorrect. The amount of $8,000 is Midland's annual sinking-fund requirement on the guaranteed debentures. Answer (B) is incorrect. The amount of $14,000 is the difference between the $20,000 due in Year 2 on the 8% note and the $6,000 due in Year 2 on the 14 1/2% note. Answer (C) is incorrect. The 14 1/2% note should be reclassified as a current liability.

12.1.15. On July 1, Dover Co. received $206,576 for $200,000 face amount, 12% bonds, a price that yields 10%. Interest expense for the 6 months ended December 31 should be

    A. $12,394

    B. $12,000

    C. $10,328

    D. $10,000

Answer (C) is correct. *(CPA, adapted)*
    REQUIRED: The amount of interest expense.
    DISCUSSION: Under the interest method, interest expense for the 6 months since the bond was issued is equal to the carrying amount of the bond multiplied by the effective interest rate for half a year. Thus, interest expense is $10,328 [$206,576 × 10% × (6 months ÷ 12 months)].
    Answer (A) is incorrect. The carrying amount multiplied by the coupon rate is $12,394. Answer (B) is incorrect. The face amount multiplied by the coupon rate is $12,000. Answer (D) is incorrect. The face amount multiplied by the yield rate is $10,000.

12.1.16. On January 2, Year 1, Kerry Co. issued $4 million of 10-year, 8% bonds at par. The bonds, dated January 1, Year 1, pay interest semiannually on January 1 and July 1. Bond issue costs were $500,000. Kerry amortizes debt issue costs using the straight-line amortization method. What amount of bond issue costs is unamortized at June 30, Year 2?

A. $475,000

B. $450,000

C. $441,600

D. $425,000

Answer (D) is correct. *(CPA, adapted)*
　　REQUIRED: The amount to be recorded as unamortized bond issue costs.
　　DISCUSSION: Debt issue costs should be amortized over the term of the debt using the interest method. But the straight-line amortization method may be applied if the results are not materially different. Thus, the amortization is $50,000 per year ($500,000 ÷ 10 years). Because the bond has been held for 18 months, $75,000 ($50,000 + $25,000) of issue costs has been amortized by 6/30/Year 2. The unamortized issue costs are $425,000 ($500,000 – $75,000). Debt issue costs are presented as a direct deduction from the debt liability.
　　Answer (A) is incorrect. An additional full year of amortization should have been claimed. Answer (B) is incorrect. Six more months of issue costs should have been amortized for the time between 1/1/Year 2 through 6/30/Year 2. Answer (C) is incorrect. The amount of $441,600 results from amortization using the interest method.

12.1.17. On January 1, Year 1, Gilson Corporation issued 1,000 of its 9%, $1,000 callable bonds for $1,030,000. The bonds are dated January 1, Year 1, and mature on December 31, Year 15. Interest is payable semiannually on January 1 and July 1. The bonds can be called by the issuer at 102 on any interest payment date after December 31, Year 5. The unamortized bond premium was $14,000 at December 31, Year 8, and the market price of the bonds was 99 on this date. In its December 31, Year 8, balance sheet, at what amount should Gilson report the carrying value of the bonds?

A. $1,020,000

B. $1,016,000

C. $1,014,000

D. $990,000

Answer (C) is correct. *(CPA, adapted)*
　　REQUIRED: The carrying amount of bonds issued at a premium.
　　DISCUSSION: The face amount of the bonds is $1,000,000 (1,000 × $1,000), and the unamortized premium is $14,000 (given). The carrying amount is thus $1,014,000. The other data are irrelevant.
　　Answer (A) is incorrect. The amount of $1,020,000 is to be paid if the bonds are called. Answer (B) is incorrect. The amount of $1,016,000 is the issue price minus the unamortized premium ($1,030,000 – $14,000). Answer (D) is incorrect. The amount of $990,000 is the market price.

12.1.18. A company issues 10-year bonds with a face amount of $1 million, dated January 1, Year 1, and bearing interest at an annual rate of 12% payable semiannually on January 1 and July 1. The full interest amount will be paid each due date. The market rate of interest on bonds of similar risk and maturity, with the same schedule of interest payments, is also 12%. If the bonds are issued on February 1, Year 1, the amount the issuing company receives from the buyers of the bonds on that date is

A. $990,000

B. $1,000,000

C. $1,010,000

D. $1,020,000

Answer (C) is correct. *(CIA, adapted)*
　　REQUIRED: The amount received when bonds are issued subsequent to the date printed on the face of the bonds.
　　DISCUSSION: The market rate of interest is equal to the stated interest rate. Thus, the amount the issuing company receives on 2/1/Year 1 is the face amount of the issue plus 1 month of accrued interest, or $1,010,000 {$1,000,000 + [($1,000,000 × 12%) ÷ 12]}.
　　Answer (A) is incorrect. The amount of $990,000 is the result if 1 month of accrued interest is deducted from, rather than added to, the face amount. Answer (B) is incorrect. The purchasers must pay for the accrued interest from the last interest date to the issue date. They will receive 6 months' interest on July 1 despite holding the bonds for 5 months. Answer (D) is incorrect. The amount of $1,020,000 results from adding 2 months of accrued interest to the face amount.

12.1.19. Mann Corp.'s liability account balances at June 30, Year 2, included a 10% note payable in the amount of $3.6 million. The note is dated October 1, Year 1, and is payable in three equal annual payments of $1.2 million plus interest. The first interest and principal payment was made on October 1, Year 2. In Mann's June 30, Year 3, balance sheet, what amount should be reported as accrued interest payable for this note?

A. $270,000

B. $180,000

C. $90,000

D. $60,000

Answer (B) is correct. *(CPA, adapted)*
REQUIRED: The amount that should be reported as accrued interest payable.
DISCUSSION: Accrued interest on the note payable at the balance sheet date is the carrying amount of the note multiplied by the interest rate on the note. Because the first payment was made 10/1/Year 2, the carrying amount of the note is $2,400,000 ($3,600,000 – $1,200,000). Also, interest has accrued for only 9 months since the first payment. As a result, accrued interest payable is $180,000 [$2,400,000 × 10% × (9 months ÷ 12 months)].
Answer (A) is incorrect. The amount of $270,000 assumes that the carrying amount of the note was not reduced by the payment of $1,200,000 made on 10/1/Year 2. Answer (C) is incorrect. The amount of $90,000 assumes that the carrying amount of the note was not reduced by the first payment of $1,200,000 and that interest was accrued for 9 months instead of 3. Answer (D) is incorrect. Interest should be accrued for 9 months instead of 3.

12.1.20. On December 31, Year 1, Arnold, Inc., issued $200,000, 8% serial bonds, to be repaid in the amount of $40,000 each year. Interest is payable annually on December 31. The bonds were issued to yield 10% per year. The bond proceeds were $190,280 based on the present values at December 31, Year 1, of the five annual payments:

	Amounts Due		
Due Date	Principal	Interest	Present Value at 12/31/Yr 1
12/31/Yr 2	$40,000	$16,000	$ 50,900
12/31/Yr 3	40,000	12,800	43,610
12/31/Yr 4	40,000	9,600	37,250
12/31/Yr 5	40,000	6,400	31,690
12/31/Yr 6	40,000	3,200	26,830
			$190,280

Arnold amortizes the bond discount by the interest method. In its December 31, Year 2, balance sheet, at what amount should Arnold report the carrying amount of the bonds?

A. $139,380

B. $149,100

C. $150,280

D. $153,308

Answer (D) is correct. *(CPA, adapted)*
REQUIRED: The carrying amount after year one of bonds issued at a discount.
DISCUSSION: The carrying amount of the bonds at the end of Year 1 equals the proceeds of $190,280. Interest expense for Year 2 at the 10% effective rate is thus $19,028. Actual interest paid is $16,000, discount amortization is $3,028 ($19,028 – $16,000), and the discount remaining at year end is $6,692 [($200,000 face amount – $190,280 issue proceeds) – $3,028 discount amortization]. Given that $40,000 in principal is paid at year end, the December 31, Year 2, carrying amount is $153,308 ($160,000 face amount – $6,692 unamortized discount).
Answer (A) is incorrect. The amount of $139,380 is the carrying amount of the bonds at December 31, Year 2, less the total amount due in Year 3. Answer (B) is incorrect. The amount of $149,100 is the difference between the face amount of the bonds and the total payment in Year 3. Answer (C) is incorrect. The amount of $150,280 results from reducing the carrying amount at December 31, Year 2, by the payment of principal during Year 3.

12.1.21. On July 1, Year 3, Lundy Company issued for $438,000 500 of its 8%, $1,000 bonds. The bonds were issued to yield 10%. The bonds are dated July 1, Year 3, and mature on July 1, Year 13. Interest is payable semiannually on January 1 and July 1. Using the interest method, how much of the bond discount should be amortized for the 6 months ended December 31, Year 3?

A. $3,800

B. $3,100

C. $2,480

D. $1,900

Answer (D) is correct. *(CPA, adapted)*
REQUIRED: The amount of bond discount to be amortized using the interest method.
DISCUSSION: Interest expense for the 6 months since the bonds were issued is $21,900 [$438,000 carrying amount × 10% effective rate × (6 ÷ 12)]. The periodic cash payment is $20,000 [$500,000 face amount × 8% stated rate × (6 ÷ 12)]. The $1,900 ($21,900 – $20,000) difference is the amount of discount to be amortized for this 6-month interest period.
Answer (A) is incorrect. The amount of $3,800 is the discount amortized for a full year. Answer (B) is incorrect. The amount of $3,100 is the difference between interest expense calculated at 10% and interest payable calculated at 10% for half a year. Answer (C) is incorrect. The amount of $2,480 is equal to the difference between interest expense calculated at 8% and interest payable calculated at 8% for half a year.

Questions 12.1.22 and 12.1.23 are based on the following information. Clare Co. issued $6 million of 12% bonds on December 1, Year 1, due on December 1, Year 6, with interest payable each December 1 and June 1. The bonds were sold for $5,194,770 to yield 16%.

12.1.22. If the discount were amortized by the straight-line method, Clare's interest expense for the fiscal year ended November 30, Year 2, related to its $6 million bond issue would be

- A. $558,954
- B. $623,372
- C. $720,000
- D. $881,046

Answer (D) is correct. *(CMA, adapted)*
REQUIRED: The interest expense under the straight-line amortization method.
DISCUSSION: Under the straight-line method, interest expense is the sum of the periodic cash flows plus the discount amortization. The periodic cash flows are equal to $720,000 ($6,000,000 face amount × 12% coupon rate). The discount at the time of issuance was $805,230 ($6,000,000 face amount − $5,194,770 issuance price). Because the term of the bonds is 5 years, amortization by the straight-line method each year will be $161,046 ($805,230 discount ÷ 5 years). Thus, interest expense is $881,046 ($720,000 + $161,046) for the fiscal year ended 11/30/Year 2. Under the straight-line method, interest expense will be the same for each year in which the bonds are outstanding. However, the straight-line method is allowable only when it does not differ materially from the interest method.
Answer (A) is incorrect. The amount of $558,954 results from subtracting the amortization of the discount. Answer (B) is incorrect. The carrying amount of the bonds multiplied by the coupon rate is $623,372. Answer (C) is incorrect. The amount of $720,000 is interest payable.

12.1.23. If the discount were amortized by the effective-interest method, Clare's interest expense for the fiscal year ended November 30, Year 2, related to its $6 million bond issue would be

- A. $623,372
- B. $720,000
- C. $831,163
- D. $835,610

Answer (D) is correct. *(CMA, adapted)*
REQUIRED: The interest expense for the first year under the effective-interest method.
DISCUSSION: Under the interest method, interest expense is equal to the carrying amount of the bonds at the beginning of the interest period times the effective interest rate. The carrying amount of the bonds at December 1, Year 1 (the issuance date), was $5,194,770. The annual yield rate was 16%. Interest expense is therefore equal to $415,582 [$5,194,770 × 16% × (6 months ÷ 12 months)] for the first 6 months of the year. For the same period, interest paid was $360,000 [$6,000,000 × 12% × (6 months ÷ 12 months)]. Hence, the semiannual discount amortization was $55,582 ($415,582 interest expense − $360,000 interest paid), and the carrying amount of the bonds for the second 6-month period was $5,250,352 ($5,194,770 + $55,582). For this period, the semiannual interest expense was $420,028 [$5,250,352 × 16% × (6 months ÷ 12 months)]. Total interest expense for the year is equal to $835,610 ($415,582 + $420,028).
Answer (A) is incorrect. The carrying amount of the bond multiplied by the coupon rate is $623,372. Answer (B) is incorrect. The amount of $720,000 is interest payable. Answer (C) is incorrect. The amount of $831,163 results from calculating interest expense as if interest is payable annually.

12.1.24. On January 2, Year 1, West Co. issued 9% bonds in the amount of $500,000, which mature on January 2, Year 11. The bonds were issued for $469,500 to yield 10%. Interest is payable annually on December 31. West uses the interest method of amortizing bond discount. In its June 30, Year 1, balance sheet, what amount should West report as bonds payable?

- A. $469,500
- B. $470,475
- C. $471,025
- D. $500,000

Answer (B) is correct. *(CPA, adapted)*
REQUIRED: The amount to be reported as bonds payable at an interim date.
DISCUSSION: Accrued interest expense is $23,475 [$469,500 carrying amount × 10% effective rate × (6 ÷ 12)]. Accrued interest payable is $22,500 [$500,000 face amount × 9% stated rate × (6 ÷ 12)]. The difference of $975 is the amount of discount amortization for the period. The amount that should be reported as bonds payable equals $470,475 ($469,500 carrying amount at January 2 + $975 current-period discount amortized).
Answer (A) is incorrect. The amount of $469,500 is the issue price unadjusted for discount amortization. Answer (C) is incorrect. The amount of $471,025 reflects a full year's discount amortization. Answer (D) is incorrect. The face amount of the bonds is $500,000.

12.1.25. On January 1, Year 4, Celt Corp. issued 9% bonds in the face amount of $1 million, which mature on January 1, Year 14. The bonds were issued for $939,000 to yield 10%, resulting in a bond discount of $61,000. Celt uses the interest method of amortizing bond discount. Interest is payable annually on December 31. At December 31, Year 4, Celt's unamortized bond discount should be

A. $51,000

B. $51,610

C. $52,000

D. $57,100

Answer (D) is correct. *(CPA, adapted)*
REQUIRED: The amount of unamortized bond discount at the end of the first year.
DISCUSSION: For the first year, interest expense is $93,900 ($939,000 carrying amount × 10% yield rate). The periodic interest payment is $90,000 ($1,000,000 face amount × 9% coupon rate). The $3,900 ($93,900 – $90,000) difference is the amount of bond discount amortized. Thus, the $61,000 unamortized bond discount at the beginning of the year should be reduced by $3,900 to a year-end balance of $57,100.
Answer (A) is incorrect. The amount of $51,000 results from reducing the discount by the face amount times the market (yield) rate, minus the interest payment. Answer (B) is incorrect. The amount of $51,610 results from reducing the discount by the carrying amount times the yield, minus the carrying amount times the coupon rate. Answer (C) is incorrect. The bond discount is reduced by the interest payment.

12.1.26. Webb Co. has outstanding a 7%, 10-year bond with a $100,000 face amount. The bond was originally sold to yield 6% annual interest. Webb uses the effective-interest method to amortize bond premium. On June 30, Year 3, the carrying amount of the outstanding bond was $105,000. What amount of unamortized premium on the bond should Webb report in its June 30, Year 4, balance sheet?

A. $1,050

B. $3,950

C. $4,300

D. $4,500

Answer (C) is correct. *(CPA, adapted)*
REQUIRED: The amount of unamortized premium.
DISCUSSION: Under the interest method, interest expense is the carrying amount of the bonds at the beginning of the interest period times the market (yield) rate of interest. Assuming interest is paid annually on June 30, interest expense for the year ended June 30, Year 4, is $6,300 ($105,000 carrying amount × 6% effective rate), and the periodic interest payment is $7,000 ($100,000 face amount × 7% stated rate). The difference ($7,000 – $6,300 = $700) is the amount of premium amortized. The remaining unamortized premium is therefore $4,300 ($5,000 – $700).
Answer (A) is incorrect. The amount of $1,050 equals 18 months of interest payments. Answer (B) is incorrect. The amount of $3,950 equals the premium minus 18 months of interest payments. Answer (D) is incorrect. The amount of $4,500 assumes straight-line amortization and a June 30, Year 3, issue date.

12.2 Convertible Debt

12.2.1. An issuer of a convertible security may attempt to induce prompt conversion of its convertible debt to equity securities by offering additional securities or other consideration as a sweetener. The additional consideration used to induce conversion should be reported as a(n)

A. Reduction of the paid-in capital recognized for the new equity securities.

B. Direct reduction of retained earnings.

C. Extraordinary item in the current income statement.

D. Expense of the current period.

Answer (D) is correct. *(CMA, adapted)*
REQUIRED: The proper treatment of a convertible debt sweetener.
DISCUSSION: A debtor may induce conversion of convertible debt by offering additional securities or other consideration to the holders of convertible debt. This convertible debt sweetener must be recognized as an expense. It is equal to the fair value of the securities or other consideration transferred in excess of the fair value of the securities that would have been issued under the original conversion privilege.
Answer (A) is incorrect. The additional consideration is expensed. Answer (B) is incorrect. The excess of the transferred consideration over the fair value of the securities issuable under the original terms is an expense. Answer (C) is incorrect. Extraordinary items are not recognized under U.S. GAAP or IFRS.

Questions 12.2.2 and 12.2.3 are based on the following information. On January 2, Year 1, Kiril Co. issued 10-year convertible bonds at 105. During Year 4, these bonds were converted into common stock having an aggregate par value equal to the total face amount of the bonds. At conversion, the market price of Kiril's common stock was 50% above its par value.

12.2.2. On January 2, Year 1, cash proceeds from the issuance of the convertible bonds should be reported as

A. Contributed capital for the entire proceeds.

B. Contributed capital for the portion of the proceeds attributable to the conversion feature and as a liability for the balance.

C. A liability for the face amount of the bonds and contributed capital for the premium.

D. A liability for the entire proceeds.

Answer (D) is correct. *(CPA, adapted)*
REQUIRED: The proper accounting for cash proceeds received from the issuance of convertible bonds.
DISCUSSION: The entire proceeds from the issuance of convertible bonds must be reported as a liability until such time as the bonds are converted into stock.
Answer (A) is incorrect. The cash proceeds from the issuance of the convertible bonds must be treated as a liability for the entire amount. Answer (B) is incorrect. Allocation of the proceeds between equity and debt is not permitted. Answer (C) is incorrect. The premium also is treated as debt.

12.2.3. Depending on whether the book-value method or the market-value method was used, Kiril should recognize gains or losses on conversion when using the

	Book-Value Method	Market-Value Method
A.	Either gain or loss	Gain
B.	Either gain or loss	Loss
C.	Neither gain nor loss	Loss
D.	Neither gain nor loss	Gain

Answer (C) is correct. *(CPA, adapted)*
REQUIRED: The accounting method(s) that recognizes gains or losses on the conversion of the convertible bonds.
DISCUSSION: Under the book-value method for recognizing the conversion of outstanding bonds payable to common stock, the stock issued is recorded at the carrying amount of the bonds with no recognition of gain or loss. Under the market-value method, the stock is recorded at the market value of the stock (or of the bonds). A gain or loss is recognized equal to the difference between the market value recorded and the carrying amount of the bonds payable. At the time of the conversion, Kiril's common stock had an aggregate par value equal to the total face amount of the bonds, and the market price of the stock was 50% above its par value. Thus, a loss should have been recognized upon conversion in accordance with the market-value method. The total of the credits to equity accounts exceeds the total of the debits to bonds payable and unamortized premium. The difference is the amount of the loss.
Answer (A) is incorrect. Under the book-value method, no gain or loss is recognized at conversion. Under the market-value method, a loss would result. Answer (B) is incorrect. Under the book-value method, no gain or loss is recognized at conversion. Answer (D) is incorrect. Under the market-value method, a loss would result.

12.2.4. What is the preferred method of accounting for unamortized discount, unamortized issue costs, and the costs of implementing a conversion of debt into common stock?

A. Expense them in the period bonds are converted.

B. Amortize them over the remaining life of the issue retired.

C. Amortize them over a period not to exceed 40 years.

D. Charge them to paid-in capital in excess of the par value of the stock issued.

Answer (D) is correct. *(Publisher, adapted)*
REQUIRED: The preferred method of accounting for unamortized discount, unamortized issue costs, and the costs of converting debt into common stock.
DISCUSSION: The conversion of debt into common stock is ordinarily based upon the carrying amount of the debt at the time of issuance. Because the carrying amount is based on all related accounts, the debit balances of unamortized bond discount, unamortized issue costs, and conversion costs should be considered reductions in the net carrying amount at the time of conversion. Consequently, these items should be reflected as reductions in the additional paid-in capital account.
Answer (A) is incorrect. Unamortized discount, issue costs, and conversion costs are not expensed. In effect, each reduces the amount at which the stock is issued. Answer (B) is incorrect. Unamortized discount, issue costs, and conversion costs are credited and additional paid-in capital is debited. Answer (C) is incorrect. No pronouncement requires amortization over 40 years.

12.2.5. On July 1, after recording interest and amortization, Lancaster Co. converted $2 million of its 12% convertible bonds into 100,000 shares of $1 par value common stock. On the conversion date, the carrying amount of the bonds was $2.6 million, the fair value of the bonds was $2.8 million, and Lancaster's common stock was publicly trading at $30 per share. Using the book-value method, what amount of additional paid-in capital should Lancaster record as a result of the conversion?

A. $1,900,000

B. $2,500,000

C. $2,700,000

D. $3,000,000

Answer (B) is correct. *(CPA, adapted)*
REQUIRED: The amount of additional paid-in capital reported on the conversion of bonds when the book-value method is used.
DISCUSSION: Under the book-value method for recognizing the conversion of outstanding bonds payable to common stock, the stock issued is recorded at the carrying amount of the bonds with no recognition of a gain or loss. Accordingly, the conversion should be recorded at $2.6 million. However, this amount must be allocated between common stock and additional paid-in capital. The common stock account is always measured at par value. Thus, $100,000 (100,000 shares × $1) will be credited to common stock and $2,500,000 to additional paid-in capital.
Answer (A) is incorrect. The face amount of the bonds minus the par value of the stock is $1,900,000. Answer (C) is incorrect. The amount of $2,700,000 is the fair value of the bonds minus the par value of the stock. Answer (D) is incorrect. The amount of $3,000,000 is the fair value of the stock.

12.2.6. On January 1, Stunt Corp. had outstanding convertible bonds with a face value of $1,000,000 and an unamortized discount of $100,000. On that date, the bonds were converted into 100,000 shares of $1 par stock. The market value on the date of conversion was $12 per share. The transaction will be accounted for with the book value method. By what amount will Stunt's stockholders' equity increase as a result of the bond conversion?

A. $100,000

B. $900,000

C. $1,000,000

D. $1,200,000

Answer (B) is correct. *(CPA, adapted)*
REQUIRED: The increase in equity as a result of a book value method bond conversion.
DISCUSSION: Under the book-value method, no gain or loss is recognized on conversion of a convertible security. The following is the entry:

Bonds payable (face amount)	$1,000,000	
Common stock (par value)		$100,000
Unamortized discount		100,000
Additional paid-in capital		800,000

The items affecting equity are the increase of $100,000 in the par value of common stock and the increase of $800,000 in additional paid-in capital, a total increase of $900,000.
Answer (A) is incorrect. The par-value of the common stock issued equals $100,000. Answer (C) is incorrect. The reduction in bonds payable is $1,000,000. Answer (D) is incorrect. The fair value of the shares issued is $1,200,000.

12.3 Bonds and Warrants

12.3.1. How should warrants attached to a debt security be accounted for?

A. No amount assigned.

B. A separate portion of paid-in capital.

C. An appropriation of retained earnings.

D. As a separate liability.

Answer (A) is correct. *(CPA, adapted)*
REQUIRED: The accounting for the value of warrants attached to a debt security.
DISCUSSION: Assuming the warrants are not detachable and the debt security must be surrendered to exercise the warrants, the securities are substantially equivalent to convertible debt. No portion of the proceeds from the issuance should be accounted for as attributable to the conversion feature or the warrants.
Answer (B) is incorrect. The portion of the proceeds allocable to the warrants should be accounted for as paid-in capital only if the warrants are detachable. Answer (C) is incorrect. Nondetachable warrants are not separately recognized, but detachable warrants are recognized as paid-in capital. Answer (D) is incorrect. The attached equity instruments are not separately recognized.

12.3.2. When bonds are issued with stock purchase warrants, a portion of the proceeds should be allocated to additional paid-in capital for bonds issued with

	Detachable Stock Purchase Warrants	Nondetachable Stock Purchase Warrants
A.	No	Yes
B.	Yes	Yes
C.	Yes	No
D.	No	No

Answer (C) is correct. *(CPA, adapted)*
REQUIRED: The warrants receiving an allocation of bond proceeds.
DISCUSSION: The proceeds from debt securities issued with detachable warrants must be allocated between the debt securities and the warrants based on their relative fair values at the time of issuance. The portion allocated to the warrants should be accounted for as additional paid-in capital. However, when debt securities are issued with nondetachable warrants, no part of the proceeds should be allocated to the warrants.
Answer (A) is incorrect. A portion of the proceeds should be allocated to additional paid-in capital for bonds issued with detachable stock purchase warrants but not nondetachable warrants. Answer (B) is incorrect. A portion of the proceeds should be allocated to additional paid-in capital for bonds issued with detachable stock purchase warrants but not nondetachable warrants. Answer (D) is incorrect. A portion of the proceeds should be allocated to additional paid-in capital for bonds issued with detachable stock purchase warrants but not nondetachable warrants.

12.3.3. Bonds with detachable stock warrants were issued by Flack Co. Immediately after issue, the aggregate market value of the bonds and the warrants exceeds the proceeds. Is the portion of the proceeds allocated to the warrants less than their market value, and is that amount recorded as contributed capital?

	Less than Warrants' Market Value	Contributed Capital
A.	No	Yes
B.	Yes	No
C.	Yes	Yes
D.	No	No

Answer (C) is correct. *(CPA, adapted)*
REQUIRED: The allocation of proceeds to detachable warrants and the recording of the allocation.
DISCUSSION: The proceeds from debt securities issued with detachable warrants must be allocated between the debt securities and the warrants based on their relative fair values at the time of issuance. The portion allocated to the warrants should be accounted for as paid-in capital. Assuming that the market values of both the bonds and the warrants are known, and that the proceeds are less than their sum, the allocation process must result in crediting additional paid-in capital from stock warrants (stock warrants outstanding) for less than their market value. If the market value of the bonds is not known, the warrants will be credited at their market value.
Answer (A) is incorrect. The warrants will be credited at less than market value. Answer (B) is incorrect. The amount allocated to the warrants is credited to paid-in (contributed) capital. Answer (D) is incorrect. The warrants will be credited at less than market value and the amount allocated to the warrants is credited to paid-in (contributed) capital.

12.3.4. On December 30, Year 4, Fort, Inc., issued 1,000 of its 8%, 10-year, $1,000 face value bonds with detachable stock warrants at par. Each bond carried a detachable warrant for one share of Fort's common stock at a specified option price of $25 per share. Immediately after issuance, the market value of the bonds without the warrants was $1,080,000, and the market value of the warrants was $120,000. In its December 31, Year 4, balance sheet, what amount should Fort report as bonds payable?

A. $1,000,000

B. $975,000

C. $900,000

D. $880,000

Answer (C) is correct. *(CPA, adapted)*
REQUIRED: The amount reported for bonds payable with detachable stock warrants.
DISCUSSION: The issue price of the bonds is allocated between the bonds and the detachable stock warrants based on their relative fair values. The market price of bonds without the warrants is $1,080,000, which is 90% [$1,080,000 ÷ ($1,080,000 + $120,000)] of the total fair value. Consequently, 90% of the issue price should be allocated to the bonds, and they should be reported at $900,000 ($1,000,000 × 90%) in the balance sheet.
Answer (A) is incorrect. The total proceeds equals $1,000,000. Answer (B) is incorrect. The amount of $975,000 is the result of deducting the option price of the stock from the issue price. Answer (D) is incorrect. The amount of $880,000 is the result of deducting the fair value of the warrants from the issue price.

12.3.5. Ray Corp. issued bonds with a face amount of $200,000. Each $1,000 bond contained detachable stock warrants for 100 shares of Ray's common stock. Total proceeds from the issue amounted to $240,000. The market value of each warrant was $2, and the market value of the bonds without the warrants was $196,000. The bonds were issued at a discount of

A. $0

B. $678

C. $4,000

D. $40,678

Answer (B) is correct. *(CPA, adapted)*
REQUIRED: The amount of the bond discount.
DISCUSSION: The proceeds of bonds issued with detachable stock warrants must be allocated based on their relative fair values at the time of issuance. The fair values are $196,000 for the bonds and $40,000 for the warrants (200 bonds × 100 shares × 1 warrant per share × $2). The bonds thus comprise 83.051% [$196,000 ÷ ($196,000 + $40,000)] of the total fair value issued, resulting in $199,322 ($240,000 × 83.051%) of the proceeds from the issue being allocated to the bonds. The discount on the bonds was thus $678 ($200,000 face amount − $199,322 allocated proceeds).
Answer (A) is incorrect. The allocation to the bonds was less than their face amount. The discount would be $0 if the market value of the bonds were unknown. Answer (C) is incorrect. The amount of $4,000 is the difference between the face amount and the market value. Answer (D) is incorrect. The amount of $40,678 is the amount allocated to the warrants.

12.3.6. On March 1, Year 4, Evan Corp. issued $1 million of 10%, nonconvertible bonds at 103. They were due on February 28, Year 14. Each $1,000 bond was issued with 30 detachable stock warrants, each of which entitled the holder to purchase, for $50, one share of Evan common stock, par value $25. On March 1, Year 4, the quoted market value of Evan's common stock was $20 per share, and the market value of each warrant was $4. What amount of the bond issue proceeds should Evan record as an increase in equity?

A. $120,000

B. $90,000

C. $30,000

D. $0

Answer (A) is correct. *(CPA, adapted)*
REQUIRED: The bond issue proceeds recorded as equity.
DISCUSSION: When bonds are issued with detachable stock warrants, the proceeds must be allocated between the warrants and the bonds on the basis of their relative fair values. When the fair value of the warrants but not the bonds is known, paid-in capital from stock warrants should be credited (increased) for the fair value of the warrants with the remainder credited to the bonds. Evan issued 1,000 bonds ($1,000,000 ÷ $1,000); therefore, 30,000 warrants (1,000 bonds × 30 warrants) must also have been issued. Their fair value was $120,000 (30,000 warrants × $4), which is the amount of the credit to paid-in capital from stock warrants. The remainder of the proceeds [($1,000,000 × 103%) − $120,000 = $910,000] is allocated to bonds payable.
Answer (B) is incorrect. The discount on the bonds equals $90,000. Answer (C) is incorrect. The amount of $30,000 is the difference between the fair value of the warrants and the discount on the bonds. Answer (D) is incorrect. Stock warrants outstanding (paid-in capital from stock warrants) is an equity account.

12.3.7. Roaster Company issued bonds with detachable stock warrants. Each warrant granted an option to buy one share of $40 par value common stock for $75 per share. Five hundred warrants were originally issued, and $4,000 was appropriately credited to warrants. If 90% of these warrants are exercised when the market price of the common stock is $85 per share, how much should be credited to capital in excess of par on this transaction?

A. $19,350

B. $19,750

C. $23,850

D. $24,250

Answer (A) is correct. *(CPA, adapted)*
REQUIRED: The credit to capital in excess of par upon exercise of 90% of the warrants.
DISCUSSION: If 90% of the warrants are exercised, 450 shares must be issued at $75 per share. The total debit to cash is $33,750. The debit to stock warrants outstanding reflects the exercise of 90% of $4,000 of warrants, or $3,600. The par value of the common stock issued is credited for $18,000 (450 shares × $40 par). The balance of $19,350 ($33,750 + $3,600 − $18,000) is credited to capital in excess of par. The transaction is based on the exercise price, not the fair value of the stock or warrants at the time of issuance.

Cash	$33,750	
Warrants	3,600	
Common stock at par		$18,000
Capital in excess of par		19,350

Answer (B) is incorrect. The amount of $19,750 results from assuming all of the warrants were exercised with the same amount of stock being issued. Answer (C) is incorrect. The amount of $23,850 results from issuing the stock for $85 per share instead of $75. Answer (D) is incorrect. The amount of $24,250 results from issuing the stock for $85 per share, instead of $75, and assuming all of the warrants were exercised with the same amount of stock being issued.

12.4 Extinguishment of Debt

12.4.1. PPF partnership purchased land for $1,000,000 on May 1, Year 1, paying $200,000 cash and giving an $800,000 note payable to Lender Bank. PPF made three annual payments on the note totaling $358,000, which included interest of $178,000. PPF then defaulted on the note. Title to the land was transferred by PPF to Lender, which canceled the note, releasing the partnership from further liability. At the time of the default, the fair value of the land approximated the note balance. In PPF's Year 4 income statement, the amount of the loss should be

    A. $558,000

    B. $442,000

    C. $380,000

    D. $200,000

Answer (C) is correct. *(CPA, adapted)*
REQUIRED: The amount of the loss after default on a note and repossession of the land.
DISCUSSION: The principal of the note had been reduced to $620,000 [$800,000 – ($358,000 total payments – $178,000 interest)] at the time of default. The resultant $380,000 loss is equal to the difference between the $1,000,000 carrying amount (cost) of the land and the $620,000 carrying amount of the note.
Answer (A) is incorrect. This amount results from subtracting the total payments ($358,000) in determining the remaining principal. Answer (B) is incorrect. The amount of $442,000 is the note payable balance after subtracting the $178,000 of interest. Answer (D) is incorrect. The amount of $200,000 is the initial payment.

12.4.2. Ray Finance, Inc., issued a 10-year, $100,000, 9% note on January 1, Year 1. The note was issued to yield 10% for proceeds of $93,770. Interest is payable semiannually. The note is callable after 2 years at a price of $96,000. Due to a decline in the market rate to 8%, Ray retired the note on December 31, Year 3. On that date, the carrying amount of the note was $94,582, and the discounted amount of its cash flows based on the market rate was $105,280. What amount should Ray report as gain (loss) from retirement of the note for the year ended December 31, Year 3?

    A. $9,280

    B. $4,000

    C. $(2,230)

    D. $(1,418)

Answer (D) is correct. *(CPA, adapted)*
REQUIRED: The amount of gain (loss) from the extinguishment of a note.
DISCUSSION: The amount of gain or loss resulting from the extinguishment of debt is the difference between the amount paid and the carrying amount of the note. Thus, a loss of $1,418 ($94,582 carrying amount – $96,000 amount paid) results from the extinguishment.
Answer (A) is incorrect. The difference between the discounted amount, based on the market rate, and the call price is $9,280. Answer (B) is incorrect. The difference between the face amount of the note and the call price is $4,000. Answer (C) is incorrect. The difference between the original amount received and the call price is $(2,230).

12.4.3. An entity should not derecognize an existing liability under which of the following circumstances?

    A. The entity exchanges convertible preferred stock for its outstanding debt securities. The debt securities are not canceled but are held as treasury bonds.

    B. Because of financial difficulties being experienced by the entity, a creditor accepts a parcel of land as full satisfaction of an overdue loan. The value of the land is less than 50% of the loan balance.

    C. The entity irrevocably places cash into a trust that will be used solely to satisfy scheduled principal and interest payments of a specific bond obligation. Because the trust investments will generate a higher return, the amount of cash is less than the carrying amount of the debt.

    D. As part of the agreement to purchase a shopping center from the entity, the buyer assumes without recourse the mortgage for which the center serves as collateral.

Answer (C) is correct. *(Publisher, adapted)*
REQUIRED: The circumstances under which an existing liability should not be derecognized.
DISCUSSION: A liability is derecognized only if it has been extinguished. Extinguishment occurs when either (1) the debtor pays the creditor and is relieved of its obligation for the liability, or (2) the debtor is legally released from being the primary obligor under the liability, either judicially or by the creditor. Thus, the recognition of a gain or loss from an in-substance defeasance (e.g., placing cash in an irrevocable trust) is prohibited.
Answer (A) is incorrect. The debt is extinguished when the entity exchanges convertible preferred stock for its outstanding debt securities. This exchange is at fair value. Debt-equity swaps are rare because they are not tax-exempt. Answer (B) is incorrect. The debt is extinguished when a creditor accepts a parcel of land as full satisfaction of an overdue loan. Answer (D) is incorrect. The debt is extinguished when a buyer assumes without recourse the mortgage for which the property sold is collateral.

12.4.4. On June 2, Year 1, Tory, Inc., issued $500,000 of 10%, 15-year bonds at par. Interest is payable semiannually on June 1 and December 1. Bond issue costs were $6,000, and Tory uses the straight-line method of amortizing bond issue costs. On June 2, Year 6, Tory retired half of the bonds at 98. What is the net carrying amount that Tory should use in computing the gain or loss on retirement of debt?

A. $250,000

B. $248,000

C. $247,000

D. $246,000

Answer (B) is correct. *(CPA, adapted)*
REQUIRED: The net amount used in computing the gain or loss on the retirement of debt.
DISCUSSION: The gain or loss on the retirement of debt is equal to the difference between the proceeds paid and the carrying amount of the debt. The carrying amount is equal to the face amount (1) plus any unamortized premium or minus any unamortized discount and (2) minus any unamortized debt issue costs. The amortization of the issue costs is $400 per year ($6,000 ÷ 15). Because accumulated amortization is $2,000 ($400 × 5), the unamortized issue costs are $4,000 ($6,000 − $2,000), of which 50% or $2,000 should be subtracted in determining the carrying amount of the bonds retired. Thus, the net carrying amount used in computing the gain or loss on this early extinguishment of debt is $248,000 ($250,000 face amount − $2,000 unamortized deferred bond issue costs).
Answer (A) is incorrect. The amount of $250,000 is half of the par value. Answer (C) is incorrect. The amount of $247,000 is half of the par value minus half of the issue costs. Answer (D) is incorrect. The amount of $246,000 results from subtracting 100% of the unamortized issue costs.

12.4.5. On July 31, Year 4, Dome Co. issued $1,000,000 of 10%, 15-year bonds at par and used a portion of the proceeds to call its 600 outstanding 11%, $1,000 face amount bonds due on July 31, Year 14, at 102. On that date, unamortized bond premium relating to the 11% bonds was $65,000. In its Year 4 income statement, what amount should Dome report as gain or loss, before income taxes, from retirement of bonds?

A. $53,000 gain.

B. $0

C. $(65,000) loss.

D. $(77,000) loss.

Answer (A) is correct. *(CPA, adapted)*
REQUIRED: The amount to be reported for the retirement of bonds.
DISCUSSION: The excess of the net carrying amount of the bonds over the reacquisition price is a gain from extinguishment. The carrying amount of the bonds equals $665,000 ($600,000 face amount + $65,000 unamortized premium). The reacquisition price is $612,000 (600 bonds × $1,000 face amount × 1.02). Thus, the gain from extinguishment is $53,000 ($665,000 − $612,000).
Answer (B) is incorrect. The excess of the carrying amount over the reacquisition cost is a gain. Answer (C) is incorrect. The unamortized premium is $65,000. Answer (D) is incorrect. The amount of $77,000 equals the reacquisition price of $612,000, minus the face amount of $600,000, plus $65,000 unamortized premium.

12.4.6. On June 30, Year 7, King Co. had outstanding 9%, $5,000,000 face value bonds maturing on June 30, Year 9. Interest was payable semiannually every June 30 and December 31. On June 30, Year 7, after amortization was recorded for the period, the unamortized bond premium and bond issue costs were $30,000 and $50,000, respectively. On that date, King acquired all its outstanding bonds on the open market at 98 and retired them. At June 30, Year 7, what amount should King recognize as gain before income taxes on redemption of bonds?

A. $20,000

B. $80,000

C. $120,000

D. $180,000

Answer (B) is correct. *(CPA, adapted)*
REQUIRED: The amount of gain from the redemption of bonds.
DISCUSSION: The amount of gain or loss on the redemption of bonds is equal to the difference between the proceeds paid and the carrying amount of the debt. The carrying amount of the bonds is equal to the face amount, plus unamortized bond premium, minus unamortized bond issue costs. Thus, the carrying amount of the bonds is $4,980,000 ($5,000,000 + $30,000 − $50,000). The $80,000 gain is the difference between the carrying amount ($4,980,000) and the amount paid $4,900,000 ($5,000,000 × 98%).
Answer (A) is incorrect. The amount of $20,000 results from subtracting the unamortized bond premium and bond issue costs from the face amount of the bond. Answer (C) is incorrect. The amount of $120,000 results from adding the unamortized bond issue costs and subtracting the issue costs to find the carrying amount. Answer (D) is incorrect. The amount of $180,000 results from adding the unamortized bond issue costs and bond premium to find the carrying amount of the bond.

12.4.7. On January 2, Year 9, Seine Corporation entered into an in-substance debt defeasance transaction by placing cash of $875,000 into an irrevocable trust. The trust assets are to be used solely for satisfying the interest and principal payments on Seine's 6%, $1.1 million, 30-year bond payable. Seine has not been legally released under the bond agreement, but the probability is remote that Seine will be required to place additional cash in the trust. On December 31, Year 8, the bond's carrying amount was $1,050,000; its fair value was $800,000. Disregarding income taxes, what amount of gain (loss) should Seine report in its Year 9 income statement?

    A. $(75,000)

    B. $0

    C. $175,000

    D. $225,000

Answer (B) is correct. *(Publisher, adapted)*
    REQUIRED: The amount of gain (loss) to be recognized on an in-substance defeasance.
    DISCUSSION: A debtor derecognizes a liability only if it has been extinguished. Extinguishment results only if (1) the debtor pays the creditor and is relieved of its obligation with respect to the liability, or (2) the debtor is legally released from being the primary obligor, either judicially or by the creditor.
    Answer (A) is incorrect. The amount of $(75,000) is the excess of cash paid over the fair value of the bond, but no loss is recognized. Seine has not been legally released under the bond agreement. Answer (C) is incorrect. An in-substance defeasance does not result in the derecognition of a liability. Answer (D) is incorrect. No gain is recognized. However, if a gain or loss were recognized, it would equal the difference between the carrying amount and the amount paid ($1,050,000 – $875,000 = $175,000).

12.4.8. A debtor should derecognize a liability in which circumstances?

  I.   The debtor pays the creditor and is relieved of its obligation with respect to the liability.

  II. The debtor is legally released from being the primary obligor.

  III. The debtor irrevocably places cash or other assets in a trust to be used solely for satisfying scheduled payments of interest and principal of a specific obligation.

    A. I only.

    B. I and II only.

    C. II and III only.

    D. I, II, and III.

Answer (B) is correct. *(Publisher, adapted)*
    REQUIRED: The circumstances in which a debtor should derecognize a liability.
    DISCUSSION: A debtor derecognizes a liability only if it has been extinguished. Extinguishment results only if (1) the debtor pays the creditor and is relieved of its obligation with respect to the liability, or (2) the debtor is legally released from being the primary obligor, either judicially or by the creditor.
    Answer (A) is incorrect. A legal release also permits derecognition. Answer (C) is incorrect. An in-substance defeasance (III) does not constitute an extinguishment. Answer (D) is incorrect. An in-substance defeasance (III) does not constitute an extinguishment.

12.4.9. Columbia Corporation extinguished an issue of bonds before its maturity date through a direct exchange of securities. The new issue of debt is best measured by the

    A. Maturity amount of the new issue.

    B. Net carrying amount of the old issue.

    C. Fair value of the new issue.

    D. Maturity amount of the old issue.

Answer (C) is correct. *(CPA, adapted)*
    REQUIRED: The best measure of a new issue of debt used to extinguish an issue of bonds.
    DISCUSSION: All extinguishments are fundamentally alike. Thus, the accounting should be the same however the extinguishment is accomplished. Any difference between the reacquisition price (e.g., the new issue of debt) and the carrying amount of the debt extinguished is recognized in current income as a loss or gain. A debtor that transfers its assets in full settlement recognizes a gain measured by the excess of the carrying amount of the payable settled over the fair value of the assets transferred. The customary estimate of the fair value of debt is present value. According to SFAC 7, *Using Cash Flow Information and Present Value in Accounting Measurements,* "The only objective of present value, when used in accounting measurements at initial recognition [e.g., for a new issue of debt] and fresh start measurements, is to estimate fair value."
    Answer (A) is incorrect. The present value of the new issue must be used. Answer (B) is incorrect. The net carrying amount of the old issue is eliminated when the extinguishment is recognized. It is not carried over. Answer (D) is incorrect. The net carrying amount of the old issue, not the maturity amount of the old issue, is relevant to accounting for the extinguishment, but it is not the measure of the new issue.

12.4.10. A 15-year bond was issued in Year 1 at a discount. During Year 10, a 10-year bond was issued at face amount with the proceeds used to retire the 15-year bond at its face amount. The net effect of the Year 10 bond transactions was to increase long-term liabilities by the excess of the 10-year bond's face amount over the 15-year bond's

A. Face amount.

B. Carrying amount.

C. Face amount minus the deferred loss on bond retirement.

D. Carrying amount minus the deferred loss on bond retirement.

Answer (B) is correct. *(CPA, adapted)*
REQUIRED: The net effect of the bond transactions.
DISCUSSION: The 10-year bond was issued at its face amount, that is, at neither a premium nor a discount. Its face amount, therefore, equaled its proceeds, which were used to retire the 15-year bond at its face amount. The 15-year bond was carried at a discount (face amount – unamortized discount). Consequently, net long-term liabilities must have increased by the amount of the unamortized discount on the 15-year bond, which is the excess of the 10-year bond's face amount over the carrying amount of the 15-year bond.
Answer (A) is incorrect. The face amount of the 10-year bond equaled the face amount of the 15-year bond. Answer (C) is incorrect. The carrying amount of the 15-year bond should be used, and the loss is not deferred. Answer (D) is incorrect. The loss on early extinguishment is not deferred.

12.5 Noncurrent Notes Payable

12.5.1. A company issued a noninterest-bearing note payable due in 1 year in exchange for land. Which of the following statements is true concerning the accounting for the transaction?

A. The land should be recorded at the future value of the note, and interest should be imputed at the prevailing rate on similar notes.

B. No interest should be recognized on the note, and the land should be recorded at the present value of the note.

C. Interest on the note should be imputed at the prime rate, and the land should be recorded at the discounted value of the note.

D. Interest on the note should be imputed at the prevailing rate for similar notes, and the land should be recorded at the present value of the note.

Answer (D) is correct. *(CIA, adapted)*
REQUIRED: The proper accounting for a noninterest-bearing note.
DISCUSSION: If interest on a note is not stated, it is imputed by recording the note at the fair value of the property, goods, or services exchanged, or at the fair value of the note itself. If these values are not determinable, an interest rate must be imputed. GAAP include certain guidelines for imputing an interest rate. The rate should be at least equal to that at which the debtor could obtain financing of a similar nature from other sources. Other considerations are the market rate for an exchange of the note, the prime or higher rate for notes discounted with banks in light of the credit standing of the maker, and the current rates for debt instruments with substantially identical terms and risks that are traded in open markets. Accordingly, if the fair value of the note or the land is not determinable, the transaction will be recorded at the present value of the note based on an imputed rate.
Answer (A) is incorrect. The land is recorded at present value. Answer (B) is incorrect. Interest should be recognized on the note. Answer (C) is incorrect. The proper discount rate is the prevailing rate for similar notes, not the prime rate.

12.5.2. On September 1, Year 1, Brok Co. issued a note payable to Federal Bank in the amount of $900,000, bearing interest at 12%, and payable in three equal annual principal payments of $300,000. On this date, the bank's prime rate was 11%. The first interest and principal payment was made on September 1, Year 2. At December 31, Year 2, Brok should record accrued interest payable of

A. $36,000

B. $33,000

C. $24,000

D. $22,000

Answer (C) is correct. *(CPA, adapted)*
REQUIRED: The amount to be recorded as accrued interest payable.
DISCUSSION: Under the interest method, accrued interest payable is equal to the face amount of the note at the beginning of the interest period, times the stated interest rate, times the portion of the interest period that is included within the accounting period. At 9/1/Yr 1, the face amount of the note was $900,000. After the first payment of $300,000 principal plus interest on 9/1/Yr 2, the face amount of the note was $600,000 ($900,000 – $300,000). Accrued interest payable for the period 9/1/Yr 2 to 12/31/Yr 2 was thus $24,000 [$600,000 face amount × 12% stated interest rate × (4 months ÷ 12 months)]. The prime rate is irrelevant to the calculation of accrued interest payable.
Answer (A) is incorrect. The accrued interest payable at 12/31/Yr 1 was $36,000. Answer (B) is incorrect. The amount of $33,000 would have been the accrued interest payable at 12/31/Yr 1 if the interest rate had been 11%. Answer (D) is incorrect. The amount of $22,000 would have been the accrued interest payable if the interest rate had been 11%.

12.5.3. When a note payable has properly been recorded at its present value, any resulting discount should be disclosed in the financial statements

A. As a separate asset or liability.

B. As a deferred charge or credit.

C. In a summary caption along with any related issue costs.

D. As a direct reduction of the face amount of the note.

Answer (D) is correct. *(Publisher, adapted)*
REQUIRED: The proper financial statement disclosure of a discount related to a note payable.
DISCUSSION: Discount or premium is not an asset or liability separable from the related note. A discount should therefore be reported in the balance sheet as a direct reduction of the face amount of the note.
Answer (A) is incorrect. The discount is disclosed as a direct adjustment to the face amount of the note. Answer (B) is incorrect. GAAP do not permit recognition of (1) a deferred charge for a discount or debt issue costs or (2) a deferred credit for a premium. Answer (C) is incorrect. A discount and issue costs are separately reported. Each is a direct reduction of the face amount of the debt.

12.5.4. Which of the following is reported as interest expense?

A. Pension cost interest.

B. Postretirement healthcare benefits interest.

C. Imputed interest on a noninterest-bearing note.

D. Interest incurred to finance construction of machinery for an entity's own use.

Answer (C) is correct. *(CPA, adapted)*
REQUIRED: The item reported as interest expense.
DISCUSSION: When a noninterest-bearing note is exchanged for property, and neither the note nor the property has a clearly determinable exchange price, the present value of the note should be determined by discounting all future payments using an appropriately imputed interest rate. Periodic interest expense must be calculated and recognized in accordance with the effective-interest method.
Answer (A) is incorrect. Interest cost for a defined benefit pension plan is reported as a component of the net periodic pension cost. Answer (B) is incorrect. Interest cost for a defined benefit postretirement plan is reported as a component of the net postretirement benefit cost. Answer (D) is incorrect. Interest incurred to finance construction of machinery for an entity's own use is capitalized.

Questions 12.5.5 and 12.5.6 are based on the following information. House Publishers offered a contest in which the winner would receive $1 million, payable over 20 years. On December 31, Year 4, House announced the winner of the contest and signed a note payable to the winner for $1 million, payable in $50,000 installments every January 2. Also on December 31, Year 4, House purchased an annuity for $418,250 to provide the $950,000 prize monies remaining after the first $50,000 installment, which was paid on January 2, Year 5.

12.5.5. In its December 31, Year 4, balance sheet, at what amount should House measure the note payable, net of current portion?

A. $368,250

B. $418,250

C. $900,000

D. $950,000

Answer (B) is correct. *(CPA, adapted)*
REQUIRED: The amount at which the note payable should be measured.
DISCUSSION: Noninterest-bearing notes payable should be measured at their present value rather than their face amount. Thus, the measure of the note payable, net of the current portion, which has a nominal amount equal to its present value at December 31, Year 4, of $50,000, is its present value of $418,250 (debit annuity cost $418,250, debit discount $531,750, credit note payable $950,000). The present value of the noncurrent portion of the note is assumed to be the cash given for the annuity ($418,250) because no other right or privilege was exchanged.
Answer (A) is incorrect. The amount of $368,250 includes a reduction of $50,000 for the first installment. Answer (C) is incorrect. The amount of $900,000 equals the face amount of the note payable minus two installments. Answer (D) is incorrect. The amount of $950,000 equals the face amount of the note payable minus the first installment.

12.5.6. In its Year 4 income statement, what should House report as contest prize expense?

A. $0

B. $418,250

C. $468,250

D. $1,000,000

Answer (C) is correct. *(CPA, adapted)*
REQUIRED: The contest prize expense.
DISCUSSION: The contest prize expense equals $468,250 ($418,250 cost of the annuity + $50,000 first installment).
Answer (A) is incorrect. The sum of the cost of the annuity and the first installment must be recognized as an expense in Year 4. Answer (B) is incorrect. The amount of $418,250 does not include the $50,000 installment due in Year 5. Answer (D) is incorrect. The face amount of the note is $1,000,000.

12.5.7. On January 1 of the current year, Parke Company borrowed $360,000 from a major customer evidenced by a noninterest-bearing note due in 3 years. Parke agreed to supply the customer's inventory needs for the loan period at less than the market price. At the 12% imputed interest rate for this type of loan, the present value of the note is $255,000 at January 1 of the current year. What amount of interest expense should be included in Parke's current-year income statement?

A. $43,200

B. $35,000

C. $30,600

D. $0

Answer (C) is correct. *(CPA, adapted)*
REQUIRED: The amount of interest expense recognized by the maker of a noninterest-bearing note.
DISCUSSION: A note issued solely for cash equal to its face amount is presumed to earn the stated rate of interest, even if that rate is zero. If, however, the parties have also exchanged stated or unstated rights or privileges, these must be recognized by determining the fair value (present value) of the note based on an appropriate interest rate. Interest income or expense should be calculated and the discount amortized using the effective interest rate. Parke agreed to supply the customer's inventory needs for the loan period at less than the market price. Hence, the initial carrying amount of the note is $255,000, with the $105,000 ($360,000 – $255,000) discount recognized as the measure of the price concession. The entry is to debit cash and credit notes payable for $360,000 and to debit discount and credit unearned revenue for $105,000. The unearned revenue is recognized as sales revenue in proportion to periodic sales to the creditor-buyer. The discount is amortized as interest expense using the effective interest method. Interest expense is equal to the carrying amount of the note at the beginning of the interest period times the 12% imputed interest rate. The interest expense for the year should therefore be $30,600 ($255,000 carrying amount × 12% imputed interest rate).
Answer (A) is incorrect. This figure results from applying the imputed interest rate to the face amount of the note instead of to the carrying amount. Answer (B) is incorrect. The amount of $35,000 results from recognizing interest expense using the straight-line method. Answer (D) is incorrect. Interest expense must be imputed on a noninterest-bearing note.

12.5.8. As of December 1, Year 2, a company obtained a $1,000,000 line of credit maturing in 1 year on which it has drawn $250,000, a $750,000 secured note due in 5 annual installments, and a $300,000 3-year balloon note. The company has no other liabilities. How should the company's debt be presented in its classified balance sheet on December 31, Year 2, if no debt repayments were made in December?

A. Current liabilities of $1,000,000; long-term liabilities of $1,050,000.

B. Current liabilities of $500,000; long-term liabilities of $1,550,000.

C. Current liabilities of $400,000; long-term liabilities of $900,000.

D. Current liabilities of $500,000; long-term liabilities of $800,000.

Answer (C) is correct. *(CPA, adapted)*
REQUIRED: The current and long-term portions of liabilities.
DISCUSSION: Current liabilities are obligations that are expected to be fulfilled within 1 year or the operating cycle, whichever is longer. Thus, the $250,000 of credit drawn and the current portion of the secured note ($750,000 ÷ 5 years = $150,000) are considered current liabilities ($250,000 + $150,000 = $400,000). The 3-year balloon note and the noncurrent portion of the secured note of $600,000 ($750,000 – $150,000) will be classified as long-term liabilities ($300,000 + $600,000). A balloon note is a loan in which only one payment is due upon maturity.
Answer (A) is incorrect. A liability (or portion of a liability) can be classified as current or noncurrent, not both. The company has total liabilities of $1,300,000. The $750,000 line of credit that has not been drawn by the company is not a liability. Answer (B) is incorrect. A liability (or portion of a liability) can be classified as current or noncurrent, not both. The company has total liabilities of $1,300,000. The $750,000 line of credit that has not been drawn by the company is not a liability. A balloon note is a loan in which only one payment is due upon maturity. As the balloon note does not mature for 3 years, no portion of the balloon note is considered current as of December 31, Year 2. Answer (D) is incorrect. A balloon note is a loan in which only one payment is due upon maturity. As the balloon note does not mature for 3 years, no portion of the balloon note is considered current as of December 31, Year 2.

12.5.9. On January 31, Year 4, Beau Corp. issued $300,000 maturity value, 12% bonds for $300,000 cash. The bonds are dated December 31, Year 3, and mature on December 31, Year 13. Interest will be paid semiannually on June 30 and December 31. What amount of accrued interest payable should Beau report in its September 30, Year 4, balance sheet?

A. $27,000

B. $24,000

C. $18,000

D. $9,000

Answer (D) is correct. *(CPA, adapted)*
REQUIRED: The amount of accrued interest payable that should be reported in the balance sheet.
DISCUSSION: Because interest is paid semiannually on June 30 and December 31, the amount of each payment is $18,000 [($300,000 face amount × 12% stated rate) × (6 ÷ 12)]. On June 30, $18,000 was paid (because the bonds were issued at par, periodic interest expense consists entirely of the cash interest payment). From July 1 to September 30, Year 4 (3 months), interest accrued for the December 31, Year 4, payment. Thus, $9,000 [$18,000 × (3 ÷ 6)] of accrued interest payable should be reported.
Answer (A) is incorrect. The amount of $27,000 includes the $18,000 already paid on June 30. Answer (B) is incorrect. The amount of $24,000 includes the $18,000 already paid on June 30 and erroneously records $6,000, which is the accrued interest for 2 months. Answer (C) is incorrect. The amount of $18,000 is the amount of the semiannual interest payable.

12.6 Troubled Debt Restructurings

12.6.1. A troubled debt restructuring (TDR) is one in which the

A. Fair value of cash, other assets, or an equity interest accepted by a creditor from a debtor in full satisfaction of its receivable at least equals the creditor's recorded investment in the receivable.

B. Creditor reduces the effective interest rate on the debt primarily to reflect a decrease in market interest rates in general.

C. Debtor issues, in exchange for its existing debt, new marketable debt having an effective interest rate that is at or near the current market interest rates for debt with similar maturity dates and stated interest rates issued by nontroubled debtors.

D. Creditor, for economic or legal reasons related to the debtor's financial difficulties, grants a concession to the debtor that it would not otherwise consider.

Answer (D) is correct. *(CMA, adapted)*
REQUIRED: The definition of a troubled debt restructuring.
DISCUSSION: A TDR occurs when the creditor, for economic or legal reasons related to the debtor's financial difficulties, grants a concession to the debtor that it would not otherwise consider. TDRs usually involve a continuation of debt with modified terms, a settlement at an amount less than the amount of the debt owed, or a combination. The concession involved may be imposed by law or a court, or it may arise from an agreement between the creditor and the debtor. The creditor's purpose is to reduce the loss it would otherwise incur if it did not grant the concession.
Answer (A) is incorrect. A TDR does not arise when the fair value of cash, other assets, or an equity interest accepted by a creditor from a debtor in full satisfaction of its receivable at least equals the creditor's recorded investment in the receivable. Answer (B) is incorrect. A TDR does not arise when the creditor reduces the effective interest rate on the debt primarily to reflect a decrease in market interest rates in general. Answer (C) is incorrect. Refunding does not constitute a TDR when the new effective rate is at or near current market rates.

12.6.2. Which of the following situations that arise because of a debtor's financial difficulties and would not otherwise be acceptable to the creditor must be accounted for as a troubled debt restructuring (TDR)?

A. Because of a court order, a creditor accepts as full satisfaction of its receivable a building the fair value of which equals the creditor's recorded investment in the receivable.

B. As part of a negotiated settlement, a creditor accepts as full satisfaction of its receivable a building the fair value of which equals the debtor's carrying amount of the payable.

C. Because of a court order, a creditor reduces the stated interest rate for the remaining original life of the debt.

D. As part of a negotiated settlement designed to maintain a relationship with a debtor, a creditor reduces the effective interest rate on debt outstanding to reflect the lower market interest rate currently applicable to debt of that risk class.

Answer (C) is correct. *(Publisher, adapted)*
REQUIRED: The situation that must be accounted for as a troubled debt restructuring.
DISCUSSION: A TDR occurs when the creditor, for economic or legal reasons related to the debtor's financial difficulties, grants a concession to the debtor that it would not otherwise consider. TDRs usually involve a continuation of debt with modified terms, a settlement at an amount less than the amount of the debt owed, or a combination. A court order reducing a creditor's interest rate creates a TDR (assuming the reduction would not be otherwise acceptable to the creditor).
Answer (A) is incorrect. No TDR exists if, because of a court order, a creditor accepts as full satisfaction of its receivable a building the fair value of which equals the creditor's recorded investment in the receivable. Answer (B) is incorrect. No TDR exists if the creditor receives full payment. Answer (D) is incorrect. If the debtor could refund the debt at the lower market rate, the creditor is not making a substantive concession.

12.6.3. All of the following disclosures are required by debtors involved in a troubled debt restructuring except disclosure of

A. A description of the major changes in terms, major features of settlement, or both.

B. The aggregate gain on restructuring and the related tax effect.

C. The aggregate net gain or loss on transfer of assets.

D. The gross interest revenue that would have been recorded in the period.

Answer (D) is correct. *(CMA, adapted)*
REQUIRED: The disclosure that is not required of debtors following a troubled debt restructuring.
DISCUSSION: Debtors must, in subsequent periods, disclose the extent to which contingent amounts are included in the carrying amount of restructured payables. The gross interest revenue that would have been recorded in the period is not a required disclosure for debtors because interest revenue is applicable to receivables, not payables.
Answer (A) is incorrect. A description of the major changes in terms or major features of settlement must be disclosed. Answer (B) is incorrect. The aggregate gain on restructuring and the related tax effect must be disclosed. Answer (C) is incorrect. The gain or loss on transfer of assets must be disclosed.

12.6.4. In Year 18, May Corp. acquired land by paying $75,000 down and signing a note with a maturity amount of $1 million. On the note's due date, December 31, Year 23, May owed $40,000 of accrued interest and $1 million principal on the note. May was in financial difficulty and was unable to make any payments. May and the bank agreed to amend the note as follows:

- The $40,000 of interest due on December 31, Year 23, was forgiven.
- The principal of the note was reduced from $1 million to $950,000 and the maturity date extended 1 year to December 31, Year 24.
- May would be required to make one interest payment totaling $30,000 on December 31, Year 24.

As a result of the troubled debt restructuring (TDR), May should report a gain, before taxes, in its Year 23 income statement of

A. $40,000

B. $50,000

C. $60,000

D. $90,000

Answer (C) is correct. *(CPA, adapted)*
REQUIRED: The amount of gain to be recognized from a troubled debt restructuring.
DISCUSSION: When a TDR is structured as a modification of terms that results in future undiscounted cash flows less than the carrying amount of the debt, a debtor should recognize a gain equal to the difference if it is material. Accordingly, May should report a gain of $60,000 ($1,000,000 principal + $40,000 accrued interest – $950,000 new principal – $30,000 interest payment). In addition, the future payments of $980,000 ($950,000 + $30,000) should be recorded as further reductions of the debt.
Answer (A) is incorrect. The amount of $40,000 is the interest forgiven. Answer (B) is incorrect. The amount of $50,000 is the reduction of the principal forgiven. Answer (D) is incorrect. The amount of $90,000 does not include the required interest payment of $30,000 in the calculation of the gain.

12.6.5. On December 30, Year 4, Hale Corp. paid $400,000 cash and issued 80,000 shares of its $1 par value common stock to its unsecured creditors on a pro rata basis pursuant to a reorganization plan under Chapter 11 of the bankruptcy statutes. Hale owed these unsecured creditors a total of $1.2 million. Hale's common stock was trading at $1.25 per share on December 30, Year 4. As a result of this transaction, Hale's total equity had a net increase of

A. $1,200,000

B. $800,000

C. $100,000

D. $80,000

Answer (B) is correct. *(CPA, adapted)*
REQUIRED: The net increase in equity immediately after the Chapter 11 reorganization.
DISCUSSION: A debtor that grants an equity interest in full settlement of a payable should account for the equity interest at fair value. The difference between the fair value of the equity interest and the carrying amount of the payable is a gain. The appropriate accounting for this troubled debt restructuring is to debit liabilities for $1,200,000 and to credit cash for $400,000, common stock at its par value of $80,000 (80,000 shares × $1), additional paid-in capital for $20,000 [80,000 shares × ($1.25 fair value per share – $1 par)], and a gain for $700,000. Accordingly, the net increase in total equity is $800,000 ($80,000 + $20,000 + $700,000).
Answer (A) is incorrect. The amount of $1,200,000 is the amount of troubled debt. Answer (C) is incorrect. The amount of $100,000 is the increase in contributed capital. Answer (D) is incorrect. The amount of $80,000 is the increase in common stock.

12.6.6. Smokey Joe Corp., a debtor-in-possession under Chapter 11 of the Federal Bankruptcy Code, granted an equity interest to a creditor in full settlement of a $56,000 debt owed to the creditor. At the date of this transaction, the equity interest had a fair value of $50,000. What amount should Smokey Joe recognize as a gain on restructuring of debt?

A. $0

B. $6,000

C. $50,000

D. $56,000

Answer (B) is correct. *(CPA, adapted)*
REQUIRED: The amount recognized as a gain on restructuring of debt by a debtor that has granted an equity interest.
DISCUSSION: A debtor that grants an equity interest in full settlement of a payable should account for the equity interest at fair value. The difference between the fair value of the equity interest and the carrying amount of the payable is a gain. Consequently, Smokey Joe will recognize a gain of $6,000 ($56,000 debt – $50,000 fair value of the equity interest).
Answer (A) is incorrect. A gain should be recognized. Answer (C) is incorrect. The amount of $50,000 is the fair value of the equity interest. Answer (D) is incorrect. The carrying amount of the debt is $56,000.

12.6.7. Franco Corporation owes Chester National Bank (CNB) on a 10-year, 15% note in the amount of $100,000, plus $30,000 accrued interest. Because of financial difficulty, Franco has been unable to make annual interest payments for the past 2 years, and the note is due today. Accordingly, CNB restructured Franco Corporation's debt as follows:

- The $30,000 of accrued interest was forgiven.
- Franco was given 3 more years to pay off the debt at 8% interest. Payments are to be made annually at year end.

Franco would properly record the restructuring and the payment for the first year as

A. An increase in interest expense of $8,000 and a gain of $2,000.

B. A decrease in accrued interest of $8,000.

C. A decrease in accrued interest of $8,000 and a gain of $2,000.

D. A decrease in accrued interest of $30,000 and a gain of $6,000.

Answer (D) is correct. *(CMA, adapted)*
REQUIRED: The entry for the restructuring of a debt if accrued interest is forgiven, the interest rate is lowered, and the payment period is extended.
DISCUSSION: When modified terms of a restructured troubled debt provide for future undiscounted cash payments that are less than the carrying amount of the debt, the debtor should record the difference as a gain if it is material. Franco's future cash payments will total $124,000 after the restructuring ($100,000 of principal + 3 years of interest at $8,000 per year). Given a $130,000 carrying amount ($100,000 principal + $30,000 interest), the result is a gain of $6,000 ($130,000 – $124,000). Following a restructuring of this type, all future payments on the debt (principal and interest) are treated as reductions of the carrying amount. Consequently, no interest expense is recorded in the years following this restructuring. The entry to recognize the restructuring and the gain is

Note payable	$100,000	
Accrued interest	30,000	
Restructured note payable		$124,000
Gain		6,000

The entry to record the first payment is to debit restructured note payable for $8,000 and credit cash for $8,000.
Answer (A) is incorrect. No interest expense is recognized on a restructuring, and the gain is $6,000. Answer (B) is incorrect. Accrued interest is reduced by $30,000 (the amount forgiven). Answer (C) is incorrect. Accrued interest is reduced by $30,000, and the gain is $6,000.

12.6.8. An entity incurs legal fees amounting to $2,000 in granting an equity interest to a creditor in a troubled debt restructuring. In its financial statements, the entity should

A. Capitalize the $2,000 and amortize it over a period not to exceed 40 years.

B. Treat the $2,000 as an expense of the period.

C. Subtract the $2,000 from the $8,000 gain resulting from the restructuring of payables.

D. Reduce by $2,000 the amount that would otherwise be recorded for the equity interest.

Answer (D) is correct. *(Publisher, adapted)*
REQUIRED: The debtor's accounting for legal fees incurred in granting an equity interest to a creditor in a troubled debt restructuring.
DISCUSSION: Legal fees and other direct costs that a debtor incurs in granting an equity interest to a creditor in a troubled debt restructuring reduce the amount otherwise recorded for the interest. Other direct costs a debtor incurs to effect a troubled debt restructuring are deducted in measuring the gain on the restructuring of the payables. If no such gain is recognized, these costs are expensed as they are incurred.
Answer (A) is incorrect. The legal fees should be applied to reduce the amount of the equity interest. Answer (B) is incorrect. Treating the $2,000 as an expense of the period is the proper accounting for direct debt restructuring costs incurred other than in granting an equity interest. Answer (C) is incorrect. Deducting the $2,000 from the $8,000 gain resulting from the restructuring of payables is the proper accounting for direct debt restructuring costs incurred other than in granting an equity interest.

12.6.9. On December 31 of the current year, X Corp. was indebted to Zyland Company on a $100,000, 10% note. Only interest had been paid to date, and the remaining life of the note was 2 years. Because X Corp. was in financial difficulties, the parties agreed that X Corp. would settle the debt on the following terms:

1. Settle one-half of the note by transferring land with a recorded amount of $40,000 and a fair value of $45,000

2. Settle one-fourth of the note by transferring 1,000 shares of $1 par common stock with a fair value of $15 per share

3. Modify the terms of the remaining one-fourth of the note by reducing the interest rate to 5% for the remaining 2 years and reducing the principal to $15,000

What total gain should X Corp. record in the current year from this troubled debt restructuring?

   A. $10,000

   B. $13,500

   C. $23,500

. D. $28,500

Answer (D) is correct. *(T. Miller)*
   REQUIRED: The total gains recorded from a troubled debt restructuring.
   DISCUSSION: A debtor must recognize a gain upon restructuring a troubled debt. X Corp. should recognize a gain of $5,000 ($45,000 fair value – $40,000 cost) when recording the land at its fair value and a gain of $5,000 when exchanging the land for a portion of the note worth $50,000 ($100,000 face amount × 50%). A gain of $10,000 should be recognized on the exchange of stock with a fair value of $15,000 (1,000 shares × $15) for the portion of the note worth $25,000 ($100,000 face amount × 25%). Accordingly, the carrying amount of the balance of the note before the modification of its terms equals the remaining $25,000 principal of the original note. Because total cash payments after the restructuring will include principal of $15,000 and 2 years of interest equal to $1,500 ($15,000 × 5% × 2 years), the difference between the $25,000 carrying amount and the total cash payments of $16,500 is a gain of $8,500. The total gain is therefore $28,500 ($5,000 + $5,000 + $10,000 + $8,500).
   Answer (A) is incorrect. The amount of $10,000 is the gain on the exchange of stock. Answer (B) is incorrect. The amount of $13,500 equals 50% of the gain that should be recognized on the transfer of land and the gain from reducing the rate on 25% of the note. Answer (C) is incorrect. The amount of $23,500 includes only 50% of the gain that should be recognized on the transfer of the land.

12.6.10. Casey Corp. entered into a troubled debt restructuring agreement with First State Bank. First State agreed to accept land with a carrying amount of $85,000 and a fair value of $120,000 in exchange for a note with a carrying amount of $185,000. Disregarding income taxes, what amount should Casey report as a gain in its income statement?

   A. $0

   B. $35,000

   C. $65,000

   D. $100,000

Answer (D) is correct. *(CPA, adapted)*
   REQUIRED: The gain reported by a debtor after a troubled debt restructuring.
   DISCUSSION: The amount of $100,000 is the total gain. It equals the carrying amount of the debt ($185,000) minus the carrying amount of the asset given ($85,000 land). This total gain is the sum of (1) a $65,000 gain on restructuring ($185,000 carrying amount of debt – $120,000 fair value of the land) and (2) a $35,000 gain on appreciation of the land recognized at its disposal ($120,000 fair value of the land – $85,000 carrying amount of the land).
   Answer (A) is incorrect. The debtor must recognize a gain as a result of the extinguishment of debt because the carrying amount of the debt is greater than the carrying amount of the asset given. Answer (B) is incorrect. The amount of $35,000 is a gain on appreciation of the land recognized at its disposal. However, the total gain also includes a gain on restructuring. Answer (C) is incorrect. The amount of $65,000 is the gain on restructuring of payables. However, the total gain also includes the gain on appreciation of the land recognized at its disposal.

12.7 Asset Retirement Obligations (AROs)

12.7.1. The guidance for asset retirement obligations prescribes the accounting for obligations related to the retirement of long-lived tangible assets. A liability for an asset retirement obligation (ARO) within the scope of this guidance may arise solely from

   A. A plan to sell a long-lived asset.

   B. The improper operation of a long-lived asset.

   C. The temporary idling of a long-lived asset.

   D. The acquisition, construction, development, or normal operation of a long-lived asset.

Answer (D) is correct. *(Publisher, adapted)*
   REQUIRED: The source of a liability for an ARO.
   DISCUSSION: An ARO is recognized for a legal obligation relating to the retirement of a long-lived tangible asset. This obligation results from the acquisition, construction, development, or normal operation of such an asset.
   Answer (A) is incorrect. The scope of the guidance for asset retirement obligations does not extend to obligations arising solely from a plan to sell or otherwise dispose of any long-lived asset. Answer (B) is incorrect. The scope of the guidance for asset retirement obligations does not extend to obligations arising from the improper operation of an asset. Answer (C) is incorrect. Retirement is the nontemporary removal of the asset from service, for example, by sale, abandonment, or recycling.

12.7.2. An entity is most likely to account for an asset retirement obligation (ARO) by

A. Recognizing the fair value of the liability using an expected present value technique.

B. Recognizing a liability equal to the sum of the net undiscounted future cash flows associated with the ARO.

C. Decreasing the carrying amount of the related long-lived asset.

D. Decreasing the liability for the ARO to reflect the accretion expense.

Answer (A) is correct. *(Publisher, adapted)*
REQUIRED: The proper accounting for an ARO.
DISCUSSION: The fair value of the ARO liability is recognized when incurred. If a reasonable estimate of the fair value cannot be made at that time, the ARO will be recognized when such an estimate can be made. An expected present value technique ordinarily should be used to estimate the fair value. A credit-adjusted risk-free rate is the appropriate discount rate.
Answer (B) is incorrect. A present value method may be used to estimate fair value. Probability-weighted present values, not undiscounted amounts, are ordinarily used to measure the ARO. Answer (C) is incorrect. The associated asset retirement cost (ARC) is debited to the carrying amount of the long-lived tangible asset when the ARO is recognized (credited). Answer (D) is incorrect. Accretion expense is debited when the ARO is credited to reflect its increase due to passage of time.

12.7.3. A business entity acquired a tangible long-lived asset with an asset retirement obligation (ARO) and included asset retirement cost (ARC) in the asset's carrying amount. The entity also recorded a liability for the ARO on the acquisition date. Subsequently, the entity should

A. Test the ARC for impairment but not amortize it.

B. Test the tangible long-lived asset for impairment and exclude ARC from the carrying amount for this purpose.

C. Recognize accretion expense before the periodic change in the ARO due to revised estimates of cash flows.

D. Discount upward revisions of the undiscounted estimated cash flows relating to the ARO by using the original credit-adjusted risk-free rate.

Answer (C) is correct. *(Publisher, adapted)*
REQUIRED: The subsequent accounting for a tangible long-lived asset with an ARO.
DISCUSSION: A change from one period to the next in the ARO due to passage of time is added to the liability. It is measured by applying an interest method of allocation to the ARO's beginning balance for the period. The rate is the credit-adjusted risk-free (CARF) rate used at the ARO's initial measurement. The offsetting debit is to accretion expense, which is classified as an operating item. After the periodic change resulting from the passage of time has been recognized, the periodic change in the ARO due to revised estimates of the timing or amount of the undiscounted cash flows is accounted for as an adjustment of the capitalized ARC and the carrying amount of the ARO. Increases in those estimated undiscounted cash flows are discounted using the current CARF rate, and decreases are discounted using the original CARF rate.
Answer (A) is incorrect. The ARC is expensed over its useful life using a systematic and rational method, but the entity is permitted to expense the amount that is capitalized in the same period. Answer (B) is incorrect. The carrying amount of the tangible long-lived asset includes ARC for the purpose of impairment testing. Answer (D) is incorrect. The original CARF rate is used to discount downward revisions of the undiscounted estimated cash flows relating to an ARO.

12.7.4. A business entity acquired a long-lived tangible asset on January 1, Year 4. On that date, it recorded a liability for an asset retirement obligation (ARO) and capitalized asset retirement cost (ARC). The estimated useful life of the long-lived tangible asset is 5 years, the credit-adjusted risk-free (CARF) rate used for initial measurement of the ARO is 10%, the initial fair value of the ARO liability based on an expected present value calculation is $250,000, and no changes occur in the undiscounted estimated cash flows used to calculate that fair value. If the entity settles the ARO on December 31, Year 8, for $420,000, what is the settlement gain or loss (rounded)?

A. $(17,372)

B. $25,000

C. $(152,628)

D. $(170,000)

Answer (A) is correct. *(Publisher, adapted)*
REQUIRED: The gain (loss) on settlement of an ARO.
DISCUSSION: Given no changes in the undiscounted estimated cash flows used to calculate the fair value of the ARO on January 1, Year 4, the only adjustment to the ARO during its useful life is for the passage of time (debit accretion expense, credit ARO). This adjustment is recognized each period in an amount equal to the beginning ARO balance times the initial CARF rate. Consequently, the ARO at December 31, Year 8, is

	Beginning Balance	Accretion Adjustment	Ending Balance
Year 4	$250,000	$25,000	$275,000
Year 5	275,000	27,500	302,500
Year 6	302,500	30,250	332,750
Year 7	332,750	33,275	366,025
Year 8	366,025	36,602.5	402,627.5

The settlement loss is $17,372 ($420,000 − $402,628 ARO balance at December 31, Year 8).
Answer (B) is incorrect. The amount of $25,000 is the accretion expense for Year 4. Answer (C) is incorrect. The amount of $(152,628) is the difference between the ARO balance at 1/1/Year 4 and the ARO balance at December 31, Year 8. Answer (D) is incorrect. The amount of $(170,000) equals the difference between the settlement amount and the initial balance.

12.7.5. Finch Co. reported a total asset retirement obligation of $257,000 in last year's financial statements. This year, Finch acquired assets subject to unconditional retirement obligations measured at undiscounted cash flow estimates of $110,000 and discounted cash flow estimates of $68,000. Finch paid $87,000 toward the settlement of previously recorded asset retirement obligations and recorded an accretion expense of $26,000. What amount should Finch report for the asset retirement obligation in this year's balance sheet?

A. $238,000

B. $264,000

C. $280,000

D. $306,000

Answer (B) is correct. *(CPA, adapted)*
REQUIRED: The amount reported for an ARO given accretion expense, acquisitions, and a payment.
DISCUSSION: An asset retirement obligation (ARO) reflects a legal obligation arising from the acquisition, construction, development, or normal operation of an asset. The ARO is recorded initially as a liability at fair value when incurred, and the liability is adjusted periodically. The liability decreases when the entity settles part of the ARO. It increases because of incurrence of a new ARO and the passage of time (accretion expense). The ARO and the asset retirement cost (the increase in the related long-lived tangible asset equal to the initial ARO) also are adjusted for changes in estimates. An expected present value technique ordinarily is used to estimate the fair value of the ARO. In this question, the fair value of the acquired ARO is meant to be approximated by the discounted cash flow estimate ($68,000). Thus, the ARO at year end is $264,000.

Beginning balance	$257,000
New ARO (FV)	68,000
Partial settlement	(87,000)
Accretion expense	26,000
Ending balance	$264,000

Answer (A) is incorrect. The amount of $238,000 does not include the accretion expense. Answer (C) is incorrect. The amount of $280,000 includes the undiscounted cash flow estimate of $110,000 instead of the discounted cash flow and does not reflect the accretion expense. Answer (D) is incorrect. The amount of $306,000 includes the undiscounted cash flow estimate instead of the discounted estimate.

12.8 IFRS

12.8.1. Debtor owes Bank on a 10-year, 15% note in the amount of $100,000, plus $30,000 accrued interest. Because of financial difficulty, Debtor has been unable to make annual interest payments for the past 2 years, and the note is due today. Accordingly, Bank legally agreed to restructure Debtor's debt as follows:

● The $30,000 of accrued interest was forgiven.

● Debtor was given 3 more years to pay off the debt at 8% interest. Payments are to be made annually at year end. The present value of the payments using the prevailing rate for similar instruments of an issuer with a similar credit rating is $84,018.

At the date of the restructuring, Debtor properly records

A. A loss of $30,000.

B. A gain of $30,000.

C. A gain of $45,982.

D. No gain or loss because no extinguishment occurred.

Answer (C) is correct. *(Publisher, adapted)*
REQUIRED: The entry for the restructuring of a debt if accrued interest is forgiven, the interest rate is lowered, and the payment period is extended.
DISCUSSION: Derecognition of a financial liability (or a part) occurs only by means of extinguishment. This condition is satisfied only when the debtor pays the creditor or is legally released from primary responsibility either by the creditor or through the legal process. An extinguishment and derecognition of the old debt and recognition of new debt occurs when the borrower and lender exchange debt instruments with substantially different terms, that is, when the respective discounted cash flows differ by at least 10%. A substantial modification of terms is also accounted for as an extinguishment. The difference between the carrying amount (including unamortized costs) of a liability (or part) that has been extinguished or transferred and the amount paid is included in profit or loss. This transaction qualifies as an extinguishment based on a substantial modification of terms because the discounted cash flow from the old debt ($130,000 due immediately) and the new debt (given as $84,018) differ by at least 10%. Hence, the amount included by Debtor in profit or loss at the date of the restructuring is a $45,982 gain ($130,000 – $84,018), that is, the difference between the carrying amount extinguished and the amount paid (the present value of the new debt instrument determined by discounting the cash outflows at the prevailing rate for similar instruments of an issuer with a similar credit rating). The entry is to debit the extinguished liability for accrued interest and principal ($130,000), debit discount on note payable ($15,982), credit note payable ($100,000), and credit gain ($45,982).
Answer (A) is incorrect. The amount of $30,000 is the difference between the sum of the existing liabilities and the face amount of the note with modified terms. Moreover, a gain should be recognized. Answer (B) is incorrect. The amount of $30,000 is the difference between the sum of the existing liabilities and the face amount of the note with modified terms. Moreover, a gain should be recognized. Answer (D) is incorrect. The terms were substantially different. Thus, an extinguishment occurred.

12.8.2. An entity most likely may derecognize a financial liability if it

A. Transfers amounts to a trust to be used to repay the obligation.

B. Exchanges debt instruments with the lender with substantially similar terms.

C. Exchanges debt instruments with the lender with substantially different terms.

D. Transfers amounts in a transaction that meets the requirements of an in-substance defeasance.

Answer (C) is correct. *(Publisher, adapted)*
REQUIRED: The circumstances in which an entity may derecognize a financial liability.
DISCUSSION: Derecognition of a financial liability (or a part) occurs only by means of extinguishment. This condition is satisfied only when the debtor pays the creditor or is legally released from primary responsibility either by the creditor or through the legal process. An extinguishment and derecognition of the old debt and recognition of new debt occurs when the borrower and lender exchange debt instruments with substantially different terms, that is, when the respective discounted cash flows differ by at least 10%.
Answer (A) is incorrect. Payment to a third party, such as a trust (also known as an in-substance defeasance), does not by itself extinguish the obligation absent a legal release. Answer (B) is incorrect. The terms should be substantially different. Answer (D) is incorrect. Payment to a third party, such as a trust (also known as an in-substance defeasance), does not by itself extinguish the obligation absent a legal release.

12.8.3. Cuddy Corp. issued bonds with a face amount of $200,000. Each $1,000 bond contained detachable share purchase warrants for 100 shares. Total proceeds from the issue equaled $240,000. The fair value of each warrant was $2, and the fair value of the bonds without the warrants was $196,000. Under IFRS, the bonds were issued at a discount of

A. $0

B. $678

C. $4,000

D. $40,678

Answer (C) is correct. *(Publisher, adapted)*
REQUIRED: The amount of the bond discount.
DISCUSSION: Under IFRS, the proceeds of bonds issued with detachable share purchase warrants must be assigned based on the residual allocation method. The liability component is measured at its fair value ($196,000), and the equity component is measured at the residual amount ($240,000 proceeds – $196,000 assigned to the liability component = $44,000). Accordingly, the bonds were issued at a discount of $4,000 ($200,000 face amount – $196,000). The entry is

Cash	$240,000	
Discount on bonds payable	4,000	
Bonds payable		$200,000
Share premium – warrants		44,000

Answer (A) is incorrect. The allocation to the bonds was less than their face amount. Answer (B) is incorrect. The total fair value of the warrants was $49,000 [($200,000 ÷ $1,000) × 100 warrants × $2]. The fair value of the bonds without warrants was given as $196,000. Thus, the amount allocated to the bonds was $199,322 {$240,000 × [$196,000 ÷ ($40,000 + $196,000)]}. The discount given an allocation based on relative fair values is therefore $678 ($200,000 – $199,322). Answer (D) is incorrect. The total fair value of the warrants was $40,000 [($200,000 ÷ $1,000) × 100 warrants × $2]. The fair value of the bonds without warrants was given as $196,000. Thus, the amount allocated to the warrants based on relative fair values is $40,678 {$240,000 × [$40,000 ÷ ($40,000 + $196,000)]}.

☑ ▬
☐ ▬   **Use Gleim Test Prep for interactive study and easy-to-use detailed analytics!**
☐ ▬

STUDY UNIT THIRTEEN
EMPLOYEE BENEFITS

This study unit addresses accounting for compensation costs recognized by employers. These costs relate to (1) pensions and similar arrangements with employees and (2) share-based payments.

The two most common types of pension plans are (1) defined contribution plans and (2) defined benefit plans. The accounting for defined contribution plans is relatively easy and rarely tested. Accordingly, most questions about pensions are on defined benefit plans.

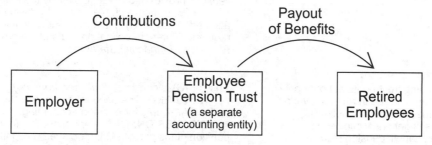

The major issues are (1) calculation of the **net periodic pension expense** (including understanding its components), (2) the calculation of pension asset or liability (including understanding the components of the **projected benefit obligation**) reported in the financial statements, and (3) required disclosure about the pension plan.

The following equations are helpful in answering questions about pensions:

Service cost	Beginning fair value of plan assets	Beginning projected benefit obligation
+ Interest cost	+ Contributions	+ Service cost
− Expected return on plan assets	− Benefits paid	+ Interest cost
± Amortization of net gain or loss	± Actual return on plan assets	+ Prior service cost
± Amortization of prior service cost or credit	**Ending fair value of plan assets**	− Prior service credit
Net periodic pension expense		− Benefits paid
		± Liability gain or loss
		Ending projected benefit obligation

Share-based payment involves obtaining goods or services in return for (1) equity instruments (e.g., share options) or (2) incurrence of liabilities based on the share price or that may require share settlement. In the typical transaction with employees, the measure of the compensation cost is the **fair value** of the equity instruments.

QUESTIONS

13.1 Pensions

13.1.1. An employer's accounting for a single-employer defined benefit pension plan is based on the fundamental assumption that such a plan is part of an employee's compensation incurred when the

- A. Defined pension benefit becomes vested.
- B. Defined pension benefit is paid.
- C. Defined pension benefit becomes a legal obligation.
- D. Employee's services are rendered.

Answer (D) is correct. *(Publisher, adapted)*
REQUIRED: The basic assumption underlying pension accounting.
DISCUSSION: The fundamental assumption of an employer's accounting for a single-employer defined benefit pension plan is that the plan is part of an employee's compensation incurred when the services provided to the employer by the employee are rendered. The defined pension benefit is provided in the form of a deferred payment. It is not precisely determinable. It can only be estimated based on the plan benefit formula and relevant future events, such as (1) future compensation levels, (2) mortality rates, (3) ages at retirement, and (4) vesting schedules.
Answer (A) is incorrect. A defined benefit pension plan is part of an employee's compensation received when the services provided to the employer by the employee are rendered. Answer (B) is incorrect. Net periodic pension cost may be accrued. Answer (C) is incorrect. Recognition of a liability requires a "present obligation" but not a legal obligation (SFAC 6, *Elements of Financial Statements*).

13.1.2. Certain accounting treatments not ordinarily allowed under GAAP are allowed in an employer's accounting for pensions. Which of the following accounting treatments is generally allowed in accounting for defined benefit pension plans?

- A. The tax basis of accounting.
- B. The cash or modified cash basis of accounting.
- C. The offsetting of assets and liabilities.
- D. The immediate recognition of all costs.

Answer (C) is correct. *(Publisher, adapted)*
REQUIRED: The accounting treatment ordinarily allowed under GAAP only for pension accounting.
DISCUSSION: GAAP for accounting for defined benefit pension plans permit (1) the delayed recognition of certain events, (2) the reporting of a net cost, and (3) the offsetting of assets and liabilities. "Delayed recognition" means that certain changes in the pension obligation and in the value of the plan assets are not recognized as they occur. They are recognized on a systematic and gradual basis over subsequent accounting periods. "Net costs" means that various pension costs (service cost, interest, actuarial gains and losses, etc.) reflected in the income statement are reported as one expense. The "offsetting feature" means that the recognized values of the plan assets contributed to the plan are offset in the statement of financial position against the recognized liabilities.
Answer (A) is incorrect. The tax basis of accounting is not appropriate under GAAP. Answer (B) is incorrect. The accrual basis of accounting is required. Answer (D) is incorrect. Delayed, rather than immediate, recognition is allowed for certain events.

13.1.3. GAAP relevant to employers' accounting for pensions apply primarily to defined benefit pension plans. It defines the projected benefit obligation as the

- A. Present value of benefits accrued to date based on future compensation levels.
- B. Present value of benefits accrued to date based on current compensation levels.
- C. Increase in retroactive benefits at the date of the amendment of the plan.
- D. Amount of the adjustment necessary to reflect the difference between actual and estimated actuarial returns.

Answer (A) is correct. *(CMA, adapted)*
REQUIRED: The definition of the projected benefit obligation.
DISCUSSION: The projected benefit obligation (PBO) as of a date is equal to the actuarial present value of all benefits attributed by the pension benefit formula to employee service rendered prior to that date. The PBO is measured using assumptions about future compensation levels.
Answer (B) is incorrect. The accumulated benefit obligation (ABO) is the present value of benefits accrued to date based on current compensation levels. Answer (C) is incorrect. Prior service cost is the increase in retroactive benefits at the date of the amendment of the plan. Answer (D) is incorrect. The gain or loss component of net periodic pension cost is the amount of the adjustment necessary to reflect the difference between actual and estimated actuarial returns.

13.1.4. Timor Co. sponsors a defined benefit pension plan. The accumulated benefit obligation (ABO) arising under the plan includes benefit obligations to <List A> employees at <List B> salary levels.

	List A	List B
A.	Vested but not nonvested	Current
B.	Vested but not nonvested	Future
C.	Vested and nonvested	Current
D.	Vested and nonvested	Future

Answer (C) is correct. *(CIA, adapted)*
REQUIRED: The nature of the ABO.
DISCUSSION: The ABO is the present value of benefits accrued to date based on past and current compensation levels. Whether benefits are vested is irrelevant to the computation. Thus, the ABO includes both vested and nonvested benefits and is calculated at current, not future, salary levels.
Answer (A) is incorrect. Vested and nonvested benefits are included in the ABO. Answer (B) is incorrect. Vested and nonvested benefits are included in the ABO at current salary levels. Answer (D) is incorrect. The PBO is measured using assumptions about future salary levels.

13.1.5. An employee's right to obtain pension benefits regardless of whether (s)he remains employed is the

A. Prior service cost.

B. Defined benefit.

C. Vested interest.

D. Minimum liability.

Answer (C) is correct. *(CIA, adapted)*
REQUIRED: The term defined as the right to obtain pension benefits regardless of future employment.
DISCUSSION: Vested benefits (vested interest) are those earned pension benefits owed to an employee regardless of the employee's continued service. The employer's vested benefit obligation (VBO) is the actuarial present value of these vested benefits.
Answer (A) is incorrect. Prior service cost relates to benefits for employee service provided prior to the adoption or amendment of a defined benefit pension plan. Answer (B) is incorrect. A defined benefit pension plan provides a defined pension benefit based on one or more factors, such as level of compensation, years of service, or age. Answer (D) is incorrect. Recognition of a minimum liability equal to the unfunded ABO was replaced by full recognition of funded status. An employer now must recognize an asset (liability) for the overfunded (underfunded) PBO.

13.1.6. Which of the following defined benefit pension plan disclosures should be made in a company's financial statements?

I. The funded status of the plans and the amounts recognized in the balance sheet

II. The amount of net periodic benefit cost recognized, showing its components separately

III. A reconciliation of beginning and ending balances of the fair value of plan assets

A. I and II.

B. I, II, and III.

C. II and III.

D. I only.

Answer (B) is correct. *(CPA, adapted)*
REQUIRED: The disclosure(s) about a defined benefit pension plan in a company's financial statements.
DISCUSSION: Many disclosures are required. One is the funded status of the plans and the amounts recognized in the balance sheet, with separate display of assets and current and noncurrent liabilities. Another required disclosure is the net periodic benefit cost recognized, showing its components separately (service cost, interest cost, expected return on plan assets, amortization of any transition amount, amortized gain or loss, amortized prior service cost, and gain or loss recognized due to a settlement or curtailment). Also required is a reconciliation of beginning and ending balances of the fair value of plan assets showing the effects of (1) the actual return, (2) exchange rate changes, (3) employer and plan participant contributions, (4) benefits paid, (5) business combinations, (6) divestitures, and (7) settlements. These are just a few of the standardized required disclosures.

13.1.7. For a defined benefit pension plan, the discount rate used to calculate the projected benefit obligation (PBO) is determined by the

	Expected Return on Plan Assets	Actual Return on Plan Assets
A.	Yes	Yes
B.	No	No
C.	Yes	No
D.	No	Yes

Answer (B) is correct. *(CPA, adapted)*
REQUIRED: The basis for determining the discount rate used to calculate the projected benefit obligation.
DISCUSSION: Assumed discount rates are used to measure the PBO. They reflect the rates at which benefits can be settled. In estimating these rates, it is appropriate to consider current prices of annuity contracts that could be used to settle pension obligations as well as the rates on high-quality fixed investments.

13.1.8. Which of the following is a true statement about the employer's reporting of the assets of a defined benefit pension plan?

A. Market-related value should be used for all purposes except determining asset gains and losses.

B. All assets should be measured at cost.

C. Plan assets that constitute plan investments should be measured at fair value for disclosure purposes.

D. Plan assets used in plan operations should be measured at market value.

Answer (C) is correct. *(Publisher, adapted)*
REQUIRED: The true statement about the measurement of plan assets.
DISCUSSION: For disclosure purposes and for determination of the plan's funded status, plan investments are measured at their fair values. For calculating the expected return on plan assets and thus for determining asset gains and losses, the market-related value is used. Market-related value may be either fair value or a calculated value that recognizes changes in fair value systematically and rationally over not more than 5 years, e.g., a 5-year moving average.
Answer (A) is incorrect. Market-related value (fair value or a calculated value) is used for calculating the expected return on plan assets and asset gains and losses (actual return – expected return). Answer (B) is incorrect. An employer discloses plan assets at fair value. Furthermore, the employer may use market-related value for certain purposes. Answer (D) is incorrect. Plan assets used in operations, e.g., an administration building, should be reported at cost minus accumulated depreciation by the plan, not the employer-sponsor.

13.1.9. Entities that sponsor defined benefit pension plans must recognize the actuarial present value of the increase in pension benefits payable to employees because of their services rendered during the current period. This element of pension expense is the

A. Amortization of prior service credit.

B. Service cost.

C. Accumulated benefit obligation (ABO).

D. Projected benefit obligation (PBO).

Answer (B) is correct. *(CMA, adapted)*
REQUIRED: The term for the actuarial present value of the pension benefits attributable to employee services during the current period.
DISCUSSION: Service cost is the present value of the future benefits earned in the current period (as calculated according to the plan's benefit formula). This amount is usually calculated by the plan's actuary. Service cost is a component of net periodic pension cost. It is also a portion of the PBO.
Answer (A) is incorrect. A plan amendment that retroactively reduces benefits results in a prior service credit. It decreases the PBO. This decrease is credited to OCI, net of tax. Any credit remaining after reducing prior service cost in accumulated OCI is amortized as part of pension expense. Answer (C) is incorrect. The ABO is the same as the PBO except that it is limited to past and current compensation levels. Answer (D) is incorrect. The PBO is the actuarial present value of all future benefits attributed to past employee service at a moment in time. It is based on assumptions as to future compensation if the plan formula is based on future compensation.

13.1.10. Interest cost included in the pension expense recognized for a period by an employer sponsoring a defined benefit pension plan represents the

A. Shortage between the expected and actual return on plan assets.

B. Increase in the projected benefit obligation resulting from the passage of time.

C. Increase in the fair value of plan assets resulting from the passage of time.

D. Amortization of prior service cost.

Answer (B) is correct. *(CPA, adapted)*
REQUIRED: The definition of interest cost.
DISCUSSION: The interest cost component of pension expense is defined as the increase in the PBO resulting from the passage of time.
Answer (A) is incorrect. The shortage between the expected and actual return on plan assets is an asset loss. Answer (C) is incorrect. The fair value of plan assets increases as a result of actual return on plan assets and not due to interest cost. Answer (D) is incorrect. Prior service cost is the cost of an amendment to a pension plan that increases pension benefits granted to employees for services already rendered. The amortization of prior service cost assigns an equal amount to each future period of service of each employee who is expected to receive benefits under the plan.

13.1.11. On July 31, Year 1, Tern Co. amended its single employee defined benefit pension plan by granting increased benefits for services provided prior to Year 1. This prior service cost will be reflected in the financial statement(s) for

    A. Years before Year 1 only.

    B. Year 1 only.

    C. Year 1 and years before and following Year 1.

    D. Year 1 and following years only.

Answer (D) is correct. *(CPA, adapted)*
    REQUIRED: The year(s) in which prior service cost will be reflected in the financial statement(s).
    DISCUSSION: Prior service cost is recognized when a plan is amended to grant additional benefits for services already rendered by employees. The amortization of prior service cost should be recognized as a component of pension expense during the future service periods of those employees active at the date of the plan amendment and who are expected to receive benefits under the plan. Thus, prior service cost is reflected in the Year 1 financial statements when the plan was amended and in the following years as it is amortized.
    Answer (A) is incorrect. Prior-service cost is not recognized as a prior period adjustment. Answer (B) is incorrect. Prior service cost is allocated to future service periods on a systematic and rational basis. Answer (C) is incorrect. Prior-service cost is not recognized as a prior period adjustment.

13.1.12. Sheen Company maintains a defined benefit pension plan for its employees. For the fiscal year ended December 31 of the current year, it reported a pension liability. This liability is the amount by which the

    A. Projected benefit obligation exceeds the fair value of plan assets.

    B. Projected benefit obligation exceeds the vested benefit obligation.

    C. Vested benefit obligation exceeds the fair value of plan assets.

    D. Accumulated benefit obligation exceeds contributions to the plan.

Answer (A) is correct. *(CPA, adapted)*
    REQUIRED: The amount that the unfunded accrued pension cost represents in a defined benefit pension plan.
    DISCUSSION: If the PBO is overfunded (fair value of plan assets > PBO), the excess is recognized in the balance sheet as an asset. If the PBO is underfunded (fair value of plan assets < PBO), the excess is recognized in the balance sheet as a liability.
    Answer (B) is incorrect. The VBO is not used to determine the funded status of the plan. Answer (C) is incorrect. The liability is the excess of the PBO over the fair value of plan assets. Answer (D) is incorrect. The factors used in measuring the funded status of the plan are the PBO and the fair value of plan assets.

13.1.13. Spencer Company sponsors a defined benefit pension plan for its employees. What pension-related information must it disclose?

	Amount of Prior Service Cost in Accumulated Other Comprehensive Income	Reclassification Adjustments of Other Comprehensive Income
A.	Yes	Yes
B.	Yes	No
C.	No	No
D.	No	Yes

Answer (A) is correct. *(CPA, adapted)*
    REQUIRED: The disclosure(s), if any, required of an employer sponsoring a defined benefit pension plan.
    DISCUSSION: A public or nonpublic entity that sponsors a defined benefit pension plan must disclose, among other things, separate amounts for (1) net gain (loss) and prior service cost (credit) recognized in OCI for the period, (2) reclassification adjustments of OCI recognized in net periodic benefit cost for the period, and (3) items still in accumulated OCI (showing separately net gain or loss, net prior service cost or credit, and net transition asset or obligation).
    Answer (B) is incorrect. Reclassification adjustments of OCI recognized in pension expense (for example, debit pension expense and credit OCI, net of tax for amortization of prior service cost recorded in a prior period) must be disclosed. Answer (C) is incorrect. Prior service cost in accumulated OCI and reclassification adjustments of OCI must be disclosed. Answer (D) is incorrect. Prior service cost in accumulated OCI must be disclosed.

13.1.14. Which of the following describes a fundamental aspect of accounting for defined benefit pension plans by employers?

- A. Changes in pension assets and obligations are recognized immediately.

- B. The amount of pension benefits is not precisely determinable.

- C. Net periodic pension cost (pension expense) may be reported within maximum and minimum limits.

- D. An employer that funds multiple pension plans may calculate its funded status based on accumulated benefit obligation if some of the plans are overfunded and others are underfunded.

Answer (B) is correct. *(Publisher, adapted)*
REQUIRED: The statement of a fundamental aspect of pension accounting.
DISCUSSION: The total pension benefit to be provided in the form of deferred payments is not precisely determinable and can only be estimated based on the plan's benefit formula and relevant future events, many of which are not controllable by the employer. Such events include how long the employee and survivors live, years of service rendered, and levels of compensation.
Answer (A) is incorrect. Certain changes in the pension obligation and in the value of the assets set aside to meet those obligations are not recognized as they occur. They are recognized on a systematic and gradual basis over subsequent accounting periods. All changes ultimately will be recognized except to the extent they may be offset by subsequent changes. Answer (C) is incorrect. A standard method (not a range) is prescribed for measuring pension expense. Answer (D) is incorrect. A defined-benefit pension plan's funded status must be measured using the projected, not accumulated, benefit obligation.

13.1.15. In a business combination, Ryan Co. acquired Pichardo Co., which sponsors a single-employer defined benefit pension plan. Ryan should

- A. Recognize any previously existing net gain or loss.

- B. Assign part of the purchase price to the prior service cost as an intangible asset.

- C. Assign part of the purchase price to the excess of plan assets over the projected benefit obligation.

- D. Recognize a previously existing transition net asset or obligation of the plan.

Answer (C) is correct. *(Publisher, adapted)*
REQUIRED: The acquiring company's accounting when the acquired company sponsors a pension plan.
DISCUSSION: In a business combination, the acquiring entity should recognize a pension liability if the PBO of the acquired entity is in excess of its plan assets. Likewise, a pension asset should be recognized if plan assets exceed the PBO.
Answer (A) is incorrect. In a business combination, previously existing net gains and losses recognized in accumulated OCI are eliminated by the assignment of part of the purchase price to a liability (excess of PBO over plan assets) or an asset (excess of plan assets over the PBO). Answer (B) is incorrect. In a business combination, previously existing prior service costs recognized in accumulated OCI are eliminated by the assignment of part of the purchase price to a liability (excess of PBO over plan assets) or an asset (excess of plan assets over the PBO). Answer (D) is incorrect. In a business combination, a previously existing transition net asset or obligation of the acquired company's defined benefit plan recognized in accumulated OCI is eliminated by the assignment of part of the purchase price to a liability (excess of PBO over plan assets) or an asset (excess of plan assets over the PBO).

13.1.16. Dawson Co. sponsors an arrangement that provides pension benefits in return for services rendered, provides an individual account for each participant, and specifies how contributions to the individual accounts are to be determined. This arrangement is a

- A. Defined benefit pension plan.

- B. Defined contribution plan.

- C. Multiemployer plan.

- D. Multiple-employer plan.

Answer (B) is correct. *(Publisher, adapted)*
REQUIRED: The type of plan defined.
DISCUSSION: A defined contribution plan specifies how contributions to an individual's account are to be determined. The benefits a participant will receive depend solely on the amount contributed, the returns earned on investments of those contributions, and forfeitures of other participants' benefits that may be allocated to his or her account. The pension expense is the contribution called for in the particular accounting period.
Answer (A) is incorrect. A defined benefit pension plan is a plan that provides a defined pension benefit based on one or more factors. Answer (C) is incorrect. A multiemployer plan is a plan to which two or more unrelated employers contribute, usually pursuant to one or more collective bargaining agreements. Assets are not segregated and may be used to provide benefits to employees of any of the participating employers. Answer (D) is incorrect. A multiple-employer plan is a pension plan to which two or more unrelated employers contribute, usually to allow pooling of assets for investment purposes and to reduce administrative costs. Assets are segregated, and contributions may be based on benefit formulas that differ.

13.1.17. The following information pertains to McNeil Co.'s defined benefit pension plan:

Actuarial estimate of projected benefit obligation at January 1	$144,000
Assumed discount rate	10%
Service cost for the year	36,000
Pension benefits paid during the year	30,000

If no change in actuarial estimates occurred during the year, McNeil's PBO at December 31 was

A. $128,400

B. $150,000

C. $158,400

D. $164,400

Answer (D) is correct. *(CPA, adapted)*
REQUIRED: The projected benefit obligation at the end of the year.
DISCUSSION: The ending balance of the PBO is the beginning balance plus the service cost and interest cost components, minus the benefits paid. The interest cost component is equal to the PBO's beginning balance times the discount rate.

Beginning PBO balance	$144,000
Service cost	36,000
Interest cost ($144,000 × 10%)	14,400
Benefits paid	(30,000)
Ending PBO balance	$164,400

Answer (A) is incorrect. The amount of $128,400 excludes the current year's service cost component. Answer (B) is incorrect. The amount of $150,000 excludes the interest cost component. Answer (C) is incorrect. The amount of $158,400 excludes both the service cost component and the benefits paid.

13.1.18. The following information pertains to Beltran Co.'s defined benefit pension plan for the current year:

Fair value of plan assets, beginning of year	$ 700,000
Fair value of plan assets, end of year	1,050,000
Employer contributions	220,000
Benefits paid	170,000

In computing pension expense, what amount should Beltran use as actual return on plan assets?

A. $130,000

B. $300,000

C. $350,000

D. $520,000

Answer (B) is correct. *(CPA, adapted)*
REQUIRED: The actual return on plan assets.
DISCUSSION: The actual return on plan assets is based on the fair value of plan assets at the beginning and end of the accounting period adjusted for contributions and payments during the period. The actual return is $300,000 ($1,050,000 − $700,000 − $220,000 + $170,000).
Answer (A) is incorrect. The amount of $130,000 results when benefits paid to employees are not included. Answer (C) is incorrect. The amount of $350,000 is the change in the fair value of plan assets without adjustment for contributions or benefits paid. Answer (D) is incorrect. The amount of $520,000 does not deduct employer contributions.

13.1.19. At the beginning of the current year, the market-related value of the plan assets of Janeway Company's defined benefit pension plan was $1,000,000. Janeway uses a 5-year weighted-average method to determine market-related values. The company, however, had not previously experienced any asset gains or losses. The expected long-term rate of return on plan assets is 10%. The actual return during the year was $50,000. Contributions and benefits paid were $150,000 and $200,000, respectively. At year end, the market-related value (MRV) of Janeway's plan assets is

A. $1,140,000

B. $1,040,000

C. $1,000,000

D. $950,000

Answer (B) is correct. *(Publisher, adapted)*
REQUIRED: The market-related value of plan assets at year end.
DISCUSSION: If market-related value is defined as fair value, the ending market-related value of the plan assets is the beginning amount, plus the actual returns, plus the contributions, minus the benefits paid. However, in this case, the company uses an alternative method to determine market-related value. This alternative includes 20% of the sum of the differences between the actual and the expected returns (asset gains and losses) over the last 5 years. The year-end market-related value is the beginning amount, plus the expected return, plus the contributions, minus the benefits paid, minus 20% of the difference between the actual return ($50,000) and the expected return ($1,000,000 × 10% = $100,000) for the current year only.

Beginning market-related value	$1,000,000
Expected return ($1,000,000 × 10%)	100,000
Contributions	150,000
Benefits paid	(200,000)
20% of $50,000 loss	(10,000)
Year-end market-related value	$1,040,000

Answer (A) is incorrect. The amount of $1,140,000 excludes the expected returns and benefits paid. Answer (C) is incorrect. The amount of $1,000,000 is the fair value and not the MRV of plan assets at year end. Answer (D) is incorrect. The amount of $950,000 excludes the expected return and 20% of the loss.

13.1.20. The following information relates to the current-year activity of the defined benefit pension plan of Kim Company, whose stock is publicly traded:

Service cost	$240,000
Expected return on plan assets	60,000
Interest cost on pension benefit obligation	80,000
Amortization of actuarial loss	20,000
Amortization of prior service cost	10,000

Kim's pension cost for the current year is

A. $240,000

B. $260,000

C. $270,000

D. $290,000

Answer (D) is correct. *(A. Oddo)*
REQUIRED: The pension expense for the year.
DISCUSSION: Components of pension expense are service cost, interest cost, the expected return on plan assets, and amortization of any (1) prior service cost or credit or (2) net gain (loss). Service cost, interest cost, and the amortization of actuarial loss and prior service cost increase the pension expense. The expected return on plan assets decreases pension expense. As indicated below, pension expense is $290,000.

Service cost	$240,000
Expected return on plan assets	(60,000)
Interest cost	80,000
Amortization of actuarial loss	20,000
Amortization of prior service cost	10,000
Pension expense	$290,000

Answer (A) is incorrect. The amount of $240,000 includes only the service cost component. Answer (B) is incorrect. The amount of $260,000 excludes the amortization of prior service cost and the actuarial loss. Answer (C) is incorrect. The amount of $270,000 excludes the amortization of the actuarial loss.

13.1.21. Schiff Co. sponsors a defined benefit pension plan. For the current year, the expected return on plan assets was $100,000. The actual return was $150,000. The company's actuary estimates an increase of $600,000 in the projected benefit obligation. The amount of the projected benefit obligation determined at year end reflected an increase of only $400,000. If no net gain (loss) was carried in accumulated OCI at the beginning of the year, the amount of net gain (loss) subject to required amortization for the current year is

A. $0

B. $400,000

C. $50,000

D. $250,000

Answer (A) is correct. *(Publisher, adapted)*
REQUIRED: The amount of net gain (loss) subject to required amortization for the current year.
DISCUSSION: Gains and losses need not be recognized in pension expense of the period in which they arise. The $50,000 asset gain ($150,000 actual return – $100,000 expected return) and the liability gain (the PBO at year end was $200,000 less than estimated) are therefore not required to be included in pension expense of the current year. Given that no net gain (loss) was carried in accumulated OCI at the beginning of the year, the required amortization for the current year is $0.

Answer (B) is incorrect. The amount of $400,000 is the year-end estimate of the PBO increase. This amount is not subject to required amortization when it occurs. Answer (C) is incorrect. The amount of $50,000 is the asset gain. No amortization is currently required. Answer (D) is incorrect. The amount of $250,000 is the sum of the asset gain and the liability gain. No amortization is currently required.

13.1.22. The following is the only information pertaining to Kane Co.'s defined benefit pension plan:

Pension asset, January 1, Year 1	$ 2,000
Service cost	19,000
Interest cost	38,000
Actual and expected return on plan assets	22,000
Amortization of prior service cost arising in a prior period	52,000
Employer contributions	40,000

In its December 31, Year 1, balance sheet, what amount should Kane report as the unfunded or overfunded projected benefit obligation (PBO)?

A. $7,000 overfunded.

B. $15,000 underfunded.

C. $45,000 underfunded.

D. $52,000 underfunded.

Answer (A) is correct. *(CPA, adapted)*
REQUIRED: The unfunded or overfunded PBO.
DISCUSSION: The employer must recognize the funded status of the plan as the difference between the fair value of plan assets and the PBO at year end. That amount is an asset or a liability. Current service cost and interest cost increase the PBO. The return on plan assets and contributions increase plan assets. Amortization of prior service cost arising in a prior period and recognized in accumulated OCI has no additional effect on the PBO or plan assets. However, it is a component of pension expense. The PBO was overfunded by $2,000 on January 1. It increased during the year by $57,000 ($19,000 + $38,000). Plan assets increased by $62,000 ($22,000 + $40,000). Accordingly, the plan is overfunded by $7,000 [$2,000 + ($62,000 – $57,000)] at year end. Kane should recognize a pension asset of $7,000 at year end.

Answer (B) is incorrect. The return on plan assets should be added to plan assets. Answer (C) is incorrect. The $45,000 underfunded includes prior service cost amortization. Prior service cost that arose in a prior period was reflected in the asset or liability recognized for the funded status of the plan at the beginning of the year. When prior service cost arises, the entry is to debit OCI, net of tax, and credit pension liability. Answer (D) is incorrect. The $52,000 underfunded is the prior service cost amortization.

13.1.23. An entity sponsors a defined benefit pension plan that is underfunded by $800,000. A $500,000 increase in the fair value of plan assets would have which of the following effects on the financial statements of the entity?

A. An increase in the assets of the entity.

B. An increase in accumulated other comprehensive income of the entity for the full amount of the increase in the value of the assets.

C. A decrease in accumulated other comprehensive income of the entity for the full amount of the increase in the value of the assets.

D. A decrease in the liabilities of the entity.

Answer (D) is correct. *(CPA, adapted)*
REQUIRED: The effects of an increase in the fair value of plan assets that is less than the underfunded amount.
DISCUSSION: If a projected benefit obligation exceeds the fair value of plan assets, the amount of the underfunding must be recognized as a liability. If the pension plan is underfunded by $800,000, an increase in the fair value of plan assets of $500,000 reduces the underfunding to $300,000. Thus, the increase in the fair value of plan assets decreases but does not eliminate the pension liability.
Answer (A) is incorrect. Given that the projected benefit obligation is underfunded by $800,000, the fair value of plan assets would have to increase by more than $800,000 to increase the assets of the entity. For example, if the fair value of the plan assets, which are not assets of the sponsor, had increased by $900,000, the entity would recognize an asset of $100,000 for the overfunding. Answer (B) is incorrect. The full over- or underfunded status of the plan is reported as an asset or liability, respectively. Unamortized gains or losses, prior service cost, and prior service credit are reported in OCI. The total OCI for the period is transferred to accumulated OCI (a component of equity in the statement of financial position). Thus, the funded status of the plan does not affect accumulated OCI. Answer (C) is incorrect. The funded status of the plan does not affect accumulated OCI.

13.1.24. A company has a defined benefit pension plan for its employees. On December 31, Year 1, the accumulated benefit obligation is $45,900, the projected benefit obligation is $68,100, and the fair value of the plan assets is $62,000. What amount, if any, related to the defined benefit plan should be recognized in the balance sheet at December 31, Year 1?

A. An asset of $16,100.

B. A liability of $6,100.

C. Nothing, as the fair value of the plan assets exceeds the accumulated benefit obligation.

D. An unrealized loss of $6,100.

Answer (B) is correct. *(CPA, adapted)*
REQUIRED: The amount, if any, recognized in relation to a defined benefit pension plan given the ABO, PBO, and fair value of plan assets.
DISCUSSION: A pension liability must be recognized for any excess of the PBO over the fair value of the plan assets at the balance sheet date. Accordingly, the balance sheet must report a liability of $6,100 ($68,100 – $62,000).
Answer (A) is incorrect. The fair value of plan assets exceeds the accumulated benefit obligation by $16,100. But the PBO, not the ABO, is used to measure the funded status of the defined benefit pension plan. Answer (C) is incorrect. The ABO was used to measure the additional minimum liability required to be recognized under prior U.S. GAAP. However, current U.S. GAAP require recognition of the full funded status of the defined benefit pension plan. Answer (D) is incorrect. The funded status of the plan is recognized as an asset or liability, and an unamortized gain or loss is recognized in OCI. Pension accounting does not use the term "unrealized loss." Amortized liability gains and losses (from changes in actuarial assumptions) and amortized asset gains and losses (from experience different from that expected) are recognized in net periodic pension cost (pension expense).

13.1.25. On January 1 of the current year, East Corp. adopted a defined benefit pension plan. The plan's service cost of $75,000 was fully funded at the end of the current year. Prior service cost was fully funded by a contribution of $30,000 in the current year. Amortization of prior service cost was $12,000 for the current year. Pension expense has no other components. What is the amount of East's pension asset at December 31 of the current year?

A. $0

B. $18,000

C. $42,000

D. $105,000

Answer (A) is correct. *(CPA, adapted)*
REQUIRED: The pension asset at year end.
DISCUSSION: The projected benefit obligation (PBO) is increased by the recognition of $30,000 of prior service cost and $75,000 of service cost, leaving a PBO of $105,000. The plan assets were increased by the full funding of both components ($30,000 + $75,000 = $105,000). Thus, the PBO is equal to the fair value of the plan assets at year end, and no pension asset or liability is reported.
Answer (B) is incorrect. The amount of $18,000 is the excess of the prior service cost over the amortization of prior service cost ($30,000 – $12,000). Answer (C) is incorrect. The amount of $42,000 is the sum of the prior service cost and the amortization of prior service cost ($30,000 + $12,000). Answer (D) is incorrect. The amount of $105,000 equals the PBO or the plan assets at year end ($30,000 + $75,000).

13.1.26. Jan Corp. amended its defined benefit pension plan, granting a total credit of $100,000 to four employees for services rendered prior to the plan's adoption. The employees, A, B, C, and D, are expected to retire from the company as follows:

"A" will retire after 3 years.
"B" and "C" will retire after 5 years.
"D" will retire after 7 years.

What is the amount of prior service cost amortization in the first year?

A. $0

B. $5,000

C. $20,000

D. $25,000

Answer (C) is correct. *(CPA, adapted)*
REQUIRED: The prior service cost amortization in the first year after amendment of a defined benefit pension plan.
DISCUSSION: The cost of retroactive benefits is the increase in the PBO at the date of the amendment (debit OCI, net of tax, and credit pension liability or asset). It should be amortized by assigning an equal amount to each future period of service of each employee active at the date of the amendment who is expected to receive benefits under the plan. However, to reduce the burden of these allocation computations, any alternative amortization approach (e.g., averaging) that more rapidly reduces the unrecognized prior service cost is acceptable provided that it is applied consistently. The total service years to be rendered by the employees equals 20 (3 + 5 + 5 + 7). Hence, the amortization percentage for the first year is 20% (4 ÷ 20), and the minimum amortization is $20,000 ($100,000 × 20%).
Answer (A) is incorrect. Amortization of prior service cost is a component of pension expense. Answer (B) is incorrect. The amount of $5,000 is the amount assigned to each period of service by each employee. Answer (D) is incorrect. The amount of $25,000 results from assigning an equal amount to each employee.

13.1.27. At end of the year, Nickel Company's projected benefit obligation (PBO) was determined to be $1,500,000, which was $200,000 higher than had been expected. The market-related value of the defined benefit plan's assets was equal to its fair value of $1,250,000. No other gains and losses have occurred. If the average remaining service life is 20 years, the minimum required amortization of the net gain (loss) in the next year will be

A. $20,000

B. $3,750

C. $2,500

D. $0

Answer (C) is correct. *(Publisher, adapted)*
REQUIRED: The minimum required amortization of net gain (loss) next year.
DISCUSSION: At a minimum, amortization of net gain or loss included in accumulated OCI at the beginning of the year (excluding asset gains and losses not yet reflected in market-related value) must be included as a component of pension expense for a year if, as of the beginning of the year, that gain or loss exceeds 10% of the greater of the PBO or the market-related value (MRV) of plan assets. At year end, Nickel's PBO was $200,000 greater than estimated (a $200,000 liability loss). Given that no other gain or loss has occurred, the net loss to be amortized beginning next year is $200,000. The corridor amount is $150,000 (10% of the greater of $1,500,000 PBO or $1,250,000 MRV of plan assets). The amount outside the corridor is $50,000 ($200,000 – $150,000), and the amount to be amortized is thus $2,500 ($50,000 ÷ 20 years of average remaining service life).
Answer (A) is incorrect. The amount of $20,000 is the result of using the full $200,000 liability loss without regard to the corridor amount. It also assumes an amortization period of 10 years instead of 20. Answer (B) is incorrect. The amount of $3,750 is the result of using $125,000 ($1,250,000 plan assets × 10%) as the corridor amount instead of $150,000. Answer (D) is incorrect. The amount of $50,000 of the liability loss must be amortized over the average remaining service life beginning the year following the loss.

13.1.28. On June 1, Year 1, Cleaver Corp. established a defined benefit pension plan for its employees. The following information was available at May 31, Year 3:

Projected benefit obligation	$29,000,000
Accumulated benefit obligation	24,000,000
Plan assets at fair value	14,000,000
Accumulated OCI – prior service cost	3,100,000

To report the proper pension liability in Cleaver's May 31, Year 3, balance sheet, what is the amount of the adjustment required?

A. $3.1 million.

B. $11.9 million.

C. $15.0 million.

D. $17.1 million.

Answer (B) is correct. *(CPA, adapted)*
REQUIRED: The amount of the adjustment required to reflect pension liability properly on the balance sheet.
DISCUSSION: A pension liability must be recognized in the amount of the underfunded PBO (PBO – fair value of plan assets). The PBO is underfunded by $15 million ($29 million PBO – $14 million FV of plan assets). However, the recording of OCI – prior service cost (a component of the PBO) required a credit to pension liability (net of tax) of $3.1 million. Accordingly, the adjustment is a credit of $11.9 million ($29 million PBO – $14 million plan assets at fair value – $3.1 million pension liability related to prior service cost).
Answer (A) is incorrect. The amount of $3.1 million equals accumulated OCI – prior service cost. Answer (C) is incorrect. The amount of $15.0 million is the total pension liability. Answer (D) is incorrect. The amount of $17.1 million is the sum of the fair value of plan assets and the accumulated OCI – prior service cost.

13.1.29. On January 2, Loch Co. established a noncontributory flat-defined-benefit pension plan covering all employees and contributed $1 million to the plan. At December 31, Loch determined that the service and interest costs of the plan were $620,000. The expected and the actual rate of return on plan assets for the year was 10%, and no benefit payments or additional contributions were made. Loch's pension expense has no other components. What amount should Loch report in its December 31 balance sheet as a pension asset?

A. $280,000

B. $380,000

C. $480,000

D. $620,000

Answer (C) is correct. *(CPA, adapted)*
   REQUIRED: The amount of prepaid pension cost.
   DISCUSSION: The funded status of a defined benefit pension plan equals the difference between the fair value of plan assets and the projected benefit obligation (PBO) at year end. Under a flat-benefit plan, benefits are based on a fixed amount for each year of service. Thus, future compensation levels are not considered in calculating the PBO. For an overfunded plan, an asset is recognized for the excess of the plan assets over the PBO. The PBO at the end of the plan's first year equals $620,000. It is the sum of the beginning PBO ($0, given no prior service cost), service and interest costs ($620,000), benefits paid ($0), prior service cost or credit ($0, given no mid-year plan amendment), and gain or loss from (1) changes in the PBO resulting from experience different from that assumed and (2) changes in actuarial assumptions ($0). This calculation assumes that the entity had no asset gain or loss (expected return = actual return) and no liability gain or loss (from changes in actuarial assumptions). Service cost is calculated for the first time at year end, so no change in actuarial assumptions could have occurred. Moreover, interest cost is $0 because the beginning PBO was $0. The plan assets equal $1,100,000 [$1,000,000 contributed + ($1,000,000 × 10%) actual return on plan assets]. Accordingly, $480,000 is the pension asset ($1,100,000 FV of plan assets – $620,000 PBO).
   Answer (A) is incorrect. The amount of $280,000 is the difference between the contributed amount and the sum of the service and interest costs, minus 10% of $1 million. Answer (B) is incorrect. The amount of $380,000 is the difference between the contributed amount and the sum of the service and interest costs. Answer (D) is incorrect. The amount of $620,000 is the sum of the service and interest costs. The return on plan assets also must be included in the calculations.

13.1.30. Worldwide Co. implemented a defined benefit pension plan for its employees on January 1, Year 4. During Year 4 and Year 5, Worldwide's contributions fully funded the plan. The following data are provided for Year 6:

	Year 6 Actual
Projected benefit obligation, December 31	$700,000
Accumulated benefit obligation, December 31	500,000
Plan assets at fair value, December 31	600,000
Projected benefit obligation in excess of plan assets	100,000

During Year 7, Worldwide recognized service cost of $120,000 and interest cost of $100,000. Its actual return on plan assets was $130,000. Worldwide had no recognized asset gain or loss and did not need to amortize prior service cost (credit), gain (loss), or a transition amount. To report a pension liability of $75,000 at December 31, Year 7, Worldwide must contribute what amount to the plan?

A. $75,000

B. $115,000

C. $165,000

D. $265,000

Answer (B) is correct. *(CPA, adapted)*
   REQUIRED: The amount contributed to report a given pension liability.
   DISCUSSION: The pension liability on January 1, Year 7, was $100,000. It increased during the year by $220,000 ($120,000 service cost + $100,000 interest cost) and decreased during the year by the actual return on plan assets of $130,000. The actual return on plan assets equaled the expected return because Worldwide had no asset gain or loss. Thus, the amount of pension liability before the adjustment for contributions is $190,000 ($100,000 + $220,000 – $130,000). To report a pension liability of $75,000, the contribution during Year 7 must be $115,000 ($190,000 – $75,000).
   Answer (A) is incorrect. A contribution of $75,000 results in a pension liability of $115,000. Answer (C) is incorrect. A contribution of $165,000 results in a pension liability of $25,000. Answer (D) is incorrect. A contribution of $265,000 results in a pension asset of $75,000.

13.1.31. On September 1, Year 1, Howe Corp. offered special termination benefits to employees who had reached the early retirement age specified in the company's pension plan. The termination benefits consisted of lump-sum and periodic future payments. Additionally, the employees accepting the company offer receive the usual early retirement pension benefits. The offer expired on November 30, Year 1. Actual or reasonably estimated amounts at December 31, Year 1, relating to the employees accepting the offer are as follows:

- Lump-sum payments totaling $475,000 were made on January 1, Year 2.
- Periodic payments of $60,000 annually for 3 years will begin January 1, Year 3. The present value at December 31, Year 1, of these payments was $155,000.
- Reduction of accrued pension costs at December 31, Year 1, for the terminating employees was $45,000.

At December 31, Year 1, Howe should report a total liability for special termination benefits of

- A. $475,000
- B. $585,000
- C. $630,000
- D. $655,000

Answer (C) is correct. *(CPA, adapted)*
REQUIRED: The total liability for special termination benefits.
DISCUSSION: The liability and expense arising from special termination benefits should be recognized by an employer when the employees accept the offer and the amount can be reasonably estimated. The amount should include the lump-sum payments and the present value of any future payments. Thus, Howe should report a total liability for special termination benefits of $630,000 ($475,000 lump-sum payments + $155,000 present value of future payments) in its 12/31/Year 1 balance sheet. The reduction of accrued pension costs is recognized by a debit for $45,000. After crediting the liability for $630,000, the debit to a loss account will be $585,000.
Answer (A) is incorrect. The amount of $475,000 omits the present value of the future benefits. Answer (B) is incorrect. The amount of $585,000 is the loss, not the liability. Answer (D) is incorrect. The amount of $655,000 is the undiscounted amount of the payments for termination benefits.

13.1.32. Which of the following components must be included in the calculation of pension expense recognized for a period by an employer sponsoring a defined benefit pension plan?

	Interest Cost	Actual Return on Plan Assets
A.	Yes	No
B.	Yes	Yes
C.	No	Yes
D.	No	No

Answer (B) is correct. *(CPA, adapted)*
REQUIRED: The component(s), if any, to be included in pension expense.
DISCUSSION: The required minimum pension expense consists of the following elements:

+	Service cost
+	Interest cost
−	Expected return on plan assets
±	Amortization of net gain or loss
±	Amortization of prior service cost of credit
	Pension expense

Thus, both interest cost and expected return on plan assets are components of pension expense.
Answer (A) is incorrect. The expected return on plan assets is an element of pension expense. Answer (C) is incorrect. Interest cost is an element of pension expense. Answer (D) is incorrect. Interest cost and the return on plan assets are elements of pension expense.

13.1.33. The following information pertains to Lee Corp.'s defined benefit pension plan for Year 1:

Service cost	$160,000
Actual and expected gain on plan assets	35,000
Unexpected loss on plan assets related to a Year 1 disposal of a subsidiary	40,000
Amortization of prior service cost	5,000
Annual interest on pension obligation	50,000

What amount must Lee report as pension expense in its Year 1 income statement?

- A. $250,000
- B. $220,000
- C. $210,000
- D. $180,000

Answer (D) is correct. *(CPA, adapted)*
REQUIRED: The pension expense for the year.
DISCUSSION: The components of the required minimum pension expense are (1) service cost, (2) interest cost, (3) return on plan assets, (4) amortization of the net gain or loss recognized in accumulated OCI, and (5) amortization of any prior service cost or credit. Accordingly, the service cost, actual and expected gain on plan assets, interest cost, and amortization of prior service cost are included in the computation. Gains and losses arising from changes in the PBO or plan assets resulting from experience different from that assumed and from changes in assumptions about discount rates, life expectancies, etc., are not required to be included in the calculation of the required minimum pension expense when they occur. Accordingly, the unexpected Year 1 loss on plan assets is included in the gain or loss recognized in OCI (debit OCI, net of tax, and credit pension liability or asset). It must be amortized beginning in Year 2. Pension expense is therefore $180,000 ($160,000 service cost – $35,000 actual and expected return on plan assets + $5,000 prior service cost amortization + $50,000 interest cost).
Answer (A) is incorrect. The amount of $250,000 results from adding, not subtracting, the expected gain on plan assets. Answer (B) is incorrect. The amount of $220,000 includes the unexpected loss. Answer (C) is incorrect. The amount of $210,000 includes the unexpected loss and subtracts instead of adding the amortization of prior service cost.

13.1.34. How should plan investments be reported in a defined benefit plan's financial statements?

- A. At actuarial present value.
- B. At cost.
- C. At net realizable value.
- D. At fair value.

Answer (D) is correct. *(CPA, adapted)*
REQUIRED: The reporting of plan investments by a defined benefit plan.
DISCUSSION: The annual financial statements of a defined benefit pension plan must include information about the net assets available for benefits at the end of the plan year. Plan investments, whether equity or debt securities, real estate, or other (excluding insurance contracts) must be presented at their fair value at the reporting date.
Answer (A) is incorrect. Accumulated plan benefits are measured at actuarial present value at the benefit information date. Answer (B) is incorrect. Plan operating assets must be presented at cost minus accumulated depreciation or amortization. Answer (C) is incorrect. The plan does not measure assets or benefits at net realizable value.

13.1.35. On January 2, Loch Co. established a noncontributory defined-benefit pension plan covering all employees and contributed $400,000 to the plan. At December 31, Loch determined that the annual service and interest costs of the plan were $720,000. The expected and the actual rate of return on plan assets for the year was 10%. Loch's pension expense has no other components. What amount should Loch report in its December 31, balance sheet as liability for pension benefits?

- A. $280,000
- B. $320,000
- C. $360,000
- D. $720,000

Answer (A) is correct. *(CPA, adapted)*
REQUIRED: The pension liability.
DISCUSSION: Service and interest costs and the return on plan assets are the entity's only components of pension expense in the plan's first year. The return on plan assets is $40,000 ($400,000 contributed to the plan × 10%). The pension expense is therefore $680,000 ($720,000 service and interest costs – $40,000 actual and expected return on plan assets). Because the actual and expected returns were the same, no gain or loss occurred. The funded status of the plan is the difference between plan assets at fair value ($400,000 + $40,000 = $440,000 at year end) and the projected benefit obligation ($720,000 service and interest costs, given no prior service cost or credit). Consequently, the liability recognized to record the unfunded status of the plan at year end is $280,000 ($720,000 – $440,000).
Answer (B) is incorrect. The amount of $320,000 is the result if the return on plan assets is not added to plan assets at year end. Answer (C) is incorrect. The amount of $360,000 results when the return on plan assets is subtracted from plan assets at year end. Answer (D) is incorrect. The amount of $720,000 is the sum of service and interest costs.

13.1.36. The following information pertains to Gali Co.'s defined benefit pension plan for Year 1:

Fair value of plan assets, beginning of year	$350,000
Fair value of plan assets, end of year	525,000
Employer contributions	110,000
Benefits paid	85,000

In computing pension expense, what amount should Gali use as actual return on plan assets?

- A. $65,000
- B. $150,000
- C. $175,000
- D. $260,000

Answer (B) is correct. *(CPA, adapted)*
REQUIRED: The actual return on plan assets.
DISCUSSION: The actual return on plan assets is based on the fair value of plan assets at the beginning and end of the accounting period adjusted for contributions and payments during the period. The actual return for Gali is $150,000 ($525,000 – $350,000 – $110,000 + $85,000).
Answer (A) is incorrect. The amount of $65,000 results when benefits paid to employees are not included. Answer (C) is incorrect. The amount of $175,000 is the change in the fair value of plan assets without adjustment for contributions or benefits paid. Answer (D) is incorrect. The amount of $260,000 does not deduct employer contributions.

13.1.37. A company sponsors two defined benefit pension plans. The following information relates to the plans at year end:

	Plan A	Plan B
Fair value of plan assets	$ 800,000	$1,000,000
Projected benefit obligation	1,000,000	700,000

What amount(s) should the company report in its balance sheet related to the plans?

- A. Liability of $200,000; asset of $300,000.
- B. Asset of $100,000.
- C. Asset of $1,800,000; liability of $1,700,000.
- D. Liability of $100,000.

Answer (A) is correct. *(CPA, adapted)*
REQUIRED: The funded status of defined benefit pension plans for an employer who sponsors multiple plans.
DISCUSSION: The balance sheet must report the full under- or overfunded status of the pension plan at year-end as a liability or asset. The funded status of a pension plan is the difference between the fair value of the plan assets and pension benefit obligation (PBO) at the reporting date. An employer that sponsors multiple defined benefit plans must recognize an asset for all overfunded plans and a liability for all underfunded plans (the asset and liability recognized cannot be netted). Plan A is underfunded by $200,000 ($800,000 FV of PA – $1,000,000 PBO), and the company must recognize a liability. Similarly, Plan B is overfunded by $300,000 ($1,000,000 FV of PA – $700,000 PBO), and the company recognizes this as an asset.
Answer (B) is incorrect. An employer that sponsors multiple defined benefit plans must recognize an asset for all overfunded plans and a liability for all underfunded plans (the asset and liability recognized cannot be netted). Answer (C) is incorrect. The funded status of a pension plan is the difference, not the sum, of the fair value of the plan assets and pension benefit obligation (PBO) at the reporting date. Answer (D) is incorrect. An employer that sponsors multiple defined benefit plans must recognize an asset for all overfunded plans and a liability for all underfunded plans. The asset and liability recognized must not be netted. Furthermore, if the plans were netted, the result would be an asset, not a liability.

13.1.38. An overfunded single-employer defined benefit postretirement plan should be recognized in a classified statement of financial position as a

- A. Noncurrent liability.
- B. Current liability.
- C. Noncurrent asset.
- D. Current asset.

Answer (C) is correct. *(CPA, adapted)*
REQUIRED: The reporting of an overfunded single-employer defined benefit postretirement plan.
DISCUSSION: If the pension is overfunded, i.e., the fair value of the plan assets at the reporting date exceeds the projected benefit obligation, the excess must be recognized in the statement of financial position as a noncurrent asset.
Answer (A) is incorrect. An overfunded defined benefit pension plan is an asset, not a liability. Answer (B) is incorrect. An overfunded defined benefit pension plan is not a liability and is not classified as current. Answer (D) is incorrect. An overfunded defined benefit pension plan is classified as a noncurrent asset.

13.2 Postretirement Benefits other than Pensions

13.2.1. Postretirement employee benefits other than pensions (OPEB) may be defined in terms of monetary amounts (e.g., a given dollar value of life insurance) or benefit coverage (e.g., amounts per day for hospitalization). The amount of benefits depends on such factors as the benefit formula, the life expectancy of the retiree and any beneficiaries and covered dependents, and the frequency and significance of events (e.g., illnesses) requiring payments. The basic elements of accounting for OPEB include

A. The expected postretirement benefit obligation (EPBO), which equals the accumulated postretirement benefit obligation (APBO) after the full eligibility date.

B. The APBO, which is the actuarial present value at a given date of the benefits projected to be earned after the full eligibility date.

C. Required recognition of a minimum liability for any excess of the EPBO over the APBO.

D. The projected benefit obligation (PBO) and the vested benefit obligation (VBO).

13.2.2. Ethelred Co. is an employer sponsoring a defined benefit postretirement healthcare plan. Which of the following components might be included in its postretirement benefit expense?

	Amortization of Prior Service Credit Remaining in Accumulated OCI	Interest Cost
A.	No	No
B.	Yes	No
C.	No	Yes
D.	Yes	Yes

13.2.3. The service cost component of the net periodic postretirement benefit cost is

A. Included in the APBO but not in the EPBO.

B. Defined as the portion of the EPBO attributed to employee service for a period.

C. Included in the EPBO but not the APBO.

D. Measured using implicit and explicit actuarial assumptions and present value techniques.

Answer (A) is correct. *(Publisher, adapted)*
REQUIRED: The true statement about the elements of accounting for OPEB.
DISCUSSION: The EPBO for an employee is the actuarial present value at a given date of the OPEB expected to be paid. Its measurement depends on the anticipated amounts and timing of future benefits, the costs to be incurred to provide those benefits, and the extent the costs are shared by the employee and others (such as governmental programs). The APBO for an employee is the actuarial present value at a given date of the future benefits attributable to the employee's service as of that date. The determination of the APBO (as well as of the EPBO and service cost) implicitly includes the consideration of future salary progression to the extent the benefit formula defines benefits as a function of future compensation levels. The full eligibility date is reached when the employee has rendered all the services necessary to earn all of the benefits expected to be received by that employee. After the full eligibility date, the EPBO and APBO are equal. Prior to that date, the EPBO exceeds the APBO.
Answer (B) is incorrect. The APBO for an employee is the actuarial present value at a given date of the future benefits attributable to the employee's service as of that date, not as of the full eligibility date. Answer (C) is incorrect. The full funded status must be recognized in the balance sheet. Answer (D) is incorrect. These terms relate to pension accounting only.

Answer (D) is correct. *(Publisher, adapted)*
REQUIRED: The true statement about the elements of postretirement benefit expense.
DISCUSSION: The six possible components of the required minimum postretirement benefit expense are (1) service cost, (2) interest on the APBO, (3) expected return on plan assets, (4) amortization of prior service cost or credit remaining in accumulated OCI, (5) amortization of the transition obligation or asset remaining in accumulated OCI, and (6) the gain or loss component. The postretirement benefit expense is very similar to pension expense.
Answer (A) is incorrect. Amortization of prior service credit remaining in accumulated OCI and interest cost should be included in the net periodic postretirement benefit cost of an employer sponsoring a defined benefit healthcare plan. Answer (B) is incorrect. Interest cost should be included in the postretirement benefit expense. Answer (C) is incorrect. Amortization of prior service credit remaining in accumulated OCI should be included in the postretirement benefit expense.

Answer (B) is correct. *(Publisher, adapted)*
REQUIRED: The definition of the service cost component of the NPPBC.
DISCUSSION: Service cost is defined as the actuarial present value of benefits attributed to services rendered by employees during the period. It is the portion of the EPBO attributed to service in the period and is not affected by the level of funding.
Answer (A) is incorrect. The service cost for the most recently completed period is included in the EPBO as well as the APBO. Answer (C) is incorrect. The service cost for the most recently completed period is included in the APBO as well as the EPBO. Answer (D) is incorrect. GAAP require the use of explicit (not implicit) assumptions, each of which is the best estimate of a particular event.

13.2.4. Li Co. is a publicly traded entity that sponsors both a pension plan and a postretirement plan providing other, nonpension benefits. The following information relates to the current year's activity of Li's defined benefit postretirement plan:

Service cost	$240,000
Return on plan assets	60,000
Interest cost on accumulated benefit obligation	80,000
Amortization of actuarial loss	20,000
Amortization of prior service cost	10,000

Li's nonpension postretirement benefit cost is

A. $240,000

B. $280,000

C. $350,000

D. $290,000

Answer (D) is correct. *(A. Oddo)*
REQUIRED: The postretirement benefit cost for the year.
DISCUSSION: The components of the postretirement benefit cost are service cost, interest cost, the expected return on plan assets, and amortization of (1) any prior service cost remaining in accumulated OCI, and (2) any net gain (loss) from prior periods remaining in accumulated OCI. Service cost, interest cost, and the amortization of actuarial loss and prior service cost increase the postretirement benefit cost. The expected return on plan assets decreases the postretirement benefit cost. As indicated below, the amount for the year is $290,000.

Service cost	$240,000
Return on plan assets	(60,000)
Interest cost	80,000
Amortization of actuarial loss	20,000
Amortization of prior service cost	10,000
Postretirement benefit cost	$290,000

Answer (A) is incorrect. The amount of $240,000 includes only the service cost component. Answer (B) is incorrect. The amount of $280,000 excludes the amortization of the prior service cost. Answer (C) is incorrect. The amount of $350,000 excludes the return on plan assets from the calculation of the postretirement benefit cost.

13.2.5. Prior service cost is defined as the cost of benefit improvements attributable to plan participants' prior service pursuant to a plan amendment or a plan initiation that provides benefits in exchange for plan participants' prior service. The general rule is that prior service cost should be recognized in NPPBC

A. By assigning an equal amount to each year of service remaining until the full eligibility date of each participant active at the amendment date who was not yet fully eligible for benefits.

B. In full in the accounting period in which the plan is amended.

C. By amortizing it over the remaining life expectancy of the participants.

D. In accordance with straight-line amortization over the average remaining years to full eligibility of the active participants.

Answer (A) is correct. *(Publisher, adapted)*
REQUIRED: The general rule for recognition of prior service cost.
DISCUSSION: The effect of a plan amendment on a participant's EPBO should be attributed to each year of service in that individual's attribution period (ordinarily from the date of hire or a later date specified by the benefit formula to the full eligibility date). This period may include years of service already rendered. The cost of benefit improvements for years of service already rendered is the increase in the APBO as a result of an amendment and measured at the date of the amendment. The general rule is that equal amounts of this cost should be assigned to each year of service remaining until the full eligibility date for each active plan participant at the date of the amendment who was not yet fully eligible.
Answer (B) is incorrect. Prior service cost is deemed to provide economic benefits to the employer in future periods. Thus, recognition in full in the year of the amendment is prohibited. Answer (C) is incorrect. Amortization over the remaining life expectancy of the participants is appropriate only if all or almost all of the participants are fully eligible. Answer (D) is incorrect. Straight-line amortization over the average remaining years to full eligibility of the active participants is a pragmatic exception to the general rule. An alternative, consistently applied amortization method that more rapidly reduces unrecognized prior service cost remaining in accumulated OCI is permitted to reduce complexity and detail.

13.2.6. Campbell Co. sponsors a single-employer defined benefit postretirement plan that provides nonpension benefits. The interest cost component of its postretirement benefit expense is the

A. Increase in the EPBO because of the passage of time.

B. Increase in the APBO because of the passage of time.

C. Product of the market-related value of plan assets and the expected long-term rate of return on plan assets.

D. Change in the APBO during the period.

Answer (B) is correct. *(Publisher, adapted)*
REQUIRED: The definition of the interest cost component of the postretirement benefit expense.
DISCUSSION: Interest cost reflects the change in the APBO during the period resulting solely from the passage of time. It equals the APBO at the beginning of the period times the assumed discount rate used in determining the present value of future cash outflows currently expected to be required to satisfy the obligation.
Answer (A) is incorrect. Interest cost is a function of the APBO. Answer (C) is incorrect. The expected return on plan assets is the product of the market-related value of plan assets and the expected long-term rate of return on plan assets. Answer (D) is incorrect. The change in the obligation reflects many factors, of which interest cost is one.

13.2.7. Which of the following items of information should be disclosed by Purpura Company, which provides healthcare benefits to its retirees under a single-employer defined benefit plan?

I. The assumed healthcare cost trend rate used to measure the expected cost of benefits covered by the plan

II. The assumptions about the discount rate, rate of compensation increase, and expected long-term rate of return on plan assets

    A. I and II.

    B. I only.

    C. II only.

    D. Neither I nor II.

Answer (A) is correct. *(CPA, adapted)*
REQUIRED: The information that should be disclosed by an entity providing healthcare benefits to its retirees.
DISCUSSION: The disclosure requirements for pensions and other postretirement employee benefits include

● "The assumed healthcare cost trend rate(s) for the next year used to measure the expected cost of benefits covered by the plan (gross eligible charges), and a general description of the direction and pattern of change in the assumed trend rates thereafter, together with the ultimate trend rate(s) and when that rate is expected to be achieved."

● "On a weighted-average basis, the following assumptions used in accounting for a plan: assumed discount rates, rates of compensation increase (for pay-related plans), and expected long-term rates of return on plan assets specifying, in a tabular format, the assumptions used to determine the benefit obligation and the assumptions used to determine net benefit cost."

Disclosures about assumed healthcare cost trend rates and certain other assumptions used in accounting for a plan must be made by public and nonpublic entities.
    Answer (B) is incorrect. The assumptions about the discount rate, rate of compensation increase, and expected long-term rate of return on plan assets also must be disclosed. Answer (C) is incorrect. The assumed healthcare cost trend rate used to measure the expected cost of benefits covered by the plan also must be disclosed. Answer (D) is incorrect. The assumed healthcare cost trend rate used to measure the expected cost of benefits covered by the plan and the assumptions about the discount rate, rate of compensation increase, and expected long-term rate of return on plan assets also must be disclosed.

13.2.8. Bounty Co. provides postretirement healthcare benefits to employees who have completed at least 10 years service and are aged 55 years or older when retiring. Employees retiring from Bounty have a median age of 62, and no one has worked beyond age 65. Fletcher is hired at 48 years old. The attribution period for accruing Bounty's expected postretirement healthcare benefit obligation to Fletcher is during the period when Fletcher is aged

    A. 48 to 65.

    B. 48 to 58.

    C. 55 to 65.

    D. 55 to 62.

Answer (B) is correct. *(CPA, adapted)*
REQUIRED: The attribution period for accruing the expected postretirement healthcare benefit obligation to an employee.
DISCUSSION: The attribution period begins on the date of hire unless the plan's benefit formula grants credit for service only from a later date. The end of the period is the full eligibility date. If the exception does not apply, Fletcher's attribution period is from age 48, the date of hire, to age 58, the date of full eligibility.
    Answer (A) is incorrect. The attribution period is 10 years from the date of hire. Answer (C) is incorrect. The attribution period is 10 years from the date of hire. Answer (D) is incorrect. The attribution period is 10 years from the date of hire.

13.2.9. Which of the following costs is unique to postretirement healthcare benefits?

    A. Per capita claims.

    B. Service.

    C. Prior service.

    D. Interest.

Answer (A) is correct. *(CPA, adapted)*
REQUIRED: The cost unique to postretirement healthcare benefits.
DISCUSSION: A per capita claim (capitation fee) is a fixed amount per individual paid periodically to a healthcare provider as payment for services for the period (ordinarily monthly).
    Answer (B) is incorrect. Service cost is an element of net periodic pension cost (pension expense) and net periodic postretirement benefit cost. Answer (C) is incorrect. Amortization of prior service cost is an element of net periodic pension cost (pension expense) and net periodic postretirement benefit cost. Answer (D) is incorrect. Interest cost is an element of net periodic pension cost (pension expense) and net periodic postretirement benefit cost.

13.3 Share-Based Payment

13.3.1. On which of the following dates is a public entity required to measure the cost of employee services in exchange for an award of equity interests, based on the fair market value of the award?

A. Date of grant.

B. Date of restriction lapse.

C. Date of vesting.

D. Date of exercise.

Answer (A) is correct. *(CPA, adapted)*
REQUIRED: The date at which a public entity must measure the cost of employee services provided in exchange for an award of equity interests.
DISCUSSION: The cost of employee services performed in exchange for an award of equity interests (share-based compensation) is recognized over the requisite service period. The beginning of this period is usually at the grant date. For equity awards, the entity estimates the fair value at the grant date of the equity instruments it is obligated to issue when employees meet the necessary conditions. The grant date is when (1) a mutual understanding of key terms of the award has been reached and (2) the employer is obligated if the employer provides the requisite service. At the grant date of an award of equity instruments, an employee begins to be affected by changes in the price of the shares. Under U.S. GAAP, this guidance applies to equity awards by public and nonpublic entities.
Answer (B) is incorrect. Sale of shares issued to employees may be restricted (prohibited) for a specified period. For example, the ability to sell vested shares or share options may be restricted. This restriction is a factor in the measurement of their fair value at the grant date. But a restriction on nonvested shares is not considered. The date of restriction lapse is not the measurement date. Answer (C) is incorrect. Measurement must precede the date of vesting. Answer (D) is incorrect. Measurement must precede the date of exercise.

13.3.2. In a share-based payment transaction (SBPT) involving the receipt of goods or services by the reporting entity,

A. Initial recognition of the goods or services occurs when the entity issues its equity instruments.

B. Equity or a liability may be credited in appropriate circumstances.

C. Measurement of the SBPT is normally at the fair value of the services provided by employees.

D. The cost of goods or services received is recognized when they are received.

Answer (B) is correct. *(Publisher, adapted)*
REQUIRED: The true statement about an SBPT involving the receipt of goods or services by the reporting entity.
DISCUSSION: The relevant guidance applies to all SBPTs involving receipt by the entity of goods or services in return for its equity instruments, e.g., most shares or share options. It also applies to incurrence of liabilities that (1) are based wholly or in part on the price of the entity's equity instruments or (2) may require share settlement. Initial recognition of goods or services occurs when they are received. The credit is to equity or a liability depending on which classification criteria are met. Cost is recognized upon disposal or consumption of the goods or services.
Answer (A) is incorrect. Initial recognition occurs when goods or services are received. Answer (C) is incorrect. In an SBPT with nonemployees, the more reliably measurable of the fair value of the equity instruments issued or the consideration received is used to measure the SBPT. In an SBPT with employees, the fair value of the equity instruments issued ordinarily is the basis for measurement. The fair value of the services they render ordinarily is not readily determinable. Answer (D) is incorrect. The cost of goods or services received is recognized when they are disposed of or consumed.

13.3.3. GAAP normally require entities to account for share-based employee compensation awards classified as equity in accordance with which of the following methods?

	Fair-Value Method	Intrinsic-Value Method
A.	Yes	Yes
B.	Yes	No
C.	No	Yes
D.	No	No

Answer (B) is correct. *(Publisher, adapted)*
REQUIRED: The method(s) prescribed for accounting for share-based employee compensations awards.
DISCUSSION: Entities must account for share-based payments classified as equity in accordance with the fair-value method except in the rare cases in which a nonpublic entity cannot reasonably estimate the fair value of the equity instruments at the grant date. In these cases, entities must account for such payments in accordance with the intrinsic-value method.
Answer (A) is incorrect. An award classified as equity must be measured at fair value except in rare cases. Answer (C) is incorrect. An award classified as equity must be measured at fair value except in rare cases. Answer (D) is incorrect. The fair-value method is required except in rare cases.

13.3.4. A reporting entity makes an award of share-based employee compensation in the form of share options classified as equity. To account for this award, the entity

A. Recognizes changes in estimated total cost by retrospective application to prior periods affected.

B. Recognizes no cost for an award with a performance condition until the condition is satisfied.

C. Credits other comprehensive income.

D. Recognizes total compensation cost based on the number of equity instruments for which the requisite service was performed.

Answer (D) is correct. *(Publisher, adapted)*
REQUIRED: The accounting for an award of share-based employee compensation in the form of share options classified as equity.
DISCUSSION: Compensation cost for an award classified as equity is recognized over the requisite service period. This period is the period during which employees must perform services. It is most often the vesting period. The requisite service period begins at the service inception date. The service required is called the requisite service. Total compensation cost at the end of the requisite service period is determined by the number of equity instruments for which the requisite service was completed and their grant-date fair value. The entity must estimate this number when initial accruals are made. The credit is usually to paid-in capital.
Answer (A) is incorrect. Changes in the estimate result in recognition of the cumulative effect on prior and current periods in calculation of compensation cost of the period of change. Answer (B) is incorrect. An accrual for an award with a performance condition is made if it is probable that the condition will be satisfied. Answer (C) is incorrect. The credit is usually to paid-in capital.

13.3.5. A reporting entity has entered into a share-based payment transaction (SBPT) with employees. In exchange for services to be performed, the entity will issue instruments properly classified as liabilities. For this SBPT,

A. The measurement date is the settlement date.

B. The measurement date is the service inception date.

C. A public entity may elect to measure the liabilities at intrinsic value.

D. A nonpublic entity must measure the liabilities at intrinsic value.

Answer (A) is correct. *(Publisher, adapted)*
REQUIRED: The true statement regarding this SBPT.
DISCUSSION: The measurement date for liabilities is the settlement date. Thus, after initial recognition, liabilities are remeasured at each reporting date.
Answer (B) is incorrect. The measurement date for liabilities is the settlement date. Answer (C) is incorrect. A public entity remeasures liabilities based on their fair values. Periodic compensation cost depends on the change (or part of the change, depending on the requisite service performed to date) in fair value. Answer (D) is incorrect. A nonpublic entity may elect to measure all such liabilities at fair value or intrinsic value. Fair value is preferable for the purpose of justifying a change in accounting principle. The percentage of fair value or intrinsic value accrued as compensation cost equals the percentage of required service rendered to date.

13.3.6. On January 1, Year 1, a company issued its employees 10,000 shares of restricted stock. On January 1, Year 2, the company issued to its employees an additional 20,000 shares of restricted stock. Additional information about the company's stock is as follows:

Date	Fair Value of Stock (per Share)
January 1, Year 1	$20
December 31, Year 1	22
January 1, Year 2	25
December 31, Year 2	30

The shares vest at the end of a 4-year period. There are no forfeitures. What amount should be recorded as compensation expense for the 12-month period ended December 31, Year 2?

A. $175,000

B. $205,000

C. $225,000

D. $500,000

Answer (A) is correct. *(CPA, adapted)*
REQUIRED: The compensation expense for an issue of stock.
DISCUSSION: The total employee compensation cost must be recognized over the requisite service period (4 years in this case). The cost of employee services performed in exchange for awards of share-based compensation (compensation expense) is measured at the grant-date fair value of the equity instruments issued. The 10,000 shares of restricted stock issued in Year 1 have a total fair value of $200,000 at the grant date (10,000 shares × $20 per share). The company should recognize compensation expense of $50,000 for each of the next 4 years ($200,000 FV ÷ 4 years). The 20,000 shares issued in Year 2 have a total fair value of $500,000 (20,000 shares × $25 per share) at the grant date. The company should recognize compensation expense related to these shares of $125,000 ($500,000 FV ÷ 4 years) for each of the next 4 years. Thus, total compensation expense for Year 2 is $175,000 ($125,000 + $50,000).
Answer (B) is incorrect. An amount of $205,000 results from using the fair value of the stock award plans at the end of their respective periods rather than their respective grant dates. Answer (C) is incorrect. An amount of $225,000 results basing employee compensation cost on the end of the current period fair value of the equity instruments granted rather than the grant-date fair value. Answer (D) is incorrect. The total compensation expense related to the 20,000 shares issued in Year 2 is not recognized entirely in Year 2. Compensation expense related to a stock award plan is recognized over the requisite service period (4 years in this case). The total compensation expense in Year 2 will include a proportionate amount of the total expense for the shares issued in Year 1 and Year 2.

Questions 13.3.7 through 13.3.10 are based on the following information. On December 21, Year 1, the board of directors of Oak Corporation approved a plan to award 600,000 share options to 20 key employees as additional compensation. Effective January 1, Year 2, each employee was granted the right to purchase 30,000 shares of the company's $2 par-value stock at an exercise price of $36 per share. The market price on that date was $32 per share. All share options vest at December 31, Year 4, the end of the 3-year requisite service period. They expire on December 31, Year 11. Based on an appropriate option-pricing formula, the fair value of the options on the grant date was estimated at $12 per option.

13.3.7. What amount of compensation expense should Oak Corporation recognize in its annual income statement for the year ended December 31, Year 2?

A. $7,200,000

B. $6,400,000

C. $2,400,000

D. $1,200,700

Answer (C) is correct. *(Publisher, adapted)*
REQUIRED: The compensation expense recognized in Year 2.
DISCUSSION: Total compensation cost recognized during the requisite service period should equal the grant-date fair value of all share options for which the requisite service is rendered. GAAP require an entity to (1) estimate the number of share options for which the requisite service is expected to be rendered, (2) measure the cost of employee services received in exchange for those options at their fair value on the grant date, and (3) allocate that cost to the requisite service period. Given that all options vest at the same time (known as cliff vesting), the $7,200,000 (600,000 shares × $12 estimated fair value) total compensation cost should be allocated proportionately to the 3-year requisite service period. Thus, $2,400,000 ($7,200,000 ÷ 3) should be expensed in the annual income statement for the year ended December 31, Year 2.
Answer (A) is incorrect. The amount of $7,200,000 is the total estimated compensation cost for the entire requisite service period. Answer (B) is incorrect. The amount of $6,400,000 is total compensation expense based on the $32 market price. Answer (D) is incorrect. The amount of $1,200,000 is 600,000 shares times the $2 par value.

13.3.8. On January 1, Year 3, five key employees left Oak Corporation. What amount of compensation expense should Oak report in the income statement for the year ended December 31, Year 3?

A. $5,400,000

B. $3,600,000

C. $2,400,000

D. $1,200,000

Answer (D) is correct. *(Publisher, adapted)*
REQUIRED: The compensation expense recognized in Year 3 after a change in estimate.
DISCUSSION: Given that all options vest at the same time (known as cliff vesting), the $7,200,000 (600,000 shares × $12 estimated fair value) total compensation cost should be allocated proportionately to the 3-year requisite service period. Thus, $2,400,000 ($7,200,000 ÷ 3) should be expensed in the annual income statement for the year ended December 31, Year 2. However, only 15 key employees are covered in Year 3. The total compensation expense for these employees is $5,400,000 [(30,000 options × 15 employees) × $12 fair value]. The amount to be recognized each year of the requisite service period is $1,800,000 ($5,400,000 ÷ 3). The revised cumulative amount to be recognized at the end of Year 3 is therefore $3,600,000 ($1,800,000 × 2 years). Because $2,400,000 was expensed in Year 2, Year 3 expense is $1,200,000 ($3,600,000 revised cumulative expense – $2,400,000).
Answer (A) is incorrect. The total compensation expense for the entire requisite service period is $5,400,000. Answer (B) is incorrect. The total compensation expense that should be recognized in Years 2 and 3 combined is $3,600,000. Answer (C) is incorrect. The amount of $2,400,000 is based on the assumption that all 20 key employees remain employed.

13.3.9. On January 1, Year 3, five key employees left Oak Corporation. During the period from January 1, Year 5, through December 31, Year 11, 400,000 of the share options that vested were exercised. At the end of this period, the cumulative amount that should have been credited to additional paid-in capital is

A. $19,200,000

B. $18,400,000

C. $13,600,000

D. $4,000,000

Answer (B) is correct. *(Publisher, adapted)*
REQUIRED: The credit to additional paid-in capital at the end of the period.
DISCUSSION: Additional paid-in capital -- share options was credited for $5,400,000 (450,000 × $12) as compensation expense was recognized during the requisite service period. During the period from January 1, Year 5, through December 31, Year 11, 400,000 options were exercised. Hence, additional paid-in capital should be credited for $18,400,000 [400,000 shares × ($36 exercise price + $12 previously credited to additional paid-in capital -- stock options – $2 par value allocated to common stock)].
Answer (A) is incorrect. The amount of $19,200,000 includes the $2 par value allocated to the common stock account. Answer (C) is incorrect. The amount of $13,600,000 does not include the $12 fair value of the options determined at the grant date. Answer (D) is incorrect. The amount of $4,000,000 does not include the $36 exercise price.

13.3.10. On January 1, Year 3, five key employees left Oak Corporation. During the period from January 1, Year 5, through December 31, Year 11, 400,000 of the share options that vested were exercised. The remaining options were not exercised. What amount of the previously recognized compensation expense should be adjusted upon expiration of the share options?

A. $2,400,000

B. $2,300,000

C. $100,000

D. $0

Answer (D) is correct. *(Publisher, adapted)*
REQUIRED: The adjustment to previously recognized compensation expense when share options are not exercised.
DISCUSSION: Total compensation expense for the requisite service period is not adjusted for expired options.
Answer (A) is incorrect. The amount of $2.4 million is the annual compensation expense recognized during each of the years of the requisite service period assuming no forfeitures. Answer (B) is incorrect. The amount of $2.3 million is the additional amount that would have been credited to additional paid-in capital if the 50,000 expired options had been exercised. Answer (C) is incorrect. The amount of $100,000 is the additional amount that would have been credited to common stock if the 50,000 expired options had been exercised.

13.3.11. On January 1, Year 1, the grant date, Public Entity entered into an equity-settled share-based payment transaction with its senior executives. This award of 1,000 share options has a 4-year vesting period. The market prices of the options and the related shares on the grant date are $20 and $80, respectively. The exercise price is $85. Assuming that the requisite service was not completed for 100 of the options because of unexpected events in Year 4, the entry to debit option expense at

A. December 31, Year 4, is for $5,000.

B. December 31, Year 3, is for $4,500.

C. December 31, Year 2, is for $5,000.

D. January 1, Year 1, is for $20,000.

Answer (C) is correct. *(Publisher, adapted)*
REQUIRED: The entry to debit option expense given that requisite service was not completed for some options.
DISCUSSION: The fair value of each share option is determined at the measurement date, which is usually the grant date for transactions with employees. Thus, the fair value of each share option was set at its market price of $20 on January 1, Year 1. The periodic expense varies only with the expected number of equity instruments for which the requisite service is expected to be completed. Because the events causing the requisite service not to be completed for 100 options occurred unexpectedly in Year 4, the entity presumably expected at each balance sheet date for the first 3 years of the requisite service period that all options would be expensed. Total expected expense was therefore $20,000, and the proportional expense recognized in each of the first 3 years was $5,000 [(1,000 options × $20) ÷ 4 years].
Answer (A) is incorrect. The Year 4 expense is $3,000 [$20,000 total expected – $15,000 recognized in the first 3 years – (100 × $20) not vested]. Answer (B) is incorrect. No retrospective adjustment is made. The Year 3 entry would have been $5,000 based on a then-expected total expense of $20,000. Answer (D) is incorrect. If the options had vested immediately, $20,000 would have been recognized at January 1, Year 1.

13.3.12. The service inception date is the date at which the requisite service period begins for a share-based payment transaction. The service inception date generally

A. Precedes the grant date.

B. Is the same as the grant date.

C. Follows the grant date.

D. Differs from the grant date.

Answer (B) is correct. *(Publisher, adapted)*
REQUIRED: The relationship between the grant date and the service inception date.
DISCUSSION: For most share-based payments, the service inception date is the same as the grant date. However, the service inception date precedes the grant date if (1) an award is authorized; (2) service begins before the employer and employee reach a mutual understanding of the terms of the award; and (3) either (a) the terms of the award do not require substantive services to be rendered after the grant date, or (b) the terms include a market or performance condition that will result in forfeiture of the award if it is not satisfied during the service period preceding the grant date.
Answer (A) is incorrect. The service inception date usually is the grant date, but it will precede the grant date under certain conditions. Answer (C) is incorrect. The service inception date usually is the grant date, but it will precede the grant date under certain conditions. Answer (D) is incorrect. The service inception date usually is the grant date, but it will precede the grant date under certain conditions.

13.3.13. On January 2, Year 1, Kine Co. granted Morgan, its president, fully vested share options to buy 1,000 shares of Kine's $10 par common stock. The options have an exercise price of $20 per share and are exercisable for 3 years following the grant date. Morgan exercised the options on December 31, Year 1. The market price of the shares was $50 on January 2, Year 1, and $70 on the following December 31. If the fair value of the options is not reasonably estimable at the grant date, by what net amount will equity increase as a result of the grant and exercise of the options? (Ignore tax considerations.)

A. $20,000

B. $30,000

C. $50,000

D. $70,000

Answer (A) is correct. *(CIA, adapted)*
REQUIRED: The amount equity increases as a result of the grant and exercise of share options.
DISCUSSION: In the rare cases in which an entity cannot reasonably estimate the fair value of equity instruments at the grant date, the measurement is based on intrinsic value (market price of an underlying share – exercise price of an option). Remeasurement is required at each reporting date and on final settlement. The initial measurement date is January 2, Year 1. At that date, the intrinsic value of the fully vested options is $30,000 [1,000 shares × ($50 market price – $20 option price)]. The entry is

Compensation expense	$30,000	
Additional paid-in capital (share options)		$30,000

When the options are exercised, compensation expense will be debited and additional paid-in capital (share options) will be credited for $20,000 [1,000 shares × ($70 – $50)] to reflect the final measure of intrinsic value.

Compensation expense	$20,000	
Additional paid-in capital (share options)		$20,000

The final entry records the receipt of payment and the issuance of shares.

Cash	$20,000	
Additional paid-in capital (share options)	50,000	
Common stock (1,000 shares × $10 par)		$10,000
Additional paid-in capital		60,000

The net effect on equity is an increase of $20,000 ($10,000 common stock + $60,000 additional paid-in capital – $50,000 compensation expense).
Answer (B) is incorrect. The amount of the initial debit to compensation expense and credit to additional paid-in capital is $30,000. Answer (C) is incorrect. The final measure of intrinsic value is $50,000. Answer (D) is incorrect. The market price of the shares issued on the settlement date is $70,000.

Use **Gleim Test Prep** for interactive study and easy-to-use detailed analytics!

STUDY UNIT FOURTEEN
LEASES

A lease is a contractual agreement in which the lessor (owner) conveys to the lessee the right to use specific property, plant, or equipment for a stated period in exchange for a stated payment. The amount and timing of lease revenue recognized by the lessor and lease expenses recognized by the lessee depend on the initial classification of the lease. Some questions test sale and leaseback transactions that involve the sale of property by the owner (seller-lessee) and a lease of the property back from the buyer-lessor. However, the FASB's guidance for lease accounting does not apply to leases of intangible assets or inventory.

QUESTIONS

14.1 Lease Classification

14.1.1. Lease M does not contain a purchase option, but the lease term is equal to 91% of the estimated economic life of the leased property. Lease P does not transfer ownership of the property to the lessee by the end of the lease term, but the lease term is equal to 77% of the estimated economic life of the leased property. How should the lessee classify these leases?

	Lease M	Lease P
A.	Finance lease	Operating lease
B.	Finance lease	Finance lease
C.	Operating lease	Finance lease
D.	Operating lease	Operating lease

Answer (B) is correct. *(CPA, adapted)*
REQUIRED: The proper classification of leases.
DISCUSSION: A lease is classified as a finance lease by the lessee and as a sales-type lease by the lessor if, at lease commencement, at least one of the following five criteria is met: (1) The ownership of the leased asset is transferred to the lessee by the end of the lease term, (2) the lease includes an option to purchase the leased asset that the lessee is reasonably certain to exercise, (3) the lease term is for the major part (generally considered as 75%) of the remaining economic life of the leased asset, (4) the present value of the sum of the lease payments and any residual value guaranteed by the lessee equals or exceeds substantially all of the fair value (generally considered as 90%) of the leased asset, and (5) the leased asset is so specialized that it is expected to have no alternative use to the lessor at the end of the lease term. When no classification criterion is met, the lease is classified as an operating lease by the lessee. Thus, both lease M (90% of the fair value of the leased asset) and lease P (75% of the economic life of the leased asset) are classified as finance leases.

14.1.2. Beal, Inc., intends to lease a machine from Paul Corp. Beal's incremental borrowing rate is 14%. The prime rate of interest is 8%. Paul's implicit rate in the lease is 10%, which is known to Beal. Beal computes the present value of the lease payments using

A. 8%

B. 10%

C. 12%

D. 14%

Answer (B) is correct. *(CPA, adapted)*
REQUIRED: The discount rate used by the lessee to determine the present value of lease payments if the incremental borrowing rate and implicit rate are known.
DISCUSSION: The discount rate for the lease is the rate implicit in the lease. If the lessee cannot determine the rate implicit in the lease, the lessee uses its incremental borrowing rate. Because the implicit rate of 10% is known to Beal, it is used as the discount rate of the lease.
Answer (A) is incorrect. The prime rate (8%) is irrelevant. Answer (C) is incorrect. The rate of 12% is the average of the implicit rate and the incremental rate. Answer (D) is incorrect. The implicit rate is known to Beal. Thus, it must be used as the discount rate for the lease.

14.1.3. GAAP list five criteria for determining when a lease should be classified as a finance lease by a lessee. Which of the following is a criterion?

A. The present value of the lease payments equals or exceeds 75% of the fair value of the leased property.

B. The lease agreement provides for the transfer of ownership of the leased property.

C. The lease term equals the remaining estimated useful life of the leased property.

D. The lessee guarantees the residual value of the leased property.

Answer (B) is correct. *(Publisher, adapted)*
REQUIRED: The criteria for determining finance lease classification.
DISCUSSION: A lease is classified as a finance lease if any of the following five criteria are met: (1) the ownership of the leased asset is transferred to the lessee by the end of the lease term, (2) the lease includes an option to purchase the leased asset that the lessee is reasonably certain to exercise, (3) the lease term is for the major part (generally considered as 75%) of the remaining economic life of the leased asset, (4) the present value of the sum of the lease payments and any residual value guaranteed by the lessee equals or exceeds substantially all of the fair value (generally considered as 90%) of the leased asset, and (5) the leased asset is so specialized that it is expected to have no alternative use to the lessor at the end of the lease term.
Answer (A) is incorrect. The present value of the lease payments should equal or exceed 90% of the fair value of the leased property. Answer (C) is incorrect. The lease term should be 75% or more of the estimated economic life of the leased property. Answer (D) is incorrect. No guarantees are made about the residual value of the leased property.

14.1.4. On January 1, a company enters into an operating lease for office space and receives control of the property to make leasehold improvements. The company begins alterations to the property on March 1 and the company's staff moves into the property on May 1. The monthly rental payments begin on July 1. The recognition of lease expense for the new offices should begin in which of the following months?

A. January.

B. March.

C. May.

D. July.

Answer (A) is correct. *(CPA, adapted)*
REQUIRED: The time to begin recognition of lease expenses.
DISCUSSION: The lease term began in January when the lessor made a leased asset available for use by a lessee. Lease expense therefore is recognized beginning in January.
Answer (B) is incorrect. Although the company did not begin alterations until March, lease expense must be recognized over the full lease term. The full lease term began when the lessor made a leased asset available for use by a lessee. Lease expense therefore is recognized beginning in January. Answer (C) is incorrect. Even though the staff did not move in until May, lease expense must be recognized over the full lease term. The full lease term began when the lessor made a leased asset available for use by a lessee. Lease expense therefore is recognized beginning in January. Answer (D) is incorrect. Lease expense must be recognized over the full lease term even though rental payments were not made until July. The full lease term began when the lessor made a leased asset available for use by a lessee. Lease expense therefore is recognized beginning in January.

14.2 Lessee Accounting -- Initial Measurement

14.2.1. The present value of lease payments should be used by the lessee in determining the amount of a lease liability under a lease classified by the lessee as a(n)

	Finance Lease	Operating Lease
A.	Yes	Yes
B.	Yes	No
C.	No	No
D.	No	Yes

Answer (A) is correct. *(CPA, adapted)*
REQUIRED: The lease(s) for which the lessee's liability is based on the present value of the lease payments.
DISCUSSION: For finance and operating leases, a lessee must recognize a lease liability and a right-of-use asset at the lease commencement date. A lease liability is measured initially at the present value of the lease payments to be made over the lease term.

14.2.2. The amount recorded initially by the lessee as a lease liability should normally

    A. Exceed the total of the lease payments.

    B. Exceed the present value of the lease payments at the beginning of the lease.

    C. Equal the total of the lease payments.

    D. Equal the present value of the lease payments at the beginning of the lease.

Answer (D) is correct. *(CPA, adapted)*
    REQUIRED: The amount recorded initially by the lessee as a lease liability.
    DISCUSSION: The lessee records a lease as an asset and a liability at the present value of the lease payments. The discount rate is the lessor's implicit interest rate (if known) or the lessee's incremental borrowing rate of interest. Lease payments include the rental payments required during the lease term and the amount of a purchase option if the lessee is reasonably certain to exercise it. If no such option exists, the lease payments equal the sum of (1) the rental payments, (2) the amount of residual value guaranteed by the lessee, and (3) any nonrenewal penalty imposed.
    Answer (A) is incorrect. The amount recorded initially should be a present value. Thus, it is less than the total of the lease payments. Answer (B) is incorrect. The amount recorded initially should be the present value of the lease payments. Answer (C) is incorrect. The amount recorded initially should be a present value. Thus, it is less than the total of the lease payments.

14.2.3. On December 29, Year 1, Action Corp. signed a 7-year lease for an airplane to transport its professional sports team around the country. The airplane's fair value was $841,500. Action made the first annual lease payment of $153,000 on December 31, Year 1. Action's incremental borrowing rate was 12%, and the interest rate implicit in the lease, which was known by Action, was 9%. The following are the rounded present value factors for an annuity due:

9% for 7 years	5.5
12% for 7 years	5.1

What amount should Action report as a lease liability in its December 31, Year 1, balance sheet?

    A. $841,500

    B. $780,300

    C. $688,500

    D. $627,300

Answer (C) is correct. *(CPA, adapted)*
    REQUIRED: The amount that should be reported as a lease liability in the balance sheet.
    DISCUSSION: The lease liability is recorded at the present value of the lease payments. The lease should be recorded at the present value of lease payments discounted at the implicit rate of 9% because this rate is known by the lessee. The amount is $841,500 ($153,000 × 5.5), which then must be reduced by the payment made at the inception of the lease of $153,000. The lease liability therefore should be $688,500 ($841,500 − $153,000) in the December 31, Year 1, balance sheet.
    Answer (A) is incorrect. The liability must be reduced by the payment made at the inception of the lease. Answer (B) is incorrect. The present value of minimum lease payments should be discounted at 9% instead of 12%. Also, the liability should be reduced by the payment made at the inception of the lease. Answer (D) is incorrect. The lease liability should be recorded at 9% instead of 12%.

14.2.4. Robbin, Inc., leased a machine from Ready Leasing Co. The lease requires 10 annual payments of $10,000 beginning immediately. The lease specifies an interest rate of 12% and a purchase option of $10,000 at the end of the tenth year, even though the machine's estimated value on that date is $20,000. Robbin expects to exercise the purchase option. Robbin's incremental borrowing rate is 14%.

    The present value of an annuity due of 1 at:
        12% for 10 years is 6.328
        14% for 10 years is 5.946

    The present value of 1 at:
        12% for 10 years is .322
        14% for 10 years is .270

What amount should Robbin record as lease liability at the beginning of the lease term?

    A. $62,160

    B. $64,860

    C. $66,500

    D. $69,720

Answer (C) is correct. *(CPA, adapted)*
    REQUIRED: The amount that should be reported as a lease liability.
    DISCUSSION: For a finance or an operating lease, a lessee initially must recognize a lease liability and a right-of-use asset. At the lease commencement date, a lease liability is measured at the present value of the lease payments to be made over the lease term. When the lease includes a purchase option that the lessee is reasonably certain to exercise, the lease is a finance lease. The lease payments therefore consist of rental payments and the exercise price of the purchase option. The discount rate for the lease is the rate implicit in the lease of 12% because it is known by Robbin. Thus, the lease liability is equal to $66,500 [($10,000 × 6.328) + ($10,000 × .322)].
    Answer (A) is incorrect. The present value of the payment required by the purchase option and the annual lease payments should be discounted at 12% instead of 14%. Answer (B) is incorrect. The amount of the purchase option is $10,000, not the estimated value at that date. Also, the discount rate for both the option amount and the annual payments should be 12% instead of 14%. Answer (D) is incorrect. The payment required by the purchase option should be included in the present value of minimum lease payments, not the estimated value of the asset at the end of the lease.

14.2.5. On December 30, Rafferty Corp. leased equipment under an operating lease. Annual lease payments of $20,000 are due December 31 for 10 years. The equipment's useful life is 10 years, and the interest rate implicit in the lease of 10% is known to Rafferty. The operating lease obligation was recorded on December 30 at $135,000, and the first lease payment was made on that date. What amount should Rafferty include in current liabilities for this lease in its December 31 balance sheet?

A. $6,500

B. $8,500

C. $11,500

D. $20,000

Answer (B) is correct. *(CPA, adapted)*
REQUIRED: The current liability for the operating lease.
DISCUSSION: In a classified balance sheet, a lease liability must be allocated between the current and noncurrent portions. The current portion at a balance sheet date is the reduction of the lease liability in the forthcoming year. The portion of the lease payment that exceeds the amount of interest expense is the reduction of the liability in the forthcoming year. At the beginning of the following year, the lease liability is $115,000 ($135,000 opening balance – $20,000 initial payment), and the following year's interest expense will be $11,500 ($115,000 lease liability × 10% effective rate). The reduction of the liability when the next payment is made will be $8,500 ($20,000 cash – $11,500 interest).
Answer (A) is incorrect. The amount of $6,500 results from assuming that the carrying amount of the lease liability in the following year will be $135,000. Answer (C) is incorrect. The interest expense component of the single periodic lease expense recognized for an operating lease is $11,500. Answer (D) is incorrect. The full payment due in the following year is $20,000.

14.3 Lessee Accounting for Finance Leases -- Subsequent Measurement

14.3.1. A 12-year finance lease expiring on December 31 specifies equal annual lease payments. Part of this payment represents interest and part represents a reduction in the lease liability. The portion of the lease payment in Year 10 applicable to the reduction of the lease liability should be

A. Less than in Year 8.

B. More than in Year 8.

C. The same as in Year 12.

D. More than in Year 12.

Answer (B) is correct. *(CPA, adapted)*
REQUIRED: The trend of the change, if any, in the periodic reduction of the lease liability for a finance lease.
DISCUSSION: A lease payment has two components: interest and the portion applied to the reduction of the lease liability. The effective interest method requires that the carrying amount of the liability at the beginning of each interest period be multiplied by the appropriate interest rate to determine the interest. The difference between the lease payment and the interest is the reduction in the carrying amount of the lease liability. Because the carrying amount declines with each payment, interest in future years also declines, resulting in an increase in the amount applied to reduce the lease liability. The Year 10 lease payment therefore will result in a greater reduction in the liability than the Year 8 payment.
Answer (A) is incorrect. More of the lease payment in Year 10 is applied to the lease liability than in Year 8. Answer (C) is incorrect. More of the lease payment in Year 12 is applied to the lease liability than in Year 10. Answer (D) is incorrect. The carrying amount of the lease liability declines with each payment, which reduces interest in future periods. As a result, more of the lease payment is applied to the lease liability in future years.

14.3.2. Quick Company's lease payments are made at the end of each period. Quick's liability for a finance lease will be reduced periodically by the

A. Lease payment less the portion of the lease payment allocable to interest.

B. Lease payment plus the amortization of the related asset.

C. Lease payment less the amortization of the related asset.

D. Lease payment.

Answer (A) is correct. *(CPA, adapted)*
REQUIRED: The reduction of the liability for a finance lease after payments at the end of each period.
DISCUSSION: The lease liability consists of the present value of the lease payments. The lease liability is reduced by the portion of the lease payment attributable to the lease liability. This amount is the lease payment minus the interest component of the payment. Thus, the liability is decreased by the lease payment each period minus the portion of the payment allocable to interest.
Answer (B) is incorrect. The lease liability cannot be reduced by an amount greater than the lease payment. Answer (C) is incorrect. The amortization of the related asset is based on the entity's depreciation policy. Answer (D) is incorrect. The portion of the lease payment allocated to interest does not reduce the liability.

14.3.3. Cott, Inc., prepared an interest amortization table for a 5-year lease payable with a purchase option having an exercise price of $2,000, effective at the end of the lease. At the end of the 5 years, the balance in the leases payable column of the spreadsheet was zero. Cott has asked Grant, CPA, to review the spreadsheet to determine the error. Only one error was made on the spreadsheet. Which of the following statements represents the best explanation for this error?

A. The beginning present value of the lease did not include the present value of the payment called for by the purchase option.

B. Cott subtracted the annual interest amount from the lease payable balance instead of adding it.

C. The present value of the payment called for by the purchase option was subtracted from the present value of the annual payments.

D. Cott discounted the annual payments as an ordinary annuity, when the payments actually occurred at the beginning of each period.

Answer (A) is correct. *(CPA, adapted)*
REQUIRED: The best explanation for an error in interest amortization for a lease with a purchase option.
DISCUSSION: Cott (the lessee) initially must record a finance lease by debiting a right-of-use asset and crediting a lease liability equal to the present value of the lease payments, which consist of (1) the rental payments and (2) the amount of the exercise price of the option to purchase the leased asset that the lessee is reasonably certain to exercise. The effect of including the present value of the purchase option is that, at the end of the 5-year amortization period, the lease liability should equal that amount.
Answer (B) is incorrect. The excess of the lease payment over the periodic interest is subtracted from the lease payable. Answer (C) is incorrect. At the lease's inception, the present value of the purchase option is added to the present value of the annual payments. Subtracting it will reduce the payable to zero before the end of 5 years (given correct amortization amounts). Answer (D) is incorrect. Treating the lease payments as an ordinary annuity results in higher annual payments and higher annual amortization. The effect is to reduce the balance below the purchase option (but not necessarily to zero).

14.3.4. Scott Co. entered into a 5-year finance lease requiring it to make equal annual payments. The reduction of the lease liability in Year 2 should equal

A. The current liability shown for the lease at the end of Year 1.

B. The current liability shown for the lease at the end of Year 2.

C. The reduction of the lease liability in Year 1.

D. One-tenth of the original lease liability.

Answer (A) is correct. *(CPA, adapted)*
REQUIRED: The reduction of a finance lease liability in the second year.
DISCUSSION: At the beginning of a finance lease, a lessee should record a right-of-use asset and a lease liability equal to the present value of the lease payments. In a classified balance sheet, the lease liability must be allocated between the current and noncurrent portions. The current portion at a balance sheet date is the reduction of the lease liability in the forthcoming year.
Answer (B) is incorrect. The current liability at the end of Year 2 is equal to the reduction that will be recorded in Year 3. Answer (C) is incorrect. The reduction of the lease liability will increase in each subsequent year. Answer (D) is incorrect. The interest method is used to determine the reduction in the lease liability.

14.3.5. Wilson leased a new machine having a total and remaining expected useful life of 30 years from Tehi. Terms of the noncancelable, 25-year lease were that Wilson would receive title to the property upon payment of a sum equal to the fair value of the machine at the termination of the lease. Wilson is reasonably certain to exercise the purchase option on the machine. For tax purposes, the depreciable life of the machine is 22.5 years. The asset recorded under this lease should properly be amortized over

A. 5 years.

B. 22.5 years.

C. 25 years.

D. 30 years.

Answer (D) is correct. *(Publisher, adapted)*
REQUIRED: The proper amortization period of a right-of-use asset given a purchase option reasonably certain to be exercised.
DISCUSSION: When a lease transfers ownership of the property to the lessee at the end of the lease or contains a purchase option that the lessee is reasonably certain to exercise, the lessee will own the asset at the end of the lease. Accordingly, the right-of-use asset is amortized over its useful life of 30 years.
Answer (A) is incorrect. Five years is the period of ownership after expiration of the lease. Answer (B) is incorrect. The right-of-use asset is amortized over its useful life when the lease contains a purchase option that the lessee is reasonably certain to exercise. Answer (C) is incorrect. The right-of-use asset is amortized over its useful life when the lease contains a purchase option that the lessee is reasonably certain to exercise.

14.3.6. On January 1, Year 1, Bay Co. acquired a land lease for a 21-year period with no option to renew. The lease required Bay to construct a building in lieu of rent. The building, completed on January 1, Year 2, at a cost of $840,000, will be depreciated using the straight-line method. At the end of the lease, the building's estimated fair value will be $420,000. What is the building's carrying amount in Bay's December 31, Year 2, balance sheet?

A. $798,000

B. $800,000

C. $819,000

D. $820,000

Answer (A) is correct. *(CPA, adapted)*
REQUIRED: The building's carrying amount after 2 years.
DISCUSSION: General improvements to leased property should be capitalized as leasehold improvements and amortized in accordance with the straight-line method over the shorter of their expected useful life or the lease term. Given no renewal option, the amortization period is 20 years, the shorter of the expected useful life or the remaining lease term at the date of completion. The amortizable base is $840,000 even though the building will have a fair value of $420,000 at the end of the lease. The latter amount is not a salvage value because the building will become the lessor's property when the lease expires. Consequently, Year 2 straight-line amortization is $42,000 ($840,000 ÷ 20 years), and the year-end carrying amount is $798,000 ($840,000 – $42,000).
Answer (B) is incorrect. The amount of $800,000 assumes a 21-year remaining lease term at 1/1/Yr 2. Answer (C) is incorrect. The amount of $819,000 assumes no amortization of an amount equal to the fair value at the end of the lease term. Answer (D) is incorrect. The amount of $820,000 assumes a 21-year remaining lease term at 1/1/Yr 2 and no amortization of an amount equal to the fair value at the end of the lease term.

14.3.7. Star Co. leases a building for its product showroom. The 10-year nonrenewable lease will expire on December 31, Year 6. In January Year 1, Star redecorated its showroom and made leasehold improvements of $48,000. The estimated useful life of the improvements is 8 years. Star uses the straight-line method of amortization. What amount of leasehold improvements, net of amortization, should Star report in its June 30, Year 1, balance sheet?

A. $45,600

B. $45,000

C. $44,000

D. $43,200

Answer (C) is correct. *(CPA, adapted)*
REQUIRED: The net amount of leasehold improvements reported in the balance sheet.
DISCUSSION: General improvements to leased property should be capitalized as leasehold improvements and amortized in accordance with the straight-line method over the shorter of their expected useful life or the lease term. Because the remaining lease term is less than the estimated life of the improvements, the cost should be amortized equally over 6 years. On 6/30/Year 1, $44,000 {$48,000 – [($48,000 ÷ 6 years) × 1/2 year]} should be reported for net leasehold improvements.
Answer (A) is incorrect. The amount of $45,600 assumes the amortization period is 10 years. Answer (B) is incorrect. The amount of $45,000 assumes the amortization period is 8 years. Answer (D) is incorrect. The amount of $43,200 assumes that 1 year's amortization has been recorded and that the amortization period is 10 years.

14.3.8. On January 1, Year 4, Harrow Co., as lessee, signed a 5-year noncancelable equipment lease with annual payments of $100,000 beginning December 31, Year 4. Harrow treated this transaction as a finance lease. The five lease payments have a present value of $379,000 at January 1, Year 4, based on interest of 10%. What amount should Harrow report as interest expense for the year ended December 31, Year 4?

A. $37,900

B. $27,900

C. $24,200

D. $0

Answer (A) is correct. *(CPA, adapted)*
REQUIRED: The interest to be recognized in the first year of a finance lease.
DISCUSSION: Under the effective-interest method, interest expense for the first year is $37,900 ($379,000 lease liability × 10% effective interest rate).
Answer (B) is incorrect. The amount of $27,900 assumes the initial payment was made immediately. Answer (C) is incorrect. The amount of $24,200 is one-fifth of the total interest ($500,000 – $379,000 PV). Answer (D) is incorrect. Interest must be accrued.

14.3.9. On January 1, Jessie Co. (lessee) entered into a 5-year lease for equipment. Jessie accounted for the acquisition as a finance lease for $120,000, which includes a $5,000 purchase option. At the end of the lease, Jessie expects to exercise the purchase option. Jessie estimates that the equipment's fair value will be $10,000 at the end of its 8-year life. For the year ended December 31, what amount should Jessie recognize as amortization of the asset recorded under the finance lease?

A. $13,750

B. $15,000

C. $23,000

D. $24,000

Answer (A) is correct. *(CPA, adapted)*
REQUIRED: The amortization of the asset recorded under a lease.
DISCUSSION: When (1) the title passes to the lessee at the end of the lease term or (2) the lease contains a purchase option that the lessee is reasonably certain to exercise, the amortization period is the estimated economic life of the underlying property. The asset recorded under the finance lease should be amortized on a straight-line basis. Accordingly, amortization is $13,750 [($120,000 asset recorded under the lease – $10,000 salvage value) ÷ 8-year economic life].
Answer (B) is incorrect. The amount of $15,000 does not consider salvage value. Answer (C) is incorrect. The amount of $23,000 subtracts the purchase option from the present value of the minimum lease payments, uses a 5-year life, and does not consider salvage value. Answer (D) is incorrect. The amount of $24,000 uses a 5-year life and does not consider salvage value.

14.4 Lessee Accounting for Operating Leases -- Subsequent Measurement

14.4.1. On January 1, Year 4, Mollat Co. signed a 6-year lease for equipment having a 10-year economic life. The present value of the monthly equal lease payments equaled 80% of the equipment's fair value. The lease agreement provides for neither a transfer of title to Mollat nor a purchase option. In its Year 4 income statement, Mollat should report

A. Lease expense equal to the Year 4 lease payments.

B. Lease expense equal to the Year 4 lease payments less interest expense.

C. Amortization expense equal to one-tenth of the equipment's fair value.

D. Amortization expense equal to one-seventh of 80% of the equipment's fair value.

Answer (A) is correct. *(CPA, adapted)*
REQUIRED: The income statement effect of the lease.
DISCUSSION: The lease is classified as an operating lease by Mollat. No criterion for classification as a financial lease is met: (1) The ownership of the leased asset is transferred to the lessee by the end of the lease term, (2) the lease includes an option to purchase the leased asset that the lessee is reasonably certain to exercise, (3) the lease term is for the major part (generally considered as 75%) of the remaining economic life of the leased asset, (4) the present value of the sum of the lease payments and any residual value guaranteed by the lessee equals or exceeds substantially all of the fair value (generally considered as 90%) of the leased asset, and (5) the leased asset is so specialized that it is expected to have no alternative use to the lessor at the end of the lease term. In an operating lease, a lessee recognizes for each period a single lease expense. It is calculated so that the total undiscounted lease payments are allocated over the lease term on a straight-line basis. Because Mollat makes equal monthly lease payments throughout the entire lease term, annual lease expense equals the annual lease payments.

14.4.2. Oak Co. leased equipment for 9 years, agreeing to pay $50,000 at the start of the lease term on December 31, Year 4, and $50,000 annually on each December 31 for the next 8 years. The present value on December 31, Year 4, of the nine lease payments over the lease term, using the rate implicit in the lease, was $316,500. Oak knows that this rate is 10%. The December 31, Year 4, present value of the lease payments using Oak's incremental borrowing rate of 12% was $298,500. Oak made a timely second lease payment. The lease was classified as an operating lease by Oak. What amount should Oak report as a lease liability in its December 31, Year 5, balance sheet?

A. $350,000

B. $243,150

C. $228,320

D. $0

Answer (B) is correct. *(CPA, adapted)*
REQUIRED: The amount to be reported as a lease liability for an operating lease.
DISCUSSION: For a finance or operating lease, a lessee initially must recognize a lease liability and a right-of-use asset. At the lease commencement date, a lease liability is measured at the present value of the lease payments to be made over the lease term. Subsequent to initial recognition, the lease liability is reduced for the excess of the periodic lease payment over the interest expense recognized during the period. Oak knows the implicit rate. Thus, the present value of the lease payments of this lease is $316,500, the amount based on the lessor's implicit rate. After the initial payment of $50,000, which contains no interest component, is deducted, the carrying amount during Year 5 is $266,500. Accordingly, the interest component of the next payment is $26,650 ($266,500 × 10% implicit rate), and the lease liability on December 31, Year 5, is $243,150 [$266,500 – ($50,000 – $26,650)].
Answer (A) is incorrect. The sum of the nine lease payments is $350,000. Answer (C) is incorrect. The amount of $228,320 is based on a 12% rate. Answer (D) is incorrect. Both finance and operating leases result in recognition of a lease liability at the lease commencement date.

14.4.3. On June 1, Oren Co. entered into a 5-year nonrenewable operating lease, commencing on that date, for office space and made the following payments to Rose Properties:

Bonus to obtain lease	$30,000
First month's rent	10,000
Last month's rent	10,000

The lease term requires monthly rent payments of $10,000. In its income statement for the year ended June 30, what amount should Oren report as rent expense?

- A. $10,000
- B. $10,500
- C. $40,000
- D. $50,000

Answer (B) is correct. *(CPA, adapted)*
REQUIRED: The amount to be reported as rent expense for an operating lease.
DISCUSSION: In an operating lease, a single lease expense is recognized in each period. It is calculated so that the total undiscounted lease payments are allocated over the lease term on a straight-line basis. The rent expense in June is $10,000, the amount to be paid each month. The bonus to obtain the lease is an initial direct cost incurred by Oren. Initial direct costs incurred by the lessee are included in the total undiscounted lease payments. Thus, they are recognized in the single periodic lease expense on a straight-line basis over the lease term. Rent expense for June is $10,500 {$10,000 for the month's rent + [($30,000 ÷ 5) ÷ 12 amortization of the bonus]}.
Answer (A) is incorrect. The expense should include amortization of the bonus. Answer (C) is incorrect. The bonus should be amortized over the lease term benefited. Answer (D) is incorrect. The last month's rent payment should be deferred and expensed in the period it benefits. Also, the bonus should be amortized over the lease term.

14.5 Lessor Accounting for Sales-Type Leases

14.5.1. In a lease that is recorded as a sales-type lease by the lessor, interest revenue

- A. Should be recognized in full as revenue at the lease's inception.
- B. Should be recognized over the period of the lease using the straight-line method.
- C. Should be recognized over the period of the lease using the effective-interest method.
- D. Does not arise.

Answer (C) is correct. *(CPA, adapted)*
REQUIRED: The proper accounting for interest income in a sales-type lease.
DISCUSSION: In a sales-type lease, each periodic lease payment received by the lessor has two components: (1) interest income and (2) the reduction of net investment in the lease. Interest income is calculated using the effective interest method. It equals the carrying amount of the net investment in the lease at the beginning of the period times the discount rate implicit in the lease.

14.5.2. The fair value of the leased asset differs from its carrying amount. What are the components of the lease receivable for a lessor involved in a sales-type lease?

- A. The lease payments plus unguaranteed residual value.
- B. The lease payments plus guaranteed residual value.
- C. The lease payments less guaranteed residual value.
- D. The lease payments less initial direct costs.

Answer (B) is correct. *(CPA, adapted)*
REQUIRED: The components of the lease receivable in a sales-type lease.
DISCUSSION: In a sales-type lease, the lease receivable recognized by the lessor at the commencement of the lease is measured at the present value of the lease payments plus the present value of residual value guaranteed by the lessee or any other third party. In sales-type leases, initial direct costs are expensed when the fair value of the leased asset differs from its carrying amount.
Answer (A) is incorrect. Unguaranteed residual value is not included in the measure of the lease receivable. Answer (C) is incorrect. The lease receivable at the lease commencement date equals the sum of the present values of (1) the lease payments and (2) any guaranteed residual value. Answer (D) is incorrect. In sales-type leases, initial direct costs are expensed when the fair value of the leased asset differs from its carrying amount.

14.5.3. Able Co. leased equipment to Baker under a noncancelable lease with a transfer of title. After recognition of the lease, will Able record any depreciation expense on the leased asset and interest revenue related to the lease?

	Depreciation Expense	Interest Revenue
A.	Yes	Yes
B.	Yes	No
C.	No	No
D.	No	Yes

Answer (D) is correct. *(CPA, adapted)*
REQUIRED: The lessor's accounting for depreciation and interest revenue related to a noncancelable lease with a transfer of title.
DISCUSSION: The lease transfers ownership. Accordingly, the lease is recognized as a sales-type lease by the lessor. The leased asset is derecognized at the lease commencement date. Thus, no depreciation expense is recognized for the leased asset by the lessor.
Answer (A) is incorrect. The lessor does not recognize depreciation expense. Answer (B) is incorrect. The lessor does not recognize depreciation expense but does recognize interest revenue. Answer (C) is incorrect. The lessor recognizes interest revenue.

14.5.4. Glade Co. leases computer equipment to customers under sales-type leases. The equipment has no residual value at the end of the lease, and the leases do not contain purchase options. At lease inception, the fair value of the leased computer equipment equals its carrying amount. Glade wishes to earn 8% interest on a 5-year lease of equipment with a fair value of $323,400. The present value of an annuity due of $1 at 8% for 5 years is 4.312. What is the total amount of interest revenue that Glade will earn over the life of the lease?

A. $51,600

B. $75,000

C. $129,360

D. $139,450

Answer (A) is correct. *(CPA, adapted)*
REQUIRED: The interest revenue earned over the life of a lease.
DISCUSSION: To earn 8% interest over the lease term, the annual payment must be $75,000 ($323,400 fair value at the inception of the lease ÷ 4.312 annuity factor). Given no residual value and no bargain purchase option, total lease payments over the lease term will be $375,000 ($75,000 payment × 5 years). The entire difference between the gross lease payments received ($375,000) and their present value ($323,400 net investment in the lease) is the interest revenue recognized over the entire lease term ($375,000 − $323,400 = $51,600).
Answer (B) is incorrect. The amount of $75,000 is the annual lease payment. Answer (C) is incorrect. Interest revenue equals the total lease payments of $375,000 minus the net investment in the lease of $323,400. Answer (D) is incorrect. Interest revenue equals the total lease payments of $375,000 minus the net investment in the lease of $323,400.

14.5.5. On January 1, Year 4, Jaffe Co. leased a machine to Pender Co. for 10 years, with $10,000 payments due at the beginning of each year effective at the inception of the lease. The machine cost Jaffe $55,000. The lease is appropriately accounted for as a sales-type lease by Jaffe. The present value of the 10 rent payments over the lease term discounted appropriately at 10% was $67,600. The estimated residual value of the machine at the end of 10 years is equal to the disposal costs. How much interest revenue should Jaffe record from the lease for the year ended December 31, Year 4?

A. $5,500

B. $5,760

C. $6,760

D. $12,600

Answer (B) is correct. *(CPA, adapted)*
REQUIRED: The interest income recognized by the lessor in the first year of a sales-type lease.
DISCUSSION: In accordance with the effective-interest method, the interest income is equal to the carrying amount of the net investment in the lease at the beginning of the interest period multiplied by the interest rate used to calculate the present value of the lease payments (rate implicit in the lease). The present value of $67,600 is reduced by the $10,000 payment made at the inception of the lease, leaving a carrying amount of $57,600. This balance multiplied by 10% yields $5,760 to be reflected as interest income for the first year of the lease.
Answer (A) is incorrect. The amount of $5,500 is 10% of the cost of the machine. Answer (C) is incorrect. The amount of $6,760 equals 10% of the present value of 10 payments. Answer (D) is incorrect. The amount of $12,600 is the profit on the sale.

14.5.6. Winn Co. manufactures equipment that is sold or leased. On December 31, Year 4, Winn leased equipment to Bart for a 5-year period ending December 31, Year 9, at which date ownership of the leased asset will be transferred to Bart. Equal payments under the lease are $22,000 and are due on December 31 of each year. The first payment was made on December 31, Year 4. The normal sales price of the equipment is $77,000, and cost is $60,000. For the year ended December 31, Year 4, what amount of selling profit should Winn realize from the lease transaction?

A. $17,000

B. $22,000

C. $50,000

D. $33,000

Answer (A) is correct. *(CPA, adapted)*
REQUIRED: The selling profit to be recognized by the lessor from a lease transaction.
DISCUSSION: Ownership of the leased equipment transfers to the lessee at the end of the lease term, so one of the five criteria to classify the lease as a sales-type lease by the lessor is satisfied. Given no residual value or initial direct costs, selling profit for a sales-type lease is recognized for the excess of the fair value of the leased equipment over its carrying amount. Thus, a selling profit of $17,000 ($77,000 − $60,000) is recognized by Winn.
Answer (B) is incorrect. The amount of a periodic payment is $22,000. Answer (C) is incorrect. The amount of $50,000 equals the sum of the five periodic payments minus the equipment's cost. Answer (D) is incorrect. The amount of $33,000 equals the sum of the five periodic payments minus the normal sales price.

14.5.7. Benedict Company leased equipment to Mark, Inc., on January 1, Year 2. The lease is for an 8-year period expiring December 31, Year 9. The first of 8 equal annual payments of $600,000 was made on January 1, Year 2. Benedict had purchased the equipment on December 29, Year 1, for $3,200,000. The lease is appropriately accounted for as a sales-type lease by Benedict. Assume that the present value at January 1, Year 2, of all rent payments over the lease term discounted at a 10% interest rate was $3,520,000. What amount of interest income should Benedict record in Year 3 (the second year of the lease period) as a result of the lease?

A. $261,200

B. $292,000

C. $320,000

D. $327,200

Answer (A) is correct. *(CPA, adapted)*
REQUIRED: The interest income during the second year of a sales-type lease.
DISCUSSION: The net investment to be recorded by the lessor at 1/1/Year 2 is given as $3,520,000, the present value of the lease payments discounted at 10%. The net investment is immediately reduced by the $600,000 lease payment on 1/1/Year 2, resulting in a carrying amount for Year 2 of $2,920,000. Interest earned for the Year 2 at a rate of 10% ($2,920,000 × 10%) is $292,000. Thus, the $600,000 1/1/Year 3 lease payment consists of the $292,000 interest component and a $308,000 reduction of the net investment. Because the Year 3 net investment balance is $2,612,000 ($2,920,000 – $308,000), interest income for Year 3 is $261,200 ($2,612,000 × 10%).
Answer (B) is incorrect. The carrying amount of the lease must be reduced by the payment on 1/1/Year 3 for the amount applied to reducing the lease obligation. Answer (C) is incorrect. The amount of $320,000 is based on original cost of the leased property. Answer (D) is incorrect. Interest income is calculated as the carrying amount of the lease multiplied by the discount rate. Thus, the amount of interest income is $261,200 [($2,920,000 – $308,000) × 10%].

14.5.8. Tau Co. manufactures machines to be sold or leased. On January 1, Tau leased machinery to Upsilon, Inc., for a 5-year period. At the end of the lease term, the machinery is to be transferred to Upsilon. Equal $25,000 payments are due at the end of each of the 5 years. The implicit rate of the lease is 7% and the cost to Tau is $90,000. The present value factor for an ordinary annuity for 5 periods at 7% is 4.100. What is the lessor's total pretax gross profit from the lease recognized on January 1?

A. $35,000

B. $0

C. $12,500

D. $7,175

Answer (C) is correct. *(Publisher, adapted)*
REQUIRED: The amount of profit on a sales-type lease.
DISCUSSION: Ownership of the leased machinery transfers to the lessee at the end of the lease term. Consequently, one of the five criteria for classifying the lease as a sales-type lease by the lessor is satisfied. The gross profit to report on the sales-type lease equals the difference between the fair value of the leased asset (the present value of the lease payments) and the cost. Thus, the profit on the sale equals $12,500 [($25,000 × 4.100) – $90,000].
Answer (A) is incorrect. The amount of $35,000 assumes the lease payments are not discounted. Answer (B) is incorrect. In a sales-type lease, the lessor recognizes a seller's profit (loss) when the fair value of the leased property at the lease's beginning differs from its cost or carrying amount. Answer (D) is incorrect. The amount of $7,175 is 7% interest on $102,500.

14.6 Lessor Accounting for Operating and Direct Financing Leases

14.6.1. On the first day of its fiscal year, Lessor, Inc., leased certain property at an annual rental of $100,000 receivable at the beginning of each year for 10 years. The first payment was received immediately. The leased property is new, had cost $650,000, and has an estimated useful life of 13 years with no salvage value. The rate implicit in the lease is 8%. The present value of an annuity of $1 payable at the beginning of the period at 8% for 10 years is 7.247. Lessor had no other costs associated with this lease. Lessor should have accounted for this lease as a sales-type lease but mistakenly treated the lease as an operating lease. Lessor depreciates all of its properties using the straight-line depreciation method. Ignoring tax effects, what was the effect on net earnings during the first year of treating this lease as an operating lease rather than as a sale?

A. Overstatement of $23,300.

B. Understatement of $74,676.

C. Understatement of $24,676.

D. Understatement of $24,700.

Answer (B) is correct. *(CPA, adapted)*
REQUIRED: The effect of accounting for a lease as an operating rather than as a sales-type lease.
DISCUSSION: Accounting for the lease as an operating lease during the first year generated $50,000 of income, the $100,000 lease payment minus $50,000 of depreciation ($650,000 ÷ 13). In a sales-type lease, the lessor recognizes two income components: profit on the sale and interest income. Total income from accounting for the lease as a sale would have been $124,676 ($74,700 + $49,976). The effect of the error on net earnings was therefore an understatement of $74,676 ($124,676 – $50,000).

Net investment		Net investment	
($100,000 × 7.247)	$724,700	($100,000 × 7.247)	$724,700
Carrying amount	(650,000)	First lease payment	(100,000)
Profit on sale	$ 74,700	Lease balance	$624,700
		Interest rate	× .08
		Interest income	$ 49,976

Answer (A) is incorrect. The effect of the accounting error is an understatement of net earnings. Answer (C) is incorrect. The amount of $24,676 ignores the depreciation expense recognized under an operating lease. Answer (D) is incorrect. The amount of $24,700 ignores the interest income recognized for a sales-type lease.

14.6.2. On January 1, Glen Co. leased a building to Dix Corp. The lease was properly classified as an operating lease by Glen for a 10-year term at an annual rental of $50,000. At the inception of the lease, Glen received $200,000 covering the first 2 years' rent of $100,000 and a security deposit of $100,000. This deposit will not be returned to Dix upon expiration of the lease but will be applied to last payment of rent for the last 2 years of the lease. What portions of the $200,000 should be shown as a current and a long-term liability, respectively, in Glen's December 31 balance sheet?

	Current Liability	Long-Term Liability
A.	$0	$200,000
B.	$50,000	$100,000
C.	$100,000	$100,000
D.	$100,000	$50,000

Answer (B) is correct. *(CPA, adapted)*
REQUIRED: The allocation of an advance payment between the liability sections of the balance sheet.
DISCUSSION: Of the $200,000 received at the inception of the lease on 1/1, $50,000 should be recognized as rental income for the year ended 12/31. At 12/31, the $50,000 attributable to rent for the following year should be classified as a current liability. Also at 12/31, the $100,000 that is applicable to the last 2 years of the lease should be classified as a long-term liability.
Answer (A) is incorrect. The rent advanced for the second year is a current liability. The last 2 years' rent is a long-term liability. Answer (C) is incorrect. The first year's rent should be recognized as rental income, not a current liability. Answer (D) is incorrect. The first year's rent should be recognized as rental income, not a current liability. The last 2 years' rent is a long-term liability.

14.6.3. On January 1, Year 4, Wren Co. leased a building to Brill under an operating lease for 10 years at $50,000 per year, payable the first day of each lease year. Wren paid $15,000 to a real estate broker as a finder's fee. The building is depreciated $12,000 per year. For Year 4, Wren incurred insurance and property tax expenses totaling $9,000. Wren's net rental income for Year 4 should be

A. $27,500

B. $29,000

C. $35,000

D. $36,500

Answer (A) is correct. *(CPA, adapted)*
REQUIRED: The net rental income in the first year.
DISCUSSION: The net rental income equals the annual payment minus expenses. The finder's fee is an initial direct cost that should be deferred and subsequently expensed over the lease term on a straight-line basis. Accordingly, the net rental income for Year 4 is $27,500 [$50,000 annual rental – $12,000 depreciation – $9,000 insurance and taxes – ($15,000 ÷ 10 years) amortization of the finder's fee].
Answer (B) is incorrect. The amount of $29,000 omits amortization of the finder's fee. Answer (C) is incorrect. The amount of $35,000 equals rental income minus the full finder's fee. Answer (D) is incorrect. The amount of $36,500 excludes insurance and property taxes from the computation.

14.6.4. Wall Co. leased office premises to Fox, Inc., for a 5-year term beginning January 2, Year 4. Under the terms of the operating lease, rent for the first year is $8,000 and rent for years 2 through 5 is $12,500 per annum. However, as an inducement to enter the lease, Wall granted Fox the first 6 months of the lease rent-free. In its December 31, Year 4, income statement, what amount should Wall report as rental income?

A. $12,000

B. $11,600

C. $10,800

D. $8,000

Answer (C) is correct. *(CPA, adapted)*
REQUIRED: The rental revenue reported for the first year of an operating lease given a varying annual rental.
DISCUSSION: For an operating lease, lease payments are recognized as rental income by the lessor. If rental payments vary from a straight-line basis, rental income should be recognized over the full lease term on a straight-line basis. Thus, an equal amount of rental income is recognized each period over the lease term. Wall therefore should report rental revenue of $10,800 {[$8,000 – ($8,000 × .5) + ($12,500 × 4)] ÷ 5 years}.
Answer (A) is incorrect. The amount of $12,000 equals the first year's rent plus, not minus, 6 months of free rent. Answer (B) is incorrect. The amount of $11,600 is the result of allocating $58,000 over 5 years. Answer (D) is incorrect. The rent must be adjusted.

14.6.5. On July 1, Year 1, Gee, Inc., leased a delivery truck from Marr Corp. under a 3-year operating lease. Total rent for the term of the lease will be $36,000, payable as follows:

$$
\begin{array}{lll}
\$ \ \ 500 & \times \ 12 \text{ months} = & \$ \ \ 6,000 \\
\$ \ \ 750 & \times \ 12 \text{ months} = & \$ \ \ 9,000 \\
\$1,750 & \times \ 12 \text{ months} = & \$21,000
\end{array}
$$

All payments were made when due. In Marr's June 30, Year 3, balance sheet, the accrued rent receivable should be reported as

A. $0

B. $9,000

C. $12,000

D. $21,000

Answer (B) is correct. *(CPA, adapted)*
REQUIRED: The amount to be included as rent receivable in the balance sheet.
DISCUSSION: For an operating lease, lease payments are recognized as rental income by the lessor. If rental payments vary from a straight-line basis, rental income should be recognized over the full lease term on a straight-line basis. Thus, an equal amount of rental income is recognized each period over the lease term. Thus, monthly rent revenue of $1,000 [($6,000 + $9,000 + $21,000) ÷ 36 months] should be recognized. At 6/30/Year 3, cumulative revenue recognized is $24,000 ($1,000 × 24 months). Because cumulative cash received is $15,000 ($6,000 + $9,000), an accrued receivable for the $9,000 ($24,000 – $15,000) difference should be recognized.
Answer (A) is incorrect. The amount of $9,000 is equal to rent received during the year ended 6/30/Year 3. Answer (C) is incorrect. The amount of $12,000 is rent revenue recognized each year. Answer (D) is incorrect. The amount of $21,000 is equal to the rent payments to be received in the following fiscal year.

14.6.6. Conn Corp. owns an office building and normally charges tenants $30 per square foot per year for office space. Because the occupancy rate is low, Conn agreed to lease 10,000 square feet to Hanson Co. at $12 per square foot for the first year of a 3-year operating lease. Rent for remaining years will be at the $30 rate. Hanson moved into the building on January 1, Year 1, and paid the first year's rent in advance. What amount of rental revenue should Conn report from Hanson in its income statement for the year ended September 30, Year 1?

A. $90,000

B. $120,000

C. $180,000

D. $240,000

Answer (C) is correct. *(CPA, adapted)*
REQUIRED: The amount of rent revenue to be included in the income statement.
DISCUSSION: In an operating lease, when payments differ from year to year, revenue is recognized by allocating the total amount of revenue to be received evenly over the lease term. At 9/30/Year 1, the amount of revenue to be recognized is for 9 months. Thus, rent revenue is $180,000 {[$10,000 square feet × ($12 + $30 + $30)] × (9 ÷ 36)}.
Answer (A) is incorrect. The amount of $90,000 recognizes rent equal to the rental payments. Answer (B) is incorrect. The amount of $120,000 recognizes rent equal to rent payments for 12 months. Answer (D) is incorrect. The amount of $240,000 recognizes rent for 12 months.

14.7 Sale and Leaseback Transactions

14.7.1. On January 1, Year 1, Entity A sold property to Entity B and simultaneously leased it back for 4 years. Which of the following statements is true if the leaseback was properly classified as a sales-type lease?

A. Entity A will continue to report the leased property and depreciate it.

B. Entity A will recognize a gain or loss on the initial transfer of the property to Entity B.

C. Entity B will recognize the property at its fair value on January 1, Year 1.

D. On January 1, Year 1, Entity A will recognize the property at the present value of the leased payments to be made to Entity B.

Answer (A) is correct. *(Publisher, adapted)*
REQUIRED: The true statement about a sale-leaseback transaction if the leaseback is a sales-type lease.
DISCUSSION: When the leaseback is classified as a sales-type lease, the initial transfer of the property to Entity B is not a sale of the property. Thus, Entity A will continue to report the transferred property and depreciate it. The initial proceeds received from Entity B are recognized as a financial liability.
Answer (B) is incorrect. When the leaseback is classified as a sales-type lease, the initial transfer of the property to Entity B is not a sale of the property. Thus, no gain or loss on sale is recognized. Answer (C) is incorrect. When the leaseback is classified as a sales-type lease, the initial transfer of the property to Entity B is not a sale of the property. Thus, Entity B will not recognize the property. The amounts paid to Entity A are recognized as a financial asset. Answer (D) is incorrect. When the leaseback is classified as a sales-type lease, the initial transfer of the property to Entity B is not a sale of the property. Thus, Entity A will continue to report the transferred property and depreciate it.

Questions 14.7.2 and 14.7.3 are based on the following information. On January 1, Year 1, White Co. sold a property with a remaining useful life of 20 years to Blue Co. for $900,000. At the same time, White entered into a contract with Blue for the right to use the property (leaseback) for a period of 6 years, with annual rental payments of $80,000 that approximate the market rental payments for similar properties. On January 1, Year 1, the carrying amount of the property was $680,000, and its fair value was $770,000. A discount rate for the lease of 10% is used by both White and Blue. The present value factor for an ordinary annuity at 10% for 6 periods is 4.3553. The lease does not transfer the property to White at the end of the lease term and does not include a purchase option.

14.7.2. What amount of gain on sale of the property was recognized by White on January 1, Year 1?

A. $0

B. $130,000

C. $90,000

D. $220,000

Answer (C) is correct. *(Publisher, adapted)*
REQUIRED: The gain on sale recognized by the seller-lessee.
DISCUSSION: The leaseback is classified by White as an operating lease because none of the five criteria for classifying the lease as a finance lease were met. When the leaseback is classified as an operating lease, the initial transfer of the asset to the buyer-lessor can be accounted for as a sale of an asset, assuming all the criteria for revenue recognition were met. When the transaction is at fair value, a gain or loss on sale recognized by the seller-lessee is the difference between the selling price and the carrying amount of the property. But this transaction is not at fair value. The selling price of the property is greater than its fair value. The gain or loss on sale therefore is the difference between the fair value of the property and its carrying amount. Accordingly, a gain on sale of $90,000 ($770,000 fair value – $880,000 carrying amount) is recognized by White on January 1, Year 1.
Answer (A) is incorrect. The leaseback is classified by White as an operating lease because none of the five criteria to classify the lease as a finance lease were met. When the leaseback is classified as an operating lease, the initial transfer of the property to the buyer-lessor can be accounted for as a sale of the property, assuming all the criteria for revenue recognition were met. Answer (B) is incorrect. The amount of $130,000 is the excess of the selling price of the property over its fair value. It is the additional financing that White received from Blue. Answer (D) is incorrect. This transaction is not at fair value, because the sales price of the machine is greater than its fair value. Thus, the gain or loss on sale is calculated as the difference between the fair value of the property and its carrying amount.

14.7.3. What amount of lease expense for the right of use of the property is recognized by White in Year 1?

A. $80,000

B. $50,151

C. $13,000

D. $58,333

Answer (B) is correct. *(Publisher, adapted)*
REQUIRED: The lease expense for the right of use of property.
DISCUSSION: The leaseback is classified by White as an operating lease because none of the five criteria for classifying the lease as a finance lease were met. Because on January 1, Year 1, the selling price of the property was greater than its fair value, White received additional financing from Blue of $130,000 ($900,000 – $770,000) for the difference. Each annual lease payment includes both (1) the payment for the additional financing of $29,849 ($130,000 ÷ 4.3553) and (2) the payment for the right of use of the property of $50,151 ($80,000 – $29,849). If the leaseback is an operating lease, the payment for the right of use of the property is recognized as lease expense.
Answer (A) is incorrect. Because on January 1, Year 1, the selling price of the property was greater than its fair value, White received additional financing from Blue for the difference. Thus, each annual lease payment includes both the payment for the additional financing and the payment for the right of use of the property (which is the lease expense). Answer (C) is incorrect. The amount of $13,000 is the interest expense recognized in Year 1 on the additional financing received from Blue. Answer (D) is incorrect. The amount of $58,333 [($80,000 – ($130,000 ÷ 6 years)] assumes that the payment for the additional financing received from Blue is $21,667 ($130,000 ÷ 6 years) each year.

14.7.4. On January 1, Year 1, Alla Co. sold a property to Mish Co. for $400,000 and simultaneously leased it back for 3 years. The carrying amount of the property was $280,000, and its fair value was $310,000. The leaseback was properly classified as an operating lease. What amount of gain on sale of the property was recognized by Alla on January 1, Year 1?

A. $0

B. $30,000

C. $90,000

D. $120,000

Answer (B) is correct. *(Publisher, adapted)*
REQUIRED: The gain on sale if the leaseback is an operating lease.
DISCUSSION: When the leaseback is classified as an operating lease, the initial transfer of the asset to the buyer-lessor can be accounted for as a sale of an asset, assuming all the criteria for revenue recognition were met. When the transaction is at fair value, a gain or loss on sale recognized by the seller-lessee is the difference between the selling price and the carrying amount of the asset. However, this transaction is not at fair value because the sales price of the property is greater than its fair value. Thus, the gain or loss on sale is calculated as the difference between the fair value of the property and its carrying amount. Accordingly, a gain on sale of $30,000 ($310,000 fair value – $280,000 carrying amount) is recognized by Alla on January 1, Year 1.
Answer (A) is incorrect. No gain or loss on sale is recognized when the leaseback is classified as a sales-type lease. Answer (C) is incorrect. The amount of $90,000 is the financial liability, not a gain on sale, recognized by Alla on January 1, Year 1. Answer (D) is incorrect. This transaction is not at fair value because the sales price of the machine is greater than its fair value. Thus, the gain or loss on sale is calculated as the difference between the fair value of the property and its carrying amount.

14.7.5. On January 1, Year 1, Abik Co. sold property with a remaining useful life of 20 years to Preston Co. for $100,000 and simultaneously leased it back for 7 years. The lease contains a purchase option that Abik is reasonably certain to exercise. Which of the following statements is true?

A. No gain or loss on sale of property is recognized by Abik.

B. Preston initially recognized the property at its purchase price of $100,000.

C. Preston depreciates the property over its remaining useful life of 20 years.

D. The leaseback of the property is classified as an operating lease by Abik and Preston.

Answer (A) is correct. *(Publisher, adapted)*
REQUIRED: The true statement about a leaseback containing a purchase option.
DISCUSSION: Because the leaseback contains a purchase option that Abik is reasonably certain to exercise, the lease is classified as a finance lease by Abik (and sales-type lease by Preston). The initial transfer of the property to Preston (buyer-lessor) is not a sale of the property if the leaseback is classified as a finance lease or a sales-type lease. The transaction therefore is accounted for as a financing transaction, and no gain or loss on sale is recognized.
Answer (B) is incorrect. Because the leaseback contains a purchase option that Abik is reasonably certain to exercise, the lease is classified as a finance lease by Abik (and sales-type lease by Preston). The transaction is accounted for as a financing transaction. Thus, Preston will not recognize the property. The amount of $100,000 paid to Abik is recognized as a financial asset (e.g., loan receivable). Answer (C) is incorrect. Because the leaseback contains a purchase option that Abik is reasonably certain to exercise, the lease is classified as a finance lease by Abik (and sales-type lease by Preston). The transaction is accounted for as a financing transaction. Thus, Preston will not recognize the property and will not depreciate it. Answer (D) is incorrect. Because the leaseback contains a purchase option that Abik is reasonably certain to exercise, the lease is classified as a finance lease by Abik and a sales-type lease by Preston.

Use **Gleim Test Prep** for interactive study and easy-to-use detailed analytics!

STUDY UNIT FIFTEEN
CORPORATE EQUITY

The basic shareholders' equity accounts are (1) retained earnings, (2) common stock, (3) preferred stock, (4) additional paid-in capital, (5) treasury stock, (6) accumulated other comprehensive income (OCI), and (7) noncontrolling interest. OCI is covered in the subunit of Study Unit 3 on comprehensive income. Noncontrolling interests result from business combinations in which the parent does not own all of a subsidiary's voting interests. They are addressed in Study Unit 24. The **statement of changes in equity** presented as part of a full set of financial statements provides disclosure of changes during the accounting period in the separate equity accounts.

Most questions about equity are on (1) dividend distribution (including cash, property, and stock dividends) and (2) the accounting for issuance and repurchase of equity securities.

QUESTIONS

15.1 General

15.1.1. Which of the following is the primary element that distinguishes accounting for corporations from accounting for other legal forms of business entity (such as partnerships)?

   A. The entity theory relates primarily to the other forms of business entity.

   B. The corporation draws a sharper distinction in accounting for sources of capital.

   C. In a corporation, retained earnings may be reduced only by the declaration of dividends.

   D. Generally accepted accounting principles apply to corporations but have relatively little applicability to other forms of business entity.

Answer (B) is correct. *(CPA, adapted)*
   REQUIRED: The primary distinguishing feature of accounting for corporations.
   DISCUSSION: The three primary forms of business entity are the corporation, the partnership, and the proprietorship. Of the three, only the corporation sharply differentiates between contributed equity and equity earned and retained in the business. Contributed capital is reflected in the various capital stock and additional paid-in capital (additional contributed capital) accounts. Earned capital is reflected in the retained earnings accounts.
   Answer (A) is incorrect. The entity theory relates primarily to the corporation. It achieves a greater degree of separation from its owners than any other form of business entity. Answer (C) is incorrect. Retained earnings may be reduced by numerous transactions, including a net operating loss. Answer (D) is incorrect. GAAP apply to all forms of business entity.

15.1.2. The issuance of shares of preferred stock to shareholders

   A. Increases preferred stock outstanding.

   B. Has no effect on preferred stock outstanding.

   C. Increases preferred stock authorized.

   D. Decreases preferred stock authorized.

Answer (A) is correct. *(CPA, adapted)*
   REQUIRED: The effect of the issuance of shares of preferred stock to shareholders.
   DISCUSSION: The charter (articles of incorporation) filed with the secretary of state of the state of incorporation indicates the classes of stock that may be issued and their authorized amounts in terms of shares and/or total dollar value. When authorized shares are issued, the effect is to increase the amount of that class of stock outstanding.
   Answer (B) is incorrect. The effect of the issuance of shares is to increase the stock outstanding. Answer (C) is incorrect. The issuance of shares has no effect on the preferred stock authorized. Answer (D) is incorrect. Preferred stock authorized is not affected by the issuance of shares.

15.1.3. Bier Corp. issued 400,000 shares of common stock when it began operations in Year 1 and issued an additional 200,000 shares in Year 2. Bier also issued preferred stock convertible to 200,000 shares of common stock. In Year 3, Bier purchased 150,000 shares of its common stock and held it in treasury. At the end of Year 3, how many shares of Bier's common stock were outstanding?

A. 800,000

B. 650,000

C. 600,000

D. 450,000

Answer (D) is correct. *(CPA, adapted)*
REQUIRED: The number of shares of outstanding common stock.
DISCUSSION: Bier issued 400,000 shares of common stock in Year 1 and 200,000 shares in Year 2. The purchase of 150,000 shares of treasury stock decreased the number of shares of common stock outstanding in Year 3 to 450,000 (400,000 + 200,000 – 150,000). The convertible preferred stock is not considered common stock.
Answer (A) is incorrect. This amount includes the convertible preferred stock and the treasury stock. Answer (B) is incorrect. This amount includes the convertible preferred stock. Answer (C) is incorrect. This amount includes the treasury stock.

15.1.4. The preemptive right of shareholders is the right to

A. Share equally in dividend distributions.

B. Purchase shares of stock on a pro rata basis when new issues are offered for sale.

C. Share in the distribution of assets on liquidation of the corporation.

D. Participate in the management of the corporation.

Answer (B) is correct. *(Publisher, adapted)*
REQUIRED: The definition of the preemptive right of shareholders.
DISCUSSION: The preemptive right refers to each shareholder's right to maintain proportionate ownership in the corporation if additional shares are offered for sale.
Answer (A) is incorrect. Sharing equally in dividend distributions is a shareholder right distinct from the preemptive right. Answer (C) is incorrect. Sharing in the distribution of assets on liquidation of the corporation is a shareholder right distinct from the preemptive right. Answer (D) is incorrect. Participating in management is a shareholder right distinct from the preemptive right. Shareholders participate in management of the corporation by electing a board of directors and by voting on referendums presented by management and the directors.

15.1.5. On December 1, Year 4, Line Corp. received a contribution of 2,000 shares of its $5 par value common stock from a shareholder. On that date, the stock's fair value was $35 per share. The stock was originally issued for $25 per share. By what amount will this contribution cause total equity to decrease if Line accounts for treasury stock using the cost method?

A. $70,000

B. $50,000

C. $20,000

D. $0

Answer (D) is correct. *(CPA, adapted)*
REQUIRED: The decrease in equity from receipt of a donation of the company's own stock.
DISCUSSION: Contributions received ordinarily are recorded as revenues or gains when received. However, adjustments or charges or credits resulting from transactions in the entity's own stock are excluded from net income or the results of operations. Thus, the receipt of a contribution of a company's own stock is recorded at fair value as increases in both contributed capital and treasury stock. Because these accounts offset, the net effect on equity is $0.
Answer (A) is incorrect. The amount of $70,000 records an effect equal to the current market price. Answer (B) is incorrect. The amount of $50,000 records an effect equal to the original issuance price. Answer (C) is incorrect. The amount of $20,000 records an effect equal to the difference between the current market price and the original issuance price.

15.1.6. Rudd Corp. had 700,000 shares of common stock authorized and 300,000 shares outstanding at December 31, Year 3. The following events occurred during Year 4:

January 31	Declared 10% stock dividend
June 30	Purchased 100,000 shares
August 1	Reissued 50,000 shares
November 30	Declared 2-for-1 stock split

At December 31, Year 4, how many shares of common stock did Rudd have outstanding?

A. 560,000

B. 600,000

C. 630,000

D. 660,000

Answer (A) is correct. *(CPA, adapted)*
REQUIRED: The number of outstanding shares of common stock.
DISCUSSION: Rudd had 300,000 shares outstanding before declaring the stock dividend. When it purchased 100,000 shares and reissued 50,000 shares, 280,000 shares (300,000 + 30,000 – 100,000 + 50,000) were left outstanding. Thus, the 2-for-1 stock split increased the shares outstanding to 560,000 (280,000 × 2).
Answer (B) is incorrect. The figure 600,000 ignores all transactions except the stock split. Answer (C) is incorrect. The figure 630,000 ignores the purchase and reissuance and assumes that the shares of the stock dividend were not split. Answer (D) is incorrect. The figure 660,000 excludes the treasury stock purchase and the reissuance of 50,000 shares.

15.1.7. East Co. issued 2,000 shares of its $5 par common stock to Krannik as compensation for 1,000 hours of legal services performed. Krannik usually bills $200 per hour for legal services. On the date of issuance, the stock was trading on a public exchange at $160 per share. By what amount should the additional paid-in capital account increase?

A. $320,000

B. $310,000

C. $200,000

D. $190,000

Answer (B) is correct. *(CPA, adapted)*
REQUIRED: The increase in additional paid-in capital.
DISCUSSION: When stock is issued for property or services, the transaction is recorded at the fair value of the stock or of the property or services received. In this case, the value of the stock is used because it is more objective. The $320,000 (2,000 shares × $160 market price) should be allocated as follows: $10,000 (2,000 shares × $5 par) to common stock and $310,000 to additional paid-in capital.
Answer (A) is incorrect. An amount of $10,000 should be allocated to common stock. Answer (C) is incorrect. Additional paid-in capital should increase by $310,000. Answer (D) is incorrect. The value of the stock should be used to record the transaction.

Questions 15.1.8 and 15.1.9 are based on the following information. Anand Co. reported the following in its statement of equity on January 1:

Common stock, $5 par value, authorized 200,000 shares, issued 100,000 shares	$ 500,000
Additional paid-in capital	1,500,000
Retained earnings	516,000
	$2,516,000
Minus: Treasury stock, at cost, 5,000 shares	(40,000)
Total equity	$2,476,000

The following events occurred during the year:

May 1	-- 1,000 shares of treasury stock were sold for $10,000.
July 9	-- 10,000 shares of previously unissued common stock sold for $12 per share.
October 1	-- The distribution of a 2-for-1 stock split resulted in the common stock's per-share par value being halved.

Anand accounts for treasury stock under the cost method. Laws in the state of Anand's incorporation protect shares held in treasury from dilution when stock dividends or stock splits are declared.

15.1.8. In Anand's December 31 statement of equity, the par value of the issued common stock should be

A. $550,000

B. $530,000

C. $275,000

D. $265,000

Answer (A) is correct. *(CPA, adapted)*
REQUIRED: The par value of the issued common stock.
DISCUSSION: At the beginning of the year, 100,000 shares with a par value of $500,000 had been issued. These shares included the treasury stock (issued but not outstanding) accounted for at cost. Under the cost method, the par value recorded in the common stock account is unaffected by purchases and sales of treasury stock. On July 9, 10,000 shares of previously unissued common stock were sold. This transaction increased the aggregate par value to $550,000 (110,000 shares issued × $5). The 2-for-1 stock split reduced the par value per share by 50% but did not affect the aggregate par value of the issued stock. Thus, state law presumably did not require capitalization of retained earnings as a result of the stock split.
Answer (B) is incorrect. The par value of the issued and outstanding shares is $530,000. Answer (C) is incorrect. Half the par value of the issued stock is $275,000. Answer (D) is incorrect. Half the par value of the issued and outstanding stock is $265,000.

15.1.9. The number of outstanding common shares at December 31 should be

A. 222,000

B. 220,000

C. 212,000

D. 210,000

Answer (C) is correct. *(CPA, adapted)*
REQUIRED: The number of outstanding shares.
DISCUSSION: On January 1, 95,000 shares (100,000 issued – 5,000 treasury shares) were outstanding. The treasury stock sale and the issuance of previously unissued shares increased that amount to 106,000 shares (95,000 + 1,000 + 10,000). The stock split doubled the shares outstanding to 212,000 (106,000 × 2).
Answer (A) is incorrect. This amount assumes 100,000 shares were outstanding on January 1. Answer (B) is incorrect. This amount assumes 100,000 shares were outstanding on January 1 but omits the treasury stock sale. Answer (D) is incorrect. This amount omits the treasury stock sale.

15.1.10. The December 31, Year 7, condensed balance sheet of Moore and Daughter, a partnership, follows:

Current assets	$280,000
Equipment (net)	260,000
	$540,000
Liabilities	$140,000
Moore and Daughter, capital	400,000
	$540,000

Fair values at December 31, Year 7, are as follows:

Current assets	$320,000
Equipment	420,000
Liabilities	140,000

On January 2, Year 8, Moore and Daughter was incorporated, with 10,000 shares of $10 par value common stock issued. How much should be credited to additional contributed capital?

A. $640,000

B. $600,000

C. $500,000

D. $400,000

Answer (C) is correct. *(CPA, adapted)*
REQUIRED: The amount credited to additional contributed capital upon incorporation.
DISCUSSION: When assets of a partnership are contributed to a corporation in exchange for par value common stock, the contributed capital account should be credited for the fair value of the net assets. The fair value of the net assets equals $600,000 ($320,000 + $420,000 – $140,000). Of this amount, $100,000 (10,000 shares × $10 par value) should be credited to the capital stock account, with the remaining $500,000 credited to additional contributed capital.
Answer (A) is incorrect. This amount equals the total fair value of the assets minus the $100,000 allocated to capital stock. Answer (B) is incorrect. This amount is the fair value of the net assets. Answer (D) is incorrect. This amount is the partnership capital at its carrying amount.

15.1.11. On February 1, Lopez Corporation issued 1,000 shares of its $10 par common and 2,000 shares of its $10 par convertible preferred stock for a lump sum of $40,000. At this date, Lopez's common stock was selling for $18 per share and the convertible preferred stock for $13.50 per share. The amount of proceeds allocated to Lopez's preferred stock should be

A. $22,000

B. $24,000

C. $27,000

D. $30,000

Answer (B) is correct. *(CPA, adapted)*
REQUIRED: The proceeds to be allocated to preferred stock in a lump-sum issuance.
DISCUSSION: Given that the 1,000 shares of common stock and 2,000 shares of preferred stock were issued for a lump sum of $40,000, the proceeds should be allocated based on the relative fair values of the securities issued. The fair value of the common stock is $18,000 (1,000 shares × $18). The fair value of the preferred stock is $27,000 (2,000 shares × $13.50). Because 60% [$27,000 ÷ ($27,000 + $18,000)] of the total fair value is attributable to the preferred stock, $24,000 ($40,000 × 60%) of the proceeds should be allocated to this stock.
Answer (A) is incorrect. This amount equals the lump sum received minus the fair value of the common stock. Answer (C) is incorrect. The fair value of the preferred stock is $27,000. Answer (D) is incorrect. The sum of the par values of the stock issued is $30,000.

15.1.12. When collectibility is reasonably assured, the excess of the subscription price over the stated value of no-par common stock subscribed should be recorded as

A. No-par common stock.

B. Additional paid-in capital when the subscription is recorded.

C. Additional paid-in capital when the subscription is collected.

D. Additional paid-in capital when the common stock is issued.

Answer (B) is correct. *(CPA, adapted)*
REQUIRED: The recording of the excess of the subscription price over the stated value of no-par common stock subscribed.
DISCUSSION: The accounting for subscriptions of no-par stock with a stated value is the same as for par value stock. When stock is subscribed, the corporation recognizes an obligation to issue stock and the subscriber undertakes the legal obligation to pay for the shares subscribed. If collectibility of the subscription price is reasonably assured on the date the subscription is received, the issuing corporation should recognize the cash collected and a subscription receivable for the remainder. In addition, the common stock subscribed account should be credited for the stated value of the shares subscribed, with the excess of the subscription price over the stated value recognized as additional paid-in capital.
Answer (A) is incorrect. The credit is to additional paid-in capital. Answer (C) is incorrect. Additional paid-in capital is credited when the subscription is recorded. Answer (D) is incorrect. The recording of additional paid-in capital is not dependent on when the stock is issued.

15.1.13. Galarraga Co. completed a number of capital transactions during the fiscal year ended September 30 as follows:

- An issue of 8% debentures was converted into common stock.
- An issue of $2.50 preferred stock was called and retired.
- A 10% common stock dividend was distributed on November 30.
- Warrants for 200,000 shares of common stock were exercised on September 20.

For the year-end financial statements to be sufficiently informative, Galarraga's most satisfactory method of presenting the effects of these events is

A. A formal retained earnings statement and general description in the notes to the financial statements.

B. A formal statement of changes in equity that discloses changes in the various equity accounts.

C. A detailed inclusion of each event or transaction in the statement of cash flows.

D. Comparative statements of income, financial position, and retained earnings for this year and last year.

Answer (B) is correct. *(CMA, adapted)*
REQUIRED: The most satisfactory method of presenting the effects of the listed capital transactions.
DISCUSSION: When both financial position and results of operations are presented, the entity must disclose changes in (1) the accounts included in equity (in addition to retained earnings) and (2) the number of shares of equity securities during at least the most recent annual fiscal period and any subsequent interim periods presented. The required disclosure may be made in the basic financial statements, in the notes, or in a formal statement of changes in equity (which is preferable).
Answer (A) is incorrect. A general description is inadequate. Answer (C) is incorrect. Events or transactions not resulting in cash flows (e.g., conversion of debt to equity or a stock dividend) are not included in the statement of cash flows. Answer (D) is incorrect. Presenting disclosures about changes in equity in a separate statement gives them greater prominence than if they were contained in the basic statements.

15.1.14. Of the 125,000 shares of common stock issued by Vey Corp., 25,000 shares were held as treasury stock at December 31, Year 3. During Year 4, transactions involving Vey's common stock were as follows:

January 1 through October 31	13,000 treasury shares were distributed to officers as part of a stock compensation plan.
November 1	A 3-for-1 stock split took effect.
December 1	Vey purchased 5,000 of its own shares to discourage an unfriendly takeover. These shares were not retired.

At December 31, Year 4, how many shares of Vey's common stock were issued and outstanding?

	Shares	
	Issued	Outstanding
A.	375,000	334,000
B.	375,000	324,000
C.	334,000	334,000
D.	324,000	324,000

Answer (A) is correct. *(CPA, adapted)*
REQUIRED: The number of shares issued and outstanding.
DISCUSSION: Given that 125,000 have been issued and that the stock has been split 3-for-1, the shares issued at year-end equal 375,000 (125,000 × 3). At the beginning of the year 100,000 shares were outstanding (125,000 issued − 25,000 treasury shares). After 13,000 treasury shares were distributed, 113,000 shares were outstanding, an amount that increased to 339,000 (113,000 × 3) after the stock split. The purchase on December 1 reduced the shares outstanding to 334,000 (339,000 − 5,000).
Answer (B) is incorrect. The 324,000 shares would be outstanding if the 5,000-share purchase had been made before the split. Answer (C) is incorrect. Shares issued exceed shares outstanding due to shares held in treasury stock. Answer (D) is incorrect. Shares issued exceed shares outstanding due to shares held in treasury stock.

15.1.15. On December 1, Year 4, shares of authorized common stock were issued on a subscription basis at a price in excess of par value. A total of 20% of the subscription price of each share was collected as a down payment on December 1, Year 4, with the remaining 80% of the subscription price of each share due in Year 5. Collectibility was reasonably assured. At December 31, Year 4, the equity section of the balance sheet should report additional paid-in capital for the excess of the subscription price over the par value of the shares of common stock subscribed and

A. Common stock issued for 20% of the par value of the shares of common stock subscribed.

B. Common stock issued for the par value of the shares of common stock subscribed.

C. Common stock subscribed for 80% of the par value of the shares of common stock subscribed.

D. Common stock subscribed for the par value of the shares of common stock subscribed.

Answer (D) is correct. *(CPA, adapted)*
REQUIRED: The proper recording of subscribed stock in the shareholders' equity section.
DISCUSSION: When stock is subscribed, the corporation recognizes an obligation to issue stock and the subscriber undertakes the legal obligation to pay for the shares subscribed. If collectibility of the subscription price is reasonably assured on the date the subscription is received, the issuing corporation should recognize the cash collected and a subscription receivable for the remainder. In addition, the common stock subscribed account should be credited for the par value of the shares subscribed, with the excess of the subscription price over the par value recognized as additional paid-in capital.
Answer (A) is incorrect. Common stock issued is credited when full payment is received. Answer (B) is incorrect. Common stock issued is credited when full payment is received. Answer (C) is incorrect. Common stock subscribed is credited for the par value of all shares subscribed.

15.1.16. During the prior year, Brad Co. issued 5,000 shares of $100 par-value convertible preferred stock for $110 per share. One share of preferred stock can be converted into three shares of Brad's $25 par-value common stock at the option of the preferred shareholder. On December 31 of the current year, when the market value of the common stock was $40 per share, all of the preferred stock was converted. What amount should Brad credit to common stock and to additional paid-in capital -- common stock as a result of the conversion?

	Common Stock	Additional Paid-In Capital
A.	$375,000	$175,000
B.	$375,000	$225,000
C.	$500,000	$50,000
D.	$600,000	$0

Answer (A) is correct. *(CPA, adapted)*
REQUIRED: The amounts credited to common stock and additional paid-in capital.
DISCUSSION: Brad recorded the issue of the convertible preferred stock with this entry:

Cash (5,000 shares × $110 market value)	$550,000	
Preferred stock (5,000 shares × $100 par value)		$500,000
Additional paid-in capital -- preferred (difference)		50,000

Brad recorded the conversion as follows:

Preferred stock (balance)	$500,000	
Additional paid-in capital -- preferred (balance)	50,000	
Common stock (5,000 shares × 3 × $25 par value)		$375,000
Additional paid-in capital -- common (difference)		175,000

Answer (B) is incorrect. The amount of $175,000 is credited to additional paid-in capital ($550,000 – $375,000). Answer (C) is incorrect. The amount of $500,000 is the par value of the preferred stock, not the common stock. Answer (D) is incorrect. The amount of $600,000 equals the fair value of the common stock at the date of conversion.

15.1.17. Sanders Company effects self-insurance against loss from fire by appropriating an amount of retained earnings each year equal to the amount that would otherwise be paid out as fire insurance premiums. According to current accounting literature, the procedure used by Sanders is

A. Prohibited for external reporting purposes.

B. Acceptable provided that fire losses are not charged against the appropriation.

C. Acceptable provided that fire losses are charged against the appropriation.

D. Acceptable if the amount is shown outside the equity section of the balance sheet.

Answer (B) is correct. *(Publisher, adapted)*
REQUIRED: The true statement about an appropriation of retained earnings to disclose self-insurance against fire loss.
DISCUSSION: An expense is not accrued prior to the occurrence of the event for which an entity self-insures. The fair value of the property diminishes only if the event actually occurs. But an appropriation of retained earnings is acceptable to disclose the self-insurance policy if, when a fire loss occurs, the entry appropriating retained earnings is reversed, and the loss is debited to income of the period of loss and not to retained earnings.
Answer (A) is incorrect. An appropriation of retained earnings for self-insurance is permissible. Answer (C) is incorrect. Fire losses may never be debited to the appropriation of retained earnings. Answer (D) is incorrect. The procedure is acceptable only if the appropriation is shown within the equity section of the balance sheet.

15.1.18. At December 31, Year 5, Chipper Corporation has the following account balances:

Common stock ($10 par, 50,000 shares issued)	$500,000
8% preferred stock ($50 par, 10,000 shares issued)	500,000
Paid-in capital in excess of par on common stock	640,000
Paid-in capital in excess of par on preferred stock	20,000
Retained earnings	600,000

The preferred stock is cumulative, nonparticipating, and has a call price of $55 per share. Chipper's journal entry to record the redemption of all preferred stock on January 2, Year 6, pursuant to the call provision is

A.
Preferred stock	$500,000	
Paid-in capital in excess of par: preferred	20,000	
Discount on preferred stock	30,000	
Cash		$550,000

B.
Preferred stock	$500,000	
Paid-in capital in excess of par: preferred	20,000	
Loss on redemption of preferred stock	30,000	
Cash		$550,000

C.
Preferred stock	$500,000	
Loss on redemption of preferred stock	50,000	
Retained earnings	300,000	
Cash		$550,000
Paid-in capital in excess of par: preferred		300,000

D.
Preferred stock	$500,000	
Paid-in capital in excess of par: preferred	20,000	
Retained earnings	30,000	
Cash		$550,000

15.1.19. In Year 1, Veras Corp. reported $3,500,000 of appropriated retained earnings for the construction of a new office building, which was completed in Year 2 at a total cost of $3,000,000. In Year 2, Veras appropriated $2,400,000 of retained earnings for the construction of a new plant. Also, $4,000,000 of cash was restricted for the retirement of bonds due in Year 3. In its Year 2 balance sheet, Veras should report what amount of appropriated retained earnings?

A. $2,400,000

B. $2,900,000

C. $5,900,000

D. $6,400,000

Answer (D) is correct. *(CIA, adapted)*
REQUIRED: The journal entry to record the redemption of preferred stock pursuant to the call provision.
DISCUSSION: The exercise of the call provision resulted in the redemption of the 10,000 shares of preferred stock issued and outstanding at the call price of $550,000 (10,000 shares × $55 call price per share). To eliminate the carrying amount of the preferred stock and recognize the cash paid in this transaction, the required journal entry is to debit preferred stock for $500,000, debit paid-in capital in excess of par: preferred for $20,000, and credit cash for $550,000. The difference of $30,000 ($550,000 cash – $520,000 carrying amount of the preferred stock) is charged to retained earnings. No loss is reported because GAAP do not permit the recognition of a gain or loss on transactions involving a company's own stock.
Answer (A) is incorrect. The $30,000 excess of cash paid over the carrying amount of the redeemed stock should not be debited to a discount on preferred stock account. Answer (B) is incorrect. The $30,000 excess of cash paid over the carrying amount of the redeemed stock should be debited to retained earnings. Answer (C) is incorrect. The $30,000 excess of cash paid over the carrying amount of the redeemed stock should be debited to retained earnings. Also, paid-in capital in excess of par: preferred, should be debited for $20,000.

Answer (A) is correct. *(CPA, adapted)*
REQUIRED: The amount of appropriated retained earnings reported.
DISCUSSION: Appropriating retained earnings is a formal way of marking a portion of retained earnings for other uses. A journal entry is used to reclassify retained earnings to appropriated retained earnings. When the appropriation is no longer necessary, the entry is reversed. The original appropriation of $3,500,000 in Year 1 would have been reversed for that amount in Year 2. The cash restriction is not included in appropriated retained earnings. If the amount is material, the restriction will require separate reporting of the cash item in the balance sheet, footnote disclosure, and reclassification as noncurrent. Thus, appropriated retained earnings in Year 2 should be reported at $2,400,000.
Answer (B) is incorrect. This amount includes the previous year's excess of appropriated retained earnings over the actual cost. Answer (C) is incorrect. This amount includes the cash restriction and subtracts the previous year's excess of appropriated retained earnings over the actual cost. Answer (D) is incorrect. This amount includes the $4,000,000 restriction on cash for bond retirement.

15.1.20. On February 1, Hyde Corp., a newly formed company, had the following stock issued and outstanding:

- Common stock, no par, $1 stated value, 10,000 shares originally issued for $15 per share
- Preferred stock, $10 par value, 3,000 shares originally issued for $25 per share

Hyde's February 1 statement of equity should report

	Common Stock	Preferred Stock	Additional Paid-In Capital
A.	$150,000	$30,000	$45,000
B.	$150,000	$75,000	$0
C.	$10,000	$75,000	$140,000
D.	$10,000	$30,000	$185,000

Answer (D) is correct. *(CPA, adapted)*
REQUIRED: The amounts of common stock, preferred stock, and additional paid-in capital to be reported in the statement of equity.
DISCUSSION: The common stock was issued for a total of $150,000 (10,000 shares × $15). Of this amount, $10,000 (10,000 shares × $1 stated value) should be allocated to the common stock, with the remaining $140,000 ($150,000 – $10,000) credited to additional paid-in capital. The preferred stock was issued for $75,000 (3,000 shares × $25), of which $30,000 (3,000 shares × $10 par value) should be allocated to the preferred stock and $45,000 ($75,000 – $30,000) should be allocated to additional paid-in capital. In the statement of equity, Hyde therefore should report $10,000 in the common stock account, $30,000 in the preferred stock account, and $185,000 ($140,000 + $45,000) as additional paid-in capital.

15.2 Cash and Property Dividends

15.2.1. On January 15, Year 5, Rico Co. declared its annual cash dividend on common stock for the year ended January 31, Year 5. The dividend was paid on February 9, Year 5, to shareholders of record as of January 28, Year 5. On what date should Rico decrease retained earnings by the amount of the dividend?

A. January 15, Year 5.

B. January 31, Year 5.

C. January 28, Year 5.

D. February 9, Year 5.

Answer (A) is correct. *(CPA, adapted)*
REQUIRED: The date to decrease retained earnings by the amount of the dividend.
DISCUSSION: On the date of declaration, a cash dividend becomes a legal liability of the corporation (unlike stock dividends, cash dividends cannot be rescinded). Thus, on January 15, a portion of retained earnings was reclassified as dividends payable.
Answer (B) is incorrect. The liability and the reduction in retained earnings should be recognized on the declaration date. Answer (C) is incorrect. The liability and the reduction in retained earnings should be recognized on the declaration date. Answer (D) is incorrect. The liability and the reduction in retained earnings should be recognized on the declaration date.

15.2.2. An entity declared a cash dividend on its common stock on December 15, Year 1, payable on January 12, Year 2. How would this dividend affect equity on the following dates?

	December 15, Year 1	December 31, Year 1	January 12, Year 2
A.	Decrease	No effect	Decrease
B.	Decrease	No effect	No effect
C.	No effect	Decrease	No effect
D.	No effect	No effect	Decrease

Answer (B) is correct. *(Publisher, adapted)*
REQUIRED: The effect on equity of a cash dividend.
DISCUSSION: When cash dividends are declared, a liability to the shareholders is created because the dividends must be paid once they are declared. At the declaration date, retained earnings must be debited, resulting in a decrease in retained earnings. The effect is to decrease total equity (assets – liabilities) because liabilities are increased with no corresponding increase in assets. At the balance sheet date, no entry is made, and there is no effect on equity. When the cash dividends are subsequently paid, dividends payable is debited and cash is credited. Thus, at the payment date, equity is also not affected.
Answer (A) is incorrect. Payment has no effect on equity. Answer (C) is incorrect. Declaration decreases equity but year-end has no effect. Answer (D) is incorrect. Declaration decreases equity but payment has no effect.

15.2.3. East Corp., a company with a fiscal year-end on October 31, had sufficient retained earnings as a basis for dividends but was temporarily short of cash. East declared a dividend of $100,000 on February 1, Year 3, and issued promissory notes to its shareholders in lieu of cash. The notes, which were dated February 1, Year 3, had a maturity date of January 31, Year 4, and a 10% interest rate. How should East account for the scrip dividend and related interest?

A. Debit retained earnings for $110,000 on February 1, Year 3.

B. Debit retained earnings for $110,000 on January 31, Year 4.

C. Debit retained earnings for $100,000 on February 1, Year 3, and debit interest expense for $10,000 on January 31, Year 4.

D. Debit retained earnings for $100,000 on February 1, Year 3, and debit interest expense for $7,500 on October 31, Year 3.

Answer (D) is correct. *(CPA, adapted)*
REQUIRED: The accounting for a scrip dividend and its related interest.
DISCUSSION: When a scrip dividend is declared, retained earnings should be debited and scrip dividends (or notes) payable should be credited for the amount of the dividend ($100,000) excluding interest. Interest accrued on the scrip dividend is recorded as a debit to interest expense up to the balance sheet date with a corresponding credit for interest payable. Thus, interest expense will be debited and interest payable credited for $7,500 [$100,000 × 10% × (9 months ÷ 12 months)] on 10/31/Year 3.
Answer (A) is incorrect. Interest expense is recognized on the balance sheet date and on the date of payment, not on the date of declaration. Answer (B) is incorrect. At year-end, $7,500 of the $10,000 interest expense should be recognized, and retained earnings should be debited on the date of declaration. Answer (C) is incorrect. At year-end, $7,500 of the $10,000 interest expense should be recognized.

15.2.4. On June 1, Ligtenberg Company's board of directors declared a cash dividend of $1.00 per share on the 50,000 shares of common stock outstanding. The company also has 5,000 shares of treasury stock. Shareholders of record on June 15 are eligible for the dividend, which is to be paid on July 1. On June 1, the company should

A. Make no accounting entry.

B. Debit retained earnings for $50,000.

C. Debit retained earnings for $55,000.

D. Debit retained earnings for $50,000 and paid-in capital for $5,000.

Answer (B) is correct. *(CMA, adapted)*
REQUIRED: The proper journal entry on the declaration date of a dividend.
DISCUSSION: Dividends are recorded on their declaration date by a debit to retained earnings and a credit to dividends payable. The dividend is the amount payable to all shares outstanding. Treasury stock is not eligible for dividends because it is not outstanding. Thus, the June 1 entry is to debit retained earnings and credit dividends payable for $50,000 (50,000 × $1).
Answer (A) is incorrect. A liability should be recorded. Answer (C) is incorrect. The treasury stock is not eligible for a dividend. Answer (D) is incorrect. Paid-in capital is not affected by the dividend declaration.

15.2.5. Arp Corp.'s outstanding capital stock at December 15, Year 4, consisted of the following:

- 30,000 shares of 5% cumulative preferred stock, par value $10 per share, fully participating as to dividends. No dividends were in arrears.

- 200,000 shares of common stock, par value $1 per share

On December 15, Year 4, Arp declared dividends of $100,000. What was the amount of dividends payable to Arp's common shareholders?

A. $10,000

B. $34,000

C. $40,000

D. $47,500

Answer (C) is correct. *(CPA, adapted)*
REQUIRED: The dividends to common shareholders.
DISCUSSION: The stated rate of dividends must be paid to preferred shareholders before any amount is paid to common shareholders. Given no dividends in arrears, this amount is $15,000 (30,000 shares × $10 par × 5%). The preferred stock will also participate equally in the cash dividend after a 5% return is paid on the common. The basic return to common shareholders is $10,000 (200,000 shares × $1 par × 5%). The remaining $75,000 ($100,000 – $15,000 – $10,000) will be shared in proportion to the par values of the shares outstanding.
The aggregate par value of the preferred is $300,000 (30,000 shares × $10 par). The aggregate par value of the common is $200,000 (200,000 shares × $1 par). The distribution will therefore be in the ratio of 3:2, and $45,000 ($75,000 × 60%) is the participating share of the preferred shareholders. The balance of $30,000 ($75,000 – $45,000) will be paid to the common shareholders. The total dividends on the common stock is $40,000 ($10,000 + $30,000).
Answer (A) is incorrect. The amount of $10,000 is the basic return to common shareholders. Answer (B) is incorrect. The amount of $34,000 results from assuming that no basic return is paid to the common shareholders. Answer (D) is incorrect. The amount of $47,500 results from dividing in half the remaining amount after the stated rate of dividends have been paid to the preferred shareholders.

15.2.6. At December 31, Year 3 and Year 4, Apex Co. had 3,000 shares of $100 par, 5% cumulative preferred stock outstanding. No dividends were in arrears as of December 31, Year 2. Apex did not declare a dividend during Year 3. During Year 4, Apex paid a cash dividend of $10,000 on its preferred stock. Apex should report dividends in arrears in its Year 4 financial statements as a(n)

A. Accrued liability of $15,000.

B. Disclosure of $15,000.

C. Accrued liability of $20,000.

D. Disclosure of $20,000.

Answer (D) is correct. *(CPA, adapted)*
REQUIRED: The accounting for preferred dividends in arrears.
DISCUSSION: Dividends in arrears on preferred stock are not obligations of the company and are not recognized in the financial statements. However, the aggregate and per-share amounts of arrearages in cumulative preferred dividends should be disclosed on the face of the balance sheet or in the notes. The aggregate amount in arrears is $20,000 [(3,000 shares × $100 par × 5% × 2 years) – $10,000 paid in Year 4].
Answer (A) is incorrect. Dividends in arrears do not meet recognition criteria. Answer (B) is incorrect. The amount of $15,000 is the arrearage for 1 year. Answer (C) is incorrect. Dividends in arrears should be disclosed on the face of the balance sheet or in the notes, not accrued.

15.2.7. Instead of the usual cash dividend, Evie Corp. declared and distributed a property dividend from its overstocked merchandise. The excess of the merchandise's carrying amount over its fair value should be

A. Ignored.

B. Reported as a separately disclosed reduction of retained earnings.

C. Reported as an item of other comprehensive income, net of income taxes.

D. Reported as a reduction in operating income.

Answer (D) is correct. *(CPA, adapted)*
REQUIRED: The accounting for the excess of the carrying amount of a property dividend over its fair value.
DISCUSSION: When a corporation declares a dividend consisting of tangible property, the property must first be remeasured to fair value. Thus, a loss should be recognized on the disposition of the asset. This loss on merchandise is an operating item.
Answer (A) is incorrect. Accounting for the property dividend at fair value gives rise to a loss that should be reported in the income statement. Answer (B) is incorrect. Accounting for the property dividend at fair value gives rise to a loss that should be reported in the income statement. Answer (C) is incorrect. The loss on remeasurement of the property to fair value is recognized in the income statement.

15.2.8. A property dividend should be recorded in retained earnings at the property's

A. Fair value at date of declaration.

B. Fair value at date of issuance (payment).

C. Carrying amount at date of declaration.

D. Carrying amount at date of issuance.

Answer (A) is correct. *(CPA, adapted)*
REQUIRED: The method of accounting for a property dividend.
DISCUSSION: When a property dividend is declared, the property to be distributed should be restated at fair value. Any gain or loss should be recognized. The declared dividend is then recorded as a debit to retained earnings and a credit to property dividends payable.
Answer (B) is incorrect. The fair value is determined as of the declaration date. Answer (C) is incorrect. Fair value at the date of declaration is used. Answer (D) is incorrect. Fair value at the date of declaration is the preferred alternative.

15.2.9. On June 27, Year 1, Marquis Co. distributed to its common shareholders 100,000 outstanding common shares of its investment in Chen Co., an unrelated party. The carrying amount on the books of Chen's $1 par common stock was $2 per share. Immediately after the distribution, the market price of Chen's stock was $2.50 per share. In its income statement for the year ended June 30, Year 1, what amount should Marquis report as gain before income taxes on disposal of the stock?

A. $250,000

B. $200,000

C. $50,000

D. $0

Answer (C) is correct. *(CPA, adapted)*
REQUIRED: The amount to be reported as gain before income taxes on disposal of stock.
DISCUSSION: When a property dividend is declared, the property to be distributed should be restated from carrying amount to fair value, with the resultant gain or loss recognized. Thus, Marquis should report a gain of $50,000 [100,000 shares × ($2.50 – $2.00)].
Answer (A) is incorrect. The fair value of the property dividend is $250,000. Answer (B) is incorrect. The book value of the property dividend is $200,000. Answer (D) is incorrect. A $50,000 gain should be recognized.

15.2.10. Orr Corporation owned 1,000 shares of Vee Corporation. These shares were purchased for $9,000. On September 15, Orr declared a property dividend of one share of Vee for every 10 shares of Orr held by a shareholder. On that date, when the market price of Vee was $14 per share, 9,000 shares of Orr were outstanding. This transaction did not constitute a spin-off or other form of reorganization or liquidation and was not part of a plan that was in substance a rescission of a prior business combination. What gain and net reduction in retained earnings would result from this property dividend?

	Gain	Net Reduction in Retained Earnings
A.	$0	$8,100
B.	$0	$12,600
C.	$4,500	$3,600
D.	$4,500	$8,100

Answer (D) is correct. *(CPA, adapted)*
REQUIRED: The gain and net reduction in retained earnings from a property dividend.
DISCUSSION: The Vee shares had a carrying amount of $9 per share ($9,000 ÷ 1,000 shares). Because 900 shares were distributed by Orr as a property dividend (9,000 shares ÷ 10), the shares used as a property dividend had a total carrying amount of $8,100. The fair value of the 900 shares on the date of declaration was $12,600 (900 shares × $14 per share). The transaction is not effectively a reorganization, liquidation, or rescission of a business combination. Thus, a nonreciprocal transfer of a nonmonetary asset to a shareholder must be recorded at the fair value of the asset transferred, and a gain or loss must be recognized on the disposition. The gain is $4,500 ($12,600 fair value – $8,100 carrying amount). The net reduction in retained earnings is $8,100 ($12,600 dividend – $4,500 gain). The journal entries are

| Retained earnings | $12,600 | |
| Property dividend payable | | $12,600 |

Property dividend payable	$12,600	
Investment in Vee		$ 8,100
Gain on Vee disposition		4,500

Answer (A) is incorrect. A gain must be recognized when the fair value of a property dividend is higher than its carrying amount. Answer (B) is incorrect. A gain must be recognized. It affects part of the reduction of retained earnings. Answer (C) is incorrect. The gain is $3,600 if the full amount of the $9,000 of Vee Corporation stock is subtracted from the $12,600 dividend.

15.3 Stock Dividends and Stock Splits

15.3.1. The following data are extracted from the equity section of the balance sheet of Ebbs Corporation:

	12/31/Yr 6	12/31/Yr 7
Common stock ($2 par value)	$100,000	$102,000
Paid-in capital in excess of par	50,000	58,000
Retained earnings	100,000	104,600

During Year 7, the corporation declared and paid cash dividends of $15,000 and also declared and issued a stock dividend. There were no other changes in stock issued and outstanding during Year 7. Net income for Year 7 was

A. $4,600

B. $19,600

C. $21,600

D. $29,600

Answer (D) is correct. *(CIA, adapted)*
REQUIRED: The net income for Year 7 after payment of cash and stock dividends.
DISCUSSION: The cash dividends reduced retained earnings by $15,000. The stock dividend reduced retained earnings by $10,000, as determined from the changes in the contributed capital accounts [($102,000 + $58,000) – ($100,000 + $50,000)]. Hence, as shown below, net income was $29,600.

	Retained earnings		
		$100,000	Beginning
Cash dividend	$15,000		
Stock dividend	10,000		
		29,600	Net income
		$104,600	Ending

Answer (A) is incorrect. The increase in retained earnings for the year is $4,600. Answer (B) is incorrect. The amount of $19,600 results from not reducing retained earnings by the stock dividend. Answer (C) is incorrect. The amount of $21,600 results from reducing retained earnings for a $2,000 stock dividend.

15.3.2. Ray Corp. declared a 5% stock dividend on its 10,000 issued and outstanding shares of $2 par value common stock, which had a fair value of $5 per share before the stock dividend was declared. This stock dividend was distributed 60 days after the declaration date. By what amount did Ray's current liabilities increase as a result of the stock dividend declaration?

A. $0

B. $500

C. $1,000

D. $2,500

Answer (A) is correct. *(CPA, adapted)*
REQUIRED: The increase in current liabilities as a result of the stock dividend declaration.
DISCUSSION: Declaration of a stock dividend is not accounted for as a liability but as a reclassification of equity. For a stock dividend that is smaller than 20 to 25% of the shares outstanding, the entry is to debit retained earnings for the fair value of the stock (10,000 shares × $5 fair value × 5% = $2,500), credit stock dividend distributable at par (10,000 shares × $2 × 5% = $1,000), and credit additional paid-in capital for the excess of fair over par value ($2,500 – $1,000 = $1,500).
Answer (B) is incorrect. No liability is recognized. Answer (C) is incorrect. No liability is recognized. Answer (D) is incorrect. No liability is recognized.

15.3.3. The following information was abstracted from the accounts of the Moore Corp. at year end:

Total income since incorporation	$840,000
Total cash dividends paid	260,000
Proceeds from sale of donated Travis Co. stock	90,000
Total value of stock dividends distributed	60,000
Excess of proceeds over cost of treasury stock sold	140,000

What should be the current balance of retained earnings?

A. $520,000

B. $580,000

C. $610,000

D. $670,000

Answer (A) is correct. *(CPA, adapted)*
REQUIRED: The current balance of retained earnings.
DISCUSSION: To compute the current balance, one must know which transactions affected retained earnings. Total income since incorporation ($840,000) increased retained earnings, whereas both the cash dividends and the stock dividends ($260,000 + $60,000) decreased it. Proceeds from the sale of the donated stock (given that it was not Moore Corp. stock) already would have been included in income to the extent of gain or loss. The excess of proceeds over the cost of treasury stock also does not affect retained earnings because the credit is to additional paid-in capital from treasury stock transactions. The current balance of retained earnings is therefore equal to $520,000 ($840,000 – $260,000 – $60,000).
Answer (B) is incorrect. This amount results from not reducing retained earnings by the value of stock dividends distributed. Answer (C) is incorrect. This amount results from adding the proceeds from the sale of donated stock. Answer (D) is incorrect. This amount results from including the proceeds from the sale of donated stock and not subtracting the total value of the stock dividends distributed.

15.3.4. A corporation issuing stock should charge retained earnings for the fair value of the shares issued in a(n)

A. Employee stock bonus.

B. Purchase of the net assets of another entity.

C. 10% stock dividend.

D. 2-for-1 stock split.

Answer (C) is correct. *(CPA, adapted)*
REQUIRED: The basis for debiting retained earnings when stock is issued.
DISCUSSION: A stock dividend in which the number of shares issued is fewer than 20 to 25% of those outstanding should be accounted for by debiting retained earnings for the fair value of the stock and crediting a capital stock account for the par value. Any excess of fair value over the par value is credited to an additional paid-in capital account. Hence, retained earnings decreases, but total equity does not change.
Answer (A) is incorrect. The debit for an employee stock bonus is to compensation expense. Answer (B) is incorrect. In a business combination, the acquirer debits the assets acquired and expenses incurred and credits the liabilities assumed and assets surrendered. It also records the shares issued (e.g., credit common stock and additional paid-in capital). Answer (D) is incorrect. A stock split has no effect on the accounts. It is recognized solely by a decrease in the par value of the common shares.

15.3.5. Effective April 27, the shareholders of Dorr Corp. approved a 2-for-1 split of its common stock and an increase in authorized common shares from 100,000 shares (par value $20 per share) to 200,000 shares (par value $10 per share). Dorr's equity accounts immediately before issuance of the stock-split shares were as follows:

Common stock, par value $20; 100,000 shares authorized; 50,000 shares outstanding	$1,000,000
Additional paid-in capital ($3 per share on issuance of common stock)	150,000
Retained earnings	1,350,000

The stock-split shares were issued on June 30. In Dorr's June 30 statement of equity, the balances of additional paid-in capital and retained earnings are

	Additional Paid-In Capital	Retained Earnings
A.	$0	$500,000
B.	$150,000	$350,000
C.	$150,000	$1,350,000
D.	$1,150,000	$350,000

Answer (C) is correct. *(CPA, adapted)*
REQUIRED: The effect of a 2-for-1 stock split on additional paid-in capital and retained earnings.
DISCUSSION: A 2-for-1 stock split is a nonreciprocal transfer of an entity's own shares to its common shareholders for the purpose of reducing the unit market price of the shares. The goal is to increase their marketability and broaden their distribution. The transaction described will increase the number of shares outstanding to 100,000 (50,000 shares × 2). The par value will be reduced to $10 ($20 ÷ 2), but the capital accounts will be unaffected. To effect a stock split, no formal entry is necessary because no capitalization of retained earnings occurs. Thus, additional paid-in capital ($150,000) and retained earnings ($1,350,000) will not change.
Answer (A) is incorrect. Additional paid-in capital and retained earnings will not change. Answer (B) is incorrect. Retained earnings will not change. Answer (D) is incorrect. Additional paid-in capital and retained earnings will not change.

15.3.6. On December 31, Year 4, the equity section of Spitz Co. was as follows:

Common stock, par value $10; authorized 30,000 shares; issued and outstanding 9,000 shares	$ 90,000
Additional paid-in capital	116,000
Retained earnings	146,000
Total equity	$352,000

On March 31, Year 5, Spitz declared a 10% stock dividend. Accordingly, 900 shares were issued when the fair value was $16 per share. For the 3 months ended March 31, Year 5, Spitz sustained a net loss of $32,000. The balance of Spitz's retained earnings as of March 31, Year 5, should be

- A. $99,600
- B. $105,000
- C. $108,600
- D. $114,000

Answer (A) is correct. *(CPA, adapted)*
REQUIRED: The retained earnings balance after a stock dividend and incurrence of a net loss.
DISCUSSION: When the number of shares issued is fewer than 20% to 25% of the outstanding stock, the issuance generally is considered a stock dividend. Retained earnings should be debited for the fair value of the stock distributed as a stock dividend. Thus, $14,400 (900 Spitz shares × $16 fair value) should be debited to retained earnings. Retained earnings should also be decreased by the net loss of $32,000. Thus, the balance of Spitz's retained earnings as of March 31 is $99,600 ($146,000 beginning balance – $14,400 stock dividend – $32,000 net loss).
Answer (B) is incorrect. The amount of $105,000 results from reducing retained earnings by the par value of the stock dividend. Answer (C) is incorrect. The amount of $108,600 results from reducing retained earnings by the difference between the fair value and the par value. Answer (D) is incorrect. The amount of $114,000 results from not reducing retained earnings for the stock dividend.

15.3.7. A company whose stock is trading at $10 per share has 1,000 shares of $1 par common stock outstanding when the board of directors declares a 30% common stock dividend. Which of the following adjustments should be made when recording the stock dividend?

- A. Treasury stock is debited for $300.
- B. Additional paid-in capital is credited for $2,700.
- C. Retained earnings is debited for $300.
- D. Common stock is debited for $3,000.

Answer (C) is correct. *(CPA, adapted)*
REQUIRED: The recording of a stock dividend.
DISCUSSION: The board of directors declared a 30% common stock dividend. As this issuance is more than 25% of the previously outstanding common shares, it should be accounted for as a stock split in the form of a dividend. Generally (depending on the state of incorporation), the company will capitalize retained earnings in an amount based on the par value. Thus, the journal entry at the date of declaration will be:

Retained earnings (1,000 shares × 30%)	$300	
Common stock dividend distributable		$300

Answer (A) is incorrect. In a stock dividend, or stock split in the form of a dividend, a portion of retained earnings is capitalized as part of paid-in capital. In this case, the treasury stock account is unaffected. Answer (B) is incorrect. This issuance is not accounted for as a regular stock dividend. Because the issuance is more than 25% of the previously outstanding common shares, it should be accounted for as a stock split in the form of a dividend. Answer (D) is incorrect. In a stock dividend, or stock split in the form of a dividend, the common stock account is increased (credited), not decreased (debited).

15.4 Treasury Stock Transactions

15.4.1. An amount representing the difference between the carrying amount and the proceeds from the purchase and resale of treasury stock may be reflected only in

- A. Paid-in capital accounts.
- B. Income, paid-in capital, and retained earnings accounts.
- C. Retained earnings and paid-in capital accounts.
- D. Income and retained earnings accounts.

Answer (C) is correct. *(Publisher, adapted)*
REQUIRED: The accounts affected by treasury stock transactions.
DISCUSSION: Adjustments, debits, or credits resulting from transactions in the entity's own stock are always excluded from earnings or the results of operations. Hence, an excess of the proceeds over the carrying amount of treasury stock must be credited to additional paid-in capital. An excess of the carrying amount over the proceeds of treasury stock may be debited to either retained earnings or additional paid-in capital, depending on the circumstances.
Answer (A) is incorrect. Retained earnings may sometimes be charged as a result of treasury stock transactions. Answer (B) is incorrect. Transactions in treasury stock do not affect income. Answer (D) is incorrect. Transactions in treasury stock may only be reflected in paid-in capital and retained earnings.

15.4.2. The acquisition of treasury stock will cause the number of shares outstanding to decrease if the treasury stock is accounted for by the

	Cost Method	Par-Value Method
A.	Yes	No
B.	No	No
C.	Yes	Yes
D.	No	Yes

Answer (C) is correct. *(CPA, adapted)*
REQUIRED: The effect of the acquisition of treasury stock on the number of shares outstanding.
DISCUSSION: When treasury stock is acquired, the effect will be to decrease the number of shares of common stock outstanding whether the treasury stock is accounted for by the cost method or the par-value method.
Answer (A) is incorrect. Outstanding shares also decrease under the cost method. Answer (B) is incorrect. Outstanding shares decrease under the both methods. Answer (D) is incorrect. Outstanding shares also decrease under the par-value method.

15.4.3. Treasury stock transactions may result in

A. Increases in the balance of retained earnings.

B. Increases or decreases in the amount of net income.

C. Decreases in the balance of retained earnings.

D. Increases or decreases in the amount of shares authorized to be issued.

Answer (C) is correct. *(J.N. McKenna)*
REQUIRED: The effect of treasury stock transactions.
DISCUSSION: Under the par-value method, when treasury shares are purchased for a price greater than the par value, retained earnings is debited for the excess of the purchase price over the par value if there is no existing paid-in capital from past treasury stock transactions or if the existing credit balance is insufficient to absorb the excess. Under the cost method, if the subsequent resale price of the treasury shares is less than the original acquisition price, it may be necessary to charge retained earnings for a portion or all of the excess of the original purchase price over the sales price.
Answer (A) is incorrect. Equity credits from treasury stock transactions would affect paid-in capital accounts, not retained earnings. Answer (B) is incorrect. Treasury stock transactions have no effect on net income. Answer (D) is incorrect. Treasury stock transactions affect only the number of outstanding shares, not the authorized number.

15.4.4. In Year 2, Fogg, Inc., issued $10 par value common stock for $25 per share. No other common stock transactions occurred until March 31, Year 4, when Fogg acquired some of the issued shares for $20 per share and retired them. Which of the following statements accurately states an effect of this acquisition and retirement?

A. Year 4 net income is decreased.

B. Year 4 net income is increased.

C. Additional paid-in capital is decreased.

D. Retained earnings is increased.

Answer (C) is correct. *(CPA, adapted)*
REQUIRED: The effect of the acquisition and retirement of a company's stock for less than the issue price.
DISCUSSION: When shares of common stock are reacquired and retired, contributed capital should be debited for the amount that was credited upon the issuance of the securities. In addition, because the acquisition of a company's own shares is an equity transaction, no gain or loss should be reflected in the determination of income. The entry is to debit common stock at par (number of shares × $10) and additional paid-in capital [number of shares × ($25 – $10)], and to credit additional paid-in capital from retirement of common stock [number of shares × ($25 – $20)] and cash (number of shares × $20). The net effect is to decrease total additional paid-in capital.
Answer (A) is incorrect. Net income is not affected. Answer (B) is incorrect. Net income is not affected. Answer (D) is incorrect. Retained earnings is only affected when a company retires its stock at a higher price than the original issue price.

15.4.5. Knight Corp. holds 20,000 shares of its $10 par value common stock as treasury stock reacquired in Year 1 for $240,000. On December 12, Year 3, Knight reissued all 20,000 shares for $380,000. Under the cost method of accounting for treasury stock, the reissuance resulted in a credit to

A. Common stock of $200,000.

B. Retained earnings of $140,000.

C. Gain on sale of investments of $140,000.

D. Additional paid-in capital of $140,000.

Answer (D) is correct. *(CPA, adapted)*
REQUIRED: The effect of the reissuance of treasury stock accounted for under the cost method.
DISCUSSION: When treasury stock accounted for under the cost method is acquired, the treasury stock account is debited for the amount of the purchase price. If it is subsequently reissued for a price greater than its carrying amount, the excess is credited to additional paid-in capital. For this transaction, the excess is $140,000 ($380,000 – $240,000).
Answer (A) is incorrect. The common stock account is unaffected by purchases and subsequent resales of treasury stock accounted for by the cost method. Answer (B) is incorrect. Gains on treasury stock transactions may not be credited to retained earnings. Answer (C) is incorrect. Gains on sale of investments may not be credited to income.

15.4.6. Cross Corp. had 2,000 outstanding shares of 11% preferred stock, $50 par. These shares were not mandatorily redeemable. On August 8, Cross redeemed and retired 25% of these shares for $22,500. On that date, Cross's additional paid-in capital from preferred stock totaled $30,000. To record this transaction, Cross should debit (credit) its capital accounts as follows:

	Preferred Stock	Additional Paid-In Capital	Retained Earnings
A.	$25,000	$7,500	$(10,000)
B.	$25,000	--	$(2,500)
C.	$25,000	$(2,500)	--
D.	$22,500	--	--

Answer (C) is correct. *(CPA, adapted)*

REQUIRED: The accounting for redemption and retirement of preferred stock.

DISCUSSION: Under the cost method, the entry to record a treasury stock purchase is to debit treasury stock at cost ($22,500) and credit cash. The entry to retire this stock is to debit preferred stock at par [(2,000 shares × 25%) × $50 = $25,000], debit additional paid-in capital from the original issuance ($30,000 × 25% = $7,500), credit treasury stock at cost ($22,500), and credit additional paid-in capital from stock retirement ($10,000). Thus, the net effect on additional paid-in capital is a $2,500 credit ($10,000 credit – $7,500 debit). No entry to retained earnings is necessary.

Answer (A) is incorrect. If the reacquisition price is less than the issuance price, a credit is made to additional paid-in capital, not retained earnings. Answer (B) is incorrect. Additional paid-in capital is debited to the extent it exists from the original issuance ($30,000 × 25% = $7,500), and a credit is made to additional paid-in capital for the stock retirement ($10,000). Retained earnings is not affected by this transaction. Answer (D) is incorrect. Preferred stock must be debited for the par value of the retired shares.

15.4.7. On December 31, Pack Corp.'s board of directors canceled 50,000 shares of $2.50 par value common stock held in treasury at an average cost of $13 per share. Before recording the cancelation of the treasury stock, Pack had the following balances in its equity accounts:

Common stock	$540,000
Additional paid-in capital	750,000
Retained earnings	900,000
Treasury stock, at cost	650,000

In its balance sheet at December 31, Pack should report common stock outstanding of

- A. $0
- B. $250,000
- C. $415,000
- D. $540,000

Answer (C) is correct. *(CPA, adapted)*

REQUIRED: The common stock outstanding after cancellation of the treasury stock.

DISCUSSION: The treasury shares had an aggregate par value of $125,000 (50,000 shares × $2.50). Consequently, the common stock outstanding after their retirement is $415,000 ($540,000 par value of issued common stock – $125,000).

Answer (A) is incorrect. The 166,000 shares ($415,000 ÷ $2.50) of common stock remain outstanding. Answer (B) is incorrect. The amount of $250,000 is the difference between retained earnings and the cost of the treasury stock. Answer (D) is incorrect. The amount of $540,000 is the par value of the issued shares prior to cancelation of the treasury stock.

15.4.8. In Year 3, Seda Corp. acquired 6,000 shares of its own $1 par value common stock at $18 per share. In Year 4, Seda reissued 3,000 of these shares at $25 per share. Seda uses the cost method to account for its treasury stock transactions. What accounts and amounts should Seda credit in Year 4 to record the reissuance of the 3,000 shares?

	Treasury Stock	Additional Paid-In Capital	Retained Earnings	Common Stock
A.	$54,000	--	$21,000	--
B.	$54,000	$21,000	--	--
C.	--	$72,000	--	$3,000
D.	--	$51,000	$21,000	$3,000

Answer (B) is correct. *(CPA, adapted)*

REQUIRED: The accounts and amounts to be credited when treasury stock is reissued.

DISCUSSION: Under the cost method, the treasury stock account should be debited for the purchase price. When this stock is subsequently reissued for an amount greater than its acquisition cost, the excess should be credited to additional paid-in capital. The 3,000 shares were purchased as treasury stock for $54,000 (3,000 shares × $18 per share). They were reissued for $75,000 (3,000 shares × $25 per share). Under the cost method, the carrying amount of the 3,000 shares was $54,000. When these shares are reissued, the treasury stock account should be credited for $54,000, with the remaining $21,000 ($75,000 – $54,000) credited to additional paid-in capital.

Answer (A) is incorrect. Additional paid-in capital, not retained earnings, should be credited. Answer (C) is incorrect. Additional paid-in capital should be credited for $21,000 and treasury stock for $54,000. Common stock is unaffected. Answer (D) is incorrect. Additional paid in capital should be credited for $21,000, and retained earnings and common stock are unaffected.

15.4.9. At its date of incorporation, Glean, Inc., issued 100,000 shares of its $10 par common stock at $11 per share. During the current year, Glean acquired 30,000 shares of its common stock at a price of $16 per share and accounted for them by the cost method. Subsequently, these shares were reissued at a price of $12 per share. Glean had made no other issuances or acquisitions of its own common stock. What effect does the reissuance of the stock have on the following accounts?

	Retained Earnings	Additional Paid-In Capital
A.	Decrease	Decrease
B.	No effect	Decrease
C.	Decrease	No effect
D.	No effect	No effect

Answer (C) is correct. *(CPA, adapted)*
REQUIRED: The effect of a reissuance of treasury stock on retained earnings and additional paid-in capital.
DISCUSSION: When shares are issued for an amount greater than their par value, the difference is credited to additional paid-in capital. Under the cost method, the treasury stock account should be debited for the price of reacquired shares. If the treasury stock is reissued for an amount less than its acquisition cost, the difference between the acquisition cost and the reissuance price should be debited to additional paid-in capital from treasury stock transactions to the extent it has a credit balance from previous transactions. However, Glean has not previously reissued treasury stock. Thus, it has a zero balance in this account. Thus, Glean must debit cash for $360,000 (30,000 shares × $12 reissuance price per share), debit retained earnings for $120,000 [30,000 shares × ($16 cost per share – $12)], and credit treasury stock for $480,000 (30,000 shares × $16 cost per share).

15.4.10. Lem Co., which accounts for treasury stock under the par-value method, acquired 100 shares of its $6 par value common stock for $10 per share. The shares had originally been issued by Lem for $7 per share. By what amount would Lem's additional paid-in capital from common stock decrease as a result of the acquisition?

A. $0

B. $100

C. $300

D. $400

Answer (B) is correct. *(CPA, adapted)*
REQUIRED: The decrease in additional paid-in capital from an acquisition of treasury stock accounted for under the par-value method.
DISCUSSION: The entry for issuance of the stock was

Cash	$700	
Common stock ($6 per share)		$600
Additional paid-in capital		100

The par-value method treats a treasury stock purchase as a constructive retirement. Assuming no balance in paid-in capital from treasury stock transactions, the entry for the treasury stock purchase using the par-value method is

Treasury stock	$600	
Additional paid-in capital	100	
Retained earnings	300	
Cash		$1,000

Answer (A) is incorrect. Under the par-value method, the acquisition of treasury stock is accounted for by reducing additional paid-in capital by the amount recorded when the shares were originally issued. Answer (C) is incorrect. The amount of $300 is the debit to retained earnings. Answer (D) is incorrect. The amount of $400 is the sum of the debit to additional paid-in capital and the debit to retained earnings.

15.4.11. Treasury stock was acquired for cash at a price in excess of its original issue price. The treasury stock was subsequently reissued for cash at a price in excess of its acquisition price. Assuming that the par value method of accounting for treasury stock transactions is used, what is the effect on total equity of each of the following events?

	Acquisition of Treasury Stock	Reissuance of Treasury Stock
A.	Decrease	No effect
B.	Decrease	Increase
C.	Increase	Decrease
D.	No effect	No effect

Answer (B) is correct. *(CPA, adapted)*
REQUIRED: The effect on total equity of each event.
DISCUSSION: The par value method treats the acquisition of treasury stock as a constructive retirement and its resale as a new issuance of stock. Thus, the acquisition of treasury stock will be reflected as a decrease in total equity. The reissuance will be accounted for as an increase in total equity.

15.4.12. Posy Corp. acquired treasury shares at an amount greater than their par value but less than their original issue price. Compared with the cost method of accounting for treasury stock, does the par-value method report a greater amount for additional paid-in capital and a greater amount for retained earnings?

	Additional Paid-In Capital	Retained Earnings
A.	Yes	Yes
B.	Yes	No
C.	No	No
D.	No	Yes

Answer (C) is correct. *(CPA, adapted)*
REQUIRED: The effect of the par-value method on additional paid-in capital and retained earnings compared with that of the cost method.
DISCUSSION: Under the cost method, the purchase of treasury stock (debit treasury stock, credit cash) has no effect on additional paid-in capital and retained earnings. Under the par-value method, given that the acquisition cost is greater than par but less than the original issue price, treasury stock is debited at par, and the additional paid-in capital associated with the original issue is also debited. Cash and paid-in capital from treasury stock transactions are credited. Hence, the par-value method does not report a greater amount for additional paid-in capital or retained earnings.

15.4.13. On incorporation, Dee, Inc., issued common stock at a price in excess of its par value. No other stock transactions occurred except that treasury stock was acquired for an amount exceeding this issue price. If Dee uses the par value method of accounting for treasury stock appropriate for retired stock, what is the effect of the acquisition on the following?

	Net Common Stock	Additional Paid-In Capital	Retained Earnings
A.	No effect	Decrease	No effect
B.	Decrease	Decrease	Decrease
C.	Decrease	No effect	Decrease
D.	No effect	Decrease	Decrease

Answer (B) is correct. *(CPA, adapted)*
REQUIRED: The effects of a purchase of treasury stock accounted for under the par value method.
DISCUSSION: Under the par value method, treasury stock is debited at par value, and the amount is reported as a reduction of common stock. The purchase also results in the removal of the additional paid-in capital associated with the original issue of the shares. Given that no other stock transactions occurred and that treasury stock was acquired for an amount exceeding the issue price, the balancing debit for the excess of the acquisition price over the issue price is to retained earnings. If paid-in capital from treasury stock had been previously recorded, the balancing debit would be to that account but only to the extent of its credit balance. Thus, retained earnings is also decreased.

15.4.14. An entity authorized 500,000 shares of common stock. At January 1, Year 2, the entity had 110,000 shares of common stock issued and 100,000 shares of common stock outstanding. The entity had the following transactions in Year 2:

March 1	Issued 15,000 shares of common stock
June 1	Resold 2,500 shares of treasury stock
September 1	Completed a 2-for-1 common stock split

What is the total number of shares of common stock that the entity has outstanding at the end of Year 2?

A. 117,500
B. 230,000
C. 235,000
D. 250,000

Answer (C) is correct. *(CPA, adapted)*
REQUIRED: The common stock outstanding at year-end.
DISCUSSION: At June 1, the entity had 117,500 shares of common stock outstanding (100,000 beginning of year + 15,000 March 1 issue + 2,500 June 1 treasury stock sale). On September 1, the entity completed a 2-for-1 common stock split, which doubles the number of shares outstanding to 235,000 shares (117,500 shares × 2).
Answer (A) is incorrect. A quantity of 117,500 shares results from failing to account for the 2-for-1 split that occurred on September 1. Answer (B) is incorrect. A quantity of 230,000 shares results from failing to include the 2,500 shares of treasury stock that were resold on June 1, Year 2. These shares are now considered outstanding since they were resold to shareholders. Answer (D) is incorrect. The question is asking for the total number of shares of common stock that the entity has outstanding, not issued. The entity only has 100,000 shares of common stock outstanding at the beginning of the year (10,000 shares are held as treasury stock and not included in the shares outstanding until they are resold).

15.5 Rights and Warrants

15.5.1. On November 2, Year 3, Finsbury, Inc., issued warrants to its shareholders giving them the right to purchase additional $20 par value common shares at a price of $30. The shareholders exercised all rights on March 1, Year 4. The shares had market prices of $33, $35, and $40 on November 2, Year 3, December 31, Year 3, and March 1, Year 4, respectively. What were the effects of the warrants on Finsbury's additional paid-in capital and net income?

	Additional Paid-In Capital	Net Income
A.	Increased in Year 4	No effect
B.	Increased in Year 3	No effect
C.	Increased in Year 4	Decreased in Year 3 and Year 4
D.	Increased in Year 3	Decreased in Year 3 and Year 4

Answer (A) is correct. *(CPA, adapted)*
REQUIRED: The effects on additional paid-in capital and net income when warrants are issued and exercised.
DISCUSSION: When stock rights are issued for no consideration, only a memorandum entry is made. Common stock and additional paid-in capital are not affected. However, when rights are exercised and stock is issued, the issuing company will reflect the proceeds as an increase in common stock and additional paid-in capital. Consequently, Finsbury will increase additional paid-in capital in Year 4 when stock is issued, and net income will not be affected.
Answer (B) is incorrect. Only a memorandum entry is made in Year 3. Answer (C) is incorrect. Net income is not affected. Answer (D) is incorrect. Only a memorandum entry is made in Year 3, and net income is not affected.

15.5.2. Quoit, Inc., issued preferred stock with detachable common stock warrants. The issue price exceeded the sum of the warrants' fair value and the preferred stocks' par value. The preferred stocks' fair value was not determinable. What amount should be assigned to the warrants outstanding?

A. Total proceeds.

B. Excess of proceeds over the par value of the preferred stock.

C. The proportion of the proceeds that the warrants' fair value bears to the preferred stocks' par value.

D. The fair value of the warrants.

Answer (D) is correct. *(CPA, adapted)*
REQUIRED: The amount assigned to outstanding warrants when the fair value of the stock is not known.
DISCUSSION: When securities are issued with detachable stock warrants, the proceeds should be allocated between the securities and the warrants based on their relative fair values at issuance. If the fair value of only the warrants is known, the warrants should be recorded at fair value with the remainder allocated to the securities.
Answer (A) is incorrect. The total proceeds need to be allocated between the warrants and the preferred stock. Answer (B) is incorrect. The preferred stock is worth more than its par value. Answer (C) is incorrect. The fair value of the warrants is not related to the par value of the preferred stock.

15.5.3. On July 1, Vail Corp. issued rights to shareholders to subscribe to additional shares of its common stock. One right was issued for each share owned. A shareholder could purchase one additional share for 10 rights plus $15 cash. The rights expired on September 30. On July 1, the market price of a share with the right attached was $40, while the market price of one right alone was $2. Vail's equity on June 30 included the following:

Common stock, $25 par value, 4,000 shares issued and outstanding	$100,000
Additional paid-in capital	60,000
Retained earnings	80,000

By what amount should Vail's retained earnings decrease as a result of issuance of the stock rights on July 1?

A. $0

B. $5,000

C. $8,000

D. $10,000

Answer (A) is correct. *(CPA, adapted)*
REQUIRED: The effect on retained earnings when stock rights are issued.
DISCUSSION: When stock rights are issued for no consideration, only a memorandum entry is made. When stock rights are exercised and stock is issued, the issuing company will reflect the proceeds as an increase in common stock and additional paid-in capital. Thus, retained earnings will not be affected when rights are either issued or exercised.
Answer (B) is incorrect. Stock rights will have no effect on retained earnings. Answer (C) is incorrect. When stock rights are issued, only a memorandum entry is made, having no effect on retained earnings. Answer (D) is incorrect. When stock rights are issued, only a memorandum entry is made.

15.5.4. On March 4, Year 4, Evan Co. purchased 1,000 shares of LVC common stock at $80 per share. On September 26, Year 4, Evan received 1,000 stock rights to purchase an additional 1,000 shares at $90 per share. The stock rights had an expiration date of February 1, Year 5. On September 26, Year 4, LVC's common stock had a fair value, ex-rights, of $95 per share, and the stock rights had a fair value of $5 each. What amount should Evan record on September 26, Year 4, for investment in stock rights?

A. $4,000

B. $5,000

C. $10,000

D. $15,000

Answer (A) is correct. *(CPA, adapted)*
REQUIRED: The amount to be recorded for the investment in stock rights on the balance sheet.
DISCUSSION: The $80 original cost of each share should be allocated between the share and the stock right based on their relative fair values at the time the rights are received.

Stock:	$80 cost × [$95 ÷ ($95 + $5)] = $76
Right:	$80 cost × [$ 5 ÷ ($95 + $5)] = $4
	$80

Thus, the stock rights should be recorded at $4,000 (1,000 rights × $4) on the balance sheet.
Answer (B) is incorrect. The amount of $5,000 is the fair value of the rights. Answer (C) is incorrect. The amount of $10,000 is the difference between the cost of the 1,000 shares and the exercise price for an additional 1,000 shares. Answer (D) is incorrect. The amount of $15,000 is the difference between the cost of the 1,000 shares and their fair value.

15.5.5. In September Year 1, Cal Corp. made a dividend distribution of one right for each of its 240,000 shares of outstanding common stock. Each right was exercisable for the purchase of 1/100 of a share of Cal's $50 variable rate preferred stock at an exercise price of $80 per share. On March 20, Year 8, none of the rights had been exercised, and Cal redeemed them by paying each shareholder $0.10 per right. As a result of this redemption, Cal's equity was reduced by

A. $240

B. $24,000

C. $48,000

D. $72,000

Answer (B) is correct. *(CPA, adapted)*
REQUIRED: The effect on shareholders' equity of the redemption of stock rights.
DISCUSSION: When rights are issued for no consideration, only a memorandum entry is made. Consequently, neither common stock nor additional paid-in capital is affected by the issuance of rights in a nonreciprocal transfer. The redemption of the rights reduces equity by the amount of their cost (240,000 × $.10 = $24,000).
Answer (A) is incorrect. The amount of $240 equals $.10 times the number of shares (2,400) that could have been purchased. Answer (C) is incorrect. If the rights were initially credited to paid-in capital at $72,000, or $.30 each [($80 exercise price – $50 par value) ÷ 100], and paid-in capital was reduced by the redemption price of $.10 each (240,000 × $.10 = $24,000), the balance remaining would be $48,000. Answer (D) is incorrect. The amount of $72,000 assumes a price per right of $.30 [($80 exercise price – $50 par value) ÷ 100].

15.5.6. Smythe Co. invested $200 in a call option for 100 shares of Gin Co. $.50 par common stock when the market price was $10 per share. The option expired in 3 months and had an exercise price of $9 per share. What was the intrinsic value of the call option at the time of initial investment?

A. $50

B. $100

C. $200

D. $900

Answer (B) is correct. *(CPA, adapted)*
REQUIRED: The intrinsic value of the call option.
DISCUSSION: The intrinsic value of an option is calculated as the market value of the underlying minus the exercise price of the option, calculated as follows: [100 shares × ($10 market price – $9 exercise price)].
Answer (A) is incorrect. The intrinsic value of an option is the difference between the market value of the underlying and the exercise price of the option. The underlying's par value is not relevant. Answer (C) is incorrect. The intrinsic value of an option is the difference between the market value of the underlying and the exercise price of the option. The amount paid for the option is not relevant. Answer (D) is incorrect. The intrinsic value of an option is the difference between the market value of the underlying and the exercise price of the option. The total market value of the underlying is not relevant.

15.6 Statement of Changes in Equity

15.6.1. Zinc Co.'s adjusted trial balance at December 31, Year 6, includes the following account balances:

Common stock, $3 par	$600,000
Additional paid-in capital	800,000
Treasury stock, at cost	50,000
Net unrealized holding loss on available-for-sale securities	20,000
Retained earnings: Appropriated for uninsured earthquake losses	150,000
Retained earnings: Unappropriated	200,000

What amount should Zinc report as total equity in its December 31, Year 6, balance sheet?

A. $1,680,000

B. $1,720,000

C. $1,780,000

D. $1,820,000

Answer (A) is correct. *(CPA, adapted)*
REQUIRED: The total equity.
DISCUSSION: Total credits to equity equal $1,750,000 ($600,000 common stock at par + $800,000 additional paid-in capital + $350,000 retained earnings). The treasury stock recorded at cost is subtracted from (debited to) total equity, and the unrealized holding loss on available-for-sale securities is debited to other comprehensive income, a component of equity. Because total debits equal $70,000 ($50,000 cost of treasury stock + $20,000 unrealized loss on available-for-sale securities), total equity equals $1,680,000 ($1,750,000 – $70,000).
Answer (B) is incorrect. The amount of $1,720,000 treats the unrealized loss as a credit. Answer (C) is incorrect. The amount of $1,780,000 treats the treasury stock as a credit. Answer (D) is incorrect. The amount of $1,820,000 treats the treasury stock and the unrealized loss as credits.

STUDY UNIT SIXTEEN
EARNINGS PER SHARE

Earnings per share (EPS) is the amount of earnings attributable to a single share of common stock. Investors commonly use this ratio to measure the performance of an entity over an accounting period. The guidance for calculation and presentation of EPS must be followed by public entities and by other entities that choose to report EPS. The two forms of EPS are basic and diluted.

Basic earnings per share (BEPS) measures earnings performance based on common stock outstanding during all or part of the reporting period.

$$BEPS = \frac{Income\ available\ to\ common\ shareholders}{Weighted\text{-}average\ number\ of\ common\ shares\ outstanding}$$

Diluted earnings per share (DEPS) measures earnings performance after considering the effect on the numerator and denominator of dilutive potential common stock (PCS).

$$DEPS = \frac{BEPS\ numerator + Effect\ of\ dilutive\ PCS}{BEPS\ denominator + Effect\ of\ dilutive\ PCS}$$

QUESTIONS

16.1 Basic Earnings per Share (BEPS)

16.1.1. With respect to the computation of earnings per share, which of the following would be most indicative of a simple capital structure?

A. Common stock, preferred stock, and convertible debt outstanding.

B. Common stock, convertible preferred stock, and debt outstanding.

C. Common stock, preferred stock, and debt outstanding.

D. Common stock, preferred stock, and stock options outstanding.

Answer (C) is correct. *(CPA, adapted)*
REQUIRED: The situation most indicative of a simple capital structure.
DISCUSSION: A simple capital structure has only common stock outstanding. A complex capital structure contains potential common stock. Potential common stock includes options, warrants, convertible securities, contingent stock requirements, and any other security or contract that may entitle the holder to obtain common stock.
Answer (A) is incorrect. A simple capital structure does not include convertible debt outstanding. Answer (B) is incorrect. A simple capital structure does not include convertible preferred stock. Answer (D) is incorrect. A simple capital structure does not include stock options.

16.1.2. The disclosure requirements for earnings per share do not apply to

A. Statements presented by corporations whose capital structures contain only common stock.

B. Statements presented by wholly owned subsidiaries.

C. Statements presented by corporations whose capital structures contain both common stock and potential common stock.

D. Summaries of financial statements that purport to present the results of operations of publicly held corporations in conformity with generally accepted accounting principles.

Answer (B) is correct. *(Publisher, adapted)*
REQUIRED: The type of capital structure or financial statement presentation to which EPS disclosure requirements do not apply.
DISCUSSION: EPS disclosure requirements apply to companies whose securities trade in a public market. Specifically exempted are investment companies (such as mutual funds) and wholly owned subsidiaries from these disclosure requirements.
Answer (A) is incorrect. EPS disclosure requirements apply to companies whose capital structures only contain common stock. Answer (C) is incorrect. EPS disclosure requirements apply to companies whose capital structures contain both common stock and potential common stock. Answer (D) is incorrect. EPS data of companies subject to EPS disclosure requirements must be presented for all periods for which an income statement or a summary of earnings is presented.

16.1.3. Earnings-per-share data must be reported on the face of the income statement for

	Income from Continuing Operations	Cumulative Effect of a Change in Accounting Principle
A.	Yes	Yes
B.	Yes	No
C.	No	No
D.	No	Yes

Answer (B) is correct. *(CPA, adapted)*
REQUIRED: The EPS data that must be reported on the face of the income statement.
DISCUSSION: EPS data for income from continuing operations and net income must be reported on the face of the income statement. EPS data for a discontinued operation may be disclosed on the face of the income statement or in a note.
Answer (A) is incorrect. EPS data is not reported for the effect of an accounting change. Answer (C) is incorrect. EPS data must be reported on the face of the income statement for income from continuing operations and net income. Answer (D) is incorrect. EPS data must be reported on the face of the income statement for income from continuing operations and net income but not for the effect of an accounting change.

16.1.4. What is the required financial statement presentation of earnings per share?

A. Restatement of EPS data of a prior period if the earnings of the prior period have been restated by a prior-period adjustment.

B. Dual presentation of BEPS and DEPS for the current period only.

C. The presentation of BEPS only for prior periods presented for comparative purposes.

D. Disclosure of the effect of a restatement of prior-period earnings from a prior-period adjustment in the current period, but not in EPS form.

Answer (A) is correct. *(Publisher, adapted)*
REQUIRED: The financial statement presentation of EPS.
DISCUSSION: When the results of operations of a prior period are restated in the financial statements, the EPS data for those prior periods must also be restated.
Answer (B) is incorrect. Both BEPS and DEPS must be disclosed for all periods presented if a corporation has a complex capital structure. Answer (C) is incorrect. BEPS must be disclosed for all periods presented if a corporation has a complex capital structure. Answer (D) is incorrect. Presentation of the effect of a prior-period adjustment on EPS is required for all prior periods affected by such restatement.

16.1.5. With regard to stock dividends and stock splits, current authoritative literature contains what general guideline for the computation of EPS?

A. If changes in common stock resulting from stock dividends, stock splits, or reverse splits have been consummated after the close of the period but before completion of the financial report, the per-share computations should be based on the new number of shares.

B. It is not necessary to give recognition to the effect on prior periods' computations of EPS for stock dividends or stock splits consummated in the current period.

C. Computations of EPS for prior periods must give recognition to changes in common shares due to stock splits, but not stock dividends, because stock dividends have an immaterial effect on EPS.

D. Footnote disclosure is necessary for anticipated stock dividends and stock splits and their effect on BEPS and DEPS.

Answer (A) is correct. *(Publisher, adapted)*
REQUIRED: The treatment of stock dividends and stock splits in the calculation of the weighted-average number of shares.
DISCUSSION: When a stock dividend, stock split, or reverse split occurs at any time before issuance of the financial statements, restatement of EPS is required for all periods presented. The purpose is to promote comparability of EPS data among reporting periods.
Answer (B) is incorrect. The effect of stock dividends and stock splits on prior-period earnings must be calculated, and EPS data should be restated for all periods presented in the financial statements. Answer (C) is incorrect. Stock dividends and stock splits are treated the same for EPS purposes regardless of their amounts. Answer (D) is incorrect. A stock dividend or stock split is not accounted for or disclosed until it occurs.

16.1.6. In computing the loss per share of common stock, cumulative preferred dividends not earned should be

A. Deducted from the loss for the year.

B. Added to the loss for the year.

C. Deducted from income in the year paid.

D. Added to income in the year paid.

Answer (B) is correct. *(CPA, adapted)*
REQUIRED: The effect of unearned cumulative preferred dividends on the loss-per-share calculation.
DISCUSSION: When preferred stock is cumulative, the dividend, whether earned or not, is deducted from income from continuing operations and net income, or added to any loss for the year, in computing earnings or loss, per share of common stock. When preferred stock is noncumulative, an adjustment is made for dividends declared. If the dividend is cumulative only if earned, no adjustment is necessary except to the extent of available income; that is, the preferred dividends accumulate only to the extent of net income.
Answer (A) is incorrect. It has the effect of reducing loss per share. Answer (C) is incorrect. Cumulative preferred dividends are a necessary adjustment for the year in which they accumulate. Answer (D) is incorrect. Cumulative preferred dividends are a necessary adjustment for the year in which they accumulate, regardless of when paid.

16.1.7. Poe Co. had 300,000 shares of common stock issued and outstanding at December 31, Year 1. No common stock was issued during Year 2. On January 1, Year 2, Poe issued 200,000 shares of nonconvertible preferred stock. During Year 2, Poe declared and paid $75,000 of cash dividends on the common stock and $60,000 on the preferred stock. Net income for the year ended December 31, Year 2, was $330,000. What should be Poe's Year 2 basic earnings per common share?

A. $1.10

B. $0.90

C. $0.85

D. $0.65

Answer (B) is correct. *(CPA, adapted)*
REQUIRED: The amount of earnings per common share.
DISCUSSION: Basic earnings per common share are equal to the amount of earnings available to the common shareholders divided by the weighted-average number of shares of common stock outstanding during the year. To calculate earnings available to holders of common stock, dividends on cumulative preferred stock must be subtracted from net income whether or not the dividends were declared. Earnings per common share for Year 2 thus amounted to $0.90.

$$\frac{\$330,000 - \$60,000}{300,000 \text{ shares}} = \$0.90$$

Answer (A) is incorrect. The amount of $1.10 assumes no preferred dividends were declared. Answer (C) is incorrect. The amount of $0.85 assumes the common but not the preferred dividends are subtracted from the numerator. Answer (D) is incorrect. The amount of $0.65 assumes all dividends are subtracted from the numerator.

16.1.8. Chape Co. had the following information related to common and preferred shares during the year:

Common shares outstanding, 1/1	700,000
Common shares repurchased, 3/31	20,000
Conversion of preferred shares, 6/30	40,000
Common shares repurchased, 12/1	36,000

Chape reported net income of $2,000,000 at December 31. What amount of shares should Chape use as the denominator in the computation of basic earnings per share?

A. 684,000

B. 700,000

C. 702,000

D. 740,000

Answer (C) is correct. *(CPA, adapted)*
REQUIRED: The denominator in the computation of basic earnings per share.
DISCUSSION: Basic earnings per share (BEPS) equals income available to common shareholders divided by the weighted average of common shares outstanding. The BEPS denominator is weighted because some shares may have been issued or reacquired during the period. The weights are the fractions of the period that different amounts of shares are outstanding.

Dates Outstanding	Shares Outstanding	Fraction of Period	Weighted-Average Shares
1/1-3/31	700,000	(3 ÷ 12)	175,000
Repurchase 3/31	(20,000)		
4/1-6/30	680,000	(3 ÷ 12)	170,000
Conversion of preferred shares 6/30	40,000		
7/1-11/30	720,000	(5 ÷ 12)	300,000
Repurchase 12/1	(36,000)		
12/1-12/31	684,000	(1 ÷ 12)	57,000
			702,000

Answer (A) is incorrect. The amount of 684,000 shares is the number outstanding during December. Answer (B) is incorrect. The amount of 700,000 shares is the number outstanding on January 1. Answer (D) is incorrect. The amount of 740,000 shares is the number that would have been deemed to be outstanding on January 1 if the conversion of preferred shares had related back to that date.

16.1.9. The following information pertains to Jet Corp.'s outstanding stock for the year just ended:

Common stock, $5 par value:
Shares outstanding, 1/1	20,000
2-for-1 stock split, 4/1	20,000
Shares issued, 7/1	10,000

Preferred stock, $10 par value, 5% cumulative:
Shares outstanding, 1/1	4,000

What are the number of shares Jet should use to calculate basic earnings per share (BEPS) for the year just ended?

A. 40,000

B. 45,000

C. 50,000

D. 54,000

Answer (B) is correct. *(CPA, adapted)*
REQUIRED: The number of shares used to calculate BEPS.
DISCUSSION: BEPS is equal to the amount of earnings available to the common shareholders divided by the weighted-average number of shares of common stock outstanding during the year. When a stock dividend, a stock split, or a reverse split occurs other than at the beginning of a year, a retroactive adjustment for the change in capital structure should be made as of the beginning of the earliest accounting period presented. Shares outstanding during the year must then be weighted by the number of months for which they were outstanding in calculating the weighted-average number of shares to be used in determining BEPS. Preferred stock is not included even if convertible because the BEPS calculation excludes the effects of potential common stock. Consequently, the BEPS denominator is 45,000, based on 40,000 shares outstanding for the entire year (20,000 beginning balance + 20,000 2-for-1 stock split) and 10,000 shares issued on July 1.

$$40,000 \times (6 \div 12) = 20,000$$
$$50,000 \times (6 \div 12) = \underline{25,000}$$
$$\underline{45,000}$$

Answer (A) is incorrect. The amount of 40,000 assumes that the stock split is not treated as though it occurred at the beginning of the period. Answer (C) is incorrect. The amount of 50,000 assumes that the shares issued on 7/1 were outstanding for 12 months. Answer (D) is incorrect. The amount of 54,000 includes the preferred stock and assumes that the shares issued on 7/1 were outstanding for 12 months.

Questions 16.1.10 through 16.1.13 are based on the following information.

Colon Co. uses a calendar year for financial reporting. The company is authorized to issue 5 million shares of $10 par common stock. At no time has Colon issued any potentially dilutive securities. A two-for-one stock split of Colon's common stock took place on March 31, Year 4. Additional information is in the next column.

Number of common shares issued and outstanding at 12/31/Year 1	1,000,000
Shares issued as a result of a 10% stock dividend on 9/30/Year 2	100,000
Shares issued for cash on 3/31/Year 3	1,000,000
Number of common shares issued and outstanding at 12/31/Year 3	2,100,000

16.1.10. The weighted-average number of common shares used in computing basic earnings per common share for Year 2 on the Year 3 comparative income statement was

A. 1,100,000

B. 1,050,000

C. 1,025,000

D. 1,000,000

Answer (A) is correct. *(CMA, adapted)*
REQUIRED: The weighted-average number of shares used in the BEPS computation for Year 2 on the Year 3 comparative income statement.
DISCUSSION: At the beginning of Year 2, 1 million shares were outstanding. Another 100,000 were issued as a result of a stock dividend on September 30. The stock dividend is assumed to have occurred at the beginning of the year. Accordingly, the number of shares outstanding throughout Year 2 would have been 1.1 million. No stock dividends or stock splits occurred in Year 3. Thus, the same 1.1 million shares used in the BEPS calculation on the Year 2 income statement would be used to determine the Year 2 BEPS in the Year 3 comparative statements.
Answer (B) is incorrect. This figure assumes the stock dividend affects shares outstanding for 6 months. Answer (C) is incorrect. This figure assumes the stock dividend affects shares outstanding for 3 months. Answer (D) is incorrect. This figure does not consider the stock dividend.

16.1.11. The weighted-average number of common shares used in computing BEPS for Year 3 on the Year 3 comparative income statement was

A. 1,600,000

B. 1,850,000

C. 2,100,000

D. 3,700,000

Answer (B) is correct. *(CMA, adapted)*

REQUIRED: The weighted-average number of shares used in computing BEPS for Year 3 on the Year 3 income statement.

DISCUSSION: At the beginning of Year 3, 1.1 million shares were outstanding. This figure remained unchanged for 3 months until March 31, when an additional 1 million shares were issued. Hence, for the last 9 months of the year, 2.1 million shares were outstanding. Weighting the shares outstanding by the amount of time they were outstanding results in a weighted average of 1,850,000 shares {[1,100,000 × (3 months ÷ 12 months)] + [2,100,000 × (9 months ÷ 12 months)]}.

Answer (A) is incorrect. The 1,000,000 shares issued on 3/31/Yr 3 are assumed to be outstanding for 6 months. Answer (C) is incorrect. The 1,000,000 shares issued on 3/31/Yr 3 are assumed to be outstanding for the entire year. Answer (D) is incorrect. This number of shares is used in computing BEPS for Year 3 on the Year 4 comparative income statement.

16.1.12. The weighted-average number of common shares to be used in computing BEPS for Year 4 on the Year 4 comparative income statement is

A. 2,100,000

B. 3,150,000

C. 3,675,000

D. 4,200,000

Answer (D) is correct. *(CMA, adapted)*

REQUIRED: The weighted-average number of shares used in computing BEPS for Year 4 on the Year 4 comparative income statement.

DISCUSSION: At the beginning of Year 4, 2.1 million shares were outstanding. Because of the March 31 two-for-one stock split, that number increased to 4.2 million. The stock split is assumed to have occurred on the first day of the year. Consequently, the number of shares outstanding throughout Year 4 was 4.2 million.

Answer (A) is incorrect. The amount of 2,100,000 ignores the 3/31/Yr 4 stock split. Answer (B) is incorrect. The amount of 3,150,000 assumes the stock split increases shares outstanding for 6 months. Answer (C) is incorrect. The amount of 3,675,000 assumes the stock split increases shares outstanding from the date the split occurred.

16.1.13. The weighted-average number of common shares to be used in computing BEPS for Year 3 on the Year 4 comparative income statement is

A. 1,850,000

B. 2,100,000

C. 3,700,000

D. 4,200,000

Answer (C) is correct. *(CMA, adapted)*

REQUIRED: The weighted-average number of shares used in computing BEPS for Year 3 on the Year 4 comparative income statement.

DISCUSSION: A stock dividend or split occurring at any time must be treated as though it occurred at the beginning of the earliest period presented for purposes of computing the weighted-average number of shares. Thus, prior-period BEPS figures presented for comparative purposes must be retroactively restated for the effects of a stock dividend or a stock split. The number of shares used in computing the Year 3 BEPS on the Year 3 income statement was 1,850,000 {[1,100,000 shares × (3 months ÷ 12 months)] + [2,100,000 × (9 months ÷ 12 months)]}. However, because of the stock split on March 31, Year 4, the number of shares doubled. Thus, the BEPS calculation for Year 3 on the Year 4 comparative income statement should be based on 3,700,000 shares (1,850,000 × 2).

Answer (A) is incorrect. The number of shares used in computing BEPS for Year 3 on the Year 3 income statement is 1,850,000. Answer (B) is incorrect. The amount of 2,100,000 is the number of shares in Year 4. It does not reflect the 3/31/Yr 4 stock split. Answer (D) is incorrect. The number of shares used in computing BEPS for Year 4 on the Year 4 comparative income statement is 4,200,000.

Question 16.1.14 is based on the following information. Smith Corporation had net income for the year of $101,504 and a simple capital structure consisting of the following common shares outstanding:

Months Outstanding	Number of Shares
January - February	24,000
March - June	29,400
July - November	36,000
December	35,040
Total	124,440

16.1.14. Smith Corporation's basic earnings per share (rounded to the nearest cent) were

A. $2.90

B. $3.20

C. $3.26

D. $3.45

Answer (B) is correct. *(CMA, adapted)*
REQUIRED: The BEPS for a company with a simple capital structure.
DISCUSSION: BEPS equals net income divided by the weighted-average number of shares outstanding. The latter is calculated as follows:

$$24,000 \times (2 \div 12) = 4,000$$
$$29,400 \times (4 \div 12) = 9,800$$
$$36,000 \times (5 \div 12) = 15,000$$
$$35,040 \times (1 \div 12) = 2,920$$
$$31,720$$

Accordingly, BEPS is $3.20 ($101,504 NI ÷ 31,720 shares).
Answer (A) is incorrect. This amount is based on the shares outstanding at year end. Answer (C) is incorrect. This amount is based on an unweighted average of the four levels of shares outstanding during the year. Answer (D) is incorrect. This amount is based on the shares outstanding March through June.

16.1.15. A company had the following outstanding shares as of January 1, Year 2:

Preferred stock,
$60 par, 4%, cumulative   10,000 shares
Common stock, $3 par   50,000 shares

On April 1, Year 2, the company sold 8,000 shares of previously unissued common stock. No dividends were in arrears on January 1, Year 2, and no dividends were declared or paid during Year 2. Net income for Year 2 totaled $236,000. What amount is basic earnings per share (BEPS) for the year ended December 31, Year 2?

A. $3.66

B. $3.79

C. $4.07

D. $4.21

Answer (B) is correct. *(CPA, adapted)*
REQUIRED: The basic earnings per share.
DISCUSSION: BEPS is computed by dividing income available to common shareholders by the weighted-average number of common shares outstanding during the period. Income in the BEPS numerator is reduced by preferred dividends declared in the current period and accumulated for the current period on cumulative preferred stock. Preferred dividends accumulated in Year 2 are $24,000 (10,000 shares × $60 par × 4%). Income available to common shareholders is $212,000 ($236,000 – $24,000). The weighted-average number of common shares outstanding for the year is 56,000 {50,000 outstanding at beginning of year + [8,000 from April 1 issue × (9 months ÷ 12 months)]}. Therefore, BEPS is $3.79 ($212,000 ÷ 56,000).
Answer (A) is incorrect. The denominator of BEPS is the weighted-average number of common shares outstanding during the period, i.e., the number of shares must be weighted by the portion of the period that the shares were outstanding. Answer (C) is incorrect. The numerator for BEPS is income available to common shareholders. To find income available to common shareholders, net income must be reduced by preferred dividends declared or accumulated during the current period. Furthermore, the denominator of BEPS is weighted average number of shares outstanding. The number of shares outstanding must be weighted by the portion of the period that the shares were outstanding. Answer (D) is incorrect. The numerator for BEPS is income available to common shareholders. To find income available to common shareholders, net income must be reduced by preferred dividends declared or accumulated during the current period.

16.2 Diluted Earnings per Share (DEPS)

16.2.1. When computing diluted earnings per share (DEPS), convertible securities that are potential common stock are

A. Ignored.

B. Recognized whether they are dilutive or antidilutive.

C. Recognized only if they are antidilutive.

D. Recognized only if they are dilutive.

Answer (D) is correct. *(CPA, adapted)*
REQUIRED: The true statement about the treatment of convertible securities in computing DEPS.
DISCUSSION: The objective of DEPS is to measure the performance of an entity during an accounting period while giving effect to all dilutive potential common shares that were outstanding during the period. Convertible securities are potential common stock.

16.2.2. In calculating annual diluted earnings per share, which of the following should not be considered?

A. The weighted-average number of common shares outstanding.

B. The amount of dividends declared on nonconvertible cumulative preferred shares.

C. The amount of cash dividends declared on common shares.

D. The number of common shares resulting from the assumed conversion of debentures outstanding.

Answer (C) is correct. *(CIA, adapted)*
REQUIRED: The information not included in the calculation of DEPS.
DISCUSSION: The numerator of the DEPS calculation represents the residual income for the period available to holders of common stock and potential common stock. A cash dividend on common stock has no effect on earnings available to common shareholders. Thus, earnings are included whether they are distributed or undistributed.
Answer (A) is incorrect. The weighted-average number of common shares outstanding is included in the denominator of DEPS. Answer (B) is incorrect. The dividend on nonconvertible cumulative preferred stock, whether declared or not, must be deducted from income from continuing operations and also from net income to arrive at earnings available to common shareholders. Answer (D) is incorrect. The assumed conversion of debentures requires adjusting both the numerator (for interest, net of tax effect) and the denominator (for the shares assumed issued) of DEPS.

16.2.3. In determining diluted earnings per share for a complex capital structure, which of the following is a potential common stock?

	Nonconvertible Preferred Stock	Stock Option
A.	Yes	No
B.	Yes	Yes
C.	No	Yes
D.	No	No

Answer (C) is correct. *(CPA, adapted)*
REQUIRED: The potential common stock.
DISCUSSION: Potential common stock is a security or other contract that may entitle its holder to obtain common stock during either the reporting period or some future accounting period. Potential common stocks include options, warrants, convertible preferred stock, convertible debt, and contingent stock agreements.
Answer (A) is incorrect. Unlike a stock option, nonconvertible preferred stock is never potential common stock. Moreover, potential common stock includes options. Answer (B) is incorrect. Unlike a stock option, nonconvertible preferred stock is never potential common stock. Answer (D) is incorrect. Potential common stock includes options.

16.2.4. In determining diluted earnings per share (DEPS), a potential common stock (PCS) was antidilutive in Year 2 and dilutive in Year 3. The potential common stock would be included in the computation for

	Year 2	Year 3
A.	Yes	Yes
B.	No	Yes
C.	No	No
D.	Yes	No

Answer (B) is correct. *(CPA, adapted)*
REQUIRED: The circumstances under which potential common stock is included in the determination of DEPS.
DISCUSSION: DEPS is based on the number of common shares outstanding during the period plus the common shares that would have been outstanding if dilutive potential common shares had been issued. Thus, in a period in which the effect of potential common stock is antidilutive, it is not included in the determination of DEPS. It is included, however, in those periods in which its effect is dilutive.
Answer (A) is incorrect. The PCS is not included in the calculation of DEPS for Year 2. Answer (C) is incorrect. The PCS is included in the calculation of DEPS for Year 3. Answer (D) is incorrect. The PCS is included in the calculation of DEPS for Year 3.

16.2.5. The nature of the adjustment for stock options in the calculation of diluted earnings per share can be described as

A. Historical because earnings are historical.

B. Historical because it indicates the firm's valuation.

C. Pro forma because it indicates potential changes in the number of shares.

D. Pro forma because it indicates potential changes in earnings.

Answer (C) is correct. *(CPA, adapted)*
REQUIRED: The nature of the adjustment required for stock options in calculating DEPS.
DISCUSSION: The denominator in the DEPS calculation is adjusted for the assumed exercise of outstanding call options and warrants issued by the entity if the exercise would have a dilutive effect. The change in the number of shares has not occurred and is only assumed, so the calculation is essentially pro forma.
Answer (A) is incorrect. The conversion of stock options into common shares has not occurred, and the required adjustment is hypothetical. Answer (B) is incorrect. The conversion of stock options into common shares has not occurred, and the required adjustment is hypothetical. Answer (D) is incorrect. The assumed exercise of the options affects only the denominator of the DEPS ratio.

16.2.6. When a company reports amounts for basic and diluted earnings per share,

A. They should be presented with equal prominence on the face of the income statement.

B. They need not be shown on the face of the income statement but must be disclosed in the notes to the financial statements.

C. They need to be reported for net income only.

D. BEPS should be presented on the face of the income statement. DEPS may be disclosed either on the face of the income statement or in the notes.

Answer (A) is correct. *(CMA, adapted)*
REQUIRED: The true statement about the reporting of BEPS and DEPS.
DISCUSSION: An entity whose stock is publicly traded must report EPS information on the face of the income statement for both income from continuing operations and net income. In addition, EPS data for any discontinued operation must be presented on the face of the income statement or in a note. When the entity does not have a simple capital structure, it must present BEPS and DEPS with equal prominence.
Answer (B) is incorrect. Certain EPS amounts must be presented on the face of the income statement. Answer (C) is incorrect. EPS must also be presented for income from continuing operations and discontinued operations. Answer (D) is incorrect. BEPS and DEPS are to be presented on the face of the income statement with equal prominence.

16.2.7. Mann, Inc., had 300,000 shares of common stock issued and outstanding at January 1. On July 1, an additional 50,000 shares of common stock were issued for cash. Mann also had unexercised stock options to purchase 40,000 shares of common stock at $15 per share outstanding at the beginning and end of the year. The average market price of Mann's common stock was $20 during the year. What is the number of shares that should be used in computing diluted earnings per share (DEPS) for the year ended December 31?

A. 325,000

B. 335,000

C. 360,000

D. 365,000

Answer (B) is correct. *(CPA, adapted)*
REQUIRED: The number of shares to be used in computing DEPS.
DISCUSSION: The weighted average shares outstanding needs to be calculated. On July 1, 50,000 shares of common stock were issued. Hence, for the purpose of calculating Mann's weighted-average number of shares, 300,000 shares should be considered outstanding for the first 6 months and 350,000 shares for the second 6 months. Therefore, the weighted average shares outstanding equals 325,000.
Dilutive call options and warrants are included in DEPS. These options are assumed to be exercised at the beginning of the period using the treasury stock method. This method assumes the options are exercised and the $600,000 of proceeds (40,000 options × $15) is used to repurchase shares. In the DEPS computation, the assumed repurchase price is the average market price for the period ($20), so 30,000 shares are assumed to be repurchased ($600,000 ÷ $20). The difference between the shares assumed to be issued and those repurchased (40,000 – 30,000 = 10,000) is added to the weighted average of common shares outstanding to determine the DEPS denominator. Thus, 335,000 (325,000 + 10,000) shares should be used in computing DEPS for the year ending December 31.
Answer (A) is incorrect. The amount of 325,000 does not include the 10,000 shares includible due to the stock option. Answer (C) is incorrect. The amount of 360,000 includes the full 50,000 shares sold on July 1 instead of the weighted-average number of shares of 25,000. Answer (D) is incorrect. The amount of 365,000 includes the full 40,000 shares covered by the stock options instead of the amount computed under the treasury stock method.

16.2.8. Under the treasury stock method, the DEPS calculation is based on the assumption that call options and warrants issued by the reporting entity and outstanding for the entire year were exercised at the

A. End of the period and that the funds obtained thereby were used to purchase common stock at the average market price during the period.

B. Beginning of the period and that the funds obtained thereby were used to purchase common stock at the average market price during the period.

C. End of the period and that the funds obtained thereby were used to purchase common stock at the current market price in effect at the end of the period.

D. Beginning of the period and that the funds obtained thereby were used to purchase common stock at the current market price in effect at the end of the period.

Answer (B) is correct. *(Publisher, adapted)*
REQUIRED: The proper application of the treasury stock method to the assumed exercise of options and warrants in the calculation of DEPS.
DISCUSSION: The treasury stock method of accounting for dilutive call options and warrants issued by the reporting entity assumes the exercise of outstanding options and warrants at the beginning of the period or at time of issuance, if later. The treasury stock method assumes that the proceeds from the exercise are used to purchase common stock at the average market price during the period. The incremental shares, that is, the excess of those assumed issued over those assumed purchased, are included in the DEPS denominator.
Answer (A) is incorrect. The options and warrants are assumed to have been exercised at the beginning of the period. Answer (C) is incorrect. The options and warrants are assumed to have been exercised at the beginning of the period, and the average market price during the period is used. Answer (D) is incorrect. The average market price during the period is used.

16.2.9. How are partially paid stock subscriptions treated in the computation of EPS?

A. By use of the treasury stock method.

B. By not including them until issuance.

C. By disclosure only.

D. By use of the if-converted method.

Answer (A) is correct. *(Publisher, adapted)*
REQUIRED: The treatment of stock subscriptions in EPS computations.
DISCUSSION: Stock purchase contracts, partially paid stock subscriptions, and nonvested stock granted to employees are equivalent to stock options and warrants. Thus, the treasury stock method is used to account for partially paid stock subscriptions.
Answer (B) is incorrect. If the stock subscriptions are dilutive, they must be included in the calculation of EPS. Answer (C) is incorrect. If the stock subscriptions are dilutive, they must be included in the calculation of EPS. Answer (D) is incorrect. The if-converted method applies to convertible securities.

16.2.10. In a diluted earnings-per-share computation, the effect of outstanding call options and warrants issued by the reporting entity is reflected by applying the treasury stock method. If the exercise price of these options or warrants exceeds the average market price, the computation would

A. Fairly present diluted earnings per share on a prospective basis.

B. Fairly present the maximum potential dilution of diluted earnings per share on a prospective basis.

C. Reflect the excess of the number of shares assumed issued over the number of shares assumed reacquired as the potential dilution of earnings per share.

D. Be antidilutive.

Answer (D) is correct. *(CPA, adapted)*
REQUIRED: The effect on DEPS of an exercise price above the average market price for options and warrants.
DISCUSSION: Under the treasury stock method, call options and warrants issued by the reporting entity are assumed to be exercised at the beginning of the period or at time of issuance, if later. The proceeds are then assumed to be used to reacquire common shares outstanding at the average market price for the period. The effect on the denominator in the DEPS calculation is the difference between the shares assumed to be issued and the treasury shares assumed to be acquired. If the exercise price exceeds the average market price, more shares would be purchased than issued. Because these assumed transactions would increase DEPS by decreasing the denominator, their effect would be antidilutive.
Answer (A) is incorrect. When the exercise price exceeds the average market price, the result is antidilutive. Answer (B) is incorrect. When the exercise price exceeds the average market price, the result is antidilutive. Answer (C) is incorrect. The number of shares reacquired would exceed the number issued.

16.2.11. Weaver Company had 100,000 shares of common stock issued and outstanding at January 1. On July 1, Weaver issued a 10% stock dividend. Unexercised call options to purchase 20,000 shares of Weaver's common stock (adjusted for the stock dividend) at $20 per share were outstanding at the beginning and end of the year. The average market price of Weaver's common stock (which was not affected by the stock dividend) was $25 per share during the year. Net income for the year ended December 31 was $550,000. What should be Weaver's diluted earnings per share (DEPS) for the year?

A. $4.82

B. $5.00

C. $5.05

D. $5.24

Answer (A) is correct. *(CPA, adapted)*
REQUIRED: The DEPS for the year given a midyear stock dividend and unexercised stock options.
DISCUSSION: A stock dividend occurring at any time before issuance of the financial statements must be reflected as a retroactive adjustment of the capital structure at the beginning of the first period presented. Hence, the 110,000 shares outstanding after the stock dividend are deemed to have been outstanding during the entire year.
The options are not antidilutive because the exercise price was less than the average market price. Accordingly, exercise of the options is assumed to have occurred at the beginning of the year at the exercise price of $20. Under the treasury stock method, the assumed proceeds of $400,000 (20,000 shares × $20) are used to repurchase 16,000 shares ($400,000 ÷ $25) at the average market price during the period. The difference between the 20,000 shares assumed to be issued and the 16,000 shares assumed to be repurchased increases the DEPS denominator from 110,000 shares to 114,000 shares. Thus, DEPS equals $4.82 ($550,000 income ÷ 114,000 shares).
Answer (B) is incorrect. Five dollars does not include the stock options in the calculation of shares outstanding for the year. Answer (C) is incorrect. The amount of $5.05 assumes the shares issued as a stock dividend were outstanding for 6 months. Answer (D) is incorrect. The amount of $5.24 assumes the shares issued as a stock dividend were outstanding for 6 months. This amount also excludes the stock options.

16.2.12. Starks Corporation has 300,000 shares of common stock outstanding. The only other securities outstanding are 10,000 shares of 9% cumulative preferred stock with detachable warrants (10 warrants per preferred share). Each warrant provides for the purchase of one share of common stock at $72. For the year, net income was $1.6 million. During the year, the average market price of common stock was $125. The price at December 31 was $120. What number of shares should be used to determine diluted earnings per share?

A. 340,000

B. 342,400

C. 357,600

D. 400,000

Answer (B) is correct. *(L. Krueger)*
REQUIRED: The number of shares to be used to determine DEPS.
DISCUSSION: The treasury stock method of accounting for the dilutive effect of call options and warrants issued by the reporting entity assumes they are exercised at the beginning of the period at the exercise price, with the proceeds being used to repurchase shares in the market. The assumed repurchase price is the average market price. Because the $7.2 million of hypothetical proceeds (10,000 shares of preferred × 10 warrants per share × $72 exercise price) can be used to purchase 57,600 shares ($7,200,000 ÷ 125), the DEPS denominator will be 342,400 shares (300,000 common shares outstanding + 100,000 assumed issued upon conversion – 57,600 assumed repurchased).
Answer (A) is incorrect. This figure is based on the 12/31 price of $120. Answer (C) is incorrect. This figure includes the 57,600 shares assumed to be repurchased. Answer (D) is incorrect. This figure does not adjust for treasury stock assumed to have been repurchased.

Questions 16.2.13 through 16.2.15 are based on the following information.

Collins Corp.'s capital structure was as follows:

	December 31	
	Year 4	Year 5
Outstanding shares of stock:		
Common	100,000	100,000
Convertible preferred	10,000	10,000
9% convertible bonds	$1,000,000	$1,000,000

During Year 5, Collins paid dividends of $3 per share on its preferred stock. The preferred shares are convertible into 20,000 shares of common stock, and the 9% bonds are convertible into 30,000 shares of common stock. Assume that the income tax rate is 30%.

16.2.13. If net income for Year 5 is $350,000, Collins should report DEPS as

A. $3.20

B. $2.95

C. $2.92

D. $2.75

Answer (D) is correct. *(CPA, adapted)*

REQUIRED: The DEPS given convertible preferred stock, convertible bonds, and net income of $350,000.

DISCUSSION: Potential common stock is included in the calculation of DEPS if it is dilutive. When two or more issues of potential common stock are outstanding, each issue is considered separately in sequence from the most to the least dilutive. This procedure is necessary because a convertible security may be dilutive on its own but antidilutive when included with other potential common shares in the calculation of DEPS. The incremental effect on EPS determines the degree of dilution. The lower the incremental effect, the more dilutive.

The incremental effect of the convertible preferred stock is $1.50 [($3 preferred dividend × 10,000) ÷ 20,000 potential common shares]. The incremental effect of the convertible debt is $2.10 {[$1,000,000 × 9% × (1.0 − .30)] ÷ 30,000 potential common shares}. Because the $1.50 incremental effect of the convertible preferred is lower, it is the more dilutive, and its incremental effect is compared with BEPS, which equals $3.20 [($350,000 − 30,000) ÷ 100,000]. Because $1.50 is lower than $3.20, the convertible preferred is dilutive and is included in a trial calculation of DEPS. The result is $2.92 [($350,000 − $30,000 + $30,000) ÷ (100,000 + 20,000)]. However, the $2.10 incremental effect of the convertible debt is lower than the $2.92 trial calculation, so the convertible debt is also dilutive and should be included in the calculation of DEPS. Thus, DEPS is $2.75 as indicated below.

$$\frac{\$350,000 - \$30,000 + \$30,000 + \$63,000}{100,000 + 20,000 + 30,000} = \$2.75$$

Answer (A) is incorrect. This amount equals BEPS. Answer (B) is incorrect. This amount excludes the convertible preferred stock. Answer (C) is incorrect. This amount excludes the convertible debt.

16.2.14. If net income for Year 5 is $245,000, Collins should report DEPS as

A. $2.15

B. $2.14

C. $2.05

D. $2.04

Answer (D) is correct. *(Publisher, adapted)*

REQUIRED: The DEPS given convertible preferred stock, convertible debt, and net income of $245,000.

DISCUSSION: The incremental effect of the convertible preferred is $1.50 and of the convertible debt is $2.10. Given net income of $245,000, BEPS equals $2.15 [($245,000 − $30,000) ÷ 100,000]. The $1.50 incremental effect of the convertible preferred stock is lower than BEPS, so it is dilutive and should be included in a trial calculation of DEPS. The result is $2.04 [($245,000 − $30,000 + $30,000) ÷ (100,000 + 20,000)]. Because the $2.10 incremental effect of the convertible debt is higher than $2.04, the convertible debt is antidilutive and should not be included in the DEPS calculation. Thus, DEPS should be reported as $2.04.

Answer (A) is incorrect. This amount equals BEPS. Answer (B) is incorrect. This amount excludes the convertible preferred stock. Answer (C) is incorrect. This amount includes the convertible debt.

16.2.15. If net income for Year 5 is $170,000, Collins should report DEPS as

A. $1.40

B. $1.42

C. $1.56

D. $1.70

Answer (A) is correct. *(Publisher, adapted)*

REQUIRED: The DEPS given convertible preferred stock, convertible debt, and net income of $170,000.

DISCUSSION: Given net income of $170,000, BEPS equals $1.40 [($170,000 − $30,000) ÷ 100,000]. This amount is lower than both the $2.10 incremental effect of the convertible debt and the $1.50 incremental effect of the convertible preferred. Thus, both convertible securities are antidilutive, and Collins should report that DEPS is equal to BEPS. This dual presentation may be displayed on one line of the income statement.

Answer (B) is incorrect. The amount of $1.42 includes the convertible preferred stock. Answer (C) is incorrect. The amount of $1.56 includes the convertible debt. Answer (D) is incorrect. The amount of $1.70 results from not adjusting the $170,000 of net income for the $30,000 of preferred dividends in determining income available to common shareholders.

16.2.16. A firm has basic earnings per share of $1.29. If the tax rate is 30%, which of the following securities would be dilutive?

    A.   Cumulative 8%, $50 par preferred stock.

    B.   Ten percent convertible bonds, issued at par, with each $1,000 bond convertible into 20 shares of common stock.

    C.   Seven percent convertible bonds, issued at par, with each $1,000 bond convertible into 40 shares of common stock.

    D.   Six percent, $100 par cumulative convertible preferred stock, issued at par, with each preferred share convertible into four shares of common stock.

Answer (C) is correct. *(CPA, adapted)*
    REQUIRED: The dilutive securities given BEPS and the tax rate.
    DISCUSSION: The calculation of dilutive EPS (DEPS) gives effect to dilutive potential common shares (e.g., options and convertible securities). Dilution is a reduction in basic EPS (BEPS) resulting from the assumption that (1) convertible securities were converted, (2) options or warrants were exercised, or (3) contingently issuable shares were issued. The conversion of the bonds would eliminate after-tax interest expense per bond of $49 [($1,000 par × 7%) × (1.0 – 30% tax rate)]. (The bonds were issued at par, so amortization of premium or discount does not affect the calculation.) The per-share effect is $1.225 ($49 ÷ 40 shares per bond). Thus, the convertible debt is dilutive ($1.225 < $1.29 BEPS).
    Answer (A) is incorrect. Unless the preferred stock is convertible, it is not dilutive. Nonconvertible preferred shares are not potential common stock and therefore are not considered in the calculation of DEPS. Answer (B) is incorrect. The conversion of the bonds would eliminate after-tax interest expense per bond of $70 [($1,000 par × 10%) × (1.0 – 30% tax rate)]. (The bonds were issued at par, so amortization of premium or discount does not affect the calculation.) The per-share effect is $3.50 ($70 ÷ 20 shares per bond). Thus, the convertible debt is antidilutive ($3.50 > $1.29 BEPS). Answer (D) is incorrect. If the preferred stock is converted, the EPS numerator increases by the dividend savings of $6 ($100 par × 6%) per share of preferred stock (the additional income available to common shareholders). The per-share effect is $1.50 ($6 ÷ 4 common shares per share of preferred stock). Thus, the preferred stock is antidilutive ($1.50 > $1.29 BEPS).

16.2.17. In determining earnings per share, interest expense, net of applicable income taxes, on dilutive convertible debt should be

    A.   Added back to net income for basic earnings per share and ignored for diluted earnings per share.

    B.   Added back to net income for both basic and diluted earnings per share.

    C.   Deducted from net income for diluted earnings per share.

    D.   Added back to net income for diluted earnings per share.

Answer (D) is correct. *(CPA, adapted)*
    REQUIRED: The correct treatment of after-tax interest on dilutive convertible debt.
    DISCUSSION: In accordance with the if-converted method, the diluted earnings per share calculation assumes that dilutive convertible debt is converted into common stock at the beginning of the period or at the time of issuance, if later. Given the assumed conversion, no debt would exist upon which interest could have been paid. Interest is a deduction in arriving at net income. Accordingly, that interest savings, net of tax effect, should be added back to net income in the diluted earnings per share computation.
    Answer (A) is incorrect. The interest, net of tax effect, should be added to the numerator for diluted earnings per share but not for basic earnings per share. Answer (B) is incorrect. The interest, net of tax effect, should be added to the numerator for diluted earnings per share. Answer (C) is incorrect. The interest, net of tax effect, should be added to the numerator for diluted earnings per share.

16.2.18. In computing diluted earnings per share (DEPS), the equivalent number of shares of convertible preferred stock is added as an adjustment to the denominator (number of shares outstanding). If the preferred stock is preferred as to dividends, which amount should be added as an adjustment to the numerator (earnings available to common shareholders)?

    A.   Annual preferred dividend.

    B.   Annual preferred dividend times (1 – the income tax rate).

    C.   Annual preferred dividend times the income tax rate.

    D.   Annual preferred dividend divided by the income tax rate.

Answer (A) is correct. *(CPA, adapted)*
    REQUIRED: The adjustment to the numerator for preferred dividends in the DEPS computation.
    DISCUSSION: If a capital structure has convertible preferred stock with a dilutive effect on DEPS, the "if-converted" method is used. This method assumes the conversion of the preferred stock occurred at the beginning of the accounting period or at issuance, if later. The annual preferred dividend is accordingly added back to earnings available to common shareholders (the numerator of the DEPS ratio).
    Answer (B) is incorrect. The tax rate is not a consideration. The preferred dividend is paid with after-tax dollars; preferred dividends are not tax deductible. Answer (C) is incorrect. The tax rate is not a consideration. The preferred dividend is paid with after-tax dollars; preferred dividends are not tax deductible. Answer (D) is incorrect. The tax rate is not a consideration. The preferred dividend is paid with after-tax dollars; preferred dividends are not tax deductible.

16.2.19. A company's convertible debt securities are both a potential common stock and dilutive in determining earnings per share. What would be the effect of these securities on the calculation of basic earnings per share (BEPS) and dilutive earnings per share (DEPS)?

	BEPS	DEPS
A.	Decrease	Decrease
B.	Increase	No effect
C.	No effect	Decrease
D.	Decrease	Increase

Answer (C) is correct. *(CPA, adapted)*
REQUIRED: The effect of dilutive convertible securities on the calculation of BEPS and DEPS.
DISCUSSION: Securities classified as potential common stock should be included in the computation of the number of common shares outstanding for DEPS if the effect of the inclusion is dilutive. Dilutive potential common stock decreases DEPS. BEPS is not affected by potential common stock.
Answer (A) is incorrect. Dilutive potential common stock has no effect on BEPS. Answer (B) is incorrect. Dilutive potential common stock decreases DEPS and has no effect on BEPS. Answer (D) is incorrect. Dilutive potential common stock decreases DEPS and has no effect on BEPS.

16.2.20. The Fleming Corporation had 200,000 shares of common stock and 10,000 shares of cumulative, 6%, $100 par preferred stock outstanding during the year just ended. The preferred stock is convertible at the rate of three shares of common per share of preferred. For the year, the company had a $30,000 net loss from continuing operations. Fleming should report loss per share for the year of

A. $(.13)

B. $(.15)

C. $(.39)

D. $(.45)

Answer (D) is correct. *(Publisher, adapted)*
REQUIRED: The loss per share given convertible preferred stock outstanding.
DISCUSSION: Potential common stock always has an antidilutive effect if an entity has a loss from continuing operations or a loss from continuing operations available to common shareholders (after an adjustment for preferred dividends). Thus, the loss per share reported should be based on common shares outstanding. When preferred stock is cumulative, the dividend, whether earned or not, is deducted from income from continuing operations and net income or added to any loss for the year in computing earnings or loss, respectively, per share of common stock. When preferred stock is noncumulative, an adjustment is made for dividends declared. If the dividend is cumulative only if earned, no adjustment is necessary except to the extent of available income; that is, the preferred dividends accumulate only to the extent of net income. Accordingly, the loss per share is $(.45) {[$30,000 + 10,000 preferred shares × ($100 × 6%)] ÷ 200,000 shares of common stock}.
Answer (A) is incorrect. This figure includes the convertible preferred stock. Answer (B) is incorrect. This figure does not include the cumulative preferred dividends in the computation. Answer (C) is incorrect. This figure includes 200,000 shares of common stock as preferred stock convertible 3-for-1 into common stock (200,000 ÷ 3 = 66,666) and the 10,000 shares of preferred stock as common stock.

16.2.21. During all of the year just ended, Littlefield, Inc., had outstanding 100,000 shares of common stock and 5,000 shares of noncumulative, $7 preferred stock. Each share of the latter is convertible into three shares of common. For the year, Littlefield had $230,000 income from continuing operations and a $575,000 loss on discontinued operations; no dividends were paid or declared. Littlefield should report diluted earnings (loss) per share (DEPS) for income from continuing operations and for net income (loss), respectively, of

A. $2.30 and $(3.45).

B. $2.00 and $(3.00).

C. $2.19 and $(3.29).

D. $2.26 and $(3.39).

Answer (B) is correct. *(CPA, adapted)*
REQUIRED: The diluted earnings (loss) per share from continuing operations and net income (loss).
DISCUSSION: The noncumulative convertible preferred stock is dilutive because its assumed conversion will have no effect on the DEPS numerator and will increase the denominator by 15,000 (5,000 × 3) shares. DEPS for income from continuing operations is $2.00 ($230,000 ÷ 115,000 shares). Net loss equals the $230,000 income from continuing operations minus the $575,000 loss on discontinued operations, or $345,000. This amount divided by the 115,000 shares results in a diluted net loss per share of $3.00.
NOTE: When a discontinued operation is reported, the control number to establish whether potential common stock are dilutive or antidilutive is BEPS from continuing operations.
Answer (A) is incorrect. The convertible preferred stock is excluded from the calculation of shares outstanding for the year. Answer (C) is incorrect. Each share of preferred stock is convertible into three shares of common stock. Answer (D) is incorrect. The number of shares outstanding is calculated as if three shares of preferred stock were convertible into one share of common stock.

Questions 16.2.22 through 16.2.28 are based on the following information.

Carolina Company is a calendar-year entity with a complex capital structure. Carolina reported a loss on discontinued operations (net of tax) of $1,200,000 in the first quarter when its income before the loss was $1,000,000.

The average market price of Carolina's common stock for the first quarter was $25, the shares outstanding at the beginning of the period equaled 300,000, and 12,000 shares were issued on March 1.

At the beginning of the quarter, Carolina had outstanding $2,000,000 of 5% convertible bonds, with each $1,000 bond convertible into 10 shares of common stock. No bonds were converted.

At the beginning of the quarter, Carolina also had outstanding 120,000 shares of preferred stock paying a dividend of $.10 per share at the end of each quarter and convertible to common stock on a one-to-one basis. Holders of 60,000 shares of preferred stock exercised their conversion privilege on February 1.

Throughout the first quarter, warrants to buy 50,000 shares of Carolina's common stock for $28 per share were outstanding but unexercised. Carolina's tax rate was 30%.

16.2.22. The weighted-average number of shares used to calculate BEPS amounts for the first quarter is

A. 444,000

B. 372,000

C. 344,000

D. 300,000

Answer (C) is correct. *(Publisher, adapted)*
REQUIRED: The weighted-average number of shares used to calculate BEPS amounts for the first quarter.
DISCUSSION: The number of shares outstanding at January 1 was 300,000, 12,000 shares were issued on March 1, and 60,000 shares of preferred stock were converted to 60,000 shares of common stock on February 1. Thus, the weighted-average number of shares used to calculate BEPS amounts for the first quarter is 344,000 {300,000 + [12,000 × (1 ÷ 3)] + [60,000 × (2 ÷ 3)]}.
Answer (A) is incorrect. The adjusted weighted-average number of shares used in the DEPS calculation is 444,000. Answer (B) is incorrect. The total outstanding at March 31 is 372,000. Answer (D) is incorrect. The shares outstanding at January 1 equals 300,000.

16.2.23. The control number for determining whether potential common shares are dilutive or antidilutive is

A. $1,000,000

B. $994,000

C. $(206,000)

D. $(1,200,000)

Answer (B) is correct. *(Publisher, adapted)*
REQUIRED: The control number for determining whether potential common shares are dilutive or antidilutive.
DISCUSSION: GAAP requires that a company use income from continuing operations (income before loss on discontinued operations in this case), adjusted for preferred dividends, as the control number for determining whether potential common shares are dilutive or antidilutive. Hence, the number of potential common shares used in calculating DEPS for income from continuing operations is also used in calculating the other DEPS amounts even if the effect is antidilutive with respect to the corresponding BEPS amounts. However, if the entity has a loss from continuing operations available to common shareholders, no potential common shares are included in the calculation of any DEPS amount. The control number for Carolina is $994,000 {$1,000,000 income before loss on discontinued operations − [(120,000 preferred shares − 60,000 preferred shares converted) × $.10 per share dividend]}.
Answer (A) is incorrect. The amount of $1,000,000 is unadjusted income from continuing operations. Answer (C) is incorrect. The amount of $(206,000) is the net loss available to common shareholders after subtracting the loss on discontinued operations. Answer (D) is incorrect. The amount of $(1,200,000) is the loss on discontinued operations.

16.2.24. BEPS for net income or loss is

A. $2.89

B. $(0.46)

C. $(0.60)

D. $(3.49)

Answer (C) is correct. *(Publisher, adapted)*
REQUIRED: The BEPS for net income or loss.
DISCUSSION: The weighted-average of shares used in the BEPS denominator is 344,000 {300,000 + [12,000 × (1 month ÷ 3 months)] + [60,000 × (2 months ÷ 3 months)]}. The numerator equals income before loss on discontinued operations minus preferred dividends of $6,000 [(120,000 preferred shares − 60,000 preferred shares converted) × $.10] minus the loss on discontinued operations. Thus, the numerator equals $(206,000) [$1,000,000 − $6,000 − $1,200,000]. BEPS for net loss is $(0.60) [$(206,000) ÷ 344,000 shares].
Answer (A) is incorrect. BEPS for income before the loss on discontinued operations is $2.89. Answer (B) is incorrect. This figure uses the denominator of the DEPS calculation. Answer (D) is incorrect. The BEPS amount for the loss on discontinued operations is $(3.49).

16.2.25. The weighted-average number of shares used to calculate DEPS amounts for the first quarter is

A. 444,000
B. 438,000
C. 372,000
D. 344,000

Answer (A) is correct. *(Publisher, adapted)*
REQUIRED: The weighted-average number of shares used to calculate DEPS amounts for the first quarter.
DISCUSSION: The denominator of DEPS equals the weighted-average number of shares used in the BEPS calculation (344,000) plus dilutive potential common shares (assuming the control number is not a loss). The incremental shares from assumed conversion of warrants is zero because they are antidilutive. The $25 market price is less than the $28 exercise price. The assumed conversion of all the preferred shares at the beginning of the quarter results in 80,000 incremental shares {[120,000 shares × (3 ÷ 3)] – [60,000 shares × (2 ÷ 3)]}. The assumed conversion of all the bonds at the beginning of the quarter results in 20,000 incremental shares [($2,000,000 ÷ $1,000 per bond) × 10 common shares per bond]. Consequently, the weighted-average number of shares used to calculate DEPS amounts for the first quarter is 444,000 (344,000 + 0 + 80,000 + 20,000).
Answer (B) is incorrect. This amount assumes the hypothetical exercise of all the warrants at the beginning of the period at a price of $28 and the repurchase of shares using the proceeds at a price of $25. Answer (C) is incorrect. The total outstanding at March 31 is 372,000. Answer (D) is incorrect. The denominator of the BEPS fraction is 344,000.

16.2.26. The difference between BEPS and DEPS for the loss on discontinued operations is

A. $2.89
B. $2.10
C. $.79
D. $.60

Answer (C) is correct. *(Publisher, adapted)*
REQUIRED: The difference between BEPS and DEPS for loss on discontinued operations.
DISCUSSION: BEPS for the loss on discontinued operations is $(3.49) [$(1,200,000) ÷ 344,000], and DEPS is $(2.70) [$(1,200,000) ÷ 444,000 shares].
Answer (A) is incorrect. The BEPS for income before the loss on discontinued operations is $2.89. Answer (B) is incorrect. The difference between DEPS for the loss on discontinued operations and the BEPS for the net loss available to common shareholders after the loss on discontinued operations is $2.10. Answer (D) is incorrect. The BEPS for the net loss available to common shareholders after the loss on discontinued operations is $.60.

16.2.27. DEPS for net income or loss is

A. $2.29
B. $(0.41)
C. $(0.53)
D. $(2.70)

Answer (B) is correct. *(Publisher, adapted)*
REQUIRED: The DEPS for net income or loss.
DISCUSSION: The numerator equals the income available to common shareholders, plus the effect of the assumed conversions, minus the loss on discontinued operations. The denominator equals the weighted-average of shares outstanding plus the dilutive potential common shares. Hence, DEPS for net loss is $(.41) [($994,000 + $23,500 – $1,200,000) ÷ 444,000].
Answer (A) is incorrect. DEPS for income before the loss on discontinued operations is $2.29. Answer (C) is incorrect. This figure is based on the BEPS denominator. Answer (D) is incorrect. DEPS for the loss on discontinued operations is $(2.70).

16.2.28. The effect of assumed conversions on the numerator of the DEPS fraction is

A. $31,000
B. $25,000
C. $23,500
D. $17,500

Answer (C) is correct. *(Publisher, adapted)*
REQUIRED: The effect of assumed conversions on the numerator of the DEPS fraction.
DISCUSSION: If all of the convertible preferred shares are assumed to be converted on January 1, $6,000 of dividends [(120,000 – 60,000) preferred shares × $.10] will not be paid. Furthermore, if the bonds are assumed to be converted on January 1, interest of $17,500 {[$2,000,000 × 5% ÷ 4] × (1.0 – .30 tax rate)} will not be paid. Accordingly, the effect of assumed conversions on the numerator of the DEPS fraction is an addition of $23,500 ($6,000 + $17,500) to the income available to common shareholders.
Answer (A) is incorrect. This amount disregards the tax shield provided by bond interest. Answer (B) is incorrect. This amount equals one quarter's bond interest payment. Answer (D) is incorrect. This amount is the effect of the assumed conversion of the bonds alone.

16.2.29. The if-converted method of computing diluted earnings per share (DEPS) amounts assumes conversion of convertible securities at the

A. Beginning of the earliest period reported (or at time of issuance, if later).

B. Beginning of the earliest period reported (regardless of time of issuance).

C. Middle of the earliest period reported (regardless of time of issuance).

D. End of the earliest period reported (regardless of time of issuance).

Answer (A) is correct. *(CPA, adapted)*
REQUIRED: The conversion assumption underlying the if-converted method.
DISCUSSION: The if-converted method of computing DEPS assumes that convertible securities are included in the determination of DEPS if dilutive. Conversion is assumed to have occurred at the beginning of the earliest period reported or, if the security was issued at a later time, at the date of issuance.
Answer (B) is incorrect. Conversion is assumed at the beginning of the earliest period reported but not regardless of time of issuance. Answer (C) is incorrect. Conversion is assumed at the beginning of the earliest period reported (or at the time of issuance, if later). Answer (D) is incorrect. Conversion is assumed at the beginning of the earliest period reported (or at the time of issuance, if later).

16.2.30. During the current year, Moore Corp. had the following two classes of stock issued and outstanding for the entire year:

- 100,000 shares of common stock, $1 par.
- 1,000 shares of 4% preferred stock, $100 par, convertible share for share into common stock. This stock is cumulative, whether or not earned, and no preferred dividends are in arrears.

Moore's current-year net income was $900,000, and its income tax rate for the year was 30%. Diluted earnings per share (DEPS) for the current year are

A. $9.00

B. $8.96

C. $8.91

D. $8.87

Answer (C) is correct. *(CPA, adapted)*
REQUIRED: The DEPS given convertible preferred stock.
DISCUSSION: DEPS is equal to the amount of earnings available to common shareholders and to holders of dilutive potential common stock, divided by the weighted-average number of shares of common stock and additional common shares that would have been outstanding if dilutive potential common shares had been issued. Dilution is tested by calculating EPS and the incremental effect of the potential common shares on EPS. BEPS equals income available to common shareholders (net income − cumulative preferred dividend) divided by the weighted average of common shares outstanding. Thus, BEPS is $8.96 {[$900,000 NI − (1,000 preferred shares × $100 par × 4%)] ÷ 100,000 common shares}. The incremental effect of the potential common shares equals the preferred dividends added back to the numerator if conversion is assumed divided by the potential common shares, or $4.00 ($4,000 ÷ 1,000). Because $4.00 is less than $8.96, the potential common shares are dilutive. Accordingly, the convertible preferred stock is assumed to be converted at the beginning of the year, and no dividends are deemed to have been paid. The DEPS calculation therefore adds the $4,000 preferred dividend to the BEPS numerator and the 1,000 common shares into which the preferred stock can be converted to the BEPS denominator. DEPS is $8.91 [($896,000 + $4,000) ÷ (100,000 + 1,000)].
Answer (A) is incorrect. Nine dollars is equal to $900,000 net income divided by 100,000 common shares. Answer (B) is incorrect. The amount of $8.96 is equal to BEPS. Answer (D) is incorrect. The amount of $8.87 is equal to $900,000 net income minus the $4,000 preferred dividend, divided by 101,000 shares.

16.2.31. At the beginning of the fiscal year, June 1, Year 3, Piotrowski Corporation had 80,000 shares of common stock outstanding. Also outstanding was $200,000 of 8% convertible bonds that had been issued at $1,000 par. The bonds were convertible into 20,000 shares of common stock; however, no bonds were converted during the year. The company's tax rate is 34%. Piotrowski's net income for the year was $107,000. Diluted earnings per share of Piotrowski common stock for the fiscal year ended May 31, Year 4, was

A. $1.07

B. $1.18

C. $1.23

D. $1.34

Answer (B) is correct. *(CMA, adapted)*
REQUIRED: The DEPS given convertible bonds outstanding.
DISCUSSION: Potential common shares that have a dilutive effect are included in the determination of DEPS. The calculation of DEPS assumes the conversion of the bonds at the beginning of the year, so the assumption is that no interest would be paid. Because bond interest was subtracted in determining net income, the DEPS numerator should be increased by the interest paid (net of tax effect). This after-tax effect was a $10,560 reduction of net income [($200,000 × 8%) × (1.0 − .34 tax rate)]. The denominator of the DEPS calculation is 100,000 shares (80,000 common shares outstanding + 20,000 shares that would be issued if the bonds were converted as of the beginning of the year). Hence, DEPS is equal to $1.18 per share [($107,000 NI + $10,560) ÷ (80,000 + 20,000)]. The convertible bonds are dilutive because their incremental inclusion reduces the corresponding BEPS amount.
Answer (A) is incorrect. The amount of $1.07 fails to adjust the numerator for the interest savings and extra taxes. Answer (C) is incorrect. The amount of $1.23 fails to consider the additional taxes that would have to be paid on the interest savings. Answer (D) is incorrect. The amount of $1.34 equals BEPS.

16.2.32. On June 30, Year 2, Lomond, Inc., issued 20, $10,000, 7% bonds at par. Each bond was convertible into 200 shares of common stock. On January 1, Year 3, 10,000 shares of common stock were outstanding. The bondholders converted all the bonds on July 1, Year 3. The following amounts were reported in Lomond's income statement for the year ended December 31, Year 3:

Revenues	$977,000
Operating expenses	(920,000)
Interest on bonds	(7,000)
Income before income tax	50,000
Income tax at 30%	(15,000)
Net income	$ 35,000

What amount should Lomond report as its Year 3 diluted earnings per share (DEPS)?

A. $2.50

B. $2.85

C. $3.00

D. $3.50

Answer (B) is correct. *(CPA, adapted)*
    REQUIRED: The DEPS given convertible bonds.
    DISCUSSION: DEPS should be calculated even though no potential common shares were outstanding at year end. The reason is that the purpose of DEPS is to measure the performance of the entity over the reporting period while giving effect to all potential common shares that were outstanding during the period. The bonds were converted into 4,000 (20 bonds × 200 shares) shares of common stock on July 1, Year 3. Thus, the weighted-average number of shares of common stock outstanding is 12,000 shares [(10,000 × 12 ÷ 12) + (4,000 × 6 ÷ 12)]. BEPS therefore equals $2.92 ($35,000 net income ÷ 12,000). To determine if the potential common shares are dilutive, their incremental effect on EPS is calculated. This effect is equal to the after-tax interest that would be added back to net income divided by the potential common shares that would be added to the denominator. After-tax interest equals $4,900 [20 shares × $10,000 par value × 7% × (1 – 30% tax rate) × (6 months ÷ 12 months)], and the dilutive potential common shares equal 2,000 [20 bonds × 200 shares × (6 months ÷ 12 months)]. The computation is based on a half-year period because the convertible bonds were outstanding for only 6 months. The incremental effect on EPS of the assumed conversion at the beginning of the year is $2.45 ($4,900 ÷ 2,000 shares). This amount is less than BEPS, so the convertible bonds are dilutive. Thus, DEPS equals $2.85 [($35,000 + $4,900) ÷ (12,000 + 2,000)].
    Answer (A) is incorrect. The amount of $2.50 is based on a numerator of $35,000. Answer (C) is incorrect. The amount of $3.00 is based on a numerator of $42,000 (not net of tax). Answer (D) is incorrect. The amount of $3.50 is based on net income of $35,000 and 10,000 shares.

16.2.33. Bilco had 10,000 shares of common stock outstanding throughout Year 3. There was no potential dilution of earnings per share except that, in Year 2, Bilco agreed to issue 2,000 additional shares of its stock to the former shareholders of an acquired company if the acquired company's earnings for any of the 5 years, Year 3 through Year 8, exceed $5,000. Results of operations for Year 3 were

Net income of Bilco	$10,000
Net income of acquired company	4,000
Consolidated net income	$14,000

Diluted earnings per share for Year 3 on a consolidated basis is

A. $14,000 ÷ 10,000 = $1.40

B. $14,000 ÷ 12,000 = $1.17

C. $15,000 ÷ 10,000 = $1.50

D. $15,000 ÷ 12,000 = $1.25

Answer (A) is correct. *(CPA, adapted)*
    REQUIRED: The consolidated DEPS when contingent shares are outstanding.
    DISCUSSION: If all necessary conditions have not been met at the end of the reporting period, the number of contingently issuable shares included in the DEPS denominator equals the number issuable if the end of the reporting period were the end of the contingency period. Because the acquired company earned only $4,000 for Year 3, no contingent shares would be issued if the end of Year 3 were the end of the contingency period. Thus, the contingent shares are disregarded. DEPS equals BEPS of $1.40 ($14,000 consolidated net income ÷ 10,000 shares issued and outstanding).
    Answer (B) is incorrect. DEPS is calculated using 10,000 common shares outstanding. Answer (C) is incorrect. Consolidated net income of $14,000 is used to calculate DEPS. Answer (D) is incorrect. Consolidated net income of $14,000 is used to calculate DEPS.

16.2.34. The senior accountant for Carlton Co., a public company with a complex capital structure, has just finished preparing Carlton's income statement for the current fiscal year. While reviewing the income statement, Carlton's finance director noticed that the earnings-per-share data has been omitted. What changes will have to be made to Carlton's income statement as a result of the omission of the earnings-per-share data?

A. No changes will have to be made to Carlton's income statement. The income statement is complete without the earnings-per-share data.

B. Carlton's income statement will have to be revised to include the earnings-per-share data.

C. Carlton's income statement will only have to be revised to include the earnings-per-share data if Carlton's market capitalization is greater than $5,000,000.

D. Carlton's income statement will only have to be revised to include the earnings-per-share data if Carlton's net income for the past 2 years was greater than $5,000,000.

Answer (B) is correct. *(CPA, adapted)*
REQUIRED: The change, if any, in the income statement because of omission of EPS data.
DISCUSSION: A public entity must report EPS data on the face of the income statement. A public entity with only common stock outstanding must report basic earnings per share (BEPS) but not diluted earnings per share (DEPS) for income from continuing operations and net income. All other public entities must present BEPS and DEPS for income from continuing operations and net income with equal prominence. A nonpublic entity must follow the guidance for calculation and presentation of EPS only if it elects to report EPS.
Answer (A) is incorrect. A public entity must report EPS data on the face of the income statement. Answer (C) is incorrect. Market capitalization does not affect whether EPS must be disclosed in the income statement. Answer (D) is incorrect. Net income does not affect whether EPS must be disclosed in the income statement.

☑ ≡
☐ ≡   Use **Gleim Test Prep** for interactive study and easy-to-use detailed analytics!
☐ ≡

STUDY UNIT SEVENTEEN
ACCOUNTING FOR INCOME TAXES

The **objectives** of accounting for income taxes are to recognize (1) the amount of taxes currently payable or refundable and (2) deferred tax liabilities and assets for the future tax consequences of events that have been recognized in the financial statements or tax returns. To achieve these objectives, an entity uses the **asset-and-liability** approach to account for (1) income taxes currently payable or deductible and (2) deferred taxes. The main issue is the timing of the recognition of tax expense or benefit (interperiod tax allocation). Intraperiod tax allocation determines where and how tax expense or benefit is presented in the income statement.

QUESTIONS

17.1 Objectives and Principles

17.1.1. Under current generally accepted accounting principles, which approach is used to determine income tax expense?

A. Asset and liability approach.

B. "With and without" approach.

C. Net-of-tax approach.

D. Deferred approach.

Answer (A) is correct. *(CPA, adapted)*

REQUIRED: The current approach used to determine income tax expense.

DISCUSSION: The asset-and-liability approach accrues liabilities or assets (taxes payable or refundable) for the current year. It also recognizes deferred tax amounts for the future tax consequences of events previously recognized in the financial statements or tax returns. These liabilities and assets recognize the effects of temporary differences measured using the tax rate(s) expected to apply when the liabilities and assets are expected to be settled or realized. Accordingly, deferred tax expense (benefit) is determined by the change during the period in the deferred tax assets and liabilities. Income tax expense (benefit) is the sum of current tax expense (benefit), that is, the amount paid or payable, and the deferred tax expense (benefit).

Answer (B) is incorrect. The "with and without" approach was an element of the deferred approach. This guidance stated that the tax effect of a timing difference should "be measured by the differential between income taxes computed with and without inclusion of the transaction creating the difference between taxable income and pretax accounting income." Answer (C) is incorrect. The net-of-tax approach accounts for the effects of taxability or deductibility on assets and liabilities as reductions in their reported amounts. Answer (D) is incorrect. The deferred method determined income tax expense by multiplying pretax financial income by the current tax rate. The difference between taxes payable (refundable) and income tax expense (benefit) was recorded as a deferred credit or charge.

17.2 Temporary and Permanent Differences

17.2.1. When accounting for income taxes, a temporary difference occurs in which of the following scenarios?

- A. An item is included in the calculation of net income but is neither taxable nor deductible.
- B. An item is included in the calculation of net income in one year and in taxable income in a different year.
- C. An item is no longer taxable due to a change in the tax law.
- D. The accrual method of accounting is used.

Answer (B) is correct. *(CPA, adapted)*
REQUIRED: The circumstances resulting in a temporary difference.
DISCUSSION: A temporary difference results when the GAAP basis and the tax basis of an asset or liability differ. The effect is that a taxable or deductible amount will occur in future years when the asset is recovered or the liability is settled. But some temporary differences are not related to an asset or liability for financial reporting. Thus, temporary differences occur when revenues or gains, or expenses or losses, are used to calculate net income under GAAP in a year before or after being used to calculate taxable income.
Answer (A) is incorrect. A permanent difference is an event that is recognized either in pretax financial income or in taxable income, but never in both. It does not result in a deferred tax amount. Answer (C) is incorrect. An item that is no longer taxable results in a permanent difference. Answer (D) is incorrect. The accrual method and the tax basis recognize many items in the same period.

17.2.2. In its income statement for the year just ended, Small Co. reported income before income taxes of $600,000. Small estimated that, because of permanent differences, taxable income for the year would be $560,000. During the year, Small made estimated tax payments of $100,000, which were debited to income tax expense. Small is subject to a 30% tax rate. What amount should Small report as income tax expense?

- A. $68,000
- B. $100,000
- C. $168,000
- D. $180,000

Answer (C) is correct. *(CPA, adapted)*
REQUIRED: The amount to be reported for income tax expense.
DISCUSSION: Income tax expense or benefit is the sum of current tax expense or benefit and deferred tax expense or benefit. A deferred tax expense or benefit is the change in an entity's deferred tax assets and liabilities. However, a permanent difference does not result in a change in a deferred tax asset or liability. Thus, income tax expense equals current income tax expense, which is the amount of taxes paid or payable for the year. Income taxes payable for the year equal $168,000 ($560,000 taxable income × 30%).
Answer (A) is incorrect. The amount of $68,000 equals the $168,000 of income taxes payable minus the $100,000 of income taxes paid. Answer (B) is incorrect. The amount of $100,000 equals income taxes paid, not the total current income tax expense. Answer (D) is incorrect. The amount of $180,000 is equal to the reported income of $600,000 times the tax rate.

17.2.3. Fern Co. has net income, before taxes, of $200,000, including $20,000 interest revenue from municipal bonds and $10,000 paid for officers' life insurance premiums where the company is the beneficiary. The tax rate for the current year is 30%. What is Fern's effective tax rate?

- A. 27.0%
- B. 28.5%
- C. 30.0%
- D. 31.5%

Answer (B) is correct. *(CPA, adapted)*
REQUIRED: The effective tax rate given interest from municipal bonds and payments for officers' life insurance premiums.
DISCUSSION: The municipal bond revenue (nontaxable) and key-person life insurance premiums (an expense that is nondeductible) are permanent differences. Thus, pretax income is adjusted to eliminate both items.

Pretax income	$200,000
Municipal bond income	(20,000)
Life insurance premiums	10,000
Taxable income	$190,000

Assuming no temporary differences and deferred taxes, total income tax expense is $57,000 ($190,000 × 30%). Accordingly, the effective tax rate is 28.5% ($57,000 income tax expense ÷ $200,000 pretax net income).
Answer (A) is incorrect. The amount of 27.0% [($180,000 × 30%) ÷ $200,000] results from treating the insurance premiums as deductible. Answer (C) is incorrect. The amount of 30.0% [($200,000 × 30%) ÷ $200,000] results from treating pretax net income as taxable income. Answer (D) is incorrect. The amount of 31.5% [($210,000 × 30%) ÷ $200,000] results from adding the insurance premiums to pretax income to determine taxable income.

17.2.4. In Year 2, Ajax, Inc., reported taxable income of $400,000 and pretax financial statement income of $300,000. The difference resulted from $60,000 of nondeductible premiums on Ajax's officers' life insurance and $40,000 of rental income received in advance. Rental income is taxable when received. Ajax's effective tax rate is 30%. In its Year 2 income statement, what amount should Ajax report as income tax expense -- current portion?

A. $90,000

B. $102,000

C. $108,000

D. $120,000

Answer (D) is correct. *(CPA, adapted)*
    REQUIRED: The current income tax expense given nondeductible insurance premiums and taxable rent received in advance.
    DISCUSSION: Current income tax expense or benefit is the amount of taxes paid or payable (or refundable) for the year based on enacted tax law applied to taxable income (or excess of deductions over revenues). Thus, current income tax expense is $120,000 ($400,000 × 30%).
    Answer (A) is incorrect. The amount of $90,000 equals the effective tax rate times pretax financial statement income. Answer (B) is incorrect. The amount of $102,000 equals the effective tax rate times the excess of reported taxable income over the nondeductible insurance premiums. Answer (C) is incorrect. The amount of $108,000 equals the effective tax rate times the excess of reported taxable income over rent received in advance.

17.2.5. Temporary differences arise when expenses are deductible for tax purposes

	After They Are Recognized in Financial Income	Before They Are Recognized in Financial Income
A.	No	No
B.	No	Yes
C.	Yes	Yes
D.	Yes	No

Answer (C) is correct. *(CPA, adapted)*
    REQUIRED: The situations in which temporary differences arise.
    DISCUSSION: A temporary difference exists when (1) the reported amount of an asset or liability in the financial statements differs from the tax basis of that asset or liability, and (2) the difference will result in taxable or deductible amounts in future years when the asset is recovered or the liability is settled at its reported amount. A temporary difference may also exist although it cannot be identified with a specific asset or liability recognized for financial reporting purposes. Temporary differences most commonly arise when either expenses or revenues are recognized for tax purposes either earlier or later than in the determination of financial income.

17.2.6. Among the items reported on Cord, Inc.'s income statement for the year ended December 31 were the following:

Compensation expense for a stock option plan	$50,000
Insurance premium on the life of an officer (Cord is the owner and beneficiary.)	25,000

Neither is deductible for tax purposes. Temporary differences amount to

A. $0

B. $25,000

C. $50,000

D. $75,000

Answer (A) is correct. *(CPA, adapted)*
    REQUIRED: The amount of temporary differences.
    DISCUSSION: Expenses for compensation expense for a stock option plan and payment of a premium for life insurance covering a key executive are recognized in the financial statements but are not deductible under the provisions of the federal tax code. Because neither will result in taxable or deductible amounts in future years, they are permanent, not temporary differences.
    Answer (B) is incorrect. The insurance premium on the life of an officer is not deductible for tax purposes. Hence, it also results in a permanent difference. Answer (C) is incorrect. The compensation expense for a stock option plan is not deductible for tax purposes. Hence, it also results in a permanent difference. Answer (D) is incorrect. Neither expense is deductible for tax purposes.

17.2.7. Which one of the following temporary differences will result in a deferred tax asset?

A. Use of the straight-line depreciation method for financial statement purposes and the Modified Accelerated Cost Recovery System (MACRS) for income tax purposes.

B. Installment sale profits accounted for on the accrual basis for financial statement purposes and on a cash basis for income tax purposes.

C. Advance rental receipts accounted for on the accrual basis for financial statement purposes and on a cash basis for tax purposes.

D. Prepaid expenses accounted for on the accrual basis for financial statement purposes and on a cash basis for income tax purposes.

Answer (C) is correct. *(CMA, adapted)*
REQUIRED: The temporary difference that will result in a deferred tax asset.
DISCUSSION: A deferred tax asset records the deferred tax consequences attributable to deductible temporary differences and carryforwards. Advance rental receipts accounted for on the accrual basis for financial statement purposes and on a cash basis for tax purposes result in a deferred tax asset. The financial statements report no income and no related tax expense because the rental payments apply to future periods. The tax return, however, reports the rent as income when the cash is received, and a tax is due in the year of receipt. Because the tax is paid prior to recording the income for financial statement purposes, it represents an asset that will be recognized as an expense when income is finally recorded.
Answer (A) is incorrect. Using accelerated depreciation on the tax return results in a deferred tax liability. Answer (B) is incorrect. Recognizing installment income on the financial statements but not the tax return results in a taxable temporary difference. Answer (D) is incorrect. Recognizing prepaid expenses earlier on the tax return than on the financial statements (a situation akin to the accelerated depreciation of fixed assets) gives rise to a deferred tax liability.

17.2.8. On December 31, Year 3, Thomas Company reported a $150,000 warranty expense in its income statement. The expense was based on actual warranty costs of $30,000 in Year 3 and expected warranty costs of $35,000 in Year 4, $40,000 in Year 5, and $45,000 in Year 6. At December 31, Year 3, deferred taxes should be based on a

A. $120,000 deductible temporary difference.

B. $150,000 deductible temporary difference.

C. $120,000 taxable temporary difference.

D. $150,000 taxable temporary difference.

Answer (A) is correct. *(Publisher, adapted)*
REQUIRED: The taxable (deductible) temporary difference resulting from a warranty expense.
DISCUSSION: At year-end Year 3, Thomas Company should report a $120,000 warranty liability in its balance sheet. The warranty liability is equal to the $150,000 warranty expense minus the $30,000 warranty cost actually incurred in Year 3. Because warranty costs are not deductible until actually incurred, the tax basis of the warranty liability is $0. The result is a $120,000 temporary difference ($120,000 carrying amount – $0 tax basis). When the liability is settled through the actual incurrence of warranty costs, the amounts will be deductible. Thus, the temporary difference should be classified as a deductible temporary difference.
Answer (B) is incorrect. The warranty expense, not the payable, equals $150,000. Answer (C) is incorrect. Warranty costs will result in a deductible amount. Answer (D) is incorrect. The warranty costs will result in a deductible amount, and the $30,000 actual warranty costs are currently deductible.

17.3 Recognition and Measurement of Deferred Income Taxes

17.3.1. West Corp. leased a building and received the $36,000 annual rental payment on June 15, Year 4. The beginning of the lease was July 1, Year 4. Rental income is taxable when received. West's tax rates are 30% for Year 4 and 40% thereafter. West had no other permanent or temporary differences. West determined that no valuation allowance was needed. What amount of deferred tax asset should West report in its December 31, Year 4, balance sheet?

A. $5,400

B. $7,200

C. $10,800

D. $14,400

Answer (B) is correct. *(CPA, adapted)*
REQUIRED: The amount of deferred tax asset reported at year end.
DISCUSSION: The $36,000 rental payment is taxable in full when received in Year 4, but only $18,000 [$36,000 × (6 ÷ 12)] should be recognized in financial accounting income for the year. The result is a deductible temporary difference (deferred tax asset) arising from the difference between the tax basis ($0) of the liability for unearned rent and its reported amount in the year-end balance sheet ($36,000 – $18,000 = $18,000). The income tax payable for Year 4 based on the rental payment is $10,800 ($36,000 × 30% tax rate for Year 4), the deferred tax asset is $7,200 ($18,000 future deductible amount × 40% enacted tax rate applicable after Year 4 when the asset will be realized), and the income tax expense is $3,600 ($10,800 current tax expense – $7,200 deferred tax benefit). The deferred tax benefit equals the net change during the year in the entity's deferred tax liabilities and assets ($7,200 deferred tax asset recognized in Year 4 – $0).
Answer (A) is incorrect. The amount of $5,400 is based on a 30% tax rate. Answer (C) is incorrect. The income tax payable is $10,800. Answer (D) is incorrect. The amount of $14,400 would be the income tax payable if the 40% tax rate applied in Year 4.

17.3.2. Rein, Inc., reported deferred tax assets and deferred tax liabilities at the end of both Year 3 and Year 4. For the year ended in Year 4, Rein should report deferred income tax expense or benefit equal to the

A. Sum of the net changes in deferred tax assets and deferred tax liabilities.

B. Decrease in the deferred tax assets.

C. Increase in the deferred tax liabilities.

D. Amount of the income tax liability plus the sum of the net changes in deferred tax assets and deferred tax liabilities.

Answer (A) is correct. *(CPA, adapted)*
REQUIRED: The method of determining deferred income tax expense or benefit.
DISCUSSION: Deferred tax expense or benefit is the net change during the year in the entity's deferred tax liabilities and assets.
Answer (B) is incorrect. The deferred tax liabilities must also be considered. Answer (C) is incorrect. The deferred tax assets must also be considered. Answer (D) is incorrect. This calculation determines the income tax expense or benefit for the year.

17.3.3. A deferred tax asset must be reduced by a valuation allowance if it is

A. Probable that some portion will not be realized.

B. Reasonably possible that some portion will not be realized.

C. More likely than not that some portion will not be realized.

D. Likely that some portion will not be realized.

Answer (C) is correct. *(Publisher, adapted)*
REQUIRED: The condition for recognizing a valuation allowance for a deferred tax asset.
DISCUSSION: A deferred tax asset shall be reduced by a valuation allowance if the weight of the available evidence, both positive and negative, indicates that it is more likely than not (that is, the probability is greater than 50%) that some portion will not be realized. The allowance should suffice to reduce the deferred tax asset to the amount that is more likely than not to be realized. The effect of a change in the beginning balance resulting from a new judgment about realizability is an item of income from continuing operations.
Answer (A) is incorrect. The FASB specifically rejected the term probable as used in the accounting for contingencies. Answer (B) is incorrect. The FASB believes that the appropriate criterion is the one that produces results that are closest to the expected outcome. A reasonable possibility does not meet that standard. Answer (D) is incorrect. The FASB rejected the term likely (probable).

17.3.4. Deferred tax assets must be reduced by a valuation allowance if, based on the weight of the evidence, it is more likely than not that some portion or all of the deferred tax assets will not be realized. Which of the following kinds of evidence is considered in making this determination?

	Positive Evidence	Negative Evidence
A.	Yes	No
B.	Yes	Yes
C.	No	Yes
D.	No	No

Answer (B) is correct. *(Publisher, adapted)*
REQUIRED: The evidence to be considered in determining whether a valuation allowance should be recognized.
DISCUSSION: In determining whether a valuation allowance is required to reduce deferred tax assets to the amount that is more likely than not to be realized, all available evidence should be considered. Available evidence includes both positive and negative evidence. In considering the relative impact of positive and negative evidence, the weight given to the potential effect of the evidence should be commensurate with the extent to which the evidence can be objectively verified. However, the more negative evidence in existence, the more positive evidence is necessary and the more difficult it is to support a conclusion that a valuation allowance is not necessary.
Answer (A) is incorrect. Negative evidence also should be considered. Answer (C) is incorrect. Positive evidence also should be considered. Answer (D) is incorrect. All available evidence should be considered in determining whether a valuation allowance is required, including both positive and negative evidence.

17.3.5. Stone Co. began operations in the current year and reported $225,000 in income before income taxes for the year. Stone's current year tax depreciation exceeded its book depreciation by $25,000. Stone also had nondeductible book expenses of $10,000 related to permanent differences. Stone's tax rate for the year was 40%, and the enacted rate for subsequent years is 35%. In its December 31 balance sheet, what amount of deferred income tax liability should Stone report?

A. $8,750

B. $10,000

C. $12,250

D. $14,000

Answer (A) is correct. *(CPA, adapted)*
REQUIRED: The deferred income tax liability reported on the balance sheet.
DISCUSSION: In measuring a deferred tax liability or asset, the objective is to use the enacted tax rate(s) expected to apply to taxable income in the periods in which the deferred tax liability or asset is expected to be settled or realized. At 12/31, the only temporary difference is the $25,000 excess of tax depreciation over the book depreciation. This temporary difference will give rise to a $25,000 taxable amount in subsequent years. Given the enacted tax rate of 35% applicable after the current year, the total tax consequence attributable to the taxable temporary difference (the deferred tax liability) is $8,750 ($25,000 × 35%).
Answer (B) is incorrect. The 35% tax rate applicable when the deferred tax liability is expected to be settled should be used. Answer (C) is incorrect. Permanent differences do not create deferred tax liabilities. Answer (D) is incorrect. Permanent differences do not create deferred tax liabilities, and the 35% tax rate applicable when the deferred tax liability is expected to be settled should be used.

17.3.6. Based on its current operating levels, Ellis Corporation estimates that its annual level of taxable income (including reversing temporary differences) in the foreseeable future will be $200,000 annually. Enacted tax rates for the tax jurisdiction in which Ellis operates are 15% for the first $50,000 of taxable income, 25% for the next $50,000 of taxable income, and 35% for taxable income in excess of $100,000. Which tax rate should Ellis use to measure a deferred tax liability or asset?

A. 15%

B. 25%

C. 27.5%

D. 35%

Answer (C) is correct. *(Publisher, adapted)*
REQUIRED: The tax rate applicable to the measurement of a deferred tax liability or asset.
DISCUSSION: In measuring a deferred tax liability or asset, the objective is to use the enacted tax rate(s) expected to apply to taxable income in the periods in which the deferred tax liability or asset is expected to be settled or realized. If graduated tax rates are a significant factor for an entity, the applicable tax rate is the average graduated tax rate applicable to the amount of estimated future annual taxable income. As indicated, the applicable tax rate is 27.5%.

Taxable Income		Tax Rate		
$ 50,000	×	15%	=	$ 7,500
50,000	×	25%	=	12,500
100,000	×	35%	=	35,000
$200,000				$55,000

$55,000 ÷ $200,000 = 27.5%

Answer (A) is incorrect. Fifteen percent is the tax rate for the first $50,000 of income. Answer (B) is incorrect. Twenty-five percent is the tax rate for income over $50,000 but less than $100,000. Answer (D) is incorrect. Thirty-five percent is the tax rate for income over $100,000.

17.3.7. In its Year 3 income statement, Noll Corp. reported depreciation of $400,000. Noll reported depreciation of $550,000 on its Year 3 income tax return. The difference in depreciation is the only temporary difference, and it will reverse equally over the next 3 years. Assume that the enacted income tax rates are 35% for Year 3, 30% for Year 4, and 25% for Year 5 and Year 6. What amount should be included in the deferred income tax liability in Noll's December 31, Year 3, balance sheet?

A. $37,500

B. $40,000

C. $45,000

D. $52,500

Answer (B) is correct. *(CPA, adapted)*
REQUIRED: The amount to be included in the deferred income tax liability at year end.
DISCUSSION: At 12/31/Year 3, the only temporary difference is the $150,000 ($550,000 – $400,000) excess of the tax depreciation over the book depreciation. This temporary difference will give rise to a $50,000 taxable amount in each of the years Year 4 through Year 6. Given the enacted tax rates of 30% in Year 4 and 25% in Year 5 and Year 6, the total tax consequences are $40,000, which is the balance that should be reported in the deferred income tax liability at year end.

Year	Taxable Amount		Enacted Tax Rates		Tax Consequences
4	$50,000	×	30%	=	$15,000
5	50,000	×	25%	=	12,500
6	50,000	×	25%	=	12,500
					$40,000

Answer (A) is incorrect. The amount of $37,500 is based on a 25% tax rate. Answer (C) is incorrect. The amount of $45,000 is based on a 30% tax rate. Answer (D) is incorrect. The amount of $52,500 is based on a 35% tax rate.

17.3.8. Taft Corp. uses the equity method to account for its 25% investment in Flame, Inc. During the year, Taft received dividends of $30,000 from Flame and recorded $180,000 as its equity in the earnings of Flame. All the undistributed earnings of Flame will be distributed as dividends in future periods. The dividends received from Flame are eligible for the 80% dividends received deduction. There are no other temporary differences. Enacted income tax rates are 30% for the current year and thereafter. In its December 31 balance sheet, what amount should Taft report for deferred income tax liability?

- A. $9,000
- B. $10,800
- C. $45,000
- D. $54,000

Answer (A) is correct. *(CPA, adapted)*
REQUIRED: The deferred income tax liability reported on the balance sheet.
DISCUSSION: The deferred tax liability constitutes the "deferred tax consequences attributable to taxable temporary differences. A deferred tax liability is measured using the applicable enacted tax rate and provisions of the enacted tax law." Taft's recognition of $180,000 of equity-based earnings creates a temporary difference that will result in taxable amounts in future periods when dividends are distributed. The deferred tax liability arising from this temporary difference is measured using the 30% enacted tax rate and the dividends received deduction. Accordingly, given that all the undistributed earnings will be distributed, a deferred tax liability of $9,000 [($180,000 equity – $30,000 dividends received) × 20% not deductible × 30% tax rate applicable after the current year] should be reported.
Answer (B) is incorrect. The amount of $10,800 equals 30% of 20% of the equity in the earnings of Flame. Answer (C) is incorrect. The amount of $45,000 is the net increase in Taft's investment in Flame account under the equity method multiplied by the 30% tax rate. Answer (D) is incorrect. The amount of $54,000 equals 30% of $180,000.

17.3.9. Black Co., organized on January 2, Year 1, had pretax accounting income of $500,000 and taxable income of $800,000 for the year ended December 31, Year 1. Black expected to maintain this level of taxable income in future years. The only temporary difference is for accrued product warranty costs, expected to be paid as follows:

Year 2	$100,000
Year 3	50,000
Year 4	50,000
Year 5	100,000

The applicable enacted income tax rate is 30%. In Black's December 31, Year 1, balance sheet, the deferred income tax asset and related valuation allowance should be

	Deferred Tax Asset	Valuation Allowance
A.	$0	$0
B.	$90,000	$90,000
C.	$90,000	$0
D.	$0	$90,000

Answer (C) is correct. *(CPA, adapted)*
REQUIRED: The deferred tax asset and valuation allowance to be recognized.
DISCUSSION: Black should report an accrued product warranty liability of $300,000. The result is a deductible temporary difference of $300,000 because the liability will be settled and related amounts will be tax deductible when the warranty costs are incurred. A deferred tax asset should be measured for deductible temporary differences using the applicable tax rate. Hence, Black should record a $90,000 ($300,000 × 30%) deferred tax asset. A valuation allowance should be used to reduce a deferred tax asset if, based on the weight of the available evidence, it is more likely than not that some portion will not be realized. In this case, Black had taxable income of $800,000 for Year 1 and expects to maintain that level of taxable income in future years. The positive evidence therefore indicates that sufficient taxable income will be available for the future realization of the tax benefit of the existing deductible temporary differences. Given no negative evidence, a valuation allowance is not necessary.
Answer (A) is incorrect. A deferred tax asset but not a valuation allowance should be recognized. Answer (B) is incorrect. A deferred tax asset but not a valuation allowance should be recognized. Answer (D) is incorrect. A deferred tax asset but not a valuation allowance should be recognized.

17.3.10. According to U.S. GAAP, which of the following items should affect current income tax expense for Year 3?

- A. Interest on a Year 1 tax deficiency paid in Year 3.
- B. Penalty on a Year 1 tax deficiency paid in Year 3.
- C. Change in income tax rate for Year 3.
- D. Change in income tax rate for Year 4.

Answer (C) is correct. *(CPA, adapted)*
REQUIRED: The item that affects current income tax expense for Year 3.
DISCUSSION: Current tax expense is the amount of income taxes paid or payable for a year (taxable income × enacted tax rate).
Answer (A) is incorrect. Interest on a Year 1 tax deficiency paid in Year 3 is applicable to Year 1. Answer (B) is incorrect. Penalty on a Year 1 tax deficiency paid in Year 3 is applicable to Year 1. Answer (D) is incorrect. A change in income tax rate for Year 4 would affect the deferred tax expense or benefit for Year 3, assuming scheduled effects of a temporary difference will occur in Year 4.

17.3.11. In preparing its December 31, Year 4, financial statements, Irene Corp. must determine the proper accounting treatment of a $180,000 loss carryforward available to offset future taxable income. There are no temporary differences. The applicable current and future income tax rate is 30%. Available evidence is not conclusive as to the future existence of sufficient taxable income to provide for the future realization of the tax benefit of the $180,000 loss carryforward. However, based on the available evidence, Irene believes that it is more likely than not that future taxable income will be available to provide for the future realization of only $100,000 of this loss carryforward. In its Year 4 statement of financial position, Irene should recognize what amounts?

	Deferred Tax Asset	Valuation Allowance
A.	$0	$0
B.	$30,000	$0
C.	$54,000	$24,000
D.	$54,000	$30,000

Answer (C) is correct. *(Publisher, adapted)*
REQUIRED: The amounts to be recognized as a deferred tax asset and related valuation allowance.
DISCUSSION: The applicable tax rate should be used to measure a deferred tax asset for an operating loss carryforward that is available to offset future taxable income. Irene should therefore recognize a $54,000 ($180,000 × 30%) deferred tax asset. A valuation allowance should be recognized to reduce the deferred tax asset if, based on the weight of the available evidence, the likelihood is more than 50% that some portion or all of a deferred tax asset will not be realized. Based on the available evidence, Irene believes that it is more likely than not that the tax benefit of only $100,000 of the operating loss will be realized. Thus, the company should recognize a $24,000 valuation allowance to reduce the $54,000 deferred tax asset to $30,000 ($100,000 × 30%).
Answer (A) is incorrect. A deferred tax asset equal to $54,000 should be recognized and a valuation allowance should be recognized equal to $24,000 to reduce the deferred tax asset to $30,000. Answer (B) is incorrect. A deferred tax asset of $30,000 results from netting the valuation allowance against the deferred tax asset. Answer (D) is incorrect. This figure is the deferred tax asset, not the valuation allowance, after the two are netted.

17.3.12. Leer Corp.'s pretax income for the current year is $100,000. The temporary differences between amounts reported in the financial statements and the tax return are as follows:

- Depreciation in the financial statements was $8,000 more than tax depreciation.

- The equity method of accounting resulted in financial statement income of $35,000.

- A $25,000 dividend was received from an equity-method investee during the year, which is eligible for the 80% dividends received deduction (DRD).

Leer's effective income tax rate is 30%. In its income statement, Leer should report a current provision for income taxes of

A. $26,400

B. $23,400

C. $21,900

D. $18,600

Answer (B) is correct. *(CPA, adapted)*
REQUIRED: The current provision for income taxes.
DISCUSSION: Current tax expense is the amount of income taxes paid or payable for a year as determined by applying the provisions of the enacted tax law to the taxable income for that year. Pretax accounting income is given as $100,000. Financial statement depreciation exceeds tax depreciation by $8,000. Accounting income includes $35,000 of income determined in accordance with the equity method, but taxable income includes only $5,000 of this amount [$25,000 dividend received – ($25,000 × 80%) dividends received deduction]. The reconciliation of pretax accounting income to taxable income is as follows:

Pretax accounting income		$100,000
Excess of fin. stmt. depreciation		8,000
Untaxed equity method income		(35,000)
Taxable portion of dividend:		
Dividend received	$ 25,000	
Dividends received deduction		
($25,000 × 80%)	(20,000)	5,000
Taxable income		$ 78,000

Accordingly, the current provision for income taxes is $23,400 ($78,000 × 30%).
Answer (A) is incorrect. The amount of $26,400 is based on the assumption that taxable income includes equity-based income minus the 80% DRD. Answer (C) is incorrect. The amount of $21,900 assumes a 100% DRD. Answer (D) is incorrect. The amount of $18,600 results from subtracting, not adding, the excess financial statement depreciation.

Questions 17.3.13 and 17.3.14 are based on the following information. Zeff Co. prepared the following reconciliation of its pretax financial statement income to taxable income for the current year, its first year of operations:

Pretax financial income	$160,000
Nontaxable interest received on municipal securities	(5,000)
Long-term loss accrual in excess of deductible amount	10,000
Depreciation in excess of financial statement amount	(25,000)
Taxable income	$140,000

Zeff's tax rate is 40%.

17.3.13. In its current-year income statement, what amount should Zeff report as income tax expense – current portion?

A. $52,000

B. $56,000

C. $62,000

D. $64,000

Answer (B) is correct. *(CPA, adapted)*
REQUIRED: The current portion of income tax expense.
DISCUSSION: Pretax financial income is adjusted for permanent and temporary differences to arrive at the current taxable income. The current portion of income tax expense equals income taxes paid or payable as determined by applying enacted tax law. Thus, the current portion of income tax expense equals $56,000 ($140,000 × 40% tax rate).
Answer (A) is incorrect. The amount of $52,000 results from using taxable income of $130,000. Answer (C) is incorrect. The amount of $62,000 excludes the temporary differences from consideration. Answer (D) is incorrect. The amount of $64,000 is based on pretax financial income.

17.3.14. In its current-year balance sheet, what should Zeff report as deferred income tax liability?

A. $2,000

B. $4,000

C. $6,000

D. $8,000

Answer (C) is correct. *(CPA, adapted)*
REQUIRED: The amount of deferred income tax liability.
DISCUSSION: A deferred income tax liability arises from a taxable temporary difference. The $10,000 long-term loss accrual (a deductible temporary difference) results in a deferred tax asset. The $25,000 excess depreciation (a taxable temporary difference) results in a deferred tax liability. These items should be netted and presented as a single noncurrent amount. Accordingly, the net deferred tax liability is $6,000 [($25,000 – $10,000) × 40%].
Answer (A) is incorrect. The amount of $2,000 is 40% times the $5,000 permanent difference. Answer (B) is incorrect. The amount of $4,000 equals 40% of the deductible temporary difference. Answer (D) is incorrect. The amount of $8,000 results from combining the temporary differences and the permanent difference (municipal bond interest).

17.4 Additional Income Tax Issues

17.4.1. When a change in the tax law or rates occurs, the effect of the change on a deferred tax liability or asset is

A. Not recognized.

B. Recognized as an adjustment as of the effective date of the change.

C. Recognized as an adjustment as of the enactment date of the change.

D. Recognized as a prior-period adjustment.

Answer (C) is correct. *(Publisher, adapted)*
REQUIRED: The effect on a deferred tax liability or asset of a change in the tax law or rates.
DISCUSSION: When a change in the tax law or rates occurs, the effect of the change on a deferred tax liability or asset is recognized as an adjustment in the period that includes the enactment date of the change. The adjustment is allocated to income from continuing operations.
Answer (A) is incorrect. The change is recognized currently and prospectively. Answer (B) is incorrect. The change is recognized in the period that includes the enactment date. Answer (D) is incorrect. A prior-period adjustment is recognized only as an error correction.

17.4.2. Because Jab Co. uses different methods to depreciate equipment for financial statement and income tax purposes, Jab has temporary differences that will reverse during the next year and add to taxable income. Deferred income taxes that are based on these temporary differences should be classified in Jab's balance sheet as a

A. Contra account to current assets.

B. Contra account to noncurrent assets.

C. Current liability.

D. Noncurrent liability.

Answer (D) is correct. *(CPA, adapted)*
REQUIRED: The classification of deferred income taxes based on temporary differences.
DISCUSSION: These temporary differences arise from use of an accelerated depreciation method for tax purposes. Future taxable amounts reflecting the difference between the tax basis and the reported amount of the asset will result when the reported amount is recovered. Accordingly, Jab must recognize a deferred tax liability to record the tax consequences of these temporary differences. Deferred taxes are classified as noncurrent amounts.
Answer (A) is incorrect. A liability is not shown as an offset to assets and it is not current. Answer (B) is incorrect. A liability is not shown as an offset to assets. Answer (C) is incorrect. Deferred tax liabilities and assets are classified as noncurrent amounts.

17.4.3. At the end of the current year, the tax effects of Scottco's temporary differences were as follows:

	Deferred Tax Assets (Liabilities)	Related Asset Classification
Accelerated tax depreciation	$(150,000)	Noncurrent asset
Additional costs in inventory for tax purposes	50,000	Current asset
	$(100,000)	

A valuation allowance was not considered necessary. Scottco anticipates that $20,000 of the deferred tax liability will reverse next year. In Scottco's current-year balance sheet, what amount should Scottco report as noncurrent deferred tax liability?

A. $80,000

B. $100,000

C. $130,000

D. $150,000

Answer (B) is correct. *(CPA, adapted)*
REQUIRED: The amount of noncurrent deferred tax liability.
DISCUSSION: In the balance sheet, deferred tax liabilities and assets are classified as noncurrent amounts. In addition, deferred tax liabilities and assets and any related valuation allowance are netted and presented as a single noncurrent amount. But they are not netted if they are attributable to different tax jurisdictions.
Answer (A) is incorrect. The amount of $80,000 equals the $100,000 net deferred tax liability minus the $20,000 expected to reverse next year. Answer (C) is incorrect. The amount of $130,000 equals the $150,000 noncurrent deferred tax liability minus the $20,000 expected to reverse next year. Answer (D) is incorrect. The amount of $150,000 is the gross, not net, balance of the noncurrent deferred tax liability.

17.4.4. On September 15, Year 4, the county in which Spirit Company operates enacted changes in the county's tax law. These changes are to become effective on January 1, Year 5. They will have a material effect on the deferred tax amounts that Spirit reported. In which of the following interim and annual financial statements issued by Spirit should the effect of the changes in tax law initially be reported?

A. The interim financial statements for the 3-month period ending September 30, Year 4.

B. The annual financial statements for the year ending December 31, Year 4.

C. The interim financial statements for the 3-month period ending March 31, Year 5.

D. The annual financial statements for the year ending December 31, Year 5.

Answer (A) is correct. *(Publisher, adapted)*
REQUIRED: The financial statements in which the effects of a change in tax law should initially be reported.
DISCUSSION: When a change in the tax law or rates occurs, the effect of the change on a deferred tax liability or asset is recognized as an adjustment in the period that includes the enactment date of the change. The adjustment is allocated to income from continuing operations in the first financial statements issued for the period that includes the enactment date.
Answer (B) is incorrect. The effect should initially be reported in the first statements issued for the period that includes the enactment date. Answer (C) is incorrect. The periods covered include the effective date, not the enactment date. Answer (D) is incorrect. The periods covered include the effective date, not the enactment date.

17.4.5. Which one of the following is true regarding disclosure of income taxes, including deferred taxes?

A. The manner of reporting the tax benefit of an operating loss carryforward or carryback is determined by the source of the income or loss in the current year.

B. The manner of reporting the tax benefit of an operating loss carryforward or carryback is determined by the source of expected future income that will result in realization of a deferred tax asset for an operating loss carryforward from the current year.

C. The tax benefit of an operating loss carryforward or carryback is disclosed only in a note to the financial statements.

D. The tax benefit of an operating loss carryforward or carryback is a component of net tax expense and is not separately disclosed.

Answer (A) is correct. *(CMA, adapted)*
REQUIRED: The true statement about disclosures relating to income taxes.
DISCUSSION: With certain exceptions, the tax benefit of an operating loss carryforward is reported in the same manner as the source of the income offset by the carryforward in the current year. Similarly, the tax benefit of an operating loss carryback is reported in the same manner as the source of the current-year loss.
Answer (B) is incorrect. The manner of reporting is controlled by the source of the income or loss in the current year. Answer (C) is incorrect. The tax benefit is recorded. Answer (D) is incorrect. Operating loss carryforwards and carrybacks should be separately disclosed.

17.4.6. Which of the following should be disclosed in an entity's financial statements related to deferred taxes?

I. The types and amounts of existing temporary differences.

II. The types and amounts of existing permanent differences.

III. The nature and amount of each type of operating loss and tax credit carryforward.

A. I and II only.

B. I and III only.

C. II and III only.

D. I, II, and III.

Answer (B) is correct. *(CPA, adapted)*
REQUIRED: The necessary disclosures about deferred taxes.
DISCUSSION: A public entity discloses the tax effects of each type of temporary difference and carryforward resulting in a significant deferred tax amount. A nonpublic entity makes the same disclosures but may omit the tax effects. Other required disclosures include the amounts and expiration dates of operating loss and tax credit carryforwards for tax purposes. No disclosure is required about the types and amounts of existing permanent differences.

17.4.7. Intraperiod income tax allocation arises because

A. Items included in the determination of taxable income may be presented in different sections of the financial statements.

B. Income taxes must be allocated between current and future periods.

C. Certain revenues and expenses appear in the financial statements either before or after they are included in taxable income.

D. Certain revenues and expenses appear in the financial statements but are excluded from taxable income.

Answer (A) is correct. *(CPA, adapted)*
REQUIRED: The accounting reason for intraperiod allocation of income taxes.
DISCUSSION: To provide a fair presentation, GAAP require that income tax expense for the period be allocated among continuing operations, discontinued operations, other comprehensive income, and items debited or credited directly to equity.
Answer (B) is incorrect. Allocation among periods is interperiod tax allocation. Answer (C) is incorrect. Differences in the timing of revenues and expenses for financial statement and tax return purposes create the need for interperiod income tax allocation. Answer (D) is incorrect. Permanent differences do not create a need for tax allocation.

17.4.8. Last year, before providing for taxes, Dixon Company had income from continuing operations of $930,000 and a gain on a discontinued operation of $104,000. The current effective tax rate on continuing operations income was 40% and the total tax liability was $398,000 ignoring any temporary differences. The amount of the gain on a discontinued operation net of tax effect was

A. $41,600

B. $62,400

C. $78,000

D. $104,000

Answer (C) is correct. *(Publisher, adapted)*
REQUIRED: The amount of gain on a discontinued operation net of the tax effect.
DISCUSSION: Given that the effective tax rate for continuing operations was 40%, the related tax expense was $372,000 ($930,000 × 40%). Because the total tax liability was $398,000, $26,000 ($398,000 – $372,000) was applicable to the gain on a discontinued operation. Accordingly, the gain on a discontinued operation net of tax effect was $78,000 ($104,000 – $26,000).
Answer (A) is incorrect. The amount of $41,600 results from multiplying the gain on a discontinued operation times the effective tax rate. Answer (B) is incorrect. The amount of $62,400 equals the gain on a discontinued operation minus the effective tax rate on continuing operations times the gain on a discontinued operation. Answer (D) is incorrect. The amount of $104,000 results from not accounting for the tax effect.

17.5 IFRS

17.5.1. Under IFRS, a deferred tax asset is

A. Required to be reduced by a valuation allowance if it is more likely than not that some portion will not be realized.

B. Measured by applying the tax rates effective when the asset is realized.

C. Recognized to the extent that realization is probable.

D. Recognized to reflect the deferred tax consequences of a taxable temporary difference.

Answer (C) is correct. *(Publisher, adapted)*
REQUIRED: The amount recorded for a deferred tax asset.
DISCUSSION: Under IFRS, a deferred tax asset is recognized for most deductible TDs and for the carryforward of unused tax losses and credits, but only to the extent it is probable that taxable profit will be available to permit the use of those amounts. Probable means more likely than not. Thus, no valuation allowance is separately recognized under IFRS.
Answer (A) is incorrect. Under U.S. GAAP, a deferred tax asset is reduced by a credit to a separate valuation allowance. This credit equals the amount needed to reduce the asset to the amount more likely than not (the probability exceeds 50%) to be realized. Under IFRS, the presentation of a separate allowance is not necessary. Instead, the deferred tax asset is recognized to the extent it is probable that taxable profit will be available against which tax deductions may be taken. Answer (B) is incorrect. According to IAS 12, deferred tax assets and liabilities ordinarily are measured using the tax rates that (1) have been enacted or substantively enacted as of the end of the reporting period and (2) apply when the asset is realized or the liability is settled. Thus, a tax rate effective when the asset is realized may not have been enacted or substantively enacted as of the end of the reporting period. Answer (D) is incorrect. A deferred tax liability is recognized to reflect the deferred tax consequences of a taxable temporary difference.

☑ ≡
□ ≡   Use **Gleim Test Prep** for interactive study and easy-to-use detailed analytics!
□ ≡

STUDY UNIT EIGHTEEN
ACCOUNTING CHANGES AND ERROR CORRECTIONS

If financial information is to have the qualities of comparability and consistency, entities must not make voluntary changes in accounting principles unless they can be justified as preferable. An **accounting change** is a change in (1) an accounting principle, (2) an accounting estimate, or (3) the reporting entity. Changes in principle or in the reporting entity are accounted for **retrospectively**. Changes in estimate are accounted for only in the period of change and in future periods. An accounting change does not include a correction of an accounting error in previously issued financial statements. Correction of **errors** in prior statements results from (1) a mathematical mistake, (2) a mistake in the application of GAAP, or (3) an oversight or misuse of facts existing when the statements were prepared. Error corrections are accounted for by restating prior-period statements.

Questions about this topic most often relate to (1) describing the accounting, (2) calculating the requested amounts, or (3) choosing the correct journal entries. Determining whether application should be prospective or retrospective is crucial.

QUESTIONS

18.1 Changes in Accounting Principle or the Reporting Entity

18.1.1. Which of the following transactions should be classified as an accounting change?

I. Change from a previously generally accepted accounting principle to a new accounting principle.

II. Change from an accounting principle not generally accepted to a generally accepted accounting principle.

III. Change in the percentage used to determine an allowance for uncollectible accounts.

  A. I, II, and III.

  B. I and II only.

  C. I and III only.

  D. II and III only.

Answer (C) is correct. *(Publisher, adapted)*
REQUIRED: The transactions properly classified as accounting changes.
DISCUSSION: An accounting change is a change in an accounting principle, an accounting estimate, or the reporting entity. A correction of an error in previously issued financial statements is not an accounting change. A transition to newly prescribed guidance is a change in accounting principle. A change from an accounting principle not generally accepted to one that is generally accepted is a correction of an accounting error. A change in the percentage used to determine an allowance for uncollectible accounts is a change in estimate.
Answer (A) is incorrect. A correction of an error is not an accounting change. Answer (B) is incorrect. A change in the percentage used to determine an allowance for uncollectible accounts is a change in accounting estimate. Furthermore, the change from an accounting principle not generally accepted to a generally accepted accounting principle is a correction of an error. Answer (D) is incorrect. A change from a previously generally accepted accounting principle to a new accounting principle is a change in accounting principle. Furthermore, the change from an accounting principle not generally accepted to a generally accepted accounting principle is a correction of an error.

18.1.2. For which of the following justified changes should previously issued financial statements be adjusted to report the effects of a newly adopted accounting principle as if the new principle had always been used?

A. A change from an accelerated method of depreciation of productive assets to the straight-line method.

B. A change from the weighted-average method of inventory measurement to the FIFO method.

C. A change in the percentages used to determine warranty expense.

D. Adoption of an accounting principle to account for a transaction clearly different in substance from previously occurring transactions.

Answer (B) is correct. *(Publisher, adapted)*
REQUIRED: The change that results in a retrospective adjustment.
DISCUSSION: Retrospective application changes previously issued financial statements to report the effects of a newly adopted accounting principle as if the new principle had always been used. It is required for all direct effects and the related income tax effects of a change in accounting principle, such as a change in inventory measurement methods, unless it is impracticable to determine either the cumulative effect or the period-specific effects of the change. An accounting principle is changed (1) to account for transition to a newly issued official pronouncement (unless the pronouncement prescribes a different method) or (2) when the entity justifies the change on the basis that it is preferable.
Answer (A) is incorrect. A change from an accelerated method of depreciation of productive assets to the straight-line method is a change in accounting estimate effected by a change in accounting principle. Answer (C) is incorrect. A change in the percentages used to determine warranty expense is a change in accounting estimate. Answer (D) is incorrect. The adoption of an accounting principle to account for a transaction clearly different in substance from previously occurring transactions is not considered a change in accounting principle.

18.1.3. When reporting a change in accounting principle, the usual approach is to report the change

A. Prospectively, in the period of change and future periods affected by the change.

B. As a cumulative effect included in net income of the period of change.

C. By retrospective application to previously issued financial statements to report the effects of the new principle.

D. As a cumulative effect included in net income of the period of change and prospective application in future periods.

Answer (C) is correct. *(CMA, adapted)*
REQUIRED: The accounting for a change in accounting principle.
DISCUSSION: A change in accounting principle is applied retrospectively to previously issued financial statements unless it is impracticable to determine either the cumulative effect or the period-specific effects of the change. However, a newly issued official pronouncement may prescribe a different transition method.
Answer (A) is incorrect. Application is prospective for changes in estimate, not changes in principle. Answer (B) is incorrect. Including the cumulative effect of a change in accounting principle in net income in the period of the change is not the generally accepted method of accounting for a change in principle. Answer (D) is incorrect. Retrospective application is required.

18.1.4. The general presumption in preparing financial statements in accordance with generally accepted accounting principles is that

A. A change in accounting principle is permissible if the entity is able to justify the new principle as preferable to the existing principle.

B. A change in accounting principle is permissible only to correct the effect of an error in previously issued financial statements.

C. A change in previously issued financial statements is never permissible.

D. A change in accounting principle is permissible only when a newly issued official pronouncement requires a change in accounting principle.

Answer (A) is correct. *(Publisher, adapted)*
REQUIRED: The general presumption regarding when changes to previously issued financial statements are permitted.
DISCUSSION: The general presumption in preparing financial statements in accordance with GAAP is that an accounting principle once adopted must be applied on a consistent basis. However, a change in principle is appropriate if the change is required by a newly issued official pronouncement, or the entity is able to justify the new principle as preferable to the existing principle. In addition, when an error is discovered, the error must be corrected by a restatement of all periods presented.
Answer (B) is incorrect. Correction of an error is not a change in accounting principle. Answer (C) is incorrect. A change in accounting principle may be justified, and a correction of an error is required. Answer (D) is incorrect. An accounting principle also may be changed if it can be justified as preferable.

18.1.5. J. Will Company has justifiably changed its method of accounting for inventory. Retrospective application of the change is practicable. The cumulative effect on all prior periods of changing to the new accounting principle is included in the first period reported as an adjustment of

A. Retained earnings at the end of the year.

B. Retained earnings at the beginning of the year.

C. Net income.

D. Comprehensive income.

Answer (B) is correct. *(Publisher, adapted)*
REQUIRED: The proper accounting for the cumulative effect of a change in accounting principle.
DISCUSSION: A change in accounting principle is accounted for by retrospective application unless it is impracticable to determine either the cumulative effect or the period-specific effects of the change. Furthermore, a newly issued official pronouncement may prescribe a different transition method. Retrospective application changes previously issued financial statements to report the effects of the newly adopted principle as if it had always been used. Retrospective application requires that the carrying amounts of assets, liabilities, and retained earnings at the beginning of the first period reported be adjusted for the cumulative effect of the new principle on periods prior to the first period reported. Moreover, all periods reported must be individually adjusted for the period-specific effects of applying the new principle.
Answer (A) is incorrect. Retained earnings at the beginning of the first period reported is adjusted. Answer (C) is incorrect. Net income is adjusted for the period-specific effects. Answer (D) is incorrect. Comprehensive income is adjusted for the period-specific effects.

18.1.6. Retrospective application of a change in accounting principle is impracticable when

I.   The costs of applying the new accounting principle to prior period financial statements are material.

II. Retrospective application requires that management's intent in a prior period be assumed without independent substantiation.

A. I only.

B. II only.

C. Both I and II.

D. Neither I nor II.

Answer (B) is correct. *(Publisher, adapted)*
REQUIRED: The condition(s) indicating that retrospective application is impracticable.
DISCUSSION: Retrospective application of a change in an accounting principle is deemed to be impracticable when (1) the entity cannot apply the new principle after making every reasonable effort; (2) assumptions about management's intent in a prior period are required that cannot be independently substantiated; or (3) significant estimates are required, and it is not possible to obtain objective evidence (a) about circumstances existing when amounts would have been recognized, measured, or disclosed and (b) that would have been available when the prior statements were issued.
Answer (A) is incorrect. Retrospective application requires that management's intent in a prior period be assumed without any independent substantiation. But whether the costs of applying the new accounting principle to prior period financial statements are material is not considered in determining impracticability. Answer (C) is incorrect. Cost is not a condition of impracticability. Answer (D) is incorrect. Retrospective application is deemed to be impracticable when management's intent in a prior period must be assumed without independent substantiation.

18.1.7. Volga Co. included a foreign subsidiary in its Year 6 consolidated financial statements. The subsidiary was acquired in Year 4 and was excluded from previous consolidations. The change was caused by the elimination of foreign currency controls. Including the subsidiary in the Year 6 consolidated financial statements results in an accounting change that should be reported

A. By note disclosure only.

B. Currently and prospectively.

C. Currently with note disclosure of pro forma effects of retrospective application.

D. By retrospective application to the financial statements of all prior periods presented.

Answer (D) is correct. *(CPA, adapted)*
REQUIRED: The reporting of the change in the subsidiaries included in consolidated financial statements.
DISCUSSION: A change in the reporting entity requires retrospective application to all prior periods presented to report information for the new entity. The following are changes in the reporting entity: (1) presenting consolidated or combined statements in place of statements of individual entities, (2) changing the specific subsidiaries included in the group for which consolidated statements are presented, and (3) changing the entities included in combined statements.
Answer (A) is incorrect. The change requires recognition in the financial statements. Answer (B) is incorrect. A change in reporting entity requires retrospective application. Answer (C) is incorrect. The change must apply to the financial statements for all periods presented.

18.1.8. P. Werner and Co. has made a justifiable change in an accounting principle. The cumulative effect of applying the change to all prior periods is determinable. However, it is not practicable to determine the period-specific effects on all prior periods presented. Consequently, the reported carrying amounts of the assets and liabilities must be adjusted for the cumulative effect of applying the new principle at the

A. Beginning of the earliest accounting period presented to which the new principle can be applied.

B. End of the latest accounting period presented for which retrospective application is impracticable.

C. Beginning of the current accounting period.

D. Beginning of the earliest accounting period presented.

Answer (A) is correct. *(Publisher, adapted)*
REQUIRED: The accounting when period-specific effects are not determinable.
DISCUSSION: When it is impracticable to determine the cumulative effect of applying a change in principle to any prior period, it must be applied prospectively at the earliest date practicable. However, it may be practicable to determine the cumulative effect but impracticable to determine the period-specific effects on all prior periods presented. In this case, cumulative effect adjustments must be made to the reported carrying amounts of assets and liabilities at the beginning of the earliest period to which the new principle can be applied. An offsetting adjustment also may need to be made to beginning retained earnings.
Answer (B) is incorrect. Cumulative-effect adjustments must be made at the beginning of the earliest accounting period presented to which the new principle can be applied. Answer (C) is incorrect. The adjustments must be made at the beginning of the current accounting period, not for any prior period applied, but only if it is the earliest period to which the new principle can be applied. Answer (D) is incorrect. The adjustments must be made at the beginning of the earliest accounting period presented when it is practicable to determine the cumulative effect on all prior periods and the period-specific effects on all prior periods presented.

18.1.9. JKC is a calendar year firm that changed its method for measuring inventory from FIFO to LIFO on January 1. Records of inventory purchases and sales were not available for certain earlier years of its existence. Thus, it was impracticable for JKC to determine the cumulative effect of applying the change in principle retrospectively. If records are available for recent years, JKC should prospectively apply LIFO at the

A. End of the latest accounting period presented for which retrospective application is impracticable.

B. Beginning of the earliest accounting period presented for which retrospective application is practicable.

C. Beginning of the current accounting period.

D. Earliest date practicable.

Answer (D) is correct. *(Publisher, adapted)*
REQUIRED: The accounting for a change in accounting principle.
DISCUSSION: When it is impracticable to determine the cumulative effect of applying a new accounting principle to any prior period, it should be applied prospectively at the earliest date practicable. For example, if JKC has all the required information for applying LIFO beginning with January 1, it will carry forward the prior year's FIFO ending inventory balance. It will then begin using LIFO on January 1 of the current year.
Answer (A) is incorrect. When it is impracticable to determine the cumulative effect of a change in accounting principle on any prior period, the change should be applied prospectively at the earliest date practicable. Answer (B) is incorrect. When it is impracticable to determine the cumulative effect of a change in accounting principle on any prior period, the change should be applied prospectively at the earliest date practicable. Answer (C) is incorrect. When it is impracticable to determine the cumulative effect of a change in accounting principle on any prior period, the change should be applied prospectively at the earliest date practicable.

Questions 18.1.10 through 18.1.12 are based on the following information. Loire Co., a calendar year-end firm, has used the FIFO method of inventory measurement since it began operations in Year 3. Loire changed to the weighted-average method for determining inventory costs at the beginning of Year 6. Justification for this change was that it better reflected inventory flow. The following schedule shows year-end inventory balances under the FIFO and weighted-average methods:

Year	FIFO	Weighted-Average
Year 3	$ 90,000	$108,000
Year 4	156,000	142,000
Year 5	166,000	150,000

In its Year 6 financial statements, Loire included comparative statements for both Year 5 and Year 4.

18.1.10. What adjustment, before taxes, should Loire make retrospectively to the balance reported for retained earnings at the beginning of Year 4?

A. $18,000 increase.

B. $18,000 decrease.

C. $4,000 increase.

D. $0.

Answer (A) is correct. *(CPA, adapted)*
REQUIRED: The pretax retrospective adjustment to retained earnings as of the beginning of the first period reported.
DISCUSSION: Retrospective application requires that the carrying amounts of assets, liabilities, and retained earnings as of the beginning of the first period reported be adjusted for the cumulative effect of the new accounting principle on periods prior to the first period reported. Moreover, all periods reported must be individually adjusted for the period-specific effects of applying the new principle. The pretax cumulative-effect adjustment to retained earnings reported at the beginning of Year 4 is equal to the $18,000 increase ($108,000 – $90,000) in inventory. If the weighted-average method had been applied in the first year of operations (Year 3), cost of goods sold would have been $18,000 lower. Pretax net income and ending retained earnings for Year 3 and beginning retained earnings for Year 4 would have been $18,000 greater.
Answer (B) is incorrect. Beginning retained earnings as of the beginning of the first period reported (Year 4) is increased. Ending inventory would have been higher and cost of goods sold lower for Year 3. Answer (C) is incorrect. The amount of $4,000 is equal to the difference between FIFO and weighted-average inventory amounts at December 31, Year 3, minus the difference at December 31, Year 4. Answer (D) is incorrect. A cumulative-effect adjustment should be recorded.

18.1.11. What amount should Loire report as inventory in its financial statements for the year ended December 31, Year 4, presented for comparative purposes?

A. $90,000

B. $108,000

C. $142,000

D. $156,000

Answer (C) is correct. *(Publisher, adapted)*
REQUIRED: The amount to be reported as inventory at December 31, Year 4.
DISCUSSION: Retrospective application results in changing previously issued financial statements to reflect the direct effects of the newly adopted accounting principle as if it had always been used. Retrospective application requires that the carrying amounts of assets, liabilities, and retained earnings as of the beginning of the first period reported be adjusted for the cumulative effect of the new principle on periods prior to the first period reported. Moreover, all periods reported must be individually adjusted for the period-specific effects of applying the new principle. Thus, the December 31, Year 4, inventory following the retrospective adjustment should be reported as the weighted-average amount of $142,000.
Answer (A) is incorrect. The FIFO amount at December 31, Year 3, is $90,000. Answer (B) is incorrect. The weighted-average amount at December 31, Year 3, is $108,000. Answer (D) is incorrect. The FIFO amount at December 31, Year 4, is 156,000.

18.1.12. By what amount should cost of sales be retrospectively adjusted for the year ended December 31, Year 5?

A. $0.

B. $2,000 increase.

C. $14,000 increase.

D. $16,000 increase.

Answer (B) is correct. *(Publisher, adapted)*
REQUIRED: The retrospective adjustment to cost of sales for the year ended December 31, Year 5.
DISCUSSION: Retrospective application changes previously issued financial statements to reflect the direct effects of the newly adopted principle as if it had always been used. Retrospective application requires that all periods reported be individually adjusted for the period-specific effects of applying the new principle. Cost of sales equals beginning inventory, plus purchases, minus ending inventory. Purchases are the same under FIFO and weighted average. Thus, the retrospective adjustment to cost of sales is equal to the change in beginning inventory resulting from the change from FIFO to weighted average minus the change in ending inventory. This adjustment equals an increase in cost of sales of $2,000 [($156,000 – $142,000) – ($166,000 – $150,000)].
Answer (A) is incorrect. Period-specific adjustments are required. Answer (C) is incorrect. The difference between FIFO and weighted-average inventory amounts at December 31, Year 4, is $14,000. Answer (D) is incorrect. The difference between FIFO and weighted-average inventory amounts at December 31, Year 5, is $16,000.

18.1.13. When the SBW Co. began business, it included such indirect costs of manufacturing as janitorial expenses, depreciation of machinery, and insurance on the factory building as inventory costs. At the beginning of the current year, SBW began expensing all insurance costs when they are incurred. SBW must justify and disclose the reason for the change. The most appropriate reason is that the new principle

    A. Constitutes an improvement in financial reporting.

    B. Has been and continues to be the treatment used for tax purposes.

    C. Is easier to apply because no assumptions about allocation must be made.

    D. Is one used by the entity for insurance costs other than those on factory-related activities.

Answer (A) is correct. *(Publisher, adapted)*
    REQUIRED: The most appropriate reason for making a change in accounting principle.
    DISCUSSION: The presumption is that, once adopted, an accounting principle should not be changed in accounting for events and transactions of a similar type. This presumption in favor of continuity may be overcome if the entity justifies the use of an alternative acceptable principle. The new principle should be preferable because it constitutes an improvement in financial reporting.
    Answer (B) is incorrect. It does not constitute sufficient justification. Answer (C) is incorrect. It does not constitute sufficient justification. Answer (D) is incorrect. It does not constitute sufficient justification.

18.2 Changes in Accounting Estimates

18.2.1. How should the effect of a change in accounting estimate be accounted for?

    A. By retrospectively applying the change to amounts reported in financial statements of prior periods.

    B. By reporting pro forma amounts for prior periods.

    C. As a prior-period adjustment to beginning retained earnings.

    D. By prospectively applying the change to current and future periods.

Answer (D) is correct. *(CPA, adapted)*
    REQUIRED: The accounting for the effect of a change in accounting estimate.
    DISCUSSION: The effect of a change in accounting estimate is accounted for in the period of change, if the change affects that period only, or in the period of change and future periods, if the change affects both. For a change in accounting estimate, the entity may not (1) restate or retrospectively adjust prior-period statements or (2) report pro forma amounts for prior periods.
    Answer (A) is incorrect. Retrospective application is required for a change in reporting entity. Answer (B) is incorrect. Retrospective application is required for a change in reporting entity. Answer (C) is incorrect. Retrospective application is required for a change in reporting entity. Disclosure of pro forma amounts is also not permitted.

18.2.2. For Year 1, Pac Co. has a standard assurance-type warranty on its equipment. It estimated its 2-year equipment warranty costs based on $100 per unit sold in Year 1. Experience during Year 2 indicated that the estimate should have been based on $110 per unit. The effect of this $10 difference from the estimate is reported

    A. In Year 2 income from continuing operations.

    B. As a cumulative amount, net of tax, below Year 2 income from continuing operations.

    C. As an accounting change retrospectively applied to the Year 1 financial statements.

    D. As a correction of an error requiring Year 1 financial statements to be restated.

Answer (A) is correct. *(CPA, adapted)*
    REQUIRED: The proper accounting for a change in estimate.
    DISCUSSION: The effect of a change in accounting estimate is accounted for prospectively, in the period of change, if the change affects that period only, or in the period of change and in future periods, if the change affects both. A change in warranty costs is considered a change in estimate and not the correction of an error. Thus, it affects current and future income from continuing operations.
    Answer (B) is incorrect. Neither a change in accounting principle nor a change in estimate is accounted for as a cumulative-effect adjustment in a separate caption of the current income statement. Answer (C) is incorrect. A change in estimate is not reported retrospectively. Answer (D) is incorrect. A change in estimate is not considered a correction of an error.

18.2.3. On July 1, Year 1, Rey Corp. purchased computer equipment at a cost of $360,000. This equipment was estimated to have a 6-year life with no residual value and was depreciated by the straight-line method. On January 3, Year 4, Rey determined that this equipment could no longer process data efficiently, that its value had been permanently impaired, and that $70,000 could be recovered over the remaining useful life of the equipment. What carrying amount should Rey report on its December 31, Year 4, balance sheet for this equipment?

A. $0

B. $50,000

C. $70,000

D. $150,000

Answer (B) is correct. *(CPA, adapted)*
    REQUIRED: The carrying amount following a change in estimate.
    DISCUSSION: At 1/3/Year 4, the carrying amount of the computer equipment should be written down to $70,000. This $70,000 is expected to be recovered over the 3.5-year remaining useful life of the equipment. Under the straight-line method, the depreciation expense for the year ending 12/31/Year 4 is $20,000 [($70,000 ÷ 42 months) × 12 months]. Thus, the carrying amount in the year-end balance sheet should be $50,000 ($70,000 – $20,000).
    Answer (A) is incorrect. The computer should have a carrying amount of $50,000. Answer (C) is incorrect. For Year 4, $20,000 of depreciation must be taken on the asset. Answer (D) is incorrect. The amount of $150,000 reflects continued depreciation based on the original assumptions.

18.2.4. Ali Co. bought a machine on January 1, Year 1, for $24,000, at which time it had an estimated useful life of 8 years, with no residual value. Straight-line depreciation is used for all of Ali's depreciable assets. On January 1, Year 3, the machine's estimated useful life was determined to be only 6 years from the acquisition date. Accordingly, the appropriate accounting change was made in Year 3. The direct effects of this change were limited to the effect on depreciation and the related provision for income tax. Ali's income tax rate was 40% in all the affected years. In Ali's Year 3 financial statements, how much should be reported as the cumulative effect on prior years because of the change in the estimated useful life of the machine?

A. $0

B. $1,200

C. $2,000

D. $2,700

Answer (A) is correct. *(CPA, adapted)*
    REQUIRED: The proper accounting for a change in estimate.
    DISCUSSION: An adjustment arising from a revision in an asset's estimated useful life is a change in accounting estimate that should be accounted for on a prospective basis. The remaining depreciable base should be allocated over the revised remaining life with no adjustment to the depreciation accumulated at the time of the change. Because no retrospective adjustment is made, the cumulative effect on prior years is $0. The remaining depreciable base of $18,000 ($24,000 cost – $6,000 accumulated depreciation based on the original 8-year life) is allocated over the remaining expected life at $4,500 per year ($18,000 ÷ 4).
    Answer (B) is incorrect. The total depreciation expense for Years 1 and 2, net of tax, for a 6-year useful life minus the amount for an 8-year life is $1,200. Answer (C) is incorrect. The total pretax depreciation for Years 1 and 2 for a 6-year useful life minus the amount for an 8-year life is $2,000. Answer (D) is incorrect. The depreciation expense, net of tax, for the current year is $2,700.

18.2.5. Tone Company is the defendant in a lawsuit filed by Witt in Year 2, disputing the validity of a copyright held by Tone. At December 31, Year 2, Tone determined that Witt would probably be successful against Tone for an estimated amount of $400,000. Appropriately, a $400,000 loss was accrued by a charge to income for the year ended December 31, Year 2. On December 15, Year 3, Tone and Witt agreed to a settlement providing for a cash payment of $250,000 by Tone to Witt and the transfer of Tone's copyright to Witt. The carrying amount of the copyright on Tone's accounting records was $60,000 at December 15, Year 3. The settlement's effect on Tone's income before income tax in Year 3 is

A. No effect.

B. $60,000 decrease.

C. $90,000 increase.

D. $150,000 increase.

Answer (C) is correct. *(CPA, adapted)*
    REQUIRED: The accounting for the effect of a settlement at an amount different from that previously accrued.
    DISCUSSION: In Year 2, a $400,000 contingent loss and an accrued liability in the amount of $400,000 were properly recognized. In Year 3, the actual loss of $310,000 ($250,000 cash + $60,000 carrying amount of the copyright) was $90,000 less than the previously estimated amount. This new information must be treated as a change in estimate and accounted for in the period of change. Consequently, the $90,000 difference will be credited to Year 3 income as a recovery of a previously recognized loss.
    Answer (A) is incorrect. Tone's income before income tax will increase by $90,000. Answer (B) is incorrect. The carrying amount of the copyright is $60,000. Answer (D) is incorrect. A $150,000 increase does not include the carrying amount of the copyright.

18.2.6. The effect of a change in accounting principle that is inseparable from the effect of a change in accounting estimate should be reported

   A. By restating the financial statements of all prior periods presented.

   B. As a correction of an error.

   C. In the period of change and future periods if the change affects both.

   D. As a separate disclosure after income from continuing operations in the period of change and future periods if the change affects both.

Answer (C) is correct. *(CPA, adapted)*
   REQUIRED: The reporting of the effect of a change in accounting principle that is inseparable from the effect of a change in accounting estimate.
   DISCUSSION: When the effect of a change in accounting principle is inseparable from the effect of a change in estimate, it must be accounted for in the same manner as a change in estimate only. An example of such a change is a change in the method of depreciation, amortization, or depletion. Because the new method is adopted to recognize a change in estimated future benefits, the effect of the change in principle is inseparable from the change in estimate. The effect of a change in accounting estimate is accounted for in the period of change if the change affects that period only or in the period of change and in future periods if the change affects both.
   Answer (A) is incorrect. A prior-period adjustment is accounted for as a correction of an error by restating the financial statements of all prior periods presented. Answer (B) is incorrect. A prior-period adjustment is accounted for as a correction of an error by restating the financial statements of all prior periods presented. Answer (D) is incorrect. This change is reflected in financial statement amounts, not merely as a disclosure. However, the effect on (1) income from continuing operations, (2) net income (or other appropriate captions), and (3) related per-share amounts for the current period should be disclosed for a change in estimate that affects several future periods. Furthermore, all disclosures required for a change in principle must be made.

18.2.7. On January 2, Year 1, Union Co. purchased a machine for $264,000 and depreciated it by the straight-line method using an estimated useful life of 8 years with no salvage value. On January 2, Year 4, Union determined that the machine had a useful life of 6 years from the date of acquisition and will have a salvage value of $24,000. An accounting change was made in Year 4 to reflect the additional data. The accumulated depreciation for this machine should have a balance at December 31, Year 4, of

   A. $179,000

   B. $160,000

   C. $154,000

   D. $146,000

Answer (D) is correct. *(CPA, adapted)*
   REQUIRED: The accumulated depreciation for a machine given changes in estimates.
   DISCUSSION: A change in the estimates for depreciation is accounted for prospectively. The new estimates are used in the year of the change, and no "catch-up" amounts are recorded. For Years 1 through 3, the amount of depreciation was $33,000 per year ($264,000 old depreciable base ÷ 8 old estimate of useful life), resulting in a balance of accumulated depreciation at December 31, Year 3, of $99,000 ($33,000 × 3 years). On January 2, Year 4, Union estimates the machine's original depreciable base to be $240,000 ($264,000 historical cost – $24,000 revised salvage value). The remaining depreciable base at January 2, Year 4, is thus $141,000 ($240,000 revised depreciable base – $99,000 accumulated depreciation), resulting in a new annual depreciation expense of $47,000 ($141,000 ÷ 3 years revised estimated life remaining). Thus, accumulated depreciation at December 31, Year 4, is $146,000 ($99,000 + $47,000).
   Answer (A) is incorrect. The amount of $179,000 does not reflect subtraction of prior depreciation in calculating depreciation for Year 4. Answer (B) is incorrect. The amount of $160,000 would be the accumulated depreciation if the revised estimates had been used from the beginning. Answer (C) is incorrect. The amount of $154,000 does not reflect subtraction of the salvage value in calculating depreciation for Year 4.

18.2.8. On January 1, Year 4, Vicar Company purchased a machine for $240,000 with a useful life of 10 years and no salvage value. The machine was depreciated using the double-declining-balance (DDB) method, and the carrying amount of the machine was $153,600 on December 31, Year 5. Vicar changed to the straight-line method on January 1, Year 6. Vicar can justify the change. What should be the depreciation expense on this machine for the year ended December 31, Year 6?

A. $15,360

B. $19,200

C. $24,000

D. $30,720

Answer (B) is correct. *(CPA, adapted)*
REQUIRED: The depreciation expense in the year in which a change in depreciation method is made.
DISCUSSION: A change in accounting estimate inseparable from (effected by) a change in accounting principle includes a change in depreciation, amortization, or depletion method. When a change in estimate and a change in principle are inseparable, the change must be accounted for as a change in estimate. The effects of a change in estimate must be accounted for prospectively. Thus, the effects should be recognized in the period of change and any future periods affected by the change. The effects should not be recognized in prior periods. Consequently, depreciation expense for the year ended December 31, Year 6, should be $19,200 ($153,600 carrying amount at December 31, Year 5 ÷ 8-year remaining useful life).
Answer (A) is incorrect. The figure of $15,360 is equal to the carrying amount at December 31, Year 5, allocated using the straight-line method and assuming a 10-year remaining useful life. Answer (C) is incorrect. The amount of $24,000 is equal to the cost of the machine allocated using the straight-line method and assuming a 10-year remaining useful life. Answer (D) is incorrect. The amount of $30,720 is the result of continuing to depreciate the machine under the DDB method.

18.2.9. On January 1, Year 4, Dickey Co. purchased a machine for $450,000 with an estimated life of 5 years with no salvage value. Dickey depreciated this machine under the sum-of-the-years'-digits method (SYD) for 2 years. At January 1, Year 6, when the carrying amount of the machine was $180,000 ($450,000 – $150,000 depreciation for Year 4 – $120,000 depreciation for Year 5), Dickey changed to the straight-line method. Dickey can justify the change. Dickey also determined that the remaining useful life of the machine had increased from 3 to 4 years. What is the amount of depreciation that Dickey should record in its income statement for the year ending December 31, Year 6?

A. $90,000

B. $75,000

C. $60,000

D. $45,000

Answer (D) is correct. *(CPA, adapted)*
REQUIRED: The depreciation expense in the year in which a change in depreciation method is made.
DISCUSSION: A change in accounting estimate inseparable from (effected by) a change in accounting principle includes a change in depreciation, amortization, or depletion method. When a change in estimate and a change in principle are inseparable, the change must be accounted for as a change in estimate. The effects of a change in estimate must be accounted for prospectively. Thus, the effects must be recognized in the period of change and any future periods affected by the change. The effects must not be recognized in prior periods. Consequently, depreciation expense for the year ended December 31, Year 6, should be $45,000 ($180,000 carrying amount at December 31, Year 5 ÷ 4-year remaining useful life).
Answer (A) is incorrect. The amount of $90,000 is based on the $450,000 original cost allocated to the 5-year useful life under the straight-line method. Answer (B) is incorrect. The amount of $75,000 is equal to the original cost of the machine allocated under the straight-line method over its revised 6-year useful life. Answer (C) is incorrect. The figure of $60,000 is equal to the December 31, Year 5, carrying amount allocated under the straight-line method over 3 years.

18.2.10. In early January of Year 6, Off-Line Co. changed its method of accounting for demo costs from writing off the costs over 2 years to expensing the costs immediately. Off-Line made the change in recognition that an increasing number of demos placed with potential customers did not result in sales. Off-Line had deferred demo costs of $500,000 at December 31, Year 5, of which $300,000 were to be written off in Year 6 and the remainder in Year 7. Off-Line's income tax rate is 30%. In its Year 6 statement of retained earnings, what amount should Off-Line report as a retrospective adjustment of its January 1, Year 6, retained earnings?

A. $0

B. $210,000

C. $300,000

D. $500,000

Answer (A) is correct. *(CPA, adapted)*
REQUIRED: The retrospective adjustment of retained earnings at the beginning of the year in which an entity changed from capitalizing a cost to expensing it as incurred.
DISCUSSION: In general, the retrospective application method is used to account for a change in accounting principle. However, a change in accounting estimate inseparable from (effected by) a change in accounting principle should be accounted for as a change in estimate. A change in estimate results from new information, such as the decreasing sales resulting from the demo placements. The effects of a change in estimate should be accounted for prospectively. Thus, the effects should be recognized in the period of change and any future periods affected. Accordingly, the write-off of the $500,000 in deferred demo costs should be reported in the Year 6 income statement. Retained earnings at the beginning of the year should not be retrospectively adjusted.
Answer (B) is incorrect. The amount of $210,000 is the after-tax effect of expensing $300,000 of the deferred costs in Year 6. Answer (C) is incorrect. The amount of $300,000 is the amount that had been scheduled to be expensed in Year 6. Answer (D) is incorrect. The amount of $500,000 is the pretax write-off to be recorded in the Year 6 income statement.

18.2.11. On January 1, Year 7, Colorado Corp. purchased a machine having an estimated useful life of 8 years and no salvage value. The machine was depreciated by the double-declining-balance (DDB) method for both financial statement and income tax reporting. On January 1, Year 9, Colorado justifiably changed to the straight-line method for both financial statement and income tax reporting. Accumulated depreciation at December 31, Year 8, was $525,000. If the straight-line method had been used, the accumulated depreciation at December 31, Year 8, would have been $300,000. The retroactive adjustment to the accumulated depreciation account on January 1, Year 9, as a result of the change in depreciation method is

A. $0

B. $225,000

C. $300,000

D. $525,000

Answer (A) is correct. *(Publisher, adapted)*
REQUIRED: The retroactive adjustment to accumulated depreciation at the beginning of the year in which a change in depreciation method was made.
DISCUSSION: A change in accounting estimate inseparable from (effected by) a change in accounting principle includes a change in depreciation, amortization, or depletion method. When a change in estimate and a change in principle are inseparable, the transaction should be accounted for as a change in estimate. The effects of a change in estimate should be accounted for prospectively. Thus, the effects should be recognized in the period of change and any future periods affected. The effects should not be recognized in prior periods. Consequently, the accumulated depreciation at January 1, Year 9, should carry forward the $525,000 balance determined in accordance with the DDB method as of December 31, Year 8.
Answer (B) is incorrect. The amount of $225,000 is the excess of the DDB over the straight-line amount. Answer (C) is incorrect. The amount of $300,000 is the balance under the straight-line method. Answer (D) is incorrect. The amount of $525,000 is the balance under the DDB method.

18.2.12. Which of the following statements is correct as it relates to changes in accounting estimates?

A. Most changes in accounting estimates are accounted for retrospectively.

B. Whenever it is impossible to determine whether a change in an estimate or a change in accounting principle occurred, the change should be considered a change in principle.

C. Whenever it is impossible to determine whether a change in accounting estimate or a change in accounting principle has occurred, the change should be considered a change in estimate.

D. It is easier to differentiate between a change in accounting estimate and a change in accounting principle than it is to differentiate between a change in accounting estimate and a correction of an error.

Answer (C) is correct. *(CPA, adapted)*
REQUIRED: The proper treatment for a change in accounting estimate.
DISCUSSION: A change in estimate inseparable from a change in principle is accounted for as a change in estimate (prospective application). An example is a change in a method of depreciation, amortization, or depletion of long-lived, nonfinancial assets.
Answer (A) is incorrect. A change in accounting estimate is accounted for prospectively. Answer (B) is incorrect. If it is impossible to determine whether a change in an estimate or a change in accounting principle occurred, it should be considered a change in estimate, not a change in principle. Answer (D) is incorrect. It is generally easier to differentiate between a change in accounting estimate and a correction of an error than it is to differentiate between a change in accounting estimate and a change in accounting principle. An error generally results from a mathematical mistake, a mistake in the application of GAAP, or an oversight or misuse of facts.

18.3 Corrections of Errors in Prior Statements

18.3.1. The correction of an error in the financial statements of a prior period should be reported, net of applicable income taxes, in the current

A. Retained earnings statement after net income but before dividends.

B. Retained earnings statement as an adjustment of the opening balance.

C. Income statement after income from continuing operations.

D. Income statement after income from continuing operations and after the results of discontinued operations.

Answer (B) is correct. *(CPA, adapted)*
REQUIRED: The recording of a prior-period adjustment (correction of an error).
DISCUSSION: Prior-period adjustments of single-period statements must be reflected net of applicable income taxes as changes in the opening balance in the statement of retained earnings of the current period. In comparative financial statements, all prior periods affected by the prior-period adjustment should be restated to reflect the adjustment.
Answer (A) is incorrect. The correction of the error should be an adjustment to beginning retained earnings. Answer (C) is incorrect. A prior-period adjustment is reported in current retained earnings, not the income statement. Answer (D) is incorrect. A prior-period adjustment is reported in current retained earnings, not the income statement.

18.3.2. Which of the following errors results in an overstatement of both current assets and equity?

A. Accrued sales expenses are understated.

B. Noncurrent note receivable principal is misclassified as a current asset.

C. Annual depreciation on manufacturing machinery is understated.

D. Holiday pay expense for administrative employees is misclassified as manufacturing overhead.

Answer (D) is correct. *(CIA, adapted)*
REQUIRED: The error that results in an overstatement of both current assets and equity.
DISCUSSION: The classification of holiday pay expense as manufacturing overhead overstates both current assets and equity. Holiday pay expense for administrative employees should be expensed as incurred. By classifying the expense as manufacturing overhead, inventory (a current asset) is overstated. If this inventory is not sold in the period, ending inventory will be overstated and expenses for the period will be understated. The effect is to overstate current assets, net income, retained earnings, and equity.
Answer (A) is incorrect. An understatement of accrued sales overstates equity but affects current liabilities, not current assets. Answer (B) is incorrect. A misclassification of a noncurrent note receivable as a current asset does not affect equity. Answer (C) is incorrect. An understatement of depreciation on equipment does not affect current assets.

18.3.3. The Year 1 financial statements of Bice Company reported net income for the year ended December 31, Year 1, of $2 million. On July 1, Year 2, subsequent to the issuance of the Year 1 financial statements, Bice changed from an accounting principle that is not generally accepted to one that is generally accepted. If the generally accepted accounting principle had been used in Year 1, net income for the year ended December 31, Year 1, would have been decreased by $1 million. On August 1, Year 2, Bice discovered a mathematical error relating to its Year 1 financial statements. If this error had been discovered in Year 1, net income for the year ended December 31, Year 1, would have been increased by $500,000. What amount, if any, should be included in net income for the year ended December 31, Year 2, because of the items noted above?

A. $0.

B. $500,000 decrease.

C. $500,000 increase.

D. $1,000,000 decrease.

Answer (A) is correct. *(CPA, adapted)*
REQUIRED: The amount that should be included in net income because of an accounting change and an accounting error.
DISCUSSION: A change from an accounting principle that is not generally accepted to one that is generally accepted should be accounted for as the correction of an error. Corrections of errors in financial statements of prior periods must be accounted for as prior-period adjustments and thus excluded from the determination of net income for the current period. Accordingly, the mathematical error and the change in accounting method have no effect on Year 2 net income.
Answer (B) is incorrect. The $500,000 decrease is the net amount by which Year 1 income should be restated. Answer (C) is incorrect. A mathematical error caused a $500,000 increase in Year 1 net income. Answer (D) is incorrect. A $1,000,000 decrease in Year 1 income was the result of using an incorrect accounting principle.

18.3.4. At the end of Year 1, Ritzcar Co. failed to accrue sales commissions earned during Year 1 but paid in Year 2. The error was not repeated in Year 2. What was the effect of this error on Year 1 ending working capital and on the Year 2 ending retained earnings balance?

	Year 1 Ending Working Capital	Year 2 Ending Retained Earnings
A.	Overstated	Overstated
B.	No effect	Overstated
C.	No effect	No effect
D.	Overstated	No effect

Answer (D) is correct. *(CPA, adapted)*
REQUIRED: The effect of failure to accrue sales commissions.
DISCUSSION: The Year 1 ending working capital (current assets – current liabilities) is overstated because the error understates current liabilities. The Year 2 ending retained earnings balance is unaffected because it is a cumulative amount. Whether the sales commission expense is recognized in Year 1 when it should have been accrued or in Year 2 when it was paid affects the net income amounts for Year 1 and Year 2 but not Year 2 ending retained earnings.
Answer (A) is incorrect. Year 2 ending retained earnings is unaffected. Answer (B) is incorrect. Year 1 ending working capital is overstated but Year 2 ending retained earnings is unaffected. Answer (C) is incorrect. Year 1 ending working capital is overstated.

18.3.5. Conn Co. reported a retained earnings balance of $400,000 at December 31, Year 2. In August Year 3, Conn determined that insurance premiums of $60,000 for the 3-year period beginning January 1, Year 2, had been paid and fully expensed in Year 2. Conn has a 30% income tax rate. What amount should Conn report as adjusted beginning retained earnings in its Year 3 statement of retained earnings?

A. $420,000

B. $428,000

C. $440,000

D. $442,000

Answer (B) is correct. *(CPA, adapted)*
REQUIRED: The adjusted beginning retained earnings after correction of an error.
DISCUSSION: Prior-period adjustments must be reflected net of applicable income taxes as changes in the opening balance in the statement of retained earnings. The $60,000 insurance prepayment in Year 2 should have been expensed ratably over the 3-year period. Consequently, Year 2 net income was understated by $40,000, net of tax effect, and $40,000 [$60,000 − ($60,000 ÷ 3)] should have been reported as a prepaid expense (an asset) at the beginning of Year 3. The prior-period adjustment to the beginning balance of retained earnings is therefore a credit of $28,000 [$40,000 × (1.0 − .30 tax rate)]. The adjusted balance is $428,000 ($400,000 + $28,000).
Answer (A) is incorrect. The sum of the beginning balance of retained earnings and the expense that should have been recognized in Year 2 is $420,000. Answer (C) is incorrect. The amount of $440,000 does not consider the tax effect. Answer (D) is incorrect. The amount of $442,000 assumes that no insurance expense should have been recognized in Year 2.

18.3.6. On January 1, Year 1, Newport Corp. purchased a machine for $100,000. The machine was depreciated using the straight-line method over a 10-year period with no residual value. Because of a bookkeeping error, no depreciation was recognized in Newport's Year 1 financial statements, resulting in a $10,000 overstatement of the book value of the machine on December 31, Year 1. The oversight was discovered during the preparation of Newport's Year 2 financial statements. What amount should Newport report for depreciation expense on the machine in the Year 2 financial statements?

A. $9,000

B. $10,000

C. $11,000

D. $20,000

Answer (B) is correct. *(CPA, adapted)*
REQUIRED: The accounting for a depreciation error in the prior period's statements.
DISCUSSION: Items of profit or loss related to corrections of errors in prior-period statements are prior-period adjustments. They are debited or credited (net of tax) to retained earnings and reported as adjustments in the statement of changes in equity or in the statement of retained earnings. They are not included in net income. Prior-period adjustments reported in single-period statements are adjustments of the opening balance of retained earnings. If comparative statements are presented, corresponding adjustments should be made to net income (and its components) and retained earnings (and other affected balances) for all periods reported. Accordingly, the error in Year 1 does not affect depreciation expense in Year 2 regardless of whether single-year or comparative statements are presented. It equals $10,000 [($100,000 − $0 residual value) ÷ 10 years].
Answer (A) is incorrect. The amount of $9,000 equals the appropriate carrying amount at the beginning of Year 2 ($90,000) divided by 10 years. Answer (C) is incorrect. The amount of $11,000 equals initial carrying amount ($100,000 divided by 9 years and rounded to the nearest thousand). Answer (D) is incorrect. The amount of $20,000 is the total depreciation expense for Years 1 and 2. However, no catch-up adjustment for the omission in Year 1 is recognized in income for Year 2.

18.3.7. An audit of Fundy Co. for its first year of operations detected the following errors made at December 31:

● Failed to accrue $50,000 interest expense

● Failed to record depreciation expense on office equipment of $80,000

● Failed to amortize prepaid rent expense of $100,000

● Failed to delay recognition of prepaid insurance expense of $60,000

The net effect of these errors was to overstate net income for the year by

A. $130,000

B. $170,000

C. $230,000

D. $290,000

Answer (B) is correct. *(CIA, adapted)*
REQUIRED: The effect of certain errors on net income.
DISCUSSION: The failure to accrue interest expense, record depreciation expense on office equipment, and amortize prepaid rent expense overstates net income. Expensing the full amount of prepaid insurance instead of deferring recognition understates net income. Thus, net income is overstated by $170,000 ($50,000 + $80,000 + $100,000 − $60,000).
Answer (A) is incorrect. The amount of $130,000 includes only the interest expense and depreciation expense. Answer (C) is incorrect. The amount of $230,000 results from not subtracting the prepaid insurance expense. Answer (D) is incorrect. The amount of $290,000 results from adding prepaid insurance expense.

Questions 18.3.8 and 18.3.9 are based on the following information. On October 1, Year 3, Eure Retailers signed a 4-month, 16% note payable to finance the purchase of holiday merchandise. At that date, there was no direct method of pricing the merchandise, and the note's market rate of interest was 11%. Eure recorded the purchase at the note's face amount. All of the merchandise was sold by December 1, Year 3. Eure's Year 3 financial statements reported interest payable and interest expense on the note for 3 months at 16%. All amounts due on the note were paid February 1, Year 4.

18.3.8. Eure's Year 3 cost of goods sold for the holiday merchandise was

A. Overstated by the difference between the note's face amount and the note's October 1, Year 3, present value.

B. Overstated by the difference between the note's face amount and the note's October 1, Year 3, present value plus 11% interest for 2 months.

C. Understated by the difference between the note's face amount and the note's October 1, Year 3, present value.

D. Understated by the difference between the note's face amount and the note's October 1, Year 3, present value plus 16% interest for 2 months.

Answer (C) is correct. *(CPA, adapted)*
REQUIRED: The cost of goods sold.
DISCUSSION: The general presumption when a note is exchanged for property, goods, or services in an arm's-length transaction is that the rate of interest is fair and adequate. If the rate is not stated or the stated rate is unreasonable, the note and the property, goods, or services should be recorded at the fair value of the property, goods, or services or the market value of the note, whichever is more clearly determinable. In the absence of these values, the present value of the note should be used as the basis for recording both the note and the property, goods, or services. This present value is obtained by discounting all future payments on the note using the market rate of interest. Because the imputed rate (11%) is less than the nominal rate (16%), the note (and the purchase) should be recorded at a premium. The face amount is the present value at the nominal rate. The face amount plus a premium is the present value at the (lower) market rate. Thus, recording the note and purchase at the face amount of the note understates the cost of the inventory sold.
Answer (A) is incorrect. The cost of goods sold was understated by the amount of the premium that should have been recognized. Answer (B) is incorrect. The cost of goods sold was understated. Answer (D) is incorrect. The understatement was equal to the note's present value at 11% on the date of purchase minus the face amount (present value at the 16% nominal rate).

18.3.9. As a result of Eure's accounting treatment of the note, interest, and merchandise, which of the following items was (were) reported correctly?

	12/31/Year 3 Retained Earnings	12/31/Year 3 Interest Payable
A.	Yes	Yes
B.	No	No
C.	Yes	No
D.	No	Yes

Answer (D) is correct. *(CPA, adapted)*
REQUIRED: The item correctly reported as a result of incorrectly recording a note payable.
DISCUSSION: If the note's rate is not stated, or the stated rate is unreasonable, the note and any related property, goods, or services should be recorded at the fair value of the property, goods, services, or the market value of the note, whichever is more clearly determinable. Because the note was recorded at its face amount, cost of goods sold was understated by the difference between the note's face amount and its present value. Interest expense should be calculated based on the present value of the note at the market rate of interest. Interest payable is the stated rate times the face amount, and amortization of premium or discount is the difference between the payable and interest expense. In this situation, interest expense and interest payable are both recorded at the stated rate multiplied by the face amount. Thus, retained earnings is misstated as a result of the error in calculating cost of goods sold and interest expense. Interest payable is correctly reported.
Answer (A) is incorrect. Retained earnings is misstated. Answer (B) is incorrect. Interest payable is correctly stated. Answer (C) is incorrect. Retained earnings is misstated, and interest payable is correctly stated.

18.3.10. For the past 3 years, Gainesville Co. has failed to accrue unpaid wages earned by workers during the last week of the year. The amounts omitted, which are considered material, were as follows:

December 31, Year 1	$56,000
December 31, Year 2	51,000
December 31, Year 3	64,000

The entry on December 31, Year 3, to correct for these omissions would include a

A. Credit to wage expense for $64,000.

B. Debit to wage expense for $51,000.

C. Debit to wage expense for $13,000.

D. Credit to retained earnings for $64,000.

Answer (C) is correct. *(CMA, adapted)*
   REQUIRED: The entry to correct for failure to accrue wages.
   DISCUSSION: Failing to record accrued wages is a self-correcting error. Expenses are understated in one year and overstated in the next. The Year 1 error overstated Year 1 earnings and understated Year 2 earnings by $56,000. The Year 2 error overstated Year 2 earnings and understated Year 3 earnings by $51,000. The Year 3 error overstated Year 3 earnings by $64,000. Thus, the net effect in Year 3 of the Year 2 and Year 3 errors is a $13,000 ($64,000 – $51,000) overstatement. The correcting entry is to debit expense for $13,000, debit retained earnings for $51,000, and credit wages payable for $64,000.
   Answer (A) is incorrect. The accrued wages payable, not the amount of the adjustment, is $64,000. Answer (B) is incorrect. The correct wage accrual for Year 2 is $51,000. Answer (D) is incorrect. Retained earnings should be debited.

18.3.11. While preparing its Year 4 financial statements, Dek Corp. discovered computational errors in its Year 3 and Year 2 depreciation expense. These errors resulted in overstatement of each year's income by $25,000, net of income taxes. The following amounts were reported in the previously issued statements:

	Year 3	Year 2
Retained earnings, 1/1	$700,000	$500,000
Net income	150,000	200,000
Retained earnings, 12/31	$850,000	$700,000

Dek's Year 4 net income is correctly reported at $180,000. Which of the following amounts should be reported as prior-period adjustments and net income in Dek's Year 4 and Year 3 comparative statements

	Year	Prior-Period Adjustment	Net Income
A.	3	--	$150,000
	4	$(50,000)	180,000
B.	3	$(50,000)	$150,000
	4	--	180,000
C.	3	$(25,000)	$125,000
	4	--	180,000
D.	3	--	$125,000
	4	--	180,000

Answer (C) is correct. *(CPA, adapted)*
   REQUIRED: The amounts that should be reported as prior-period adjustments and net income in comparative financial statements.
   DISCUSSION: A prior-period adjustment is necessary to correct an error. In the comparative financial statements presented for Year 3 and Year 4, all prior periods affected by the prior-period adjustment should be restated to reflect the adjustment. Consequently, the beginning balance of retained earnings for Year 3 should be debited to correct the $25,000 overstatement of after-tax income for Year 2, a year for which financial statements are not presented. Because the statements for Year 3 should be restated to reflect the correction of the error in Year 3 net income, this amount will be correctly reported in the Year 4 and Year 3 comparative financial statements as $125,000 ($150,000 in the previously issued Year 3 statements – $25,000 overstatement). No prior-period adjustment to the Year 4 financial statements is necessary. The Year 3 statements, including the ending retained earnings balance, will have been revised to correct the errors. Hence, the Year 4 beginning retained earnings (Year 3 ending retained earnings) will need no further revision.
   Answer (A) is incorrect. Year 3 net income is $125,000, and the prior-period adjustment is made to the beginning balance of retained earnings for Year 3. Answer (B) is incorrect. The prior-period adjustment is for $25,000 (the overstatement of Year 2 net income). Answer (D) is incorrect. A prior-period adjustment must be made in the Year 3 statements.

18.3.12. Which of the following should be reflected, net of applicable income taxes, in the statement of equity as an adjustment of the opening balance in retained earnings?

A. Correction of an error in previously issued financial statements.

B. Cumulative effect of a change in depreciation method.

C. Loss on disposal of a material component of an entity.

D. A material transaction that an entity considers to be unusual in nature.

Answer (A) is correct. *(CPA, adapted)*
   REQUIRED: The item treated as an adjustment to beginning retained earnings.
   DISCUSSION: The correction of an error occurring in a prior period should be accounted for as a prior-period adjustment. It should be charged or credited net of tax to retained earnings and reported as an adjustment in the statement of equity. It is not included in net income for the current period.
   Answer (B) is incorrect. A change in depreciation method is a change in estimate that is accounted for prospectively. Answer (C) is incorrect. A discontinued operation is reported under a separate caption in the income statement. Answer (D) is incorrect. A material transaction that is unusual in nature or infrequent in occurrence is reported as a separate component of income from continuing operations.

18.3.13. Cuthbert Industrials, Inc., prepares 3-year comparative financial statements. In Year 3, Cuthbert discovered an error in the previously issued financial statements for Year 1. The error affects the financial statements that were issued in Years 1 and 2. How should the company report the error?

A. The financial statements for Years 1 and 2 should be restated; an offsetting adjustment to the cumulative effect of the error should be made to the comprehensive income in the Year 3 financial statements.

B. The financial statements for Years 1 and 2 should not be restated; financial statements for Year 3 should disclose the fact that the error was made in prior years.

C. The financial statements for Years 1 and 2 should not be restated; the cumulative effect of the error on Years 1 and 2 should be reflected in the carrying amounts of assets and liabilities as of the beginning of Year 3.

D. The financial statements for Years 1 and 2 should be restated; the cumulative effect of the error on Years 1 and 2 should be reflected in the carrying amounts of assets and liabilities as of the beginning of Year 3.

Answer (D) is correct. *(CPA, adapted)*
REQUIRED: The reporting of errors from prior periods when presenting comparative financial statements.
DISCUSSION: Any error related to a prior period discovered after the statements are used must be reported as an error correction by restating the prior-period statements. If comparative statements are presented, corresponding adjustments must be made to net income (and its components) and retained earnings (and other affected balances) for all periods reported. As such, the cumulative effect of the error on Years 1 and 2 will be reflected in the carrying amounts of assets and liabilities as of the beginning of Year 3.
Answer (A) is incorrect. Corrections of prior-period errors (cumulative effect of the error) must not be included in the comprehensive income of the current period. Answer (B) is incorrect. Any error related to a prior period discovered after the statements are used must be reported as an error correction by restating the prior-period statements. Answer (C) is incorrect. Any error related to a prior period discovered after the statements are used must be reported as an error correction by restating the prior-period statements.

18.4 IFRS

18.4.1. Under IAS 8, *Accounting Policies, Changes in Accounting Estimates and Errors*, an impracticability exception applies to which of the following?

I. Retrospective application of a new accounting policy

II. Retrospective application of a change in estimate

III. Retrospective restatement of a prior period error

A. I and II only.

B. I and III only.

C. II and III only.

D. I only.

Answer (B) is correct. *(Publisher, adapted)*
REQUIRED: The item(s) to which an impracticability exception applies.
DISCUSSION: Retrospective application of a new accounting policy is not done if it is impracticable to determine period-specific effects or the cumulative effect. Impracticable means that the entity cannot apply a requirement after making every reasonable effort. Accordingly, retrospective application to a prior period is impracticable unless the cumulative effects on the opening and closing statements of financial position for the period are practicably determinable. The impracticability exception also applies to retrospective restatement of a prior period error. However, a change in estimate is applied prospectively in profit or loss.
Answer (A) is incorrect. A change in estimate is applied prospectively, and retrospective restatement of a prior period error is subject to an impracticability exception. Answer (C) is incorrect. Retrospective application of a new accounting policy is subject to an impracticability exception, and a change in estimate is applied prospectively. Answer (D) is incorrect. Retrospective restatement of a prior period error is subject to an impracticability exception.

18.4.2. Under IFRS, changes in accounting policies are

A. Permitted if the change will result in a more reliable and more relevant presentation of the financial statements.

B. Permitted if the entity encounters new transactions, events, or conditions that are substantively different from existing or previous transactions.

C. Required on material transactions if the entity had previously accounted for similar, though immaterial, transactions under an unacceptable accounting method.

D. Required if an alternate accounting policy gives rise to a material change in assets, liabilities, or the current-year net income.

Answer (A) is correct. *(CPA, adapted)*
REQUIRED: The true statement about changes in accounting policies.
DISCUSSION: A change in policy must be made only if it (1) is required by a new standard or interpretation or (2) results in reliable and more relevant information about transactions, financial condition, financial performance, and cash flows.
Answer (B) is incorrect. Applying a new policy to new transactions, events, or conditions that are substantively different from existing or previous transactions is not a change in policy. Answer (C) is incorrect. A change in policy does not occur when a new policy is applied to transactions that were immaterial. Answer (D) is incorrect. A change is made only if required by a pronouncement or the result is reliable and more relevant information.

☑ ▬
☐ ▬   Use **Gleim Test Prep** for interactive study and easy-to-use detailed analytics!
☐ ▬

STUDY UNIT NINETEEN
STATEMENT OF CASH FLOWS

A statement of cash flows is required as part of a full set of financial statements of most business and not-for-profit entities. If an entity reports financial position and results of operations, it must present a statement of cash flows for any period for which results of operations are presented. The **primary purpose** is to provide information about the cash receipts and payments of an entity during a period. To achieve its primary purpose, the statement should provide information about cash inflows and outflows from **operating, investing, and financing activities**. This format reconciles the cash balance at the beginning of the period with the balance at the end of the period. The following is an example of the summarized format of the statement of cash flows (headings only). The amounts of cash, cash equivalents, and restricted cash at the beginning and end of the year are taken from the balance sheet.

Entity A's Statement of Cash Flows for the Year Ended December 31, Year 1

Net cash provided by (used in) operating activities	$XXX
Net cash provided by (used in) investing activities	XXX
Net cash provided by (used in) financing activities	XXX
Net increase (decrease) in cash, cash equivalents, and restricted cash during the year	$XXX
Cash, cash equivalents, and restricted cash at beginning of year (January 1, Year 1)	XXX
Cash, cash equivalents, and restricted cash at end of year (December 31, Year 1)	$XXX

The two ways of presenting the statement of cash flows are the direct method and the indirect method. The only difference between these two methods is their presentation of net cash flows from operating activities. The total cash flows from operating activities is the same regardless of which method is used. Under the **direct method**, the entity presents major classes of gross operating cash receipts and payments and their sum (net cash flow from operating activities). Under the **indirect method** (also called the reconciliation method), the net cash flow from operating activities is determined by adjusting the net income for the period.

QUESTIONS

19.1 Statement of Cash Flows -- General

19.1.1. A statement of cash flows is to be presented in general-purpose external financial statements by which of the following?

    A. Publicly held businesses only.

    B. Privately held businesses only.

    C. All businesses.

    D. All businesses and nongovernmental not-for-profit entities.

Answer (D) is correct. *(Publisher, adapted)*
    REQUIRED: The entities required to present a statement of cash flows.
    DISCUSSION: A statement of cash flows is required as part of a full set of financial statements of all business entities (both publicly held and privately held) and nongovernmental not-for-profit entities.

19.1.2. The primary purpose of a statement of cash flows is to provide relevant information about

    A. Differences between net income and associated cash receipts and disbursements.

    B. An entity's ability to generate future positive net cash flows.

    C. The cash receipts and cash disbursements of an entity during a period.

    D. An entity's ability to meet cash operating needs.

Answer (C) is correct. *(CPA, adapted)*
    REQUIRED: The primary purpose of a statement of cash flows.
    DISCUSSION: The primary purpose is to provide information about the cash receipts and cash payments of a business entity during a period. This information helps investors, creditors, and other users to assess the entity's ability to generate net cash inflows, meet its obligations, pay dividends, and secure external financing. It also helps assess reasons for the differences between net income and net cash flow and the effects of cash and noncash financing and investing activities.
    Answer (A) is incorrect. Reconciling net income with cash flows is a secondary purpose. Answer (B) is incorrect. Assessing the ability to generate cash flows is a secondary purpose. Answer (D) is incorrect. The ability to meet cash needs is a secondary purpose.

19.1.3. A corporation issues a balance sheet and income statement for the current year. It also issues comparative income statements for each of the 2 previous years and a comparative balance sheet for 1 previous year. A statement of cash flows

    A. Must be issued for the current year only.

    B. Must be issued for the current and the previous year only.

    C. Must be issued for all 3 years.

    D. May be issued at the company's option for any or all of the 3 years.

Answer (C) is correct. *(Publisher, adapted)*
    REQUIRED: The circumstances in which a statement of cash flows must be issued.
    DISCUSSION: When a business provides a set of financial statements that reports both financial position and results of operations, it also must present a statement of cash flows for each period for which the results of operations are provided.
    Answer (A) is incorrect. A statement of cash flows must be provided for all 3 years. Answer (B) is incorrect. An income statement was issued for the 2 previous years. Answer (D) is incorrect. The statement of cash flows is mandatory when an income statement is issued.

19.1.4. Which of the following cash flows per share should be reported in a statement of cash flows?

    A. Primary cash flows per share only.

    B. Fully diluted cash flows per share only.

    C. Both basic and diluted cash flows per share.

    D. Cash flows per share should not be reported.

Answer (D) is correct. *(CPA, adapted)*
    REQUIRED: The cash flows per share reported in a statement of cash flows.
    DISCUSSION: Financial statements must not report cash flow per share. Reporting per-share amounts might improperly imply that cash flow is an alternative to net income as a performance measure.

19.1.5. Bay Manufacturing Co. purchased a 3-month U.S. Treasury bill. In preparing Bay's statement of cash flows, this purchase would

A. Have no effect.

B. Be treated as an outflow from financing activities.

C. Be treated as an outflow from investing activities.

D. Be treated as an outflow from lending activities.

Answer (A) is correct. *(CPA, adapted)*
REQUIRED: The effect of purchasing a 3-month T-bill.
DISCUSSION: Cash equivalents are short-term, highly liquid investments that are both readily convertible to known amounts of cash and so near their maturity that they present insignificant risk of changes in value because of changes in interest rates. Moreover, cash equivalents ordinarily include only investments with original maturities to the holder of 3 months or less. The T-bill is therefore a cash equivalent and has no effect on the statement of cash flows.

19.2 Classification of Cash Flows

19.2.1. Which collection is reported as an investing activity in statement of cash flows?

A. Proceeds from a note payable.

B. A note receivable from a related party.

C. An overdue account receivable from a customer.

D. A tax refund.

Answer (B) is correct. *(CPA, adapted)*
REQUIRED: The collection reported as an investment activity.
DISCUSSION: Investing activities include making and collecting loans. Whether the debtor is a related party affects disclosure requirements, not the classification of the cash inflow.
Answer (A) is incorrect. Collection of proceeds from a note payable is an incurrence of debt. It is reported as a financing activity. Answer (C) is incorrect. Collection of an overdue account receivable from a customer is not related to the financing or investing activities of the business. Thus, it is reported in the operating activities section. Answer (D) is incorrect. Collection of a tax refund is not related to the financing or investing activities of the business. Thus, it is reported in the operating activities.

19.2.2. Which of the following transactions should be classified as investing activities on an entity's statement of cash flows?

A. Increase in accounts receivable.

B. Sale of property, plant, and equipment.

C. Payment of cash dividend to the shareholders.

D. Issuance of common stock to the shareholders.

Answer (B) is correct. *(CPA, adapted)*
REQUIRED: The investing activity.
DISCUSSION: Investing activities include (1) making and collecting loans; (2) acquiring and disposing of debt or equity instruments; and (3) acquiring and disposing of property, plant, and equipment and other productive assets (but not materials in inventory) held for or used in the production of goods and services.
Answer (A) is incorrect. An increase in accounts receivable affects cash flows from operating activities. Answer (C) is incorrect. Payment of dividends is a financing activity. Answer (D) is incorrect. Issuance of stock is a financing activity.

19.2.3. Alp, Inc., had the following activities during the current year:

- Acquired 2,000 shares of stock in Maybel, Inc., for $26,000
- Sold an investment in bonds classified as available for sale for $35,000 when the carrying amount was $33,000
- Acquired a $50,000, 4-year certificate of deposit from a bank that was classified as held to maturity. (During the year, interest of $3,750 was paid to Alp.)
- Collected dividends of $1,200 on stock investments

In Alp's current-year statement of cash flows, net cash used in investing activities should be

A. $37,250

B. $38,050

C. $39,800

D. $41,000

Answer (D) is correct. *(CPA, adapted)*
REQUIRED: The net cash used in investing activities.
DISCUSSION: Investing activities include the lending of money; the collection of those loans; and the acquisition, sale, or other disposal of (1) loans and other securities that are not cash equivalents and that have not been acquired specifically for resale and (2) property, plant, equipment, and other productive assets. Thus, the purchase of debt and equity securities, sale of debt and equity securities, and acquisition of a long-term certificate of deposit (not a cash equivalent) are investing activities assuming the debt securities are not trading securities. The receipts of interest and dividends are cash flows from operating activities. The net cash used in investing activities therefore equals $41,000 ($26,000 – $35,000 + $50,000).
Answer (A) is incorrect. The amount of $37,250 treats interest received as an investing cash inflow. Answer (B) is incorrect. The amount of $38,050 treats interest and dividends received as investing cash inflows and uses the carrying amount of the investment sold. Answer (C) is incorrect. The amount of $39,800 treats dividends received as an investing cash inflow.

19.2.4. On July 1, Year 1, Dewey Co. signed a 20-year building lease that it reported as a finance lease. Dewey paid the monthly lease payments when due. How should Dewey report the effect of the lease payments in the financing activities section of its Year 1 statement of cash flows?

A. An inflow equal to the present value of future lease payments at July 1, Year 1, less Year 1 principal and interest payments.

B. An outflow equal to the Year 1 principal and interest payments on the lease.

C. An outflow equal to the Year 1 principal payments only.

D. The lease payments should not be reported in the financing activities section.

Answer (C) is correct. *(CPA, adapted)*
REQUIRED: The effect of lease payments on the financing activities section in the statement of cash flows.
DISCUSSION: Financing activities include the repayment or settlement of debt obligations. Financing activities do not include the payment of interest. Thus, the payment of principal is an outflow from financing activities. The payments for interest are operating cash flows.
Answer (A) is incorrect. The payments made in Year 1 are cash outflows, but the present value of future payments is not a cash item. Answer (B) is incorrect. The interest payments should not be included as cash flows from a financing activity. Answer (D) is incorrect. Lease payments are considered cash outflows from financing activities.

19.2.5. Abbott Co. is preparing its statement of cash flows for the year. Abbott's cash disbursements during the year included the following:

Payment of interest on bonds payable	$500,000
Payment of dividends to stockholders	300,000
Payment to acquire 1,000 shares of Marks Co. common stock	100,000

What should Abbott report as total cash outflows for financing activities in its statement of cash flows under U.S. GAAP?

A. $0

B. $300,000

C. $800,000

D. $900,000

Answer (B) is correct. *(CPA, adapted)*
REQUIRED: The total cash outflows from financing activities under U.S. GAAP.
DISCUSSION: The $300,000 dividend should be classified as a financing cash outflow. The payment of interest is an operating cash outflow under U.S. GAAP, and the payment to acquire the common stock of Marks is an investing cash outflow. Under IFRS, payment of dividends may be classified as an operating or a financing activity.
Answer (A) is incorrect. The $300,000 dividend is classified as a financing cash outflow. Answer (C) is incorrect. The $500,000 payment of interest, although related to a financing activity, is reported under U.S. GAAP as an operating cash outflow. Answer (D) is incorrect. The $100,000 payment to acquire another entity's common stock is classified as an investing activity.

19.2.6. The following information was taken from the accounting records of Gorky Corporation for the year ended December 31, Year 1:

Proceeds from issuance of preferred stock	$8,000,000
Dividends paid on preferred stock	800,000
Bonds payable converted to common stock	4,000,000
Payment for purchase of machinery	1,000,000
Proceeds from sale of plant building	2,400,000
2% stock dividend on common stock	600,000
Gain on sale of plant building	400,000

The net cash flows from investing and financing activities that should be presented on Gorky's statement of cash flows for the year ended December 31, Year 1, are respectively

A. $1,400,000 and $7,200,000.

B. $1,400,000 and $7,800,000.

C. $1,800,000 and $7,800,000.

D. $1,800,000 and $7,200,000.

Answer (A) is correct. *(CMA, adapted)*
REQUIRED: The respective net cash flows from investing and financing activities.
DISCUSSION: Investing activities include (1) making and collecting loans; (2) acquiring and disposing of debt and equity instruments; and (3) acquiring and disposing of property, plant, equipment, and other productive assets held for, or used in, the production of goods or services (excluding inventory). However, transactions in cash equivalents and certain loans or other instruments acquired specifically for resale are operating, not investing, activities. Financing activities include the issuance of stock, the payment of dividends, treasury stock transactions, the issuance of debt, the receipt of donor-restricted resources to be used for long-term purposes, and the repayment or other settlement of debt obligations. Investing activities include the purchase of machinery and the sale of a building. The net inflow from these activities is $1,400,000 ($2,400,000 – $1,000,000). Financing activities include the issuance of preferred stock and the payment of dividends. The net inflow is $7,200,000 ($8,000,000 – $800,000). The conversion of bonds into common stock and the stock dividend do not affect cash.
Answer (B) is incorrect. The stock dividend has no effect on cash flows from financing activities. Answer (C) is incorrect. The gain on the sale of the building is double counted in determining the net cash flow from investing activities, and the stock dividend has no effect on cash flows from financing activities. Answer (D) is incorrect. The gain on the sale of the building is double counted in determining the net cash flow from investing activities.

19.2.7. In a statement of cash flows, which of the following items is reported as a cash outflow from financing activities by a nongovernmental not-for-profit organization?

I. Payments to retire real estate mortgage notes
II. Interest payments on real estate mortgage notes
III. Payments on the principal of seller-financed debt related to a purchase of equipment

    A. I, II, and III.

    B. II and III.

    C. I only.

    D. I and III.

Answer (D) is correct. *(CPA, adapted)*
REQUIRED: The cash outflows from financing activities.
DISCUSSION: Financing activities include issuance of stock, payment of dividends and other distributions to owners, treasury stock transactions, issuance of debt, receipt of donor-restricted resources to be used for long-term purposes, and repayment or other settlement of debt obligations. Thus, payment of the principal of a real estate mortgage note and payment on the principal of seller-financed debt related to a purchase of equipment are outflows from financing activities.
Answer (A) is incorrect. Interest payments are outflows from operating activities. Answer (B) is incorrect. Interest payments are outflows from operating activities. Answer (C) is incorrect. Payments on the principal of seller-financed debt related to a purchase of equipment are outflows from financing activities.

19.2.8. In preparing its statement of cash flows, if Harlingen Co. omits the payment of cash dividends, the net cash provided by <List A> activities will be <List B>.

	List A	List B
A.	Operating	Understated
B.	Investing	Understated
C.	Investing	Overstated
D.	Financing	Overstated

Answer (D) is correct. *(CIA, adapted)*
REQUIRED: The effect of omitting payment of cash dividends.
DISCUSSION: Cash flows from financing activities include (1) obtaining resources from owners and providing them with a return on their investment, (2) borrowing from and repaying creditors, and (3) receiving restricted resources that by donor stipulation must be used for long-term purposes. This category of cash flows will be overstated if the use of cash to pay dividends to equity holders is omitted from the statement of cash flows.
Answer (A) is incorrect. Cash flows from operating activities ordinarily arise from transactions that enter into the determination of net income. Cash dividends paid do not affect the cash flows from operating activities. Answer (B) is incorrect. Cash flows from investing activities arise from making and collecting loans and acquiring and disposing of investments (both debt and equity) and property, plant, and equipment. Cash dividends do not affect the cash flows from investing activities. Answer (C) is incorrect. Cash dividends do not affect the cash flows from investing activities and therefore do not misstate the net cash provided by investing activities.

19.2.9. A company calculated the following data for the period:

Cash received from customers	$25,000
Cash received from sale of equipment	1,000
Interest paid to bank on note	3,000
Cash paid to employees	8,000

What amount should the company report as net cash provided by operating activities in its statement of cash flows?

    A. $14,000

    B. $15,000

    C. $18,000

    D. $26,000

Answer (A) is correct. *(CPA, adapted)*
REQUIRED: The net cash provided by operating activities.
DISCUSSION: Operating activities are all transactions and other events that are not financing or investing activities. In general, operating activities involve the production and delivery of goods and the provision of services. Their effects normally are reported in earnings. Cash inflows from operating activities include receipts from collection or sale of accounts and notes resulting from sales to customers. Cash outflows from operating activities include cash payments to employees for services and creditors for interest. Thus, the net cash provided by operating activities is ($25,000 – $8,000 – $3,000) $14,000.
Answer (B) is incorrect. The amount of $15,000 includes cash received from sale of equipment, an investing cash inflow. Answer (C) is incorrect. The amount of $18,000 excludes interest paid but includes cash from the equipment sale. Answer (D) is incorrect. The amount of $26,000 equals cash from customers plus cash from sale of equipment.

19.2.10. Fara Co. reported bonds payable of $47,000 on December 31, Year 1, and $50,000 on December 31, Year 2. During Year 2, Fara issued $20,000 of bonds payable in exchange for equipment. There was no amortization of bond premium or discount during the year. What amount should Fara report in its Year 2 statement of cash flows for redemption of bonds payable?

    A. $3,000

    B. $17,000

    C. $20,000

    D. $23,000

Answer (B) is correct. *(CPA, adapted)*
REQUIRED: The amount reported in the statement of cash flows for redemption of bonds payable.
DISCUSSION: Assuming no amortization of premium or discount, the net amount of bonds payable reported was affected solely by the issuance of bonds for equipment and the redemption of bonds. Given that $20,000 of bonds were issued and that the amount reported increased by only $3,000, $17,000 of bonds must have been redeemed. This amount should be reported in the statement of cash flows as a cash outflow from a financing activity.
Answer (A) is incorrect. The amount of $3,000 equals the increase in bonds payable. Answer (C) is incorrect. The amount of bonds issued is $20,000. Answer (D) is incorrect. The amount of $23,000 is the sum of the bonds issued and the increase in bonds payable.

19.3 Operating Activities -- Indirect Presentation

19.3.1. How should a gain from the sale of used equipment for cash be reported in a statement of cash flows using the indirect method?

    A. In investment activities as a reduction of the cash inflow from the sale.

    B. In investment activities as a cash outflow.

    C. In operating activities as a deduction of income.

    D. In operating activities as an addition to income.

Answer (C) is correct. *(CPA, adapted)*
REQUIRED: The presentation of a gain on the sale of used equipment in a statement of cash flows (indirect method).
DISCUSSION: Cash received from the sale of equipment is ordinarily classified in a statement of cash flows as a cash inflow from an investing activity. The cash inflow is equal to the carrying amount of the equipment plus any gain or minus any loss realized. Because the gain will be included in the determination of income from continuing operations, it must be subtracted from the net income figure presented in the statement of cash flows (indirect method) in the reconciliation of net income to net cash flow from operating activities. The purpose of the adjustment is to remove the effect of the gain from both net income and the cash inflows from operating activities. In the cash flows from investing activities section, the amount reported is the sum of the gain and the carrying amount of the equipment.

19.3.2. In a statement of cash flows (indirect method) of a business, an increase in inventories should be presented as a(n)

    A. Outflow of cash.

    B. Inflow and outflow of cash.

    C. Addition to income from continuing operations.

    D. Deduction from income from continuing operations.

Answer (D) is correct. *(CPA, adapted)*
REQUIRED: The presentation of an increase in inventories in a statement of cash flows (indirect method).
DISCUSSION: The objective of a statement of cash flows is to explain the cash receipts and cash disbursements of an entity during an accounting period. In a statement of cash flows of a business in which operating activities are presented on an indirect or reconciliation basis, cash flows from operating activities are determined by adjusting net income (which includes income from continuing operations) to remove the effects of all (1) non-cash items, (2) deferrals of past operating cash receipts and payments, (3) accruals of expected future operating cash receipts and payments, and (4) items whose cash effects are investing or financing activities. Cost of goods sold is included in the determination of net income. Cash paid to suppliers, however, should be the amount included in determining net cash flows from operating activities. To adjust net income to cash flow from operating activities for the difference between cost of goods sold and cash paid to suppliers, a two-step adjustment is necessary. The first step is to adjust net income for the change in the inventory account. This step adjusts for the difference between cost of goods sold and purchases. The second step is to adjust for the changes in the accounts payable account. This step adjusts for the difference between purchases and the amounts disbursed to suppliers. An increase in inventories indicates that purchases were greater than cost of goods sold. Thus, as part of the first step, an increase in inventories should be presented in a statement of cash flows (indirect method) as a deduction from net income.
Answer (A) is incorrect. An increase in inventory should be presented as a deduction from income from continuing operations under the indirect method. Answer (B) is incorrect. An increase in inventory implies that cost of goods sold is less than purchases. Answer (C) is incorrect. An addition to income from continuing operations results from a decrease in inventory.

19.3.3. If the indirect method is used to present the statement of cash flows of a business, depreciation expense is

A. Presented as an addition to net income in the operating section of the statement.

B. Presented as a deduction from net income in the operating section of the statement.

C. Reported as a cash outflow in the investing section of the statement.

D. Not disclosed on the statement.

Answer (A) is correct. *(R. Derstine)*
REQUIRED: The presentation of depreciation when the indirect method is used.
DISCUSSION: In an indirect presentation of net cash flows from operating activities by a business, the statement of cash flows should begin with net income adjusted for certain items, including those recognized in the determination of net income that did not affect cash during the period. The recognition of depreciation expense reduces net income without directly affecting cash. Thus, depreciation must be added back to net income in the determination of cash flows from operating activities.
Answer (B) is incorrect. Depreciation is an addition to net income. Answer (C) is incorrect. Depreciation is not a cash flow. Answer (D) is incorrect. Depreciation is disclosed as an adjustment to net income.

19.3.4. Ionia Company reports operating activities in its statement of cash flows using the indirect method. Which of the following items, if any, should Ionia add back to net income to arrive at net operating cash flow?

	Excess of Treasury Stock Acquisition Cost over Sales Proceeds (Cost Method)	Bond Discount Amortization
A.	Yes	Yes
B.	No	No
C.	No	Yes
D.	Yes	No

Answer (C) is correct. *(CPA, adapted)*
REQUIRED: The item(s), if any, added back to net income when a business reports net operating cash flow by the indirect method.
DISCUSSION: Bond discount amortization is a noncash component of interest expense. Because the amortization decreases net income, it is added back in the reconciliation of net income to net operating cash flow. Treasury stock transactions involve cash flows that do not affect net income. They are also classified as financing activities, not operating activities.
Answer (A) is incorrect. Cash flows from treasury stock transactions do not affect net income. Answer (B) is incorrect. The bond discount amortization should be added to net income. Answer (D) is incorrect. The bond discount amortization should be added to net income, and cash flows from treasury stock transactions do not affect net income.

19.3.5. Kresley Co. has provided the following current account balances for the preparation of the annual statement of cash flows:

	January 1	December 31
Accounts receivable	$11,500	$14,500
Allowance for uncollectible accounts	400	500
Prepaid rent expense	6,200	4,100
Accounts payable	9,700	11,200

Kresley's current-year net income is $75,000. Net cash provided by operating activities in the statement of cash flows should be

A. $72,700

B. $74,300

C. $75,500

D. $75,700

Answer (D) is correct. *(CPA, adapted)*
REQUIRED: The net cash provided by operating activities.
DISCUSSION: The net income of a business should be adjusted for the effects of items properly included in the determination of net income but having either a different effect or no effect on net operating cash flow. The increase in gross accounts receivable should be subtracted from net income. The increase indicates that sales exceeded cash received. The increase in the allowance for uncollectible accounts should be added to net income. This amount reflects a noncash expense. The decrease in prepaid rent expense should be added to net income. The cash was disbursed in a prior period, but the expense was recognized currently as a noncash item. The increase in accounts payable indicates that liabilities and related expenses were recognized without cash outlays. Thus, the change in this account should be added to net income. The net cash provided by operating activities is $75,700 ($75,000 NI – $3,000 change in A/R + $100 change in allowance + $2,100 decrease in prepaid rent + $1,500 increase in A/P).
Answer (A) is incorrect. The amount of $72,700 results from subtracting the increase in accounts payable. Answer (B) is incorrect. The amount of $74,300 results from adding the change in accounts receivable and subtracting the changes in the other balances. Answer (C) is incorrect. The amount of $75,500 results from subtracting the change in the allowance.

Questions 19.3.6 and 19.3.7 are based on the following information. NFP, a nongovernmental not-for-profit entity, reported a change in net assets of $300,000 for the current year. Changes occurred in several balance sheet accounts as follows:

Equipment	$25,000 increase
Accumulated depreciation	40,000 increase
Note payable	30,000 increase

Additional Information:

- During the current year, NFP sold equipment costing $25,000, with accumulated depreciation of $12,000, for a gain of $5,000.
- In December of the current year, NFP purchased equipment costing $50,000 with $20,000 cash and a 12% note payable of $30,000.
- Depreciation expense for the year was $52,000.

19.3.6. In Ithaca's current-year statement of cash flows, net cash provided by operating activities should be

A. $340,000

B. $347,000

C. $352,000

D. $357,000

Answer (B) is correct. *(CPA, adapted)*
REQUIRED: The net cash provided by operating activities in the statement of cash flows.
DISCUSSION: A business should adjust net income for the effects of items included in the determination of net income that have no effect on net cash provided by operating activities. Depreciation is included in the determination of net income but has no cash effect. Thus, depreciation should be added to net income. The sale of equipment resulted in a gain included in the determination of net income, but the cash effect is classified as an inflow from an investing activity. Thus, the gain should be subtracted from net income. The cash outflow for the purchase of equipment is from an investing activity and has no effect on net income. Hence, it requires no adjustment. Thus, the net cash provided by operating activities is $347,000 ($300,000 NI + $52,000 depreciation – $5,000 gain).
Answer (A) is incorrect. The amount of $340,000 reflects addition of the accumulated depreciation. Answer (C) is incorrect. The amount of $352,000 results from not deducting the gain. Answer (D) is incorrect. The amount of $357,000 results from adding the gain.

19.3.7. In Ithaca's current-year statement of cash flows, net cash used in investing activities should be

A. $2,000

B. $12,000

C. $18,000

D. $20,000

Answer (A) is correct. *(CPA, adapted)*
REQUIRED: The net cash used in investing activities.
DISCUSSION: Cash flows from investing activities include the cash inflow from the sale of equipment and the cash outflow from the purchase of equipment. The issuance of a note payable as part of the acquisition price of equipment is classified as a noncash financing and investing activity. The cash inflow from the sale of equipment (carrying amount + gain) is $18,000 [($25,000 – $12,000) + $5,000]. The cash outflow from the purchase of equipment is $20,000. Thus, net cash used is $2,000 ($20,000 – $18,000).
Answer (B) is incorrect. The amount of $12,000 assumes a $30,000 cash payment for the equipment. Answer (C) is incorrect. The amount of $18,000 is the cash inflow from the sale of equipment. Answer (D) is incorrect. The cash outflow from the purchase of equipment is $20,000.

19.3.8. In its statement of cash flows issued for the year ending June 30, Prince Company reported a net cash inflow from operating activities of $123,000. The following adjustments were included in the supplementary schedule reconciling cash flow from operating activities with net income:

Depreciation	$38,000
Increase in net accounts receivable	31,000
Decrease in inventory	27,000
Increase in accounts payable	48,000
Increase in interest payable	12,000

Net income is

   A. $29,000

   B. $41,000

   C. $79,000

   D. $217,000

Answer (A) is correct. *(Publisher, adapted)*
REQUIRED: The net income given cash flow from operating activities and reconciling adjustments.
DISCUSSION: To derive net income from net cash inflow from operating activities, various adjustments are necessary. The depreciation of $38,000 should be subtracted because it is a noncash item included in the determination of net income. The increase in net accounts receivable of $31,000 should be added because it signifies that sales revenue was greater than the cash collections from customers. The increase in accounts payable should be subtracted because it indicates that purchases were $48,000 greater than cash disbursements to suppliers. The second step of the transformation from cash paid to suppliers to cost of goods sold is to subtract the decrease in inventory. This change means that cost of goods sold was $27,000 greater than purchases. The $12,000 increase in interest payable also should be subtracted because it indicates that interest expense was greater than the cash paid to the lenders. Thus, the net adjustment to net cash inflow from operating activities is –$94,000 (–$38,000 + $31,000 – $27,000 – $48,000 – $12,000). Net income is $29,000 ($123,000 net cash inflow – $94,000 net adjustment).
Answer (B) is incorrect. The increase in interest payable should be subtracted. Answer (C) is incorrect. Depreciation and the increase in interest payable should be subtracted. Answer (D) is incorrect. Depreciation, the increase in accounts payable, the decrease in inventory, and the increase in interest payable should be subtracted, and the increase in net accounts receivable should be added.

19.3.9. In the indirect presentation of cash flows from operating activities, net income of a business is adjusted for noncash revenues, gains, expenses, and losses to determine the cash flows from operating activities. A reconciliation of net cash flows from operating activities to net income

   A. Must be reported in the statement of cash flows.

   B. Must be presented separately in a related disclosure.

   C. May be either reported in the statement of cash flows or presented separately in a related disclosure.

   D. Need not be presented.

Answer (C) is correct. *(Publisher, adapted)*
REQUIRED: The reporting of a reconciliation of net cash flows from operating activities to net income.
DISCUSSION: When an indirect presentation of net cash flows from operating activities is made by a business, a reconciliation with net income must be provided for all noncash revenues, gains, expenses, and losses. This reconciliation may be either (1) reported in the statement of cash flows or (2) provided separately in related disclosures, with the statement of cash flows presenting only the net cash flows from operating activities.
Answer (A) is incorrect. A reconciliation may be presented in a related disclosure. Answer (B) is incorrect. A reconciliation may be reported in the statement of cash flows. Answer (D) is incorrect. A reconciliation must be reported in an indirect presentation of the statement of cash flows.

19.3.10. Reed Co.'s Year 1 statement of cash flows reported cash provided from operating activities of $400,000. For Year 1, depreciation of equipment was $190,000, impairment of goodwill was $5,000, and dividends paid on common stock were $100,000. In Reed's Year 1 statement of cash flows, what amount was reported as net income?

   A. $105,000

   B. $205,000

   C. $305,000

   D. $595,000

Answer (B) is correct. *(CPA, adapted)*
REQUIRED: The net income reported in the statement of cash flows.
DISCUSSION: Depreciation expense and the loss from goodwill impairment are noncash items that are added to net income to arrive at net cash provided by operating activities. Hence, they are subtracted from net cash provided by operating activities to arrive at net income. The payment of cash dividends is not a reconciling item because it is a financing cash flow that does not affect net income. Net income was therefore $205,000 ($400,000 net cash provided by operating activities – $190,000 depreciation – $5,000 goodwill impairment).
Answer (A) is incorrect. Payment of dividends on common stock does not affect net income or operating cash flows. Answer (C) is incorrect. Payment of dividends on common stock does not affect net income or operating cash flows. Answer (D) is incorrect. Depreciation and the impairment loss are subtracted from net cash provided by operating activities to arrive at net income.

19.3.11. In its statement of cash flow for the current year, Ness Co. reported cash paid for interest of $70,000. Ness did not capitalize any interest during the current year. Changes occurred in several balance sheet accounts as follows:

Accrued interest payable	$17,000 decrease
Prepaid interest	23,000 decrease

In its income statement for the current year, what amount should Ness report as interest expense?

- A. $30,000
- B. $64,000
- C. $76,000
- D. $110,000

Answer (C) is correct. *(CPA, adapted)*
REQUIRED: The interest expense given cash paid for interest and changes in interest payable and prepaid interest.
DISCUSSION: To reconcile cash paid for interest ($70,000) to interest expense, the decrease in interest payable (a prior-period expense and a current-period cash outflow) is subtracted. The decrease in prepaid interest (a prior-period cash outflow and a current-period expense) is added. Current interest expense is $76,000 ($70,000 – $17,000 + $23,000).
Answer (A) is incorrect. A decrease in prepaid interest must be added to cash paid to arrive at interest expense. Answer (B) is incorrect. A decrease in interest payable must be subtracted and a decrease in prepaid interest must be added to arrive at interest expense. Answer (D) is incorrect. A decrease in accrued interest payable must be subtracted, not added, to arrive at interest expense.

19.3.12. A company is preparing its year-end cash flow statement using the indirect method. During the year, the following transactions occurred:

Dividends paid	$300
Proceeds from the issuance of common stock	250
Borrowings under a line of credit	200
Proceeds from the issuance of convertible bonds	100
Proceeds from the sale of a building	150

What is the company's increase in cash flows provided by financing activities for the year?

- A. $50
- B. $150
- C. $250
- D. $550

Answer (C) is correct. *(CPA, adapted)*
REQUIRED: The net cash increase from financing activities.
DISCUSSION: Cash flows from financing activities generally involve the cash effects of transactions and other events that relate to the issuance, settlement, or reacquisition of the entity's debt and equity instruments. The proceeds from the sale of a building is an investing cash flow. All of the other transactions represent cash flows from financing activities. Thus, the company's increase in cash flows provided by financing activities is $250 [($300) + $250 + $200 + $100].
Answer (A) is incorrect. An amount of $50 results from failing to consider the borrowing under a line of credit, which is classified as a cash inflow from a financing activity. Answer (B) is incorrect. An amount of $150 results from failing to consider the proceeds from the issuance of convertible bonds, which is classified as a cash inflow from financing activities. Answer (D) is incorrect. Dividends paid represent a cash outflow from financing activities that must be considered in determining the company's cash flows from financing activities.

19.4 Operating Activities -- Direct Presentation

19.4.1. The Marburg Corporation owns extensive rental property. For some of this property, rent is paid in advance. For other property, rent is paid following the end of the year. In the income statement for the year ended December 31, Year 2, Marburg reported $140,000 in rental income. The following data are included in Marburg's December 31 balance sheets:

	Year 2	Year 1
Rent receivable	$95,000	$120,000
Deferred rent income	40,000	50,000

In its statement of cash flows for the year ended December 31, Year 2, Marburg should report cash receipts from rental properties totaling

- A. $105,000
- B. $125,000
- C. $155,000
- D. $175,000

Answer (C) is correct. *(K.M. Boze)*
REQUIRED: The amount of total rental cash receipts.
DISCUSSION: No write-offs of rent receivables are mentioned. Consequently, a decrease in the rent receivable asset account implies that Marburg collected more in cash receipts from rental customers than it recognized as rental income in Year 2. In contrast, a decrease in the deferred rent income liability account signifies that Marburg recognized more rental income than it received in cash payments. To determine cash receipts from rental properties, the rental income of $140,000 should be increased by the $25,000 change in the rent receivable account and decreased by the $10,000 reduction in the deferred rent income account. Cash receipts from rental properties were therefore $155,000.
Answer (A) is incorrect. The $25,000 decrease in rent receivable should be added to rental income, not subtracted. Answer (B) is incorrect. The $25,000 decrease in rent receivable should be added to rental income, not subtracted, and the $10,000 decrease in deferred rental income should be subtracted, not added. Answer (D) is incorrect. The $10,000 decrease in deferred rental income should be subtracted from rental income, not added.

19.4.2. In a statement of cash flows of a business enterprise, which of the following will increase reported cash flows from operating activities using the direct method? (Ignore income tax considerations.)

A. Dividends received from investments.

B. Gain on sale of equipment.

C. Gain on early retirement of bonds.

D. Change from straight-line to accelerated depreciation.

Answer (A) is correct. *(CPA, adapted)*
REQUIRED: The item that increases reported cash flows from operating activities using the direct method.
DISCUSSION: Operating activities are transactions and other events not classified as investing and financing activities. In general, the cash effects of operating activities (other than gains and losses) enter into the determination of the net income of a business enterprise or the change in net assets of a not-for-profit entity. Thus, cash receipts from dividends are cash flows from an operating activity.
Answer (B) is incorrect. The sale of equipment is an investing activity. Answer (C) is incorrect. An early retirement of bonds is a financing activity. Answer (D) is incorrect. A change in accounting principle is a noncash event.

19.4.3. Lane Company acquired copyrights from authors, in some cases paying advance royalties and in others paying royalties within 30 days of year-end. Lane reported royalty expense of $375,000 for the year ended December 31, Year 2. The following data are included in Lane's balance sheet:

	Year 1	Year 2
Prepaid royalties	$60,000	$50,000
Royalties payable	75,000	90,000

In its Year 2 statement of cash flows, Lane should report cash payments for royalties of

A. $350,000

B. $370,000

C. $380,000

D. $400,000

Answer (A) is correct. *(CPA, adapted)*
REQUIRED: The cash payments for royalty payments.
DISCUSSION: A decrease in a prepaid royalties asset account implies that royalty expense was greater than the related cash payments. Similarly, an increase in a royalties payable liability account indicates that royalties expense exceeded cash payments. Royalty expense therefore exceeds the amount of cash payments for royalty payments by the amount of the decrease in the prepaid royalties account plus the increase in the royalties payable account. Thus, Lane's Year 2 cash payments for royalty payments total $350,000 ($375,000 royalty expense – $10,000 decrease in prepaid royalties – $15,000 increase in royalties payable).
Answer (B) is incorrect. The $10,000 decrease in prepaid royalties should be subtracted, not added. Answer (C) is incorrect. The $15,000 increase in royalties payable should be subtracted from royalty expense, not added. Answer (D) is incorrect. The decrease in prepaid royalties and the increase in royalties payable should be subtracted, not added.

19.4.4. The statement of cash flows may be presented in either a direct or an indirect (reconciliation) format. In which of these formats would cash collected from customers be presented as a gross amount?

	Direct	Indirect
A.	No	No
B.	No	Yes
C.	Yes	Yes
D.	Yes	No

Answer (D) is correct. *(Publisher, adapted)*
REQUIRED: The format in which cash collected from customers is presented as a gross amount.
DISCUSSION: The statement of cash flows may report cash flows from operating activities in either an indirect (reconciliation) or a direct format. The direct format reports the major classes of operating cash receipts and cash payments as gross amounts. The indirect presentation reconciles net income to the same amount of net cash flow from operations that would be determined in accordance with the direct method. To arrive at net operating cash flow, the indirect method adjusts net income by removing the effects of (1) all deferrals of past operating cash receipts and payments, (2) all accruals of expected future operating cash receipts and payments, (3) all financing and investing activities, and (4) all noncash operating transactions.

19.4.5. Duke Co. reported cost of goods sold of $270,000 for the current year. Additional information is as follows:

	December 31	January 1
Inventory	$60,000	$45,000
Accounts payable	26,000	39,000

If Duke uses the direct method, what amount should Duke report as cash paid to suppliers in its current year statement of cash flows?

A. $242,000

B. $268,000

C. $272,000

D. $298,000

Answer (D) is correct. *(CPA, adapted)*
REQUIRED: The amount of cash paid to suppliers.
DISCUSSION: To reconcile cost of goods sold to cash paid to suppliers, a two-step adjustment is needed. First, determine purchases by adding the increase in inventory to cost of goods. Second, determine cash paid for goods sold by adding the decrease in accounts payable to purchases. Thus, cash paid for goods sold equals $298,000 [$270,000 + ($60,000 – $45,000) + ($39,000 – $26,000)].
Answer (A) is incorrect. The amount of $242,000 results from subtracting the changes in inventory and accounts payable. Answer (B) is incorrect. The amount of $268,000 results from subtracting the change in inventory. Answer (C) is incorrect. The amount of $272,000 results from subtracting the change in accounts payable.

Questions 19.4.6 through 19.4.9 are based on the following information.

Pimlico Corp. uses the direct method to prepare its statement of cash flows. Pimlico's trial balances at December 31, Year 2 and Year 1, are as follows:

	December 31	
	Year 2	Year 1
Debits		
Cash	$ 35,000	$ 32,000
Accounts receivable	33,000	30,000
Inventory	31,000	47,000
Property, plant, & equipment	100,000	95,000
Unamortized bond discount	4,500	5,000
Cost of goods sold	250,000	380,000
Selling expenses	141,500	172,000
General and administrative expenses	137,000	151,300
Interest expense	4,300	2,600
Income tax expense	20,400	61,200
	$756,700	$976,100

Credits		
Allowance for uncollectible accounts	$ 1,300	$ 1,100
Accumulated depreciation	16,500	15,000
Trade accounts payable	25,000	17,500
Income taxes payable	21,000	27,100
Deferred income taxes	5,300	4,600
8% callable bonds payable	45,000	20,000
Common stock	50,000	40,000
Additional paid-in capital	9,100	7,500
Retained earnings	44,700	64,600
Sales	538,800	778,700
	$756,700	$976,100

- Pimlico purchased $5,000 in equipment during Year 2.
- Pimlico allocated one-third of its depreciation expense to selling expenses and the remainder to general and administrative expenses.

19.4.6. What amounts should Pimlico report in its statement of cash flows for the year ended December 31, Year 2, for cash collected from customers?

A. $541,800

B. $541,600

C. $536,000

D. $535,800

Answer (D) is correct. *(CPA, adapted)*
REQUIRED: The cash collected from customers.
DISCUSSION: Collections from customers equal sales minus the increase in gross accounts receivable, or $535,800 ($538,800 – $33,000 + $30,000).
Answer (A) is incorrect. This amount results from adding the increase in receivables. Answer (B) is incorrect. This amount results from adding the increase in receivables and subtracting the increase in the allowance for uncollectible accounts, that is, from adding net accounts receivable. Answer (C) is incorrect. This amount results from subtracting net accounts receivable.

19.4.7. What amounts should Pimlico report in its statement of cash flows for the year ended December 31, Year 2, for cash paid for interest?

A. $4,800

B. $4,300

C. $3,800

D. $1,700

Answer (C) is correct. *(CPA, adapted)*
REQUIRED: The cash paid for interest.
DISCUSSION: Interest expense is $4,300. This amount includes $500 of discount amortization, a noncash item. Hence, the cash paid for interest was $3,800 ($4,300 – $500).
Answer (A) is incorrect. This figure results from adding the amortized discount. Answer (B) is incorrect. This figure is the total interest expense. Answer (D) is incorrect. This figure is the increase in interest expense.

19.4.8. What amounts should Pimlico report in its statement of cash flows for the year ended December 31, Year 2, for cash paid for income taxes?

A. $25,800

B. $20,400

C. $19,700

D. $15,000

Answer (A) is correct. *(CPA, adapted)*
REQUIRED: The cash paid for income taxes.
DISCUSSION: To reconcile income tax expense to cash paid for income taxes, a two-step adjustment is needed. The first step is to add the decrease in income taxes payable. The second step is to subtract the increase in deferred income taxes. Hence, cash paid for income taxes equals $25,800 [$20,400 + ($27,100 – $21,000) – ($5,300 – $4,600)].
Answer (B) is incorrect. This amount is income tax expense. Answer (C) is incorrect. This amount equals income tax expense minus the increase in deferred income taxes. Answer (D) is incorrect. This amount results from subtracting the decrease in income taxes payable and adding the increase in deferred taxes payable.

19.4.9. What amounts should Pimlico report in its statement of cash flows for the year ended December 31, Year 2, for cash paid for selling expenses?

A. $142,000

B. $141,500

C. $141,000

D. $140,000

Answer (C) is correct. *(CPA, adapted)*
REQUIRED: The cash paid for selling expenses.
DISCUSSION: Cash paid for selling expenses equals selling expenses minus the depreciation allocated to selling expenses. Total depreciation expense equals the $1,500 ($16,500 – $15,000) change in accumulated depreciation. Thus, cash paid for selling expenses equals $141,000 ($141,500 expense for Year 2 – $1,500 depreciation for Year 2 × 33 1/3% allocated to selling).
Answer (A) is incorrect. The amount of $142,000 results from adding the depreciation allocated to selling expenses. Answer (B) is incorrect. The amount of $141,500 equals the selling expenses for Year 2. Answer (D) is incorrect. The amount of $140,000 results from subtracting 100% of depreciation expense from selling expenses.

19.4.10. The following information was taken from the financial statements of Planet Corp. for the year just ended:

Accounts receivable, January 1	$ 21,600
Accounts receivable, December 31	30,400
Sales on account and cash sales	438,000
Uncollectible accounts	1,000

No accounts receivable were written off or recovered during the year. If the direct method is used in the statement of cash flows, Planet should report cash collected from customers as

A. $447,800

B. $446,800

C. $429,200

D. $428,200

Answer (C) is correct. *(CPA, adapted)*
REQUIRED: The cash collected from customers.
DISCUSSION: This question requires the assumption that accounts receivable is a gross amount. Collections from customers equal sales revenue adjusted for the change in gross accounts receivable and write-offs and recoveries. Because no accounts receivable were written off or recovered during the year, no adjustment for these transactions is needed. Accounts receivable increased by $8,800 ($30,400 – $21,600), an excess of revenue recognized over cash received. Planet therefore should report cash collected from customers of $429,200 ($438,000 – $8,800).
Answer (A) is incorrect. The amount of $447,800 results from adding the increase in accounts receivable and the uncollectible accounts balance. Answer (B) is incorrect. The amount of $446,800 results from adding the increase in accounts receivable. Answer (D) is incorrect. The amount of $428,200 results from subtracting the uncollectible accounts balance.

19.4.11. The following balances were reported by Mall Co. at December 31, Year 2 and Year 1:

	12/31/Year 2	12/31/Year 1
Inventory	$260,000	$290,000
Accounts payable	75,000	50,000

Mall paid suppliers $490,000 during the year ended December 31, Year 2. What amount should Mall report for cost of goods sold in Year 2?

A. $545,000

B. $495,000

C. $485,000

D. $435,000

Answer (A) is correct. *(CPA, adapted)*
REQUIRED: The cost of goods sold.
DISCUSSION: If trade accounts increased by $25,000, purchases must have been $25,000 higher than the disbursements for purchases. Purchases thus are $515,000 ($490,000 + $25,000). The decrease in merchandise inventory indicates that cost of goods sold must have been $30,000 higher than purchases. Hence, COGS equals $545,000 ($515,000 + $30,000).
Answer (B) is incorrect. The amount of $495,000 results from subtracting the increase in accounts payable. Answer (C) is incorrect. The amount of $485,000 results from subtracting the decrease in inventory. Answer (D) is incorrect. The amount of $435,000 results from subtracting the decrease in inventory and the increase in accounts payable.

19.5 IFRS

19.5.1. In accordance with IFRS, which combination below explains the effect of credit card interest incurred and paid during the period on (1) equity on the statement of financial position and (2) the statement of cash flows?

	(1) Effect on Equity on Balance Sheet	(2) Reflected on Statement of Cash Flows as a(n)
A.	Decrease	Investing outflow
B.	Decrease	Operating or financing outflow
C.	No effect	Financing or investing outflow
D.	No effect	Operating outflow

Answer (B) is correct. *(CIA, adapted)*
REQUIRED: The effect of interest paid on the balance sheet and cash flow statement under IFRS.
DISCUSSION: Interest incurred is classified as interest expense on the income statement, which in turn reduces equity on the statement of financial position by reducing retained earnings. According to IAS 7, cash payments for interest made by an entity that is not a financial institution may be classified on the statement of cash flows as an outflow of cash from operating or financing activities.
Answer (A) is incorrect. Interest payments are classified as an operating or financing outflow on the statement of cash flows. Answer (C) is incorrect. Credit card interest charges reduce equity. Answer (D) is incorrect. Credit card interest charges reduce equity.

19.5.2. In accordance with IFRS, in the statement of cash flows, the payment of cash dividends appears in the <List A> activities section as a <List B> of cash.

	List A	List B
A.	Operating or investing	Source
B.	Operating or financing	Use
C.	Investing or financing	Use
D.	Investing	Source

Answer (B) is correct. *(CIA, adapted)*
REQUIRED: The treatment of cash dividends in a statement of cash flows under IFRS.
DISCUSSION: According to IAS 7, dividends paid may be treated as a cash outflow from financing activities because they are a cost of obtaining resources from owners. However, they also may be treated as operating items to help determine the entity's ability to pay dividends from operating cash flows.

19.5.3. The comparative balance sheet for an entity that had profit of $150,000 for the year ended December 31, Year 2, and paid $125,000 of dividends during Year 2 is as follows:

	12/31/Yr 2	12/31/Yr 1
Cash	$150,000	$180,000
Accounts receivable	200,000	220,000
Total assets	$350,000	$400,000
Payables	$ 80,000	$160,000
Share capital	130,000	125,000
Retained earnings	140,000	115,000
Total	$350,000	$400,000

If dividends paid are treated as an operating item, the amount of net cash from operating activities during Year 2 was

A. $(35,000)

B. $90,000

C. $150,000

D. $210,000

Answer (A) is correct. *(CIA, adapted)*
REQUIRED: The amount of net cash from operating activities during Year 2.
DISCUSSION: Profit is adjusted to determine the net cash from operations. The payment of cash dividends is regarded as a cash flow from an operating activity. Hence, it is a reconciling item requiring a $125,000 reduction of profit. However, the decrease in accounts receivable ($220,000 – $200,000 = $20,000) during the period represents a cash inflow (collections of pre-Year 2 receivables) not reflected in Year 2 profit. Moreover, the decrease in payables ($160,000 – $80,000 = $80,000) indicates a cash outflow (payment of pre-Year 2 liabilities) that also is not reflected in Year 2 profit. Accordingly, net cash from operations was –$35,000 ($150,000 – $125,000 + $20,000 – $80,000).
Answer (B) is incorrect. The amount of $90,000 assumes that dividends paid were a financing item. Answer (C) is incorrect. The amount of $150,000 is profit. Answer (D) is incorrect. The amount of $210,000 subtracts the reduction in receivables and adds the reduction in payables.

STUDY UNIT TWENTY
FINANCIAL STATEMENT DISCLOSURES

This study unit presents the **disclosure** requirements for the seven topics in the listing of subunits. The disclosure requirements for all other financial reporting topics are covered in the appropriate study units throughout the book.

QUESTIONS

20.1 Disclosure of Accounting Policies

20.1.1. The specific accounting policies and methods considered to be appropriate by management and used for reporting purposes

A. Should be disclosed parenthetically in the tabular portion of the financial statements.

B. Should be disclosed in a separate summary of significant accounting policies preceding the notes to the financial statements or in the initial note to the financial statements.

C. Should be disclosed in management's discussion of operations.

D. Need not be disclosed unless they are at variance with generally accepted accounting principles.

Answer (B) is correct. *(CMA, adapted)*
REQUIRED: The most appropriate statement concerning disclosure of accounting policies.
DISCUSSION: All significant accounting policies of a reporting entity must be disclosed as an integral part of its financial statements. The preferred presentation is inclusion of a summary of accounting policies in a separate section preceding the notes or in the initial note. Disclosure should encompass those principles and methods that involve a selection from existing acceptable alternatives, those methods peculiar to the industry in which the entity operates, and any unusual or innovative applications of GAAP.
Answer (A) is incorrect. Specific accounting policies and methods should not be disclosed parenthetically in the tabular portion of the financial statements. Answer (C) is incorrect. Specific accounting policies and methods should not be disclosed in management's discussion of operations. Answer (D) is incorrect. Accounting policies and methods must be disclosed.

20.1.2. Which of the following facts concerning fixed assets should be included in the summary of significant accounting policies?

	Depreciation Method	Composition
A.	No	Yes
B.	Yes	Yes
C.	Yes	No
D.	No	No

Answer (C) is correct. *(CPA, adapted)*
REQUIRED: The fact(s) concerning fixed assets disclosed in the summary of significant accounting policies.
DISCUSSION: Disclosure of significant accounting policies is required when (1) a selection has been made from existing acceptable alternatives; (2) a policy is unique to the industry in which the entity operates, even if the policy is predominantly followed in that industry; and (3) GAAP have been applied in an unusual or innovative way. A depreciation method is a selection from existing acceptable alternatives and should be included in the summary of significant accounting policies. Financial statement disclosure of accounting policies should not duplicate details presented elsewhere in the financial statements, such as composition of plant assets.

20.1.3. Disclosure of accounting policies is not necessary when

A. Selection of an accounting principle or method has been made from existing acceptable alternatives.

B. The accounting principles and methods used by an entity are peculiar to the entity's industry, provided that such principles and methods are predominantly followed in that industry.

C. Unaudited financial statements are issued as of a date between annual reporting dates and the reporting entity has not changed its accounting policies since the end of its preceding fiscal year.

D. An entity makes unusual or innovative applications of GAAP.

Answer (C) is correct. *(Publisher, adapted)*
REQUIRED: The situation in which disclosure of accounting policies is not necessary.
DISCUSSION: Disclosure of accounting policies is not required in unaudited interim financial statements when the reporting entity has not changed its policies since the end of the preceding fiscal year. Users of such interim statements will presumably consult the disclosure concerning significant accounting policies in the statements issued at the close of the preceding fiscal year.
Answer (A) is incorrect. Disclosure is required when an accounting principle or method has been selected from existing acceptable alternatives. Answer (B) is incorrect. Disclosure is required when the accounting principles and methods used are peculiar to the entity's industry. Answer (D) is incorrect. Disclosure is required when an entity makes unusual or innovative applications of GAAP.

20.1.4. Which of the following information should be disclosed in the summary of significant accounting policies?

A. Refinancing of debt subsequent to the balance sheet date.

B. Guarantees of indebtedness of others.

C. Criteria for determining which investments are treated as cash equivalents.

D. Adequacy of pension plan assets relative to vested benefits.

Answer (C) is correct. *(CPA, adapted)*
REQUIRED: The disclosure of the summary of significant accounting policies.
DISCUSSION: All significant accounting policies should be disclosed as an integral part of the financial statements. Disclosure of the policy for determining which investments are treated as cash equivalents is required.
Answer (A) is incorrect. The refinancing of debt subsequent to the balance sheet date is not an accounting policy but is an item disclosed in the notes. Answer (B) is incorrect. Guaranteeing the indebtedness of others is not an accounting policy but an item that should be disclosed in the notes. Answer (D) is incorrect. The adequacy of pension plan assets is not an accounting policy, but rather is an item that should be disclosed in the notes.

20.1.5. Which of the following information should be included in Mariah Company's current-year summary of significant accounting policies?

A. Property, plant, and equipment is recorded at cost with depreciation computed principally by the straight-line method.

B. During the current year, the consulting services operating segment was sold.

C. Operating segment current-year sales are $2 million for the software segment, $4 million for the book production segment, and $6 million for the technical services segment.

D. Future common share dividends are expected to approximate 60% of earnings.

Answer (A) is correct. *(CPA, adapted)*
REQUIRED: The item properly disclosed in the summary of significant accounting policies.
DISCUSSION: The commonly required disclosures in a summary of significant accounting policies include (1) the basis of consolidation, (2) depreciation methods, (3) amortization of intangible assets, (4) inventory pricing, (5) recognition of profit on long-term construction-type contracts, (6) recognition of revenue from franchising and leasing operations, and (7) the policy for defining cash equivalents. Hence, the summary of significant accounting policies should include information about property, plant, and equipment depreciated by the straight-line method.
Answer (B) is incorrect. The sale of an operating segment is a transaction, not an accounting principle. It is reflected in the discontinued operations section of the income statement. Answer (C) is incorrect. Specific operating segment information does not constitute an accounting policy. An accounting policy is a specific principle or a method of applying it. Answer (D) is incorrect. Future dividend policy is not an accounting policy.

20.1.6. Which of the following should be disclosed in the summary of significant accounting policies?

	Composition of Inventories	Maturity Dates of Noncurrent Debt
A.	Yes	Yes
B.	Yes	No
C.	No	No
D.	No	Yes

Answer (C) is correct. *(CPA, adapted)*
    REQUIRED: The item(s) properly disclosed.
    DISCUSSION: Certain items are commonly required disclosures in a summary of significant accounting policies. These items include (1) the basis of consolidation, (2) depreciation methods, (3) amortization of intangibles, (4) inventory pricing, (5) recognition of revenue from contracts with customers, and (6) recognition of revenue from leasing operations. But financial statement disclosure of accounting policies should not duplicate details presented elsewhere in the financial statements. Details about the composition of inventories and the maturity dates of long-term debts are disclosed elsewhere in the financial statements. Thus, the summary of significant accounting policies should refer to these details but need not duplicate them.
    Answer (A) is incorrect. Neither the composition of inventories nor the maturity dates of long-term debt should be disclosed in the summary of significant accounting policies. Answer (B) is incorrect. Neither the composition of inventories nor the maturity dates of long-term debt should be disclosed in the summary of significant accounting policies. Answer (D) is incorrect. Neither the composition of inventories nor the maturity dates of long-term debt should be disclosed in the summary of significant accounting policies.

20.1.7. When financial statements are issued, a statement identifying the accounting policies adopted by the reporting entity preferably should be presented as part of the financial statements. All of the following are required to be disclosed with respect to accounting policies except the

A. Depreciation methods used for plant assets.

B. Accounting for long-term construction contracts.

C. Estimated lives of depreciable assets.

D. Principles of consolidation.

Answer (C) is correct. *(CMA, adapted)*
    REQUIRED: The item not a required disclosure.
    DISCUSSION: Disclosure of accounting policies is required to be made in a separate summary of significant accounting policies or in the initial note to the financial statements. The disclosures should identify the principles followed and the methods of applying them that materially affect the statements. Moreover, the disclosures should encompass (1) principles and methods involving a selection from acceptable alternatives, (2) accounting principles unique to a particular industry, and (3) innovative or unusual applications of GAAP. However, the disclosures should not repeat details presented elsewhere, e.g., the estimated lives of depreciable assets.
    Answer (A) is incorrect. Examples of required disclosures include depreciation and amortization methods. Answer (B) is incorrect. Examples of required disclosures include means of accounting for long-term construction contracts. Answer (D) is incorrect. Examples of required disclosures include basis of consolidation.

20.1.8. The summary of significant accounting policies should disclose the

A. Reasons that retrospective application of a change in an accounting principle is impracticable.

B. Basis of profit recognition on long-term construction contracts.

C. Adequacy of pension plan assets in relation to vested benefits.

D. Future minimum lease payments in the aggregate and for each of the 5 succeeding fiscal years.

Answer (B) is correct. *(CPA, adapted)*
    REQUIRED: The item disclosed in the summary of significant accounting policies.
    DISCUSSION: Certain items are commonly required disclosures in a summary of significant accounting policies: (1) the basis of consolidation, (2) depreciation methods, (3) amortization of intangibles, (4) inventory pricing, (5) recognition of revenue from contracts with customers, and (6) recognition of revenue from franchising and leasing operations.
    Answer (A) is incorrect. If retrospective application of a change in accounting principle is impracticable, disclosure of the reasons and the alternative method of reporting the change is required. The reasons are not policies. Answer (C) is incorrect. The adequacy of pension plan assets in relation to vested benefits is not a disclosure required by GAAP. Answer (D) is incorrect. The future minimum lease payments in the aggregate and for each of the 5 succeeding fiscal years should be disclosed but not in the summary of significant accounting policies.

20.2 Development Stage Entities

20.2.1. A statement of cash flows for a development stage entity

A. Is the same as that of an established operating entity and, in addition, reports cumulative amounts from the entity's inception.

B. Reports only cumulative amounts from the entity's inception.

C. Is the same as that of an established operating entity, but does not show cumulative amounts from the entity's inception.

D. Is not presented.

Answer (A) is correct. *(CPA, adapted)*
REQUIRED: The true statement about a statement of cash flows for a development stage entity.
DISCUSSION: A development stage entity must present financial statements in conformity with GAAP together with certain additional information accumulated since the entity's inception. The additional disclosures include (1) cumulative net losses in the equity section of the balance sheet, (2) cumulative amounts of revenue and expense in the income statement, (3) cumulative amounts of cash inflows and outflows in the statement of cash flows, and (4) information about each issuance of stock in the statement of equity.
Answer (B) is incorrect. The statement of cash flows also must conform with GAAP applicable to established entities. Answer (C) is incorrect. The statement of cash flows also must report cumulative amounts from the entity's inception. Answer (D) is incorrect. A statement of cash flows is required as part of a full set of financial statements.

20.2.2. An entity is considered to be in the development stage if

A. 12 months of operations have not been completed.

B. Planned principal operations have commenced but have not yet begun to produce significant revenue.

C. The entity has not previously shown a profit from operations.

D. The entity has not obtained 50% of the initial planned activity level.

Answer (B) is correct. *(Publisher, adapted)*
REQUIRED: The statement that describes the development stage of an entity.
DISCUSSION: An entity is considered to be in the development stage if planned principal operations have not yet commenced or if they have not yet begun to generate significant revenue.
Answer (A) is incorrect. The development stage has no time limit. Answer (C) is incorrect. Amounts of profit or loss do not define the development stage. Answer (D) is incorrect. The development stage is not defined by a level of planned activity.

20.2.3. Juris Corp. was a development stage entity from October 10, Year 1, (inception) through December 31, Year 2. The year ended December 31, Year 3, was the first year in which Juris qualified as an established operating entity. The following are among the costs incurred by Juris:

	For the Period 10/10/Yr 1 through 12/31/Yr 2	For the Year Ended 12/31/Yr 3
Leasehold improvements, equipment, and furniture	$1,000,000	$ 300,000
Security deposits	60,000	30,000
Research and development	750,000	900,000
Laboratory operations	175,000	550,000
General and administrative	225,000	685,000
Depreciation	25,000	115,000
	$2,235,000	$2,580,000

From its inception through the period ended December 31, Year 3, what is the total amount of costs incurred by Juris that should be charged to operations?

A. $3,425,000

B. $2,250,000

C. $1,775,000

D. $1,350,000

Answer (A) is correct. *(CPA, adapted)*
REQUIRED: The total amount of costs that a development stage entity should charge to operations.
DISCUSSION: A development stage entity must use the same GAAP as an established operating entity. An established operating entity would have capitalized the entire $1,300,000 of leasehold improvements, equipment, and furniture, as well as the $90,000 of security deposits. Consequently, Juris Corp., a development stage entity, should also capitalize these costs. An established operating entity would have expensed the $1,650,000 of research and development costs, the $725,000 of laboratory operations costs, the $910,000 of general and administrative costs, and the $140,000 of depreciation. Juris Corp. should also expense these costs. The total to be expensed by Juris therefore equals $3,425,000 ($1,650,000 + $725,000 + $910,000 + $140,000).
Answer (B) is incorrect. The amount of $2,250,000 equals costs incurred in Year 3 minus security deposits and leasehold improvements, equipment, and furniture. Answer (C) is incorrect. The amount of $1,775,000 excludes R&D costs. Answer (D) is incorrect. The amount of $1,350,000 equals costs incurred during the development stage, minus leasehold improvements, equipment, and furniture, plus Year 3 depreciation.

20.2.4. Financial reporting by a development stage entity differs from financial reporting for an established operating entity in regard to note disclosures

A. Only.

B. And expense recognition principles only.

C. And revenue recognition principles only.

D. And revenue and expense recognition principles.

Answer (A) is correct. *(CPA, adapted)*
REQUIRED: The way in which financial reporting by a development stage entity differs from financial reporting for an established operating entity.
DISCUSSION: A development stage entity must present financial statements in conformity with GAAP together with certain additional information accumulated since the entity's inception. The additional disclosures include (1) cumulative net losses in the equity section of the balance sheet, (2) cumulative amounts of revenue and expense in the income statement, (3) cumulative amounts of cash inflows and outflows in the statement of cash flows, and (4) information about each issuance of stock in the statement of equity.

20.3 Related Party Disclosures

20.3.1. Dex Co. has entered into a joint venture with an affiliate to secure access to additional inventory. Under the joint venture agreement, Dex will purchase the output of the venture at prices negotiated on an arm's-length basis. Which of the following is (are) required to be disclosed about the related party transaction?

I. The amount due to the affiliate at the balance sheet date.

II. The dollar amount of the purchases during the year.

A. I only.

B. II only.

C. Both I and II.

D. Neither I nor II.

Answer (C) is correct. *(CPA, adapted)*
REQUIRED: The disclosures for a related party transaction.
DISCUSSION: Required disclosures include (1) the nature of the relationship involved; (2) a description of the transactions for each period an income statement is presented and such other information as is deemed necessary to an understanding of the effects of the transactions; (3) the dollar amounts of transactions for each period an income statement is presented and the effects of any change in the method of establishing their terms; (4) amounts due from or to related parties as of the date of each balance sheet, including the terms of settlement; and (5) certain tax information if the entity is part of a group that files a consolidated tax return.
Answer (A) is incorrect. The dollar amount of the purchases during the year must be disclosed. Answer (B) is incorrect. The amount due to the affiliate at the balance sheet date must be disclosed. Answer (D) is incorrect. The amount due to the affiliate at the balance sheet date and the dollar amount of the purchases during the year must be disclosed.

20.3.2. Related party transactions include transactions between the entity and

A. The principal owners, management, and any of their relatives.

B. Affiliates.

C. Trusts for the benefit of employees whether or not the trustee is independent of management.

D. Beneficial owners of at least 5% of the voting interests of the entity.

Answer (B) is correct. *(Publisher, adapted)*
REQUIRED: The parties to related party transactions.
DISCUSSION: Related party transactions include transactions between

1. A parent and its subsidiaries
2. Subsidiaries of a common parent
3. An entity and employee trusts managed by or under the trusteeship of the entity's management
4. An entity and its principal owners, management, or members of their immediate families
5. Affiliates
6. An entity and (a) its equity-based investees or (b) investees that would be accounted for using the equity method if not for the election of the fair value option
7. An entity and any other entity if one party can significantly influence the other to the extent that one party may be prevented from fully pursuing its own interests
8. Parties all of which can be significantly influenced by another party

Answer (A) is incorrect. Only immediate family members of the principal owners and management are considered related parties. Answer (C) is incorrect. Employee benefit trusts that are not managed by the entity are not related parties. Answer (D) is incorrect. Only those owners of record or known beneficial owners of more than 10% of the voting interests of the entity are related parties.

20.3.3. For purposes of related party disclosures, principal owners are

A. Parties that, directly or indirectly, through one or more intermediaries, control, are controlled by, or are under common control with an entity.

B. Owners of record or known beneficial owners of more than 10% of the voting interests of that entity.

C. Owners of record or known beneficial owners of more than 30% of the voting interests of that entity.

D. Persons who are responsible for achieving the objectives of the entity and who have the authority to establish policies and make decisions by which those objectives are pursued.

Answer (B) is correct. *(Publisher, adapted)*
REQUIRED: The definition of a principal owner for the purpose of disclosing related party transactions.
DISCUSSION: Principal owners are owners of record or known beneficial owners of more than 10% of the voting interests of the entity.
Answer (A) is incorrect. Affiliates are parties that, directly or indirectly, through one or more intermediaries, control, are controlled by, or are under common control with an entity. Answer (C) is incorrect. The threshold percentage of ownership is 10%, not 30%. Answer (D) is incorrect. Management consists of persons who are responsible for achieving the objectives of the entity and who have the authority to establish policies and make decisions by which those objectives are pursued.

20.3.4. The disclosure of certain related party transactions is required. Which of the following is not a related party transaction?

A. The Eli Company borrowed money from the Peyton Company at the prevailing market rate of interest. Both companies are subsidiaries of the Arch Corporation.

B. The Kerwin Corporation established a profit-sharing trust fund administered by an independently owned bank located in the same community. The trustees invested part of the trust fund in Kerwin Corporation's outstanding bonds.

C. The Perry Company provided management services to its subsidiary without charge.

D. The Peace Company lent $25,000 to the son of the company's president at the prevailing market rate of interest.

Answer (B) is correct. *(Publisher, adapted)*
REQUIRED: The transaction not between related parties.
DISCUSSION: Related parties include

1. A parent and its subsidiaries
2. Subsidiaries of a common parent
3. An entity and employee trusts managed by or under the trusteeship of the entity's management
4. An entity and its principal owners, management, or members of their immediate families
5. Affiliates
6. An entity and (a) its equity-based investees or (b) investees that would be accounted for using the equity method if not for the election of the fair value option
7. An entity and any other entity if one party can significantly influence the other to the extent that one party may be prevented from fully pursuing its own interests
8. Parties, all of which can be significantly influenced by another party

If a trust fund established to benefit employees is administered by an independent party (the bank), the investment of trust assets in the bonds of the reporting entity is not a transaction between related parties.
Answer (A) is incorrect. Subsidiaries of a common parent are related parties even if they do business at arm's length and at prevailing market interest rates. Answer (C) is incorrect. Transactions between a parent and subsidiary are considered related party transactions even if they are not recorded when they occur. Answer (D) is incorrect. A reporting entity and a member of the immediate family of one of its policy makers are related parties.

20.3.5. The material transaction between related parties that must be disclosed in financial statements is the

A. Compensation arrangement between a company and its president.

B. Loan made by a parent to its consolidated subsidiary.

C. Loan between a parent entity and its unconsolidated equity-based investee.

D. Expense allowance provided by a company to its chief executive officer.

Answer (C) is correct. *(Publisher, adapted)*
REQUIRED: The transaction between related parties that must be disclosed.
DISCUSSION: The disclosure of material related party transactions is required. Exceptions are compensation arrangements, expense allowances, and other similar items in the ordinary course of business. Related party transactions that are eliminated in the preparation of consolidated or combined financial statements also are not required to be disclosed in those financial statements. A loan made by a parent to an unconsolidated equity-based investee (or vice versa) is not eliminated, so the transaction must be disclosed.
Answer (A) is incorrect. A compensation agreement in the ordinary course of business need not be disclosed. Answer (B) is incorrect. Transactions that will be eliminated in the preparation of consolidated statements need not be disclosed. Answer (D) is incorrect. Expense allowances in the ordinary course of business need not be disclosed.

20.3.6. The disclosure of certain related party transactions is considered useful to financial statement users in formulating their investment and credit decisions. Which of the following statements about related party transactions is true?

A. A reporting company need only disclose that it is the subsidiary of another company when transactions have taken place between it and its parent.

B. Representations about transactions between related parties may not imply that they were equivalent to arm's-length transactions.

C. Transactions between related parties are not considered to be related party transactions unless they are given accounting recognition.

D. Transactions between related parties cannot ordinarily be presumed to be carried out on an arm's-length basis.

Answer (D) is correct. *(Publisher, adapted)*
REQUIRED: The true statement about related party transactions.
DISCUSSION: Transactions reflected in financial statements are usually presumed to have been consummated between independent parties on an arm's-length basis. When transactions occur between related parties, the required conditions of competitive, free-market dealings may not be present and this general presumption is not applicable.
Answer (A) is incorrect. Even if there were no transactions between the entity, disclosure of the control relationship is required when common ownership or management control could result in financial position or operating results of a reporting entity materially different from those obtainable if the entities were independent. Answer (B) is incorrect. Such representations may be made if they can be substantiated. Answer (C) is incorrect. Accounting recognition is not a requirement of a related party transaction.

20.3.7. Julia Co. acquired 100% of Amsterdam Corp. prior to the current year. During the current year, the individual companies included in their financial statements the following:

	Julia	Amsterdam
Officers' salaries	$150,000	$100,000
Officers' expenses	40,000	20,000
Loans to officers	250,000	100,000
Intercompany sales	300,000	--

What amount should be reported as related party disclosures in the notes to Julia's current year consolidated financial statements?

A. $300,000

B. $310,000

C. $350,000

D. $660,000

Answer (C) is correct. *(CPA, adapted)*
REQUIRED: The amount to be reported as related party disclosures.
DISCUSSION: The disclosure of material related party transactions is required. Exceptions are compensation arrangements, expense allowances, and other similar items in the ordinary course of business. Related party transactions that are eliminated in the preparation of consolidated or combined financial statements also are not required to be disclosed in those financial statements. Accordingly, the compensation arrangements (officers' salaries and expenses) and the intercompany sales, which will be eliminated in the consolidated financial statements, need not be disclosed. However, other transactions between an entity and its management, such as borrowings and lendings, must be disclosed. Julia should therefore report as related party disclosures the $350,000 ($250,000 + $100,000) of loans to officers.
Answer (A) is incorrect. The intercompany sales equals $300,000. Answer (B) is incorrect. The officers' salaries and officers' expenses equal $310,000. Answer (D) is incorrect. The officers' salaries and officers' expenses plus the loans to officers equal $660,000.

20.3.8. Lemu Co. and Young Co. are under the common management of Ego Co. Ego can significantly influence the operating results of both Lemu and Young. While Lemu had no transactions with Ego during the year, Young sold merchandise to Ego under the same terms given to unrelated parties. In the notes to their respective financial statements, should Lemu and Young disclose their relationship with Ego?

	Lemu	Young
A.	Yes	Yes
B.	Yes	No
C.	No	Yes
D.	No	No

Answer (A) is correct. *(CPA, adapted)*
REQUIRED: The disclosure(s), if any, by entities under common management regarding an entity that can significantly influence them.
DISCUSSION: Financial statements should disclose material related party transactions. A related party is essentially any party that controls or can significantly influence the management or operating policies of the reporting entity. Moreover, two or more entities may be under common ownership or management control such that the results of the reporting entity might vary significantly from those obtained if the entities were autonomous. In these circumstances, the relationship should be disclosed even though no transactions occurred between the parties.

20.4 Segment Information

20.4.1. GAAP require the disclosure of information about operating segments in financial statements of

A. Public business entities.

B. Public and nonpublic business entities.

C. Public business entities, nonpublic business entities, and not-for-profit entities.

D. Public business entities and not-for-profit entities.

Answer (A) is correct. *(Publisher, adapted)*
REQUIRED: The entities for which operating segment disclosures are required in annual financial statements.
DISCUSSION: GAAP require public business entities to disclose information about operating segments in their financial statements.
Answer (B) is incorrect. Required disclosure of segment information is not applicable to nonpublic business entities. Answer (C) is incorrect. Required disclosure of segment information is not applicable to nonpublic business entities or not-for-profit entities. Answer (D) is incorrect. Required disclosure of segment information is not applicable to not-for-profit entities.

20.4.2. The disclosure of information about major customers is required when the amount of sales to a single customer is 10% or more of the revenue of an entity. Which of the following must be disclosed?

A. The identity of the major customer.

B. The amount of revenues that each segment reports from that customer.

C. The operating segment or segments making the sale.

D. The geographic area or areas from which the sales were made.

Answer (C) is correct. *(Publisher, adapted)*
REQUIRED: The required disclosure for sales to major customers.
DISCUSSION: If 10% or more of the revenue of an entity is derived from sales to any single customer, that fact and the amount of revenue from each such customer (without disclosing the identity of the customer) must be disclosed. The identity of the operating segment or segments making the sales must also be disclosed.
Answer (A) is incorrect. The identity of a major customer is not a required disclosure. Answer (B) is incorrect. The amount of revenues that each segment reports from that customer is not a required disclosure. Answer (D) is incorrect. The geographic area from which a major sale is made is not a required disclosure.

20.4.3. Which of the following is not one of the three criteria used to define an operating segment?

A. Discrete financial information about the segment is available.

B. The segment's operating results are regularly reviewed by the chief operating decision maker (CODM).

C. The segment is involved with business activities from which it may earn revenues and incur expenses.

D. The segment is primarily involved in business activities with unaffiliated entities.

Answer (D) is correct. *(Publisher, adapted)*
REQUIRED: The criterion not included in the definition of an operating segment.
DISCUSSION: An operating segment is a component of an entity (1) engaged in business activities from which it may earn revenues and incur expenses, (2) whose operating results regularly are reviewed by the chief operating officer as a basis for allocating resources and assessing performance, and (3) for which discrete information is available. The segment's business activities may involve affiliated components as well as unaffiliated entities.
Answer (A) is incorrect. Availability of discrete financial information about a segment is one of the three definitional criteria of an operating segment. Answer (B) is incorrect. The CODM's regular review of operating results is one of the three definitional criteria of an operating segment. Answer (C) is incorrect. Involvement in revenue-generating and expense-incurring activities is one of the three definitional criteria of an operating segment.

20.4.4. YIV, Inc., is a multidivisional corporation that makes both intersegment sales and sales to external customers. If each division qualifies as an operating segment, YIV should report segment financial information for each division when it meets which of the following criteria?

A. Segment profit or loss is 10% or more of consolidated profit or loss.

B. Segment profit or loss is 10% or more of combined profit or loss of all operating segments.

C. Segment revenue is 10% or more of combined revenue of all the operating segments.

D. Segment revenue is 10% or more of consolidated revenue.

Answer (C) is correct. *(CPA, adapted)*
REQUIRED: The criterion used to identify the reportable operating segments.
DISCUSSION: An entity separately reports information about an operating segment if it satisfies one of three tests: (1) Its revenue (including sales to external customers and intersegment sales or transfers) is equal to at least 10% of the combined revenue, internal and external, of all the entity's operating segments; (2) its assets are equal to at least 10% of the combined assets of all operating segments; and (3) the absolute amount of its reported profit or loss is equal to at least 10% of the greater, in absolute amount, of the combined reported profit of all operating segments that did not report a loss or the combined reported loss of all operating segments that did report a loss.
Answer (A) is incorrect. The profit or loss test is that the absolute amount must be equal to at least 10% of the greater, in absolute amount, of the combined profit of all operating segments that did not report a loss or the combined loss of all operating segments that did incur a loss. Answer (B) is incorrect. The profit or loss test is that the absolute amount must be equal to at least 10% of the greater, in absolute amount, of the combined profit of all operating segments that did not report a loss or the combined loss of all operating segments that did incur a loss. Answer (D) is incorrect. Segment revenue must be 10% or more of the combined revenue of all operating segments. Consolidated revenue is used in the test of foreign operations.

20.4.5. The following information pertains to revenue earned by Meadows Co.'s operating segments for the year ended December 31:

Segment	Sales to Unaffiliated Customers	Intersegment Sales	Total Revenue
Alpha	$ 5,000	$ 3,000	$ 8,000
Beta	8,000	4,000	12,000
Delta	4,000	--	4,000
Gamma	43,000	16,000	59,000
Combined	60,000	$23,000	83,000
Elimination	--	(23,000)	(23,000)
Consolidated	$60,000	--	$60,000

In conformity with the revenue test, the entity's reportable segments were

A. Only Gamma.

B. Only Beta and Gamma.

C. Only Alpha, Beta, and Gamma.

D. Alpha, Beta, Delta, and Gamma.

Answer (B) is correct. *(CPA, adapted)*
REQUIRED: The reportable segments in conformity with the revenue test.
DISCUSSION: For the purpose of identifying reportable operating segments, revenue includes sales to unaffiliated customers and intersegment sales. In accordance with the revenue test, a reportable operating segment has revenue equal to 10% or more of the total combined revenue of all of the entity's operating segments. Given combined revenue of $83,000, only Beta ($12,000) and Gamma ($59,000) qualify because their revenues are at least $8,300 ($83,000 × 10%). Moreover, their total external revenue of $51,000 ($8,000 + $43,000) is not less than 75% of total consolidated revenue of $45,000 ($60,000 × 75%).
Answer (A) is incorrect. Beta also qualifies. Answer (C) is incorrect. Alpha does not qualify. Answer (D) is incorrect. Alpha and Delta do not qualify.

20.4.6. An enterprise must separately report information about an operating segment when the segment's revenue meets what minimum percentage of the combined revenue of all reported operating segments?

A. 5%

B. 10%

C. 20%

D. 50%

Answer (B) is correct. *(CPA, adapted)*
REQUIRED: The minimum percentage of the combined revenue of all operating segments at which an operating segment must be separately reported.
DISCUSSION: Reportable segments are operating segments that must be separately disclosed if (1) reported revenue is at least 10% of the combined revenue of all operating segments, (2) assets are at least 10% of the combined assets of all operating segments, and (3) the absolute amount of reported profit or loss is at least 10% of the greater (in absolute amount) of either (a) the combined profit of all profitable operating segments or (b) the combined loss of all operating segments that reported a loss.

20.4.7. Greque Co. operates in four industries. Which of the following operating segments should be identified as a reportable segment under the operating profit or loss test?

Segment	Operating Profit (Loss)
Rho	$ 90,000
Sigma	(100,000)
Tau	910,000
Upsilon	(420,000)

A. Segment Tau only.

B. Segments Tau and Upsilon.

C. Segments Sigma, Tau, and Upsilon.

D. Segments Rho, Sigma, Tau, and Upsilon.

Answer (C) is correct. *(Publisher, adapted)*
REQUIRED: The reportable segments under the operating profit or loss test.
DISCUSSION: An operating segment is identified as a reportable segment if it meets the profit or loss test (among others). The segment is reportable if the absolute amount of the operating profit or loss equals at least 10% of the greater, in absolute amount, of (1) the combined operating profit of all operating segments not reporting an operating loss or (2) the combined operating loss of all operating segments reporting an operating loss.
Segments Sigma, Tau, and Upsilon are reportable operating segments. As shown below, the sum of the operating profits of Rho and Tau ($1,000,000) is greater than the sum of the operating losses of Sigma and Upsilon ($520,000). Consequently, the test criterion is $100,000 ($1,000,000 × 10%).

Segment	Operating Profit	Operating Loss
Rho	$ 90,000	$ 0
Sigma	0	100,000
Tau	910,000	0
Upsilon	0	420,000
	$1,000,000	$520,000

Answer (A) is incorrect. Segments Sigma and Upsilon also meet the operating profit or loss test. Answer (B) is incorrect. Segment Sigma also meets the operating profit or loss test. Answer (D) is incorrect. Segment Rho does not meet the operating profit or loss test.

20.4.8. Salaam Co.'s four operating segments have revenues and identifiable assets expressed as percentages of Salaam's total revenues and total assets as follows:

	Revenues	Assets
Un	64%	66%
Deux	14%	18%
Trois	14%	4%
Quatre	8%	12%
	100%	100%

Which of these operating segments are deemed to be reportable segments?

A. Un only.

B. Un and Deux only.

C. Un, Deux, and Trois only.

D. Un, Deux, Trois, and Quatre.

Answer (D) is correct. *(CPA, adapted)*
REQUIRED: The operating segment(s) deemed to be reportable.
DISCUSSION: An operating segment is a reportable segment if it satisfies one or more of three criteria. One test is whether its revenue is 10% or more of the combined revenue of all the entity's operating segments. According to the identifiable assets test, an operating segment with identifiable assets equal to 10% or more of the combined identifiable assets of all operating segments is a reportable segment. Un, Deux, and Trois meet the revenue test, and Un, Deux, and Quatre meet the identifiable assets test.
Answer (A) is incorrect. Deux, Trois, and Quatre also meet at least one of the criteria. Answer (B) is incorrect. Trois and Quatre also meet at least one of the criteria. Answer (C) is incorrect. Quatre also meets at least one of the criteria.

20.4.9. Correy Corp. and its divisions are engaged solely in manufacturing operations. The following data (consistent with prior years' data) pertain to the industries in which operations were conducted for the year ended December 31, Year 2:

Operating Segment	Total Revenue	Profit	Assets at 12/31/Yr 2
A	$10,000,000	$1,750,000	$20,000,000
B	8,000,000	1,400,000	17,500,000
C	6,000,000	1,200,000	12,500,000
D	3,000,000	550,000	7,500,000
E	4,250,000	675,000	7,000,000
F	1,500,000	225,000	3,000,000
	$32,750,000	$5,800,000	$67,500,000

In its segment information for Year 2, how many reportable segments does Correy have?

A. Three.

B. Four.

C. Five.

D. Six.

Answer (C) is correct. *(CPA, adapted)*
REQUIRED: The number of reportable operating segments.
DISCUSSION: Four operating segments (A, B, C, and E) have revenue equal to or greater than 10% of the $32,750,000 total revenue of all operating segments. These four segments also have profit equal to or greater than 10% of the $5,800,000 total profit. Five segments (A, B, C, D, and E) have assets greater than 10% of the $67,500,000 total assets. Because an operating segment is reportable if it meets one or more of the three tests, Correy Corp. has five reportable segments for Year 2.
Answer (A) is incorrect. Segments A, B, C, D, and E, but not F, meet at least one of the tests. Answer (B) is incorrect. Segments A, B, C, D, and E, but not F, meet at least one of the tests. Answer (D) is incorrect. Segments A, B, C, D, and E, but not F, meet at least one of the tests.

20.4.10. Which of the following materiality tests is required to determine whether the operating segments of an entity that have been identified as reportable operating segments represent a substantial portion of the total operations of the entity?

A. The combined revenue of all reportable segments equals or exceeds 75% of the combined revenue of all operating segments.

B. The combined revenue from sales to unaffiliated customers by all reportable segments equals or exceeds 75% of the combined revenue of all operating segments.

C. The combined revenue from sales to unaffiliated customers by all reportable segments equals or exceeds 75% of total consolidated revenue.

D. The combined revenue of all reportable segments equals or exceeds 75% of the combined revenue from sales to unaffiliated customers by all operating segments.

Answer (C) is correct. *(Publisher, adapted)*
REQUIRED: The test for determining whether the reportable segments represent a substantial portion of the entity's total operations.
DISCUSSION: The reportable segments must represent a substantial portion of the entity's total operations. To determine materiality, the combined revenue from sales to unaffiliated customers by all reportable segments must equal or exceed 75% of total consolidated revenue. The test should be applied separately for each fiscal year for which financial statements are presented. When the test criterion is not met, additional segments must be identified as reportable until the criterion is met.

20.4.11. Zan Corp., a publicly owned corporation, is subject to the requirements for segment reporting. In its income statement for the current year end, Zan reported revenues of $100,000,000, operating expenses of $94,000,000, and net income of $6,000,000. Operating expenses include payroll costs of $30,000,000. Zan's combined identifiable assets of all operating segments in the current year were $80,000,000. In its current-year financial statements, Zan should disclose major customer data if sales to any single customer amount to at least

A. $600,000

B. $3,000,000

C. $8,000,000

D. $10,000,000

Answer (D) is correct. *(CPA, adapted)*
REQUIRED: The sales level requiring disclosure of major customer data.
DISCUSSION: If 10% or more of the revenue of an entity is derived from sales to any single customer, that fact and the amount of revenue from each such customer (without disclosing the identity of the customer) must be disclosed. The identity of the operating segment or segments making the sales also must be disclosed. Hence, Zan's sales to a single customer of $10,000,000 ($100,000,000 total revenue × 10%) will necessitate disclosure of major customer data.
Answer (A) is incorrect. The amount of $600,000 is 10% of net income. Answer (B) is incorrect. The amount of $3,000,000 is 10% of payroll costs. Answer (C) is incorrect. The amount of $8,000,000 is 10% of combined identifiable assets of all industry segments.

20.4.12. Listed below are the most recent year's sales to the three largest customers of the Oxford Company, a publicly held firm.

Federal government	$5,000,000
State of Florina	4,000,000
State of Carolida	3,000,000

If Oxford's total revenue amounts to $44,000,000, Oxford should disclose the total amount of sales to major customers as which of the following amounts?

A. $0

B. $5,000,000

C. $9,000,000

D. $12,000,000

Answer (B) is correct. *(Publisher, adapted)*
REQUIRED: The total amount of sales to major customers required to be separately reported.
DISCUSSION: An entity should disclose information about the extent of its reliance on its major customers. If 10% or more of the revenue of an entity is derived from sales to any single customer, that fact, the identity of the operating segment or segments making the sale, and the amount of revenue from such customer must be disclosed. A single customer includes a group of entities under common control, the federal government, a state government, a local government, or a foreign government. Total revenue for Oxford is $44,000,000. Thus, Oxford should disclose the amount of sales to any major customer from whom sales revenue totals $4,400,000 ($44,000,000 × 10%). Because the year's sales to the federal government totaled $5,000,000, such disclosure must be made (but not necessarily identifying the customer).
Answer (A) is incorrect. Sales to the federal government of $5,000,000 meet or exceed the 10% of total revenues test. Answer (C) is incorrect. Sales to the state of Florina do not meet or exceed the 10% of total revenues test. Answer (D) is incorrect. Sales to the states of Florina and Carolida do not meet or exceed the 10% of total revenues test.

20.5 Risks and Uncertainties

20.5.1. Neely Co. disclosed in the notes to its financial statements that a significant number of its unsecured trade account receivables are with companies that operate in the same industry. This disclosure is required to inform financial statement users of the existence of

A. Concentration of credit risk.

B. Concentration of market risk.

C. Risk of measurement uncertainty.

D. Off-balance-sheet risk of accounting loss.

Answer (A) is correct. *(CPA, adapted)*
REQUIRED: The risk of having significant unsecured receivables from entities in the same industry.
DISCUSSION: Credit risk is the risk of accounting loss from a financial instrument because of the possible failure of another party to perform. An entity must disclose most significant concentrations of credit risk arising from instruments. Group concentrations arise when multiple counterparties have similar characteristics that cause their ability to meet obligations to be similarly affected by change in conditions. An example of such a group is an industry.
Answer (B) is incorrect. Market risk is the risk of loss from the change in market value of assets or liabilities. Answer (C) is incorrect. That a significant number of unsecured trade accounts receivable are with companies that operate in the same industry has no bearing on the risk of measurement uncertainty. Answer (D) is incorrect. The entity's trade accounts receivable are on the balance sheet. Moreover, the risk of accounting loss is reflected in the recognition of an allowance for bad debts.

20.6 Unconditional Purchase Obligations

20.6.1. Denmark Corp. has unconditional purchase obligations associated with product financing arrangements. These obligations are reported as liabilities on Denmark's balance sheet, with the related assets also recognized. In the notes to Denmark's financial statements, the aggregate amount of payments for these obligations should be disclosed for each of how many years following the date of the balance sheet?

A. 0

B. 1

C. 5

D. 10

Answer (C) is correct. *(CPA, adapted)*
REQUIRED: The disclosure about reported unconditional purchase obligations.
DISCUSSION: The following disclosures must be made for recorded unconditional purchase obligations for each of the 5 years after the date of the latest balance sheet: (1) the aggregate amount of the payments for the recognized obligations and (2) the combined amount of maturities and sinking fund requirements for all noncurrent borrowing.
Answer (A) is incorrect. Disclosures are required for 5 years. Answer (B) is incorrect. Disclosures are required for 5 years, not 1 year. Answer (D) is incorrect. Disclosures are required for 5 years, not 10 years.

20.6.2. Witt Corp. has outstanding at December 31, Year 3, two long-term borrowings with annual sinking-fund requirements and maturities as follows:

	Sinking-Fund Requirements	Maturities
Year 4	$1,000,000	$ --
Year 5	1,500,000	2,000,000
Year 6	1,500,000	2,000,000
Year 7	2,000,000	2,500,000
Year 8	2,000,000	3,000,000
	$8,000,000	$9,500,000

In the notes to its December 31, Year 3, balance sheet, how should Witt report the above data?

A. No disclosure is required.

B. Only sinking-fund payments totaling $8,000,000 for the next 5 years detailed by year need be disclosed.

C. Only maturities totaling $9,500,000 for the next 5 years detailed by year need be disclosed.

D. The combined aggregate of $17,500,000 of maturities and sinking-fund requirements detailed by year should be disclosed.

Answer (D) is correct. *(CPA, adapted)*
REQUIRED: The required note disclosure of sinking fund payments and maturities for long-term borrowings.
DISCUSSION: The following information for recorded obligations for each of the 5 years following the date of the latest balance sheet presented must be disclosed: (1) the aggregate amount of payments for unconditional purchase obligations and (2) the aggregate amount of maturities and sinking-fund requirements for all long-term borrowings. Thus, Witt Corp. should disclose in the notes to the December 31, Year 3, balance sheet the combined aggregate of $17,500,000 ($8,000,000 + $9,500,000) of maturities and sinking-fund requirements detailed by year.
Answer (A) is incorrect. The combined aggregate amount of maturities and sinking-fund payments for all borrowings must be disclosed. Answer (B) is incorrect. The amount of maturities also must be disclosed. Answer (C) is incorrect. The sinking-fund payments also must be disclosed.

20.6.3. A purchase obligation is not unconditional if it is cancelable under which of the following conditions?

A. Upon the occurrence of a remote contingency.

B. With the permission of the other party.

C. If a replacement agreement is signed between the same parties.

D. Upon payment of a nominal penalty.

Answer (D) is correct. *(Publisher, adapted)*
REQUIRED: The condition preventing a purchase obligation from being unconditional.
DISCUSSION: An unconditional purchase obligation

1. Was negotiated as part of the financing arrangement for (a) facilities that will provide contracted goods or services or (b) costs related to those goods or services,

2. Has a remaining term of more than 1 year, and

3. Is either noncancelable or cancelable only under specific terms that make continuation or replacement of the agreement reasonably assured.

A purchase obligation cancelable upon the payment of a nominal penalty is not unconditional.
Answer (A) is incorrect. Cancelability only upon the occurrence of a remote contingency is a condition indicating that the obligation is noncancelable in substance. Answer (B) is incorrect. Cancelability only with the permission of the other party is a condition indicating that the obligation is noncancelable in substance. Answer (C) is incorrect. Cancelability only if a replacement agreement is signed between the same parties is a condition indicating that the obligation is noncancelable in substance.

20.6.4. An entity discloses the imputed interest rate necessary to reduce an unconditional purchase obligation, not recorded in the balance sheet, to its present value. The interest rate disclosed should be

A. If known by the purchaser, the effective initial rate of the debt that financed the facilities providing the contracted goods or services.

B. The purchaser's incremental borrowing rate.

C. The prime rate.

D. The current AA bond interest rate.

Answer (A) is correct. *(Publisher, adapted)*
REQUIRED: The interest rate to be used in determining the present value of an unconditional purchase obligation.
DISCUSSION: GAAP encourage, but do not require, disclosure of the imputed interest rate. If known by the purchaser, the rate disclosed should be the initial effective rate of the debt that financed the facilities providing the contracted goods or services. If that rate cannot be determined by the purchaser, the purchaser's incremental borrowing rate should be used.
Answer (B) is incorrect. The purchaser's incremental borrowing rate is used only if the purchaser does not know the initial rate on the debt that financed the facilities providing the contracted goods or services. Answer (C) is incorrect. The prime rate is not relevant. Answer (D) is incorrect. The current AA bond interest rate is not relevant.

20.7 Subsequent Events

20.7.1. Zero Corp. suffered a loss that would have a material effect on its financial statements on an uncollectible trade account receivable due to a customer's bankruptcy. This occurred suddenly due to a natural disaster 10 days after Zero's balance sheet date but 1 month before the issuance of the financial statements. Under these circumstances,

	The Loss Must Be Recognized in the Financial Statements	The Event Requires Financial Statement Disclosure Only
A.	Yes	Yes
B.	Yes	No
C.	No	No
D.	No	Yes

Answer (D) is correct. *(CPA, adapted)*

REQUIRED: The effect on the financial statements of a customer's bankruptcy after the balance sheet date but before the issuance of the statements.

DISCUSSION: Certain subsequent events may provide additional evidence about conditions at the date of the balance sheet, including estimates inherent in the preparation of statements. These events require recognition in the statements at year end. Other subsequent events provide evidence about conditions not existing at the date of the balance sheet but arising subsequent to that date and before the issuance of the statements or their availability for issuance. These events may require disclosure but not recognition in the statements. Thus, the loss must not be recognized in Zero's statements, but disclosure must be made.

20.7.2. On January 15, Year 2, before the Mapleview Co. released its financial statements for the year ended December 31, Year 1, it settled a long-standing lawsuit. A material loss resulted and no prior liability had been recorded. How should this loss be disclosed or recognized in the Year 1 financial statements?

A. The loss should be disclosed, but the financial statements themselves need not be adjusted.

B. The loss should be disclosed in an explanatory paragraph in the auditor's report.

C. No disclosure or recognition is required.

D. The loss must be recognized in the financial statements.

Answer (D) is correct. *(Publisher, adapted)*

REQUIRED: The proper treatment of a material loss on an existing lawsuit after year end.

DISCUSSION: Subsequent events that provide additional evidence with the respect to conditions that existed at the balance sheet date, including the estimates inherent in preparing the financial statements, must be recognized in the financial statements of the year affected by the subsequent event. Settlement of a lawsuit is indicative of conditions existing at year end and calls for recognition in the statements.

Answer (A) is incorrect. The loss must be recognized in the financial statements. Answer (B) is incorrect. The audit report need not be modified. Answer (C) is incorrect. Failure to recognize a material loss on an asset that existed at year end is a departure from GAAP.

Use **Gleim Test Prep** for interactive study and easy-to-use detailed analytics!

STUDY UNIT TWENTY-ONE
NEW REVENUE RECOGNITION STANDARD:
REVENUE FROM CONTRACTS WITH CUSTOMERS

This study unit answers questions about the major provisions of the revenue recognition standard issued jointly by the FASB and the IASB. The converged new standard was issued as ASU 2014-09, *Revenue from Contracts with Customers* (Topic 606), by the FASB and as IFRS 15 by the IASB. It provides a **single, principles-based** revenue recognition model that can be applied to all contracts with customers regardless of the industry-specific or transaction-specific fact pattern. The main reasons for issuing the new standard were to

- Improve **globally** the comparability of the top line in the income statement (i.e., revenue) by converging revenue recognition guidance under U.S. GAAP and IFRS.

- Improve comparability of revenue recognition practices **across industries** and entities. Currently, revenue can be recognized based on different industry-specific guidance, for example, for real estate or software. The new single revenue recognition model eliminates most current industry-specific guidance.

- Provide more useful financial statement information through improved disclosure.

Core Principle

The core principle of this standard is that an entity recognizes revenue to depict the transfer of promised goods or services to customers in an amount that reflects the consideration to which the entity expects to be entitled in exchange for those goods or services. To achieve this purpose, the standard requires an entity to perform the **following five steps**:

Step 1: Identify the contract(s) with a customer.
Step 2: Identify the performance obligations in the contract.
Step 3: Determine the transaction price.
Step 4: Allocate the transaction price to the performance obligations in the contract.
Step 5: Recognize revenue when (or as) the entity satisfies a performance obligation.

This **five-step approach** helps the entity determine the **amount** and the **timing** of revenue recognized. But it requires significant management judgment.

QUESTIONS

21.1 Introduction

21.1.1. The scope of the FASB's standard on revenue from contracts with customers (ASC 606) includes

A. Product or service warranty contracts.

B. Loan guarantee contracts.

C. Lease contracts.

D. Insurance contracts.

Answer (A) is correct. *(Publisher, adapted)*
REQUIRED: The scope of the FASB's revenue recognition standard.
DISCUSSION: An entity must apply the guidance on revenue from contracts with customers to all contracts with customers except for (1) lease contracts, (2) insurance contracts, (3) financial instruments, (4) guarantees (other than product or service warranties), and (5) nonmonetary exchanges between entities in the same line of business to facilitate sales to customers. Accordingly, product or service warranties are within the scope of the new standard.
Answer (B) is incorrect. Loan guarantee contracts are outside the scope of the revenue recognition standard. Answer (C) is incorrect. Lease contracts are outside the scope of the revenue recognition standard. They include those between entities in the same line of business to facilitate sales to customers. Answer (D) is incorrect. Insurance contracts are outside the scope of the revenue recognition standard.

21.1.2. The revenue recognition standard for revenue from contracts with customers improves comparability because it

	Retains Most Industry-Specific Guidance	Converges U.S. GAAP and IFRS
A.	Yes	Yes
B.	Yes	No
C.	No	Yes
D.	No	No

Answer (C) is correct. *(Publisher, adapted)*
REQUIRED: The improvement(s), if any, resulting from the new revenue recognition standards.
DISCUSSION: The converged revenue recognition standard was jointly issued by the FASB and IASB. Because the same standard will be applied under U.S. GAAP and IFRS, comparability will be globally improved. Moreover, the new standard provides a single, principles-based revenue recognition model that eliminates most of the current industry-specific guidance. Thus, comparability across industries will be improved.
Answer (A) is incorrect. The revenue recognition standard provides a single, principles-based revenue recognition model that can be applied to all contracts with customers regardless of the industry-specific or transaction-specific fact pattern. Thus, comparability across industries will be improved. Answer (B) is incorrect. The same revenue recognition standard will be applied under U.S. GAAP and IFRS, improving comparability globally. It also eliminates most industry-specific guidance. Answer (D) is incorrect. The revenue recognition standard improves comparability of revenue recognition by converging U.S. GAAP and IFRS.

21.1.3. The revenue recognition from contracts with customers standard (ASC 606) provides a <List A> model that <List B>.

	List A	List B
A.	Rules-based	Can be applied differently across specific industries
B.	Single principles-based	Eliminates most current industry-specific guidance
C.	Principles-based	Can be applied differently under U.S. GAAP and IFRS
D.	Rules-based	Eliminates most current industry-specific guidance

Answer (B) is correct. *(Publisher, adapted)*
REQUIRED: The provisions of the standard for recognition of revenue from contracts with customers
DISCUSSION: The revenue recognition standard provides a single principles-based model (the five-step approach) that can be applied to all contracts with customers regardless of the industry-specific or transaction-specific fact pattern.
Answer (A) is incorrect. The revenue recognition standard provides a single principles-based model that can be applied to all contracts with customers regardless of the industry-specific or transaction-specific fact pattern. Answer (C) is incorrect. The revenue recognition standard basically converges revenue recognition guidance under U.S. GAAP and IFRS. The converged standard requires the application of the same five-step approach to revenue recognition from customers under both U.S. GAAP and IFRS. Answer (D) is incorrect. The revenue recognition standard provides a single principles-based, not rules-based, revenue recognition model (the five-step approach).

21.2 Identifying the Contract with a Customer

21.2.1. When applying the guidance for revenue recognition from contracts with customers, which of the following is a criterion for combining two contracts with a customer into a single contract?

A. The contracts are negotiated as a package with a single commercial objective.

B. The consideration to be paid in one contract is independent of the price of the other contract.

C. The two contracts are expected to be executed within a short time of each other.

D. The contracts contain two or more performance obligations.

Answer (A) is correct. *(Publisher, adapted)*
REQUIRED: The criterion for combining two contracts with a customer.
DISCUSSION: The entity must combine two or more contracts entered into at or near the same time with the same customer if at least one of the following criteria is met:

● The contracts are negotiated as a package with a single commercial objective.
● The consideration to be paid in one contract depends on the price or performance of the other contract.
● The goods or services to be provided in the contracts are a single performance obligation.

Answer (B) is incorrect. When the consideration to be paid in one contract depends on the price or performance of the other contract, the two contracts must be combined into a single contract. Answer (C) is incorrect. The timing of execution of the contracts is not considered when determining whether the contracts should be combined into a single contract. Answer (D) is incorrect. When the goods or services to be provided in the contracts are a single performance obligation, the two contracts must be combined into a single contract.

21.2.2. Under ASC 606, a contract modification is accounted for as a separate contract if the additional promised goods are <List A> and the price for these additional goods is <List B>.

	List A	List B
A.	Distinct	Based on the price of the original contract
B.	Not distinct	Their incremental selling price
C.	Distinct	Their standalone selling price
D.	Not distinct	Cumulative catch-up adjustment to revenue

Answer (C) is correct. *(Publisher, adapted)*
REQUIRED: The criteria to account for a contract modification as a separate contract.
DISCUSSION: A contract modification exists when the parties approve a change in the scope or price of a contract. A contract modification is accounted for as a separate contract if (1) it results in the addition to the contract of promised goods or services that are distinct and (2) the price for these additional goods or services is their standalone selling price.
Answer (A) is incorrect. A contract modification is accounted for as a separate contract when (1) the additional promised goods are distinct and (2) the price of the contract increases their standalone selling price. Answer (B) is incorrect. The promised goods or services must be distinct, and the increase in price must reflect the standalone selling price of the additional goods or services. Answer (D) is incorrect. A contract modification is accounted for as a cumulative catch-up adjustment to revenue, not a separate contract, when the remaining goods to be delivered (1) are not distinct and (2) are part of a single performance obligation that is partially satisfied at the date of the contract modification.

21.2.3. Which of the following is not a criterion that must be met for a contract with a customer to be accounted for under the revenue recognition standard (ASC 606)?

A. The contract must have commercial substance.

B. The payment terms can be identified.

C. The costs to fulfill the contract are expected to be recovered.

D. Each party's rights regarding goods or services to be transferred can be identified.

Answer (C) is correct. *(Publisher, adapted)*
REQUIRED: The item not a criterion for applying the revenue recognition standard (ASC 606).
DISCUSSION: One of the criteria for capitalizing the costs to fulfill a contract is that such costs are expected to be recovered. A contract is accounted for under the revenue recognition standard if all the following criteria are met: (1) The contract was approved by both parties, (2) the contract has commercial substance, (3) each party's rights regarding (a) goods or services to be transferred and (b) the payment terms can be identified, and (4) it is probable that the entity will collect the consideration to which it is entitled according to the contract.
Answer (A) is incorrect. The contract must have commercial substance to be accounted for under the revenue recognition standard. Answer (B) is incorrect. An entity accounts for a contract with a customer under the revenue recognition standard only if it can identify the payment terms for goods or services to be transferred. Answer (D) is incorrect. An entity accounts for a contract with a customer under the revenue recognition standard only if it can identify each party's rights regarding goods or services to be transferred.

Questions 21.2.4 and 21.2.5 are based on the following information. On May 1, Year 1, an entity entered into a contract to deliver 100 units of its product to a customer for $150,000. The units are transferred to the customer over a 9-month period. On November 1, Year 1, after 80 units were transferred to the customer, the contract was modified to require the delivery of an additional 30 units for an additional $30,000. The entity determined that (1) the price for the additional 30 units does not reflect the standalone selling price of the product and (2) the remaining units to be delivered are distinct from those already transferred. During Year 1, the entity delivered a total of 90 units to the customer.

21.2.4. What amount of revenue per unit was recognized by the entity for the 10 units delivered to the customer between November 1, Year 1, and December 31, Year 1?

A. $1,500

B. $1,000

C. $1,385

D. $1,200

Answer (D) is correct. *(Publisher, adapted)*
   REQUIRED: The revenue per unit delivered in Year 1 after the contract was modified.
   DISCUSSION: Because the price for the additional 30 units does not reflect their standalone selling price, the contract modification must not be accounted for as a separate contract. However, the remaining units to be delivered are distinct from those already transferred. Accordingly, the entity must account for the modification as (1) a termination of the original contract and (2) the creation of a new contract. The modified total transaction price of $60,000 [($1,500 × 20) + $30,000] is allocated to all of the remaining 50 units to be delivered. Consequently, the amount recognized as revenue for each unit delivered after the contract modification is a blended price of $1,200 ($60,000 ÷ 50).
   Answer (A) is incorrect. The amount of $1,500 is the revenue recognized per unit delivered before the modification of the contract. Because the price for the additional 30 units does not reflect their standalone selling price, the contract modification must not be accounted for as a separate contract. Answer (B) is incorrect. The amount of $1,000 is the selling price per unit for the additional 30 units to be delivered assuming that the contract modification is accounted for as a separate contract. Because the price for the additional 30 units does not reflect their standalone selling price, the contract modification must not be accounted for as a separate contract. Answer (C) is incorrect. The remaining units to be delivered are distinct from those already transferred. Thus, the entity must account for the modification of the contract as a termination of the original contract and a creation of a new contract. The total remaining transaction price should be allocated prospectively to the remaining performance obligation in the contract.

21.2.5. What is the total amount of revenue that was recognized by the entity in Year 2 upon the delivery of the remaining units?

A. $48,000

B. $45,000

C. $36,000

D. $30,000

Answer (A) is correct. *(Publisher, adapted)*
   REQUIRED: The revenue per unit delivered in Year 2 after the contract was modified.
   DISCUSSION: In Year 2, the entity delivered 40 units (100 units from the initial contract + 30 units from the contract modification – 90 units delivered in Year 1 to the customer). The price for the additional 30 units resulting from the contract modification does not reflect their standalone selling price, and the remaining units to be delivered are distinct from those already transferred. Accordingly, the entity must account for the modification of the contract as (1) a termination of the original contract and (2) the creation of a new contract. The modified total transaction price of $60,000 [($1,500 × 20) + $30,000] is allocated to all the remaining 50 units to be delivered. Thus, the blended price per unit to be delivered is $1,200 ($60,000 ÷ 50). The total revenue recognized in Year 2 is $48,000 ($1,200 × 40).
   Answer (B) is incorrect. The amount of $45,000 is based on the assumption that the contract modification was accounted for as a separate contract. But the price for the additional 30 units does not reflect their standalone selling price, so the contract modification must not be accounted for as a separate contract. Answer (C) is incorrect. In Year 2, the entity delivered to the customer 40 units (100 + 30 – 90), not 30. Answer (D) is incorrect. The amount of $30,000 is the total price of the contract modification, not the amount of revenue recognized in Year 2.

21.3 Identifying the Performance Obligations in the Contract

21.3.1. A software developer enters into a contract with a new customer to sell a software license and perform installation services. The entity sometimes sells the license and installation services separately. The installation service is routinely performed by other entities and does not significantly modify the software. The entity historically provided to new customers technical support for a 5-year period for no additional consideration. The contract does not specify the terms or conditions for the technical support services. Under ASC 606, which of the following represents the performance obligations identified by the entity in this contract?

  A. One performance obligation: (1) Software license plus installation services.

  B. Two performance obligations: (1) Software license and (2) installation services.

  C. Three performance obligations: (1) Software license, (2) installation services, and (3) technical support services.

  D. Two performance obligations: (1) Software license plus installation services and (2) technical support services.

Answer (C) is correct. *(Publisher, adapted)*
  REQUIRED: The performance obligation.
  DISCUSSION: The transfer of the software license and the performance of installation services are separately identifiable from other promises in the contract. The installation services do not significantly modify or customize the software itself. In addition, on the basis of the entity's customary business practice, at contract inception, it made an implicit promise to provide technical support services. The entity's past practice of providing these services creates a valid expectation that the customer will receive these services. Consequently, the entity identifies the following performance obligations in the contract: (1) software license, (2) installation services, and (3) technical support services.
  Answer (A) is incorrect. The transfer of a software license and the installation services are separately identifiable from other promises in the contract. The installation services do not significantly modify or customize the software itself. On the basis of the entity's customary business practice, at contract inception, it made an implicit promise to provide technical support services. Answer (B) is incorrect. Although not explicitly stated in the contract, technical support service is a performance obligation. On the basis of the entity's customary business practice, at contract inception, it made an implicit promise to provide technical support services. The entity's past practice of providing these services creates a valid expectation of the customer to receive these services. Answer (D) is incorrect. The transfer of a software license and the installation services are separately identifiable from other promises in the contract. The installation services do not significantly modify or customize the software itself.

21.4 Determining the Transaction Price

21.4.1. Under ASC 606, which of the following, if any, determines the transaction price of a contract with a significant financing component?

	Undiscounted Cash Flows	Variable Consideration
A.	Yes	Yes
B.	Yes	No
C.	No	Yes
D.	No	No

Answer (C) is correct. *(Publisher, adapted)*
  REQUIRED: The determinant(s), if any, of the transaction price with a significant financing component.
  DISCUSSION: The revenue recognized must reflect the price that a customer would have paid for the promised goods or services if the cash payment had been made when the goods or services were transferred to the customer (the cash selling price). Thus, the transaction price should be adjusted for the effect of the time value of money when the contract includes a significant financing component. Also, an entity must estimate the amount of consideration to which it will be entitled in exchange for transferring the promised goods or services to a customer. For example, the transaction price may vary due to discounts, refunds, incentives, or contingencies (uncertainties based on the occurrence or nonoccurence of a future event). Thus, variable consideration also determines the transaction price. In this case, variable consideration must be estimated at the inception of the contract.
  Answer (A) is incorrect. The revenue recognized must reflect the price that a customer would have paid for the promised goods or services if the cash payment had been made when the goods or services were transferred to the customer (the cash selling price). Thus, the transaction price should be adjusted for the effect of the time value of money (discounted cash flows) when the contract includes a significant financing component. Answer (B) is incorrect. In determining the transaction price, an entity should consider the effects of (1) the time value of money (discounted cash flows) and (2) variable consideration. Answer (D) is incorrect. Variable consideration also determines the transaction price.

21.4.2. For recognition of revenue from contracts with customers, which of the following methods, if any, is (are) acceptable for estimating the amount of variable consideration?

	Present Value	Minimum Amount in the Range of Possible Amounts
A.	Yes	Yes
B.	Yes	No
C.	No	Yes
D.	No	No

Answer (D) is correct. *(Publisher, adapted)*
REQUIRED: The acceptable method(s), if any, for estimating variable consideration.
DISCUSSION: The amount of variable consideration must be estimated by applying consistently throughout the contract period one of two methods: (1) expected value or (2) most likely amount. The expected value method may provide an appropriate estimate if an entity has a large number of contracts with similar characteristics. The expected value is the sum of probability-weighted amounts in the range of possible consideration amounts. The most likely amount method may provide an appropriate estimate if the contract has only two possible outcomes. The most likely amount is the single most likely amount in a range of possible consideration amounts.
Answer (A) is incorrect. The expected value method and the most likely amount method are the appropriate means of estimating the amount of variable consideration. Answer (B) is incorrect. The expected value method, not the present value (discounted cash flow) method, is an acceptable means of estimating the amount of variable consideration. It may provide an appropriate estimate if an entity has a large number of contracts with similar characteristics. Answer (C) is incorrect. The most likely amount method, not the minimum amount in the range of possible amounts, is an acceptable means of estimating the amount of variable consideration. It may provide an appropriate estimate if the contract has only two possible outcomes.

21.4.3. Under the FASB's standard for recognition of revenue from contracts with customers, the transaction price may

A. Not include the effect of the time value of money.

B. Include coupons payable to the customer.

C. Not include variable consideration.

D. Not include amounts collected on behalf of third parties.

Answer (D) is correct. *(Publisher, adapted)*
REQUIRED: The item that is or is not included in the transaction price.
DISCUSSION: The transaction price is the amount of consideration to which an entity expects to be entitled in exchange for transferring promised goods or services to a customer. It excludes amounts collected on behalf of third parties. Thus, the amount collected for taxes must not be included in the transaction price. Furthermore, any consideration payable to the customer, such as coupons, credit, or vouchers, reduces the transaction price. Also, the effect of the time value of money and variable consideration should be considered in determining the transaction price.
Answer (A) is incorrect. The transaction price must reflect the time value of money when the contract contains a significant financing component. Answer (B) is incorrect. Any consideration payable to the customer, such as coupons, credit, or vouchers, reduces the transaction price. Answer (C) is incorrect. The transaction price must reflect the time value of money and variable consideration.

21.4.4. Under ASC 606, adjustment of the transaction price to reflect the time value of money results in

A. Revenue from contracts with customers in the income statement.

B. An item of other comprehensive income.

C. Interest income or expense that is presented in the income statement separately from revenue.

D. An unusual item in the income statement.

Answer (C) is correct. *(Publisher, adapted)*
REQUIRED: The effect of adjusting the transaction price for the time value of money.
DISCUSSION: The transaction price should be adjusted for the effect of the time value of money when the contract includes a significant financing component. The interest income or expense is recognized using the effective interest method. Interest income or expense must be presented in the income statement separately from revenue from contracts with customers.
Answer (A) is incorrect. Interest income or expense recognized when the transaction price is adjusted to reflect the time value of money must be presented in the income statement separately from revenue from contracts with customers. Answer (B) is incorrect. Interest income or expense recognized on the adjustment of the contract price to reflect the time value of money is not an item of other comprehensive income. It must be recognized separately from revenue in the income statement. Answer (D) is incorrect. Interest income or expense recognized when the transaction price is adjusted to reflect the time value of money is not an unusual item.

21.4.5. On January 1, Year 1, an entity receives a payment of $20,000 for delivering a product to a customer at the end of Year 3. Based on the contract's terms, the performance obligation will be satisfied at a point in time (upon delivery of the product). The entity determined that (1) the contract includes a significant financing component and (2) a financing rate of 6% is an appropriate discount rate. What amount of interest expense and contract liability will be recognized in the entity's December 31, Year 2, financial statements?

	Year 2 Interest Expense	Contract Liability on December 31, Year 2
A.	$1,200	$21,200
B.	$2,400	$22,400
C.	$1,272	$22,472
D.	$1,348	$0

Answer (C) is correct. *(Publisher, adapted)*
REQUIRED: The interest expense and contract liability recognized for a performance obligation satisfied at a point in time.
DISCUSSION: Until the product is delivered to the customer, all payments received are recognized as a contract liability. Because the contract includes a significant financing component, interest expense is recognized using the effective interest method. The contract liability at the beginning of Year 2 equals $21,200 ($20,000 × 1.06). Thus, Year 2 interest expense equals $1,272 ($21,200 × 6%), and the contract liability at the end of Year 2 equals $22,472 ($21,200 × 1.06).
Answer (A) is incorrect. The amounts of $1,200 and $21,200 are the Year 1 interest expense and the December 31, Year 1, contract liability, respectively. Answer (B) is incorrect. The contract includes a significant financing component, so interest expense is recognized using the effective interest method, not a simple interest method. Answer (D) is incorrect. The amounts of $1,348 and $0 are the Year 3 interest expense and December 31, Year 3, contract liability, respectively.

21.4.6. Under ASC 606, the transaction price generally should be adjusted for the effect of the time value of money when

A. The selling price of the product and the consideration promised in the contract differ significantly.

B. The time between the payment and the delivery of the promised goods in the contract to the customer is 6 months.

C. After the customer is billed, it has 2 years to request a delivery of the goods.

D. A royalty contract with a distribution in which the consideration to be received depends on sales to end customers.

Answer (A) is correct. *(Publisher, adapted)*
REQUIRED: The reason for adjusting the transaction price for the time value of money.
DISCUSSION: The transaction price should be adjusted for the effect of the time value of money when the contract includes a significant financing component. A significant difference between (1) the selling price of the product and (2) the consideration promised in the contract may indicate that the financing component is significant.
Answer (B) is incorrect. The transaction price should not be adjusted for the effect of the time value of money if the time between the payment and the delivery of the promised good or service to the customer is 1 year or less. Answer (C) is incorrect. The transaction price should not be adjusted for the effect of the time value of money when the transfer of goods or services is at the discretion of the customer (e.g., a bill-and-hold contract). Answer (D) is incorrect. The transaction price should not be adjusted for the effect of the time value of money when (1) a substantial amount of the consideration promised is variable and (2) the amount or timing of the consideration varies on the basis of future circumstances that are not within the control of the entity or the customer.

21.4.7. On November 1, Year 1, an entity sold 50 machines to a customer for $100 each. The cost of each machine is $20. The entity allows customers to return any unused machine within 6 months and receive a full refund. The entity uses the expected value method to estimate the variable consideration. Based on the entity's experience and other relevant factors, it reasonably estimates that 10 machines (6 in Year 1 and 4 in Year 2) will be returned. What amount of revenue is recognized by the entity from the sale of these machines on November 1, Year 1?

A. $5,000

B. $4,400

C. $0

D. $4,000

Answer (D) is correct. *(Publisher, adapted)*
REQUIRED: The revenue recognized using the expected value method to estimate the variable consideration.
DISCUSSION: Because the contract allows the customer a right of return, the consideration received from the customer is variable. Revenue from variable consideration is recognized only to the extent that it is probable that a significant reversal will not occur. The entity estimates that 10 machines will be returned. Thus, it recognizes revenue only for the sale of 40 (50 – 10) machines, and on November 1, Year 1, a revenue of $4,000 (40 × $100) is recognized.
Answer (A) is incorrect. Because the contract allows a customer the right of return, the consideration received from the customer is variable. Revenue from variable consideration is recognized only to the extent that it is probable that a significant reversal will not occur. Because some machines are expected to be returned, the full amount of revenue from the sale must not be recognized. Answer (B) is incorrect. At the inception of the contract, the entity recognizes revenue from the sale of only 40 (50 – 10) machines. Based on its reasonable estimate, 10 machines are expected to be returned. Answer (C) is incorrect. The entity recognizes no revenue until the right of return expires only if it cannot reasonably estimate the probability and the amount of a refund.

21.4.8. The transaction price from contracts with customers generally should not be adjusted for the effect of the time value of money when

A. The transfer of goods is at the discretion of the seller.

B. A substantial amount of the consideration is contingent on a future event that is not within the control of the seller.

C. The time between the payment and the delivery of the promised goods in the contract to the customer is 18 months.

D. The selling price of the product and the consideration promised in the contract differ significantly.

Answer (B) is correct. *(Publisher, adapted)*
REQUIRED: The reason not to adjust the transaction price for the time value of money.
DISCUSSION: The transaction price should not be adjusted for the effect of the time value of money if

● The time between the payment and the delivery of the promised good or service to the customer is 1 year or less.

● The transfer of goods or services is at the discretion of the customer (e.g., a bill-and-hold contract in which the seller provides storage services for goods it sold to the buyer).

● A substantial amount of the consideration promised is variable, and its amount or timing varies on the basis of future circumstances that are not within the control of the entity or the customer. An example is a sales-based royalty contract in which the amount of consideration depends on sales by the customer to third parties.

Answer (A) is incorrect. The transaction price should not be adjusted when the transfer of goods or services is at the discretion of the customer. Answer (C) is incorrect. The transaction price should not be adjusted for the effect of the time value of money if the time between the payment and the delivery of the promised good or service to the customer is 1 year or less. Answer (D) is incorrect. The transaction price should be adjusted for the effect of the time value of money when the contract includes a significant financing component. A significant difference between (1) the selling price of the product and (2) the consideration promised in the contract may indicate that the financing component is significant.

21.5 Allocating the Transaction Price to the Performance Obligations in the Contract

21.5.1. Which of the following can be used to estimate the standalone selling price of a performance obligation in a contract with customers when that price is not directly observable?

	Adjusted Market Assessment	Expected Cost Plus an Appropriate Margin
A.	Yes	No
B.	Yes	Yes
C.	No	No
D.	No	Yes

Answer (B) is correct. *(Publisher, adapted)*
REQUIRED: The method(s), if any, of estimating the standalone selling price when the price is not directly observable.
DISCUSSION: The transaction price is allocated to performance obligations in the contract based on their standalone selling prices. The best evidence of a standalone selling price is the observable price of a good or service when it is sold separately in similar circumstances and to similar customers. The adjusted market assessment and the expected cost plus an appropriate margin are acceptable estimates of the standalone selling price of a performance obligation when that price is not directly observable. Using the adjusted market assessment approach, an entity evaluates the market in which it sells goods or services and estimates the price that a customer in that market would be willing to pay for them. Using the expected cost plus an appropriate margin approach, an entity forecasts its expected costs of satisfying a performance obligation and adds an appropriate margin for that cost.

Answer (A) is incorrect. The expected cost plus an appropriate margin approach also is an acceptable estimate of the standalone selling price of a performance obligation when that price is not directly observable. Answer (C) is incorrect. If the standalone price of a performance obligation is not directly observable, it can be estimated by the following approaches: (1) adjusted market assessment, (2) expected cost plus an appropriate margin, and (3) residual. Answer (D) is incorrect. The adjusted market assessment also is an acceptable estimate of the standalone selling price of a performance obligation when that price is not directly observable.

21.5.2. The best evidence of a standalone selling price, given different performance obligations in the contract, is

A. Expected cost.

B. Expected cost plus an appropriate margin.

C. An observable price.

D. Competitor's selling price.

Answer (C) is correct. *(Publisher, adapted)*
REQUIRED: The best evidence of a standalone selling price.
DISCUSSION: The standalone selling price is the price at which an entity would sell a promised good or service separately to a customer. The best evidence of a standalone selling price is the observable price of a good or service when it is sold separately in similar circumstances and to similar customers (e.g., a contractually stated price or list price of a good or service).
Answer (A) is incorrect. An observable price that is evidence of a standalone selling price is preferable to an estimate. If the standalone price is not directly observable, possible approaches to estimation include an adjusted market assessment or an expected cost plus an appropriate margin. Answer (B) is incorrect. Only when the selling price is not directly observable may an entity use the expected cost plus an appropriate margin approach to estimate the standalone selling price. Answer (D) is incorrect. Only when the selling price is not directly observable may an entity use the adjusted market assessment approach to estimate the standalone selling price.

21.5.3. A contract with a customer has more than one performance obligation. The transaction price most likely is allocated to the performance obligations based on

A. A residual approach.

B. Expected gross profit of performance obligations.

C. Directly observable prices.

D. Expected costs of satisfying performance obligations.

Answer (C) is correct. *(Publisher, adapted)*
REQUIRED: The most likely basis for allocating the transaction price to performance obligations.
DISCUSSION: After separate performance obligations are identified and the transaction price is determined, the transaction price is allocated to performance obligations in the contract based on their standalone selling prices. The standalone selling price is the price at which an entity would sell a promised good or service separately to a customer. The best evidence of a standalone selling price is the observable price of a good or service when it is sold separately in similar circumstances and to similar customers (e.g., a contractually stated price or list price of a good or service).
Answer (A) is incorrect. A residual approach is an approach used only in limited circumstances to estimate standalone prices that are not directly observable. Answer (B) is incorrect. The transaction price must be allocated to performance obligations in the contract based on their standalone selling prices. Answer (D) is incorrect. The expected cost plus an appropriate margin approach may be used to estimate the standalone selling price of a performance obligation that is not directly observable.

21.5.4. The standalone selling price of a performance obligation in a contract with a customer may not be directly observable. Alternatives for estimating the standalone selling price include

	Estimation of the Price in the Seller's Market	Residual Approach
A.	No	Yes
B.	No	No
C.	Yes	No
D.	Yes	Yes

Answer (D) is correct. *(Publisher, adapted)*
REQUIRED: The way(s), if any, of estimating the standalone selling price.
DISCUSSION: The adjusted market assessment, the expected cost plus an appropriate margin, and a residual are among the acceptable estimates of the standalone selling price of a performance obligation when that price is not directly observable. Using the adjusted market assessment approach, an entity evaluates the market in which it sells goods or services and estimates the price that a customer in that market would be willing to pay for them. Using the expected cost plus an appropriate margin approach, an entity forecasts its expected costs of satisfying a performance obligation and adds an appropriate margin for that cost. In limited circumstances, a residual approach also may be used. A residual is the total transaction price minus the observable prices for other items promised in the contract. The residual approach may be applied only when the standalone price is (1) highly variable or (2) uncertain.
Answer (A) is incorrect. The adjusted market assessment also is an acceptable estimate of the standalone selling price of a performance obligation when that price is not directly observable. Answer (B) is incorrect. If the standalone price of a performance obligation is not directly observable, it can be estimated by the following approaches: (1) adjusted market assessment, (2) expected cost plus an appropriate margin, and (3) residual. Answer (C) is incorrect. The residual approach may be used but only in limited circumstances.

21.6 Recognizing Revenue when (or as) the Entity Satisfies a Performance Obligation

21.6.1. A promised asset is transferred in full satisfaction of a performance obligation in a contract when the customer

A. Obtains control of the asset.

B. Can direct use of the product.

C. Has physical possession of the asset.

D. Pays for the asset in full.

Answer (A) is correct. *(Publisher, adapted)*
REQUIRED: The time when an asset transfer fully satisfies a performance obligation.
DISCUSSION: Revenue is recognized when a performance obligation is satisfied by transferring a promised good or service to a customer. It happens when the customer obtains control of the good or service (i.e., an asset). Control of an asset is transferred to the customer when the customer (1) has the ability to direct the use of the asset and (2) obtains substantially all of the remaining benefits (potential cash flows) from the asset.
Answer (B) is incorrect. Control of the asset is not transferred to the customer unless the customer also obtains substantially all of the remaining benefits from the asset. Answer (C) is incorrect. Transfer of a physical possession is only one of the indicators for transfer of control. However, according to the terms of some contracts, the control of an asset may be transferred to a customer even when the product is still physically in the seller's warehouse. An example is a bill-and-hold contract in which the transfer of goods or services is at the discretion of the customer. Answer (D) is incorrect. Control of an asset is transferred to the customer when the customer (1) has the ability to direct the use of the asset and (2) obtains substantially all of the remaining benefits (potential cash flows) from the asset. Control can be transferred to a customer before (installment sale contract) or after (prepaid contract) the full payment is made.

21.6.2. Which of the following situations may result in recognition over time of revenue from a contract with a customer by an entity?

A. The entity can enforce payment for work completed to date on an asset with an alternative use to the entity.

B. The customer simultaneously receives and consumes the benefits from performance as the entity performs.

C. The customer has accepted the asset, and the entity has a present right to payment.

D. The entity's performance creates or enhances an asset not controlled by the customer during the process.

Answer (B) is correct. *(Publisher, adapted)*
REQUIRED: The basis for recognizing revenue over time.
DISCUSSION: An entity recognizes revenue when (or as) it satisfies each performance obligation in the contract by transferring the promised good or service (an asset) to a customer. An asset is transferred when the customer obtains control of that asset. When the customer simultaneously receives and consumes the benefits from performance as the entity performs, revenue is recognized over time.
Answer (A) is incorrect. When (1) the asset created has no alternative use to the entity and (2) the entity can enforce payment for performance completed to date, revenue is recognized over time. Answer (C) is incorrect. The customer's acceptance of the asset and the entity's present right to payment are indicators of a transfer of control when a performance obligation is satisfied at a point in time. Answer (D) is incorrect. When the entity's performance creates or enhances an asset (for example, work in process) that the customer controls as the asset is created or enhanced, revenue is recognized over time (e.g., over a construction period).

21.6.3. When revenue from contracts with customers is recognized over time, the progress toward complete satisfaction of a performance obligation may be measured using the

A. Point-in-time method.

B. Zero-profit-margin method.

C. Estimated gross profit method.

D. Input method.

Answer (D) is correct. *(Publisher, adapted)*
REQUIRED: The method for measuring the progress toward complete satisfaction of a performance obligation.
DISCUSSION: When revenue is recognized over time, the progress toward complete satisfaction of a performance obligation must be measured. This progress must be measured either by the output method or the input method. To determine the appropriate method, an entity must consider the nature of the good or service that it promised to transfer to the customer. The chosen method should measure the entity's performance in transferring control of the promised asset to the customer. The input method recognizes revenue on the basis of (1) the entity's inputs to the satisfaction of the performance obligation relative to (2) the total expected inputs to the satisfaction of that performance obligation. Examples of input methods include (1) resources consumed, (2) labor hours expended, (3) costs incurred, (4) time elapsed, or (5) machine hours used. When an entity's inputs are incurred evenly over time, recognition of revenue on a straight-line basis may be appropriate.
Answer (A) is incorrect. A performance obligation can be satisfied either over time or at a point in time. Thus, point in time is not a method used to measure satisfaction of the obligation over time. Answer (B) is incorrect. An entity recognizes revenue only to the extent of the cost incurred (zero profit margin) when (1) progress cannot be measured reasonably but (2) the entity expects to recover its costs. Answer (C) is incorrect. The estimated gross profit method is used to determine inventory for interim statements. Progress must be measured either by the output method or the input method.

21.6.4. An entity entered into a contract to construct a building. Based on the contract's terms, the entity appropriately determined that the performance obligation in the contract will be satisfied over time. At an early stage of the contract, the entity cannot reasonably measure the outcome of the contract, but it expects to recover the costs incurred in the construction of the building. The revenue from the contract should be recognized

A. Only to the extent of the costs incurred.

B. Only upon completion of the construction.

C. Evenly over the contract period on a straight-line basis.

D. Based on the progress toward completion of the project.

Answer (A) is correct. *(Publisher, adapted)*
REQUIRED: The revenue recognized for a performance obligation satisfied over time if the outcome cannot be reasonably measured but cost recovery is expected.
DISCUSSION: When the outcome of the contract is not reasonably measurable but the costs incurred in satisfying the performance obligation are expected to be recovered, revenue must be recognized only to the extent of the costs incurred. Revenue recognized is based on a zero profit margin until the entity can reasonably measure the outcome of the performance obligation.
Answer (B) is incorrect. Revenue can be recognized before the completion of the construction, but only to the extent of costs incurred. Answer (C) is incorrect. When the outcome of the contract is not reasonably measurable but the costs incurred in satisfying the performance obligation are expected to be recovered, revenue must be recognized only to the extent of the costs incurred. Answer (D) is incorrect. When the outcome of the contract is not reasonably measurable but the costs incurred in satisfying the performance obligation are expected to be recovered, revenue must be recognized only to the extent of the costs incurred. Thus, neither the input nor the output method is used until the entity can reasonably measure the outcome of the performance obligation.

21.6.5. An entity recognizes revenue from a long-term contract over time. However, early in the performance of the contract, it cannot reasonably measure the outcome, but it expects to recover the costs incurred. Revenue should be recognized based on

A. The output method.

B. A straight-line calculation.

C. A zero profit margin.

D. The completed-contract method.

Answer (C) is correct. *(Publisher, adapted)*
REQUIRED: The basis for recognizing revenue for a performance obligation satisfied over time if the outcome cannot be reasonably measured but cost recovery is expected.
DISCUSSION: When the outcome of the contract is not reasonably measurable but the costs incurred in satisfying the performance obligation are expected to be recovered, revenue must be recognized only to the extent of the costs incurred. Revenue recognized is based on a zero profit margin until the entity can reasonably measure the outcome of the performance obligation.
Answer (A) is incorrect. When the outcome of the contract is not reasonably measurable but the costs incurred in satisfying the performance obligation are expected to be recovered, revenue must be recognized only to the extent of the costs incurred. Thus, neither the input nor the output method is used until the entity can reasonably measure the outcome of the performance obligation. Answer (B) is incorrect. When the outcome of the contract is not reasonably measurable but the costs incurred in satisfying the performance obligation are expected to be recovered, revenue must be recognized only to the extent of the costs incurred. Answer (D) is incorrect. When the outcome of the contract is not reasonably measurable but the costs incurred in satisfying the performance obligation are expected to be recovered, revenue is recognized to the extent of the costs incurred.

21.6.6. On January 1, Year 1, an entity enters into a contract with a customer to build a robot. The construction of the robot is expected to be completed at the end of Year 2. The entity also determines that

● It has no alternative use for the robot.

● It has an enforceable right to payment for the performance completed to date.

● The progress toward complete construction of the robot is reasonably measurable using the input method based on costs incurred.

The contract price is $800,000, and expected total costs are $500,000. The following additional information relates to the actual and expected costs incurred:

	Year 1	Year 2
Costs incurred during each year	$250,000	$350,000
Costs expected in future	$250,000	$ 0

What amounts of revenue, cost of goods sold, and gross profit are recognized by the entity for Year 2?

	Revenue	Cost of Goods Sold	Gross Profit
A.	$400,000	$350,000	$50,000
B.	$400,000	$250,000	$150,000
C.	$800,000	$350,000	$450,000
D.	$800,000	$600,000	$200,000

Answer (A) is correct. *(Publisher, adapted)*
REQUIRED: The revenue, cost of goods sold, and gross profit recognized if the asset has no alternative use to the entity, the entity has an enforceable right to payment for completed performance, and progress is reasonably measurable using the input method.
DISCUSSION: Revenue must be recognized over time, that is, over the 2 years of the construction period, because (1) the robot has no alternative use to the entity and (2) the entity has an enforceable right to payment for the performance completed to date. In Year 1, 50% ($250,000 ÷ $500,000) of expected costs has been incurred. Using the input method based on costs incurred, the entity recognizes 50% of the expected revenue from the contract for Year 1 ($800,000 contract price × 50% = $400,000). The total gross profit from the contract is expected to be $300,000 ($800,000 – $500,000). Thus, $150,000 ($300,000 × 50%) of gross profit ($400,000 revenue – $250,000 cost of goods sold) is recognized in Year 1. In Year 2, the contract is completed, and the total gross profit from the contract is $200,000 [$800,000 contract price – ($250,000 + $350,000) total costs incurred]. Because $150,000 of gross profit was recognized in Year 1, $50,000 ($200,000 – $150,000) of gross profit is recognized in Year 2. The total revenue from the contract is $800,000. Revenue of $400,000 was recognized in Year 1, so Year 2 revenue is $400,000 ($800,000 – $400,000). Cost of goods sold in Year 2 equals the actual costs incurred of $350,000.
Answer (B) is incorrect. The revenue of $400,000, cost of goods sold of $250,000, and gross profit of $150,000 are recognized in Year 1, not Year 2. Answer (C) is incorrect. Some revenue from the contract was recognized in Year 1. Also, the total gross profit from the project is $200,000 [$800,000 contract price – ($250,000 + $350,000) total costs incurred]. Answer (D) is incorrect. The amounts of revenue ($800,000), cost of goods sold ($600,000), and gross profit ($200,000) are the totals recognized over the entire contract period (Year 1 and Year 2).

21.6.7. A building contractor has a fixed-price contract to construct a building on the customer's land. The building is expected to be completed in 2 years. Progress billings will be sent to the customer at quarterly intervals. Which of the following describes the preferable point for revenue recognition for this contract if its outcome can be reasonably measured?

A. After the contract is signed.

B. As progress is made toward completion of the contract.

C. As cash is received.

D. As and only to the extent of costs incurred.

Answer (B) is correct. *(Publisher, adapted)*
REQUIRED: The preferable point for revenue recognition for a contract to instruct an asset on the customer's land if the outcome can be reasonably measured.
DISCUSSION: An entity must recognize revenue when (or as) it satisfies each performance obligation in the contract by transferring the promised good or service to a customer. Because the customer controls the building as it is constructed, the contract meets the criteria for recognition of revenue over time. Thus, the contractor must recognize revenue as progress is made toward completion of the contract.
Answer (A) is incorrect. Revenue is not recognized until progress has been made toward complete satisfaction of the contract. Answer (C) is incorrect. A cash method of accounting is inappropriate. An accrual method, that is, the input or the output method, must be used to measure the progress toward complete satisfaction of the contract. Answer (D) is incorrect. Recognition of revenue is limited to the extent of costs incurred when the outcome of the contract is not reasonably measurable, but costs incurred are expected to be recovered. If the outcome of the contract can be reasonably measured, the input or the output method must be used.

21.6.8. A building contractor has a contract to construct a large building. It is estimated that the building will take 2 years to complete. Progress billings will be sent to the customer at quarterly intervals. Which of the following describes the preferable point for revenue and gross profit recognition for this contract?

A. After the contract is signed.

B. As progress is made toward completion of the contract.

C. As cash is received.

D. When the contract is completed.

Answer (B) is correct. *(CIA, adapted)*
REQUIRED: The timing of recognition of revenue and gross profit.
DISCUSSION: Two methods are used for revenue and gross profit recognition for long-term construction-type contracts: the percentage-of-completion method and the completed-contract method. Under the percentage-of-completion method, revenue and gross profit are recognized each period based upon the progress of the construction. The presumption is that the percentage-of-completion approach is the better method and that the completed-contract method should be used only when the percentage-of-completion method is inappropriate.
Answer (A) is incorrect. Revenue and gross profit are not earned until progress has been made toward completion. Answer (C) is incorrect. An accrual method, such as the percentage-of-completion method, should be used. Answer (D) is incorrect. The completed-contract method should be used only if conditions for using the percentage-of-completion method cannot be met.

21.6.9. Saskia Company's construction projects extend over several years, and collection of receivables is reasonably certain. Each project has a firm contract price, reliable estimates of the extent of progress and cost to finish, and a contract that is specific as to the rights and obligations of all parties. The contractor and the buyer are expected to fulfill their contractual obligations on each project. Saskia should recognize revenue from the projects

A. As cash is collected from customers.

B. Based on the progress toward complete satisfaction of the performance obligation for each project.

C. Only to the extent of the costs incurred.

D. At a point in time.

Answer (B) is correct. *(CIA, adapted)*
REQUIRED: The method appropriate to account for construction revenue.
DISCUSSION: For each performance obligation satisfied over time, an entity must recognize revenue over time. For this purpose, the entity measures the progress toward complete satisfaction using the output method or the input method.
Answer (A) is incorrect. When a performance obligation is satisfied over time, revenue is recognized over time based on the progress toward complete satisfaction of the performance obligation (contract). Answer (C) is incorrect. When the performance obligation is satisfied over time, revenue can be recognized to the extent of the cost incurred only if (1) the outcome of a performance obligation or the progress toward satisfaction of that obligation cannot be reasonably measured and (2) the costs incurred in satisfying the performance obligation are expected to be recovered. Answer (D) is incorrect. When a performance obligation is satisfied over time, revenue is recognized over time based on the progress toward complete satisfaction of the performance obligation (contract).

21.6.10. The calculation of the gross profit recognized in the third year of a 5-year construction contract accounted for by the input method based on the costs incurred (cost-to-cost) method includes the ratio of

A. Total costs incurred to date to total estimated costs.

B. Total costs incurred to date to total billings to date.

C. Costs incurred in Year 3 to total estimated costs.

D. Costs incurred in Year 3 to total billings to date.

Answer (A) is correct. *(CPA, adapted)*
REQUIRED: The ratio used in the calculation of gross profit recognized for a construction contract using the percentage-of-completion method.
DISCUSSION: The input method based on costs incurred (cost-to-cost) method provides for the recognition of gross profit based on the relationship between costs incurred to date and estimated total costs for completion of the contract. (But other measures of progress are permitted.) The amount recognized in the third year of a 5-year contract is calculated as follows: The total anticipated gross profit (based on the latest available estimated costs) is multiplied by the ratio of costs incurred to date to the latest available total estimated costs, and the product is reduced by previously recognized gross profit.
Answer (B) is incorrect. The ratio of total costs incurred to date to total billings to date is not relevant. Answer (C) is incorrect. Total costs incurred must be used. Answer (D) is incorrect. Neither the issuance nor the collection of billings results in income recognition.

21.6.11. A company used the input method based on costs incurred to measure the progress toward completion of a 4-year construction contract. Which of the following items should be used to calculate the gross profit recognized in the second year?

	Gross Profit Previously Recognized	Amounts Billed to Date
A.	Yes	Yes
B.	No	Yes
C.	Yes	No
D.	No	No

Answer (C) is correct. *(CPA, adapted)*
REQUIRED: The item(s) used in computing gross profit in the second year.
DISCUSSION: The cost-to-cost method provides for the recognition of gross profit based on the relationship between the costs incurred to date and estimated total costs for the completion of the contract. The amount of gross profit (based on the latest available estimated costs) recognized in the second year of a 4-year contract is calculated as follows: The total anticipated gross profit is multiplied by the ratio of the costs incurred to date to the total estimated costs, and the product is reduced by previously recognized gross profit. Gross profit previously recognized is therefore used to calculate gross profit to be recognized in the second year. However, amounts billed to date have no effect on the amount of gross profit to be recognized in the second year.
Answer (A) is incorrect. Amounts billed to date are not used to calculate the gross profit recognized. Answer (B) is incorrect. Gross profit previously recognized is used to calculate the amount recognized, but amounts billed are not. Answer (D) is incorrect. The gross profit previously recognized must be included in the calculation of current period gross profit.

21.6.12. Lake Construction Company has consistently used the input method based on costs incurred to measure the progress toward completion of the contract. During Year 1, Lake entered into a fixed-price contract to construct an office building for $10 million. Information relating to the contract is as follows:

	December 31	
	Year 1	Year 2
Percentage of completion	20%	60%
Estimated total costs at completion	$7,500,000	$8,000,000
Gross profit recognized (cumulative)	500,000	1,200,000

Contract costs incurred during Year 2 were

A. $3,200,000

B. $3,300,000

C. $3,500,000

D. $4,800,000

Answer (B) is correct. *(CPA, adapted)*
REQUIRED: The contract cost incurred during the second year of a long-term contract.
DISCUSSION: The progress toward completion of the project is based on the relationship of the cumulative costs incurred to date to estimated total costs at completion. Thus, the cumulative amount incurred at December 31, Year 1, was $1,500,000 ($7,500,000 × 20%). At December 31, Year 2, the cumulative amount incurred was $4,800,000 ($8,000,000 × 60%). The difference of $3,300,000 ($4,800,000 – $1,500,000) equals the contract costs incurred during Year 2.
Answer (A) is incorrect. The amount of $3,200,000 results from calculating costs incurred in Year 1 based on estimated costs at completion using Year 2 figures. Answer (C) is incorrect. The amount of $3,500,000 results from calculating the difference between total costs at the end of Year 2 based on $7,500,000 and costs incurred during Year 1, then adding the increase in estimated total costs of $500,000. Answer (D) is incorrect. The amount of $4,800,000 is the total costs incurred after Year 2.

21.6.13. Kechara Corp. started a long-term construction project on a customer's land in Year 1. The following data relate to this project:

Contract price	$4,200,000
Costs incurred in Year 1	1,750,000
Estimated costs to complete	1,750,000
Progress billings	900,000
Collections on progress billings	800,000

The project is accounted for using the input method based on costs incurred to measure progress toward completion of the contract. In Kechara's Year 1 income statement, what amount of gross profit should be reported for this project?

A. $350,000

B. $150,000

C. $133,333

D. $100,000

Answer (A) is correct. *(CPA, adapted)*
    REQUIRED: The gross profit for the first year of a long-term construction contract accounted for using the cost-to-cost method.
    DISCUSSION: In Year 1, one-half of the estimated costs of this construction project were incurred [$1,750,000 ÷ ($1,750,000 + $1,750,000)]. The company should therefore recognize one-half of the estimated gross profit in Year 1. At year-end, the estimated gross profit is $700,000, equal to the contract price minus total estimated costs [$4,200,000 – ($1,750,000 + $1,750,000)]. In Year 1, $350,000 should be recognized as gross profit ($700,000 × 50%).
    Answer (B) is incorrect. The amount of $150,000 results from multiplying the estimated gross profit by the ratio of amounts billed to the contract price. Amounts billed are not used in the calculation of gross profit. Answer (C) is incorrect. The amount of $133,333 results from multiplying the estimated gross profit by the ratio of collections on amounts billed to the contract price. Amounts billed are not used in the calculation of gross profit. Answer (D) is incorrect. Uncollected amounts billed of $100,000 have no effect on the gross profit.

21.6.14. Ailouros Construction, Inc., has consistently used the input method based on costs incurred to measure the progress toward completion of a project. During Year 1, Ailouros started work on a $6 million fixed-price construction contract. The accounting records disclosed the following data for the year ended December 31, Year 1:

Costs incurred	$1,860,000
Estimated costs to complete	4,340,000
Accounts receivable	600,000
Collections	1,400,000

How much loss should Ailouros have recognized in Year 1?

A. $460,000

B. $200,000

C. $60,000

D. $0

Answer (B) is correct. *(CPA, adapted)*
    REQUIRED: The loss to be recorded in the first year of a long-term construction contract.
    DISCUSSION: As soon as an estimated loss on any project becomes apparent, it must be recognized in full. The total of the costs incurred in Year 1 plus estimated costs to complete is $6,200,000 ($1,860,000 + $4,340,000). Because this sum exceeds the $6 million fixed-price construction contract amount, a $200,000 loss should be recognized.
    Answer (A) is incorrect. The difference between the costs incurred and the collections ($1,860,000 – $1,400,000) is $460,000. Answer (C) is incorrect. The amount of $60,000 results from multiplying the loss that should be recognized by the ratio of estimated costs incurred to total costs [$1,860,000 ÷ ($1,860,000 + $4,340,000) × $200,000 = $60,000]. Answer (D) is incorrect. A loss is recognized in the period in which it occurs.

21.6.15. A company uses the completed-contract method to account for a long-term construction contract. Revenue and gross profit are recognized when recorded progress billings

	Are Collected	Exceed Recorded Costs
A.	Yes	Yes
B.	No	No
C.	Yes	No
D.	No	Yes

Answer (B) is correct. *(CPA, adapted)*
    REQUIRED: The effect of the completed-contract method on revenue recognition.
    DISCUSSION: Under the completed-contract method of accounting for long-term construction contracts, recorded progress billings have no effect on the recognition of revenue and gross profit.
    Answer (A) is incorrect. Progress billings are accrued until the end of the project. Answer (C) is incorrect. Collection of progress billings have no effect on the completed contract's revenue recognition. Answer (D) is incorrect. The excess of billings over costs will be closed out at the completion of the contract.

21.6.16. Frame Construction Company's contract requires the construction of a bridge in 3 years. The expected total cost of the bridge is $2,000,000, and Frame will receive $2,500,000 for the project. The actual costs incurred to complete the project were $500,000, $900,000, and $600,000, respectively, during each of the 3 years. Progress payments received were $600,000, $1,200,000, and $700,000, respectively. Frame uses the input method based on costs incurred to recognize revenue from a performance obligation satisfied over time. What amount of gross profit should Frame report during the last year of the project?

A. $120,000

B. $125,000

C. $140,000

D. $150,000

Answer (D) is correct. *(CPA, adapted)*
REQUIRED: The recognized gross profit during the last year of the project.
DISCUSSION: The expected gross profit is $500,000 ($2,500,000 price – $2,000,000 expected cost). Cumulative recognized gross profit in Year 2 is $350,000 {$500,000 × [($500,000 + $900,000) ÷ $2,000,000]}. Recognized gross profit in Year 3 is $150,000 [($2,500,000 price – $500,000 – $900,000 – $600,000) actual gross profit – $350,000 previously recognized].
Answer (A) is incorrect. The amount of $120,000 is the recognized gross profit in the first year based on the percentage of the price paid ($600,000 ÷ $2,500,000). Answer (B) is incorrect. The amount of $125,000 is the amount recognized in the first year. Answer (C) is incorrect. The amount of $140,000 is the recognized gross profit in the third year based on the percentage of the price paid ($700,000 ÷ $2,500,000).

21.6.17. Haft Construction Co. has consistently used the input method based on costs incurred to measure progress toward completion of the project. On January 10, Year 3, Haft began work on a $3 million construction contract. At the inception date, the estimated cost of construction was $2,250,000. The following data relate to the progress of the contract:

Gross profit recognized at 12/31/Yr 3 $ 300,000
Costs incurred 1/10/Yr 3 through
    12/31/Yr 4   1,800,000
Estimated cost to complete at 12/31/Yr 4   600,000

In its income statement for the year ended December 31, Year 4, what amount of gross profit should Haft report?

A. $450,000

B. $300,000

C. $262,500

D. $150,000

Answer (D) is correct. *(CPA, adapted)*
REQUIRED: The amount of gross profit reported using the input method based on costs incurred to measure progress toward completion of the project.
DISCUSSION: The input method based on costs incurred provides for the recognition of gross profit based on the relationship between the costs incurred to date and estimated total costs for the completion of the contract. The total anticipated gross profit is multiplied by the ratio of the costs incurred to date to the total estimated costs, and the product is reduced by previously recognized gross profit. The percentage-of-completion at 12/31/Yr 4 is 75% [$1,800,000 ÷ ($1,800,000 + $600,000)]. The total anticipated gross profit is $600,000 ($3,000,000 contract price – $2,400,000 expected total costs). Consequently, a gross profit of $150,000 [($600,000 total gross profit × 75%) – $300,000 previously recognized gross profit] is recognized for Year 4.
Answer (A) is incorrect. The current year's profit equals the cumulative income minus the previously recognized gross profit. Answer (B) is incorrect. The amount of $300,000 is the previously recognized gross profit. Answer (C) is incorrect. The amount of $262,500 assumes the total estimated gross profit is $750,000 ($3,000,000 price – $2,250,000 originally estimated total cost).

Questions 21.6.18 and 21.6.19 are based on the following information. Data pertaining to Catus Co.'s long-term construction jobs, which commenced during Year 1, are as follows:

	Project 1	Project 2
Contract price	$420,000	$300,000
Costs incurred during Year 1	240,000	280,000
Estimated costs to complete	120,000	40,000
Billed to customers during Year 1	150,000	270,000
Received from customers during Year 1	90,000	250,000

21.6.18. If Catus cannot reasonably measure the progress toward completion of the projects but expects to recover the costs incurred, what amount of gross profit (loss) should Catus report in its Year 1 income statement?

A. $(20,000)

B. $0

C. $40,000

D. $420,000

Answer (A) is correct. *(CPA, adapted)*
REQUIRED: The amount of gross profit (loss) reported in the income statement under the completed-contract method.
DISCUSSION: Catus is not able to reasonably measure the progress toward satisfaction of the performance obligation (contract) but expects to recover the costs incurred. Accordingly, it recognizes revenue from the contracts to the extent of the cost incurred (zero profit margin). For Project 1, no gross profit is recognized in Year 1. However, as soon as an estimated loss on any project becomes apparent, it must be recognized in full. Catus therefore recognizes a loss of $20,000 on Project 2 ($300,000 contract price – ($280,000 + $40,000) estimated contract costs).
Answer (B) is incorrect. As soon as an estimated loss on any project becomes apparent, it must be recognized in full. Answer (C) is incorrect. The amount of $40,000 is the total estimated gross profit from the two projects, not what is recognized in Year 1. Answer (D) is incorrect. Gross profit is not recognized for the amounts billed to customers.

21.6.19. If Catus uses the input method based on costs incurred to measure the progress toward completion of the project, what amount of gross profit (loss) should Catus report in its Year 1 income statement?

A. $(20,000)

B. $20,000

C. $22,500

D. $40,000

Answer (B) is correct. *(CPA, adapted)*
REQUIRED: The amount of gross profit (loss) reported in the income statement using the input method.
DISCUSSION: The input method based on costs incurred provides for the recognition of gross profit based on the relationship between the costs incurred to date and estimated total costs for the completion of the contract. The total anticipated gross profit is multiplied by the ratio of the costs incurred to date to the total estimated costs, and the product is reduced by previously recognized gross profit. At the end of Year 1, Project 1 is 66 2/3% complete [$240,000 ÷ ($240,000 + $120,000)] and Project 2 is 87 1/2% complete [$280,000 ÷ ($280,000 + $40,000)]. Each project's percentage of completion is multiplied by its expected total gross profit. Accordingly, Catus recognizes $40,000 [($420,000 contract price – $240,000 costs incurred – $120,000 additional estimated costs) × 66 2/3%] of gross profit for Project 1. However, Project 2 estimates indicate a loss of $20,000 ($300,000 – $280,000 – $40,000). Because the full amount of a loss is reported immediately irrespective of the accounting method used, a gross profit of $20,000 [$40,000 Project 1 + $(20,000) Project 2] is recognized.
Answer (A) is incorrect. The amount of $(20,000) does not include the gross profit from Project 1. Answer (C) is incorrect. The entire loss projected for Project 2 is reported. Answer (D) is incorrect. The amount of $40,000 excludes the loss on Project 2.

21.7 Costs to Obtain or Fulfill a Contract with a Customer

21.7.1. Under the accounting for revenue recognition from contracts with customers ,which of the following must be amortized after their initial capitalization?

	Incremental Costs of Obtaining a Contract	Costs Incurred to Fulfill a Contract
A.	Yes	No
B.	Yes	Yes
C.	No	Yes
D.	No	No

Answer (B) is correct. *(Publisher, adapted)*

REQUIRED: The costs, if any, that must be amortized.

DISCUSSION: Costs incurred to fulfill a contract may be capitalized if certain criteria are met. The incremental costs of obtaining a contract with a customer must be capitalized if they are expected to be recovered. The amount capitalized for both types of costs must be amortized on a systematic basis that is consistent with the transfer to the customer of the goods or services to which the capitalized asset relates.

Answer (A) is incorrect. Costs incurred to fulfill a contract may be capitalized if certain criteria are met. The amount capitalized must be amortized on a systematic basis that is consistent with the transfer to the customer of the goods or services to which the asset relates. Answer (C) is incorrect. The amount capitalized for the incremental costs of obtaining a contract with a customer must be amortized on a systematic basis that is consistent with the transfer to the customer of the goods or services to which the capitalized asset relates. Answer (D) is incorrect. Incremental capitalized costs of (1) obtaining a contract or (2) fulfilling a contract must be amortized on a systematic basis that is consistent with the transfer to the customer of the goods or services to which the capitalized asset relates.

21.7.2. Which of the following costs with respect to a 5-year construction contract, if any, must be recognized as an asset whenever the entity expects to recover them?

	Incremental Costs of Obtaining a Contract	Costs Incurred to Fulfill a Contract
A.	Yes	No
B.	Yes	Yes
C.	No	Yes
D.	No	No

Answer (A) is correct. *(Publisher, adapted)*

REQUIRED: The costs, if any, recognized as an asset whenever the entity expects their recovery.

DISCUSSION: The incremental costs of obtaining a contract with a customer must be capitalized (recognized as an asset) if the entity expects to recover them. These costs would not have been incurred if the contract had not been obtained. Sales commissions are an example. However, costs incurred to fulfill a contract must be capitalized (recognized as an asset) only if they meet all of the following criteria:

- The costs relate directly to a current or anticipated contract.
- The costs generate or enhance resources of the entity that will be used in satisfying performance obligations in the future.
- The costs are expected to be recovered.

Answer (B) is incorrect. Costs incurred to fulfill a contract must meet two additional criteria. Answer (C) is incorrect. The incremental costs of obtaining a contract with a customer must be capitalized (recognized as an asset) if the entity expects to recover them. However, costs incurred to fulfill a contract must meet two additional criteria. Answer (D) is incorrect. The incremental costs of obtaining a contract with a customer must be capitalized (recognized as an asset) if the entity expects to recover them.

21.7.3. The incremental costs of obtaining a contract with a customer

A. Would have been incurred regardless of whether the contract was obtained.

B. Always must be capitalized.

C. Should not be capitalized if the performance obligations in the obtained contract are expected to be satisfied over a period of less than 1 year.

D. Always must be expensed as incurred.

Answer (C) is correct. *(Publisher, adapted)*

REQUIRED: The incremental costs of fulfilling a contract with a customer.

DISCUSSION: The incremental costs of obtaining a contract with a customer must be capitalized (recognized as an asset) if the entity expects to recover them. The cost capitalized (the asset recognized) must be amortized on a systematic basis that is consistent with the transfer to the customer of the goods or services to which the asset relates. But no cost should be capitalized to an asset if its amortization period is 1 year or less.

Answer (A) is incorrect. The incremental costs of obtaining a contract with a customer would not have been incurred if the contract had not been obtained. Answer (B) is incorrect. The incremental costs of obtaining a contract with a customer must be expensed if they are not expected to be recovered. Answer (D) is incorrect. The incremental costs of obtaining a contract with a customer must be capitalized (recognized as an asset) if the entity expects to recover them.

21.7.4. The incremental costs of obtaining a contract with a customer that are expected to be recovered must be

A. Reported as a direct deduction from the revenue recognized from the contract.

B. Recognized as an item of equity.

C. Recognized as an asset and amortized in subsequent periods.

D. Recognized in the income statement.

Answer (C) is correct. *(Publisher, adapted)*
REQUIRED: The accounting for incremental costs of obtaining a contract with a customer.
DISCUSSION: The incremental costs of obtaining a contract with a customer must be capitalized (recognized as an asset) if the entity expects to recover them. These costs would not have been incurred if the contract had not been obtained. The cost capitalized (asset recognized) must be amortized on a systematic basis that is consistent with the transfer to the customer of the goods or services to which the asset relates.
Answer (A) is incorrect. The incremental costs of obtaining a contract with a customer must be capitalized if the entity expects to recover them. Answer (B) is incorrect. The incremental costs of obtaining a contract with a customer are not an item of equity. These costs must be capitalized if they are expected to be recovered. Answer (D) is incorrect. The incremental costs of obtaining a contract with a customer must be capitalized (recognized as an asset) if those costs are expected to be recovered.

21.7.5. Which of the following is a criterion for capitalization of costs incurred to fulfill a contract with a customer?

A. The costs would have been incurred whether or not the contract was obtained.

B. The costs must be related to a satisfied performance obligation.

C. The costs relate to any future contract.

D. The costs generate or enhance resources of the entity that will be used in satisfying performance obligations in the future.

Answer (D) is correct. *(Publisher, adapted)*
REQUIRED: The criterion capitalization of costs incurred to fulfill a contract with a customer
DISCUSSION: Costs incurred to fulfill a contract must be capitalized (recognized as an asset) only if the costs meet all of the following criteria: (1) The costs relate directly to a current or anticipated contract that is specifically identifiable, (2) the costs generate or enhance resources of the entity that will be used in satisfying performance obligations in the future, and (3) the costs are expected to be recovered.
Answer (A) is incorrect. Costs to obtain a contract that would have been incurred whether or not the contract was obtained are expensed as incurred. Answer (B) is incorrect. Costs that relate to satisfied performance obligation in the contract must be expensed as incurred. Answer (C) is incorrect. One of the criteria for capitalization of costs incurred to fulfill a contract is that the costs must be related directly to a current contract or an anticipated contract that is specifically identifiable.

Use **Gleim Test Prep** for interactive study and easy-to-use detailed analytics!

STUDY UNIT TWENTY-TWO
FINANCIAL STATEMENT ANALYSIS

The most common form of financial statement analysis is **ratio analysis**, in which two financial statement measures are compared. Ratio analysis helps investors and managers to estimate and measure the firm's

- Liquidity -- a firm's ability to pay its current obligations as they come due and remain in business in the short run.

- Activity -- a measure of how quickly major noncash assets are converted to cash.

- Solvency -- a firm's ability to pay its noncurrent obligations as they come due and remain in business in the long run.

- Leverage -- the relative amount of fixed cost in a firm's overall cost structure.

- Profitability -- a measure of how effectively the firm is using its resource base to generate a return.

Questions often test the student's ability to determine the effect that a specific transaction has on one or more ratios.

QUESTIONS

22.1 General

22.1.1. A useful tool in financial statement analysis is the common-size financial statement. What does this tool enable the financial analyst to do?

A. Evaluate financial statements of companies within a given industry of approximately the same value.

B. Determine which companies in the same industry are at approximately the same stage of development.

C. Compare the mix of assets, liabilities, capital, revenue, and expenses within a company over time or between companies within a given industry without respect to relative size.

D. Ascertain the relative potential of companies of similar size in different industries.

Answer (C) is correct. *(CPA, adapted)*
 REQUIRED: The purposes of a common-size financial statement.
 DISCUSSION: A common-size financial statement presents the items in a financial statement as percentages of a common base. The items in a balance sheet are usually stated in percentages of total assets. The items in the income statement are usually expressed as a percentage of sales. Thus, comparisons among firms in the same industry are possible despite differences in size. Comparison of firms in different industries has drawbacks because the optimal mix of assets, liabilities, etc., will vary from industry to industry.
 Answer (A) is incorrect. Common-size statements are designed to permit comparison of different-sized companies. Answer (B) is incorrect. Common-size statements do not reveal the stage of development of a company. Answer (D) is incorrect. Common-size statements are not useful for comparing companies in different industries.

22.1.2. In financial statement analysis, expressing all financial statement items as a percentage of base-year amounts is called

A. Horizontal common-size analysis.

B. Vertical common-size analysis.

C. Trend analysis.

D. Ratio analysis.

Answer (A) is correct. *(CMA, adapted)*
REQUIRED: The term for expressing all financial statement items as a percentage of base-year amounts.
DISCUSSION: Expressing financial statement items as percentages of corresponding base-year figures is a horizontal form of common-size (percentage) analysis that is useful for evaluating trends. The base amount is assigned the value of 100%, and the amounts for other years are denominated in percentages compared to the base year.
Answer (B) is incorrect. Vertical common-size (percentage) analysis presents figures for a single year expressed as percentages of a base amount on the balance sheet (e.g., total assets) and on the income statement (e.g., sales). Answer (C) is incorrect. The term "trend analysis" is most often applied to the quantitative techniques used in forecasting to fit a curve to given data. Answer (D) is incorrect. It is a general term.

22.1.3. The relationship of the total debt to the total equity of a corporation is a measure of

A. Liquidity.

B. Profitability.

C. Creditor risk.

D. Solvency.

Answer (C) is correct. *(CMA, adapted)*
REQUIRED: The information provided by the debt-to-equity ratio.
DISCUSSION: The ratio of total debt to total equity is a measure of risk to creditors. It helps in the evaluation of a company's relative reliance on debt and equity financing (leverage).
Answer (A) is incorrect. Liquidity measures describe the ability of a company to meet its short-term obligations. Answer (B) is incorrect. Profitability ratios measure the relative success of a firm in earning a return on its assets, sales, equity, etc. Answer (D) is incorrect. Solvency measures describe the ability of a company to meet its short-term obligations.

22.1.4. What type of ratio is earnings per share?

A. Profitability ratio.

B. Activity ratio.

C. Liquidity ratio.

D. Leverage ratio.

Answer (A) is correct. *(Publisher, adapted)*
REQUIRED: The proper classification of the earnings-per-share ratio.
DISCUSSION: Earnings per share is a profitability ratio. It measures the level of profitability of the entity on a per-share basis.
Answer (B) is incorrect. Activity ratios measure management's efficiency in using specific resources. Answer (C) is incorrect. Liquidity ratios indicate the ability of an entity to meet short-term obligations. Answer (D) is incorrect. Leverage ratios concern the relationship of debt to equity and measure the impact of the debt on profitability and risk.

22.1.5. Are the following ratios useful in assessing the liquidity position of a company?

	Defensive-Interval Ratio	Return on Equity
A.	Yes	Yes
B.	Yes	No
C.	No	Yes
D.	No	No

Answer (B) is correct. *(CPA, adapted)*
REQUIRED: The ratio(s) useful in assessing the liquidity position of a company.
DISCUSSION: The defensive-interval ratio is equal to defensive assets divided by average daily expenditures for operations. Defensive assets include cash, short-term marketable securities, and net short-term receivables. This ratio provides information about a company's ability to survive in the absence of external cash flows. It is therefore useful in assessing liquidity (the ability to meet obligations as they mature). In contrast, return on equity is equal to net income minus preferred dividends, divided by average common equity. Return on equity provides information about the profitability of the firm. It does not provide information that is useful in assessing liquidity.
Answer (A) is incorrect. Return on equity is useful in measuring the profitability, not the liquidity, of a company. Answer (C) is incorrect. Return on equity is not useful in assessing the liquidity position. Answer (D) is incorrect. The defensive-interval ratio is useful in assessing the liquidity position.

22.2 Quick (Acid-Test) Ratio

22.2.1. Which of the following ratios is(are) useful in assessing a company's ability to meet currently maturing or short-term obligations?

	Acid-Test Ratio	Debt-to-Equity Ratio
A.	No	No
B.	No	Yes
C.	Yes	Yes
D.	Yes	No

Answer (D) is correct. *(CPA, adapted)*
REQUIRED: The ratio(s) useful in assessing the ability to meet currently maturing obligations.
DISCUSSION: The acid-test, or quick, ratio measures liquidity, which is the ability of a company to meet its short-term obligations. The debt-to-equity ratio is a leverage ratio. Leverage ratios measure the impact of debt on profitability and risk.
Answer (A) is incorrect. The acid-test ratio measures liquidity and is therefore useful in assessing a company's ability to meet currently maturing or short-term obligations. Answer (B) is incorrect. The acid-test ratio but not the debt-to-equity ratio is useful in assessing a company's ability to meet currently maturing or short-term obligations. Answer (C) is incorrect. The debt-to-equity ratio measures leverage and therefore is not useful in assessing a company's ability to meet currently maturing or short-term obligations.

22.2.2. How is the average inventory used in the calculation of each of the following?

	Acid-Test (Quick) Ratio	Inventory Turnover Ratio
A.	Numerator	Numerator
B.	Numerator	Denominator
C.	Not used	Denominator
D.	Not used	Numerator

Answer (C) is correct. *(CPA, adapted)*
REQUIRED: The use of average inventories in the acid-test (quick) ratio and the inventory turnover ratio.
DISCUSSION: Assets included in the numerator of the acid-test (quick) ratio include cash, short-term investment securities, and net accounts receivable. The inventory turnover rate is equal to cost of goods sold divided by average inventory. Thus, average inventory is included in the denominator of the inventory turnover rate but is not used in the acid-test ratio.
Answer (A) is incorrect. Average inventory is not used to calculate the acid-test ratio and it is the denominator of the inventory turnover rate. Answer (B) is incorrect. Average inventory is not used to calculate the acid-test ratio. Answer (D) is incorrect. Average inventory is the denominator of the inventory turnover rate.

22.2.3. Selected financial data from Drew Company follow:

	As of December 31
Cash	$ 75,000
Accounts receivable (net)	225,000
Merchandise inventory	270,000
Trading securities	40,000
Land and building (net)	500,000
Mortgage payable -- current portion	30,000
Accounts payable and accrued liabilities	120,000
Short-term notes payable	50,000

	Year Ended December 31
Sales	$1,500,000
Cost of goods sold	900,000

Drew's quick (acid-test) ratio as of December 31 is

A. 3.6 to 1.

B. 3.1 to 1.

C. 2.0 to 1.

D. 1.7 to 1.

Answer (D) is correct. *(CPA, adapted)*
REQUIRED: The quick (acid-test) ratio.
DISCUSSION: The quick or acid-test ratio is a measure of the firm's ability to pay its maturing liabilities in the short run. It is defined as quick assets (cash, short-term investment securities, and net receivables) divided by current liabilities. Drew Company's quick assets equal $340,000 ($75,000 + $40,000 + $225,000). The current liabilities equal $200,000 ($30,000 + $120,000 + $50,000). Dividing the $340,000 of quick assets by the $200,000 of current liabilities results in a quick (acid-test) ratio of 1.7 to 1.
Answer (A) is incorrect. The ratio 3.6 to 1 results from including inventory in quick assets and excluding the mortgage payable--current portion from current liabilities. Answer (B) is incorrect. The ratio 3.1 to 1 is the current ratio. Answer (C) is incorrect. The ratio 2.0 to 1 results from excluding the mortgage payable--current portion from current liabilities.

22.2.4. North Bank is analyzing Belle Corp.'s financial statements for a possible extension of credit. Belle's quick ratio is significantly better than the industry average. Which of the following factors should North consider as a possible limitation of using this ratio when evaluating Belle's creditworthiness?

A. Fluctuating market prices of short-term investments may adversely affect the ratio.

B. Increasing market prices for Belle's inventory may adversely affect the ratio.

C. Belle may need to sell its available-for-sale investments to meet its current obligations.

D. Belle may need to liquidate its inventory to meet its long-term obligations.

Answer (A) is correct. *(CPA, adapted)*
REQUIRED: The possible limitation of using the quick ratio to evaluate creditworthiness.
DISCUSSION: The quick ratio equals cash plus short-term investment securities plus net receivables, divided by current liabilities. Because short-term investment securities are included in the numerator, fluctuating market prices of these investments may adversely affect the ratio if Belle holds a substantial amount of such current assets.
Answer (B) is incorrect. Inventory is excluded from the calculation of the quick ratio. Answer (C) is incorrect. If the available-for-sale securities are not current, they are not included in the calculation of the ratio. If they are classified as current, their sale to meet current obligations is consistent with normal current assets management practices. Answer (D) is incorrect. Inventory and noncurrent obligations are excluded from the calculation of the quick ratio.

22.2.5. Given an acid-test ratio of 2.0, current assets of $5,000, and inventory of $2,000, and assuming no prepaid expenses, the value of current liabilities is

A. $1,500

B. $2,500

C. $3,500

D. $6,000

Answer (A) is correct. *(CIA, adapted)*
REQUIRED: The value of current liabilities given the acid-test ratio, current assets, and inventory.
DISCUSSION: The acid-test or quick ratio equals the ratio of the quick assets divided by current liabilities. Current assets equal the quick assets plus inventory and prepaid expenses. This question assumes that the entity has no prepaid expenses. Given current assets of $5,000, inventory of $2,000, and no prepaid expenses, the quick assets must be $3,000. Because the acid-test ratio is 2.0, the quick assets are double the current liabilities. Current liabilities therefore are equal to $1,500 ($3,000 quick assets ÷ 2.0).
Answer (B) is incorrect. The amount of $2,500 results from dividing the current assets by 2.0. Current assets include inventory, which should not be included in the calculation of the acid-test ratio. Answer (C) is incorrect. The amount of $3,500 results from adding inventory to current assets rather than subtracting it. Answer (D) is incorrect. The amount of $6,000 results from multiplying the quick assets by 2 instead of dividing by 2.

22.3 Current Ratio and Net Working Capital

22.3.1. Heath Co.'s current ratio is 4:1. Which of the following transactions will normally increase its current ratio?

A. Purchasing inventory on account.

B. Selling inventory on account.

C. Collecting an account receivable.

D. Purchasing machinery for cash.

Answer (B) is correct. *(CPA, adapted)*
REQUIRED: The transaction that increases a current ratio.
DISCUSSION: The current ratio is equal to current assets divided by current liabilities. An increase in current assets (the numerator) or decrease in current liabilities (the denominator) would cause the ratio to increase. If the company sold merchandise on open account that earned a normal gross margin, receivables would be increased at the time of recording the sales revenue in an amount greater than the decrease in inventory from recording the cost of goods sold. The effect would be an increase in the current assets and no change in the current liabilities. Thus, the current ratio would be increased.
Answer (A) is incorrect. The purchase of inventory on open account increases current assets and current liabilities by the same amount. Equal increases in the numerator and denominator of a fraction that exceeds one decrease the fraction. Answer (C) is incorrect. Collecting an account receivable decreases one current asset and increases another by the same amount. Answer (D) is incorrect. Purchasing machinery for cash decreases a current asset and increases a noncurrent asset, thereby decreasing the ratio.

22.3.2. Information from Dominic Company's year-end financial statements is as follows:

	Year 1	Year 2
Current assets	$ 4,000,000	$ 4,200,000
Current liabilities	2,000,000	1,800,000
Equity	5,000,000	5,400,000
Net sales	16,600,000	17,600,000
Cost of goods sold	12,400,000	12,800,000
Operating income	1,000,000	1,100,000

What is the current ratio at December 31, Year 2?

A. 1.38 to 1.

B. 2.94 to 1.

C. 2.33 to 1.

D. 3.00 to 1.

Answer (C) is correct. *(CPA, adapted)*
REQUIRED: The current ratio at the end of the second year.
DISCUSSION: The current ratio equals current assets divided by current liabilities. For Year 2, the current ratio equals $4,200,000 divided by $1,800,000, or 2.33. The other information is irrelevant.
Answer (A) is incorrect. The current ratio is not net sales divided by cost of goods sold. Answer (B) is incorrect. The current ratio does not include income. Answer (D) is incorrect. The current ratio does not include equity.

22.3.3. At December 30, Vida Co. had cash of $200,000, a current ratio of 1.5:1, and a quick ratio of .5:1. On December 31, all cash was used to reduce accounts payable. How did these cash payments affect the ratios?

	Current Ratio	Quick Ratio
A.	Increased	Decreased
B.	Increased	No effect
C.	Decreased	Increased
D.	Decreased	No effect

Answer (A) is correct. *(CPA, adapted)*
REQUIRED: The effect of the cash payments on the current and quick ratios.
DISCUSSION: The current ratio (1.5) equals current assets (cash, marketable securities, and net accounts receivable) divided by current liabilities (accounts payable, etc.). If a ratio is greater than 1.0, equal decreases in the numerator and denominator (debit accounts payable and credit cash for $200,000) increase the ratio. The quick ratio (.5) equals quick assets (cash, trading securities, net accounts receivable) divided by current liabilities. If a ratio is less than 1.0, equal decreases in the numerator and denominator (debit accounts payable and credit cash for $200,000) decrease the ratio.
Answer (B) is incorrect. The quick ratio decreased. Answer (C) is incorrect. The current ratio increased and the quick ratio decreased. Answer (D) is incorrect. The current ratio increased and the quick ratio decreased.

22.3.4. In comparing the current ratios of two companies, why is it invalid to assume that the company with the higher current ratio is the better company?

A. The current ratio includes assets other than cash.

B. A high current ratio may indicate inadequate inventory on hand.

C. A high current ratio may indicate inefficient use of various assets and liabilities.

D. The two companies may define working capital in different terms.

Answer (C) is correct. *(CPA, adapted)*
REQUIRED: The reason comparison of firms' current ratios does not indicate the better company.
DISCUSSION: The current ratio measures only the ratio of current assets to current liabilities. It does not measure the efficiency of handling the individual current asset accounts. A high ratio may indicate, for example, holding of excess inventory, or retention of more cash than needed for the cash flow requirements of the firm. The weaker and less efficient company may have the higher current ratio.
Answer (A) is incorrect. The composition of the assets in the current ratio does not, by itself, indicate whether a higher or lower ratio is preferable. Answer (B) is incorrect. A high ratio more likely indicates excess inventory on hand. Answer (D) is incorrect. Working capital is always defined as the excess of current assets over current liabilities.

22.3.5. Zenk Co. wrote off obsolete inventory of $100,000 during the year. What was the effect of this write-off on Zenk's ratio analysis?

A. Decrease in current ratio but not in quick ratio.

B. Decrease in quick ratio but not in current ratio.

C. Increase in current ratio but not in quick ratio.

D. Increase in quick ratio but not in current ratio.

Answer (A) is correct. *(CPA, adapted)*
REQUIRED: The effect of writing off obsolete inventory.
DISCUSSION: Inventory is included in the numerator of the current ratio but not the quick ratio. Consequently, an inventory write-off decreases the current ratio but not the quick ratio.
Answer (B) is incorrect. The write-off decreases the current but not the quick ratio. Answer (C) is incorrect. The write-off decreases the current but not the quick ratio. Answer (D) is incorrect. The write-off decreases the current but not the quick ratio.

22.3.6. Galad Corp. has current assets of $180,000 and current liabilities of $360,000. Which of the following transactions would improve Galad's current ratio?

A. Refinancing a $60,000 long-term mortgage with a short-term note.

B. Purchasing $100,000 of merchandise inventory with a short-term account payable.

C. Paying $40,000 of short-term accounts payable.

D. Collecting $20,000 of short-term accounts receivable.

Answer (B) is correct. *(CPA, adapted)*
REQUIRED: The transaction that improves the current ratio.
DISCUSSION: If a current ratio is less than 1.0, a transaction that results in equal increases in the numerator and denominator will improve the ratio. The current ratio is .5 ($180,000 ÷ $360,000). Debiting inventory and crediting accounts payable increases the ratio to .61 ($280,000 ÷ $460,000).
Answer (A) is incorrect. Refinancing a $60,000 long-term mortgage with a short-term note results in an increase in the denominator and no change in the numerator. Answer (C) is incorrect. Decreasing the denominator and the numerator by the same amount decreases a current ratio that is lower than 1.0. Answer (D) is incorrect. Collecting $20,000 of short-term accounts receivable has no effect on the amount of the numerator or denominator.

22.3.7. A company has a current ratio of 2 to 1. This ratio will decrease if the company

A. Receives a 5% stock dividend on one of its marketable securities.

B. Pays a large account payable which had been a current liability.

C. Borrows cash on a 6-month note.

D. Sells merchandise for more than cost and records the sale using the perpetual inventory method.

Answer (C) is correct. *(CPA, adapted)*
REQUIRED: The transaction reducing a positive current ratio.
DISCUSSION: If a ratio is greater than 1.0, an equal increase in the numerator (current assets) and denominator (current liabilities), like borrowing cash on a short-term basis, decreases the ratio.
Answer (A) is incorrect. Stock dividends do not affect the carrying value of the securities. Answer (B) is incorrect. Paying a current liability decreases current assets and liabilities equally, thereby increasing the ratio. Answer (D) is incorrect. This transaction increases the numerator with no effect on the denominator, which causes the ratio to increase.

22.3.8. Austen, Inc., uses the allowance method to account for uncollectible accounts. An account receivable that was previously determined to be uncollectible and written off was collected during September. The effect of the collection on Austen's current ratio and total working capital is

	Current Ratio	Working Capital
A.	None	None
B.	Increase	Increase
C.	Decrease	Decrease
D.	None	Increase

Answer (A) is correct. *(CMA, adapted)*
REQUIRED: The effect of the collection of a previously written off account receivable on the current ratio and total working capital.
DISCUSSION: The current ratio is the ratio of current assets to current liabilities. Working capital is equal to the difference between current assets and current liabilities. When an account receivable is written off, the allowance for uncollectible accounts and the gross receivables are decreased by the same amount. Thus, there is no effect on net accounts receivable. When an account receivable that was previously determined to be uncollectible and written off is collected, the amounts previously written off must be reestablished (debit accounts receivable, credit the allowance). This entry also has no net effect on net accounts receivable. The collection is then recorded as an equal increase in cash and a decrease in accounts receivable. The changes in these accounts are equal, so net current assets is unchanged. Because the net amount of current assets remains the same, neither the current ratio nor working capital is affected.
Answer (B) is incorrect. There is no increase in either of these accounts. Answer (C) is incorrect. There is no decrease in either of these accounts. Answer (D) is incorrect. The net amount of current assets remains the same, so neither the current ratio nor the working capital is affected.

22.3.9. If a company converts a short-term note payable into a long-term note payable, this transaction will

A. Decrease working capital only.

B. Decrease both working capital and the current ratio.

C. Increase working capital only.

D. Increase both working capital and the current ratio.

Answer (D) is correct. *(CPA, adapted)*
REQUIRED: The effect of converting a short-term note to a long-term note.
DISCUSSION: Converting a short-term note to a long-term note reduces current liabilities but not current assets. Thus, the transaction increases both working capital and the current ratio.
Answer (A) is incorrect. A reduction in current liabilities increases working capital. Answer (B) is incorrect. A reduction in current liabilities with no change in current assets increases both working capital and the current ratio. Answer (C) is incorrect. A decrease in current liabilities increases the current ratio as well as working capital.

Questions 22.3.10 and 22.3.11 are based on the following information. Calculation of ratios and the determination of other factors are considered important in analysis of financial statements. Prior to the independent events described below, the corporation concerned had current and quick ratios in excess of one to one and reported a net income (as opposed to a loss) for the period just ended. Income tax effects are to be ignored. The corporation had only one class of shares outstanding.

22.3.10. The effect of recording a 2-for-1 stock split is to

A. Decrease the current ratio, decrease working capital, and decrease book value per share.

B. Leave inventory turnover unaffected, decrease working capital, and decrease book value per share.

C. Leave working capital unaffected, decrease earnings per share, and decrease book value per share.

D. Leave working capital unaffected, decrease earnings per share, and decrease the debt-to-equity ratio.

Answer (C) is correct. *(CPA, adapted)*
REQUIRED: The effect of recording a 2-for-1 stock split.
DISCUSSION: A 2-for-1 stock split involves an increase in shares outstanding with no increase in the capital stock account. Thus, the par or stated value of the shares is adjusted so that the total is unchanged. It has no effect on assets, liabilities, working capital, or total equity. Thus, the current ratio, the working capital, and the debt-to-equity ratio are unaffected. EPS and book value per share decline because more shares are outstanding.
Answer (A) is incorrect. The current ratio, the working capital, and the debt-to-equity ratio are unaffected. Answer (B) is incorrect. None of these accounts change. Answer (D) is incorrect. The debt-to-equity ratio is unaffected.

22.3.11. Recording the payment (as distinguished from the declaration) of a cash dividend, the declaration of which was already recorded, will

A. Increase the current ratio but have no effect on working capital.

B. Decrease both the current ratio and working capital.

C. Increase both the current ratio and working capital.

D. Have no effect on the current ratio or earnings per share.

Answer (A) is correct. *(CPA, adapted)*
REQUIRED: The effect of the payment of a cash dividend.
DISCUSSION: The payment of a previously declared cash dividend reduces current assets and current liabilities equally. An equal reduction in current assets and current liabilities causes an increase in a positive (greater than 1.0) current ratio.
Answer (B) is incorrect. Working capital is not affected by the dividend payment. Answer (C) is incorrect. Paying a dividend does not increase working capital. Answer (D) is incorrect. The current ratio is increased.

22.4 Receivable and Inventory Ratios

22.4.1. The following information is available from Timber Corp.'s financial records for the current year:

Sales	
Net credit sales	$500,000
Net cash sales	250,000
	$750,000

Accounts Receivable	
Balance, January 1	$ 75,000
Balance, December 31	50,000

How many times did Timber's accounts receivable turn over during the year?

A. 15

B. 12

C. 10

D. 8

Answer (D) is correct. *(CPA, adapted)*
REQUIRED: The accounts receivable turnover.
DISCUSSION: The accounts receivable turnover is equal to net credit sales divided by the average accounts receivable. Net credit sales is $500,000 and average accounts receivable is $62,500 [($75,000 + $50,000) ÷ 2]. Accounts receivable turnover is thus 8 × ($500,000 ÷ $62,500).
Answer (A) is incorrect. A turnover of 15 times results from including total sales (credit and cash) divided by ending accounts receivable. Answer (B) is incorrect. A turnover of 12 times results from dividing total sales (credit and cash) by the average accounts receivable. Answer (C) is incorrect. A turnover of 10 times results from dividing net credit sales by ending accounts receivable.

22.4.2. Kline Co. had the following sales and accounts receivable balances at the end of the current year:

Cash sales	$1,000,000
Net credit sales	3,000,000
Net accounts receivable, 1/1	100,000
Net accounts receivable, 12/31	400,000

Assuming a 360-day year, what is Kline's average collection period for its accounts receivable?

- A. 48.0 days.
- B. 30.0 days.
- C. 22.5 days.
- D. 12.0 days.

Answer (B) is correct. *(CPA, adapted)*
REQUIRED: The average collection period for accounts receivable.
DISCUSSION: The average collection period for accounts receivable is calculated by dividing 360 days by the accounts receivable turnover. Accounts receivable turnover is equal to net credit sales divided by average accounts receivable. Average accounts receivable equals $250,000 [($100,000 beginning balance + $400,000 ending balance) ÷ 2]. Accounts receivable turnover is 12 times ($3,000,000 ÷ $250,000). Thus, the average collection period for accounts receivable is 30 days (360 days ÷ 12).
Answer (A) is incorrect. The figure of 48 days is based on a turnover rate calculated using ending accounts receivable instead of average accounts receivable. Answer (C) is incorrect. Cash sales should not be included when calculating the turnover ratio. Answer (D) is incorrect. The receivables turnover ratio is 12.

22.4.3. During the current year, Rand Co. purchased $960,000 of inventory. The cost of goods sold was $900,000, and the ending inventory at December 31 was $180,000. What was the inventory turnover?

- A. 6.4
- B. 6.0
- C. 5.3
- D. 5.0

Answer (B) is correct. *(CPA, adapted)*
REQUIRED: The inventory turnover given cost of sales, purchases, and ending inventory.
DISCUSSION: Inventory turnover is equal to cost of goods sold divided by the average inventory. Beginning inventory equals cost of goods sold, plus ending inventory, minus purchases ($900,000 + $180,000 – $960,000 = $120,000). Average inventory is equal to the average of beginning inventory and ending inventory [($120,000 + $180,000) ÷ 2 = $150,000]. Inventory turnover is thus 6.0 ($900,000 cost of goods sold ÷ $150,000 average inventory).
Answer (A) is incorrect. This figure equals purchases divided by average inventory. Answer (C) is incorrect. This figure equals purchases divided by ending inventory. Answer (D) is incorrect. This figure equals COGS divided by ending inventory.

22.4.4. On December 31, Northpark Co. collected a receivable due from a major customer. Which of the following ratios would be increased by this transaction?

- A. Inventory turnover ratio.
- B. Receivable turnover ratio.
- C. Current ratio.
- D. Quick ratio.

Answer (B) is correct. *(CPA, adapted)*
REQUIRED: The ratio increased by collection of a receivable.
DISCUSSION: The accounts receivable turnover is equal to net credit sales divided by the average accounts receivable. Collection of a receivable decreases the denominator and thus increases the ratio.
Answer (A) is incorrect. The inventory turnover ratio equals the cost of goods sold divided by the average inventory. Collection of a receivable does not affect it. Answer (C) is incorrect. A decrease in a receivable and an equal increase in cash have no effect on the current ratio. Answer (D) is incorrect. A decrease in a receivable and an equal increase in cash have no effect on the quick ratio.

22.4.5. Selected data from Baez Corporation's year-end financial statements are presented below. The difference between average and ending inventory is immaterial.

Current ratio	3.0
Quick ratio	2.0
Current liabilities	$120,000
Inventory turnover (based on cost of goods sold)	6 times
Gross profit margin	50%

Net sales for the year were

- A. $1,440,000
- B. $720,000
- C. $1,800,000
- D. $360,000

Answer (A) is correct. *(CMA, adapted)*
REQUIRED: The net sales for the year.
DISCUSSION: Net sales may be calculated indirectly from the inventory turnover ratio and the other ratios given. If the current ratio is 3.0 and current liabilities are $120,000, current assets must be $360,000 (3.0 × $120,000). Similarly, if the quick ratio is 2.0, the total quick assets must be $240,000 (2.0 × $120,000). The major difference between quick assets and current assets is that inventory is not included in the definition of quick assets. Consequently, ending inventory must be $120,000 ($360,000 – $240,000). The inventory turnover ratio (COGS ÷ average inventory) is 6. Thus, cost of goods sold must be 6 times average inventory, or $720,000, given no material difference between average and ending inventory. If the gross profit margin is 50%, the cost of goods sold percentage is 50%, cost of goods sold equals 50% of sales, and sales must be $1,440,000 ($720,000 ÷ 50%).
Answer (B) is incorrect. Cost of goods sold is $720,000. Answer (C) is incorrect. The amount of $1,800,000 is based on a 60% gross profit margin. Answer (D) is incorrect. Current assets equals $360,000.

22.4.6. Which one of the following inventory cost flow assumptions will result in a higher inventory turnover ratio in an inflationary economy?

A. FIFO.

B. LIFO.

C. Weighted average.

D. Specific identification.

Answer (B) is correct. *(CMA, adapted)*
REQUIRED: The cost flow assumption that will result in a higher inventory turnover ratio in an inflationary economy.
DISCUSSION: The inventory turnover ratio equals the cost of goods sold divided by the average inventory. LIFO assumes that the last goods purchased are the first goods sold and that the oldest goods purchased remain in inventory. The result is a higher cost of goods sold and a lower average inventory than under other inventory cost flow assumptions if prices are rising. Because cost of goods sold (the numerator) will be higher and average inventory (the denominator) will be lower than under other inventory cost flow assumptions, LIFO produces the highest inventory turnover ratio.
Answer (A) is incorrect. When prices are rising, FIFO results in a lower cost of goods sold and a higher average inventory than LIFO. Answer (C) is incorrect. When prices are rising, weighting the average dilutes the cost effect on total inventory. Answer (D) is incorrect. When prices are rising, LIFO results in a higher cost of goods sold and a lower average inventory than under other inventory cost flow assumptions.

22.4.7. Selected information from the accounting records of Bolingbroke Company follows:

Net sales	$1,800,000
Cost of goods sold	1,200,000
Inventories at January 1	336,000
Inventories at December 31	288,000

Assuming there are 300 working days per year, what is the number of days' sales in average inventories for the year?

A. 78

B. 72

C. 52

D. 48

Answer (A) is correct. *(CPA, adapted)*
REQUIRED: The number of days' sales in average inventories.
DISCUSSION: The number of days' sales in average inventories (average number of days to sell inventories) equals the number of working days in the year (300) divided by the inventory turnover ratio (COGS ÷ average inventory). COGS is given as $1,200,000, and average inventory is $312,000 [($336,000 + $288,000) ÷ 2]. The number of days' sales in average inventories is therefore 78 [300 ÷ ($1,200,000 ÷ $312,000)].
Answer (B) is incorrect. This figure results from using ending inventory rather than average inventory in the inventory turnover ratio. Answer (C) is incorrect. This figure results from using net sales rather than cost of goods sold in the inventory turnover ratio. Answer (D) is incorrect. This figure results from using net sales and ending inventory rather than cost of goods sold and average inventory in the inventory turnover ratio.

22.4.8. Which of the following ratios should be used in evaluating the effectiveness with which the company uses its assets?

	Receivables Turnover	Dividend Payout Ratio
A.	Yes	Yes
B.	No	No
C.	Yes	No
D.	No	Yes

Answer (C) is correct. *(CPA, adapted)*
REQUIRED: The ratios that should be used in evaluating the effectiveness with which assets are used by a company.
DISCUSSION: The receivables turnover is equal to net credit sales divided by average accounts receivable, which is an estimate of the number of times a year that receivables are collected. It may indicate the quality of receivables and the success of collection efforts. Accordingly, this ratio is a measure of the effectiveness with which a company uses its assets. In contrast, the dividend payout ratio is equal to the declared cash dividends divided by income available to common shareholders (net income – preferred dividends). It measures the extent to which a company distributes its assets and may be useful to investors desiring regular income from equity securities. However, the payout ratio does not reflect the efficiency and effectiveness of management.
Answer (A) is incorrect. The dividend payout ratio is not useful in evaluating the effectiveness with which the company uses its assets. Answer (B) is incorrect. The receivables turnover is useful in evaluating the effectiveness with which the company uses its assets. Answer (D) is incorrect. The receivables turnover is useful in evaluating the effectiveness with which the company uses its assets, but the dividend payout ratio is not.

22.4.9. Selected information from the accounting records of the Blackwood Company is as follows:

Net A/R at December 31, Year 7	$ 900,000
Net A/R at December 31, Year 8	$1,000,000
Accounts receivable turnover	5 to 1
Inventories at December 31, Year 7	$1,100,000
Inventories at December 31, Year 8	$1,200,000
Inventory turnover	4 to 1

All of the company's sales are on credit. What was the gross margin for Year 8?

A. $150,000

B. $200,000

C. $300,000

D. $400,000

Answer (A) is correct. *(CPA, adapted)*
REQUIRED: The gross margin given inventory, receivables, and the related turnover ratios.
DISCUSSION: Gross margin is net sales minus cost of goods sold. Net sales are equal to sales on credit and may be calculated from the accounts receivable turnover ratio, which is net sales divided by average receivables. The average accounts receivable is $950,000 [($900,000 + $1,000,000) ÷ 2]. Sales equal average receivables multiplied by the related turnover ratio, or $4,750,000 (5 × $950,000).
Cost of goods sold may be calculated from the inventory turnover ratio, which is cost of goods sold divided by average inventory. Average inventory is $1,150,000 [($1,100,000 + $1,200,000) ÷ 2]. Cost of goods sold equals average inventory multiplied by the inventory turnover ratio, or $4,600,000 (4 × $1,150,000). Thus, the gross margin is $150,000 ($4,750,000 net sales − $4,600,000 cost of goods sold).
Answer (B) is incorrect. The amount of $200,000 results from subtracting the ending inventory times the inventory turnover from the ending accounts receivable times the accounts receivable turnover. Answer (C) is incorrect. The amount of $300,000 results from subtracting the sum of the beginning and ending inventories times the inventory turnover from the sum of the beginning and ending accounts receivable times the accounts receivable turnover. Answer (D) is incorrect. The amount of $400,000 results from subtracting the sum of the beginning and ending accounts receivable from the sum of the beginning and ending inventories.

22.4.10. In a comparison of the two most recent years, Neir Co.'s inventory turnover ratio increased substantially, although sales and inventory amounts were essentially unchanged. Which of the following statements explains the increased inventory turnover ratio?

A. Cost of goods sold decreased.

B. Accounts receivable turnover increased.

C. Total asset turnover increased.

D. Gross profit percentage decreased.

Answer (D) is correct. *(CPA, adapted)*
REQUIRED: The statement that explains the increased inventory turnover ratio.
DISCUSSION: The inventory turnover ratio is equal to cost of goods sold divided by average inventory. If inventory is unchanged, an increase in cost of goods sold (the numerator) increases the ratio. A decrease in the gross profit percentage [(sales − cost of goods sold) ÷ sales] signifies an increase in cost of goods sold, given that the amount of sales is constant.
Answer (A) is incorrect. A decrease in cost of goods sold results in a decrease in the inventory turnover ratio. Answer (B) is incorrect. The accounts receivable turnover does not affect the inventory turnover ratio. Answer (C) is incorrect. Total asset turnover does not affect the inventory turnover ratio.

22.4.11. Blasso Company's net accounts receivable were $500,000 at December 31, Year 3, and $600,000 at December 31, Year 4. Net cash sales for Year 4 were $200,000. The accounts receivable turnover for Year 4 was 5.0. What were Blasso's total net sales for Year 4?

A. $2,950,000

B. $3,000,000

C. $3,200,000

D. $5,500,000

Answer (A) is correct. *(CPA, adapted)*
REQUIRED: The net sales given accounts receivable, net cash sales, and the accounts receivable turnover.
DISCUSSION: Total sales equal cash sales plus credit sales. Blasso's cash sales were $200,000. Credit sales may be determined from the accounts receivable turnover formula, which equals net credit sales divided by average accounts receivable. Net credit sales are equal to 5.0 times average receivables [($500,000 + $600,000) ÷ 2], or $2,750,000. Total sales were equal to $2,950,000 ($2,750,000 + $200,000).
Answer (B) is incorrect. Ending accounts receivable multiplied by the accounts receivable turnover ratio equals $3,000,000. Answer (C) is incorrect. Cash sales plus the product of ending accounts receivable and the accounts receivable turnover ratio equals $3,200,000. Answer (D) is incorrect. Beginning accounts receivable plus ending accounts receivable multiplied by the accounts receivable turnover ratio equals $5,500,000.

22.4.12. If a company changes from the first-in, first-out (FIFO) inventory method to the last-in, first-out (LIFO) method during a period of rising prices, its

A. Current ratio will be reduced.

B. Inventory turnover ratio will be reduced.

C. Cash flow will be decreased.

D. Debt-to-equity ratio will be decreased.

Answer (A) is correct. *(CMA, adapted)*
REQUIRED: The effect of changing from FIFO to LIFO during a period of rising prices.
DISCUSSION: Changing from FIFO to LIFO during a period of rising prices will result in a lower inventory valuation and a higher cost of goods sold. Thus, the current ratio will be reduced because current assets are lower under LIFO.
Answer (B) is incorrect. Inventory turnover will increase. Cost of goods sold (the numerator) will increase, and the average inventory (the denominator) will decline. Answer (C) is incorrect. Cash flow will be unchanged except for the tax savings from switching to LIFO. The tax savings will result in increased cash flow. Answer (D) is incorrect. The debt-to-equity ratio will increase. Assets and equity will be lower, but debt will be unchanged.

22.4.13. Based on the data presented below, what is the cost of sales for the Canfield Corporation for Year 5?

Current ratio	3.5
Acid-test ratio	3.0
Current liabilities 12/31/Year 5	$600,000
Inventory 12/31/Year 4	$500,000
Inventory turnover	8.0

A. $1,600,000

B. $2,400,000

C. $3,200,000

D. $6,400,000

Answer (C) is correct. *(CMA, adapted)*
REQUIRED: The cost of sales given various ratios, ending liabilities, and beginning inventory.
DISCUSSION: Inventory turnover equals cost of sales divided by average inventory. The turnover ratio and the beginning inventory are known. If ending inventory can be determined, average inventory and cost of sales can also be calculated. The relationship among the current ratio, acid-test ratio, and current liabilities facilitates this calculation. The current ratio is the ratio of current assets to current liabilities. Thus, current assets are 3.5 times current liabilities. Given that current liabilities at year end are $600,000, current assets at year end must be $2,100,000 (3.5 × $600,000). The acid-test ratio is equal to the ratio of the sum of cash, net accounts receivable, and short-term marketable securities to current liabilities. Accordingly, quick assets are 3.0 times current liabilities. If current liabilities at year end are $600,000, the quick assets are $1,800,000 (3.0 × $600,000). The difference between current assets and quick assets is equal to inventory (assuming no prepaid expenses are included in current assets). Because current assets at year end are $2,100,000 and quick assets are $1,800,000, ending inventory must be $300,000. Average inventory is equal to $400,000 [($500,000 beginning inventory + $300,000 ending inventory) ÷ 2]. An inventory turnover (cost of sales ÷ average inventory) of 8.0 indicates that cost of sales is 8.0 times average inventory. Cost of sales is therefore equal to $3,200,000 (8.0 × $400,000).
Answer (A) is incorrect. The amount of $1,600,000 incorrectly uses half of average inventory in the denominator. Answer (B) is incorrect. The amount of $2,400,000 incorrectly uses ending, not average, inventory in the denominator. Answer (D) is incorrect. The amount of $6,400,000 incorrectly uses the sum, rather than the average, of beginning and ending inventory.

22.4.14. The following computations were made from Bruckner Co.'s current-year books:

Number of days' sales in inventory	55
Number of days' sales in trade accounts receivable	26

What was the number of days in Bruckner's current-year operating cycle?

A. 26

B. 40.5

C. 55

D. 81

Answer (D) is correct. *(CPA, adapted)*
REQUIRED: The number of days in the operating cycle.
DISCUSSION: The operating cycle is the time needed to turn cash into inventory, inventory into receivables, and receivables back into cash. It is equal to the sum of the number of days' sales in inventory (average number of days to sell inventory) and the number of days' sales in receivables (the average collection period). The number of days' sales in inventory is given as 55 days. The number of days' sales in receivables is given as 26 days. Hence, the number of days in the operating cycle is 81 (55 + 26).
Answer (A) is incorrect. The number of days' sales in receivables is 26. Answer (B) is incorrect. The figure of 40.5 equals the sum of the number of days' sales in inventory and the number of days' sales in receivables, divided by 2. Answer (C) is incorrect. The number of days' sales in inventory is 55.

22.5 Leverage and Profitability Ratios

22.5.1. Boe Corp.'s equity balances, which include no accumulated other comprehensive income, were as follows at December 31:

6% noncumulative preferred stock, $100 par (liquidation value $105 per share)	$100,000
Common stock, $10 par	300,000
Retained earnings	95,000

At December 31, Boe's book value per common share was

A. $13.17

B. $13.00

C. $12.97

D. $12.80

Answer (B) is correct. *(CPA, adapted)*
REQUIRED: The book value per share of common stock at year-end.
DISCUSSION: The preferred stock is noncumulative, so the equity of the preferred shareholders equals the liquidation value of $105,000 (1,000 shares × $105 per share). Given total equity of $495,000 ($100,000 + $300,000 + $95,000), common equity is $390,000 ($495,000 – $105,000). Therefore, book value per common share equals $13.00 ($390,000 ÷ 30,000 shares).
Answer (A) is incorrect. The sum of common stock and retained earnings divided by the shares outstanding of common stock equals $13.17. Answer (C) is incorrect. The sum of common stock and retained earnings, minus the preferred stock dividend, divided by the number of common stock shares outstanding equals $12.97. Answer (D) is incorrect. The amount of $12.80 results from deducting the preferred stock dividend from common equity and dividing by the number of common shares outstanding.

22.5.2. The ratio of earnings before interest and taxes to total interest expense is a measure of

A. Liquidity.

B. Solvency.

C. Activity.

D. Profitability.

Answer (B) is correct. *(CPA, adapted)*
REQUIRED: The function of the times-interest-earned ratio.
DISCUSSION: The ratio of earnings before interest and taxes to total interest expense is the times-interest-earned ratio. This ratio assists a creditor in estimating risk by measuring a firm's ability to pay interest expense.
Answer (A) is incorrect. The current (liquidity) ratio measures the ability to pay short-term liabilities out of current assets. Answer (C) is incorrect. Turnover ratios measure a firm's activity. Answer (D) is incorrect. EPS measures return to owners.

22.5.3. The following data pertain to Cowl, Inc., for the year ended December 31, Year 4:

Net sales	$ 600,000
Net income	150,000
Total assets, January 1, Year 4	2,000,000
Total assets, December 31, Year 4	3,000,000

What was Cowl's rate of return on assets for Year 4?

A. 5%

B. 6%

C. 20%

D. 24%

Answer (B) is correct. *(CPA, adapted)*
REQUIRED: The rate of return on assets.
DISCUSSION: Return on assets equals net income ($150,000) divided by average total assets [($2,000,000 + $3,000,000) ÷ 2 = $2,500,000], or 6%.
Answer (A) is incorrect. A return of 5% results from using ending total assets instead of the average total assets. Answer (C) is incorrect. A return of 20% results from dividing net sales by ending total assets. Answer (D) is incorrect. A return of 24% results from using net sales rather than net income in the numerator.

22.5.4. If Day Company has a higher rate of return on assets than Night Company, the reason may be that Day has a <List A> profit margin on sales, or a <List B> asset turnover ratio, or both.

	List A	List B
A.	Higher	Higher
B.	Higher	Lower
C.	Lower	Higher
D.	Lower	Lower

Answer (A) is correct. *(CIA, adapted)*
REQUIRED: The reason for a higher rate of return on assets.
DISCUSSION: The return on assets equals the product of the profit margin and the asset turnover.

$$Return\ on\ assets = Profit\ margin \times Asset\ turnover$$

$$\frac{Net\ income}{Assets} = \frac{Net\ income}{Sales} \times \frac{Sales}{Assets}$$

If one company has a higher return on assets than another, it may have a higher profit margin, a higher asset turnover, or both.
Answer (B) is incorrect. The asset turnover ratio does not explain a higher return on assets. Answer (C) is incorrect. A lower profit margin on sales does not explain a higher return on assets. Answer (D) is incorrect. A higher profit margin on sales or a higher asset turnover ratio may explain a higher return on assets.

22.5.5. Hoyt Corp.'s current balance sheet reports the following equity:

5% cumulative preferred stock, par value $100 per share; 2,500 shares issued and outstanding	$250,000
Common stock, par value $3.50 per share; 100,000 shares issued and outstanding	350,000
Additional paid-in capital in excess of par value of common stock	125,000
Retained earnings	300,000
Accumulated other comprehensive income	100,000

Dividends in arrears on the preferred stock amount to $25,000. If Hoyt were to be liquidated, the preferred shareholders would receive par value plus a premium of $50,000. The book value per share of common stock is

A. $8.75

B. $8.50

C. $8.25

D. $8.00

Answer (D) is correct. *(CPA, adapted)*
REQUIRED: The book value per share of common stock upon liquidation.
DISCUSSION: Given that the preferred stock is cumulative, the liquidation value of the preferred stock equals the par value ($250,000), plus the premium ($50,000), plus the dividends in arrears ($25,000), or $325,000. Given total equity of $1,125,000 ($250,000 + $350,000 + $125,000 + $300,000 + $100,000), common equity is $800,000 ($1,125,000 – $325,000). Thus, book value per share of common stock equals $8.00 ($800,000 ÷ 100,000 shares outstanding).
Answer (A) is incorrect. The amount of $8.75 does not include the dividends in arrears or the premium. Answer (B) is incorrect. The amount of $8.50 does not include the premium. Answer (C) is incorrect. The amount of $8.25 does not include the dividends in arrears.

22.5.6. Selected information for Dayan Company is as follows:

	December 31,	
	Year 5	Year 6
Preferred stock, 8%, par $100, nonconvertible, noncumulative	$125,000	$125,000
Common stock	300,000	400,000
Retained earnings	75,000	185,000
Accumulated other comprehensive income	0	40,000
Dividends paid on preferred stock for year ended	10,000	10,000
Net income for year ended	60,000	120,000

Dayan's return on common equity, rounded to the nearest percentage point, for Year 6 is

A. 16%

B. 17.6%

C. 22%

D. 24%

Answer (C) is correct. *(CPA, adapted)*
REQUIRED: The return on common equity for the year.
DISCUSSION: Return on common equity is equal to the earnings available to common shareholders divided by the average common equity. The numerator is therefore net income ($120,000) minus preferred dividends ($125,000 × 8% = $10,000), that is, $110,000. Average common equity is equal to the average of beginning and ending common equity, or $500,000 [($375,000 + $625,000) ÷ 2]. Thus, return on common equity equals 22% ($110,000 ÷ $500,000).
Answer (A) is incorrect. Sixteen percent results from dividing net income for Year 6 by total equity. Answer (B) is incorrect. This percentage results from dividing earnings available to common shareholders by ending common equity. Answer (D) is incorrect. This percentage results from dividing net income for Year 6 by average common equity without subtracting the preferred dividends from net income.

22.5.7. Barr Co. has total debt of $420,000 and equity of $700,000. Barr is seeking capital to fund an expansion. Barr is planning to issue an additional $300,000 in common stock and is negotiating with a bank to borrow additional funds. The bank requires a debt-to-equity ratio of .75. What is the maximum additional amount Barr will be able to borrow?

A. $225,000

B. $330,000

C. $525,000

D. $750,000

Answer (B) is correct. *(CPA, adapted)*
REQUIRED: The maximum additional borrowing allowed to satisfy a specific debt-to-equity ratio.
DISCUSSION: Barr will have $1,000,000 ($700,000 + $300,000) in total equity. The debt-to-equity restriction allows up to $750,000 ($1,000,000 × .75) in debt. Barr already has $420,000 in debt, so the additional borrowing cannot exceed $330,000 ($750,000 – $420,000).
Answer (A) is incorrect. The amount of $225,000 results from multiplying the $300,000 of additional common stock by the debt-to-equity ratio. Answer (C) is incorrect. The amount of $525,000 equals the $700,000 of shareholders' equity times the debt-to-equity ratio. Answer (D) is incorrect. The amount of $750,000 is the total debt allowed.

22.5.8. A company has 100,000 outstanding common shares with a market value of $20 per share. Dividends of $2 per share were paid in the current year, and the company has a dividend-payout ratio of 40%. The price-earnings (P-E) ratio of the company is

A. 2.5

B. 4

C. 10

D. 50

Answer (B) is correct. *(CIA, adapted)*
REQUIRED: The P-E ratio.
DISCUSSION: The P-E ratio equals the share price divided by EPS. If the dividends per share equaled $2 and the dividend-payout ratio was 40%, EPS must have been $5 ($2 ÷ .4). Accordingly, the P-E ratio is 4 ($20 share price ÷ $5 EPS).
Answer (A) is incorrect. This ratio equals EPS divided by dividends per share. Answer (C) is incorrect. Share price divided by dividends per share equals 10. Answer (D) is incorrect. Price per share divided by the dividend-payout percentage equals 50.

22.5.9. How are the following used in the calculation of the dividend-payout ratio for a company with only common stock outstanding?

	Dividends per Share	Earnings per Share	Book Value per Share
A.	Denominator	Numerator	Not used
B.	Denominator	Not used	Numerator
C.	Numerator	Denominator	Not used
D.	Numerator	Not used	Denominator

Answer (C) is correct. *(CPA, adapted)*
REQUIRED: The components of the dividend-payout ratio.
DISCUSSION: In the absence of preferred stock, the dividend-payout ratio may be stated as the dividends per share (numerator) divided by the earnings per share (denominator).
Answer (A) is incorrect. Dividends per share is the numerator and earnings per share is the denominator in the dividend-payout ratio. Answer (B) is incorrect. Dividends per share is the numerator, earnings per share is the denominator, and book value per share is not used in the dividend-payout ratio. Answer (D) is incorrect. Earnings per share is the denominator and book value per share is not used in the dividend-payout ratio.

22.5.10. Ehrenburg Company had net income of $5.3 million and earnings per share on common stock of $2.50. Included in the net income was $500,000 of bond interest expense related to its long-term debt. The income tax rate was 50%. Dividends on preferred stock were $300,000. The dividend-payout ratio on common stock was 40%. What were the dividends on common stock?

A. $1,000,000

B. $1,900,000

C. $2,000,000

D. $2,120,000

Answer (C) is correct. *(CPA, adapted)*
REQUIRED: The dividends on common stock given the dividend-payout ratio.
DISCUSSION: The dividend-payout ratio is equal to the dividends on common stock divided by the earnings available to common. If earnings available to common were $5,000,000 ($5,300,000 net income – $300,000 preferred dividends) and the payout ratio was 40%, the dividends on common stock were $2,000,000.
Answer (A) is incorrect. Taxes should not be included in this calculation. Answer (B) is incorrect. The dividends on common stock are determined by multiplying the earnings available to common shareholders by the dividend-payout ratio. Answer (D) is incorrect. The preferred dividends must be subtracted out.

22.5.11. Information concerning Rashad Company's common stock is presented below for the fiscal year ended May 31, Year 9.

Common shares outstanding	750,000
Stated value per share	$15.00
Market price per share	45.00
Year 8 dividends paid per share	4.50
Year 9 dividends paid per share	7.50
Basic earnings per share	11.25
Diluted earnings per share	9.00

The price-earnings ratio for Rashad's common stock is

A. 3.0 times.

B. 4.0 times.

C. 5.0 times.

D. 6.0 times.

Answer (C) is correct. *(CMA, adapted)*
REQUIRED: The price-earnings ratio for the common stock.
DISCUSSION: The price-earnings ratio is calculated by dividing the current market price of the stock by the earnings per share. Diluted earnings per share is used if disclosed. Thus, Rashad's price-earnings ratio is 5.0 ($45 market price ÷ $9 DEPS).
Answer (A) is incorrect. The 3.0 figure is based on the stated value per share in the denominator. Answer (B) is incorrect. The ratio of 4.0 is based on the basic earnings per share in the denominator. Answer (D) is incorrect. The ratio of 6.0 is derived by using Year 9 dividends per share in the denominator.

22.5.12. Selected financial data of Draco Corporation for the year ended December 31 are as follows. Common stock dividends were $120,000.

Operating income	$900,000
Interest expense	(100,000)
Income before income tax	$800,000
Income tax expense	(320,000)
Net income	$480,000
Preferred stock dividends	(200,000)
Net income available to common shareholders	$280,000

The times-interest-earned ratio is

A. 2.8 to 1.

B. 4.8 to 1.

C. 8.0 to 1.

D. 9.0 to 1.

Answer (D) is correct. *(CPA, adapted)*
REQUIRED: The times-interest-earned ratio.
DISCUSSION: The times-interest-earned ratio is a measure of the firm's ability to pay interest on debt. It equals earnings before interest and taxes divided by the amount of interest.

$$\frac{\$900,000}{\$100,000} = 9.0$$

Answer (A) is incorrect. The ratio of 2.8 to 1 results from dividing net income available to common shareholders by interest expense. Answer (B) is incorrect. The ratio of 4.8 to 1 results from dividing net income by interest expense. Answer (C) is incorrect. The ratio of 8.0 to 1 results from dividing income before income tax by interest expense.

22.6 Questions on More than One Ratio

Questions 22.6.1 and 22.6.2 are based on the following information. Selected data pertaining to Castile Co. for the current calendar year is as follows:

Net cash sales	$ 3,000
Cost of goods sold	18,000
Inventory at beginning of year	6,000
Purchases	24,000
Accounts receivable at beginning of year	20,000
Accounts receivable at end of year	22,000

22.6.1. The accounts receivable turnover for the current year was 5.0 times. What were Castile's current-year net credit sales?

A. $105,000

B. $107,000

C. $110,000

D. $210,000

Answer (A) is correct. *(CPA, adapted)*
REQUIRED: The net credit sales.
DISCUSSION: Credit sales may be determined from the accounts receivable turnover formula (credit sales ÷ average accounts receivable). Credit sales are equal to 5.0 times average receivables [($20,000 + $22,000) ÷ 2], or $105,000.
Answer (B) is incorrect. Ending accounts receivable multiplied by the accounts receivable turnover ratio, minus cash sales equals $107,000. Answer (C) is incorrect. Ending accounts receivable multiplied by the accounts receivable turnover ratio equals $110,000. Answer (D) is incorrect. Beginning accounts receivable plus ending accounts receivable, multiplied by the accounts receivable turnover ratio equals $210,000.

22.6.2. What was the inventory turnover for the current year?

A. 1.2 times.

B. 1.5 times.

C. 2.0 times.

D. 3.0 times.

Answer (C) is correct. *(CPA, adapted)*
REQUIRED: The inventory turnover ratio.
DISCUSSION: Inventory turnover is equal to cost of goods sold divided by average inventory. Ending inventory equals beginning inventory, plus purchases, minus cost of goods sold, or $12,000 ($6,000 + $24,000 – $18,000). Average inventory is $9,000 [($6,000 + $12,000) ÷ 2]. Inventory turnover is 2.0 times ($18,000 cost of goods sold ÷ $9,000 average inventory).
Answer (A) is incorrect. This figure uses the average of beginning inventory and purchases. Answer (B) is incorrect. This figure uses ending inventory instead of average inventory. Answer (D) is incorrect. This figure uses beginning inventory instead of average inventory.

22.6.3. Obsolete inventory of $125,000 was written off during the year. This transaction

A. Decreased the quick ratio.

B. Increased the quick ratio.

C. Increased net working capital.

D. Decreased the current ratio.

Answer (D) is correct. *(CMA, adapted)*
REQUIRED: The effect of writing off obsolete inventory.
DISCUSSION: Writing off obsolete inventory reduced current assets but not quick assets (cash, receivables, and marketable securities). Thus, the current ratio was reduced, and the quick ratio was unaffected.
Answer (A) is incorrect. Inventory is not included in the quick ratio calculation. Answer (B) is incorrect. The quick ratio was not affected. Answer (C) is incorrect. Working capital was decreased.

22.6.4. The issuance of new shares in a five-for-one split of common stock

A. Decreases the book value per share of common stock.

B. Increases the book value per share of common stock.

C. Increases total equity.

D. Decreases total equity.

Answer (A) is correct. *(CMA, adapted)*
REQUIRED: The effect of a five-for-one split of common stock.
DISCUSSION: Given that five times as many shares of stock are outstanding after the split, the book value per share of common stock is one-fifth of the former value.
Answer (B) is incorrect. The book value per share is decreased. Answer (C) is incorrect. The stock split does not change the amount of equity. Answer (D) is incorrect. The stock split has no effect on the amount of equity it represents.

22.6.5. The early liquidation of a noncurrent note with cash affects the

A. Current ratio to a greater degree than the quick ratio.

B. Quick ratio to a greater degree than the current ratio.

C. Current and quick ratio to the same degree.

D. Current ratio but not the quick ratio.

Answer (B) is correct. *(CMA, adapted)*
REQUIRED: The effect of an early liquidation of a noncurrent note with cash.
DISCUSSION: The numerators of the quick and current ratios are decreased when cash is expended. Early payment of a noncurrent liability has no effect on the denominator (current liabilities). Because the numerator of the quick ratio, which includes cash, net receivables, and marketable securities, is less than the numerator of the current ratio, which includes all current assets, the quick ratio is affected to a greater degree.
Answer (A) is incorrect. This is the opposite of what happens. Answer (C) is incorrect. The quick ratio is affected to a greater degree than the current ratio. Answer (D) is incorrect. The quick ratio is affected.

Questions 22.6.6 through 22.6.8 are based on the following information. Ellington Company reports the following account balances at year end:

Account	Balance
Long-term debt	$200,000
Cash	50,000
Net sales	600,000
Fixed assets (net)	370,000
Tax expense	67,500
Inventory	25,000
Common stock	100,000
Interest expense	20,000
Administrative expense	35,000
Retained earnings	150,000
Accumulated other comprehensive income	50,000
Accounts payable	65,000
Accounts receivable	120,000
Cost of goods sold	400,000
Depreciation expense	10,000

Additional Information:

- The opening balance of common stock was $100,000.
- The opening balance of retained earnings was $82,500.
- The opening balance of accumulated other comprehensive income was $17,500.
- The company had 10,000 common shares outstanding all year.
- No dividends were paid during the year.

22.6.6. For the year just ended, Ellington has times-interest-earned of

A. 3.375 times.

B. 6.75 times.

C. 7.75 times.

D. 9.5 times.

Answer (C) is correct. *(CIA, adapted)*
REQUIRED: The times-interest-earned ratio (TIE).
DISCUSSION: The TIE ratio is a leverage ratio. It indicates the company's ability to pay interest expense. The ratio equals income before interest and taxes divided by interest.

$$= \frac{(\text{Sales} - \text{COGS} - \text{Administrative expense} - \text{Depreciation})}{(\text{Interest expense})}$$

$$= \frac{\$600,000 - \$400,000 - \$35,000 - \$10,000}{\$20,000}$$

$$= 7.75 \text{ times}$$

Answer (A) is incorrect. This number results from including deductions for taxes and interest in the numerator. Answer (B) is incorrect. This number results from including a deduction for interest in the numerator. Answer (D) is incorrect. This number results from failing to deduct the administrative expenses from the numerator.

22.6.7. At year end, Ellington has a book value per share of

A. $15

B. $20

C. $25

D. $30

Answer (D) is correct. *(CIA, adapted)*
REQUIRED: The book value per share at year end.
DISCUSSION: Book value per share, based on balance sheet amounts, measures the per-share amount that would be received if the company were liquidated. The ratio is calculated as common equity divided by the number of outstanding shares.

$$= \frac{\text{Common stock} + \text{Retained earnings} + \text{AOCI}}{\text{Outstanding shares}}$$

$$= \frac{\$100,000 + \$150,000 + \$50,000}{10,000 \text{ shares}}$$

$$= \$30$$

Answer (A) is incorrect. The amount of $15 excludes retained earnings from the numerator. Answer (B) is incorrect. The amount of $20 excludes common stock from the numerator. Answer (C) is incorrect. The amount of $25 is based on average equity.

22.6.8. For the year just ended, Ellington had a rate of return on common equity, rounded to two decimals, of

A. 27.00%

B. 45.00%

C. 50.47%

D. 62.00%

Answer (A) is correct. *(CIA, adapted)*
REQUIRED: The rate of return on common equity for the year just ended.
DISCUSSION: Rate of return on common equity, a profitability ratio, measures the rate of return on investment. The ratio equals net income divided by average equity.

$$= \frac{(\text{Sales} - \text{COGS} - \text{Adm. expense} - \text{Deprec.} - \text{Interest} - \text{Tax})}{(\text{Beginning equity} + \text{Ending equity}) \div 2}$$

$$= \frac{\$600,000 - \$400,000 - \$35,000 - \$10,000 - \$20,000 - \$67,500}{(\$200,000 + \$300,000) \div 2}$$

$$= \frac{\$67,500}{\$250,000}$$

$$= 27.00\%$$

Answer (B) is incorrect. Forty-five percent excludes common stock from the denominator. Answer (C) is incorrect. This percentage excludes retained earnings from the denominator. Answer (D) is incorrect. Sixty-two percent excludes interest expense and tax expense from the numerator.

Questions 22.6.9 through 22.6.11 are based on the following information. The following inventory and sales data are available for the current year for Dylan Company, which uses a 365-day year when computing ratios.

	November 30, Year 2	November 30, Year 1
Net credit sales	$6,205,000	
Gross receivables	350,000	$320,000
Inventory	960,000	780,000
Cost of goods sold	4,380,000	

22.6.9. Dylan Company's average number of days to collect accounts receivable for the current year is

A. 18.82 days.

B. 19.43 days.

C. 19.71 days.

D. 20.59 days.

Answer (C) is correct. *(CMA, adapted)*
REQUIRED: The average collection period.
DISCUSSION: The average collection period (the number of days' sales in receivables) equals 365 days divided by the receivables turnover (net credit sales ÷ average accounts receivable). Turnover is 18.52 times {$6,205,000 sales ÷ [($350,000 + $320,000) ÷ 2]}. Hence, the average collection period is 19.71 days (365 ÷ 18.52).
Answer (A) is incorrect. The number of 18.82 days is based on receivables of $320,000. Answer (B) is incorrect. The number of 19.43 days is based on a 360-day year. Answer (D) is incorrect. The number of 20.59 days is based on receivables of $350,000.

22.6.10. Dylan Company's average number of days to sell inventory for the current year is

A. 51.18 days.

B. 65.00 days.

C. 71.51 days.

D. 72.50 days.

Answer (D) is correct. *(CMA, adapted)*
REQUIRED: The average days to sell inventory.
DISCUSSION: The average number of days to sell inventory (the number of days' sales in inventory) equals 365 days divided by the inventory turnover (cost of goods sold ÷ average inventory). Thus, turnover is 5.0345 times {$4,380,000 COGS ÷ [($960,000 + $780,000) ÷ 2]}. The average number of days to sell inventory is 72.5 days (365 ÷ 5.0345).
Answer (A) is incorrect. The number of 51.18 days is based on sales, not cost of sales. Sales are recorded at retail prices. Answer (B) is incorrect. The number of 65.00 days is based on the beginning inventory. Answer (C) is incorrect. The number of 71.51 days is based on a 360-day year, not a 365-day year.

22.6.11. Dylan Company's operating cycle for the current year is

A. 70.61 days.

B. 93.09 days.

C. 92.21 days.

D. 99.71 days.

Answer (C) is correct. *(CMA, adapted)*
REQUIRED: The length of the firm's operating cycle.
DISCUSSION: The operating cycle is the length of time required to complete normal operating activities. Thus, the operating cycle is a cash-to-cash cycle equivalent to the average time that inventory is held plus the average time that receivables are held. Dylan holds its inventory 72.50 days [365 days ÷ ($4,380,000 COGS ÷ $870,000 average inventory)] and its receivables 19.71 days [365 days ÷ ($6,205,000 sales ÷ $335,000 average receivables)]. Its operating cycle is 92.21 days (72.50 + 19.71).
Answer (A) is incorrect. The inventory alone is held for 72.50 days. Answer (B) is incorrect. The number of 93.09 days is based on the ending receivables balance. Answer (D) is incorrect. The number of 99.71 days is based on the ending inventory.

Questions 22.6.12 through 22.6.14 are based on the following information. The selected data below pertain to Patel Company at December 31:

Quick assets	$208,000
Acid-test ratio	2.6 to 1
Current ratio	3.5 to 1
Net sales for the year	$1,800,000
Cost of sales for the year	$990,000
Average total assets for the year	$1,200,000

22.6.12. Patel's current liabilities at December 31 amount to

A. $59,429

B. $80,000

C. $311,538

D. $231,429

Answer (B) is correct. *(CIA, adapted)*
REQUIRED: Current liabilities at year end.
DISCUSSION: The acid-test ratio is equal to quick assets divided by current liabilities. Thus, current liabilities equal the $208,000 of quick assets divided by the 2.6 acid-test ratio. Hence, current liabilities equal $80,000.
Answer (A) is incorrect. The amount of $59,429 improperly divides the $208,000 of quick assets by the current ratio instead of by the acid-test ratio. Answer (C) is incorrect. The current liabilities at year end are not determined using the gross margin. Answer (D) is incorrect. The current liabilities at year end are not determined using the gross margin or the current ratio.

22.6.13. Patel's asset turnover for the year is

A. 0.667

B. 1.82

C. 0.825

D. 1.50

Answer (D) is correct. *(CIA, adapted)*
REQUIRED: The asset turnover for the year.
DISCUSSION: Asset turnover equals $1,800,000 of net sales divided by $1,200,000 of average total assets. The asset turnover for the year is therefore equal to 1.5.
Answer (A) is incorrect. Asset turnover does not equal average total assets divided by net sales. Answer (B) is incorrect. Asset turnover does not equal net sales divided by cost of sales. Answer (C) is incorrect. Asset turnover does not equal cost of sales divided by average total assets.

22.6.14. Patel's inventory balance at December 31 is

A. $72,000

B. $282,857

C. $280,000

D. $342,857

Answer (A) is correct. *(CIA, adapted)*
REQUIRED: The inventory balance at year end.
DISCUSSION: Inventory is equal to the difference between current assets and quick assets (assuming no prepaid expenses are included in current assets). The current ratio is equal to current assets divided by current liabilities. Accordingly, multiplying the current liabilities of $80,000 (determined by dividing the quick assets by the acid-test ratio) by the current ratio of 3.5 gives current assets of $280,000. Subtracting the $208,000 of quick assets from the $280,000 of current assets results in an inventory balance of $72,000.
Answer (B) is incorrect. Inventory does not equal cost of sales divided by current ratio. Answer (C) is incorrect. Inventory equals the difference between current assets and quick assets (assuming no prepaid expenses). Multiplying the current liabilities by the current ratio gives the current assets. Answer (D) is incorrect. Inventory does not equal the average assets divided by the current ratio.

Questions 22.6.15 and 22.6.16 are based on the following information. Eisenstein Co. had the following account information:

Accounts receivable	$200,000
Accounts payable	80,000
Bonds payable, due in 10 years	300,000
Cash	100,000
Interest payable, due in 3 months	10,000
Inventory	400,000
Land	250,000
Notes payable, due in 6 months	50,000
Prepaid expenses	40,000

The company has an operating cycle of 5 months.

22.6.15. The current ratio for Eisenstein is

A. 1.68

B. 2.14

C. 5.00

D. 5.29

Answer (D) is correct. *(CMA, adapted)*
REQUIRED: The current ratio.
DISCUSSION: The current ratio equals current assets divided by current liabilities. This company's current assets consist of accounts receivable, cash, inventory, and prepaid expenses, which total $740,000 ($200,000 + $100,000 + $400,000 + $40,000). The current liabilities consist of accounts payable, interest payable, and notes payable, which total $140,000 ($80,000 + $10,000 + $50,000). Thus, the current ratio is 5.29 ($740,000 ÷ $140,000).
Answer (A) is incorrect. The ratio of 1.68 treats bonds payable as a current liability. Answer (B) is incorrect. The quick ratio is 2.14. Answer (C) is incorrect. This ratio excludes prepaid expenses from current assets.

22.6.16. What is the company's acid-test (quick) ratio?

A. 0.68

B. 1.68

C. 2.14

D. 2.31

Answer (C) is correct. *(CMA, adapted)*
REQUIRED: The acid-test (quick) ratio.
DISCUSSION: The acid-test, or quick, ratio equals quick assets divided by current liabilities. Quick assets consist of cash ($100,000) and accounts receivable ($200,000), for a total of $300,000. The current liabilities consist of accounts payable, interest payable, and notes payable, for a total of $140,000 ($80,000 + $10,000 + $50,000). Hence, the quick ratio is 2.14 ($300,000 ÷ $140,000).
Answer (A) is incorrect. This ratio equals the quick assets divided by the sum of the current liabilities and the bonds payable. Answer (B) is incorrect. This ratio equals current assets divided by the sum of current liabilities and the bonds payable. Answer (D) is incorrect. This ratio omits interest payable from the current liabilities.

22.6.17. The issuance of serial bonds in exchange for an office building, with the first installment of the bonds due late this year,

A. Decreases net working capital.

B. Decreases the current ratio.

C. Decreases the quick ratio.

D. Decreases net working capital, the current ratio, and the quick ratio.

Answer (D) is correct. *(CMA, adapted)*
REQUIRED: The effect of issuing serial bonds with the first installment due late this year.
DISCUSSION: The first installment is a current liability; thus, the amount of current liabilities increases with no corresponding increase in current assets. The effect is to decrease working capital, the current ratio, and the quick ratio.
Answer (A) is incorrect. The bond issuance also decreases the current ratio and the quick ratio. Answer (B) is incorrect. The bond issuance also decreases the quick ratio and net working capital. Answer (C) is incorrect. The bond issuance also decreases the current ratio and net working capital.

Questions 22.6.18 through 22.6.20 are based on the following information. Hopper Company is a manufacturer of industrial products and employs a calendar year for financial reporting purposes. These questions present several of Hopper's transactions during the year. Assume that total quick assets exceeded total current liabilities both before and after each transaction described. Further assume that Hopper has positive profits during the year and a credit balance throughout the year in its retained earnings account.

22.6.18. Hopper's payment of a trade account payable of $64,500 will

A. Increase the current ratio, but the quick ratio would not be affected.

B. Increase the quick ratio, but the current ratio would not be affected.

C. Increase both the current and quick ratios.

D. Decrease both the current and quick ratios.

Answer (C) is correct. *(CMA, adapted)*
REQUIRED: The effect of paying a trade account payable on the current and quick ratios.
DISCUSSION: Given that the quick assets exceed current liabilities, both the current and quick ratios exceed one because the numerator of the current ratio includes other current assets in addition to the quick assets of cash, net accounts receivable, and short-term marketable securities. An equal reduction in the numerator and the denominator, such as a payment of a trade payable, will cause each ratio to increase.
Answer (A) is incorrect. The quick ratio also would increase. Answer (B) is incorrect. The current ratio also would increase. Answer (D) is incorrect. Both the current ratio and the quick ratio would increase.

22.6.19. Hopper's purchase of raw materials for $85,000 on open account will

A. Increase the current ratio.

B. Decrease the current ratio.

C. Increase net working capital.

D. Decrease net working capital.

Answer (B) is correct. *(CMA, adapted)*
REQUIRED: The effect of a credit purchase of raw materials on the current ratio and working capital.
DISCUSSION: The purchase increases both the numerator and denominator of the current ratio by adding inventory to the numerator and payables to the denominator. Because the ratio before the purchase was greater than one, the ratio is decreased.
Answer (A) is incorrect. The current ratio is decreased. Answer (C) is incorrect. The purchase of raw materials on account has no effect on working capital. Answer (D) is incorrect. Current assets and current liabilities change by the same amount.

22.6.20. Hopper's collection of a current accounts receivable of $29,000 will

A. Increase the current ratio.

B. Decrease the current ratio and the quick ratio.

C. Increase the quick ratio.

D. Not affect the current or quick ratios.

Answer (D) is correct. *(CMA, adapted)*
REQUIRED: The effect of collection of a current account receivable on the current and quick ratios.
DISCUSSION: Collecting current accounts receivable has no effect on either the current ratio or the quick ratio because current assets, quick assets, and current liabilities are unchanged by the collection.
Answer (A) is incorrect. Collecting current accounts receivable does not change the current ratio. Answer (B) is incorrect. Collecting current accounts receivable does not change current assets, quick assets, or current liabilities, which means the current and quick ratios are not changed. Answer (C) is incorrect. Collecting current accounts receivable does not change quick assets or current liabilities, so the quick ratio is not changed.

Use **Gleim Test Prep** for interactive study and easy-to-use detailed analytics!

STUDY UNIT TWENTY-THREE
GAAP ACCOUNTING FOR PARTNERSHIPS

A **partnership**, as defined by the Revised Uniform Partnership Act, is "the association of two or more persons to carry on as co-owners a business for profit." Partnership accounting is essentially the same as for any other profit-oriented entity, except that the accounts reflecting ownership of the entity differ. The partners' capital accounts replace common stock and other shareholders' equity accounts. **Capital accounts** record the partners' initial contributions, additional investments, shares of profits and losses, withdrawals, and adjustments for ownership changes. They facilitate the accounting for partnership interests when partners elect to share differently in profits or losses. Partners' withdrawals are recorded in **drawing accounts**. Drawing accounts are nominal accounts that are closed to partnership capital at the end of each period.

QUESTIONS

23.1 Partnership Formation

23.1.1. The Revised Uniform Partnership Act defines a partnership as

A. Any association of two or more persons or entities.

B. An association of two or more persons to carry on as co-owners a business for profit.

C. A separate legal entity for most legal purposes.

D. An entity created by following statutory requirements.

Answer (B) is correct. *(Publisher, adapted)*
REQUIRED: The definition of a partnership.
DISCUSSION: A partnership, as defined by the Revised Uniform Partnership Act, is "the association of two or more persons to carry on as co-owners a business for profit."
Answer (A) is incorrect. A partnership must be a profit-oriented business arrangement among co-owners. Answer (C) is incorrect. A partnership is viewed for most legal purposes as a group of individuals rather than a separate entity. Answer (D) is incorrect. No statutory requirements need be met to create a general partnership. A partnership may arise regardless of the intent of the parties when an arrangement satisfies the definition. However, specific statutory requirements must be followed to create a limited partnership.

23.1.2. Cor-Eng Partnership was formed on January 2 of the current year. Under the partnership agreement, each partner has an equal initial capital balance accounted for under the goodwill method. Partnership net income or loss is allocated 60% to Cor and 40% to Eng. To form the partnership, Cor originally contributed assets costing $30,000 with a fair value of $60,000 on January 2 of the current year, while Eng contributed $20,000 in cash. Drawings by the partners during the current year totaled $3,000 by Cor and $9,000 by Eng. The partnership's current-year net income was $25,000. Eng's initial capital balance in the partnership is

A. $20,000

B. $25,000

C. $40,000

D. $60,000

Answer (D) is correct. *(CPA, adapted)*
REQUIRED: The initial capital balance credited to Eng based on the goodwill method.
DISCUSSION: If $60,000 (the fair value of Cor's original contribution) is 50% of the partnership capital, the total initial capital is $120,000, and goodwill of $40,000 should be recognized ($120,000 – $60,000 – $20,000 cash contributed by Eng). Thus, Eng's initial capital is $60,000.
Answer (A) is incorrect. Eng's initial cash contribution is $20,000. Answer (B) is incorrect. The amount of $25,000 equals 50% of the cost of assets contributed by Cor plus the cash contributed by Eng. Answer (C) is incorrect. The goodwill recorded is $40,000.

23.1.3. Pilates and Wesson drafted a partnership agreement that lists the following assets contributed at the partnership's formation:

	Contributed by	
	Pilates	Wesson
Cash	$40,000	$60,000
Inventory	--	30,000
Building	--	80,000
Furniture and equipment	30,000	--

The building is subject to a mortgage of $20,000, which the partnership has assumed. The partnership agreement also specifies that profits and losses are to be distributed evenly. What amounts should be recorded as capital for Pilates and Wesson at the formation of the partnership?

	Pilates	Wesson
A.	$70,000	$170,000
B.	$70,000	$150,000
C.	$110,000	$110,000
D.	$120,000	$120,000

Answer (B) is correct. *(CPA, adapted)*
REQUIRED: The capital balances of partners at the formation of the partnership.
DISCUSSION: The balances should reflect the fair values of the assets contributed. The building should be valued net of the mortgage. Hence, the capital balances for Pilates and Wesson are $70,000 ($40,000 + $30,000) and $150,000 ($60,000 + $30,000 + $80,000 – $20,000), respectively.
Answer (A) is incorrect. The building should be included net of the mortgage. Answer (C) is incorrect. The partners did not agree to divide capital equally. Answer (D) is incorrect. The partners did not agree to divide capital equally, and the building should be included net of the mortgage.

23.1.4. Byrd and Katt formed a partnership and agreed to divide initial capital equally, even though Byrd contributed $200,000 and Katt contributed $168,000 in identifiable assets. Under the bonus approach to adjust the capital accounts, Katt's unidentifiable asset should be debited for

A. $92,000

B. $32,000

C. $16,000

D. $0

Answer (D) is correct. *(CPA, adapted)*
REQUIRED: The unidentifiable asset debited under the bonus approach.
DISCUSSION: The goodwill and the bonus methods are two means of adjusting for differences between the carrying amount and the fair value of partnership net assets. Under the goodwill method, assets are revalued. Under the bonus method, assets are not revalued. Instead, adjustments are made to partnership capital accounts. Consequently, total partnership capital differs between the two methods, and an unidentifiable asset may be debited under the goodwill but not the bonus method.
Answer (A) is incorrect. The amount of $92,000 is 50% of the balance in each partner's capital account under the bonus method. Answer (B) is incorrect. The unidentifiable asset recognized under the goodwill method is $32,000. Answer (C) is incorrect. The amount transferred from Byrd's capital account to Katt's capital account under the bonus method is $16,000.

23.1.5. When property other than cash is invested in a partnership, at what amount should the noncash property be credited to the contributing partner's capital account?

A. Fair value at the date of contribution.

B. Contributing partner's original cost.

C. Assessed valuation for property tax purposes.

D. Contributing partner's tax basis.

Answer (A) is correct. *(CPA, adapted)*
REQUIRED: The credit to the contributing partner's capital account when noncash assets are invested.
DISCUSSION: The capital account should be credited for the current fair value of the assets at the date of the contribution.
Answer (B) is incorrect. Cost does not reflect depreciation or appreciation of the property. Answer (C) is incorrect. Fair value best reflects the economic substance of the transaction. Answer (D) is incorrect. Tax basis is determined differently than the true economic value of the property.

23.1.6. Partnership capital and drawing accounts are similar to the corporate

A. Paid-in capital, retained earnings, and dividends accounts.

B. Retained earnings account.

C. Paid-in capital and retained earnings accounts.

D. Preferred and common stock accounts.

Answer (A) is correct. *(Publisher, adapted)*
REQUIRED: The corporate accounts similar to partnership capital and drawing accounts.
DISCUSSION: Partnership capital accounts are similar to corporate paid-in capital and retained earnings accounts. Partnership drawing accounts are similar to corporate dividends accounts. They are nominal accounts that are closed to partnership capital and corporate retained earnings, respectively, at the end of each period.

23.2 Distribution of Income

23.2.1. The partnership agreement of Axel, Berg, & Cobb provides for the year-end allocation of net income in the following order:

- First, Axel is to receive 10% of net income up to $100,000 and 20% over $100,000.
- Second, Berg and Cobb are to receive 5% each of the remaining income over $150,000.
- The balance of income is to be allocated equally among the three partners.

The partnership's net income for the year was $250,000 before any allocations to partners. What amount should be allocated to Axel?

- A. $101,000
- B. $106,667
- C. $108,000
- D. $110,000

Answer (C) is correct. *(CPA, adapted)*
REQUIRED: The amount of partnership net income allocated to Axel.
DISCUSSION: Axel initially receives $40,000 {($100,000 × 10%) + [($250,000 – $100,000) × 20%]}. The remaining income is $210,000 ($250,000 – $40,000). Of this amount, Berg and Cobb receive $3,000 each [($210,000 – $150,000) × 5%], a total of $6,000. The balance is allocated equally [($250,000 – $40,000 – $6,000) ÷ 3 = $68,000]. Thus, Axel receives a total of $108,000 ($40,000 + $68,000).
Answer (A) is incorrect. The amount of $101,000 omits the 10% of net income up to $100,000 paid to Axel. Answer (B) is incorrect. The amount of $106,667 assumes, in the calculation of amounts paid to Berg and Cobb, that the remaining income over $150,000 is $100,000. Answer (D) is incorrect. The amount of $110,000 omits the 5% of remaining income over $150,000 paid to both Berg and Cobb.

23.2.2. If the partnership agreement does not specify how income is to be allocated, profits should be allocated

- A. Equally.
- B. In proportion to the weighted average of capital invested during the period.
- C. Equitably so that partners are compensated for the time and effort expended on behalf of the partnership.
- D. In accordance with an established ratio.

Answer (A) is correct. *(Publisher, adapted)*
REQUIRED: The profit and loss allocation among partners absent a provision in the partnership agreement.
DISCUSSION: Under the RUPA, profits are to be distributed equally among partners, and losses are to be distributed in the same manner as profits unless the partnership agreement provides otherwise. This equal distribution should be based on the number of partners rather than in proportion to the partners' capital balances.
Answer (B) is incorrect. The RUPA assumes that the partners intended an equal distribution if their agreement is silent on the issue. Answer (C) is incorrect. An equitable distribution depends on the circumstances of the individual partnership. Thus, a distribution on all equitable basis must be defined in the partnership agreement. Answer (D) is incorrect. Whenever a partnership agreement is silent on the matter, profits and losses are distributed equally.

23.2.3. Beck, the active partner in Beck & Cris, receives an annual bonus of 25% of partnership net income after deducting the bonus. For the year ended December 31, partnership net income before the bonus amounted to $300,000. Beck's bonus for the year should be

- A. $56,250
- B. $60,000
- C. $75,000
- D. $62,500

Answer (B) is correct. *(CPA, adapted)*
REQUIRED: The amount of a bonus defined as a percentage of income after deduction of the bonus.
DISCUSSION: Calculating the bonus requires formulating an equation with one unknown. The bonus (B) is equal to 25% of net income ($300,000) minus the bonus.

$$B = .25(NI – B)$$
$$B = .25($300,000 – B)$$
$$B = $75,000 – .25B$$
$$1.25B = $75,000$$
$$B = $60,000$$

Answer (A) is incorrect. This figure is a nonsense number. Answer (C) is incorrect. The amount of $75,000 is 25% of net income before deducting the bonus. Answer (D) is incorrect. This figure is a nonsense number.

23.2.4. Kaspar and Karp formed a partnership on January 2 and agreed to share profits 90% and 10%, respectively. Kaspar contributed capital of $25,000. Karp contributed no capital but has a specialized expertise and manages the firm full-time. There were no withdrawals during the year. The partnership agreement provides that capital accounts are to be credited annually with interest at 5% of beginning capital; Karp is to be paid a salary of $1,000 a month; Karp is to receive a bonus of 20% of income calculated before deducting her salary, the bonus, and interest on both capital accounts; and bonus, interest, and Karp's salary are to be considered partnership expenses. The partnership annual income statement follows:

Revenues	$96,450
Expenses (including salary, interest, and bonus)	(49,700)
Net income	$46,750

What is Karp's bonus?

- A. $11,688
- B. $12,000
- C. $14,687
- D. $15,000

Answer (D) is correct. *(CPA, adapted)*
REQUIRED: The amount of a bonus calculated as a percentage of income before salary and interest.
DISCUSSION: The bonus payable to Karp is equal to 20% of the income before deduction of her salary and interest on both capital accounts. Net income after deduction of salary, interest, and the bonus is $46,750. The solution requires adding back salary ($1,000 × 12 months), interest ($25,000 × 5%), and the bonus (B) to the net income. The bonus (B) equals 20% of the sum of these items.

$$
\begin{aligned}
B &= .2(\$46,750 + \$12,000 + \$1,250 + B) \\
B &= .2(\$60,000 + B) \\
B &= \$12,000 + .2B \\
.8B &= \$12,000 \\
B &= \$15,000
\end{aligned}
$$

Answer (A) is incorrect. The amount of $11,688 results from omitting salary and interest from the bonus computation. Answer (B) is incorrect. The salary is $12,000. Answer (C) is incorrect. The amount of $14,687 results from omitting interest from the bonus computation.

23.2.5. The Flat and Iron partnership agreement provides for Flat to receive a 20% bonus on profits before the bonus. Remaining profits and losses are divided between Flat and Iron in the ratio of 2 to 3, respectively. Which partner has a greater advantage when the partnership has a profit and when it has a loss?

	Profit	Loss
A.	Flat	Iron
B.	Flat	Flat
C.	Iron	Flat
D.	Iron	Iron

Answer (B) is correct. *(CPA, adapted)*
REQUIRED: The partner with a greater advantage when the partnership has a profit and when it has a loss.
DISCUSSION: When the partnership has a loss, Iron is allocated 60% and Flat 40%. Hence, Flat has the advantage when the partnership has a loss. When the partnership has a profit, Flat receives 20% plus 40% of the remaining 80%, a total of 52% [20% + (40% × 80%)]. Thus, Flat also has the advantage in this situation.
Answer (A) is incorrect. Flat has the advantage in the case of a loss. Answer (C) is incorrect. Flat has the advantage in the case of a profit. Answer (D) is incorrect. Flat has the advantage in the case of either a profit or a loss. Flat's bonus is computed before any distribution of profit or loss.

23.2.6. The partnership agreement of Orion and Hunt provides that interest at 10% per year is to be credited to each partner on the basis of weighted-average capital balances. A summary of Hunt's capital account for the current year ended December 31 is as follows:

Balance, January 1	$280,000
Additional investment, July 1	80,000
Withdrawal, August 1	(30,000)
Balance, December 31	330,000

What amount of interest should be credited to Hunt's capital account for the current year?

- A. $28,000
- B. $30,750
- C. $33,000
- D. $36,000

Answer (B) is correct. *(CPA, adapted)*
REQUIRED: The amount of interest credited to Hunt's capital account.
DISCUSSION: Hunt's balance was $280,000 for 6 months, $360,000 for 1 month, and $330,000 for 5 months. Consequently, the weighted-average balance was $307,500, as shown below, and interest was $30,750 ($307,500 × 10%).

$280,000 × (6 ÷ 12)	=	$140,000
$360,000 × (1 ÷ 12)	=	30,000
$330,000 × (5 ÷ 12)	=	137,500
		$307,500

Answer (A) is incorrect. The amount of $28,000 is based on the beginning balance. Answer (C) is incorrect. The amount of $33,000 is based on the year-end balance. Answer (D) is incorrect. The amount of $36,000 is based on the July 1 balance.

23.2.7. Porter and Saint-Lucie are partners who share profits and losses in the ratio of 6:4, respectively. Porter's salary is $20,000 and Saint-Lucie's is $10,000. The partners also are paid interest on their average capital balances. In the year just ended, Porter received $10,000 of interest and Saint-Lucie $4,000. The profit and loss allocation is determined after deductions for the salary and interest payments. If Saint-Lucie's share of partnership income was $40,000 for the year, what was the total partnership income?

  A. $65,000

  B. $95,000

  C. $100,000

  D. $109,000

Answer (D) is correct. *(P. Lockett)*
   REQUIRED: The partnership income given the distribution of income to one partner.
   DISCUSSION: Given that Saint-Lucie's share of partnership income was $40,000, her share of residual income must have been $26,000 ($40,000 – $10,000 salary – $4,000 interest on his average capital balance). This amount represents 40% of the residual income, so total residual income was $65,000 ($26,000 ÷ 40%). Consequently, Porter's share of residual income was $39,000 ($65,000 × 60%). Moreover, Porter's share of partnership income was equal to $69,000 ($10,000 interest + $20,000 salary + $39,000 residual income). Total partnership income was therefore $109,000 ($69,000 + $40,000).
   Answer (A) is incorrect. The residual income was $65,000. Answer (B) is incorrect. The sum of residual income and salaries was $95,000. Answer (C) is incorrect. Assuming Saint-Lucie's share of residual income was $40,000, the residual income was $100,000.

23.2.8. During the current year, Young and Zinc maintained average capital balances in their partnership of $160,000 and $100,000, respectively. The partners receive 10% interest on average capital balances, and residual profit or loss is divided equally. Partnership profit before interest was $4,000. By what amount should Zinc's capital balance change for the year?

  A. $1,000 decrease.

  B. $2,000 increase.

  C. $11,000 decrease.

  D. $12,000 increase.

Answer (A) is correct. *(CPA, adapted)*
   REQUIRED: The change in a partner's capital account.
   DISCUSSION: The partners are to receive 10% interest and then split the residual profit or loss. Because interest exceeds partnership profit before interest, the residual loss is $22,000 {[($160,000 + $100,000) × 10%] – $4,000}. Zinc's capital balance is increased by $10,000 ($100,000 × 10%) and decreased by $11,000 ($22,000 loss × 50%), a net decrease of $1,000.
   Answer (B) is incorrect. The amount of $2,000 is 50% of the partnership profit before interest. Answer (C) is incorrect. An $11,000 decrease does not include the $10,000 of interest owed to Zinc. Answer (D) is incorrect. A $12,000 increase equals 10% of capital plus 50% of residual profit.

23.3 Admission of New Partners

23.3.1. The goodwill and bonus methods are two means of adjusting for differences between the net book value and the fair value of partnerships when new partners are admitted. Which of the following statements about these methods is true?

  A. The bonus method does not revalue assets to market values.

  B. The bonus method revalues assets to market values.

  C. Both methods result in the same balances in partner capital accounts.

  D. Both methods result in the same total value of partner capital accounts, but the individual capital accounts vary.

Answer (A) is correct. *(Publisher, adapted)*
   REQUIRED: The true statement about the bonus and goodwill methods.
   DISCUSSION: The goodwill method revalues assets to adjust the total value of partnership capital. The bonus method simply readjusts capital accounts and makes no changes in existing asset accounts.
   Answer (B) is incorrect. The bonus method does not revalue assets. Answer (C) is incorrect. The goodwill method revalues assets and the bonus method adjusts capital accounts. Answer (D) is incorrect. The goodwill method revalues assets where bonus method adjusts capital accounts. Consequently, total partnership capital differs between the two methods.

23.3.2. Presented below is the condensed balance sheet of the partnership of Kane, Clark, and Lane, who share profits and losses in the ratio of 6:3:1, respectively:

Cash	$ 85,000
Other assets	415,000
	$500,000
Liabilities	$ 80,000
Kane, capital	252,000
Clark, capital	126,000
Lane, capital	42,000
	$500,000

Assume that the partners agree to sell to Bayer 20% of their respective capital and profit and loss interests for a total payment of $90,000. The payment by Bayer is to be made directly to the individual partners. The partners agree that implied goodwill is to be recorded prior to the acquisition by Bayer. What are the capital balances of Kane, Clark, and Lane, respectively, after the acquisition by Bayer?

A. $198,000; $99,000; $33,000

B. $201,600; $100,800; $33,600

C. $216,000; $108,000; $36,000

D. $270,000; $135,000; $45,000

23.3.3. Kern and Pate are partners with capital balances of $60,000 and $20,000, respectively. Profits and losses are divided in the ratio of 60:40. Kern and Pate decided to form a new partnership with Grant, who invested land valued at $15,000 for a 20% capital interest in the new partnership. Grant's cost of the land was $12,000. The partnership elected to use the bonus method to record the admission of Grant into the partnership. Grant's capital account should be credited for

A. $12,000

B. $15,000

C. $16,000

D. $19,000

23.3.4. Dunn and Grey are partners with capital account balances of $60,000 and $90,000, respectively. They agree to admit Zorn as a partner with a one-third interest in capital and profits, for an investment of $100,000, after revaluing the assets of Dunn and Grey. Goodwill to the original partners should be

A. $0

B. $33,333

C. $50,000

D. $66,667

Answer (C) is correct. *(CPA, adapted)*
REQUIRED: The capital balances of the original partners after recording goodwill and selling an interest to a new partner.
DISCUSSION: If Bayer is to purchase a 20% interest in the partnership for $90,000, the partnership is estimated to be worth $450,000 ($90,000 ÷ 20%). But the sum of the original capital balances is only $420,000. Because goodwill is to be recognized prior to the purchase, $30,000 must be allocated to the capital accounts of the original partners. This amount will be shared in the profit and loss ratio of 6:3:1. The final step is to debit the capital accounts of the original partners for 20% of their respective interests and to credit the new partner's account for $90,000.

	Kane	Clark	Lane	Bayer
Beginning capital	$252	$126	$42	
Goodwill	18	9	3	
	$270	$135	$45	
Minus 20% sold	(54)	(27)	(9)	$90
Ending capital	$216	$108	$36	$90

Answer (A) is incorrect. The amounts of $198,000, $99,000, and $33,000 equal the balances of Kane, Clark, and Lane, respectively, if $90,000 is allocated according to the profit-and-loss ratio from the partners' original balances to Bayer's account. Answer (B) is incorrect. The amounts of $201,600, $100,800, and $33,600 are the original partners' balances if no goodwill is recognized and if 20% of the original balances ($420,000 × 20% = $84,000) is deemed to have been sold. Answer (D) is incorrect. The amounts of $270,000, $135,000, and $45,000 are the original partners' balances after allocation of goodwill but before deduction of the interest sold.

Answer (D) is correct. *(CPA, adapted)*
REQUIRED: The amount to be credited to a new partner's capital account.
DISCUSSION: This transaction is to be accounted for under the bonus method. The incoming partner invests $15,000 fair value of land for a 20% interest in the capital of the new partnership. Hence, the incoming partner's capital account should be credited for 20% of the total capital following the investment. The total capital following the investment by the new partner equals $95,000 ($60,000 + $20,000 + $15,000). Because 20% of this amount is $19,000, Grant's capital account should be credited for $19,000.
Answer (A) is incorrect. The amount of $12,000 is the cost of the land. Answer (B) is incorrect. The amount of $15,000 is the fair value of the land. Answer (C) is incorrect. The amount of $16,000 equals 20% of the capital of the original partners.

Answer (C) is correct. *(CPA, adapted)*
REQUIRED: The goodwill to the original partners.
DISCUSSION: If a one-third interest is worth an investment of $100,000, the fair value of the partnership must be $300,000 ($100,000 ÷ 33 1/3%). The total of the existing capital balances and Zorn's investment is $250,000 ($60,000 + $90,000 + $100,000). Thus, goodwill is $50,000 ($300,000 − $250,000). The entry will be to debit cash (or property at fair value) for $100,000 and goodwill for $50,000, and to credit Zorn's capital balance for $100,000 and the capital balances of Dunn and Grey for a total of $50,000.
Answer (A) is incorrect. Goodwill should be recognized and credited to the capital balances of Dunn and Grey. Answer (B) is incorrect. The amount of $33,333 is one-third of the new partner's investment. Answer (D) is incorrect. The amount of $66,667 is two-thirds of the new partner's investment.

23.3.5. Presented below is the condensed balance sheet for the partnership of Lever, Polen, and Quint, who share profits and losses in the ratio of 4:3:3, respectively.

Cash	$ 90,000
Other assets	830,000
Lever, loan	20,000
	$940,000
Accounts payable	$210,000
Quint, loan	30,000
Lever, capital	310,000
Polen, capital	200,000
Quint, capital	190,000
	$940,000

Assume that the assets and liabilities are fairly valued on the balance sheet and that the partnership decides to admit Fahn as a new partner with a 20% interest. No goodwill or bonus is to be recorded. How much should Fahn contribute in cash or other assets?

A. $140,000

B. $142,000

C. $175,000

D. $177,500

Answer (C) is correct. *(CPA, adapted)*
REQUIRED: The amount to be contributed by a new partner when neither goodwill nor bonus is to be recorded.
DISCUSSION: The carrying amount of the partnership is the sum of the capital accounts of Lever, Polen, and Quint, i.e., $700,000. If Fahn is to have a 20% interest without recording goodwill or bonus, the current sum of the capital accounts will be equal to 80% of the carrying amount after the admission of Fahn. Dividing the original carrying amount of $700,000 by 80% yields the new carrying amount after Fahn's admission ($875,000). The difference between the respective carrying amounts is the amount the new partner must contribute.

New partnership ($700,000 ÷ 80%)	$875,000
Old partnership	(700,000)
Fahn's contribution	$175,000

Answer (A) is incorrect. The amount of $140,000 equals 20% of the $700,000 carrying amount. Answer (B) is incorrect. The amount of $142,000 equals 20% of the $700,000 carrying amount plus the $10,000 excess of the Quint payable over the Lever receivable. Answer (D) is incorrect. The amount of $177,500 assumes that the $10,000 excess of the Quint payable over the Lever receivable is added to the sum of the existing capital accounts before being divided by 80%.

23.3.6. Max Blau and Harry Rubi are partners who share profits and losses in the ratio of 6:4, respectively. On May 1, their respective capital accounts were as follows:

Blau	$60,000
Rubi	50,000

On that date, Joe Lind was admitted as a partner with a one-third interest in capital and profits for an investment of $40,000. The new partnership began with total capital of $150,000. Immediately after Lind's admission, Blau's capital should be

A. $50,000

B. $54,000

C. $46,000

D. $60,000

Answer (B) is correct. *(CPA, adapted)*
REQUIRED: The capital balance of an existing partner following the admission of a new partner.
DISCUSSION: Following the entrance of Lind, the partnership began with total capital of $150,000, the sum of the capital balances of Blau and Rubi and Lind's investment. Thus, no goodwill was recognized. Lind received a one-third interest, and his capital balance must be credited for $50,000 ($150,000 × 33 1/3). But Lind contributed only $40,000, so the $10,000 bonus ($50,000 – $40,000) must be allocated to the existing partners in the ratio of 6:4. The result will be debits to the capital accounts of Blau and Rubi of $6,000 ($10,000 × 60%) and $4,000 ($10,000 × 40%), respectively. Consequently, immediately after Lind's admission, Blau's capital is $54,000 ($60,000 – $6,000).
Answer (A) is incorrect. The amount of $50,000 is Lind's initial capital balance. Answer (C) is incorrect. The amount of $46,000 is Rubi's capital balance after the admission of Lind. Answer (D) is incorrect. The amount of $60,000 is Blau's initial capital balance.

23.3.7. Orange and Blue have a partnership with capital balances of $50,000 and $70,000, respectively. They wish to admit Jeri White into the partnership partly because of the prestige that she will bring to the partnership. If White purchases a one-fourth interest in capital and future profit and loss for $25,000, her capital account should reflect assigned goodwill in what amount?

A. $10,000

B. $11,250

C. $15,000

D. $25,000

Answer (C) is correct. *(Publisher, adapted)*
REQUIRED: The goodwill assigned to a new partner.
DISCUSSION: The partnership capital is $120,000 prior to the admission of White, and she is to receive 25% of the capital for her contribution of cash and goodwill. Thus, $120,000 equals 75% of the new capital after her admission. The total capital will therefore be $160,000 ($120,000 ÷ 75%), and White's capital account will be credited for $40,000. Because she contributed only $25,000 in cash, a debit to goodwill of $15,000 also is required.
Answer (A) is incorrect. The amount of $10,000 is the difference between the cash contribution and the goodwill assigned. Answer (B) is incorrect. The amount of $11,250 equals 25% of the capital excluding goodwill, minus the cash contribution. Answer (D) is incorrect. The cash contribution equals $25,000.

23.3.8. In the Adel-Brick partnership, Adel and Brick had a capital ratio of 3:1 and a profit and loss ratio of 2:1, respectively. The bonus method was used to record Colter's admittance as a new partner. What ratio would be used to allocate, to Adel and Brick, the excess of Colter's contribution over the amount credited to Colter's capital account?

A. Adel and Brick's new relative capital ratio.

B. Adel and Brick's new relative profit and loss ratio.

C. Adel and Brick's old capital ratio.

D. Adel and Brick's old profit and loss ratio.

Answer (D) is correct. *(CPA, adapted)*
REQUIRED: The ratio used to allocate to the original partners the excess of the new partner's contribution over the amount credited to his or her capital account.
DISCUSSION: The bonus method makes no changes in existing asset accounts. Capital accounts of existing partners are adjusted in accordance with the old profit and loss ratio to reflect the bonus. The entry will be to debit cash (or the fair value of the property) contributed and to credit Colter's capital account for a lesser amount. The excess will be credited in the ratio of 2:1 to the original partners' capital balances.
Answer (A) is incorrect. The bonus to the original partners should not be allocated based on the new capital ratio.
Answer (B) is incorrect. The bonus to the original partners should be allocated based on the old profit and loss ratio. Answer (C) is incorrect. The bonus to the original partners should be allocated based on the old profit and loss ratio, not the old capital ratio.

23.4 Withdrawal of Partners

23.4.1. Hi Shade, a partner in an accounting firm, decided to withdraw from the partnership. Shade's share of the partnership profits and losses was 20%. Upon withdrawing from the partnership, he was paid $74,000 in final settlement of his interest. The total of the partners' capital accounts before recognition of partnership goodwill prior to Shade's withdrawal was $210,000. After his withdrawal, the remaining partners' capital accounts, excluding their share of goodwill, totaled $160,000. The total agreed upon goodwill of the firm was

A. $120,000

B. $160,000

C. $210,000

D. $250,000

Answer (A) is correct. *(CPA, adapted)*
REQUIRED: The amount of goodwill agreed upon prior to Shade's withdrawal.
DISCUSSION: The balance in Shade's account prior to recognition of goodwill was $50,000 ($210,000 − $160,000). Given that he was paid $74,000 upon withdrawing, Shade's account must have been credited with $24,000 in goodwill. If his share of partnership profits and losses was 20%, the total agreed upon goodwill equals $120,000 ($24,000 ÷ 20%).
Answer (B) is incorrect. The amount of $160,000 was the sum of the remaining partners' capital balances exclusive of goodwill. Answer (C) is incorrect. The amount of $210,000 was the sum of the partners' capital balances prior to Shade's withdrawal. Answer (D) is incorrect. The amount of $250,000 assumes that Shade was assigned $50,000 of goodwill.

23.4.2. On June 30, the condensed balance sheet for the partnership of Eddy, Fox, and Grimm, together with their respective profit and loss sharing percentages, was as follows:

Assets, net of liabilities	$320,000
Eddy, capital (50%)	$160,000
Fox, capital (30%)	96,000
Grimm, capital (20%)	64,000
	$320,000

Eddy decided to retire from the partnership and, by mutual agreement, is to be paid $180,000 out of partnership funds for his interest. Total goodwill implicit in the agreement is to be recorded. After Eddy's retirement, what are the capital balances of the other partners?

	Fox	Grimm
A.	$84,000	$56,000
B.	$102,000	$68,000
C.	$108,000	$72,000
D.	$120,000	$80,000

Answer (C) is correct. *(CPA, adapted)*
REQUIRED: The capital balances of the remaining partners following the retirement of a partner.
DISCUSSION: The $180,000 paid to Eddy represents Eddy's 50% interest in the partnership. The total fair value of the partnership is therefore $360,000 ($180,000 ÷ 50%), and the goodwill implicit in the retirement agreement is $40,000 ($360,000 total value − $320,000 net assets prior to the recording of goodwill). This $40,000 should be allocated 50% ($20,000) to Eddy, 30% ($12,000) to Fox, and 20% ($8,000) to Grimm. Fox's capital balance following the recording of goodwill is $108,000 ($96,000 + $12,000), and Grimm's is $72,000 ($64,000 + $8,000).
Answer (A) is incorrect. Under the bonus method, Fox and Grimm's capital balances would be $84,000 and $56,000, respectively. The payment of 50% of the goodwill to Eddy would be shared 3:2 by the remaining partners. Answer (B) is incorrect. The amount of goodwill shared by Fox and Grimm is $20,000, not $10,000. Answer (D) is incorrect. The amount of goodwill shared by Fox and Grimm is $20,000, not $40,000.

23.4.3. When Mill retired from the partnership of Mill, Yale, and Lear, the final settlement of Mill's interest exceeded Mill's capital balance. Under the bonus method, the excess

   A. Was recorded as goodwill.

   B. Was recorded as an expense.

   C. Reduced the capital balances of Yale and Lear.

   D. Had no effect on the capital balances of Yale and Lear.

Answer (C) is correct. *(CPA, adapted)*
   REQUIRED: The treatment of the excess of the settlement of a partner's interest over the capital balance.
   DISCUSSION: The bonus method reduces the capital accounts of the other partners because the bonus, that is, the excess of settlement value over the retiring partner's capital balance, is deemed to be paid to the withdrawing partner by the remaining partners.
   Answer (A) is incorrect. Goodwill is not recorded under the bonus method. Answer (B) is incorrect. The excess is not an expense. Answer (D) is incorrect. The excess reduces the capital accounts.

23.4.4. On June 30, the balance sheet for the partnership of Ace, Deuce, and Trey, including their respective profit-and-loss ratios, was as follows:

Assets, at cost	$300,000
Ace, loan	$ 15,000
Ace, capital (20%)	70,000
Deuce, capital (20%)	65,000
Trey, capital (60%)	150,000
Total	$300,000

Ace has decided to retire from the partnership and by mutual agreement the assets are to be adjusted to their fair value of $360,000 at June 30. It was agreed that the partnership would pay Ace $102,000 cash for Ace's partnership interest exclusive of the amount due on the loan, which is to be repaid in full. No goodwill is to be recorded in this transaction. After Ace's retirement, what are the capital account balances of Deuce and Trey, respectively?

   A. $65,000 and $150,000.

   B. $72,000 and $171,000.

   C. $73,000 and $174,000.

   D. $77,000 and $186,000.

Answer (B) is correct. *(CPA, adapted)*
   REQUIRED: The capital account balances of the remaining partners after a partner's retirement.
   DISCUSSION: The first step is to record $60,000 to reflect the appreciation of the assets. This amount should be allocated according to the profit-and-loss ratio of 2:2:6. Writeup of specific assets has nothing to do with the recording of goodwill.
   After the distribution, Ace has an account balance of $82,000. If Ace is to be paid $102,000, exclusive of the repayment of the loan and without recording goodwill, a $20,000 bonus must be deducted from the capital accounts of Deuce and Trey. Because they share profits and losses in the ratio of 2:6, their accounts will be reduced by $5,000 and $15,000, respectively.

	Ace	Deuce	Trey
Beginning capital	$ 70	$65	$150
Appreciation	12	12	36
	$ 82	$77	$186
Bonus	20	(5)	(15)
Ending capital	$102	$72	$171

   Answer (A) is incorrect. The accounts must be adjusted for appreciation and bonus. Answer (C) is incorrect. The accounts must be increased for appreciation in the ratio of 2:2:6 and decreased in Deuce's and Trey's accounts for the bonus in the ratio of 2:6. Answer (D) is incorrect. The accounts must be reduced by the amount of the bonus.

23.5 Liquidation of Partnerships

23.5.1. The following condensed balance sheet is presented for the partnership of Smith and Johnson, who share profits and losses in the ratio of 60:40, respectively:

Other assets	$450,000
Smith, loan	20,000
	$470,000
Accounts payable	$120,000
Smith, capital	195,000
Johnson, capital	155,000
	$470,000

The partners have decided to liquidate the partnership. If the other assets are sold for $385,000, what amount of the available cash should be distributed to Smith?

   A. $136,000

   B. $156,000

   C. $159,000

   D. $195,000

Answer (A) is correct. *(CPA, adapted)*
   REQUIRED: The amount of cash to be distributed to a partner.
   DISCUSSION: When the partnership sells the other assets, it must recognize a loss of $65,000 ($450,000 – $385,000). This loss must be allocated to the partners based on their loss ratio of 60:40. Thus, Smith's capital account is reduced to $156,000 [$195,000 – ($65,000 × 60%)] and Johnson's to $129,000 [$155,000 – ($65,000 × 40%)]. The accounts payable are then paid, leaving assets of $265,000. Finally, the balance of the loan is subtracted from Smith's capital account balance, and each partner receives the balance in his or her capital account. Thus, Smith should receive $136,000 in cash ($156,000 – $20,000).
   Answer (B) is incorrect. The amount of $156,000 results from not subtracting the loan from Smith's capital account. Answer (C) is incorrect. The amount of $159,000 equals 60% of the assets remaining after the liabilities have been settled. Answer (D) is incorrect. Smith's unadjusted capital balance equals $195,000.

Questions 23.5.2 and 23.5.3 are based on the following information.

December 31 balance sheet accounts of the Dan, Jim, and Mary Partnership follow:

Cash	$ 20,000
Inventory	120,000
Plant assets – net	300,000
Accounts payable	170,000
Dan, capital	100,000
Jim, capital	90,000
Mary, capital	80,000

The partners' profit and loss percentages are Dan, 50%; Jim, 30%; and Mary, 20%.

On January 1 of the next year, the partners decide to liquidate the partnership. They agree that all cash should be distributed as soon as it becomes available during the liquidation process. They also agree that a cash predistribution plan is necessary to facilitate the distribution of cash.

23.5.2. If cash of $220,000, including the $20,000 cash on hand, becomes available, it should be distributed in accordance with the cash predistribution plan. How much should be distributed to the creditors and partners respectively?

	Creditors	Dan	Jim	Mary
A.	$170,000	$25,000	$15,000	$10,000
B.	$170,000	$0	$26,000	$24,000
C.	$170,000	$10,000	$32,000	$8,000
D.	$170,000	$0	$18,000	$32,000

Answer (D) is correct. *(Publisher, adapted)*
REQUIRED: The distribution of cash to partners and creditors using a cash predistribution plan.
DISCUSSION: To prepare a cash predistribution plan, the smallest projected loss that will eliminate the partner most vulnerable to losses is allocated in the profit-loss ratio. Then, based on the newly calculated capital balances, the projected loss that will eliminate the next most vulnerable partner is allocated. The projected loss and its allocation are based on a profit-and-loss ratio adjusted for the previous elimination of more vulnerable partners. Once projected losses to eliminate all partners are calculated, the plan sets forth a distribution of cash that prevents an overpayment to an insolvent partner. Liabilities to outside creditors must be satisfied before cash is distributed to the partners. After satisfying the accounts payable of $170,000, $50,000 remains to be distributed to partners. The first $20,000 is to be distributed to Mary. Of the remaining $30,000, 60% ($18,000) will be distributed to Jim and 40% ($12,000) to Mary. The $50,000 should therefore be distributed $0 to Dan, $18,000 to Jim, and $32,000 to Mary.

Cash Predistribution Plan

Projected Loss	Dan-50%	Jim-30%	Mary-20%
	$100,000	$90,000	$80,000
$200,000	(100,000)	(60,000)	(40,000)
	$ --	$30,000	$40,000
$ 50,000		(30,000)	(20,000)
		$ --	$20,000
$ 20,000			(20,000)
			$ --

Cash Distribution		Creditors	Dan	Jim	Mary
First	$170,000	100%			
Next	20,000				100%
Next	50,000			60%	40%
Then			50%	30%	20%

Answer (A) is incorrect. A 5:3:2 distribution is appropriate only for amounts in excess of $240,000. Answer (B) is incorrect. The first $170,000 must go to creditors, the next $20,000 must go to Mary, and the remaining $30,000 should be distributed to Jim and Mary in the ratio of 3:2. Answer (C) is incorrect. Mary did not receive the $20,000 distribution, Dan does not receive a distribution until Jim and Mary receive theirs, and Jim and Mary have not fulfilled a 3:2 distribution of $50,000.

23.5.3. The predistribution plan should be based on relative vulnerability to losses. For the Dan, Jim, and Mary Partnership, the relative vulnerability should show that

A. Dan is the most vulnerable.

B. Dan is the least vulnerable.

C. Jim is the most vulnerable.

D. Jim is the least vulnerable.

Answer (A) is correct. *(Publisher, adapted)*
REQUIRED: The true statement about relative vulnerability.
DISCUSSION: A cash predistribution plan is based on the partners' relative vulnerability to losses under the assumption that a partner would not repay a deficit capital balance. This vulnerability is determined by projecting the loss that, in accordance with the profit-and-loss ratio, would eliminate each partner's account. Because Dan would be allocated 50% of each loss, a projected loss of $200,000 ($100,000 capital balance ÷ 50%) would eliminate his account. Projected losses of $300,000 ($90,000 ÷ 30%) and $400,000 ($80,000 ÷ 20%) would eliminate Jim's and Mary's balances, respectively. Accordingly, Dan is the most vulnerable because his capital balance would be eliminated by the smallest projected loss.

23.5.4. On January 1, the partners of Cobb, Davis, and Eddy, who share profits and losses in the ratio of 5:3:2, respectively, decided to liquidate their partnership. On this date, the partnership condensed balance sheet was as follows:

Assets

Cash	$ 50,000
Other assets	250,000
	$300,000

Liabilities and Capital

Liabilities	$ 60,000
Cobb, capital	80,000
Davis, capital	90,000
Eddy, capital	70,000
	$300,000

On January 15, the first cash sale of other assets with a carrying amount of $150,000 realized $120,000. Safe installment payments to the partners were made the same date. How much cash should be distributed to each partner?

	Cobb	Davis	Eddy
A.	$15,000	$51,000	$44,000
B.	$40,000	$45,000	$35,000
C.	$55,000	$33,000	$22,000
D.	$60,000	$36,000	$24,000

Answer (A) is correct. *(CPA, adapted)*
REQUIRED: The safe installment payments to partners after the initial sale of assets.
DISCUSSION: When the liquidation of a partnership proceeds over time, a conservative approach must be taken to the distribution of assets (cash) to partners. This conservative approach incorporates three steps. In the first step, a gain or loss realized from the actual sale of assets ($120,000 – $150,000 = $30,000 loss) is allocated to the partners' capital accounts in accordance with the profit-and-loss ratio. In the second step, remaining assets are assumed to have a fair value of $0, which results in an assumed loss equal to their carrying amount. For this partnership, an assumed loss of $100,000 ($250,000 of other assets – $150,000 of other assets sold) results. This assumed loss is also allocated to the partners' accounts in accordance with the profit-and-loss ratio. The third step is taken only if at least one of the partners' capital accounts has a deficit balance. If a deficit results, the conservative approach requires allocation of the deficit to the remaining partners' accounts. This step is not necessary in this example. The final balances in the partnership accounts equal the amounts of cash that may be distributed in a safe installment payment schedule.

	Cobb	Davis	Eddy
Beginning capital	$80,000	$90,000	$70,000
Realized loss ($30,000)	(15,000)	(9,000)	(6,000)
Assumed loss ($100,000)	(50,000)	(30,000)	(20,000)
Resulting capital	$15,000	$51,000	$44,000

Answer (B) is incorrect. A maximum of $110,000 in cash can be distributed given available cash of $170,000 and liabilities of $60,000. Answer (C) is incorrect. The amounts of $55,000, $33,000, and $22,000 are equal to 50%, 30%, and 20%, respectively, of the excess of the total cash available over the liabilities. Answer (D) is incorrect. The amounts of $60,000, $36,000, and $24,000 are equal to 50%, 30%, and 20%, respectively, of the $120,000 of cash realized from the sale of other assets.

23.5.5. The following condensed balance sheet is presented for the partnership of Axel, Barr, and Cain, who share profits and losses in the ratio of 4:3:3, respectively:

Cash	$100,000
Other assets	300,000
Total	$400,000

Liabilities	$150,000
Axel, capital	40,000
Barr, capital	180,000
Cain, capital	30,000
Total	$400,000

The partners agreed to dissolve the partnership after selling the other assets for $200,000. Upon dissolution of the partnership, Axel should have received

A. $0

B. $40,000

C. $60,000

D. $150,000

Answer (A) is correct. *(CPA, adapted)*
REQUIRED: The amount Axel should receive upon liquidation.
DISCUSSION: When the other assets with a carrying amount of $300,000 were sold for $200,000, a loss of $100,000 resulted. When this loss is distributed in the ratio of 4:3:3 to the capital balances, Axel's and Cain's capital balances are eliminated. Thus, upon dissolution of the partnership, neither Axel nor Cain will receive any cash. Of the $300,000 available ($100,000 cash on hand + $200,000 proceeds from the sale of other assets), $150,000 will be distributed to creditors (liabilities) and $150,000 will be distributed to Barr.

	Axel	Barr	Cain
Beginning capital	$40,000	$180,000	$30,000
Loss on sale	(40,000)	(30,000)	(30,000)
Distribution of cash	$ 0	$150,000	$ 0

Answer (B) is incorrect. The amount of $40,000 is Axel's capital balance before dissolution. Answer (C) is incorrect. The amount of $60,000 is 40% of the assets remaining after payment of liabilities. Answer (D) is incorrect. The amount of $150,000 is the amount distributed to Barr.

23.5.6. Prior to partnership liquidation, a schedule of possible losses is frequently prepared to determine the amount of cash that may be safely distributed to the partners. The schedule of possible losses

A. Consists of each partner's capital account plus loan balance, divided by that partner's profit-and-loss sharing ratio.

B. Shows the successive losses necessary to eliminate the capital accounts of partners (assuming no contribution of personal assets by the partners).

C. Indicates the distribution of successive amounts of available cash to each partner.

D. Assumes contribution of personal assets by partners unless there is a substantial presumption of personal insolvency by the partners.

Answer (B) is correct. *(Publisher, adapted)*
REQUIRED: The true statement about a schedule of possible losses.
DISCUSSION: A schedule of possible losses presents a series of incremental losses to indicate the amount of loss in a liquidation that will eliminate each partner's capital account. The presumption is that losses or partners' capital deficits will not be repaid by individual partners. The schedule is used to determine the amount of cash that may be safely distributed to the individual partners without potential impairment of the rights of any party.
Answer (A) is incorrect. It describes the computation that determines the order in which partners' capital accounts will be eliminated by losses, not the amounts thereof. Answer (C) is incorrect. It describes a cash distribution schedule. Answer (D) is incorrect. The presumption (for the schedule) is that losses or deficits will not be repaid by individual partners.

Use **Gleim Test Prep** for interactive study and easy-to-use detailed analytics!

STUDY UNIT TWENTY-FOUR
BUSINESS COMBINATIONS AND
CONSOLIDATED FINANCIAL REPORTING

A business combination is a transaction or other event in which an investor obtains **control** of one or more businesses. When the investor holds more than 50% of the total outstanding voting interests of the investee, the investor has control of the investee. The investee is deemed to be a subsidiary of the investor (parent).

The accounting for the combination is based on the acquisition method. The investor must (1) determine the acquirer and the acquisition date and (2) recognize and measure (a) identifiable assets acquired, (b) liabilities assumed, (c) any noncontrolling interest, and (d) goodwill or a gain from a bargain purchase.

At the end of each reporting period, the parent must report consolidated financial statements. These statements report the parent and the subsidiaries as if they were one economic entity. Thus, the effects of intraentity transactions must be eliminated in full during the preparation of the consolidated financial statements.

QUESTIONS

24.1 Nature of a Business Combination

24.1.1. A parent-subsidiary relationship most likely arises from a

A. Tax-free reorganization.

B. Vertical business combination.

C. Horizontal business combination.

D. Greater than 50% ownership of the voting interests of another entity.

Answer (D) is correct. *(Publisher, adapted)*
   REQUIRED: The situation creating a parent-subsidiary relationship.
   DISCUSSION: A parent-subsidiary relationship usually arises from an effective ownership of more than 50% of the voting interests of another entity. The financial statements for the two entities must be presented on a consolidated basis unless control does not rest with the majority owner. To the extent the acquiree is not wholly owned, a noncontrolling interest is presented.
   Answer (A) is incorrect. A tax-free reorganization may or may not be a combination, and it may or may not result in a parent-subsidiary relationship. Answer (B) is incorrect. Vertical combinations also may be accomplished by a merger or a consolidation, in which case the combining entities become one. A vertical combination combines a supplier and customer. Answer (C) is incorrect. Horizontal combinations also may be accomplished by a merger or a consolidation, in which case the combining entities become one. A horizontal combination combines competitors.

24.1.2. Primor, a manufacturer, owns 75% of the voting interests of Sublette, an investment firm. Sublette owns 60% of the voting interests of Minos, an insurer. In Primor's consolidated financial statements, should consolidation accounting or equity method accounting be used for Sublette and Minos?

A. Consolidation used for Sublette and equity method used for Minos.

B. Consolidation used for both Sublette and Minos.

C. Equity method used for Sublette and consolidation used for Minos.

D. Equity method used for both Sublette and Minos.

Answer (B) is correct. *(CPA, adapted)*
REQUIRED: The method of accounting used by an entity that has a direct controlling interest in one entity and an indirect interest in another.
DISCUSSION: All entities in which a parent has a controlling financial interest through direct or indirect ownership of a majority voting interest ordinarily must be consolidated. However, a subsidiary is not consolidated when control does not rest with the majority owner. Primor has direct control of Sublette and indirect control of Minos and should consolidate both.
Answer (A) is incorrect. Primor has a controlling interest in Minos as well. Answer (C) is incorrect. Primor has a controlling interest in Sublette as well. Answer (D) is incorrect. Primor should consolidate both Sublette and Minos.

24.1.3. According to GAAP, a business must

A. Have goodwill.

B. Generate a return.

C. Be capable of being managed to provide economic benefits.

D. Have inputs, outputs, and processes.

Answer (C) is correct. *(CPA, adapted)*
REQUIRED: The element of a business.
DISCUSSION: The activities and assets of a business are capable of being managed to provide economic benefits (returns such as dividends, and lower costs). Processes are applied to inputs to generate outputs. Outputs are direct returns to investors and other participants.
Answer (A) is incorrect. A set of activities and assets that includes goodwill is presumed to be a business. However, a business need not have goodwill. Answer (B) is incorrect. A business must be capable of being managed to provide economic benefits (a return). It need not have outputs or returns. Answer (D) is incorrect. A business need not have outputs if it is capable of being managed to provide them.

24.2 Acquisition Method

24.2.1. Parent Co. acquires a controlling financial interest in Sub Co., a business entity. However, part of the equity in Sub is not attributable, directly or indirectly, to Parent. The NCI must be

A. Measured at its acquisition-date fair value.

B. Greater if goodwill is recognized.

C. Lower if the acquirer previously held an equity interest in the acquiree.

D. Excluded from the measurement of goodwill.

Answer (A) is correct. *(Publisher, adapted)*
REQUIRED: The accounting for an NCI.
DISCUSSION: A business combination has occurred because the acquirer has obtained control of a business. The acquirer measures the identifiable assets acquired, liabilities assumed, and any NCI in the acquiree at their acquisition-date fair values.
Answer (B) is incorrect. NCI is measured at its fair value on the acquisition date regardless of whether goodwill is recognized. Answer (C) is incorrect. The amount of the NCI initially recognized bears no necessary relationship to the acquirer's equity interest held prior to the combination. Answer (D) is incorrect. The acquisition-date fair value of the NCI is an element of the calculation of goodwill.

24.2.2. For the past several years, Mozza Company has invested in the common stock of Chedd Company, a wholesaler of imported cheeses. As of July 1, Mozza owned approximately 13% of the total of Chedd's outstanding voting common stock. Recently, managements of the two companies have discussed a possible combination of the two entities. However, no public announcement has been made, and no notice to owners has been given. The business combination that may result must be accounted for using the

A. Pooling-of-interests method.

B. Acquisition method.

C. Part pooling, part acquisition method.

D. Joint venture method.

Answer (B) is correct. *(Publisher, adapted)*
REQUIRED: The accounting for a business combination.
DISCUSSION: A business combination is "a transaction or other event in which an acquirer obtains control of one or more businesses" (FASB Codification). An entity must account for a combination using the following steps of the acquisition method: (1) identify the acquirer; (2) determine the acquisition date; (3) recognize and measure the identifiable assets acquired, liabilities assumed, and any noncontrolling interest; and (4) recognize and measure goodwill or a gain from a bargain purchase.
Answer (A) is incorrect. The pooling-of-interests method may no longer be used to account for a business combination. Answer (C) is incorrect. Accounting for a business combination as part pooling and part acquisition is not allowed. Answer (D) is incorrect. A joint venture does not meet the definition of a business combination.

24.2.3. Rolan Corporation issued 10,000 shares of common stock in exchange for all of Sandin Corporation's outstanding stock on September 1. Rolan's common stock had a market price of $60 per share on September 1. The market price of Sandin's stock was not readily ascertainable. Condensed balance sheets of Rolan and Sandin immediately prior to the combination are indicated below.

	Rolan	Sandin
Total assets	$1,000,000	$500,000
Liabilities	$ 300,000	$150,000
Common stock ($10 par)	200,000	100,000
Retained earnings	500,000	250,000
Total liabilities and shareholders' equities	$1,000,000	$500,000

Rolan's investment in Sandin's stock will be stated in Rolan's parent-only balance sheet immediately after the combination in the amount of

A. $100,000

B. $350,000

C. $500,000

D. $600,000

Answer (D) is correct. *(CPA, adapted)*
REQUIRED: The recorded amount of the acquired entity.
DISCUSSION: In a parent-only balance sheet, the acquirer recognizes only an investment in subsidiary and the issuance of equity. The fair value of the consideration transferred (10,000 shares × $60 = $600,000) is the measure of the investment immediately after the combination. (In a consolidated balance sheet, no investment in the subsidiary would be recognized.)
Answer (A) is incorrect. The par value of the stock issued equals $100,000. Answer (B) is incorrect. The carrying amount of Sandin's net assets equals $350,000. Answer (C) is incorrect. The fair value of the stock issued minus its par value equals $500,000.

24.2.4. Acquirer Co. and Acquiree Co. are in negotiations for a business combination. Acquirer suggested to Acquiree that it reach agreements with certain key executives to make payments with a total amount of $5,000,000 if negotiations succeed. Acquiree already had a contract with its chief executive to make a $10,000,000 payment if the company was acquired. This contract was agreed to several years before any acquisition was contemplated. What amount, if any, of these payments most likely is part of the exchange for the acquiree?

A. $15,000,000

B. $10,000,000

C. $5,000,000

D. $0

Answer (B) is correct. *(CPA, adapted)*
REQUIRED: The payment, if any, part of the exchange for the acquiree.
DISCUSSION: Under the acquisition method, one recognition condition is that assets and liabilities be part of the exchange (part of the consideration transferred for the acquiree). The assumption of the $10,000,000 liability to the chief executive of Acquiree is not part of a separate arrangement with Acquirer reached before or during the negotiations for the combination. Moreover, the purpose was apparently to obtain (or retain) the services of the chief executive, a benefit to Acquiree. However, the agreement with other key executives was made by Acquiree at the suggestion of Acquirer to provide termination payments, a likely benefit to Acquirer. Accordingly, the acquisition-date fair value of the $10,000,000 liability is included in the accounting for the combination. The $5,000,000 of other termination payments will be accounted for separately.
Answer (A) is incorrect. The $5,000,000 in payments apparently is for the benefit of Acquirer. Answer (C) is incorrect. The assumption of the $10,000,000 liability to the chief executive is part of the consideration transferred for the acquiree. The assumption of the $5,000,000 liability is postcombination compensation for the departures of certain key executives. Answer (D) is incorrect. The assumption of the $10,000,000 liability to the chief executive is part of the consideration transferred for the acquiree.

24.2.5. Damon Co. purchased 100% of the outstanding common stock of Smith Co. in an acquisition by issuing 20,000 shares of its $1 par common stock that had a fair value of $10 per share and providing contingent consideration that had a fair value of $10,000 on the acquisition date. Damon also incurred $15,000 in direct acquisition costs. On the acquisition date, Smith had assets with a book value of $200,000, a fair value of $350,000, and related liabilities with a book and fair value of $70,000. What amount of gain should Damon report related to this transaction?

    A. $55,000

    B. $70,000

    C. $80,000

    D. $250,000

Answer (B) is correct. *(CPA, adapted)*
REQUIRED: The gain on acquisition of all of the common stock of another entity given contingent consideration and direct acquisition costs.
DISCUSSION: The gain on a bargain purchase arising from a business combination equals the excess of 1. over 2.:

1) The net of the acquisition-date fair value of

    ●   The identifiable assets acquired and
    ●   Liabilities assumed

2) The sum of the acquisition-date fair value of

    ●   The consideration transferred
    ●   Any noncontrolling interest
    ●   Any previously held equity interest in the acquiree

The net of the acquisition-date fair value of the identifiable assets acquired and the liabilities assumed was $280,000 ($350,000 FV of assets – $70,000 FV of liabilities). The acquisition-date fair value of the consideration transferred was $210,000 [(20,000 shares × $10 FV per share) + $10,000 FV of contingent consideration]. Contingent consideration given in exchange for the acquiree is usually an obligation to transfer something to the former owners if a specified condition is met. Because the acquirer received 100% of the voting interests of the acquiree, no controlling interest or previously held equity interest in the acquiree existed. Consequently, the acquiree recognizes an ordinary gain in earnings of $70,000 ($280,000 FV net identifiable assets – $210,000 FV consideration transferred).
    Answer (A) is incorrect. The amount of $55,000 includes $15,000 of direct acquisition costs, an expense not included in the calculation of the gain on a bargain purchase. Answer (C) is incorrect. The amount of $80,000 omits the fair value of the contingent consideration. Answer (D) is incorrect. The amount of $250,000 equals the $280,000 fair value of the net identifiable assets acquired, minus the $20,000 par value of the common stock issued, minus the $10,000 fair value of the contingent consideration.

24.2.6. Acquirer and Acquiree are the combining entities in a business combination. As part of the bargain, Acquirer assumed a contingent liability based on a suit brought against Acquiree because of a defect in one of its products. However, the former owner of Acquiree has agreed to pay the amount of any damages in excess of $5,000,000. In the consolidated balance sheet issued on the acquisition date, the contingent liability is reported at acquisition-date fair value. Accordingly,

    A. An indemnification asset is recognized at acquisition-date fair value.

    B. A valuation allowance is reported for the indemnification asset.

    C. An exception to the customary accounting for a business combination applies.

    D. No indemnification asset is recognized until the contingency is resolved.

Answer (A) is correct. *(CPA, adapted)*
REQUIRED: The effect of the acquiree's agreement to pay excess damages related to a contingent liability assumed by the acquirer.
DISCUSSION: The contingent liability for damages resulting from a lawsuit is noncontractual. However, if it is more likely than not at the acquisition date that a noncontractual contingency will result in a liability or an asset, it will be measured at acquisition-date fair value. Moreover, the indemnification asset and the indemnified item are recognized at the same time and on the same basis. Thus, the indemnification asset also is recognized at acquisition-date fair value.
    Answer (B) is incorrect. No valuation allowance is necessary when an item is recognized at acquisition-date fair value. The effects of uncertainty are reflected in the fair value measurement. Answer (C) is incorrect. The asset is recognized at acquisition-date fair value. The exception for items measured using GAAP relative to accounting for contingencies does not apply. Answer (D) is incorrect. The indemnification asset and the indemnified item are recognized at the same time.

24.3 Goodwill and Bargain Purchases

24.3.1. On November 30, Pindar Co. purchased for cash at $30 per share all 250,000 shares of the outstanding common stock of Shimoda Co., a business entity. Shimoda reported net assets on that date with a carrying amount of $6 million. This amount reflected acquisition-date fair value except for property, plant, and equipment, which had a fair value that exceeded its carrying amount by $800,000. In its November 30 consolidated balance sheet, what amount should Pindar report as goodwill?

A. $1,500,000

B. $800,000

C. $700,000

D. $0

Answer (C) is correct. *(CPA, adapted)*
   REQUIRED: The amount reported as goodwill.
   DISCUSSION: A business combination is accounted for as an acquisition. Under the acquisition method, the entity recording the transaction is based on fair values. Goodwill is the excess of (1) the sum of the acquisition-date fair values of (a) the consideration transferred, (b) any noncontrolling interest in the acquiree, and (c) the acquirer's previously held equity interest in the acquiree over (2) the net of the acquisition-date fair values of the identifiable assets acquired and liabilities assumed. Pindar's goodwill is therefore calculated as follows:

Consideration transferred (250,000 shares × $30 market price)	$7,500,000
Acquisition-date fair value of the net assets acquired:	
Carrying amount	(6,000,000)
Undervaluation of PP&E	(800,000)
Goodwill	$ 700,000

   Answer (A) is incorrect. The excess of the consideration transferred over the carrying amount equals $1,500,000. Answer (B) is incorrect. The fair value in excess of the carrying amount of the acquired net assets is $800,000. Answer (D) is incorrect. Goodwill must be recognized. The consideration transferred exceeds the fair value of the net assets acquired.

24.3.2. When should goodwill be recognized?

A. Costs have been incurred in the development of goodwill.

B. Goodwill has been created in the purchase of a business.

C. The company expects a future benefit from the creation of goodwill.

D. The fair market value of the company's assets exceeds the book value of the company's assets.

Answer (B) is correct. *(CPA, adapted)*
   REQUIRED: The time of recognition of goodwill.
   DISCUSSION: Goodwill can be recognized only in a business combination. Goodwill is an asset representing the future economic benefits arising from other assets acquired in a business combination that are not individually identified and separately recognized.
   Answer (A) is incorrect. Internally generated goodwill may not be recognized as an asset on the balance sheet. Answer (C) is incorrect. Internally generated goodwill may not be recognized as an asset on the balance sheet, even if the company expects a future benefit. Answer (D) is incorrect. Goodwill is recognized only in a business combination.

24.3.3. Pellew Corp. paid $600,000 for all of the outstanding common stock of Samos Co. in a business combination initiated and completed in December. At that time, Samos had the following condensed balance sheet:

	Carrying Amounts
Current assets	$ 80,000
Plant and equipment, net	760,000
Liabilities	400,000
Equity	440,000

The acquisition-date fair value of the plant and equipment was $120,000 more than its carrying amount. The acquisition-date fair values and carrying amounts were equal for all other assets and liabilities. What amount of goodwill, related to Samos's acquisition, must Pellew report in its December 31 consolidated balance sheet?

A. $40,000

B. $80,000

C. $120,000

D. $160,000

Answer (A) is correct. *(CPA, adapted)*
   REQUIRED: The amount of goodwill reported in the consolidated balance sheet.
   DISCUSSION: A business combination is accounted for as an acquisition. Under the acquisition method, the entry recording the transaction is based on the fair values exchanged. Goodwill is the excess of (1) the sum of the acquisition-date fair values of (a) the consideration transferred, (b) any noncontrolling interest in the acquiree, and (c) the acquirer's previously held equity interest in the acquiree over (2) the net of the acquisition-date fair values of the identifiable assets acquired and liabilities assumed. Pellew's goodwill is therefore calculated as follows:

Consideration transferred	$600,000
Acquisition-date fair value of net assets acquired:	
Current assets	(80,000)
Plant and equipment, fair value ($760,000 + $120,000)	(880,000)
Liabilities	400,000
Goodwill	$ 40,000

   Answer (B) is incorrect. The amount of current assets is $80,000. Answer (C) is incorrect. The amount of plant and equipment is undervalued is $120,000. Answer (D) is incorrect. The difference between the $600,000 cost and the $440,000 carrying amount of the net assets is $160,000.

24.3.4. Plume Co. acquired all of the outstanding voting stock of Sumir Co. for $6 million. The identifiable net assets of Sumir were appropriately measured at an acquisition-date fair value of $7.5 million. Moreover, the business combination was completed in the period in which it was initiated, and no contingent consideration or preacquisition contingency existed. Below are Sumir's only assets. They are measured at acquisition-date fair values.

Financial assets (not accounted for by the equity method)	$3 million
Deferred tax assets	.5 million
Assets to be disposed of by sale	3 million
Other current assets	2 million
Property, plant, and equipment	1 million

The consolidated income statement for the period in which the combination was completed must reflect

    A. An extraordinary gain of $500,000.

    B. A gain of $1.5 million.

    C. Goodwill of $150,000.

    D. No gain or goodwill.

Answer (B) is correct. *(Publisher, adapted)*
    REQUIRED: The accounting for a business combination.
    DISCUSSION: In a bargain purchase, the gain is recognized in earnings. The gain equals the excess of (1) the net of the acquisition-date fair values (with some exceptions) of the identifiable assets acquired and liabilities assumed over (2) the sum of the acquisition-date fair values (with some exceptions) of (a) the consideration transferred, (b) any NCI in the acquiree, and (c) the acquirer's previously held equity interest in the acquiree. Consequently, the gain was $1.5 million ($7.5 million – $6 million).
    Answer (A) is incorrect. Extraordinary items are not recognized under U.S. GAAP or IFRS. Answer (C) is incorrect. Goodwill is the excess of (1) the sum of the acquisition-date fair values (with some exceptions) of (a) the consideration transferred, (b) any NCI in the acquiree, and (c) the acquirer's previously held equity interest in the acquiree over (2) the net of the acquisition-date fair values (with some exceptions) of the identifiable assets acquired and liabilities assumed. Answer (D) is incorrect. A gain is recognized.

24.3.5. MAJ Corporation acquired 90% of the common stock of Min Co. for $420,000. MAJ previously held no equity interest in Min. On the date of acquisition, the carrying amount of Min's identifiable net assets equaled $300,000. The acquisition-date fair values of Min's inventory and equipment exceeded their carrying amounts by $60,000 and $40,000, respectively. The carrying amounts of the other assets and liabilities were equal to their acquisition-date fair values, and the fair value of the noncontrolling interest was $45,000. What amount should MAJ recognize as goodwill immediately after the acquisition?

    A. $150,000

    B. $90,000

    C. $65,000

    D. $114,000

Answer (C) is correct. *(Publisher, adapted)*
    REQUIRED: The goodwill recognized given an NCI.
    DISCUSSION: Goodwill is the excess of (1) the sum of the acquisition-date fair values of (a) the consideration transferred, (b) any NCI in the acquiree, and (c) the acquirer's previously held equity interest in the acquiree over (2) the net of the acquisition-date fair values (with some exceptions) of the identifiable assets acquired and liabilities assumed. Goodwill is therefore $65,000.

Consideration transferred	$ 420,000
Noncontrolling interest	45,000
Previous equity interest	0
Carrying amount of net assets	(300,000)
Fair value adjustment of inventory	(60,000)
Fair value adjustment of equipment	(40,000)
Goodwill	$ 65,000

    Answer (A) is incorrect. The amount of $150,000 is the difference between the consideration transferred and 90% of the carrying amount of the identifiable net assets. Answer (B) is incorrect. The amount of $90,000 is the excess of the consideration transferred over the carrying amount of 90% of the identifiable net assets, minus the amount allocated to inventory. Answer (D) is incorrect. The amount of $114,000 is the excess of the consideration transferred over 90% of the carrying amount of the identifiable net assets, minus 90% of the excess fair value of the equipment.

24.3.6. Practicum Co. paid $1.2 million for an 80% interest in the common stock of Sarong Co. Practicum had no previous equity interest in Sarong. On the acquisition date, Sarong's identifiable net assets had a $1.3 million carrying amount, and their fair value equaled $1.4 million. The fair value of the noncontrolling interest (NCI) equals 20% of the implied fair value of the acquiree. Practicum should record goodwill of

A. $(200,000)

B. $(100,000)

C. $100,000

D. $160,000

Answer (C) is correct. *(Publisher, adapted)*
REQUIRED: The calculation of goodwill recorded using the acquisition method.
DISCUSSION: In a business combination, goodwill is the excess of (1) the sum of the acquisition-date fair values (with some exceptions) of (a) the consideration transferred, (b) any NCI in the acquiree, and (c) the acquirer's previously held equity interest in the acquiree over (2) the net of the acquisition-date fair values (with some exceptions) of the identifiable assets acquired and liabilities assumed. Goodwill is therefore $100,000.

Consideration transferred	$1,200,000
NCI [($1,200,000 ÷ 80%) × 20%]	300,000
Previously held equity interest	0
Fair value of identifiable net assets acquired	(1,400,000)
Goodwill	$ 100,000

Answer (A) is incorrect. The amount of $(200,000) is the difference between the fair value of Sarong's identifiable net assets and the consideration transferred. Answer (B) is incorrect. The amount of $(100,000) is the difference between the carrying amount of Sarong's identifiable net assets and their fair value. Answer (D) is incorrect. The amount of $160,000 is the difference between the consideration transferred and 80% of the carrying amount of the identifiable net assets.

24.3.7. A company is completing its annual impairment analysis of the goodwill included in one of its cash generating units (CGUs). The recoverable amount of the CGU is $32,000. The company noted the following related to the CGU:

	Goodwill	Patents	Other Assets	Total
Historical cost	$15,000	$10,000	$35,000	$60,000
Depreciation and amortization	0	3,333	11,667	15,000
Carrying amount, December 31	$15,000	$ 6,667	$23,333	$45,000

Under IFRS, which of the following adjustments should be recognized in the company's consolidated financial statements?

A. Decrease goodwill by $13,000.

B. Decrease goodwill by $15,000.

C. Decrease goodwill by $3,250; patents by $2,167; and other assets by $7,583.

D. Decrease goodwill by $4,333; patents by $1,926; and other assets by $6,741.

Answer (A) is correct. *(CPA, adapted)*
REQUIRED: The adjustment for the impairment of goodwill under IFRS.
DISCUSSION: Under IFRS, the test for impairment of a CGU to which goodwill has been allocated is whether the carrying amount of the CGU (including allocated goodwill) exceeds its recoverable amount. The carrying amount of the CGU (including goodwill) is $45,000. The recoverable amount of the CGU is $32,000. Thus, the impairment loss is equal to $13,000 ($45,000 − $32,000). An impairment loss for a CGU is allocated first to reduce allocated goodwill to zero and then pro rata to the other assets. As such, goodwill is decreased by $13,000.
Answer (B) is incorrect. Goodwill is decreased only by the amount of the impairment loss ($13,000). Answer (C) is incorrect. Under IFRS, an impairment loss for a CGU is allocated first to reduce allocated goodwill to zero and then pro rata to the other assets. Since the impairment loss is less than the $15,000 carrying amount of goodwill, there is no need to pro rate the loss to other assets of the CGU. Answer (D) is incorrect. Under IFRS, an impairment loss for a CGU is allocated first to reduce allocated goodwill to zero before it is allocated to the other assets. Since the impairment loss is less than the $15,000 carrying amount of goodwill, there is no need to pro rate the loss to other assets of the CGU.

24.3.8. How should the acquirer recognize a bargain purchase in a business acquisition?

A. As negative goodwill in the statement of financial position.

B. As goodwill in the statement of financial position.

C. As a gain in earnings at the acquisition date.

D. As a deferred gain that is amortized into earnings over the estimated future periods benefited.

Answer (C) is correct. *(CPA, adapted)*
REQUIRED: The recognition of a bargain purchase acquisition.
DISCUSSION: A bargain purchase is recognized in the consolidated financial statements as an ordinary gain at the acquisition date. A bargain purchase occurs when the net of the acquisition-date fair values of identifiable assets acquired and liabilities assumed exceeds the sum of the acquisition-date fair values of the consideration transferred, any noncontrolling interest recognized, and any previously held equity interest in the acquiree.
Answer (A) is incorrect. A bargain purchase is reported in the consolidated financial statements as an ordinary gain. Answer (B) is incorrect. A bargain purchase is recognized when the net of the acquisition-date fair values of identifiable assets acquired and liabilities assumed is less than the sum of the acquisition-date fair values of the consideration transferred, any noncontrolling interest recognized, and any previously held equity interest in the acquiree. Goodwill arises in the opposite case. Answer (D) is incorrect. A bargain purchase is reported in the consolidated financial statements as an ordinary gain.

24.4 Acquisition-Related Costs

24.4.1. Pendragon Co. issues 200,000 shares of $5 par value common stock to acquire Squire Co. in a business combination. The market value of Pendragon's common stock is $12. Legal and consulting fees incurred in relationship to the combination are $110,000. Direct registration and issuance costs for the common stock are $35,000. What should be recorded in Pendragon's additional paid-in capital (APIC) for this business combination?

A. $1,545,000

B. $1,400,000

C. $1,365,000

D. $1,255,000

Answer (C) is correct. *(CPA, adapted)*
REQUIRED: The effect of the business combination on APIC.
DISCUSSION: Acquisition-related costs, such as finder's fees, professional (e.g., legal) and consulting fees, and general administrative costs (e.g., for an acquisitions department), are expensed as incurred. The one exception is for the issuance costs of debt or equity securities. These are accounted for under other GAAP. Thus, direct issuance costs of equity (underwriting, legal, accounting, tax, registration, etc.) are debited to additional paid-in capital. Accordingly, the amount recorded in APIC for the combination should be $1,365,000 {[200,000 shares × ($12 market value – $5 par value)] – $35,000 direct issuance costs}.
Answer (A) is incorrect. The amount of $1,545,000 equals $1,400,000 [200,000 × ($12 – $5)] plus legal and consulting fees ($110,000) and direct issuance costs ($35,000). Answer (B) is incorrect. APIC without an adjustment for direct issuance costs equals $1,400,000. Answer (D) is incorrect. The amount of $1,255,000 equals $1,400,000 [200,000 × ($12 – $5)], minus legal and consulting fees ($110,000), minus direct issuance costs ($35,000).

24.4.2. In a business combination, Major Corporation issued nonvoting, nonconvertible preferred stock with a fair value of $8 million in exchange for all of the outstanding common stock of Minor Corporation. On the acquisition date, Minor had identifiable net assets with a carrying amount of $4 million and a fair value of $5 million. In addition, Major issued preferred stock with a fair value of $800,000 to an individual as a finder's fee in arranging the transaction. As a result of this transaction, Major should record an increase in net assets of

A. $4,000,000

B. $5,000,000

C. $8,000,000

D. $8,800,000

Answer (C) is correct. *(CPA, adapted)*
REQUIRED: The increase in net assets recorded.
DISCUSSION: Based on fair value, goodwill is the excess of (1) the sum of (a) the consideration transferred ($8,000,000), (b) any noncontrolling interest in the acquiree ($0), and (c) the acquirer's previously held equity interest in the acquiree ($0) over (2) the net of the identifiable assets acquired and liabilities assumed ($5,000,000). Thus, goodwill is $3,000,000, and the increase in net assets is $8,000,000. The acquisition-related cost (the finder's fee) is expensed.
Answer (A) is incorrect. The amount of $4,000,000 is the carrying amount of Minor's identifiable net assets. Answer (B) is incorrect. The amount of $5,000,000 is the fair value of Minor's identifiable net assets. Answer (D) is incorrect. The amount of $8,800,000 includes the preferred stock issued as a finder's fee.

24.4.3. On August 31, Planar Corp. exchanged 100,000 shares of its $40 par value common stock for all of the net assets of Sistrock Co. The fair value of Planar's common stock on August 31 was $72 per share. Planar paid a fee of $320,000 to the consultant who arranged this acquisition. Direct costs of registering and issuing the equity securities amounted to $160,000. No goodwill or bargain purchase was involved in the acquisition. At what amount should Planar record the acquisition of Sistrock's net assets?

A. $7,200,000

B. $7,360,000

C. $7,520,000

D. $7,680,000

Answer (A) is correct. *(CPA, adapted)*
REQUIRED: The fair value of the net assets acquired.
DISCUSSION: Acquisition-related costs, such as the $320,000 consultant's fee, are expensed as incurred. But exceptions are made for direct issue costs of securities accounted for under other GAAP. Thus, the direct issue costs of equity ($160,000) are debited to additional paid-in capital. The consideration transferred is measured at its fair value of $7,200,000 (100,000 shares of common stock issued × $72). Given that no goodwill or bargain purchase was involved, neither goodwill nor a gain is recognized. Consequently, the identifiable assets acquired and liabilities assumed are recorded at their net amount of $7,200,000. The journal entries are

Investment in Sistrock (100,000 × $72)	$7,200,000	
Common stock (100,000 × $40)		$4,000,000
Additional paid-in capital (difference)		3,200,000
Business combination expense	$ 320,000	
Additional paid-in capital	160,000	
Cash		$ 480,000

Answer (B) is incorrect. The fair value of the net assets acquired plus the registration and issuance costs equals $7,360,000. Answer (C) is incorrect. The fair value of the net assets acquired plus the consultant's fee equals $7,520,000. Answer (D) is incorrect. The fair value of the net assets acquired plus the registration and issuance costs and the consultant's fee equals $7,680,000.

24.4.4. The following costs were incurred by the acquirer in business combinations:

Legal fees	$ 3,000,000
Cost of an internal acquisitions department	10,000,000
Issuance cost of debt securities	180,000

Which costs related to effecting business combinations are expensed in full by the controlled group for the period in which they are incurred?

A. $180,000

B. $3,180,000

C. $13,000,000

D. $13,180,000

Answer (C) is correct. *(Publisher, adapted)*
REQUIRED: The amount of costs related to business combinations that are fully expensed.
DISCUSSION: Acquisition-related costs, such as finder's fees, professional and consulting fees, and general administrative costs (e.g., for an acquisitions department), are expensed as incurred. The one exception is for issuance costs of debt or equity securities. These are accounted for under other GAAP. Issue costs of debt should be reported in the balance sheet as a direct deduction from the face amount of the debt and amortized over the life of the debt using the interest method. They are not commingled with premium or discount. Thus, the amount expensed as incurred is $13,000,000 ($3,000,000 + $10,000,000).
Answer (A) is incorrect. Costs to register and issue debt securities are reported as a deferred charge and amortized over the life of the debt using the interest method. Answer (B) is incorrect. The amount of $3,180,000 results from failing to include the cost of the acquisitions department and from improperly including the cost of the debt securities. Answer (D) is incorrect. The amount of $13,180,000 results from improperly including the cost of issuing the debt securities.

24.4.5. Bale Co. incurred $100,000 of acquisition costs related to the purchase of the net assets of Dixon Co. The $100,000 should be

A. Allocated on a pro rata basis to the nonmonetary assets acquired.

B. Capitalized as part of goodwill and tested annually for impairment.

C. Capitalized as an other asset and amortized over 5 years.

D. Expensed as incurred in the current period.

Answer (D) is correct. *(CPA, adapted)*
REQUIRED: The accounting for acquisition costs of a purchase of net assets.
DISCUSSION: In a business combination, acquisition-related costs, such as finder's fees, professional and consulting fees, and general administrative costs, are expensed as incurred. If this transaction were an acquisition of a group of assets (and not a business combination), the direct acquisition costs would be allocated on a pro rata basis to the assets acquired.
Answer (A) is incorrect. Acquisition-related costs, such as finder's fees, professional and consulting fees, and general administrative costs, are expensed as incurred. Answer (B) is incorrect. Acquisition-related costs, such as finder's fees, professional and consulting fees, and general administrative costs, are expensed as incurred. Answer (C) is incorrect. Acquisition-related costs, such as finder's fees, professional and consulting fees, and general administrative costs, are expensed as incurred.

24.5 Consolidated Reporting

24.5.1. When a parent-subsidiary relationship exists, consolidated financial statements are prepared in recognition of the accounting concept of

- A. Reliability.
- B. Materiality.
- C. Legal entity.
- D. Economic entity.

Answer (D) is correct. *(CPA, adapted)*
REQUIRED: The accounting concept recognized in consolidated financial statements.
DISCUSSION: Consolidated financial statements should reflect the economic activities of an entity measured without regard to the boundaries of the legal entity. Accounting information pertains to an entity, the boundaries of which are not necessarily those of the legal entity. For instance, a parent and subsidiary are legally separate but are treated as a single entity in consolidated statements.
Answer (A) is incorrect. Reliability reflects the quality of information assuring that it is reasonably free from error and bias and faithfully represents what it purports to represent. Answer (B) is incorrect. Materiality requires reporting of information that has a value significant enough to affect decisions of those using the financial statements. Answer (C) is incorrect. The boundaries of the legal entity are disregarded in the preparation of consolidated financial statements.

24.5.2. A parent need not consolidate a subsidiary for financial reporting purposes if

- A. The subsidiary's operations differ greatly from those of the parent.
- B. The subsidiary operates in a country different from that of the parent.
- C. A noncontrolling interest holds 45% of the subsidiary's outstanding common stock.
- D. It is in legal reorganization.

Answer (D) is correct. *(N. Powell)*
REQUIRED: The exception to mandatory consolidation.
DISCUSSION: A parent is defined as an entity that holds a controlling financial interest in a subsidiary. The usual condition for a controlling financial interest is a majority voting interest. Thus, consolidation of all majority-owned subsidiaries ordinarily is required unless control does not rest with the majority owner. Circumstances in which control does not rest with the majority owner include when the subsidiary is (1) in bankruptcy, (2) in legal reorganization, or (3) subject to severe government-imposed uncertainties.
Answer (A) is incorrect. Whether the subsidiary's operations differ greatly from those of the parent does not affect the consolidation requirements. Answer (B) is incorrect. Whether the subsidiary operates in a country different from that of the parent does not affect the consolidation requirements. Answer (C) is incorrect. A noncontrolling interest does not prevent the need for consolidation.

24.5.3. Which subsidiary is most likely to meet the criteria for mandatory consolidation?

- A. A 55%-owned subsidiary in bankruptcy.
- B. A 49%-owned domestic subsidiary.
- C. A 51%-owned foreign subsidiary.
- D. A 90%-owned subsidiary subject to severe governmentally imposed uncertainties.

Answer (C) is correct. *(Publisher, adapted)*
REQUIRED: The subsidiary most likely to be consolidated.
DISCUSSION: All entities in which a parent has a controlling financial interest through direct or indirect ownership of a majority voting interest ordinarily must be consolidated. However, a subsidiary is not consolidated when control does not rest with the majority owner. Circumstances in which control does not rest with the majority owners include when the subsidiary is (1) in bankruptcy, (2) in legal reorganization, or (3) subject to foreign exchange restrictions or other government imposed restrictions that preclude exercise of control.
Answer (A) is incorrect. The majority-owned subsidiary is in bankruptcy. Answer (B) is incorrect. Over 50% of the outstanding voting interests are not owned by this investor. Answer (D) is incorrect. The government-imposed restrictions preclude exercise of control.

24.5.4. Consolidated financial statements are typically prepared when one entity has a majority voting interest in another unless

- A. The subsidiary is a finance entity.
- B. The fiscal year ends of the two entities are more than 3 months apart.
- C. Control does not rest with the majority owner(s).
- D. The two entities are in unrelated industries, such as manufacturing and real estate.

Answer (C) is correct. *(CPA, adapted)*
REQUIRED: The circumstance in which a majority-owned entity is not consolidated.
DISCUSSION: Consolidated financial reporting is required when one entity owns, directly or indirectly, more than 50% of the outstanding voting interests of another entity. However, a majority-owned subsidiary is not consolidated if control does not rest with the majority owner.
Answer (A) is incorrect. The nature of the subsidiary's business is irrelevant. Answer (B) is incorrect. A difference in fiscal periods is irrelevant. Answer (D) is incorrect. Whether the parent and subsidiary are in related industries is irrelevant.

24.5.5. According to GAAP relative to consolidation of variable interest entities,

A. A not-for-profit organization may not be treated as a variable interest entity.

B. A variable interest entity has an equity investment of more than 10% of its total assets.

C. A variable interest entity is consolidated by its primary beneficiary when the beneficiary becomes involved with the entity.

D. Corporations may not be organized as variable interest entities.

Answer (C) is correct. *(Publisher, adapted)*
REQUIRED: The true statement about VIEs.
DISCUSSION: In essence, a variable interest entity (VIE) is any legal structure (including, but not limited to, those previously described as special-purpose entities) with insufficient equity investment or whose equity investors lack one of the essential characteristics of financial control. When an entity becomes involved with a VIE, it must determine whether it is the primary beneficiary and therefore must consolidate the VIE. A primary beneficiary holds a variable interest(s) that will absorb a majority of the VIE's expected losses or receive a majority of its expected residual returns (or both).
Answer (A) is incorrect. The guidance for VIEs applies to NPOs if they are used to avoid the requirements of GAAP. Answer (B) is incorrect. An entity qualifies as a VIE if the equity at risk does not suffice to finance entity activities without additional subordinated financial support. An equity investment of less than 10% of total assets is usually considered to be insufficient. But a greater investment also may not suffice if, for example, assets or entity activities are high risk. Answer (D) is incorrect. A VIE may take any form.

24.6 Consolidated Reporting -- Balance Sheet

24.6.1. Pent Corp. acquired 100% of Subtle Corp.'s outstanding capital stock for $890,000 cash. Immediately before the acquisition, the balance sheets of both corporations reported the following:

	Pent	Subtle
Assets	$4,000,000	$1,500,000
Liabilities	$1,400,000	$ 720,000
Common stock	2,000,000	620,000
Retained earnings	500,000	80,000
Accumulated other comprehensive income	100,000	80,000
Liabilities and equity	$4,000,000	$1,500,000

At the date of purchase, the fair value of Subtle's assets was $100,000 more than the aggregate carrying amounts. In the consolidated balance sheet prepared immediately after the purchase, the consolidated equity should equal

A. $3,490,000

B. $3,480,000

C. $3,380,000

D. $2,600,000

Answer (D) is correct. *(CPA, adapted)*
REQUIRED: The consolidated equity after the purchase.
DISCUSSION: A business combination is an acquisition of net assets, and the subsidiary's equity balances are not included. Thus, in the absence of a bargain purchase and NCIs, total equity of the consolidated entity immediately after acquisition is the same as the total equity of the parent. Consequently, equity reported in the consolidated balance sheet prepared immediately after the acquisition of Subtle by Pent is $2,600,000 ($2,000,000 common stock + $500,000 retained earnings + $100,000 accumulated OCI).
Answer (A) is incorrect. The sum of the equity of Pent plus the cash price is $3,490,000. Answer (B) is incorrect. The sum of the equity of Pent and Subtle plus the excess fair value of Subtle's assets is $3,480,000. Answer (C) is incorrect. The sum of the equity of Pent and Subtle is $3,380,000.

Questions 24.6.2 through 24.6.6 are based on the following information. On January 2, Parma borrowed $60,000 and used the proceeds to purchase 90% of the outstanding common shares of Seville. Parma had no prior equity interest in Seville. Ten equal principal and interest payments begin December 30. The excess of the implied fair value of Seville over the carrying amount of its identifiable net assets should be assigned 60% to inventory and 40% to goodwill. Moreover, the fair value of the noncontrolling interest (NCI) is 10% of the implied fair value of the acquiree.

The following are the balance sheets of Parma and Seville on January 1:

	Parma	Seville
Current assets	$ 70,000	$20,000
Noncurrent assets	90,000	40,000
Total assets	$160,000	$60,000
Current liabilities	$ 30,000	$10,000
Noncurrent liabilities	50,000	--
Equity	80,000	50,000
Total liabilities and equity	$160,000	$60,000

24.6.2. On Parma's January 2 consolidated balance sheet, current assets equal

A. $100,000

B. $96,000

C. $90,000

D. $80,000

Answer (A) is correct. *(CPA, adapted)*
REQUIRED: The consolidated current assets.
DISCUSSION: The implied fair value of the subsidiary is $66,667 ($60,000 cash paid by the parent ÷ 90%). The excess of this amount over the carrying amount of the subsidiary's identifiable net assets is $16,667 ($66,667 – $50,000). This amount is allocated $10,000 to inventory ($16,667 × 60%) and $6,667 to goodwill ($16,667 × 40%). Thus, the reported amount of the current assets is $100,000.

Current assets of Parma	$ 70,000
Current assets of Seville	20,000
Understatement of inventory	10,000
Consolidated current assets	$100,000

Answer (B) is incorrect. The amount of $96,000 assumes an assignment of $6,000 to inventory. Answer (C) is incorrect. The amount of $90,000 ignores the $10,000 excess of the fair value of inventory over its carrying amount. Answer (D) is incorrect. The amount of $80,000 excludes the carrying amount of Seville's current assets.

24.6.3. On Parma's January 2 consolidated balance sheet, noncurrent assets equal

A. $130,000

B. $134,000

C. $136,667

D. $140,000

Answer (C) is correct. *(CPA, adapted)*
REQUIRED: The consolidated noncurrent assets.
DISCUSSION: The implied fair value of the subsidiary is $66,667 ($60,000 cash paid by the parent ÷ 90%). The excess of this amount over the carrying amount of the subsidiary's identifiable net assets is $16,667 ($66,667 – $50,000). This amount is allocated $10,000 to inventory ($16,667 × 60%) and $6,667 to goodwill ($16,667 × 40%). Thus, reported noncurrent assets equal $136,667.

Noncurrent assets of Parma	$ 90,000
Noncurrent assets of Seville	40,000
Goodwill	6,667
Consolidated noncurrent assets	$136,667

Answer (A) is incorrect. The amount of $130,000 ignores goodwill. Answer (B) is incorrect. The amount of $134,000 assumes that a 100% interest was acquired and that goodwill was therefore $4,000 [($60,000 – $50,000) × 40%]. Answer (D) is incorrect. The amount of $140,000 assumes that a 100% interest was acquired and that goodwill was $10,000.

24.6.4. On Parma's January 2 consolidated balance sheet, current liabilities equal

A. $50,000

B. $46,000

C. $40,000

D. $30,000

Answer (B) is correct. *(CPA, adapted)*
    REQUIRED: The consolidated current liabilities.
    DISCUSSION: Consolidated current liabilities contain the current portion of the debt issued by Parma to finance the acquisition ($60,000 ÷ 10 equal principal payments = $6,000). Reported current liabilities equal $46,000.

Current liabilities of Parma	$30,000
Current liabilities of Seville	10,000
Current component of new debt	6,000
Consolidated current liabilities	$46,000

Answer (A) is incorrect. The pre-existing noncurrent debt is $50,000. Answer (C) is incorrect. The amount of $40,000 ignores the new borrowing. Answer (D) is incorrect. The amount of Parma's pre-existing current liabilities is $30,000.

24.6.5. On Parma's January 2 consolidated balance sheet, the sum of the noncurrent liabilities and the NCI equal

A. $116,667

B. $110,667

C. $104,000

D. $50,000

Answer (B) is correct. *(CPA, adapted)*
    REQUIRED: The sum of the noncurrent liabilities and the NCI.
    DISCUSSION: Consolidated noncurrent liabilities include the noncurrent portion of the debt issued by Parma to finance the acquisition ($60,000 – $6,000 = $54,000). Thus, reported noncurrent liabilities equal $104,000.

Noncurrent liabilities of Parma	$ 50,000
Noncurrent component of new debt	54,000
Consolidated noncurrent liabilities	$104,000

The implied fair value of the subsidiary is $66,667 ($60,000 cash paid by the parent ÷ 90%), and the NCI is $6,667 ($66,667 × 10%). The sum of the noncurrent liabilities and the NCI is therefore $110,667 ($104,000 + $6,667).
    Answer (A) is incorrect. The amount of $116,667 is the sum of noncurrent liabilities (excluding the new borrowing) and the implied fair value of the subsidiary. Answer (C) is incorrect. The amount of $104,000 omits the NCI. Answer (D) is incorrect. The amount of $50,000 ignores the new borrowing and the NCI.

24.6.6. On Parma's January 2 consolidated balance sheet, Parma's shareholders' equity should be

A. $80,000

B. $86,667

C. $90,000

D. $130,000

Answer (A) is correct. *(CPA, adapted)*
    REQUIRED: The equity in the consolidated balance sheet.
    DISCUSSION: In the absence of a bargain purchase, the total equity of the consolidated entity immediately after acquisition is the equity of the parent just prior to acquisition plus the fair value of the NCI. An NCI is the equity in a subsidiary not attributable to the parent. Thus, the portion of the total consolidated equity that is attributable to the shareholders of the parent (Parma) equals the parent's (Parma's) equity just prior to the acquisition of $80,000.
    Answer (B) is incorrect. Parma's equity at 1/1 plus the fair value of the noncontrolling interest equals $86,667. Answer (C) is incorrect. The total liabilities of the two entities at 1/1 equal $90,000. Answer (D) is incorrect. The sum of the equity amounts for Parma and Seville at 1/1 is $130,000.

Questions 24.6.7 through 24.6.9 are based on the following information. The separate condensed balance sheets and income statements of Pater Corp. and its wholly owned subsidiary, Subito Corp., are as follows:

BALANCE SHEETS
As of December 31

	Pater	Subito
Assets		
Current assets		
Cash	$ 80,000	$ 60,000
Accounts receivable (net)	140,000	25,000
Inventories	90,000	50,000
Total current assets	$ 310,000	$135,000
Property, plant, and equipment (net)	515,000	280,000
Intangible assets	100,000	--
Investment in Subito (equity method)	400,000	--
Total assets	$1,325,000	$415,000
Liabilities and Equity		
Current liabilities		
Accounts payable	$ 160,000	$ 95,000
Accrued liabilities	110,000	30,000
Total current liabilities	$ 270,000	$125,000
Equity		
Common stock ($10 par)	$ 300,000	$ 50,000
Additional paid-in capital		10,000
Retained earnings	755,000	230,000
Total equity	$1,055,000	$290,000
Total liabilities and equity	$1,325,000	$415,000

INCOME STATEMENTS
For the Year Ended December 31

	Pater	Subito
Sales	$2,000,000	$750,000
Cost of goods sold	1,540,000	500,000
Gross margin	$ 460,000	$250,000
Operating expenses	260,000	150,000
Operating income	$ 200,000	$100,000
Equity in earnings of Subito	70,000	--
Income before income taxes	$ 270,000	$100,000
Provision for income taxes	70,000	30,000
Net income	$ 200,000	$ 70,000

Additional Information:

- On January 1, Pater purchased for $360,000 all of Subito's $10 par, voting common stock. On January 1, the fair value of Subito's assets and liabilities equaled their carrying amounts of $410,000 and $160,000, respectively, except that the fair values of certain items in Subito's inventory were $10,000 more than their carrying amounts. These items were still on hand on December 31. Pater amortizes intangible assets over a 10-year period.

- During the year, Pater and Subito paid cash dividends of $100,000 and $30,000, respectively. For tax purposes, Pater receives the 100% exclusion for dividends received from Subito.

- There were no intraentity transactions, except for Pater's receipt of dividends from Subito and Pater's recording of its share of Subito's earnings.

- No transactions affected other comprehensive income.

- Both Pater and Subito paid income taxes at the rate of 30%.

- Pater treats Subito as a reporting unit, and all goodwill acquired in the business combination is assigned to Subito for the purpose of testing impairment. However, goodwill was not impaired on December 31.

- Assume that the consolidation did not affect the net incomes of Pater and Subito.

24.6.7. In the December 31 consolidated financial statements of Pater and its subsidiary, total current assets should be

A. $455,000

B. $445,000

C. $310,000

D. $135,000

Answer (A) is correct. *(CPA, adapted)*
REQUIRED: The total current assets.
DISCUSSION: Consolidated current assets are calculated as follows:

Current assets of Pater	$310,000
Current assets of Subito	135,000
Undervalued inventory	10,000
Consolidated current assets	$455,000

Answer (B) is incorrect. The amount of $445,000 does not reflect the fair value of the inventory. Answer (C) is incorrect. The parent's current assets equal $310,000. Answer (D) is incorrect. The unadjusted current assets of the subsidiary equal $135,000.

24.6.8. In the December 31 consolidated financial statements of Pater and its subsidiary, total assets should be

A. $1,740,000

B. $1,450,000

C. $1,350,000

D. $1,325,000

Answer (B) is correct. *(CPA, adapted)*
REQUIRED: The total assets.
DISCUSSION: Goodwill is the excess of (1) the sum of the acquisition-date fair values (with some exceptions) of (a) the consideration transferred, (b) any NCI in the acquiree, and (c) the acquirer's previously held equity interest in the acquiree over (2) the net of the acquisition-date fair values (with some exceptions) of the identifiable assets acquired and liabilities assumed. Goodwill is therefore $100,000.

Consideration transferred	$360,000
Carrying amount of net assets acquired	(250,000)
Undervaluation of inventory	(10,000)
Goodwill	$100,000

December 31 consolidated total assets are calculated as follows:

Assets of Pater	$1,325,000
Assets of Subito	415,000
Investment in Subito	(400,000)
Undervalued inventory	10,000
Goodwill	100,000
Consolidated total assets	$1,450,000

Answer (A) is incorrect. The unadjusted sum of the assets of Pater and Subito is $1,740,000. Answer (C) is incorrect. The amount of $1,350,000 excludes goodwill. Answer (D) is incorrect. The parent's total assets equal $1,325,000.

24.6.9. In the December 31 consolidated financial statements of Pater and its subsidiary, total retained earnings should be

A. $985,000

B. $825,000

C. $795,000

D. $755,000

Answer (D) is correct. *(CPA, adapted)*
REQUIRED: The total retained earnings.
DISCUSSION: Pater acquired Subito in a business combination and properly accounts for the investment in its separate statements using the equity method. Subito's separate net income for the year is reflected in full in consolidated net income and in Pater's retained earnings. It is given that the consolidation did not affect Subito's separate net income. Thus, consolidated retained earnings consist only of Pater's $755,000 of retained earnings.
Answer (A) is incorrect. The amount of $985,000 includes the subsidiary's retained earnings. Answer (B) is incorrect. The amount of $825,000 includes the subsidiary's net income, an amount already reflected in the parent's retained earnings under the equity method. Answer (C) is incorrect. The amount of $795,000 includes the subsidiary's net income minus the dividends paid, an amount already accounted for using the equity method.

24.6.10. On December 31, Poe Corporation exchanged 200,000 shares of its $10 par common stock, with a market price of $18 per share, for all of Saxe Corporation's common stock. The equity section of each entity's balance sheet immediately before the combination is presented below:

	Poe	Saxe
Common stock	$3,000,000	$1,500,000
Additional paid-in capital	1,300,000	150,000
Retained earnings	2,500,000	850,000
Totals	$6,800,000	$2,500,000

In the December 31 consolidated balance sheet, additional paid-in capital should be reported at

A. $950,000

B. $1,300,000

C. $1,450,000

D. $2,900,000

Answer (D) is correct. *(CPA, adapted)*
REQUIRED: The additional paid-in capital to be reported in the consolidated balance sheet.
DISCUSSION: A business combination is an acquisition of net assets, and the subsidiary's equity accounts are eliminated. Thus, the additional paid-in capital of $2,900,000 after acquisition is the acquirer's before the acquisition plus the additional paid-in capital from the new issuance of stock {$1,300,000 + [200,000 × ($18 – $10)]}.
Answer (A) is incorrect. The amount of $950,000 is the additional paid-in capital reported under the pooling-of-interests method, a method no longer applied to business combinations. Answer (B) is incorrect. The amount reported by the acquirer immediately before the combination is $1,300,000. Answer (C) is incorrect. The amount of $1,450,000 is the sum of the amounts reported by the acquirer and acquiree immediately before the combination.

Questions 24.6.11 and 24.6.12 are based on the following information. On January 1, Pathan Corp. purchased 80% of Samoa Corp.'s $10 par common stock for $975,000. Pathan had no prior equity interest in Samoa. The remaining 20% of this stock is held by NCI Co., an unrelated party. On the acquisition date for this business combination, the carrying amount of Samoa's net assets was $1 million. The fair values of the assets acquired and liabilities assumed were the same as their carrying amounts on Samoa's balance sheet except for plant assets (net), the fair value of which was $100,000 in excess of the carrying amount. The fair value of the noncontrolling interest (NCI) is 20% of the implied fair value of the acquiree's net assets at the acquisition date. (No exceptions to the recognition or measurement principles apply.) For the year ended December 31, Samoa's net income included in consolidated net income was $190,000, and Samoa paid cash dividends totaling $125,000.

24.6.11. In the December 31 consolidated balance sheet, the NCI is reported at

A. $200,000

B. $213,000

C. $243,750

D. $256,750

Answer (D) is correct. *(CPA, adapted)*

REQUIRED: The amount of the NCI at year end.

DISCUSSION: An NCI is the equity of a subsidiary not directly or indirectly attributable to the parent. Thus, the NCI is equal to the 20% (100% – 80%) interest in Samoa not held by Pathan. The fair value of the NCI at the acquisition date was $243,750 [($975,000 ÷ 80%) implied fair value of acquiree × 20%]. The NCI to be reported in the year-end balance sheet equals its fair value at the beginning of the year, plus 20% of the net income, minus 20% of the dividends. Thus, the NCI is reported at $256,750.

Fair value on 1/1	$243,750
NCI in subsidiary's net income included in consolidated net income ($190,000 × 20%)	38,000
NCI in subsidiary's dividends paid ($125,000 × 20%)	(25,000)
Noncontrolling interest at 12/31	$256,750

Answer (A) is incorrect. The amount of $200,000 equals 20% of the carrying amount of Samoa's net assets on 1/1. Answer (B) is incorrect. The amount of $213,000 equals 20% of the carrying amount of the net assets on 1/1, plus 20% of net income, minus 20% of dividends. Answer (C) is incorrect. The NCI measured at fair value at 1/1 was $243,750.

24.6.12. The goodwill recognized by Pathan at the date of the business combination is

A. $0

B. $98,750

C. $118,750

D. $243,750

Answer (C) is correct. *(CPA, adapted)*

REQUIRED: The initial goodwill recognized.

DISCUSSION: Goodwill is the excess of (1) the sum of the acquisition-date fair values of (a) the consideration transferred, (b) any NCI in the acquiree, and (c) the acquirer's previously held equity interest in the acquiree over (2) the net of the acquisition-date fair values of the identifiable assets acquired and liabilities assumed.

Consideration transferred		$ 975,000
NCI [($975,000 ÷ 80%) × 20%]		243,750
Acquisition-date fair value of net assets acquired:		
Carrying amount:	$1,000,000	
Understatement of plant assets:	100,000	(1,100,000)
Goodwill		$ 118,750

Answer (A) is incorrect. The sum of the acquisition-date fair values of the consideration transferred and the NCI (the acquirer had no previously held equity interest in the acquiree) exceeds the net of the acquisition-date fair values of the identifiable assets acquired and liabilities assumed (no exceptions to the recognition and measurement principles apply). Answer (B) is incorrect. The amount of $98,750 equals $118,750 minus 20% of $100,000. Answer (D) is incorrect. The amount of $243,750 is the acquisition-date fair value of the NCI.

24.6.13. Rowe, Inc., owns 80% of Cowan Co.'s outstanding capital stock. On November 1, Rowe advanced $100,000 in cash to Cowan. What amount should be reported related to the advance in Rowe's consolidated balance sheet as of December 31?

A. $0

B. $20,000

C. $80,000

D. $100,000

Answer (A) is correct. *(CPA, adapted)*
REQUIRED: The amount reported related to an advance to a subsidiary.
DISCUSSION: Because consolidated statements present amounts for the parent and subsidiary as if they were one economic entity, the effects of intraentity transactions must be eliminated. Thus, reciprocal balances, e.g., a receivable and a payable for an advance, between the parent and subsidiary are eliminated in full. This procedure is followed even if a noncontrolling interest exists. Accordingly, no amount for the advance is reported in the consolidated statements.
Answer (B) is incorrect. The amount of $20,000 is based on the assumption that a portion of the transaction is allocated to the noncontrolling interest. Answer (C) is incorrect. The amount of $80,000 is based on the assumption that only the portion of the transaction allocated to the noncontrolling interest is eliminated. Answer (D) is incorrect. The amount of $100,000 is based on the assumption that the transaction was with an external party.

24.7 Consolidated Reporting -- Net Income and Retained Earnings

24.7.1. To effect a business combination, Proper Co. acquired all the outstanding common shares of Scapula Co., a business entity, for cash equal to the carrying amount of Scapula's net assets. The carrying amounts of Scapula's assets and liabilities approximated their fair values at the acquisition date, except that the carrying amount of its building was more than fair value. In preparing Proper's year-end consolidated income statement, what is the effect of recording the assets acquired and liabilities assumed at fair value, and should goodwill amortization be recognized?

	Depreciation Expense	Goodwill Amortization
A.	Lower	Yes
B.	Higher	Yes
C.	Lower	No
D.	Higher	No

Answer (C) is correct. *(CPA, adapted)*
REQUIRED: The effects of the combination on depreciation and goodwill amortization.
DISCUSSION: A business combination is accounted for as an acquisition. Under the acquisition method, the entry recording the transaction is based on the fair values exchanged. Accordingly, the identifiable assets acquired and liabilities assumed ordinarily are recorded at their acquisition-date fair values. The differences between those fair values and carrying amounts will affect net income when related expenses are incurred. The effect of recording the building at fair value in the consolidated balance sheet instead of its higher carrying amount on Scapula's books will be to decrease future depreciation. Goodwill is the excess of (1) the sum of the acquisition-date fair values of (a) the consideration transferred, (b) any noncontrolling interest in the acquiree, and (c) the acquirer's previously held equity interest in the acquiree over (2) the net of the acquisition-date fair values of the identifiable assets acquired and liabilities assumed. Thus, Proper recognizes goodwill for the excess of the cash paid over the fair value of the net assets acquired (given an acquisition of 100% of Scapula's common shares). This amount will be tested for impairment, not amortized.
Answer (A) is incorrect. Goodwill will be recognized but not amortized. Answer (B) is incorrect. Depreciation will decrease, and goodwill will be recognized but not amortized. Answer (D) is incorrect. Depreciation will decrease.

24.7.2. Jane Co. owns 90% of the common stock of Dun Corp. and 100% of the common stock of Beech Corp. On December 30, Dun and Beech each declared a cash dividend of $100,000 for the current year. What is the total amount of dividends that should be reported in the December 31 consolidated financial statements of Jane and its subsidiaries, Dun and Beech?

A. $10,000

B. $100,000

C. $190,000

D. $200,000

Answer (A) is correct. *(CPA, adapted)*
REQUIRED: The total dividends reported in the consolidated financial statements.
DISCUSSION: The only dividends declared by the subsidiaries that are reported are those paid to noncontrolling interests. Beech has no NCIs because the parent (Jane) owns 100% of its shares. Accordingly, the dividends reported equal $10,000 ($100,000 declared by Dun × 10% noncontrolling ownership interest in Dun).
Answer (B) is incorrect. The amount of $100,000 is the amount declared by Dun or Beech. Answer (C) is incorrect. The amount of $190,000 is the amount eliminated in the consolidation. Answer (D) is incorrect. The amount of $200,000 is the total declared by Dun and Beech.

24.7.3. A 70%-owned subsidiary declares and pays a cash dividend. What effect does the dividend have on the retained earnings and noncontrolling interest balances in the consolidated balance sheet?

A. No effect on either retained earnings or the noncontrolling interest.

B. No effect on retained earnings and a decrease in the noncontrolling interest.

C. Decreases in both retained earnings and the noncontrolling interest.

D. A decrease in retained earnings and no effect on the noncontrolling interest.

Answer (B) is correct. *(CPA, adapted)*
REQUIRED: The effect of payment of a cash dividend by a subsidiary.
DISCUSSION: The parent's investment in subsidiary, intraentity dividends, and the subsidiary's equity accounts, which include retained earnings, are among the eliminations in a consolidation. The equity (net assets) of the subsidiary not directly or indirectly attributable to the parent is reported separately in consolidated equity as the noncontrolling interest. Consolidated retained earnings equals the accumulated earnings of the consolidated group not distributed to the owners of, or capitalized by, the parent. Thus, it equals the parent's retained earnings. Accordingly, the subsidiary's cash dividend reduces retained earnings reported in the subsidiary-only statements and the noncontrolling interest reported in the consolidated statements. But it does not affect consolidated retained earnings.
Answer (A) is incorrect. Cash dividends from a subsidiary decrease the noncontrolling interest. Answer (C) is incorrect. Cash dividends from a subsidiary have no effect on consolidated retained earnings but decrease the noncontrolling interest. Answer (D) is incorrect. Cash dividends from a subsidiary have no effect on consolidated retained earnings.

24.7.4. On January 1, Year 4, Pane Corp. exchanged 150,000 shares of its $20 par value common stock for all of Sky Corp.'s common stock. At that date, the fair value of Pane's common stock issued was equal to the fair value of the identifiable assets acquired and liabilities assumed. Both corporations continued to operate as separate businesses, maintaining accounting records with years ending December 31. In its separate statements, Pane accounts for the investment using the equity method. Information from separate company operations follows:

	Pane	Sky
Retained earnings – 12/31/Yr 3	$3,200,000	$925,000
Dividends paid – 3/25/Yr 4	750,000	200,000

If consolidated net income was $800,000, what amount of retained earnings should Pane report in its December 31, Year 4, consolidated balance sheet?

A. $4,925,000

B. $4,125,000

C. $3,050,000

D. $3,250,000

Answer (D) is correct. *(CPA, adapted)*
REQUIRED: The consolidated retained earnings.
DISCUSSION: Retained earnings of the consolidated entity at the acquisition date consist solely of the retained earnings of the parent. The consolidated entity does not report any equity amounts of the subsidiary. Retained earnings of the consolidated entity at the reporting date consist of acquisition-date retained earnings, plus consolidated net income (no NCI exists), minus consolidated dividends paid. Sky's dividends, if any, are paid solely to Pane. Thus, consolidated dividends (those paid outside the entity) consist entirely of those paid by Pane.

Acquisition-date retained earnings of Pane	$3,200,000
Consolidated net income since acquisition date	800,000
Consolidated dividends paid since acquisition date	(750,000)
Consolidated retained earnings at reporting date	$3,250,000

Answer (A) is incorrect. The amount of $4,925,000 includes Sky's retained earnings at 12/31/Yr 3 and does not reflect an adjustment for the dividends paid. Answer (B) is incorrect. The amount of $4,125,000 is the sum of the retained earnings of Pane and Sky at 12/31/Yr 3. Answer (C) is incorrect. The amount of $3,050,000 results from treating Sky's dividends as consolidated dividends.

Question 24.7.5 is based on the following information. The separate condensed balance sheets and income statements of Pater Corp. and its wholly owned subsidiary, Subito Corp., are as follows:

BALANCE SHEETS
As of December 31

Assets	Pater	Subito
Current assets		
Cash	$ 80,000	$ 60,000
Accounts receivable (net)	140,000	25,000
Inventories	90,000	50,000
Total current assets	$ 310,000	$135,000
Property, plant, and equipment (net)	515,000	280,000
Intangible assets	100,000	--
Investment in Subito (equity method)	400,000	--
Total assets	$1,325,000	$415,000
Liabilities and Equity		
Current liabilities		
Accounts payable	$ 160,000	$ 95,000
Accrued liabilities	110,000	30,000
Total current liabilities	$ 270,000	$125,000
Equity		
Common stock ($10 par)	$ 300,000	$ 50,000
Additional paid-in capital		10,000
Retained earnings	755,000	230,000
Total equity	$1,055,000	$290,000
Total liabilities and equity	$1,325,000	$415,000

INCOME STATEMENTS
For the Year Ended December 31

	Pater	Subito
Sales	$2,000,000	$750,000
Cost of goods sold	1,540,000	500,000
Gross margin	$ 460,000	$250,000
Operating expenses	260,000	150,000
Operating income	$ 200,000	$100,000
Equity in earnings of Subito	70,000	--
Income before income taxes	$ 270,000	$100,000
Provision for income taxes	70,000	30,000
Net income	$ 200,000	$ 70,000

Additional Information:

- On January 1, Pater purchased for $360,000 all of Subito's $10 par, voting common stock. On January 1, the fair value of Subito's assets and liabilities equaled their carrying amounts of $410,000 and $160,000, respectively. Pater amortizes intangible assets over a 10-year period.

- During the year, Pater and Subito paid cash dividends of $100,000 and $30,000, respectively. For tax purposes, Pater receives the 100% exclusion for dividends received from Subito.

- There were no intraentity transactions, except for Pater's receipt of dividends from Subito and Pater's recording of its share of Subito's earnings.

- No transactions affected other comprehensive income.

- Both Pater and Subito paid income taxes at the rate of 30%.

- Pater treats Subito as a reporting unit, and all goodwill acquired in the business combination is assigned to Subito for the purpose of testing impairment. However, goodwill was not impaired on December 31.

- Assume that no eliminations or adjustments in the consolidation procedure affect the amount of Pater's or Subito's net income included in consolidated net income.

24.7.5. In the December 31 consolidated financial statements of Pater and its subsidiary, net income should be

A. $270,000

B. $200,000

C. $190,000

D. $170,000

Answer (B) is correct. *(CPA, adapted)*
REQUIRED: The consolidated net income.
DISCUSSION: Because Pater owns 100% of Subito, all of Subito's net income for the period since acquisition is included in Pater's separate net income. Also, given that no eliminations or adjustments affect the separate net income of Pater and Subito, consolidated net income for the year is $200,000.

Answer (A) is incorrect. The sum of the net incomes of Pater and Subito equals $270,000. Answer (C) is incorrect. Pater's net income minus goodwill amortization ($100,000 ÷ 10 years) equals $190,000. However, goodwill is tested for impairment but not amortized. Goodwill was not impaired at December 31. Answer (D) is incorrect. Pater's net income minus the dividend payment, which does not affect equity-based net income, equals $170,000.

24.7.6. On January 2 of the current year, Peace Co. paid $310,000 to purchase 75% of the voting shares of Surge Co. Surge held no shares in Peace. Peace reported retained earnings of $80,000, and Surge reported contributed capital of $300,000 and retained earnings of $100,000. The purchase differential was attributed to depreciable assets with a remaining useful life of 10 years. Peace used the equity method in accounting for its investment in Surge. Surge reported net income of $20,000 and paid dividends of $8,000 during the current year. Peace reported income, exclusive of its income from Surge, of $30,000 and paid dividends of $15,000 during the current year. What amount will Peace report as dividends declared and paid in its current year's consolidated statement of changes in equity?

A. $8,000

B. $15,000

C. $17,000

D. $23,000

Answer (C) is correct. *(CPA, adapted)*
    REQUIRED: The consolidated dividends declared and paid.
    DISCUSSION: Peace acquired a greater than 50% share of the voting interests in Surge. Accordingly, Peace must consolidate Surge unless it does not have control. Moreover, the equity method is not appropriate except in parent-only statements. The consolidated statements should report only dividends paid to parties outside the consolidated entity. Because Peace acquired only 75% of the voting shares of Surge, a 25% noncontrolling interest exists. Thus, 25% of Surge's dividends were paid to parties outside the consolidated entity. Furthermore, all of Peace's dividends were paid to parties outside of the consolidated entity. Accordingly, consolidated dividends paid are calculated as follows:

Dividends declared and paid by Peace	$15,000
Dividends declared and paid by Surge	8,000
Intraentity dividends ($8,000 × 75%)	(6,000)
Consolidated dividends declared and paid	$17,000

    Answer (A) is incorrect. The amount of $8,000 equals the dividends declared by Surge. Answer (B) is incorrect. The amount of $15,000 equals the dividends paid by Peace. Answer (D) is incorrect. The amount of $23,000 includes $6,000 of intraentity dividends.

24.7.7. Purvis Company acquired a 100% interest in Smith Company on January 1, Year 1, at a price $200,000 in excess of its carrying amount. Of this excess, $40,000 was attributable to inventory (FIFO) and $70,000 to equipment with a 5-year remaining useful life that was depreciated on the straight-line basis. The remainder was attributable to goodwill. Condensed income statements for the year for Purvis and Smith are presented below:

	Purvis	Smith
Sales	$530,000	$440,000
COGS	(80,000)	(60,000)
Depreciation	(140,000)	(80,000)
Other expenses	(156,000)	(100,000)
Investment income	146,000	-0-
Net income	$300,000	$200,000

No intraentity transactions occurred during the year, and no other eliminations or adjustments were required in the consolidation procedure. Assuming Purvis applied the equity method in its parent-only statements, at what amount should net income be included in the December 31, Year 1, consolidated income statement?

A. $200,000

B. $300,000

C. $446,000

D. $500,000

Answer (B) is correct. *(Publisher, adapted)*
    REQUIRED: The consolidated net income.
    DISCUSSION: Equity in the earnings of a subsidiary is recorded on the parent-only income statement in accordance with the equity method. Purvis has a 100% interest in Smith. Hence, it recognizes $146,000 of investment income, consisting of 100% of Smith's net income ($200,000), minus the $40,000 increase in cost of goods sold (the FIFO inventory is presumed to have been sold) and additional depreciation of $14,000 ($70,000 ÷ 5 years). Consolidated net income thus equals the parent's separate net income of $300,000.
    Answer (A) is incorrect. Smith's net income is $200,000. Answer (C) is incorrect. The amount of $446,000 results from double counting investment income. Answer (D) is incorrect. The total of Purvis's net income and Smith's net income is $500,000.

24.7.8. Parr Company acquired 80% of Syd Co. for $800,000. On the date of acquisition, September 1 of the current year, the fair value of the consideration transferred equaled 80% of the fair value and the carrying amount of the acquired net assets of Syd. Syd earned $600,000 of net income evenly throughout the calendar year and paid dividends of $90,000 on December 30. At what amount will the preacquisition earnings of Syd be included in consolidated net income for the calendar year of the acquisition?

A. $400,000

B. $320,000

C. $160,000

D. $0

Answer (D) is correct. *(Publisher, adapted)*
REQUIRED: The amount at which the preacquisition earnings will be included in consolidated net income.
DISCUSSION: When a subsidiary is initially consolidated during the year, its revenues, expenses, gains, and losses are included in the consolidated statements only from the initial consolidation date. Thus, Syd's earnings prior to September 1 are excluded from consolidated net income of the year of acquisition.
Answer (A) is incorrect. The amount of income Syd earned before the acquisition is $400,000. Answer (B) is incorrect. The amount of $320,000 is 80% of the amount of income that Syd earned before the acquisition. Answer (C) is incorrect. This amount of $160,000 is 80% of the amount of income that Syd earned after the acquisition.

24.8 Consolidated Reporting -- Intraentity Transactions

24.8.1. Wright Corp. has several subsidiaries that are included in its consolidated financial statements. In its December 31 trial balance, Wright had the following intraentity balances before eliminations:

	Debit	Credit
Current receivable due from Main Co.	$ 32,000	
Noncurrent receivable from Main Co.	114,000	
Cash advance to Corn Corp.	6,000	
Cash advance from King Co.		$ 15,000
Payable to King Co.		101,000

In its December 31 consolidated balance sheet, what amount should Wright report as intraentity receivables?

A. $152,000

B. $146,000

C. $36,000

D. $0

Answer (D) is correct. *(CPA, adapted)*
REQUIRED: The amount reported as intraentity receivables.
DISCUSSION: In a consolidated balance sheet, reciprocal balances, such as receivables and payables, between a parent and a consolidated subsidiary are eliminated in their entirety, regardless of the portion of the subsidiary's stock held by the parent. Thus, Wright should report $0 as intraentity receivables.
Answer (A) is incorrect. The amount of $152,000 includes intraentity transactions in the consolidated financial statements. Answer (B) is incorrect. The effects of intraentity transactions should be completely eliminated in consolidated financial statements. Answer (C) is incorrect. Intraentity transactions should not be netted out in the consolidated financial statements.

24.8.2. Shep Co. has a receivable from its parent, Pep Co. Should this receivable be separately reported in Shep's balance sheet and in Pep's consolidated balance sheet.

	Shep's Balance Sheet	Pep's Consolidated Balance Sheet
A.	Yes	No
B.	Yes	Yes
C.	No	No
D.	No	Yes

Answer (A) is correct. *(CPA, adapted)*
REQUIRED: The reporting of a subsidiary's receivable from its parent.
DISCUSSION: In a consolidated balance sheet, reciprocal balances, such as receivables and payables, between a parent and a consolidated subsidiary are eliminated in their entirety, regardless of the portion of the subsidiary's stock held by the parent. However, intraentity transactions should not be eliminated from the separate financial statements of the entities.
Answer (B) is incorrect. The receivable should be eliminated from the consolidated statements. Answer (C) is incorrect. The receivable should be reported on the subsidiary's balance sheet. Answer (D) is incorrect. The receivable should be eliminated from the consolidated statements but not from the subsidiary's balance sheet.

24.8.3. Parker Corp. owns 80% of Smith, Inc.'s common stock. During the year, Parker sold Smith $250,000 of inventory on the same terms as sales made to third parties. Smith sold all of the inventory purchased from Parker during the year. The following information pertains to Smith's and Parker's sales for the year:

	Parker	Smith
Sales	$1,000,000	$700,000
Cost of sales	(400,000)	(350,000)
Gross Profit	$ 600,000	$350,000

What amount should Parker report as cost of sales in its consolidated income statement?

- A. $750,000
- B. $680,000
- C. $500,000
- D. $430,000

Answer (C) is correct. *(CPA, adapted)*
REQUIRED: The cost of sales in the consolidated income statement.
DISCUSSION: In the consolidated income statement, the cost of sales must be reported at the amount as if the intraentity transaction had never occurred. Given that Smith purchased inventory from Parker for $250,000 and sold all of it during the year, $250,000 must be eliminated from consolidated cost of goods sold. Hence, the cost of sales in the consolidated income statement can be calculated as follows:

Cost of sales of Parker	$400,000
Cost of sales of Smith	350,000
Cost of sales on intraentity sales	(250,000)
Consolidated cost of sales	$500,000

Answer (A) is incorrect. This figure is the total of the amounts reported separately by Parker and Smith. Answer (B) is incorrect. This figure equals Parker's COGS plus 80% of Smith's. Answer (D) is incorrect. This figure equals Parker's COGS plus 80% of Smith's, minus $250,000.

24.8.4. Clark Co. had the following transactions with affiliated parties during the year just ended:

- Sales of $50,000 to Dean, Inc., with $20,000 gross profit. Dean had $15,000 of this inventory on hand at year-end. Clark owns a 15% interest in Dean and does not exert significant influence.

- Purchases of raw materials totaling $240,000 from Kent Corp., a wholly owned subsidiary. Kent's gross profit on the sale was $48,000. Clark had $60,000 of this inventory remaining on December 31.

Before eliminating entries, Clark had consolidated current assets of $320,000. What amount should Clark report in its December 31 consolidated balance sheet for current assets?

- A. $320,000
- B. $314,000
- C. $308,000
- D. $302,000

Answer (C) is correct. *(CPA, adapted)*
REQUIRED: The amount reported on the consolidated balance sheet for current assets.
DISCUSSION: When an investor buys inventory from an investee that is neither a consolidated subsidiary nor an equity-method investee, no adjustment for intraentity profit is made. Thus, no adjustment is made to the inventory purchased from Dean. When a parent buys inventory from a subsidiary, the inventory on the consolidated balance sheet must be adjusted to remove any intraentity profit. Hence, the inventory must be reduced by the pro rata share of intraentity profit made on the sale by Kent.

Inventory remaining on Clark's books	$60,000
Kent's gross profit percentage ($48,000 ÷ $240,000)	× 20%
Unrealized intraentity gross profit	$12,000

Current assets can thus be calculated as follows:

Pre-elimination current assets	$320,000
Intraentity gross profit eliminated	(12,000)
Consolidated current assets	$308,000

Answer (A) is incorrect. The amount of $320,000 does not eliminate intraentity transactions. Answer (B) is incorrect. The amount of $314,000 does not eliminate the effect of the transactions with Kent but subtracts the gross profit included in the inventory held by Dean. Answer (D) is incorrect. The amount of $302,000 treats the sales between Clark and Dean as an intraentity transaction.

24.8.5. Perez, Inc., owns 80% of Senior, Inc. During the year just ended, Perez sold goods with a 40% gross profit to Senior. Senior sold all of these goods during the year. In its consolidated financial statements for the year, how should the summation of Perez and Senior income statement items be adjusted?

- A. Sales and cost of goods sold should be reduced by the intraentity sales.

- B. Sales and cost of goods sold should be reduced by 80% of the intraentity sales.

- C. Net income should be reduced by 80% of the gross profit on intraentity sales.

- D. No adjustment is necessary.

Answer (A) is correct. *(CPA, adapted)*
REQUIRED: The adjustment for intraentity inventory sales.
DISCUSSION: Given that all of the goods were sold, no adjustment is necessary for intraentity profit in ending inventory. Accordingly, the parent's cost should be included in consolidated cost of goods sold, and the price received by the subsidiary should be included in consolidated sales. The required adjustment is to eliminate the sale recorded by the parent and the cost of goods sold recorded by the subsidiary.
Answer (B) is incorrect. The elimination is made without regard to the noncontrolling interest. Answer (C) is incorrect. No profit should be eliminated. All of the goods sold to Senior have been resold. Answer (D) is incorrect. Sales and cost of sales should be reduced.

Questions 24.8.6 and 24.8.7 are based on the following information. Scroll, Inc., a wholly owned subsidiary of Pirn, Inc., began operations on January 1, Year 4. The following information is from the condensed Year 4 income statements:

	Pirn	Scroll
Sales to Scroll	$100,000	$ --
Sales to others	400,000	300,000
	$500,000	$300,000
Cost of goods sold:		
Acquired from Pirn	--	80,000
Acquired from others	350,000	190,000
Gross profit	$150,000	$ 30,000
Depreciation	40,000	10,000
Other expenses	60,000	15,000
Income from operations	$ 50,000	$ 5,000
Gain on sale of equipment to Scroll	12,000	--
Income before income taxes	$ 38,000	$ 5,000

Additional Information

- Sales by Pirn to Scroll are made on the same terms as those made to third parties.
- Equipment purchased by Scroll from Pirn for $36,000 on January 1, Year 4, is depreciated using the straight-line method over 4 years.

24.8.6. In Pirn's December 31, Year 4, consolidating worksheet, how much intraentity profit should be eliminated from Scroll's inventory?

A. $30,000

B. $20,000

C. $10,000

D. $6,000

Answer (D) is correct. *(CPA, adapted)*
   REQUIRED: The intraentity profit eliminated from a subsidiary's inventory.
   DISCUSSION: Intraentity profit to be eliminated can be calculated as follows:

Sales by Pirn to Scroll	$100,000
Related cost of goods sold	(80,000)
Inventory remaining	$ 20,000
Pirn's gross profit rate ($150,000 ÷ $500,000)	× 30%
Intraentity gross profit eliminated	$ 6,000

   Answer (A) is incorrect. The amount of $30,000 is Scroll's total gross profit. Answer (B) is incorrect. The amount of $20,000 is the inventory of items obtained from Pirn. Answer (C) is incorrect. The amount of $10,000 equals the total gross profit minus the inventory obtained from Pirn.

24.8.7. What amount should be reported as depreciation expense in Pirn's Year 4 consolidated income statement?

A. $50,000

B. $47,000

C. $44,000

D. $41,000

Answer (B) is correct. *(CPA, adapted)*
   REQUIRED: The depreciation expense in the consolidated income statement.
   DISCUSSION: The depreciation on the gain on sale of equipment to Scroll must be eliminated. If the original useful life and the deprecation method remain the same, the depreciation expense eliminated is equal to the amount of gain on intraentity sale of equipment divided by the years of useful life remaining. Total consolidated depreciation expense can be calculated as follows:

Pirn's depreciation expense	$40,000
Scroll's depreciation expense	10,000
Depreciation expense eliminated ($12,000 ÷ 4 years)	(3,000)
Consolidated depreciation expense	$47,000

   Answer (A) is incorrect. The amount of $50,000 does not eliminate the effect of the gain. Answer (C) is incorrect. The amount of $44,000 equals total depreciation minus the inventory profit. Answer (D) is incorrect. The amount of $41,000 equals total depreciation minus the inventory profit and the effect of the gain.

24.8.8. Power Co. is a manufacturer and Slack Co., its 100%-owned subsidiary, is a retailer. The companies are vertically integrated. Thus, Slack purchases all of its inventory from Power. On January 1, Slack's inventory was $30,000. For the year ended December 31, its purchases were $150,000, and its cost of sales was $166,500. Power's sales to Slack reflect a 50% markup on cost. Slack then resells the goods to outside entities at a 100% markup on cost. At what amount should the intraentity inventory purchase be reported in the consolidated balance sheet at December 31?

A. $16,500

B. $9,000

C. $13,500

D. $6,750

Answer (B) is correct. *(E. Milacek)*
REQUIRED: The amount to report as intraentity inventory on the consolidated balance sheet.
DISCUSSION: Based on beginning inventory and purchases, Slack had $180,000 in inventory that was available to sell. If cost of goods sold is $166,500, $13,500 ($180,000 – $166,500) is still in Slack's inventory. As shown below, after the elimination of intraentity profit, Slack's inventory has a balance of $9,000 at the end of the year.

$$EI + 0.50EI = \$13,500$$
$$1.50EI = \underline{13,500}$$
$$EI = \underline{\$\ 9,000}$$

Answer (A) is incorrect. The difference between $166,500 and $150,000 is $16,500. Answer (C) is incorrect. Slack's ending inventory before the elimination of intraentity profits is $13,500. Answer (D) is incorrect. The amount of $6,750 is 50% of Slack's ending inventory before the elimination of intraentity profits.

24.8.9. During the current year, Pard Corp. sold goods to its 80%-owned subsidiary, Seed Corp. At December 31, one-half of these goods were included in Seed's ending inventory. Reported selling expenses were $1.1 million and $400,000 for Pard and Seed, respectively. Pard's selling expenses included $50,000 in freight-out costs for goods sold to Seed. What amount of selling expenses should be reported in Pard's consolidated income statement?

A. $1,500,000

B. $1,480,000

C. $1,475,000

D. $1,450,000

Answer (D) is correct. *(CPA, adapted)*
REQUIRED: The selling expenses reported in the consolidated income statement.
DISCUSSION: The effects of intraentity transactions should be eliminated from consolidated financial statements in their entirety regardless of the parent's percentage of ownership. Consequently, consolidated selling expense is $1,450,000 ($1,100,000 + $400,000 – $50,000 of freight-out incurred on a sale by Pard to Seed). Seed's inventory balance is not relevant to this calculation because selling expenses, including freight-out, are not inventoried.
Answer (A) is incorrect. The amount of $1,500,000 assumes no elimination of the effects of the intraentity transaction. Answer (B) is incorrect. The amount of $1,480,000 assumes that the selling expense eliminated is related to the inventory held by Seed and that a noncontrolling interest in the remainder ($25,000 × 20%) also is not eliminated. Answer (C) is incorrect. The amount of $1,475,000 assumes that the selling expense eliminated is related to the inventory held by Seed.

24.8.10. Pelota Co. owns 80% of Saginaw Co.'s outstanding common stock. Saginaw, in turn, owns 10% of Pelota's outstanding common stock. What percentage of the common stock cash dividends declared by the individual companies should be reported as dividends declared in the consolidated financial statements?

	Dividends Declared by Pelota	Dividends Declared by Saginaw
A.	90%	0%
B.	90%	20%
C.	100%	0%
D.	100%	20%

Answer (A) is correct. *(CPA, adapted)*
REQUIRED: The dividends declared by a parent and its subsidiary reported in the consolidated statements.
DISCUSSION: Because the parent owns 80% of the subsidiary and the subsidiary owns 10% of the parent, 80% of the dividends declared by the subsidiary and 10% of the dividends declared by the parent are not transferred outside of the consolidated group. These amounts are eliminated as intraentity transactions. Consequently, 90% of the parent's and 20% of the subsidiary's dividend payments are to third parties. Only the 90% declared by the parent will be reported as dividends declared. The 20% declared by the subsidiary is treated as a reduction of noncontrolling interest.
Answer (B) is incorrect. Zero percent of the subsidiary's dividends are treated as consolidated dividends declared. Answer (C) is incorrect. Ninety percent of the parent's dividends are treated as consolidated dividends declared. Answer (D) is incorrect. Ninety percent of the parent's dividends and 0% of the subsidiary's are treated as consolidated dividends declared.

24.8.11. Port, Inc., owns 100% of Salem, Inc. On January 1, Port sold Salem delivery equipment at a gain. Port had owned the equipment for 2 years and used a 5-year straight-line depreciation rate with no residual value. Salem is using a 3-year straight-line depreciation rate with no residual value for the equipment. In the consolidated income statement, Salem's recorded depreciation expense on the equipment for the year will be decreased by

A. 20% of the gain on sale.

B. 33 1/3% of the gain on sale.

C. 50% of the gain on sale.

D. 100% of the gain on sale.

Answer (B) is correct. *(CPA, adapted)*
REQUIRED: The consolidated depreciation expense on equipment sold by a parent to a subsidiary.
DISCUSSION: The effects of intraentity transactions are eliminated. If the original useful life and depreciation method remain the same, the depreciation expense eliminated is equal to the amount of gain on sale of equipment divided by the years of useful life remaining. Thus, depreciation expense on the equipment for the year will be decreased by 33 1/3% of the gain on sale (gain on sale ÷ useful life remaining).
Answer (A) is incorrect. The percentage of 20% is based on the assumption of a 5-year life. Answer (C) is incorrect. The percentage of 50% is based on the assumption of a 2-year life. Answer (D) is incorrect. The percentage of 100% is based on the assumption of a 1-year life.

24.8.12. Moss Corp. owns 20% of Dobro Corp.'s preferred stock and 80% of its common stock. Dobro's stock outstanding at December 31, Year 1, is as follows:

10% cumulative preferred stock	$100,000
Common stock	700,000

Dobro reported net income of $60,000 for the year ended December 31, Year 1. What amount should Moss record as equity in earnings of Dobro for the year ended December 31, Year 1?

A. $42,000

B. $48,000

C. $48,400

D. $50,000

Answer (A) is correct. *(CPA, adapted)*
REQUIRED: The equity of a parent in the earnings of a subsidiary.
DISCUSSION: Moss must consolidate Dobro because it holds more than 50% of Dobro's outstanding voting interests. A subsidiary's dividends (whether or not declared) on outstanding cumulative preferred stock held by parties outside the consolidated entity are included in the calculation of the parent's share of the subsidiary's earnings. The parent determines its share of the subsidiary's earnings after adjusting for dividends on such stock and the share of the noncontrolling interest (NCI). Thus, the equity of Moss in Dobro's earnings is $42,000.

Earnings		$60,000
NCI's share of earnings available		
to common shareholders		
Earnings	$60,000	
Preferred dividends ($100,000 × 10%)	(10,000)	
	$50,000	
	× 20%	(10,000)
Earnings available to common shareholders		$50,000
Preferred dividends payable outside		
consolidated entity ($10,000 × 80%)		(8,000)
		$42,000

Answer (B) is incorrect. The amount of $48,000 equals 80% of Dobro's net income. Answer (C) is incorrect. The amount of $48,400 equals 80% of Dobro's net income plus 20% of a 20% share of the preferred dividends. Answer (D) is incorrect. The amount of $50,000 equals Dobro's net income minus the preferred dividends.

24.8.13. On January 1, Poe Corp. sold a machine for $900,000 to Saxe Corp., its wholly owned subsidiary. Poe paid $1.1 million for this machine, which had accumulated depreciation of $250,000. Poe estimated a $100,000 salvage value and depreciated the machine on the straight-line method over 20 years, a policy that Saxe continued. In Poe's December 31 consolidated balance sheet, this machine should be included in cost and accumulated depreciation as

	Cost	Accumulated Depreciation
A.	$1,100,000	$300,000
B.	$1,100,000	$290,000
C.	$900,000	$40,000
D.	$850,000	$42,500

Answer (A) is correct. *(CPA, adapted)*
REQUIRED: The cost and accumulated depreciation in the consolidated balance sheet.
DISCUSSION: All the accounts related to the plant asset transferred must be reported in the consolidated financial statements at the amounts that would have been reported if the intraentity transaction had never occurred. Annual depreciation expense on the machine is calculated as follows:

Historical cost	$1,100,000
Salvage value	(100,000)
Depreciable base	$1,000,000
Useful life	÷ 20
Straight-line depreciation expense	$ 50,000

Accumulated depreciation at December 31 thus equals $300,000 ($250,000 + $50,000).
Answer (B) is incorrect. The amount of $290,000 assumes that depreciation is based on a $900,000 cost, $100,000 salvage value, and a remaining 20-year life. Answer (C) is incorrect. The amount of $900,000 is the sales price, and $40,000 is the depreciation based on a $900,000 cost, $100,000 salvage value, and a remaining 20-year life. Answer (D) is incorrect. The amount of $850,000 was the carrying amount at the time of sale, and $42,500 would be the depreciation in Saxe's separate financial statements assuming the $850,000 cost, a 20-year life, and no salvage value.

24.8.14. Wagner, a holder of a $1 million Palmer, Inc., bond, collected the interest due on March 31, and then sold the bond to Seal, Inc., for $975,000. On that date, Palmer, a 75% owner of Seal, had a $1,075,000 carrying amount for this bond. What was the effect of Seal's purchase of Palmer's bond on the retained earnings and noncontrolling interest amounts reported in Palmer's March 31 consolidated balance sheet?

	Retained Earnings	Noncontrolling Interest
A.	$100,000 increase	$0
B.	$75,000 increase	$25,000 increase
C.	$0	$25,000 increase
D.	$0	$100,000 increase

Answer (A) is correct. *(CPA, adapted)*
REQUIRED: The effect of the purchase by the subsidiary of the parent's debt.
DISCUSSION: The purchase was in substance a retirement of debt by the consolidated entity for less than its carrying amount. The transaction resulted in a constructive gain of $100,000 ($1,075,000 carrying amount – $975,000 price) and therefore a $100,000 increase in consolidated retained earnings. The noncontrolling interest was unaffected. The noncontrolling interest is based on the subsidiary's carrying amounts adjusted for subsidiary income and dividends. This transaction did not result in gain or loss for Seal.
Answer (B) is incorrect. The gain is not allocated. Answer (C) is incorrect. The noncontrolling interest is not affected. Answer (D) is incorrect. Retained earnings is increased by $100,000.

24.8.15. Sun, Inc., is a wholly owned subsidiary of Patton, Inc. On June 1, Year 4, Patton declared and paid a $1 per share cash dividend to shareholders of record on May 15, Year 4. On May 1, Year 4, Sun bought 10,000 shares of Patton's common stock for $700,000 on the open market, when the book value per share was $30. What amount of gain should Patton report from this transaction in its consolidated income statement for the year ended December 31, Year 4?

A. $0

B. $390,000

C. $400,000

D. $410,000

Answer (A) is correct. *(CPA, adapted)*
REQUIRED: The amount of gain to be reported from the purchase of parent's stock by a subsidiary.
DISCUSSION: Consolidated financial statements report financial position, results of operations, and cash flows as if the consolidated entities were a single economic entity. Thus, subsidiary shareholdings in a parent are normally treated as treasury stock on the consolidated balance sheet. Gains and losses on treasury stock are not recognized. Thus, no gain is recognized in the consolidated income statement when a subsidiary purchases the parent's stock on the open market.
Answer (B) is incorrect. The amount of $390,000 equals the $700,000 paid, minus the $300,000 carrying amount, minus the $10,000 dividend. Answer (C) is incorrect. The amount of $400,000 equals the $700,000 paid minus the $300,000 carrying amount. Answer (D) is incorrect. The amount of $410,000 equals the $700,000 paid, minus the $300,000 carrying amount, plus the $10,000 dividend.

24.9 Combined Financial Statements

24.9.1. Combined statements may be used to present the results of operations of

	Entities under Common Management	Commonly Controlled Entities
A.	No	Yes
B.	Yes	No
C.	No	No
D.	Yes	Yes

Answer (D) is correct. *(CPA, adapted)*
REQUIRED: The use(s) of combined financial statements.
DISCUSSION: Combined (as distinguished from consolidated) statements of commonly controlled entities may be more meaningful than separate statements. For example, combined statements may be used (1) to combine the statements of several entities with related operations when one individual owns a controlling financial interest in them or (2) to combine the statements of entities under common management.
Answer (A) is incorrect. Common management justifies use of combined statements. Answer (B) is incorrect. Common control justifies use of combined statements. Answer (C) is incorrect. Either common management or common control justifies use of combined statements.

24.9.2. Ahm Corp. owns 90% of Bee Corp.'s common stock and 80% of Cee Corp.'s common stock. The remaining common shares of Bee and Cee are owned by their respective employees. Bee sells exclusively to Cee, Cee buys exclusively from Bee, and Cee sells exclusively to unrelated companies. Selected information for Bee and Cee for the year follows:

	Bee Corp.	Cee Corp.
Sales	$130,000	$91,000
Cost of sales	100,000	65,000
Beginning inventory	None	None
Ending inventory	None	65,000

What amount should be reported as gross profit in Bee and Cee's combined income statement for the year ended December 31?

A. $26,000

B. $41,000

C. $47,800

D. $56,000

Answer (B) is correct. *(CPA, adapted)*
REQUIRED: The amount reported as gross profit in the combined income statement.
DISCUSSION: Cee buys exclusively from Bee. Thus, Cee's cost of sales equals the sales price charged by Bee, which represented a 30% [($130,000 − $100,000) ÷ $100,000] markup on the cost to the combined entity. Consequently, the gross profit of the combined entity on sales to unrelated companies should include Bee's markup as well as Cee's gross profit. Because Bee's sales were 130% of its cost, the cost to the entity of Cee's sales was $50,000 ($65,000 cost of sales ÷ 130%). The gross profit in the combined income statement was therefore $41,000 ($91,000 − $50,000).
Answer (A) is incorrect. The amount of $26,000 was Cee's gross profit. Answer (C) is incorrect. The amount of $47,800 is the sum of 90% of Bee's and 80% of Cee's gross profits. Answer (D) is incorrect. The amount of $56,000 is the sum of Bee's and Cee's gross profits.

24.9.3. At December 31, S Corp. owned 80% of J Corp.'s common stock and 90% of C Corp.'s common stock. J's net income for the year was $200,000 and C's net income was $400,000. C and J had no interentity ownership or transactions during the year. Combined financial statements are being prepared for C and J in contemplation of their sale to an outside party. In the combined income statement, combined net income should be reported at

A. $420,000

B. $520,000

C. $560,000

D. $600,000

Answer (D) is correct. *(CPA, adapted)*
REQUIRED: The combined net income.
DISCUSSION: Combined financial statements are appropriate when common management or common control exists for two or more entities not subject to consolidation. The calculation of combined net income is similar to the calculation for consolidated net income. Thus, combined net income should be recorded at the total of the net income reported by the combined entities, adjusted for any profits or losses from transactions between the combined entities. In the combined income statement issued for J Corp. and C Corp., net income should be reported at $600,000 ($200,000 + $400,000).
Answer (A) is incorrect. The amount of $420,000 is 70% of the combined net income. Answer (B) is incorrect. The amount of $520,000 equals 80% of the net income of J and 90% of the net income of C. Answer (C) is incorrect. The amount of $560,000 equals 80% of J's net income and 100% of C's net income.

24.9.4. Selected data for two subsidiaries of Dunn Corp. taken from December 31 preclosing trial balances are as follows:

	Banks Co. Debit	Lamm Co. Credit
Shipments to Banks	--	$150,000
Shipments from Lamm	$200,000	--
Intraentity inventory profit on total shipments	--	50,000

Additional data relating to the December 31 inventory are as follows:

Inventory acquired from outside parties	$175,000	$250,000
Inventory acquired from Lamm	60,000	--

At December 31, the inventory reported on the combined balance sheet of the two subsidiaries should be

- A. $425,000
- B. $435,000
- C. $470,000
- D. $485,000

Answer (C) is correct. *(CPA, adapted)*
REQUIRED: The inventory to be reported on the combined balance sheet of two subsidiaries.
DISCUSSION: When combined financial statements are prepared for unconsolidated subsidiaries, intraentity profits should be eliminated. The $60,000 of ending inventory acquired by Banks from Lamm is equal to 30% ($60,000 inventory remaining ÷ $200,000 shipments) of the total received from Lamm. Accordingly, $15,000 ($50,000 inventory profit on total shipments × 30%) should be eliminated. Given that $425,000 ($175,000 + $250,000) of the ending inventory held by Banks and Lamm was obtained from outside parties, the combined balance sheet of the two subsidiaries should report inventory of $470,000 ($425,000 + $60,000 − $15,000).
Answer (A) is incorrect. The total inventory acquired from outside parties is $425,000. Answer (B) is incorrect. The amount of $435,000 excludes the profit on inventory acquired from Lamm and subsequently sold. Answer (D) is incorrect. The amount of $485,000 does not exclude the intraentity inventory profit.

24.9.5. Mr. Cord owns four corporations. Combined financial statements are being prepared for these corporations, which have intraentity loans of $200,000 and intraentity profits of $500,000. What amount of these loans and profits should be included in the combined financial statements?

	Intraentity Loans	Profits
A.	$200,000	$0
B.	$200,000	$500,000
C.	$0	$0
D.	$0	$500,000

Answer (C) is correct. *(CPA, adapted)*
REQUIRED: The amount of intraentity loans and profits that should be included in combined financial statements.
DISCUSSION: Combined financial statements are appropriately issued when two or more entities are under common control or common management. When combined financial statements are issued, intraentity loans and profits should be eliminated in their entirety. Thus, $200,000 in loans and $500,000 in profits should not be included in the combined financial statements.
Answer (A) is incorrect. The loans equaling $200,000 should not be included in the combined financial statements. Answer (B) is incorrect. When combined financial statements are issued, intraentity loans and profits should be eliminated in their entirety. Answer (D) is incorrect. The profits of $500,000 should not be included in the combined financial statements.

☑ ▬
☐ ▬ Use **Gleim Test Prep** for interactive study and easy-to-use detailed analytics!
☐ ▬

STUDY UNIT TWENTY-FIVE
INTERIM FINANCIAL REPORTING

Reporting of **interim information** (reports covering less than 1 year) is not required unless the entity is an issuer subject to federal securities law. Issuers must file quarterly reports on Form 10-Q. U.S. GAAP apply whenever entities (public or private) issue interim financial information. Moreover, minimum disclosure requirements apply when publicly traded companies issue summarized interim information.

Each interim period is treated primarily as an integral part of an annual period. Ordinarily, the results for an interim period should be based on the same accounting principles the entity uses in preparing annual statements. But certain principles and practices used for annual reporting may require modification at interim dates.

QUESTIONS

25.1 Basic Concepts

25.1.1. Which of the following is not a required disclosure when a publicly traded company elects to issue a financial summary of interim operations?

A. Basic and diluted earnings per share.

B. Significant changes in estimates or provisions for income tax.

C. Changes in accounting principles or estimates.

D. Changes in investment policy.

Answer (D) is correct. *(CMA, adapted)*
REQUIRED: The interim financial reporting disclosures not required.
DISCUSSION: Presentation of interim income statements, statements of financial position, statements of cash flows, and disclosure of changes in investment policy are not required. However, when a publicly traded company elects to issue a financial summary of interim operations, minimum required disclosures include

1) Sales or gross revenues, provision for income taxes, net income, and comprehensive income
2) Basic and diluted EPS
3) Seasonal revenues, costs, or expenses
4) Significant changes in estimates or provisions for income taxes
5) Disposal of a component of an entity and unusual or infrequent items
6) Contingent items
7) Changes in accounting principles or estimates
8) Significant changes in financial position (disclosure of balance sheet and cash flow data is encouraged)
9) Certain information about reportable operating segments
10) Certain information about defined benefit postretirement benefit plans
11) Certain information about fair value measurement of assets and liabilities

A change in investment policy is not required to be disclosed because it is not an accounting change.
Answer (A) is incorrect. Required interim disclosures include BEPS and DEPS. Answer (B) is incorrect. Required interim disclosures include estimates or provisions for income tax. Answer (C) is incorrect. Required interim disclosures include changes in estimates and principles.

25.1.2. In considering interim financial reporting, how should such reporting be viewed?

A. As a "special" type of reporting that need not follow generally accepted accounting principles.

B. As useful only if activity is evenly spread throughout the year so that estimates are unnecessary.

C. As reporting for a basic accounting period.

D. As reporting for an integral part of an annual period.

Answer (D) is correct. *(CPA, adapted)*
REQUIRED: The perspective of interim financial reporting.
DISCUSSION: Each interim period is viewed primarily as an integral part of an annual period. Ordinarily, the results for an interim period should be based on the same accounting principles the enterprise uses in preparing annual statements. Certain principles and practices used for annual reporting, however, may require modification at interim dates so that interim reports may relate more closely to the results of operations for the annual period.
Answer (A) is incorrect. Interim reporting is not a "special" type of reporting, and GAAP should be followed. Answer (B) is incorrect. Interim reports may be useful for seasonal and unevenly spread activities. Answer (C) is incorrect. The view that the interim period is a discrete accounting period is not generally accepted.

25.1.3. The Hoity-Toity Country Club offers membership privileges for a 3-year period under the following arrangements:

1) The applicant pays the entire $200,000 membership fee in eight quarterly installments during the first 2 years of the contract period.

2) The applicant is entitled to unlimited use of the facilities during the 3-year contract period.

Based on experience, Hoity-Toity is able to reasonably estimate uncollectible receivables. It prepares quarterly financial statements. In which accounting period(s) should Hoity-Toity recognize the membership fee as revenue for financial statement reporting?

A. In the quarter that the membership contract is signed.

B. Evenly over the eight quarters in which the installment payments are to be received.

C. In the quarter that the membership period terminates.

D. Evenly over the 12-quarter membership period.

Answer (D) is correct. *(CIA, adapted)*
REQUIRED: The accounting period in which revenue should be recognized.
DISCUSSION: In general, the results for an interim period should be based on the same accounting principles that the entity uses in preparing annual statements. SFAC 5 states that revenue should be recognized when it is realized or realizable and earned. For revenue associated with membership privileges, the earning process is completed in proportion to the amount of the membership period elapsed. This principle is applicable in both annual and interim periods. Thus, the membership fee should be allocated evenly over the 12-quarter membership period.
Answer (A) is incorrect. Only one-twelfth of the fee should be accrued in the quarter that the membership contract is signed. Answer (B) is incorrect. The membership revenue should be prorated evenly over the membership period. Answer (C) is incorrect. Only one-twelfth of the fee should be accrued in the quarter that the membership period terminates.

25.1.4. How should material seasonal variations in revenue be reflected in interim financial statements?

A. The seasonal variation should be disclosed by showing pro forma financial statements for subsequent interim periods within the fiscal year.

B. Because the total revenue pattern of the current annual period is not known with certainty, any statements about seasonal patterns may be misleading and must be omitted from interim statements.

C. Disclosures should warn the statement reader that revenues are subject to seasonal variation, but no supplemental schedules of past seasonality should be shown.

D. The seasonal nature should be disclosed. Revenue information for 12-month periods ended at the interim date may be disclosed.

Answer (D) is correct. *(Publisher, adapted)*
REQUIRED: The proper method of reflecting material seasonal variations in revenue in interim financial statements.
DISCUSSION: If businesses issue interim information, certain disclosures are mandatory if they have material seasonal fluctuations. Such disclosures safeguard the user of the statements from being misled into believing that interim results from such businesses are fairly representative of annual results. Businesses must disclose the seasonal nature of their activities and should consider supplementing interim reports with information for the 12-month period that ended at the interim date for the current and preceding years.
Answer (A) is incorrect. The disclosure requirement may be met by providing financial data for prior, not subsequent, interim periods within the fiscal year. Answer (B) is incorrect. Businesses must disclose the seasonal nature of their activities. Answer (C) is incorrect. Supplemental schedules with information for the 12-month period ending at the interim date for the current and preceding years are proper disclosures.

25.1.5. On June 30, Tun Corp. incurred a $200,000 net loss from disposal of a component. Also on June 30, Tun paid $80,000 for property taxes assessed for the calendar year. What amount of the foregoing items should be included in the determination of Tun's net income or loss for the 6-month interim period ended June 30?

A. $280,000

B. $240,000

C. $180,000

D. $140,000

Answer (B) is correct. *(CPA, adapted)*
REQUIRED: The amount of property taxes and loss from disposal of a component that should be included in the determination of net income or loss for the interim period.
DISCUSSION: Costs other than product costs, such as rent, interest, or property taxes, that will clearly benefit two or more interim periods should be allocated among those periods based on estimates of time expired, the benefit received, or the activity associated with each period. Thus, Tun should allocate $40,000 [$80,000 × (6 ÷ 12)] of the property taxes to the 6-month interim period ended June 30. Gains and losses that arise in an interim period that are similar to gains and losses that would not be deferred at year end should not be deferred to later interim periods within the same fiscal year. Consequently, gains or losses from disposal of a component should not be prorated over the balance of the fiscal year, so the loss on disposal ($200,000) should be recognized in full for the interim period ended June 30. The total included in the interim income statement for the two items is therefore $240,000 ($40,000 + $200,000).
Answer (A) is incorrect. The amount of $280,000 reflects a failure to prorate the property taxes. Answer (C) is incorrect. The amount of $180,000 reflects proration of the loss on disposal of a segment and the full amount of the property taxes. Answer (D) is incorrect. The amount of $140,000 reflects proration of the loss on disposal of a component.

25.1.6. For interim financial reporting, a gain on disposal of property occurring in the second quarter should be

A. Recognized ratably over the last three quarters.

B. Recognized ratably over all four quarters, with the first quarter being restated.

C. Recognized in the second quarter.

D. Disclosed in the notes only in the second quarter.

Answer (C) is correct. *(CPA, adapted)*
REQUIRED: The appropriate recognition of an extraordinary gain in an interim report.
DISCUSSION: Gains and losses similar to those that would not be deferred at year end should not be deferred to later interim periods of the same year. Accordingly, a gain on disposal of an asset should not be prorated. It is recognized in full in the quarter in which it occurs.
Answer (A) is incorrect. The gain should be recognized in the quarter in which it occurs. Answer (B) is incorrect. The gain should be recognized in the quarter in which it occurs. Answer (D) is incorrect. The gain should be recognized in income. Disclosure in footnotes is not sufficient.

25.1.7. On March 15 of the current year, Chen Company paid property taxes of $120,000 on its factory building for the current calendar year. On April 1, Chen made $240,000 in unanticipated repairs to its plant equipment. The repairs will benefit operations for the remainder of the calendar year. What total amount of these expenses should be included in Chen's quarterly income statement for the 3 months ended June 30?

A. $60,000

B. $110,000

C. $150,000

D. $270,000

Answer (B) is correct. *(CPA, adapted)*
REQUIRED: The proper accounting for payments of property taxes and major repair costs in a quarterly income statement.
DISCUSSION: The benefit from the payment of the property taxes relates to all four quarters of the current year and should be prorated at $30,000 ($120,000 ÷ 4) per quarter. The benefit from the unanticipated repairs to plant equipment relates to the second, third, and fourth quarters. It should be spread evenly over these quarters at $80,000 ($240,000 ÷ 3) per quarter. The total amount of expenses that should be included in the quarterly income statement for the 3 months ended June 30 is therefore $110,000.
Answer (A) is incorrect. The amount of $60,000 results from not prorating the property taxes and from prorating the repair cost over all four quarters. Answer (C) is incorrect. The amount of $150,000 assumes that the entire repair cost is allocated to the first two quarters. Answer (D) is incorrect. The amount of $270,000 results from not allocating the repair expense.

25.1.8. Napier Corp. has estimated that total depreciation expense for the year ending December 31 will amount to $120,000 and that year-end bonuses to employees will total $240,000. In Napier's interim income statement for the 6 months ended June 30, what is the total amount of expense relating to these two items that should be reported?

A. $0

B. $60,000

C. $180,000

D. $360,000

Answer (C) is correct. *(CPA, adapted)*
REQUIRED: The amount of expenses related to depreciation and year-end bonuses that should be reported in the 6-month income statement.
DISCUSSION: Costs and expenses other than product costs should be either charged to income in interim periods as incurred or allocated among interim periods based on the benefits received. The depreciation and the bonuses to employees clearly provide benefits throughout the year, and they should be allocated ratably to all interim periods. In the interim income statement for the 6 months ended June 30, the total amount of expense that should be recorded is $180,000 [($360,000 ÷ 12 months) × 6 months].
Answer (A) is incorrect. Depreciation and bonus expenses should be allocated ratably. Answer (B) is incorrect. The amount of $60,000 excludes the allocation of bonuses. Answer (D) is incorrect. The amount of $360,000 allocates the expenses entirely to the 6-month interim period ending June 30.

25.1.9. In October Year 3, Snow Company spent $300,000 on an advertising campaign for subscriptions to the magazine it publishes concerning preparing for the winter sports season. The only two issues appear in October and in November. The magazine is sold only on a subscription basis, and the subscriptions started in October Year 3. Assuming Snow's fiscal year ends on March 31, Year 4, what amount of expense should be included in Snow's quarterly income statement for the 3 months ended December 31, Year 3, as a result of this expenditure?

A. $75,000

B. $100,000

C. $150,000

D. $300,000

Answer (D) is correct. *(CPA, adapted)*
REQUIRED: The amount of advertising expense included in the third quarter's income statement.
DISCUSSION: Advertising costs should be expensed, either as incurred or when advertising first occurs. Because the magazine is published only during October and November, and the expenses were incurred in October, recognition of subscription revenue and related expenses is appropriate only during that quarter. Accordingly, the entire advertising expense of $300,000 should be recognized in that period.
Answer (A) is incorrect. The amount of $75,000 results from allocating the $300,000 expense ratably to four quarters. Answer (B) is incorrect. The amount of $100,000 results from allocating 33 1/3% of the $300,000 expense. Answer (C) is incorrect. The amount of $150,000 results from allocating 50% of the $300,000 expense.

25.1.10. How are discontinued operations and material unusual or infrequently occurring items that occur at midyear initially reported?

A. Disclosed only in the notes to the year-end financial statements.

B. Included in net income and disclosed in the notes to the year-end financial statements.

C. Included in net income and disclosed in the notes to interim financial statements.

D. Disclosed only in the notes to interim financial statements.

Answer (C) is correct. *(CPA, adapted)*
REQUIRED: The initial reporting of discontinued operations and extraordinary items occurring at midyear.
DISCUSSION: Material unusual or infrequent items, and gains or losses from disposal of a component of an entity are (1) separately disclosed in the interim statements, (2) included in interim-period net income, and (3) not prorated over the year.
Answer (A) is incorrect. Material unusual or infrequently occurring items and gains or losses from disposal of a component of an entity are separately disclosed in the interim-period financial statements and included in interim-period net income. Answer (B) is incorrect. Material unusual or infrequently occurring items and gains or losses from disposal of a component of an entity are separately disclosed in the interim statements. Answer (D) is incorrect. Discontinued operations and material unusual or infrequently occurring items also are included in interim-period net income.

25.2 Costs and Expenses

25.2.1. Which of the following reporting practices is permissible for interim financial reporting?

A. Use of the gross profit method for interim inventory pricing.

B. Use of the direct costing method for determining manufacturing inventories.

C. Deferral of unplanned variances under a standard cost system until year end.

D. Deferral of inventory market declines until year end.

Answer (A) is correct. *(CPA, adapted)*
REQUIRED: The inventory reporting practice permissible in interim financial reporting.
DISCUSSION: Certain accounting principles and practices followed for annual reporting purposes may be modified for interim reporting. For example, the gross profit method may be used for estimating cost of goods sold and inventory because a physical inventory count at the interim date may not be feasible.
Answer (B) is incorrect. The direct costing method is never permissible for external financial reporting. Answer (C) is incorrect. Only variances that are planned and expected to be absorbed by the end of the annual period may be deferred. Answer (D) is incorrect. Only market declines that can reasonably be expected to be restored within the fiscal year may be deferred.

25.2.2. A store uses the gross profit method to estimate inventory and cost of goods sold for interim reporting purposes. Past experience indicates that the average gross profit rate is 25% of sales. The following data relate to the month of June:

Inventory cost, June 1	$25,000
Purchases during the month at cost	67,000
Sales	84,000
Sales returns	3,000

Based on the data above, what is the estimated ending inventory at June 30?

A. $20,250

B. $21,000

C. $29,000

D. $31,250

Answer (D) is correct. *(CIA, adapted)*
REQUIRED: The estimated ending inventory under the gross profit method.
DISCUSSION: The gross profit rate is 25% of sales. Thus, estimated cost of goods sold is 75% $(1.0 - .25)$ of sales. Subtracting estimated cost of goods sold from total goods available for sale leaves an estimated ending inventory of $31,250.

Beginning inventory	$25,000
Purchases	67,000
Goods available for sale	$92,000
Estimated COGS ($84,000 – $3,000) × (1.0 – .25)	(60,750)
Estimated ending inventory	$31,250

Answer (A) is incorrect. The gross profit is $20,250. Answer (B) is incorrect. Purchases are subtracted from beginning inventory, and cost of goods sold ($84,000 × 75% = $63,000) is not adjusted for sales returns and is added to beginning inventory ($25,000 – $67,000 + $63,000 = $21,000). Answer (C) is incorrect. Cost of goods sold is not adjusted for sales returns.

25.2.3. A loss from a market price decline on inventory accounted for under the LIFO method occurred in the first quarter. The loss was not expected to be restored in the fiscal year. However, in the third quarter the inventory had a market price recovery that exceeded the market price decline that occurred in the first quarter. For interim financial reporting, the dollar amount of net inventory should

A. Decrease in the first quarter by the amount of the market price decline and increase in the third quarter by the amount of the market price recovery.

B. Decrease in the first quarter by the amount of the market price decline and increase in the third quarter by the amount of decrease in the first quarter.

C. Decrease in the first quarter by the amount of the market price decline and not be affected in the third quarter.

D. Not be affected in either the first quarter or the third quarter.

Answer (B) is correct. *(CPA, adapted)*
REQUIRED: The proper interim financial reporting of a market decline and a market price recovery.
DISCUSSION: A market price decline in inventory must be recognized in the interim period in which it occurs unless it is expected to be temporary, i.e., unless the decline is expected to be restored by the end of the fiscal year. This loss was not expected to be restored in the fiscal year, and the company should report the dollar amount of the market price decline as a loss in the first quarter. Inventory may never be written up to an amount above its original cost. Accordingly, the market price recovery recognized in the third quarter is limited to the extent of losses previously recognized in a prior interim period.
Answer (A) is incorrect. The recovery recognized in the third quarter is limited to the amount of the losses previously recognized. Answer (C) is incorrect. Assuming no market price decline had been recognized prior to the current year, the first quarter loss and the third quarter recovery would be offsetting. The recognized third quarter gain is limited to the amount of the first quarter loss, and the year-end results would not be affected. Answer (D) is incorrect. The inventory amount is affected in both the first and third quarters.

25.2.4. When a standard cost system of accounting is used to determine costs for valuation of inventory in interim financial statements,

   A. Unanticipated variances should be spread prospectively to the remaining interim periods in the current annual reporting period.

   B. Unplanned variances should be recognized in the interim period in which they are incurred.

   C. Unplanned volume variances should be retroactively allocated to prior interim periods in the current annual reporting period if they occur after the first quarter.

   D. Unplanned variances should be deferred to the fourth quarter and recognized as a component of year-end adjustments.

Answer (B) is correct. *(Publisher, adapted)*
REQUIRED: The true statement about interim reporting of unplanned variances when using standard costs.
DISCUSSION: Planned standard cost variances may be deferred if they are expected to be absorbed in subsequent interim periods of a year. Unplanned or unanticipated variances, however, should be recognized in the interim period in which they are incurred.
Answer (A) is incorrect. Unanticipated variances should be expensed in the interim period in which they are incurred. Answer (C) is incorrect. An unplanned volume variance is not a basis for a retroactive restatement. Answer (D) is incorrect. Unplanned variances are not deferred.

25.3 Accounting Changes

25.3.1. In the third quarter of calendar Year 6, Li Co. documented justification for a change in accounting principle. Li also determined the cumulative effects of applying the new principle at January 1, Year 3, and the period-specific effects of applying it to the current quarter and the previously reported quarterly interim periods of the current and previous 3 fiscal years. If Li makes this change in the third quarter, the cumulative effect of applying the change to periods prior to the periods presented should be

   A. Included in net income in the first quarter of calendar Year 6.

   B. Included in net income in the third quarter of calendar Year 6.

   C. Included in net income in the first period presented.

   D. Reflected in the balance sheet at the beginning of the first period presented.

Answer (D) is correct. *(Publisher, adapted)*
REQUIRED: The proper treatment of the cumulative effect of applying the change to periods prior to the periods presented.
DISCUSSION: Retrospective application is generally required when it is practicable to determine the cumulative effect and the period-specific effects of a change in accounting principle in an interim period. Retrospective application results in changing previously issued financial statements to reflect the effects of the newly adopted accounting principle as if the new principle had always been used. Retrospective application requires that (1) the carrying amounts of assets, liabilities, and retained earnings as of the beginning of the first period reported be adjusted for the cumulative effect of the new principle on periods prior to the first period reported, and (2) each period reported be adjusted for the period-specific effects of applying the new principle.
Answer (A) is incorrect. The cumulative effect is not included in net income directly. Answer (B) is incorrect. The amount will not be reported in the third quarter. Answer (C) is incorrect. The cumulative effect must be reflected in the carrying amounts of assets and liabilities at the beginning of the first period reported.

25.3.2. Andrews Corp.'s $190,000 net income for the quarter ended September 30, Year 6, included the following after-tax items:

- A $120,000 gain on disposal of a material operating segment, realized on April 30, Year 6, was allocated equally to the second, third, and fourth quarters of Year 6.
- A $32,000 loss (a period-specific effect of a change in accounting principle during the quarter) was recognized on September 30, Year 6. While the cumulative effect of the change at July 1, Year 6, could be determined, it was not practicable to determine the period-specific effects of the change on first and second quarter net income of Year 6.

In addition, Andrews paid $96,000 on February 1, Year 6, for Year 6 calendar-year property taxes. Of this amount, $24,000 was allocated to the third quarter of Year 6. For the quarter ended September 30, Year 6, Andrews should report net income of

- A. $222,000
- B. $206,000
- C. $182,000
- D. $150,000

Answer (C) is correct. *(CPA, adapted)*
REQUIRED: The net income reported for the quarter.
DISCUSSION: Gains and losses similar to those that would not be deferred at year-end should not be deferred to later interim periods of the same year. Consequently, the $120,000 gain on disposal of a material operating segment should be recognized in net income for the second quarter. It has no effect on third quarter income. A change in accounting principle is not permitted to take effect in an interim period if it is impracticable to differentiate between the cumulative effect of the change on prior years and the period-specific effects on prior interim periods of the year of the change. Thus, Andrews is not permitted to change this accounting principle until January 1, Year 7. Accordingly, the $32,000 loss should not be included in third quarter income. Because property taxes were proportionally allocated among the four quarters, the $24,000 is properly included in third quarter income. As a result, Andrews should report third quarter net income of $182,000 [$190,000 – ($120,000 ÷ 3) + $32,000].

Answer (A) is incorrect. The amount of $222,000 does not include the adjustment for the proportionate gain on disposal of a material operating segment. Answer (B) is incorrect. The amount of $206,000 includes an adjustment for the $24,000 allocation of property taxes. However, property taxes were already correctly allocated over the four quarters. Thus, no adjustment should be made for them. Answer (D) is incorrect. The amount of $150,000 does not include an adjustment for the $32,000 period-specific effects of the accounting change.

25.3.3. The following information is applicable to a change in accounting principle made in the second quarter of the year from FIFO to LIFO. The firm is able to apply the new principle retrospectively. For all relevant periods, prices have risen. The effect of the change is limited to the effects on the inventory balance and income tax provisions (a 40% tax rate).

Period	Net Income on the Basis of FIFO	Gross Effect of Change	Gross Effect Minus Income Taxes
Prior to 1st Qtr	$6,262,000	$300,000	$180,000
1st Qtr	1,032,400	60,000	36,000
2nd Qtr	1,282,400	60,000	36,000
3rd Qtr	1,298,600	90,000	54,000
4th Qtr	1,164,800	120,000	72,000

Net income for the first quarter should be restated as

- A. $1,068,400
- B. $1,032,400
- C. $816,400
- D. $996,400

Answer (D) is correct. *(Publisher, adapted)*
REQUIRED: The restated net income for the first quarter resulting from a change in principle in the second quarter.
DISCUSSION: The change in accounting principle should be effected by retrospective application unless determination of the cumulative effect or the period-specific effects is impracticable. (However, the impracticability exception is not applicable to prior interim periods of the year of change.) The period-specific effects are adjustments made to the individual periods reported. Beginning balances of the first period reported are adjusted to reflect the cumulative effects of the change on all prior periods. Accordingly, given the period-specific effects for the first quarter, restated net income based on retrospective application is $996,400 ($1,032,400 – $36,000 gross after-tax effect of applying the new principle). Changing to LIFO when prices are rising decreases net income.

Answer (A) is incorrect. The amount of $1,068,400 results from adding, not subtracting, the gross effect minus income taxes. Given rising prices, the change to LIFO lowers after-tax income. Answer (B) is incorrect. First quarter net income must be adjusted. Answer (C) is incorrect. The amount of $816,400 results from subtracting the cumulative after-tax effect on prior periods as well as the adjustment for the first quarter.

25.4 Adjustments Related to Prior Interim Periods of the Current Year

25.4.1. During the third quarter of Year 10, the accountant at the Laurie Company discovered that a machine purchased January 2, Year 8, for $120,000 had been erroneously charged against first quarter net income in Year 8. The machine should have been depreciated at a rate of $2,000 per month. If Laurie issues interim statements, the correction of this error should include

- A. A charge of $66,000 to income before taxes of the third quarter of Year 10.

- B. An adjustment of $48,000 to the previously declared income before taxes of the first quarter of Year 10.

- C. An adjustment of $54,000 to the previously declared income before taxes of the first quarter of Year 10.

- D. An adjustment of $6,000 to the previously declared income before taxes of the first quarter of Year 10.

Answer (D) is correct. *(Publisher, adapted)*
REQUIRED: The treatment of an accounting error.
DISCUSSION: An error was committed when the full cost of the asset was expensed in the period of acquisition. Instead, the cost should have been capitalized and the asset depreciated over its useful life. The correction of this error should be accounted for by restatement. Ignoring tax effects, this requires an entry to beginning retained earnings for the year to correct the understatement of income (and of retained earnings) that resulted from the error. If comparative statements are issued, a restatement of prior-period financial statements is also necessary. The previously reported income of the first quarter of Year 10 (as well as that for the second quarter) should be restated to reflect the $6,000 ($2,000 × 3 months) depreciation that should have been taken on the asset during that period.
Answer (A) is incorrect. The adjustment must be recorded in the first quarter of Year 10. Answer (B) is incorrect. The adjustment should be $6,000. Answer (C) is incorrect. The adjustment should only be for Year 10, not the entire life of the machine.

25.4.2. On June 15, Year 6, a court of law found the Panther Corporation, a calendar-year company, guilty of patent infringement and awarded damages of $5,000,000 to the plaintiff. Of this amount, $2,000,000 related to Year 4 and $2,000,000 to Year 5, and $500,000 related to each of the first two quarters of Year 6. No provision for loss had been recorded previously. If the applicable tax rate is 40%, this event should result in a

- A. Charge of $3,000,000 to income reported for the second quarter of Year 6.

- B. Restatement of the previously reported net income for the first quarter of Year 6 to include a charge of $300,000.

- C. Restatement of the previously reported net income for the first quarter of Year 6 to include a charge of $2,700,000.

- D. Restatement of the previously reported net income for the first quarter of Year 6 to include a charge of $3,000,000.

Answer (C) is correct. *(Publisher, adapted)*
REQUIRED: The proper treatment of the settlement of litigation related to a prior interim period and prior fiscal years.
DISCUSSION: The judgment is an item of profit or loss that relates to settlement of litigation occurring in other than the first interim period of the fiscal year. Moreover, all or a part of the item meets the criteria for an adjustment related to prior interim periods of that fiscal year. Thus, the financial statements for the prior interim periods should be restated to include their allocable portions of the adjustment. The portion of the adjustment directly related to prior fiscal years also should be included in the determination of net income of the first interim period of the current fiscal year. The settlement in this case occurred in the second quarter, so the first quarter should be restated for the $500,000 directly related to first-quarter operations and the $4,000,000 directly related to prior years' operations. The restated net income for the first quarter of Year 6 should therefore include a $2,700,000 adjustment ($4,500,000 – the tax savings of $1,800,000).
Answer (A) is incorrect. An after-tax loss of $300,000 is reported in the second quarter. Answer (B) is incorrect. The amount of the restatement is $2,700,000. Answer (D) is incorrect. The sum of the restatements for the first two quarters equals $3,000,000.

25.4.3. On June 1, Year 5, the Adipose Corporation, a calendar-year company, settled a patent infringement lawsuit. The court awarded Adipose $3,000,000 in damages. Of this amount, $1,000,000 related to each of Year 3 and Year 4, and $500,000 related to each of the first two quarters in Year 5. The applicable tax rate is 40%. What effect does the settlement have on the net income of the second quarter of Year 5?

- A. $200,000

- B. $300,000

- C. $600,000

- D. $1,800,000

Answer (B) is correct. *(Publisher, adapted)*
REQUIRED: The effect of a patent lawsuit settlement on second quarter net income.
DISCUSSION: If an item of profit related to settlement of litigation occurs in other than the first interim period of the fiscal year (here, the second quarter of a calendar-year company), and all or part of the item of profit meets the criteria for an adjustment related to a prior interim period of the current fiscal year, the portion of the item allocable to the current interim period should be included in the determination of net income for that period. Prior interim periods should be restated to include their allocable portions of the adjustment. Accordingly, $500,000 of the settlement should be included in the determination of net income for the second quarter. Given a tax rate of 40%, the settlement increases net income of the second quarter by $300,000.
Answer (A) is incorrect. The amount of the income tax is $200,000. Answer (C) is incorrect. The adjustment to be made to each year (Year 4 and Year 3) is $600,000. Answer (D) is incorrect. The income should not be recognized entirely in Year 5.

25.4.4. On September 30, Year 3, the Cantata Corporation, a calendar-year company, reached an agreement with the Internal Revenue Service. The company agreed to pay additional income taxes of $2,000,000 that directly related to a loss claimed in the third quarter of Year 1. In accordance with current authoritative guidance, this transaction should be recorded as a

A. Component of the net income reported for the third quarter of Year 3.

B. Restatement of the net income previously reported for the first quarter of Year 3.

C. Restatement of the beginning retained earnings previously reported for the third quarter of Year 3.

D. Restatement of the beginning retained earnings previously reported for the first quarter of Year 3.

Answer (A) is correct. *(Publisher, adapted)*
REQUIRED: The proper recording of an income tax settlement reached in the third quarter of the current year relating to the third quarter of a prior year.
DISCUSSION: A prior interim period adjustment may be required for (1) an adjustment or settlement of litigation, (2) income taxes (except for the effects of retroactive tax legislation), (3) renegotiation proceedings, and (4) utility revenue under rate-making processes. All or part of the adjustment or settlement must relate specifically to a prior interim period of the current year, its effect must be material, and the amount must have become reasonably estimable only in the current interim period. XYZ's transaction does not qualify as a prior interim period adjustment because no portion of the item is related to prior interim periods of the current fiscal year. Thus, the tax settlement liability should be included in net income in the third quarter of Year 3.
Answer (B) is incorrect. The item does not qualify for treatment as a prior interim period adjustment in the current fiscal year. Answer (C) is incorrect. The item should be a component of net income in the current fiscal year. Answer (D) is incorrect. A tax settlement related to a prior fiscal year is not treated as a prior-period adjustment.

25.5 Interim Income Taxes

25.5.1. For interim financial reporting, a company's income tax provision for the second quarter should be determined using the

A. Statutory tax rate for the year.

B. Effective tax rate expected to be applicable for the full year as estimated at the end of the first quarter.

C. Effective tax rate expected to be applicable for the full year as estimated at the end of the second quarter.

D. Effective tax rate expected to be applicable for the second quarter.

Answer (C) is correct. *(CPA, adapted)*
REQUIRED: The tax rate used to determine the interim income tax provision.
DISCUSSION: At the end of each interim period, the entity should estimate the annual effective tax rate. This rate is used in providing for income taxes on a current year-to-date basis.
Answer (A) is incorrect. The quarterly tax provision should be based on the rate expected to be applicable for the full year as determined at the end of the quarter. Answer (B) is incorrect. The quarterly tax provision should be based on the rate expected to be applicable for the full year as determined at the end of the quarter. Answer (D) is incorrect. The quarterly tax provision should be based on the rate expected to be applicable for the full year as determined at the end of the quarter.

25.5.2. For interim financial reporting, the computation of a company's second quarter provision for income taxes uses an effective tax rate expected to be applicable for the full fiscal year. The effective tax rate should reflect anticipated

	Foreign Tax Rates	Available Tax Planning Alternatives
A.	No	Yes
B.	No	No
C.	Yes	No
D.	Yes	Yes

Answer (D) is correct. *(CPA, adapted)*
REQUIRED: The factors used to estimate the annual effective tax rate for interim statements.
DISCUSSION: The estimated annual effective tax rate should be based upon the statutory rate adjusted for the current year's expected conditions. These conditions include anticipated investment tax credits, foreign tax rates, percentage depletion, capital gains rates, and other tax planning alternatives. The rate should also include "the effect of any valuation allowance expected to be necessary at year end for deferred tax assets related to originating deductible temporary differences and carryforwards during the year."

25.5.3. The computation of a company's third quarter provision for income taxes should be based upon "ordinary" income (loss)

A. For the quarter at an expected annual effective income tax rate.

B. For the quarter at the statutory rate.

C. To date at an expected annual effective income tax rate, minus prior quarters' provisions.

D. To date at the statutory rate, minus prior quarters' provisions.

Answer (C) is correct. *(CPA, adapted)*
REQUIRED: The correct computation of a third quarter provision for income taxes.
DISCUSSION: The income tax provision for an interim period should be calculated by applying the estimated annual effective tax rate to the "ordinary" income (loss) for the year to date and then deducting the prior interim periods' income tax provisions. "Ordinary" in this context means excluding unusual or infrequent items and discontinued operations.
Answer (A) is incorrect. The calculation must apply the expected annual effective income tax rate to the cumulative "ordinary" income (loss) for the year to date and then subtract prior quarters' tax provisions. Answer (B) is incorrect. The company must use an expected annual effective income tax rate. Answer (D) is incorrect. The company must use an estimated tax rate.

25.5.4. During the first quarter of Year 4, Tech Co. had income before taxes of $200,000, and its effective income tax rate was 15%. Tech's Year 3 effective annual income tax rate was 30%, but Tech expects its Year 4 effective annual income tax rate to be 25%. In its first quarter interim income statement, what amount of income tax expense should Tech report?

A. $0

B. $30,000

C. $50,000

D. $60,000

Answer (C) is correct. *(CPA, adapted)*
REQUIRED: The provision for income taxes for the first interim period.
DISCUSSION: At the end of each interim period, the entity should estimate the annual effective tax rate. This rate is used in providing for income taxes on a current year-to-date basis. Tech's income before taxes for the first quarter is $200,000, and the estimated annual effective tax rate for Year 4 is 25%. The provision for income taxes for the first interim period is therefore $50,000 ($200,000 × 25%).
Answer (A) is incorrect. Zero excludes any income tax expense. Answer (B) is incorrect. The amount of $30,000 uses Tech's quarterly effective income tax rate. Answer (D) is incorrect. The amount of $60,000 uses Tech's Year 3 effective annual income tax rate.

25.5.5. Bard Co., a calendar-year corporation, reported income before income tax expense of $10,000 and income tax expense of $1,500 in its interim income statement for the first quarter of the year. Bard had income before income tax expense of $20,000 for the second quarter and an estimated effective annual rate of 25%. What amount should Bard report as income tax expense in its interim income statement for the second quarter?

A. $3,500

B. $5,000

C. $6,000

D. $7,500

Answer (C) is correct. *(CPA, adapted)*
REQUIRED: The income tax expense reported in the second quarter interim income statement.
DISCUSSION: Interim period tax expense equals the estimated annual effective tax rate, times year-to-date "ordinary income," minus the tax expense recognized in previous interim periods. Accordingly, the income tax expense reported in the interim income statement for the second quarter is calculated as follows:

First quarter pre-tax income	$10,000
Second quarter pre-tax income	20,000
Total year-to-date income	$30,000
Times: Estimated effective annual tax rate	25%
Total tax expense	$ 7,500
Minus: Income tax expense for first quarter	(1,500)
Income tax expense for second quarter	$ 6,000

Answer (A) is incorrect. The amount of $3,500 equals the second quarter pre-tax income, times the estimated annual tax rate, minus the income tax expense for the first quarter. Answer (B) is incorrect. The amount of $5,000 equals the second quarter pre-tax income times the estimated annual tax rate. Answer (D) is incorrect. The amount of $7,500 is the total tax expense for the first two quarters.

25.5.6. The following information was used in preparing Nocturne Company's quarterly income statements during the first half of the current year:

Quarter	Income before Income Taxes	Estimated Effective Annual Income Tax Rate
1	$80,000	45%
2	70,000	45%

For the third quarter of the current year, income before income taxes was $50,000, and the estimated effective annual income tax rate was 40%. The income statement for the third quarter of the current year should include a provision for income taxes of

A. $12,500

B. $17,500

C. $20,000

D. $22,500

Answer (A) is correct. *(CIA, adapted)*
REQUIRED: The income taxes reported in the interim income statement for the third quarter.
DISCUSSION: The reported tax for the third quarter is calculated by multiplying the estimated annual effective tax rate determined at the end of the third quarter times the cumulative year-to-date ordinary income (loss). The cumulative tax reported for the first two quarters is then subtracted. At the end of the third quarter, the year-to-date ordinary income is $200,000 ($80,000 + $70,000 + $50,000), and the cumulative tax provision is $80,000 ($200,000 × 40%). Because the cumulative tax provision at the end of the second quarter was $67,500 [($80,000 + $70,000) × 45%], $12,500 ($80,000 – $67,500) should be reported as a provision for income taxes in the income statement for the third quarter.
Answer (B) is incorrect. The amount of $17,500 adds the estimated income tax of $50,000 at 40% to the cumulative tax provision and then subtracts $150,000 (80,000 + 70,000) × 40%. Answer (C) is incorrect. The amount of $20,000 is the third-quarter effective annual income tax rate multiplied by income before taxes ($50,000 × 40%). Answer (D) is incorrect. The amount of $22,500 is the second-quarter effective annual income tax rate multiplied by income before taxes ($50,000 × 45%).

25.5.7. During the first quarter of the calendar year, Worth Co. had income before taxes of $100,000, and its effective income tax rate was 15%. Worth's effective annual income tax rate for the previous year was 30%. Worth expects that its effective annual income tax rate for the current year will be 25%. The statutory tax rate for the current year is 35%. In its first quarter interim income statement, what amount of income tax expense should Worth report?

A. $15,000

B. $25,000

C. $30,000

D. $35,000

Answer (B) is correct. *(CPA, adapted)*
REQUIRED: The amount of income tax expense to report.
DISCUSSION: At the end of each interim period, the entity should estimate the annual effective tax rate. This tax rate is used in providing for income taxes on a current year-to-date basis. Since the estimated annual effective tax rate for the current year is 25% and the income before taxes is $100,000, the provision for income taxes for the first interim period is $25,000 ($100,000 × 25%).
Answer (A) is incorrect. Worth's actual effective tax rate for the first quarter is not the rate used to calculate interim-period tax expense. Answer (C) is incorrect. Worth's previous-year effective annual income tax rate is not the rate used to calculate interim-period tax expense for the current year. Answer (D) is incorrect. The statutory tax rate is not the rate used to calculate interim-period tax expense. The estimated annual effective tax rate is used in providing for income taxes on a current year-to-date basis. This rate is based on the statutory rate adjusted for the current year's expected conditions, such as capital gain rates, foreign tax rates, etc.

25.6 IFRS

25.6.1. Wilson Corp. experienced a decline in the net realizable value (NRV) of its inventory to an amount $50,000 below cost. The loss occurred in the first quarter of its fiscal year. Wilson had expected this decline to reverse in the third quarter, and, in fact, the third quarter recovery exceeded the previous decline by $10,000. Wilson's inventory did not experience any other changes in NRV during the fiscal year. What amounts of loss or gain should Wilson report in its interim financial statements for the first and third quarters?

	First Quarter	Third Quarter
A.	$0	$0
B.	$0	$10,000 gain
C.	$50,000 loss	$50,000 gain
D.	$0	$60,000 gain

Answer (C) is correct. *(CPA, adapted)*
REQUIRED: The loss or gain reported for changes in the NRV of inventory in interim financial statements.
DISCUSSION: Under IFRS, inventory is measured at the lower of cost or NRV, regardless of whether it is expected to be recovered within the fiscal year. If the loss is recovered later during the fiscal year (in another quarter), it should be treated as a change in estimate. The price recovery recognized is limited to the extent of the losses previously recognized because inventory may be written up only to the lower of cost or NRV as a result of a new assessment of NRV each period.
Answer (A) is incorrect. The first quarter decline and the third quarter recovery (limited to lower of cost or revised NRV) must be recognized when they occurred. Answer (B) is incorrect. A first quarter loss of $50,000 and a third quarter gain of $50,000 must be recognized. Answer (D) is incorrect. A first quarter loss of $50,000 must be recognized. The third quarter gain is limited to the increase in the revised NRV that is not above cost.

25.6.2. Cox Co. accounts for its inventory using the LIFO cost method. An inventory loss from a permanent market decline of $360,000 occurred in May. Cox appropriately recorded this loss in May after its March 31 quarterly report was issued. What amount of inventory loss should be reported in Cox's quarterly income statement for the 3 months ended June 30?

A. $0

B. $90,000

C. $180,000

D. $360,000

Answer (D) is correct. *(CPA, adapted)*
REQUIRED: The permanent inventory loss from market decline reported in a quarterly income statement.
DISCUSSION: An inventory loss from market decline must not be deferred beyond the interim period in which it occurs, unless it is expected to be recovered within the fiscal year. The $360,000 market decline occurring in the quarter ended 6/30 is not considered temporary. Thus, it should be recognized in full in that quarter.
Answer (A) is incorrect. The amount of $0 assumes no loss should be recognized in the quarter ended 6/30. Answer (B) is incorrect. The amount of $90,000 assumes proration over four quarters. Answer (C) is incorrect. The amount of $180,000 assumes proration over two quarters.

25.6.3. A company determined the following information for its FIFO basis inventory at the end of an interim period on June 30, Year 2:

Historical cost	$80,000
Net realizable value (NRV)	77,000
Current replacement cost	76,000
Normal profit margin	2,000

The company expects that on December 31, Year 2, the inventory's NRV will be at least $81,000. What amount of inventory should the company report in its interim financial statements under IFRS and under U.S. GAAP on June 30, Year 2?

	IFRS	U.S. GAAP
A.	$77,000	$80,000
B.	$77,000	$77,000
C.	$80,000	$80,000
D.	$80,000	$81,000

Answer (A) is correct. *(Publisher, adapted)*
REQUIRED: The amount of inventory reported in interim statements under U.S. GAAP and IFRS.
DISCUSSION: Under U.S. GAAP, inventory that is accounted for using the FIFO method is measured at the lower of cost or net realizable value. Although the NRV is lower than the historical cost, the inventory is reported in the interim financial statements at its historical cost of $80,000 because no write-down of inventory is reasonably anticipated for the year. Under IFRS, the inventory is measured at the lower of cost ($80,000) and NRV ($77,000) for each interim reporting period. Whether a market decline is expected to be reversed by the end of the annual period is not considered. Thus, the inventory is reported at its NRV of $77,000.
Answer (B) is incorrect. Under U.S. GAAP, the inventory loss on write-down below cost is deferred if no loss is reasonably anticipated for the year. Answer (C) is incorrect. Under IFRS, the inventory is measured at the lower of cost and NRV ($77,000), regardless of whether the write-down of inventory is expected to be reversed at year end. Answer (D) is incorrect. Under U.S. GAAP, the inventory cannot be reported above its historical cost. Under IFRS, the inventory should not be reported at its historical cost when its NRV is lower.

☑ ≡
☐ ≡   **Use Gleim Test Prep** for interactive study and easy-to-use detailed analytics!
☐ ≡

STUDY UNIT TWENTY-SIX
FOREIGN CURRENCY
TRANSLATION AND TRANSACTIONS

Foreign currency issues include foreign currency translation and foreign currency transactions. A consolidated entity may consist of separate entities operating in different economic and currency environments. Translation is necessary in these circumstances so that all amounts are presented in the reporting currency used in the consolidated statements.

Foreign currency translation uses a current exchange rate to express in the reporting currency amounts that are (1) fixed in units of a different currency or (2) measured in a different currency. For example, a U.S. entity may have a liability fixed in euros that it measures in U.S. dollars. Translation adjustments are reported directly in other comprehensive income (OCI). The **functional currency** is the currency of the primary economic environment in which the entity operates. Normally, that environment is the one in which it primarily generates and expends cash. For example, the functional currency of a foreign subsidiary is more likely to be the parent's currency if its cash flows directly and currently affect the parent's cash flows. If the books of a foreign entity are maintained in a currency not the functional currency, foreign currency amounts must be **remeasured** into the functional currency using (1) historical rates for nonmonetary balance sheet (and related) items and (2) current rates for monetary items (the temporal method). Remeasurement gains and losses on monetary items are recognized in earnings.

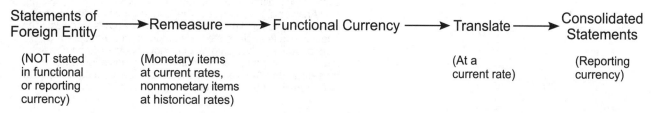

The terms of **foreign currency transactions** are stated in a currency different from the entity's functional currency. For example, if an entity whose functional currency is the U.S. dollar purchases inventory on credit from a German entity, payment is to be in euros. Initial measurement is in the functional currency using the exchange rate at the date of the transaction. A gain or loss is recognized in earnings for a change in the exchange rate between the transaction date, the statement date, and the settlement date.

QUESTIONS

26.1 Foreign Currency Translation

26.1.1. The financial results of three foreign subsidiaries are included along with those of a U.S. parent in consolidated financial statements. The subsidiaries are distinct and separable from the parent and from each other. If the four operations are conducted in four different economic environments, how many different functional currencies most likely are necessary to measure these operations?

A. One.

B. Two.

C. Three.

D. Four.

Answer (D) is correct. *(Publisher, adapted)*
REQUIRED: The number of functional currencies involved in measuring the financial activities of a parent and three distinct subsidiaries operating in different environments.
DISCUSSION: The activities of an entity must be measured in terms of the currency of the primary economic environment in which the entity operates, that is, the functional currency. Because the four operations (parent and three subsidiaries) are distinct and separable from each other and are conducted in four different economic environments, each entity's assets, liabilities, and operations are measured using a different functional currency.
Answer (A) is incorrect. The operations are not all reported using the parent's functional currency. Answer (B) is incorrect. Each of the four operations (most likely) has its own functional currency. Answer (C) is incorrect. Each of the four operations (most likely) has its own functional currency.

26.1.2. The assets, liabilities, and operations of a foreign subsidiary are presented in the consolidated financial statements of a U.S.-based parent. They must be measured in

A. The functional currency of the subsidiary.

B. The local currency of the subsidiary.

C. The reporting currency.

D. The local currency of the parent.

Answer (A) is correct. *(Publisher, adapted)*
REQUIRED: The conversion of foreign subsidiary financial statements for consolidation purposes.
DISCUSSION: The assets, liabilities, and operations of a foreign entity must be measured using its functional currency. Thus, translation into the reporting currency should reflect in the consolidated statements the financial results of the consolidated entities measured in their functional currencies. The steps in the translation process include (1) identifying the functional currency of the entity (the currency of the primary economic environment in which the entity operates), (2) remeasuring the entity's financial statements into the functional currency if they are measured in another currency, and (3) translating (using a current rate) the entity's financial statements into the reporting currency if it differs from the functional currency.
Answer (B) is incorrect. The local currency of the subsidiary may not be its functional currency. Answer (C) is incorrect. The subsidiary's financial statement amounts are measured (or remeasured) in its functional currency. They are then translated into the reporting currency (if different). Translation is not measurement. Answer (D) is incorrect. The local currency of the parent may not be the functional currency of the subsidiary.

26.1.3. GAAP provide specific guidelines for translating foreign currency financial statements. The translation process begins with a determination of whether a foreign affiliate's functional currency is also its local reporting currency. Which one of the following factors indicates that a foreign affiliate's functional currency is the U.S. dollar?

A. Cash flows are primarily in foreign currency and do not affect parent's cash flows.

B. Financing is primarily obtained from local foreign sources and from the affiliate's operations.

C. Sales prices are responsive to short-term changes in exchange rates and worldwide competition.

D. Labor, materials, and other costs consist primarily of local costs to the foreign affiliate.

Answer (C) is correct. *(CMA, adapted)*
REQUIRED: The factor indicating that a foreign affiliate's functional currency is the U.S. dollar.
DISCUSSION: The functional currency is the currency of the primary economic environment in which an entity operates. It is normally the currency of the environment in which an entity primarily generates and expends cash. If a U.S. entity's foreign affiliate's sales prices respond to short-term changes in exchange rates and worldwide competition, its functional currency is likely to be the U.S. dollar.
Answer (A) is incorrect. Cash flows that are primarily in a foreign currency indicate that the foreign currency is the functional currency. Answer (B) is incorrect. When financing is obtained primarily from foreign sources and operations, the foreign currency is likely to be the functional currency. Answer (D) is incorrect. When costs are primarily paid in the foreign country, the foreign currency is likely to be the functional currency.

26.1.4. A wholly owned subsidiary of Ward, Inc., has certain expense accounts for the year ended December 31, Year 4, stated in local currency units (LCU) as follows:

	LCU
Depreciation of equipment (related	
assets purchased Jan. 1, Year 2)	120,000
Provision for doubtful accounts	80,000
Rent	200,000

The exchange rates at various dates are as follows:

	Dollar Equivalent of 1 LCU
December 31, Year 4	$.40
Average for year ended 12/31/Yr 4	.44
January 1, Year 2	.50

Assume that the LCU is the subsidiary's functional currency and that the charges to the expense accounts occurred approximately evenly during the year. What total dollar amount should be included in Ward's Year 4 consolidated income statement to reflect these expenses?

A. $160,000

B. $172,000

C. $176,000

D. $200,000

Answer (C) is correct. *(CPA, adapted)*
REQUIRED: The amount of expenses in the consolidated income statement.
DISCUSSION: When the local currency of the subsidiary is the functional currency, translation into the reporting currency is necessary. Assets and liabilities are translated at the exchange rate at the balance sheet date, and revenues, expenses, gains, and losses are usually translated at average rates for the period. Thus, the 400,000 LCU in total expenses should be translated at the average exchange rate of $.44, resulting in expenses reflected in the consolidated income statement of $176,000 (400,000 LCU × $.44).
Answer (A) is incorrect. The average exchange rate, not the current year-end rate, should be used. Answer (B) is incorrect. The average exchange rate, not a combination of rates, should be used. Answer (D) is incorrect. It values all assets at the January 1, Year 2, rate.

26.1.5. A wholly owned foreign subsidiary of Union Corporation has certain expense accounts for the year ended December 31, Year 10, stated in local currency units (LCUs) as follows:

	LCU
Amortization of patent (related	
patent acquired Jan. 1, Year 8)	40,000
Provision for doubtful accounts	60,000
Rent	100,000

The exchange rates at various dates are as follows:

	Dollar Equivalent of 1 LCU
December 31, Year 10	$.20
Average for year ended	
12/31/Year 10	.22
January 1, Year 8	.25

The subsidiary's operations were an extension of the parent company's operations. What total dollar amount should be included in Union's income statement to reflect the above expenses for the year ended December 31, Year 10?

A. $40,000

B. $42,000

C. $44,000

D. $45,200

Answer (D) is correct. *(CPA, adapted)*
REQUIRED: The dollar amount of remeasured expenses of a foreign subsidiary whose operations are an extension of the parent's.
DISCUSSION: Given that the foreign subsidiary's operations are an extension of the parent's, the functional currency of the subsidiary is considered to be the U.S. dollar. Thus, remeasurement from the local currency to the U.S. dollar is required for financial statement purposes.
Nonmonetary balance sheet items and related revenues and expenses (e.g., cost of sales, depreciation, and amortization) should be remeasured using historical rates to produce the same results as if those items had been initially recorded in the functional currency (U.S. dollar). Accordingly, the amortization of patent expense (LCUs = 40,000) should be remeasured at the rate of exchange in effect at the date the patent was acquired, $.25. Monetary and current value items should be remeasured at a current rate. Thus, provision for doubtful accounts and rent should be remeasured at the average Year 10 exchange rate of $.22, which is the customary approximation of the current rate used to remeasure expenses not related to nonmonetary items.

Patent amortization	40,000 × $.25	=	$10,000
Provision for doubtful accounts	60,000 × $.22	=	13,200
Rent	100,000 × $.22	=	22,000
Total remeasured expenses			$45,200

Answer (A) is incorrect. The amount of $40,000 results from applying the year-end exchange rate to the total expenses. Answer (B) is incorrect. The amount of $42,000 results from applying the average rate to the patent and the year-end rate to the rent. Answer (C) is incorrect. The amount of $44,000 results from applying the average rate to the total expenses.

26.1.6. Which of the following is not part of foreign currency translation?

A. The functional currency of each foreign operation must be identified.

B. All elements of the financial statements of a foreign operation must be measured in the functional currency.

C. If the functional currency of a foreign operation differs from the reporting currency, translation using the current exchange rate method is required.

D. The gain or loss arising from translation must be included in earnings of the current period.

Answer (D) is correct. *(Publisher, adapted)*
REQUIRED: The item that is not part of foreign currency translation.
DISCUSSION: A gain or loss arising from translation from the functional currency into the reporting currency is not included in the current period's earnings. Translation adjustments are reported in OCI.
Answer (A) is incorrect. One step in the process is identifying the functional currency of each operation. Answer (B) is incorrect. One step in the process is measuring the elements of the financial statements of a foreign operation in the functional currency. Answer (C) is incorrect. One step in the process is translating functional currency amounts into the reporting currency using the current exchange rate method.

26.1.7. In preparing consolidated financial statements of a U.S. parent company with a foreign subsidiary, the foreign subsidiary's functional currency is the currency

A. In which the subsidiary maintains its accounting records.

B. Of the country in which the subsidiary is located.

C. Of the country in which the parent is located.

D. Of the environment in which the subsidiary primarily generates and expends cash.

Answer (D) is correct. *(CPA, adapted)*
REQUIRED: The foreign subsidiary's functional currency.
DISCUSSION: The method used to convert foreign currency amounts into units of the reporting currency is the functional currency translation approach. It is appropriate for use in accounting for and reporting the financial results and relationships of foreign subsidiaries in consolidated statements. This method (1) identifies the functional currency of the entity (the currency of the primary economic environment in which the foreign entity operates), (2) measures all elements of the financial statements in the functional currency, and (3) uses a current exchange rate for translation from the functional currency to the reporting currency. The currency indicated by the relevant economic indicators, such as cash flows, sales prices, sales markets, expenses, financing, and intraentity transactions, may not be (1) the currency in which the subsidiary maintains its accounting records, (2) the currency of the country in which the subsidiary is located, or (3) the currency of the country in which the parent is located.
Answer (A) is incorrect. The currency in which the subsidiary maintains its accounting records may not be the currency indicated by the relevant economic indicators. Answer (B) is incorrect. The currency of the country in which the subsidiary is located may not be the currency indicated by the relevant economic indicators. Answer (C) is incorrect. The currency of the country in which the parent is located may not be the currency indicated by the relevant economic indicators.

26.1.8. Which of the following is included in other comprehensive income?

A. Unrealized holding gains and losses on trading debt securities.

B. Unrealized holding gains and losses that result from a debt security being transferred into the held-to-maturity category from the available-for-sale category.

C. Foreign currency translation adjustments.

D. The difference between the accumulated benefit obligation and the fair value of pension plan assets.

Answer (C) is correct. *(CPA, adapted)*
REQUIRED: The item included in OCI.
DISCUSSION: Other comprehensive income (OCI) includes all items of comprehensive income not included in net income. Foreign currency translation adjustments for a foreign operation that is relatively self-contained and integrated within its environment do not affect cash flows of the reporting entity. Thus, they are excluded from earnings and reported in OCI.
Answer (A) is incorrect. Unrealized holding gains and losses on available-for-sale (not trading) debt securities are included in OCI. Answer (B) is incorrect. When a debt security is transferred to the held-to-maturity category from the available-for sale category, amounts previously recognized in OCI are not reversed. However, they are amortized to earnings in the same way as premium or discount. Moreover, the transfer does not result in recognition of any new amounts in OCI. If the transfer is to available-for-sale from held-to-maturity, any unrealized gains or losses that were previously unrecognized are recognized in OCI. Answer (D) is incorrect. The difference between the projected benefit obligation and the fair value of pension plan assets is the amount by which a defined benefit pension plan is over- or underfunded. It is reported as an asset or a liability. The excess of the ABO over the fair value of plan assets was the measure of the liability required to be recognized according to prior guidance.

26.1.9. If an entity's books of account are not maintained in its functional currency, GAAP require remeasurement into the functional currency prior to the translation process. An item that should be remeasured by use of the current exchange rate is

A. An investment in bonds to be held until maturity.

B. A plant asset and the associated accumulated depreciation.

C. A patent and the associated accumulated amortization.

D. The revenue from a long-term construction contract.

Answer (A) is correct. *(CMA, adapted)*
REQUIRED: The item that should be remeasured into the functional currency using the current exchange rate.
DISCUSSION: Common nonmonetary balance sheet items and their related revenues, expenses, gains, and losses are remeasured at historical rates. All others are remeasured using the current rate. Thus, most monetary items, such as an investment in bonds, are remeasured at the current exchange rate.
Answer (B) is incorrect. Plant assets are remeasured at historical rates. Answer (C) is incorrect. A patent is remeasured at historical rates. Answer (D) is incorrect. The revenue from a long-term construction contract is one of the exceptions for which the current rate is not to be used.

26.1.10. Certain balance sheet accounts of a foreign subsidiary of Rowan, Inc., at December 31, have been translated into U.S. dollars as follows:

	Translated at	
	Current Rates	Historical Rates
Note receivable, long-term	$240,000	$200,000
Prepaid rent	85,000	80,000
Patent	150,000	170,000
	$475,000	$450,000

The subsidiary's functional currency is the currency of the country in which it is located. What total amount should be included in Rowan's December 31 consolidated balance sheet for the above accounts?

A. $450,000

B. $455,000

C. $475,000

D. $495,000

Answer (C) is correct. *(CPA, adapted)*
REQUIRED: The total translated amount to be included in the consolidated balance sheet.
DISCUSSION: When the currency used to prepare a foreign entity's financial statements is its functional currency, the current-rate method is used to translate the foreign entity's financial statements into the reporting currency. This method applies the current exchange rate at the balance sheet date to assets and liabilities and historical rates to shareholders' equity. The translation gains and losses arising from applying this method are reported in other comprehensive income in the consolidated statements and are not reflected in earnings. Because Rowan's listed assets should be translated at current rates, $475,000 is the total amount that should be included in the consolidated balance sheet.
Answer (A) is incorrect. The amount of $450,000 results from translating all listed items at historical rates. Answer (B) is incorrect. The amount of $455,000 results from translating all listed items except prepaid rent at historical rates. Answer (D) is incorrect. The amount of $495,000 results from translating all listed items except the patent at current rates.

26.1.11. A foreign subsidiary's functional currency is its local currency, which has not experienced significant inflation. The weighted-average exchange rate for the current year is an appropriate exchange rate for translating

	Wages Expense	Sales to Customers
A.	Yes	No
B.	Yes	Yes
C.	No	Yes
D.	No	No

Answer (B) is correct. *(CPA, adapted)*
REQUIRED: The item(s) translated at the weighted-average exchange rate for the current year.
DISCUSSION: When an entity's local currency is the functional currency and this currency has not experienced significant inflation, translation into the reporting currency of all elements of the financial statements must be at a current exchange rate. Assets and liabilities are translated at the exchange rate at the balance sheet date. Revenues (e.g., sales), expenses (e.g., wages), gains, and losses should be translated at the rates in effect when they were recognized. However, translation of income statement items at a weighted-average rate for the period is permitted.
Answer (A) is incorrect. Wages expense and sales to customers are appropriately translated using the weighted-average exchange rate for the current year. Answer (C) is incorrect. Wages expense and sales to customers are appropriately translated using the weighted-average exchange rate for the current year. Answer (D) is incorrect. Wages expense and sales to customers are appropriately translated using the weighted-average exchange rate for the current year.

26.1.12. If all assets and liabilities of a firm's foreign subsidiary are translated into the parent's currency at the current exchange rate (the rate in effect at the date of the balance sheet), the extent of the parent firm's translation gain or loss is based on the subsidiary's

A. Current assets minus current liabilities.

B. Total assets minus total liabilities.

C. Monetary assets minus monetary liabilities.

D. Operating cash flows.

Answer (B) is correct. *(CIA, adapted)*
REQUIRED: The basis for the parent's translation gain or loss if all assets and liabilities of the foreign subsidiary are translated at the current exchange rate.
DISCUSSION: When the functional currency of a foreign subsidiary is the local (foreign) currency, translation of all assets and liabilities is required at the current rate as of the balance sheet date.

26.1.13. The economic effects of a change in foreign exchange rates on a relatively self-contained and integrated operation within a foreign country relate to the net investment by the reporting entity in that operation. Consequently, translation adjustments that arise from the consolidation of that operation

A. Directly affect the reporting entity's cash flows but must not be included in earnings.

B. Directly affect the reporting entity's cash flows and must be included in earnings.

C. Do not directly affect the reporting entity's cash flows and must not be included in earnings.

D. Do not directly affect the reporting entity's cash flows but must be included in earnings.

Answer (C) is correct. *(Publisher, adapted)*
REQUIRED: The true statement about translation adjustments arising from consolidation of a self-contained foreign operation.
DISCUSSION: Foreign currency translation adjustments for a foreign operation that is relatively self-contained and integrated within its environment do not affect cash flows of the reporting entity and must be excluded from earnings. When an operation is relatively self-contained, the cash generated and expended by the entity is normally in the currency of the foreign country, and that currency is deemed to be the operation's functional currency.
Answer (A) is incorrect. When an operation is relatively self-contained, the assumption is that translation adjustments do not affect cash flows. Answer (B) is incorrect. When an operation is relatively self-contained, the assumption is that translation adjustments do not affect cash flows, and translation adjustments must be included in other comprehensive income, not earnings. Answer (D) is incorrect. Translation adjustments must be included in OCI, not earnings.

26.1.14. U.S. GAAP require the current rate of exchange to be used for remeasuring certain balance sheet items and the historical rate of exchange for other balance sheet items. An item that should be remeasured using the historical exchange rate is

A. Accounts and notes receivable.

B. Accounts and notes payable.

C. Taxes payable.

D. Prepaid expenses.

Answer (D) is correct. *(CMA, adapted)*
REQUIRED: The item that should be remeasured using the historical exchange rate.
DISCUSSION: Financial statements are remeasured using the temporal rate method. In general, this method adjusts monetary items at the current rate and nonmonetary items at the historical rate. Prepaid expenses is a nonmonetary item that should be remeasured using the historical rate.
Answer (A) is incorrect. They are monetary items. Thus, they should be remeasured using the current rate of exchange. Answer (B) is incorrect. They are monetary items. Thus, they should be remeasured using the current rate of exchange. Answer (C) is incorrect. They are monetary items. Thus, they should be remeasured using the current rate of exchange.

26.1.15. Park Co.'s wholly owned subsidiary, Schnell Corp., maintains its accounting records in euros. Because all of Schnell's branch offices are in London, its functional currency is the British pound. Remeasurement of Schnell's Year 4 financial statements resulted in a $7,600 gain, and translation of its financial statements resulted in an $8,100 gain. What amount should Park report as a foreign currency transaction gain in its income statement for the year ended December 31, Year 4?

A. $0

B. $7,600

C. $8,100

D. $15,700

Answer (B) is correct. *(CPA, adapted)*
REQUIRED: The amount of foreign currency transaction gain that should be included in the income statement.
DISCUSSION: The financial statements must be remeasured into the functional currency using the temporal method and then translated into the reporting currency using the current rate method. The $7,600 gain arising from remeasurement should be reported in current income. The $8,100 translation gain should be reported in other comprehensive income and is not reflected in income.
Answer (A) is incorrect. The gain on remeasurement should be reported in the income statement. Answer (C) is incorrect. The $8,100 translation gain is reported in other comprehensive income, and the $7,600 gain should be reported as part of continuing operations. Answer (D) is incorrect. The $8,100 translation gain is reported in other comprehensive income.

26.1.16. When remeasuring foreign currency financial statements into the functional currency, which of the following items would be remeasured using historical exchange rates?

A. Inventories carried at cost.

B. Equity securities reported at fair values.

C. Bonds payable.

D. Accrued liabilities.

Answer (A) is correct. *(CPA, adapted)*
REQUIRED: The item remeasured using historical exchange rates.
DISCUSSION: The current rate of exchange is used for remeasuring certain balance sheet items and the historical rate for other balance sheet items. Nonmonetary balance sheet items and related revenue, expense, gain, and loss accounts are remeasured at the historical rate. Monetary accounts are remeasured at the current rate. Inventories valued at cost are nonmonetary items and are measured at historical rates.
Answer (B) is incorrect. Equity securities reported at fair values are monetary items valued at the current rate. Answer (C) is incorrect. Bonds payable are monetary items valued at the current rate. Answer (D) is incorrect. Accrued liabilities are monetary items valued at the current rate.

26.1.17. The Brinjac Company owns a foreign subsidiary. Included among the subsidiary's liabilities for the year just ended are 400,000 LCUs of revenue received in advance, recorded when $.50 was the dollar equivalent per LCU, and a deferred tax liability for 187,500 LCU, recognized when $.40 was the dollar equivalent per LCUs. The rate of exchange in effect at year end was $.35 per LCU. If the dollar is the functional currency, what total should be included for these two liabilities on Brinjac's consolidated balance sheet at year end?

A. $205,625

B. $215,000

C. $265,625

D. $275,000

Answer (D) is correct. *(C.J. Skender)*
REQUIRED: The total of two liabilities of a foreign subsidiary in the consolidated statements if the functional currency is the U.S. dollar.
DISCUSSION: When a foreign entity's functional currency is the U.S. dollar, the financial statements of the entity recorded in a foreign currency must be remeasured in terms of the U.S. dollar. Revenue received in advance (deferred income) is considered a nonmonetary balance sheet item and is remeasured at the applicable historical rate (400,000 LCUs × $.50 per LCU = $200,000). Deferred charges and credits (except policy acquisition costs for life insurance companies) also are remeasured at historical exchange rates. Consequently, the deferred tax liability (a deferred credit) is remeasured at the historical rate (187,500 LCUs × $.40 per LCU) = $75,000). The total for these liabilities is therefore $275,000 ($200,000 + $75,000).
Answer (A) is incorrect. The amount of $205,625 results from applying the year-end rate to the total liabilities. Answer (B) is incorrect. The historical, not current, rate must be used to remeasure the deferred income. Answer (C) is incorrect. The historical rate is used to remeasure nonmonetary balance sheet items, including deferred tax assets and liabilities.

26.1.18. The Dease Company owns a foreign subsidiary with 3,600,000 local currency units (LCUs) of property, plant, and equipment before accumulated depreciation on December 31, Year 7. The subsidiary's functional currency is the U.S. dollar. Of this amount, 2,400,000 LCUs were acquired in Year 0 when the rate of exchange was 1.6 LCUs to $1, and 1,200,000 LCUs were acquired in Year 3 when the rate of exchange was 1.8 LCUs to $1. The rate of exchange in effect at December 31, Year 7, was 2 LCUs to $1. The weighted average of exchange rates in effect during Year 7 was 1.92 LCUs to $1. Assuming that the property, plant, and equipment are depreciated using the straight-line method over a 10-year period with no salvage value, how much depreciation expense relating to the foreign subsidiary's property, plant, and equipment should be charged in Dease's income statement for Year 7?

A. $180,000

B. $187,500

C. $200,000

D. $216,667

Answer (D) is correct. *(CPA, adapted)*
REQUIRED: The amount of remeasured depreciation expense recognized in consolidating a foreign subsidiary whose functional currency is the U.S. dollar.
DISCUSSION: Given that the subsidiary's functional currency is the U.S. dollar, the financial statements of the subsidiary must be remeasured in terms of the dollar. Nonmonetary assets and the related revenues and expenses are remeasured based on the historical rates in effect at the dates of the transactions. Depreciation expense relates to the property, plant, and equipment (nonmonetary assets), so the rate of exchange in effect when these fixed assets were acquired is used in remeasuring depreciation expense for the period.
Because 2,400,000 LCUs of fixed assets were acquired when the rate of exchange was 1.6, depreciation expense can be remeasured by multiplying the LCU depreciation by $1 ÷ 1.6, resulting in $150,000 of remeasured depreciation expense [(2,400,000 ÷ 10) × ($1 ÷ 1.6)]. Depreciation related to the asset that cost 1,200,000 LCUs is $66,667 in remeasured terms [(1,200,000 ÷ 10) × ($1 ÷ 1.8)]. Total depreciation expense equals $216,667 ($150,000 + $66,667).
Answer (A) is incorrect. The amount of $180,000 results from applying the current (year-end) rate to the total depreciation expense. Answer (B) is incorrect. The amount of $187,500 results from applying the average rate to the total depreciation expense. Answer (C) is incorrect. The rate prevailing at the time the assets were acquired should be used for each group of assets.

26.1.19. A foreign subsidiary of a U.S. parent reports its financial statements in its local currency although its functional currency is the U.S. dollar. In the consolidated financial statements, all of the following accounts of the subsidiary are remeasured into the functional currency at the historical rate except

A. Marketable securities carried at cost.

B. Inventories carried at market.

C. Property, plant, and equipment.

D. Goodwill.

Answer (B) is correct. *(J.W. Mantooth)*
REQUIRED: The account that is not remeasured at the historical rate.
DISCUSSION: When a foreign subsidiary's functional currency is the U.S. dollar, all elements of its financial statements reported in a foreign currency must be remeasured as if they had been recorded in the U.S. dollar. Nonmonetary balance sheet items and related revenue, expense, gain, and loss amounts are remeasured at the historical rate. Monetary items are remeasured at the current rate. Inventories carried at market are classified as monetary assets and must be remeasured at the current rate.
Answer (A) is incorrect. Marketable securities carried at cost are remeasured using historical exchange rates. Answer (C) is incorrect. Property, plant, and equipment are remeasured using historical exchange rates. Answer (D) is incorrect. Goodwill is remeasured using historical exchange rates.

26.2 Foreign Currency Transactions

26.2.1. On October 1, Year 5, Mild Co., a U.S. company, purchased machinery from Grund, a German company, with payment due on April 1, Year 6. If Mild's Year 5 operating income included no foreign currency transaction gain or loss, the transaction could have

A. Resulted in an extraordinary gain.

B. Been denominated in U.S. dollars.

C. Caused a foreign currency transaction gain to be reported as a contra account against machinery.

D. Caused a foreign currency translation gain to be reported in OCI.

Answer (B) is correct. *(CPA, adapted)*
REQUIRED: The reason no foreign currency transaction gain or loss occurred when a U.S. company purchased machinery from a German company.
DISCUSSION: A foreign currency transaction results in a receivable or a payable fixed in terms of the amount of foreign currency. A change in the exchange rate between the functional currency and the currency in which the transaction is stated is a gain or loss that ordinarily should be included as a component of income from continuing operations in the period in which the exchange rate changes. If Mild Co.'s functional currency is the U.S. dollar and the transaction was stated in U.S. dollars, the transaction is a foreign transaction, not a foreign currency transaction. Thus, no foreign currency transaction gain or loss occurred.
Answer (A) is incorrect. Extraordinary items are not reported under U.S. GAAP or IFRS. Answer (C) is incorrect. Foreign currency transaction gains and losses are included in earnings. Answer (D) is incorrect. Foreign currency translation gains and losses result from translating functional currency amounts into the reporting currency. If the transaction was stated in U.S. dollars, no translation was needed.

26.2.2. Ball Corp. had the following foreign currency transactions during Year 4:

● Merchandise was purchased from a foreign supplier on January 20, Year 4, for the U.S. dollar equivalent of $90,000. The invoice was paid on March 20, Year 4, at the U.S. dollar equivalent of $96,000.

● On July 1, Year 4, Ball borrowed the U.S. dollar equivalent of $500,000 evidenced by a note that was payable in the lender's local currency on July 1, Year 6. On December 31, Year 4, the U.S. dollar equivalents of the principal amount and accrued interest were $520,000 and $26,000, respectively. Interest on the note is 10% per annum.

In Ball's Year 4 income statement, what amount should be included as a foreign currency transaction loss?

A. $0

B. $6,000

C. $21,000

D. $27,000

Answer (D) is correct. *(CPA, adapted)*
REQUIRED: The amount to be included as a foreign currency transaction loss.
DISCUSSION: When a foreign currency transaction gives rise to a receivable or a payable that is fixed in terms of the foreign currency, a change in the exchange rate between the functional currency and the currency in which the transaction is denominated is a gain or loss that ordinarily should be included as a component of income from continuing operations in the period in which the exchange rate changes. In the Year 4 income statement, the foreign currency transaction loss should include the $6,000 difference between the $90,000 initially recorded as a payable and the $96,000 payment amount, the $20,000 difference between the $500,000 equivalent amount of the principal of the note at December 31 and its $520,000 equivalent at July 1, and the $1,000 difference between the $26,000 equivalent of the interest accrued and the $25,000 [$500,000 × 10% × (6 ÷ 12 months)] interest on the initially recorded amount of the loan. The foreign currency transaction loss therefore equals $27,000 ($6,000 + $20,000 + $1,000).
Answer (A) is incorrect. A foreign currency transaction loss would result from the purchase of merchandise and the note payable. Answer (B) is incorrect. The amount of $6,000 results from not accounting for the loss that results on the note. Answer (C) is incorrect. The amount of $21,000 results from not accounting for the loss that results from the purchase of merchandise.

26.2.3. Shore Co. records its transactions in U.S. dollars. A sale of goods resulted in a receivable denominated in Japanese yen, and a purchase of goods resulted in a payable denominated in euros. Shore recorded a foreign currency transaction gain on collection of the receivable and an exchange loss on settlement of the payable. The exchange rates are expressed as so many units of foreign currency to one dollar. Did the number of foreign currency units exchangeable for a dollar increase or decrease between the contract and settlement dates?

	Yen Exchangeable for $1	Euros Exchangeable for $1
A.	Increase	Increase
B.	Decrease	Decrease
C.	Decrease	Increase
D.	Increase	Decrease

Answer (B) is correct. *(CPA, adapted)*
   REQUIRED: The movements in exchange rates.
   DISCUSSION: When a foreign currency transaction results in a receivable or a payable, fixed in terms of the amount of foreign currency, a change in the exchange rate between the functional currency and the currency in which the transaction is denominated is a gain or loss that ordinarily should be included as a component of income from continuing operations in the period in which the exchange rate changes. A gain on a receivable denominated in a foreign currency results when the fixed amount of the foreign currency can be exchanged for a greater number of dollars at the date of collection, that is, when the number of foreign currency units exchangeable for a dollar decreases. A loss on a payable denominated in a foreign currency results when the number of dollars needed to purchase the fixed amount of the foreign currency increases, that is, when the number of foreign currency units exchangeable for a dollar decreases.
   Answer (A) is incorrect. A gain on a foreign currency receivable and a loss on a foreign currency payable result when the dollar weakens. Answer (C) is incorrect. A gain on a foreign currency receivable and a loss on a foreign currency payable result when the dollar weakens. Answer (D) is incorrect. A gain on a foreign currency receivable and a loss on a foreign currency payable result when the dollar weakens.

26.2.4. On October 1, Velec Co., a U.S. company, contracted to purchase foreign goods requiring payment in euros 1 month after their receipt at Velec's factory. Title to the goods passed on December 15. The goods were still in transit on December 31. Exchange rates were one dollar to 1.06 euros, 1.04 euros, and 1.05 euros on October 1, December 15, and December 31 respectively. Velec should account for the exchange rate fluctuation for the year as

A. A loss included in net income.

B. A gain included in net income.

C. Other comprehensive gain.

D. Other comprehensive loss.

Answer (B) is correct. *(CPA, adapted)*
   REQUIRED: The classification of a gain or loss due to exchange rate fluctuations.
   DISCUSSION: A receivable or payable stated in a foreign currency is adjusted to its current exchange rate at each balance sheet date. The transaction gain or loss arising from this adjustment should ordinarily be reflected in current income. Because title passed on December 15, the liability fixed in euros should have been recorded on that date at the 1.04 euro exchange rate. The increase to 1.05 euros per dollar at year-end decreases the dollar value of the liability and results in a transaction gain. Such a gain is reported as a component of income from continuing operations.
   Answer (A) is incorrect. The strengthening of the dollar from the date the liability was recorded (December 15) to year end resulted in a gain. Answer (C) is incorrect. Foreign currency transaction gains or losses are recognized in the income statement. Answer (D) is incorrect. Foreign currency transaction gains or losses are recognized in the income statement.

26.2.5. Toigo Co. purchased merchandise from a vendor in England on November 20 for 500,000 British pounds. Payment was due in British pounds on January 20. The spot rates to purchase 1 pound were as follows:

November 20	$1.25
December 31	1.20
January 20	1.17

How should the foreign currency transaction gain be reported on Toigo's financial statements at December 31?

A. A gain of $40,000 as a separate component of stockholders' equity.

B. A gain of $40,000 in the income statement.

C. A gain of $25,000 as a separate component of stockholders' equity.

D. A gain of $25,000 in the income statement.

Answer (D) is correct. *(CPA, adapted)*
   REQUIRED: The reporting of a foreign currency transaction gain.
   DISCUSSION: Foreign currency transactions are recorded at the spot rate in effect at the transaction date. Transaction gains and losses are included in the income statement in the period the exchange rate changes. On November 20, the entity made the following entry:

Inventory (500,000 pounds × $1.25)	$625,000	
Accounts payable (pounds)		$625,000

On December 31, the entity made the following entry:

Accounts payable [500,000 pounds × ($1.25 – $1.20)]	$25,000	
Transaction gain		$25,000

   Answer (A) is incorrect. The entity recognizes a gain in earnings of $15,000 [500,000 pounds × ($1.20 – $1.17)] on January 20. Answer (B) is incorrect. The only effect of the change in the spot rate during the period is recognized at the balance sheet date. Answer (C) is incorrect. The gain is recognized in earnings. Translation adjustments are recognized in OCI.

26.2.6. Transaction gains and losses have direct cash flow effects when foreign-denominated monetary assets are settled in amounts greater or less than the functional currency equivalent of the original transactions. These transaction gains and losses should be reflected in income

    A. At the date the transaction originated.

    B. On a retroactive basis.

    C. In the period the exchange rate changes.

    D. Only at the year-end balance sheet date.

Answer (C) is correct. *(CMA, adapted)*
    REQUIRED: The time when foreign currency transaction gains and losses should be reflected in income.
    DISCUSSION: When a foreign currency transaction gives rise to a receivable or a payable that is fixed in terms of the amount of foreign currency to be received or paid, a change in the exchange rate between the functional currency and the currency in which the transaction is stated results in a gain or loss that ordinarily should be included as a component of income from continuing operations in the period in which the exchange rate changes.
    Answer (A) is incorrect. The extent of any gain or loss cannot be known at the date of the original transaction. Answer (B) is incorrect. Retroactive recognition is not permitted. Answer (D) is incorrect. Gains and losses are to be recognized in the period of the rate change.

26.2.7. On September 1, Year 2, Cano & Co., a U.S. corporation, sold merchandise to a foreign firm for 250,000 local currency units (LCUs). Terms of the sale require payment in LCUs on February 1, Year 3. On September 1, Year 2, the spot exchange rate was $0.20 per LCU. On December 31, Year 2, Cano's year-end, the spot rate was $0.19, but the rate increased to $0.22 by February 1, Year 3, when payment was received. How much should Cano report as foreign currency transaction gain or loss in its Year 3 income statement?

    A. $0.

    B. $2,500 loss.

    C. $5,000 gain.

    D. $7,500 gain.

Answer (D) is correct. *(CPA, adapted)*
    REQUIRED: The foreign currency transaction gain or loss in the Year 3 income statement.
    DISCUSSION: A receivable or payable stated in a foreign currency should be recorded at the current exchange rate and then adjusted to the current exchange rate at each balance sheet date. That adjustment is a foreign currency transaction gain or loss that is ordinarily included in earnings for the period of change. Furthermore, a gain or loss measured from the transaction date or the most recent intervening balance sheet date is recognized when the transaction is settled. Accordingly, Cano should recognize a foreign currency transaction gain of $7,500 [250,000 LCUs receivable × ($0.22 – $0.19)] in Year 3.
    Answer (A) is incorrect. The exchange rate changed between the balance sheet date and the settlement date. Answer (B) is incorrect. A $2,500 loss was incurred in Year 2. Answer (C) is incorrect. The net transaction gain is $5,000.

26.2.8. Fay Corp. had a realized foreign currency transaction loss of $15,000 for the year ended December 31, Year 5, and must also determine whether the following items will require year-end adjustment:

- Fay had an $8,000 loss resulting from the translation of the accounts of its wholly owned foreign subsidiary for the year ended December 31, Year 5.
- Fay had an account payable to an unrelated foreign supplier payable in the supplier's local currency. The U.S. dollar equivalent of the payable was $64,000 on the October 31, Year 5, invoice date and $60,000 on December 31, Year 5. The invoice is payable on January 30, Year 6.

In Fay's Year 5 consolidated income statement, what amount should be included as foreign currency transaction loss?

    A. $11,000

    B. $15,000

    C. $19,000

    D. $23,000

Answer (A) is correct. *(CPA, adapted)*
    REQUIRED: The amount to be included as foreign currency transaction loss.
    DISCUSSION: Translation adjustments are reported in OCI. Translation adjustments are therefore not included in earnings. Furthermore, a receivable or payable fixed in terms of a foreign currency is recorded at the date of the transaction at the current rate of exchange. This receivable or payable must then be adjusted to the current rate at each balance sheet date. The gain or loss from this adjustment is included in earnings. Accordingly, the $4,000 ($64,000 – $60,000) gain adjustment arising from the foreign currency transaction should be included along with the realized foreign currency transaction loss of $15,000 in the Year 5 consolidated income statement. The amount to be reported is an $11,000 ($15,000 loss – $4,000 gain) foreign currency transaction loss.
    Answer (B) is incorrect. The amount of $15,000 excludes the $4,000 gain. Answer (C) is incorrect. The gain was added to, rather than subtracted from, the loss. Answer (D) is incorrect. The translation loss is added to the loss, and the transaction gain is not included.

☑ ☰
☐ ☰   Use **Gleim Test Prep** for interactive study and easy-to-use detailed analytics!
☐ ☰

STUDY UNIT TWENTY-SEVEN
STATE AND LOCAL GOVERNMENTS

Accountability (fiscal and operational) is the primary objective of all governmental financial reporting. It is a broad concept that is based on the public's right to know. The diversity of governmental activities and the need for legal compliance require multiple accounting entities (funds). A **fund** is an independent, distinct fiscal and accounting entity with a self-balancing set of accounts. Items in a fund are segregated because they relate to activities or objectives that are subject to special regulations or limitations.

Governmental funds emphasize fiscal accountability. They account for the nonbusiness activities of a government and its current, expendable resources (most often taxes). They have a current financial resources measurement focus and use modified accrual accounting. They do not report capital assets and long-term liabilities. They do report deferred inflows and outflows of resources. The general fund accounts for all financial resources except those required to be accounted for in another fund. Special revenue funds account for restricted or committed inflows from specific revenue sources. Capital projects funds account for financial resources restricted, committed, or assigned to be expended for capital purposes. Debt service funds account for resources restricted, committed, or assigned to paying principal and interest. But these funds do not account for the debt itself. Permanent funds account for resources that are restricted to the use of earnings (not principal) for the benefit of the government or its citizens. An example is a perpetual-care fund for a public cemetery.

Proprietary funds provide operational information about the business-type activities of a government. They generally are financed through fees. They (1) have an economic resources measurement focus; (2) use accrual accounting; and (3) report capital assets, long-term liabilities, and deferred flows of resources. Enterprise funds account for activities that benefit outside parties who are willing to pay for them, such as parking garages and utilities. Internal service funds account for activities performed primarily for the benefit of other agencies, such as a centralized IT department.

Fiduciary funds provide operational information about the **fiduciary activities** of a government. They (1) have an economic resources measurement focus; (2) use accrual accounting; and (3) report capital assets, long-term liabilities, and deferred flows of resources. (But custodial funds do not report capital assets and long-term liabilities.) Pension (and other employee benefit) trust funds report fiduciary activities for pensions, other postemployment benefit plans, and certain other employee benefit programs. Investment trust funds report fiduciary activities involving (1) the external portion of investment pools and (2) individual investment accounts held in a trust meeting certain criteria. Private-purpose trust funds report all fiduciary activities (1) not reported in the other fiduciary trust funds and (2) accounted for in a trust meeting certain criteria. Custodial funds report fiduciary activities not required to be reported in the other fiduciary funds, such as tolls that will be paid to a private business.

Fund Classification

Governmental Funds	Proprietary Funds	Fiduciary Funds
General Fund	Enterprise Funds	Pension (and other employee
Special Revenue Funds	Internal Service Funds	benefit) Trust Funds
Capital Projects Funds		Investment Trust Funds
Debt Service Funds		Private-Purpose Trust Funds
Permanent Funds		Custodial Funds

Government-wide financial statements provide information about the operational accountability of the governmental activities and business-type activities of the government as a whole. They have the same general scope of reporting as proprietary funds.

Summary

	Governmental Funds Financial Statements	Proprietary Funds Financial Statements	Fiduciary Funds Financial Statements	Government-Wide Financial Statements
Measurement Focus	Current financial resources	Economic resources	Economic resources	Economic resources
Basis of Accounting	Modified accrual	Accrual	Accrual	Accrual
Capital Assets	No	Yes	Trust funds only	Yes
Long-Term Liabilities	No	Yes	Trust funds only	Yes
Deferred Inflows and Outflows of Resources	Yes	Yes	Yes	Yes

A **comprehensive annual financial report (CAFR)** covers all funds and activities of the primary government and provides an overview of the component units of the reporting entity. The CAFR includes introductory, financial, and statistical sections. The **introductory section** contains (1) a letter of transmittal from the appropriate officials, (2) an organization chart, and (3) names of principal officers. The **financial section** contains (1) the independent auditor's report, (2) management's discussion and analysis (MD&A), (3) the basic financial statements (government-wide statements, fund statements, and notes), (4) required supplementary information (budgetary schedules), and (5) certain other statements.

Minimum Requirements for General-Purpose External Financial Reporting

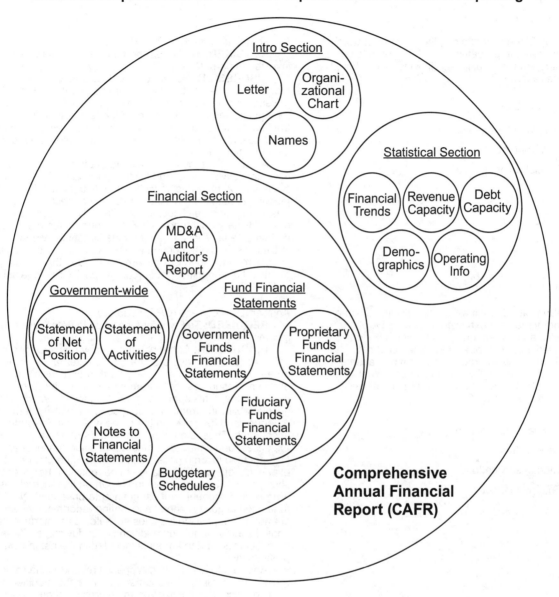

QUESTIONS

27.1 Objective

27.1.1. Roy City received a gift, the principal of which is to be invested in perpetuity with the income to be used to support the local library. In which fund should this gift be recorded?

    A. Permanent fund.

    B. Investment trust fund.

    C. Private-purpose trust fund.

    D. Special revenue fund.

Answer (A) is correct. *(CPA, adapted)*
REQUIRED: The fund reporting the principal of a gift to be invested in perpetuity.
DISCUSSION: Permanent funds account for resources that are restricted to the use of earnings for the benefit of the government or its citizens. An example is a perpetual-care fund for a public cemetery. Permanent funds are not private-purpose trust funds, which benefit individuals, private organizations, or other governments. Private-purpose trust funds are reported with the other fiduciary funds.
Answer (B) is incorrect. Investment trust funds report fiduciary activities involving (1) the external portion of investment pools and (2) individual investment accounts held in a trust meeting certain criteria. Answer (C) is incorrect. Private-purpose trust funds report all fiduciary activities (1) not reported in the other fiduciary trust funds and (2) accounted for in a trust meeting certain criteria. These arrangements benefit individuals, private individuals, and other governments. Answer (D) is incorrect. A special revenue fund is a governmental fund that accounts for restricted or committed resources of specific revenue sources.

27.1.2. King City Council will be establishing a library fund. Library fees are expected to cover 55% of the library's annual resource requirements. King has decided that an annual determination of net income is desirable in order to maintain management control and accountability over the library. What type of fund should King establish in order to meet its measurement objectives?

    A. Special revenue fund.

    B. General fund.

    C. Internal service fund.

    D. Enterprise fund.

Answer (D) is correct. *(CPA, adapted)*
REQUIRED: The type of fund used to determine annual net income.
DISCUSSION: Enterprise funds may be used for any activities for which fees are charged to external users. Moreover, an enterprise fund (a proprietary fund) reports using the economic resources measurement focus and the accrual basis of accounting. This approach provides longer-term operational accountability information about economic activity. It measures revenues and expenses in the same way as in for-profit accounting. Thus, the enterprise fund's statement of revenues, expenses, and changes in fund net position presents amounts for (1) operating income (loss); (2) income before other revenues, expenses, etc.; and (3) change in net position. Because the library fund will charge fees and report on the accrual basis, King should account for it using an enterprise fund. NOTE: No fund used in governmental accounting reports net income. The change in net position includes such items as interfund transfers, capital contributions, and additions to endowments. These items do not correspond to amounts included in the net income of a for-profit entity.
Answer (A) is incorrect. A special revenue fund (a governmental fund) is accounted for using the modified accrual basis of accounting. However, measures of income are based on the accrual basis of accounting. Answer (B) is incorrect. The general fund (a governmental fund) is accounted for using the modified accrual basis of accounting. However, measures of income are based on the accrual basis of accounting. Answer (C) is incorrect. An internal service fund (a proprietary fund) is used for activities that provide goods and services to other subunits of the primary government and its component units or to other governments on a cost-reimbursement basis. It is not used for activities for which fees are charged to external users.

27.1.3. Government financial reporting should provide information to assist users in which situation(s)?

I. Making social and political decisions

II. Assessing whether current-year citizens received services but shifted part of the payment burden to future-year citizens

    A. I only.

    B. II only.

    C. Both I and II.

    D. Neither I nor II.

Answer (C) is correct. *(CPA, adapted)*
REQUIRED: The information, if any, that governments should provide.
DISCUSSION: Interperiod equity is an important component of accountability that is fundamental to public administration. Financial resources received during a period should suffice to pay for the services during that period. Moreover, debt should be repaid during the probable period of usefulness of the assets required. Thus, financial reporting should help taxpayers assess whether future taxpayers will have to assume burdens for services already provided. Furthermore, governmental financial reporting also should assist users (e.g., the citizenry and legislative and oversight bodies) in making economic, political, and social decisions. For example, revenue forecasts may help advocates for increased expenditures for education or transportation.
Answer (A) is incorrect. Financial reporting also should help taxpayers assess whether future taxpayers will have to assume burdens for services already provided. Answer (B) is incorrect. Financial reporting also should assist users (e.g., the citizenry and legislative and oversight bodies) in making economic, political, and social decisions. Answer (D) is incorrect. Financial reporting should help taxpayers assess whether future taxpayers will have to assume burdens for services already provided. Furthermore, it should assist users (e.g., the citizenry and legislative and oversight bodies) in making economic, political, and social decisions.

27.1.4. The primary authoritative body for determining the measurement focus and basis of accounting standards for governmental fund operating statements is the

    A. Governmental Accounting Standards Board (GASB).

    B. National Council on Governmental Accounting (NCGA).

    C. Governmental Accounting and Auditing Committee of the AICPA (GAAC).

    D. Financial Accounting Standards Board (FASB).

Answer (A) is correct. *(CPA, adapted)*
REQUIRED: The authoritative body that issues pronouncements on GAAP for state and local governments.
DISCUSSION: The GASB is the primary body that establishes authoritative accounting and reporting standards, including those on measurement focus and basis of accounting, for state and local governments. However, pronouncements in effect when the GASB was created remain in force until changed by a subsequent GASB pronouncement.
Answer (B) is incorrect. The NCGA was a predecessor to the GASB. Answer (C) is incorrect. The GAAC is not currently an active committee of the AICPA. Answer (D) is incorrect. The FASB is the primary standard-setting body for private-sector accounting.

27.1.5. The statement of activities of the government-wide financial statements is designed primarily to provide information to assess which of the following?

    A. Operational accountability.

    B. Financial accountability.

    C. Fiscal accountability.

    D. Functional accountability.

Answer (A) is correct. *(CPA, adapted)*
REQUIRED: The primary form of accountability provided by government-wide financial statements.
DISCUSSION: Fiscal accountability is the responsibility of governments to justify that their actions currently comply with public decisions concerning the raising and spending of public resources in the short term. Operational accountability is a government's responsibility to report the extent to which it has met accounting objectives efficiently and effectively, using all resources available, and whether it can continue to do so in the near future. The governmental funds financial statements focus on the fiscal accountability of governmental activities. However, government-wide financial statements focus on the operational accountability of the governmental and business-type activities of the government as a whole. The financial statements of fiduciary funds and proprietary funds provide information about operational accountability.
Answer (B) is incorrect. The government-wide statements focus on operational accountability. Moreover, financial accountability is not as accurate a phrase as fiscal accountability. The term "fiscal" is preferable because it means having to do with the public treasury or revenues. Answer (C) is incorrect. Fiscal accountability is the main focus of governmental funds financial statements. Answer (D) is incorrect. Operational accountability includes but is not limited to functional accountability.

27.2 Fund Accounting

27.2.1. State and local governments report various funds to the extent their activities meet the fund criteria. Governmental funds include

    A. Internal service funds.

    B. Nonexpendable trust funds.

    C. Enterprise funds.

    D. Permanent funds.

Answer (D) is correct. *(Publisher, adapted)*
    REQUIRED: The governmental funds.
    DISCUSSION: Governmental funds (the general fund, special revenue funds, capital projects funds, debt service funds, and permanent funds) emphasize sources, uses, and balances of current financial resources, often with use of budgetary accounts. Expendable assets are assigned to funds based on their intended use, liabilities are assigned to the funds from which they will be paid, and the difference (fund equity) is the fund balance. Permanent funds report resources legally restricted so that earnings only, not principal, may be expended for the benefit of the government or its citizenry, that is, to support the government's programs. An example is a perpetual-care fund for a public cemetery. Permanent funds should be distinguished from private-purpose trust funds.
    Answer (A) is incorrect. Internal service funds are proprietary funds. Answer (B) is incorrect. The expendable and nonexpendable trust fund types are no longer permitted. Answer (C) is incorrect. Enterprise funds are proprietary funds.

27.2.2. The accounting systems of state and local governmental entities should be organized and operated using which structure?

    A. Proprietary fund.

    B. Fiduciary fund.

    C. Governmental fund.

    D. Fund.

Answer (D) is correct. *(Publisher, adapted)*
    REQUIRED: The structure of governmental accounting systems of state and local governments.
    DISCUSSION: An accounting system should permit state and local governments to (1) present fairly and with full disclosure the funds and activities of state and local governments in conformity with GAAP and (2) demonstrate compliance with finance-related legal and contractual provisions. To satisfy these objectives, state and local government accounting systems use funds. A fund is a fiscal and accounting entity with a self-balancing set of accounts. It records (1) financial resources (including cash), (2) related liabilities, (3) residual equities or balances, and (4) changes in all of the above. Items in a fund are separated because they relate to specific activities or certain objectives that are subject to special regulations or limitations. The three categories of funds used by state and local governments are governmental, proprietary, and fiduciary.
    Answer (A) is incorrect. Proprietary funds are only one of the categories of funds used by state and local governments. Answer (B) is incorrect. Fiduciary funds are only one of categories of funds used by state and local governments. Answer (C) is incorrect. Governmental funds are only one of the categories of funds used by state and local governments.

27.2.3. A government may report which fiduciary funds?

    A. Private-purpose trust funds.

    B. Expendable trust funds.

    C. Nonexpendable trust funds.

    D. Permanent funds.

Answer (A) is correct. *(Publisher, adapted)*
    REQUIRED: The fiduciary funds reportable by a government.
    DISCUSSION: Fiduciary funds report assets held as a fiduciary activity. They include (1) pension (and other employee benefit) trust funds, (2) investment trust funds, (3) private-purpose trust funds, and (4) custodial funds. Private-purpose trust funds report all fiduciary activities (1) not reported in the other fiduciary trust funds and (2) accounted for in a trust meeting certain criteria.
    Answer (B) is incorrect. Expendable trust funds no longer are part of the fund structure. Answer (C) is incorrect. Nonexpendable trust funds no longer are part of the fund structure. Answer (D) is incorrect. Permanent funds are governmental funds.

27.2.4. A local governmental unit could use which of the following types of funds?

	Fiduciary	Proprietary
A.	Yes	No
B.	Yes	Yes
C.	No	Yes
D.	No	No

Answer (B) is correct. *(CPA, adapted)*
REQUIRED: The types of funds that could be used by a local government.
DISCUSSION: The three categories of fund types that can be used by a state or local government are (1) governmental (general, special revenue, debt service, capital projects, and permanent funds), (2) proprietary (internal service and enterprise funds), and (3) fiduciary (pension and other employee benefit trust, investment trust, private-purpose trust, and custodial funds).

27.2.5. The city of Cal maintains several fund types. The following were among Cal's cash receipts during the current year:

State grant received in a voluntary
nonexchange transaction $1,000,000
Interest on bank accounts held for
employees' pension plan   200,000

What amount of these cash receipts should be accounted for in Cal's general fund?

A. $1,200,000

B. $1,000,000

C. $200,000

D. $0

Answer (B) is correct. *(CPA, adapted)*
REQUIRED: The amount of cash receipts to be accounted for in the general fund.
DISCUSSION: The general fund is used to account for all financial resources of a governmental unit that are not accounted for in another fund. The interest is accounted for in a pension trust fund. Thus, the general fund accounts for the $1 million grant only.
Answer (A) is incorrect. The amount of $1,200,000 incorrectly includes the interest. Answer (C) is incorrect. The amount of $200,000 incorrectly includes the interest and excludes the unrestricted state grant. Answer (D) is incorrect. Zero excludes the unrestricted state grant.

27.2.6. Revenues that are restricted or committed to expenditure for specified purposes should be accounted for in special revenue funds, including

A. Accumulation of resources for payment of general long-term debt principal and interest.

B. Pension trust fund additions.

C. Gasoline taxes to finance road repairs.

D. Proprietary fund revenues.

Answer (C) is correct. *(Publisher, adapted)*
REQUIRED: The revenue accounted for in special revenue funds.
DISCUSSION: A special revenue fund is used to account for the proceeds of specific revenue sources that are restricted or committed to expenditure for specified purposes other than debt service or capital projects. Gasoline taxes levied to finance road repair are revenues restricted to expenditure for specified purposes that are accounted for in special revenue funds.
Answer (A) is incorrect. Resources for payment of general long-term debt principal and interest are accounted for in the debt service fund. Answer (B) is incorrect. Pension trust fund additions are accounted for in the pension trust fund. Answer (D) is incorrect. Proprietary fund revenues are accounted for in either enterprise or internal service funds.

27.2.7. Bay Creek's municipal motor pool maintains all city-owned vehicles and charges the various departments for the cost of rendering those services. In which of the following funds should Bay Creek account for the cost of such maintenance?

A. General fund.

B. Internal service fund.

C. Special revenue fund.

D. Special assessment fund.

Answer (B) is correct. *(CPA, adapted)*
REQUIRED: The fund in which to account for the cost of vehicle maintenance provided by a motor pool.
DISCUSSION: Internal service funds generally are used for activities that provide goods and services to other subunits of the primary government and its component units or to other governments on a cost-reimbursement basis.
Answer (A) is incorrect. Activities similar to those of profit-seeking businesses are best accounted for on the accrual basis. The general fund uses the modified accrual basis. Answer (C) is incorrect. A special revenue fund is used to account for certain restricted or committed categories of revenue. Answer (D) is incorrect. An ongoing activity like a motor pool should not be accounted for in a special assessment fund.

27.2.8. Kew City received a $15,000,000 federal grant to finance the construction of a center for rehabilitation of drug addicts. The proceeds of this grant should be accounted for in the

A. Special revenue funds.

B. General fund.

C. Capital projects funds.

D. Trust funds.

Answer (C) is correct. *(CPA, adapted)*
REQUIRED: The fund used to account for a federal grant to finance the construction of a center for rehabilitation of drug addicts.
DISCUSSION: A capital projects fund is used to account for the receipt and disbursement of resources restricted to the acquisition of major capital facilities (other than those financed by proprietary and trust funds) through purchase or construction.
Answer (A) is incorrect. Special revenue funds do not record resources to be used for major capital facilities. Answer (B) is incorrect. The general fund does not record resources to be used for major capital facilities. Answer (D) is incorrect. A grant for a drug rehabilitation center is not accounted for in a trust fund. A trust fund accounts for assets held as a fiduciary activity.

27.2.9. The following equity balances are among those maintained by Cole City:

Enterprise funds	$1,000,000
Internal service funds	400,000

Cole's proprietary equity balances amount to

A. $1,400,000

B. $1,000,000

C. $400,000

D. $0

Answer (A) is correct. *(CPA, adapted)*
REQUIRED: The amount of proprietary equity balances.
DISCUSSION: Proprietary funds include enterprise funds and internal service funds. Thus, the proprietary equity balances equal $1,400,000 ($1,000,000 + $400,000).
Answer (B) is incorrect. The amount of $1,000,000 excludes the equity balance of the internal service funds. Answer (C) is incorrect. The amount of $400,000 excludes the equity balance of the enterprise funds. Answer (D) is incorrect. The amount of $0 excludes the equity balances of the enterprise funds and the internal service funds.

27.2.10. A state government had the following activities:

I. State-operated lottery
II. State-operated hospital

Which of the above activities may be accounted for in an enterprise fund?

A. Neither I nor II.

B. I only.

C. II only.

D. Both I and II.

Answer (D) is correct. *(CPA, adapted)*
REQUIRED: The activities to be accounted for in the enterprise fund.
DISCUSSION: Enterprise funds may be used to account for any activity of a state or local government that provides goods or services to external users for a fee. Both a state-operated hospital and a state-operated lottery are typical enterprise fund activities.
Answer (A) is incorrect. A state-run hospital and a state-run lottery provide services to external users for a fee. Answer (B) is incorrect. A state-run hospital provides services to external users for a fee. Answer (C) is incorrect. A state-run lottery provides services to external users for a fee.

27.2.11. An activity that provides goods to other subunits of the primary government on a cost-reimbursement basis should be reported as a(n)

A. Fiduciary fund.

B. Custodial fund.

C. Enterprise fund in some cases.

D. Internal service fund in all cases.

Answer (C) is correct. *(Publisher, adapted)*
REQUIRED: The fund used to report an activity providing goods to other subunits of the primary government on a cost-reimbursement basis.
DISCUSSION: Internal service funds may be used for activities that provide goods and services to other subunits of the primary government and its component units or to other governments on a cost-reimbursement basis. However, if the reporting government is not the predominant participant, the activity should be reported as an enterprise fund.
Answer (A) is incorrect. Fiduciary fund reporting emphasizes net position and changes in net position. Fiduciary funds report fiduciary activities. The criteria for identifying these activities ordinarily emphasize (1) whether the government controls the assets of the activity and (2) the beneficiaries in the fiduciary relationship. Answer (B) is incorrect. Custodial funds report fiduciary activities not required to be reported in the other fiduciary funds, such as tolls that will be paid to a private business. Answer (D) is incorrect. Use of an internal service fund is inappropriate if the reporting government is not the predominant participant.

27.2.12. Grants that are to be transferred to secondary recipients by a local government should be accounted for in which fund if the government has no administrative or direct involvement in the program?

A. Investment trust fund.

B. Private-purpose trust fund.

C. Custodial fund.

D. Special assessment fund.

Answer (C) is correct. *(Publisher, adapted)*
REQUIRED: The funds that account for grants to be transferred to secondary recipients.
DISCUSSION: Custodial funds may account for certain grants and other financial assistance to be transferred to, or spent on behalf of, secondary recipients. The custodial fund receives the grants and passes them through to the ultimate recipients. However, if the recipient government has administrative or direct financial involvement in the program, the pass-through grant is accounted for in an appropriate governmental, proprietary, or trust fund.
Answer (A) is incorrect. Investment trust funds report fiduciary activities involving (1) the external portion of investment pools and (2) individual investment accounts held in a trust meeting certain criteria. Answer (B) is incorrect. Private-purpose trust funds report all fiduciary activities (1) not reported in the other fiduciary trust funds and (2) accounted for in a trust meeting certain criteria. Answer (D) is incorrect. A special assessment fund is not permitted for general-purpose external reporting purposes.

27.3 Measurement Focus and Basis of Accounting

27.3.1. In the fund financial statements of which of the following fund types of a city government are revenues and expenditures recognized on the same basis of accounting as the general fund?

A. Private-purpose trust.

B. Internal service.

C. Enterprise.

D. Debt service.

Answer (D) is correct. *(CPA, adapted)*
REQUIRED: The fund that recognizes revenues and expenditures in the same manner as the general fund.
DISCUSSION: A debt service fund is the only type of fund listed that is classified as a governmental fund. The other funds are proprietary or fiduciary. The modified accrual basis is used to prepare the financial statements for governmental funds. Proprietary and fiduciary funds are reported on the accrual basis.
Answer (A) is incorrect. Private-purpose trust funds report all fiduciary activities (1) not reported in the other fiduciary trust funds and (2) accounted for in a trust meeting certain criteria. Answer (B) is incorrect. An internal service fund is a proprietary fund. Its financial statements are prepared using the accrual basis of accounting. Answer (C) is incorrect. An enterprise fund is a proprietary fund. Its financial statements are prepared using the accrual basis of accounting.

27.3.2. A major exception to the general rule of expenditure accrual for governmental funds of a state or local government relates to unmatured

	Principal of General Long-Term Debt	Interest on General Long-Term Debt
A.	Yes	Yes
B.	Yes	No
C.	No	Yes
D.	No	No

Answer (A) is correct. *(CPA, adapted)*
REQUIRED: The major exception to the general rule of expenditure accrual for governmental units.
DISCUSSION: According to the modified accrual basis of accounting, expenditures are recognized when liabilities are incurred. For general long-term debt, however, principal and interest expenditures ordinarily are recognized when payments on the debt are due.
Answer (B) is incorrect. The interest on general long-term debt is recognized when due, not when incurred. Answer (C) is incorrect. The principal of general long-term debt is recognized when due. Answer (D) is incorrect. The principal and interest of general long-term debt are recognized when due, not when incurred.

27.3.3. When a snowplow purchased by a governmental unit is received, it should be recorded in the general fund as a(n)

A. Encumbrance.

B. Expenditure.

C. General capital asset.

D. Appropriation.

Answer (B) is correct. *(CPA, adapted)*
REQUIRED: The effect of receipt of equipment.
DISCUSSION: When previously ordered goods are received, the entry includes a debit to expenditures for the actual amount to be paid. An expenditure is recognized when a liability is incurred, that is, when an executory contract is complete or virtually complete.

Answer (A) is incorrect. An encumbrance is recorded to account for the purchase commitment. Answer (C) is incorrect. General capital assets are reported only in the governmental activities column of the government-wide statement of net position. Answer (D) is incorrect. Appropriations are accounted for when recording the budget.

27.3.4. Expenditures of a government for insurance extending over more than one accounting period

A. Must be accounted for as expenditures of the period of acquisition.

B. Must be accounted for as expenditures of the periods subsequent to acquisition.

C. Must be allocated between or among accounting periods.

D. May be allocated among periods or accounted for as expenditures when acquired.

Answer (D) is correct. *(CPA, adapted)*
REQUIRED: The proper treatment of expenditures extending over more than one period.
DISCUSSION: In the governmental fund financial statements, prepaid insurance may be reported under either (1) the purchases method, in which an expenditure is reported when the policy is purchased, or (2) the consumption method, in which an expenditure is reported when the asset is consumed.

27.3.5. Government-wide financial statements are prepared using the

	Economic Resources Measure- ment Focus	Current Financial Resources Measure- ment Focus	Accrual Basis	Modified Accrual Basis
A.	Yes	No	Yes	No
B.	No	Yes	No	Yes
C.	Yes	No	No	Yes
D.	No	Yes	Yes	No

Answer (A) is correct. *(Publisher, adapted)*
REQUIRED: The measurement focus and basis of accounting used in government-wide financial statements.
DISCUSSION: Government-wide financial statements are prepared using the economic resources measurement focus and the accrual basis of accounting and should report all of the government's assets, liabilities, revenues, expenses, gains, and losses. The economic resources focus measures revenues and expenses in the same way as in for-profit accounting. It also emphasizes a longer-range measure of revenues earned or levied (and accrued immediately if measurable) and cost of services. The accrual basis recognizes most transactions when they occur, regardless of when cash is received or paid.

Answer (B) is incorrect. Government-wide financial statements use the economic resources measurement focus and the accrual basis of accounting. Only governmental fund financial statements use the current financial resources measurement focus and the modified accrual basis of accounting. Answer (C) is incorrect. Government-wide financial statements use the economic resources measurement focus and the accrual basis of accounting. Only governmental fund financial statements use the current financial resources measurement focus and the modified accrual basis of accounting. Answer (D) is incorrect. Government-wide financial statements use the economic resources measurement focus and the accrual basis of accounting. Only governmental fund financial statements use the current financial resources measurement focus and the modified accrual basis of accounting.

27.3.6. Proprietary fund financial statements are prepared using the

	Economic Resources Measurement Focus	Current Financial Resources Measurement Focus	Accrual Basis	Modified Accrual Basis
A.	Yes	No	Yes	No
B.	No	Yes	No	Yes
C.	Yes	No	No	Yes
D.	No	Yes	Yes	No

Answer (A) is correct. *(Publisher, adapted)*
REQUIRED: The measurement focus and basis of accounting used in proprietary fund financial statements.
DISCUSSION: The economic resources measurement focus and the accrual basis of accounting are required in the proprietary fund financial statements. The economic resources measurement focus differs from the shorter-term flow-of-current-financial-resources approach used in governmental funds. It measures revenues and expenses in the same way as in commercial accounting. The emphasis is on a longer-range measure of revenues earned or levied (and accrued immediately if measurable). Moreover, the economic resources model focuses on cost of services. The accrual basis of accounting recognizes most transactions when they occur, regardless of when cash is received or paid.
Answer (B) is incorrect. Proprietary fund financial statements use the economic resources measurement focus and the accrual basis of accounting. Only governmental fund financial statements use the current financial resources measurement focus and the modified accrual basis of accounting. Answer (C) is incorrect. Proprietary fund financial statements use the accrual basis of accounting. Answer (D) is incorrect. Proprietary fund financial statements use the economic resources measurement focus.

27.3.7. Which of the following funds, if any, of a governmental unit recognize revenues in the accounting period in which they become available and measurable?

	General Fund	Enterprise Fund
A.	Yes	No
B.	No	Yes
C.	Yes	Yes
D.	No	No

Answer (A) is correct. *(CPA, adapted)*
REQUIRED: The funds, if any, of a governmental unit that recognize revenues in the accounting period in which they become available and measurable.
DISCUSSION: The general fund is accounted for on the modified accrual basis. This basis of accounting recognizes revenues in the period in which they are measurable and available. The enterprise fund is a proprietary fund and is accounted for on the accrual basis.
Answer (B) is incorrect. The general fund recognizes revenues when they are available and measurable, and the enterprise fund is accounted for on the accrual basis. Answer (C) is incorrect. The enterprise fund is accounted for on the accrual basis. Answer (D) is incorrect. The general fund recognizes revenues when they are available and measurable.

27.3.8. Liabilities of a defined benefit pension plan for benefits and refunds are reported in a state or local government's fiduciary fund financial statements using the

	Economic Resources Measurement Focus	Current Financial Resources Measurement Focus	Accrual Basis	Modified Accrual Basis
A.	Yes	No	Yes	No
B.	No	Yes	No	Yes
C.	Yes	No	No	Yes
D.	No	Yes	Yes	No

Answer (A) is correct. *(Publisher, adapted)*
REQUIRED: The measurement focus and basis of accounting used in fiduciary fund financial statements.
DISCUSSION: The economic resources measurement focus and the accrual basis of accounting are required in the fiduciary fund financial statements. Liabilities of defined benefit pension plans and of postemployment benefit plans other than pensions are recognized on the accrual basis, that is, when the transaction or event occurs. For plan liabilities for benefits and refunds, the transaction occurs when the benefits and refunds become due and payable under the terms of the plan.
Answer (B) is incorrect. Fiduciary fund financial statements ordinarily use the economic resources measurement focus and the accrual basis of accounting. Only governmental fund financial statements use the current financial resources measurement focus and the modified accrual basis of accounting. Answer (C) is incorrect. Fiduciary fund financial statements ordinarily use the economic resources measurement focus and the accrual basis of accounting. Only governmental fund financial statements use the current financial resources measurement focus and the modified accrual basis of accounting. Answer (D) is incorrect. Fiduciary fund financial statements ordinarily use the economic resources measurement focus and the accrual basis of accounting. Only governmental fund financial statements use the current financial resources measurement focus and the modified accrual basis of accounting.

27.3.9. Which of the following fund types used by a government most likely would have a fund balance classification used for an inventory of supplies?

    A. General.

    B. Internal service.

    C. Private-purpose trust.

    D. Capital projects.

Answer (A) is correct. *(CPA, adapted)*
    REQUIRED: The fund type most likely to have a fund balance classification used for an inventory of supplies.
    DISCUSSION: Governmental units normally record the purchases of supplies inventory in the general fund. In accounting for supplies, the expenditure account may be debited when the materials and supplies are purchased or when they are consumed. Under either method, the inventory of supplies remaining at year-end must be recorded on the balance sheet as an asset. In addition, under the purchases method, resources already have been expended to acquire these supplies. Accordingly, an appropriate amount of fund balance-nonexpendable must be credited to indicate the unavailability of resources in this amount for other expenditures.
    Answer (B) is incorrect. An internal service fund is a proprietary fund. Thus, net position, not fund balance, is reported. Answer (C) is incorrect. A private-purpose trust is a fiduciary fund. Thus, net position, not fund balance, is reported. Answer (D) is incorrect. Supplies generally are not recognized as an asset of a capital projects fund.

27.3.10. In which situations, if any, should property taxes due to a governmental unit be recorded as deferred inflows of resources?

  I.   Property taxes receivable are recognized in advance of the year for which they are levied.

  II. Property taxes receivable are collected in advance of the year in which they are levied.

    A. I only.

    B. Both I and II.

    C. II only.

    D. Neither I nor II.

Answer (B) is correct. *(CPA, adapted)*
    REQUIRED: The situations, if any, when taxes due should be recorded as deferred inflows of resources.
    DISCUSSION: A property tax assessment is made to finance the budget of a specific period. Thus, the revenue produced should be recognized in the period for which the assessment was levied. When property taxes are recognized or collected in advance, they should be recorded as deferred inflows of resources in a governmental fund. They are not recognized as revenue until the period for which they are levied. A property tax assessment is an imposed nonexchange revenue transaction. In such a transaction, assets should be recognized when (1) an enforceable legal claim arises or (2) resources are received, whichever is earlier. Thus, recognition of a receivable in a year prior to that for which the property taxes were levied implies that, under the enabling statute, the enforceable legal claim existed in that prior year.
    Answer (A) is incorrect. Property taxes collected in advance also should be initially recorded as deferred inflows of resources. Answer (C) is incorrect. Property taxes recognized in advance also should be initially recorded as deferred inflows of resources. Answer (D) is incorrect. Property taxes recognized or collected in advance should be initially recorded as deferred inflows of resources.

27.3.11. A public school district should recognize revenue from property taxes levied for its debt service fund when

    A. Bonds to be retired by the levy are due and payable.

    B. Assessed valuations of property subject to the levy are known.

    C. Funds from the levy are measurable and available to the district.

    D. Proceeds from collection of the levy are deposited in the district's bank account.

Answer (C) is correct. *(CPA, adapted)*
    REQUIRED: The timing of property tax recognition.
    DISCUSSION: Debt service funds apply the modified accrual basis of accounting. Thus, revenues are recognized when they are measurable and available. Property tax revenues are recognized in the period for which the taxes are levied if the availability criterion is met. For property taxes, this criterion is met if they are collected within the current period or soon enough thereafter (not exceeding 60 days) to pay current liabilities.
    Answer (A) is incorrect. Revenues are recognized when property taxes are levied. Answer (B) is incorrect. The assessed valuations are necessary for calculating the amount of tax but do not make the tax revenue available. Answer (D) is incorrect. Revenue recognition is not on the cash basis.

27.3.12. Governmental fund financial statements are prepared using the

	Economic Resources Measurement Focus	Current Financial Resources Measurement Focus	Accrual Basis	Modified Accrual Basis
A.	Yes	No	Yes	No
B.	No	Yes	No	Yes
C.	Yes	No	No	Yes
D.	No	Yes	Yes	No

Answer (B) is correct. *(Publisher, adapted)*
REQUIRED: The measurement focus and basis of accounting used in governmental fund financial statements.
DISCUSSION: The current financial resources measurement focus and the modified accrual basis of accounting are required in the financial statements of governmental funds. The emphasis is on determination of financial position and changes in it (sources, uses, and balances of financial resources). Revenues should be recognized when they become available and measurable. Expenditures should be recognized when the fund liability is incurred, if measurable. However, unmatured interest on general long-term liabilities is recognized when due.
Answer (A) is incorrect. The economic resources measurement focus and the accrual basis are used in (1) the government-wide statements; (2) the fund statements for proprietary funds; and (3), with certain exceptions, the fund statements for fiduciary funds. Answer (C) is incorrect. The current financial resources measurement focus is used in the governmental fund financial statements. Answer (D) is incorrect. The modified accrual basis is used in the governmental fund financial statements.

27.4 General Capital Assets and Long-Term Liabilities

27.4.1. Which of the following capital assets are least likely to be considered infrastructure assets of a state or local government?

A. Buildings.

B. Sewer systems.

C. Roads.

D. Lighting systems.

Answer (A) is correct. *(Publisher, adapted)*
REQUIRED: The capital assets least likely to be considered infrastructure assets.
DISCUSSION: Infrastructure assets are capital assets that normally are stationary and can be preserved for a longer time than most capital assets, e.g., roads, bridges, water and sewer systems, drainage systems, and lighting systems. However, buildings, other than those that are ancillary parts of a network of infrastructure assets, are not deemed to be infrastructure assets. Answer (B) is incorrect. Sewer systems are considered infrastructure assets. Answer (C) is incorrect. Roads are considered infrastructure assets. Answer (D) is incorrect. Lighting systems are considered infrastructure assets.

27.4.2. If a capital asset is donated to a governmental unit, the asset is accounted for in an enterprise fund, and eligibility requirements are met, it should be recorded

A. At the donor's carrying amount as revenue.

B. At acquisition value as revenue.

C. At the lower of the donor's carrying amount or estimated fair value as deferred inflows of resources.

D. As a memorandum entry only.

Answer (B) is correct. *(CPA, adapted)*
REQUIRED: The recording of capital assets accounted for in an enterprise fund that are donated to a governmental unit.
DISCUSSION: If a capital asset is donated to a governmental unit, it should be recorded at its acquisition value (an entry price). It is the price that would be paid to acquire an asset with equivalent service potential in an orderly market transaction at the acquisition date. In any voluntary nonexchange transaction, assets and revenues are recognized when all eligibility requirements (including time requirements) are met. Because an enterprise fund uses the accrual basis, the resources need not be available.
Answer (A) is incorrect. The donor's carrying amount may not reflect the asset's acquisition value at the time of the governmental unit's receipt of the asset. Answer (C) is incorrect. The asset should be recorded at acquisition value as revenue. Answer (D) is incorrect. The acquisition value of the donated asset should be recognized.

27.4.3. The government-wide financial statements report purchased capital assets

A. In the general fixed assets account group.

B. At historical cost, including ancillary charges.

C. Only in the notes if they are donated.

D. At acquisition value.

Answer (B) is correct. *(Publisher, adapted)*
REQUIRED: The reporting of purchased capital assets in the government-wide financial statements.
DISCUSSION: General capital assets are all capital assets not reported in the proprietary funds or the fiduciary funds. Purchased capital assets are reported at historical cost, including ancillary charges (e.g., for freight and site preparation) only in the governmental activities column of the government-wide statement of net position.
Answer (A) is incorrect. Presentation of government-wide financial statements eliminates the need for the general fixed assets account group and the general long-term debt account group. Answer (C) is incorrect. Purchased capital assets are reported at historical cost, including ancillary charges, in the statements. Answer (D) is incorrect. Only donated capital assets, donated works of art, historical treasures and certain other items are reported at acquisition value at the time of acquisition.

27.4.4. Tree City reported a $1,500 net increase in fund balance for governmental funds for the current year. During the year, Tree purchased general capital assets of $9,000 and recorded depreciation expense of $3,000. What amount should Tree report as the change in net position for governmental activities?

A. $(4,500)

B. $1,500

C. $7,500

D. $10,500

Answer (C) is correct. *(CPA, adapted)*
REQUIRED: The change in net position for governmental activities.
DISCUSSION: The $1,500 net increase in the fund balance for governmental funds reflects a $9,000 expenditure (modified accrual basis of accounting) for general capital assets. These assets are not reported in governmental funds. The effect of the expenditure is a decrease in current financial resources of $9,000. However, the government-wide statements report an expense of $3,000 (accrual basis of accounting) for depreciation and a depreciated asset with a carrying amount of $6,000 ($9,000 cost – $3,000 depreciation). The effect is a decrease in economic resources of $3,000. Reconciling the net increase in fund balance to the change in net position therefore requires adding $6,000 ($9,000 modified accrual basis expenditure – $3,000 accrual basis expense). The change in net position is $7,500 ($1,500 + $6,000 reconciling item).
Answer (A) is incorrect. The amount of $(4,500) is the excess of the expenditure over the sum of the expense and the increase in fund balance. Answer (B) is incorrect. The amount of $1,500 is the increase in fund balance. Answer (D) is incorrect. The amount of $10,500 assumes depreciation is not recognized.

27.4.5. A state or local government's general capital assets and general long-term liabilities must be reported in the

A. Governmental funds financial statements.

B. General account groups.

C. General fund's balance sheet.

D. Governmental activities column of the government-wide statement of net position.

Answer (D) is correct. *(Publisher, adapted)*
REQUIRED: The reporting of general capital assets and general long-term liabilities.
DISCUSSION: General capital assets are all capital assets not reported in proprietary funds or fiduciary funds. They usually result from expenditure of governmental fund financial resources, and should be reported in the governmental activities column of the government-wide statement of net position. However, they are not reported as assets in governmental funds because they apply to all governmental activities. Likewise, general long-term liabilities are not reported as liabilities in governmental funds because they apply to all governmental activities. They should be reported in the governmental activities column of the government-wide statement of net position.
Answer (A) is incorrect. General capital assets and general long-term liabilities traditionally have not been reported in any given fund or funds because they apply to all governmental activities. Answer (B) is incorrect. Account groups are no longer used in governmental accounting. Answer (C) is incorrect. General capital assets and general long-term liabilities should be reported in the statement of net position.

27.4.6. Which capital assets must be depreciated in the government-wide financial statements?

    A. All capitalized collections of works of art.

    B. All infrastructure assets.

    C. All noncapitalized collections of historical treasures.

    D. All capitalized collections that are exhaustible.

Answer (D) is correct. *(Publisher, adapted)*
    REQUIRED: The capital assets that must be depreciated.
    DISCUSSION: Individual items or collections of works of art, historical treasures, and similar assets ordinarily must be capitalized. However, if a collection is (1) held in furtherance of public service and not for gain; (2) protected, preserved, cared for, and kept unencumbered; and (3) subject to a policy that sale proceeds are to be used to obtain other collection items, capitalization is not required. If capitalized collections or individual items are exhaustible, for example, because their useful lives are reduced by display, educational, or research uses, they must be depreciated.
    Answer (A) is incorrect. Capitalized collections or individual items that are inexhaustible need not be depreciated. Answer (B) is incorrect. Infrastructure assets that are part of a network or a subsystem of a network need not be depreciated if the assets are managed using a system with certain characteristics and if the government documents preservation of the assets at an established and disclosed condition. Answer (C) is incorrect. Capitalization is needed for depreciation.

27.4.7. If a government reports eligible infrastructure assets using the modified approach,

    A. Complete condition assessments must be performed annually.

    B. Expenditures for the assets are capitalized.

    C. No depreciation expense is required to be recognized.

    D. The assets are not being preserved at or above the established and disclosed condition level.

Answer (C) is correct. *(Publisher, adapted)*
    REQUIRED: The implication of reporting eligible infrastructure assets using the modified approach.
    DISCUSSION: Under the modified approach, infrastructure assets that are part of a network or subsystem of a network (eligible infrastructure assets) need not be depreciated if the government uses an asset management system with certain characteristics and documents that the assets are being preserved approximately at (or above) a condition level established and disclosed by the government. An asset management system should (1) include an updated inventory of eligible infrastructure assets, (2) perform condition assessments and summarize results using a measurement scale, and (3) make annual estimates of the annual amounts needed to maintain the assets at the established condition level.
    Answer (A) is incorrect. A government using the modified approach must document that (1) complete condition assessments are performed in a consistent manner every 3 years and (2) the three most recent assessments provide reasonable assurance that the assets are being preserved at or above the established and disclosed condition level. Answer (B) is incorrect. Under the modified approach, expenditures (except those for additions and improvements) are expensed when incurred. Answer (D) is incorrect. If the assets are not being preserved at or above the established and disclosed condition level, the modified approach must be abandoned, and depreciation must be recognized.

27.4.8. Jonn City entered into a capital lease for equipment during the year. How should the asset obtained through the lease be reported in Jonn City's government-wide statement of net position?

    A. General capital asset.

    B. Other financing use.

    C. Expenditure.

    D. Not reported.

Answer (A) is correct. *(CPA, adapted)*
    REQUIRED: The reporting of a leased asset in the government-wide statement of net position.
    DISCUSSION: In the government-wide financial statements, a capital lease obligation associated with general governmental activities is recorded as a general capital asset and a liability under the accrual basis of accounting. In governmental fund financial statements, the asset financed by a capital lease is debited to an expenditure, and the lease financing is credited to another financing source under the modified accrual basis of accounting.
    Answer (B) is incorrect. The leased asset is debited to an asset and credited to a liability in the government-wide statements. It is debited to an expenditure and credited to another financing source in the governmental funds statements. Answer (C) is incorrect. Expenditures are recognized only in the governmental funds statements. Answer (D) is incorrect. The acquisition of a leased asset must be reported.

27.4.9. In Soan County's general fund statement of revenues, expenditures, and changes in fund balances, which of the following has an effect on the excess of revenues over expenditures?

    A. Purchase of fixed assets.

    B. Payment to a debt-service fund.

    C. Special items.

    D. Proceeds from the sale of capital assets.

Answer (A) is correct. *(CPA, adapted)*
    REQUIRED: The item affecting the excess of revenues over expenditures.
    DISCUSSION: The general fund is a governmental fund. Governmental funds report capital outlays as expenditures. Thus, the purchase of fixed assets affects the excess of revenues over expenditures.
    Answer (B) is incorrect. In the general fund, the entry to record the earmarking of resources for debt service is to debit other financing uses--interfund transfer to debt service fund and to credit due to debt service fund. The transfer is recorded by a debit to due to debt service fund and a credit to cash. These entries do not affect revenues or expenditures. Answer (C) is incorrect. Special items are significant transactions or other events that are (1) unusual or infrequent and (2) within the control of management. They are reported separately after other financing sources and uses and do not affect revenues or expenditures. Answer (D) is incorrect. Proceeds from the sale of capital assets are recorded by a debit to cash and a credit to other financing sources (unless the sale is a special item). The sale does not affect revenues or expenditures.

27.5 Budgetary Accounting

27.5.1. Assuming no outstanding encumbrances at year end, closing entries for which of the following situations would increase the general fund's unassigned fund balance at year end?

    A. Actual revenues were less than estimated revenues.

    B. Estimated revenues exceed actual appropriations.

    C. Actual expenditures exceed appropriations.

    D. Appropriations exceed actual expenditures.

Answer (D) is correct. *(CPA, adapted)*
    REQUIRED: The reason to increase unassigned fund balance at year end.
    DISCUSSION: Unassigned fund balance (the residual balance of the general fund) is a real account. It is the fund balance of a general fund that is spendable but not restricted, committed, or assigned. Appropriations (public funds set aside for a specific purpose) are recognized in the budgetary entry at the beginning of the fiscal period. If they exceed the government's actual expenditures for the year, unassigned fund balance increases. The reason is that no reclassifications to committed or assigned fund balance are recorded for encumbered amounts not already restricted, committed, or assigned.
    Answer (A) is incorrect. If actual revenues were less than estimated revenues, the effect would be to decrease unassigned fund balance. Answer (B) is incorrect. Appropriations is an anticipatory liability credited at the beginning of the period and reversed at the end of the period. However, actual appropriations is not an account used in governmental accounting. Answer (C) is incorrect. If actual expenditures exceed appropriations, the effect is to decrease unassigned fund balance.

27.5.2. Park City uses encumbrance accounting and formally integrates its budget into the general fund's accounting records. For the year ending July 31, Year 1, the following budget was adopted:

Estimated revenues	$30,000,000
Appropriations	27,000,000
Estimated transfer to debt service fund	900,000

Park's budgetary fund balance is a

    A. $3,000,000 credit balance.

    B. $3,000,000 debit balance.

    C. $2,100,000 credit balance.

    D. $2,100,000 debit balance.

Answer (C) is correct. *(CPA, adapted)*
    REQUIRED: The budgetary fund balance when a budget is adopted and recorded.
    DISCUSSION: Park City's budgetary entry for the Year 1 fiscal year:

Estimated revenues	$30,000,000	
Appropriations		$27,000,000
Estimated other financing uses		
-- transfer to debt service fund		900,000
Budgetary fund balance		2,100,000

    Answer (A) is incorrect. The $900,000 estimated transfer to debt service fund must be credited. Answer (B) is incorrect. The estimated revenues must be debited and the transfer to debt service must be credited. Answer (D) is incorrect. The estimated revenues should be debited.

27.5.3. For the budgetary year ending December 31, Maple City's general fund expects the following inflows of resources:

Property taxes, licenses, and fines	$9,000,000
Proceeds of debt issue	5,000,000
Interfund transfers for debt service	1,000,000

In the budgetary entry, what amount should Maple record for estimated revenues?

- A. $9,000,000
- B. $10,000,000
- C. $14,000,000
- D. $15,000,000

Answer (A) is correct. *(CPA, adapted)*
REQUIRED: The amount of estimated revenues.
DISCUSSION: Estimated revenues is an anticipatory asset and is debited for the amount expected to be collected from a governmental body's main sources of revenue. In the general fund, the main sources of revenue are taxes, fees, penalties, etc. ($9,000,000). Expected proceeds from the issuance of debt is an other financing source. An expected transfer from a different fund is an other financing source.
Answer (B) is incorrect. The amount of $10,000,000 incorrectly includes the interfund transfers to the debt source fund (an other financing use). Answer (C) is incorrect. The amount of $14,000,000 incorrectly includes the debt issue proceeds (an other financing source). Answer (D) is incorrect. The amount of $15,000,000 incorrectly includes the debt issue proceeds (an other financing source) and interfund transfers to the debt service fund (an other financing use).

27.5.4. In the current year, New City issued purchase orders and contracts of $850,000 that were chargeable against current-year budgeted appropriations of $1 million. The journal entry in the general fund to record the issuance of the purchase orders and contracts should include a

- A. Credit to vouchers payable of $1,000,000.
- B. Credit to encumbrances outstanding of $850,000.
- C. Debit to expenditures of $1 million.
- D. Debit to appropriations of $850,000.

Answer (B) is correct. *(CPA, adapted)*
REQUIRED: The entry for issuance of purchase orders and contracts in the general fund.
DISCUSSION: When a purchase order is approved or a contract is signed, an estimated liability is recorded in a budgetary account for the amount of the purchase order. The entry is a debit to encumbrances and a credit to encumbrances outstanding.
Answer (A) is incorrect. Vouchers payable are credited for $850,000 when the liability has been incurred. Answer (C) is incorrect. Expenditures will be debited for $850,000 when the liability has been incurred. Answer (D) is incorrect. Appropriations is debited when the budgetary accounts are closed.

27.5.5. Which of the following amount(s) is(are) included in a general fund's encumbrances account?

I. Outstanding vouchers payable amounts

II. Outstanding purchase order amounts

III. Excess of the amount of a purchase order over the actual expenditure for that order

- A. I only.
- B. I and III only.
- C. II only.
- D. II and III only.

Answer (C) is correct. *(CPA, adapted)*
REQUIRED: The amounts included in a general fund's encumbrances.
DISCUSSION: When a purchase order is approved, an encumbrance is recognized. When the goods are delivered or the services are performed, the entry is reversed, effectively eliminating the purchase order amount. Thus, encumbrances include only outstanding purchase orders.
Answer (A) is incorrect. The encumbrance is eliminated when the expenditure and the voucher payable relating to the purchase order are recorded. Answer (B) is incorrect. The encumbrance includes only outstanding purchase order amounts. Answer (D) is incorrect. When the goods are delivered or the services are performed, the original encumbrance entry is reversed. The actual amount owed is recorded in expenditures, so any excess is not reflected in encumbrances.

27.5.6. Gold County received goods that had been approved for purchase but for which payment had not yet been made. Should the accounts in the general fund listed below be increased?

	Encumbrances	Expenditures
A.	No	No
B.	No	Yes
C.	Yes	No
D.	Yes	Yes

Answer (B) is correct. *(CPA, adapted)*
REQUIRED: The effect of receipt of previously ordered goods on encumbrances and expenditures.
DISCUSSION: The initial encumbrance entry (debit encumbrances, credit encumbrances outstanding) is reversed (credit encumbrances, debit encumbrances outstanding) when an expenditure is recognized and the liability is incurred. Thus, encumbrances is decreased and expenditures increased (debit expenditures, credit vouchers payable) when previously ordered goods have been received. Expenditures and vouchers payable are increased for the actual amount to be paid for the goods.
Answer (A) is incorrect. Expenditures is debited (increased) upon receipt of goods previously ordered, i.e., when the liability is incurred. Answer (C) is incorrect. Encumbrances is decreased and expenditures is increased. Answer (D) is incorrect. Encumbrances is decreased.

27.5.7. During its fiscal year ended June 30, Cliff City issued purchase orders totaling $5 million, which were properly charged to encumbrances at that time. Cliff received goods and related invoices at the encumbered amounts totaling $4.5 million before year end. The remaining goods of $500,000 were not received until after year end. Cliff paid $4.2 million of the invoices received during the year. The amount of Cliff's encumbrances outstanding in the general fund at June 30 was

A. $0

B. $300,000

C. $500,000

D. $800,000

Answer (C) is correct. *(CPA, adapted)*
REQUIRED: The amount of encumbrances outstanding.
DISCUSSION: When a commitment is made to expend general fund resources, encumbrances is debited and encumbrances outstanding is credited. When the goods or services are received and the liability is recognized, this entry is reversed, and an expenditure is recorded. Because goods totaling $500,000 were not received at year end, encumbrances outstanding total $500,000 ($5,000,000 – $4,500,000).
Answer (A) is incorrect. Not all of the goods related to the encumbrance amounts were received during the year. Answer (B) is incorrect. The amount of $300,000 is the excess of goods received over the amount actually paid on the invoices during the year. Answer (D) is incorrect. The amount of $800,000 is the excess of total encumbrances over the amount paid on the invoices.

27.5.8. Elm City issued a purchase order for supplies with an estimated cost of $5,000. When the supplies were received, the accompanying invoice indicated an actual price of $4,950. What amount should Elm debit (credit) to encumbrances outstanding in its general fund after the supplies and invoice were received?

A. $(50)

B. $50

C. $4,950

D. $5,000

Answer (D) is correct. *(CPA, adapted)*
REQUIRED: The debit (credit) to encumbrances outstanding after the supplies and invoice were received.
DISCUSSION: When supplies are received by or services are rendered to a governmental unit, a journal entry is made to debit expenditures and to credit vouchers payable. Also, the previously recorded encumbrance must be reversed by debiting encumbrances outstanding and crediting encumbrances. Because the original encumbrance entry is reversed in full, encumbrances outstanding must be debited for the estimated cost of $5,000.
Answer (A) is incorrect. Encumbrances outstanding is debited, not credited, for original estimated cost. Answer (B) is incorrect. The amount of $50 is the difference between the estimated and actual price. Answer (C) is incorrect. The amount of $4,950 is the actual price, not the estimated price.

27.5.9. Should a special revenue fund with a legally adopted budget prepare its financial statements using the accrual basis and integrate budgetary accounts into its accounting system?

	Fund Statements Use Accrual Basis	Integrate Budgetary Accounts
A.	Yes	Yes
B.	Yes	No
C.	No	Yes
D.	No	No

Answer (C) is correct. *(CPA, adapted)*
REQUIRED: The accounting by a special revenue fund with a legally adopted budget.
DISCUSSION: Use of the modified accrual basis is required for the fund financial statements of all governmental funds. Thus, a special revenue fund should prepare its financial statements using the modified accrual basis. The integration of budgetary accounts into the formal accounting system is a control used to assist in controlling expenditures and enforcing revenue provisions. The extent to which the budgetary accounts should be integrated varies among governmental fund types and according to the nature of fund transactions. However, integration is necessary in the general, special revenue, and other annually budgeted governmental funds with many revenues, expenditures, and transfers. Thus, a special revenue fund with a legally adopted budget should integrate its budgetary accounts into its accounting system.
Answer (A) is incorrect. The financial statements of special revenue funds are prepared using the modified accrual basis. Answer (B) is incorrect. The financial statements of special revenue funds are prepared using the modified accrual basis, but budgetary accounts should be integrated. Answer (D) is incorrect. The special revenue fund with a legally adopted budget should integrate its budgetary accounts into its accounting system.

27.5.10. The following information pertains to Park Township's general fund at December 31:

Total assets, including $200,000 of cash	$1,000,000
Total liabilities	600,000
Encumbrances	100,000

Appropriations do not lapse at year end. At December 31, what amount should Park report as unassigned fund balance in its general fund balance sheet?

A. $200,000

B. $300,000

C. $400,000

D. $500,000

Answer (B) is correct. *(CPA, adapted)*
REQUIRED: The amount to be reported as unassigned fund balance in the general fund.
DISCUSSION: Appropriations encumbered at year end are reported in the balance sheet as committed or assigned fund balance (as appropriate). Accordingly, the amount of the unassigned fund balance in the general fund is equal to the amount of assets available to finance expenditures of the current or succeeding year. Funds that are (1) nonspendable, (2) restricted, (3) committed, or (4) assigned must be removed from the unassigned fund balance. Because $600,000 is needed to cover liabilities and $100,000 is reported in assigned or committed fund balance, the unassigned fund balance is $300,000 ($1,000,000 total assets – $600,000 liabilities – $100,000 assigned or committed).
Answer (A) is incorrect. The amount of $200,000 is the cash available. Answer (C) is incorrect. The amount of $400,000 does not reflect the amount encumbered. Answer (D) is incorrect. The amount of $500,000 is net position (assets – liabilities), plus the amount encumbered.

27.5.11. Encumbrances would not appear in which fund?

A. Capital projects.

B. Special revenue.

C. General.

D. Enterprise.

Answer (D) is correct. *(CPA, adapted)*
REQUIRED: The fund in which encumbrances do not appear.
DISCUSSION: Encumbrance accounting is used only for internal purposes in governmental funds, especially general and special revenue funds. An enterprise fund is a proprietary fund. The accounts and reports of proprietary funds are maintained and prepared in essentially the same way as those of businesses. Thus, such budgetary control accounts as encumbrances are not used in enterprise funds.
Answer (A) is incorrect. The capital projects fund is a governmental fund. Answer (B) is incorrect. The special revenue fund is a governmental fund. Answer (C) is incorrect. The general fund is a governmental fund.

27.5.12. A budgetary fund balance of a government's general fund is classified for encumbrances in excess of a balance of encumbrances. This accounting indicates

A. An excess of vouchers payable over encumbrances.

B. An excess of purchase orders over invoices received.

C. An excess of appropriations over encumbrances.

D. A recording error.

Answer (D) is correct. *(CPA, adapted)*
REQUIRED: The reason a budgetary fund balance exceeds the encumbrance balance.
DISCUSSION: The budgetary fund balance account is a general ledger budgetary account sometimes used to record the anticipated change in fund balance at the beginning of the period. Encumbrances is debited and encumbrances outstanding is credited to record commitments related to unperformed executory contracts and unfulfilled purchase orders. When the expenditure is recorded, the encumbrance entry is reversed. At year end, any remaining encumbrances may be eliminated if the legal authority of appropriations expires. If (1) encumbrances will be honored by the entity, and (2) encumbered amounts have not been restricted, committed, or assigned, they are reclassified from unassigned fund balance to committed or assigned fund balance, as appropriate. They are not reported as encumbrances in the financial statements. (But significant encumbrances should be disclosed.) However, none of these entries involves budgetary fund balance, a nominal account that is (1) debited (credited) at the beginning of the year and (2) credited (debited) at year end for the budgeted change in fund balance. Thus, a recording error must exist if a budgetary fund balance is classified for any purpose.
Answer (A) is incorrect. An excess of vouchers payable over encumbrances indicates that expenditures exceeded encumbrances. Answer (B) is incorrect. An excess of purchase orders over invoices received indicates an excess of encumbrances over expenditures. Answer (C) is incorrect. An excess of appropriations over encumbrances equals the amount of permissible expenditures.

27.5.13. A county's balances in the general fund included the following:

Appropriations	$435,000
Encumbrances	18,000
Expenditures	164,000
Vouchers payable	23,000

What is the remaining amount available for use by the county?

A. $230,000

B. $248,000

C. $253,000

D. $271,000

Answer (C) is correct. *(CPA, adapted)*
REQUIRED: The remaining amount available in the general fund.
DISCUSSION: An appropriation is a budgetary account. It is the total authorized to be expended for the period. An encumbrance also is a budgetary account. It is debited and encumbrances outstanding is credited to recognize a commitment to expand resources. An expenditure is recognized by the general fund when the liability has been incurred. Accordingly, comparison of appropriations, encumbrances, and expenditures determines that the unencumbered amount of appropriations that still may be expended is $253,000 ($435,000 – $18,000 – $164,000).
Answer (A) is incorrect. Vouchers payable are credited when expenditures are debited. Thus, $230,000 double counts $23,000 of expenditures. Answer (B) is incorrect. The amount of $248,000 results from subtracting vouchers payable, not encumbrances, from appropriations. Answer (D) is incorrect. The amount of $271,000 results from not subtracting encumbrances from appropriations.

27.6 Sources of Financing

27.6.1. Chase City imposes a 2% tax on hotel charges. Revenues from this tax will be used to promote tourism in the city. Chase should record this tax as what type of nonexchange transaction?

A. Derived tax revenue.

B. Imposed nonexchange revenue.

C. Government-mandated transaction.

D. Voluntary nonexchange transaction.

Answer (A) is correct. *(CPA, adapted)*
REQUIRED: The type of nonexchange transaction.
DISCUSSION: Derived tax revenues are assessments on exchange transactions, for example, income, sales, and, in this case, hotel room rentals. The government recognizes assets when the underlying exchange occurs (or when resources are received, if earlier). Revenues (net of estimated refunds) are recognized when the underlying exchange occurs. The requirements to use the proceeds for promotion of tourism is a purpose restriction, and the resulting net assets, equity, or fund balance is restricted until used.
Answer (B) is incorrect. Imposed nonexchange revenues (e.g., property taxes and fines) are assessments on nongovernmental entities, including individuals, that are not based on exchange transactions. Answer (C) is incorrect. Government-mandated nonexchange transactions occur when one government provides resources to a government at another level and requires that they be used for a specific purpose (e.g., federal programs that state or local governments are required to implement). Answer (D) is incorrect. Voluntary nonexchange transactions arise from legislative or contractual agreements, other than exchanges, entered into willingly by the parties (e.g., certain grants and private donations).

27.6.2. State University received two contributions during the current year that must be used to provide scholarships. Contribution A for $10,000 was collected during the year, and $8,000 was spent on scholarships. Contribution B is a pledge for $30,000 to be received next fiscal year. What amount of contribution revenue should the university report in its statement of activities?

A. $8,000

B. $10,000

C. $38,000

D. $40,000

Answer (D) is correct. *(CPA, adapted)*
REQUIRED: The contribution revenue reported in the statement of activities of a public university.
DISCUSSION: The contributions are voluntary nonexchange transactions (legislative or contractual agreements, other than exchanges, entered into willingly by the parties). No eligibility requirements (such as types of recipients) must be met, so the donee recognizes cash and revenue in the amount of $10,000 when Contribution A is received. However, Contribution B was announced 1 fiscal year in advance. Nevertheless, if the promise is verifiable, the resources are measurable, and collection is deemed to be probable, State University should debit a receivable and credit contribution revenue in the amount of $30,000 at the time of the announcement. Total contribution revenue is therefore $40,000 ($10,000 + $30,000).
Answer (A) is incorrect. The amount of $8,000 may be reclassified as unrestricted net assets (or fund balance) as a result of its use for the purpose to which it was restricted. Answer (B) is incorrect. The pledge may be recognized as revenue if its collection is probable. Answer (C) is incorrect. The full amount of Contribution A may be reported although part was not spent.

27.6.3. Resources received as a result of revenue-generating activities, such as interest and rents, are recognized as revenues in a governmental fund when they are measurable and available. Revenues received as a result of an imposed nonexchange transaction, such as property taxes or fines, are recognized when the

A. Resources to be received are measurable and available.

B. Governmental body has a legally enforceable right to the resources.

C. Time period in which the resources can be used begins.

D. Resources are received.

Answer (C) is correct. *(Publisher, adapted)*
REQUIRED: The timing of revenue recognition for an imposed nonexchange transaction.
DISCUSSION: A governmental fund is accounted for on the modified accrued basis. Thus, revenues are recognized when the resources to be received are susceptible to accrual (measurable and available). Furthermore, imposed nonexchange revenues also cannot be recognized until (1) the period in which the resources must be used or (2) the first period in which use is permitted. But a receivable may be accrued when the governmental body has a legally enforceable right to the resources.
Answer (A) is incorrect. For an imposed nonexchange transaction, additional criteria apply. Answer (B) is incorrect. The receivable, not the revenue, for an imposed nonexchange transaction is recognized when the governmental body has a legally enforceable right to it. Answer (D) is incorrect. An asset is recognized at the earlier of when the legally enforceable claim arises or when resources are received.

27.6.4. During the year just ended, Todd City received two state grants: one to buy a bus and one for bus operation. During the year, 90% of the capital grant was used for the bus purchase, but 100% of the operating grant was disbursed. Todd accounts for its bus operations in an enterprise fund. Todd is liable for general obligation bonds issued for the water and sewer fund, which will service the debt, and for revenue bonds to be repaid from admission fees collected from users of the municipal recreation center. Both issues are expected to be paid from enterprise funds and to be secured by Todd's full faith and credit, as well as its taxing power. In reporting the state grants for the bus purchase and operation, what should Todd include as grant revenues for the year ended December 31?

	90% of the Capital Grant	100% of the Capital Grant	Operating Grant
A.	Yes	No	No
B.	No	Yes	No
C.	No	Yes	Yes
D.	Yes	No	Yes

Answer (C) is correct. *(CPA, adapted)*
REQUIRED: The grant revenues for the year.
DISCUSSION: The grants for bus purchase and operation are voluntary nonexchange transactions. Revenues are recognized in such transactions when all eligibility requirements, including time requirements, are met. If the modified accrual method is used to account for the transaction, resources also should be "available." Todd has apparently met the eligibility requirements because it has what are presumably the characteristics of a recipient (it is a local government with a bus operation), and the period when the resources are required to be used or when use is first permitted has begun. Other eligibility requirements are not relevant based on the stated facts. The availability criterion has been met but is not relevant because the bus operation is accounted for in an enterprise fund, which uses the accrual method. The requirement to use the grants for bus purchase and operation is a purpose restriction and has no bearing on revenue recognition. Its effect is to cause the recipient to classify the unused resources as restricted. Thus, 100% of both grants should be recognized as revenues.
Answer (A) is incorrect. One hundred percent of both grants should be recognized. Answer (B) is incorrect. One hundred percent of the operating grant should be recognized. Answer (D) is incorrect. One hundred percent of the capital grant should be recognized.

27.6.5. A capital projects fund for a new city courthouse recorded a receivable of $300,000 for a state grant and a $450,000 transfer from the general fund. What amount should be reported as revenue by the capital projects fund?

A. $0

B. $300,000

C. $450,000

D. $750,000

Answer (B) is correct. *(CPA, adapted)*
REQUIRED: The revenue reported by a capital projects fund that received a state grant and an interfund transfer.
DISCUSSION: Governmental fund revenues are increases in fund financial resources other than from interfund transfers, debt issue proceeds, and redemptions of demand bonds. Thus, revenues of a capital projects fund include grants. The grant (a voluntary nonexchange transaction) is recognized when all eligibility requirements, including time requirements, have been met. When modified accrual accounting is used, as in a capital projects fund, the grant also must be available. Other financing sources include proceeds from bonds and interfund transfers.
Answer (A) is incorrect. The grant is a revenue. Answer (C) is incorrect. The interfund transfer is an other financing source. Answer (D) is incorrect. The interfund transfer is an other financing source.

27.6.6. The renovation of Fir City's municipal park was accounted for in a capital projects fund. Financing for the renovation, which was begun and completed during the current year, came from the following sources:

Grant from state government	$400,000
Proceeds from general obligation bond issue	500,000
Transfer from Fir's general fund	100,000

In its governmental fund statement of revenues, expenditures, and changes in fund balances for the current year, Fir should report these amounts as

	Revenues	Other Financing Sources
A.	$1,000,000	$0
B.	$900,000	$100,000
C.	$400,000	$600,000
D.	$0	$1,000,000

Answer (C) is correct. *(CPA, adapted)*
REQUIRED: The amounts to be reported in the governmental fund statement of revenues, expenditures, and changes in fund balances.
DISCUSSION: Governmental fund revenues are increases in fund financial resources other than from (1) interfund transfers, (2) debt issue proceeds, and (3) redemptions of demand bonds. Thus, revenues of a capital projects fund include grants. The grant (a voluntary nonexchange transaction) is recognized when all eligibility requirements, including time requirements, have been met. When modified accrual accounting is used, as in a capital projects fund, the grant also must be available. Other financing sources include proceeds from bonds and interfund transfers in. Thus, revenues of $400,000 and other financing sources of $600,000 ($500,000 + $100,000) are reported in the governmental fund statement of revenues, expenditures, and changes in fund balances.
Answer (A) is incorrect. The proceeds from the bond issue and the transfer from the general fund should be reported under other financing sources. Answer (B) is incorrect. The proceeds from bond issue should be reported under other financing sources. Answer (D) is incorrect. The grant should be reported under revenues.

27.6.7. In Year 8, Menton City received $5,000,000 of bond proceeds to be used for capital projects. Of this amount, $1,000,000 was expended in Year 8 with the balance expected to be expended in Year 9. When should the bond proceeds be recorded in a capital projects fund?

A. $5,000,000 in Year 8.

B. $5,000,000 in Year 9.

C. $1,000,000 in Year 8 and $4,000,000 in Year 9.

D. $1,000,000 in Year 8 and in the general fund for $4,000,000 in Year 8.

Answer (A) is correct. *(CPA, adapted)*
REQUIRED: The date(s) bond proceeds should be recorded in a capital projects fund.
DISCUSSION: The capital projects fund is a governmental fund. In this fund, the face amount of (1) long-term debt, (2) issuance premium or discount, and (3) certain other items are reported as other financing sources and uses. Thus, the entry in the capital projects fund to record receipt of the bond proceeds in Year 8 is a debit to cash and a credit to other financing sources -- bond issue proceeds for $5,000,000.
Answer (B) is incorrect. The $5,000,000 in bond proceeds should have been recognized in Year 8 when the proceeds were received. Answer (C) is incorrect. The $5,000,000 in bond proceeds should have been recognized in Year 8 when the proceeds were received. Answer (D) is incorrect. The $5,000,000 in bond proceeds should have been recognized in Year 8 when the proceeds were received.

27.6.8. Grove Township issued $50,000 of bond anticipation notes at face amount and placed the proceeds in its capital projects fund. All legal steps were taken to refinance the notes, but Grove was unable to consummate refinancing. In the capital projects fund, which account should be credited to record the $50,000 proceeds?

A. Other financing sources control.

B. Revenues control.

C. Deferred inflows of resources.

D. Bond anticipation notes payable.

Answer (D) is correct. *(CPA, adapted)*
REQUIRED: The account to be credited to record the proceeds from bond anticipation notes.
DISCUSSION: Bond anticipation notes of governmental funds are reported only as general long-term liabilities in the governmental activities column of the government-wide statement of net position if (1) all legal steps have been taken to refinance them, and (2) the intent is supported by an ability to consummate the refinancing on a long-term basis. If the government fails to meet both criteria, the bond anticipation notes must be reported as a liability in (1) the governmental fund in which the proceeds are recorded and (2) the government-wide statement of net position. Thus, given an inability to consummate the refinancing, the proceeds should be recorded as a bond anticipation note payable in the capital projects fund.
Answer (A) is incorrect. The notes should be recorded in the capital projects fund by a debit to cash and a credit to bond anticipation notes payable. Answer (B) is incorrect. Bond proceeds are not revenues. Answer (C) is incorrect. The notes should be recorded as a liability. A deferred inflows of resources is an acquisition of net assets that applies to a future reporting period.

27.6.9. What is the major difference between an exchange transaction and a nonexchange transaction for governmental units?

A. The relationship between the amount of value given and received.

B. Time requirements and whether the transaction is required by law.

C. Purpose restrictions placed upon fund balances.

D. Whether resources acquired can be further exchanged.

Answer (A) is correct. *(CPA, adapted)*
    REQUIRED: The major difference between an exchange transaction and a nonexchange transaction.
    DISCUSSION: In a nonexchange transaction, a government either gives or receives value without directly receiving or giving equal value in return.
    Answer (B) is incorrect. Time requirements affect recognition, and whether the transaction is required by law determines whether the transaction is imposed, government-mandated, or voluntary. Answer (C) is incorrect. Purpose restrictions on fund balances affect the classification of those funds as unrestricted, temporarily restricted, or permanently restricted. They determine how those amounts are to be used. Answer (D) is incorrect. Whether resources acquired can be further exchanged relates to time requirements and purpose restrictions.

27.6.10. During the year, Public College received the following:

- An unrestricted $50,000 pledge to be paid the following year.
- A $25,000 cash gift restricted for scholarships.
- A notice from a recent graduate that the college is named as a beneficiary of $10,000 in that graduate's will.

What amount of contribution revenue should Public College report in its statement of activities?

A. $25,000

B. $35,000

C. $75,000

D. $85,000

Answer (C) is correct. *(CPA, adapted)*
    REQUIRED: The contribution revenue reported by a public college.
    DISCUSSION: Private donations are voluntary nonexchange transactions. They result from agreements, other than exchanges, entered into willingly by the parties (e.g., certain grants and private donations). Revenues are recognized by recipients when all eligibility requirements are met. Eligibility requirements are that (1) the recipient has certain characteristics (e.g., it is a public college); (2) any time requirements are satisfied (e.g., use in a given period); (3) the donation is on an expenditure-driven basis, and the recipient has incurred costs; and (4) a contingent recipient action required by the provider has occurred. In this case, only the first requirement applies, and it has been satisfied. The promise of $50,000 in cash to be paid the following year is recognizable as current revenue if, in addition to meeting eligibility requirements, (1) the promise is verifiable and (2) the resources are measurable and probable of collection. The $25,000 of restricted cash already received also is revenue. The testamentary gift is not revenue because of verifiability and collectibility issues. For example, the gift may not be received for many years if the recent graduate is young, and the will may be changed.
    Answer (A) is incorrect. The $50,000 pledge should be recognized. Answer (B) is incorrect. The $50,000 pledge should be recognized, but the testamentary gift should not. Answer (D) is incorrect. The testamentary gift should not be recognized.

27.7 Reporting Entity and the CAFR

27.7.1. Financial reporting by general-purpose governments includes presentation of management's discussion and analysis as

A. Required supplementary information after the notes to the financial statements.

B. Part of the basic financial statements.

C. A description of currently known facts, decisions, or conditions expected to have significant effects on financial activities.

D. Information that may be limited to highlighting the amounts and percentages of change from the prior to the current year.

Answer (C) is correct. *(Publisher, adapted)*
    REQUIRED: The nature of MD&A.
    DISCUSSION: MD&A is required supplementary information (RSI) that precedes the basic financial statements and provides an overview of financial activities. It is based on currently known facts, decisions, or conditions and includes comparisons of the current and prior years, with an emphasis on the current year, based on government-wide information. Currently known facts are those of which management is aware at the audit report date.
    Answer (A) is incorrect. MD&A precedes the basic financial statements. Answer (B) is incorrect. MD&A is not part of the basic financial statements. Answer (D) is incorrect. MD&A should state the reasons for change from the prior year, not merely the amounts or percentages of change.

27.7.2. What is the correct approach to presentation of the notes to the financial statements?

A. The notes are essential for fair presentation of the statements.

B. The notes are required supplementary information.

C. The notes have the same status as MD&A.

D. The notes give equal focus to the primary government and its discretely presented component units.

Answer (A) is correct. *(Publisher, adapted)*
REQUIRED: The approach to presentation of the notes to the financial statements.
DISCUSSION: Notes to the financial statements are an integral part of the basic financial statements. They disclose information essential to fair presentation that is not reported on the face of the statements. The focus is on the primary government's (1) governmental activities, (2) business-type activities, (3) major funds, and (4) nonmajor funds in the aggregate.
Answer (B) is incorrect. Notes are not merely RSI. Answer (C) is incorrect. RSI includes MD&A, budgetary comparison schedules for governmental funds, and information about infrastructure assets reported using the modified approach. Answer (D) is incorrect. The notes focus on the primary government.

27.7.3. Budgetary comparison schedules must

A. Be reported for the general fund.

B. Be presented instead of budgetary comparison statements included in the basic statements.

C. Convert the appropriated budget information to the GAAP basis for comparison with actual amounts reported on that basis.

D. Compare only the final appropriated budget with actual amounts.

Answer (A) is correct. *(Publisher, adapted)*
REQUIRED: The true statement about budgetary comparison schedules.
DISCUSSION: Certain information must be presented as RSI in addition to MD&A. Budgetary comparison schedules must be reported only for the general fund and each major special revenue fund with a legally adopted annual budget. A schedule includes (1) the first complete appropriated budgets; (2) the final appropriated budgets; and (3) the actual inflows, outflows, and balances stated on the budgetary basis of accounting.
Answer (B) is incorrect. A government may elect to report budgetary comparison information in a statement as part of the basic statements. Answer (C) is incorrect. The budgetary comparison schedules compare the budgets with actual inflows, outflows, and balances stated on the government's budgetary basis. However, a reconciliation to GAAP is required. Answer (D) is incorrect. The original and final appropriated budgets are compared with the actual inflows, outflows, and balances.

27.7.4. Users of a government's financial statements should be able to distinguish between the primary government and its component units. Furthermore, an overview of the discretely presented component units should be provided. Accordingly,

A. The government-wide statements provide discrete presentation of component unit data, including data for fiduciary component units.

B. Condensed financial statements for major component units must be presented in the notes to the basic statements.

C. Information about each major component unit must be provided in the reporting entity's basic statements.

D. Major component unit information must be provided in the form of combining statements.

Answer (C) is correct. *(Publisher, adapted)*
REQUIRED: The presentation of component unit data.
DISCUSSION: To provide an overview of component units, discrete presentation of component unit data is required in the government-wide statements. Each major component unit should be reported in the basic statements by presentation (1) in a separate column in the government-wide statements, (2) in combining statements of major component units after the fund statements, or (3) of condensed statements (a statement of net position and a statement of activities) in the notes. However, major component unit information is not required for fiduciary component units. NOTE: An entity that meets the criteria for classification as a component unit must meet additional criteria to be classified as a fiduciary activity.
Answer (A) is incorrect. Information for fiduciary component units is presented only in the fund statements. Answer (B) is incorrect. Major component units also may be presented in combining statements after the fund statements or in separate columns in the government-wide statements. Answer (D) is incorrect. Major component units also may be presented in separate columns or in condensed statements in the notes.

27.7.5. How should state appropriations to a state university choosing to report as engaged only in business-type activities be reported in its statement of revenues, expenses, and changes in net position?

A. Operating revenues.

B. Nonoperating revenues.

C. Capital contributions.

D. Other financing sources.

Answer (B) is correct. *(CPA, adapted)*
REQUIRED: The classification of state appropriations received by a state university reporting as engaged only in business-type activities.
DISCUSSION: Receipt of a state appropriation is recognized as a revenue from a government-mandated nonexchange transaction. This kind of transaction occurs when one government provides resources to a government at another level and requires that they be used for a specific purpose. These activities ordinarily are reported in an enterprise fund (a proprietary fund). A proprietary fund reports all revenues, including capital contributions, in its statement of revenues, expenses, and changes in fund net position. This statement separately displays operating revenues, nonoperating revenues, capital contributions, and various other items. Grants (appropriations) made for operating purposes are generally classified as nonoperating revenues rather than operating revenues.
Answer (A) is incorrect. Revenues from providing educational services, not operating grants, are reported as operating revenues. Answer (C) is incorrect. The state appropriations are not reported as capital contributions if they are operating grants. Answer (D) is incorrect. Other financing sources are recognized in governmental, not proprietary, funds.

27.7.6. Which of the following statements are required to be presented for special-purpose governments engaged only in business-type activities (such as utilities)?

A. Statement of net position only.

B. Management's discussion and analysis (MD&A) and required supplementary information (RSI) only.

C. The financial statements required for governmental funds, including MD&A.

D. The financial statements required for enterprise funds, including MD&A and RSI.

Answer (D) is correct. *(CPA, adapted)*
REQUIRED: The statements required for special-purpose governments (SPGs) engaged only in business-type activities.
DISCUSSION: SPGs are legally separate entities that are component units or other stand-alone governments. If an SPG is engaged only in business-type activities, it presents only the financial statements for enterprise funds. For an SPG, the basic financial statements and RSI include (1) MD&A, (2) enterprise (proprietary) fund statements (statement of net position; statement of revenues, expenses, and changes in fund net position; and statement of cash flows), (3) notes, and (4) RSI other than MD&A.
Answer (A) is incorrect. The SPG also must present MD&A, RSI other than MD&A, and the other statements presented by enterprise funds. Answer (B) is incorrect. An SPG engaged only in business-type activities also must present the financial statements required for enterprise funds. Answer (C) is incorrect. The SPG presents the statements for enterprise funds.

27.7.7. If a city government is the primary reporting entity, which of the following is an acceptable method to present component units in its combined financial statements?

A. Consolidation.

B. Cost method.

C. Discrete presentation.

D. Government-wide presentation.

Answer (C) is correct. *(CPA, adapted)*
REQUIRED: The presentation of component units in the combined financial statements of the primary reporting entity.
DISCUSSION: The reporting entity consists of the primary government and its component units. A component unit is a legally separate entity for which the primary government is financially accountable. A component unit must be blended or discretely presented. A blended component unit is in effect the same as the primary government. Thus, its balances and transactions are reported in a manner similar to those of the primary government. Discrete presentation involves reporting component unit information in columns and rows separate from the information of the primary government.
Answer (A) is incorrect. Consolidation is a means of accounting for a combination in which a nongovernmental acquirer obtains control of a nongovernmental acquiree. Blending is not the same as consolidation. For example, the general fund of a blended component unit is presented as a special revenue fund of the primary government. Answer (B) is incorrect. The cost method is an accounting principle. Answer (D) is incorrect. Government-wide financial statements report information for the government as a whole. They do not display funds or fund types.

27.8 Government-Wide Reporting

27.8.1. Which of the following would be reported as program revenues on a local government's government-wide statement of activities?

A. Charges for services.

B. Taxes levied for a specific function.

C. Proceeds from the sale of a capital asset used for a specific function.

D. Interest revenues.

Answer (A) is correct. *(CPA, adapted)*
REQUIRED: The program revenue reported on a government-wide statement of activities.
DISCUSSION: The statement of activities presents operations in a format that displays net (expense) revenue for each function. The purpose is to report the relative financial burden to the taxpayers for that function. The net (expense) revenue for each governmental or business-type function equals expenses (at a minimum, the direct expenses of the function) minus program revenues. Charges for services are program revenues resulting from charges to customers, applicants, or others who directly benefit from what is provided (goods, services, or privileges) or who are otherwise directly affected.
Answer (B) is incorrect. General revenues are revenues that are not required to be reported as program revenues. They are reported separately after total net (expense) revenue for all functions. All taxes, including those levied for a special purpose, are general revenues. Answer (C) is incorrect. Proceeds from the sale of a capital asset used for a specific function are not revenues. Answer (D) is incorrect. Interest revenues are general revenues.

27.8.2. Government-wide financial statements

A. Display individual funds.

B. Display aggregated information about fund types.

C. Exclude information about discretely presented component units.

D. Use separate columns to distinguish between governmental and business-type activities.

Answer (D) is correct. *(Publisher, adapted)*
REQUIRED: The reporting in government-wide financial statements.
DISCUSSION: The basic financial statements include government-wide statements, fund statements, and the notes to the statements. Government-wide statements do not display funds or fund types but instead report information about the overall government. They distinguish between the primary government and its discretely presented component units and between the governmental activities and business-type activities of the primary government.
Answer (A) is incorrect. Fund information is reported in the fund financial statements. Answer (B) is incorrect. Fund information is reported in the fund financial statements. Answer (C) is incorrect. Separate rows and columns report information about discretely presented component units.

27.8.3. During the year just ended, Todd City received two state grants: one to buy a bus and one for bus operation. During the year, 90% of the capital grant was used for the bus purchase, but 100% of the operating grant was disbursed. Todd accounts for its bus operations in an enterprise fund. Todd is liable for general obligation bonds issued for the water and sewer fund, which will service the debt, and for revenue bonds to be repaid from admission fees collected from users of the municipal recreation center. Both issues are expected to be paid from enterprise funds and to be secured by Todd's full faith and credit, as well as its taxing power. Which of Todd's noncurrent obligations should be accounted for only in the government-wide financial statements?

	General Obligation Bonds	Revenue Bonds
A.	Yes	Yes
B.	Yes	No
C.	No	Yes
D.	No	No

Answer (D) is correct. *(CPA, adapted)*
REQUIRED: The bonds reported in the government-wide financial statements.
DISCUSSION: Noncurrent liabilities directly related to and expected to be paid from a proprietary fund, such as an enterprise fund, are not general noncurrent liabilities. They should be reported in the proprietary fund statement of net position as well as the government-wide statement of net position. They are specific fund liabilities even though they are backed by the full faith and credit of the governmental unit. The water and sewer fund and the municipal recreation center fund are both enterprise funds.
Answer (A) is incorrect. The bond issues are not general noncurrent liabilities and should be reported in the government-wide statement of net position and in the proprietary fund statement of net position. Answer (B) is incorrect. The general obligation bonds are reported in the government-wide statement of net position and in the proprietary fund statement of net position. Answer (C) is incorrect. The revenue bonds are reported in the government-wide statement of net position and in the proprietary fund statement of net position.

27.8.4. The government-wide statement of net position must

A. Be presented in a classified format.

B. Present assets and liabilities in order of liquidity.

C. Use the balance sheet format.

D. Display net position in three components.

Answer (D) is correct. *(Publisher, adapted)*
REQUIRED: The required presentation of the government-wide statement of net position.
DISCUSSION: The GASB requires that the government-wide statement of net position display net position in three components: net investment in capital assets, net of related debt, accumulated depreciation, and deferred inflows and outflows of resources; restricted net position; and unrestricted net position.
Answer (A) is incorrect. A classified format is acceptable but not required. Answer (B) is incorrect. The GASB encourages but does not require governments to present assets and liabilities in order of liquidity. Answer (C) is incorrect. The GASB permits governments to use the balance sheet format, although it prefers the net position format.

27.8.5. In the government-wide statement of net position, restricted capital assets should be included in the

A. Expendable component of restricted net position.

B. Nonexpendable component of restricted net position.

C. Net investment in capital assets, net of related debt, component of net position.

D. Designated component of net position.

Answer (C) is correct. *(Publisher, adapted)*
REQUIRED: The classification of restricted capital assets in the statement of net position.
DISCUSSION: Net position has three components: (1) net investment in capital assets, net of related debt, accumulated depreciation, and deferred inflows and outflows of resources; (2) restricted net position; and (3) unrestricted net position. Net investment in capital assets includes unrestricted and restricted capital assets. However, debt related to significant unspent proceeds is classified in the same net position component as those proceeds.
Answer (A) is incorrect. Restricted net position is subject to constraints imposed by external entities (creditors, grantors, or other governments) or by law (constitutional provisions or enabling legislation). If permanent endowments or permanent fund principal amounts are included, restricted net position should be displayed as expendable and nonexpendable. Nonexpendable means that the restriction is retained in perpetuity. However, capital assets must be included in net investment in capital assets even if they are restricted and expendable. Answer (B) is incorrect. Capital assets must be included in the net investment in capital assets even if they are restricted and nonexpendable. Answer (D) is incorrect. Designations of net position are not reported on the face of the statement.

27.8.6. The government-wide statement of activities reports

A. Activities accounted for in governmental funds at least at the segment level of detail.

B. Activities accounted for in the enterprise funds at least at the fund level of detail.

C. Net (expense) revenue for each function equal to expenses minus program revenues.

D. Net (expense) revenue for each function equal to expenses minus general revenues.

Answer (C) is correct. *(Publisher, adapted)*
REQUIRED: The reporting in the government-wide statement of activities.
DISCUSSION: The statement of activities presents operations in a format that displays net (expense) revenue for each function. The net (expense) revenue for each governmental or business-type function equals expenses minus program revenues. The minimum levels of detail for activities of governmental funds and enterprise funds are by function and by different identifiable activities, respectively.
Answer (A) is incorrect. The minimum level of detail for activities of governmental funds is by function. Answer (B) is incorrect. The minimum level of detail for activities of enterprise funds is different identifiable activities. Answer (D) is incorrect. General revenues are reported separately after total net (expense) revenue for all functions.

27.8.7. How are expenses reported in the government-wide statement of activities?

A. Interest on general long-term liabilities is ordinarily treated as a direct expense.

B. At a minimum, direct expenses should be reported for each function.

C. Indirect expenses are not allocated.

D. Indirect expenses are reported for each function.

Answer (B) is correct. *(Publisher, adapted)*
    REQUIRED: The reporting of expenses in the statement of activities.
    DISCUSSION: Direct expenses are specifically associated with a service, program, or department. Thus, they are clearly identifiable with a given function. The net (expense) revenue for each function equals expenses (at a minimum, the direct expenses of the function) minus program revenues. Indirect expenses need not be allocated and included in the determination of net (expense) revenue for each function.
    Answer (A) is incorrect. Interest on general long-term liabilities is a direct expense only in unusual circumstances, that is, when the borrowing is essential to a program and omitting the interest would be misleading. Answer (C) is incorrect. Direct expenses must be reported by function, but indirect expenses may or may not be allocated. Answer (D) is incorrect. Direct expenses are reported for each function.

27.8.8. The government-wide statement of activities should report which of the following categories of program revenues?

I.   Charges for services

II. Earnings for permanent funds that finance general fund programs

III. Program-specific capital grants and contributions

A. I only.

B. I and III only.

C. II and III only.

D. I, II, and III.

Answer (B) is correct. *(Publisher, adapted)*
    REQUIRED: The category(ies) of program revenues.
    DISCUSSION: Program revenues include (1) charges for services, (2) program-specific operating grants and contributions, and (3) program-specific capital grants and contributions. They may also include earnings on (1) endowments, (2) permanent fund investments, or (3) other investments restricted to a given program. Earnings of endowments or permanent funds that finance general fund programs or general operating expenses are not program revenues. However, when earnings on a program's invested accumulated resources are legally restricted for use by the program, those earnings are program revenues.
    Answer (A) is incorrect. Program revenues also include program-specific grants and contributions, both operating and capital. Answer (C) is incorrect. Earnings of endowments or permanent funds that finance general fund programs or general operating expenses are not program revenues. Answer (D) is incorrect. Earnings of endowments or permanent funds that finance general fund programs or general operating expenses are not program revenues.

27.8.9. General revenues reported in the government-wide statement of activities

A. Include all taxes.

B. Exclude taxes levied for a specific purpose.

C. Are aggregated with contributions, special and extraordinary items, and transfers in a line item.

D. Exclude interest and grants.

Answer (A) is correct. *(Publisher, adapted)*
    REQUIRED: The true statement about general revenues.
    DISCUSSION: General revenues are revenues not required to be reported as program revenues. They are reported separately after total net (expense) revenue for all functions in the government-wide statement of activities. All taxes, including those levied for a special purpose, are general revenues.
    Answer (B) is incorrect. All taxes are general revenues but should be reported by type of tax, e.g., income, sales, and property. Answer (C) is incorrect. (1) Contributions to endowments, (2) contributions to permanent fund principal, (3) transfers between governmental and business-type activities, and (4) special and extraordinary items are reported separately in the same manner as general revenues (at the bottom of the statement of activities to determine the change in net position for the period). Answer (D) is incorrect. General revenues are all revenues not required to be reported as program revenues.

27.8.10. Preparation of government-wide financial statements requires elimination of

A. Receivables from fiduciary funds from the statement of net position.

B. The effects on the statement of activities of interfund services provided and used between functions.

C. Internal balances from the total primary government column in the statement of net position.

D. Net residual amounts due between governmental and business-type activities from those columns in the statement of net position.

Answer (C) is correct. *(Publisher, adapted)*
REQUIRED: The elimination necessary in the preparation of government-wide financial statements.
DISCUSSION: Numerous eliminations and reclassifications are necessary in preparing the government-wide statements. Thus, interfund receivables and payables are eliminated in the governmental and business-type activities columns of the statement of net position, except for net residual amounts due (presented as internal balances). However, the total primary government column excludes internal balances.
Answer (A) is incorrect. Fund receivables from, or payables to, fiduciary funds are treated in the statement of net position as resulting from transactions with external parties, not as internal balances. Answer (B) is incorrect. Eliminations are not made in the statement of activities for the effects of interfund services provided and used between functions (e.g., the sale of power by a utility to the general government). Answer (D) is incorrect. Net residual amounts due between governmental and business-type activities are presented as interfund balances in the appropriate columns but are eliminated in the total primary government column.

27.8.11. In preparing Chase City's reconciliation of the statement of revenues, expenditures, and changes in fund balances to the government-wide statement of activities, which of the following items should be subtracted from changes in fund balances?

A. Capital assets purchases.

B. Payment of long-term debt principal.

C. Internal service fund increase in net assets.

D. Book value of capital assets sold during the year.

Answer (D) is correct. *(CPA, adapted)*
REQUIRED: The subtraction from changes in fund balances in the reconciliation to the government-wide statement of activities.
DISCUSSION: In the statement of activities, only the gain or loss on the sale of a capital asset is reported. (The acquisition was recorded in the governmental funds as an expenditure for its full amount.) But in the governmental funds, the proceeds are recorded as an increase in resources. Consequently, the change in net position (statement of activities) differs from the change in fund balances by the carrying amount of the capital assets sold. This item requires a reconciling subtraction from the change in fund balance.
Answer (A) is incorrect. Governmental funds report capital outlays as expenditures (decreases in the fund balance). The reconciling item is the amount by which these expenditures exceeded the depreciation recognized in the statement of activities for the current period. This item is added to the net change in fund balances. Answer (B) is incorrect. The payment of long-term debt principal is an expenditure in the governmental funds (debt service fund). This transaction does not affect the change in net position reported in the statement of activities. Thus, this item is added to the net change in fund balances. Answer (C) is incorrect. Internal service funds are proprietary funds that account for activities performed primarily for the benefit of agencies accounted for in other funds. Examples are a motor pool and an information technology department. In the preparation of the statement of activities, the effects of internal service activities must be eliminated to avoid double counting. The purpose is to prevent recognition of both the activities of the internal service fund and the charges made to the participating funds or functions. Thus, the preparation of the statement of activities essentially involves reducing (through an intraentity elimination) the balance of the internal service fund to zero. The effect on the reconciliation is an addition to the net change in fund balances because of the elimination of charges to governmental funds by a proprietary fund.

27.8.12. In the government-wide statement of activities, special items are transactions or other events that are

A. Unusual in nature and infrequent in occurrence.

B. Unusual in nature or infrequent in occurrence but not within management's control.

C. Unusual in nature and infrequent in occurrence and within management's control.

D. Unusual in nature or infrequent in occurrence and within management's control.

Answer (D) is correct. *(Publisher, adapted)*
   REQUIRED: The characteristics of special items.
   DISCUSSION: Extraordinary items are both unusual in nature and infrequent in occurrence. Special items are significant transactions or other events within the control of management that are either unusual or infrequent. They are reported separately after extraordinary items.
   Answer (A) is incorrect. Extraordinary items are unusual in nature and infrequent in occurrence. Answer (B) is incorrect. Special items are within management's control. Answer (C) is incorrect. Extraordinary items are unusual in nature and infrequent in occurrence.

27.8.13. A summary reconciliation of the government-wide and fund financial statements

A. Must be presented at the bottom of the fund statements or in an accompanying schedule.

B. Must be presented as required supplementary information.

C. Must be presented in the notes.

D. Is recommended but not required.

Answer (A) is correct. *(Publisher, adapted)*
   REQUIRED: The presentation of a summary reconciliation of the government-wide and fund financial statements.
   DISCUSSION: A government must provide a summary reconciliation to the government-wide statements at the bottom of the fund statements or in a schedule. Brief explanations on the face of the statements may suffice, but a more detailed explanation in the notes may be necessary.
   Answer (B) is incorrect. RSI consists of MD&A, budgetary comparison schedules, and information about infrastructure assets reported using the modified approach. Answer (C) is incorrect. The summary reconciliation must be presented at the bottom of the fund statements or in an accompanying schedule. Additional detail may need to be given in the notes. Answer (D) is incorrect. The summary reconciliation is required.

27.8.14. Which of the following activities should be excluded when governmental fund financial statements are converted to government-wide financial statements?

A. Proprietary activities.

B. Fiduciary activities.

C. Government activities.

D. Enterprise activities.

Answer (B) is correct. *(CPA, adapted)*
   REQUIRED: The activities excluded from government-wide financial statements.
   DISCUSSION: The government-wide financial statements include the primary government and its component units but exclude fiduciary activities. Fiduciary funds, including fiduciary component units, should be reported only in the statements of fiduciary net position and changes in fiduciary net position. However, in some circumstances, business-type activities (including enterprise funds) may report assets and a corresponding liability that ordinarily should be reported in a custodial fund. This reporting is permitted if the assets normally are expected to be held for no more than 3 months.
   Answer (A) is incorrect. Proprietary activities presumably include activities of proprietary funds (enterprise funds and internal service funds). Proprietary fund activities of internal service funds are usually reported in the governmental activities column. Activities of enterprise funds are reported in the business-type activities column. Answer (C) is incorrect. The government-wide statement of activities displays columns for governmental activities and business-type activities. Answer (D) is incorrect. Business-type activities are reported in enterprise funds and in the government-wide statements.

27.9 Governmental Funds Reporting

27.9.1. Which financial statement must be presented for governmental funds?

A. A statement of activities.

B. A statement of cash flows.

C. A statement of revenues, expenses, and changes in fund net assets.

D. A financial statement in balance sheet format.

Answer (D) is correct. *(Publisher, adapted)*
   REQUIRED: The governmental fund financial statement.
   DISCUSSION: A balance sheet is required for governmental funds. It should be in balance sheet format (assets = liabilities + fund balances) with a total column and segregation of fund balances into reserved and unreserved amounts.
   Answer (A) is incorrect. A statement of activities is a required government-wide statement. Answer (B) is incorrect. A statement of cash flows is required for proprietary funds. Answer (C) is incorrect. A statement of revenues, expenses, and changes in fund net assets is required for proprietary funds.

27.9.2. Tott City's serial bonds are serviced through a debt service fund with cash provided by the general fund. In the governmental funds financial statements, how are cash receipts and cash payments reported?

	Cash Receipts	Cash Payments
A.	Revenues	Expenditures
B.	Revenues	Interfund transfers
C.	Interfund transfers	Expenditures
D.	Interfund transfers	Interfund transfers

Answer (C) is correct. *(CPA, adapted)*
REQUIRED: The reporting of cash flows in a debt service fund's financial statements.
DISCUSSION: An interfund transfer is a nonreciprocal interfund activity because no repayment is required. Accordingly, cash receipts of a debt service fund from the general fund are recorded as interfund transfers. Furthermore, these resources already have been recorded as revenues in the general fund. An expenditure is recognized in accordance with the modified accrual basis of accounting used in the governmental funds when the fund liability is incurred, if measurable. Exceptions are the unmatured principal and interest on general long-term debt (e.g., the serial bonds), which are recognized when due. Thus, maturing amounts of principal and interest on serial bonds are recorded as expenditures when they are due, whether or not the cash payments are made. The actual credit for a cash payment is therefore offset by a debit to expenditures or to a liability.
Answer (A) is incorrect. The cash receipts from the general fund by the debt service fund are other financing sources (interfund transfers). Answer (B) is incorrect. The cash receipts from the general fund by the debt service fund are other financing sources (interfund transfers). The cash payments by a debt service fund to pay principal and interest are expenditures. Answer (D) is incorrect. The cash payments by a debt service fund to pay principal and interest are expenditures.

27.9.3. Wood City, which is legally obligated to maintain a debt service fund, issued the following general obligation bonds on July 1:

Term of bonds	10 years
Face amount	$1,000,000
Issue price	$101
Stated interest rate	6%

Interest is payable January 1 and July 1. What amount of bond issuance premium should be amortized in Wood's debt service fund for the year ended December 31?

A. $1,000

B. $500

C. $250

D. $0

Answer (D) is correct. *(CPA, adapted)*
REQUIRED: The amount of bond premium amortized in the debt service fund.
DISCUSSION: The debt service fund of a governmental unit is a governmental fund used to account for the accumulation of resources for, and the payment of, general long-term debt principal and interest. Bond issuance premium is accounted for as an other financing source in the fund out of which the proceeds are spent. Thus, bond issuance premium is not amortized.

27.9.4. Dale City is accumulating financial resources that are legally restricted to payments of general long-term debt principal and interest maturing in future years. At December 31 of the current year, $5,000,000 has been accumulated for principal payments, and $300,000 has been accumulated for interest payments. These restricted funds should be accounted for in the

	Debt Service Fund	General Fund
A.	$0	$5,300,000
B.	$300,000	$5,000,000
C.	$5,000,000	$300,000
D.	$5,300,000	$0

Answer (D) is correct. *(CPA, adapted)*
REQUIRED: The funds in which to account for financial resources reserved for principal and interest.
DISCUSSION: Debt service funds account for resources restricted, committed, or assigned to paying principal and interest. But these funds do not account for the debt itself. They also account for resources being accumulated for future principal and interest payments. The general fund does not account for these transactions, except to record transfers to the debt service fund.
Answer (A) is incorrect. The debt service fund, not the general fund, accounts for resources restricted, committed, or assigned to paying principal and interest. But these funds do not account for the debt itself. They also account for resources being accumulated for future principal and interest payments. Answer (B) is incorrect. The debt service fund also accounts for the accumulation of principal. Answer (C) is incorrect. The debt service fund also accounts for the accumulation of interest.

27.9.5. The focus of certain fund financial statements of a local government is on major funds. Accordingly,

A. Major internal service funds must be presented separately in the statement of net position for proprietary funds.

B. The main operating fund is always reported as a major fund.

C. Combining statements for nonmajor funds are required.

D. Enterprise funds not meeting the quantitative criteria are not eligible for presentation as major funds.

Answer (B) is correct. *(Publisher, adapted)*
    REQUIRED: The true statement about major fund reporting.
    DISCUSSION: The focus of reporting of governmental and proprietary funds (but not internal service funds) is on major funds. The main operating fund (e.g., the general fund) is always reported as a major fund, and any governmental or enterprise funds believed to be particularly important to users also may be reported in this way. These funds must be reported as major if they meet the quantitative thresholds.
    Answer (A) is incorrect. Major fund reporting requirements apply to governmental and enterprise funds but not to internal service funds. Answer (C) is incorrect. Combining statements for nonmajor funds are not required but may be reported as supplementary information. Answer (D) is incorrect. A government may report any governmental or enterprise individual fund as major if it is particularly important.

27.9.6. A capital projects fund of a local government must be reported as major if

A. Total assets of that fund are 5% of the total assets of all governmental funds and 2% of the total assets of all governmental and enterprise funds combined.

B. Total expenditures of that fund are 10% of the total expenditures of all governmental funds and 2% of the total expenditures of all governmental and enterprise funds combined.

C. Total liabilities of that fund are 10% of the total liabilities of all governmental funds and 5% of the total liabilities of all governmental and enterprise funds combined.

D. Total revenues of that fund are 6% of the total revenues of all governmental funds and 3% of the total revenues of all governmental and enterprise funds combined.

Answer (C) is correct. *(Publisher, adapted)*
    REQUIRED: The criteria for requiring major fund reporting of a capital projects fund.
    DISCUSSION: Any governmental or enterprise fund must be reported as major if total revenues, expenditures or expenses, assets, or liabilities (excluding extraordinary items) of the fund (1) are at least 10% of the corresponding element total (assets, etc.) for all funds of the same category or type, that is, for all governmental or all enterprise funds, and (2) the same element that met the 10% standard is at least 5% of the corresponding element total for all governmental and enterprise funds in the aggregate.
    Answer (A) is incorrect. The appropriate percentages are 10% of the corresponding element total for governmental funds and 5% of the corresponding element total for governmental funds and enterprise funds in the aggregate. Answer (B) is incorrect. The appropriate percentages are 10% of the corresponding element total for governmental funds and 5% of the corresponding element total for governmental funds and enterprise funds in the aggregate. Answer (D) is incorrect. The appropriate percentages are 10% of the corresponding element total for governmental funds and 5% of the corresponding element total for governmental funds and enterprise funds in the aggregate.

27.9.7. A statement of revenues, expenditures, and changes in fund balances must be reported for governmental funds. In that statement,

A. Debt refundings are treated as extraordinary items.

B. Revenues are classified, at a minimum, by function.

C. Proceeds of long-term debt should be reported in the other financing sources and uses classification.

D. Expenditures are classified by major expenditure source.

Answer (C) is correct. *(Publisher, adapted)*
    REQUIRED: The appropriate reporting in the statement of revenues, expenditures, and changes in fund balances.
    DISCUSSION: A statement of revenues, expenditures, and changes in fund balances is required for governmental funds. It reports inflows, outflows, and balances of current financial resources for each major fund, for nonmajor funds in the aggregate, and in a total column. In this statement, the other financing sources and uses classification appears after excess (deficiency) of revenues over expenditures. Other financing sources and uses include the face amount of long-term debt, issuance premium or discount, some payments to escrow agents for bond refundings, transfers, and sales of capital assets (unless the sale is a special item).
    Answer (A) is incorrect. Debt refundings in governmental funds are not extraordinary items. They result in other financing sources or uses, not gains or losses. Answer (B) is incorrect. Revenues are classified in this statement by major source. Answer (D) is incorrect. Expenditures are classified in this statement by, at a minimum, function.

27.9.8. Brandon County's general fund had the following transactions during the year:

Transfer to a debt service fund	$100,000
Payment to a pension trust fund	500,000
Purchase of equipment	300,000

What amount should Brandon County report for the general fund as other financing uses in its governmental funds statement of revenues, expenditures, and changes in fund balances?

A. $100,000

B. $400,000

C. $800,000

D. $900,000

Answer (A) is correct. *(CPA, adapted)*
REQUIRED: The amount reported for the general fund as other financing uses.
DISCUSSION: Other financing sources and uses are reported in the governmental funds statement of revenues, expenditures, and changes in fund balances. They include (1) the face amount of long-term debt, (2) issuance premium or discount, (3) some payments to escrow agents for bond refundings, (4) interfund transfers, and (5) sales of capital assets. Accordingly, the only item reported in the general fund as other financing uses is the $100,000 transfer to a debt service fund.
Answer (B) is incorrect. The amount of $400,000 includes the purchase of equipment. It should be reported as an expenditure for a capital asset in the statement of revenues, expenditures, and changes in fund balances. Answer (C) is incorrect. The amount of $800,000 omits the transfer. It includes the purchase of equipment. This purchase should be reported as an expenditure for a capital asset in the statement of revenues, expenditures, and changes in fund balances. The payment to the pension trust fund also is reported as an expenditure. Answer (D) is incorrect. The amount of $900,000 includes the purchase of equipment. It should be reported as an expenditure for a capital asset in the statement of revenues, expenditures, and changes in fund balances. The payment to a pension trust fund also is reported as an expenditure.

27.9.9. How should a city's general fund report the acquisition of a new police car in its governmental fund statement of revenues, expenditures, and changes in fund balances?

A. Noncurrent asset.

B. Expenditure.

C. Expense.

D. Property, plant, and equipment.

Answer (B) is correct. *(CPA, adapted)*
REQUIRED: The treatment of an asset acquisition in the general fund.
DISCUSSION: Governmental funds have a current financial resources measurement focus. Thus, the full cost of the capital asset is reported as an expenditure.
Answer (A) is incorrect. Governmental funds have a current financial resources measurement focus. They do not report capital assets as noncurrent assets. Answer (C) is incorrect. Governmental funds report expenditures, not expenses. Answer (D) is incorrect. Governmental funds have a current financial resources measurement focus. They do not report capital assets as property, plant, and equipment.

27.10 Proprietary Funds Reporting

27.10.1. The following transactions were among those reported by Corfe City's electric utility enterprise fund for the year just ended:

Capital contributed by subdividers	$ 900,000
Cash received from customer households	2,700,000
Proceeds from sale of revenue bonds	4,500,000

In the proprietary funds statement of cash flows for the year ended December 31, what amount should be reported as cash flows from the electric utility enterprise fund's capital and related financing activities?

A. $4,500,000

B. $5,400,000

C. $7,200,000

D. $8,100,000

Answer (B) is correct. *(CPA, adapted)*
REQUIRED: The amount reported as cash flows from capital and related financing activities.
DISCUSSION: Cash flows should be classified as operating, noncapital financing, capital and related financing, or investing. Operating activities include producing and delivering goods and providing services. Thus, cash from customer households is a revenue item reported under cash flows from operating activities. Capital and related financing activities include acquiring and disposing of capital assets, borrowing and repaying money related to capital asset transactions, etc. Assuming the sale of revenue bonds and the capital contributions by subdividers are for the acquisition or improvement of capital assets, the amount to report under capital and related financing activities is $5,400,000 ($900,000 + $4,500,000).
Answer (A) is incorrect. The amount of $4,500,000 omits the capital contributed by subdividers. Answer (C) is incorrect. The amount of $7,200,000 includes customer fees revenue and omits capital contributed by subdividers. Answer (D) is incorrect. The amount of $8,100,000 includes customer fees.

27.10.2. The statement of revenues, expenses, and changes in fund net position for proprietary funds

A. Combines special and extraordinary items in a subtotal presented before nonoperating revenues and expenses.

B. Must report revenues at gross amounts, with discounts and allowances disclosed parenthetically.

C. Distinguishes between operating and nonoperating revenues and expenses.

D. Must define operating items in the same way as in the statement of cash flows.

Answer (C) is correct. *(Publisher, adapted)*
REQUIRED: The true statement about the statement of revenues, expenses, and changes in fund net position.
DISCUSSION: A statement of revenues, expenses, and changes in fund net position is the required operating statement for proprietary funds. Operating and nonoperating revenues and expenses should be distinguished, and separate subtotals should be presented for operating revenues, operating expenses, and operating income.
Answer (A) is incorrect. Nonoperating revenues and expenses are presented immediately after operating income (loss). Moreover, special and extraordinary items are reported separately. Answer (B) is incorrect. Revenues are reported by major source either net with disclosure of discounts and allowances or gross with discounts and allowances reported beneath the revenue amounts. Answer (D) is incorrect. A government should consistently follow appropriate definitions of operating items. Considerations in defining these items are (1) the principal purpose of the fund and (2) their presentation in a cash flows statement. However, the classification in the statement of cash flows is not controlling.

27.10.3. Dogwood City's water enterprise fund received interest of $10,000 on long-term investments. How should this amount be reported on the statement of cash flows?

A. Operating activities.

B. Noncapital financing activities.

C. Capital and related financing activities.

D. Investing activities.

Answer (D) is correct. *(CPA, adapted)*
REQUIRED: The classification of interest received on long-term investments in the statement of cash flows.
DISCUSSION: Reporting of cash flows of proprietary funds and entities engaged in business-type activities, e.g., governmental utilities, is required. Cash inflows should be classified as operating, noncapital financing, capital and related financing, and investing. Investing activities include making and collecting loans (other than program loans) and acquiring and disposing of debt and equity instruments. Cash inflows from investing activities include interest and dividends received as returns on loans (not program loans), debt of other entities, equity securities, and cash management or investment pools.
Answer (A) is incorrect. Operating activities are all transactions and other events that are not classified as either financing or investing activities. In general, operating activities involve transactions and other events the effects of which are included in the determination of operating income. Answer (B) is incorrect. Noncapital financing activities include borrowings for purposes other than acquiring, constructing, or improving capital assets and debt. Answer (C) is incorrect. Capital and related financing activities include borrowings and repayments of debt related to (1) acquiring, constructing, or improving capital assets; (2) acquiring and disposing of capital assets used to provide goods or services; and (3) paying for capital assets obtained on credit.

27.10.4. In a statement of net position for proprietary funds,

A. Net position must be reported in two components: restricted or unrestricted.

B. Capital contributions must be reported in a separate component of net position.

C. Designations must be shown on the face of the statement.

D. Assets, deferred inflows or outflows of resources, and liabilities must be classified.

Answer (D) is correct. *(Publisher, adapted)*
REQUIRED: The appropriate display in the statement of net position for proprietary funds.
DISCUSSION: A statement of net position is required for proprietary funds, and assets and liabilities must be classified as current or noncurrent. Either a net position format [(assets + deferred outflows of resources) – (liabilities + deferred inflows of resources) = net position] or a balance sheet format [(assets + deferred outflows of resources) = (liabilities + deferred inflows of resources) + net position] may be used. Furthermore, net position should be reported in three components (net investment in capital assets, restricted, and unrestricted).
Answer (A) is incorrect. Net position should be reported in three components, including net investment in capital assets. Answer (B) is incorrect. One of the three components of net position is not capital contributions. Answer (C) is incorrect. Designations are removable at the discretion of the reporting government and should not be reported in the statement.

27.10.5. A state or local government must present which financial statements for proprietary funds?

I. A statement of activities
II. A statement in net position or balance sheet format
III. A statement of cash flows

   A. I only.

   B. I and III only.

   C. II and III only.

   D. I, II, and III.

Answer (C) is correct. *(Publisher, adapted)*
   REQUIRED: The statement(s) required for proprietary funds.
   DISCUSSION: Proprietary funds emphasize determination of operating income, changes in net assets (or cost recovery), financial position, and cash flows. A statement of net position is required for proprietary funds, with assets and liabilities classified as current or noncurrent (but a balance sheet format is permitted). Either a net position format [(assets + deferred outflows of resources) – (liabilities + deferred inflows of resources) = net position] or a balance sheet format [(assets + deferred outflows of resources) = (liabilities + deferred inflows of resources) + net position] may be used. A statement of revenues, expenses, and changes in fund net position is the required operating statement for proprietary funds. A statement of cash flows also is required for proprietary funds. However, the direct method (including a reconciliation of operating cash flows to operating income) must be used. The direct method reports major classes of gross operating cash receipts and payments and their sum (net cash flow from operating activities). The minimum classes to be reported are cash receipts from customers, cash receipts from interfund services provided, other operating cash receipts, cash payments to employees for services, cash payments to other suppliers, cash payments for interfund services used, and other operating cash payments.
   Answer (A) is incorrect. A statement of activities is a government-wide statement. Answer (B) is incorrect. Proprietary funds also must report a statement in net position or balance sheet format. Answer (D) is incorrect. Proprietary funds report a statement in net assets or balance sheet format; a statement of revenues, expenses, and changes in fund net position; and a statement of cash flows. However, a statement of activities is a government-wide statement.

27.10.6. An interfund transfer

   A. Is the internal counterpart to an exchange or an exchange-like transaction.

   B. Results in a receivable and a payable.

   C. Is reported in a proprietary fund's statement of revenues, expenses, and changes in fund net position after nonoperating revenues and expenses.

   D. Is reported in a proprietary fund as an other financing source or use.

Answer (C) is correct. *(Publisher, adapted)*
   REQUIRED: The treatment of an interfund transfer.
   DISCUSSION: Interfund transfers are one-way asset flows with no repayment required. In a governmental fund, a transfer is an other financing use (source) in the transferor (transferee) fund. In a proprietary fund's statement of revenues, expenses, and changes in fund net position, transfers should be reported separately after nonoperating revenues and expenses. This component includes (1) capital contributions, (2) additions to endowments, and (3) special and extraordinary items.
   Answer (A) is incorrect. Nonreciprocal interfund activity is similar to nonexchange transactions. Answer (B) is incorrect. Reciprocal interfund activity results in a receivable and a payable. Answer (D) is incorrect. In a governmental fund, a transfer is an other financing use (source) in the transferor (transferee) fund.

27.10.7. A statement of cash flows for proprietary funds

   A. Is optional.

   B. Must be prepared using either the direct method or the indirect method.

   C. Must be prepared using the direct method.

   D. Need not reconcile operating cash flows to operating income if the direct method is used.

Answer (C) is correct. *(Publisher, adapted)*
   REQUIRED: The true statement about the statement of cash flows for proprietary funds.
   DISCUSSION: A statement of cash flows is required for proprietary funds, and the direct method (including a reconciliation of operating cash flows to operating income) is required. The direct method reports major classes of gross operating cash receipts and payments and their sum (net cash flow from operating activities). The minimum classes to be reported are cash receipts from customers, cash receipts from interfund services provided, other operating cash receipts, cash payments to employees for services, cash payments to other suppliers, cash payments for interfund services used, and other operating cash payments.
   Answer (A) is incorrect. A statement of cash flows for proprietary funds is required. Answer (B) is incorrect. The direct method is required. Answer (D) is incorrect. The reconciliation is required.

27.10.8. The summary of significant accounting policies makes which of the following general disclosures?

A. The policy for applying FASB pronouncements issued before November 30, 1989, to business-type activities.

B. The policy for defining operating and nonoperating revenues of proprietary funds.

C. The measurement focus and basis of accounting of the fund financial statements.

D. The capital acquisitions for the period presented by major classes.

Answer (B) is correct. *(Publisher, adapted)*
REQUIRED: The general disclosure required to be made in the summary of significant accounting policies.
DISCUSSION: A government should have a policy that defines operating items in a way that is consistent with the nature of the activity, disclose that policy in the summary of significant accounting policies, and apply it consistently. How transactions are classified in a statement of cash flows is a consideration in defining operating items for proprietary funds.
Answer (A) is incorrect. Proprietary fund statements should be based on (1) GASB pronouncements and (2) certain FASB and other pronouncements issued on or before November 30, 1989 that do not conflict with GASB pronouncements. An enterprise fund also may apply certain nonconflicting FASB pronouncements issued after that date if they were developed for businesses. This policy should be disclosed in the notes. Answer (C) is incorrect. A government must disclose in the summary of significant accounting policies the measurement focus and basis of accounting used in the government-wide financial statements. Answer (D) is incorrect. The capital acquisitions for the period presented by major classes are details required to be disclosed in a note but not in the summary of significant accounting policies.

27.10.9. Lily City uses a pay-as-you-go approach for funding postemployment benefits other than pensions. The city reports no other postemployment benefits (OPEB) liability at the beginning of the year. At the end of the year, Lily City reported the following information related to OPEB for the water enterprise fund:

Benefits paid	$100,000
Annual required contribution	500,000
Unfunded actuarial accrued liability	800,000

What amount of expense for OPEB should Lily City's water enterprise fund report in its fund level statements?

A. $100,000

B. $500,000

C. $600,000

D. $1,400,000

Answer (B) is correct. *(CPA, adapted)*
REQUIRED: The OPEB expense reported in the fund level statements.
DISCUSSION: Lily City's water enterprise fund should report the amount of the annual required contribution (ARC) of $500,000 as an expense in its fund level statements. The ARC is the employer's periodic required contribution to a defined benefit OPEB plan. The ARC is the sum of the normal cost and an amortization payment for the unfunded actuarial accrued liability.
Answer (A) is incorrect. The postretirement benefit obligation is accrued during the period of employment. The amount of the benefits paid does not equal the current expense. Answer (C) is incorrect. The amount of benefits paid is not the total current expense. A postretirement benefit obligation is accrued during the period of employment. Answer (D) is incorrect. The full amount of the unfunded actuarial accrued liability is not expensed in the current period. An unfunded actuarial accrued liability is amortized, and the current amortization payment is included in the annual required contribution. The benefits paid of $100,000 do not constitute a current expense. Under GASB, entities are not required actually to pay the annual required contribution each year.

27.11 Fiduciary Funds Reporting

27.11.1. The debt service transactions of a special assessment bond issue for which the government is not obligated in any manner should be reported in a(n)

A. Custodial fund.

B. Enterprise fund.

C. Special revenue fund.

D. Debt service fund.

Answer (A) is correct. *(CPA, adapted)*
REQUIRED: The reporting of debt service transactions of a special assessment bond issue for which the government is not obligated.
DISCUSSION: The debt service transactions of a special assessment issue for which the government is not obligated in any manner should be reported in a custodial fund rather than a debt service fund. Custodial funds report fiduciary activities not required to be reported in the other fiduciary funds, such as tolls that will be paid to a private business.
Answer (B) is incorrect. An enterprise fund is a proprietary fund used to account for activities for which fees are charged to external users. Answer (C) is incorrect. A special revenue fund is a governmental fund used to account for the proceeds of specific revenue sources that are legally restricted and expended for a specific purpose. Answer (D) is incorrect. The government is not obligated for this special assessment bond issue.

27.11.2. Glen County uses governmental fund accounting and is the administrator of a multiple-jurisdiction deferred compensation plan covering both its own employees and those of other governments participating in the plan. This plan is an eligible deferred compensation plan under the U.S. Internal Revenue Code and Income Tax Regulations and meets the criteria for a pension (and other employee benefit) trust fund. Glen has legal access to the plan's $40 million in assets, of which $2 million pertain to Glen and $38 million pertain to the other participating governments. In Glen's balance sheet, what amount should be reported in a custodial fund for plan assets and as a corresponding liability?

A. $0

B. $2,000,000

C. $38,000,000

D. $40,000,000

Answer (A) is correct. *(CPA, adapted)*
REQUIRED: The deferred compensation plan assets and liability to record in an agency fund.
DISCUSSION: The plan should be reported in a pension (and other employee benefit) trust fund in the statements of fiduciary net position and changes in fiduciary net position if it meets the criteria for that fund type. Pension (and other employee benefit) trust funds report fiduciary activities for pensions, other postemployment benefit plans, and certain other employee benefit programs. This treatment is in accordance with a tax law amendment that required all assets and income of the plan to be held in trust for the exclusive benefit of participants and their beneficiaries. Consequently, no amounts should be reported in a custodial fund.
Answer (B) is incorrect. The plan must be reported as a pension (and other employee benefit) trust fund. Answer (C) is incorrect. The plan must be reported as a pension (and other employee benefit) trust fund. Answer (D) is incorrect. The plan must be reported as a pension (and other employee benefit) trust fund.

27.11.3. Which of the following is a required financial statement for an investment trust fund?

A. Statement of revenues, expenditures, and changes in fiduciary net position.

B. Statement of activities.

C. Statement of revenues, expenses, and changes in fiduciary net position.

D. Statement of changes in fiduciary net position.

Answer (D) is correct. *(CPA, adapted)*
REQUIRED: The required financial statement for an investment trust fund.
DISCUSSION: A sponsoring governmental entity should report the external portion of each of its external investment pools as an investment trust fund. Investment trust funds report fiduciary activities involving (1) the external portion of investment pools and (2) individual investment accounts held in a trust meeting certain criteria. Separate statements of fiduciary net position and changes in fiduciary net position should be presented for each such fund. The external portion belongs to legally separate entities not included in the reporting entity.
Answer (A) is incorrect. Fiduciary funds emphasize net position and changes in net position, not revenues and expenditures. Answer (B) is incorrect. A statement of activities is presented in the government-wide financial statements. Answer (C) is incorrect. Fiduciary funds emphasize net position and changes in net position, not revenues and expenses.

27.11.4. Items reported only in the fund financial statements of the primary government are those arising from

A. Proprietary activities.

B. Fiduciary activities.

C. Exchange-like transactions.

D. Nonexchange-like transactions.

Answer (B) is correct. *(Publisher, adapted)*
REQUIRED: The items reported only in the fund financial statements.
DISCUSSION: Fiduciary activities are reported only in the fund financial statements. Fiduciary funds, including fiduciary component units, should be reported only in the statements of fiduciary net position and changes in fiduciary net position.
Answer (A) is incorrect. Government-wide statements report governmental and business-type (proprietary) activities. Answer (C) is incorrect. Government-wide statements recognize exchange or exchange-like transactions when the exchange occurs. Answer (D) is incorrect. Government-wide statements recognize nonexchange-like transactions.

27.11.5. Which financial statements must be reported for fiduciary funds?

I.   Statement of fiduciary net position

II. Statement of changes in fiduciary net position

III. Statement of revenues, expenditures, and changes in fund balances

IV. Statement of cash flows

    A.   I and II only.

    B.   I, II, and III only.

    C.   II, III, and IV only.

    D.   I, II, III, and IV.

Answer (A) is correct. *(Publisher, adapted)*
    REQUIRED: The financial statements reported by fiduciary funds.
    DISCUSSION: Fiduciary funds, including fiduciary component units, should be reported only in the statements of fiduciary net position and changes in fiduciary net position. The statement of fiduciary net position should be used to report the (1) assets, (2) deferred outflows of resources, (3) liabilities, (4) deferred inflows of resources, and (5) fiduciary net position of fiduciary funds: (a) pension (and other employee benefit) trust funds, (b) investment trust funds, (c) private-purpose trust funds, and (d) custodial funds. With certain exceptions, a liability to the beneficiaries of a fiduciary activity should be recognized if the government must disburse fiduciary resources. The statement of changes in fiduciary net position should be used to report additions to and deductions from fiduciary funds. This statement ordinarily disaggregates additions by source.
    Answer (B) is incorrect. The statement of revenues, expenditures, and changes in fund balances is required for governmental funds. Answer (C) is incorrect. The statement of revenues, expenditures, and changes in fund balances is required for governmental funds, and the statement of cash flows is required for proprietary funds. Answer (D) is incorrect. The statement of revenues, expenditures, and changes in fund balances is required for governmental funds, and the statement of cash flows is required for proprietary funds.

27.11.6. River City has a defined contribution pension plan. How should River report the pension plan in its financial statements?

    A.   Amortize any transition asset over the estimated number of years of current employees' service.

    B.   Disclose in the notes to the financial statements the amount of the pension benefit obligation and the net position available for benefits.

    C.   Disclose in the notes to the financial statements the classes of employees covered and the employer's and employees' obligations to contribute to the fund.

    D.   Accrue a liability for benefits earned but not paid to fund participants.

Answer (C) is correct. *(CPA, adapted)*
    REQUIRED: The method for reporting a defined contribution pension plan.
    DISCUSSION: A defined contribution pension plan must report (1) a plan description, (2) a summary of significant accounting policies, and (3) information about investment concentrations. The plan description should identify the plan as a defined contribution plan and disclose the number of participating employers and other contributing entities. The description also should include (1) the classes of employees covered, (2) the total current membership, (3) a brief description of plan provisions, (4) the authority under which they are established (or may be amended), and (5) contribution requirements.
    Answer (A) is incorrect. No transition asset is recognized under a defined contribution plan. Answer (B) is incorrect. A pension benefit obligation is recognized under a defined benefit pension plan. Answer (D) is incorrect. Under a defined contribution plan, the governmental employer's obligation is for contributions, not benefits.

27.11.7. Fiduciary fund financial statements report

    A.   Information by major fund.

    B.   Three components of net position.

    C.   A separate column for each fund type.

    D.   No separate statements for individual pension plans.

Answer (C) is correct. *(Publisher, adapted)*
    REQUIRED: The reporting in fiduciary fund financial statements.
    DISCUSSION: Fiduciary fund financial statements include information about all fiduciary funds and similar component units. The statements report information in a separate column for each fund type but not by major fund. The notes present financial statements for individual pension plans and postemployment healthcare plans unless separate GAAP reports have been issued.
    Answer (A) is incorrect. Major funds are reported only in governmental and enterprise fund statements. Answer (B) is incorrect. Three components of net position are reported only in the government-wide statement of net position and in the proprietary fund statement of net position. Answer (D) is incorrect. Separate financial statements for individual pension plans and postemployment healthcare plans are reported in the notes. However, if separate GAAP financial statements have been issued for such plans, information is given in the notes about how those statements may be obtained.

27.12 Interfund Activity

27.12.1. On December 31, Year 1, Elm Village paid a contractor $4.5 million for the total cost of a new Village Hall built in Year 1 on Village-owned land. Financing for the capital project was provided by a $3 million general obligation bond issue sold at face amount on December 31, Year 1, with the remaining $1.5 million transferred from the general fund. What account and amount should be reported in Elm's Year 1 financial statements for the general fund?

A. Other financing sources control, $4,500,000.

B. Expenditures control, $4,500,000.

C. Other financing sources control, $3,000,000.

D. Other financing uses control, $1,500,000.

Answer (D) is correct. *(CPA, adapted)*
REQUIRED: The account and amount to be reported for the general fund.
DISCUSSION: Nonreciprocal interfund activity is similar to nonexchange transactions. Interfund transfers are one-way asset flows with no repayment required. In a governmental fund, a transfer is an other financing use (source) in the transferor (transferee) fund. Consequently, the one-way asset flow from the general fund (a governmental fund) to the capital projects fund (also a governmental fund) requires a debit to other financing uses -- interfund transfer for $1.5 million. The cash inflow from the general obligation bond issue is recorded in the capital projects fund by a credit for $3 million to other financing sources -- bond issue proceeds. Capital projects funds account for financial resources, including general obligation bond proceeds, intended for acquiring or constructing major capital facilities, except for those financed through proprietary and trust funds.
Answer (A) is incorrect. The capital projects fund credits other financing sources -- interfund transfers for the $1.5 million transfer from the general fund. It also credits other financing sources -- bond proceeds for the $3 million provided by the general obligation bond issue. Answer (B) is incorrect. The expenditure for the sum paid to the contractor is recognized in the capital projects fund. Answer (C) is incorrect. The capital projects fund credits other financing sources for receipt of the $3 million from the bond issue.

27.12.2. During the year, a city's electric utility, which is operated as an enterprise fund, rendered billings for electricity supplied to the general fund. Which of the following accounts should be debited by the general fund?

A. Appropriations.

B. Expenditures.

C. Due to electric utility enterprise fund.

D. Other financing uses -- interfund transfer.

Answer (B) is correct. *(CPA, adapted)*
REQUIRED: The account debited in the general fund for receipt of services supplied by an enterprise fund.
DISCUSSION: Enterprise funds are used to account for operations similar to those of private businesses. The services provided by the enterprise fund to the general fund are (1) most likely at prices equivalent to external exchange values and (2) classified as interfund services provided and used. The result is revenue to the seller and an expenditure to the buyer, a governmental fund. Unpaid amounts are interfund receivables or payables. The entry is to debit expenditures and credit due to enterprise fund.
Answer (A) is incorrect. Appropriations is debited when the budgetary accounts are closed. Answer (C) is incorrect. Due to enterprise fund should be credited. Answer (D) is incorrect. This transaction is an interfund service provided and used, not an interfund transfer.

27.12.3. The following pertains to Grove City's interfund receivables and payables at December 31:

Due to special revenue fund from general fund	$10,000
Due to agency fund from special revenue fund	4,000

How should Grove report these interfund amounts for the special revenue fund in its governmental fund balance sheet at December 31?

A. As an asset of $6,000.

B. As a liability of $6,000.

C. As an asset of $4,000 and a liability of $10,000.

D. As an asset of $10,000 and a liability of $4,000.

Answer (D) is correct. *(CPA, adapted)*
REQUIRED: The reporting of interfund amounts in the special revenue fund.
DISCUSSION: In a special revenue fund, funds due to the special revenue fund are receivables (assets), and funds due to another fund from the special revenue fund are payables (liabilities). Thus, Grove should report a $10,000 asset and a $4,000 liability in the special revenue fund.
Answer (A) is incorrect. In a special revenue fund, assets are not reported net of liabilities. Answer (B) is incorrect. The amount of $6,000 is the amount of net assets. Answer (C) is incorrect. "Due to special revenue fund" is a receivable (asset), and "due from special revenue fund" is a payable (liability).

27.12.4. The standards for reporting interfund activity classifies such activity as

A. Operating transfers and residual equity transfers.

B. Operating transfers, residual equity transfers, and reimbursements.

C. Quasi-external transfers and residual equity transfers.

D. Reciprocal and nonreciprocal.

Answer (D) is correct. *(Publisher, adapted)*
REQUIRED: The classification of interfund activity.
DISCUSSION: Interfund activity may be reciprocal or nonreciprocal. Reciprocal interfund activity is similar to exchange and exchange-like transactions, for example, interfund loans and services provided and used. Nonreciprocal interfund activity is similar to nonexchange transactions, for example, interfund transfers and reimbursements.
Answer (A) is incorrect. Operating transfers and residual equity transfers were classifications in superseded authoritative guidance. Answer (B) is incorrect. Operating transfers, residual equity transfers, and reimbursements were classifications in superseded authoritative guidance. Answer (C) is incorrect. Quasi-external transfers and residual equity transfers were classifications in superseded authoritative guidance.

27.12.5. An internal service provided and used by a state or local government

A. Is the internal counterpart to a nonexchange transaction.

B. Results in expenditures or expenses to buyer funds and revenues to seller funds.

C. Normally is displayed in the financial statements as a reimbursement.

D. Requires recognition of an other financing source by the transferee fund and an other financing use by the transferor fund.

Answer (B) is correct. *(Publisher, adapted)*
REQUIRED: The treatment of an internal service provided and used.
DISCUSSION: Interfund services provided and used are reciprocal interfund activities. They are sales and purchases of goods and services at prices equivalent to external exchange values. Thus, they result in revenues to seller funds and expenditures or expenses to buyer funds. Unpaid amounts are interfund receivables or payables.
Answer (A) is incorrect. An internal service provided and used is similar to an exchange transaction. Answer (C) is incorrect. Reimbursements are not displayed in the statements. Answer (D) is incorrect. An interfund transfer (nonreciprocal interfund activity) is an other financing source (use) in a transferee (transferor) governmental fund. An internal service provided and used is reciprocal interfund activity.

27.12.6. Through an internal service fund, New County operates a centralized data processing center to provide services to New's other governmental units. This internal service fund billed New's parks and recreation fund $150,000 for data processing services. What account should New's internal service fund credit to record this $150,000 billing to the parks and recreation fund?

A. Data processing department expenses.

B. Interfund transfers.

C. Interfund reimbursements.

D. Operating revenues control.

Answer (D) is correct. *(CPA, adapted)*
REQUIRED: The account to be credited by an internal service fund to record a billing to other governmental units.
DISCUSSION: Interfund services provided and used are sales and purchases of goods and services at prices equivalent to external exchange values. They result in revenues to seller funds and expenditures or expenses to buyer funds. Unpaid amounts are interfund receivables or payables. Thus, billings issued for services rendered by an internal service data processing center to other governmental units should be recorded as a debit to a receivable and a credit to operating revenues control.
Answer (A) is incorrect. The services provided should be recorded as a revenue, not a decrease in an expense. Answer (B) is incorrect. Interfund services provided and used are reciprocal interfund activities. Interfund transfers are nonreciprocal interfund activities. Answer (C) is incorrect. Interfund services provided and used are reciprocal interfund activities. Interfund reimbursements are nonreciprocal interfund activities.

STUDY UNIT TWENTY-EIGHT
NOT-FOR-PROFIT ENTITIES

This study unit addresses accounting and reporting by **nongovernmental not-for-profit entities (NFPs)** in accordance with GAAP. An NFP has the following characteristics: (1) contributors of significant resources to the NFP do not expect a proportionate financial return, (2) the NFP has operating purposes other than providing goods or services for profit, and (3) the NFP has no ownership interests similar to those of a business entity. Among the many kinds of NFPs are (1) educational institutions, (2) healthcare entities, (3) cultural organizations, (4) voluntary health and welfare entities, (5) federated fundraising organizations, (6) unions, (7) political parties, and (8) public broadcasting stations.

General-purpose financial reporting of an NFP is based on a **net assets model**. Net assets equals the residual interest in the assets of an NFP that remains after subtracting its liabilities. Net assets is classified as follows depending on whether assets are donor-restricted: (1) with donor restrictions or (2) without donor restrictions. An NFP's general-purpose financial statements are the statements of (1) financial position (equivalent to a balance sheet), (2) activities (an operating statement), and (3) cash flows (similar to what is reported by for-profit entities). Furthermore, a statement of activities or the notes must provide information about expenses by **functional** classification (program services and supporting activities). An analysis must be presented that disaggregates functional expense classifications by **natural** expense classifications (e.g., salaries, rent, interest, and depreciation). Also, an NFP must report information about **all** expenses in one place: (1) the statement of activities, (2) a schedule in the notes, or (3) a separate statement.

NOTE: The guidance on revenue recognition from contracts with customers applies to not-for-profit, business-oriented healthcare entities. This subject is covered in Study Unit 21.

QUESTIONS

28.1 Introduction

28.1.1. Which of the following is ordinarily not considered one of the major distinguishing characteristics of not-for-profit entities (NFPs)?

A. Significant amounts of resources are provided by donors in nonreciprocal transactions.

B. Defined, transferable ownership interests do not exist.

C. Performance indicators similar to a business enterprise's profit are readily available.

D. The primary operating purpose is not to provide goods or services at a profit.

Answer (C) is correct. *(Publisher, adapted)*
REQUIRED: The statement not ordinarily considered a major characteristic of NFPs.
DISCUSSION: The objectives of financial reporting are derived from the common interests of those who provide the resources to NFPs. Such entities ordinarily have no single indicator of performance comparable to a business enterprise's profit. Thus, their performance is usually evaluated in terms of management stewardship.
Answer (A) is incorrect. According to SFAC 4, significant amounts of resources are provided by donors in nonreciprocal transactions with NFPs. Answer (B) is incorrect. According to SFAC 4, defined, transferable ownership interests are absent from NFPs. Answer (D) is incorrect. According to SFAC 4, NFPs do not primarily provide goods or services at a profit.

28.1.2. Which of the following is a characteristic of nongovernmental not-for-profit entities (NFPs)?

A. Noneconomic reasons seldom underlie the decision to provide resources to NFPs.

B. Business entities and NFPs usually obtain resources in the same way.

C. Both NFPs and business entities use scarce resources in the production and distribution of goods and services.

D. The operating environment of NFPs ordinarily differs from that of business entities.

Answer (C) is correct. *(Publisher, adapted)*
REQUIRED: The characteristic of NFPs.
DISCUSSION: The operating environments of NFPs and business entities are similar in many ways. Both produce and distribute goods and services using scarce resources.
Answer (A) is incorrect. Many noneconomic factors affect decisions to provide resources to NFPs. Answer (B) is incorrect. Business entities obtain resources by providing goods and services. Many NFPs obtain resources from contributors and are accountable to the providers of those resources or to their representatives. Answer (D) is incorrect. The operating environments of NFPs and business entities are similar.

28.1.3. Net assets is an element of the financial statements of nongovernmental not-for-profit entities (NFPs). It

A. Is the residual interest in the assets of an NFP after subtracting its liabilities.

B. Is the change in equity during a period from transactions and other events and circumstances not involving resource providers.

C. Differs from equity in businesses because it is not a residual interest.

D. Consists of the probable future economic benefits obtained or controlled by a particular entity as a result of past transactions or events.

Answer (A) is correct. *(Publisher, adapted)*
REQUIRED: The definition of the net assets element of the financial statements of NFPs.
DISCUSSION: Net assets equals the residual interest in the assets of an entity that remains after subtracting its liabilities. In an NFP, which has no ownership interest in the same sense as a business, net assets is classified at a minimum as net assets without donor restrictions and net assets with donor restrictions.
Answer (B) is incorrect. Comprehensive income is the change in equity of a business during a period from transactions and other events and circumstances from nonowner sources. Answer (C) is incorrect. Equity and net assets are residuals. Answer (D) is incorrect. Assets, not net assets, are probable future economic benefits obtained or controlled by a particular entity as a result of past transactions or events.

28.1.4. For external reporting purposes, the not-for-profit reporting model requires information about

A. Individual funds of the entity but not about the entity as a whole.

B. The entity as a whole but not about individual funds.

C. Individual funds of the entity and the entity as a whole.

D. The entity and precludes reporting individual fund information.

Answer (B) is correct. *(Publisher, adapted)*
REQUIRED: The information required by the not-for-profit reporting model.
DISCUSSION: The not-for-profit reporting model emphasizes information about the entity as a whole, not individual funds. Consequently, fund accounting is not required for external reporting but is not precluded.

28.2 Financial Statements

28.2.1. The guidance for reporting the financial statements of nongovernmental not-for-profit entities focuses on

A. Basic information for the entity as a whole.

B. Standardization of funds nomenclature.

C. Inherent differences of not-for-profit entities that affect reporting presentations.

D. Distinctions between current fund and noncurrent fund presentations.

Answer (A) is correct. *(CPA, adapted)*
REQUIRED: The focus of reporting by NFPs.
DISCUSSION: This guidance is intended to promote the relevance, understandability, and comparability of financial statements issued by NFPs by requiring that certain basic information be reported. The focus of the required financial statements is on the entity as a whole. It is also on (1) reporting assets, liabilities, and net assets; (2) changes in net assets; (3) flows of economic resources; (4) cash flows, borrowing and repayment of borrowing, and other factors affecting liquidity; and (5) service efforts.
Answer (B) is incorrect. Fund accounting is not required. Answer (C) is incorrect. Answer (C) is incorrect. Answer (D) is incorrect. The emphasis of reporting by NFPs is basic information for the entity as a whole. Also, fund accounting is not required.

28.2.2. Forkin Manor, a nongovernmental not-for-profit entity (NFP), wants to reformat its financial statements using terminology that is more readily associated with for-profit entities. The director believes that the term "operating profit" and the practice of segregating recurring and nonrecurring items more accurately depict the NFP's activities. Under what condition will Forkin be allowed to use "operating profit" and to segregate its recurring items from its nonrecurring items in its statement of activities?

A. The NFP reports the change in net assets without donor restrictions for the period.

B. A parenthetical disclosure in the notes implies that the NFP is seeking for-profit entity status.

C. Forkin receives special authorization from the Internal Revenue Service that this wording is appropriate.

D. At a minimum, the NFP reports the change in net assets with donor restrictions for the period.

Answer (A) is correct. *(CPA, adapted)*
REQUIRED: The condition allowing an NFP to use the term "operating profit" and to segregate recurring and nonrecurring items in its statement of activities.
DISCUSSION: In its statement of activities, an NFP may use such classifications as (1) operating and nonoperating, (2) expendable and nonexpendable, (3) recognized and unrecognized, and (4) recurring and nonrecurring. Furthermore, if an intermediate operating measure (e.g., operating income or operating profit) is used, it must be in a financial statement that at a minimum reports the change in net assets without donor restrictions.
Answer (B) is incorrect. The NFP need not seek for-profit status to report in the described manner. Answer (C) is incorrect. The NFP need not obtain IRS authorization to report in the described manner. Answer (D) is incorrect. The NFP must report the changes in the two classes of net assets regardless of whether additional classifications are included in the statement of activities.

28.2.3. In a statement of financial position, a nongovernmental not-for-profit entity must at a minimum report amounts for which of the following classes of net assets?

I. Without donor restrictions
II. With donor restrictions
III. Permanently restricted

A. I, II, and III.

B. I and II only.

C. I and III only.

D. II and III only.

Answer (A) is correct. *(Publisher, adapted)*
REQUIRED: The classes of net assets reported in a statement of financial position of a not-for-profit entity.
DISCUSSION: A not-for-profit entity should report amounts only for net assets without donor restrictions and net assets with donor restrictions.
Answer (B) is incorrect. A not-for-profit entity must at a minimum report amounts for two classes: net assets without donor restrictions and net assets with donor restrictions. Information regarding the nature and amounts of restrictions must be provided on the face of the statement or in the notes. Also, separate line items may be included in (1) net assets with donor restrictions or (2) the notes. Answer (C) is incorrect. A not-for-profit entity should report amounts only for net assets without donor restrictions and net assets with donor restrictions. Answer (D) is incorrect. A not-for-profit entity should report amounts only for net assets without donor restrictions and net assets with donor restrictions.

28.2.4. In Year 3, Gamma, a nongovernmental not-for-profit entity, deposited at a bank $1 million given to it by a donor to purchase endowment securities. The securities were purchased January 2, Year 4. At December 31, Year 3, the bank recorded $2,000 interest on the deposit. In accordance with the bequest, this $2,000 was used to finance ongoing program expenses in March Year 4. At December 31, Year 3, what amount of the bank balance should be included as current assets in Gamma's classified statement of financial position?

 A. $0

 B. $2,000

 C. $1,000,000

 D. $1,002,000

Answer (B) is correct. *(CPA, adapted)*
 REQUIRED: The amount of the bank balance classified as current assets.
 DISCUSSION: An NFP may classify its assets and liabilities as current or noncurrent. Current assets are defined as those reasonably expected to be realized in cash, sold, or consumed during the operating cycle or within 1 year, whichever is longer. Accordingly, the $2,000 of interest recorded at December 31, Year 3, should be classified as current because the bequest stipulated that it be used for ongoing program expenses. However, the $1 million restricted to the purchase of endowment securities is not classified as current. Assets received with a donor-imposed restriction limiting their use to long-term purposes must not be classified with assets available for current use.
 Answer (A) is incorrect. The interest should be included in current assets. Answer (C) is incorrect. The interest, not the principal, should be included in current assets. Answer (D) is incorrect. The principal should not be included in current assets.

28.2.5. Pharm, a nongovernmental not-for-profit entity, is preparing its year-end financial statements. Which of the following statements is required?

 A. Statement of changes in fiduciary net position.

 B. Statement of cash flows.

 C. Statement of revenues, expenses, and changes in fund net position.

 D. Statement of revenues, expenditures, and changes in fund balances.

Answer (B) is correct. *(CPA, adapted)*
 REQUIRED: The statement required in a complete set of financial statements of NFPs.
 DISCUSSION: A complete set of financial statements of an NFP must include (1) a statement of financial position as of the end of the reporting period, (2) a statement of activities and a statement of cash flows for the reporting period, and (3) accompanying notes to financial statements.
 Answer (A) is incorrect. A statement of changes in fiduciary net position is reported for the fiduciary funds of a state or local government. Answer (C) is incorrect. A statement of revenues, expenses, and changes in fund net position is reported for the proprietary funds of a state or local government. Answer (D) is incorrect. A statement of revenues, expenditures, and changes in fund balances is reported for the governmental funds of a state or local government.

28.2.6. For which of the following assets held by a religious entity should depreciation be recognized in the entity's general purpose external financial statements?

 A. The house of worship.

 B. A priceless painting.

 C. A nationally recognized historical treasure.

 D. Land used for a building site.

Answer (A) is correct. *(Publisher, adapted)*
 REQUIRED: The asset held by a religious entity for which depreciation should be recognized.
 DISCUSSION: Not-for-profit entities recognize the cost of using up long-lived tangible assets (depreciation) in their general purpose external financial statements. Thus, a building used for religious activity is ordinarily depreciable.
 Answer (B) is incorrect. Depreciation does not have to be recognized for certain works of art whose economic benefit or service potential is used up so slowly that their estimated useful lives are extraordinarily long. Answer (C) is incorrect. Depreciation does not have to be recognized for certain historical treasures whose service potential is used up so slowly that their estimated useful lives are exceptionally long. Answer (D) is incorrect. Land is normally not depreciated by any organization.

28.2.7. Health Policy Foundation (HPF), a voluntary health and welfare entity supported by contributions from the general public, included the following costs in its statement of functional expenses for the year:

Fundraising	$1,000,000
Administrative (including data processing)	600,000
Research	200,000

HPF's functional expenses for program services included

- A. $1,800,000
- B. $1,000,000
- C. $600,000
- D. $200,000

Answer (D) is correct. *(CPA, adapted)*
REQUIRED: The amount of functional expenses for program services incurred by a VHWE.
DISCUSSION: An NFP's statement of activities or notes thereto should classify expenses by function. The major functional classes include program services and supporting services. Management and general expenses, along with fundraising expenses, are classified in the supporting services category. Program services expenses are those directly related to the administration of programs. Of the costs given, only the research costs ($200,000) are program services expenses.
Answer (A) is incorrect. The amount of $1,800,000 includes $1,000,000 of fundraising expenses and $600,000 of administrative expenses that should be included in supporting services expenses. Answer (B) is incorrect. The amount of $1,000,000 of fundraising expenses should be classified as supporting services expenses. Answer (C) is incorrect. The amount of $600,000 of administrative expenses should be classified as supporting services expenses.

28.2.8. Functional expenses recorded in the general ledger of ABC, a nongovernmental not-for-profit entity, are as follows:

Soliciting prospective members	$45,000
Printing membership benefits brochures	30,000
Soliciting membership dues	25,000
Maintaining donor list	10,000

What amount should ABC report as fundraising expenses?

- A. $10,000
- B. $35,000
- C. $70,000
- D. $110,000

Answer (A) is correct. *(CPA, adapted)*
REQUIRED: The fundraising expenses.
DISCUSSION: The major functional classes of expenses for an NFP are program services and supporting activities. An analysis also must be presented that disaggregates functional expense classifications by natural expense classifications (e.g., salaries, interest, rent, and depreciation). Supporting activities include (1) management and general, (2) fundraising, and (3) membership-development activities. Fundraising expenses include maintaining donor lists ($10,000). Soliciting members and dues and printing membership benefits brochures are membership-development activities.
Answer (B) is incorrect. The amount of $35,000 includes the cost of soliciting dues, a membership-development activity. Answer (C) is incorrect. The amount of $70,000 is the cost of soliciting members and dues. Answer (D) is incorrect. Only the cost of the donor list is an expense of fundraising.

28.2.9. For the fall semester of the current year, Micanopy University, a private not-for-profit institution, assessed its students $3,000,000 for tuition and fees. The net amount realized was only $2,500,000 because scholarships of $400,000 were granted to students and tuition remissions of $100,000 were allowed to faculty members' children attending Micanopy. What amount should Micanopy report for the period as revenues for tuition and fees?

- A. $2,500,000
- B. $2,600,000
- C. $2,900,000
- D. $3,000,000

Answer (D) is correct. *(CPA, adapted)*
REQUIRED: The amount reported as revenues for tuition and fees.
DISCUSSION: Revenues from exchange transactions are recognized in accordance with GAAP. Tuition and fees for private, not-for-profit colleges and universities are received in an exchange transaction. Thus, the full amount of the tuition assessed is reported as revenue. Tuition waivers, scholarships, and like items are recorded as expenses if given in exchange transactions. Refunds are handled by merely debiting revenues and crediting cash, so tuition is automatically reported net of refunds.
Answer (A) is incorrect. The amount of $2,500,000 assumes that only net tuition is recorded. Answer (B) is incorrect. The amount of $2,600,000 assumes that scholarships are deducted before recording tuition revenues. Answer (C) is incorrect. The amount of $2,900,000 assumes that tuition remissions are deducted before recording tuition revenues.

28.2.10. Cancer Educators, a nongovernmental not-for-profit entity, incurred costs of $10,000 in its combined program services and fundraising activities. Which of the following cost allocations might Cancer Educators report in its statement of activities?

	Program Services	Fund Raising	General Services
A.	$0	$0	$10,000
B.	$0	$6,000	$4,000
C.	$6,000	$4,000	$0
D.	$10,000	$0	$0

Answer (C) is correct. *(CPA, adapted)*
REQUIRED: The allocation of costs for combined functions.
DISCUSSION: NFPs must provide information about expenses reported by functional classification. An analysis also must be presented that disaggregates functional expense classifications by natural expense classifications (e.g., salaries, interest, rent, and depreciation). The $10,000 of costs should therefore be divided between program services and fundraising.
Answer (A) is incorrect. The costs were incurred in program services and fundraising activities. Answer (B) is incorrect. The costs resulted from program services and fundraising. The entire $10,000 should be allocated between those classifications. Answer (D) is incorrect. The costs must be allocated between program services and fundraising.

28.2.11. In Year 1, a nonprofit trade association enrolled five new member companies, each of which was obligated to pay nonrefundable initiation fees of $1,000. These fees were receivable by the association in Year 2. Three of the new members paid the initiation fees in Year 2, and the other two new members paid their initiation fees in Year 3. Annual dues (excluding initiation fees) received by the association from all of its members have always covered the entity's costs of services provided to its members. It can be reasonably expected that future dues will cover all costs of the entity's future services to members. Average membership duration is 10 years because of mergers, attrition, and economic factors. What amount of initiation fees from these five new members should the association recognize as revenue in Year 2?

A. $5,000

B. $3,000

C. $500

D. $0

Answer (A) is correct. *(CPA, adapted)*
REQUIRED: The amount of initiation fees to be reported as revenue.
DISCUSSION: Membership dues received or receivable in exchange transactions that relate to several accounting periods should be allocated and recognized as revenue in those periods. Nonrefundable initiation and life membership fees are recognized as revenue when they are receivable if future dues and fees can be reasonably expected to cover the costs of the entity's services. Otherwise, they are amortized to future periods. Accordingly, given that future dues are expected to cover the entity's costs, the $5,000 in nonrefundable initiation fees should be recognized as revenue when assessed and reported as such in the Year 2 statement of activities.
Answer (B) is incorrect. The full amount of nonrefundable initiation fees that are receivable in Year 2 also are recognized as revenue, provided that future dues and fees can be reasonably expected to cover costs of the entity's services. Answer (C) is incorrect. The full amount of nonrefundable initiation fees are not recognized by being allocated across the average membership duration. Answer (D) is incorrect. The full amount of all nonrefundable initiation fees is recognized as revenue, provided that future dues and fees can be reasonably expected to cover costs of the entity's services.

28.2.12. Molko, a community foundation, incurred $10,000 in management and general expenses during Year 4. In Molko's statement of activities for the year ended December 31, Year 4, the $10,000 should be reported as

A. A direct reduction of fund balance.

B. Part of supporting services.

C. Part of program services.

D. A contra account to offset revenue.

Answer (B) is correct. *(CPA, adapted)*
REQUIRED: The expense classification for management and general expenses in the statement of activities.
DISCUSSION: Two functional categories of expenses for an NFP are program services expenses and supporting activities expenses. An analysis also must be presented that disaggregates functional expense classifications by natural expense classifications (e.g., salaries, interest, rent, and depreciation). Supporting activities expenses, which do not relate to the primary mission of the organization, may be further subdivided into (1) management and general expenses, (2) fundraising expenses, and (3) membership development costs.
Answer (A) is incorrect. A direct reduction of fund balance would be the result of a transfer or a refund to a donor. Moreover, fund accounting information is not required to be externally reported. Answer (C) is incorrect. Program services expenses relate directly to the primary mission of the NFP. Answer (D) is incorrect. Only costs directly related to a certain source of support, such as a special event or estimated uncollectible pledges, may be offset against revenue.

28.2.13. The following expenditures were made by Green Services, a society for the protection of the environment:

Printing of the annual report	$12,000
Unsolicited merchandise sent to encourage contributions	25,000
Cost of an audit performed by a CPA firm	3,000

What amount should be classified as fundraising costs in the society's statement of activities?

- A. $37,000
- B. $28,000
- C. $25,000
- D. $0

28.2.14. On January 1, Year 4, a nongovernmental not-for-profit botanical society received a gift of an exhaustible fixed asset with an estimated useful life of 10 years and no salvage value. The donor's cost of this asset was $20,000, and its fair value at the date of the gift was $30,000. What amount of depreciation of this asset should the society recognize in its Year 4 financial statements?

- A. $3,000
- B. $2,500
- C. $2,000
- D. $0

28.2.15. A large nongovernmental not-for-profit entity's statement of activities must report the net change for net assets that are

	Without Donor Restrictions	With Donor Restrictions
A.	Yes	Yes
B.	Yes	No
C.	No	No
D.	No	Yes

Answer (C) is correct. *(CPA, adapted)*
REQUIRED: The amount to be reported as fundraising costs in the statement of activities.
DISCUSSION: The major classifications of expenses for an NFP are program services and supporting activities. An analysis also must be presented that disaggregates functional expense classifications by natural expense classifications (e.g., salaries, interest, rent, and depreciation). Program service expenses relate directly to the primary purpose or mission of the organization. Supporting activities expenses are further classified as management and general expenses, fundraising expenses, and membership development costs. The only fundraising-related cost is the unsolicited merchandise sent to encourage contributions.
Answer (A) is incorrect. The amount of $37,000 classifies all of the expenses as fundraising expenses when only the unsolicited merchandise is related to fundraising. Answer (B) is incorrect. The cost of an audit is a management-related expense. Answer (D) is incorrect. The unsolicited merchandise is a fundraising expense.

Answer (A) is correct. *(CPA, adapted)*
REQUIRED: The amount of depreciation to be recognized in the financial statements.
DISCUSSION: NFPs must recognize depreciation. Moreover, contributions are recorded at their fair value when received. Assuming the straight-line method is used, the amount of depreciation that the NFP should recognize is $3,000 [($30,000 fair value – $0 salvage value) ÷ 10 years].
Answer (B) is incorrect. Annual straight-line depreciation for this asset is $3,000. Answer (C) is incorrect. The amount of $2,000 results from using cost as the depreciable basis of the asset. Answer (D) is incorrect. NFPs recognize depreciation on most property and equipment.

Answer (A) is correct. *(CPA, adapted)*
REQUIRED: The changes in net assets reported in a large NFP's statement of activities.
DISCUSSION: The statement of financial position must at a minimum report the amounts of net assets without donor restrictions, net assets with donor restrictions, and total net assets. The statement of activities should report the changes in each category.

Questions 28.2.16 through 28.2.18 are based on the following information. United Together, a labor union, had the following receipts and expenses for the current year ended December 31:

Receipts:		Expenses:	
Per capita dues	$680,000	Labor negotiations	$500,000
Initiation fees	90,000	Fundraising	100,000
Sales of organizational supplies	60,000	Membership development	50,000
Gift restricted by donor for loan		Administrative and general	200,000
purposes for 10 years	30,000		
Gift restricted by donor for loan			
purposes in perpetuity	25,000		

Additional information: The union's constitution provides that 10% of the per capita dues are designated for the Strike Insurance Fund to be distributed for strike relief at the discretion of the union's executive board.

28.2.16. In United Together's statement of activities for the year ended December 31, what amount should be reported as revenue?

A. $795,000

B. $830,000

C. $825,000

D. $885,000

Answer (D) is correct. *(CPA, adapted)*
REQUIRED: The amount classified as revenue.
DISCUSSION: NFPs generate resources through contributions, exchange transactions, and agency transactions. Revenues are recognized on contributions and exchange transactions. Contributions of resources by donors result from nonreciprocal transactions. Thus, revenue includes not only the resources provided as membership dues, initiation fees, sales revenue, investment income, gains and losses on the disposal of fixed assets and investments, and fees for services rendered but also the contributions received with donor restrictions. United Together should recognize $885,000 ($680,000 dues + $90,000 initiation fees + $60,000 sales + $30,000 gift + $25,000 gift) of revenue.
Answer (A) is incorrect. The initiation fees of $90,000 should be included as revenue. Answer (B) is incorrect. The revenue should include the amounts for gifts. Answer (C) is incorrect. The amount for sales of organizational supplies should be included as revenue.

28.2.17. In United Together's statement of activities for the year ended December 31, what amount should be reported as program services expenses?

A. $850,000

B. $600,000

C. $550,000

D. $500,000

Answer (D) is correct. *(CPA, adapted)*
REQUIRED: The amount to be reported.
DISCUSSION: Program services include the expenses that relate directly to the primary missions of the NFP. These expenses include both the direct expenses clearly identified with the program and a systematic and rational allocation of indirect costs. Because the $500,000 labor negotiation expenses are the only expenses that relate directly to the primary mission of the labor union, $500,000 should be reported in the statement of activities.
Answer (A) is incorrect. Fundraising, membership development, and administrative costs relate to supporting services. Answer (B) is incorrect. The fundraising amount should be supporting services expenses. Answer (C) is incorrect. The expenses for membership development are supporting services expenses.

28.2.18. In United Together's statement of activities for the year ended December 31, what amount should be reported as donor-restricted support?

A. $55,000

B. $30,000

C. $25,000

D. $0

Answer (A) is correct. *(CPA, adapted)*
REQUIRED: The amount of donor-restricted support.
DISCUSSION: Donor-restricted support consists of contribution revenues or gains that increase net assets with donor restrictions. A donor-restricted endowment fund is created by a donor stipulation requiring a gift to be invested for a specified period or in perpetuity. Consequently, donor-restricted support equals $55,000 ($30,000 donor-restricted for 10 years + $25,000 donor-restricted in perpetuity).
Answer (B) is incorrect. The amount of $30,000 omits the nonexpendable gift in perpetuity. Answer (C) is incorrect. The amount of $25,000 omits the nonexpendable gift for loan purposes that is donor-restricted for 10 years. Answer (D) is incorrect. Both gifts are donor-restricted.

28.2.19. In the preparation of the statement of activities for a nongovernmental NFP, most expenses are reported as decreases in which of the following minimum required net asset classes?

A. Total net assets.

B. Net assets without donor restrictions.

C. Net assets with donor restrictions.

D. Permanently restricted net assets.

Answer (B) is correct. *(CPA, adapted)*
REQUIRED: The net asset class in which expenses are recorded by a nongovernmental NFP.
DISCUSSION: Most expenses of an NFP must be reported as decreases in net assets without donor restrictions. An exception is investment expense. It must be netted against investment return and reported in the same net assets category.
Answer (A) is incorrect. Total net assets is the sum of net assets without donor restrictions and net assets with donor restrictions. Answer (C) is incorrect. Revenues, gains, and losses are reported in net assets with donor restrictions in appropriate cases. Answer (D) is incorrect. Permanently restricted net assets is not one of the two minimum required net asset classes.

28.2.20. At the beginning of the year, the Baker Fund, a nongovernmental not-for-profit corporation, received a $125,000 contribution restricted to youth activity programs. During the year, youth activities generated revenues of $89,000 and had program expenses of $95,000. What amount should Baker report as net assets released from restrictions for the current year?

A. $0

B. $6,000

C. $95,000

D. $125,000

Answer (C) is correct. *(CPA, adapted)*
REQUIRED: The net assets released from restrictions for the current year.
DISCUSSION: At the time the contribution was made, net assets with donor restrictions increased by $125,000. The restriction stated that the funds were to be used for youth activity programs. The amount of actual program expenses for the year ($95,000) is reported under net assets released from restrictions.
Answer (A) is incorrect. The incurrence of program expenses reduced net assets with donor restrictions by fulfilling the purpose of the restriction to the extent the resources were used. Answer (B) is incorrect. The amount of $6,000 is the excess of program expenses over revenues generated by youth activities. Answer (D) is incorrect. The purpose of the restriction was fulfilled only to the extent the contribution was used for the stated purpose.

28.2.21. A nongovernmental not-for-profit entity borrowed $5,000, which it used to purchase a truck. In which section of the entity's statement of cash flows should the transaction be reported?

A. In cash inflow and cash outflow from investing activities.

B. In cash inflow and cash outflow from financing activities.

C. In cash inflow from financing activities and cash outflow from investing activities.

D. In cash inflow from operating activities and cash outflow from investing activities.

Answer (C) is correct. *(CPA, adapted)*
REQUIRED: The section of the statement of cash flows in which the purchase of a truck is reported by an NFP.
DISCUSSION: The borrowing is a cash inflow from a financing activity because it results from issuing debt. The purchase of the truck is a cash outflow from an investing activity because it involves the acquisition of property, plant, or equipment or other productive assets.
Answer (A) is incorrect. The cash inflow is from a financing activity. Answer (B) is incorrect. The cash outflow is from an investing activity. Answer (D) is incorrect. Although the cash outflow is from an investing activity, the cash inflow is from a financing activity.

28.2.22. Which of the following assets of a nongovernmental not-for-profit charitable entity must be depreciated?

A. A freezer costing $150,000 for storing food for the soup kitchen.

B. Building costs of $500,000 for construction in progress for senior citizen housing.

C. Land valued at $1 million being used as the site of the new senior citizen home.

D. A bulk purchase of $20,000 of linens for its nursing home.

Answer (A) is correct. *(CPA, adapted)*
REQUIRED: The asset of an NFP charity that must be depreciated.
DISCUSSION: NFPs recognize depreciation for most property and equipment. Exceptions are land used as a building site and certain individual works of art and historical treasures with extremely long useful lives. A freezer is a long-lived tangible asset that is depreciable equipment.
Answer (B) is incorrect. Construction in progress is inventory. Inventory is not depreciated. Answer (C) is incorrect. Land is not depreciated. Answer (D) is incorrect. Linens are inventory. Inventory is not depreciated.

28.2.23. In a nongovernmental not-for-profit entity, which of the following should be included in total expenses?

	Grants to Other Organizations	Depreciation
A.	Yes	Yes
B.	Yes	No
C.	No	No
D.	No	Yes

Answer (A) is correct. *(CPA, adapted)*
REQUIRED: The item(s), if any, included in total expenses by an NFP.
DISCUSSION: Depreciation expense is recognized for most property and equipment. It decreases net assets without donor restrictions. Other types of expenses based on a natural classification recognized by NFPs may include (1) salaries, (2) rent, (3) electricity, (4) interest, (5) awards and grants to others, (6) supplies, and (7) professional fees. But NFPs must report expenses by functional classification (major classes of program services and supporting activities). They also must provide an analysis that disaggregates functional classifications by their natural classifications.
Answer (B) is incorrect. An NFP recognizes depreciation expense. Answer (C) is incorrect. An NFP recognizes depreciation and grants to other organizations as expenses. Answer (D) is incorrect. An NFP recognizes expenses for grants to other organizations.

28.2.24. How should operating expenses for a nongovernmental not-for-profit organization be reported?

A. Change in net assets with donor restrictions.

B. Change in net assets without donor restrictions.

C. Change in permanently restricted net assets.

D. Contra-account to associated revenues.

Answer (B) is correct. *(CPA, adapted)*
REQUIRED: The reporting of an NFP's operating expenses.
DISCUSSION: Revenues are reported as increases in net assets without donor restrictions unless the use of the assets received is donor restricted. Expenses ordinarily are reported as decreases in net assets without donor restrictions. An exception is investment expenses. They must be netted against investment return and reported in the same net asset category. Investment expenses are not operating expenses of an NFP.
Answer (A) is incorrect. Expenses are reported as decreases in net assets without donor restrictions. An exception is investment expense. Also, revenues may be donor restricted. Answer (C) is incorrect. Operating expenses are never reported as changes in net assets with donor restrictions. Moreover, permanently restricted net assets is not one of the two minimum required classes of net assets. Answer (D) is incorrect. Operating expenses are never reported as a contra-account to associated revenues. But the entity may report an amount for excess or deficit of operating revenues over expenses if the statement reports the changes in net assets without donor restrictions.

28.2.25. Nongovernmental not-for-profit organizations are required to provide which of the following external financial statements?

A. Statement of financial position, statement of activities, and statement of cash flows.

B. Statement of financial position, statement of comprehensive income, and statement of cash flows.

C. Statement of comprehensive income, statement of cash flows, and statement of gains and losses.

D. Statement of cash flows, statement of comprehensive income, and statement of unrelated business income.

Answer (A) is correct. *(CPA, adapted)*
REQUIRED: The external financial statements provided by nongovernmental NFPs.
DISCUSSION: Nongovernmental NFPs must provide external financial statements that include a statement of financial position based on a net assets model. Changes in the classes of net assets, including the effects of reclassification, must be reported in a statement of activities. A statement of cash flows also must be presented. It must follow the same guidance as that applicable to cash flow statements of for-profit entities. Furthermore, a statement of activities or the notes should provide information about expenses reported by functional classification, e.g., by major classes of program services and supporting activities. An analysis also must be presented that disaggregates functional expense classifications by natural expense classifications (e.g., salaries, interest, rent, and depreciation).
Answer (B) is incorrect. A statement of comprehensive income must be presented by for-profit entities. NFPs and for-profit entities that do not have items of other comprehensive income are not subject to the requirement. Answer (C) is incorrect. An NFP does not present a statement of comprehensive income or a statement of gains and losses. Answer (D) is incorrect. An NFP does not present a statement of comprehensive income or a statement of unrelated business income.

28.2.26. Fenn Museum, a nongovernmental not-for-profit organization, had the following expense balances in its statement of activities:

Education	$300,000
Fundraising	250,000
Management and general	200,000
Research	50,000

What amount should Fenn report as expenses for support services?

- A. $350,000
- B. $450,000
- C. $500,000
- D. $800,000

Answer (B) is correct. *(CPA, adapted)*

REQUIRED: The amount of expenses for support services.

DISCUSSION: The expenses of not-for-profit entities (NFPs) are classified by function: program services or support services. Program services relate to the NFP's mission or service delivery objectives. Support services are all other activities of an NFP: management and general, fundraising, and membership development. Thus, the amount of expenses for support services is $450,000 ($250,000 fundraising + $200,000 management and general). Education and research are most likely program services of the Fenn Museum.

Answer (A) is incorrect. The amount of $350,000 is the sum of education and research expenses. Answer (C) is incorrect. The amount of $500,000 is the sum of either (1) education and management and general expenses or (2) management and general, fundraising, and research expenses. Education and research are program services. Answer (D) is incorrect. The amount of $800,000 includes the expenses incurred for the program services (education and research).

28.2.27. Which of the following types of information would be included in total net assets in the statement of financial position for a nongovernmental not-for-profit organization?

- A. Total current net assets and total other assets.
- B. Total current assets and restricted assets.
- C. Net assets without donor restrictions and net assets with donor restrictions.
- D. Unrestricted net assets, restricted net assets, and total current assets.

Answer (C) is correct. *(CPA, adapted)*

REQUIRED: The information included in total net assets in the statement of financial position.

DISCUSSION: Net assets are reported in the statement of financial position at a minimum as net assets without donor restrictions and net assets with donor restrictions.

Answer (A) is incorrect. Net assets are reported in the statement of financial position as net assets without donor restrictions and net assets with donor restrictions. Assets, not net assets, are presented as current and noncurrent. Answer (B) is incorrect. Net assets that are required to be used for a specified purpose based on donor restrictions are reported as net assets with donor restrictions, not as current or noncurrent. Answer (D) is incorrect. Net assets that are required to be used for a specified purpose based on donor restrictions are reported as net assets with donor restrictions. Moreover, assets, not net assets, are presented as current or noncurrent.

28.3 Contributions

28.3.1. According to GAAP applying to accounting for contributions received and contributions made, what classification(s), if any, should be used by nongovernmental not-for-profit entities (NFPs) to report receipts of contributions?

	Net Assets with Donor Restrictions	Net Assets without Donor Restrictions
A.	No	No
B.	No	Yes
C.	Yes	No
D.	Yes	Yes

Answer (D) is correct. *(Publisher, adapted)*

REQUIRED: The classification(s), if any, of contributions received by NFPs.

DISCUSSION: Contributions received by NFPs must be reported as net assets with donor restrictions or net assets without donor restrictions. Contributions with donor restrictions are reported as revenues or gains that increase net assets with donor restrictions. Contribution revenues or gains without donor restrictions increase net assets without donor restrictions.

Answer (A) is incorrect. NFPs must record contributions as net assets with donor restrictions or net assets without donor restrictions. Answer (B) is incorrect. NFPs also must record contributions as net assets with donor restrictions when applicable. Answer (C) is incorrect. NFPs also must record contributions as net assets without donor restrictions when applicable.

28.3.2. Pica, a nongovernmental not-for-profit entity, received unconditional promises of $100,000 expected to be collected within 1 year. Pica received $10,000 prior to year end. Pica anticipates collecting 90% of the contributions and has a June 30 fiscal year end. What amount should Pica record as contribution revenue as of June 30?

    A. $10,000

    B. $80,000

    C. $90,000

    D. $100,000

Answer (C) is correct. *(CPA, adapted)*
    REQUIRED: The contribution revenue recorded at fiscal year end.
    DISCUSSION: An unconditional promise to give may be recognized as a contribution given sufficient verifiable documentation. Contributions received ordinarily are accounted for at fair value as credits to revenues or gains and as debits to assets, liabilities, or expenses. For an unconditional promise to give, the present value of estimated future cash flows is an appropriate measure of fair value. However, unconditional promises to give expected to be collected in less than 1 year may be recognized at net realizable value. The latter amount equals $90,000 ($100,000 unconditionally promised × 90% collection percentage).
    Answer (A) is incorrect. The amount collected is $10,000. Answer (B) is incorrect. The amount collected also should be recognized as revenue. Answer (D) is incorrect. Revenue equals the net realizable value, not the gross amount promised.

28.3.3. On December 31, Year 3, Dahlia, a nongovernmental not-for-profit entity, purchased a vehicle with $15,000 unrestricted cash and received a donated second vehicle having a fair value of $12,000. Dahlia expects each vehicle to provide it with equal service value over each of the next five years and then to have no residual value. The donor stipulated a 5-year time restriction on the donated vehicle. In Dahlia's Year 4 statement of activities, what depreciation expense should be included under changes in net assets without donor restrictions?

    A. $0

    B. $2,400

    C. $3,000

    D. $5,400

Answer (D) is correct. *(CPA, adapted)*
    REQUIRED: The depreciation expense included under changes in net assets without donor restrictions.
    DISCUSSION: The expiration of a donor restriction is recognized in the accounting records. Expiration occurs when the stipulated time has elapsed, the purpose of the restriction has been fulfilled, or both. All amounts released during the period are reported in the statement of activities as net assets released from restrictions. The effect is to increase one class of net assets (net assets without donor restrictions) and decrease another (net assets with donor restrictions). In the case of a long-lived depreciable asset, the donor's time restriction expires as the economic benefits are used. Depreciation expense then is reported as a decrease in net assets without donor restrictions. Consequently, the NFP should record a decrease in net assets without donor restrictions related to depreciation of $5,400 [($15,000 + $12,000) ÷ 5-year useful life], given no residual value.
    Answer (A) is incorrect. Depreciation on both vehicles decreases net assets without donor restrictions. Answer (B) is incorrect. The amount of $2,400 results from failing to include the depreciation on the purchased vehicle. Answer (C) is incorrect. The amount of $3,000 results from failing to include the depreciation on the donated vehicle.

28.3.4. The Pel Museum, a nongovernmental not-for-profit entity (NFP), received a contribution of historical artifacts. It need not recognize the contribution if the artifacts are to be sold and the proceeds used to

    A. Support general museum activities.

    B. Acquire other items for collections.

    C. Repair existing collections.

    D. Purchase buildings to house collections.

Answer (B) is correct. *(CPA, adapted)*
    REQUIRED: The circumstance under which a contribution of artifacts to be sold need not be recognized.
    DISCUSSION: Contributions of such items as art works and historical treasures need not be capitalized and recognized as revenues if they are added to collections that are (1) held for public exhibition, education, or research for public service purposes rather than financial gain; (2) protected, kept unencumbered, cared for, and preserved; and (3) subject to a policy that requires the proceeds of sale of collection items to be used to acquire other collection items.
    Answer (A) is incorrect. If the proceeds are used to support general museum activities, the contribution must be recognized. Answer (C) is incorrect. If the proceeds are used to repair existing collections, the contribution must be recognized. Answer (D) is incorrect. If the proceeds are used to purchase buildings to house collections, the contribution must be recognized.

28.3.5. A family lost its home in a fire. On December 25, Year 3, a philanthropist sent money to the Benevolent Society to purchase furniture for the family. The resource provider did not explicitly grant the Society the unilateral power to redirect the use of the assets. During January Year 4, the Society purchased this furniture for the family. The Society, a not-for-profit entity, should report the receipt of the money in its Year 3 financial statements as a

A. Contribution without donor restrictions.

B. Contribution with donor restrictions.

C. Permanently restricted contribution.

D. Liability.

Answer (D) is correct. *(CPA, adapted)*
REQUIRED: The reporting of a transfer to an NFP with a direction that the money be used to aid a specific beneficiary.
DISCUSSION: Assets may be transferred to an NFP or a charitable trust that raises or holds contributions for others. The relevant guidance applies when a donor makes a contribution of cash or other financial assets to a recipient entity that agrees either to use the assets on behalf of, or to transfer the assets to, a specified beneficiary. In these circumstances, the recipient should debit cash or other financial assets and credit a liability. However, if the assets received are nonfinancial, the recipient is permitted but not required to recognize the assets and a liability. Furthermore, if the recipient is explicitly granted variance power to redirect the use of transferred assets, it recognizes a contribution. Also, if (1) the recipient and the specified beneficiary are financially interrelated and (2) the recipient is not a trustee, the recipient recognizes a contribution when it receives financial or nonfinancial assets.
Answer (A) is incorrect. Reporting a contribution without donor restrictions is required when the recipient has been granted variance power, or the recipient and beneficiary are financially interrelated. Answer (B) is incorrect. Reporting a contribution with donor restrictions is required when the recipient has been granted variance power, or the recipient and beneficiary are financially interrelated entities. Answer (C) is incorrect. The minimum required classes of net assets are net assets with donor restrictions and net assets without donor restrictions.

28.3.6. During Year 4, Jones Foundation received the following support:

- A cash contribution of $875,000 to be used at the board of directors' discretion
- A promise to contribute $500,000 in Year 5 from a supporter who has made similar contributions in prior periods
- Contributed legal services with a value of $100,000, which Jones would have otherwise purchased

At what amounts should Jones classify and record these transactions?

	Revenue Increasing Net Assets without Donor Restrictions	Revenue Increasing Net Assets with Donor Restrictions
A.	$1,375,000	$0
B.	$875,000	$500,000
C.	$975,000	$0
D.	$975,000	$500,000

Answer (D) is correct. *(CPA, adapted)*
REQUIRED: The amounts recorded for revenues from contributions with donor-imposed restrictions and without donor-imposed restrictions.
DISCUSSION: The cash contribution ($875,000) was a revenue received in Year 4 that was without donor-imposed restrictions. Thus, it is classified as support that increases net assets without donor restrictions. The unconditional promise to give ($500,000) with the amount due in Year 5 meets the definition of a contribution (assuming sufficient evidence in the form of verifiable documentation exists to recognize a promise to give). The NFP should recognize an asset and contribution revenue. Because (1) the amount is to be received in a future period and (2) the donor did not indicate clearly that the support was to be used for current activities, the $500,000 should be reported as net assets with donor restrictions. Contributions of services are recognized as revenues at fair value ($100,000) if they (1) require special skills (e.g., legal training), (2) are provided by those having such special skills, and (3) usually would be purchased if not donated. They are classified as support that increases net assets without donor restrictions because the services presumably have been rendered, and any purpose for which the resource was restricted has been fulfilled. Consequently, revenue increasing net assets without donor restrictions is $975,000 ($875,000 + $100,000), and revenue increasing net assets with donor restrictions is $500,000.
Answer (A) is incorrect. The promise to contribute is donor-restricted support until actually received, and the contribution of legal services should be reported as an increase in net assets without donor restrictions. Answer (B) is incorrect. Contributions of services are recognized as revenues at fair value if they require special skills, are provided by those having such special skills, and would usually be purchased if not obtained by donations. Answer (C) is incorrect. The promise to contribute is donor-restricted support.

28.3.7. Foundation, a nongovernmental not-for-profit entity, receives free electricity on a continuous basis from a local utility company. The contribution is made subject to cancelation by the donor. Foundation should account for this contribution as a

A. Revenue only without donor-imposed restrictions.

B. Revenue only with donor-imposed restrictions.

C. Revenue without donor-imposed restrictions and an expense.

D. Revenue with donor-imposed restrictions and an expense.

Answer (C) is correct. *(Publisher, adapted)*
REQUIRED: The amount at which a contribution of electricity should be recorded by the donee.
DISCUSSION: A contribution of utilities, such as electricity, is a contribution of other assets, not a contribution of services. A simultaneous receipt and use of utilities should be recognized as revenue that increases net assets without donor restrictions and expense in the period of receipt and use. The revenue and expense should be measured at estimated fair value. This estimate can be obtained from the rate schedule used by the utility company to determine rates charged to a similar customer.
Answer (A) is incorrect. An expense also should be recognized for the simultaneous receipt and use of electricity. Answer (B) is incorrect. The simultaneous receipt and use of electricity should be recorded as a revenue without donor-imposed restrictions and an expense in the period of receipt and use. Answer (D) is incorrect. The simultaneous receipt and use of electricity should be recorded as a revenue without donor-imposed restrictions and an expense in the period of receipt and use.

28.3.8. Following the destruction of its house of worship by fire, a religious organization held a rebuilding party. Part of the labor was donated by professional carpenters. The remainder was donated by members of the organization. Recognition is required for the value of the services provided by

A. The professional carpenters only.

B. The members only.

C. The professional carpenters and the members.

D. Neither the professional carpenters nor the members.

Answer (C) is correct. *(Publisher, adapted)*
REQUIRED: The contributed services to be recognized.
DISCUSSION: Contributions of services by the professional carpenters should be recognized because they require (1) special skills, (2) that are provided by those having such skills, and (3) that usually would be purchased if not donated. Moreover, donated services creating or enhancing nonfinancial assets must be recognized even though specialized skills are not involved. Because the members' labor helped rebuild the church (a nonfinancial asset), their contributions of services also should be recognized.
Answer (A) is incorrect. The church members' donated labor and the services of the professional carpenters should be recognized. Answer (B) is incorrect. The church members' donated labor and the services of the professional carpenters should be recognized. Answer (D) is incorrect. The church members' donated labor and the services of the professional carpenters should be recognized.

28.3.9. Nongovernmental not-for-profit entities recognize a conditional promise to give when

A. The promise is received.

B. The promise is received in writing.

C. The conditions are met.

D. It is reasonably possible that the conditions will be met.

Answer (C) is correct. *(Publisher, adapted)*
REQUIRED: The timing of recognition of a conditional promise to give.
DISCUSSION: A conditional promise to give depends on the occurrence of a specified future uncertain event to establish the promisor's obligation. It is recognized when the conditions are substantially met, i.e., when the conditional promise becomes unconditional. If the possibility is remote that the condition will not be met, the recognition criterion is satisfied.
Answer (A) is incorrect. Receipt of the promise is not sufficient for recognition of a contribution. Answer (B) is incorrect. Even if it is in writing, receipt of a promise is not sufficient for recognition of a contribution. Answer (D) is incorrect. The possibility that the condition will not be met must be remote before a contribution is recognized.

Questions 28.3.10 through 28.3.12 are based on the following information. On June 30 of the current year, Older Relatives Community Assistance (ORCA), a not-for-profit entity, received a building and the land on which it was constructed as a gift from Sapient Corporation. The building is intended to support the entity's education and training mission or any other purpose consistent with the entity's mission. Immediately prior to the contribution, the fair values of the building and land had been appraised as $700,000 and $300,000, respectively. Carrying amounts on Sapient's books at June 30 of the current year were $580,000 and $150,000, respectively.

28.3.10. If ORCA does not have a policy of implying time restrictions on gifts of long-lived assets, the gift should be recorded by the entity as net assets

	Without Donor Restrictions	With Donor Restrictions
A.	$300,000	$700,000
B.	$1,000,000	$0
C.	$0	$1,000,000
D.	$150,000	$580,000

Answer (B) is correct. *(Publisher, adapted)*
REQUIRED: The donee's recorded amount of a contribution of long-lived assets.
DISCUSSION: The terms of this contribution allow the long-lived assets to be used for any purpose consistent with the NFP's mission. Moreover, the NFP is not permitted to imply time restrictions on gifts of long-lived assets. Thus, the building and land on which it was constructed should be recorded at fair value as net assets without donor restrictions.
Answer (A) is incorrect. The building also should be recorded as net assets without donor restrictions. Answer (C) is incorrect. The building and land should be recorded as net assets without donor restrictions. Answer (D) is incorrect. The building and land should be recorded at fair value as net assets without donor restrictions.

28.3.11. Assume that Sapient gave ORCA a gift of $1,000,000 to acquire the building and land with no time restriction on their use. Also assume that ORCA has a policy of implying time restrictions on gifts of long-lived assets. When the assets are placed in service, the gift should be recorded by the entity as net assets

	Without Donor Restrictions	With Donor Restrictions
A.	$300,000	$700,000
B.	$1,000,000	$0
C.	$0	$1,000,000
D.	$150,000	$580,000

Answer (B) is correct. *(Publisher, adapted)*
REQUIRED: The amount at which a contribution of cash to acquire long-lived assets should be recorded by the donee when the assets are placed in service.
DISCUSSION: The terms of the gift allow the long-lived assets to be acquired to be used for any purpose consistent with the NFP's mission. A contribution of cash may be restricted to acquisition (or construction) of property, plant, or equipment. The entire amount then is reclassified when the asset is placed in service given no subsequent time restriction. Moreover, the NFP is not permitted to imply time restrictions on gifts of long-lived assets. Thus, when the building and land are placed in service, and the purpose restriction expires, $1,000,000 is reclassified from net assets with donor restrictions to net assets without donor restrictions.
Answer (A) is incorrect. The building also should be recorded as net assets without donor restrictions. Answer (C) is incorrect. The building and land should be recorded as net assets without donor restrictions. Answer (D) is incorrect. The building and land should be recorded at fair value as net assets without donor restrictions.

28.3.12. Sapient Corporation should record its contribution of the building and land as a

A. $730,000 reduction in contributed capital.

B. $1,000,000 reduction in contributed capital.

C. $730,000 expense.

D. $1,000,000 expense.

Answer (D) is correct. *(Publisher, adapted)*
REQUIRED: The amount at which a contribution of long-lived assets should be recorded by the donor.
DISCUSSION: Contributions should be recognized when made as (1) expenses and (2) decreases in assets or increases in liabilities. They should be measured at the fair value of the assets contributed.
Answer (A) is incorrect. The contribution should be recorded as an expense and measured at the fair value of the assets contributed. Answer (B) is incorrect. The contribution should be recorded as an expense. Answer (C) is incorrect. The contribution should be measured at the fair value of the assets contributed.

28.3.13. Oz, a nongovernmental not-for-profit entity, received $50,000 from Ame Company to sponsor a play given by Oz at the local theater. Oz gave Ame 25 tickets, which generally cost $100 each. Ame received no other benefits. What amount of ticket sales revenue should Oz record?

A. $0

B. $2,500

C. $47,500

D. $50,000

Answer (B) is correct. *(CPA, adapted)*
REQUIRED: The amount of ticket sales revenue.
DISCUSSION: This transaction involves both a contribution and an exchange. In an exchange, the parties receive and sacrifice something of approximately equal value. Oz therefore should recognize $2,500 of ticket revenue (25 tickets × $100), the fair value of the exchange element of the transaction. The fair value of the contribution element ($50,000 − $2,500) is recorded as contribution revenue in the period received. It is classified as net assets with donor restrictions until it is expended in fulfillment of the donor restriction.
Answer (A) is incorrect. Ticket sales revenue is recorded to account for the exchange element of the transaction. Answer (C) is incorrect. The amount of $47,500 is the contribution revenue. Answer (D) is incorrect. The amount of $50,000 is the ticket sales revenue plus the contribution revenue.

28.3.14. During the current year, a voluntary health and welfare entity received $300,000 in pledges without donor-imposed restrictions. Of this amount, $100,000 has been designated by donors for use next year to support operations. If 15% of the pledges without donor-imposed restrictions are expected to be uncollectible, what amount of support that increases net assets without donor restrictions should the entity recognize in its current-year financial statements?

A. $300,000

B. $270,000

C. $200,000

D. $170,000

Answer (D) is correct. *(CPA, adapted)*
REQUIRED: The current-year support that increases net assets without donor restrictions to be recognized.
DISCUSSION: Only $200,000 of the pledged total constitutes support that increases net assets without donor restrictions. These pledges may be recognized at net realizable value (NRV) if their collection is expected in less than 1 year. The NRV of these pledges is $170,000 [$200,000 × (1.0 − .15 estimated uncollectible)].
Answer (A) is incorrect. The amount of $300,000 is the total amount of pledges. Answer (B) is incorrect. The amount of $100,000 of the pledges is restricted until the next year. Answer (C) is incorrect. The amount of $200,000 does not reflect the estimated uncollectible pledges.

28.3.15. A nongovernmental not-for-profit entity (NFP) required an audit. The fair value of the service was $60,000, but the auditor accepted only $10,000, effectively donating $50,000 worth of services. The journal entry made by the NFP after completion of the audit and payment of the reduced fee is

A.	Expense	$60,000	
	Revenue		$50,000
	Cash		10,000
B.	Expense	$10,000	
	Cash		$10,000
C.	Expenditure	$60,000	
	Revenue		$50,000
	Cash		10,000
D.	Expenditure	$10,000	
	Cash		$10,000

Answer (A) is correct. *(K. Putnam)*
REQUIRED: The entry to record donated accounting services.
DISCUSSION: Contributions of services that require specialized skills and would have to be paid for if not donated are recognized. Contributions received are recognized as (1) revenues or gains when received and (2) assets, decreases in liabilities, or expenses given the form of the benefits. Thus, the donated audit services, which do not result in capitalization of an asset, are recognized as an expense because their benefits are used up as they are provided. The entry is to debit expense and credit cash and contribution revenue.
Answer (B) is incorrect. The donated services are recognized as an expense and a revenue. Answer (C) is incorrect. NFPs are required to use full accrual accounting. These entities use the term expense rather than expenditure. Expenditures are recognized in the governmental funds of state and local governments. These funds use the modified accrual basis of accounting. Answer (D) is incorrect. An expense and revenue are recognized for donated professional services that otherwise would have to be paid for.

28.3.16. In its fiscal year ended June 30, Year 4, Barr College, a large nongovernmental not-for-profit entity, received $100,000 designated by the donor for scholarships for superior students. On July 26, Year 4, Barr selected the students and awarded the scholarships. How should the July 26 transaction be reported in Barr's statement of activities for the year ended June 30, Year 5?

A. As both an increase and a decrease of $100,000 in net assets without donor restrictions.

B. As a decrease only in net assets without donor restrictions.

C. By footnote disclosure only.

D. Not reported.

Answer (A) is correct. *(CPA, adapted)*
REQUIRED: The treatment by a private not-for-profit entity of funds received and used for a designated purpose.
DISCUSSION: When the NFP received the contribution, it should have been classified as net assets with donor restrictions because it was to be used for a specified purpose. When the purpose is fulfilled, the restriction expires. The amount then should be reclassified as a decrease in net assets with donor restrictions and an increase in net assets without donor restrictions. When the scholarships are awarded, net assets without donor restrictions is decreased.
Answer (B) is incorrect. Net assets without donor restrictions also must be increased. Answer (C) is incorrect. A donation must be reported on the face of the statement of activities. Answer (D) is incorrect. This donation must be reported as (1) an increase and a decrease in net assets without donor restrictions and (2) a decrease in net assets with donor restrictions when its purpose is fulfilled and the scholarships are awarded.

28.3.17. Stanton College, a nongovernmental not-for-profit entity, received a building with no donor stipulations as to its use. Stanton does not have an accounting policy implying a time restriction on donated assets. What type of net assets should be increased when the building was received?

I. Without donor restrictions
II. Temporarily restricted
III. Permanently restricted

A. I only.

B. II only.

C. III only.

D. II or III.

Answer (A) is correct. *(CPA, adapted)*
REQUIRED: The classification(s) of net assets affected by a contribution of a building with no donor use stipulation.
DISCUSSION: The required minimum categories of net assets are net assets with donor restrictions and net assets without donor restrictions. Contributions without donor restrictions are reported as increases in net assets without donor restrictions. Furthermore, an entity is not permitted to imply a time restriction on gifts of long-lived assets (or assets for acquiring them).
Answer (B) is incorrect. Temporarily restricted net assets are now reported as net assets with donor restrictions; however, the contribution did not contain restrictions. Answer (C) is incorrect. Permanently restricted net assets are now reported as net assets with donor restrictions; however, the contribution did not contain restrictions. Answer (D) is incorrect. The contribution was without donor restrictions.

28.3.18. A storm damaged the roof of a new building owned by K-9 Shelters, a nongovernmental not-for-profit entity. A supporter of K-9, a professional roofer, repaired the roof at no charge. In K-9's statement of activities, the damage and repair of the roof should

A. Be reported by note disclosure only.

B. Be reported as an increase in both expenses and contributions.

C. Be reported as an increase in both net assets and contributions.

D. Not be reported.

Answer (B) is correct. *(CPA, adapted)*
REQUIRED: The treatment of services received at no charge by a not-for-profit entity.
DISCUSSION: Contributions of services at fair value are recognized if they (1) create or enhance nonfinancial assets or (2) (a) require special skills, (b) are provided by individuals having those skills, and (c) usually would be purchased if not donated. Thus, K-9 should report an expense and contribution revenue for the services received.
Answer (A) is incorrect. Note disclosure does not adequately record the contributions received. Answer (C) is incorrect. The repair of a roof is an expense, not an asset. Answer (D) is incorrect. Contributions received must be recorded in the accounts.

28.3.19. The Turtle Society, a nongovernmental not-for-profit entity (NFP), receives numerous contributed hours from volunteers during its busy season. Chris, a clerk at the local tax collector's office, volunteered 10 hours per week for 24 weeks transferring turtle food from the port to the turtle shelter. His rate of pay at the tax office is $10 per hour, and the prevailing wage rate for laborers is $6.50 per hour. What amount of contribution revenue should Turtle Society record for this service?

A. $0

B. $840

C. $1,560

D. $2,400

Answer (A) is correct. *(CPA, adapted)*
REQUIRED: The amount of contribution revenue recorded for a volunteer's service.
DISCUSSION: Contributions of services are recognized if they (1) create or enhance nonfinancial assets or (2) (a) require special skills, (b) are provided by those having such skills, and (c) usually would be purchased if not donated. The volunteer's efforts meet neither of these criteria. Thus, no contribution revenue is recognized.
Answer (B) is incorrect. The amount of $840 equals 24 weeks, times 10 hours per week, times $3.50 per hour ($10 – $6.50). Answer (C) is incorrect. The amount of $1,560 equals 24 weeks, times 10 hours per week, times $6.50 per hour. Answer (D) is incorrect. The amount of $2,400 equals 24 weeks, times 10 hours per week, times $10 per hour.

28.3.20. Janna Association, a nongovernmental not-for-profit entity, received a cash gift with the stipulation that the principal be held for at least 20 years. How should the cash gift be recorded?

A. Net assets with donor restrictions.

B. An asset restricted in perpetuity.

C. Net assets without donor restrictions.

D. A temporary liability.

Answer (A) is correct. *(CPA, adapted)*
REQUIRED: The classification of a cash gift with a time restriction.
DISCUSSION: Net assets with donor restrictions result from restrictions removable by the passage of time or by the actions of the NFP unless they are imposed in perpetuity. A stipulation that the principal be held for at least 20 years is a time restriction.
Answer (B) is incorrect. After 20 years, the asset is no longer restricted. Answer (C) is incorrect. The cash gift is donor-restricted for at least 20 years. Answer (D) is incorrect. Cash is an asset.

28.3.21. In July Year 3, Katie irrevocably donated $200,000 cash to be invested and held in trust by a church. Katie stipulated that the revenue generated from this gift be paid to Katie during Katie's lifetime. After Katie dies, the principal is to be used by the church for any purpose chosen by its governing body. The church received interest of $16,000 on the $200,000 for the year ended June 30, Year 4, and the interest was remitted to Katie. In the church's June 30, Year 4, annual financial statements,

A. $200,000 should be reported as revenue.

B. $184,000 should be reported as revenue.

C. $16,000 should be reported as revenue.

D. The gift and its terms should be disclosed only in notes to the financial statements.

Answer (A) is correct. *(CPA, adapted)*
REQUIRED: The accounting for a donation of cash to be invested to pay income to the donor for life and then to pay the principal to the donee.
DISCUSSION: An NFP should report an irrevocable split-interest agreement. Assets under the control of the NFP are recorded at fair value at the time of initial recognition, and the contribution is recognized as revenue. Because the NFP has a remainder interest, it should not recognize revenue from receipt of the income of the trust. Thus, the NFP should recognize revenue of $200,000 (the presumed fair value of the contributed cash).
Answer (B) is incorrect. The contribution is not reduced by the income paid to the donor. Answer (C) is incorrect. The income paid to the donor is not revenue of the NFP. Answer (D) is incorrect. The contribution should be recognized at fair value.

28.3.22. Pann, a nongovernmental not-for-profit organization, provides food and shelter to the homeless. Pann received a $15,000 gift with the stipulation that the funds be used to buy beds. In which net asset class should Pann report the contribution?

A. Endowment.

B. Net assets with donor restrictions.

C. Net assets without donor restrictions.

D. Unrestricted.

Answer (B) is correct. *(CPA, adapted)*
REQUIRED: The net asset class in which a nongovernmental NFP reports a cash gift with a specified use.
DISCUSSION: A statement of financial position of an NFP must report at a minimum net assets in two classes: (1) net assets without donor restrictions and (2) net assets with donor restrictions. The cash gift is reported in net assets with donor restrictions because it will be expended for the stated purpose.
Answer (A) is incorrect. A perpetual endowment requires resources to be maintained permanently. Moreover, an endowment is not a net asset class. Answer (C) is incorrect. The cash gift is donor-restricted support. Answer (D) is incorrect. The cash gift is donor-restricted support because the funds must be used to buy beds.

28.3.23. Whitestone, a nongovernmental not-for-profit organization, received a contribution in December, Year 1. The donor restricted use of the contribution until March, Year 2. How should Whitestone record the contribution?

A. Footnote the contribution in Year 1 and record as income when it becomes available in Year 2.

B. No entry required in Year 1 and record as income in Year 2 when it becomes available.

C. Report as income in Year 1.

D. Report as deferred income in Year 1.

Answer (C) is correct. *(CPA, adapted)*
REQUIRED: The recording of a contribution with a time restriction.
DISCUSSION: A nongovernmental NFP recognizes contributions received as revenues or gains in its statement of activities. A contribution is unconditional, voluntary, and not reciprocal, and the donor does not act as an owner. Thus, it does not result from an exchange transaction. A donor restriction does not preclude recognition of contribution revenue or gain (income). It merely limits the use of contributed assets.
Answer (A) is incorrect. The contribution should be recognized. A donor restriction merely limits the use of contributed assets. Answer (B) is incorrect. The contribution should be recognized when received if it is unconditional, voluntary, and nonreciprocal, and the donor does not act as an owner. Answer (D) is incorrect. By definition, a contribution does not result in deferred revenue (income). Deferred revenue results from exchange transactions with service beneficiaries for specific activities that have not yet occurred.

28.3.24. A nongovernmental not-for-profit animal shelter receives contributed services from the following individuals valued at their normal billing rate:

Veterinarian provides volunteer animal care	$8,000
Board members volunteer to prepare books for audit	4,500
Registered nurse volunteers as receptionist	3,000
Teacher provides volunteer dog walking	2,000

What amount should the shelter record as contribution revenue?

- A. $8,000
- B. $11,000
- C. $12,500
- D. $14,500

Answer (C) is correct. *(CPA, adapted)*
REQUIRED: The contribution revenue recorded for contributed services.
DISCUSSION: Contributions of services are recognized if they (1) create or enhance nonfinancial assets or (2) (a) require special skills, (b) are provided by those having such skills, and (c) would usually be purchased if not donated. The services provided by the veterinarian and the board members are recognized as contribution revenue. The services provided by the registered nurse and the teacher are not. Veterinary services and bookkeeping (1) require special skills, (2) are provided by persons with such skills (assuming the board members have accounting experience or training), and (3) usually would be paid for by an animal shelter if not donated. Thus, the animal shelter should record $12,500 ($8,000 + $4,500) as contribution revenue.
Answer (A) is incorrect. The amount of $8,000 includes only the value of services provided by the veterinarian. Answer (B) is incorrect. The amount of $11,000 includes the value of services provided by the registered nurse and excludes the value of the services provided by the board members. Answer (D) is incorrect. The amount of $14,500 includes the value of the services provided by the teacher.

28.3.25. How should a nongovernmental not-for-profit organization classify gains and losses on investments purchased with net assets with donor restrictions?

- A. Gains may not be netted against losses in the statement of activities.
- B. Gains and losses can only be reported net of expenses in the statement of activities.
- C. Unless explicitly restricted by donor or law, gains and losses should be reported in the statement of activities as increases or decreases in net assets without donor restrictions.
- D. Unless explicitly restricted by donor or law, gains and losses should be reported in the statement of activities as increases or decreases in net assets with donor restrictions.

Answer (C) is correct. *(CPA, adapted)*
REQUIRED: The classification by an NFP of gains and losses on net assets with donor restrictions.
DISCUSSION: Unless explicitly restricted by the donor or law, gains and losses on net assets with donor restrictions should be reported in the statement of activities as increases or decreases in net assets without donor restrictions.
Answer (A) is incorrect. Gains and losses may be reported as net amounts if they result from (1) peripheral or incidental transactions or (2) other events and circumstances largely beyond the control of management. Answer (B) is incorrect. Expenses ordinarily are not netted against gains and losses. But investment returns not related to program services must be reported net of external, and direct internal, expenses. Answer (D) is incorrect. Gains and losses should not be reported as increases or decreases in net assets with donor restrictions unless explicitly restricted by donor or law.

28.3.26. Which of the following resources increases the net assets with donor restrictions of a nongovernmental, not-for-profit voluntary health and welfare organization?

- A. Refundable advances for purchasing playground equipment.
- B. Donor contributions to fund a resident camp program.
- C. Membership fees to fund general operations.
- D. Participants' deposits for an entity-sponsored trip.

Answer (B) is correct. *(CPA, adapted)*
REQUIRED: The resources that increase net assets with donor restrictions.
DISCUSSION: An NFP recognizes contributions received (1) with donor restrictions and (2) without donor restrictions. Donor-restricted support consists of contribution revenues or gains that increase net assets with donor restrictions. Donor contributions subject to a purpose restriction are classified as net assets with donor restrictions.
Answer (A) is incorrect. Refundable advances are recorded as assets with a corresponding liability until the conditions are substantially met. Net assets does not change. Answer (C) is incorrect. Membership fees received in exchange transactions that fund general operations are not subject to donor restrictions. They are classified as increases in net assets without donor restrictions. Answer (D) is incorrect. Receipts of participants' deposits for an entity-sponsored trip are exchange transactions. Resources received in exchange transactions are classified as net assets without donor restrictions.

28.3.27. During the current year, Mill Foundation, a nongovernmental not-for-profit entity, received $100,000 in unrestricted contributions from the general public. Mill's board of directors stipulated that $75,000 of these contributions would be used to create an endowment. At the end of the current year, how should Mill report the $75,000 in the net assets section of the statement of financial position?

A. Permanently restricted.

B. Net assets without donor restrictions.

C. Temporarily restricted.

D. Donor restricted.

Answer (B) is correct. *(CPA, adapted)*
REQUIRED: The reporting of unrestricted contributions designated as an endowment.
DISCUSSION: An internal decision to designate a portion of net assets without donor restrictions as an endowment is not a restriction. The minimum required classes of net assets are (1) net assets with donor restrictions and (2) net assets without donor restrictions. Moreover, an NFP must report amounts for those classes and total assets. Accordingly, if the contributions had been restricted by the donor, the classification of the assets would have been net assets with donor restrictions.
Answer (A) is incorrect. The contributions were not restricted by the donors. Also, permanently restricted is not a minimum required class of net assets for which an amount must be reported. Answer (C) is incorrect. The contributions were not restricted because the endowment was designated by the board. Also, temporarily restricted is not a minimum required class of net assets for which an amount must be reported. Answer (D) is incorrect. The board of directors, not the donors, designated a portion of the contributions as an endowment.

28.4 Investments

28.4.1. Midtown Church received a donation of equity securities with readily determinable fair values from a church member. The securities had appreciated in value after they were purchased by the donor and continued to appreciate through the end of Midtown's fiscal year. At what amount should Midtown report its investment in donated securities in its year-end balance sheet?

A. Donor's cost.

B. Fair value at the date of receipt.

C. Fair value at the balance sheet date.

D. Fair value at either the date of receipt or the balance sheet date.

Answer (C) is correct. *(CPA, adapted)*
REQUIRED: The year-end measure of donated equity securities.
DISCUSSION: In its statement of financial position, an NFP initially should measure equity securities at fair value if received as contributions. Subsequent measurement of equity securities with readily determinable fair values also is at fair value. Thus, the total change in the fair value of the donated securities from the date of receipt to the balance sheet date must be reported in the statement of activities.
Answer (A) is incorrect. All investments are reported at fair value. Answer (B) is incorrect. All investments are reported at fair value but not fair value at the date of receipt. Answer (D) is incorrect. All investments are reported at fair value at the balance sheet date.

28.4.2. On December 31 of the current year, Communities Organized for Social Improvement (COSI), a not-for-profit entity, holds an investment in common stock of one publicly traded entity and an investment in debt securities of another. The not-for-profit entity holds the common stock as a long-term investment and has the intent and the ability to hold the debt securities until maturity.

	Investment in Common Stock	Investment in Debt Securities
Original cost	$50,000	$35,000
Amortized cost		28,000
Fair value	63,000	40,000

In the December 31 statement of financial position for the current year, COSI should value these investments as

	Investment in Common Stock	Investment in Debt Securities
A.	$50,000	$28,000
B.	$50,000	$40,000
C.	$63,000	$28,000
D.	$63,000	$40,000

Answer (D) is correct. *(Publisher, adapted)*
REQUIRED: The amount to be recorded by an NFP for investments in equity and debt securities.
DISCUSSION: GAAP applying to accounting for certain investments held by NFPs require them to measure investments in equity securities with readily determinable fair values and all investments in debt securities at fair value in the statement of financial position.
Answer (A) is incorrect. The investment in common stock should not be measured at original cost. The investment in debt securities should not be measured at amortized cost. Answer (B) is incorrect. The investment in common stock should not be measured at original cost. Answer (C) is incorrect. The investment in debt securities should not be measured at amortized cost.

28.4.3. In Year 1, a not-for-profit voluntary health and welfare entity received a $500,000 perpetual endowment. The applicable state law is based on the Uniform Prudent Management of Institutional Funds Act (UPMIFA). The donor stipulated that the income be used for a mental health program. The endowment fund reported $60,000 net decrease in fair value and $30,000 investment income. The entity spent $45,000 on the mental health program during the year. What amount of change in net assets with donor restrictions should the entity report in its statement of activities for Year 1?

A. $75,000 decrease.

B. $15,000 decrease.

C. $60,000 decrease.

D. $425,000 increase.

Answer (C) is correct. *(CPA, adapted)*
REQUIRED: The change in net assets with donor restrictions.
DISCUSSION: The contribution of $500,000 to be maintained in a perpetual endowment as a source of income is classified as an increase in net assets with donor restrictions. The income is donor restricted for the purpose of supporting a mental health program. However, the donor restriction expired in the reporting period when the investment income was recognized. Under U.S. GAAP, the NFP may recognize an increase in net assets without donor restrictions, provided that it (1) has a similar policy for reporting contributions received, (2) reports on a consistent basis from period to period, and (3) adequately discloses its accounting policy. Moreover, UPMIFA extended the restriction to the use of the assets, including the investment return, until appropriation for expenditures. Appropriation is implied because more than the $30,000 of investment income was spent for the stipulated purpose. Consequently, the legal extension of the donor restriction also expired. Under U.S. GAAP, an underwater endowment fund has a reporting-date fair value less than the amount (1) of the gift or (2) required by the donor or a law that extends donor restrictions. The accumulated losses are included with that fund in net assets with donor restrictions. Thus, the decrease in net fair value below the amount of the gift resulted in an underwater endowment fund. The effect was a decrease in net assets with donor restrictions of $60,000. The NFP presumably elected to treat the $30,000 of income (included in program support) as an increase in net assets without donor restrictions (and a decrease of the same amount upon expenditure in the same period). The net effect on net assets with donor restrictions is therefore a decrease of $60,000.
Answer (A) is incorrect. The amount of $75,000 is the sum of the fair value decrease and the excess of expenditures over income. Answer (B) is incorrect. The amount of $15,000 is the excess of the amount spent over income. Answer (D) is incorrect. The amount of $425,000 equals the contribution minus the sum of the fair value decrease and the excess of expenditures over income.

28.4.4. RST Charities received equity securities valued at $100,000 as a gift without donor-imposed restrictions. During the year, RST received $5,000 in dividends from these securities; at year end, the securities had a fair market value of $110,000. By what amount did these transactions increase RST's net assets?

A. $100,000

B. $105,000

C. $110,000

D. $115,000

Answer (D) is correct. *(CPA, adapted)*
REQUIRED: The increase in net assets from a contribution without donor-imposed restrictions of securities that paid dividends and appreciated after receipt.
DISCUSSION: NFPs must measure investments in equity securities at fair value. Unrealized holding gains or losses (changes in fair value) are reported in the statement of activities as changes in net assets without donor restrictions given no donor-imposed restriction or law that extends donor restrictions. Investment income (e.g., dividends) also increases net assets without donor restrictions (given no donor-imposed restriction or law that extends donor restrictions). Accordingly, RST's net assets without donor restrictions increased by $115,000 [$100,000 fair value of contribution + $5,000 in dividends + $10,000 ($110,000 – $100,000) unrealized holding gain in fair value].
Answer (A) is incorrect. The amount of $100,000 excludes the dividends and the unrealized holding gain. Answer (B) is incorrect. The amount of $105,000 excludes the unrealized holding gain. Answer (C) is incorrect. The amount of $110,000 excludes the dividends.

Questions 28.4.5 through 28.4.9 are based on the following information. Early in Year 2, a nongovernmental not-for-profit entity (NFP) received a $2,000,000 gift. The donor specified that the gift be invested in a perpetual endowment, with income restricted to provide speaker fees for a lecture series named for the benefactor. The NFP is responsible for all other costs associated with initiating and administering this series. The donor's stipulation does not address gains and losses on this perpetual endowment, and the NFP reports only the minimum required classes of net assets. In Year 2, the investments purchased with the gift earned $50,000 in dividend income. The fair value of the investments increased by $120,000. The applicable state law is based on the Uniform Prudent Management of Institutional Funds Act (UPMIFA).

28.4.5. The $2 million gift from the benefactor should be recorded in the Year 2 statement of activities as an increase in

    A. Net assets without donor restrictions.

    B. Temporarily restricted net assets.

    C. Net assets with donor restrictions.

    D. Permanently restricted net assets.

Answer (C) is correct. *(Publisher, adapted)*
REQUIRED: The classification of a gift to be invested in perpetuity.
DISCUSSION: A donor-imposed restriction limits the use of contributed assets. This gift is unconditional in the sense that no condition is imposed on the transfer, but it includes a perpetual restriction on the use of the assets. Because the NFP reports only the minimum required classes of net assets (net assets without donor restrictions and net assets with donor restrictions), the gift therefore should be classified as an increase in net assets with donor restrictions.
Answer (A) is incorrect. The donor stipulated that the gift be invested in perpetuity, a donor-imposed restriction. Answer (B) is incorrect. Temporarily restricted net assets is not one of the minimum required classes of net assets. Answer (D) is incorrect. Permanently restricted net assets is not one of the minimum required classes of net assets.

28.4.6. The total of speaker fees for the lectures was $90,000. The board of the not-for-profit entity appropriated the $50,000 of dividend income to pay part of the total fees. Because the board did not wish to sell any of the investments, the entity used $40,000 of other resources to pay the remainder of the speaker fees. In the NFP's Year 2 statement of activities, the $50,000 of dividend income should be recorded as an increase in

    A. Net assets without donor restrictions, followed by a decrease in net assets without donor restrictions.

    B. Temporarily restricted net assets, followed by a decrease in temporarily restricted net assets.

    C. Permanently restricted net assets, followed by a decrease in permanently restricted net assets.

    D. Either net assets without donor restrictions or net assets with donor restrictions, followed by a decrease in net assets without donor restrictions or net assets with donor restrictions, respectively.

Answer (D) is correct. *(Publisher, adapted)*
REQUIRED: The accounting for expended dividend income from investments held in perpetuity.
DISCUSSION: Income from donor-restricted endowment funds must be classified as an increase in net assets with donor restrictions if the donor restricts its use. A donor restriction (paying speaker fees) existed on the divided income. It expired on the $50,000 of dividend income used to pay part of the speaker fees in the period (1) the income was recognized and (2) the board appropriated that income for expenditure. Most donor-restricted endowment funds are subject to the UPMIFA. This statute extends a donor restriction to use of the assets, including the return, until appropriation for expenditure by the NFP's governing board. In the period of the expiration, the NFP therefore may choose to report an increase in either net assets without donor restrictions or net assets with donor restrictions, followed by a decrease in net assets without donor restrictions or net assets with donor restrictions, respectively. But if the NFP chooses to report an increase in net assets without donor restrictions, it must (1) apply the same policy to contributions, (2) report consistently, and (3) disclose the policy chosen.
Answer (A) is incorrect. Investment income may be reported as an increase in either net assets without donor restrictions or net assets with donor restrictions in these circumstances. Answer (B) is incorrect. The minimum required classes of net assets are net assets without donor restrictions and net assets with donor restrictions. Answer (C) is incorrect. The minimum required classes of net assets are net assets without donor restrictions and net assets with donor restrictions.

28.4.7. The NFP's accounting policy is to record gains and investment income, for which a donor-imposed restriction is met in the same accounting period as the gains and investment income are recognized, as increases in net assets without donor restrictions. In the Year 2 statement of activities, the $120,000 unrealized gain should be recorded as

A. A $40,000 increase in net assets without donor restrictions and an $80,000 increase in temporarily restricted net assets.

B. A $120,000 increase in net assets with donor restrictions.

C. A $120,000 increase in temporarily restricted net assets.

D. A $120,000 increase in permanently restricted net assets.

Answer (B) is correct. *(Publisher, adapted)*
REQUIRED: The classification of an unrealized gain from investments held in perpetuity.
DISCUSSION: Without a donor or legal restriction, investment return generally is free of donor restrictions. But most donor-restricted endowment funds are subject to the UPMIFA. This statute extends a donor restriction to use of the assets, including the return, until appropriation for expenditure by the governing board. Without contrary language in the gift instrument, the assets in the endowment fund (including the return) are net assets with donor restrictions until appropriation. An appropriation reduces net assets with donor restrictions if all time and purpose restrictions have been met. The result is a reclassification to net assets without donor restrictions. Appropriation occurs upon approval for expenditure unless a legal interpretation states otherwise. Thus, without an appropriation of the gain (part of the investment return), the donor's perpetual restriction on the investment extends to the gain. The NFP therefore recognizes a $120,000 increase in net assets with donor restrictions.
Answer (A) is incorrect. The entire $120,000 unrealized gain should be recorded as an increase in net assets with donor restrictions. Answer (C) is incorrect. The unrealized gain should be recorded as an increase in net assets with donor restrictions, not temporarily restricted net assets. Answer (D) is incorrect. The unrealized gain should be recorded as an increase in net assets with donor restrictions, not permanently restricted net assets.

28.4.8. Assume that the UPMIFA does not apply and that the lecture series is not scheduled to begin until Year 3. The $50,000 of dividend income should be recorded in the NFP's Year 2 statement of activities as an increase in

A. Net assets without donor restrictions.

B. Net assets with donor restrictions.

C. Temporarily or permanently restricted net assets.

D. Either net assets without donor restrictions or net assets with donor restrictions.

Answer (B) is correct. *(Publisher, adapted)*
REQUIRED: The accounting for unexpended dividend income from investments held in perpetuity.
DISCUSSION: Gains and investment income from donor-restricted perpetual endowments must be classified as increases in net assets with donor restrictions if the donor restricts the use of these resources to a specific purpose. Because the restriction cannot expire until the income is expended in a future period, the NFP does not have the option to report the income as an increase in net assets without donor restrictions.
Answer (A) is incorrect. The restriction expires when the income is expended. But the income cannot be classified as an increase in net assets without donor restrictions. Recognition and the expiration of the restriction do not occur in the same period. Answer (C) is incorrect. Temporarily and permanently restricted net assets are not minimum required classes of net assets. Answer (D) is incorrect. The restriction expires when the income is expended. But the income cannot be classified as an increase in net assets without donor restrictions. Recognition and the expiration of the restriction do not occur in the same period.

28.4.9. If the lecture series is not scheduled to begin until Year 3, the $120,000 unrealized gain should be recorded in the NFP's Year 2 statement of activities as an increase in

A. Net assets without donor restrictions.

B. Net assets with donor restrictions.

C. Permanently restricted net assets.

D. Either net assets with donor restrictions or temporarily restricted net assets.

Answer (B) is correct. *(Publisher, adapted)*
REQUIRED: The classification of an unrealized gain on investments held in perpetuity.
DISCUSSION: Investment return (income and gains) generally is free of donor restrictions unless its use is limited by (1) a donor-imposed restriction or (2) a law. Most donor-restricted endowment funds are subject to the UPMIFA. This statute extends a donor restriction to use of the assets, including the return, until appropriation for expenditure by the NFP's governing board. Thus, without other language in the gift instrument, the assets in the fund (including the return) are net assets with donor restrictions until appropriation. Without a contrary legal interpretation, appropriation occurs upon approval for expenditure. No approval for expenditure of the increase in fair value of the investments has been made. Accordingly, the unrealized gain is an increase in net assets with donor restrictions.
Answer (A) is incorrect. The UPMIFA extends the donor restriction to the gain. Answer (C) is incorrect. Permanently restricted net assets is not a minimum required class of net assets. Answer (D) is incorrect. Temporarily restricted net assets is not a minimum required class of net assets.

28.4.10. During the current year, the local humane society, a nongovernmental not-for-profit organization, received a $100,000 perpetual endowment from Cobb. Cobb stipulated that the income must be used to care for older horses that can no longer race. The endowment reported income of $8,000 in the current year. What amount of contribution revenue should the humane society report as an increase in net assets without donor restrictions for the current year?

   A. $108,000

   B. $100,000

   C. $8,000

   D. $0

Answer (D) is correct. *(CPA, adapted)*
   REQUIRED: The contribution revenue reported as an increase in net assets without donor restrictions.
   DISCUSSION: The donor stipulated that the income from the perpetual endowment fund be used to care for older horses. Thus, the $100,000 contribution is donor-restricted support reported as contribution revenue that increases net assets with donor restrictions. The $8,000 of income from the donor-restricted perpetual endowment fund is investment income, not contribution revenue. Furthermore, the purpose restriction on the income has not expired. Consequently, the increase in net assets without donor restrictions is $0.
   Answer (A) is incorrect. The amount of $108,000 includes the contribution to the perpetual endowment fund and the income. Answer (B) is incorrect. The amount of $100,000 equals the contribution to the perpetual endowment fund. Answer (C) is incorrect. The amount of $8,000 equals the investment income.

28.4.11. During the current year, the Finn Foundation, a nongovernmental not-for-profit organization, received a $1,000,000 perpetual endowment from Chris. Chris stipulated that the income must be used to provide recreational activities for the elderly. The endowment reported income of $80,000 in the current year. What amount of contribution revenue should Finn report as an increase in net assets with donor restrictions at the end of the current year?

   A. $1,080,000

   B. $1,000,000

   C. $80,000

   D. $0

Answer (A) is correct. *(CPA, adapted)*
   REQUIRED: The contribution revenue reported by a nongovernmental NFP as an increase in net assets with donor restrictions.
   DISCUSSION: A perpetual endowment is a donation restricted by the donor to generate investment income in perpetuity. Thus, the $1,000,000 contribution is an addition to net assets with donor restrictions. Moreover, a contribution to an NFP is recognized as a revenue or a gain. Assuming that the NFP's ongoing major or central operations include soliciting contributions, the donation is classified as a revenue. Because the endowment is perpetual, it is also classified as donor-restricted support. The income also increases net assets with donor restrictions. The restriction on the income does not expire until the purpose restriction (use of recreational activities for the elderly) is satisfied. Accordingly, the increase in net assets with donor restrictions is $1,080,000 ($1,000,000 endowment gift + $80,000 income not expensed).
   Answer (B) is incorrect. The amount of $1,000,000 excludes income. Answer (C) is incorrect. The amount of $80,000 excludes the perpetually restricted contribution. Answer (D) is incorrect. The amount of $0 does not include the contribution or income.

28.4.12. A nongovernmental, not-for-profit organization received the following donations of corporate stock during the year:

	Donation 1	Donation 2
Number of shares	2,000	3,000
Adjusted basis	$ 8,000	$5,500
Fair market value at time of donation	8,500	6,000
Fair market value at year end	10,000	4,000

What net value of investments will the organization report at the end of the year?

   A. $12,000

   B. $13,500

   C. $14,000

   D. $14,500

Answer (C) is correct. *(CPA, adapted)*
   REQUIRED: The net value of the investments reported at year end.
   DISCUSSION: Investments in equity securities (corporate stock) with readily determinable fair values are measured at fair value in the statement of financial position. Accordingly, the net value of the investments at the end of the year is $14,000 ($10,000 FV at year end + $4,000 FV at year end).
   Answer (A) is incorrect. The amount of $12,000 equals the sum of the adjusted basis of Donation 1 and the fair value of Donation 2 at year end. Answer (B) is incorrect. The amount of $13,500 equals the sum of the adjusted bases of Donations 1 and 2. Answer (D) is incorrect. The amount of $14,500 equals the sum of the fair values of Donations 1 and 2 at the time of the donation.

28.4.13. A nongovernmental not-for-profit organization received a $2 million gift from a donor who specified it be used to create an endowment fund that would be invested in perpetuity. The income from the fund is to be used to support a specific program in the second year and beyond. An investment purchased with the gift earned $40,000 during the first year. At the end of the first year, the fair value of the investment was $2,010,000. What is the net effect on net assets with donor restrictions at year end?

A. $0

B. $10,000 increase.

C. $40,000 increase.

D. $50,000 increase.

Answer (D) is correct. *(CPA, adapted)*
REQUIRED: The effect on net assets with donor restrictions of investment income and a change in fair value of a perpetual endowment.
DISCUSSION: Investment return (e.g., income and gains) generally is free of donor restrictions unless its use is limited by (1) a donor-imposed restriction or (2) a law. Most donor-restricted endowment funds are subject to a statute that extends a donor restriction to use of the assets, including the return, until appropriation for expenditure by the NFP's governing board. Thus, without other language in the gift instrument, the assets in the fund (including the return) are net assets with donor restrictions until appropriation. Without a contrary legal interpretation, appropriation occurs upon approval for expenditure. No approval for expenditure of the increase in fair value of the investments has been made. Accordingly, the unrealized gain is an increase in net assets with donor restrictions. Given that the income is to be used for the purpose specified by the donor, the income also is an increase in net assets with donor restrictions. The NFP does not have the option of reporting the income as an increase in net assets without donor restrictions when it is recognized because the restriction will not expire in the same period. Accordingly, the $10,000 gain on the perpetual endowment and the $40,000 of income increase net assets with donor restrictions by $50,000.
Answer (A) is incorrect. The gain and the income increase net assets with donor restrictions. Answer (B) is incorrect. The income also is an increase in net assets with donor restrictions. Answer (C) is incorrect. The gain also is an increase in net assets with donor restrictions.

28.4.14. At which of the following amounts should a nongovernmental not-for-profit organization report investments in debt securities?

A. Potential proceeds from liquidation sale.

B. Discounted expected future cash flows.

C. Quoted market prices.

D. Historical cost.

Answer (C) is correct. *(CPA, adapted)*
REQUIRED: The amounts at which NFPs should report investments in debt securities.
DISCUSSION: A nongovernmental NFP should report investments in debt securities at the quoted market prices. Equity securities with readily determinable fair values and all debt securities are to be measured at fair value in the statement of financial position.
Answer (A) is incorrect. Debt securities are not reported at their potential proceeds from liquidation sale by nongovernmental not-for-profit organizations. Answer (B) is incorrect. Debt securities are not reported at their discounted expected future cash flows by nongovernmental not-for-profit organizations. Answer (D) is incorrect. Debt securities are not reported at their historical cost by nongovernmental not-for-profit organizations.

28.5 Healthcare Entities (HCEs)

28.5.1. Which of the following should normally be considered ongoing or central transactions for a not-for-profit hospital?

I. Room and board fees from patients
II. Recovery room fees

A. Neither I nor II.

B. Both I and II.

C. II only.

D. I only.

Answer (B) is correct. *(CPA, adapted)*
REQUIRED: The fees, if any, that are ongoing or central transactions for a not-for-profit hospital.
DISCUSSION: Revenues result from an entity's ongoing major or central operations. Revenues of an HCE include (1) patient services revenue, (2) premium revenue, and (3) other revenue. Room and board fees and recovery room fees are patient services revenues.
Answer (A) is incorrect. Providing room and board and recovery room services are ongoing or central activities. Answer (C) is incorrect. Providing room and board and recovery room services are ongoing or central activities. Answer (D) is incorrect. Providing room and board and recovery room services are ongoing or central activities.

28.5.2. In healthcare accounting, net assets with donor restrictions are

A. Not available unless the directors remove the restrictions.

B. Restricted as to use only for board-designated purposes.

C. Not available for current operating use; however, the income generated is available for current operating use.

D. Restricted as to use by the donor, grantor, or other source of the resources.

Answer (D) is correct. *(CPA, adapted)*
REQUIRED: The definition of net assets with donor restrictions.
DISCUSSION: All NFPs, including healthcare entities, divide the excess or deficiency of assets over liabilities into two mutually exclusive classes of net assets: (1) net assets with donor restrictions and (2) net assets without donor restrictions. Donors include other contributors, including certain grantors.
Answer (A) is incorrect. Donor restrictions are not removable by the board. Answer (B) is incorrect. Board-designated restrictions are board-removable. Answer (C) is incorrect. Income generated by net assets with donor restrictions are subject to purpose and time restrictions.

28.5.3. In April, Delta Hospital purchased medicines from Field Pharmaceutical Co. at a cost of $5,000. However, Field notified Delta that the invoice was being canceled and that the medicines were being donated to Delta. Delta should record this donation of medicines as

A. A memorandum entry only.

B. A $5,000 credit to nonoperating expenses.

C. A $5,000 credit to operating expenses.

D. Other operating revenue of $5,000.

Answer (D) is correct. *(CPA, adapted)*
REQUIRED: The accounting for a donation of medicine.
DISCUSSION: Contributions of noncash assets that are not long-lived are reported at fair value in the statement of operations. Thus, when a supplier cancels an invoice, the HCE debits the payable and credits other operating revenue.
Answer (A) is incorrect. Donated assets should be recorded at their fair value when received. Answer (B) is incorrect. This donation should be credited to another revenue account or a gain account. Answer (C) is incorrect. This donation should be credited to another revenue account or a gain account.

28.5.4. A voluntary health and welfare entity received a $700,000 perpetual endowment during the year. The donor stipulated that the income and investment appreciation be used to maintain its senior center. The endowment fund reported a net investment appreciation of $80,000 and investment income of $50,000. The entity appropriated and spent $60,000 to maintain its senior center during the year. What amount of change in net assets with donor restrictions should the entity report?

A. $50,000

B. $70,000

C. $130,000

D. $770,000

Answer (B) is correct. *(CPA, adapted)*
REQUIRED: The change in net assets with donor restrictions reported by a VHWE that received a perpetual endowment with a use restriction on appreciation and income.
DISCUSSION: The contribution to a perpetual endowment is an increase in net assets with donor restrictions. Income or appreciation from the endowment is an increase in donor-restricted support if the donor restricts its use. However, if the restriction expires in the period the income is recognized, it may be reported as an increase in net assets without donor restrictions if the entity (1) has a similar policy for reporting contributions received, (2) reports consistently, and (3) makes adequate disclosure. The restriction on the income and appreciation expired only to the extent it was expended during the year. Accordingly, the change in net assets with donor restrictions was $70,000 ($80,000 appreciation + $50,000 income – $60,000 spent). The same result is reached under the law applicable in the majority of jurisdictions. The extension of the donor restriction under that law to the use of the assets expires upon appropriation for expenditure.
Answer (A) is incorrect. The amount of $50,000 is the VHWE's investment income. Answer (C) is incorrect. The amount of $130,000 is the sum of appreciation and income. Answer (D) is incorrect. The amount of $770,000 is the sum of the appreciation and the perpetual endowment.

28.5.5. General purpose external financial reporting by a healthcare entity requires presentation of

A. Fund group information by a not-for-profit entity.

B. A statement of operations.

C. A separate statement of changes in equity, net assets, or fund balance.

D. A performance indicator only by for-profit entities.

Answer (B) is correct. *(Publisher, adapted)*
REQUIRED: The true statement about external reporting by a healthcare entity.
DISCUSSION: The basic financial statements of a healthcare entity include a balance sheet; a statement of operations; a statement of changes in equity or net assets; and a statement of cash flows.
Answer (A) is incorrect. Fund accounting may be used for internal purposes but is not required or encouraged for external reporting. Answer (C) is incorrect. The statement of changes in equity, net assets, or fund balance may be combined with the statement of operations. Answer (D) is incorrect. The statement of operations of all HCEs, including NFPs, should report a performance indicator and other changes in net assets.

28.5.6. An organization of high school seniors performs services for patients at Leer Hospital. These students are volunteers and perform services that the hospital would not otherwise provide, such as wheeling patients in the park and reading to patients. They donated 5,000 hours of service to Leer in Year 4. At a minimum wage rate, these services would amount to $18,750, while it is estimated that the fair value of these services was $25,000. In Leer's Year 4 statement of activities, what amount should be reported as nonoperating revenue?

- A. $25,000
- B. $18,750
- C. $6,250
- D. $0

Answer (D) is correct. *(CPA, adapted)*

REQUIRED: The nonoperating revenue to record for services by volunteers.

DISCUSSION: Contributed services are recognized if they (1) create or enhance nonfinancial assets or (2) (a) require special skills, (b) are provided by those having such skills, and (c) ordinarily would be purchased if not donated. Thus, the hospital should report no revenue. Nonfinancial assets are not involved, and no special skills, such as those of professionals, are required.

Answer (A) is incorrect. The volunteered services do not meet the criteria for revenue recognition of contributions. Answer (B) is incorrect. The volunteered services do not meet the criteria for revenue recognition of contributions. Answer (C) is incorrect. The volunteered services do not meet the criteria for revenue recognition of contributions.

☑ ☰
☐ ☰   Use **Gleim Test Prep** for interactive study and easy-to-use detailed analytics!
☐ ☰

APPENDIX A

SUBUNIT CROSS-REFERENCES TO INTERMEDIATE AND ADVANCED FINANCIAL ACCOUNTING TEXTBOOKS

This section contains the tables of contents of current intermediate and advanced financial accounting textbooks with cross-references to the related subunits or study units in this study manual. The texts are listed in alphabetical order by the first author. As you study a particular chapter in your intermediate or advanced textbook, you can easily determine which subunit(s) to study in your Gleim EQE material.

Professors and students should note that, even though new editions of the following texts may be published as you use this study material, the new tables of contents usually will be very similar, if not the same. Thus, this edition of *Financial Accounting Exam Questions and Explanations* will remain current and useful.

If you are using a textbook that is not included in this list or if you have any suggestions on how we can improve these cross-references to make them more relevant/useful, please submit your request/feedback at www.gleim.com/crossreferences/FIN or email them to FINcrossreferences@gleim.com.

INTERMEDIATE ACCOUNTING TEXTBOOKS

Gordon, Raedy, and Sannella, *Intermediate Accounting*, Second Edition, Pearson, 2019.

Kieso, Weygandt, and Warfield, *Intermediate Accounting*, Sixteenth Edition, Wiley, 2016.

Libby, Libby, and Hodge, *Financial Accounting*, Ninth Edition, McGraw-Hill, 2017.

Miller-Nobles, Mattison, and Matsumura, *Horngren's Accounting: The Financial Chapters*, Twelfth Edition, Pearson, 2018.

Needles and Powers, *Principles of Financial Accounting*, Twelfth Edition, South-Western, Cengage Learning, 2014.

Revsine, Collins, Johnson, Mittelstaedt, and Soffer, *Financial Reporting and Analysis*, Seventh Edition, McGraw-Hill, 2018.

Spiceland, Nelson, and Thomas, *Intermediate Accounting*, Ninth Edition, McGraw-Hill, 2018.

Stice and Stice, *Intermediate Accounting*, Nineteenth Edition, South-Western, Cengage Learning, 2014.

Wahlen, Jones, and Pagach, *Intermediate Accounting: Reporting and Analysis*, Second Edition, 2017 Update, Cengage Learning, 2017.

Warren and Jones, *Corporate Financial Accounting*, Fifteenth Edition, Cengage Learning, 2019.

ADVANCED ACCOUNTING TEXTBOOKS

Beams, Anthony, Bettinghaus, and Smith, *Advanced Accounting*, Thirteenth Edition, Pearson, 2018.

Christensen, Cottrell, and Budd, *Advanced Financial Accounting*, Twelfth Edition, McGraw-Hill, 2019.

Copley, *Essentials of Accounting for Governmental and Not-for-Profit Organizations*, Thirteenth Edition, McGraw-Hill, 2018.

Fischer, Taylor, and Cheng, *Advanced Accounting*, Twelfth Edition, Cengage Learning, 2016.

Freeman, Shoulders, McSwain, and Scott, *Governmental and Nonprofit Accounting*, Eleventh Edition, Pearson, 2018.

Granof, Khumawala, Calabrese, and Smith, *Government and Not-for-Profit Accounting: Concepts and Practices*, Seventh Edition, Wiley, 2016.

Halsey and Hopkins, *Advanced Accounting*, Third Edition, Cambridge Business Publishers, 2017.

Hamlen, *Advanced Accounting*, Fourth Edition, Cambridge Business Publishers, 2018.

Hoyle, Schaefer, and Doupnik, *Advanced Accounting*, Thirteenth Edition, McGraw-Hill, 2017.

Hoyle, Schaefer, and Doupnik, *Fundamentals of Advanced Accounting*, Seventh Edition, McGraw-Hill, 2018.

Jeter and Chaney, *Advanced Accounting*, Sixth Edition, Wiley, 2015.

Reck, Lowensohn, and Neely, *Accounting for Governmental & Nonprofit Entities*, Eighteenth Edition, McGraw-Hill Education, 2019.

INTERMEDIATE ACCOUNTING TEXTBOOKS

Gordon, Raedy, and Sannella, *Intermediate Accounting*, Second Edition, Pearson, 2019.

Chapter   1 - The Financial Reporting Environment - SU 1
Chapter   2 - Financial Reporting Theory - SU 1
Chapter   3 - Judgment and Applied Financial Accounting Research - N/A
Chapter   4 - Review of the Accounting Cycle - SU 2
Chapter   5 - Statements of Net Income and Comprehensive Income - SU 3
Chapter   6 - Statements of Financial Position and Cash Flows and the Annual Report - 1.8, SUs 5-15, SUs 17-20
Chapter   7 - Accounting and the Time Value of Money - SU 4
Chapter   8 - Revenue Recognition - SU 3, SU 21
Chapter   9 - Short-Term Operating Assets: Cash and Receivables - 5.2-5.5
Chapter 10 - Short-Term Operating Assets: Inventory - SU 6
Chapter 11 - Long-Term Operating Assets: Acquisition, Cost Allocation, and Derecognition - SU 7
Chapter 12 - Long-Term Operating Assets: Departures from Historical Cost - SUs 7-8
Chapter 13 - Operating Liabilities and Contingencies - SU 11
Chapter 14 - Financing Liabilities - SU 12
Chapter 15 - Accounting for Stockholders' Equity - SU 15
Chapter 16 - Investments in Financial Assets - SU 10
Chapter 17 - Accounting for Income Taxes - SU 17
Chapter 18 - Accounting for Leases - SU 14
Chapter 19 - Accounting for Employee Compensation and Benefits - SU 13
Chapter 20 - Earnings Per Share - SU 16
Chapter 21 - Accounting Changes and Error Analysis - SU 18
Chapter 22 - The Statement of Cash Flows - SU 19

Kieso, Weygandt, and Warfield, *Intermediate Accounting*, Sixteenth Edition, Wiley, 2016.

Chapter   1 - Financial Accounting and Accounting Standards - 1.7-1.9
Chapter   2 - Conceptual Framework for Financial Reporting - 1.1-1.5
Chapter   3 - The Accounting Information System - 2.1-2.4
Chapter   4 - Income Statement and Related Information - SU 3
Chapter   5 - Balance Sheet and Statement of Cash Flows - SUs 5-15, SUs 17-20
Chapter   6 - Accounting and the Time Value of Money - SU 4
Chapter   7 - Cash and Receivables - 5.2-5.6
Chapter   8 - Valuation of Inventories: A Cost-Basis Approach - 6.1-6.4
Chapter   9 - Inventories: Additional Valuation Issues - 6.5-6.7
Chapter 10 - Acquisition and Disposition of Property, Plant, and Equipment - SU 7
Chapter 11 - Depreciation, Impairments, and Depletion - 7.4, SU 8
Chapter 12 - Intangible Assets - SU 9
Chapter 13 - Current Liabilities and Contingencies - SU 11
Chapter 14 - Long-Term Liabilities - SU 12
Chapter 15 - Stockholders' Equity - SU 15
Chapter 16 - Dilutive Securities and Earnings per Share - SU 16
Chapter 17 - Investments - SU 10
Chapter 18 - Revenue Recognition - 1.5, SU 21
Chapter 19 - Accounting for Income Taxes - SU 17
Chapter 20 - Accounting for Pensions and Postretirement Benefits - 11.4, SU 13
Chapter 21 - Accounting for Leases - SU 14
Chapter 22 - Accounting Changes and Error Analysis - SU 18, 25.3
Chapter 23 - Statement of Cash Flows - SU 19
Chapter 24 - Full Disclosure in Financial Reporting - SU 20

Libby, Libby, and Hodge, *Financial Accounting*, Ninth Edition, McGraw-Hill, 2017.

Chapter   1 - Financial Statements and Business Decisions - SU 1
Chapter   2 - Investing and Financing Decisions and the Accounting System - SU 2, SU 10, SU 22
Chapter   3 - Operating Decisions and the Accounting System - SU 2
Chapter   4 - Adjustments, Financial Statements, and the Quality of Earnings - 1.3, 2.5, SU 3, SU 18
Chapter   5 - Communicating and Interpreting Accounting Information - SU 1, SU 22
Chapter   6 - Reporting and Interpreting Sales Revenue, Receivables, and Cash - SU 5, SU 21
Chapter   7 - Reporting and Interpreting Cost of Goods Sold and Inventory - SU 6
Chapter   8 - Reporting and Interpreting Property, Plant, and Equipment; Intangibles; and Natural Resources - SUs 7-9
Chapter   9 - Reporting and Interpreting Liabilities - SU 11, SU 12
Chapter 10 - Reporting and Interpreting Bond Securities - SU 12
Chapter 11 - Reporting and Interpreting Stockholders' Equity - SU 15
Chapter 12 - Statement of Cash Flows - SU 19
Chapter 13 - Analyzing Financial Statements - SU 22
Appendix A - Reporting and Interpreting Investments in Other Corporations - SU 10
Appendix B - American Eagle Outfitters, Inc., Form 10-K Annual Report - 1.8
Appendix C - Urban Outfitters, Inc., Form 10-K Annual Report - 1.8
Appendix D - Industry Ratio Report - SU 22
Appendix E - Present and Future Value Tables - SU 4

Miller-Nobles, Mattison, and Matsumura, *Horngren's Accounting: The Financial Chapters*, Twelfth Edition, Pearson, 2018.

Chapter   1 - Accounting and the Business Environment - SU 1
Chapter   2 - Recording Business Transactions - SU 2
Chapter   3 - The Adjusting Process - SU 2
Chapter   4 - Completing the Accounting Cycle - SU 2
Chapter   5 - Merchandising Operations - SU 6
Chapter   6 - Merchandise Inventory - SU 6
Chapter   7 - Accounting Information Systems - 2.1-2.4
Chapter   8 - Internal Control and Cash - 5.2
Chapter   9 - Receivables - 5.3-5.6
Chapter 10 - Plant Assets, Natural Resources, and Intangibles - SUs 7-9
Chapter 11 - Current Liabilities and Payroll - SU 11
Chapter 12 - Partnerships - SU 23
Chapter 13 - Corporations - SU 15
Chapter 14 - Long-Term Liabilities - SU 12
Chapter 15 - Investments - SU 10
Chapter 16 - The Statement of Cash Flows - SU 19
Chapter 17 - Financial Statement Analysis - SU 22

Needles and Powers, *Principles of Financial Accounting*, Twelfth Edition, South-Western, Cengage Learning, 2014.

Chapter   1 - Accounting Principles and the Financial Statements - SU 1
Chapter   2 - Analyzing and Recording Business Transactions - SU 2
Chapter   3 - Adjusting the Accounts - SU 2, SU 18
Chapter   4 - Completing the Accounting Cycle - SU 2
Chapter   5 - Foundations of Financial Reporting and the Classified Balance Sheet - SU 2, SUs 5-15, SUs 17-18, SU 20
Chapter   6 - Accounting for Merchandising Operations - SU 6
Chapter   7 - Inventories - SU 6
Chapter   8 - Cash and Internal Control - 5.2
Chapter   9 - Receivables - 5.3-5.6
Chapter 10 - Long-Term Assets - SUs 7-9
Chapter 11 - Current Liabilities and Fair Value Accounting - 1.6, SU 11
Chapter 12 - Accounting for Partnerships - SU 23
Chapter 13 - Accounting for Corporations - SU 15
Chapter 14 - Long-Term Liabilities - SU 12
Chapter 15 - The Statement of Cash Flows - SU 19
Chapter 16 - Financial Statement Analysis - SU 22
Appendix A - Investments - SU 10
Appendix B - Present Value Tables - SU 4

Revsine, Collins, Johnson, Mittelstaedt, and Soffer, *Financial Reporting and Analysis*, Seventh Edition, McGraw-Hill, 2018.

Chapter   1 - The Economic and Institutional Setting for Financial Reporting - 1.7-1.9
Chapter   2 - Accrual Accounting and Income Determination - 1.1-1.5, SU 2
Chapter   3 - Revenue Recognition - SU 3, SU 21
Chapter   4 - Structure of the Balance Sheet and Statement of Cash Flows - SUs 5-15, SUs 17-20
Chapter   5 - Essentials of Financial Statement Analysis - SU 22
Chapter   6 - The Role of Financial Information in Valuation and Credit Risk Assessment - 1.6
Chapter   7 - The Role of Financial Information in Contracting - N/A
Chapter   8 - Receivables - 5.3-5.6
Chapter   9 - Inventories - SU 6
Chapter   10 - Long-Lived Assets - SUs 7-9
Chapter   11 - Financial Instruments and Liabilities - SUs 10-12, 26.2
Chapter   12 - Financial Reporting for Leases - SU 14
Chapter   13 - Income Tax Reporting - SU 17
Chapter   14 - Pensions and Postretirement Benefits - SU 13
Chapter   15 - Financial Reporting for Owners' Equity - SU 15
Chapter   16 - Intercorporate Investments - SU 10, SU 24
Chapter   17 - Statement of Cash Flows - SU 19
Appendix A - Time Value of Money - SU 4
Appendix B - Segment Reporting - 20.4

Spiceland, Nelson, and Thomas, *Intermediate Accounting*, Ninth Edition, McGraw-Hill, 2018.

Chapter   1 - Environment and Theoretical Structure of Financial Accounting - SU 1
Chapter   2 - Review of the Accounting Process - 2.1-2.4
Chapter   3 - The Balance Sheet and Financial Disclosures - SUs 5-15, SUs 17-18, SU 20
Chapter   4 - The Income Statement, Comprehensive Income, and the Statement of Cash Flows - SU 3, SU 19
Chapter   5 - Revenue Recognition - 1.5, SU 3, SU 21, 22.5
Chapter   6 - Time Value of Money Concepts - SU 4
Chapter   7 - Cash and Receivables - 5.2-5.5
Chapter   8 - Inventories: Measurement - 6.1-6.5
Chapter   9 - Inventories: Additional Issues - 6.6-6.8
Chapter   10 - Property, Plant, and Equipment and Intangible Assets: Acquisition - 7.1-7.2, SU 9
Chapter   11 - Property, Plant, and Equipment and Intangible Assets: Utilization and Disposition - 7.3-7.6, SU 8
Chapter   12 - Investments - SU 10
Chapter   13 - Current Liabilities and Contingencies - SU 11
Chapter   14 - Bonds and Long-Term Notes - SU 12
Chapter   15 - Leases - SU 14
Chapter   16 - Accounting for Income Taxes - SU 17
Chapter   17 - Pensions and Other Postretirement Benefits - 11.4, SU 13
Chapter   18 - Shareholders' Equity - SU 15
Chapter   19 - Share-Based Compensation and Earnings Per Share - 13.3, SU 16
Chapter   20 - Accounting Changes and Error Corrections - SU 18
Chapter   21 - Statement of Cash Flows Revisited - SU 19

Stice and Stice, *Intermediate Accounting*, Nineteenth Edition, South-Western, Cengage Learning, 2014.

Chapter   1 - Financial Reporting - SU 1
Chapter   2 - A Review of the Accounting Cycle - 2.1-2.4
Chapter   3 - The Balance Sheet and Notes to the Financial Statements - SUs 5-15, SUs 17-18, SU 20
Chapter   4 - The Income Statement - SU 3
Chapter   5 - Statement of Cash Flows and Articulation - SU 19
Chapter   6 - Earnings Management - N/A
Chapter   7 - The Revenue/Receivables/Cash Cycle - 5.2-5.6, SU 21
Chapter   8 - Revenue Recognition - 1.5, SU 21
Chapter   9 - Inventory and Cost of Goods Sold - SU 6
Chapter   10 - Investments in Noncurrent Operating Assets--Acquisition - 7.1-7.2, SU 9
Chapter   11 - Investments in Noncurrent Operating Assets--Utilization and Retirement - 7.3-7.6, SU 8
Chapter   12 - Debt Financing - SUs 11-12
Chapter   13 - Equity Financing - SU 15
Chapter   14 - Investments in Debt and Equity Securities - SU 10

Wahlen, Jones, and Pagach, *Intermediate Accounting: Reporting and Analysis*, Second Edition, 2017 Update, Cengage Learning, 2017.

Warren and Jones, *Corporate Financial Accounting*, Fifteenth Edition, Cengage Learning, 2019.

ADVANCED ACCOUNTING TEXTBOOKS

Beams, Anthony, Bettinghaus, and Smith, *Advanced Accounting*, Thirteenth Edition, Pearson, 2018.

Chapter   1 - Business Combinations - 24.1-24.4
Chapter   2 - Stock Investments–Investor Accounting and Reporting - 10.1-10.3
Chapter   3 - An Introduction to Consolidated Financial Statements - 24.5-24.8
Chapter   4 - Consolidation Techniques and Procedures - 24.5-24.8
Chapter   5 - Intercompany Profit Transactions–Inventories - 24.5, 24.8
Chapter   6 - Intercompany Profit Transactions–Plant Assets - 24.5, 24.8
Chapter   7 - Intercompany Profit Transactions–Bonds - 24.5, 24.8
Chapter   8 - Consolidations–Changes in Ownership Interests - N/A
Chapter   9 - Indirect and Mutual Holdings - N/A
Chapter 10 - Subsidiary Preferred Stock, Consolidated Earnings per Share, and Consolidated Income Taxation - N/A
Chapter 11 - Consolidation Theories, Push-Down Accounting, and Corporate Joint Ventures - 24.1, 24.3-24.5
Chapter 12 - Derivatives and Foreign Currency: Concepts and Common Transactions - 10.7, SU 26
Chapter 13 - Accounting for Derivatives and Hedging Activities - 10.7, SU 26
Chapter 14 - Foreign Currency Financial Statements - SU 26
Chapter 15 - Segment and Interim Financial Reporting - 20.4, SU 25
Chapter 16 - Partnerships–Formation, Operations, and Changes in Ownership Interests - SU 23
Chapter 17 - Partnership Liquidation - 23.5
Chapter 18 - Corporate Liquidations and Reorganizations - N/A
Chapter 19 - An Introduction to Accounting for State and Local Governmental Units - 27.1-27.3
Chapter 20 - Accounting for State and Local Governmental Units–Governmental Funds - 27.5-27.9
Chapter 21 - Accounting for State and Local Governmental Units–Proprietary and Fiduciary Funds - 27.10-27.11
Chapter 22 - Accounting for Not-for-Profit Organizations - SU 28
Chapter 23 - Estates and Trusts - N/A

Christensen, Cottrell, and Budd, *Advanced Financial Accounting*, Twelfth Edition, McGraw-Hill, 2019.

Chapter   1 - Intercorporate Acquisitions and Investments in Other Entities - SU 10, SU 24
Chapter   2 - Reporting Intercorporate Investments and Consolidation of Wholly Owned Subsidiaries with No Differential - SU 24
Chapter   3 - The Reporting Entity and the Consolidation of Less-Than-Wholly-Owned Subsidiaries with No Differential - SU 24
Chapter   4 - Consolidation of Wholly Owned Subsidiaries Acquired at More than Book Value - SU 24
Chapter   5 - Consolidation of Less-than-Wholly-Owned Subsidiaries Acquired at More than Book Value - SU 24
Chapter   6 - Intercompany Inventory Transactions - 24.8
Chapter   7 - Intercompany Transfers of Services and Noncurrent Assets - 24.8
Chapter   8 - Intercompany Indebtedness - 24.8
Chapter   9 - Consolidation Ownership Issues - 24.1-24.2
Chapter 10 - Additional Consolidation Reporting Issues - 24.4-24.8
Chapter 11 - Multinational Accounting: Foreign Currency Transactions and Financial Instruments - SU 26
Chapter 12 - Multinational Accounting: Issues in Financial Reporting and Translation of Foreign Entity Statements - SU 26
Chapter 13 - Segment and Interim Reporting - 20.4, SU 25
Chapter 14 - SEC Reporting - 1.8
Chapter 15 - Partnerships: Formation, Operation, and Changes in Membership - SU 23
Chapter 16 - Partnerships: Liquidation - 23.5
Chapter 17 - Governmental Entities: Introduction and General Fund Accounting - 27.1-27.3
Chapter 18 - Governmental Entities: Special Funds and Governmentwide Financial Statements - SU 27
Chapter 19 - Not-for-Profit Entities - SU 28
Chapter 20 - Corporations in Financial Difficulty - N/A

Copley, *Essentials of Accounting for Governmental and Not-for-Profit Organizations*, Thirteenth Edition, McGraw-Hill, 2018.

Fischer, Taylor, and Cheng, *Advanced Accounting*, Twelfth Edition, Cengage Learning, 2016.

Freeman, Shoulders, McSwain, and Scott, *Governmental and Nonprofit Accounting*, Eleventh Edition, Pearson, 2018.

Chapter   1 - Governmental and Nonprofit Accounting: Environment and Characteristics - 27.1, 28.1
Chapter   2 - State and Local Government Accounting and Financial Reporting Model: The Foundation - 27.2, 27.3
Chapter   3 - Budgeting, Budgetary Accounting, and Budgetary Reporting - 27.5
Chapter   4 - The General Fund and Special Revenue Funds - 27.9
Chapter   5 - Revenue Accounting–Governmental Funds - 27.9
Chapter   6 - Expenditure Accounting–Governmental Funds - 27.9
Chapter   7 - Capital Projects Funds - 27.9
Chapter   8 - Debt Service Funds - 27.9
Chapter   9 - General Capital Assets; General Long-Term Liabilities; Permanent Funds: Introduction to Interfund-GCA-GLTL Accounting - 27.4, 27.9
Chapter 10 - Enterprise Funds - 27.10
Chapter 11 - Internal Service Funds - 27.10
Chapter 12 - Trust and Agency (Fiduciary) Funds: Summary of Interfund-GCA-GLTL Accounting - 27.11
Chapter 13 - Financial Reporting: The Basic Financial Statements and Required Supplementary Information - 27.8-27.11
Chapter 14 - Financial Reporting: Deriving Government-Wide Financial Statements and Required Reconciliations - 27.8
Chapter 15 - Financial Reporting: The Comprehensive Annual Financial Report and the Financial Reporting Entity - 27.7
Chapter 16 - Non-SLG Not-for-Profit Organizations - 28.1-28.4
Chapter 17 - Accounting for Colleges and Universities - 28.2, 28.3, 28.4
Chapter 18 - Accounting for Health Care Organizations - 28.5
Chapter 19 - Federal Government Accounting - N/A
Chapter 20 - Auditing Governments and Not-for-Profit Organizations - N/A

Granof, Khumawala, Calabrese, and Smith, *Government and Not-for-Profit Accounting: Concepts and Practices*, Seventh Edition, Wiley, 2016.

Chapter   1 - The Government and Not-for-Profit Environment - 27.1, 28.1
Chapter   2 - Fund Accounting - 27.2, 27.12
Chapter   3 - Issues of Budgeting and Control - 27.5
Chapter   4 - Recognizing Revenues in Governmental Funds - 27.3, 27.6
Chapter   5 - Recognizing Expenditures in Governmental Funds - 27.3, 27.6
Chapter   6 - Accounting for Capital Projects and Debt Service - 27.2, 27.6
Chapter   7 - Capital Assets and Investments in Marketable Securities - 27.4, 27.6
Chapter   8 - Long-Term Obligations - 27.4
Chapter   9 - Business-Type Activities - 27.2, 27.10
Chapter 10 - Pensions and Other Fiduciary Activities - 27.2, 27.11
Chapter 11 - Issues of Reporting, Disclosure, and Financial Analysis - 27.7-27.11
Chapter 12 - Not-for-Profit Organizations - 28.1-28.4
Chapter 13 - Colleges and Universities - 28.1-28.4
Chapter 14 - Health Care Providers - 28.5
Chapter 15 - Managing for Results - 27.5
Chapter 16 - Auditing Governments and Not-for-Profit Organizations - N/A
Chapter 17 - Federal Government Accounting - N/A

Halsey and Hopkins, *Advanced Accounting*, Third Edition, Cambridge Business Publishers, 2017.

Chapter   1 - Accounting for Intercorporate Investments - SU 24
Chapter   2 - Introduction to Business Combinations and the Consolidation Process - 24.1-24.5
Chapter   3 - Consolidated Financial Statements Subsequent to the Date of Acquisition - 24.5-24.8
Chapter   4 - Consolidated Financial Statements and Intercompany Transactions - 24.5, 24.8
Chapter   5 - Consolidated Financial Statements with Less than 100% Ownership - SU 24
Chapter   6 - Consolidation of Variable Interest Entities and Other Intercompany Investments - 24.5-24.8
Chapter   7 - Accounting for Foreign Currency Transactions and Derivatives - 10.7, SU 26
Chapter   8 - Consolidation of Foreign Subsidiaries - SU 26
Chapter   9 - Government Accounting: Fund-Based Financial Statements - 27.7, 27.9-27.11
Chapter 10 - Government Accounting: Government-Wide Financial Statements - 27.7-27.8
Chapter 11 - Accounting for Not-for-Profit Organizations - SU 28
Chapter 12 - Segment Disclosures and Interim Financial Reporting - 20.4, SU 25
Chapter 13 - Accounting for Partnerships - SU 23

Hamlen, *Advanced Accounting*, Fourth Edition, Cambridge Business Publishers, 2018.

Chapter 1 - Intercorporate Investments: An Overview - SU 24
Chapter 2 - Mergers and Acquisitions - SU 24
Chapter 3 - Consolidated Financial Statements: Date of Acquisition - 24.2-24.5
Chapter 4 - Consolidated Financial Statements Subsequent to Acquisition - 24.5-24.8
Chapter 5 - Consolidated Financial Statements: Outside Interests - 24.5-24.8
Chapter 6 - Consolidated Financial Statements: Intercompany Transactions - 24.5, 24.8
Chapter 7 - Consolidating Foreign Currency Financial Statements - SU 26
Chapter 8 - Foreign Currency Transactions and Hedging - 10.7, SU 26
Chapter 9 - Futures, Options and Interest Rate Swaps - 10.7
Chapter 10 - State and Local Governments: Introduction and General Fund Transactions - 27.1-27.3, 27.6, 27.9
Chapter 11 - State and Local Governments: Other Transactions - SU 27
Chapter 12 - State and Local Governments: External Financial Reporting - 27.7-27.11
Chapter 13 - Private Not-For-Profit Organizations - SU 28
Chapter 14 - Partnership Accounting and Reporting - SU 23
Chapter 15 - Bankruptcy and Reorganization - N/A
Chapter 16 - The SEC and Financial Reporting - N/A

Hoyle, Schaefer, and Doupnik, *Advanced Accounting*, Thirteenth Edition, McGraw-Hill, 2017.

Chapter 1 - The Equity Method of Accounting for Investments - 10.4
Chapter 2 - Consolidation of Financial Information - SU 24
Chapter 3 - Consolidations–Subsequent to the Date of Acquisition - 24.5-24.8
Chapter 4 - Consolidated Financial Statements and Outside Ownership - 24.5-24.8
Chapter 5 - Consolidated Financial Statements–Intra-Entity Asset Transactions - 24.5, 24.8
Chapter 6 - Variable Interest Entities, Intra-Entity Debt, Consolidated Cash Flows, and Other Issues - 24.5, 24.8-24.9
Chapter 7 - Consolidated Financial Statements–Ownership Patterns and Income Taxes - N/A
Chapter 8 - Segment and Interim Reporting - 20.4, SU 25
Chapter 9 - Foreign Currency Transactions and Hedging Foreign Exchange Risk - SU 26
Chapter 10 - Translation of Foreign Currency Financial Statements - 26.1
Chapter 11 - Worldwide Accounting Diversity and International Standards - N/A
Chapter 12 - Financial Reporting and the Securities and Exchange Commission - 1.8
Chapter 13 - Accounting for Legal Reorganizations and Liquidations - N/A
Chapter 14 - Partnerships: Formation and Operation - 23.1-23.4
Chapter 15 - Partnerships: Termination and Liquidation - 23.4-23.5
Chapter 16 - Accounting for State and Local Governments (Part I) - SU 27
Chapter 17 - Accounting for State and Local Governments (Part II) - SU 27
Chapter 18 - Accounting and Reporting for Private Not-for-Profit Entities - SU 28
Chapter 19 - Accounting for Estates and Trusts - N/A

Hoyle, Schaefer, and Doupnik, *Fundamentals of Advanced Accounting*, Seventh Edition, McGraw-Hill, 2018.

Chapter 1 - The Equity Method of Accounting for Investments - 10.4
Chapter 2 - Consolidation of Financial Information - SU 24
Chapter 3 - Consolidations–Subsequent to the Date of Acquisition - 24.5-24.8
Chapter 4 - Consolidated Financial Statements and Outside Ownership - 24.1-24.5
Chapter 5 - Consolidated Financial Statements–Intra-Entity Asset Transactions - 24.5, 24.8
Chapter 6 - Variable Interest Entities, Intra-Entity Debt, Consolidated Cash Flows, and Other Issues - 24.5-24.9
Chapter 7 - Foreign Currency Transactions and Hedging Foreign Exchange Risk - 10.7, 26.2
Chapter 8 - Translation of Foreign Currency Financial Statements - 26.1
Chapter 9 - Partnerships: Formation and Operation - 23.1-23.4
Chapter 10 - Partnerships: Termination and Liquidation - 23.4-23.5
Chapter 11 - Accounting for State and Local Governments (Part I) - SU 27
Chapter 12 - Accounting for State and Local Governments (Part II) - SU 27

Jeter and Chaney, *Advanced Accounting*, Sixth Edition, Wiley, 2015.

Chapter   1 - Introduction to Business Combinations and the Conceptual Framework - 1.1, 24.1
Chapter   2 - Accounting for Business Combinations - SU 24
Chapter   3 - Consolidated Financial Statements--Date of Acquisition - 24.2-24.5
Chapter   4 - Consolidated Financial Statements After Acquisition - 24.5-24.8
Chapter   5 - Allocation and Depreciation of Differences Between Implied and Book Values - 24.2-24.3
Chapter   6 - Elimination of Unrealized Profit on Intercompany Sales of Inventory - 24.5, 24.8
Chapter   7 - Elimination of Unrealized Gains or Losses on Intercompany Sales of Property and Equipment - 24.5, 24.8
Chapter   8 - Changes in Ownership Interest - N/A
Chapter   9 - Intercompany Bond Holdings and Miscellaneous Topics--Consolidated Financial Statements - 24.5, 24.8
Chapter 10 - Insolvency--Liquidation and Reorganization - N/A
Chapter 11 - International Financial Reporting Standards - 1.9
Chapter 12 - Accounting for Foreign Currency Transactions and Hedging Foreign Exchange Risk - 10.7, SU 26
Chapter 13 - Translation of Financial Statements of Foreign Affiliates - 26.1
Chapter 14 - Reporting for Segments and for Interim Financial Periods - 20.4, SU 25
Chapter 15 - Partnerships: Formation, Operation, and Ownership Changes - 23.1-23.4
Chapter 16 - Partnership Liquidation - 23.4-23.5
Chapter 17 - Introduction to Fund Accounting - 27.2
Chapter 18 - Introduction to Accounting for State and Local Governmental Units - 27.1-27.3
Chapter 19 - Accounting for Nongovernment Nonbusiness Organizations: Colleges and Universities, Hospitals and Other Health Care Organizations - SU 28

Reck, Lowensohn, and Neely, *Accounting for Governmental & Nonprofit Entities*, Eighteenth Edition, McGraw-Hill Education, 2019.

Chapter   1 - Introduction to Accounting and Financial Reporting for Government and Not-for-Profit Entities - 27.1-27.3, 28.1
Chapter   2 - Principles of Accounting and Financial Reporting for State and Local Governments - 27.2, 27.3
Chapter   3 - Governmental Operating Statement Accounts; Budgetary Accounting - 27.5, 27.8
Chapter   4 - Accounting for Governmental Operating Activities--Illustrative Transactions and Financial Statements - 27.6-27.12
Chapter   5 - Accounting for General Capital Assets and Capital Projects - 27.4
Chapter   6 - Accounting for General Long-term Liabilities and Debt Service - 27.4
Chapter   7 - Accounting for the Business-type Activities of State and Local Governments - 27.10
Chapter   8 - Accounting for Fiduciary Activities--Custodial and Trust Funds - 27.11
Chapter   9 - Financial Reporting of State and Local Governments - 27.7-27.11
Chapter 10 - Analysis of Governmental Financial Performance - N/A
Chapter 11 - Auditing of Government and Not-for-Profit Organizations - N/A
Chapter 12 - Budgeting and Performance Measurement - N/A
Chapter 13 - Not-for-Profit Organizations--Regulatory, Taxation, and Performance Issues - N/A
Chapter 14 - Accounting for Not-for-Profit Organizations - 28.1-28.4
Chapter 15 - Accounting for Colleges and Universities - 28.1-28.4
Chapter 16 - Accounting for Health Care Organizations - 28.5
Chapter 17 - Accounting and Reporting for the Federal Government - N/A

INDEX